Automotive Principles and Service

second edition

Automotive Principles and Service

Second Edition

Frank J. Thiessen   **Davis N. Dales**

 Reston Publishing Company, Inc.
A Prentice-Hall Company
Reston, Virginia

Cover photo copyright 1984 by Bill Agee

Library of Congress Cataloging in Publication Data

Thiessen, F. J.
  Automotive principles and service.

  1. Automobiles. 2. Automobiles—Maintenance and
repair. I. Dales, D. N. II. Title.
TL145.T337 1984   629.2′222   83-16114
ISBN 0-8359-0331-1

10 9 8 7 6 5 4 3 2 1

Printed and bound in Canada by
The Bryant Press Limited

Contents

Chapter 6 Engine Components 93

Chapter 7 Lubrication Systems 145

Chapter 8 Cooling Systems 163

Chapter 9 Engine Diagnosis and Service Procedure 183

SECTION 3   AIR, FUEL, AND
EXHAUST SYSTEMS   243

Daily Book Scanning Log

Name: Krystal Rangel   # of Scanners: 2

Date: 7/9/24

BIN #	BOOKS COMPLETED	# OF PAGES	NOTES / EXCEPTIONS
Bin 1			
Bin 2			
Bin 3			
Bin 4			
Bin 5			
Bin 6			
Bin 7			
Bin 8			
Bin 9			
Bin 10			
Bin 11			
Bin 12			
Bin 13			
Bin 14			
Bin 15			
Bin 16			
Bin 17			
Bin 18			
Bin 19			
Bin 20			
Bin 21			
Bin 22			
Bin 23			
Bin 24			
Bin 25			
Bin 26			
Bin 27			
Bin 28			
Bin 29			
Bin 30			
Bin 31			
Bin 32			
Bin 33			
Bin 34			
Bin 35			
Bin 36			
Bin 37			
Bin 38			
Bin 39			
Bin 40			

(BOOKS/LIBROS) TOTAL:_____ / 600

(PAGES/PAGINAS) TOTAL:_____

x Contents

Preface

The automotive industry is continually undergoing rapid technological change. Constant development of and improvement to the automobile make an automotive service career challenging and rewarding. In spite of these changes, however, much of the automobile remains the same.

This second edition of the popular and widely accepted first edition of Automotive Principles and Service retains most of the relevant subject matter of the first edition; it includes increased coverage of basic principles and technical depth, and relevant new material covering the latest technological changes. The broader coverage and the new material contribute to making this edition among the most current and comprehensive automotive texts available.

The subject matter has been divided into nine sections and forty chapters. The first four chapters present information that is necessary throughout all other subject areas. The remaining chapters are arranged to cover the eight categories of NIASE (National Institute for Automotive Service Excellence) certification and testing as well as Canadian Interprovincial testing and certification.

The presentation of the subject matter is arranged to describe, in the following order, the purpose, construction, operation, and service of each system or unit.

- *Purpose* and function of each system or component.

  Why is the system or unit needed in the automobile and what function does it perform?
- *Construction* of the system or unit.

System design and layout; individual component design and construction including design differences and operating requirements.

- *Operation* of the system or unit.

  How the system operates as a whole, and how each component in the system operates; the effects of long-term normal operation, and the effects of abnormal and severe operating conditions; deterioration, wear, and damage to the system or component resulting from both normal and abnormal operating conditions.
- *Service* of the system or unit.

  Routine maintenance; diagnosis; repair and overhaul of the system or unit.

Service procedures recommended follow the generally accepted practices common to the trade.

The text is abundantly illustrated; many new illustrations are added. Each illustration is accompanied by a brief caption tying the illustration to the text.

The authors are deeply grateful to all the readers of the first edition who generously contributed the time to make constructive comments and suggestions. These suggestions are reflected in this new text. The authors are also grateful to all the various vehicle manufacturers, tool and equipment manufacturers, fuel and other product manufacturers who kindly contributed to the development of this text. We are particularly grateful to the local representatives of these companies for their help.

The authors are especially grateful to Linda Zuk and Diane Anderson for the fine work done on the design and layout of this text as well as all our other texts. The assistance and cooperation provided by the Reston Publishing Company staff is also deeply appreciated.

A great number of instructors have contributed suggestions for improvements in this revision. In particular, we are indebted to Roy Baker and Murray E. Williams of Lincoln Technical Institute, David Spear of Niagara College, Norman Storms of Loyalist College, Henry Burgess of St. Clair College, Harry Thomas of Technichron Vocational Institute, William Routley of Ferris State College, John Berry of College of the Canyons, and Graham Johnston of Northern Alberta Institute of Technology, who were most helpful during the preparation of this edition.

IMPORTANT SAFETY NOTICE

Proper service and repair are important for the safe, reliable operation of all motor vehicles. The service procedures described and recommended in this text

xiii

are effective methods of performing service operations. Some of these service operations require the use of tools specially designed for the purpose. These special tools should be used as recommended in the manufacturers' service manuals.

It is important to note that this text contains various general precautions that should be read carefully in order to minimize the risk of personal injury or damage to the vehicle resulting from improper service methods. It is also important to understand that these general precautions are not exhaustive. The authors could not possibly know, evaluate, and advise the service trade of all conceivable ways in which service might be carried out or of the possible hazardous consequences of each method. Accordingly, anyone who uses any given service procedure or tool must first satisfy himself thoroughly that neither his safety nor the safety of the vehicle will be jeopardized by the service method he selects.

Textbooks by the Same Authors and Reston Publishing Co.

1. Automotive Principles and Service
   Study Guide and Workbook for Automotive Principles and Service
   Instructor's Manual for Automotive Principles and Service

2. Diesel Fundamentals—Principles and Service
   Instructor's Manual for Diesel Fundamentals

3. Automotive Engines—Principles and Service

4. Automotive Steering, Suspension, and Braking Systems

5. Automatic Transmissions

6. Automotive Drive Trains

7. Automotive Electronics and Engine Performance

Introduction

PART 1 AUTOMOTIVE SERVICE CAREERS

The automotive service industry is one of the largest industries worldwide. In industrialized countries, employment in this industry is as high as one out of every seven working people.

The size and diversity of the industry offer many opportunities for interesting, challenging, and rewarding careers. Continuing technological change in the automobile demands that the service technician continue to learn and update his knowledge and skills.

Career choices include becoming a specialist in one or more specific subject areas such as the following:

- Light service and lubrication
- Tires
- Brakes
- Wheel alignment and balance
- Manual transmissions and differentials
- Automatic transmissions
- Engines
- Tune up
- Air conditioning
- Electrical
- Diesel injection
- Trim
- Diagnostics

Someone who has mastered all of these subject areas may be known as a master mechanic.

In addition to these, there are career opportunities in automotive rebuilding plants as engine rebuilders, transmission rebuilders, carburetor rebuilders, and the like.

Service career opportunities are also available in the body repair and frame alignment fields.

Supervisory Careers

Larger automotive shops, dealers, vehicle manufacturers, fleet owners, and public and private technical schools offer opportunities for supervisory careers in the automotive service industry. Among these are:

- Service sales
- Service control operator
- Shop foreman
- Service manager
- Garage manager or proprietor
- Manufacturer's district service representative
- Manufacturer's technical training instructor
- Manufacturer's factory quality control inspector
- Manufacturer's regional service manager
- Automotive instructor in public or private schools, high schools, vocational-technical schools, and community colleges
- Fleet maintenance manager in industry, federal or local governments

Some of these positions require additional experience and training.

Related Career Opportunities

Many related career opportunities exist both inside and outside of the automotive service industry. Some of these are:

- Parts sales
- Parts manager
- New and used car sales
- Used parts sales (auto wreckers)
- Recreational vehicle sales and service
- Agricultural equipment sales and service
- Highway transport sales and service
- Off road industrial and construction equipment sales and service
- Government vehicle safety inspection
- Government emissions control inspection

PART 2 PREPARING FOR AN AUTOMOTIVE SERVICE CAREER

The degree of success achieved in the chosen career is dependent on a number of factors, not the least of which is desire—the kind that results in determination, effort, and achievement.

It is a good idea to "stay with it" in high school to gain the necessary skills in communications, mathematics, and science. Knowledge of the basic principles of the following subject matter should be acquired either prior to taking an automotive course, or during the automotive course. Some automotive courses may require a knowledge of these principles as prerequisites, while others may provide related class instruction in science, mathematics, and communication.

Some of the major areas in which knowledge of basic principles is required are:

- Matter
- Mass
- Atmospheric Pressure
- Weight
- Gravity
- Absolute Pressure
- Vacuum
- Density
- Hydraulics
- Pneumatics
- Friction
- Work
- Force
- Force Multiplication
- Energy
- Power
- Torque
- Heat
- Electricity
- Refrigeration
- Areas
- Volumes
- Ratios
- Speed

Also required is the ability to calculate these as they relate to the automobile by means of addition, subtraction, multiplication, and division using whole numbers, fractions, decimals, and percentages.

This text deals with each of these topics in their respective chapters where necessary. However, it is assumed that the needed skills in mathematics have already been acquired.

Understanding the Measurement System

The modern automobile consists of many individual parts and components held together by a variety of fasteners of different shapes and sizes.

Some automotive components are dimensioned in the customary U.S. system of measurement while others are dimensioned in the SI metric system. The modern technician and the modern automotive shop must, therefore, be equipped with tools and measuring devices designed to be used on U.S. dimensioned components and on SI metric components as well. The technician must also be able to distinguish between the two. The importance of this is obvious when fasteners (bolts, nuts, screws, etc.) used in the automobile are considered. It is critical to the safety of the vehicle and its passengers that only replacement fasteners of original equipment size, type, and quality be used. Metric dimensioned fasteners should never be used when U.S. dimensioned fasteners were originally used. Nor should U.S. dimensioned fasteners be used where metric fasteners were originally used. Even though they may appear to be similar, they do not fit properly and are not interchangeable.

Current manufacturer's service repair manuals, as well as other types of service manuals, are not confined to using one system of measurement for vehicle specifications. U.S. measurements, metric measurements, or both, may appear in any given service manual.

This text will give most measurements and specifications in the customary units, with metric equivalents in brackets following. Metric equivalents will be stated in figures that are rounded off to the most appropriate value. This avoids the cumbersome figures with three or four decimals which result from stating exact equivalents.

The U.S. system of measurement is the same as the Imperial system used earlier in Canada, with the exception of liquid volume measurements such as the gallon, quart, and pint. Reference charts in the Appendix for this text provide comparative equivalent measurements in the U.S. system, the SI metric system, and the Imperial system, as well as the appropriate conversion factors, should conversion be necessary.

Schools and Courses

Many different types of schools offer a variety of automotive service training programs and courses.

High schools in many areas offer courses which allow the student to major in automotive service.

Courses may be of two or three years duration and may offer an in-school service shop as well as some "industry" experience through cooperative training programs. These types of courses are of the job entry or pre-employment type, meaning that sufficient skills training is provided to allow a student to become employable in the industry. Additional experience and/or training are required to become a certified technician or mechanic.

Vocational-technical schools, community colleges, and universities may offer similar job entry type courses, usually of one or two years duration, and may offer more advanced, more technical courses as well.

The job entry type courses normally offer a certificate after successful completion of the course. The more technical courses offer a diploma or a degree.

Community colleges and vocational-technical schools may also offer short courses for apprentices leading to eligibility for certification as a licensed journeyman mechanic.

High schools, community colleges, and vocational-technical schools also usually offer short courses in theory only for those experienced in the trade but not yet certified. These courses are designed to help the student in taking certification exams. Automobile manufacturers also offer a variety of courses on basic principles as well as the more technical and product improvement courses.

PART 3 BECOMING CERTIFIED

Reasons for Certification

Doctors, lawyers, accountants, nurses, plumbers, electricians, dentists, and other professions are licensed or certified in order to practice their profession.

In order to become certified, certain strict uniform requirements must be met. This protects the general public and the practitioner or profession. Licensing or certification tells the general public and the prospective employer that certain minimum standards of performance have been met. Standards for knowledge and skill are established. Usually the certified technician receives higher pay than the non-certified operator. The certified technician is recognized as a professional by the public, by the employer, and by his peers.

Kinds of Certification

The National Institute for Automotive Service Excellence (NIASE), with headquarters in Washington D.C., has offered a program of voluntary certification since 1972. This certification program is rec-ommended by the major vehicle manufacturers in the U.S. In Canada, most provincial departments of labor include an apprenticeship division responsible for apprenticeship training and certification. An interprovincial agreement has set up standards for certification as an Interprovincial Motor Vehicle Mechanic.

NIASE Certification (New Logo–ASE)

NIASE certification tests fall into eight categories or specialties as follows:

- Engine repairs
- Electrical systems
- Engine performance
- Front end
- Brakes
- Manual drive train and rear axle
- Automatic transmissions/transaxles
- Heating and air conditioning

This arrangement permits two types of certification:

1. Specialist technician
2. General technician

To become certified, you must have at least two years of experience. If you wish to be certified as a Specialist Technician, you need to pass only the examination that pertains to your work speciality. If you want to be certified as a General Technician, you must pass examinations in all eight areas.

A mechanic who passes at least one examination receives a gear-shaped patch for the shoulder of his shirt or coveralls. Additional bar-shaped patches are issued for each test area passed. Two gear-shaped patches indicate that the mechanic has passed all eight test categories and is a General Technician meeting minimum standards in all eight categories.

A mechanic must have a minimum of two years experience to be eligible to take the tests. A nominal fee is charged for each test taken.

Canadian Interprovincial Certification

The Interprovincial Standards Committee representing the various provincial apprenticeship training programs has established testing standards and tests for certification as an Interprovincial Motor Vehicle Mechanic. These tests cover all phases of automotive service similar to the eight areas used by NIASE. This certificate is recognized interprovincially.

A passing grade of at least 70% is required on a single comprehensive examination covering all phases of service. A nominal fee is charged for writing the test. Some provinces will issue a provincial journeyman certificate if the test writer does not achieve the required 70% but is above a minimum passing grade.

To be eligible to write the test the technician must have completed all provincial apprenticeship levels successfully (usually four years), or a minimum of five years of experience acceptable to the apprenticeship review board.

PART 4   HOW TO PASS A TEST

Be Confident

If you didn't think you could pass the test, you would not have spent the time studying. You know you can pass the test because you have done your work and have studied the subject.

Review Your Notes

You should have made a set of notes during your studies listing key points. Review these a day or two before the test. Don't cram the night before. This will only cause you mental and physical fatigue and perhaps rob you of needed sleep. Cramming can also upset you emotionally.

Get a Good Night's Rest

Get to bed at a respectable time the night before the exam. Don't go out on the town or entertain until all hours. You need the rest in order to be calm and relaxed.

Eat Properly

Don't skip supper, breakfast, or lunch before a test. Keep your normal, regular eating routine. Don't attempt to fortify your courage with stimulants—you want to be clear headed and able to think.

Bring Pencils

Pencils are often not provided for the examination so bring two or three so you won't have to sharpen a broken pencil.

Be on Time

Allow yourself enough time to eat and arrive calm and relaxed. If you don't, you may be emotionally upset before you start. If the test is to be written at a location unfamiliar to you, be sure you know how to get there. It may be worthwhile to check it out a day or two before test time by going there.

Listen to Instructions

Be sure you pay attention to any verbal instructions that may be given by the examiner. If you fail to hear or understand, be sure to ask for clarification.

Read Test Instructions Carefully

Make sure you understand all written instructions for the test. If you do not understand the written instructions fully, raise your hand and ask the test supervisor to explain them to you.

Write the Test

If there is a time limit on the test, allocate your time. For example, if the test has 200 questions and you are allowed two hours, you need to pace yourself to about 50 questions every 30 minutes. However, don't rush yourself. If necessary, read the question twice. If you are still baffled, you should go on to the next question and come back to this one later. By then, some of the other questions may have helped you to understand. Don't assume that there are trick questions. Trying to figure out what you may think is a trick question is a waste of time. Test questions are not intentionally tricky. If you think the question is tricky, perhaps you did not fully understand the instructions. Read them again.

Try to answer every question. Most tests have a choice of one answer out of four, so you have a 25% chance of being correct before you start.

When you have finished, review your questions and answers briefly. Do not try to read unintended meanings into them. Correct any errors or missed questions.

Test Types

Most examination questions you will face in certification tests are of the multiple choice type. There may also be a few true or false questions and some fill-in-the-blank-to-complete-the-statement types.

There are several types of multiple choice questions to be considered. First there is the "simple choice" question in which there is only one correct answer among the four choices. Based on your knowledge of the subject, you must be able to select that one correct answer.

Another type is the "best choice" or the "one best answer" type. In this type of question, you must be able to decide which of the answers given is the most correct or the most complete. This requires careful consideration of and discrimination between each of the answers given, to choose the one best answer based on your knowledge of the subject.

A third type of question is the "all except one is correct" type. In this type of question all the answers given are correct except for one which is wrong. You must select the one wrong answer. Make sure you understand that, to answer the question correctly, you must select the one wrong answer.

A fourth type of question is the one in which "comparative statements" are given. A lead statement is given describing some operation or repair procedure. Then two more statements are given which comment on the first statement. This is usually in the form of "Mechanic A says . . . and Mechanic B says . . . ." These statements must be evaluated to determine the correct answer to a question about the statements made by Mechanic A and Mechanic B. The question is usually "Who is correct?"

(a) Mechanic A

(b) Mechanic B

(c) Both Mechanic A and Mechanic B are correct

(d) Neither A nor B

If you understand the type of question you are faced with and you have read the question correctly, then you should be able to come up with the correct answer based on your knowledge of the subject.

PART 5   HOW TO STUDY

Decide on a definite study plan. When you are faced with a repair job in the shop, you follow a definite plan of procedure with the proper tools and a specific allocation of time. Then you proceed to do one thing at a time in the right sequence until the job is successfully completed. The same methods must be applied to study habits in order to be successful. Here are some suggestions that have proved to work well.

1. Establish a definite time period for study. Set aside at least one hour for study, but don't try to overdo it. More than two hours at one sitting is too much.

2. Find a place for study that will allow you to concentrate on what you are doing. Distractions caused by children, the TV or hi-fi, the telephone, or disturbing noise should be avoided.

3. Decide on a definite time of day for your study. You may function best in your studies sometime in the afternoon or early evening, or you may be a morning person. Make sure it is a time during which you are alert and during which there will be minimum interruptions or distractions.

4. Study and learn in small chunks. Like eating an elephant, it must be done one bite at a time; it cannot be swallowed whole. Concentrate on the specific subject matter at hand until you have grasped it fully. When you have learned all the smaller chunks well, the larger concept or subject matter will easily fall into place without gaps or grey areas.

5. Underline key points in your text as you read. This helps you to better remember them and allows you to review material easier and quicker.

6. Take notes during class of key points made by your instructor. Don't try to write down every-

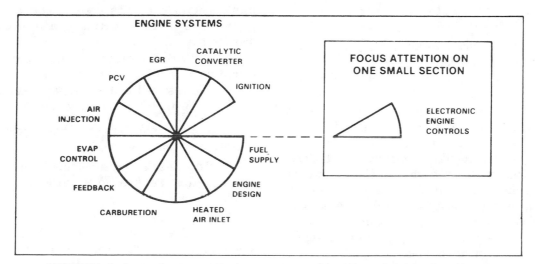

FIGURE I-1. Learn to concentrate on one small section of subject matter at a time. When you have all the individual sections mastered, they will fit together to form a complete unit. All professionals acquire their expertise in this manner. *(Courtesy of Chrysler Corporation)*

thing the instructor says, a few words to remind you of what was said about each point is enough.

7. If you were given a course outline, use it. It is a summary of the subject matter being covered and is very useful in developing a good set of notes.

8. Make sure you understand the diagrams and schematics, such as wiring diagrams and test instrument connections. Don't guess—you must understand the reason why connections are made a certain way.

9. Keep fit physically and mentally. Poor physical health can lower mental ability and efficiency. Be on time for all classes and be prepared to pay attention and participate in class activities, such as discussions and projects. Complete assignments on time.

Good study habits, a healthy body and mind, a keen desire to succeed, and confidence in yourself and your ability are key elements to success.

PART 6   THE AUTOMOTIVE SHOP

Several different types of automotive repair shops or garages are engaged in automotive service. Some of the most common are:

- The service station
- The general repair garage
- The specialized repair shop
- The dealership

The Service Station

Service stations usually consist of an office, a combined display room and reception area, one or more service bays equipped with one or more hoists, and a stockroom.

Service stations are engaged in selling motor fuels, lubricants, tires, batteries, accessories, and light service, such as tire repairs, lubrication services, tune ups, and the like. Some service stations are also equipped with car wash facilities and wheel alignment equipment. Some may perform heavier service, such as valve grinds, clutch repairs, and brake repairs. Many service stations are also equipped with a tow truck to provide emergency road service or to tow in a disabled vehicle.

Service station employees, including mechanics, usually are involved in direct contact with the customer.

The General Repair Garage

This type of garage is usually independently owned and offers all types of automotive repair. It can be a relatively small operation where the technicians must be able to diagnose and repair all types of malfunctions. Others are quite large and employ a larger staff allowing technicians to be more specialized.

This type of garage is usually equipped with all types of equipment used to test, diagnose, overhaul, and recondition most vehicle components.

The Specialized Shop

A number of different types of specialized automotive service shops are engaged in the automotive service industry. These shops restrict themselves to performing a narrow range of services. Among these are the following:

- Tire shops
- Muffler shops
- Tune up shops
- Brake and clutch shops
- Automatic transmission shops
- Wheel alignment and balance shops
- Diagnostic centers

Some speciality shops combine two or more of these specialties; for example, mufflers and brakes, tires, wheel alignment and balance, and other combinations.

The Dealership

Automotive dealerships are there to sell and service the car manufacturer's products. They usually consist of a showroom, offices, a new car sales department, a used car sales department, a service department, a parts department, and an accounting department.

The service department in the larger urban dealership usually includes all types of mechanical repair service as well as body repair. Service department staff usually includes the following:

1. *Service manager* - responsible for the overall operation of the service department.

2. *Service sales* - responsible for customer contact regarding service work and writing up service repair orders.

3. *Control operator* - responsible for allocating work to all service technicians and ensuring a smooth flow of work through the shop.

4. *Shop foreman* - responsible for all phases of work being performed by all service technicians; oversees quality of work and solves problems.

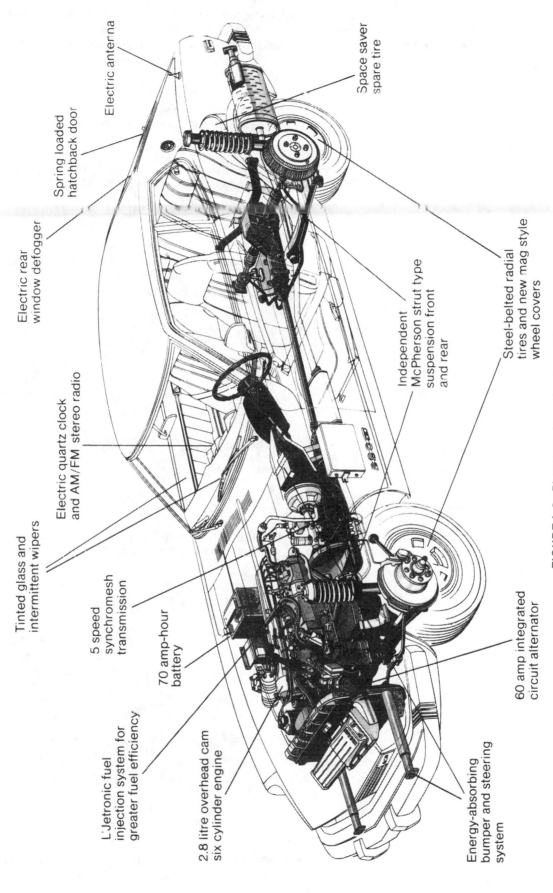

Electric antenna

Spring loaded hatchback door

Electric rear window defogger

Space saver spare tire

Tinted glass and intermittent wipers

Electric quartz clock and AM/FM stereo radio

Independent McPherson strut type suspension front and rear

Steel-belted radial tires and new mag style wheel covers

L'Jetronic fuel injection system for greater fuel efficiency

5 speed synchromesh transmission

70 amp-hour battery

2.8 litre overhead cam six cylinder engine

60 amp integrated circuit alternator

Energy-absorbing bumper and steering system

FIGURE I–2. Phantom view of automobile.

5. *Service technicians* - may perform one or several of the following service functions:

- New car pre-delivery inspection
- Car clean up—inside and out
- Lubrication
- Tires
- Wheel alignment and balance
- Tune up
- Electrical—radio, etc.
- Trim—interior and exterior
- Mechanical—transmissions, engine repair, etc.

PART 7   WORKING CONDITIONS

Automotive shops today usually are modern facilities which provide clean, well-lighted working conditions. Good equipment is provided for the type of service work done by the shop.

Employees often work eight hours a day for five and a half days a week, though this varies somewhat in the different shops. Some shift work may be required.

Most of the larger dealerships provide cafeteria facilities or lunch rooms, showers, and specific types of clothing.

In many of the larger shops, technicians work "flat rate." This means that there is a given time, obtained from a "flat rate manual," allotted to each repair job. If, for example, the flat rate time for a carburetor overhaul is two hours, the technician would be paid for two hours of work for doing that job. This would be so whether the job took more or less than the two hour flat rate time.

Other technicians work on "straight time"—an hourly, weekly, or monthly rate. However, productivity remains a factor in maintaining job security.

The automotive service industry offers many rewarding and challenging career opportunities as well as the opportunity for advancement and a good standard of living.

PART 8   THE AUTOMOBILE

The automobile can be divided into three major sections:

- The body
- The chassis
- The drive train

The body consists of the passenger compartments, the trunk, hood, fenders, grill, and all the external metal and plastic parts. The body may be mounted on a separate frame, or it may be a unitized body which has reinforced frame sections as part of the body.

The chassis consists of the frame, suspension, steering, and wheels.

The drive train consists of the engine, transmis-

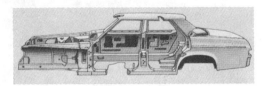

FIGURE I-3. The automobile consists of two major components, the body and the chassis. The chassis includes the drive train and the running gear. This picture shows a typical four-door body assembly.

FIGURE I-4. The running gear includes the wheels, suspension, steering, and braking systems, as well as the frame.

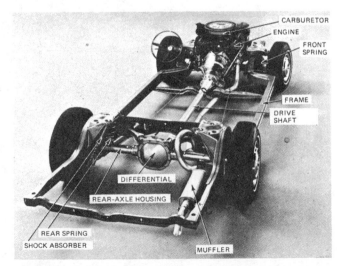

FIGURE I-5. The drive train shows the engine, transmission, drive shaft, differential, and rear axle assemblies.

sion, drive line, and drive axles. The drive train is also known as the power train. This text deals only with the chassis and drive train components, not the body.

Automobiles may be classified as rear wheel drive, front wheel drive, and four wheel drive, depending on which wheels do the actual driving.

Automobiles may be further classified as to engine location and position. They may be of the type with the engine in the front (most common), or the engine may be in the rear. Prototypes produced with the engine approximately in the middle are known as mid-engine vehicles.

Front-engine vehicles may have the engine mounted longitudinally or in a transverse position.

Automobiles are also classified into four approximate size categories: full size, intermediate size, compact, and sub-compact.

Trucks are classified as light duty, medium duty, and heavy duty. Highway transports are known as tractor-trailer units. Heavy duty off-road trucks are used in the mining and construction industries.

SHOP ROUTINE

Chapter 1

Safety

Performance Objectives

After thorough study of this chapter and your school shop or service shop, you should be able to do the following:

1. Recognize and practice safety in selecting and using proper clothing for work in an automotive shop.
2. Follow the required procedures in case of fire in the shop.
3. Use proper ventilation and shop exhaust equipment whenever needed.
4. Follow the first-aid procedures given for the shop in which you are working.
5. Complete the self-check and the test questions with at least 80 percent accuracy.

If you are the type of person who likes a variety of work, you will find it in shop work, where a large number of different service jobs and procedures are carried out. The variety of jobs and procedures, however, requires a high degree of awareness of the importance of safety. Safety is your job, everyone's job.

Safety in the shop includes avoiding injury to yourself and to others working near you. It also includes avoiding damage to vehicles in the shop and damage to shop equipment and parts. The following are some of the factors to consider in practicing shop safety.

PART 1   PERSONAL SAFETY

1. Wear proper clothing. Loose clothing, ties, uncontrolled long hair, rings, etc., can get caught in rotating parts or equipment and cause injury. Wear the kind of shoes that provide protection for your feet; steel-capped work boots with nonskid soles are best. Keep clothing clean.

2. Use protective clothing and equipment where needed. Use rubber gloves and apron as well

FIGURE 1–1. Protective leather gloves should be worn for welding. Rubber gloves protect hands when working with batteries. *(Courtesy of Mac Tools Inc.)*

FIGURE 1–2. Safety goggles shield the eyes from injury. *(Courtesy of Mac Tools Inc.)*

FIGURE 1-3. Face shields protect the face from possible injury resulting from acid, Freon, flying particles from grinding wheels, chipping metal, and the like. *(Courtesy of Mac Tools Inc.)*

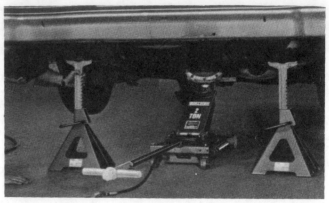

FIGURE 1-5. Always support the car on properly placed jack stands before working under it. *(Courtesy of Walker)*

FIGURE 1-6. Use a creeper for working under a vehicle. *(Courtesy of Mac Tools Inc.)*

as a face mask for handling batteries. Protective goggles or safety glasses are recommended at all times.

3. Keep hands and tools clean to avoid injury to hands and to avoid falling due to slipping when pulling on a wrench.

4. Do not use compressed air to clean your clothes. This can cause dirt particles to be embedded in your skin and cause infection. Do not point the compressed air hose at anyone. Compressed shop air, used for cleaning, should not exceed 30psi.

5. Be careful when using compressed air to blow away dirt from parts. You should not use compressed air to blow dirt from brake parts since cancer-causing asbestos dust may be inhaled as a result.

FIGURE 1-4. Those requiring glasses to correct a visual defect should use glasses with safety lenses. *(Courtesy of Mac Tools Inc.)*

FIGURE 1-7. Dirty shop floors can cause major injury.

6. Do not carry screwdrivers, punches, or other sharp objects in your pockets. You could injure yourself or damage the car you are working on.

7. Never get involved in horseplay or other practical jokes. They can lead to injury.

8. Make sure you use the proper tool for the job and use it the right way. The wrong tool or its incorrect use can damage the part you are working on or cause injury or both.

9. Never work under a car or under anything

FIGURE 1-8. Proper lifting methods are a must to avoid back injury.

FIGURE 1-9. Avoid getting clothing caught in rotating parts such as fans, pulleys, grinders, and drills. Do not stand in the plane of rotating parts that are not shielded.

FIGURE 1-10. Electrical cords and connectors must be in good condition to avoid injury.

else that is not properly supported. Use safety stands properly placed to work under a car. Also, use a creeper.

10. Do not jack a car while someone is under it.

11. Never run a car engine without proper ventilation and adequate means of getting rid of exhaust gases. Exhaust gas contains deadly carbon monoxide. It can and does kill.

12. Keep your work area clean at all times. Your safety and the quality of work you do depend on it.

13. Lifting and carrying should be done properly to avoid injury. Heavy objects should be lifted and moved with the right equipment for the job.

14. Do not stand in the plane of rotating parts such as fans, etc.

15. Never smoke while working on any vehicle.

16. When working with others, note any unsafe practices and report them.

PART 2   SHOP SAFETY

1. Familiarize yourself with the way the shop is laid out. Find out where things are in the shop. You will need to know where the shop manuals are kept in order to obtain specifications and service procedures. Make sure you know the route to the exit in case of fire.

2. Find out whether there are certain stalls that are reserved for special jobs. Abide by these rules.

3. Take note of all the warning signs around the shop. No smoking signs, special instructions for some shop tools and equipment, danger zones, etc., are all there to help the shop run smoothly and safely.

4. Note the location of fire extinguishers. Take time to read their operating instructions and the type of fire they are meant to be used on.

5. Follow local regulations with regard to storing gasoline and other flammable liquids. Gasoline should be stored only in approved containers and locations.

6. Never use gasoline to clean parts. Never pour gasoline into a carburator air horn to start the car.

7. Always immediately wipe up any gasoline that has been spilled.

8. Fuel vapors are highly explosive. If vapors are present in the shop, have the doors open and the

ventilating system turned on to get rid of these dangerous vapors.

9. Repair any fuel leak immediately. The potential fire hazard is very high. The smallest spark can set off an uncontrollable or fatal fire or explosion.

10. Dirty and oily rags should be stored in closed metal containers to avoid catching fire.

11. Keep the shop floor and work benches clean and tidy. Oil on the floor can cause serious personal injury.

12. Do not operate shop tools or equipment that are in unsafe condition. Electrical cords and connectors must be in good condition. Bench grinding wheels and wire brushes should be replaced if defective. Floor jacks and hoist must be in safe operating condition and should not be used above their rated capacity. The same applies to mechanical and hydraulic presses, drills, and drill presses. Draw the attention of your instructor or shop foreman to any unsafe equipment or conditions.

13. Extension cords should not pose a hazard by being strung across walkways.

14. Do not leave jack handles in the down position across the floor. Someone could trip over them.

15. Do not drive cars over electrical cords. This could cause short circuits.

PART 3   FIRST AID

1. Make sure you are aware of the location and contents of the first-aid kit in your shop.

2. Find out if there is a resident nurse in your shop or school, and find out where the nurse's office is.

3. If there are any specific first-aid rules in your school or shop, make sure you are aware of them and follow them. You should be able to locate emergency telephone numbers quickly, such as ambulance, doctor, and police.

4. There should be an eye-wash station in the shop to thoroughly rinse your eye should you get acid or some other irritant into it.

5. Burns should be cooled immediately by rinsing with water and then treating as recommended.

6. If someone is overcome by carbon monoxide, immediately get him or her to fresh air.

7. In case of severe bleeding, try to stop blood loss by applying pressure with clean gauze on or around the wound, and summon medical aid.

8. Do not move someone who may have broken bones unless life is further endangered. Moving a person may cause additional injury. Call for medical assistance.

Safety is the responsibility of everyone. The following is a good procedure to use:

• Study safety regulations
• Set up a safe working area
• Report any unsafe working conditions
• Be safety conscious
• Practice safety on every job

PART 4   SELF-CHECK

1. What type of shoes are best for automotive shop use?

2. Why is adequate ventilation of such critical importance in an automotive shop?

3. Make a list of as many safety rules as you can think of regarding the use of shop tools and equipment.

4. List three safety rules that should be practiced when using power tools.

5. What is the purpose of jack stands?

PART 5   TEST QUESTIONS

Select the one best answer for each question.

1. Automotive shop safety includes:
   (a) avoiding injury to yourself
   (b) avoiding injury to others in the shop
   (c) avoiding injury to vehicles and equipment
   (d) all of the above

2. The type of clothing that should be worn in the automotive shop includes:
   (a) shoes with non-slip soles
   (b) shoes with steel-capped toes
   (c) clothing that is not loose, baggy, or torn
   (d) all of the above

3. Compressed air can be used to:
   (a) blow dirt from clothing
   (b) dry hands after washing
   (c) clean the floor

or the above

(e) none of the above

4. Automobile exhaust gases contain deadly:
   (a) carbon dioxide
   (b) nitric oxides
   (c) carbon monoxide
   (d) hydrocarbon

5. Face shields should be used when working with:
   (a) grinders
   (b) cold chisels
   (c) batteries
   (d) all of the above
   (e) none of the above

(d) all of the above
(e) none of the above

4. Automobile exhaust gases contain deadly:
    (a) carbon dioxide
    (b) nitric oxides
    (c) carbon monoxide
    (d) hydrocarbon

5. Face shields should be used when working with:
    (a) grinders
    (b) cold chisels
    (c) batteries
    (d) all of the above
    (e) none of the above

Chapter 2

Tools and Fasteners

Performance Objectives

Study this chapter and the proper use of the various tools and shop equipment used in the automotive shop. After having had enough opportunity to practice using the tools and equipment in a safe and efficient manner, you should be able to accomplish the following:

1. Select and use the correct hand tools and power equipment in a safe and efficient manner.
2. Select the appropriate shop manual, and locate and use the required information for the job being done.
3. Interpret work order information correctly.
4. Prepare a parts list with all the required information necessary for correct replacement.
5. Select and use the correct type of fastener.
6. Complete the self-check and the test questions with at least 80 percent accuracy.

PART 1 SHOP MANUALS, WORK ORDERS, PARTS LISTS

Shop Manuals

Shop manuals are a necessary part of the automotive service shop. They are needed to obtain the desired specifications and for specific service procedures. Mistakes and comebacks can be almost eliminated by the proper use of the correct shop manual.

Manufacturers' shop manuals are the most reliable source of information. Other shop manuals are

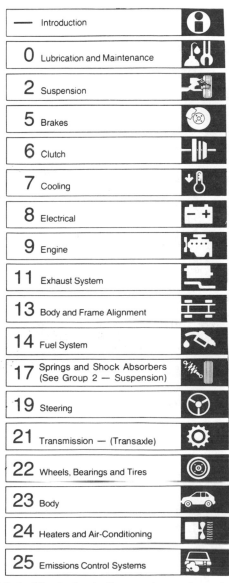

FIGURE 2–1. The index is the road map to a shop manual. It gets you where you want to go for information, specifications, and procedures. This is an example of a shop manual sectional index. It directs you to the appropriate section in the manual.

19

STEERING

CONTENTS

INDEX

FIGURE 2-2. Another index appears at the front of each section in a shop manual as shown here. *(Courtesy of Chrysler Corporation)*

SPECIFICATIONS
MANUAL STEERING GEAR

Fill gear with 0.11—0.14 litre (1/4 pint) of S.A.E. 90 hypoid oil
Apply silicone grease to tie rod bellows groove to prevent rotation of bellows.

TIGHTENING REFERENCE	Newton metres	Foot-Pounds
Clamp and Housing Pad Bolts	23-54	17-25
Tie Rod End Nut	34-70	25-50
Tie Rod End Lock Nut	60-90	45-65

POWER STEERING GEAR

Apply silicone grease to tie rod bellows groove to prevent rotation of bellows.

TIGHTENING REFERENCE	Newton metres	Foot-Pounds
Clamp and Housing Pad Bolts	23-54	17-25
Tie Rod End Nut	34-70	25-50
Tie Rod End Lock Nut	60-90	45-65
Inner Tie Rod	95	70

POWER STEERING PUMP

OUTPUT FLOW
88.3 to 114 ML/S (1.4 to 1.8 GPM)
at 1500 RPM and minimum pressure.

PRESSURE RELIEF
6.20 to 6.90 MPa
(900 to 1000 PSI)

Power Steering Oil Return Hose   LENGTH 254 mm (10 in.)

IF RETURN HOSE IS CHANGED, USE ONLY HYPALON MATERIAL, MOPAR PART NUMBER 3879925 OR EQUIVALENT.

POWER STEERING HOSES

	Newton metres	Foot-Pounds
Pressure Hose Tube Nuts (Both Ends)	20	15
Return Tube Nut	20	15
Pressure Hose Locating Bracket At Pump	40	30
Pressure Hose Locating Bracket At Crossmember	12	9
Return Tube Locating Bracket At Gear	28	21

POWER STEERING PUMP

	Newton metres	Foot-Pounds
Discharge Fitting	55	40
Relief Valve Ball Seat	6	4
Bracket Mounting Fasteners:		
3/8—16 Stud	48	35
3/8—16 Bolt and Nuts	40	30
M8 Bolts	28	21

FIGURE 2-3. Part of the specifications from a recent shop manual. *(Courtesy of Chrysler Corporation)*

also available that often provide helpful hints and suggestions.

Figure 2–1 shows the index of three different sections in a manual. This directs the reader to the desired section, where there is another index (Figure 2–2). This index leads to the particular area for which information is being sought, for example, the manual and power steering gear specifications (Figure 2–3).

Work Orders

The sample work order illustrated in Figure 2–4 has room for the following information:

- Place of business
- Name of customer
- Date of work order
- Work order number
- Vehicle identification
- Type of service required
- Customer's signature
- List of parts used and their cost
- Labor costs
- Tax

- Responsibilities and liabilities of place of business and of customer

The work order serves as a means of communication between the various parties involved in the repair procedure, such as the service writer, customer, technician, shop foreman, parts department, cashier, and accounting department. The technician usually gets the hard copy, on which he records the time used to repair the vehicle and the parts required. The original copy is given to the customer on receipt of payment, and the remaining copies stay with the place of business for its records.

Parts Lists

Whether the hard copy of the work order is used for a parts list or a separate requisition is used, the parts department requires at least the following information to be able to provide the correct parts for the unit being serviced: vehicle make, year, and model must be provided in every case.

Further information is included depending on which component of the vehicle is being serviced. For example:

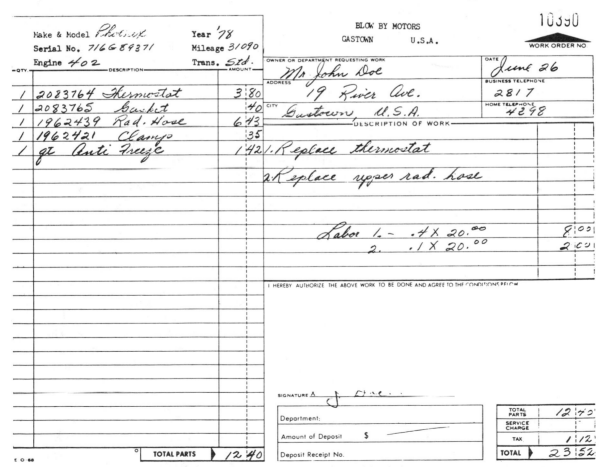

FIGURE 2–4. Sample copy of a work order or repair order.

- Suspension—standard or heavy duty.
- Steering—manual or power.
- Brakes—standard or power, drum diameter, shoe width, wheel cylinder or caliper piston diameter.
- Rear axle—standard or traction type, ratio.
- Engine: displacement, engine number, two- or four-barrel carburetor, single or dual exhaust, with or without air conditioning.
- Carburetor—make, model, number of barrels.
- Transmission—type (standard or automatic transmission) number, and model.
- Clutch—diameter, number of springs in pressure plate.

Naturally, the correct names of the parts required must be used when ordering or requisitioning parts. When the correct name is not known, it usually becomes quite difficult to communicate with the parts department. Learning the correct name for each part is one of the first things a prospective technician should do if he expects to function in the service industry.

PART 2   HAND TOOLS

The technician's job is made easier by a good selection of quality tools and equipment. The quality and speed of work are also increased. Fast and efficient work is necessary to satisfy the customer and the employer. An efficient, productive technician also experiences greater job satisfaction and earns more money as a result. The technician should not jeopardize his ability by selecting tools that are inadequate or of poor quality. Good tools are easier to keep clean and last longer than tools of inferior quality.

Good tools deserve good care. Select a good roll cabinet and a good tool box to properly store your tools. They represent a fairly large investment and should be treated accordingly. Measuring instruments and other precision tools require extra care in handling and storage to prevent damage. Keeping your tools clean and orderly is time well spent. It increases your speed and efficiency on each job you do.

Wrenches

Open end, box end, combination, and Allen wrenches are used to turn bolts, nuts, and screws. The open end wrench holds the nut or bolt only on two flat sides. They slip or round off the nut more readily

FIGURE 2–5. Typical roll cabinet with tool box on top providing good storage, easy access, and portability of tools. *(Courtesy of Mac Tools Inc.)*

than do box end wrenches. It is better to use box end wrenches wherever possible. Various offsets are available to make it easier to get at tight places. Both six- and twelve-point box end wrenches are available.

Sizes range from 3/8 to $1\frac{1}{4}$ inches in the average set and in 1/16-inch steps. Ignition wrench sets come in a smaller range of sizes. Metric wrench sets range from 6 to 32 millimeters. Allen wrench sizes generally range from 2 to 20 millimeters and from 1/8 to 7/16 inch. Other sizes are also available.

Ratcheting box end wrenches are very handy and come in similar size ranges as open end and box end wrenches. For tubing fittings, flare nut wrenches should be used rather than open end wrenches. The technician should also have an adjustable wrench, but this wrench should not be used in place of the proper open end or box end wrench.

Sockets and Drives

The well-equipped automotive technician should have a 1/4-inch drive socket set, a 3/8-inch drive set, and a 1/2- inch drive set with standard and metric

FIGURE 2-6. Example of a well-stocked roll cabinet and tool box for the professional technician. Can you name all the items shown? *(Courtesy of Proto Canada, Div. Ingersoll-Rand Canada Inc.)*

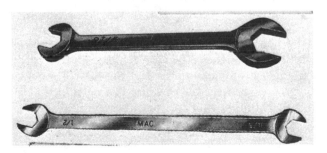

FIGURE 2-7. Heavy open-end wrench (above) and thinner open-end wrench (below). *(Courtesy of Mac Tools Inc.)*

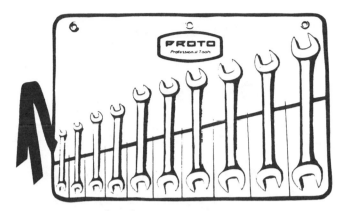

FIGURE 2-8. Open-end wrench set of various sizes in storage pouch. *(Courtesy of Proto Canada, Div. Ingersoll-Rand Canada Inc.)*

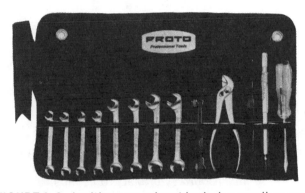

FIGURE 2-9. Ignition wrench set includes smaller open-end wrenches and small pliers. *(Courtesy of Proto Canada, Div. Ingersoll-Rand Canada Inc.)*

FIGURE 2-10. Box-end wrenches are available in many sizes in both 6- and 12-point styles. Various offset styles are also available. *(Courtesy of Mac Tools Inc.)*

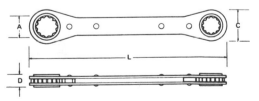

FIGURE 2-11. Ratcheting box wrenches can be a handy addition to any tool kit. *(Courtesy of Mac Tools Inc.)*

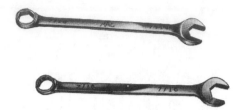

FIGURE 2-12. Combination wrenches have an open-end wrench on one end and a box end on the other.

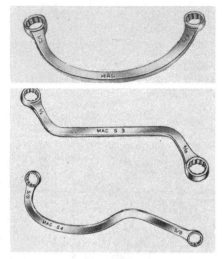

FIGURE 2-13. A number of special wrenches of various shapes for hard-to-get-at places, such as manifolds, distributors, front end, and starters, are available and often essential. *(Courtesy of Mac Tools Inc.)*

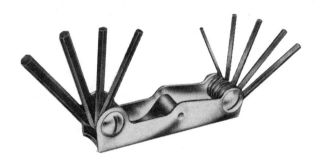

FIGURE 2-14. Hex or Allen wrenches are a must in the technician's tool kit.

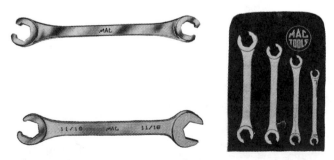

FIGURE 2-15. Flare nut or tubing wrenches should be used on tubing fittings to avoid rounding off the fittings.

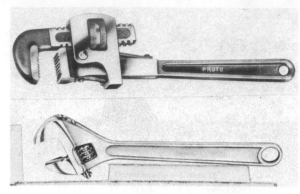

FIGURE 2-16. The adjustable wrench and the pipe wrench are necessary parts of a tool kit but should not be used in place of wrenches or sockets. *(Courtesy of Proto Canada, Div. Ingersoll-Rand Canada Inc.)*

sockets. Socket wrenches are fast and convenient to use. Both six- and twelve-point sockets should be included in the well-equipped tool kit, as well as deep sockets and flex sockets. Socket sizes are similar to wrench sizes and metric sizes. Other drive sizes such as 3/4 or 1 inch are used for heavy duty work.

Socket drives include universal joints, extensions of different lengths, ratchets, flex handles, T-handles, and speed handles. Drive sizes are available, as mentioned above. Drive adapters are also available to increase or reduce drive sizes to fit available sockets.

A number of other socket attachments are available and are handy to have. Both electric and air-operated impact wrenches are used to drive sockets to speed up the work; however, the sockets used are of a special design to withstand the continuous impacts of the driver.

Torque Wrenches

To tighten a bolt or nut to specifications, it is necessary to use a torque wrench. If a bolt or nut is overtightened, it puts excessive strain on the parts and damages the bolt or nut as well. On the other hand, if not tightened enough the unit may come apart during use. Torque can be defined as twisting force. A 1-pound pull on a 1-foot wrench (center of bolt to point of pull) equals 1 pound-foot. Force times distance equals torque ($F \times D = T$) or 1 pound $\times$ 1 foot = 1 pound-foot of torque.

When an adapter is used on a torque wrench, this increases the effective length of the torque wrench thereby changing the actual torque from that which is read on the dial. To calculate actual torque, the following formula may be used:

A = Torque reading on dial
B = Length of torque wrench without adapter
C = Length of adapter

$$\frac{A \times B + C}{B} = \text{Actual torque}$$

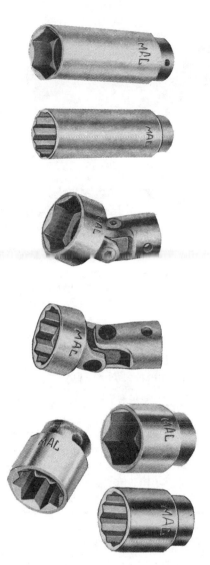

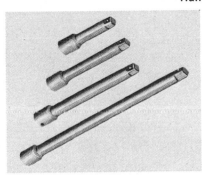

FIGURE 2-19. Drive extensions allow access to hard-to-get-at bolts and nuts. Extensions are available in various lengths. *(Courtesy of Mac Tools Inc.)*

meters. This system is also currently being used by domestic manufacturers.

Use the appropriate type of torque wrench for the specifications given. If specifications are given in centimeter-kilograms, then a torque wrench with a centimeter-kilogram scale should be used. If torque values stated do not match the values on your torque wrench, use the metric conversion chart in the Appendix to convert the values given.

FIGURE 2-17. Standard, flex, and deep sockets are available in both 6- and 12-point types, as well as 8 point. *(Courtesy of Mac Tools Inc.)*

Other values for force are used, such as kilograms (kiloponds) or newtons. In this case, the values used for distance are centimeter and meter. The amount of torque, depending on the type of torque wrench used, was measured in inch-pounds or foot-pounds for domestic cars in the past. For imports, the centimeter-kilogram and meter-kilogram torque values are used. Another term for kilogram is kilopond when used in connection with torque values. The current SI torque values are given in newton-

FIGURE 2-18. A ratchet allows turning the fastener without repeated removal of the wrench, thereby speeding up the work. Common drive sizes are ¼, ⅜, ½, and ¾ inch. *(Courtesy of Mac Tools Inc.)*

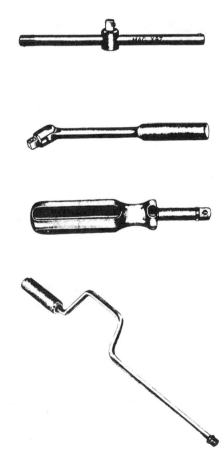

FIGURE 2-20. Other socket drives include (from top to bottom) T bar handle, flex handle, spinner, and speed handle.

FIGURE 2-21. A universal joint converts the standard socket drive to a flex drive for hard-to-get-at places.

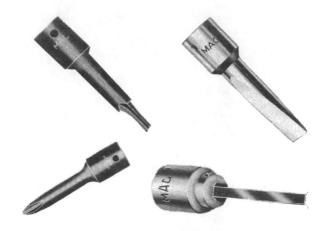

FIGURE 2-24. Other socket attachments include a standard screwdriver tip, a Phillips screwdriver, clutch screwdriver, and hex wrench. *(Courtesy of Mac Tools Inc.)*

Abbreviations for the various torque values given are as follows:

- Pound-inches: lb-in
- Pound-feet: lb-ft
- Centimeter kilograms: cm kg or cm kp

- Meter kilograms: m kg or m kp
- Newton meters: N • m

Screwdrivers

Screwdrivers are probably abused more than any other tool. Use them only for the purpose for which they were intended. There is no all-purpose screwdriver. Use the right type and size of screwdriver for the job. Slotted screws require flat-blade screwdrivers. Select a screwdriver with a tip that is as wide as the screw slot is long.

Use the correct size of Phillips, Reed and Prince,

FIGURE 2-22. Drive size adapters convert socket drives up or down in size. Care must be exercised when using a large driver on a small socket. Breakage can result. *(Courtesy of Mac Tools Inc.)*

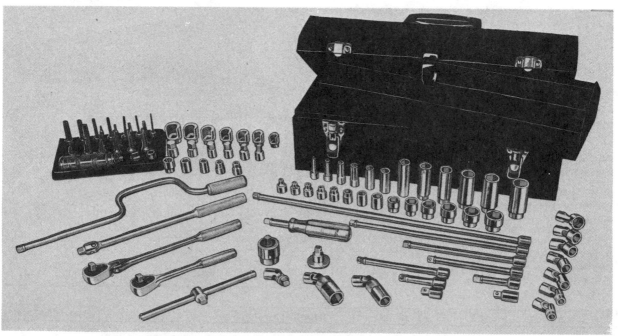

FIGURE 2-23. A complete ⅜-inch drive socket set including a swivel head ratchet and other special attachments.

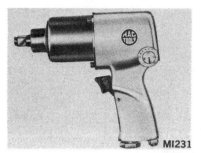

FIGURE 2-25. Impact tools speed the technician's work. Both air-operated (top) and electric impact tools (bottom) are available. *(Courtesy of Mac Tools Inc.)*

FIGURE 2-26. Special sockets such as these should be used with impact tools. They are able to withstand the heavier use and continuous impacts. *(Courtesy of Mac Tools Inc.)*

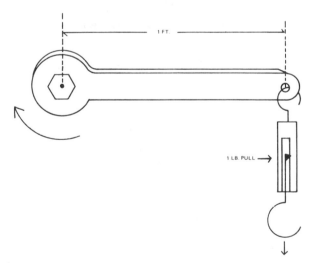

FIGURE 2-27. Torque is twisting force. Amount of torque is calculated by multiplying force times distance. $F \times D = T$.

FIGURE 2-28. The dial-type torque wrench is available in various drive sizes. Dials are read directly and must be closely observed to torque fasteners correctly.

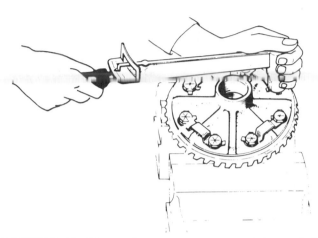

FIGURE 2-29. The scale-type torque wrench is read directly, just as the dial type. A feelable-audible click attachment is provided on some models that signals when predetermined-preset torque has been reached.

FIGURE 2-30. Another click-type torque wrench has a micrometer-type adjustment. There is no direct reading scale. Desired torque must be set on the micrometer adjustment. Preset torque is reached when the wrench clicks. *(Courtesy of Mac Tools Inc.)*

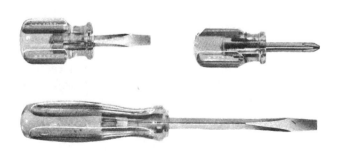

FIGURE 2-31. Common screwdriver types. The square socket type is also known as the Robertson screwdriver.

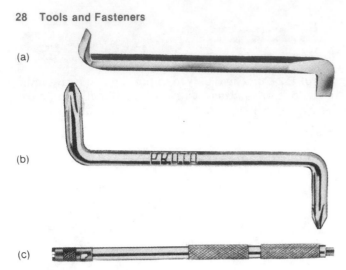

(a)

(b)

(c)

FIGURE 2-32. (A) Offset tip, (B) Phillips screwdrivers, (C) screw-holding screwdriver for starting screws. *(Courtesy of Proto Canada, Div. Ingersoll-Rand Canada Inc.)*

Robertson, or clutch-type screwdriver. Never make do with the wrong size.

Pliers

There are two groups of pliers. One is used for gripping and the other for cutting. Diagonal cutting pliers are sometimes called side-cutting pliers or side cutters. Gripping pliers should not be used in place of wrenches or sockets since this damages nuts and bolts. Do not grip machined or hardened surface parts with pliers; it will damage the surface.

Hammers

Ball-peen hammers and soft hammers are the type used by automotive technicians. Soft hammers such as plastic, rawhide, lead, or brass types are used on easily damaged surfaces.

A hammer should be held at the end of the handle. The hammer should land flat on the surface being struck.

Handles should be kept secure in the hammer head to avoid injury and damage. Select the right size (weight) of hammer for the job.

Punches

Pins and rivets are removed with punches. A tapered starting punch is used to start rivet removal after the rivet head has been chiseled or ground off. The rivet is then driven out the rest of the way with the pin punch. A long tapered punch is used for aligning parts. A center punch is used to mark parts before disassembly and to mark the spot where a hole is to be drilled.

Punches should be kept in good condition. Do not allow mushrooming to take place.

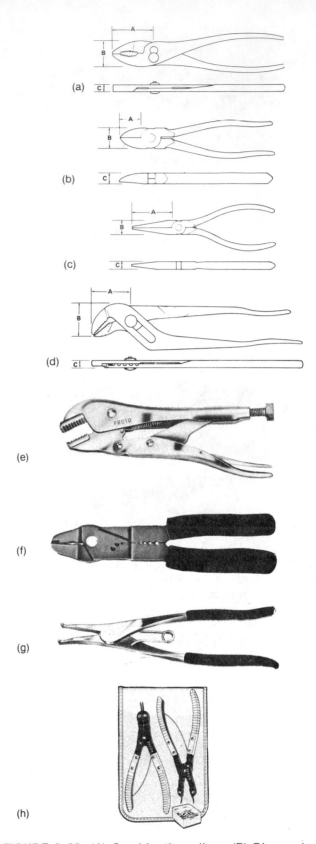

(a)

(b)

(c)

(d)

(e)

(f)

(g)

(h)

FIGURE 2-33. (A) Combination pliers. (B) Diagonal or side cutting pliers. (C) Needle-nose pliers. (D) Channel lock pliers. (E) Lock grip pliers. (F) Wire cutting and stripping tool. (G) External snap ring pliers. (H) Lock ring plier set with interchangeable tips.

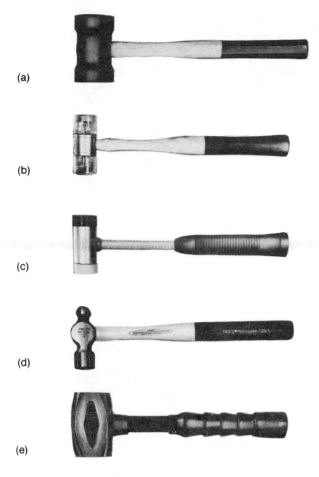

FIGURE 2-34. (A) Rubber mallet. (B) Plastic-faced hammer. (C) Rubber- or plastic-faced hammer. (D) Ball-peen hammer. (E) Sledge hammer. *(Courtesy of Proto Canada, Div. Ingersoll-Rand Canada Inc.)*

Chisels

Chisels are used to cut rivet heads and other metal. A chisel holder can be used for heavy work. Chisels should be kept sharp. Sharpen at approximately a 60° included angle.

Any sign of mushrooming should be ground off. Use safety goggles or a face mask when using a chisel.

Files

Files are cutting tools used to remove metal, to smooth metal surfaces, etc. Many types of files are available for different jobs, with different sizes, shapes, and coarse or fine cutting edges. Size is determined as shown in Figure 2-40, which also shows some different shapes. The range of coarseness in order from coarse to fine is rough, coarse, bastard, second cut, and dead smooth. Never use a file without a handle. Do not use a file as a pry. Files are brittle and break easily.

Hacksaws

A hacksaw consists of an adjustable frame with a handle and a replaceable hacksaw blade. Blades are commonly available in 10- and 12-inch lengths. The coarseness of the cutting teeth is stated in number of teeth per inch, usually 14, 18, 24, or 32 teeth per inch. The finer blades are used for materials of thin cross section. Select a blade for the job that will have at least two teeth cutting at all times.

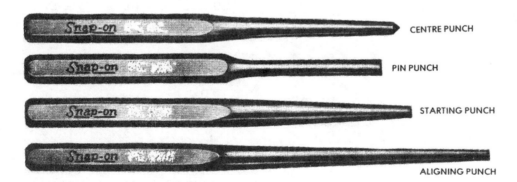

CENTRE PUNCH

PIN PUNCH

STARTING PUNCH

ALIGNING PUNCH

FIGURE 2-35. Common types of punches used by automotive technicians. *(Courtesy of Snap-on Tools Corporation)*

FIGURE 2-36. Punch or chisel holder avoids injury to hands in heavy work.

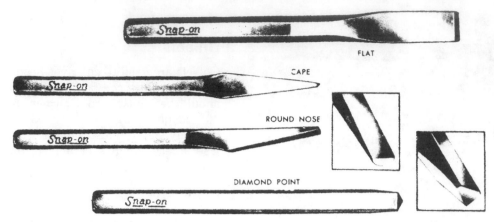

FLAT

CAPE

ROUND NOSE

DIAMOND POINT

FIGURE 2-37. Common chisel types that should be included in the technician's tool kit. *(Courtesy of Snap-on Tools Corporation)*

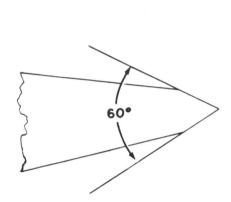

60°

FIGURE 2-38. Chisel sharpening angle.

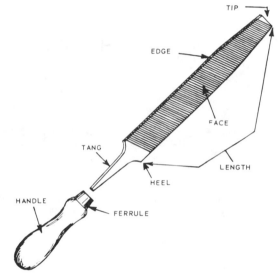

TIP

EDGE

FACE

TANG

LENGTH

HEEL

HANDLE

FERRULE

FIGURE 2-40. Parts of a file. Size is determined by length.

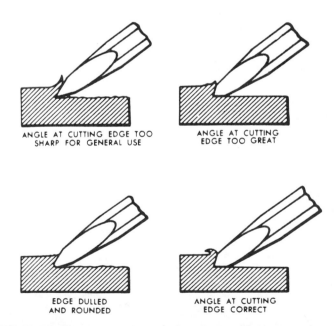

ANGLE AT CUTTING EDGE TOO SHARP FOR GENERAL USE

ANGLE AT CUTTING EDGE TOO GREAT

EDGE DULLED AND ROUNDED

ANGLE AT CUTTING EDGE CORRECT

FIGURE 2-39. Incorrect and correctly sharpened chisel angles. *(Courtesy of Ford Motor Co. of Canada Ltd.)*

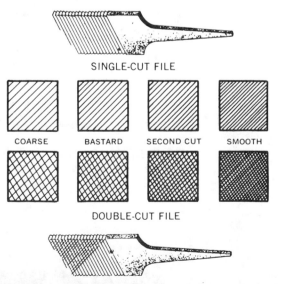

SINGLE-CUT FILE

COARSE   BASTARD   SECOND CUT   SMOOTH

DOUBLE-CUT FILE

FIGURE 2-41. Coarse to fine files, left to right. Single-cut (upper) and double-cut (lower) file types.

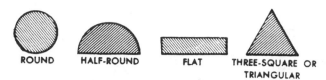

ROUND   HALF-ROUND   FLAT   THREE-SQUARE OR
                                      TRIANGULAR

FIGURE 2-42. Cross-sectional shapes of files *(Courtesy of Ford Motor Co. of Canada Ltd.)*

FIGURE 2-43. Adjustable frame hack saw.

Apply light pressure on the forward stroke and release the pressure on the return stroke. When replacing a hacksaw blade, install it with the teeth pointing away from the handle.

Cleaning Tools

Hand-held scrapers are used to scrape gasket or other material from flat surfaces. This should be followed by a light sanding.

The wire brush is used to clean rough surfaces. A soft bristle brush is used to help clean parts being

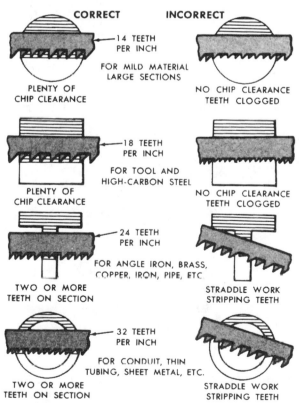

FIGURE 2-44. Correct and incorrect use of different hack saw blades. *(Courtesy of Ford Motor Co. of Canada Ltd.)*

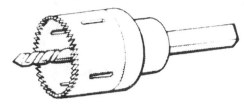

FIGURE 2-45. Power-driven hole saw. *(Courtesy of Ford Motor Co. of Canada Ltd.)*

(a)

(b)

FIGURE 2-46. Parts cleaning scrapers: (A) for irregular surfaces; (B) for flat surfaces. *(Courtesy of Proto Canada, Div. Ingersoll-Rand Canada, Inc.)*

washed in solvent. Rotary wire carbon brushes are used to remove carbon from combustion chambers and the like.

Tubing Tools

Steel and copper tubing should be cut with a tubing cutter. Avoid applying two much pressure during cutting. This can collapse the tube. Low-pressure lines need only a single flare, whereas brake lines require double-lap flaring.

After cutting, ream the tubing and then flare as required. The reamer is usually part of the tubing

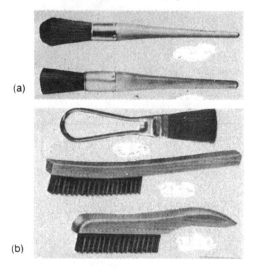

(a)

(b)

FIGURE 2-47. (A) Brushes for cleaning parts in solvent; (B) Wire brushes. *(Courtesy of Proto Canada, Div. Ingersoll-Rand Canada, Inc.)*

FIGURE 2-48. Power-driven rotary wire brushes. *(Courtesy of Proto Canada, Div. Ingersoll-Rand Canada, Inc.)*

FIGURE 2-49. Flaring tool kit required to flare tubular lines. *(Courtesy of Proto Canada, Div. Ingersoll-Rand Canada, Inc.)*

FIGURE 2-50. Tubing cutter with reamer attached. *(Courtesy of Proto Canada, Div. Ingersoll-Rand Canada, Inc.)*

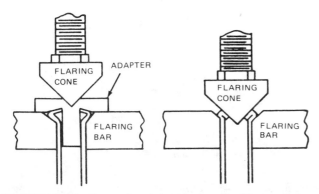

FIGURE 2-51. Example of double-lap flaring procedure required for high-pressure lines such as brake lines.

cutter. Make sure there are no metal chips left in the tubing.

Threading Tools

Tools used for cutting threads are called taps and dies. Taps are used to cut inside threads and dies for outside threads. The most common thread types are (1) coarse, known as UNC, NC, or Unified National Coarse, (2) fine, known as UNF, NF, or Unified National Fine, and (3) extra fine, known as UNEF, NEF, or Unified National Extra Fine. In ad-

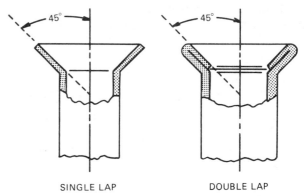

SINGLE LAP   DOUBLE LAP

FIGURE 2-52. Completed single-lap flare for low-pressure lines and double-lap flare for high-pressure lines.

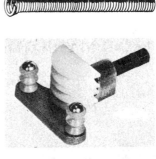

FIGURE 2-53. Two types of tubing benders. Tubing benders must be used when bending tubing to avoid collapsing or kinking of tubing. A collapsed tube reduces flow. *(Courtesy of Proto Canada, Div. Ingersoll-Rand Canada, Inc.)*

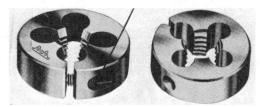

FIGURE 2-54. Adjustable round dies for threading bolts and studs.

dition, there are machine-thread taps and dies and metric taps and dies.

Always make sure that the correct taps and dies are being used to fit the fastener threads. Mistakes can be costly and time consuming. The taper tap is used to thread a hole through a piece of metal. The bottoming tap is used to thread a hole that does not go all the way through. In this case the taper tap should be used first, followed by the bottoming tap to complete the job. The plug tap is used to thread a hole partway through for a plug. To ensure that smooth, undamaged threads are produced, use a good lubricant and frequently back up the threading tool to remove metal chips. Chamfer rods or other round stock to be threaded. This makes it easier to start the die.

Drills and Reamers

Drills used by automotive technicians are known as twist drills. Drill sizes or diameters are identified in five ways: by number, by letter, in fractions, in decimals, and in millimeters. Refer to the Appendix for cross reference.

Fractional sizes range from 1/64 inch and up in 1/64-inch steps. There are 80 numbered sizes from 0.0135 to 0.228 inch. Sizes identified by letter range from 0.234 to 0.413 inch. Metric drill sizes range from less than 1 millimeter and up.

The point to be drilled should first be marked with a center punch. This prevents the drill from wandering. Drill speed varies with drill size; in general, the larger the drill, the slower the drill speed should be. The type of material being drilled also affects drill speed.

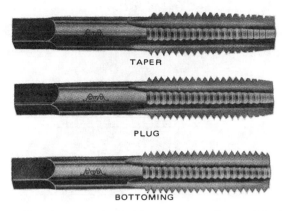

FIGURE 2-56. Three types of taps for threading holes: taper tap for threading right through a hole, plug tap to thread holes for plugs such as drain and fill plug holes, bottoming tap for threading holes that do not go all the way through.

A good drilling lubricant should be used on the material being drilled. High-speed carbon drills should be used on harder metals.

Reamers are used to produce a smooth, perfectly round hole. First use a drill 1/64 inch smaller than the desired finished size; then finish by reaming. Turn the reamer slowly and only in a forward direction until the desired size is reached.

Screw Extractors

Several methods are used to remove broken screws or studs. If the stud is not very tight, it can sometimes be removed by turning it with a center punch and hammer. If enough of the stud extends above the surface, saw a slot in it and turn it out with a screwdriver. Another method is to drill the stud in the exact center with a drill that leaves only a thin shell of the stud in the hole. Then turn the extractor into the hole in a counterclockwise direction. Penetrating oil helps to loosen the threads. Be careful

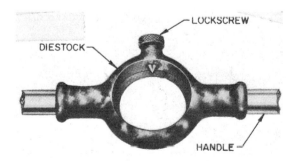

FIGURE 2-55. Die holder required to use dies.

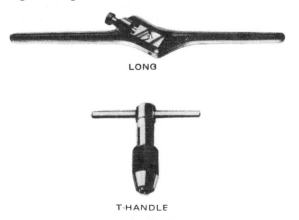

FIGURE 2-57. Handle types for taps.

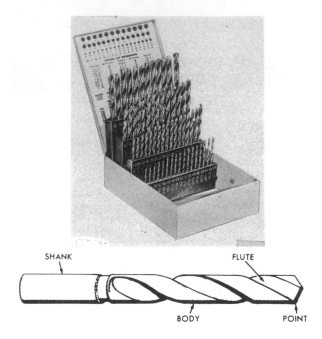

FIGURE 2-58. A good drill index showing drill sizes and a good selection of drill bits. *(Courtesy of Mac Tools Inc.)*

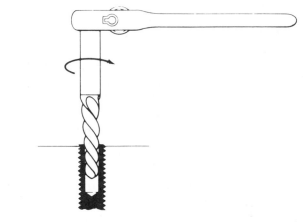

SHANK FLUTE BODY POINT

FIGURE 2-59. Parts of a drill bit.

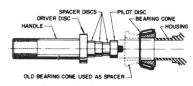

FIGURE 2-60. Using a screw extractor to remove a broken stud after it has been properly drilled.

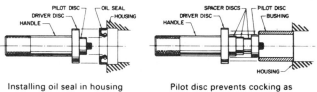

PILOT DISC, OIL SEAL	SPACER DISCS, PILOT DISC	SPACER DISC, PILOT DISC	SPACER DISCS, PILOT DISC
DRIVER DISC HOUSING	DRIVER DISC BUSHING	DRIVER DISC BEARING CUP	DRIVER DISC BEARING CONE
HANDLE	HANDLE	HANDLE	HANDLE HOUSING
	HOUSING	HOUSING	OLD BEARING CONE USED AS SPACER
Installing oil seal in housing is easily accomplished here.	Pilot disc prevents cocking as bushing is installed with tool.	Bearing cup driven into housing. Alignment is maintained.	Here, a bearing cone is being installed on a shaft correctly.

FIGURE 2-61. A universal bushing, bearing, and seal tool kit for removing and installing bushings, bearings, and seals. A variety of disc sizes and combinations can be used for different jobs as illustrated. *(Courtesy of Owatonna Tool Company)*

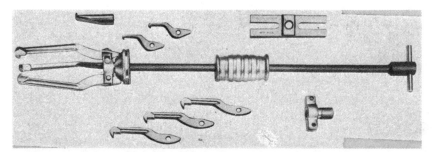

FIGURE 2-62. A slide hammer puller kit with attachments. Inside and outside jaws are interchangeable. *(Courtesy of Owatonna Tool Company)*

FIGURE 2-63. A long-handle, flex-head magnet for retrieving parts.

not to break the screw extractor in the hole. It is extremely hard and cannot be drilled out.

Bushing and Seal Tools

There are many different types of bushing and seal drivers and pullers. Some automotive jobs require very special types of pullers or drivers. Pullers are either of the threaded type or the slide hammer type. Care must be exercised in selecting the correct type for the job. Bushings and seals are very easily damaged if an improper tool or method is used. Refer to the tool maker's instructions and the shop manual for specific information.

Miscellaneous Tools

A great variety of miscellaneous tools is available to the automotive service industry. Many such tools can lighten and speed up the task of the technician.

A magnetic retrieving tool is very handy to have. A stethoscope helps to localize and identify abnormal knocks and other noises in a vehicle. Essential miscellaneous tools include extension lights and cords, a good creeper, and fender covers.

A good technician should be aware of any new developments in tools and equipment that will improve the quality and productivity of his work.

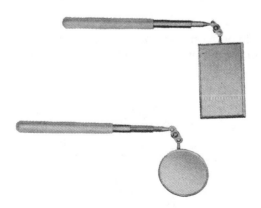

FIGURE 2-64. Mirrors with flex heads and long handles allow the technician to look at otherwise inaccessible places.

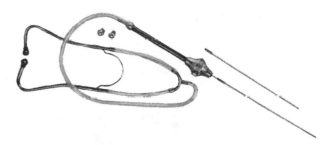

FIGURE 2-65. The stethoscope is used to determine the exact location of knocks and other abnormal noises.

PART 3   SOLDERING TOOLS

The technician may be required to solder such items as radiators and wiring connections. To do a good job of soldering, the surfaces must be smooth and absolutely clean. A good soldering iron of the proper size should be used: heavier irons for heavier work, a soldering gun for electrical work, etc. The soldering iron should be thoroughly cleaned and tinned (coated with solder). Solder is available in bar or wire form. The correct flux must also be used. Rosin flux must be used for electrical work to prevent corrosion. Acid flux is used on other work. Acid-core and rosin-core wire solder are most frequently used.

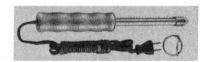

FIGURE 2-66. Electric soldering iron. *(Courtesy of Snap-on Tools Corporation)*

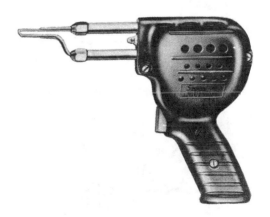

FIGURE 2-67. Electric soldering gun used for soldering electrical connections. *(Courtesy of Snap-on Tools Corporation)*

BAR

FIGURE 2-68. Bar- and wire-type solder.

Soldering irons should be placed in holders during heating and cooling.

PART 4   MEASURING TOOLS

All measuring tools should be treated as precision instruments. They should be properly used, cared for, and stored. Tools provided with special storage cases should be put back in the case when no longer being used. Be careful not to drop precision tools. Do not have them lying around among or under other tools. Precision surfaces, such as straight edges, micrometer anvils, and caliper jaws, should not be marred, scratched, or dented. The accuracy of measuring instruments should be checked if any doubt exists. They can be checked against other tools known to be accurate. Gauge blocks for micrometers determine micrometer accuracy. If no means of checking are available in the shop, they should be sent out to be checked.

Feeler Gauges

Feeler gauges are precision measuring tools used to measure small clearances. Various blade lengths are available. Flat feeler gauges have their thickness marked in thousandths of an inch or in millimeters or both. Nonmagnetic feeler gauges are used for

FIGURE 2-69. Standard English feeler gauge with ten blades from 0.002 to 0.015 inch. (Courtesy of Mac Tools Inc.)

FIGURE 2-70. Go-no-go gauge with stepped feeler blades.

checking clearances where magnetic force exists. Stepped feeler gauges have the tip of the blade two thousandths of an inch thinner than the rest of the blade. These are used for "go-no go" quick measurements. Wire feeler gauges are used to measure spark-plug gaps.

Never bend, twist, force, or wedge feeler gauges since this destroys their accuracy. Wipe blades clean with an oily cloth to prevent rust.

Calipers

Inside and outside calipers are useful in measuring to an accuracy of approximately 1/100 inch. Vernier calipers measure inside and outside dimensions. English, metric, and combination types are available. English vernier calipers measure to an accuracy of 0.001 inch, while metric calipers measure to

FIGURE 2-71. Nonmagnetic feeler gauge with brass blades in both English and metric size identification for electronic ignition distributors. (Courtesy of Mac Tools Inc.)

FIGURE 2-72. Round spark-plug gap gauge with wire-type gauges and gap adjuster. (Courtesy of Mac Tools Inc.)

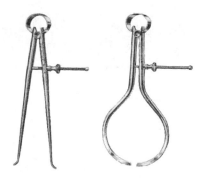

FIGURE 2-73. Inside and outside calipers. *(Courtesy of The L.S. Starrett Company)*

an accuracy of 0.02 millimeters. Most vernier calipers also have a depth measuring rod attached.

Straight Edges

Straight edges are used to measure surface irregularities. A feeler gauge is needed to determine the amount of warpage shown by the straight edge. Cylinder heads, valve bodies, and other machined surfaces are checked with a straight edge.

Micrometers

Outside micrometers are used to measure the size of parts, such as diameter and thickness. The size of a micrometer is determined by the distance between the face of the anvil and the face of the spindle when the micrometer is adjusted to its minimum and maximum adjustments. A 1- to 2-inch micrometer

would not be able to measure anything less than 1 inch or anything more than 2 inches. A 25- to 50-millimeter micrometer would not be able to measure anything less than 25 millimeters or anything more than 50 millimeters.

Digital micrometers measure inside and outside diameters, are available in sizes and types similar to conventional micrometers, and are read directly.

English Micrometer Scale

Each division on the sleeve represents 0.025 or 25/1000 inch. From 0 to 1 represents four such divisions (4 × 0.025 inch) or 0.100 inch (100/1000 inch). Each division on the thimble represents 0.001 or 1/1000 inch. There are 25 such divisions on the thimble. Therefore, one turn of the thimble moves the spindle 0.025 or 25/1000 inch. To read the micrometer in thousandths, multiply the number of divisions visible on the sleeve by 0.025, then add the number of thousandths indicated by the line on the thimble that coincides with the long reading line on the sleeve.

Example: Refer to Figure 2-76.

The 1 line on sleeve is visible representing	0.100
There are three additional lines visible, each representing 0.025 inch	0.075
Line 3 on the thimble coincides with the reading line on the sleeve, each line representing 0.001 inch	0.003
The micrometer reading is	0.178 inch

Metric Micrometer Scale

One revolution of the thimble advances the spindle toward or away from the anvil 0.5 millimeter distance.

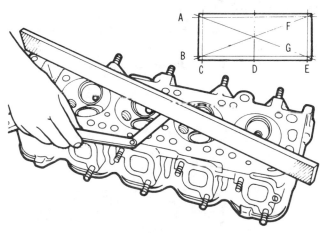

FIGURE 2-74. The straight edge is used to determine whether a flat surface is warped. Here it is used with a feeler gauge to check the amount of head warpage. If head is warped beyond manufacturer's specifications, it must be machined or ground to restore the surface.

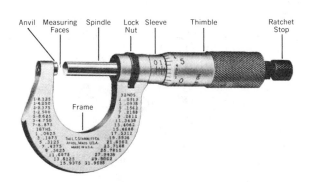

FIGURE 2-75. Outside micrometer with major parts identified. A piece of work is measured by placing it between the anvil and the spindle faces and turning the spindle by means of the thimble until both faces contact the work. The micrometer reading is then taken. *(Courtesy of The L.S. Starrett Company)*

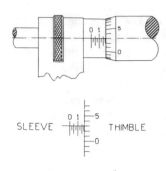

SLEEVE ⊢ THIMBLE

READING .178"

FIGURE 2-76. Micrometer reading (English scale).

The reading line on the sleeve is graduated in millimeters (1.0 millimeter) from 0 to 25. Each millimeter is also divided in half (0.5 millimeter). It requires two revolutions of the thimble to advance the spindle 1.0 millimeter. The beveled edge of the thimble is graduated in 50 divisions from 0 to 50. One revolution of the thimble moves the spindle 0.5 millimeter. Each thimble graduation equals 1/50 of 0.5 millimeter or 0.01 millimeter.

To read the micrometer, add the number of millimeters and half-millimeters visible on the sleeve to

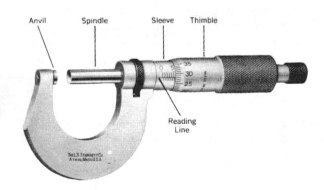

FIGURE 2-77. The metric micrometer is similar in appearance to the English micrometer. *(Courtesy of The L.S. Starrett Company)*

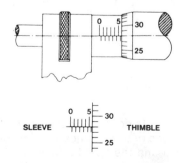

SLEEVE   THIMBLE

Reading 5.78 mm

FIGURE 2-78. Metric micrometer scale.

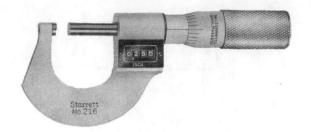

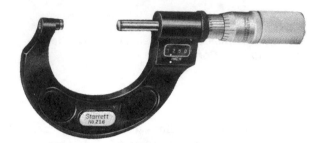

FIGURE 2-79. Digital read-out micrometers are quicker to read but are more expensive.

the number of hundredths of a millimeter indicated by the thimble graduation that coincides with the reading line on the sleeve.

Example: Refer to Figure 2-78.

The 5-millimeter sleeve graduation is visible	5.00
One additional 0.5-millimeter line is visible on the sleeve	0.50
Line 28 on the thimble coincides with the reading line on the sleeve; 28 × 0.01	0.28
The micrometer reading is	5.78 millimeters

Telescoping Gauges

Telescoping gauges can be used, in conjunction with outside micrometers, for measuring inside diameters, instead of using inside micrometers.

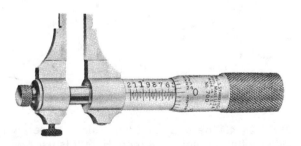

FIGURE 2-80. Inside micrometers in English and metric are read the same as outside micrometers. *(Courtesy of The L.S. Starrett Company)*

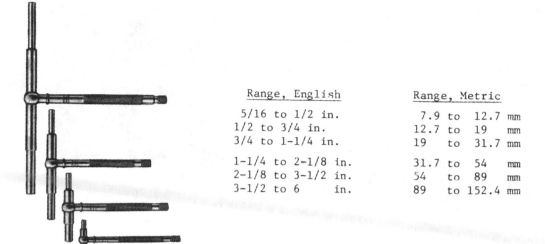

Range, English	Range, Metric
5/16 to 1/2 in.	7.9 to 12.7 mm
1/2 to 3/4 in.	12.7 to 19 mm
3/4 to 1-1/4 in.	19 to 31.7 mm
1-1/4 to 2-1/8 in.	31.7 to 54 mm
2-1/8 to 3-1/2 in.	54 to 89 mm
3-1/2 to 6 in.	89 to 152.4 mm

FIGURE 2–81. Telescoping gauges are used to measure inside diameters when used in conjunction with an outside micrometer. The knurled handle releases the spring-loaded plungers to diameter size; then they are locked by turning the knurled handle. The telescoping gauge is then carefully removed and measured with an outside micrometer. *(Courtesy of The L.S. Starrett Company)*

FIGURE 2–82. This dial indicator set takes care of many measuring requirements in the shop. Dial indicators are used to measure differential gear backlash, disc and flywheel run-out, crankshaft and transmission shaft end play, and so on. (A) hole attachment or wiggle bar; (B) clamp; (C) toolpost holder; (D) upright spindle; (E) universal clamp. *(Courtesy of The L.S. Starrett Company)*

Dial Indicators

The dial indicator is needed to perform many of the measurements required in the shop. Graduations on the scale are in either 0.001 inch (1/1000 inch) or in 0.01 millimeter (1/100 millimeter) for general shop use.

The measurement range of the dial indicator is determined by the amount of plunger travel provided. Special dial indicators are available for measuring cylinder taper and out of round, as shown in Chapter 9.

PART 5   POWER TOOLS

Bench Grinder

The bench grinder is an indispensable item in any shop. Usually one end of the motor shaft has a grinding wheel and the other has a wire wheel. The grinder can then be used for sharpening tools and cleaning parts. Other jobs for the grinder are grinding rivets or removing stock from metal parts. Grinding wheels of different types and sizes are available for specific jobs.

Grinding and cleaning require skill and careful handling to avoid injury to the operator or the tools and parts being reworked.

Electric Drills

Hand-held electric drills perform a variety of jobs, as listed in Figure 2–85. When using a hand-held drill, a few general rules will make the job easier. Do not apply any side pressure when drilling since this

FIGURE 2–84. Wire wheel and grinding wheel attachments for the bench grinder.

can break drill bits. Apply only enough pressure for good drilling; too much pressure can cause overheating and destroy the drill bit. Ease up on the pressure just before the drill breaks through to prevent grabbing. Keep a firm grasp on the drill at all

FIGURE 2–85. Hand-held electric drill. Common types include ¼, ⅜, and ½ inch. Available in low-speed, high-speed, and variable-speed models. Common uses are for drilling, honing, and driving and for cleaning brushes, hole saws, and rotary files. (Courtesy of Sioux Tools Inc.)

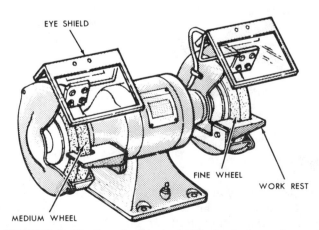

FIGURE 2–83. Bench grinder with tool supports and protective shields in place. (Courtesy of Ford Motor Co. of Canada Ltd.)

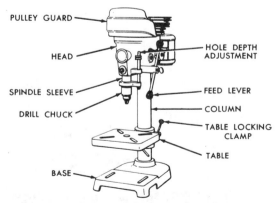

FIGURE 2–86. The drill press provides for a number of drilling speeds by changing the drive belt to different pulley positions. The drill press is used for precision drilling of parts that can be carried by hand. (Courtesy of Ford Motor Co. of Canada Ltd.)

times. Use a small amount of cutting oil when drilling steel. Make sure the piece of work being drilled is held securely. These general rules apply to the drill press as well. The drill press has a movable table which can be raised, lowered, and turned sideways. A drilling block should be used on top of the table to avoid drilling into the table.

PART 6   SHOP TOOLS

Hydraulic Jacks

Hydraulic floor jacks, transmission jacks, and bumper jacks are used in the automotive shop. The floor jack is used to raise a vehicle at the front, rear, or sides. The jack should be properly placed so that under-vehicle parts are not damaged. The floor jack can also be used to help move cars in tight places.

The bumper jack should only be used on bumpers that can withstand the strain. Place pads at bumper brackets. Do not work under a car supported only on a jack. Always use jack stands properly placed.

The transmission jack is indispensable for transmission removal and installation. The platform adjusts by tilting forward, back, or sideways, and can be raised or lowered hydraulically. The hold-down chain should always be fastened securely to prevent the transmission from falling off the jack. Use of the transmission jack allows proper alignment of transmission and bell housing for removal and installation.

FIGURE 2–88. Always support raised vehicle with properly placed jack stands before doing any work under vehicle.

FIGURE 2–89. Bumper jack can be used to raise vehicles. Pads must be properly positioned and bumper must be of adequate strength; commonly used when changing wheels and tires in the shop.

Hoists

Different types of hoists are used to raise vehicles for under-vehicle work. Transmission removal, drive line work, and exhaust system repairs are usually done on a hoist. A good hoist is one that allows easy vehicle positioning and has minimal under-vehicle obstruction. Single-post, frame-contact hoists, and twin-post and drive-on hoists are commonly used in automotive shops.

Chassis Lubrication Equipment

Chassis lubrication equipment is located in the lube bay and provides a motor oil dispenser, gear oil dispenser, grease gun, and air pressure hose. Different car manufacturers recommend lubrication at different mileage intervals. Lubrication points generally

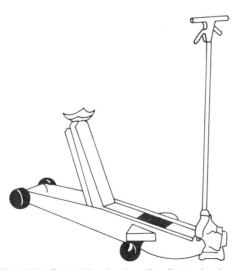

FIGURE 2–87. Portable hydraulic floor jack used to raise vehicles.

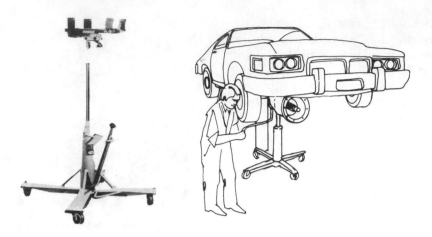

FIGURE 2-90. Hydraulic transmission jack, with adjustable platform and hold-down chain, assures proper transmission alignment and avoids heavy lifting.

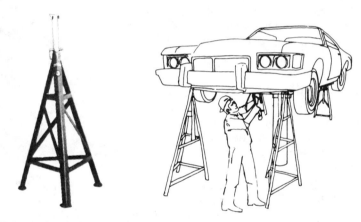

FIGURE 2-91. Under-hoist stands. Used to spread springs, unload ball joints, facilitate exhaust system replacement, and as a safety device.

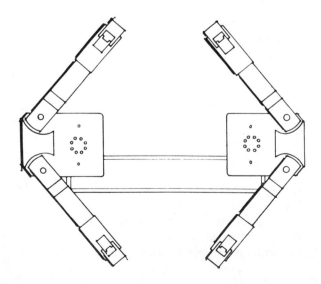

FIGURE 2-92. Twin-post frame contact hoist. Arms and pads pivot for positioning under proper lift points of vehicle.

FIGURE 2-93. One type of drive-on hoist with frame lift attachment extended.

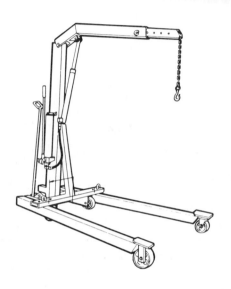

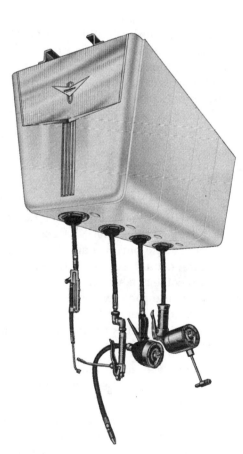

FIGURE 2-94. Common type of overhead lubrication dispensing equipment. This unit has an air hose, grease gun, gear oil dispenser, and motor oil dispenser. This type of equipment is located in the lube bay, which is also equipped with a hoist. *(Courtesy of Lincoln, St. Louis)*

TILTS LOAD
TO ANY ANGLE

FIGURE 2-95. Portable hydraulic shop crane used for a variety of automotive lifting jobs. Sling adapter at right allows tilting of load as required for engine removal and installation.

FIGURE 2-96. Chain hoist used for lifting heavy objects. Mechanical gear reduction makes lifting heavy objects easier.

include tie rod ends, ball joints, and some suspension components. The number of points requiring lubrication varies among different vehicle makes. Some makes have lubrication fittings already installed; others have plugs which must be removed and lube fittings installed before lubrication can be done.

Follow manufacturer's recommendations and specifications for periodic lubrication and types of lubricants required.

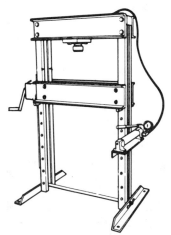

FIGURE 2-97. Floor-type and bench-top hydraulic shop presses. Floor model has an adjustable press bed for different working positions. Presses are used to remove and install bearings, gears, bushing, piston pins, and so on.

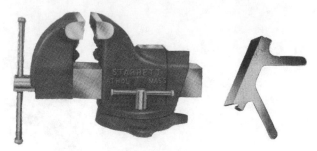

FIGURE 2-98. The bench vise is used to hold items on which work is being done. The soft jaw at right must be used when clamping easily damaged surfaces. *(Courtesy of The L.S. Starrett Company)*

Portable Cranes

Cranes are used to lift and transport heavy components. The crane should not be adjusted beyond its designed adjustment limits. For transporting a component with a crane, the load should be lowered to avoid upsetting.

Hydraulic Presses

The hydraulic press should not be used beyond its rated capacity. All work should be properly positioned and supported, and all recommended shields and protective equipment should be used. The hydraulic press exerts tremendous pressure and can cause parts under pressure to literally explode, causing serious injury.

PART 7 FASTENERS

A great variety of types and sizes of fasteners is used in the automotive industry. Each fastener is designed for a specific purpose and for specific conditions that are encountered in vehicle operation.

Using an incorrect fastener or a fastener of inferior quality for the job can result in early failure and even injury to driver and passengers.

Some precautions to observe when replacing fasteners are the following:

• Always use the same diameter, length, and type of fasteners as were used originally by the vehicle manufacturer.

• Never thread a fastener of one thread type to a fastener of a different thread type.

• Always use the same number of fasteners as were originally used by the manufacturer of the vehicle.

• Always observe the vehicle manufacturer's recommendations for tightening sequence, tightening steps (increments), and torque values.

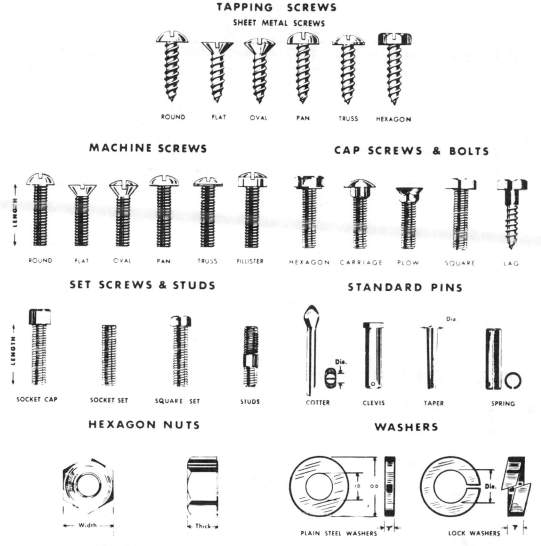

TAPPING SCREWS

SHEET METAL SCREWS

ROUND   FLAT   OVAL   PAN   TRUSS   HEXAGON

MACHINE SCREWS

LENGTH

ROUND   FLAT   OVAL   PAN   TRUSS   FILLISTER

CAP SCREWS & BOLTS

HEXAGON   CARRIAGE   PLOW   SQUARE   LAG

SET SCREWS & STUDS

LENGTH

SOCKET CAP   SOCKET SET   SQUARE SET   STUDS

STANDARD PINS

Dia.

Dia.

COTTER   CLEVIS   TAPER   SPRING

HEXAGON NUTS

Width   Thick

WASHERS

ID   OD

PLAIN STEEL WASHERS   T

Dia.

LOCK WASHERS   T

FIGURE 2-99. Many of the common types of fasteners used in the automotive industry. *(Courtesy of H. Paulin & Co. Limited)*

• Always use the correct washers, pins, and locks as specified by the vehicle manufacturer.

• Always replace stretched fasteners or fasteners with damaged threads.

• Never use a cotter pin more than once.

Damaged threads in threaded parts can be restored by the use of helically coiled thread inserts. Replace damaged snap rings and keys with new ones. The completed work is only as good as the technician's desire and ability to do a professional job with the use of correct parts and fasteners.

A number of terms have been used over the years to identify the various types of threads. Some of these have been replaced with new terms. The terms most commonly used in the automotive trade are as follows:

The United States Standard (USS), the American National Standard (ANS), and the Society of

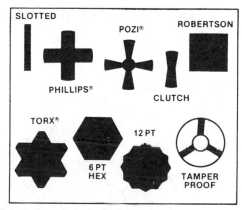

SLOTTED   POZI®   ROBERTSON

PHILLIPS®   CLUTCH

TORX®   12 PT

6 PT HEX   TAMPER PROOF

FIGURE 2-100. Various types of fastener head drive designs. *(Courtesy of Mac Tools Inc.)*

Automotive Engineers Standard (SAE) have all been replaced by the Unified National Series. The Unified National Series consists of four basic classifications.

45

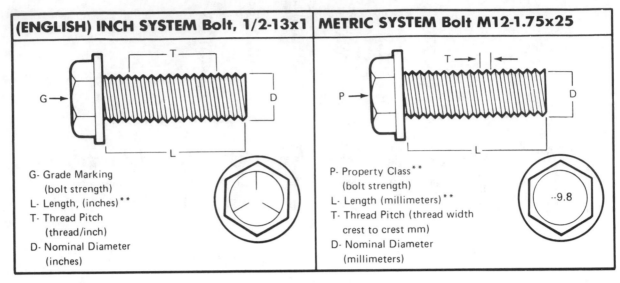

(ENGLISH) INCH SYSTEM Bolt, 1/2-13x1	METRIC SYSTEM Bolt M12-1.75x25
G- Grade Marking (bolt strength) L- Length, (inches)** T- Thread Pitch (thread/inch) D- Nominal Diameter (inches)	P- Property Class** (bolt strength) L- Length (millimeters)** T- Thread Pitch (thread width crest to crest mm) D- Nominal Diameter (millimeters)

*The property class is an Arabic numeral distinguishable from the slash SAE English grade system.

**The length of all bolts is measured from the underside of the head to the end.

BOLT STRENGTH IDENTIFICATION

(ENGLISH) INCH SYSTEM

Grade 1 or 2   Grade 5   Grade 8

(English) Inch bolts - Identification marks correspond to bolt strength - increasing number of slashes represent increasing strength.

METRIC SYSTEM

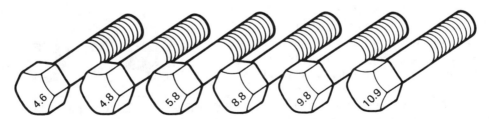

Metric bolts - Identification class numbers correspond to bolt strength - increasing numbers represent increasing strength. Common metric fastener bolt strength property are 9.8 and 10.9 with the class identification embossed on the bolt head.

FIGURE 2-101. Bolt terminology. *(Courtesy of Ford Motor Co. of Canada Ltd.)*

(ENGLISH) INCH SYSTEM		METRIC SYSTEM	
Grade	Identification	Class	Identification
Hex Nut Grade 5	3 Dots	Hex Nut Property Class 9	Arabic 9
Hex Nut Grade 8	6 Dots	Hex Nut Property Class 10	Arabic 10
Increasing dots represent increasing strength.		May also have blue finish or paint daub on hex flat. Increasing numbers represent increasing strength.	

OTHER TYPES OF PARTS

Metric identification schemes vary by type of part, most often a variation of that used of bolts and nuts. Note that many types of English and metric fasteners carry no special identification if they are otherwise unique.

—Stamped "U" Nuts

—Tapping, thread forming and certain other case hardened screws

—Studs, Large studs may carry the property class number. Smaller studs use a geometric code on the end.

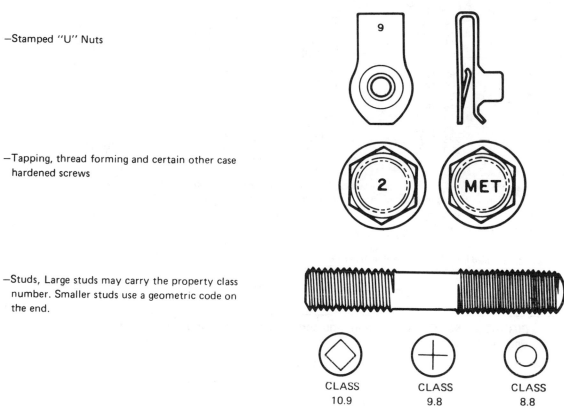

FIGURE 2-102. Nut and stud terminology. (*Courtesy of Ford Motor Co. of Canada Ltd.*)

Current Usage	Much Used	Much Used	Used at Times	Used at Times
Minimum Tensile Strength PSI MPa	To 1/2–69,000 [476] To 3/4–64,000 [421] To 1–55,000 [379]	To 3/4–120,000 [827] To 1–115,000 [793]	To 5/8–140,000 [965] To 3/4–133,000 [917]	150,000 [1 034]
Quality of Material	Indeterminate	Minimum Commercial	Medium Commercial	Best Commercial
SAE Grade Number	1 or 2	5	6 or 7	8

Capscrew Head Markings

Manufacturer's marks may vary

These are all SAE Grade 5 (3 line)

   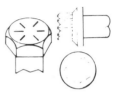

Capscrew Body Size (Inches) – (Thread)	Torque Ft-Lbs [N·m]	Torque Ft-Lbs [N·m]	Torque Ft-Lbs [N·m]	Torque Ft-Lbs [N·m]
1/4 – 20	5 [7]	8 [11]	10 [14]	12 [16]
– 28	6 [8]	10 [14]		14 [19]
5/16 – 18	11 [15]	17 [23]	19 [26]	24 [33]
– 24	13 [18]	19 [26]		27 [37]
3/8 – 16	18 [24]	31 [42]	34 [46]	44 [60]
– 24	20 [27]	35 [47]		49 [66]
7/16 – 14	28 [38]	49 [66]	55 [75]	70 [95]
– 20	30 [41]	55 [75]		78 [106]
1/2 – 13	39 [53]	75 [102]	85 [115]	105 [142]
– 20	41 [56]	85 [115]		120 [163]
9/16 – 12	51 [69]	110 [149]	120 [163]	155 [210]
– 18	55 [75]	120 [163]		170 [231]
5/8 – 11	83 [113]	150 [203]	167 [226]	210 [285]
– 18	95 [129]	170 [231]		240 [325]
3/4 – 10	105 [142]	270 [366]	280 [380]	375 [508]
– 16	115 [156]	295 [400]		420 [569]
7/8 – 9	160 [217]	395 [536]	440 [597]	605 [820]
– 14	175 [237]	435 [590]		675 [915]
1 – 8	235 [319]	590 [800]	660 [895]	910 [1234]
– 14	250 [339]	660 [895]		990 [1342]

Notes:

1. Always use the torque values listed above when specific torque values are not available.
2. Do not use above values in place of those specified in manufacturer's manual; special attention should be observed when using SAE Grade 6, 7, and 8 capscrews.
3. The above is based on use of clean, dry threads.
4. Reduce torque by 10% when engine oil is used as a lubricant.
5. Reduce torque by 20% if new plated capscrews are used.
6. Capscrews threaded into aluminum may require reductions in torque of 30% or more of Grade 5 capscrews torque and must attain two capscrew diameters of thread engagement.

Caution: If replacement capscrews are of a higher grade than originally supplied, adhere to torque specifications for that placement.

FIGURE 2-103. Capscrew markings and torque values. *(Courtesy of Cummins Engine Company)*

REUSE OF PREVAILING TORQUE NUT(S) AND BOLT(S)

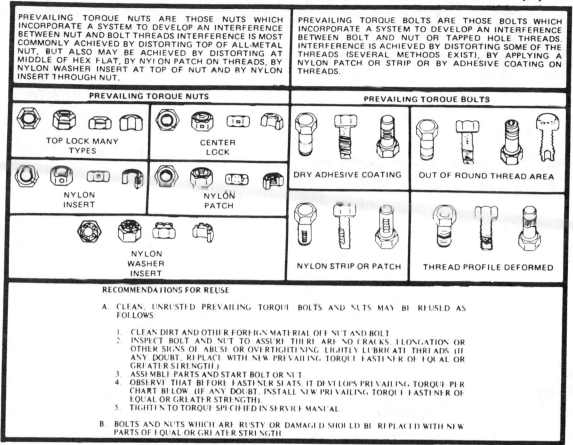

PREVAILING TORQUE NUTS ARE THOSE NUTS WHICH INCORPORATE A SYSTEM TO DEVELOP AN INTERFERENCE BETWEEN NUT AND BOLT THREADS INTERFERENCE IS MOST COMMONLY ACHIEVED BY DISTORTING TOP OF ALL-METAL NUT, BUT ALSO MAY BE ACHIEVED BY DISTORTING AT MIDDLE OF HEX FLAT, BY NYLON PATCH ON THREADS, BY NYLON WASHER INSERT AT TOP OF NUT AND BY NYLON INSERT THROUGH NUT.

PREVAILING TORQUE BOLTS ARE THOSE BOLTS WHICH INCORPORATE A SYSTEM TO DEVELOP AN INTERFERENCE BETWEEN BOLT AND NUT OR TAPPED HOLE THREADS. INTERFERENCE IS ACHIEVED BY DISTORTING SOME OF THE THREADS (SEVERAL METHODS EXIST), BY APPLYING A NYLON PATCH OR STRIP OR BY ADHESIVE COATING ON THREADS.

PREVAILING TORQUE NUTS

TOP LOCK MANY TYPES

CENTER LOCK

NYLON INSERT

NYLON PATCH

NYLON WASHER INSERT

PREVAILING TORQUE BOLTS

DRY ADHESIVE COATING

OUT OF ROUND THREAD AREA

NYLON STRIP OR PATCH

THREAD PROFILE DEFORMED

RECOMMENDATIONS FOR REUSE

A. CLEAN, UNRUSTED PREVAILING TORQUE BOLTS AND NUTS MAY BE REUSED AS FOLLOWS:

1. CLEAN DIRT AND OTHER FOREIGN MATERIAL OFF NUT AND BOLT
2. INSPECT BOLT AND NUT TO ASSURE THERE ARE NO CRACKS, ELONGATION OR OTHER SIGNS OF ABUSE OR OVERTIGHTENING LIGHTLY LUBRICATE THREADS (IF ANY DOUBT, REPLACE WITH NEW PREVAILING TORQUE FASTENER OF EQUAL OR GREATER STRENGTH)
3. ASSEMBLE PARTS AND START BOLT OR NUT
4. OBSERVE THAT BEFORE FASTENER SEATS, IT DEVELOPS PREVAILING TORQUE PER CHART BELOW. (IF ANY DOUBT, INSTALL NEW PREVAILING TORQUE FASTENER OF EQUAL OR GREATER STRENGTH).
5. TIGHTEN TO TORQUE SPECIFIED IN SERVICE MANUAL.

B. BOLTS AND NUTS WHICH ARE RUSTY OR DAMAGED SHOULD BE REPLACED WITH NEW PARTS OF EQUAL OR GREATER STRENGTH

FIGURE 2-104. Reuse of prevailing torque nut(s) and bolt(s). *(Courtesy of General Motors Corporation)*

1. Unified National Coarse (UNC or NC).
2. Unified National Fine (UNF or NF).
3. Unified National Extrafine (UNEF or NEF).
4. Unified National Pipe Thread (UNPT or NPT).

The two common metric classifications are coarse and fine and can be identified by the letters SI (Système International d'Unités or International System of Units) or ISO (International Standards Organization).

Bolt Size

Bolt size is determined by two measurements. This is true of both English and metric bolts. Bolt length is the distance measured (in inches for English bolts and in millimeters or centimeters for S.I. metric bolts) from the bottom of the head to the tip of the bolt. Bolt diameter is the measurement across (in inches or fractions of an inch in the English system and in millimeters (mm) in the metric system) the major diameter of the threaded area.

Thread Pitch

The thread pitch of a bolt in the English system is determined by the number of threads there are in one inch of threaded bolt length and is expressed in "number of threads per inch." The thread pitch in the metric system is determined by the distance in millimeters between two adjacent threads. To check the thread pitch of a bolt or stud, a thread pitch gauge is used. Gauges are available in both English and metric dimensions.

Tensile Strength

The tensile strength of a bolt is the amount of stress or stretch it is able to withstand. The type of bolt material and the diameter of the bolt determine its tensile strength. In the English system, the tensile strength of a bolt is identified by the number of radial lines of the bolt head. More lines means higher tensile strength. See Figure 2-101. In the metric system tensile strength of a bolt can be identified by a number on the bolt head. See Figure 2-101. The higher the number, the greater the tensile strength.

HEXAGON   HEXAGON WASHER FACED   SQUARE (CHAMFER)   PLAIN

SELF LOCKING NUT   WHEEL NUT   WING NUT   HEX. CAP

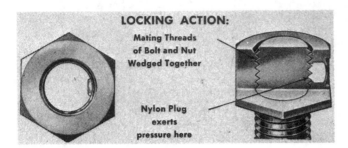

LOCKING ACTION:
Mating Threads of Bolt and Nut Wedged Together

Nylon Plug exerts pressure here

FIGURE 2-105. Several types of automotive nuts (above). Cutaway view of one type of self-locking nut action.

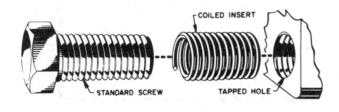

COILED INSERT

STANDARD SCREW   TAPPED HOLE

FIGURE 2-106. Damaged threads can be restored in a threaded part by the use of a helically coiled insert. The damaged hole is drilled to a precise oversize, tapped, and a coiled insert installed. This provides new threads of original diameter and type.

FLAT   COMMON LOCK   EXTERNAL LOCK   INTERNAL LOCK   EXTERNAL-INTERNAL LOCK   COUNTER-SUNK LOCK

FIGURE 2-107. Common types of washers as used on the automobile. Lock washers prevent loosening of fasteners and should be used wherever original equipment was so equipped.

CONTRACTING   EXPANDING

FIGURE 2-108. Several types of commonly used snap rings. Snap rings are used to prevent endwise movement of shafts and bearings. Damaged or distorted snap rings must be replaced. *(Courtesy of Ford Motor Co. of Canada Ltd.)*

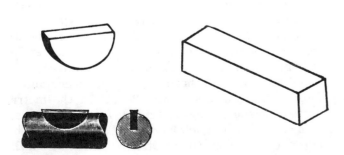

FIGURE 2-109. Woodruff keys (left) and straight keys are used to hold parts to shafts so that part and shaft rotate as a unit. In other cases splined shaft and parts are used to accomplish the same result.

PART 8 SELF-CHECK

1. Why are shop manuals necessary in the automotive shop?

2. What information is necessary about a vehicle in order to obtain correct replacement parts for it?

3. What is torque?

4. Why is a torque wrench necessary?

5. A well-equipped technician will have a good range of English or U.S. size wrenches as well as _____ sizes.

6. To measure with an outside micrometer, the part being measured must be placed between the ___ and the _____.

7. The straight edge is not a precision measuring tool. True or false?

8. A hoist used to raise a car may be positioned to contact any point under the car. True or false?

9. Why should the load on a portable floor crane be lowered for movement from one place to another?

PART 9 TEST QUESTIONS

Select the one best answer for each question.

1. The automotive shop manual is essential to good shop practice in order to:
   (a) obtain accurate specifications and procedures
   (b) give the mechanic broad general information
   (c) provide the maximum number of short cuts
   (d) increase parts and service sales

2. The technician's productivity and earning power are increased by:
   (a) buying a minimum selection of tools that are the least expensive
   (b) buying incomplete sets of tools at bargain prices
   (c) borrowing tools from a fellow worker as often as possible
   (d) having a complete set of good quality tools kept in an adequate storage cabinet

3. Torque is measured in:
   (a) pound feet
   (b) pound inches
   (c) newton meters
   (d) all of the above
   (e) none of the above

4. The five major parts of a micrometer are the:
   (a) frame, anvil, spindle, swivel, sleeve
   (b) swivel, anvil, sleeve, spindle, thimble
   (c) thimble, swivel, spindle, anvil, sleeve
   (d) anvil, frame, spindle, sleeve, thimble

5. The thread pitch on an English-dimensioned bolt is determined by:
   (a) a number on the bolt head
   (b) radial lines on the bolt head
   (c) the required wrench size
   (d) the number of threads per inch

6. The property class or strength of a metric bolt is determined by:
   (a) a number on the bolt head
   (b) radial lines on the bolt head
   (c) the required wrench size
   (d) the number of threads per inch

7. Prevailing torque bolts use:
   (a) an adhesive coating
   (b) an out of round thread
   (c) a deformed thread
   (d) a nylon strip or patch
   (e) all of the above
   (f) none of the above

8. Bolt size is determined by:
   (a) wrench size
   (b) nut size
   (c) length and diameter
   (d) thread pitch and tensile strength

Chapter 3

Gaskets, Seals, and Bearings

Performance Objectives

After thorough study of this chapter and the appropriate gaskets, seals, and bearings, you should be able to do the following:

1. State the purpose of gaskets and sealants.
2. Identify the different types of gaskets and sealants and state their use.
3. State the purposes of static and dynamic seals.
4. Identify different types of seals and state their use.
5. State the purposes of friction and antifriction bearings.
6. Describe the basic construction and design differences of various bearing types.
7. Complete the self-check and the test questions with at least 80 percent accuracy.

PART 1 GASKETS AND SEALANTS

Gaskets are used to prevent leakage of gases or liquids between two parts bolted together. The gasket is placed between the two mating machined surfaces; the bolts or fasteners are then tightened in the recommended sequence, and to the specified torque. The gasket is designed for the particular job it is required to do. Different materials, such as cork, synthetic rubber, Vellumoid®, steel, copper, and asbestos, are used. In some cases special sealant is used with the gasket.

Gasket Requirements

Gaskets are required to function without deterioration, over long periods of time, and in various conditions. The type of gasket that is used in any given application is carefully chosen to achieve the proper results. Determining factors include:

- High and low temperature extremes that will be encountered
- Type of material to be sealed, gases, liquids, etc.
- Pressure of confined material
- Finish or smoothness of mating parts
- Clearance required between assembled mating parts

Different applications require a variety of different materials and designs.

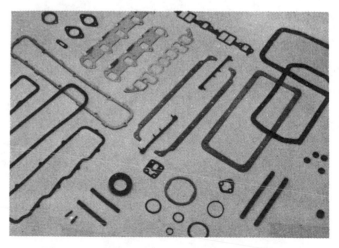

FIGURE 3–1. Various types of gaskets as shown here are used in the automotive industry. Materials used are embossed steel (for cylinder heads and manifolds), cork and synthetic rubber (for oil pans and valve covers), fiber (for thermostat housings and timing covers), felt (for wheel dust seals), and others. Gaskets for particular applications are dealt with in the appropriate chapters.

Gasket Qualities

Good gasket qualities include the following:

• *Compressibility* and *extrudability*—required to allow the gasket to "flow" slightly to conform to the minor irregularities of the mating surfaces.

• *Resilience* - the ability of the gasket material to contract and expand with the changes in temperature and still provide good sealing.

• *Permeability*—the degree to which the gasket material is able to prevent liquids or gases from passing through the material itself.

These qualities are required to a greater or lesser degree depending on the particular application for which the gasket is designed.

Gasket Storage

Many gaskets are encapsulated in plastic and cardboard packages to prevent deterioration and breakage. These gaskets are more easily stored than single gaskets that are not packaged. Loose gaskets should be stored lying flat. Other parts should not be laid on top of them. Nevertheless, cork and paper or fiber may still deteriorate and shrink due to drying out. They may be restored, however, by being soaked in warm water until original size has returned.

Sealants

There are two types of sealants used in automotive service. One type is used with gaskets and is applied directly to the gasket or to the mating surfaces to be sealed by the gasket. A great variety of materials is available for this purpose. The manufacturer's service manual recommendations should be followed as to whether to use a sealer with the gasket, and if so, which type of sealer to use (i.e., hardening or nonhardening, compatibility, and the like). Another type of sealant used is the "form-in-place gasket material." There are two basic types of this material available. They are not interchangeable and should not be so used.

Aerobic Sealant (RTV Sealant)

Aerobic or Room Temperature Sealant cures when exposed to moisture in the air. It has a shelf storage life of one year and should not be used if the expiration date on the package has passed. Always inspect the date on the package before use. This material is normally used on flexible metal flanges.

Anaerobic Sealant

This type of sealant cures in the absence of air (as when squeezed between two metal surfaces). It will not cure if left in an uncovered tube. This material is used between two smooth machined surfaces. It should not be used on flexible metal flanges.

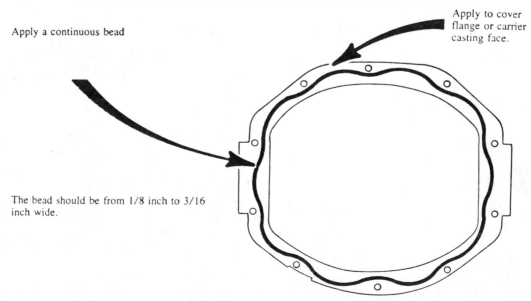

FIGURE 3-2. Typical use of gasket making type of sealant on differential cover. Other applications include valve covers, oil pans, and the like. *(Courtesy of Ford Motor Co. of Canada Ltd.)*

To use either of these form-in-place gasket materials, be sure to follow the material supplier and vehicle manufacturer's recommendations, including preparation of mating surfaces, application methods, and maximum exposure time allowed before assembly.

PART 2 SEALS

Oil seals are classified as static or dynamic. The static seal is used between two stationary parts. The dynamic seal provides a seal between a stationary and a moving part. One example of a static seal is the O ring seal between a transmission hydraulic pump and the transmission case. The rear main bearing crankshaft oil seal is an example of a dynamic seal.

Some seals are designed to withstand high pressures. Piston rings, for instance, are designed to withstand high combustion pressures and seal both gases and liquids. Other seals use felt, synthetic, rubber, fiber, or leather. Many seals have a metal case and a tension spring. Both single- and double-lip seals are used.

Seals should always be installed according to manufacturer's specifications. In general, though, the sealing lip should be installed toward the fluid or gas being contained. Felt dust seals should be installed with the felt toward the outside.

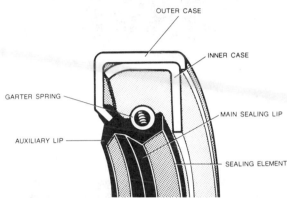

FIGURE 3-4. A typical seal (above) and common seal terminology (below). Seals are used to keep in oils, fluids, and grease or to exclude dirt, or both. The main sealing element can be synthetic rubber, leather, or felt. Some seals have both an inner and outer case; others have only an outer case. Some seals include a bolt-on flange. Special seals will be dealt with in the appropriate chapters.

FIGURE 3-3. A great variety of seals of various shapes and designs is required in the automobile. Some examples are shown above. *(Courtesy of National Seal)*

PART 3 BEARINGS

Bearings reduce the friction of rotating parts. Overhauling and reconditioning are easier and less expensive when bearings can be replaced.

There are two basic classifications of bearings: friction and antifriction bearings.

Friction Bearings

Friction bearings rely on sliding friction with a film of oil between the bearing and bearing journal. A friction bearing is a thin-walled cylindrical part located between the rotating part and the supporting part. It can be of one-piece construction or it may consist of several pieces. The one-piece friction bearing is often called a bushing; the terms bearing inserts or bearing shells are used for multiple-piece friction bearings. Various types of combinations of metals are used for friction bearings. Sintered bronze, brass, steel, Babbitt metal, lead, tin, nylon, and aluminum are examples. There are no balls or rollers in friction-type bearings.

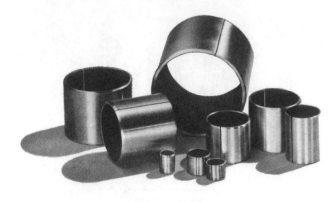

Concentric Wall Bearing
(uniform wall thickness)

Eccentric Wall Bearing
(wall heavier at crown than at parting faces)

FIGURE 3-5. Several types of friction bearings and bushings. Two-piece bearings are needed on applications such as an engine crankshaft. Eccentric bearing design improves the ability to maintain an oil film between the bearing and bearing journal. One-piece bushings are used on distributor shafts, camshafts, and other parts. Some bushings of a porous material are permanently lubricated with a special lubricant that saturates the bushing.

Thrust Washers

Thrust washers are also a type of friction bearing. They are designed to absorb an axial load or thrust load. They may be designed to rotate with a rotating part against a stationary part, they may be "lugged" to the stationary part, or they may "float"—be free to rotate between two parts, not being lugged to either part.

Thrust washers are designed to reduce wear on adjacent parts and to maintain specified clearances between parts. Various metals, metal combinations, and plastics are used in thrust washer design including steel, bronze, steel-backed bronze, aluminized steel, nylon, and teflon. Thrust washer surfaces are often grooved for improved lubrication.

Antifriction Bearings

Antifriction bearings rely on rolling friction for operation. Rolling friction requires less effort to rotate a part than does sliding friction. The greater the load, the more evident this fact becomes.

Antifriction bearings include various designs of ball bearings and roller bearings.

Shielded Bearings

Some ball bearing designs include a shield on one side. The shield is attached to the outer race and shields or hides the balls with only a small opening around the inner race. This restricts the amount of lubrication that can pass through the bearing. In this way it is possible to prevent overloading a seal with lubricant, which reduces the chances of leakage past the seal.

Sealed Bearings

Sealed bearings are not to be confused with shielded bearings. Sealed bearings appear similar but are completely sealed to prevent any lubricant from escaping from the bearing or past the bearing. Some designs are sealed on one side only allowing bearing lubrication from the open side of the bearing. The open side of the bearing is installed toward the lubricant being confined. Other designs are sealed on both sides; they are pre-lubricated for life during the manufacturing process.

Needle Thrust Bearings

The needle thrust bearing or Torrington type bearing is designed to absorb thrust loads. Compared to a thrust washer, it provides reduced friction. It consists of a series of small diameter rollers or "needle" rollers arranged radially and held in position in a washer-shaped cage. The assembly may include separate washer type thrust surfaces—one on each side—or the thrust surfaces may be incorporated into the adjacent parts.

Bearing Loads

Bearings are designed to carry radial loads, axial loads, or both. A radial load is a load imposed at

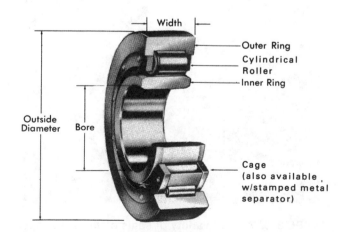

FIGURE 3-6. Cutaway view of a straight roller bearing with parts identified. This bearing is designed to carry a radial load (90° to the shaft).

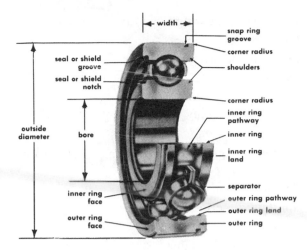

FIGURE 3-7. Cutaway view of a ball bearing with parts identified. This bearing is also designed to carry a radial load.

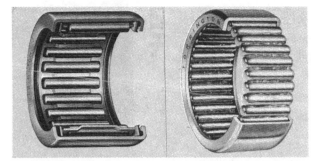

FIGURE 3-9. Common types of needle bearings designed to carry radial loads.

right angles to the shaft. An axial load is a load imposed parallel to the shaft.

A straight roller bearing is able to carry a radial load, whereas a thrust bearing is able to absorb an axial load. A tapered roller bearing can carry both a radial load and a unidirectional axial load. A double row opposed tapered roller bearing is able to carry a radial load as well as axial loads in both directions.

Specific types of friction and antifriction bearings are dealt with in different chapters as they apply.

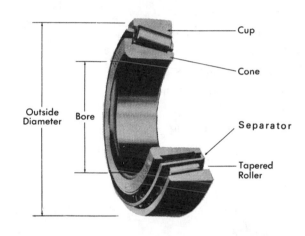

FIGURE 3-8. Tapered roller bearing and component part names. This bearing is able to carry a radial load as well as an axial load in one direction. *(Courtesy of General Motors Corporation)*

PART 4   SELF-CHECK

1. Why are gaskets required?
2. List four factors that determine the type of gasket required for a particular application.
3. How should gaskets be stored to prevent damage?
4. Explain the use of aerobic and anaerobic sealants.
5. List two classifications of seals.
6. The two basic classifications of bearings are the _____type and the _____type.
7. Define radial loads and axial loads on bearings.

FIGURE 3-10. Several types of thrust bearings. Thrust bearings are designed to absorb axial loads.

PART 5   TEST QUESTIONS

Select the one best answer for each question.

1. Good gasket qualities include:
   (a) compressibility
   (b) extrudability
   (c) resilience
   (d) permeability
   (e) only (a), (c), and (d) are right
   (f) all of the above

2. Mechanic A says that aerobic and anaerobic seal-ants can be used interchangeably. Mechanic B says that each must only be used for particular applications. Who is right?
   (a) Mechanic A
   (b) Mechanic B
   (c) both A and B
   (d) neither A nor B

3. A dynamic seal is used to seal:
   (a) dust from entering
   (b) oil from escaping
   (c) between a stationary and a moving part
   (d) (a) and (b) only
   (e) (a), (b), and (c)

4. Antifriction bearings include:
   (a) shielded bearings
   (b) sealed bearings
   (c) bushings
   (d) thrust washers
   (e) (a) and (b) only
   (f) (c) and (d) only

5. A single tapered roller bearing is able to carry the following load:
   (a) radial load
   (b) a unidirectional axial load
   (c) both (a) and (b)
   (d) none of the above

6. Axial load carrying bearings include:
   (a) friction bearings
   (b) needle bearings
   (c) thrust washers
   (d) all of the above
   (e) none of the above

7. Shielded bearings are:
   (a) permanently lubricated
   (b) sealed bearings
   (c) friction bearings
   (d) all of the above
   (e) none of the above

Chapter 4

Lines, Fittings, and Belts

Performance Objectives

After a thorough study of this chapter and the appropriate training aids, you should be able to do the following:

1. Identify various types of lines, tubing, and fittings, and state their general uses.

2. Properly cut tubing and perform satisfactory single- and double-lap flares with fittings properly installed.

3. Bend tubing using a tubing bender to fit a given application, without cracking or kinking the tubing.

4. Identify various types of belt drives, belts, and pulleys, and state their general automotive applications.

5. Properly adjust belt tension as specified by the service manual.

6. Complete the self-check and test questions with at least 80 percent accuracy.

PART 1   LINES AND FITTINGS

Lines and fittings are used to carry liquids and gases in such engine systems as the cooling system, the lubrication system, the fuel system, the exhaust system, and so on. Some lines are subjected to relatively low pressures while other lines are required to withstand very high pressures.

It is essential to only use the recommended type and size of line for any particular application in order to avoid trouble and failure. These lines should be only used with the recommended fittings installed in the correct manner.

Lines include relatively thick walled pipes, which do not lend themselves readily to bending; thin walled tubing, which is easier to bend; and flexible hoses.

Copper, aluminum, plastic, and steel tubing is used. Only the seamless steel tubing is suitable for

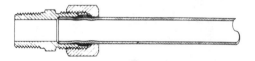

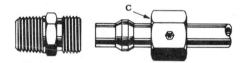

Use long nut when excessive vibration may be encountered.

FIGURE 4-1. Compression-type brass fittings used with copper and steel lines. *(Courtesy of The Weatherhead Company of Canada Ltd.)*

Use long nut when excessive vibration may be encountered.

FIGURE 4-2. One type of plastic tubing and fittings uses a sleeve type of seal as shown here. *(Courtesy of The Weatherhead Company of Canada Ltd.)*

FIGURE 4-3. Slip-on type of plastic tubing and fitting often used with a clamp. *(Courtesy of The Weatherhead Company of Canada Ltd.)*

UNION   COUPLING

FIGURE 4-4. The union shown connects two lines, using compression sleeves, while the coupling on the right connects two threaded lines. *(Courtesy of the Weatherhead Company of Canada Ltd.)*

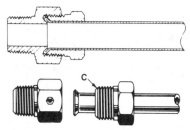

FIGURE 4-5. Inverted flare type of fittings. *(Courtesy of the Weatherhead Company of Canada Ltd.)*

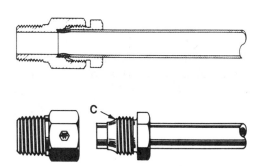

FIGURE 4-6. Threaded sleeve type of fitting. *(Courtesy of The Weatherhead Company of Canada Ltd.)*

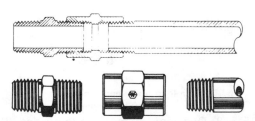

FIGURE 4-7. Pipe thread type of fittings. *(Courtesy of The Weatherhead Company of Canada Ltd.)*

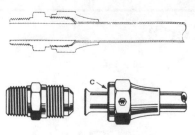

Use long nut when excessive vibration may be encountered.

FIGURE 4-8. Flare nut type of fittings. Note the difference between this fitting and the inverted flare type of fittings shown in Figure 4-5. *(Courtesy of The Weatherhead Company of Canada Ltd.)*

high-pressure applications such as fuel injection lines and brakes.

Care must be taken not to kink or flatten tubing when it is necessary to bend it to required shape. Kinks or flattened sections restrict flow in the tubing. Use a good type of tubing bender to avoid damage to the tubing.

It is essential that the different thread types in fittings be recognized. Never mix thread types or seal types in fittings. Do not cross thread fittings. Route lines and fittings in such a way as to avoid abrasion, which can cause a line to leak. Use all original brackets and clamps to ensure that lines are properly supported. Do not allow lines to twist dur-

HOSE INSTALLATION

RIGHT	WRONG

FIGURE 4-9. Right and wrong methods of hose installation. Installation should not result in twisted or kinked hose after fittings are tightened.

FIGURE 4-10. Flaring tool kit required to flare tubular lines. *(Courtesy of Proto Canada, Div. Ingersoll-Rand Canada, Inc.)*

ing removal or installation. Route lines to avoid damage from exhaust heat.

Flexible lines and hoses are used for various pressure ranges. Hose construction and flexible line construction is different for low- or high-pressure use. Always use the recommended hose for a particular application.

Flaring Tubing

Steel and copper tubing should be cut with a tubing cutter. Avoid applying too much pressure during

FIGURE 4-11. Tubing cutter with reamer attached. *(Courtesy of Proto Canada, Div. Ingersoll-Rand Canada, Inc.)*

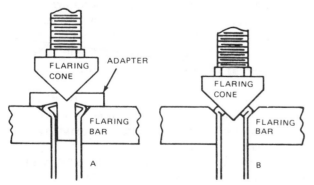

FIGURE 4-12. Example of double-lap flaring procedure required for high-pressure lines such as brake lines.

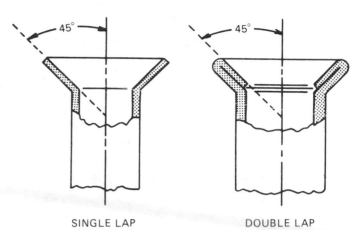

SINGLE LAP DOUBLE LAP

FIGURE 4-13. Completed single-lap flare for low-pressure lines and double-lap flare for high-pressure lines.

FIGURE 4-14. Two types of tubing benders. Tubing benders must be used when bending tubing to avoid collapsing or kinking of tubing. A collapsed tube reduces flow. *(Courtesy of Proto Canada, Div. Ingersoll-Rand Canada, Inc.)*

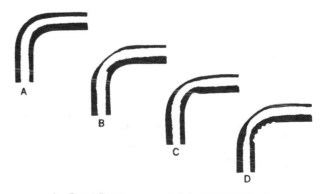

A—Good Bend   C—Kinked Bend
B—Flattened Bend D—Wrinkled Bend

FIGURE 4-15. When bending tubing, make sure that the result does not restrict flow due to kinked, flattened, or wrinkled bends.

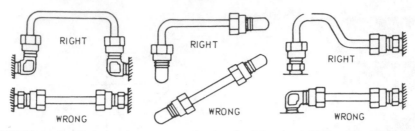

FIGURE 4-16. Right and wrong methods of tubing installation. Sufficient tubing length must always be allowed to prevent the tubing from cracking due to expansion and contraction as well as vibration.

HOW TO TIGHTEN FLARE-TYPE TUBE FITTINGS

Line Size (Outside Diameter)	Flare Nut Size (Across Flats)	Tightness (Ft-lbs)	Recommended Turns of Tightness (After Finger Tightening)	
			Original Assembly	Re-assembly
3/16"	7/16"	10	1/3 Turn	1/6 Turn
1/4"	9/16"	10	1/4 Turn	1/12 Turn
5/16"	5/8"	10-15	1/4 Turn	1/6 Turn
3/8"	11/16"	20	1/4 Turn	1/6 Turn
1/2"	7/8"	30-40	1/6 to 1/4 Turn	1/12 Turn
5/8"	1"	80-110	1/4 Turn	1/6 Turn
3/4"	1 1/4"	100-120	1/4 Turn	1/6 Turn

FIGURE 4-17. General tightening specifications which may be used if manufacturer's specifications for tightening tubing fittings are not available.

cutting. This can collapse the tube. Low-pressure lines need only a single flare, whereas brake lines require double-lap flaring or International Standards Organization (ISO) flaring. Some vehicles have the double-lap flared brake lines while others have the ISO-type flared lines and fittings. Fittings and lines of different designs should never be mixed, used together, or interchanged.

After cutting, ream the tubing and then flare as required. The reamer is usually part of the tubing cutter. Make sure that no metal chips are left in the tubing.

PART 2 BELTS AND PULLEYS

A system of belts and pulleys is used to drive such engine accessories as the alternator, water pump, fan, power steering pump, air conditioning compressor, air injection pump, and the like. None of these needs to be timed to rotate in a precise relationship to the engine crankshaft.

However, such items as overhead camshafts and

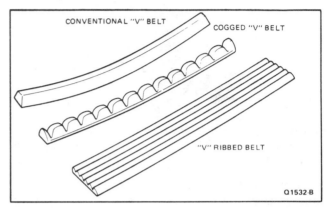

FIGURE 4-18. Three types of belts used to drive engine accessories. *(Courtesy of Ford Motor Co. of Canada Ltd.)*

diesel fuel injection pumps require precise timing to the engine crankshaft on a continuing basis and, therefore, require more positive drive mechanisms. Among these is the toothed or cog belt and sprocket drive.

"V" Belts

Several different designs of V belts are used to drive engine accessories. These are the conventional V belt, the cogged V belt, and the poly V or ribbed V belt, also known as a serpentine belt (Figure 4-19).

All of these belts are constructed of a combination of rubber, fabric, and rubber-impregnated fabric. Reinforcing fabric or steel cords are used in some belts that are required to drive heavier loads, and to reduce stretch and slippage (such as air conditioning compressors). Conventional and cogged V belt drives may be of the single belt or dual matched belt type.

In some cases a single, poly "V", serpentine belt is used to drive all accessories while in many other applications two, three, or more belt drive systems may be used.

All V belt drives rely on proper belt tension to provide the necessary wedging action of the belt in the pulleys to keep belt slippage at a minimum. However, excessive belt tension will cause early

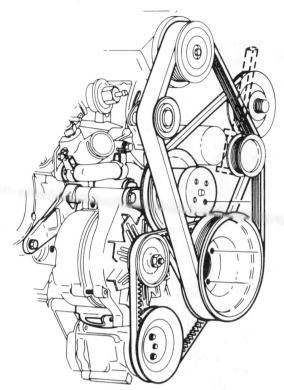

FIGURE 4-19. Example of use of three types of belts shown in Figure 4-18. *(Courtesy of Ford Motor Co. of Canada Ltd.)*

bearing failure in engine driven accessories, as well as excessive belt and pulley wear. Belts that are too loose will allow slippage, causing engine accessories to be driven too slowly. Loose belts will also cause overheating and rapid wear of belts and pulleys, as well as engine overheating due to insufficient fan and water pump speeds.

Belt tension adjustment is provided by means of an adjustable idler pulley or by one or more of the accessories (usually the alternator and power steering pump) being on a sliding adjustable mounting.

"V" Belt Size

Efficient belt drive operation is dependent on proper belt size to match pulley V width. A belt that is too narrow will not result in good side gripping action since it will bottom out in the pulleys. A belt that is too wide will ride too high in the pulleys resulting in slippage, belt damage, and possibly in the belt jumping off the pulleys during operation.

Belts that are worn, glazed, oil or grease contaminated, cracked or torn, should be replaced.

Belt squeal is usually the result of glazed and slipping belts. Adjusting belt tension may not eliminate the squeal since the belt may be glazed or worn, in which case the belt should be replaced. Dual matched belts should always be replaced in matched pairs

"V" Pulleys

The crankshaft drive pulley may be a single, dual, triple, or quadruple V design, depending on how many belt drive systems the engine has. Pulleys on accessories may be of single or dual V design.

Pulley construction varieties include stamped steel, cast iron, steel alloy, and die cast aluminum.

Pulley diameters determine the speed ratio between engine crankshaft and driven accessories. A crankshaft drive pulley and a driven accessory pulley of the same size would drive the accessory at crankshaft speed minus some minor slippage. An accessory pulley that is smaller than the drive pulley would result in the accessory being driven at greater than crankshaft speed.

Proper pulley size is determined by the manufacturer to insure the best of a wide range of operating speeds for all engine accessories.

Pulleys may be mounted in several different ways: press fit on the shaft, keyed to the shaft, splined to the shaft, tapered shaft, and hub. Any one of these mountings may also include a retaining bolt and washer.

Pulleys must run straight and true and be in alignment with each other for efficient belt drive operation. Bent, damaged, cracked, worn, or broken pulleys must be replaced with pulleys equivalent to original equipment type and size.

Poly "V" Belts

Poly "V," ribbed "V," or serpentine belts are more flexible than conventional V belts since they are of smaller cross sectional dimension. They are also constructed of a combination of rubber and fabric. The poly V belt consists of a series of small inner surface Vs that grip corresponding V grooves in poly V pulleys.

A unique feature of this type of belt is that it can be routed in a variety of ways including looping the back of the belt over a flat surfaced pulley. This is not possible with the conventional V belt since it would crack and tear if routed in this manner.

Similar operating principles regarding belt tension, belt condition, pulley condition, and pulley ratios apply as they do to conventional V belt drives discussed earlier.

Cog Belt Drives

Cog belt drives, in some cases, are used to drive overhead camshafts, auxiliary shafts, and diesel fuel injection pumps.

In all of these cases, a precise drive relationship

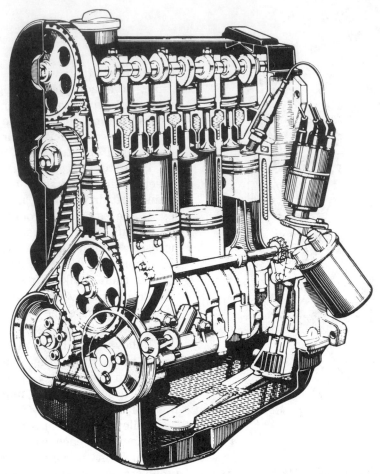

FIGURE 4-20. Overhead camshaft cog belt drive. Note auxiliary shaft used to drive oil pump, distributor, and fuel pump. *(Courtesy of Chrysler Corporation)*

must be maintained between the engine crankshaft and the driven component.

On a four-stroke-cycle engine for example, the camshaft and the diesel injection pump must be driven at exactly half the speed of the crankshaft. They must also be precisely timed to the engine crankshaft and piston position. This timing and speed ratio relationship must be continuously maintained during all phases of the operating life of the engine. This places more rigorous requirements on the cog belt drive than are required for other V belt drives.

The cog belt must not stretch or lose its tension. Belt construction such as fiber glass reinforcement provides this characteristic. The cog belt must not slip. Teeth or cogs on the inner circumference of the belt, and corresponding teeth on the drive and driven sprockets, prevent slippage. The cog belt must not deteriorate over long periods of time from slight oil or water contamination. Synthetic rubber compounds assure long life under these conditions. The cog belt must not encounter foreign objects such as twigs, stones, ice, or snow during operation which

could cause the drive to fail. A shield almost completely enclosing the cog belt drive prevents entry of such foreign objects.

Proper cog belt tension is provided by a belt tensioner adjustment. Proper cog belt operation (and engine operation) requires that precise belt tension specifications be followed when making adjustments.

PART 3   SELF-CHECK

1. What materials are used for automotive lines and fittings?
2. Kinked or flattened sections in tubing _____ flow.
3. Name three types of automotive drive belts.
4. All belt drives rely on proper belt _____ to prevent slippage.
5. Cogged or toothed drive belts are used where no _____ can be tolerated.

PART 4   TEST QUESTIONS

Select the one best answer for each question.

1. Mechanic A says that only seamless steel tubing is used for fuel injection lines. Mechanic B says seamless steel tubing is used for hydraulic brake lines. Who is right?
   (a) Mechanic A
   (b) Mechanic B
   (c) neither A nor B
   (d) both A and B

2. A tubing bender must be used when bending tubing to:
   (a) prevent flattening
   (b) prevent flow restriction
   (c) reduce flow
   (d) (a) and (c) only
   (e) (a) and (b) only

3. Automotive drive belts include:
   (a) V belts, seat belts, cog belts
   (b) seat belts, poly V belts, cog belts
   (c) cog belts, V belts, poly V belts
   (d) poly V belts, seat belts, V belts

4. Proper belt drive operation relies on:
   (a) belt condition
   (b) belt tension
   (c) pulley condition
   (d) all of the above

5. Accessory drive speed is determined by:
   (a) pulley size
   (b) belt type and size
   (c) belt tension
   (d) accessory load
   (e) all of the above

ENGINES

Chapter 5

Engine Principles

Performance Objectives

After sufficient study of this chapter and the appropriate training aids and models, you should be able to do the following:

1. Describe energy conversion in the internal combustion engine.
2. Identify basic engine components by name.
3. Describe basic four-stroke-cycle gasoline and diesel engine operation.
4. Describe basic two-stroke-cycle gasoline and diesel engine operation.
5. Identify ten engine operating systems.
6. Use seven methods to classify engine type and size.
7. Define and calculate engine bore, stroke, displacement, and compression ratios.
8. Define force, pressure, vacuum, and atmospheric pressure.
9. Define energy, work, and power.
10. Define and calculate engine brake power, indicated power, and friction power.
11. Define engine torque.
12. Describe engine volumetric, thermal, mechanical, and fuel efficiency.
13. Describe dynamometer operation.
14. Complete the self-check with at least 80 percent accuracy.
15. Complete the test questions with at least 80 percent accuracy.

The engine is required to produce the power to drive the vehicle under varying conditions of speed and load. Vehicle size and weight, as well as performance requirements, determine the size of the power plant that a vehicle will have.

Both two- and four-stroke-cycle engines are used in automotive applications. The two-stroke-cycle engine is used in some trucks, and the four-stroke-cycle engine is used in cars as well as in trucks.

Engines may be fueled by gasoline, propane (LPG—Liquefied Petroleum Gas), or diesel fuel. Compressed Natural Gas (CNG) may also be used in some vehicles.

Multicylinder reciprocating piston engines with four, five, six, eight, twelve, or sixteen cylinders have been used. The four-, six- and eight-cylinder engines are the most common. A limited number of rotary engines are also being used.

Regardless of the type of engine, the demands placed on the engine to perform are rigorous. Speed and load are constantly being changed during op-

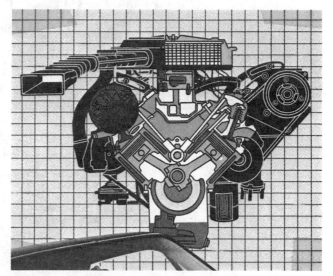

FIGURE 5-1. Cross-sectional view of a General Motors V8 engine. (*Courtesy of General Motors Corporation*)

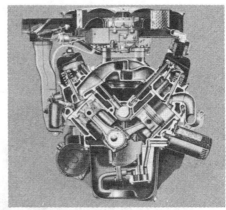

FIGURE 5-2. Ford V8 engine cross-sectional view. (*Courtesy of Ford Motor Co. of Canada Ltd.*)

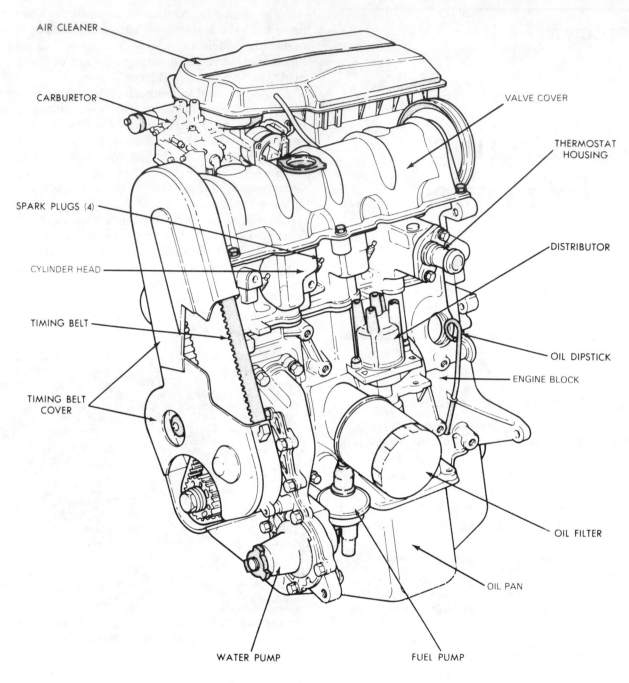

AIR CLEANER

CARBURETOR

SPARK PLUGS (4)

CYLINDER HEAD

TIMING BELT

TIMING BELT COVER

VALVE COVER

THERMOSTAT HOUSING

DISTRIBUTOR

OIL DIPSTICK

ENGINE BLOCK

OIL FILTER

OIL PAN

WATER PUMP

FUEL PUMP

FIGURE 5-3. Major exterior components of transverse four-cylinder engine. *(Courtesy of Chrysler Corporation)*

FIGURE 5-4. Chrysler's transverse-mounted overhead cam engine.

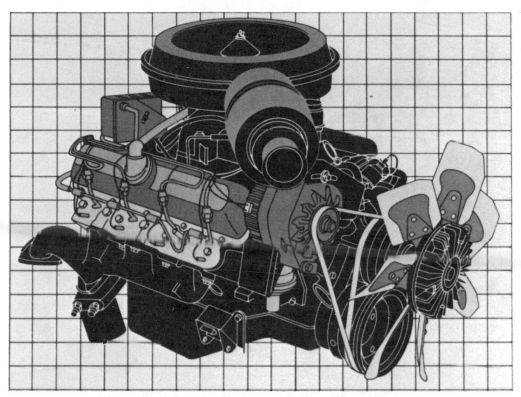

FIGURE 5-5. General Motors 350 C.I.D. (5.7-liter) V8 diesel engine. *(Courtesy of General Motors Corporation)*

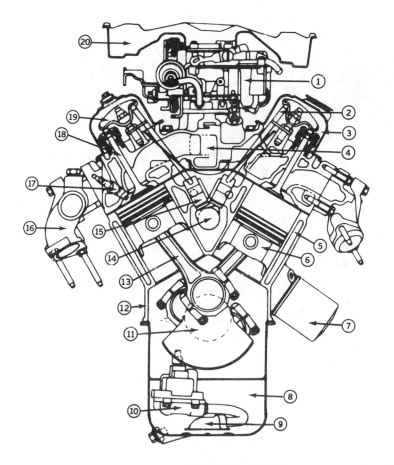

1. Carburetor	11. Crankshaft
2. Pushrod	12. Cylinder block
3. Valve cover	13. Connecting rod
4. Intake manifold	14. Camshaft
5. Water jacket	15. Valve lifter
6. Piston	16. Exhaust manifold
7. Oil filter	17. Spark plug
8. Oil pan	18. Valve
9. Oil pick-up screen	19. Rocker arm
10. Oil pump	20. Air cleaner

FIGURE 5-6. Major components of 65° V6 engine.

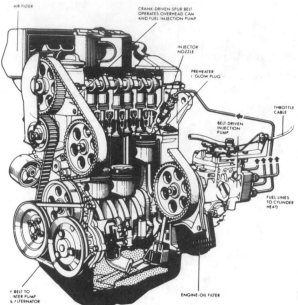

FIGURE 5-7. Cutaway view of Volkswagen four-cylinder diesel engine.

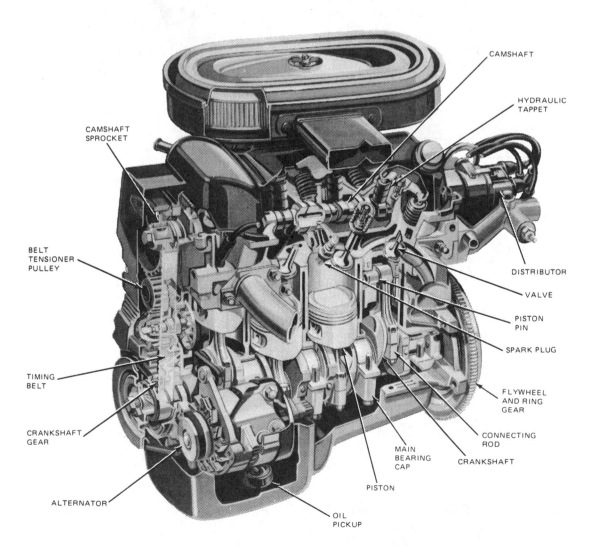

FIGURE 5-8. Cutaway view and components of transverse four-cylinder overhead cam engine. (*Courtesy of Ford Motor Co. of Canada Ltd.*)

eration. Seasonal and regional temperature extremes are encountered, which also must be considered in engine operation.

Engine location is in the front of most vehicles and in the rear of others. The front-mounted engine is the most common and can be either in a front wheel drive, rear wheel drive, or four wheel drive vehicle.

To diagnose engine problems or service engines effectively, it is necessary to have a thorough understanding of the operating principles and construction features of the internal combustion engine.

PART 1   ENERGY CONVERSION

The internal combustion engine is a device used to convert the chemical energy of the fuel (gasoline or diesel fuel) into heat energy, and then to convert this heat energy into usable mechanical energy. This is achieved by combining the appropriate amounts of air and fuel, and burning the mixture in an enclosed cylinder at a controlled rate. A movable piston in the cylinder is forced down by the expanding gases of combustion.

An average air-fuel ratio for good combustion is about 15 parts of air to 1 part of fuel by weight. This means that for every gallon of gasoline burned, the oxygen in about 9000 to 10,000 gallons of air is required. Air is about 20 percent oxygen and 80 percent nitrogen.

Diesel engines operate on a much wider air to fuel ratio, since air intake is not regulated on most diesels. Ratios may range from about 20 to 1 to about 100 to 1. This fact, plus the high compression of the diesel, makes it a very fuel-efficient engine.

The movable piston in the cylinder is connected to the top of a connecting rod. The bottom of the

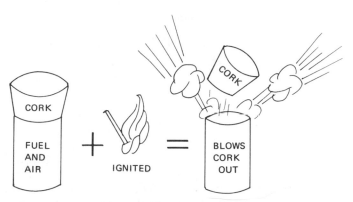

FIGURE 5-10. When gasoline and air are burned in a confined area, heat and pressure are created (internal combustion). This is the chemical energy of the fuel and air converted into heat energy.

connecting rod is attached to the offset portion of a crankshaft. As the piston is forced down, this force is transferred to the crankshaft, causing the crankshaft to rotate. The reciprocating (back and forth or up and down) movement of the piston is converted to rotary (turning) motion of the crankshaft, which supplies the power to drive the vehicle.

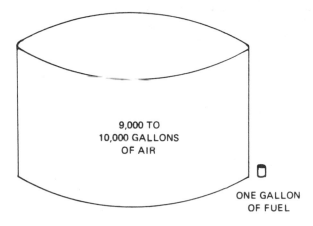

FIGURE 5-9. Approximately 9,000 to 10,000 gallons of air are required to burn one gallon of gasoline in an automobile engine.

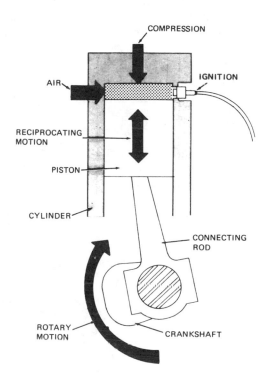

FIGURE 5-11. Pressure from the expanding gases of combustion in the cylinder forces the piston down. Downward movement of the piston is converted to rotary motion of the crankshaft. This is heat energy converted into mechanical energy.

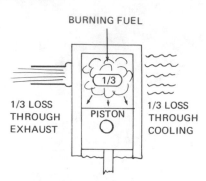

FIGURE 5-12. Of the available heat energy in the gasoline, only about one third is usable energy in the internal combustion engine.

The efficiency of the internal combustion, reciprocating piston engine in converting the potential energy in fuel into mechanical energy is only about 33 percent. Of the available heat energy in the fuel, about one-third is lost through the exhaust system and one-third is absorbed and dissipated by the cooling system. Of the remaining one-third, about one-half is lost through friction in the engine and drive train parts. This leaves only about 15 percent of the energy in the fuel available at the vehicle's drive wheels.

The overall efficiency of the diesel engine is considerably higher than that of the gasoline engine. The reasons for this are: the higher compression ratio, the higher air to fuel ratio, and the higher heat value of the fuel. The useful power developed at the drive wheels by a diesel engine is about 25 percent, as compared to 15 percent by a gasoline engine.

PART 2 BASIC ENGINE COMPONENTS

The basic single-cylinder engine consists of a cylinder (engine block), a movable piston inside this cylinder, a connecting rod attached at the top end to the piston and at the bottom to the offset portion of a crankshaft, a camshaft to operate the two valves (intake and exhaust), and a cylinder head. A flywheel is attached to one end of the crankshaft. The other end of the crankshaft has a gear to drive the camshaft gear. The camshaft gear is twice as large as the crankshaft gear. This drives the camshaft at half the speed of the crankshaft.

PART 3 FOUR-STROKE-CYCLE GASOLINE ENGINE OPERATION

The movement of the piston from its upper-most position (TDC, top dead center) to its lowest position (BDC, bottom dead center) is called a *stroke*. Most automobile engines operate on the four-stroke-cycle principle. A series of events involving four strokes of the piston completes one cycle. These events are

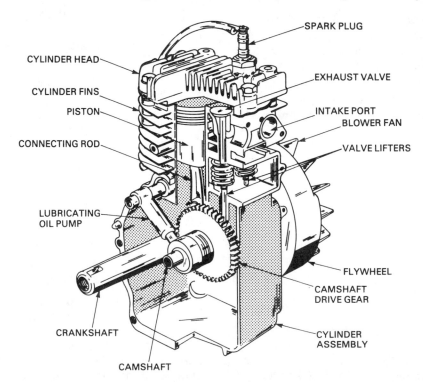

FIGURE 5-13. Basic components of a single-cylinder four-stroke-cycle engine.

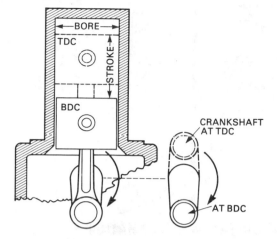

FIGURE 5–14. The distance the piston travels from its highest position in the cylinder (TDC, top dead center) to its lowest position in the cylinder (BDC, bottom dead center) is known as the stroke. The length of the stroke is determined by crankshaft design.

(1) the intake stroke, (2) the compression stroke, (3) the power stroke, and (4) the exhaust stroke. Two revolutions of the crankshaft and one revolution of the camshaft are required to complete one cycle.

On the intake stroke the piston is pulled down in the cylinder by the crankshaft and connecting rod. During this time the intake valve is held open by the camshaft. Since the piston has moved down in the cylinder, creating a low pressure area (vacuum), atmospheric pressure forces a mixture of air and fuel past the intake valve into the cylinder. Atmospheric pressure is approximately 14.7 pounds per square inch (about 101.35 kilopascals) at sea level. Pressure in the cylinder during the intake stroke is considerably less than this. The pressure difference is the force that causes the air-fuel mixture to flow into the cylinder, since a liquid or a gas (vapor) will always flow from a high- to a low-pressure area.

As the piston is moved up by the crankshaft from BDC, the intake valve closes. The air-fuel mixture is trapped in the cylinder above the piston. Further piston travel compresses the air-fuel mixture to approximately one-eighth of its original volume (approximately 8:1 compression ratio) when the piston has reached TDC. This completes the compression stroke.

When the piston is at or near TDC, the air-fuel mixture is ignited. The burning of the air-fuel mixture (*combustion*) takes place at a controlled rate. Expansion of the burning mixture causes a rapid rise in pressure. This increased pressure forces the piston down on the power stroke, causing the crankshaft to rotate.

At the end of the power stroke the camshaft opens the exhaust valve, and the exhaust stroke begins. Remaining pressure in the cylinder, and upward movement of the piston, force the exhaust

gases out of the cylinder. At the end of the exhaust stroke, the exhaust valve closes and the intake valve opens, repeating the entire cycle of events over and over again.

To start the engine, some method of cranking the engine is required to turn the crankshaft and cause piston movement. This is done by the starter motor when the ignition key is in the start position. When sufficient air-fuel mixture has entered the cylinders and is ignited, the power strokes create enough energy to continue crankshaft rotation. At this point, the ignition key is released to the run position and the starter is disengaged.

Sufficient energy is stored in the flywheel and other rotating parts on the power strokes to move the pistons and related parts through the other three strokes (exhaust, intake, and compression). The amount of air-fuel mixture allowed to enter the cylinders determines the power and speed developed by the engine.

PART 4 TWO-STROKE-CYCLE GASOLINE ENGINE OPERATION

Two-stroke-cycle engine operation, as the name implies, requires only two strokes of the piston to complete all four events: intake, compression, power, and exhaust. There are several types of two-stroke-cycle engines. One type uses ports and a reed valve to perform the function of the intake and exhaust valves of the four-stroke-cycle engine. A specially designed piston head helps to control the flow of intake and exhaust gases. This type of engine is used mostly on small engine power applications. A mix-

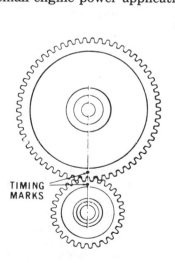

FIGURE 5–15. The crankshaft drives the camshaft at one-half crankshaft speed. (Crankshaft to camshaft ratio = 2:1)

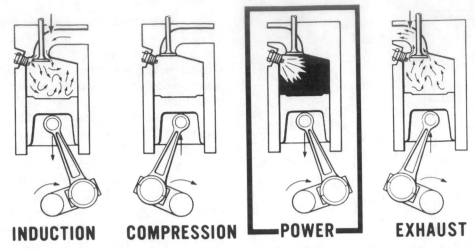

INDUCTION   **COMPRESSION**   **POWER**   **EXHAUST**

FIGURE 5-16. The four-stroke-cycle engine requires four strokes to complete one cycle of events: intake stroke, compression stroke, power stroke, and exhaust stroke. This cycle of events requires two complete revolutions of the crankshaft. *(Courtesy of Ford Motor Co. of Canada Ltd.)*

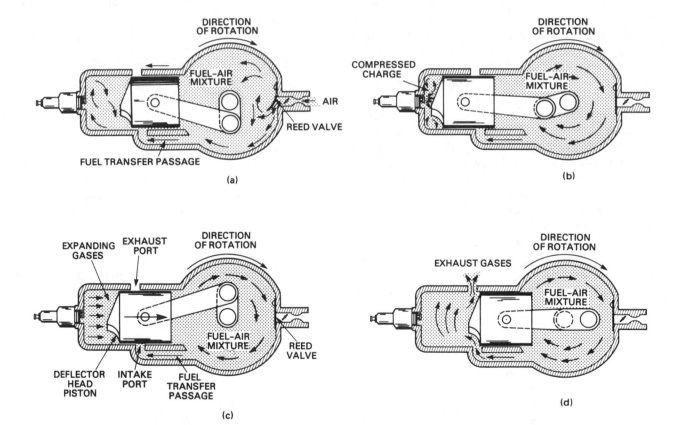

FIGURE 5-17. The two-stroke-cycle engine requires two strokes of the piston and one revolution of the crankshaft to complete one cycle of events: intake, compression, power, exhaust. (A) Movement of the piston from BDC to TDC completes both intake and compression. (B) When the piston nears TDC, the compressed air-fuel mixture is ignited, causing expansion of the gases. Note that the reed valve is closed. (C) Expanding gases in the cylinder force the piston down, rotating the crankshaft. Downward movement of the piston compresses the air-fuel mixture in the crankcase. (D) With the piston at BDC, the intake and exhaust ports are both open, allowing exhaust gases to leave the cylinder and air-fuel mixture to enter the cylinder.

ture of air-fuel and oil in correct proportion is used. There is no separate lubrication system. The oil in the mixture provides the lubrication required.

PART 5 FOUR-STROKE-CYCLE DIESEL ENGINE OPERATION

The diesel engine is easily recognized by the absence of such components as spark plugs, ignition wires, coil, and distributor, common to gasoline engines.

In the diesel engine the movement of the piston from its uppermost position (TDC, top dead center) to its lowest (BDC, bottom dead center) position is called a stroke. Many engines operate on the four-stroke-cycle principle. A series of events involving four strokes of the piston completes one cycle. These events are: (1) the intake stroke, (2) the compression stroke, (3) the power stroke, and (4) the exhaust stroke. Two revolutions of the crankshaft and one revolution of the camshaft are required to complete one cycle.

On the intake stroke the piston is pulled down in the cylinder by the crankshaft and connecting rod. During this time the intake valve is held open by the camshaft. Since the piston has moved down in the cylinder, creating a low-pressure area (vacuum), atmospheric pressure forces air past the intake valve into the cylinder. Atmospheric pressure is approximately 14.7 pounds per square inch (about 101.35 kilopascals) at sea level. Pressure in the cylinder during the intake stroke is considerably less than this. The pressure difference is the force that causes the air to flow into the cylinder, since a liquid or a gas (vapor) will always flow from a high- to a low-pressure area.

As the piston is moved up by the crankshaft from BDC, the intake valve closes. The air is trapped in the cylinder above the piston. Further piston travel compresses the air to approximately 1/20 of its original volume (approximately 20:1 compression ratio) when the piston has reached TDC. This completes the compression stroke. (Compression ratios vary from about 13:1 to about 22:1.) Compressing the air to this extent creates a great deal of friction between the air molecules, which creates sufficient heat to ignite the fuel when it is injected. This temperature could be in the area of 800°F (426.6°C) to 1200°F (648.8°C). For this reason, a spark ignition system is not required on a diesel engine.

The burning of the air-fuel mixture (combustion) occurs at a controlled rate. Expansion of the burning mixture increases pressure. This increased pressure forces the piston down on the power stroke, causing the crankshaft to rotate.

At the end of the power stroke, the camshaft opens the exhaust valve, and the exhaust stroke begins. Remaining pressure in the cylinder and upward movement of the piston force the exhaust gases out of the cylinder. At the end of the exhaust stroke, the exhaust valve closes and the intake valve opens, continually repeating the entire cycle of events.

To start the engine, some method of cranking the engine is required to turn the crankshaft and cause piston movement. This is done by the starting

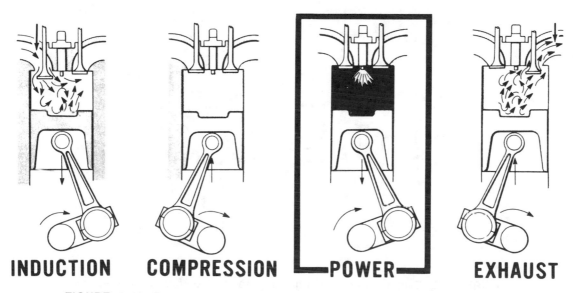

INDUCTION   **COMPRESSION**   **POWER**   **EXHAUST**

FIGURE 5–18. Four-stroke-cycle diesel engine operation consists of four strokes of the piston to complete one cycle of events. This cycle is repeated over and over as the engine runs.

motor when the key is turned to the start position. When sufficient air has entered the cylinders and fuel injected, the power strokes create enough energy to continue crankshaft rotation. At this point the key is released and the starter is disengaged.

Sufficient energy is stored in the fly-wheel and other rotating parts on the power strokes to move the pistons and related parts through the other three strokes (exhaust, intake, and compression). The amount of fuel allowed to enter the cylinders will determine the power and speed developed by the engine.

PART 6 TWO-STROKE-CYCLE DIESEL ENGINE OPERATION

The two-stroke- cycle diesel engine completes all four events, (intake, compression, power, and exhaust) in one revolution of the crankshaft (or two strokes of the piston).

A series of ports or openings is arranged around the cylinder in such a position that the ports are open when the piston is at the bottom of its stroke. A blower forces air into the cylinder through the open ports, expelling all remaining exhaust gases past the open exhaust valves and filling the cylinder with air. This is called scavenging.

As the piston moves up, the exhaust valves close and the piston covers the ports. The air trapped above the piston is compressed since the exhaust valve is closed. Just before the piston reaches top dead center, the required amount of fuel is injected into the cylinder. The heat generated by compressing the air immediately ignites the fuel. Combustion continues until the injected fuel has been burned. The pressure resulting from combustion forces the piston downward on the power stroke. When the piston is approximately halfway down, the exhaust valves are opened, allowing the exhaust gases to es-

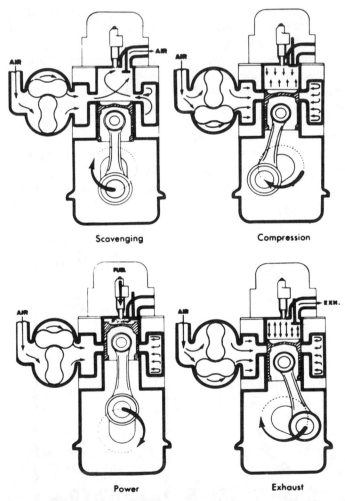

Scavenging

Compression

Power

Exhaust

FIGURE 5-19. Two-stroke-cycle engine operation. All four events—intake (scavenging), compression, power, and exhaust—are completed in only two strokes of the piston (one turn of the crankshaft). *(Courtesy of Detroit Diesel Allison Division of General Motors Corporation)*

cape. Further downward movement uncovers the inlet ports, causing fresh air to enter the cylinder and expel the exhaust gases. The entire procedure is then repeated, as the engine continues to run.

PART 7 ENGINE SYSTEMS

For an engine to operate, a number of systems must perform their function in an efficient manner. These are as follows:

• The *fuel system* provides fuel to the cylinders.

• The *induction system* provides the air to the cylinders.

• The *compression system* sufficiently compresses the air, or the air-fuel mixture, to provide a controlled rate of combustion and expansion.

• The *ignition system* provides the means for igniting the air-fuel mixture on gas engines.

• The *exhaust system* provides the means to efficiently dispose of the burned gases.

• The *lubrication system* reduces friction and wear and helps in cooling, sealing, and cleaning.

• The *cooling system* maintains the engine's most efficient operating temperature.

• The *ventilation system* removes harmful crankcase vapors.

• The *emission control systems* control the amount of harmful pollutants emitted into the atmosphere by the automobile.

PART 8 ENGINE CLASSIFICATIONS

Engines can be classified in a number of different ways, depending on engine design.

By Cycles. Two-stroke- and four-stroke-cycle engines.

By Cooling Systems. Liquid-cooled engines and air-cooled engines are being used. Liquid-cooled engines are the most common in the automotive industry.

By Fuel System. Gasoline, diesel and propane fuel systems are currently used in automobile engines.

By Ignition System. Gas engines use the spark (electrical) ignition system. The electrical ignition system causes a spark across the spark plug electrodes in the cylinder at the end of the compression stroke which ignites the vaporized fuel and air mixture.

Diesel engines use the heat from compressing the air to ignite the fuel when it is injected into the cylinder at the end of the compression stroke. Since diesel engine compression ratios (about 22:1) are much higher than gasoline engine compression ratios, sufficient heat is generated by compressing the air to immediately ignite the fuel upon injection.

By Valve Arrangement. Four types of valve arrangements have been used, as shown in Figure 5-20. Of the four types (L, T, F, and I heads), the I head is the most common on both in-block and overhead camshaft designs.

By Cylinder Arrangement. Engine block configuration or cylinder arrangement depends on cylinder block design. Cylinders may be arranged in a straight line one behind the other. The most common *in-line* designs are the four- and six-cylinder engines.

The V type of cylinder arrangement uses two *banks* of cylinders arranged in a 60° or 90° V design. The most common examples are the V-8, with two banks of four cylinders each in a 90° design, and the V-6, with two banks of three cylinders each in either a 60° or 90° design. The horizontal opposed engine uses two banks of cylinders opposite each other with the crankshaft in between and all

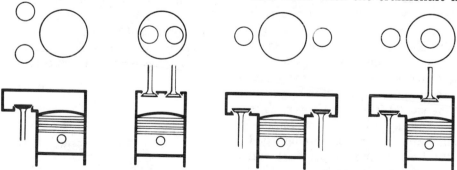

FIGURE 5-20. Engines can be classified by valve arrangement, as shown above. From left to right: L head, I head, T head, and F head. The most common arrangement is the I head or valve-in-head type.

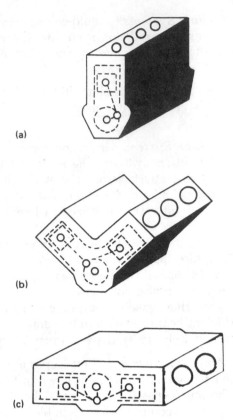

(a)

(b)

(c)

FIGURE 5-21. Engines are also classified by cylinder arrangement or configuration: (A) in-line cylinders; (B) V types; (C) horizontal opposed cylinders.

cylinders in a horizontal position. Both four- and six-cylinder types have been used.

By Displacement. Engine displacement is the amount of air displaced by the piston when it moves from BDC to TDC; it varies with cylinder bore size, length of piston stroke, and number of cylinders.

PART 9   ENGINE MEASUREMENTS

A number of factors determine the ability of an engine to produce usable power. Some of these factors are determined by the manufacturer, such as cylinder bore, stroke, displacement, and compression ratio. Other factors such as force, pressure, vacuum, and atmospheric pressure also affect the power output of an engine. The amount of power an engine is able to produce is measured in several ways, as is the efficiency of an engine. All of these factors, terms, and conditions must be properly understood to gain an understanding of their individual and combined effects on engine performance.

The following definitions are not intended to be highly technical or comprehensive in scope. They are, however, meant to be adequate for the purpose

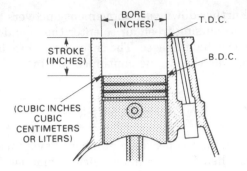

FIGURE 5-22. Length of stroke and bore diameter are stated in inches or millimeters (mm). Displacement is stated in cubic inches, cubic centimeters (cc), or liters (l). Displacement is calculated as follows: $\pi r^2 \times$ stroke $\times$ number of cylinders.

intended—to help the student gain competence in the understanding of an engine's operating principles, its ability to produce power, and some of its limitations.

Cylinder Bore

Cylinder bore is the diameter of the engine's cylinder measured in inches or millimeters. Cylinder bore size is a major factor in determining engine displacement.

Piston Stroke

The engine's stroke is the distance travelled by the piston from its bottom dead center position to its top dead center position measured in inches or millimeters. The distance travelled by the piston is determined by crankshaft design and is exactly twice the crank throw measurement.

The engine's stroke is also a major factor in engine displacement.

Displacement

The displacement of an engine is determined by cylinder bore diameter, length of stroke, and number of cylinders. Simply stated, it is the amount or volume of air pushed out of the cylinder (displaced) by one piston as it moves from BDC to TDC, multiplied by the number of cylinders in the engine.

Displacement is calculated as follows:

$$\pi r^2 \times \text{stroke} \times \text{no. of cylinders}$$

$$\pi = \frac{22}{7}$$

$$r^2 = \text{radius} \times \text{radius}$$

$$(\text{radius} = 1/2 \text{ of cylinder bore})$$

Therefore, a six-cylinder engine with a 3.800-inch bore and a 3.4-inch stroke would have a displacement of:

$$\frac{22}{7} \times (1.9 \times 1.9) \times (3.4 \times 6) = \frac{22}{7} \times 3.61 \times 20.4$$

$$\frac{22}{7} \times 73.644 = \frac{1620.168}{7} = 231.45 \text{ CID}$$

(cubic inches of displacement)

In metric terms, a six-cylinder engine with a 100.0-millimeter bore and a stroke of 80 millimeters, would be calculated as follows. First, since metric displacement is stated in cubic centimeters, it is necessary to convert the bore and stroke dimensions to centimeters.

100 mm = 10-cm bore   80 mm = 8-cm stroke

$$\frac{22}{7} \times (5 \times 5) \times (8 \times 6) = \frac{22}{7} \times 25 \times 48$$

or

$$\frac{22}{7} \times 1200 = \frac{26,400}{7} = 3771 \text{ cubic centimeters of displacement or 3.771 liters (L)}$$

The power an engine is able to produce depends very much on its displacement. Engines with more displacement are able to take in a greater amount of air-fuel mixture on each intake stroke and can therefore produce more power. Engine displacement can be increased by engine design in three ways: (1) increasing cylinder bore diameter, (2) lengthening the stroke, and (3) increasing the number of cylinders.

Compression Ratio-Gas Engine

The compression ratio of an engine is a comparison of the total volume of one cylinder (cylinder displacement plus combustion chamber volume) to combustion chamber volume. To calculate compression ration, *divide the combustion chamber volume into the total cylinder volume.* For example, if the combustion chamber volume is 5 cubic inches and the cylinder displacement is 36 cubic inches, the total cylinder volume is 41 cubic inches.

$$41 \div 5 = 8.2{:}1$$

Metric Example. If combustion chamber volume is 90 cubic centimeters and cylinder displacement is 650 cubic centimeters, the total cylinder volume is 740 cubic centimeters.

$$740 \div 90 = 8.22{:}1$$

These are typical compression ratios for gasoline engines.

An engine with an 8.2 compression ratio will produce approximately 150 pounds per square inch (psi) of compression pressure (1034.25 kilopascals, kPa). This rises to approximately 600 psi of combustion pressure (4137 kPa).

The compression ratio of an engine can be changed in several ways. To raise the compression ratio, the combustion chamber volume can be reduced and the cylinder volume left unchanged, or the cylinder volume can be increased (increased bore or stroke) and the combustion chamber volume left unchanged.

To lower the compression ratio, increase combustion chamber volume and leave cylinder volume unchanged or reduce cylinder volume (decrease bore or stroke) and leave combustion chamber volume unchanged.

The approximate maximum compression ratio for gasoline engines is about 14:1. Detonation and serious engine damage are the result of too high a compression ratio. Combustion chamber design and type of gasoline (octane or anti-knock rating) also affect the point at which detonation will occur. Detonation is the ignition of the fuel due to the high temperature caused by the high pressure in the combustion chamber. Fuel may be ignited before the spark occurs at the spark plug, and burning is rapid and uncontrolled. This causes parts to be subjected to excessive heat and stress.

Compression ratios must be high enough to produce adequate pressures and power. Compression ratios in passenger car engines prior to emission-

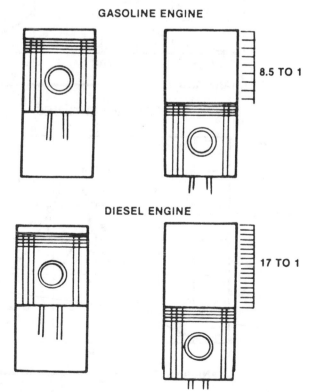

FIGURE 5-23. Comparison of compression ratios of typical gasoline and diesel engines. *(Courtesy of Ford Motor Co. of Canada Ltd.)*

control legislation were at approximately 12:1. This resulted in good power production but caused high exhaust emissions. One method of reducing exhaust emissions includes lowering the compression ratio to reduce combustion temperatures. High combustion temperatures cause excessive nitric oxide exhaust emissions.

Compression Ratio-Diesel Engines

The compression ratio of a diesel engine is much higher than that of a gasoline engine. This is possible since air only is compressed. Compressing air at diesel compression ratios causes air molecules to collide rapidly with each other. The friction caused by these collisions creates heat. Temperatures of 1000° Fahrenheit (540°C) or higher can be reached depending on the compression ratio. This is hot enough to ignite the fuel when it is injected near the top of the compression stroke.

Compression ratios are determined by cylinder displacement and combustion chamber volume. To calculate compression ratio, divide the combustion chamber volume into the total cylinder volume. For example, if the combustion chamber volume is 2 cubic inches and the cylinder displacement is 36 cubic inches, the total cylinder volume is 38 cubic inches.

$$38 \div 2 = 19:1$$

Metric Example. If combustion chamber volume is 36 cubic centimeters and cylinder displace-

GASOLINE ENGINES

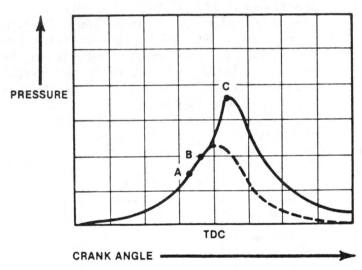

GASOLINE ENGINES:

Point A: The spark ignition is conducted. (Before the top dead center point when the compression process finishes)

Point B: The mixture starts to burn on a full scale.

At the instant it enters into a combustible state at the point B, the explosive combustion starts, and reaches the maximum (point C) at the 20-degree crank angle.

DIESEL ENGINES

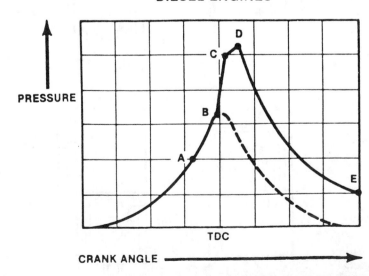

DIESEL ENGINE:

A-D: Fuel injection time

A-B: Retarded time of ignition (formation of igniting conditions)

B-C: Flame transmission time (increase of pressure)

C-D: Direct combustion time (late burning)

D-E: Later combustion time (combustion of unburned gas)

FIGURE 5-24. Comparison of pressure rise in gasoline engine and diesel engine cylinders. *(Courtesy of Ford Motor Co. of Canada Ltd.)*

ment is 650 cubic centimeters, the total cylinder volume is 686 cubic centimeters.

$$686 \div 36 = 19{:}1$$

There are typical compression ratios for diesel engines.

An engine with a 19:1 compression ratio will produce approximately 500 pounds per square inch (psi) of compression pressure (3447.5 kilopascals [kPa]). This rises to approximately 2000 psi of combustion pressure (13,790 kPa) when the piston reaches the top dead center position.

The compression ratio of an engine can be changed in several ways. To raise the compression ratio, the combustion chamber volume can be reduced and the cylinder volume left unchanged, or the cylinder volume can be increased (increased bore or stroke) and the combustion chamber volume left unchanged.

To lower the compression ratio, the combustion chamber volume can be increased and the cylinder volume left unchanged, or the cylinder volume can be reduced (decreased bore or stroke) and the combustion chamber volume left unchanged.

Compression ratios in diesel engines must be high enough to create sufficient heat for good ignition and adequate power.

PART 10 Force and Pressure

Force and Force Measurement

A force is a push, pull, or twist that acts on something. The push or pull attempts to change the state of motion of that thing or the at rest state of that thing. In other words, a force is something that can try to stop something that is moving or it can try to keep it moving. It can try to move something that is stopped, or it can try to prevent its movement.

The force of expanding gases in a cylinder causes the piston to move down on the power stroke. The force of a brake pad against a brake disc tries to stop the disc from turning.

The automobile uses the principle of force in a great variety of applications. The degree or magnitude of a force can be measured and is stated in pounds in the English system and in newtons in the metric system. For example, an engine weighing 300 pounds exerts a pulling force of 300 pounds on the hook of a portable engine lift on which it is suspended. The same engine, in metric terms, exerts a pulling force of 1334.4 newtons on that hook.

A twisting force (called torque) exerted on a drive shaft by an engine might be in the area of 50

pound feet under certain driving conditions. In metric terms this would be 67.79 newton meters (N m).

Pressure and Pressure Measurement

Pressure can be defined as a force applied over a specific area. For example, 100 pounds of metal resting on a 10 square inch area exerts a pressure of 100 pounds over the 10 square inches of area. The pressure exerted on one square inch is, therefore, 100 pounds divided by 10 square inches, (100 ÷ 10), which is 10 pounds per square inch of pressure.

Compression pressure in the engine's cylinder is measured in pounds per square inch. A typical example could be a compression pressure of 100 pounds per square inch.

In metric terms pressure is stated in kilopascals (kPa). For purposes of comparison, one pound per square inch is equal to 6.895 kPa. A typical compression pressure could be 700 kPa.

To understand the metric term *kilopascals*, we know that the prefix *kilo* means one thousand. Therefore, the term *kilopascals* means 1000 pascals. A pascal is a force of one newton over an area of one square meter ($1N/m^2$).

Atmospheric Pressure

The atmosphere is a layer of air surrounding the earth's surface. This layer of air exerts a force against the earth's surface because of the earth's force of gravity. This force or pressure of the atmosphere against the earth's surface is called atmospheric pressure.

Atmospheric pressure is greatest at sea level, since there is more atmosphere above a given point at sea level than there is at a given point on a high mountain. The air is, therefore, also less dense (air molecules not packed together as tightly) at higher altitudes.

A one square inch column of atmosphere at sea level weighs 14.7 pounds. Atmospheric pressure at sea level is, therefore, 14.7 pounds per square inch. However, at the top of a 10,000-foot-high mountain, a one square inch column of air weighs only 12.2 pounds; therefore, atmospheric pressure is 12.2 pounds per square inch at that altitude.

It is important to recognize this fact since the air intake of an engine is affected adversely by increased altitude.

It should also be remembered that the atmosphere consists of approximately 20 percent oxygen and nearly 80 percent nitrogen, with a small percentage of other elements. It is the oxygen in the air that is needed to combine with fuel to support combustion.

The air at sea level is more dense, or more tightly compacted, than it is at higher altitudes. For this reason, an engine is able to produce more power at sea level than at higher altitudes.

The temperature of air also has a bearing on an engine's ability to produce power. When air is heated, it expands and becomes less dense. The engine is not able to take in as much air on the intake stroke because of this and will, therefore, produce less power. Today's engines, however, are equipped with intake air temperature control systems which more closely control inlet air temperatures. Air density is stated as lb/ft^3 or as kg/m^3.

The humidity of the air is the percentage of moisture the air is able to keep in suspension at a given temperature. At 100 percent humidity, the air cannot support any additional moisture. At 50 percent humidity, there is half as much moisture in the air as it is able to support at that temperature. Moisture in the air improves engine performance since it has a cooling effect. Engines do not perform as well in hot dry air.

Atmospheric Pressure Measurement

Atmospheric pressure is measured with a barometer and is expressed in inches or millimeters of mercury (or hg).

A simple barometer is a glass tube closed at one end and open at the other. The tube is filled with mercury. The open end is then held shut while the tube is inverted and the open end is submerged in an open top dish filled with mercury. With the mercury-filled tube fixed in this position, the mercury level in the tube will drop slightly, leaving part of the tube empty at the top. As atmospheric pressure is able to act on the mercury in the open dish, the mercury level in the tube will rise or fall as atmospheric pressure rises or falls. The height of the mercury in the tube above the surface of the mercury in the dish is measured in inches; this is the barometric pressure. At sea level, 14.7 pounds per square inch of atmospheric pressure results in 29.92 inches of mercury in the barometer. In metric terms, barometric pressure at sea level is expressed as 101.35 kilopascals (kPa) since one inch of mercury is equal to 3.38 kPa. Or to put it another way, atmospheric pressure at sea level is 14.7 pounds per square inch, or 101.35 kilopascals, since one pound per square inch of pressure is equal to 6.895 kPa. Another unit of pressure measurement is the bar. One bar is equal to 0.986923 atmosphere.

A kilopascal is 1000 pascals since the prefix kilo represents 1000. A pascal is equal to a newton of force applied over one square meter.

Measuring Other Pressures

Pressure testing gauges used in the automotive industry register zero at atmospheric pressure. All pressure measurements taken are, therefore, actually pressures above atmospheric pressure, except for vacuum measurements.

Vacuum Measurements

Any pressure which is less than atmospheric pressure is called a vacuum. Actually, it is a partial vacuum.

Vacuum is measured as a difference in pressure. The difference in pressure between atmospheric pressure and the pressure being measured (intake manifold vacuum for instance) is expressed in inches of mercury or millimeters of mercury. This is so since the measurement is taken with a "U" tube mercury manometer.

A "U" tube manometer is a measuring device that indicates a pressure difference by the difference in the height of fluid in the two columns of the "U" tube. A mercury manometer is used to measure a relatively large pressure difference from atmospheric pressure. A water manometer is used to measure minor differences, and it can measure more accurately since water is lighter than mercury. Manometers are used to measure such items as intake manifold pressure (or vacuum), exhaust back pressure, crankcase pressure, and boost pressure (turbocharger output pressure).

Dial type automotive vacuum gauges are commonly used to measure intake manifold vacuum. These gauges are calibrated to indicate inches or millimeters of mercury on the dial and can be read directly.

PART 11   ENERGY, WORK, AND POWER

Energy

Energy can be defined as the potential or ability to do work. The fuel in an automobile has the potential for doing work if it is placed in the engine's cylinders, combined with compressed air, and ignited. When these conditions are met, the potential energy of the raw fuel becomes the kinetic energy of rapidly expanding gases caused by combustion.

This kinetic energy of the burning fuel forces the piston downward in the cylinder, which results in usable crankshaft rotation.

From this we can see that there are two basic

forms of energy—potential energy, which does not result in any action or motion until proper conditions are met, and kinetic energy, which is the ability to do work because of motion.

Another example of kinetic energy is the energy of a vehicle moving at road speed. The vehicle continues to move even after the source of power (engine) is disconnected from the drive train.

The vehicle continues to move because of the kinetic energy stored in the moving vehicle. When the brakes are applied, the kinetic energy of the moving vehicle is converted, by friction, to heat energy.

Work

To do work requires energy. Work is said to be done when an applied force overcomes a resistance and moves through a distance. Work produces measurable results. When sufficient energy is expended through an application of force (push, pull, or twist) to overcome the resistance to motion of any particular object, movement is the result.

Pulling a one pound object a distance of one foot results in one foot pound of work being done (if friction is ignored). In other words, force times distance equals work ($W = F \times D$).

Units of measurement for work in the English system include foot pounds and inch pounds—both being the most commonly used in the automotive industry.

In metric terms, the formula $W = F \times D$ also applies. The unit of force measurement is the newton (N), and the unit of distance measurement is the meter (m). Therefore, when a force of one newton is required to move an object a distance of one meter, the unit measurement of work done is one newton meter (1N m), which is equal to one joule (J). The relationship of the joule to the kilowatt is discussed under engine power.

Power

Power is the rate at which work is being done. Power can also be defined as the ability to do a specific amount of work in a specific amount of time.

Engine power in the English system is stated in horsepower and in the metric system in kilowatts. Both systems are explained here. The formula for calculating power is $P = F \times D \div T$, where F = force, D = distance, and T = time.

Engine Power—Brake Power

A man named Watt, observing the ability of a horse to do work in a mine, decided arbitrarily that this ability to do work was the equivalent of raising 33,000 pounds of coal a distance of one foot in one

minute. This became the standard measurement of a unit of power called horsepower (HP).

This can be expressed as a formula.

1HP = 33,000 pounds $\times$ 1 foot $\times$ 1 minute.

This formula allows the horsepower of an engine to be calculated if certain factors are known. These factors are: the force produced by an engine and the distance through which that force moves in one minute.

A device known as the prony brake can be used to obtain these factors. Since the prony brake is a braking device, the output of an engine is stated in terms of brake power.

To determine the brake horsepower of an engine, we need to calculate the engine's force times the distance through which that force travels in one minute, and divide Watt's formula for one horsepower into the result of that calculation.

A prony brake uses a drum attached to the engine flywheel. A contracting brake band surrounds the drum. The band can be tightened to increase the load on the engine. An arm is attached at one end to the band. The other end of the arm is connected to a scale through a knife edge device. This assures accuracy of arm length from the center of crankshaft rotation to the scale.

With the engine running, the band is slowly tightened. This causes the arm to exert pressure on the scale. The brake horsepower output of an engine can be calculated using Watt's formula for one horsepower and the prony brake test results. Simply divide Watt's formula into the prony brake test results.

Let's calculate the brake horsepower of a theoretical engine, assuming the following conditions.

• Engine speed: 2000 revolutions per minute (rpm).

• Arm length: 3 feet (radius of circle arm would make if allowed to turn)

• Reading on scale: 100 pounds

Don't forget the formula: $F \times D \times T$ divided by 33,000 pounds $\times$ 1 ft. $\times$ 1 minute = Brake Horsepower (BHP).

And, don't forget that, to determine the circumference of a circle, we calculate $2\pi \times$ radius or $2\pi r$, and we know that π is 22/7.

Therefore:

$$F = 100 \text{ pounds}$$
$$D = 3 \text{ ft.} \times 2\pi \times 2000$$
$$T = 1 \text{ minute}$$

Using this information produces this formula.

$$\frac{2\pi \times 3 \times 2000 \times 100 \times 1}{33,000 \times 1 \times 1} =$$

$$\frac{3 \times 2000 \times 100 \times 1}{5250} = \frac{600,000}{5250} = 114.28 \text{ BHP}$$

Dividing 2π into 33,000 gives us the denominator of 5,250. Multiplying the remaining numerator figures results in 600,000. One horsepower is equal to 0.746 kilowatts (kW). Therefore, 114.28 BHP = 85.25 kW.

Indicated Power

Indicated power is the theoretical power an engine is able to produce. It is calculated by using the following factors:

- P = mean effective pressure in the cylinder in pounds per square inch
- L = length of piston stroke in feet
- A = area of cylinder cross section in square inches
- N = number of power strokes per minute for one cylinder
- K = number of cylinders in the engine.

The formula for calculating indicated horsepower is, therefore,

$$\frac{\text{PLANK}}{33,000} = \text{IP}$$

Using this formula, it is possible to calculate the IP of an engine if the number of cylinders in the engine, the engine's bore and stroke, the engine's speed, and the mean effective pressure in the cylinder are known.

Friction Power

Friction power is the power required to overcome the friction of the various moving parts of the engine as it runs. Friction power increases as engine size and speed are increased.

The friction power of an engine can be calculated (if the indicated power and brake power are known) by subtracting the BP from the IP (IP − BP = FP).

SAE Power

SAE power is the power of an engine as determined by the Society of Automotive Engineers. Tests are performed under rigorously controlled conditions including the inlet air temperature, ambient temperature, humidity, and the like. A number of specific conditions, such as inlet air restriction and exhaust restriction are also stated, since these are determining factors. Other factors and conditions must also be met.

Aside from all these factors and conditions, SAE power is measured at the transmission output shaft, with all normal engine accessories mounted and operating. This includes the air cleaner and exhaust system.

Since a particular engine model may be used by a vehicle manufacturer for several different applications and may be equipped differently on different models, the SAE power for a particular engine varies depending on how it is equipped.

Engine Power—Kilowatts (kW)

In the metric system engine power is stated in kilowatts.

The power output of an engine is calculated, as stated earlier, by using the formula $P = W \div T$, where P = power, W = work, and T = time. We also know that work represents force × distance.

Force in the metric system is measured in newtons or N. Distance, for our purposes here, is measured in meters or m. Therefore, work can be expressed in terms of newton meters (Nm).

Time is stated in minutes. To determine the power of an engine, we calculate force times distance divided by time (F × D ÷ T).

The electrical unit for measuring work is the joule. One joule is the equivalent of one ampere of current under one volt of pressure for one second. One joule is also the equivalent of one newton of force moving one meter of distance in one second.

The watt is the unit of electrical power and is the equivalent of one joule per second. One kilowatt is one thousand watts.

To summarize:

1 N m = 1 joule

1 joule per second = 1 watt (W)

1000 watts = 1 kilowatt (kW)

It would be possible to determine the power output in kilowatts of an engine by using a prony brake described earlier.

If, for example, the prony brake had a torque arm length of one meter, and the scale upon which it acted measured the applied force in newtons, the resultant power would be stated in newton meters. The newton meter output, at a given engine speed measured in revolutions per minute, could then be used to calculate engine power in kilowatts.

Assuming an engine speed of 2000 rpm, we would obtain the engine speed per second by dividing 2000 by 60, since kilowatts is joules per second.

$$2000 \div 60 = 33.33$$

Assuming further that the applied force at the end of the torque arm is 1000 newtons and the length of the torque arm is one meter, we calculate as follows:

$$2\pi \times 1 \times 33.33 = 209.5 \text{ kW}$$

or

$$\frac{2000}{60} \times 2\pi \times 1 = 209.5 \text{ kW}$$

or

$$2\pi \times 1 \times \frac{2000}{60} = 209.5 \text{ kW}$$

One kilowatt is 1.341 horsepower. Therefore, 209.5 kW is equal to 280 horsepower.

Friction

A certain amount of force (push or pull) is required to slide one object over the surface of another. This resistance to motion between two objects in contact with each other is called friction. Friction increases with load. It requires more effort to slide a heavy object across a surface than it does to slide a lighter object over the same surface.

The condition of the two surfaces in contact also affects the degree of friction. Smooth surfaces produce less friction than rough surfaces. Dry surfaces cause more friction than surfaces that are lubricated or wet.

Residual oil clinging to the cylinder walls, rings, and pistons of an engine that has been stopped for some time will produce a greasy friction when the engine is started. Of course, as soon as the engine starts, the lubrication system supplies increased lubrication, which results in viscous friction.

Viscous comes from the word *viscosity*, which is a measure of an oil's ability to flow or its resistance to flow. Some energy is still required to slide a well-lubricated object over the surface of another. Although the layer of lubricant separates the two surfaces, the lubricant itself provides some resistance to motion. This is called viscous friction. Friction bearings provide a sliding friction action, while ball and roller bearings provide rolling friction. Rolling friction offers less resistance to motion than sliding friction.

Inertia

Inertia is the tendency of an object in motion to stay in motion or the tendency of an object at rest to stay at rest. The first can be called *kinetic inertia* and the latter *static inertia*. The moving parts of an engine are affected by kinetic inertia. A piston moving in one direction tries to keep moving in that direction because of kinetic inertia. The crankshaft and connecting rod must overcome this kinetic inertia by stopping the piston at its travel limit and reversing its direction. The static inertia of a car that is stopped must be overcome by engine power to cause the car to move.

Engine Torque and Brake Power

As an engine runs, the crankshaft is forced to turn by the series of pushes or power impulses imposed on the crank pins by the pistons and rods. This twisting force is called *torque*.

Engine torque and engine power are closely related. For instance, as we learned earlier, if we know the torque and speed of an engine, we can calculate its power.

Torque is equal to F × R where F is the force applied to the end of a lever and R is the length of the lever from the center of the turning shaft to the point on the lever at which force is being applied. R

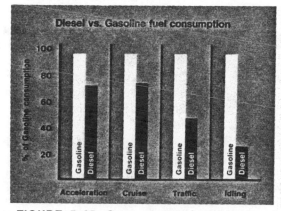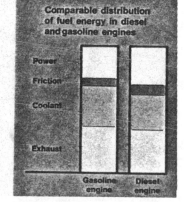

FIGURE 5-25. Comparison of efficiency of gasoline and diesel engines. *(Courtesy of Ford Motor Co. of Canada Ltd.)*

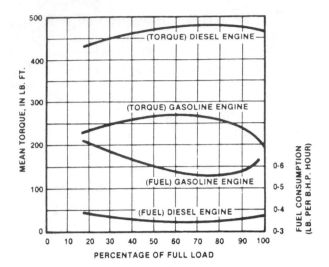

**BOTH ENGINES ARE 6-CYLINDER
150 HORSEPOWER**

**MAX. RPM 1,700 DIESEL
3,700 GASOLINE**

FIGURE 5-26. Comparison of torque and fuel consumption between typical gasoline and diesel engines of the same size. *(Courtesy of Ford Motor Co. of Canada Ltd.)*

represents the radius of a circle through which the applied force would move, if moved through a complete revolution. Therefore, $T = F \times R$.

Engine torque is expressed in terms of pound feet in the English system and in newton meters in the metric system.

Maximum torque is produced in an engine when there is maximum pressure in the cylinders. Peak

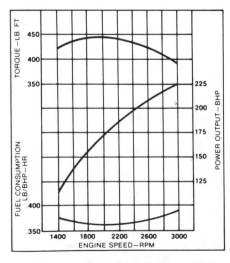

FIGURE 5-27. This chart shows the relationship between torque in lb.-ft., brake power, and fuel consumption over the operating speed range of one typical diesel engine. *(Courtesy of Cummins Engine Company Inc.)*

torque is, therefore, reached when there is maximum air and fuel delivery to the engine. This normally occurs at a somewhat lower engine speed than that at which maximum brake power is produced.

Engine torque drops off as engine speed increases to the point where cylinders take in less air. At this point, engine brake power is still increasing due to the increased number of power impulses per minute. Engine brake power drops off when the effect of an increased number of power impulses is offset by the reduced air intake of the cylinders.

As can be seen from this, engine torque and engine brake power are closely related to the volumetric efficiency of the engine.

PART 12   ENGINE EFFICIENCY

The degree of engine efficiency is expressed in percentage figures resulting from a comparison of the theoretical power of an engine without any power losses, to the actual power available from the engine.

Mechanical efficiency and thermal efficiency are two ways used to express engine efficiency.

Mechanical Efficiency

Indicated power is the theoretical power an engine is able to produce as discussed earlier. It is expressed as horsepower or as kilowatts. Brake power is the actual power delivered by an engine expressed in horsepower or kilowatts.

The formula for calculating the mechanical efficiency of an engine compares the brake power to the indicated power and is calculated by dividing IP into BP.

$$BP \div IP = \text{mechanical efficiency}$$

For example, an engine that produces 72 brake horsepower and has an indicated power of 90 hp, would have a mechanical efficiency of 72/90 or 80 percent. This means that, although 90 BHP is produced in the cylinders, only 72 BHP is being delivered at the flywheel.

Or, using the metric units, if an engine has an indicated power of 120 kW but delivers only 102 kW, the mechanical efficiency would be 102/120 or 85 percent.

Thermal Efficiency

The thermal efficiency of an engine is the degree to which the engine is successful in converting the energy of the fuel into usable heat energy or power. It is the heat energy in the cylinder that forces the pistons to move which results in crankshaft rotation.

The engine is not able to burn 100 percent of the fuel delivered to the cylinders. Some of it remains unburned in colder areas of the cylinder and as a result of not having enough oxygen to burn. Theoretically, an air/fuel mixture of 14.7 parts air to one part fuel by weight, is capable of 100 percent complete combustion. This is known as a stoichiometric mixture, a chemically correct mixture for complete combustion in a gasoline engine.

Some of the heat energy produced by the fuel that has burned in the cylinder is removed from the engine by the exhaust system. Some heat energy is removed from the engine by the cooling system. The lubrication system and the effects of heat radiation carry additional heat from the engine.

Approximately 35 percent of heat energy is lost through the cooling system and another 35 percent through the exhaust system. This leaves only 30 percent of heat energy as usable power from which another 5 percent is lost through engine friction.

Gasoline engine thermal efficiency ranges from about 20 to 30 percent. The thermal efficiency of a diesel engine can approach 40 percent. The diesel engine is able to operate on a leaner air/fuel mixture than a gasoline engine and has a higher thermal efficiency because it has a much higher compression ratio. Since most diesel engines do not have a throttle plate to restrict air intake, there always is an excess of air intake. Only air is compressed in the cylinder, and only the required amount of fuel is injected after compression. Fuel is ignited by the heat of compressed air.

Other Efficiency Factors

Additional energy losses occur due to such factors as drive train friction, rolling resistance, air resistance, and vehicle speed. As much as 5 percent of the heat energy of the fuel may be lost through drive train friction.

Rolling resistance varies depending on tire type used, tire inflation pressures, and condition of road surfaces. Radial tires have less rolling resistance than bias ply tires. Underinflated tires increase rolling resistance, as do soft road surfaces.

Air resistance is directly related to vehicle speed, vehicle body design, and direction and speed of wind. Aerodynamically designed car bodies have less wind resistance than square box-like designs. Larger frontal body areas increase wind resistance. Increased vehicle speed dramatically increases wind resistance. Increased wind velocity and driving into the wind cause greater air resistance. All of these factors have a bearing on how much heat energy (and therefore fuel) will be required to operate the vehicle.

Driving habits such as frequent and rapid acceleration and braking increase the fuel consumption of any vehicle.

Fuel Efficiency

Fuel efficiency is actually the rate of fuel consumption over a distance travelled. It is expressed in miles travelled per gallon of fuel consumed or in liters of fuel consumed per 100 kilometers travelled. Fuel efficiency is dependent on all the foregoing factors as well as vehicle weight, size, and load.

Volumetric Efficiency

The amount of air an engine is able to take into the cylinder on the intake stroke, compared to filling the cylinder completely with air at atmospheric pressure, is known as the volumetric efficiency of an engine.

Another way to describe it would be to say that volumetric efficiency is the engine's ability to get rid of exhaust gases and take in the air/fuel mixture, as compared to the displacement of the engine.

The engine is not able to take in a 100 percent fill on each intake stroke because of design limitations. Such factors as valve and port diameters, manifold runner configuration, valve timing, engine speed, and atmospheric pressure all affect volumetric efficiency.

An engine running at 3000 rpm will have only half the time to fill the cylinder on each intake stroke as it would have at 1500 rpm. Since this is the case, volumetric efficiency drops as engine speed increases. As a result, engine torque also decreases (when engine speed exceeds a certain range).

An engine operating in an area that is 5000 feet above sea level will have less volumetric efficiency than the same engine at sea level because atmospheric pressure is lower at 5000 feet above sea level than at sea level. Since it is atmospheric pressure that forces the air/fuel mixture into the cylinder, it is easy to see that there will be a corresponding decrease in volumetric efficiency as the altitude (at which an engine operates) increases.

To achieve 100 percent volumetric efficiency in an engine, it is necessary to use a blower to force the air/fuel mixture into the cylinders. A turbocharger or a supercharger can be used for this. The turbocharger uses exhaust gas pressure to drive a turbine, and the turbine drives the blower. A supercharger uses a mechanically driven blower to do the job. Turbochargers and superchargers must have precise controls to prevent overcharging of the cylinders and consequent engine damage. Turbochargers are described later in this text.

PART 13 DYNAMOMETERS

The dynamometer is a reliable tool of the trade used to measure all aspects of vehicle performance. This can be done by simulating road load and driving conditions without taking the vehicle being tested out of the service shop.

Steep grades, level roads, stop-and-go city driving, acceleration and deceleration, and a wide range of load conditions all can be simulated in the shop. With the proper diagnostic equipment connected to the vehicle during these tests, engine condition and performance can be accurately determined in a very few minutes. This kind of diagnosis and testing cannot be done on the road nor can it be done in the shop without a dynamometer. In addition to the test results obtained from the auxiliary test equipment, the dynamometer indicates vehicle or engine speed and power.

A simple type of test equipment called a *prony brake* can be used to measure engine brake power. This device uses a slipping friction type of brake with an arm attached to it. The other end of the arm is attached to a scale. If the length of this arm is 4 feet from the center of the brake drum shaft to the point at which the scale is attached, and the brake is applied to provide a reading on the scale of 30 pounds, the torque would be: 30 pounds × 4 feet = 120 pound-feet of torque.

If engine speed under these conditions is 1500 revolutions per minute, the brake horsepower can be calculated as follows: torque (in lb.-ft) × rpm ÷ 5250 = bhp or (120 × 1500) ÷ 5250 = 34.28 brake power. This can be converted to kilowatts (kW) by multiplying 34.28 × 0.746 = 25.57 kilowatts.

Most dynamometers, whether of the engine type or the chassis type, convert the torque and speed factors automatically to a brake power or road power reading on a dial.

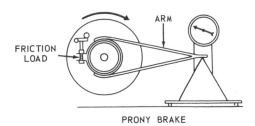

PRONY BRAKE

FIGURE 5-28. The prony brake uses a friction device to apply a load to an engine. An arm connected to the friction device deflects in proportion to the load applied and actuates the gauge, which indicates load in pounds or newtons of force. Engine speed and load figures are then used to calculate brake power.

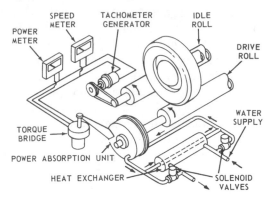

FIGURE 5-29. Major components of dynamometer used to test the road power of a vehicle. Road power is the available power at the drive wheels.

The engine converts the heat energy of combustion to mechanical energy to drive a drive shaft or drive wheels. The drive shaft or drive wheels transfer this mechanical energy to the dynamometer by means of a shaft in the case of an engine dynamometer, and by means of rollers mounted in the shop floor in the case of a chassis dynamometer. This mechanical energy is transmitted to the dynamometer's power absorption unit, which converts the mechanical energy back to heat energy.

The power absorption unit, the torque bridge, and the connecting arm serve the same function as the prony brake. The torque bridge, however, converts the applied force to an electrical signal, which varies with the amount of force applied. This electrical signal provides a reading on the brake horsepower dial. The dynamometer also measures speed, which is indicated on a second dial.

Chassis and engine dynamometers used in service shops are generally of the hydraulic type. The power absorption unit consists basically of two units: a drive unit and a driven unit. The drive unit is a drum with vanes attached to it internally. The driven unit is also a drum with vanes attached to its interior. The driven unit has an arm attached to it. The other end of the arm is connected to the torque bridge. The drive unit and driven unit are enclosed in a sealed housing, which can be filled and emptied of fluid.

The fluid used in some dynamometers is water; others may use oil. In either case, the amount of load applied is in direct proportion to the amount of fluid permitted to enter the power absorption unit. This is controlled by electrically operated solenoid valves. The solenoids are operated by a hand-held control device.

As fluid is allowed to enter the power absorption unit, the rotating drive member throws the fluid against the driven member, which is held by the connecting arm. As more fluid is allowed to enter the unit (more load applied), the force against the driven member is increased, causing the arm to move slightly. This arm movement is converted to an electrical signal by the torque bridge, which then is indicated on the dial in brake horsepower. In this manner any combination of vehicle or engine speed and load can be observed.

As a load is applied to the dynamometer, the fluid in the power absorption unit heats up. This heat must be dissipated in order to prevent overheating. In the open water-type dynamometers, the absorption unit is connected to a cool-water pressure source that is constant (city main water) in order to keep the unit cool and dissipate the heat. The heated water is directed to the floor drain.

In the closed hydraulic-type of absorption unit, the oil is circulated through a heat exchanger, which is water cooled. This type requires less water.

Many dynamometers are equipped with an inertia flywheel, usually belt-driven from the rollers in the floor. The inertia flywheel can be used to simulate vehicle inertia during acceleration, deceleration, and coasting modes. It is useful in diagnosing engine and drive train problems. The flywheel can be engaged or disengaged by a manually operated lever.

When doing any type of dynamometer testing, make sure that the engine or vehicle is in a safe condition to be tested. Serious damage to the engine or vehicle can result from improper testing methods.

Be sure to follow all procedures recommended by the vehicle manufacturer and by the manufacturer of the equipment (dynamometer) being used.

It must be remembered that all test results observed during dynamometer testing are valid only for the conditions that existed at the time of the test, including engine and vehicle condition.

PART 14   SELF-CHECK

1. The internal combustion engine converts _____ energy of the fuel into _____ energy and to usable _____ energy.

2. What is the approximate air/fuel ratio of a gasoline engine?

3. What is the approximate air/fuel ratio of a diesel engine?

4. List the major components that make up the internal combustion engine.

5. List the four strokes of a four-stroke-cycle engine and describe the basic operation of each.

6. Describe the basic operating principle of a two-stroke-cycle engine.

7. The diesel engine compresses the air/fuel mixture on the compression stroke. True or false.

8. List the ten engine systems required for engine operation.

9. List seven methods of classifying engine types and sizes.

10. Define engine bore, stroke, and displacement.

11. How is the compression ratio of an engine calculated?

12. Describe atmospheric pressure.

13. What is a vacuum?

14. Define energy and work.

15. What is the formula for calculating power?

16. Engine power is measured in units of _____ or _____.

17. How would you calculate engine brake power when indicated power and friction power are known?

18. What is kinetic inertia?

19. Define engine torque.

20. What is the mechanical efficiency of an engine with 72 bhp and 90 ihp?

21. Which engine has the higher thermal efficiency, the gasoline engine or the diesel engine?

22. Volumetric efficiency increases with engine speed. True or false.

23. What are the advantages of using a dynamometer for engine testing?

PART 15   TEST QUESTIONS

1. The reciprocating motion of the piston is changed to rotary motion by the:
   (a) connecting rod
   (b) camshaft
   (c) crankshaft
   (d) valves

2. The air/fuel ratio of a diesel engine is approximately:
   (a) 20:1 to 100:1
   (b) 10:1 to 50:1
   (c) 50:1 to 200:1
   (d) 10:1 to 15:1

3. The four strokes of a four-stroke-cycle engine occur in the following order:
   (a) power, exhaust, intake, compression
   (b) intake, compression, power, exhaust
   (c) exhaust, intake, compression, power
   (d) compression, power, exhaust, intake

(e) all of the above

(f) none of the above

4. Mechanic A says the diesel engine compresses air only in the cylinder. Mechanic B says that diesel fuel is injected directly into the cylinder in a diesel engine. Who is right?

   (a) Mechanic A

   (b) Mechanic B

   (c) both A and B

   (d) neither A nor B

5. Mechanic A says the I head engine has the valves in the block. Mechanic B says the L head engine has the valves in the block. Who is right?

   (a) Mechanic A

   (b) Mechanic B

   (c) both A and B

   (d) neither A nor B

6. A four-cylinder engine with a three-inch bore and a 3.25-inch stroke has a displacement in cubic inches of:

   (a) 91.92

   (b) 89.91

   (c) 191.92

   (d) 189.91

7. One joule is equivalent to:

   (a) 1Nm/s

   (b) 1Wm/s

   (c) 1ms/W

   (d) 1N/s

8. Three kinds of friction are:

   (a) dry, rough, and smooth

   (b) smooth, wet, and dry

   (c) rough, greasy, and viscous

   (d) viscous, greasy, and dry

9. Engine torque is defined as:

   (a) brake power

   (b) indicated power

   (c) twisting force

   (d) all of the above

10. The power absorption unit in a hydraulic dynamometer is a:

    (a) friction device

    (b) fluid coupling

    (c) heat-producing device

    (d) all of the above

Chapter 6

Engine Components

The automobile engine consists of a great number of parts, each of which is identified by a particular name. Each part is distinguishable from every other part, in some way—even if it is a bolt or a snap ring. They are distinguished by their size and type as well as their particular application. In addition, a single part may consist of a number of components (e.g., a piston). Although the piston is only a single part, it consists of ring grooves, lands, pin bosses, skirts, head, thrust surfaces, and oil drain back holes. It is essential that proper names be used to identify parts. No discussion of engine construction and operation is possible without being fully acquainted by name with all engine parts.

Figure 6-1 to 6-5 illustrate and name most of the common engine components. Further identification of special parts and components is covered in the remainder of the chapter and in Chapters 7 and 8.

Performance Objectives

After adequate study of this chapter and the appropriate engine components you should be able to do the following:

1. Complete the self-check and the test questions with at least 80 percent accuracy.
2. State the purposes of engine components a–g below.
3. Describe the construction and design differences of engine components a–g below.
4. Describe the operation, wear, and deterioration of engine components a–g below.
   (a) cylinder block and all its components
   (b) crankshaft assembly and balance shafts
   (c) piston and connecting rod assembly
   (d) camshafts and camshaft drives
   (e) valve operating mechanisms
   (f) cylinder heads and valves
   (g) externally mounted engine parts

PART 1   CYLINDER BLOCK

Construction

The engine block is the main supporting structure to which all other engine parts are attached. The cylinders guide the pistons and the lifter bores guide the lifters. The block houses the crankshaft and, in many cases, the camshaft, too. The block is heavily constructed; such strength is necessary in maintaining correct alignment of all engine parts. Cooling and lubrication passages are provided in the block; the lower part of the block forms the upper part of the crankcase.

Cylinder blocks are manufactured by a casting process. Materials used are cast iron alloys and cast aluminum alloys. The cast iron block is fairly heavy but is also very rigid and not subject to much distortion. Aluminium blocks have the advantages of less weight and superior heat conductivity. Aluminum, however, has a higher expansion rate and is more subject to distortion than cast iron.

Cylinder blocks are formed by pouring the molten metal into a mold with a sand-based core. When the metal has cooled and hardened, the mold and sand core are removed. Removing the sand core leaves openings for cylinders, water jackets, crankcase, and bearing bores. Rough holes in the side of the block through which the sand core was supported are machined and closed with soft metal plugs. These core hole plugs are also known as expansion plugs or frost plugs. They are either of the dished type or the cup type.

Oil galleries are either cast in the block or drilled and plugged during the machining process.

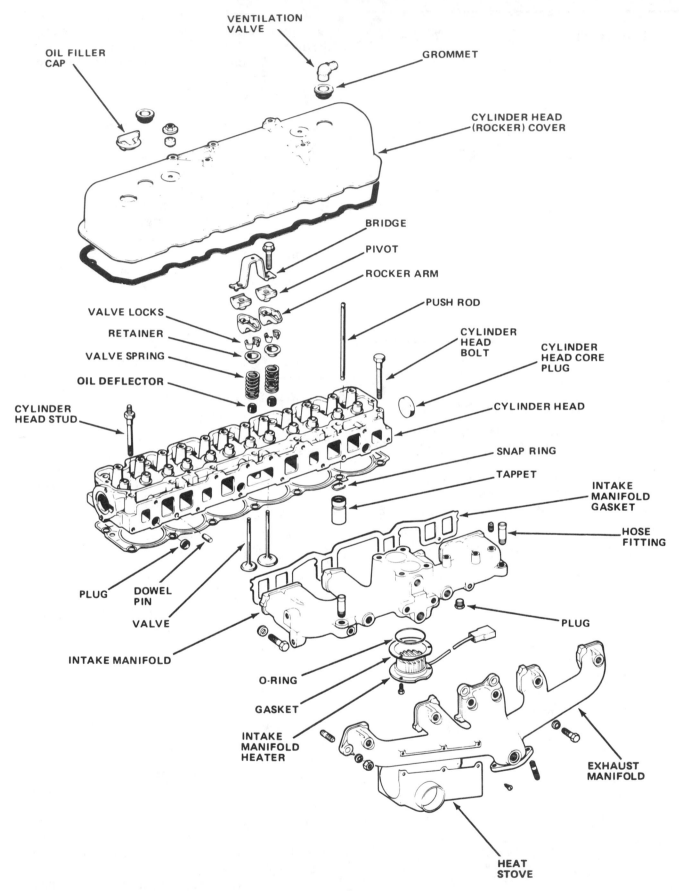

FIGURE 6-1. Exploded view of typical six-cylinder gasoline engine head assembly. *(Courtesy of American Motors Corporation)*

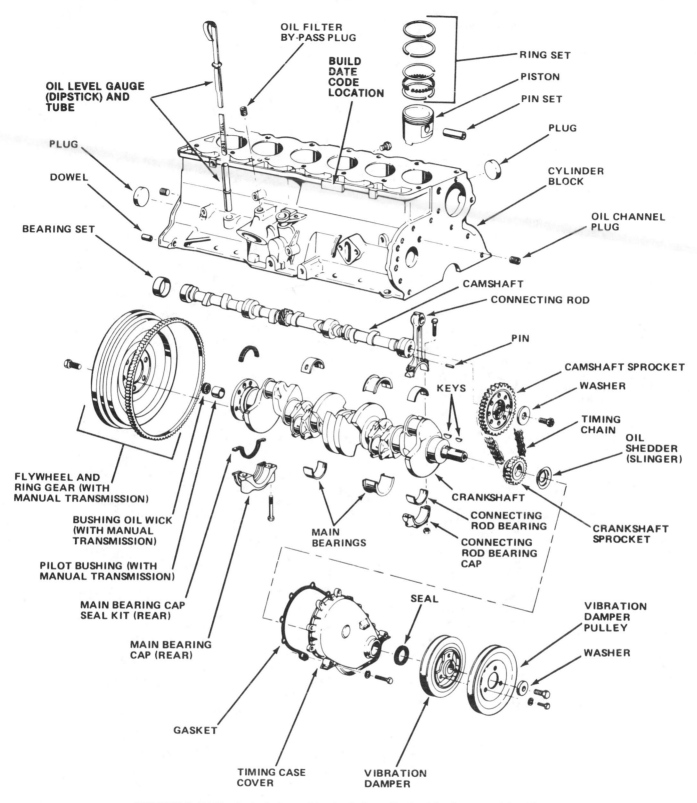

FIGURE 6-2. Exploded view of typical six-cylinder block assembly. *(Courtesy of American Motors Corporation)*

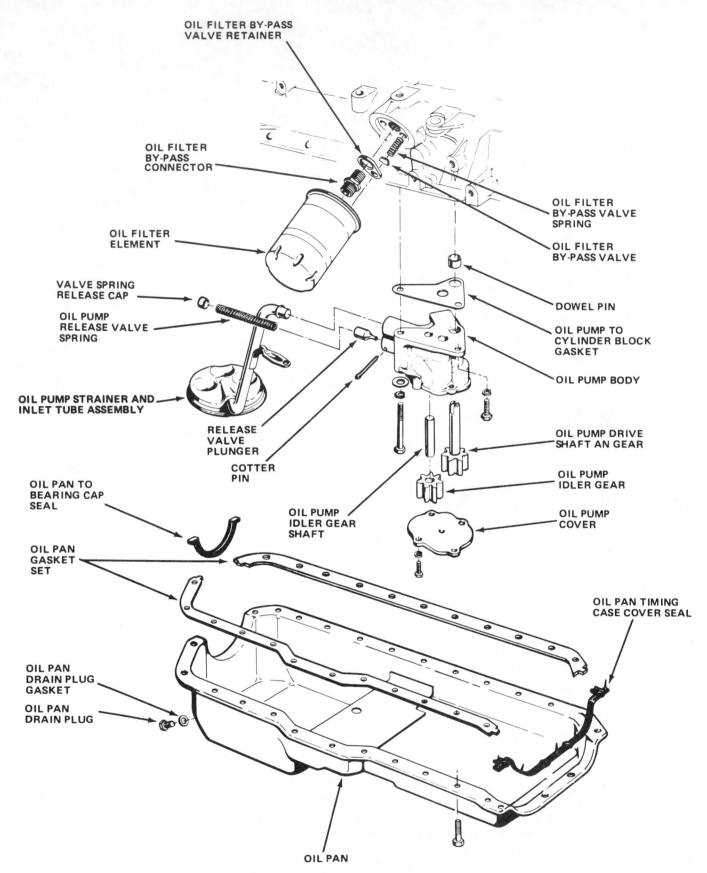

FIGURE 6-3. Exploded view of oil pan, oil pump, and oil filter components of typical six-cylinder engine. *(Courtesy of American Motors Corporation)*

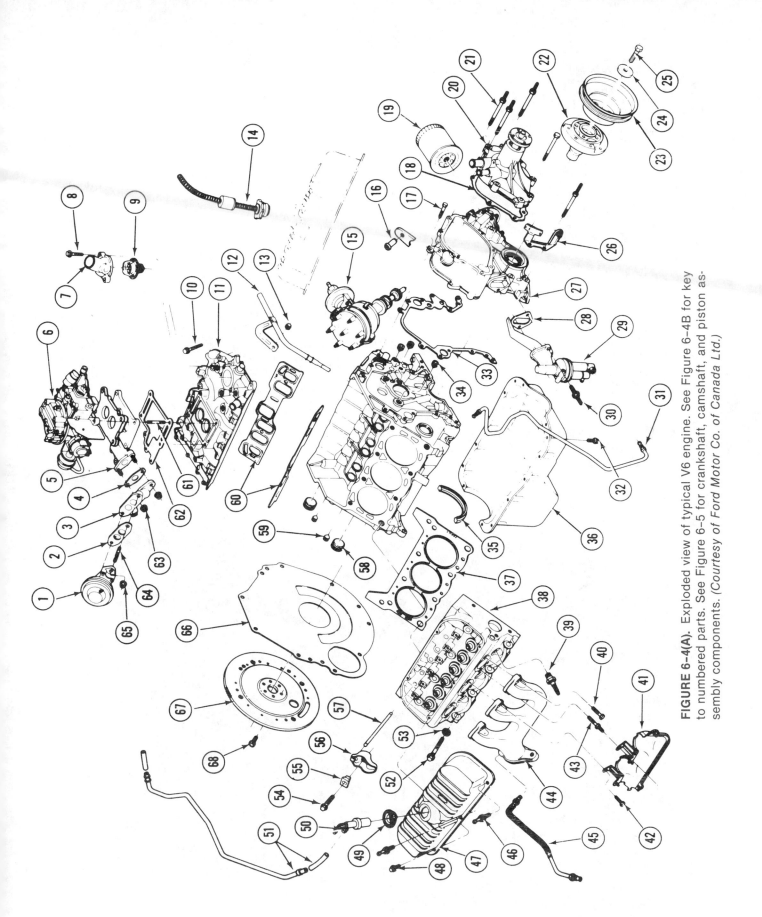

FIGURE 6-4(A). Exploded view of typical V6 engine. See Figure 6-4B for key to numbered parts. See Figure 6-5 for crankshaft, camshaft, and piston assembly components. *(Courtesy of Ford Motor Co. of Canada Ltd.)*

1. EGR VALVE
2. GASKET, VALVE
3. ADAPTOR, EGR VALVE
4. GASKET, ADAPTOR
5. SPACER, CARBURETOR
6. CARBURETOR
7. THERMOSTAT HOUSING
8. BOLT, HOUSING ATTACHING (3)
9. THERMOSTAT
10. BOLT, MANIFOLD ATTACHING (14)
11. INTAKE MANIFOLD
12. OIL LEVEL INDICATOR TUBE
13. NUT, TUBE ATTACHING (1)
14. OIL FILL CAP, TUBE AND FILTER ASSEMBLY
15. IGNITION DISTRIBUTOR
16. CLAMP AND BOLT, DISTRIBUTOR HOLD DOWN
17. BOLT, COVER ATTACHING (7)
18. GASKET, PUMP (WATER)
19. OIL FILTER
20. WATER PUMP
21. BOLTS, WATER PUMP ATTACHING (8)
22. CRANKSHAFT DAMPER
23. CRANKSHAFT PULLEY
24. WASHER, DAMPNER BOLT
25. BOLT, DAMPNER ATTACHING
26. IGNITION TIMING INDICATOR
27. FRONT COVER
28. GASKET, PUMP
29. FUEL PUMP
30. STUD/BOLT, PUMP ATTACHING (2)
31. FUEL LINE – PUMP TO CARBURETOR
32. BOLT, PAN ATTACHING (14)
33. GASKET, COVER
34. PLUG, OIL GALLERY

35. SEAL, OIL PAN REAR
36. OIL PAN
37. GASKET, CYLINDER HEAD
38. CYLINDER HEAD
39. SPARKPLUG
40. BOLTS, MANIFOLD ATTACHING (6 EACH SIDE)
41. SHROUD, HOT AIR INTAKE
42. STUD/BOLT, SHROUD AND MANIFOLD ATTACHING
43. BOLT W/STUD MANIFOLD AND SHROUD ATTACHING
44. EXHAUST MANIFOLD
45. EGR TUBE
46. BOLT W/STUD, COVER ATTACHING (2 EACH SIDE)
47. VALVE COVER
48. BOLT, COVER ATTACHING (3 EACH SIDE)
49. GROMMET, VALVE
50. PCV VALVE
51. HOSE AND TUBE, PCV VALVE
52. BOLT, CYLINDER HEAD ATTACHING (8 EACH SIDE)
53. WASHER, CYLINDER HEAD BOLT
54. BOLT, FULCRUM ATTACHING (12 EACH SIDE)
55. ROCKER ARM FULCRUM
56. ROCKER ARM
57. PUSH ROD
58. PLUG, WATER JACKET
59. PLUG, OIL GALLERY
60. GASKET, MANIFOLD
61. STUD, CARBURETOR ATTACHING (4)
62. GASKET, CARBURETOR
63. NUT, ADAPTOR ATTACHING (2)
64. STUD, VALVE ATTACHING (2)
65. NUT, VALVE ATTACHING (2)
66. REAR COVER PLATE
67. DRIVE PLATE
68. BOLT, PLATE ATTACHING (5)

FIGURE 6-4(B). Key to numbered components in Figure 6-4A. *(Courtesy of Ford Motor Co. of Canada Ltd.)*

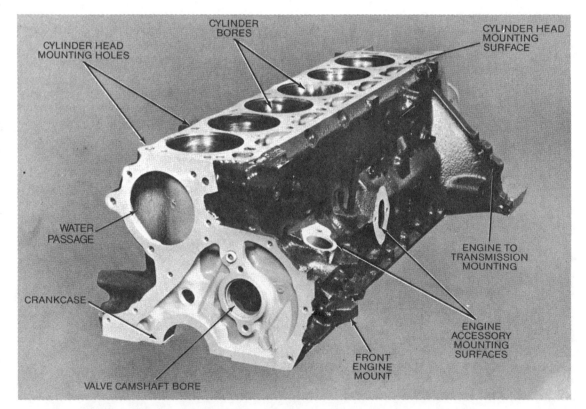

FIGURE 6-5. Six-cylinder engine block with all engine parts removed. *(Courtesy of Ford Motor Co. of Canada Ltd.)*

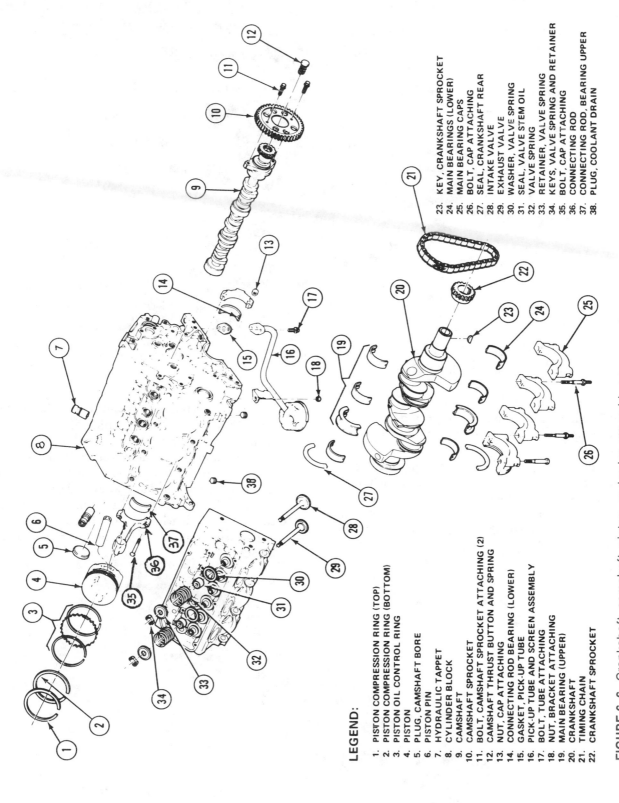

LEGEND:

1. PISTON COMPRESSION RING (TOP)
2. PISTON COMPRESSION RING (BOTTOM)
3. PISTON OIL CONTROL RING
4. PISTON
5. PLUG, CAMSHAFT BORE
6. PISTON PIN
7. HYDRAULIC TAPPET
8. CYLINDER BLOCK
9. CAMSHAFT
10. CAMSHAFT SPROCKET
11. BOLT, CAMSHAFT SPROCKET ATTACHING (2)
12. CAMSHAFT THRUST BUTTON AND SPRING
13. NUT, CAP ATTACHING
14. CONNECTING ROD BEARING (LOWER)
15. GASKET, PICK-UP TUBE
16. PICK-UP TUBE AND SCREEN ASSEMBLY
17. BOLT, TUBE ATTACHING
18. NUT, BRACKET ATTACHING
19. MAIN BEARING (UPPER)
20. CRANKSHAFT
21. TIMING CHAIN
22. CRANKSHAFT SPROCKET
23. KEY, CRANKSHAFT SPROCKET
24. MAIN BEARINGS (LOWER)
25. MAIN BEARING CAPS
26. BOLT, CAP ATTACHING
27. SEAL, CRANKSHAFT REAR
28. INTAKE VALVE
29. EXHAUST VALVE
30. WASHER, VALVE SPRING
31. SEAL, VALVE STEM OIL
32. VALVE SPRING
33. RETAINER, VALVE SPRING
34. KEYS, VALVE SPRING AND RETAINER
35. BOLT, CAP ATTACHING
36. CONNECTING ROD
37. CONNECTING ROD, BEARING UPPER
38. PLUG, COOLANT DRAIN

FIGURE 6-6. Crankshaft, camshaft, piston, and valve assembly components of a V6 engine. *(Courtesy of Ford Motor Co. of Canada Ltd.)*

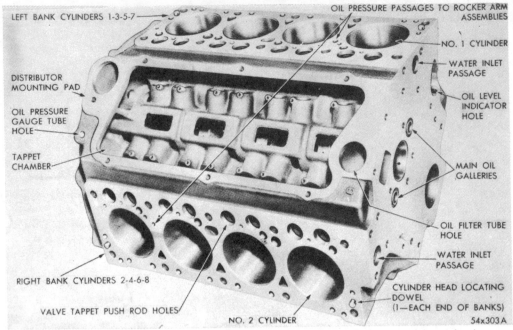

FIGURE 6-7. V8-type cylinder block with all components removed (top view). *(Courtesy of Chrysler Corporation)*

Oil galleries are required to provide lubrication for bearings and valve lifters as well as other engine parts.

Block mating surfaces are carefully machined to provide proper sealing surfaces for attaching cylinder heads, timing covers, oil pans, and bell housings. Main bearing caps are installed, and main bearing bores and camshaft bearing bores are align-bored to allow shafts to rotate freely.

Particular attention is paid to such items as the block deck surface and to crankshaft center line dimensions. The cylinder center line must also be at exactly 90 degrees to the crankshaft center line to ensure free piston movement without creating side stresses on pistons, rods, and cylinders.

Valve lifter bores are machined at right angles to the camshaft bearing bores. Holes are drilled and threaded to allow attachment of parts and accessories.

FIGURE 6-8. V8-type engine block (bottom view) showing main bearing caps in place. *(Courtesy of Chrysler Corporation)*

100

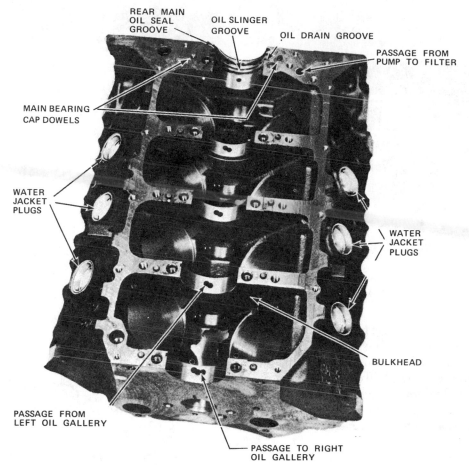

FIGURE 6-9. V8-type engine block with main bearing caps removed. (Courtesy of General Motors Corporation)

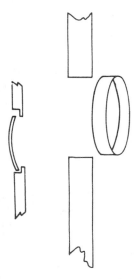

FIGURE 6-10. Two types of core hole plugs (frost plugs) are used to seal holes left in the block from the casting process: the dish type (left), and the cut type (right).

Diesel Engine Blocks

Cylinder blocks for diesel engines are made of cast iron and are of heavier construction than similar size gasoline engine blocks. The extra strength and rig-idity is required due to the much higher combustion pressures produced by the diesel engine. This results in heavier loads being imposed on cylinders, crankshafts, and main bearing supports. Main bearing caps are also heavier for the same reason, and may be of four-bolt design.

It may be said of any engine that cylinder pressures acting on the engine try to push the cylinder head off the top and try to push the crankshaft out of the bottom. The force of this cylinder pressure, being much greater in diesel engines, requires increased strength in the crankshaft and main bearing area, as well as in the cylinder head and the cylinder bolt holes in the block.

Other than the increased strength required for diesel engine blocks, construction is generally the same as that for gasoline engines. Some engines have replaceable cylinder liners while others do not.

Block Design

In-line cylinder block designs have all cylinders arranged in line—one behind the other. V-type blocks have cylinders arranged in a V shape. A variation of the V block is the Y block. On a Y block, the sides of the block extend down, well past the crankshaft center line. This type of block is heavier and re-

101

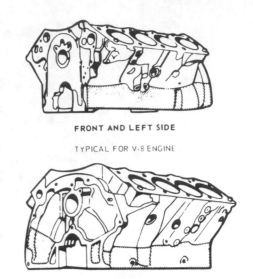

FRONT AND LEFT SIDE

TYPICAL FOR V-8 ENGINE

REAR AND RIGHT SIDE

FIGURE 6-11. Several different types of engine blocks.

quires only a shallow oil pan. The V block oil pan mounting surfaces are at the same level as the crankshaft center line. This requires a deeper oil pan but reduces engine weight. The horizontal opposed engine block has cylinders arranged in a horizontal position on each side of the crankshaft. This type of engine is air cooled and has separately cast, finned cylinder pots.

Cylinders and Cylinder Liners

Cylinders may be cast integrally with the block, or a provision may be made for replaceable cylinder liners. Most automotive engines in cars and light trucks do not have replaceable cylinder liners. Larger engines usually have cylinder liners. Both wet- and dry-type liners are used. The dry-type liner is in full length metal-to-metal contact with the cylinder block. The wet-type liner is in contact with the block only at the top and at the bottom, where they are sealed to prevent coolant from leaking into the crankcase or into the combustion chamber. One aluminum block engine has free-standing cylinder liners that seal midway up the outside of the liners against the block but are sealed at the top only against the cylinder head. Another small engine aluminum block uses silicone-impregnated cylinder walls to prevent wear, since bare aluminum cylinders would wear very rapidly.

Wet cylinder liners are usually made of cast iron alloy, whereas dry liners are made of steel.

Cylinders are machined and honed to a very precise finish to aid in good lubrication and proper ring seating. Cylinder walls are finished to a 25 to 30 micro-inch finish with a fine rotary hone. The light visible "scratches" produced by the hone form an intersecting crosshatch pattern of from 50 to 60 degrees.

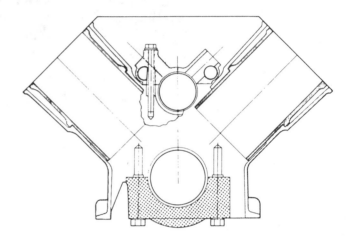

FIGURE 6-12. Cross section of aluminum block V8 engine with cast iron cylinder liners and separately cast aluminum lifter bore assembly. Main bearing caps are cast iron. Note cylinder liners are free standing at top. (*Courtesy of General Motors Corporation*)

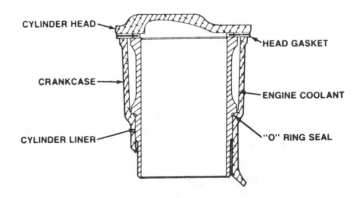

FIGURE 6-13. Details of cast iron cylinder liner mounting and seals as used in aluminum block V8 gasoline engine. (*Courtesy of General Motors Corporation*)

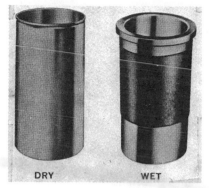

DRY   WET

FIGURE 6-14. Some engines have removable cylinder sleeves such as these. The dry type does not contact the engine coolant, but the wet sleeve does. The wet sleeve is a heavy thick-walled sleeve, whereas the dry sleeve is much lighter. *(Courtesy of TRW)*

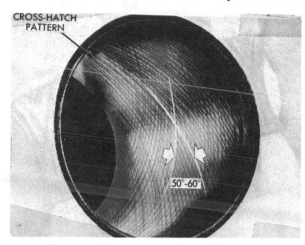

FIGURE 6-15. All cylinders, whether integral or removable, are machined to provide a surface with a 50° to 60° crosshatch pattern of 25- to 30-microinch finish, which is visible but cannot be felt by hand. *(Courtesy of Chrysler Corporation)*

Cylinder Numbering and Firing Order

Cylinder numbering is usually done from the front to the back, or from the end opposite to the flywheel, on in-line engines. (This is not always the case.)

On V-type engines, the farthest forward cylinder is usually the number one position. Remaining cylinders may be numbered from 1 to 4 down the right bank, and from 5 to 8 down the left bank, or they may be numbered alternately from side to side in sequence, as the connecting rods are mounted on the crankshaft.

The manufacturer decides the type of cylinder firing order the engine will have. The cylinder numbering system used and the crankshaft design will determine the firing order of an engine.

Cylinder Wear

In operation, the cylinder block is subject to great changes in temperature, pressure of combustion, stress from expansion and contraction, cylinder wear from piston thrust, ring pressure, abrasives (possible scoring), and distortion.

Major thrust forces of the piston against the cylinder wall occur as a result of combustion pressures against the piston and the angle of the connecting rod during the power stroke. See Figure 6-18. Piston thrust is considerably less during the

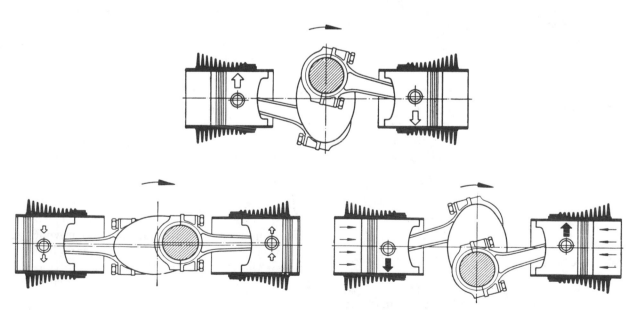

FIGURE 6-16. Removable, finned cylinder pots are used on some air-cooled engines. Note arrows indicating major and minor thrust of piston against cylinder walls. *(Courtesy of General Motors Corporation)*

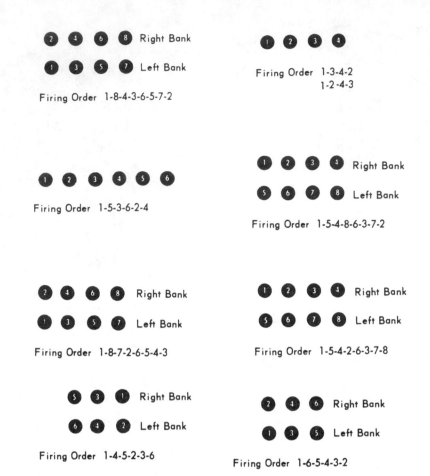

Firing Order 1-8-4-3-6-5-7-2

Firing Order 1-3-4-2
1-2-4-3

Firing Order 1-5-3-6-2-4

Firing Order 1-5-4-8-6-3-7-2

Firing Order 1-8-7-2-6-5-4-3

Firing Order 1-5-4-2-6-3-7-8

Firing Order 1-4-5-2-3-6

Firing Order 1-6-5-4-3-2

FIGURE 6-17. Engine manufacturers use a variety of cylinder numbering systems and firing orders. Some of the most common types are shown here. Some manufacturers number the cylinders starting with No. 1 at the flywheel end. A firing order for a V6 engine (not shown here) is 1-2-3-4-5-6 with No. 1 being at the front and No. 6 at the back.

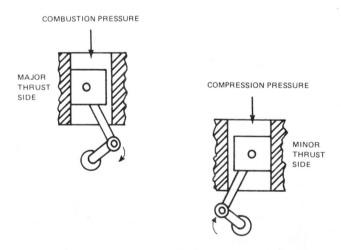

FIGURE 6-18. Combustion pressures force the piston against the major thrust side due to connecting rod angle and the crankshaft's resistance to rotation during the power stroke (above left). Compression pressures resisting piston movement during the compression stroke result in less thrust on the opposite side of the cylinder.

other strokes. Piston thrust contributes to cylinder wear.

Piston rings push and slide against cylinder walls as the piston moves up and down. Small particles of carbon and other abrasives that may enter the lubricating oil can cause wear.

Heat and pressure are most severe when the piston is near the top on the power stroke. Lubrication at this point and under these conditions is also least effective. Consequently, most cylinder wear resulting in cylinder taper takes place at the very top of ring travel in the cylinder. This wear results in a cylinder ridge developing at the top of the cylinder.

Hot spots can develop as a result of rust and scale buildup in the water jacket. This prevents good heat transfer to the engine coolant and causes this area of the cylinder to overheat. Distortion and a wavy cylinder surface can result. If severe, metal from the piston ring can be transferred to the cylinder wall and cause piston, cylinder, and ring scoring.

A *loose piston pin, broken rings, dirt,* and *car-*

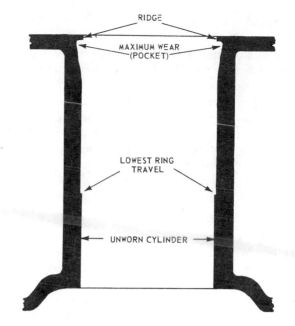

FIGURE 6-19. The greatest amount of cylinder wear takes place near the top of the cylinder. This is where there is more heat, less lubrication, and more ring pressure against the cylinder walls due to high combustion pressures. *(Courtesy of General Motors Corporation)*

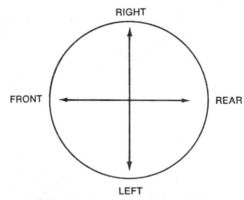

FIGURE 6-20. Major and minor thrust (Figure 6-18) results in cylinders wearing out of round. Cylinders can also become distorted due to thermal shock, hot spots, and incorrect tightening of cylinder head bolts. *(Courtesy of Ford Motor Co. of Canada Ltd.)*

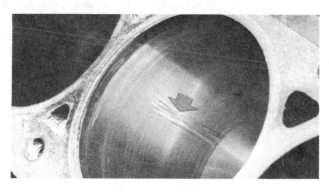

FIGURE 6-21. Cylinders can become scored due to broken rings, dirt or carbon, hot spots, a loose piston pin, lubrication breakdown, or incorrect piston-to-cylinder clearance. *(Courtesy of Ford Motor Co. of Canada Ltd.)*

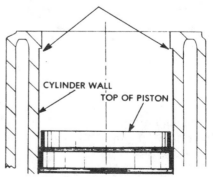

FIGURE 6-22. Cylinder wear results in the development of a ridge at the top of the cylinder since rings do not travel to the top of the cylinder. *(Courtesy of General Motors Corporation)*

105

bon can also damage cylinder walls. An *excessively rich fuel mixture* can cause lubrication to be washed away and increase cylinder wear.

Incorrectly tightened cylinder head bolts or *thermal shock* (sudden and extreme temperature change) can cause cylinder distortion. Coolant seepage into the combustion chamber can cause corrosion, as can combustion by product acids, especially if the engine is not serviced frequently enough.

Main Bearing Bores

Main bearing bores support the crankshaft and main bearings. Main bearing caps must absorb all the force imposed by all the power impulses of the engine. These loads are quite high and can cause out of round and misalignment in time. Radial loads of approximately three tons per power impulse are imposed on the crankshaft and main bearing caps. At a speed of 3000 rpm, an eight-cylinder engine would subject the main bearing caps to 12,000 such impacts per minute. To withstand such punishment, engine tolerances and torque values must be very precise. Larger engines use larger-diameter main bearings and four-bolt main bearing caps.

Camshaft Bearing Bores

Camshaft bores support the camshaft and are subjected to loads imposed by valve springs during valve operation. Bearing bores must be in alignment to allow proper camshaft rotation and even wear distribution. In-block camshaft bearing bores are not distorted due to normal operation, but may distort due to block distortion.

Lifter Bores

Lifter bores are subject to wear and scoring due to abrasives such as carbon and varnish, particularly if engine oil is not changed at regular intervals.

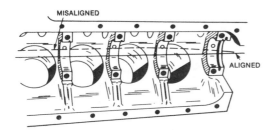

FIGURE 6-23. Main bearing bores should be in perfect alignment. Misalignment can result from overloading, thermal shock, incorrect tightening of main bearing cap bolts, overheating, and so on.

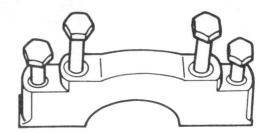

FIGURE 6-24. Typical four-bolt main bearing cap. *(Courtesy of Ford Motor Co. of Canada Ltd.)*

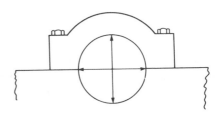

FIGURE 6-25. Main bearing bores can become out of round due to normal operation and incorrect tightening of bolts, and can wear due to a bearing becoming loose and moving in the bore.

Oil Galleries

Oil galleries can become restricted due to sludge buildup. Reduced lubrication of moving parts can result from partially plugged passages.

Water Jackets

Water jackets surrounding the cylinders can collect sludge, scale, and rust, which reduces heat-transfer ability and coolant circulation, resulting in overheating and block distortion. Core hole plugs in water jackets may look good on the outside, but may be corroded and nearly rusted through from the inside.

PART 2   CRANKSHAFT ASSEMBLY

The crankshaft assembly includes the crankshaft and bearings, the flywheel, harmonic balancer, gear or sprocket (to drive the camshaft), and the front and rear oil seals.

The crankshaft converts the reciprocating motion of the pistons to rotary motion. All the power produced by all the cylinders is transferred to the crankshaft. The crankshaft transmits it to the flywheel or torque converter.

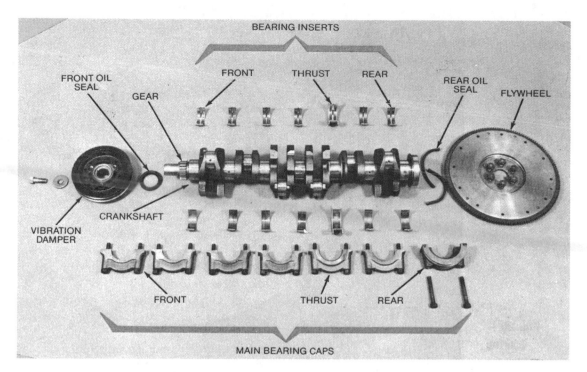

FIGURE 6-26. Exploded view of crankshaft assembly components of six-cylinder in-line engine with seven main bearings. *(Courtesy of Ford Motor Co. of Canada Ltd.)*

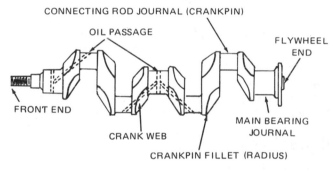

FIGURE 6-27. Crankshaft terminology and phantom view of oil passages. *(Courtesy of Ford Motor Co. of Canada Ltd.)*

The *flywheel* or *torque converter* helps the engine to run smoothly by absorbing some of the energy during the power stroke and releasing it during the other three strokes.

The *vibration damper* (harmonic balancer) dampens crankshaft torsional vibrations that result from the power impulses. As each cylinder fires, it causes the crank throw for that cylinder to speed up. The rest of the crankshaft tends to stay slightly behind, causing a twist. This causes torsional vibrations, which are dampened or partially absorbed by the vibration damper.

The *crankshaft* is supported by split-type (two-piece) precision bearing inserts that reduce wear and friction.

The front and rear crankshaft seals prevent oil leakage past the rotating crankshaft.

Crankshaft Construction

Automotive crankshafts are either cast steel or cast iron. Some crankshafts are forged. Forging is a more expensive procedure. The casting process has been improved considerably over the years, and a cast crankshaft does a very satisfactory job.

Main bearing journals are machined to a highly polished finish and are in perfect alignment with each other. The main bearing journals are mounted in the cylinder block with split-type precision bearing inserts, which are held in place by the main bearing caps. The crankshaft rotates freely in these bearings.

The *connecting rod journals* are offset from the crankshaft center line, which causes the crankpin journals to orbit the crankshaft center line as the shaft rotates. The distance from the main bearing journal center to the connecting rod bearing journal center is exactly one half the engine's stroke. This is sometimes called the *crank throw*.

A *flange* at the rear of the crankshaft provides the means for mounting the flywheel or converter drive plate. A seal journal is machined just ahead of the flange to allow the rear main oil seal to effectively prevent oil leakage past the seal. An in-

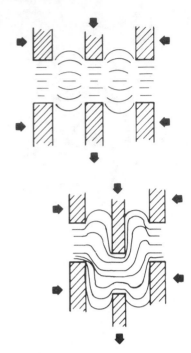

FIGURE 6-28. Crankshaft being shaped by the forging process.

tegral oil slinger is also provided just ahead of the seal journal to deflect oil away from the seal. This increases the effectiveness of the seal.

The front of the crankshaft is machined with a keyway for the camshaft drive gear and the vibration damper. The front oil seal, located in the timing cover, seals between the cover and the vibration damper hub. An oil slinger deflects oil away from the seal.

Thrust surfaces are machined on the side of one of the main bearing journals. These thrust surfaces and the flanged main bearing control crankshaft end play.

Oil holes are drilled from the main bearing jour-

nals to the connecting rod journals to lubricate the connecting rod bearings. The main bearings receive their lubrication from the oil galleries in the engine block.

Crankshafts have heavy sections of metal, or *counterweights,* opposite the crank throws. Counterweights offset the weight of the crank throws and connecting rods to provide crankshaft balance. Finish balancing is achieved by drilling the counterweights or sometimes also the connecting rod journals to remove some metal. This provides for a smoother running engine and longer crankshaft and bearing life. Some engines use balance shafts to improve engine balance.

Crankshaft configuration varies from engine to engine. Four-cylinder crankshafts have four connecting rod journals and usually three or five main bearing journals. Connecting rod journals are indexed (positioned) 180° apart to provide evenly spaced power impulses.

Six-cylinder in-line crankshafts have six connecting rod bearing journals and either four or seven main bearing journals. The four-main-bearing crankshaft must be of heavier construction than the seven-main-bearing crankshaft. Connecting rod journals are spaced 120° apart for even cylinder firing.

The V-6 crankshaft has four main journals and six crank throws spaced for even firing. The V-8 crankshaft has five main journals and four connecting rod journals. Each connecting rod journal has two connecting rods attached to it. Crank throws are spaced 90° apart for even cylinder firing.

Diesel Engine Crankshafts

Diesel engine crankshafts are forged rather than cast. The forging process, although a more expensive manufacturing process, is needed to provide greater strength.

Main and rod bearing journals on diesel crankshafts are generally larger in diameter and may be wider than those for a similar sized gasoline engine. Bearing journals are also usually induction hardened to increase wear resistance and service life.

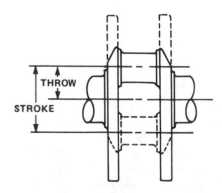

FIGURE 6-29. The stroke of an engine is determined by crankshaft design and is exactly twice the distance of the crank throw measurement.

FIGURE 6-30. V8 engine crankshaft showing counterweights and five main bearing journals. *(Courtesy of Ford Motor Co. of Canada Ltd.)*

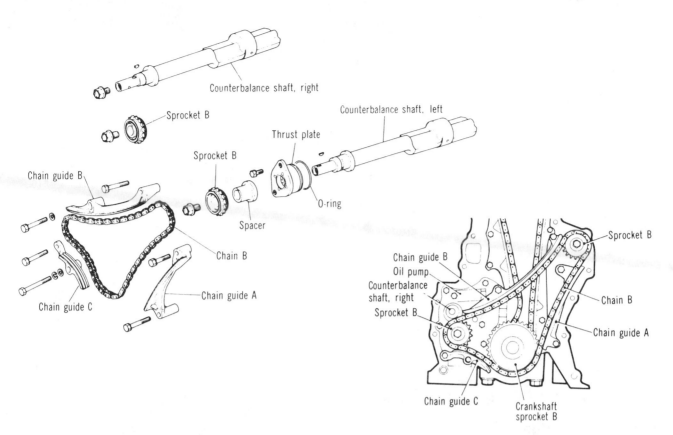

FIGURE 6-31. Details of counterbalance shaft system of one four-cylinder engine design. Balance shafts rotate in opposite directions to provide equal but opposing forces to engine vertical forces. Note that right balance shaft is driven indirectly through oil pump gears to provide opposite rotation to crankshaft. Balance shafts rotate at twice crankshaft speed and are timed to crankshaft position. (Courtesy of Chrysler Corporation)

FIGURE 6-32. Close-up of crank pin journal (connecting rod bearing journal) and main bearing journal. Note spiral grooves on oil seal journal at rear of crankshaft. Spiral grooves help prevent oil seepage past the rear main oil seal. (Courtesy of Ford Motor Co. of Canada Ltd.)

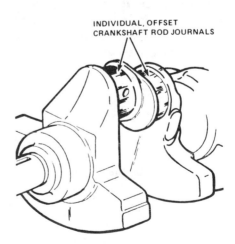

FIGURE 6-33. Crankshaft with connecting rod journals offset 30 degrees as used in a 90-degree block V6 engine to provide even firing intervals (120 degrees of crankshaft rotation between all cylinder firings). This makes for a smoother running engine. Another 90-degree V6 has a 15-degree offset and fires unevenly.

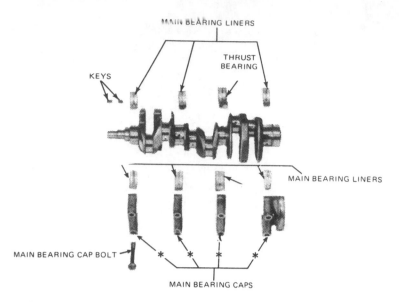

FIGURE 6-34. Crankshaft assembly for 60-degree V block six-cylinder engine.

Other than these differences, the general design and construction features of the diesel engine crankshaft are similar to those of the gasoline engine.

Crankshaft Bearings

Crankshaft main bearings and *connection rod bearings* are of the precision insert split type. Bearings are steel-backed and have laminated layers of softer bearing liner materials. Alloys, including such materials as babbitt, copper, aluminum, and lead, are used as bearing liners.

Bearings have a number of characteristics and design features that extend their service life. One of the main bearings is flanged (has thrust surfaces) to control crankshaft end play. Lubrication holes and grooves facilitate maintaining a good oil film between the bearing and the journal. Locating lugs align the bearing location in the bore. Crush height ensures good radial pressure of the bearing against

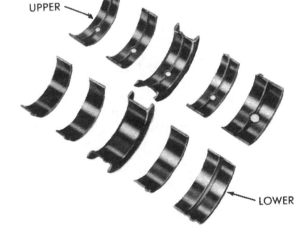

FIGURE 6-36. Complete set of precision main bearing inserts. Note flanged main bearing and difference between upper and lower bearing shells. *(Courtesy of Chrysler Corporation)*

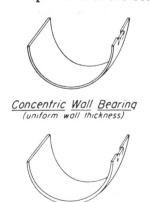

Concentric Wall Bearing
(uniform wall thickness)

Eccentric Wall Bearing
(wall heavier at crown than at parting faces)

FIGURE 6-35. Two types of precision bearing inserts. *(Courtesy of Federal Mogul)*

FIGURE 6-37. Machined surfaces on crankshaft bear against flanged main bearing to control crankshaft end play. *(Courtesy of General Motors Corporation)*

110

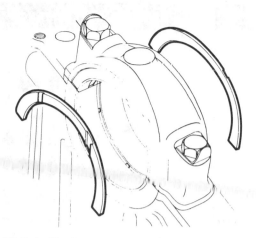

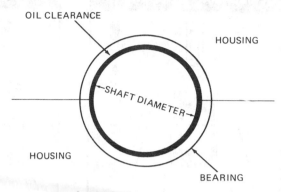

FIGURE 6-38. Some types of engines use separate thrust washers instead of a flanged main bearing to control crankshaft end play.

FIGURE 6-41. A specified amount of clearance between the bearing journal and the bearing surface must be provided to maintain a film of oil between these two parts to reduce friction and wear.

the bore for good heat transfer. Bearing spread keeps the bearing in position during assembly. Good bearing characteristics include conformability, embedability, fatigue resistance, corrosion resistance, and long life.

The *clearance* between bearing journals and bearings must be of precise dimension to be able to maintain a good oil film and prevent metal-to-metal contact. As soon as this oil film breaks down, rapid wear on the crankshaft and bearings results.

Bearing clearances on journals up to $2\frac{1}{2}$ inches in diameter (62.5 millimeters) are generally from 0.001 to 0.003 inches (0.025 to 0.080 millimeters). The rotating journal forces the oil between the journal and the bearing on the loaded side in the direction of journal rotation when bearing clearances are correct. This is known as *hydrodynamic lubrication*. The ability to maintain hydrodynamic lubrication decreases rapidly with increased bearing clearances.

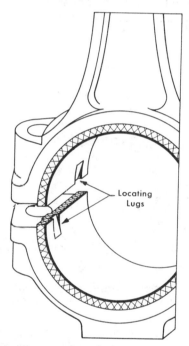

FIGURE 6-39. Locating lugs (bearing tangs) fit into notches in the bearing bore to prevent fore and aft movement of the bearing inserts. Rotation of the bearing in its bore is also prevented by these lugs. *(Courtesy of Sunnen Products Co. Ltd.)*

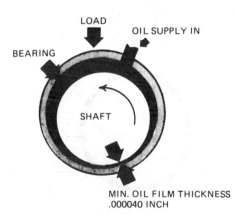

FIGURE 6-42. Oil is fed to the lightly loaded side of the bearing. Shaft rotation forces oil around the bearing to maintain an oil film around the entire bearing journal. This is called hydrodynamic lubrication. *(Courtesy of Sunnen Products Co. Ltd.)*

FIGURE 6-40. Bearing spread makes it necessary to snap the bearing into place when installing. The bearing is slightly out of round before installation, but it becomes round when snapped into place in the connecting rod or main bearing bore. This helps keep bearings in place during assembly. *(Courtesy of Sunnen Products Co. Ltd.)*

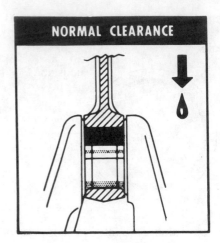 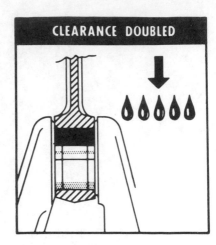 

NORMAL CLEARANCE | **CLEARANCE DOUBLED** | **FOUR TIMES CLEARANCE**

FIGURE 6-43. With correct bearing clearance, the amount of oil throw-off from the rotating shaft is minimal. When clearance is doubled, oil throw-off is five times greater; if clearance is four times as great, oil throw-off is 25 times as great. Piston rings are unable to scrape this excessive oil from the cylinder walls, and oil then enters the combustion chamber and is burned. *(Courtesy of Hastings Ltd., Toronto, Canada)*

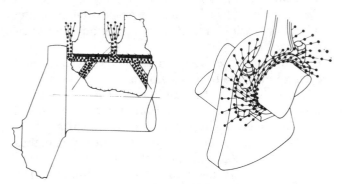

FIGURE 6-44. A controlled amount of oil throw-off is normal and is dependent on bearing clearances being correct. Oil throw-off helps lubricate cylinder walls, piston pins, and cam lobes. *(Courtesy of Sunnen Products Co. Ltd.)*

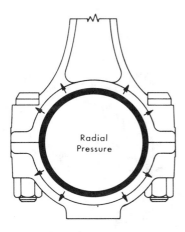

FIGURE 6-46. Proper bearing crush creates a radial pressure of the bearing against its bore for good heat transfer and load-carrying ability. Any dirt or foreign matter between the bearing insert and bearing bore would destroy these qualities and reduce bearing inside diameter. *(Courtesy of Sunnen Products Co. Ltd.)*

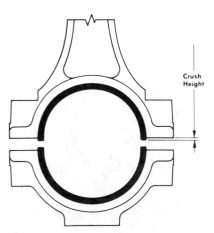

FIGURE 6-45. With the bearings in place and before tightening, the bearing extends slightly past the mating surfaces of the connecting rod or main bearing bores and caps. This is called crush height. *(Courtesy of Sunnen Products Co. Ltd.)*

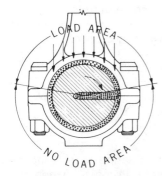

FIGURE 6-47. As the oil hole in the crankshaft sweeps past the load area, no oil is being fed into the bearing. Oil already there is forced between bearing and journal by journal rotation (hydrodynamic lubrication). *(Courtesy of Sunnen Products Co. Ltd.)*

112

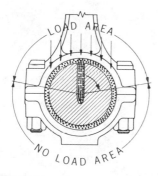

FIGURE 6-48. As the oil hole reaches the no-load area, oil is again fed into the bearing to replace oil being thrown off at the edges. As the shaft rotates to the loaded area, the process in Figure 6-47 is repeated. *(Courtesy of Sunnen Products Co. Ltd.)*

FIGURE 6-51. Oil diluted by fuel caused this bearing condition.

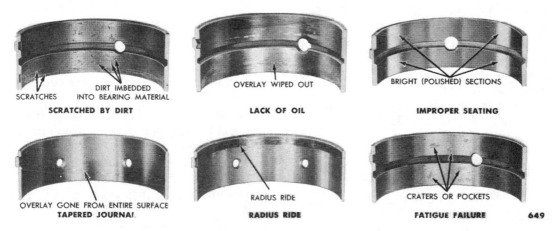

FIGURE 6-49. Several types and causes of bearing failures. *(Courtesy of Ford Motor Co. of Canada Ltd.)*

FIGURE 6-50. Type of bearing failure caused by antifreeze leakage into crankcase.

FIGURE 6-52. Incorrect crankshaft end play caused thrust flange failure on this main bearing.

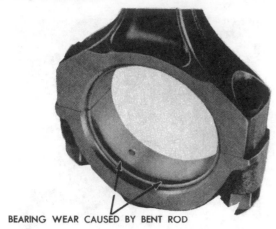

BEARING WEAR CAUSED BY BENT ROD

FIGURE 6-53. Upper half of bearing would show similar wear on opposite side. Other results of this condition are increased oil throw-off, bearing journal wear, and connecting rod (big end) out of round. *(Courtesy of Ford Motor Co. of Canada Ltd.)*

Excessive bearing clearances also increase the amount of oil throw-off from the bearings. A certain amount of oil throw-off is needed for oil circulation and for lubrication of other internal engine parts. However, if oil throw-off is excessive, the amount of oil thrown up on the cylinder walls is more than the rings are able to remove. As a result of this, oil passes by the rings into the combustion chamber where it is burned.

Close examination of bearings will indicate reasons for bearing failure, as shown in Figures 6-49 to 6-53.

Crankshaft Oil Seals

Main bearing oil seals are subjected to wear and heat. When seals become hardened, they lose their flexibility and their sealing ability. Excessive main bearing clearance will also reduce the ability of the rear main bearing seal to function properly. Both lip-

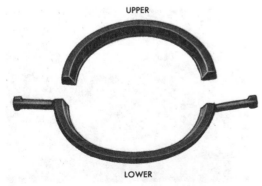

UPPER

LOWER

FIGURE 6-54. Rear main bearing oil seal, split type. *(Courtesy of General Motors Corporation)*

DAMPER

SEALING SURFACE

FIGURE 6-55. The vibration damper (harmonic balancer) dampens torsional vibrations of the crankshaft caused by power impulses. The timing cover seal will eventually wear a groove into the sealing surface of the damper hub. *(Courtesy of Ford Motor Co. of Canada Ltd.)*

type synthetic rubber seals and graphite-impregnated wick- or rope-type seals are used.

The front crankshaft seal can wear a groove into the hub of the harmonic balancer over a long period of time. Sometimes the inertia ring will slip on the harmonic balancer. This will change crankshaft balance and the location of the ignition timing mark in relation to the crankshaft. Replacement of the balancer can correct this condition. Another repair method uses a thin-walled sleeve to cover the vibration damper hub if it is worn.

PART 3   PISTON AND ROD ASSEMBLY

The piston and rod assembly (in conjunction with the cylinder and valves) acts as a pump on the intake and exhaust strokes. On the power stroke, it transmits the pressure of expanding gases to the crankshaft, forcing it to turn.

Connecting Rod

The *connecting rod* is attached to the crankshaft at one end (big end) and to the piston at the other end (small end). The tapered I-beam type of connecting rod is the most common. The big end of the rod is split to make it possible to connect it to the crankshaft. The cap and yoke are a matched pair, and their relationship must not be altered. Both rod and cap are numbered. Special precision connecting rod bolts and nuts keep the cap in proper alignment with the rod. Some connecting rods have an oil spurt hole in the yoke or at the cap mating surface to provide cylinder wall lubrication. Notches in the yoke and cap provide proper bearing positioning.

The small end of the connecting rod is attached to the piston by a piston pin, which is a press fit in the connecting rod. In some cases, the small end of the rod is clamped to the pin or has a bushing in it to allow pin and rod oscillation.

The connecting rod undergoes high loads and speeds as well as constant change of direction. Overloading the engine can cause bent connecting rods and bearing failure. The big end of the connecting rod can also become out of round as a result of high loads and high mileage.

FIGURE 6-57. Assembled view of piston and rod assembly. *(Courtesy of Chrysler Corporation)*

Diesel Connecting Rods

Connecting rods for most gasoline engines are cast, whereas those for diesel engines are forged. High performance gasoline engines also have forged connecting rods. Many diesel engine connecting rods are rifle drilled the length of the rod to provide good piston pin lubrication. In some cases, this oil passage is also utilized to provide piston cooling. In this case, the top of the rod has a spray nozzle aimed at the underside of the piston.

The split in the big end of the rod is offset in many cases to allow clearance for rod removal through the cylinder. Some rod caps are attached by means of cap screws rather than bolts and nuts. The yoke of the rod is threaded in this case. Yokes and caps are often provided with a precisely machined tongue and groove to provide perfect alignment of upper and lower bearing bore halves.

The diesel engine connecting rod is subjected to the same types of loads and stresses as the gasoline engine rod but loads and stresses are much greater.

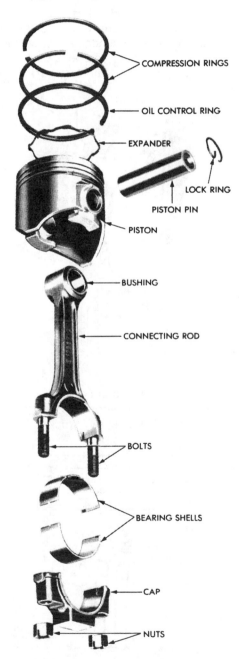

FIGURE 6-56. Exploded view of piston and rod assembly with parts identified. *(Courtesy of Chrysler Corporation)*

FIGURE 6-58. Tapered I-beam connecting rod (left) and tubular rod (right). *(Courtesy of Sunnen Products Co. Ltd.)*

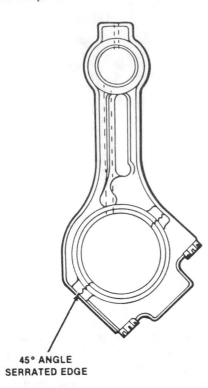

**45° ANGLE
SERRATED EDGE**

FIGURE 6-59. Rifle drilled rod (dotted lines) provides pin lubrication and piston cooling on diesel engine. Note serrated offset split. Offset provides increased strength and clearance for removal through cylinder. Serrations insure cap-to-rod alignment. *(Courtesy of Ford Motor Co. of Canada Ltd.)*

Pistons and Pins

The piston forms the movable bottom of the cylinder and combustion chamber. It is designed to withstand normal loads and temperatures, and provides long service life under these conditions. The piston must absorb all the thrust a cylinder is able to produce. Most automotive pistons are made of a special alloy of aluminum because of its lighter weight.

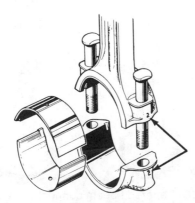

FIGURE 6-60. Connecting rods and caps are numbered for identification and proper assembly.

FIGURE 6-61. Some connecting rods have an oil squirt hole in the yoke, as shown here. This hole squirts oil to the major thrust side of the cylinder. Other designs have a squirt hole in the cap mating surface, while some designs have no oil squirt hole. *(Courtesy of Chrysler Corporation)*

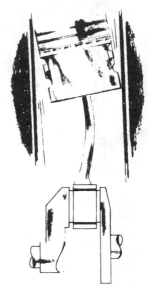

FIGURE 6-62. Connecting rods can become bent due to overloading as a result of detonation and preignition. *(Courtesy of Sunnen Products Co. Ltd.)*

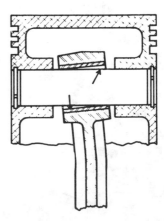

FIGURE 6-63. Bent connecting rods cause bushing and pin wear on full floating piston pins and rods. *(Courtesy of Sunnen Products Co. Ltd.)*

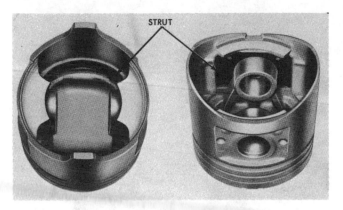

FIGURE 6-64. A steel strut is used in some aluminum pistons to help control expansion.

Several *piston designs* are used in gasoline engines. Piston head designs include domed, dished, flat, and notched types. Eyebrow-type notches are provided for valve clearance. A small notch at the front edge of the piston head or an arrow indicates proper installation position of the piston.

Three or *four grooves* are provided for the piston rings. Lands separate the ring grooves. Round or slotted holes are located in or just below the bottom ring groove to allow oil scraped from the cylinder walls by the rings to return to the crankcase.

The *piston head diameter* (which includes the

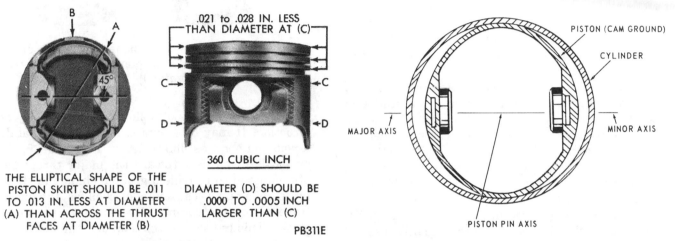

THE ELLIPTICAL SHAPE OF THE PISTON SKIRT SHOULD BE .011 TO .013 IN. LESS AT DIAMETER (A) THAN ACROSS THE THRUST FACES AT DIAMETER (B)

.021 to .028 IN. LESS THAN DIAMETER AT (C)

360 CUBIC INCH

DIAMETER (D) SHOULD BE .0000 TO .0005 INCH LARGER THAN (C)

PB311E

FIGURE 6-65. Pistons are cam ground to prevent piston slap when the engine is cold. As the engine warms up, expansion of the piston takes place across the pin axis. At operating temperature, the piston becomes round. *(Courtesy of Chrysler Corporation)*

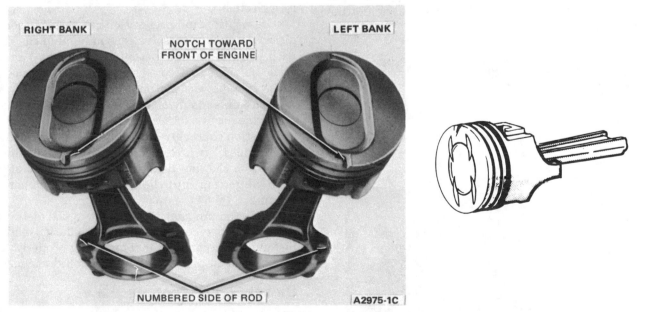

FIGURE 6-66. Some piston head designs as used in automotive engines. Piston head design affects combustion chamber design and provides for valve head clearance.

ring area) usually is approximately 0.030 inch smaller (0.76 millimeter) than the skirt diameter. This is necessary since the top of the piston is subjected to the hottest temperatures, approximately 500°F (260°C), and the most expansion. The piston head is round, whereas the piston skirt is cam ground (slight oval shape).

The *horizontal slot* in the piston just above the skirt acts as a heat dam to prevent piston head heat from having a direct path of travel to the skirt area. Clearance between the piston skirt and cylinder wall must be maintained at precise low tolerances.

Cam ground piston skirts (slight oval shaped) are larger in diameter across the thrust surfaces as compared to the diameter parallel to the piston pin. This allows the piston to fit the cylinder better when cold as well as at operating temperatures. In other words, clearance between the piston skirt and the cylinder on the thrust sides remains relatively constant whether the engine is cold or at operating temperature. Since the slot above the skirt directs heat away from the skirt area and to the pin relief (pin boss) area, expansion takes place parallel to the pin. As the piston expands and becomes more round, a wider area of the thrust sides (skirts) of the piston comes in contact with the cylinder wall.

A *steel strut* is used in many piston designs to help control the direction of piston expansion as well as to strengthen the piston.

A *tapered skirt* piston design is also used for expansion control. Since the top of the skirt runs at a higher temperature than the bottom of the skirt, some pistons are designed to be slightly smaller in diameter at the top of the skirt than at the bottom of the skirt.

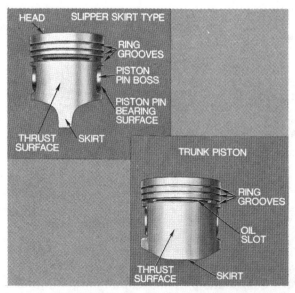

FIGURE 6-67. Piston features.

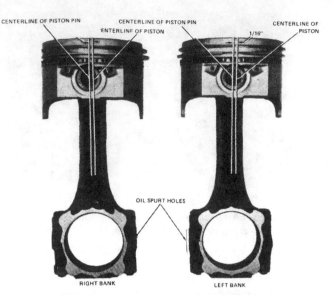

FIGURE 6-68. Pistons are designed with some pin offset to help reduce piston slap and thrust. *(Courtesy of General Motors Corporation)*

The *piston pin* is of hollow tempered steel construction. It may be mounted in one of several different manners, as illustrated in Figure 6-69. The pin is slightly offset toward the major thrust side of the piston to provide a gradual change in thrust pressure against the cylinder wall as the piston travels from the compression stroke to the power stroke. This reduces piston slap and thrust.

In *operation*, the piston is subjected to wide temperature variations, high combustion pressures, rapid changes in speed and direction, friction, and the effects of improper combustion, improper cooling, and incorrect ignition timing if engine service is neglected.

Detonation and preignition can result in serious piston damage. Excessive carbon buildup can cause both preignition and detonation. Carbon can also cause the rings to become seized in their grooves and cause cylinder and piston scoring.

Carbon is a soft or hard deposit that builds up on engine parts such as rings, pistons, spark plugs, combustion chambers, and valves. It is the result of the residues left after combustion. Some of this results from the fuel being burned, but most of it is from oil getting into the combustion chamber and burning.

A piston pin that is too tight in the piston can prevent proper connecting rod oscillation and the piston from expanding or contracting properly. This could result in piston slap and piston damage.

Diesel Engine Pistons

Diesel engine pistons are generally of heavier design than gasoline engine pistons due to higher combustion pressure loads. Diesel pistons also are steel

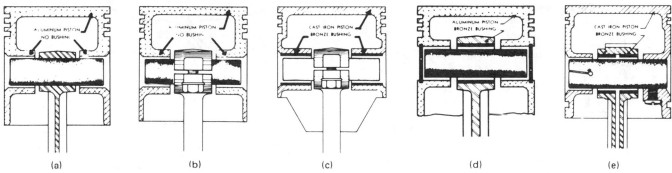

(a)　(b)　(c)　(d)　(e)

FIGURE 6-69. Different methods of piston pin mounting: (A) press fit in rod, no bushings; (B) clamped in rod, no bushings; (C) clamped in rod, bushings in piston; (D) full floating, bushing in rod; (E) pin held in piston (on one side only), bushing in rod. *(Courtesy of Sunnen Products Co. Ltd.)*

FIGURE 6-70. Examples of piston damage due to overheating caused by preignition or detonation.

reinforced for increased strength. Heavier piston pins are used for the same reason. Piston head design varies depending on combustion chamber design and valve clearance required. Diesel pistons also are usually designed with more skirt area than gasoline engine pistons since they are subjected to greater side thrust. Many diesel engine pistons are oil cooled from a spray nozzle in the connecting rod or from a separate tube type spray nozzle aimed at the underside of the piston and connected to the engine oil gallery. Many diesel pistons have the top

ring groove equipped with a chrome steel insert to reduce groove wear.

Diesel engine pistons are subjected to similar types of loads and stresses as are gasoline engine pistons, but loads and stresses are much greater.

Piston Rings

Piston rings provide a dynamic seal between the piston and the cylinder wall. Their purpose is to prevent combustion pressures from entering the crankcase and crankcase oil from entering the combustion chamber. They also control the degree of cylinder wall lubrication.

Types of piston rings include compression rings and oil control rings. Most automobile engines have two compression rings at the top of the piston and one oil control ring just below the compression rings. Some engines, including diesel engines, may use four piston rings on each piston.

Chrome-faced cast-iron compression rings are commonly used in automobile engines. The chrome face provides a very smooth, wear-resistant surface. Figures 6-71 to 6-75 show a number of ring designs.

The oil control ring commonly used consists of a slotted expander-spacer and two chrome-faced steel rails, one on each side of the expander-spacer. The slotted expander-spacer keeps the steel scraper

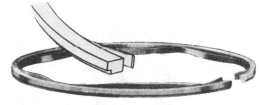

FIGURE 6-71. One type of compression ring with a ring expander to increase static pressure of the ring against the cylinder wall. *(Courtesy of Hastings Ltd., Toronto, Canada)*

119

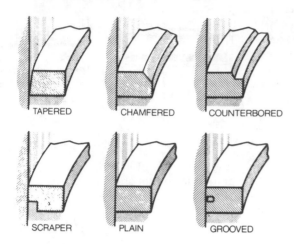

FIGURE 6-72. Various types of compression ring designs. *(Courtesy of Ford Motor Co. of Canada Ltd.)*

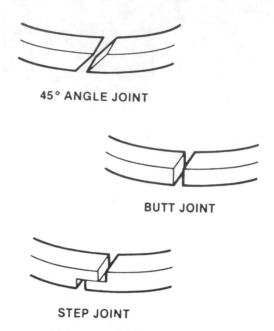

FIGURE 6-74. Piston ring end gap designs. *(Courtesy of Ford Motor Co. of Canada Ltd.)*

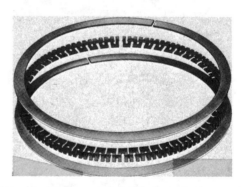

FIGURE 6-75. Three-piece oil ring design using two steel scrapers and an expander spacer between. *(Courtesy of Hastings Ltd., Toronto, Canada)*

rails in position and allows oil scraped from the cylinder walls to return through it and the piston to the crankcase. The steel rails scrape oil from the cylinder walls and help prevent oil from the crankcase from passing into the combustion chamber.

Two compression rings are needed since the top compression ring is not able to seal all the combustion pressures. The second compression ring seals off most of the remaining combustion pressures. Some combustion gases and unburned fuel (hydrocarbons) will inevitably get past the rings and into the crankcase. If the rings, pistons, cylinders, and fuel and lubrication systems are in good condition, this will be minimal.

Since motor oil from the lubrication system helps seal the rings, any decrease in lubrication system efficiency will affect the rings' ability to seal and will increase ring and cylinder wear.

FIGURE 6-73. Cross section of barrel-faced ring (top) and keystone ring (bottom).

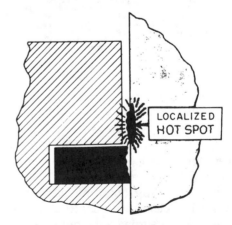

FIGURE 6-76. Example of damage caused by a localized hot spot. Metal from ring is deposited (welded) to cylinder wall, causing further damage as piston moves up and down. Localized hot spots can result from cooling system scale buildup on water jackets or manufacturing defect in block. *(Courtesy of General Motors Corporation)*

FIGURE 6-77. Piston rings seized in grooves. Ring pressure against cylinder wall is lost by this condition and oil consumption is excessive. *(Courtesy of General Motors Corporation)*

FIGURE 6-79. Piston damage as a result of broken rings. *(Courtesy of General Motors Corporation)*

Counterbores and chamfers on compression rings assist the rings to slide over the oil on the cylinder walls during upward movement of the piston and scrape the oil off the cylinder walls on downward movement. Tapered-face and barrel-face ring designs are also used for this purpose.

Expanders used behind specially designed compression rings increase ring pressure against the cylinder walls for increased sealing ability. Rings without expanders rely on ring tension alone for static pressure against the cylinder wall. Static tension is caused by the fact that the piston ring in its relaxed state is larger in diameter than the cylinder

and must be compressed to be installed. In its relaxed state, the ring is slightly out of round; however, when it is installed, it becomes round and seals against the surface of the cylinder wall. The ring face and the 60° crosshatch pattern of the cylinder wall *wear in* during the first period of engine operation to form a good seal. On the power stroke, the dynamic pressure of combustion increases ring pressure against the cylinder wall. This is the result of combustion pressure getting in between the top compression ring and the piston.

Ring side clearance is provided in the ring grooves to prevent rings from sticking or binding in the grooves due to expansion. A *gap* at the ring ends is provided to prevent ring ends from butting and causing the ring to become tight in the cylinder due to expansion from heat.

During *operation*, piston rings are subjected to dynamic pressures, friction, heat, constant change of direction and speed, and inertia. Since there is some side clearance between the ring and the land, the piston ring moves up and down in the ring groove on the different strokes of the engine. Due to ring pressure against the cylinder wall and the inertia of the piston ring, the ring tends to stay be-

FIGURE 6-78. Example of excessive ring groove wear. This causes improper ring operation and excessive oil consumption, as well as ring breakage. *(Courtesy of General Motors Corporation)*

FIGURE 6-80. Clogged and seized oil ring causes excessive oil consumption and carbon. The carbon is an abrasive, which causes piston and cylinder scoring. *(Courtesy of General Motors Corporation)*

hind when the piston changes direction. This causes the ring to move up and down in the groove and eventually causes ring groove wear. The ring itself also wears, increasing ring side clearance even further. When excessive, ring breakage can occur.

Another factor concerning ring and groove wear is cylinder condition. When a cylinder wears, it becomes tapered (larger diameter at the top of ring travel than at the bottom of ring travel). As a result, the piston rings are forced deeper into the ring grooves as the piston moves down in the cylinder. As the piston moves up in the cylinder, ring tension causes the ring to expand to fit the worn part of the cylinder. The rings continuously expand and contract in the ring grooves as the piston moves up and down in the worn cylinder.

PART 4   CAMSHAFTS AND DRIVES

The camshaft assembly includes the camshaft, bearings, and drive mechanism. The camshaft and drive assembly are required to control the opening and closing of the valves. The design of the camshaft and drive assembly results in valves being opened and closed at a controlled rate of speed, as well as at a precise time in relation to piston position. In-block camshafts also drive the distributor and oil pump and operate the fuel pump. Overhead-mounted camshaft engines usually have an auxiliary shaft to do this job. Camshafts are driven at one-half crankshaft speed on four-stroke-cycle engines by gears, by a chain and sprockets, or by a cog belt and sprockets.

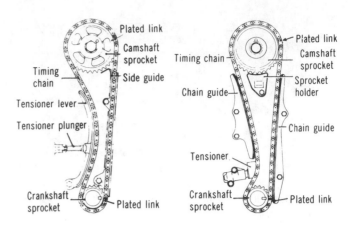

FIGURE 6-82. Typical overhead camshaft roller chain drive with chain tensioner and chain guides. Tensioner provides automatic chain tension adjustment as normal wear takes place. Two types are shown here; one acts on the chain guide, and the other acts independently. The chain guides prevent chain whip. (Courtesy of Chrysler Corporation)

Camshafts and Bearings

Camshafts are constructed from a hardened cast-iron alloy. A number of integral bearing journals support the shaft in the bearings and bearing bores. Bearing journals fit in the bores with approximately 0.002- to 0.005-inch (0.05- to 0.127-millimeter) clearance to provide room for lubrication and metal expansion. Bearing journals are machined and polished to reduce friction and wear. Diesel camshafts may be forged steel.

Camshaft bearings are of the bushing type and are similar in construction to crankshaft bearings. On some engines the camshaft bearings are all of

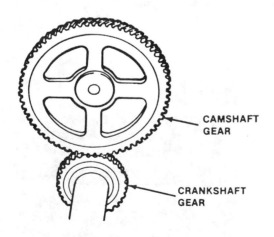

DIRECT DRIVE

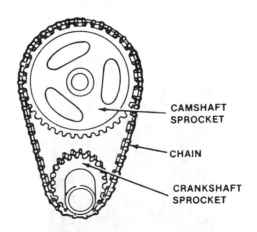

INDIRECT DRIVE

FIGURE 6-81. Direct gear drive and indirect chain drives for in-block camshafts. (Courtesy of Ford Motor Co. of Canada Ltd.)

FIGURE 6-83. Details of chain tensioner. Note oil hole which lubricates chain as it slides over the tensioner. *(Courtesy of Chrysler Corporation)*

equal diameter. On other engines the front camshaft bearing and journal are the largest, and the remaining bearings and journals are of progressively smaller diameter, with the smallest at the rear of the engine. This makes it easier to remove and install. Camshaft bearings are lubricated from oil galleries in the block or cylinder head.

Some camshafts have an integral spiral toothed gear to drive the distributor and oil pump. An integral eccentric or a bolt-on eccentric operates the fuel pump.

Endwise movement of the camshaft is limited by a thrust plate located between the front bearing journal and the drive gear or sprocket. The thrust plate is bolted to the engine. On some engines there

is no thrust plate to hold the camshaft in place. This arrangement relies on the effects of the spiral teeth of the distributor oil pump drive to keep the camshaft in the block. Thrust is absorbed between the inner surface of the sprocket and the front of the block.

Camshafts normally have two lobes for each cylinder of the engine: one to operate the intake valve and one to operate the exhaust valve. The cam lobes convert the rotary motion of the camshaft to reciprocating motion of the valve train and valves.

The *design of the cam lobe contour* has a major effect on engine performance. The amount of valve opening, how long the valve remains open (duration), when the valves open and close (valve timing), and the speed at which valves open and close are all determined by cam lobe design. The tapered cam lobe nose and convex lifter base promote even wear distribution on these parts.

The difference between the diameter of the lobe base circle and the nose-to-heel diameter plus rocker arm ratio (about 1.6:1) determines the amount of valve opening. In other words, lobe lift times rocker arm ratio equals valve lift.

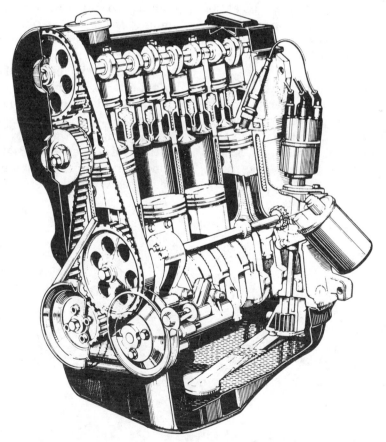

FIGURE 6-84. Overhead camshaft valve train and cog belt camshaft drive. Note auxiliary shaft used to drive oil pump, distributer, and fuel pump. *(Courtesy of Chrysler Corporation)*

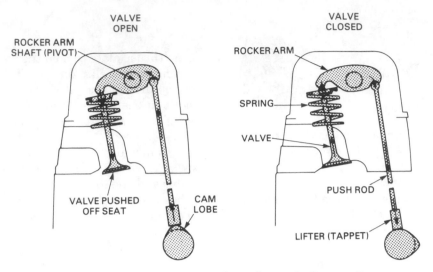

FIGURE 6-85. I-head valve train and camshaft operation.

Valve Timing

The *time* at which valves open and close (valve timing) and the duration of valve opening is stated in degrees of crankshaft rotation. For example, the intake valve normally begins to open just before the piston has reached top dead center. The valve remains open as the piston travels down to BDC and even past BDC. This is intake valve duration. An example of this could be stated as follows: IO at 20° BTDC, IC at 50° ABDC, (or, intake opens 20° before top dead center, intake closes 50° after bottom dead center). Intake valve duration in this case is 250° of crankshaft rotation.

This leaves 130° duration for the compression stroke since compression ends when the piston reaches TDC. At this point the power stroke begins. The power stroke ends when the exhaust valve begins to open approximately at 50° before bottom dead center. The duration of the power stroke in this case is also 130°.

Since the exhaust valve is opening at 50° BBDC, this begins the exhaust stroke. The exhaust stroke continues as the piston passes BDC and moves upward to and past TDC. With the exhaust valve closing at 20° ATDC, the duration of the exhaust stroke is 250°.

It is apparent from this description that the exhaust valve stays open for a short period of time during which the intake valve is also open. In other words, the end of the exhaust stroke and the beginning of the intake stroke overlap for a short period of time. This is called *valve overlap*. Valve timing and valve overlap vary on different engines.

Opening the intake valve before TDC and closing it after BDC increases the fill of air-fuel mixture in the cylinder. Opening the intake valve early helps overcome the static inertia of the air-fuel mixture at the beginning of the intake stroke, while leaving the intake valve open after BDC takes advantage of the kinetic inertia of the moving air-fuel mixture. This increases volumetric efficiency.

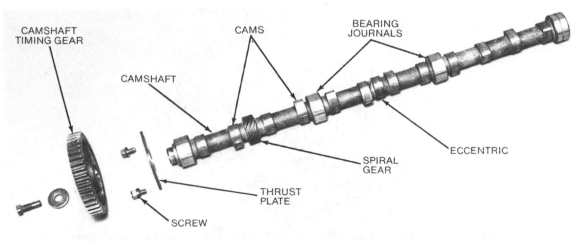

FIGURE 6-86. Exploded view of camshaft and drive gear with camshaft parts named. *(Courtesy of Ford Motor Co. of Canada Ltd.)*

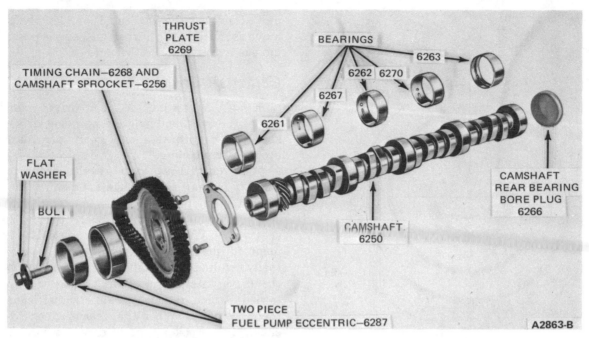

FIGURE 6-87. Chain drive camshaft and related parts. Note removable fuel pump eccentric and rear bearing bore plug. *(Courtesy of Ford Motor Co. of Canada Ltd.)*

As the piston moves down on the power stroke past the 90° ATDC position, pressure in the cylinder has dropped, and the leverage to the crankshaft has decreased due to connecting rod angle and crankshaft position. This ends the effective length of the power stroke, and the exhaust valve can now be opened to begin expelling the burned gases. The exhaust valve remains open until the piston has

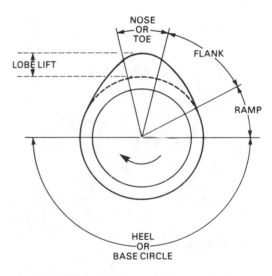

FIGURE 6-89. Cam lobe terminology.

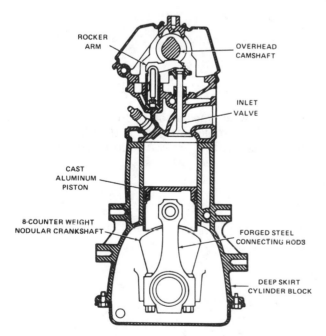

FIGURE 6-88. Overhead camshaft valve-train design using rocker arms. *(Courtesy of General Motors Corporation)*

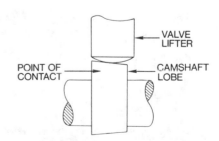

FIGURE 6-90. Exaggerated sketch of tapered cam lobe and convex lifter base, which causes lifter to rotate in its bore for even wear distribution.

125

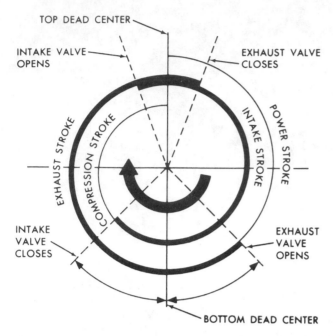

FIGURE 6-91. Typical valve timing diagram in relation to crankshaft rotation. *(Courtesy of General Motors Corporation)*

moved up past the TDC position. This helps to remove as much of the burned gases as is possible and increases volumetric efficiency.

Camshaft Drives

Camshaft drives include gear drives, chain and sprocket drives, and belt and sprocket drives. Camshaft drive sprockets and gears are marked for proper valve timing.

Camshaft drive wear results from torsional loads of driving the camshaft. Opening the valves against spring pressure causes a reverse twist on the camshaft, which has to be overcome by the camshaft drive. When the cam lobe passes the high lift point, torque is reversed. This torque reversal eventually results in camshaft drive mechanism wear. As the drive mechanism wears, valve timing is retarded, which reduces volumetric efficiency and therefore power. When the wear is excessive on the chain and sprocket type of drive, it can cause the drive to jump one or more teeth and change valve timing. If valve timing is sufficiently affected, the valves will not close in time, and the piston will hit the valves and can cause valve and piston damage. This is also the case when cam drive gear teeth are

FIGURE 6-92. Gear-type camshaft drive with fiber camshaft gear, steel crankshaft gear, and helical (angled) gear teeth. *(Courtesy of General Motors Corporation)*

NU269A

FIGURE 6-93. Chain drive for camshaft showing camshaft timing marks. *(Courtesy of Chrysler Corporation)*

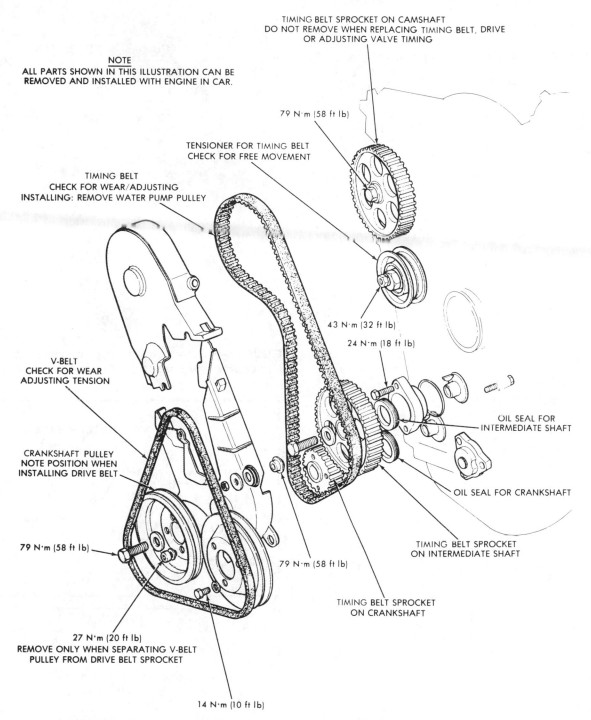

TIMING BELT SPROCKET ON CAMSHAFT
DO NOT REMOVE WHEN REPLACING TIMING BELT, DRIVE
OR ADJUSTING VALVE TIMING

79 N·m (58 ft lb)

TENSIONER FOR TIMING BELT
CHECK FOR FREE MOVEMENT

TIMING BELT
CHECK FOR WEAR/ADJUSTING
INSTALLING: REMOVE WATER PUMP PULLEY

V-BELT
CHECK FOR WEAR
ADJUSTING TENSION

43 N·m (32 ft lb)
24 N·m (18 ft lb)

OIL SEAL FOR
INTERMEDIATE SHAFT

CRANKSHAFT PULLEY
NOTE POSITION WHEN
INSTALLING DRIVE BELT

OIL SEAL FOR CRANKSHAFT

79 N·m (58 ft lb)

79 N·m (58 ft lb)

TIMING BELT SPROCKET
ON INTERMEDIATE SHAFT

TIMING BELT SPROCKET
ON CRANKSHAFT

27 N·m (20 ft lb)
REMOVE ONLY WHEN SEPARATING V-BELT
PULLEY FROM DRIVE BELT SPROCKET

14 N·m (10 ft lb)

FIGURE 6-94. Cog belt drive for camshaft and related parts. *(Courtesy of Chrysler Corporation)*

broken or when a cam drive belt jumps a cog or more.

Cam Lobe Wear

Camshaft lobe wear is caused by friction between the cam lobe and the lifter or cam follower base. Insufficient lubrication, excessive valve spring tension, excessive valve lash, hydraulic lifter failure, and dirty oil will contribute to early and rapid wear. Worn cam lobes retard valve timing, reduce valve opening, and decrease duration. This reduces volumetric efficiency and therefore engine power.

PART 5   VALVE OPERATING ASSEMBLY

The valve operating assembly includes the lifters or cam followers, pushrods, rocker arms and shafts or pivot, valves, springs, retainers, rotators, seals, and

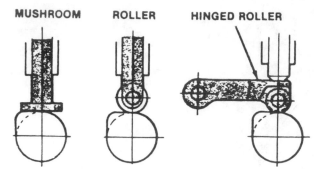

FIGURE 6-95. Typical mechanical valve lifter designs. Roller lifters have less friction. *(Courtesy of Ford Motor Co. of Canada Ltd.)*

locks. The purpose of this assembly is to open and close the intake and exhaust ports that lead to the combustion chamber.

Valve Lifters

Lifter types include mechanical lifters and hydraulic lifters. Mechanical-lifter-equipped engines require periodic valve lash adjustment, whereas hydraulic lifters are self-adjusting. The main oil galleries in the engine are connected to the lifter bores supplying engine oil pressure to the lifters.

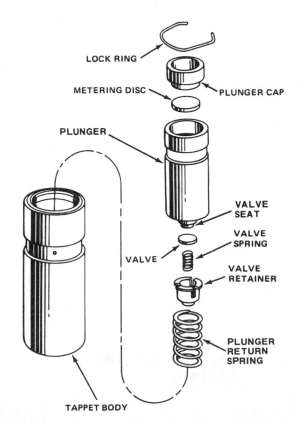

FIGURE 6-96. Exploded view of hydraulic valve lifter. *(Courtesy of Ford Motor Co. of Canada Ltd.)*

FIGURE 6-97. Overhead cam type of hydraulic valve lifter. *(Courtesy of Ford Motor Co. of Canada Ltd.)*

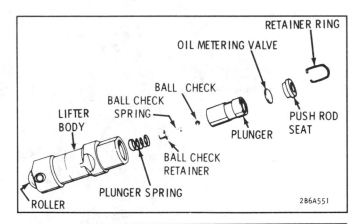

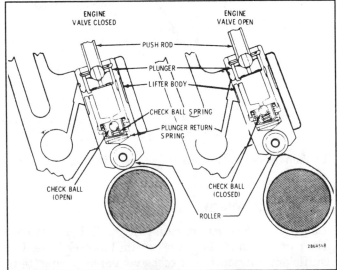

FIGURE 6-98. Exploded view of hydraulic roller type valve lifter (top) and operation (bottom). *(Courtesy of Ford Motor Co. of Canada Ltd.)*

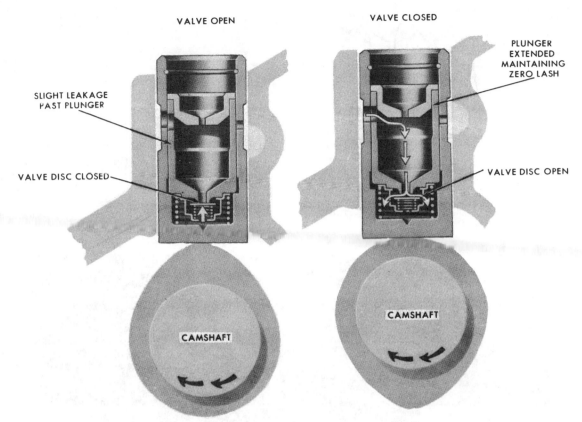

VALVE OPEN

SLIGHT LEAKAGE PAST PLUNGER

VALVE DISC CLOSED

CAMSHAFT

VALVE CLOSED

PLUNGER EXTENDED MAINTAINING ZERO LASH

VALVE DISC OPEN

CAMSHAFT

FIGURE 6-99. Hydraulic valve lifter operation. *(Courtesy of Ford Motor Co. of Canada Ltd.)*

Hydraulic lifter operation relies on engine oil pressure. When the intake or exhaust valve is closed, and the lifter is on the base circle or heel of the cam lobe, engine oil pressure is fed into the lifter body and the lifter plunger. Oil flows through the check valve and fills the area below the lifter plunger. This takes up all valve lash. As the camshaft rotates, the cam lobe begins to push against the bottom of the lifter body. Valve spring pressure through the rocker arm and pushrod attempts to keep the lifter plunger down. This causes pressure in the lifter below the plunger to increase and close the check valve. The oil is trapped below the plunger, and the lifter, in effect, becomes solid, since oil is not compressible.

A small amount of oil leakage past the plunger allows the lifter to *leak down*, should the lifters *pump up*. Lifter pump up is caused by anything that causes even momentary clearance anywhere in the valve operating train. Valves that are sticky in the valve guides, weak valve springs, and overspeeding of an engine can cause lifter pump up. Another reason for this slight leakage past the plunger is to allow oil to escape as parts expand as their temperatures increase. If oil could not escape, the valves would not be able to seal. On some models, a metering disc just below the pushrod seat meters the amount of oil delivered through the pushrod to the

rocker arm. On others, the oil is fed down from the rocker arm through the pushrod to the lifter.

Lifter wear is most evident on the lifter base, which is subjected to the friction of the cam lobe. Excessive leaking past the lifter plunger, or a leaking check valve, can cause lifters to bottom out. This causes valve-train noise or clatter. Varnish buildup

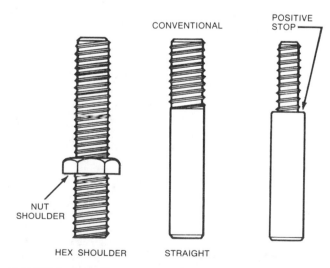

CONVENTIONAL

POSITIVE STOP

NUT SHOULDER

HEX SHOULDER

STRAIGHT

FIGURE 6-100. Three types of rocker arm studs. *(Courtesy of Ford Motor Co. of Canada Ltd.)*

129

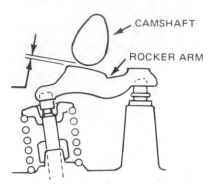

FIGURE 6-101. Nonhydraulic overhead cam valve train requires clearance at A. *(Courtesy of Ford Motor Co. of Canada Ltd.)*

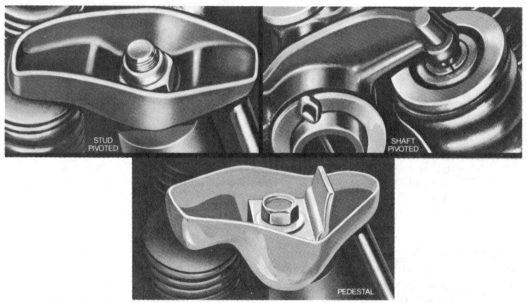

STUD PIVOTED

SHAFT PIVOTED

PEDESTAL

FIGURE 6-102. Rocker arm designs vary and are mounted in several different ways. *(Courtesy of Ford Motor Co. of Canada Ltd.)*

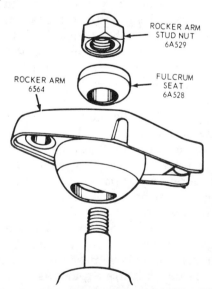

ROCKER ARM STUD NUT 6A529

ROCKER ARM 6564

FULCRUM SEAT 6A528

FIGURE 6-103. Exploded view of positive stop stud-mounted rocker arm. Adjustment of this valve train requires changing to different length pushrods. *(Courtesy of Ford Motor Co. of Canada Ltd.)*

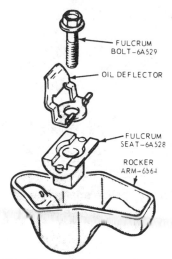

FIGURE 6-104. Exploded view of pedestal-mounted rocker arm. *(Courtesy of Ford Motor Co. of Canada Ltd.)*

inside the lifter can cause the lifter to stick and cause valve-train noise and wear.

Pushrods

Bent pushrods can be the result of incorrect valve adjustment, valve sticking, or valve timing. Bent pushrods can reduce the amount of valve opening and increase valve lash and wear on valve operating parts. Pushrod balls and seats are also subject to wear, which results in changes in valve-train adjustment.

Rocker Arms and Shafts

Rocker arms, shafts, and *pivots wear* owing to friction from valve-train operation. Rocker shaft wear is easily detected at the bottom of the shaft. Rocker arms wear at the valve stem, as well as at the pushrod end. The bottom of the rocker shaft hole in the rocker arm will also wear. Stud-mounted rocker arms will wear at both ends and at the pivot. In some cases, the rocker arm stud can also wear owing to improper rocker arm alignment. The same types of wear can be found on pedestal-mounted rocker arms and pivots.

PART 6   CYLINDER HEAD ASSEMBLY

The cast iron or aluminum cylinder head assembly forms the top or lid for the cylinders. It includes the valves that open and close the passages (ports) that lead from the combustion chamber to the exhaust manifold and from the intake manifold to the combustion chamber. The head includes the valve guides, valve seats, ports, combustion chambers, water jackets, threaded holes for spark plugs, other threaded

holes for attaching parts, and a number of machined surfaces. A number of nonthreaded holes are provided for attaching the head to the block. On overhead camshaft engines, the cylinder head includes provision for mounting the camshaft and related parts.

The *valve assemblies* open and close the intake and exhaust ports that connect the intake and exhaust manifolds to the combustion chamber. The valve assembly includes the valve, valve seat, spring, spring retainer, locks, valve guide, and seal. A rotator is sometimes used instead of a retainer.

Poppet-type intake and exhaust valves are used in automotive engines. The intake valve head diameter is usually larger than the exhaust valve head, because the intake valve and port handle the slow-moving air-fuel mixture, whereas the piston moves the exhaust gases out with more positive force.

The valve stem passes through the valve guide in the port, and the valve head closes the port when the valve is seated. The valve seat is located at the combustion chamber end of the ports. The valve spring is located on the spring seat and keeps the valve seated until the camshaft causes the valve to open against spring pressure. The spring is held in place by a spring retainer that is locked to the valve stem by two split locks. The valve stem seal is located on the valve stem to prevent motor oil from entering the combustion chamber or exhaust manifold through the valve guide.

Valves, Seats, and Guides

Intake and exhaust valves are designed to operate over a long period of time with relatively little attention or problems. Valve heads are sufficiently heavy for good heat capacity, yet light enough not to cause valve float very readily. Valve face and seat angles are usually 45°, while some valve face and seat angles may be 30°. Seating angles are required to provide a positive seal. The wiping action of angled seating surfaces helps clear minor carbon particles that could prevent proper sealing. The wedging action of the angled surfaces also contributes to better sealing. Valves are made of high-grade steel alloy for long service life.

Intake and exhaust valve materials include alloy steel valves with an aluminized face and chrome stem, Silchrome valve with an aluminized face, austenitic steel with aluminized face and chrome stem, and SAE 21-2 steel with a nickel-plated face. On some engines, exhaust valves with sodium-filled stems are used for better valve cooling. At operating temperature, the sodium is liquefied. Valve movement causes the sodium to transfer heat from

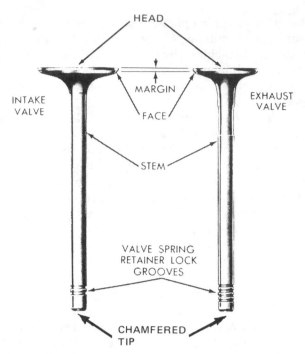

FIGURE 6-105. Valve terminology. *(Courtesy of Chrysler Corporation)*

the head of the valve to the valve stem and then to the valve guide.

Valve Temperatures

Exhaust valve temperature may reach approximately 1300° to 1500°F (704° to 815°C). This means that they are in fact running red hot. Good heat transfer, therefore, is essential.

It is important that valves be fully seated when they are closed. The exhaust valve is closed approximately two-thirds of the time while the engine is running. It is during this time that a large part of

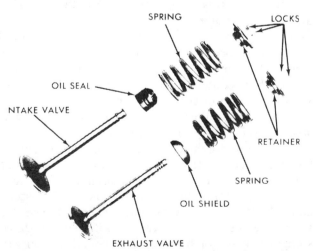

FIGURE 6-106. Exploded view of valve retaining parts and stem seals. *(Courtesy of Chrysler Corporation)*

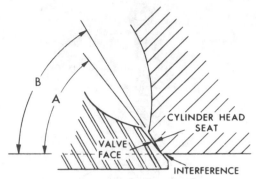

FIGURE 6-107. Valve face angle A is ½° to 2° less than seat angle B. This interference angle provides a positive seal on the combustion chamber side of the valve and seat. *(Courtesy of General Motors Corporation)*

the heat transfer from the valve head to the seat takes place. The heat from the seat is transferred to the engine coolant. The remaining heat transfer takes place from the valve stem to the valve guide to the engine coolant. The sodium-filled valve increases the amount of heat transfer from the valve head to the stem, which helps the valve head to run cooler.

Intake valve temperatures are considerably lower than exhaust valve temperatures. Incoming air-fuel gases cool the intake valve while the valve is open.

The *valve seat* has a great deal to do with good heat transfer. A valve seat that is too narrow will not absorb sufficient heat from the valve head and will wear both seat and valve more rapidly. A seat that is too wide is not able to clear carbon particles as readily; it will, therefore, not seal as well, and can cause valve seat burning. Many engines have integral valve seats that are induction hardened. Other engines have replaceable alloy-steel valve seat inserts.

Valve guides keep the valves in proper alignment with the valve seat during operation. Valve guides are either integral or replaceable.

Valve, Seat, and Guide Wear

Normal Wear

Valves, seats, and guides will wear from normal friction, heat, and pressures. Valve stems and valve guides will wear, resulting in increased valve stem-to-guide clearance. Valve seats and valve faces will also eventually wear from continued opening and closing of the valves. Rocker arm action causes both rocker arms and valve stem tips to wear. The rocking action of the rocker arm also creates a side pressure on the valve stem which contributes to valve stem and guide wear. By-products from normal combustion, such as carbon, acids, and moisture, also have a bearing on the wear of these parts.

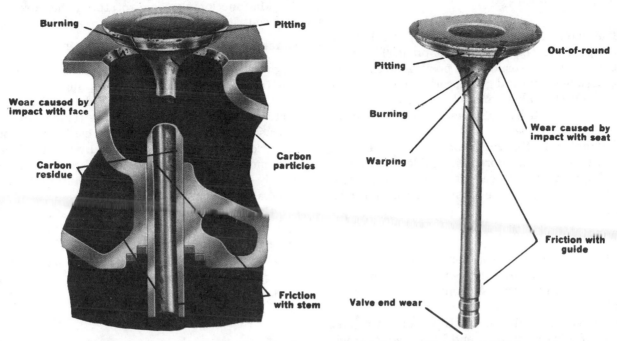

FIGURE 6-108. Valve face, seat, stem, and guide wear. *(Courtesy of Sioux Tools Inc.)*

Even in normal use, the intake and the exhaust valves absorb a fantastic amount of punishment. During a quick 15-minute trip to the shopping center, a single valve may open and close 10,000 times. Extreme temperatures scorch it many times each second. Violent explosions and powerful spring tension pound the red hot valve head. Hot gases under tremendous pressure swirl past it. Carbon deposits form on the face, preventing the valve from seating properly or cooling efficiently. As a result, the valves (particularly the exhaust valves) become pitted, burned, warped, and grooved. No longer concentric with the valve seat, they leak compression and fail to dissipate heat. Engine efficiency and economy nosedive.

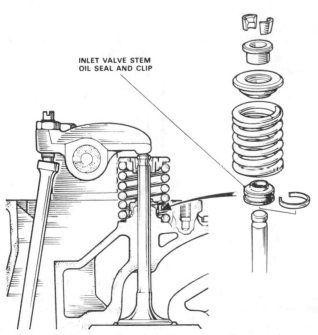

FIGURE 6-109. Positive type of valve stem seal. *(Courtesy of Chrysler Corporation)*

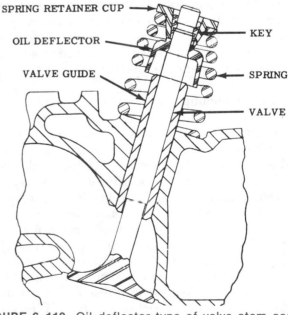

FIGURE 6-110. Oil deflector type of valve stem seal. Another type of valve stem seal uses an O ring between the valve stem and the spring retainer, which makes the retainer act as an oil shedder. *(Courtesy of General Motors Corporation)*

133

The valve seat also wears. Hot gases burn it. Carbon particles that retain heat pit it. The valve guide wears in a corresponding position to the valve stem. Between stem and guide, carbon residues form which cause the valves to stick. To ensure top performance, valve face, valve seat, and valve guide must be reconditioned.

But not only the valve face wears. The valve stem travels a mile or more in its guides during that short shopping trip. It wears at the top of the guides and at the bottom. Valve tips also wear and must be trued.

Abnormal Wear

The rate of wear on valves, valve seats, and valve guides will increase owing to any abnormal conditions that may exist in the engine that affect valve operation.

An overly rich air-fuel mixture can cause some dilution of lubricating oils, and increased wear will result. While it is true that in general a leaner mixture will increase combustion temperatures and therefore increase valve, seat, and guide wear and deterioration, it is also true that further leaning out of the mixture to 16:1 or leaner will decrease combustion temperatures considerably. Other reasons for excessive combustion temperatures include retarded valve timing, incorrect ignition timing, detonation, and preignition.

Valve timing becomes retarded as a result of valve-train wear and excessive valve lash adjustment. Retarded ignition timing will cause increased combustion chamber temperatures. Excessively advanced ignition timing can cause detonation and preignition, both of which cause extremely high combustion temperatures and early piston and valve failure.

Carbon buildup in the combustion chamber can also cause preignition and detonation. Excessive valve lash or excessive valve spring pressures can cause high-velocity valve seating and rapid valve and seat wear. Valves can stick in the guides as a result of bent valves, insufficient stem-to-guide clearance, incorrect cylinder head tightening, guide distortion, varnish, and carbon deposits.

Valve float refers to the condition when a valve is not closing fast enough. Weak or broken valve springs can cause valve float, which reduces the time a valve is seated and therefore increases valve temperatures. Valve float can also result in bent valves from pistons hitting slow-closing valves. If the valve is not out of the way by the time the piston comes up, it may hit the valve and bend it. This condition is usually experienced at high engine speeds.

Malfunctioning valve rotators (when used) can also contribute to increased valve and seat wear.

Cracked, Burned, and Broken Valves

High engine speeds and loads, poor valve seating due to carbon deposits, warpage, alignment, or insufficient lash, preignition, and detonation are all factors that cause excessive valve temperature and cracked or burned or broken valves. High temperatures combined with combustion by-products (acids and moisture) and high-velocity gases can sufficiently erode the valve stem, resulting in valve breakage.

Carbon deposits on the valves are a result of fuel residues and engine oil being burned. Engine oil can enter the combustion chamber past the valve stems if valve stem and guide wear are excessive. Engine oil can also get past worn cylinders and piston rings. Carbon deposits in the combustion chamber can

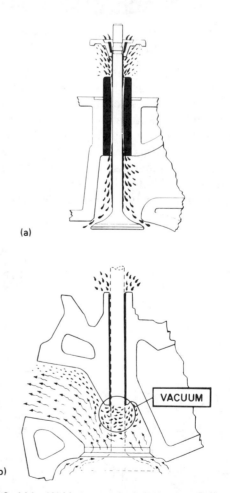

FIGURE 6-111. (A) Vacuum during the intake stroke can draw oil into the combustion chamber past the valve guide if clearance is excessive or stem seals are faulty or missing. (B) As exhaust gases are expelled past the valve guide area, a low-pressure area is created, causing oil to pass by the valve guide into the exhaust gases.

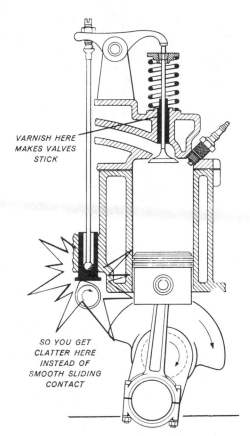

VARNISH HERE
MAKES VALVES
STICK

SO YOU GET
CLATTER HERE
INSTEAD OF
SMOOTH SLIDING
CONTACT

FIGURE 6-112. Varnish buildup causes valves to stick and close too late. This causes noise in the valve train. Insufficient stem-to-guide clearance can cause the same problem.

cause preignition and detonation, which increase combustion and valve temperatures.

Poorly seated valves allow hot-burning gases to escape past the valve with a cutting torch effect and can cause valves to be burned and cracked. Severely cracked valves can have pieces break away and cause piston and cylinder damage. A valve head that has separated from the stem also causes severe piston, cylinder, and cylinder head damage. Stem erosion and acid etching can cause this kind of valve breakage.

Excessive oil consumption can be caused by excessive valve stem-to-guide clearance or hardened and cracked valve stem seals. Excessive guide and valve stem wear will allow too much heat to get to the seals and cause them to harden and crack.

Valve Springs

Valve springs are needed to close the valves. A spiral winding of high-grade spring steel is ground flat at each end for square seating and even pressure distribution. Valve spring rates are designed to cause the valve operating mechanism to follow the

cam lobe profile for controlled opening and closing of the valve. A valve spring that is not square (tilted) will cause a valve to only close on one side of the seat.

Valve spring action is dampened by spring design or by a separate spring dampener to reduce spring vibrations. A variable-rate valve spring (coned spring or unequally spaced coils) is one method of spring dampening. A friction type of cup placed between the retainer and spring reduces vibrations by spring coil friction in the cup. A reverse-wound secondary spring inside the main valve spring reduces spring vibration by friction as well as different vibration frequencies.

Valve Rotators

Valve rotators are used in some engines to cause the valve to rotate slightly each time the valve is operated. Some engines use rotators only on the exhaust valves; others have them on both intake and exhaust valves. Slight rotation of the valve promotes even wear distribution on the seat, valve, and tip, and helps in removing small particles from between the valve and seat. Better valve seating and longer valve life are the result.

Several types of rotators are in use. Positive rotator types include the spring-loaded ball and ramp type and the single circular coil spring type. These two types ensure some valve rotation each time the valve is operated. The spring-loaded ball and ramp type will cause the valve to be rotated in one direction only. The single circular coil spring type can cause the valve to rotate in either direction.

The free type of valve rotator momentarily releases spring tension from the valve during opening so that the valve is free to rotate. This type does not cause positive valve rotation. Engine vibration and turbulence of gases contribute to valve rotation during the time the valve is free to rotate.

Some positive rotators are designed to operate between the valve spring and the cylinder head. Others are designed to operate at the valve tip in place of the spring retainer. The free-type rotator also operates at the valve tip.

Uneven wear patterns develop at the valve stem tip if rotators are not functioning.

Combustion Chambers

The shape of a combustion chamber depends on the shape of the depression in the cylinder head and the shape of the piston head. Combustion is affected by the shape of the combustion chamber to a large extent.

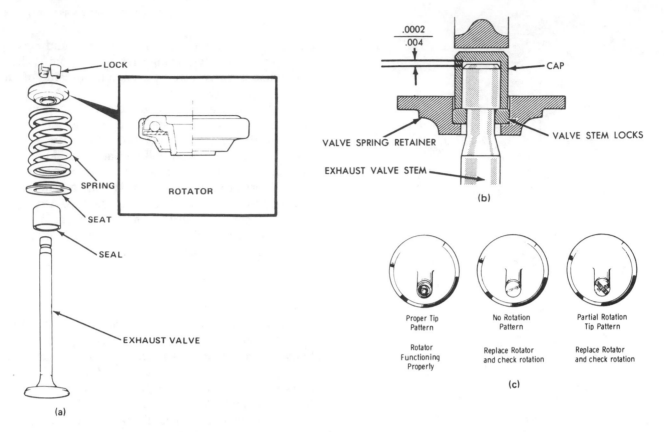

FIGURE 6-113. (A) Positive type of valve rotator. Valve rotation helps the valve and seat to maintain a positive seal. (B) Free type of valve rotator. (C) Wear patterns on the valve tip are good indicators of rotator malfunction.

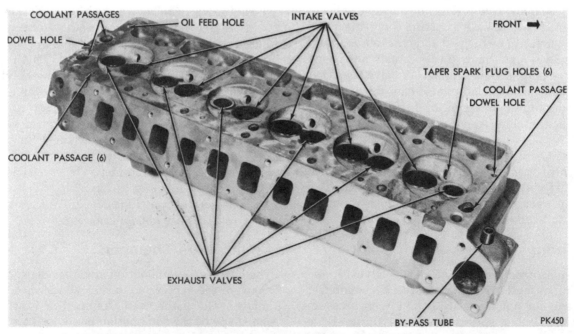

FIGURE 6-114. Cylinder head with individual exhaust and intake ports. *(Courtesy of Chrysler Corporation)*

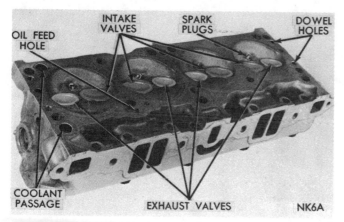

FIGURE 6-115. V8 cylinder head. (Courtesy of Chrysler Corporation)

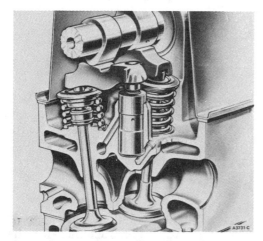

FIGURE 6-116. Overhead camshaft valve train and cross flow porting. (Courtesy of Ford Motor Co. of Canada Ltd.)

The two most common combustion chambers are the wedge type and the hemispherical type. The wedge type is also known as a turbulent combustion chamber. The hemispherical chamber is a nonturbulent type (Fig. 6-119 and 6-120).

FIGURE 6-117. Integral valve guides.

FIGURE 6-118. Wedge-type combustion chamber.

In the wedge type of combustion chamber, the spark plug is located at the wide part of the wedge. The opposite side of the wedge has a shallow area called the *squish area*. As the piston nears TDC, the air-fuel mixture is squished in this area, forcing it into the wider part of the wedge. This creates turbulence, which helps keep fuel particles in suspension and promotes smooth progressive combustion. However, in this type of combustion chamber, flame propagation proceeds from the spark plug across the combustion chamber. This increases the pressure and temperature of end gases in the chamber, which makes it more prone to detonation than the hemispherical combustion chamber.

In the hemispherical combustion chamber, the spark plug is centrally located. Flame propagation proceeds smoothly and evenly in all directions. This reduces the tendency for detonation.

Diesel Engine Combustion Chambers

In order to burn all the fuel injected into the cylinder, there must be adequate atomization and vaporization of the fuel. There must also be enough air around each fuel particle to allow complete combustion.

The injectors spray fuel into the cylinders in a

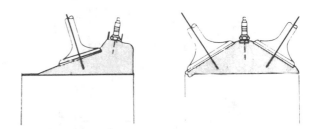

FIGURE 6-119. Cross-sectional shape of wedge type of combustion chamber (left) and hemispherical combustion chamber (right).

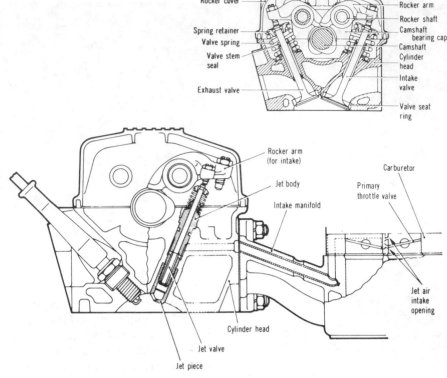

FIGURE 6-120. Double rocker shaft hemihead engine valve train and jet valve. *(Courtesy of Chrysler Corporation)*

very fine mist or spray under very high pressures (up to 20,000 pounds per square inch or 137,900 kPa). This provides the necessary vaporization; turbulence is provided by the combustion chamber design.

Open Combustion Chamber

In the open combustion chamber design, fuel is injected directly into the combustion chamber. The cylinder head and valves provide a flat cover or top for the chamber. The design of the piston causes the turbulence of the air in the cylinder. Various piston head designs are used to accomplish this action.

Piston designs for the open combustion chamber include a flanged-domed design, a dished design

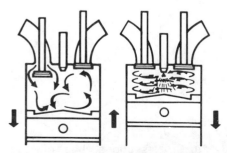

FIGURE 6-121. Action in open combustion chamber, direct injection four-stroke-cycle engine.

with a raised center area, and other irregularly shaped designs. Advantages claimed for the open combustion direct injection design include good fuel economy and simplicity of design.

Precombustion Chamber

The precombustion chamber design consists of two interconnected chambers. The smaller chamber is located in the cylinder head or block close to the top of the cylinder. The fuel injector is mounted so that fuel is injected into the precombustion chamber where combustion begins. The precombustion chamber is connected to the area above the piston and, as fuel injection and combustion continue, pressure is forced through the connecting passage to the top of the piston. The precombustion chamber design allows the use of a wider range of fuels and provides for very smooth combustion.

Turbulence Chamber

The turbulence chamber resembles the precombustion chamber in that a separate turbulence chamber is connected to the area above the piston. There is very little room above the piston when it is at TDC. As the piston moves up on the compression stroke, compressed air is forced into the turbulence cham-

138

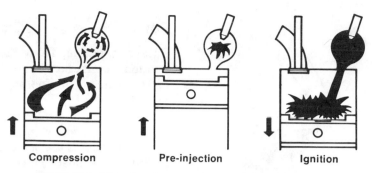

Compression | Pre-injection | Ignition

FIGURE 6-122. Prechamber indirect injection action.

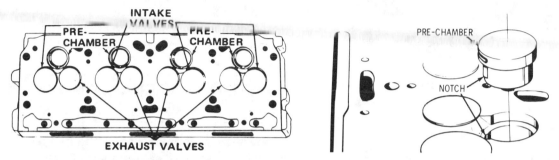

FIGURE 6-123. Precombustion chamber details in GM automotive diesel engine. *(Courtesy of General Motors Corporation)*

ber. The turbulent air promotes good mixing of fuel and air and provides good combustion.

Energy Cell

The energy cell is a combination of the precombustion chamber and the turbulence chamber. It is also known as the Lanova combustion chamber. Combustion takes place mostly in the main figure-eight chamber. This design depends on a great deal of tur-

bulence to provide the necessary mixing of air and fuel and the distribution of the air fuel mixture in the cylinder. Most of the combustion chamber is in the direct path of the intake and exhaust valves. Turbulence in this design is dependent on thermal action rather than piston speed as in the case of the open chamber.

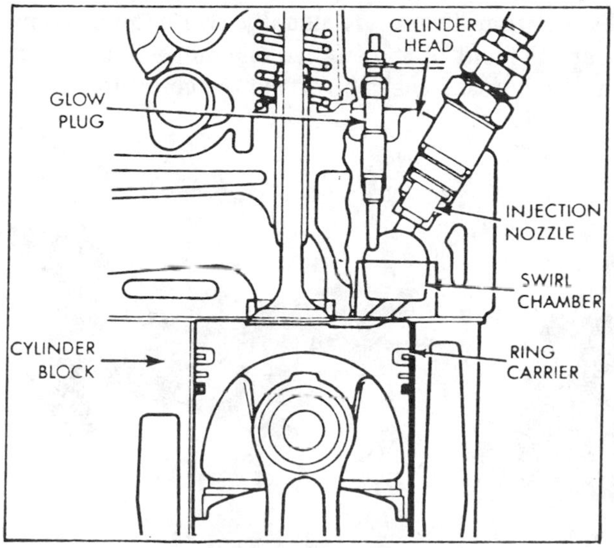

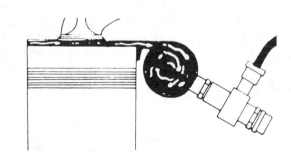

FIGURE 6-125. Swirl chamber action with indirect injection.

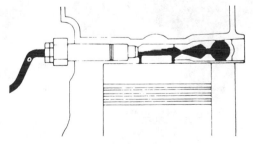

FIGURE 6-126. Power cell (energy cell) type of combustion chamber and injection.

FIGURE 6-124. Precombustion chamber on 2.3-liter four-cylinder overhead cam turbocharged diesel engine. Note glow plug which heats prechamber for cold engine starting. *(Courtesy of Chrysler Corporation)*

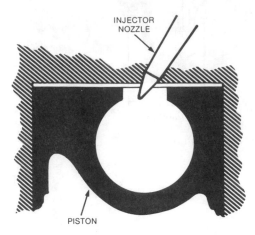

INJECTOR
NOZZLE

PISTON

FIGURE 6-127. M type of combustion chamber.

M-Type Chamber

The M type of combustion chamber consists of a spherical chamber in the head of the piston. This chamber has a small opening at the top. The fuel injector is positioned so that fuel will be injected into this chamber. This type of chamber has the advantage of eliminating the well-known diesel knock. It is also capable of using a variety of different fuels such as diesel fuels, kerosene, gasoline, etc.

Regardless of the type of combustion chamber used on any given engine, it should be remembered that the combustion chamber and injector are matched and work as a team. The combination of combustion chamber design (shape), engine compression ratio, fuel injection spray pattern, and fuel injection pressure is very carefully selected by the engine and fuel system manufacturers for good combustion, power, fuel economy, and low exhaust emissions.

Ports

Passages leading from the manifolds to the combustion chamber (called *ports*) may be all on one side of the head on in-line engines, or they may be of cross-flow design. The cross-flow design contributes to greater volumetric efficiency; V-type engines are of the cross-flow design.

Intake ports are sometimes siamesed (two ports joined in the head) since cylinders use them alternately on intake strokes. Individual alternate porting contributes to more even temperature control and better heat distribution. This is important since the combustion chamber area is the most critical area of engine temperature control.

PART 7   EXTERNALLY MOUNTED PARTS

Aside from components of the fuel, electrical, and cooling systems, a number of engine parts are mounted externally. Included are motor mounts, valve covers, oil pans, timing covers, and flywheel housings.

Motor mounts consist of two metal brackets with a heavy piece of rubber fused between them. One bracket is attached to a point on the engine that has relatively little vibration. The other part is attached to the frame. This insulates the engine from the frame and consequently reduces the noise and vibration transmitted to the passenger compartment. Motor mounts carry the entire weight of the engine—350 to 650 pounds (160 to 295 kilograms). They must also absorb and withstand the torque and torque reaction caused by acceleration and deceleration. There are usually two engine mounts near the front of the engine, one on each side, and a third mount at the rear of the transmission.

INTER LOCK METALS
TYPE MOUNT

BUSHING OR CAPTURED
TYPE MOUNT

RESTRAINING STUD
TYPE MOUNT

FIGURE 6-128. Several types of engine mounts. *(Courtesy of Ford Motor Co. of Canada Ltd.)*

FIGURE 6-129. Flywheel housing (bell housing) and cover.

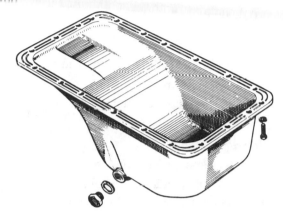

FIGURE 6-130. Stamped steel oil pan, gasket, and drain plug. *(Courtesy of Chrysler Corporation)*

FIGURE 6-131. Overhead camshaft cylinder head cover for four-cylinder engine. *(Courtesy of Ford Motor Co. of Canada Ltd.)*

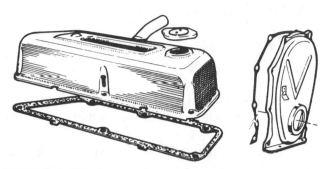

FIGURE 6-132. Stamped steel valve cover and timing cover. *(Courtesy of Chrysler Corporation)*

Engine mounts can cause chatter and vibration if deteriorated or broken. This is most evident on standard transmission cars and can even be mistaken for clutch chatter.

Valve covers, oil pans, and *timing covers* are usually made of stamped steel, plastic, or die-cast aluminum. They cover otherwise exposed moving engine parts. The oil pan also serves as a sump to hold a reserve of motor oil for engine lubrication. The timing cover incorporates a seal to prevent oil leakage past the front of the rotating crankshaft and vibration damper. The timing or camshaft drive cover sometimes includes provisions for mounting the distributor, oil pump, fuel pump, and water pump. All are attached with gaskets to prevent entry of dirt and escape of fluids from the engine.

The *bell housing* (clutch housing or torque converter housing) is bolted to the rear of the engine and encloses the clutch and flywheel assembly or torque converter. It is either of cast-iron or die-cast aluminum construction. Dowel pins keep the housing in proper alignment with the engine block. In some instances, the bell housing may be integral with the transmission case. An inspection cover is located at the bottom or lower front of the bell housing. In some cases the starting motor is bolted to the bell housing.

PART 8   SELF-CHECK

1. Engine blocks are made of _____ or _____.

2. The minor thrust side of an engine is on the opposite side of the crank throw when the piston is on the _____ stroke.

3. List the three major reasons for cylinders wearing to a taper.

4. State the purpose of the crankshaft.

5. What three functions are performed by the flywheel?

6. The V-8 crank throws are indexed every _____ degrees.

7. The purpose of the connecting rod is to _____.

8. List three methods of controlling piston expansion.

9. Three methods used to mount piston pins are _____.

10. What is the purpose of piston pin offset?

11. Why are piston rings needed?

12. Why are ring side clearance and ring gap clearance required?

13. The camshaft-to-crankshaft speed ratio is _____ to one.

14. Camshafts are manufactured from _____.

15. The camshaft controls the _____and the _____of the valves.

16. List three types of camshaft drives.

17. What is the advantage of hydraulic lifters as compared to mechanical valve lifters?

18. Rocker arms pivot on _____, _____, or _____.

19. List all the major components of the I-type cylinder head.

20. What is the purpose of the valve in the cylinder head?

21. The two most common valve face and seat angles are _____degrees and _____degrees.

22. Describe how the valves are cooled.

23. List four reasons for valve failure.

24. What is valve float?

25. Why are valve rotators used on some engines?

26. Name the two most common types of combustion chambers and state which is turbulent or nonturbulent.

PART 9 TEST QUESTIONS

1. The cylinder block manufacturing process includes:
   (a) casting
   (b) line boring
   (c) machining
   (d) honing
   (e) all of the above

2. Mechanic A says gasoline engine blocks and diesel engine blocks are the same. Mechanic B says that they are similar in design but diesel blocks are of heavier construction. Who is right?
   (a) Mechanic A
   (b) Mechanic B
   (c) both A and B
   (d) neither A nor B

3. Cylinder bores must be at an angle of _____ degrees to the crankshaft centerline.
   (a) 60°
   (b) 90°
   (c) 120°
   (d) 180°

4. Cylinder liner designs include the following:
   (a) wet or dry liners
   (b) cast iron or steel liners
   (c) integral cylinders
   (d) all of the above

5. Cylinder taper refers to:
   (a) angle of cylinder to crankshaft
   (b) angle between cylinders on V block
   (c) cylinder wear larger at the top
   (d) cylinder wear larger at the bottom

6. Crank throw indexing refers to:
   (a) cylinder numbering
   (b) firing order
   (c) piston stroke
   (d) relative position of rod journals

7. Balance shafts are used in some engines to balance:
   (a) engine weight
   (b) valve timing
   (c) engine torque
   (d) engine crankshaft assembly

8. Offset or splayed connecting rod journals are used in the following engine designs:
   (a) 90°V-8
   (b) 90°V-6
   (c) 60°V-8
   (d) 60°V-6

9. Crankshaft bearing materials include the following:
   (a) copper, aluminum, lead, steel, babbitt
   (b) aluminum, copper, rhodium, molybdenum
   (c) molybdenum, copper, rhodium, steel, aluminum
   (d) steel, platinum, aluminum, copper, lead

10. Four causes of bearing failure are:

(a) bent connecting rod

(b) antifreeze contamination

(c) dirt

(d) excessive clearance

(e) all of the above

11. Mechanic A says the connecting rod cap must be installed on the rod from which it was removed. Mechanic B says the connecting rod cap should only be installed in one position on the rod. Who is right?

(a) Mechanic A

(b) Mechanic B

(c) both are wrong

(d) both are right

12. Piston pins on some engines are offset to the:

(a) right side

(b) left side

(c) major thrust side

(d) minor thrust side

(e) both (a) and (c)

(f) both (b) and (d)

13. The purpose of piston rings is to control:

(a) combustion pressures

(b) cylinder wall lubrication

(c) oil consumption

(d) all of the above

14. During engine operation piston rings are subjected to:

(a) constantly changing direction and speed

(b) heat and friction

(c) dynamic pressures

(d) all of the above

15. Camshaft drive types include:

(a) cog belt, V-belt, chain

(b) gear, cog belt, chain

(c) V-belt, serpentine belt, gear

(d) serpentine belt, gear, chain

16. The camshaft controls:

(a) valve opening

(b) valve closing

(c) valve timing

(d) all of the above

17. Valve overlap occurs between the following strokes:

(a) intake, compression

(b) compression, power

(c) power, exhaust

(d) exhaust, intake

18. At 2000 rpm each valve on a four-stroke engine opens and closes how many times in 3 minutes?

(a) 6000

(b) 8000

(c) 3000

(d) 2000

19. Rocker arms pivot on a:

(a) shaft

(b) ball stud

(c) pedestal

(d) all of the above

20. Mechanic A says rocker arms reverse reciprocating motion. Mechanic B says rocker arms convert rotating motion to reciprocating motion. Who is right?

(a) Mechanic A

(b) Mechanic B

(c) both are right

(d) both are wrong

21. Mechanic A says that intake valves are cooled while they are open. Mechanic B says that exhaust valves are heated when they are open. Who is right?

(a) Mechanic A

(b) Mechanic B

(c) both are right

(d) both are wrong

22. Mechanic A says that only the valve and seat must be concentric for good valve sealing. Mechanic B says that the valve, seat, and guide must be concentric. Who is right?

(a) Mechanic A

(b) Mechanic B

(c) both are right

(d) both are wrong

23. Of the following answers, select the one that does not cause retarded valve opening.

(a) cam lobe wear

(b) valve face and seat wear

(c) rocker arm wear

(d) camshaft drive train wear

24. Excessive oil consumption may be caused by:

(a) excessive valve stem to guide clearance

(b) cracked or missing valve stem seals

(c) excessive cylinder wear

(d) all of the above

25. Valve rotator designs include the following:

(a) ball type, spring type, free type

(b) free type, enclosed type, open type

(c) open type, spring type, ball type

(d) spring type, free type, closed type

Chapter 7

Lubrication Systems

PART 1 LUBRICATION PRINCIPLES

The lubrication system of an engine is required to perform a number of very important functions. How successfully these jobs are done depends on a variety of factors. This section deals with a number of the more important jobs and features of the lubrication system.

Reducing friction to minimize wear and loss of power is one of the jobs a lubrication system must perform. Residual oil on engine parts also provides lubrication for engine start-up.

The engine oil forms a seal between the pistons, rings, and cylinders. It also helps to cool engine parts. Without the cleaning action of the lubricating system, carbon and varnish buildup would be excessive. The engine oil also absorbs the shock and dampens the noise of moving parts.

How successful the lubrication system is in performing all these functions depends on a number of factors and conditions. There must be an adequate supply of good-quality lubricant delivered to all moving engine parts under sufficient pressure to

FIGURE 7-1. *(Courtesy of Chrysler Corporation)*

FIGURE 7-2. *(Courtesy of Chrysler Corporation)*

FIGURE 7-3. *(Courtesy of Chrysler Corporation)*

OIL MUST KEEP PARTS CLEAN

FIGURE 7-5. *(Courtesy of Chrysler Corporation)*

PROTECT AGAINST ACID AND MOISTURE

FIGURE 7-4. *(Courtesy of Chrysler Corporation)*

ANTI-SCUFF ADDITIVES PROMOTE POLISHING

FIGURE 7-6. *(Courtesy of Chrysler Corporation)*

FIGURE 7-7. Heat destroys antiscuff additives. Antiscuff additives have a limited life expectancy; therefore, oil must be changed regularly. *(Courtesy of Chrysler Corporation)*

provide hydrodynamic lubrication for rotating parts and oil adhesion to surfaces subject to sliding friction.

- The oil and filter must be changed at frequent intervals.
- The engine must operate at its most efficient temperature.
- Engine oil temperatures must not be excessively hot or cold.

PART 2   LUBRICATING OILS

Motor oils for four-stroke-cycle engines fall into two basic categories: petroleum-based oils and synthetic oils. Petroleum-based oils, however, contain a variety of additives; so in fact they, too, are partly synthetic. Some of the major additives include those described here.

Additives

Antiscuff additives help to polish moving parts, including cams, pistons, and cylinder walls. This is particularly important during new engine break-in and after an engine overhaul. Since heat is the prime enemy of antiscuff additives, operating conditions

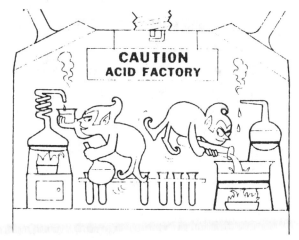

FIGURE 7-8. Corrosive acids from combustion by-products cause abnormal engine wear if oil is not changed as recommended. (Courtesy of Chrysler Corporation)

FIGURE 7-10. Sludge is also a by-product of combustion. (Courtesy of Chrysler Corporation)

that produce excessively high engine temperatures reduce the life expectancy of these additives. This type of operation requires more frequent oil changes than does normal operation.

Corrosion inhibitors reduce the formation of harmful acids by attacking the acid-forming ingredients. Combustion produces a number of by-products, including acids and water. Corrosion inhibitors neutralize these combustion by-products before they can do any harm to the engine. A cold engine, rich fuel mixtures, a poorly tuned engine; and much short-trip, cold-weather driving increases the amount of acids produced.

Oxidation inhibitors reduce the formation of sludge and varnish in an engine. Sludge is a heavy, thick, dirty substance that is formed from combustion by-products including partially burned gasoline, soot, moisture, and carbon. Varnish is produced when high engine temperatures cook some of the sludge ingredients, which then adhere to engine sur-

faces such as hydraulic lifters, pistons and rings, valves, and rocker arms. Sludge and varnish restrict oil flow and the movement of some engine parts.

Short-trip, cold-weather driving increases sludge formation, whereas high-speed, high-load, high-temperature driving increases varnish formation (i.e., oxidation). Oxidation inhibitors react chemically with sludge and varnish materials to render them relatively harmless.

Detergent-dispersants clean engine parts during operation and keep these contaminants in suspension in the oil. As the oil is forced through the filter, the majority of these contaminants are trapped by the filter.

Foam inhibitors reduce the tendency of oil to foam. Heat and agitation mix the oil with air to create foam. Oil foam reduces the lubricating ability of the oil and causes oil starvation and failure of engine parts. Loss of oil pressure due to foaming increases this problem.

Viscosity index improvers tend to stabilize or

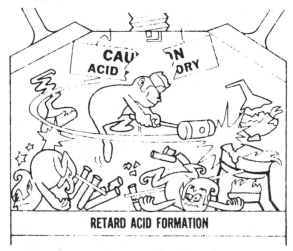

FIGURE 7-9. Corrosion inhibitors reduce acids formed in the engine. (Courtesy of Chrysler Corporation)

FIGURE 7-11. Heat that cooks the sludge produces varnish. (Courtesy of Chrysler Corporation)

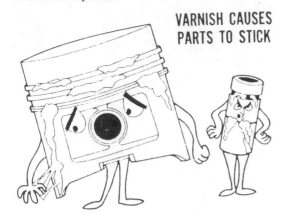

VARNISH CAUSES PARTS TO STICK

FIGURE 7-12. *(Courtesy of Chrysler Corporation)*

improve the viscosity of engine oils at various temperatures. They tend to give the oil more body when the oil temperature is high and increase its fluidity when the oil is cold. In other words, they improve the body and fluidity of the oil. The ability of the oil to carry a load at high temperatures is improved by this additive, and the ability of the oil to flow when cold is also improved.

Pour point depressants improve the ability of oil to flow (fluidity) when cold. This reduces the effort required to crank a cold engine and improves lubrication during warm-up.

Synthetic Oils

Synthetic oils are a chemically compounded lubricating oil. Manufacturers of these oils claim a number of benefits and advantages over petroleum-based oils, such as the following:

• Higher viscosity stability over a wider operating temperature range

• Greatly reduced effects of oxidation (reduced oil thickening)

• Reduced wear and increased loading-carrying ability

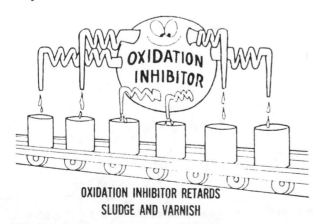

OXIDATION INHIBITOR RETARDS SLUDGE AND VARNISH

FIGURE 7-13. *(Courtesy of Chrysler Corporation)*

HEAT AND AGITATION CAUSE FOAM

FIGURE 7-14. *(Courtesy of Chrysler Corporation)*

• Reduced loss through evaporation
• Reduced crankcase oil temperatures
• Considerably reduced oil consumption
• Less engine deposits
• Less frequent oil changes
• Increased fuel economy

Oil Dilution

Oil dilution is a result of unburned fuel getting past the rings into the oil. An overly rich air-fuel mixture or a poorly tuned engine can cause unburned fuel to dilute the oil and seriously affect its ability to lubricate, seal, and reduce wear.

Oil Ratings

Service ratings for motor oils are determined by the American Petroleum Institute (API), American Society for Testing Materials (ASTM), and the Society of Automotive Engineers (SAE) in cooperation with each other.

ADDITIVES PREVENT DEPOSITS

FIGURE 7-15. *(Courtesy of Chrysler Corporation)*

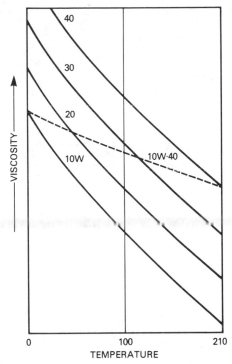

FIGURE 7-16. Viscosity (SAE) oil classification comparisons.

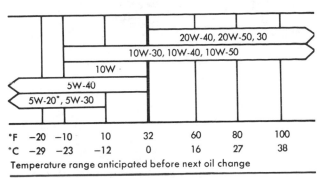

Temperature range anticipated before next oil change

*SAE 5W-20 Not recommended for sustained high speed vehicle operation.

FIGURE 7-18. Example of recommended oil viscosity ratings for different temperatures. *(Courtesy of Chrysler Corporation)*

The service rating of motor oils currently recommended for gasoline engines is the SF rating. SF oils supersede the previously recommended SA, SB, SC, SD, and SE oils. The types and quantities of additives used in blending motor oils determine their service rating.

Car manufacturer recommendations for the type of oil to be used and frequency of oil changes must be followed for the warranty to remain in effect.

The service ratings for compression ignition diesel engines are CA, CB, CC, and CD (the last being the one recommended for severe service).

Viscosity ratings of motor oils designate the body and fluidity of the oil. Both single-viscosity and multiviscosity oils are available. The lower the viscosity number of a single-viscosity oil, the greater the fluidity of the oil. The higher the viscosity number of a single-viscosity oil, the more body and load-carrying ability it will have. A multiviscosity oil will have the fluidity of the low number in its designa-

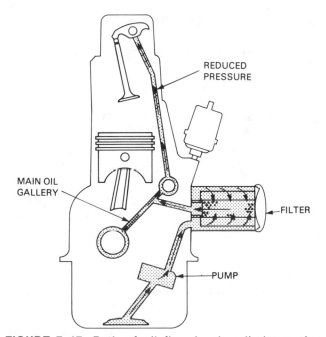

FIGURE 7-17. Path of oil flow in six-cylinder engine with camshaft in block.

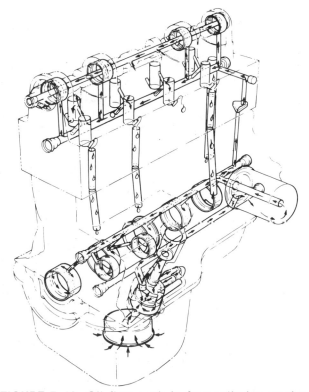

FIGURE 7-19. Oil flow path in four-cylinder overhead cam engine. *(Courtesy of Ford Motor Co. of Canada Ltd.)*

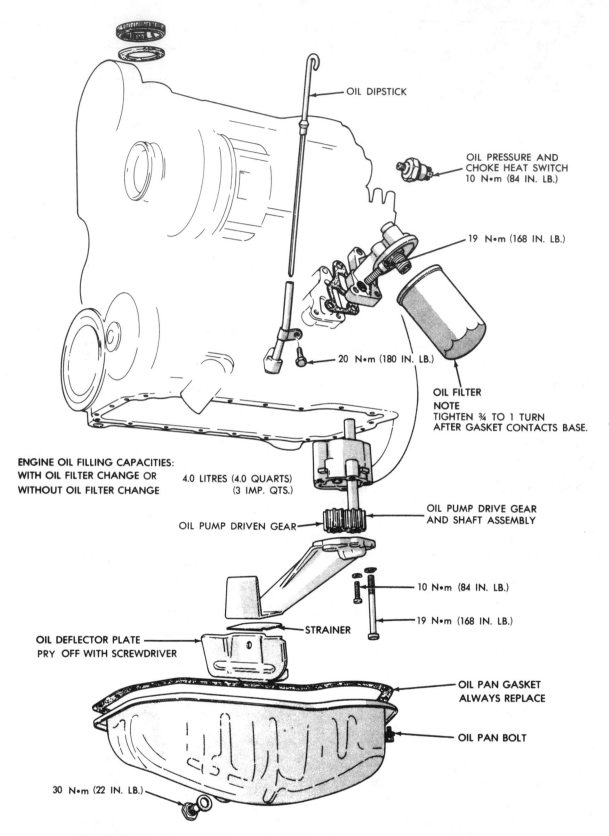

OIL DIPSTICK

OIL PRESSURE AND
CHOKE HEAT SWITCH
10 N•m (84 IN. LB.)

19 N•m (168 IN. LB.)

20 N•m (180 IN. LB.)

OIL FILTER
NOTE
TIGHTEN ¾ TO 1 TURN
AFTER GASKET CONTACTS BASE.

ENGINE OIL FILLING CAPACITIES:
WITH OIL FILTER CHANGE OR   4.0 LITRES (4.0 QUARTS)
WITHOUT OIL FILTER CHANGE   (3 IMP. QTS.)

OIL PUMP DRIVE GEAR
AND SHAFT ASSEMBLY

OIL PUMP DRIVEN GEAR

10 N•m (84 IN. LB.)

19 N•m (168 IN. LB.)

STRAINER

OIL DEFLECTOR PLATE
PRY OFF WITH SCREWDRIVER

OIL PAN GASKET
ALWAYS REPLACE

OIL PAN BOLT

30 N•m (22 IN. LB.)

FIGURE 7–20. Four-cylinder engine lubrication system components. Oil galleries to engine bearings and valve train are not shown here. (Courtesy of Chrysler Corporation)

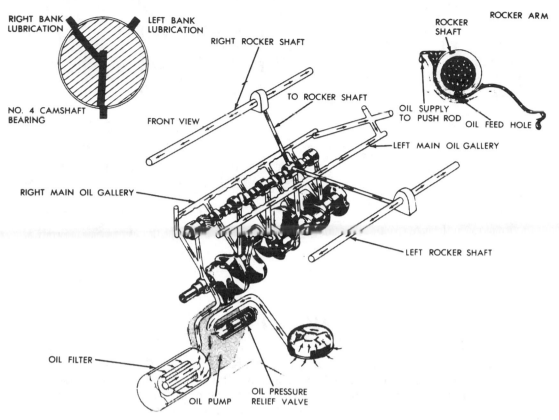

FIGURE 7–21. V8 engine path of oil flow. *(Courtesy of Chrysler Corporation)*

tion and the load-carrying ability of the high number in its designation. For example, a 10W-40 oil would have the fluidity of a 10W oil and the body and load-carrying capacity of a 40 viscosity oil.

The viscosity of engine oils is tested at 210°F (99°C). If the viscosity designation includes a W, this indicates the viscosity of the oil was also tested at 0°F (-18°C). The W stands for motor oils recommended for winter driving.

Manufacturer's recommendations for the viscosity of engine oil to be used for different ambient temperatures should be followed.

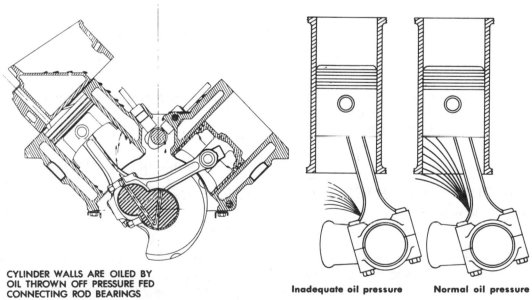

CYLINDER WALLS ARE OILED BY OIL THROWN OFF PRESSURE FED CONNECTING ROD BEARINGS

Inadequate oil pressure   Normal oil pressure

FIGURE 7–22. Cylinder wall and camshaft lobe oiling. *(Courtesy of Hastings Ltd., Toronto, Canada, and General Motors Corporation)*

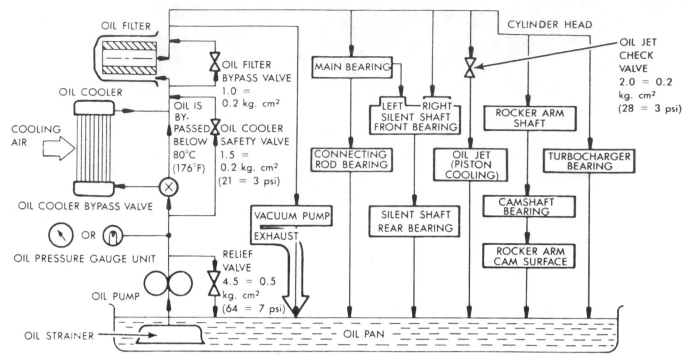

FIGURE 7-23. Lubrication system schematic for four-cylinder turbocharged diesel engine with air-cooled oil cooler. This type of oil cooler is usually located in front of the radiator. *(Courtesy of Chrysler Corporation)*

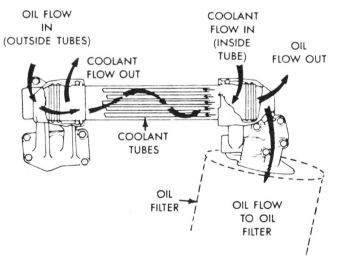

FIGURE 7-24. Typical diesel engine oil cooler cooled by engine coolant. Note coolant flow and engine oil flow paths. *(Courtesy of Chrysler Corporation)*

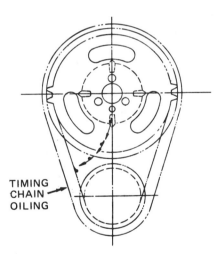

FIGURE 7-25. *(Courtesy of General Motors Corporation)*

PART 3 OIL PUMPS AND PRESSURE REGULATION

The engine oil pump must provide a continuous supply of oil at sufficient pressure and in sufficient quantity to provide adequate lubrication to the entire engine. The oil pump is mounted on the engine block on either the outside or inside. It picks up oil from the reserve in the oil pan through the inlet screen and pickup tube. The oil is forced out of the pump outlet to the pressure regulator valve, which limits maximum oil pressure.

Two types of oil pumps are used: the rotor type and the gear type. One of the rotors or gears is driven by a shaft from the camshaft or accessory shaft.

Since there is no direct path or opening for oil to flow through between the pump inlet and outlet, the pump is a positive displacement pump. Bearing clearances and metered oil holes restrict the flow of oil from the pump. This results in back pressure and

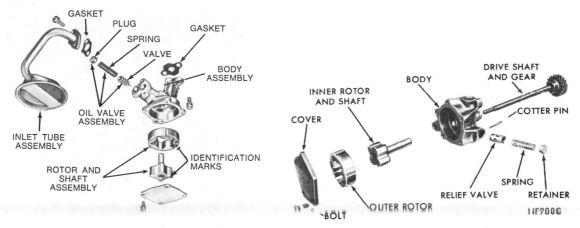

FIGURE 7-26. Rotor-type oil pumps. *(Courtesy of Ford Motor Co. of Canada Ltd. [left] and [right] Chrysler Corporation)*

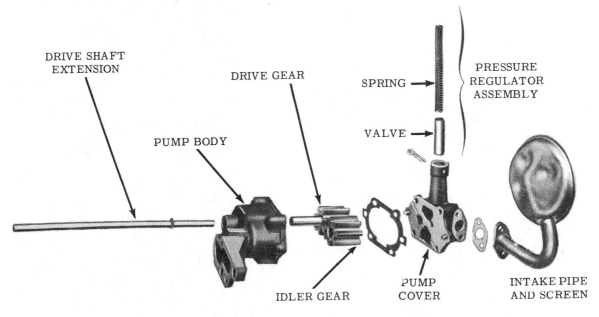

FIGURE 7-27. Gear-type oil pump components. *(Courtesy of Ford Motor Co. of Canada Ltd.)*

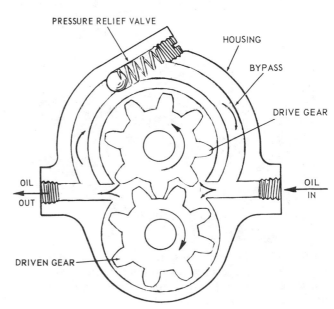

FIGURE 7-28. Gear pump operation. As operating oil pressure is reached, relief valve unseats, allowing excess oil pressure to return to oil inlet of pump.

153

pressure buildup. To limit maximum pressure, a pressure regulator valve is incorporated into the oil pump. Excess oil pressure is vented to the pump inlet or to the oil pan. It is therefore apparent that engine oil pressure is dependent on pressure regulator valve spring tension and restriction to flow on the outlet side of the pump. It follows, then, that excessive bearing clearances will cause a drop in oil pressure. A sticking regulator valve or damaged regulator valve spring will also affect oil pressure.

Internal wear in the oil pump allowing oil to bypass back to the inlet side will cause oil pressure to drop correspondingly. Oil pumps are designed to have sufficient reserve capacity to allow for normal wear.

PART 4   OIL FILTERS

Oil filters are designed to trap foreign particles suspended in the oil and prevent them from getting to engine bearings and other parts. Modern engines use the full-flow filtering system in which all the oil delivered by the pump must pass through the filter before reaching the engine bearings.

Should the filter be neglected and become completely clogged, a bypass valve allows oil to flow directly from the oil pump to the bearings. Another valve prevents the oil from draining out of the filter when the engine is stopped. This ensures oil delivery to engine parts immediately after the engine is started.

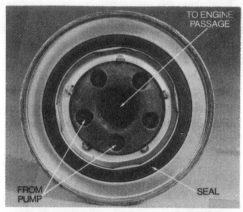
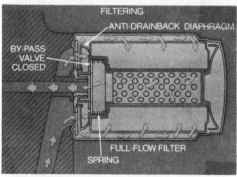
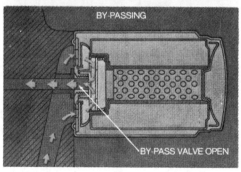

FIGURE 7-30. Spin-on type of oil filter. Note path of oil flow through filter when filter is in operation and when filter is plugged. *(Courtesy of Ford Motor Co. of Canada Ltd.)*

FIGURE 7-29. One type of in-block filter bypass valve. When filter is plugged, valve opens to allow unfiltered oil to be fed to lubrication system. *(Courtesy of General Motors Corporation)*

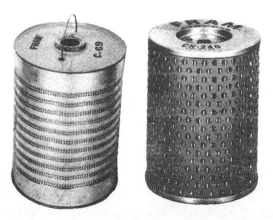

FIGURE 7-31. Replaceable filter elements: depth type (left), surface type (right). *(Courtesy of Fram)*

FIGURE 7-32. Spin-on type of filter showing paper bellows element (surface type). *(Courtesy of Fram)*

PART 5 CRANKCASE VENTILATION

Positive crankcase ventilation (PCV) systems are required to (1) prevent pressure buildup in the crankcase due to combustion pressure blow-by; (2) remove harmful crankcase vapors and remove condensa-

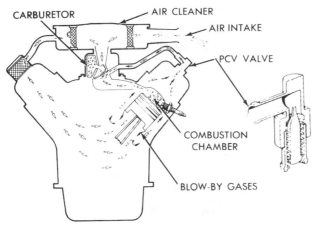

FIGURE 7-33. Positive crankcase ventilation system. *(Courtesy of Chrysler Corporation)*

tion; (3) prevent crankcase vapors from being emitted into the atmosphere, where they would contribute to atmospheric pollution harmful to health; and (4) prevent backfire gases from entering the crankcase.

Crankcase vapors are directed to the intake manifold through the PCV valve. These vapors are then burned in the normal process of combustion. This creates a low-pressure area in the crankcase and causes fresh, clean air to flow from the carburetor air cleaner into the crankcase.

A PCV valve stuck in the closed position causes crankcase pressures to build up and the flow of vapors to reverse. A similar condition can develop under heavy acceleration and load.

A malfunctioning PCV valve will also affect the engine's ability to idle properly, since some of the air for engine idle is supplied through the PCV system.

PART 6 OIL PRESSURE INDICATORS

Oil pressure indicators inform the driver whether or not the lubrication system is functioning normally. Direct-reading gauges that indicate actual oil pressure are used in some instances. These are either pressure-sensitive, direct-acting gauges or electric gauges that respond to a pressure-sensitive, variable-resistance sending unit switch.

Oil warning lights that indicate inadequate oil pressure when they light up are also used.

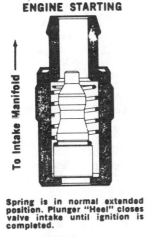

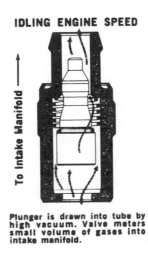

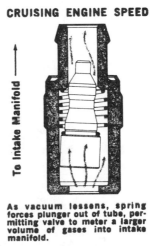

FIGURE 7-34. Normal PCV valve operation. Under heavy acceleration (low vacuum and high crankcase pressures), crankcase vapors will also pass through the crankcase breather to the air cleaner and can cause oily deposits on the air cleaner filter element. *(Courtesy of Fram)*

PROBLEM	CAUSE	CORRECTION
External oil leaks	1. Fuel pump gasket broken or improperly seated. 2. Cylinder head cover RTV sealant broken or improperly seated. 3. Oil filler cap leaking or missing. 4. Oil filter gasket broken or improperly seated. 5. Oil pan gasket broken or improperly seated; or opening in RTV sealant. 6. Oil pan gasket broken or improperly seated. 7. Oil pan rear oil seal broken or improperly seated. 8. Timing case cover oil seal broken or improperly seated. 9. Excess pressure because of restricted PCV valve. 10. Oil pan drain plug loose or has stripped threads. 11. Rear oil gallery plug loose. 12. Rear camshaft plug loose or improperly seated. 13. Distributor base gasket damaged.	1. Replace gasket. 2. Replace sealant; inspect cylinder head cover sealant flange, and cylinder head sealant surface for distortion and cracks. 3. Replace cap. 4. Replace oil filter. 5. Replace gasket or repair opening in sealant; inspect oil pan gasket flange for distortion. 6. Replace seal; inspect timing case cover and oil pan seal flange for distortion. 7. Replace seal; inspect oil pan rear oil seal flanges; inspect rear main bearing cap for cracks, plugged oil return channels, or distortion in seal groove. 8. Replace seal. 9. Replace PCV valve. 10. Repair as necessary and tighten. 11. Use appropriate sealant on gallery plug and tighten. 12. Seat camshaft plug or replace and seal, as necessary. 13. Replace gasket.
Excessive oil consumption	1. Oil level too high. 2. Oil with wrong viscosity being used. 3. PCV valve stuck closed. 4. Valve stem oil deflectors (or seals) are damaged, missing, or incorrect type. 5. Valve stems or valve guides worn. 6. Poorly fitted or missing valve cover baffles. 7. Piston rings broken or missing. 8. Scoffed piston. 9. Incorrect piston ring gap. 10. Piston rings sticking or excessively loose in grooves. 11. Compression rings installed upside down. 12. Cylinder walls worn, scored, or glazed. 13. Piston ring gaps not properly staggered. 14. Excessive main or connecting rod bearing clearance.	1. Drain oil to specified level. 2. Replace with specified oil. 3. Replace PCV valve. 4. Replace valve stem oil deflectors. 5. Measure stem-to-guide clearance and repair as necessary. 6. Replace valve cover. 7. Replace broken or missing rings. 8. Replace piston. 9. Measure ring gap, repair as necessary. 10. Measure ring side clearance, repair as necessary. 11. Repair as necessary. 12. Repair as necessary. 13. Repair as necessary. 14. Measure bearing clearance, repair as necessary.
No oil pressure	1. Low oil level. 2. Oil pressure gauge, warning lamp, or sending unit inaccurate. 3. Oil pump malfunction. 4. Oil pressure relief valve sticking. 5. Oil passages on pressure side of pump obstructed. 6. Oil pickup screen or tube obstructed. 7. Loose oil inlet tube.	1. Add oil to correct level. 2. Replace oil pressure gauge or warning lamp 3. Replace oil pump. 4. Remove and inspect oil pressure relief valve assembly. 5. Inspect oil passages for obstructions. 6. Inspect oil pickup for obstructions. 7. Tighten or seal inlet tube.
Low oil pressure	1. Low oil level. 2. Inaccurate gauge, warning lamp, or sending unit. 3. Oil excessively thin because of dilution, poor quality, or improper grade. 4. Excessive oil temperature. 5. Oil pressure relief spring weak or sticking. 6. Oil inlet tube and screen assembly has restriction or air leak.	1. Add oil to correct level. 2. Replace oil pressure gauge warning lamp or sending unit. 3. Drain and refill crankcase with recommended oil. 4. Correct cause of over heating engine. 5. Remove and inspect oil pressure relief valve assembly. 6. Remove and inspect oil inlet tube and screen assembly. (Fill inlet tube with lacquer thinner to locate leaks.)

PROBLEM	CAUSE	CORRECTION
Low oil pressure (cont.)	7. Excessive oil pump clearance. 8. Excessive main, rod, or camshaft bearing clearance.	7. Replace oil pump. 8. Measure bearing clearances, repair as necessary.
High oil pressure	1. Improper oil viscosity. 2. Oil pressure gauge or sending unit inaccurate. 3. Oil pressure relief valve sticking closed.	1. Drain and refill crankcase with correct viscosity oil. 2. Replace oil pressure gauge or sending unit. 3. Remove and inspect oil pressure relief valve assembly.

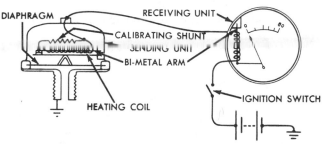

FIGURE 7-35. Schematic of electric oil pressure indicator. *(Courtesy of Ford Motor Co. of Canada Ltd.)*

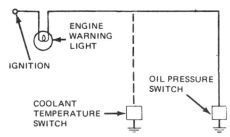

FIGURE 7-36. Schematic of oil pressure and coolant temperature warning light. *(Courtesy of Ford Motor Co. of Canada Ltd.)*

PART 7   LUBRICATION SYSTEM DIAGNOSIS AND SERVICE PROCEDURE

General Precautions

All the usual personal and shop safety practices should be followed. Some additional precautions should also be followed, such as the following:

1. Be sure engine has adequate oil and coolant before running engine for tests.

2. Be sure to keep hands, tools, and clothing clear of all rotating parts such as fans, belts, and pulleys.

3. Never stand in the direct plane of a rotating fan. Fan blades have been known to separate and fly off in any direction causing injury, death, or damage. Be sure to inspect fans for possible cracks that could lead to failures of this type.

4. Beware of hot engine parts and hot motor oil.

5. Do not disconnect any lubricating system parts from the pressure system while the engine is running. Doing this will cause hot engine oil to be discharged under high pressure.

6. Be sure entire lubricating system is leak free after service has been performed.

Checking Oil Level and Condition

It is important that the engine oil level be checked in a consistent manner in order to be able to accurately determine the level of oil in an engine. It is equally important that the engine oil level not be allowed to fall below the recommended level and not be overfilled.

If the oil level is too low, the oil pump may, at times, pick up air rather than oil. If the oil level is too high, oil foaming may occur. In either case, the lubrication system is not able to provide sufficient oil to the various engine bearings and hydraulic lifters. Increased wear and noisy lifters can result.

A good method of checking engine oil level is to do it in the morning before the engine is started. The vehicle should be level to avoid a false reading. This method assures the consistency needed to determine if an oil loss or oil consumption problem actually exists. It is not necessary to add oil until the oil level has dropped to the add-oil mark on the dip stick. Normally, when the oil level is at the add-oil mark, adding 1 quart or 1 liter will bring it up to the correct level.

If the oil level is checked at a service station immediately after the engine is turned off, the oil has not had sufficient time to drain back into the oil pan and a false reading may be obtained. Adding oil under these circumstances may overfill the crankcase.

Oil Consumption, Oil Leaks

A certain amount of oil consumption is normal. It is, therefore, also normal that oil may have to be added between oil changes. For warranty purposes, vehicle manufacturers usually consider oil consumption of 1 quart in 500 miles (1 liter in 600 kilometers) not to be excessive. These figures will vary somewhat among different manufacturers. To determine whether a vehicle is using an excessive amount of oil, the method of checking the oil level must be applied consistently over a period of time and mileage.

Oil consumption may be the result of worn piston rings, worn valve guides, excessive bearing clearance, and oil leakage. If an oil consumption problem exists, any oil leakage must be corrected first before the condition of the engine is blamed. If no oil leakage exists, a thorough diagnosis of the engine's mechanical condition should be performed to determine the cause. A wet and dry compression test can help to decide whether the piston rings, valve guides, or seals may be at fault.

Oil and Filter Change Intervals

The oil and filter change intervals should be followed as outlined in the vehicle owner's manual or shop service manual. The SAE rating (viscosity) and the service rating of the oil used, should comply with the vehicle manufacturer's recommendations.

The frequency of oil and filter changes may vary depending on the type of service the vehicle is required to provide. Under severe operating conditions, such as driving in dusty conditions, trailer towing, extensive idling, frequent short trips (especially in cold weather), and sustained high-speed driving (especially in hot weather), more frequent oil changes are required.

In some cases, manufacturers may recommend a special antiscuff additive be used with the engine oil after an engine overhaul or after severe service. Special conditions may have to be observed to use such additives. The manufacturer's recommendations should be followed in every case.

Oil Pressure Testing

If for any reason an oil pressure problem is suspected, a master test gauge with a range of 0 to 100 psi (0 to 689.5 kilopascals) should be used to verify actual oil pressure produced by the engine.

Generally, procedures include bringing the engine oil to operating temperature. The engine is then turned off and the test gauge installed at the point indicated in the service manual (usually a plug in the main oil gallery). The engine is restarted and readings are taken at specified engine speeds. These readings are then compared to those provided in the shop manual.

If the oil pressure is too high, the problem is usually a stuck oil pump pressure relief valve. The relief valve should be removed and polished with crocus cloth to correct this condition. Relief valve spring pressure should also be checked at this time.

If the oil pressure is too low, the cause may be any of the following:

- Worn oil pump
- Excessive bearing clearances (camshaft or crankshaft)
- Weak or broken pressure relief valve spring
- Relief valve stuck in the open position
- Excessive oil dilution
- Plugged oil pickup screen
- Air leak into oil pump inlet

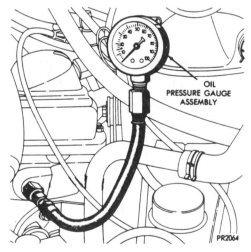

Oil Pressure Check:
Oil temperature —80°C (176°F)
Engine speed —2000 rpm
Min. pressure —193 KPa (28 psi)

FIGURE 7-38. Using test gauge to check engine oil pressure. Specifications shown are only one example. For specific engines, refer to manufacturer's manual. *(Courtesy of Chrysler Corporation)*

FIGURE 7-37. Removing spin-on type of oil filter with a special tool. *(Courtesy of Chrysler Corporation)*

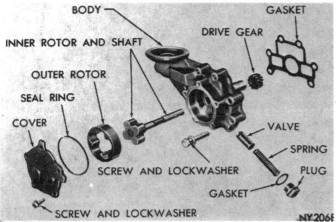

FIGURE 7-39. Exploded view of rotor-type oil pump (Courtesy of Chrysler Corporation)

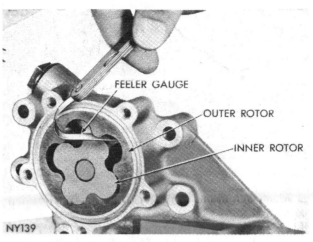

FIGURE 7-41. Measuring inner-to-outer rotor clearance. (Courtesy of Chrysler Corporation)

If the oil pump is worn, it is usually replaced. The oil pump must be removed and checked as outlined in the following section to determine its condition.

If the bearing clearances are excessive, they must be corrected to bring clearances to specified limits. This requires replacement of the bearings, and may require replacing the camshaft and crankshaft as well. If the relief valve or spring is at fault, it should be cleaned or replaced.

Excessive oil dilution requires changing the engine oil and filter and correcting the cause of oil dilution. This may require adjusting or replacing the automatic choke or correcting any fuel delivery system problems resulting in excessive fuel delivery to the cylinders.

If the oil pickup tube or screen is faulty, it should be cleaned or replaced.

Oil Pump Service

If the oil pump is suspected of being faulty, it must be removed and checked for wear. Both gear and ro-

tor-type pumps are similarly measured to determine if wear is excessive.

The relationship of the pump parts to each other must be maintained during this procedure if the pump is to be used again. Do not mark pump parts with a center punch. Use a felt pen or chalk to mark parts for correct reassembly. Some pumps have the gears or rotors marked during manufacture. Procedures for measuring pump clearances are illustrated, and results should be compared to limits specified in the service shop manual.

The oil pump should be assembled properly lubricated and primed to ensure immediate lubrication on engine start up. The correct thickness of the cover plate gasket must be used (where applicable) to ensure correct gear or rotor tolerances and adequate oil pump pressure. Install the pump and oil pan as outlined in Chapter 9. All bolts should be tightened to specified torque.

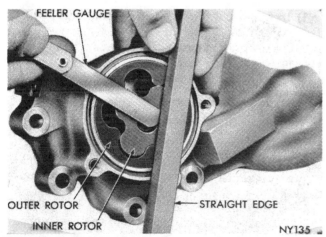

FIGURE 7-40. Measuring rotor end clearance with straight edge and feeler gauge. (Courtesy of Chrysler Corporation)

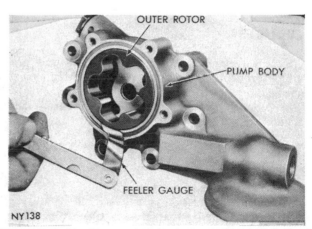

FIGURE 7-42. Measuring outer rotor-to-pump body clearance. If clearances are excessive, replace oil pump. (Courtesy of Chrysler Corporation)

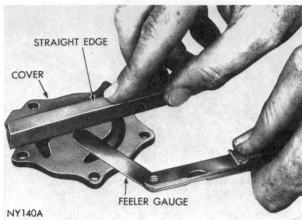

FIGURE 7-43. Measuring pump cover plate for wear or warpage. *(Courtesy of Chrysler Corporation)*

PART 8   PCV SYSTEM DIAGNOSIS AND SERVICE PROCEDURE

Inspection and Service Procedure

A. With Engine Idling.

1. Remove PCV valve from rocker cover. If the valve is not plugged, a hissing noise will be heard as air passes through the valve, and a strong vacuum should be felt when a finger is placed over the valve inlet.

2. Reinstall the PCV valve, and then remove the crankcase inlet air cleaner. Loosely hold a piece of stiff paper, such as parts tag, over the opening in the rocker cover. After allowing about a minute for the crankcase pressure to decrease, the paper should be sucked against the opening in the rocker cover with noticeable force.

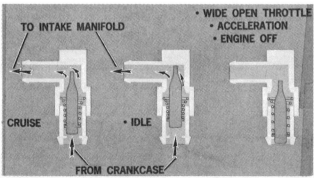

FIGURE 7-44. Operation of the positive crankcase ventilation system valve during different modes of vehicle operation. *(Courtesy of Chrysler Corporation)*

B. With Engine Stopped. Remove PCV valve from rocker cover and shake. A clicking noise should be heard to indicate that the valve is free.

C. If the ventilation system meets the tests in steps A and B, no further service is required; if not, the PCV valve should be replaced and the system rechecked. Install a new PCV valve. *Do not attempt to clean the old PCV valve.*

D. With a new PCV valve installed (and engine running), if the paper is not sucked against the crankcase inlet air cleaner opening in the rocker cover, it will be necessary to clean the PCV valve hose and passage in the lower part of the carburetor.

Special PCV system testers are available. These should be used according to tester manufacturer's instructions.

PART 9   SELF-CHECK

1. What four jobs are done by the lubrication system?

2. Name at least five common additives used in compounding motor oils.

3. Give one example of the SAE rating and the service rating of engine oils.

4. Two types of engine oil pumps are ____, and ____.

5. Why is the engine oil filter needed?

6. The positive crankcase ventilation system is required to ____, ____, ____and ____.

PART 10   TEST QUESTIONS

1. The lubrication system performs the following tasks in the engine:
   (a) cleans the engine
   (b) cools engine parts
   (c) seals engine parts
   (d) all of the above
   (e) none of the above

2. Hydrodynamic lubrication is:
   (a) hydraulic lifter lubrication
   (b) hydraulic brake lubrication
   (c) hydraulic pump lubrication
   (d) wedging of oil between a bearing and a journal

3. Sludge is a formation of:
   (a) water, dirt, and oil
   (b) water, fuel, and dirt

(c) fuel, oil, and water

(d) dirt, fuel, and water

4. Mechanic A says varnish is caused by excessively high lubricating oil temperatures. Mechanic B says varnish causes hydraulic lifters to stick. Who is right?

(a) Mechanic A

(b) Mechanic B

(c) both are right

(d) both are wrong

5. Mechanic A says sludge is caused by short-trip, cold weather driving. Mechanic B says varnish is caused by long-trip, high speed, high temperature driving. Who is right?

(a) Mechanic A

(b) Mechanic B

(c) both are right

(d) both are wrong

6. Mechanic A says viscosity ratings and SAE ratings of oil refer to the same rating. Mechanic B says service ratings and API ratings refer to the same rating. Who is right?

(a) Mechanic A

(b) Mechanic B

(c) both are right

(d) both are wrong

7. Oil pump types include the following:

(a) gear type, rotor type, chain type

(b) chain type, belt type, gear type

(c) rotor type, gear type, belt type

(d) rotor type, gear type

8. Excessive internal oil pump wear causes:

(a) low oil pressure

(b) increased wear

(c) lifter noise

(d) all of the above

9. Crankcase vapors are directed to the:

(a) induction system

(b) exhaust system

(c) vapor canister

(d) atmosphere

10. Oil pressure tests should be performed:

(a) at specified engine speed

(b) at operating temperature

(c) with a master pressure gauge

(d) all of the above

Chapter 8

Cooling Systems

Performance Objectives

After thorough study of this chapter and sufficient practice on the appropriate engine components, you should be able to:

1. Complete the self-check and test questions with at least 80 percent accuracy.
2. Describe the purpose, construction, and operation of the cooling system and its components.
3. Diagnose cooling system problems.
4. Recondition or replace the faulty components.
5. Test the reconditioned system to determine the success of the service performed.
6. Prepare the vehicle for customer acceptance.

PART 1   COOLING SYSTEM PRINCIPLES

The engine cooling system is designed to bring the engine to its most efficient operating temperature (as soon as possible after starting) and to maintain that temperature through all operating conditions. Some of the heat absorbed by the cooling system is used to heat the car's interior in cold weather and to keep windows clear of moisture and frost. Although some manufacturers have produced engines with air cooling systems, the vast majority of engines have liquid cooling systems.

The cooling system of an engine relies on the principles of conduction, convection, and radiation. Heat is conducted from the metal surrounding the cylinders, from valves, and from cylinder heads to the coolant in the water jackets of the block and head. The hot coolant is forced out of the block and cylinder heads by the water pump to the radiator, where the heat is removed by convection. Some cooling of the engine takes place through radiation. Air flow around the engine carries this heat away.

Since about one-third of the heat energy of the burning fuel in an engine, as well as heat from friction, is absorbed by the cooling system, all components involved must be of sufficient capacity, and they must be in good operating condition.

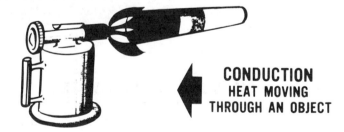

CONDUCTION
HEAT MOVING THROUGH AN OBJECT

FIGURE 8-1. (Courtesy of Ford Motor Co. of Canada Ltd.)

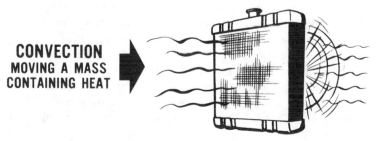

CONVECTION
MOVING A MASS CONTAINING HEAT

FIGURE 8-2. (Courtesy of Ford Motor Co. of Canada Ltd.)

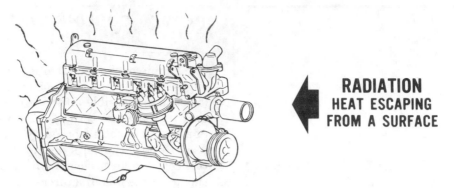

RADIATION
HEAT ESCAPING
FROM A SURFACE

FIGURE 8-3. Radiation: Heat escaping from a surface.

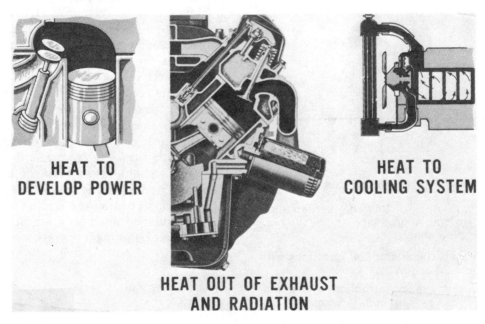

HEAT TO DEVELOP POWER

HEAT TO COOLING SYSTEM

HEAT OUT OF EXHAUST AND RADIATION

FIGURE 8-4. Approximately one-third of the available heat energy must be dissipated by the cooling system. One-third is disposed of by the exhaust system and by radiation, while about one-third is used to develop power. (*Courtesy of Ford Motor Co. of Canada Ltd.*)

PART 2   LIQUID COOLING SYSTEM

In the liquid cooling system, the coolant circulates through the cylinder block, up through the cylinder head, and back through the bypass to the water pump when the thermostat is closed. When the temperature of the coolant reaches thermostat-opening temperature, coolant circulates from the water pump to the block, and the cylinder head, through the open thermostat to the radiator inlet, through the radiator and the radiator oulet, and back to the water pump. Coolant circulates through the heater core at all times on some vehicles, and only when the heater temperature control is turned on in others.

Antifreeze

Liquid coolant is the medium used to absorb heat while it is in the engine and transfer it to the radiator, where it is dissipated to the atmosphere. Although water is a satisfactory liquid to use for absorbing and transferring heat, it has several deficiencies. It has a relatively low boiling point and freezes readily. Also, inhibitors must be added to water to prevent rust and scale formation and for water pump seal lubrication. For these reasons, an ethylene glycol-based liquid is used for year-round service.

Ethylene glycol-based antifreeze coolant has a higher boiling point than water; it has the necessary inhibitors and additives required to retard the

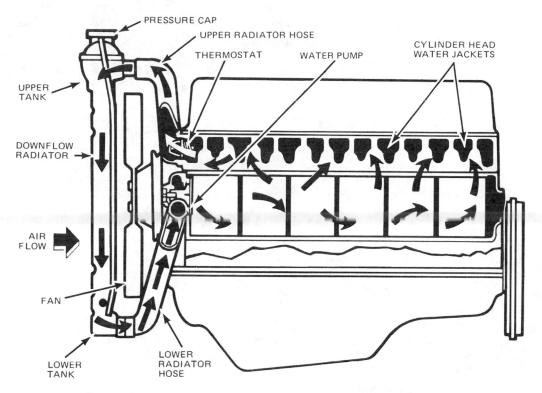

PRESSURE CAP

UPPER RADIATOR HOSE

THERMOSTAT   WATER PUMP

CYLINDER HEAD
WATER JACKETS

UPPER
TANK

DOWNFLOW
RADIATOR

AIR
FLOW

FAN

LOWER
TANK

LOWER
RADIATOR
HOSE

FIGURE 8-5. Schematic of coolant flow through the cooling system with the thermostat open. *(Courtesy of Ford Motor Co. of Canada Ltd.)*

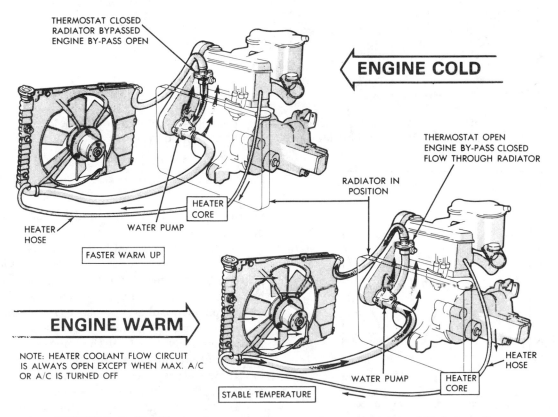

THERMOSTAT CLOSED
RADIATOR BYPASSED
ENGINE BY-PASS OPEN

ENGINE COLD

THERMOSTAT OPEN
ENGINE BY-PASS CLOSED
FLOW THROUGH RADIATOR

RADIATOR IN
POSITION

HEATER
CORE

HEATER
HOSE   WATER PUMP

FASTER WARM UP

ENGINE WARM

NOTE: HEATER COOLANT FLOW CIRCUIT
IS ALWAYS OPEN EXCEPT WHEN MAX. A/C
OR A/C IS TURNED OFF

HEATER
HOSE

WATER PUMP   HEATER
CORE

STABLE TEMPERATURE

FIGURE 8-6. Cooling system operation on a transverse-mounted, four-cylinder, front-wheel-drive engine. This engine uses an electrically driven radiator fan. *(Courtesy of Chrysler Corporation)*

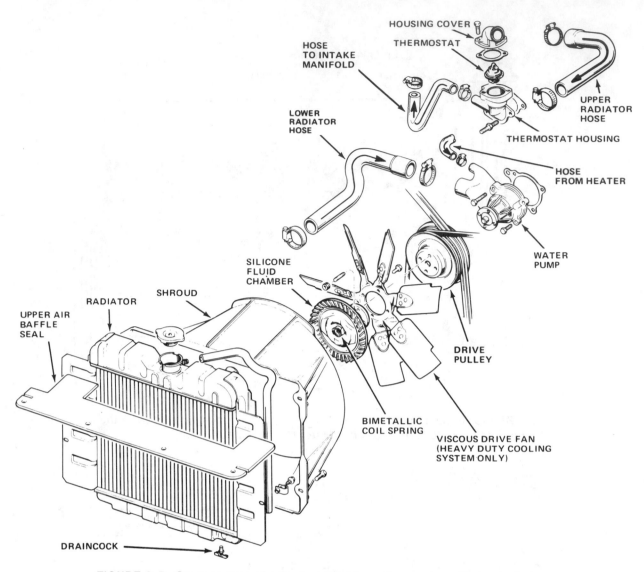

FIGURE 8-7. Components of a typical liquid cooling system. Water jackets in the cylinder block and head are also part of the cooling system.

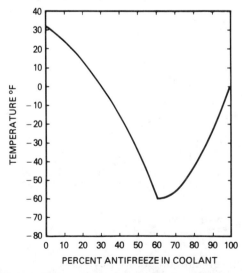

FIGURE 8-8. This graph shows the degree of freeze protection with various precentages of ethylene glycol in the coolant.

buildup of rust and scale, and it also has a water pump seal lubricant.

A mix of 50 percent undiluted ethylene glycol antifreeze and 50 percent water will provide freeze protection at approximately -34°F (-36°C) and will have a boiling point of approximately 230°F (110°C) at 14.7 psi atmospheric pressure (101.4 kilopascals). A greater than 60 percent ethylene glycol content is not practical, since further increasing the antifreeze content can cause the antifreeze to thicken at low temperatures, restrict coolant circulation, and cause antifreeze in the engine to boil.

In operation, antifreeze additives and inhibitors tend to lose their effectiveness. For this reason, car manufacturers and antifreeze manufacturers recommend changing the coolant every 12 to 24 months.

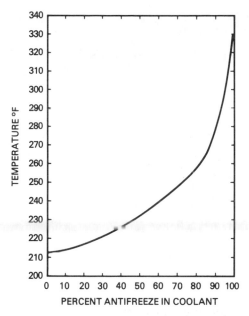

FIGURE 8-9. This graph shows the boiling point of coolant in relation to the percentage of ethylene glycol in the coolant.

Radiators

Radiators are designed to allow rapid heat dissipation and good air flow through the radiator core. On cars equipped with automatic transmissions, a heat exchanger, in the outlet tank connected to the transmission, regulates transmission fluid temperature.

A radiator consists of two metal tanks connected to each other by a core consisting of a series of thin tubes and fins. Coolant flows from the inlet tank through the tubes to the outlet tank whenever the thermostat in the engine is open. The tubes and fins radiate heat from the hot coolant, and the air flow created by the fan, or ram air, dissipates the heat to the atmosphere.

The inlet tank is equipped with a filler neck and radiator cap as well as an overflow tube. The overflow tube allows excess pressure to escape either to the ground or to the coolant reserve tank.

The radiator is made of aluminum or copper-brass. Both of these metals have good heat conductivity. Some radiators have the inlet tank at the top and the outlet tank at the bottom. This is a vertical-flow radiator. The horizontal-flow radiator has one tank at each side. The inlet tank is connected to the thermostat housing, while the outlet tank is connected to the water pump inlet. Hoses are used to make these connections.

The *radiator cap* incorporates two valves. The pressure relief valve limits pressure in the cooling system to a predetermined level. By using a pressure cap, the system becomes pressurized as a result of coolant expansion. Engine heat causes the coolant to expand. Pressurizing the cooling system

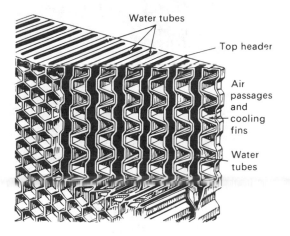

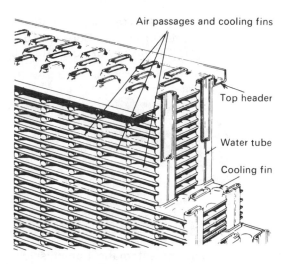

FIGURE 8-10. Two types of radiator core construction: honeycomb or cellular type (above) and tube and fin (below). *(Courtesy of Ford Motor Co. of Canada Ltd.)*

raises the boiling point of the coolant by approximately 3.25°F (1.8°C) for every pound per square inch (6.895 kilopascals) of pressure increase. This reduces the tendency for coolant to boil.

A 10-psi (68.95-kPa) radiator pressure cap would increase the boiling point of a 50:50 solution of antifreeze from 230°F (110°C) to 262.5°F (128°C).

If the coolant expands sufficiently to cause system pressure above radiator cap design relief pressure, the pressure valve opens and allows coolant to escape, via the overflow tube, to the reservoir, until pressure in the system is stabilized.

When the engine is shut off, the coolant cools down and contracts. This creates a low pressure in the cooling system and allows coolant to re-enter from the reservoir through the vacuum valve in the radiator pressure cap. This prevents radiator hoses from collapsing and allows the cooling system to remain full of coolant at all times. Reduced oxidation

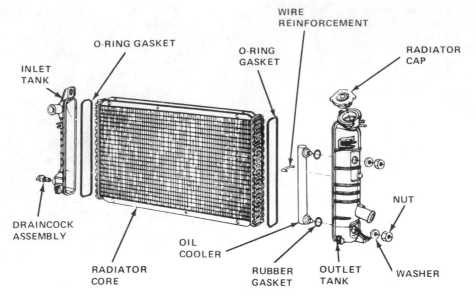

FIGURE 8-11. Typical horizontal flow radiator components. Tanks may be metal or plastic. Core may be made of copper-brass or aluminum construction. *(Courtesy of Ford Motor Co. of Canada Ltd.)*

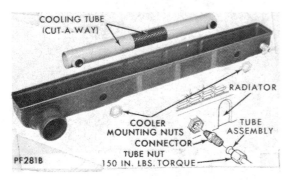

FIGURE 8-12. Detail of automatic transmission fluid cooler in outlet tank of radiator. *(Courtesy of Chrysler Corporation)*

and rust formation are benefits of the constant full cooling system.

Radiator capacity is determined by core size, thickness, and surface area. Engine size, number of accessories such as air conditioning, and type of service (e.g. trailer towing) determine the radiator capacity of different vehicles.

Water Pumps

The *water pump* is belt driven from the crankshaft pulley. Water pump capacity must be sufficient to provide adequate coolant circulation. Centrifugal,

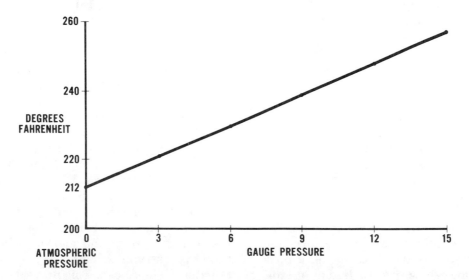

FIGURE 8-13. Effects of pressure in the cooling system on the boiling point of the coolant. *(Courtesy of Ford Motor Co. of Canada Ltd.)*

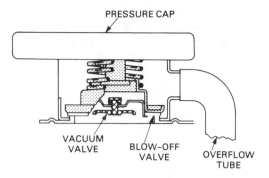

FIGURE 8-14. Cross-sectional view of radiator pressure cap.

vane-type, nonpositive displacement pumps are commonly used. The impeller, shaft, fan hub, and pulley are supported in the water pump housing by one or more bearings. A water pump seal prevents coolant from leaking.

The water pump forces coolant into the engine block as the impeller rotates. Coolant enters the center area of the impeller from the radiator outlet and is thrown outward centrifugally to create a flow into the block. Coolant flow returns to the water pump through the bypass when the thermostat is closed, and through the radiator when the thermostat is open.

Radiator Hoses

Radiator hoses include straight, molded, and flexible types. The straight type and the molded type should not be distorted when installed. The flexible hose can be bent to suit. The lower radiator hose has a wire coil in it to prevent collapsing. Several types of hose clamps are used to secure the hoses.

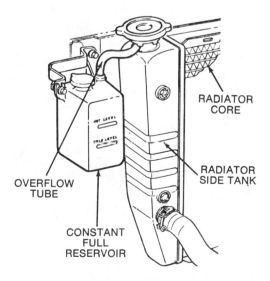

FIGURE 8-15. Coolant reserve tank ensures that air will not enter radiator during normal operation. *(Courtesy of Ford Motor Co. of Canada Ltd.)*

FIGURE 8-16. Cross-sectional view of vane type of water pump. *(Courtesy of General Motors Corporation)*

Radiator Fan and Shroud

The *fan* is designed to provide sufficient air flow through the radiator core to provide adequate cooling at all engine speeds. The fan is bolted to the water pump shaft and driven by a V-type belt from the crankshaft pulley, or it is attached to an electric motor mounted on brackets at the radiator. Some fans incorporate a fluid drive clutch to control fan speeds in relation to cooling demands.

Fan capacity depends on the number of fan blades, total fan diameter, and fan speed. A shroud surrounding the fan increases fan effectiveness by reducing air recirculation back through the fan. The pitch or angle of the fan blades also affects fan capacity. Flatter fan blades (less pitch) move less air than blades with more pitch. Variable-pitch fans

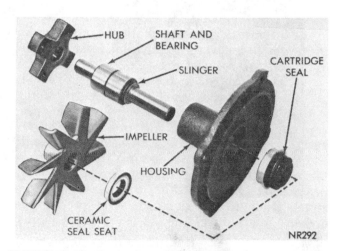

FIGURE 8-17. Exploded view of water pump components. *(Courtesy of Chrysler Corporation)*

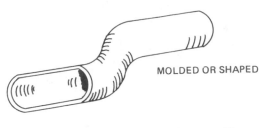

COMMON HOSE

MOLDED OR SHAPED

ACCORDION TYPE

FIGURE 8-18. Types of radiator hoses. *(Courtesy of Ford Motor Co. of Canada Ltd.)*

FIGURE 8-19. Radiator hose deterioration.

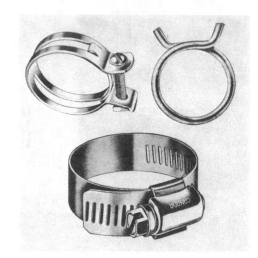

FIGURE 8-20. Three types of radiator hose clamps.

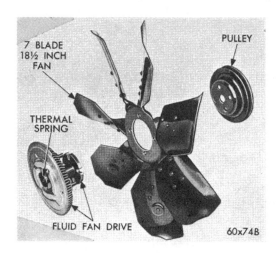

FIGURE 8-21. Seven-blade silicone fluid drive fan as used on larger air-conditioning-equipped cars. *(Courtesy of General Motors Corporation)*

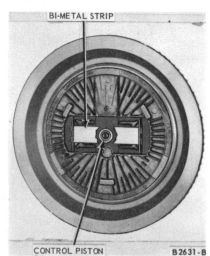

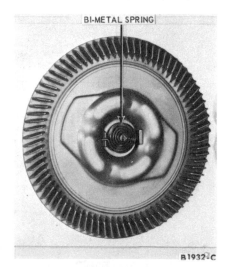

FIGURE 8-22. Location of fan drive clutch (left) and two types of fan clutches. The bimetal strip or spring deflects with engine temperature change. This operates a piston that controls the amount of silicone fluid entering the clutch for positive drive when engine temperature is high and little fan drive when engine is cold. *(Courtesy of Ford Motor Co. of Canada Ltd.)*

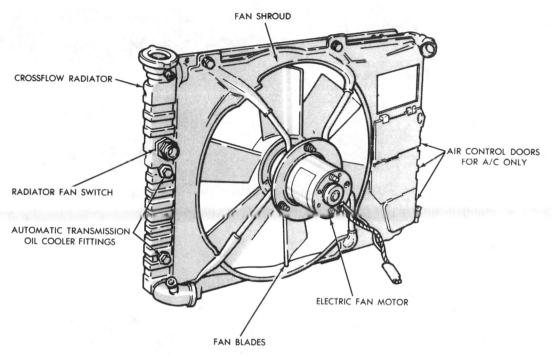

FIGURE 8-23. Cross-flow radiator and electrically driven fan assembly. Fan switch completes electrical circuit to fan motor when coolant temperature increases to above normal. *(Courtesy of Chrysler Corporation)*

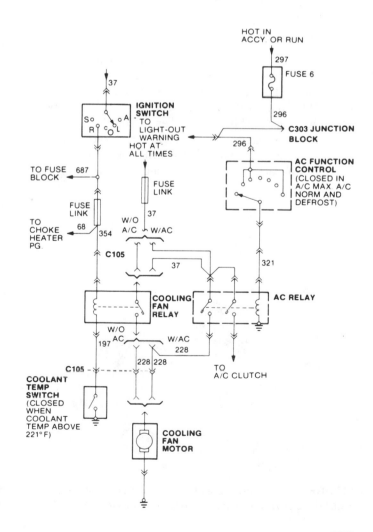

FIGURE 8-24. Typical electric-motor-driven fan control circuit. *(Courtesy Ford Motor Company)*

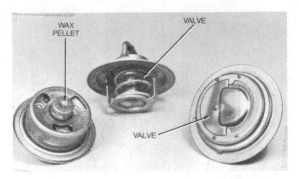
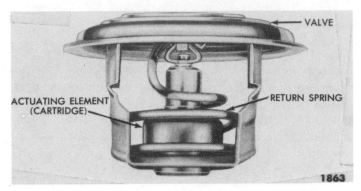

FIGURE 8-25. Several types of thermostat (left) and thermostat components (right). *(Courtesy of Ford Motor Co. of Canada Ltd.)*

have flexible fan blades that tend to flatten out as engine speed increases. The increased speed still creates sufficient air flow even though the fan blades have less pitch. The variable-pitch fan drive and the variable-speed fan drive reduce the horsepower required to drive the fan. This increases fuel economy. Fan blades are curved at the tip and are often unevenly spaced to reduce the noise level. Fan efficiency is increased by the use of a fan shroud. The shroud prevents recirculation of air around the tips of the fan blades.

Thermostats

The *thermostat* is a temperature-sensitive valve located in the thermostat housing at the front of the engine. The thermostat remains closed until the engine reaches operating temperature. As the temperature increases, the thermostat opens. This allows coolant to be circulated through the radiator for cooling. When the engine coolant falls below operating temperature, the thermostat closes once again.

FIGURE 8-27. Variable-pitch flexible-blade fan. *(Courtesy of Ford Motor Co. of Canada Ltd.)*

Coolant circulation is restricted to the engine block and cylinder heads and the car's interior heater when the thermostat is closed. A bypass provides the passage for coolant return to the pump.

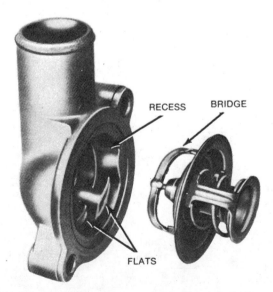

FIGURE 8-26. Thermostat housing with recess for thermostat. *(Courtesy of Ford Motor Co. of Canada Ltd.)*

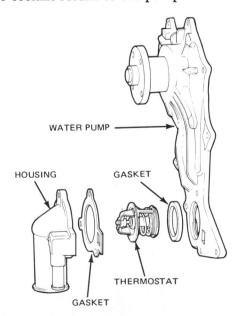

FIGURE 8-28. Location of thermostat is in bottom of water pump housing on one type of V6 engine. *(Courtesy of Ford Motor Co. of Canada Ltd.)*

Several types of thermostats are in use. The butterfly-valve and poppet-valve thermostats have a wax crystal element exposed to engine coolant. As the wax crystals are heated they expand, forcing a rod out of the element. The rod is attached to the valve and opens it. As the wax crystals cool and contract, the valve spring closes the valve and allows the rod to move back into the element.

Opening and closing temperatures of thermostats range from approximately 160°F (70°C) to 200°F (93°C). A 160°F thermostat should be wide open at about 170°F.

Temperature Indicators

Coolant temperature indicators mounted in the dash inform the driver whether engine temperature is normal. A direct-reading temperature gauge or hot and cold temperature-indicating lights are mounted in the instrument panel. A temperature-sensitive switch, (sending unit) mounted in the engine cylinder head or in a coolant passage in the intake manifold connected to the dash unit, provides the temperature signal.

PART 3   SHUTTERS AND SHUTTER CONTROLS

The automatic shutter controls engine temperature by regulating air flow through the radiator. It provides faster engine warm-up and less variation in operating temperature.

There are three methods of operating the shutters. A thermostatically operated system is used on some trucks. An air operated system is used on trucks with air brakes. A vacuum operated system is used on trucks with vacuum-boosted hydraulic brakes.

Thermostat Operated System

The thermostat operated system consists of a shutter control assembly, a shutter control rod or a shutter control cable and a shutter assembly. The shutter control assembly has a power element which works much like a thermostat. When the coolant temperature is below operating temperature, the

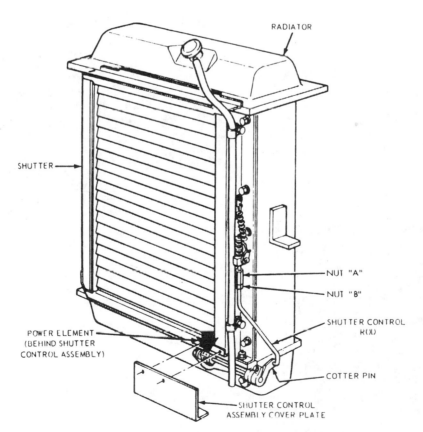

FIGURE 8-29. Typical thermostat operated radiator shutters. *(Courtesy of Ford Motor Co. of Canada Ltd.)*

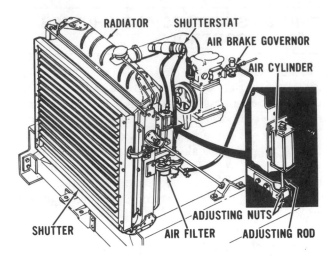

FIGURE 8-30. Air-operated truck type of radiator shutters. Automatically controlled shutters maintain relatively constant engine operating temperatures. *(Courtesy of Ford Motor Co. of Canada Ltd.)*

shutters are closed because of the spring tension at the end of the control rod or cable. As the coolant reaches operating temperature, the power element expands and opens the shutters by working against the spring tension.

Air Operated System

The air operated shutter system consists of the shutter assembly, an air cylinder which operates the shutter, and a thermostatically controlled air valve called a shutterstat. With no air pressure on the system, springs in the shutter assembly will hold the shutter blades in the open position. With normal air pressure and the engine below operating temperature, the shutter blades close. As the engine coolant heats to the operating temperature setting of the shutterstat, an air valve in the shutterstat closes, cutting off air to the air cylinder. The air in the air cylinder is then exhausted through the shutterstat and the shutter assembly springs open the shutter blades.

Vacuum Operated System

The vacuum-operated shutter system consists of the shutter assembly, a vacuum powered cylinder which operates the shutter, and a thermostatically controlled vacuum valve called a shutterstat. Operation of this system is the same as for air with the exception that vacuum power is the operating medium.

Interior Heaters

Interior heaters utilize excess engine heat absorbed by the cooling system to heat the car's interior. A

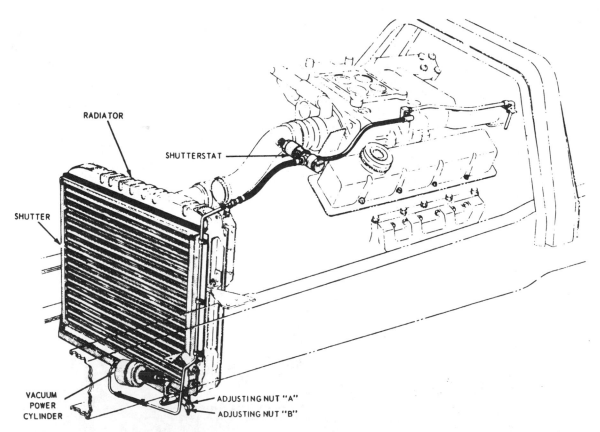

FIGURE 8-31. Vacuum operated shutter system used on trucks with vacuum-hydraulic brakes. *(Courtesy of Ford Motor Co. of Canada Ltd.)*

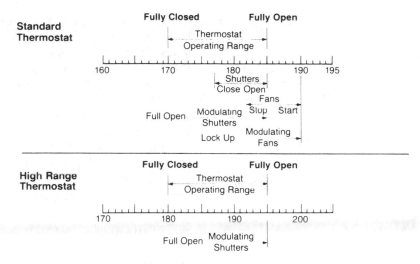

FIGURE 8-32. Operating range of typical thermostats, shutters, and fans in relation to each other.

heater core similar in construction to a radiator but much smaller is mounted on the firewall. An inlet hose from a hot area of the engine is connected to one side of the heater core, and another hose joins the heater core outlet to the engine water pump to provide good circulation of the heated liquid.

A housing and ductwork provide air circulation through the heater core for heat. Air circulation bypasses the heater core when no heat is required. An electric-motor-driven drum-type blower provides air circulation at several blower speeds. When the blower is not turning, and the car is moving fast enough, ram air provides circulation.

A control valve to regulate liquid circulation through the heater core and a series of doors controlling air circulation provide comfort control. Either manual controls on the dash or manual and automatic controls operate the flow control valves and doors. See Chapter 40 for more on heating and air conditioning.

PART 4   AIR COOLING SYSTEM

The air cooling system uses air as the medium to transfer heat from the engine parts to the atmosphere. Engine heads and cylinders are finned for greater heat radiation. Shrouds and ducts direct air

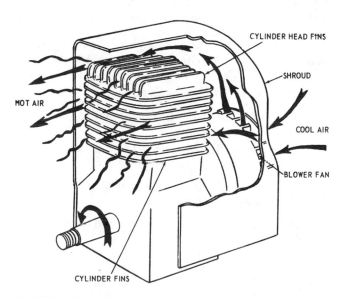

FIGURE 8-33. Components of air-type cooling system. Cylinders and heads have fins and are enclosed in a shroud to control air flow. Fins expose more surface area to air flow for better heat dissipation.

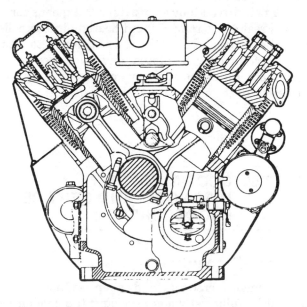

FIGURE 8-34. V-type air-cooled diesel engine cross-sectional view. (Courtesy of Chrysler Corporation)

175

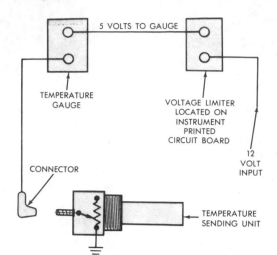

FIGURE 8-35. Schematic of electric temperature gauge including voltage limiter. *(Courtesy of Ford Motor Co. of Canada Ltd.)*

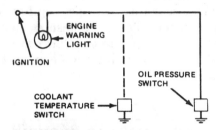

FIGURE 8-36. Schematic of coolant and oil pressure warning light. *(Courtesy of Ford Motor Co. of Canada Ltd.)*

flow over the engine parts, especially over the hotter cylinder head area.

A belt-driven blower provides the means for air flow. Fresh air is taken in and heated air is expelled into the atmosphere. A thermostat linked to a control valve or door regulates air flow to control engine temperature. Stationary engines have a blower attached to the engine crankshaft rather than being belt driven.

PART 5 COOLING SYSTEM DIAGNOSIS AND SERVICE PROCEDURE

General Precautions

All normal, personal, and shop safety practice should be followed when servicing the cooling system. Some special precautions should also be observed, including the following:

1. Never remove the radiator cap under any conditions while the engine is operating. Failure to follow these instructions could result in damage to the cooling system or engine and in personal injury. To avoid having scalding hot coolant or steam blow out of the radiator, use extreme care when removing the cap from a hot radiator. If possible, wait until the engine has cooled, then wrap a thick cloth around the radiator cap and turn it slowly to the first stop. Step back while the pressure is released from the cooling system. When you are sure all the pressure has been released, press down on the cap (still with the cloth), turn, and remove it.

2. Always be careful not to make contact with rotating parts such as fans, pulleys, and belts. Contact can easily be made if careful attention is not given to staying clear of these items with hands, tools, or clothing.

3. Never stand in the plane of a fast turning fan. Fan blades have been known to separate from a turning fan, flying off in any direction at a very high speed. This could cause injury, death, or damage to vehicles. The fan should always be closely examined for any cracks (sometimes barely visible) before running the engine during underhood testing and diagnosis.

4. Always be aware of the danger of burns and scalding from hot engine parts and hot coolant. Never remove any parts from the cooling system that will release hot coolant unexpectedly.

5. Be careful of electric-drive cooling fans. Many of them will start turning at any time after the engine has been shut down due to heat soak.

Cooling system problems are usually confined to either of two conditions: overheating or overcooling.

To avoid needless time and cost in diagnosing cooling system complaints, the customer should be questioned about driving conditions that place abnormal loads on the cooling system.

1. Does overheating occur while pulling a trailer?

2. Is car equipped with add-on or aftermarket air conditioning (AC) system?

3. Is overheating occurring after prolonged idle in gear; AC system operating?

Driving techniques that avoid overheating should be practiced:

1. Idle in neutral as much as possible; increase engine rpm to get higher air flow and coolant flow through radiator.

2. Turn AC system off during extended idles if overheating is indicated by hot light or temperature gauge.

PROBLEM	CAUSE	CORRECTION
High temperature gauge indication-overheating	1. Coolant level low. 2. Fan belt loose. 3. Radiator hose(s) collapsed. 4. Radiator airflow blocked. 5. Faulty radiator cap. 6. Ignition timing incorrect. 7. Idle speed low. 8. Air trapped in cooling system. 9. Heavy traffic driving. 10. Incorrect cooling system component(s) installed. 11. Faulty thermostat. 12. Water pump shaft broken or impeller loose. 13. Radiator tubes clogged. 14. Cooling system clogged. 15. Casting flash in cooling passages. 16. Brakes dragging. 17. Excessive engine friction. 18. Antifreeze concentration over 68%. 19. Missing air seals. 20. Faulty gauge or sending unit. 21. Loss of coolant flow caused by leakage or foaming. 22. Viscous fan drive failed.	1. Replenish coolant. 2. Adjust fan belt tension. 3. Replace hose(s). 4. Remove restriction (bug screen, fog lamps, etc.) 5. Replace radiator cap. 6. Adjust ignition timing. 7. Adjust idle speed. 8. Purge air. 9. Operate at fast idle in neutral intermittently to cool engine. 10. Install proper components(s). 11. Replace thermostat. 12. Replace water pump. 13. Flush radiator. 14. Flush system. 15. Repair or replace as necessary. Flash may be visible by removing cooling system components or removing core plugs. 16. Repair brakes. 17. Repair engine. 18. Lower antifreeze concentration percentage. 19. Replace air seals. 20. Repair or replace faulty component. 21. Repair or replace leaking component, replace coolant. 22. Replace unit.
Low temperature indication undercooling	1. Thermostat stuck open. 2. Faulty gauge or sending unit.	1. Replace thermostat. 2. Repair or replace faulty component.
Coolant loss-boilover	Refer to Overheating Causes in addition to the following items. 1. Overfilled cooling system. 2. Quick shutdown after hard (hot) run. 3. Air in system resulting in occasional "burping" of coolant. 4. Insufficient antifreeze allowing coolant boiling point to be too low. 5. Antifreeze deteriorated because of age or contamination. 6. Leaks due to loose hose clamps, loose nuts, bolts, drain plugs, faulty hoses, or defective radiator. 7. Faulty head gasket. 8. Cracked head, manifold, or block. 9. Faulty radiator cap.	1. Reduce coolant level to proper specification. 2. Allow engine to run at fast idle prior to shutdown. 3. Purge system. 4. Add antifreeze to raise boiling point. 5. Replace coolant. 6. Pressure test system to locate source of leak(s) then repair as necessary. 7. Replace head gasket. 8. Replace as necessary. 9. Replace cap.
Coolant entry into crankcase or cylinder(s)	1. Faulty head gasket. 2. Crack in head, manifold, or block.	1. Replace head gasket. 2. Replace as necessary.
Coolant recovery system inoperative	1. Coolant level low. 2. Leak in system. 3. Pressure cap not tight or seal missing or leaking. 4. Pressure cap defective. 5. Overflow tube clogged or leaking. 6. Recovery bottle vent restricted.	1. Replenish coolant to FULL mark. 2. Pressure test to isolate leak and repair as necessary. 3. Repair as necessary. 4. Replace cap. 5. Repair as necessary. 6. Remove restriction.
Noise	1. Fan contacting shroud. 2. Loose water pump impeller. 3. Glazed fan belt. 4. Loose fan belt.	1. Reposition shroud and inspect engine mounts. 2. Replace pump. 3. Apply silicone or replace belt. 4. Adjust fan belt tension.

(Continued)

177

PROBLEM	CAUSE	CORRECTION
Noise (contd)	5. Rough surface on drive pulley. 6. Water pump bearing worn. 7. Belt alignment.	5. Replace pulley. 6. Remove belt to isolate. Replace pump. 7. Check pulley alignment. Repair as necessary.
No coolant flow through heater core	1. Restricted return inlet in water pump. 2. Heater hose collapsed or restricted. 3. Restricted heater core. 4. Restricted outlet in thermostat housing. 5. Intake manifold bypass hole in cylinder head restricted. 6. Faulty heater control valve. 7. Intake manifold coolant passage restricted.	1. Remove restriction. 2. Remove restriction or replace hose. 3. Remove restriction or replace core. 4. Remove flash or restriction. 5. Remove restriction. 6. Replace valve. 7. Remove restriction or replace intake manifold.

Overcooling

Overcooling is caused by a defective thermostat, a thermostat of too low a temperature range, too much heat loss through radiation, or a combination of these conditions.

To correct an overcooling problem, remove the thermostat and test it as shown in Figure 8–42. If the thermostat does not remain closed until the specified temperature is reached, it should be replaced with a thermostat of the correct temperature range.

In areas where extremely low ambient temperatures are experienced, some vehicles may lose sufficient heat through radiation to prevent the engine from reaching proper operating temperature. To reduce the amount of heat loss from this cause, a recommended type of *winter front* should be used to cover the radiator grille. This reduces the amount of cold air flow over the engine and resultant heat loss. As soon as ambient temperature increases sufficiently, the winter front should be opened or removed to avoid overheating.

Overheating

Overheating can be caused by a number of factors, all of which may require inspection and testing. Inspect coolant level and condition. Coolant should be of the correct type and at the proper level. Antifreeze should be tested for proper strength and corrected if necessary. Several different types of testers are available for this purpose. Coolant should also be clean. Rust or contamination can reduce flow and the ability to absorb heat.

If the coolant is contaminated, it should be drained and the entire cooling system thoroughly flushed to remove as much of the contamination as possible. A wide variety of methods are employed to flush cooling systems depending on the particular repair shop's preferences. The degree of success varies with the type of equipment used.

Flushing with water, if done thoroughly, will be

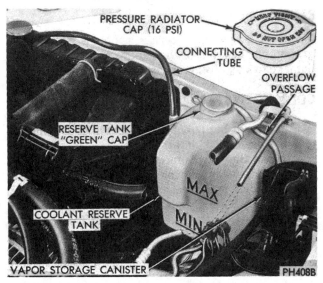

FIGURE 8–37. Coolant level must be maintained between maximum and minimum levels indicated on reserve tank. *(Courtesy of Chrysler Corporation)*

of some benefit, but this method cannot dislodge heavy deposits. Pressure flushing in reverse of normal coolant flow is more successful.

Commercial preparation can be used to help loosen deposits in the system, after which thorough flushing must be done. In some cases, this type of chemical cleaner requires neutralizing with another chemical before flushing. When using flushing equipment and flushing chemicals, the instructions supplied with the equipment or the product should be followed carefully.

The coolant can also become contaminated and forced out of the system by a combustion leak into the cooling system. The most accurate method of checking for this type of leak uses a chemical that changes color when used for testing. Leakage of this type is not visible externally and may be hard to detect without the proper test equipment. The causes could include head gasket leakage or small cracks in the block or cylinder head. Both of these require fairly extensive engine disassembly to correct.

Obstructions restricting air circulation through the radiator can also cause overheating. Obstruction can be caused by insects, leaves, or even mud plugging the radiator. Thorough cleaning with compressed air or water will correct this problem. A net type of bug screen mounted on the radiator or air-conditioning condenser can sufficiently reduce air flow to cause overheating in hot weather. The type of bug screen mounted in front of the grille is preferable.

Fan belts should be checked to be sure they are in good condition (not glazed, cracked, or worn) and adjusted to the proper tension. Glazed belts or belts not adjusted to the correct tension may slip and cause overheating. Replace belts that are damaged and adjust to specifications with a belt tension gauge.

Hoses and clamps should be inspected to assure that there is neither leakage of coolant out of the system nor leakage of air into the system. Swollen hoses or internal hose deterioration can cause restricted coolant circulation and overheating. Such hoses should be replaced and installed with properly tightened hose clamps.

If hose clamps are not tight, air may be drawn into the cooling system by the water pump thereby reducing the effectiveness of the cooling system. This may happen even when there is no apparent coolant leak at the problem point. Air in the cooling system will contribute to rust and oxidation, contaminating the coolant. Particular attention should be paid to the inlet hose of the water pump to avoid this problem.

The *water pump* should be checked for leakage and for a loose or noisy bearing. This can be done by relieving the belt tension and then grasping the fan to see if there is any radial movement of the water pump shaft and pulley. Feel for any roughness by rotating the fan and pump shaft with a radially applied load. A water pump that leaks or has a rough or loose bearing should be replaced.

Pressure testing the entire cooling system will help in locating external leaks. Internal leaks will show up on the tester if the system is left pressurized (with the tester in place) by a drop in pressure on the test gauge. Inspect all cooling system components for external leaks while the system is pressurized. Do not pressurize the system above rated capacity. Leaks should be corrected as required.

The radiator cap should also be pressure tested to assure that the cap will hold system design pressure and open at the specified pressure. A radiator cap that does not meet specifications must be replaced. A cap that does not hold the pressure it was designed to hold lowers the boiling point of the coolant and can cause boiling and overheating.

The *thermostat*, if suspected, should be removed and tested. The thermostat should remain closed until heated to the rated temperature, and it should be wide open at approximately 10° to 15°F above the temperature stamped on it. If the thermostat does not meet the required specifications, it should be replaced, using a new gasket.

Care should be exercised when replacing a thermostat not to clamp it between the thermostat housing flange and the cylinder head. If this happens, the thermostat housing will crack when the bolts are tightened. Be sure the thermostat is installed with the temperature-sensitive element toward the engine.

Filling the System with Coolant

After all necessary flushing and cooling system repairs are made, the system should be filled with the recommended coolant as follows:

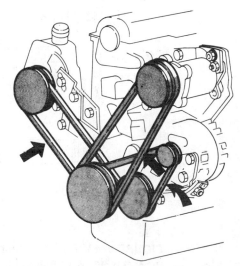
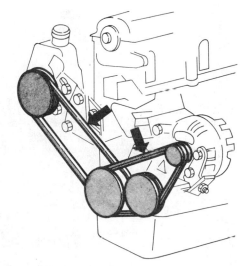

FIGURE 8–38. Belt tension gauge (left) is used to check belt tension as indicated by arrows. *(Courtesy of Chrysler Corporation)*

FIGURE 8-39. Testing radiator pressure cap. *(Courtesy of General Motors Corporation)*

FIGURE 8-40. Testing cooling system for internal and external leaks by pressurizing system with special tester. *(Courtesy of Chrysler Corporation)*

FIGURE 8-41. Removing or replacing thermostat. *(Courtesy of General Motors Corporation)*

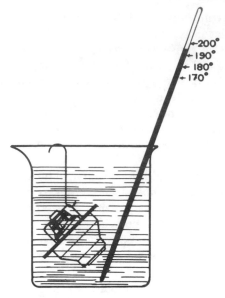

FIGURE 8-42. Testing a thermostat in a container with water. Water is heated until opening temperature has been reached. If thermostat does not open at specified temperature, replace thermostat. *(Courtesy of General Motors Corporation)*

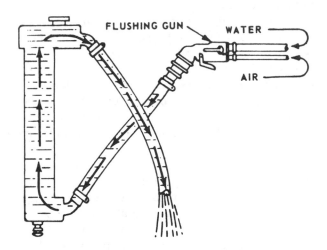

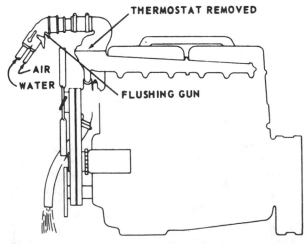

FIGURE 8-43. Reverse flushing the radiator with shop air and water with a special flushing gun (top). Reverse flushing head and block (bottom).

1. Close drain cocks and install drain plugs.

2. Turn heater temperature control to high.

3. Add coolant to system until radiator remains full.

4. Add additional coolant to the required level in the coolant reserve tank.

5. Install radiator cap.

6. Start engine and run until operating temperature is reached.

7. Switch heater blower fan on; if heater produces heat, heater core is full; if not, accelerate engine several times to remove air lock from heater until heat is produced.

8. Switch engine off.

9. Correct coolant level in reserve tank.

10. Make sure there are no coolant leaks.

PART 6   SELF-CHECK

1. The engine cooling system is designed to _____.

2. Describe the path of coolant flow (a) when the thermostat is closed; (b) when the thermostat is open.

3. The sole purpose of using antifreeze as a coolant is for freeze protection. True or false?

4. The radiator cap has two valves. What is the purpose of each?

5. Three factors that determine the capacity of a radiator fan are (a)_____, (b)_____, and (c)_____.

PART 7   TEST QUESTIONS

1. The cooling system removes heat from the engine by the following methods:
   (a) conduction, convection, radiation
   (b) radiation, evacuation, precipitation
   (c) evacuation, conduction, convection
   (d) convection, precipitation, evacuation

2. Coolant circulation is as follows:
   (a) pump to block to head to radiator
   (b) pump to head to block to radiator
   (c) pump to radiator to block to head
   (d) pump to radiator to head to block

3. Mechanic A says antifreeze is used to provide freeze protection. Mechanic B says antifreeze is used to provide a higher boiling point. Who is right?

   (a) Mechanic A
   (b) Mechanic B
   (c) both are right
   (d) both are wrong

4. Water pumps are of what design?
   (a) vane
   (b) centrifugal
   (c) nonpositive displacement
   (d) all of the above

5. Radiator caps are designed to provide:
   (a) increased boiling point
   (b) pressure relief and vacuum relief
   (c) increased pressure
   (d) all of the above

6. The thermostat regulates:
   (a) coolant flow in the engine
   (b) engine temperature
   (c) coolant flow in the radiator
   (d) all of the above

7. Cooling fans are driven:
   (a) electrically and by belts
   (b) by gears and belts
   (c) by belts, gears, and electrically
   (d) all of the above

8. Mechanic A says the cooling system should be pressure tested to determine engine internal leakage. Mechanic B says the cooling system should be pressure tested to determine external leakage. Who is right?
   (a) Mechanic A
   (b) Mechanic B
   (c) both are right
   (d) both are wrong

9. Mechanic A says the thermostat should be installed with the thermal element toward the radiator. Mechanic B says the thermostat should be pressure tested to determine whether it operates properly. Who is right?
   (a) Mechanic A
   (b) Mechanic B
   (c) both are right
   (d) both are wrong

10. Incorrect belt tension can result in:
    (a) water pump failure
    (b) alternator failure
    (c) overheating
    (d) all of the above

Chapter 9

Engine Diagnosis and Service Procedure

Performance Objectives

After thorough study of this chapter and sufficient practical work on the appropriate components, and with the appropriate shop manuals, tools, and equipment, you should be able to do the following:

1. Complete the self-check and test questions with at least 80 percent accuracy.
2. Follow the accepted general precautions as outlined in this chapter.
3. Diagnose basic engine problems according to the diagnostic chart provided.
4. Safely remove and properly disassemble the engine.
5. Properly clean, inspect, and accurately measure all engine components.
6. Recondition or replace all engine parts required.
7. Correctly assemble and adjust all engine components.
8. Properly install the engine assembly.
9. Follow all required start-up procedures.
10. Follow required road test and break-in procedures accurately.
11. Perform the necessary inspection to determine the success of the engine overhaul.
12. Prepare the vehicle for customer acceptance.

PART 1   GENERAL PROCEDURE

Automotive shops differ considerably in their appoach to engine service. Some fully equipped shops will perform most of the service operations required to completely overhaul an engine; others rely on rebuilt unit replacement.

Service procedures such as crack detection and repair, cylinder reboring, block deck machining, main bearing bore line boring, connecting rod straightening and resizing, and crankshaft and camshaft rebuilding are normally done by rebuilding shops. These operations require specialized equipment normally not found in automotive shops. Although many shops do their own work on valve guides, valve seats, and valves, other shops replace the complete cylinder head with a rebuilt unit. This is also true of the short block assembly. A short block assembly normally includes a rebuilt block with new pistons, rings, camshaft bearings, crankshaft bearings, a rebuilt camshaft, crankshaft, and connecting rods. A new oil pump is also usually included, as well as a new camshaft drive (chain and sprocket or gears).

Complete rebuilt engines, sometimes called remanufactured engines, are also available from engine rebuilding shops. These include the complete block assembly and cylinder heads, as well as the oil pan, valve covers, and water pump.

Drop-in engines available from engine rebuilders include a completely rebuilt engine assembly with starter, generator, carburetor, fuel pump, manifolds, fan and belts, distributor, high-tension wiring, coil, spark plugs, and flywheel.

A complete overhaul of an engine should be accompanied by cleaning and servicing of the starter, generator, fuel system, air cleaner, oil filter, and distributor; and it may require replacement of the fuel and water pumps, high-tension wiring, spark plugs, and motor mounts for proper performance and a long trouble-free service life.

Service shops that do not overhaul engines but do replace them usually base their decision for replacing cylinder heads on the results of a compression test and (or) leak-down test. Cylinder wear is usually measured as soon as the heads have been removed. If wear is excessive, a short block or a complete rebuilt engine is installed.

It is essential that a thorough understanding of the purpose, construction, and operation of the engine and all of its components (as well as the engine support systems) be acquired before any intelligent diagnosis and service can be performed.

The course of action to be taken in any repair work is decided by following a systematic approach to problem diagnosis. The diagnostic chart in Part

3 will assist in the procedure of identifying the source of the problem and the extent of work required to correct the problem. The items identified by an asterisk on the diagnostic chart are covered in this chapter. The other items require corrections to engine support systems and are covered elsewhere in this text.

In general, the problem must be isolated as follows:

- A noise problem only
- A performance problem only
- A noise problem and a performance problem
- An engine mechanical problem
- An engine support system problem

A number of test procedures must be performed to determine where the problem exists.

- Fuel and induction system tests
- Electrical system tests
- Compression tests and cylinder leakage tests
- Exhaust system tests
- Emission-control system tests
- Cooling system tests
- Lubrication system tests

Refer to the appropriate section of this text for these procedures.

It must also be determined whether the service required can be done without removing the engine. If engine removal is not required, perform only those service procedures in this chapter that apply to the unit being serviced. Should engine removal be required, proceed as outlined in this chapter.

Engine Repair in Vehicle

Many engine repair jobs can be done without removing the engine from the vehicle. Whether a particular repair can be done without engine removal will depend on the vehicle make and model, since accessibility and clearances vary considerably.

Other factors are also considered such as:

1. Expected service life of the engine after proposed repair.

2. Available "down time." Sometimes the owner of the vehicle prefers to assume the risk of service life expectancy in order to put the vehicle back in service as quickly as possible, even though it may be advisable to perform additional service to extend the expected service life. This practice, however, is definitely not to be recommended.

3. Cost of the repair. The cost of the repair must be justifiable in relation to the expected service life of the vehicle after the repair. There is no point in performing costly repairs on a vehicle that will soon be scrapped because of age and general deterioration, or will soon require other costly engine repairs.

Consult the appropriate manufacturer's service manual to determine whether the desired repair can be done without engine removal. In many cases, other vehicle components may have to be removed to gain access to the desired component to be repaired or replaced. Typical examples are steering linkage and exhaust pipes to allow for oil pan removal; radiator removal to allow access to the water pump, timing cover, or camshaft drive parts; air cleaner and carburetor to allow access to the intake manifold and the like.

Many of the following engine repair jobs can be done without engine removal, depending on the make and the model of the vehicle.

- Renew valve seals, spring, or covers
- Renew rocker arms, push rods, studs, and rocker shafts
- Renew valve lifters
- Grind valves and seats
- Renew cylinder heads
- Renew intake and exhaust manifolds
- Renew fuel pump
- Renew water pump
- Renew timing cover and seal
- Renew camshaft drive gears, chain, or camshaft drive belt
- Renew camshaft and bearings
- Renew engine mounts
- Renew oil pump and oil pan
- Renew main and connecting rod bearings
- Renew main bearing seals
- Renew pistons, piston rings, and connecting rods.

Refer to the appropriate section in this chapter for procedures to follow in each case.

PART 2 GENERAL PRECAUTIONS

Follow all normal personal and shop safety precautions. The following general precautions should also be observed during engine service.

- Be aware of the danger of causing electrical system damage.

• Be careful when handling hot cooling systems (system is pressurized and radiator cap removal can cause system to boil and overflow, causing burns to hands and face). Turn cap to *first notch only* to relieve system pressure (use rag) and then remove cap.

• Be careful of hot engine parts.

• Engine oil and transmission fluid may be hot enough to cause burns; handle with care to avoid injury.

• Engine parts are heavy. Use proper methods and equipment for handling parts to avoid personal injury and parts damage.

• Engine parts have many precision machined surfaces. They must be handled with extreme care to avoid damage.

• For accuracy, all measurements should be taken with the engine components at room temperature, approximately 70°F (21°C).

• Absolute cleanliness of all parts and the entire area is essential during engine assembly. A very small piece of dirt can cause complete engine failure. Abrasives damage friction surfaces severely. Extremely close tolerances are destroyed by small particles of dirt or foreign material.

• Store such components as the hood, radiator, and battery in a safe manner so they will not be damaged during engine overhaul.

• Do not damage the radiator or AC condenser during engine service. They are easily dented or ruptured, causing a leak.

Diesel Engine Precautions

Even though diesel fuel is not as combustible as gasoline, it is a flammable liquid. All safety precautions used for working on a gasoline engine should be exercised when working on a diesel engine. Diesel fuel should be stored in a container made (approved) for diesel fuel. Do not store diesel fuel in a container approved for gasoline. The following is a list of safety precautions that should be followed:

1. *Never* attempt to remove an injector, an injector line, or an injection pump with the engine running. *Do not loosen injection pump flange bolts with engine running.*

2. *Always* double-check that all components have been properly torqued before starting the engine.

3. Be sure to prime the injection pump completely before engine start-up. *Never* run a dry pump.

4. Be sure to drain all visible traces of water from the fuel system. Check water separators and fuel filters.

5. If you encounter an air or fuel leak, stop the engine to tighten fittings.

6. When working in an enclosed area, be sure to follow all regulations concerning ventilation, smoking, and use of electric tools.

7. When working with high-pressure injector test equipment (like "pop testers"):

   (a) Be sure to wear safety glasses.

   (b) Follow the equipment manufacturer's directions concerning the set-up of test equipment.

   (c) Follow all test procedures exactly.

   (d) Follow all safety precautions and practices. A mandatory safety practice is to use the glass safety bottle to cover the injector tip and to catch all fuel sprayed. The pressure of fuel delivery is so great that diesel fuel could be sprayed directly through your skin into the blood. Once in the bloodstream, diesel additives cause irreversible damage to the liver and pancreas. In extreme cases, they can cause paralysis, loss of the injured limb, or even death.

8. Whenever working with turbochargers, be sure to cap all lubrication lines and passages. Be sure also to cover all air intake passages on the turbo and on the engine so that no dirt enters them.

9. *Never* attempt to stop a diesel engine by covering the opening in the intake manifold with your hand. Although this may work with some gasoline engines, it can cause serious injury.

10. *Never run a diesel faster than maximum governed speed.*

11. *Never* use a bent, frayed, or kinked fuel injection line.

12. When removing injectors and/or injection pump, *always* cap all openings and put component in clean plastic bag. Dust destroys injection systems.

13. *Always* cover all injection lines and block openings which arise when injectors or pumps are removed. Do not allow dust to enter this way.

14. *Never* grind, sand, or raise large amounts of dust or grit near any injection pump, injectors, or open engines. Keep all engines covered with plastic or cloth if grinding is done.

15. *Never* use any kind of hammer, wrench, or wooden handle to tap on injectors or pump housings.

16. Never drop any injection system components.

17. *Always* use proper tools when working on injectors. Do not use non-metric wrenches or adjustable wrenches on metric fasteners.

18. Adhere to all torque specifications exactly. Do not use a ratchet when a torque wrench is required. Adhere to all bolt tightening patterns where specified. This is more critical on diesels than on gas engines.

19. When connecting lines to injectors or pumps, double-check the lines and flares for cracks and dirt. Also check for threads without burrs. Improperly connected lines either bring air into the system or cause high-pressure fuel leaks that may lead to poor engine performance or even fires. Remember that fuel line pressures are 6000 to 8000 psi, (42,000 to 55,000 kPa).

20. When replacing fuel filters, be sure to fill the replacement filter to prevent air from entering the system.

21. Be sure to bleed the fuel injection system according to proper procedures before starting the engine. Some pumps may need hand priming.

22. Prior to working on a vehicle engine in a garage, both the vehicle and the engine should be washed down (steam cleaned).

Propane Engine Precautions

Avoid Fire or Explosion Hazards

Warning: Do not park or service a propane-fueled vehicle near any source of fire, such as open flame, cigarettes or smoking materials, sparks, excessive heat, welding, or body grinding. Avoid placing the vehicle near electrical equipment that discharges sparks through normal operation, for example, motor electrical switches, and radio transmission equipment. Avoid storing or servicing a vehicle over sewer drains, lubrication pits, sub-floor level rooms, or other low-lying areas. If any source of fire or ignition contacts propane vapor, a fire could result. If the fuel is confined and ignited in a confined, unventilated area, an explosion could result.

Propane is a flammable substance similar to gasoline and diesel fuel. However, at room temperatures and normal barometric pressures, propane is a gas, or vapor—like natural gas used for heating

homes. Although the propane fuel system is closed to the atmosphere, two relief valves are used to vent excess pressure in the event of high ambient temperatures, as specified by National Fire Protection Association Standard #58. If liquid propane leaks or is released to the atmosphere through the normal function of a relief valve, the fuel will immediately vaporize and expand to approximately 270 times its volume as a liquid. Therefore, even a small amount of liquid fuel can become a large area of flammable propane gas.

Propane gas is also heavier than air. So any fuel present will settle to low spots and remain until ventilated or until the fuel gradually dissipates in the air. Always park a propane-fueled vehicle in a well-ventilated area that is free of the fire hazards described above.

Avoid Health Hazard

Warning: Avoid inhaling propane gas or occupying confined areas containing propane gas. Propane gas is heavier than air. The heavier gas can displace or "push" fresh air out of an area. In large quantities, propane can displace enough oxygen to make the surrounding air unfit to breathe, and possibly cause illness. If a person breathes propane gas (or air which lacks oxygen due to the presence of propane gas) headache, dizziness, and weakness in the extremities can result. In severe cases, prolonged breathing of propane-fouled air can cause suffocation.

In the event of illness from inhaling propane gas, move the victim immediately to fresh air and contact a physician or medical emergency personnel for artificial respiration and further treatment.

If a confined area, such as a lubrication pit, has been subject to propane gas leakage, the area should be checked for adequate oxygen levels by local health department personnel before being entered. Otherwise, illness or suffocation, as described above, can result.

Be Alert For Venting Fuel Pressure

Note: During high ambient temperatures, like those experienced in desert locations, the fuel system is designed to relieve excess fuel vapor pressure. The pressure relief valve will vent fuel and automatically reset itself. This will normally occur as long as high temperatures persist. If the manual shut off valve is closed and the vehicle is parked in high ambient temperatures, the hydrostatic relief valve will vent excess liquid pressure and reset automatically.

Warning: Be alert for situations which can cause the propane fuel system to vent fuel—extremely hot days, parking by a space heater, or hoisting a vehicle up near a ceiling heater. As previously described under "Avoid Fire or Explosion Hazards," the normal pressure of propane fuel could result in a fire, if ignited, and lead to personal injury.

Give Warning of Fuel Leaks

Warning: When servicing a propane system fuel leak, or if the odor of propane or a quantity of propane is present in an area, warn all persons in the area to:

- Extinguish all flames and lighted tobacco
- Shut off electrical and air power equipment
- Evacuate the area immediately
- Ventilate the area until the odor of gas is no longer present

Use care not to confuse propane gas odor and propane exhaust gas odor. Both are similar, but a leak odor will linger in the area and exhaust gas odor will normally dissipate after the engine is stopped. (A hydrocarbon "sniffer" can also be used to distinguish the two gases.)

Do Not Vent Fuel Needlessly

Warning: Don't needlessly release propane fuel during service, and don't open the 80 percent stop-fill-valve while a vehicle is inside a building. When servicing the fuel system, follow recommended procedures to shut off the fuel tanks; run the engine out of fuel before disconnecting fuel system components. If the fuel tank is being serviced, have the fuel evacuated by trained personnel at a local fuel station. Liquid propane fuel vaporizes at normal barometric pressures and temperatures above -44°F (-42°C) and expands to 270 times its volume as a liquid. Unnecessary venting of propane fuel can create the fire and health hazards previously described in this section and lead to personal injury or illness.

Do Not Drain the Fuel Tanks

Warning: Do not attempt to use shop air pressure to force propane fuel from the tanks. Normal system pressure is about 160 psi (1724 kPa). Connecting a shop air hose to the fuel system could result in fuel flowing back into the service air system and result in a fire or an explosion. Fuel tanks should be drained by trained personnel only.

Shut Off the Fuel Tank

Warning: Close the fuel tank manual shut-off valve securely before performing any service on a propane-fueled vehicle. If the fuel system is to be serviced, also run the engine out of fuel before disconnecting any components. (This should take 2 to 3 minutes. If the engine continues to run, reset the shut-off valve hand-tight.) Failure to close the shut-off valve could result in fuel leakage during fuel system service, creating a fire hazard.

Note: The above *warning* is based on National Fire Protection Association (NFPA) Standard #58. NFPA #58 describes technical standards for the design of propane fuel systems and recommends certain precautions for servicing propane-fueled vehicles. The Canadian Gas Association (CGA) has also adopted similar technical standards.

Many states and provinces regard as law NFPA #58 or the CGA standards, respectively. There are other local laws which apply to propane fuel systems, and they should be observed. In particular, all service personnel should observe the above *Warning* about closing the fuel tank manual shut-off valve on any propane vehicle being serviced inside a building. This practice is a requirement for safety and is law in most areas.

Note: Open the shut-off valve very slowly after completing service. Listen for the sound of fuel filling the lines. When the filling sound stops, open the valve fully. If the shut-off valve is opened too quickly, the sudden flow of fuel will cause the excess flow valve in the tank to block fuel flow. If this occurs, close the manual shut-off valve for 10 seconds. You should hear a faint "click" from inside the tank when the excess flow valve resets. Then slowly open the manual shut-off valve.

Specification and Measurements

It is important that students record all the required information regarding specifications and measurements as obtained from the appropriate service repair manual for the unit being studied or repaired. Results of all measurements and adjustments made during disassembly, repair, and reassembly should also be recorded, as well as the general condition or serviceability of each component. Work sheets with this information recorded provide both the student and the instructor with required information to assess the progress and quality of work being performed.

PART 3   GASOLINE ENGINE DIAGNOSTIC CHARTS

PROBLEM	CORRECTION

Engine fails to start.

1. Clean and tighten loose battery terminal connections. Using battery hydrometer, check specific gravity; if low, recharge battery.
2. Check for broken or loose ignition wires and/or ignition switch and repair or replace as necessary.
3. Remove moisture from spark-plug wires and/or distributor cap.
4. Inspect condition of distributor cap and rotor. Replace if damaged or cracked.
5. Check, inspect, and regap spark plugs. Replace as necessary.
6. Check for weak or faulty ignition system coil.
7. Check carburetor float level.
8. Inspect carburetor fuel filter for presence of water and/or impurities. Correct as necessary.
9. Check choke mechanism for proper operation. Any binding condition that may have developed owing to petroleum gum formation on the choke shaft or from damage should be corrected.
10. Check fuel pump for leaks and proper operation. Correct as necessary.
11. Check operation of starter motor and solenoid. Repair or replace as necessary.
12. Inspect park or neutral safety switch. Adjust or replace as necessary.
*13. Check for air or vacuum leaks. Correct as necessary.

Engine lopes while idling.

*1. Check for vacuum leaks and correct as necessary.
*2. Check for blown head gasket and repair as necessary.
*3. Inspect condition of camshaft, timing belt, and/or sprockets. Replace as necessary.
*4. Check engine operating temperature and correct as necessary.
*5. Check the PCV system for satisfactory operation. Correct as necessary.
6. Check fuel pump for leaks and proper operation. Correct as necessary.
7. Check operation of exhaust gas recirculation valve. Repair or replace as necessary.
8. Check ignition timing and operation. Correct as necessary.
9. Check carburetor for incorrect idle speed, sticking choke, and adjust, repair, or replace as necessary.
10. Check, inspect, and regap spark plugs. Replace if necessary.

Engine misses while idling.

1. Check, inspect, and regap spark plugs. Replace as necessary.
2. Remove moisture from spark-plug wires and/or distributor cap.
3. Check for broken or loose ignition wires. Repair or replace as necessary.
*4. Check condition of cylinders for uneven compression. Repair as necessary.
5. Check for weak or faulty ignition system coil.
6. Inspect condition of distributor cap and rotor. Replace if damaged or cracked.
7. Check carburetor for internal obstructions, incorrect idle speed, sticking choke, and adjust, repair, or replace as necessary.
8. Inspect carburetor fuel filter for presence of water and/or impurities and correct as necessary.
9. Check carburetor mounting gasket for air leaks. Repair as necessary.
10. Check distributor spark advance mechanism for proper operation. Repair or replace as necessary.
*11. Inspect valve-train components. Adjust, repair, and/or replace as necessary.
*12. Check engine for low compression. Repair as necessary.
13. Check operation of exhaust gas recirculation valve. Repair or replace as necessary.
14. Check ignition timing and condition of ignition system. Correct as necessary.
*15. Check for vacuum leaks. Correct as necessary.

Engine misses at various speeds.

1. Inspect carburetor fuel filter for presence of water and/or impurities. Correct as necessary.
2. Check fuel system for leaks, plugged fuel lines, incorrect fuel pump pressure, and/or plugged carburetor jets. Correct as necessary.
3. Check ignition timing. Correct as necessary.
4. Check for excessive play in distributor shaft. Repair or replace as necessary.
*5. Check for weak valve springs and condition of camshaft lobes. Repair or replace as necessary.
6. Check, inspect, and regap spark plugs. Replace as necessary.
*7. Detonation and preignition may be caused by using substandard fuel. Correct as necessary.
*8. Check for weak valve springs and condition of camshaft lobes. Repair or replace as necessary.
*9. Check engine operating temperature. Correct as necessary.
10. Check operation of exhaust gas recirculation valve. Repair or replace as necessary.
11. Inspect distributor cap for evidence of carbon tracking. Replace if necessary.

Engine stalls.

1. Check carburetor for incorrect and/or misadjusted idle speed, float level, leaking needle and seat, air valve, sticking choke. Adjust, repair, or replace as necessary.
2. Inspect carburetor fuel filter for presence of water and/or impurities. Correct as necessary.
3. Check ignition system.
4. Check, inspect, and regap spark plugs. Replace as necessary.
5. Check distributor spark advance mechanism for proper operation. Repair or replace as necessary.
*6. Inspect exhaust system for restrictions. Correct as necessary.
7. Check carburetor mounting gasket for air leaks. Repair as necessary.
*8. Check for burned, warped, or sticking valves. Repair as necessary.

PROBLEM	CORRECTION

*9. Check engine for low compression. Repair as necessary.
*10. Check engine operating temperature. Correct as necessary.
11. Check for loose, corroded, or leaking wiring connections (bulkhead connectors and the like). Repair as necessary.
12. Check operation of exhaust gas recirculation system. Repair or replace as necessary.
13. Check fuel system for leaks and/or obstructions. Repair as necessary.
*14. Check for vacuum leaks. Correct as necessary.

Engine has low power.
1. Check for weak or faulty ignition system coil.
2. Check ignition timing. Correct as necessary.
3. Check for excessive play in distributor shaft. Repair or replace as necessary.
4. Check, inspect, and regap spark plugs. Replace as necessary.
5. Check carburetor for incorrect and/or misadjusted idle speed, float level, leaking needle and seat, air valve, and sticking choke. Adjust, repair, or replace as necessary.
6. Inspect carburetor fuel filter for presence of water and/or impurities. Correct as necessary.
7. Check fuel pump for leaks and proper operation. Correct as necessary.
*8. Check for sticking valves, weak valve springs, incorrect valve timing, lash adjuster noise, and worn camshaft lobes. Adjust, repair, or replace as necessary.
*9. Check for insufficient piston-to-bore clearance. Correct as necessary.
*10. Check condition of cylinders for uneven compression and/or blown head gasket. Repair as necessary.
11. Check for clutch slippage (vehicles with manual transmissions) and adjust or replace as necessary.
12. Check hydraulic brake system for proper operation. Correct as necessary.
*13. Check engine operating temperature. Correct as necessary.
14. Check pressure regulator valve (automatic transmission) for proper operation. Repair as necessary.
15. Check transmission fluid level. Correct as necessary.
16. Loss of power may be caused by using substandard fuel. Correct as necessary.
17. Check operation of diverter valve (AIR system). Repair or replace as necessary.
*18. Check for engine vacuum leaks. Correct as necessary.

Engine dieseling on shut off.
1. Check base idle speed for improper adjustment and correct as necessary.
2. Check ignition timing and reset to specifications if required.
3. Chect idle mixture setting and correct as necessary.
4. Check accelerator and choke linkage operation and correct as necessary.
*5. Check engine operating temperature and correct as necessary.

Engine detonation.
1. Check for overadvanced ignition timing and/or faulty ignition system and correct as necessary.
2. Check for loose or improper application of spark plugs or spark plugs with cracked or broken ceramic cores and replace as necessary.
3. Check for the use of substandard fuel and correct as necessary.
4. Check for foreign material in fuel lines and/or carburetor and correct as necessary.
5. Check for restricted fuel delivery to carburetor (pinched lines, faulty fuel tank cap or pickup) and correct as necessary.
6. Check fuel pump operation and replace if necessary.
7. Check EGR system operation and correct as necessary.
8. Check thermostatically controlled air cleaner operation and correct as necessary.
9. Check PCV system operation and correct as necessary.
*10. Check for vacuum leaks and repair or replace as necessary.
*11. Check engine operating temperature and correct as necessary.
*12. Check for excessive combustion chamber deposits and correct as necessary.
*13. Check for leaking, sticking, or broken valves and repair or replace as necessary.

External oil leakage.
1. Check for improperly seated or broken fuel pump gasket. Replace as necessary.
*2. Check for improperly seated or broken cam cover gasket. Replace as necessary.
*3. Check for improperly seated or broken oil filter gasket. Replace as necessary.
*4. Check for broken or improperly seated oil pan gasket. Replace as necessary.
*5. Inspect gasket surface of oil pan to see if bent or distorted. Repair or replace as necessary.
*6. Check for improperly seated or broken crankcase front cover gasket. Replace as necessary.
*7. Inspect crankcase front cover oil seal. Replace if necessary.
*8. Check for worn or improperly seated rear main bearing oil seal. Replace if necessary.
*9. Inspect for loose oil line plugs. Repair or replace if necessary.
*10. Check for engine oil pan drain plug improperly seated. Correct as necessary.

Excessive oil consumption due to oil entering combustion chamber through head area.
*1. Replace valve stem seals.
*2. Check for worn valve stems or guides. Correct as necessary.
*3. Inspect oil drainback holes in cylinder head for obstructions. Correct as necessary.
4. Inspect PCV system operation. Correct as necessary.

PROBLEM	CORRECTION
Excessive oil consumption due to oil entering combustion chamber by passing piston rings.	*1. Check engine oil level too high. Correct as necessary. *2. Check for excessive main or connecting rod bearing clearance and correct as necessary. *3. Check for piston ring gaps not staggered and correct as necessary. *4. Check for incorrect-sized rings installed and correct as necessary. *5. Check for piston rings out of round, broken, or scored and replace as necessary. *6. Inspect for insufficient piston ring tension due to engine overheating and replace as necessary. *7. Check for ring grooves or oil-return slots clogged and correct as necessary. *8. Inspect rings sticking in ring grooves of piston and correct as necessary. *9. Inspect ring grooves worn excessively in piston and correct as necessary. *10. Inspect compression rings installed upside down and correct as necessary. *11. Check for excessively worn or scored cylinder walls and correct as necessary. *12. Inspect for oil too thin and replace if necessary. *13. Inspect for mismatch of oil ring expander and rail and correct as necessary.
No oil pressure while idling.	*1. Check faulty oil gauge sending unit and correct as necessary. *2. Check for oil pump not functioning properly. *3. Inspect for excessive clearance at main, cam, and connecting rod bearings and correct as necessary. *4. Inspect leakage at internal oil passages and correct as necessary.
No oil pressure while accelerating.	*1. Check low oil level in oil pan and correct as necessary. *2. Inspect leakage at internal oil passages and correct as necessary. *3. Check to see if oil pump suction screen is loose or has fallen off and correct as necessary.
Burned, sticking, or broken valves.	*1. Check for weak valve springs and replace as necessary. *2. Check for improper valve guide clearance and/or worn valve guides and correct as necessary. *3. Check for out-of-round valve seats or incorrect valve seat width and correct as necessary. *4. Check for deposits on valve seats and/or gum formation on stems or guides and correct as necessary. *5. Check for warped valves or faulty valve forgings and correct as necessary. *6. Check for exhaust back pressure and correct as necessary. 7. Check improper spark timing and correct as necessary.
Noisy valves.	*1. Check for excessively worn, dirty, or faulty valve-lash adjusters. Replace if necessary. *2. Check for worn valve guides. Repair as necessary. *3. Check for excessive run-out of valve seat or valve face. Repair as necessary. *4. Check for worn camshaft lobes. Replace camshaft if necessary. *5. Inspect for broken valve spring. Replace if necessary.
Noisy lash adjusters.	*1. Check for broken valve springs and replace as necessary. *2. Check for worn rocker arms and repair or replace as necessary. *3. Check for lash adjusters incorrectly fitted to bore size and correct as necessary. *4. Check for excessively worn camshaft lobes and replace if necessary. *5. Check if lash adjuster oil feed holes are plugged, causing internal breakdown and correct as necessary.
Noisy pistons and rings.	*1. Check for excessive piston-to-bore clearance. Correct as necessary. *2. Inspect for improper fit of piston pin. Correct as necessary. *3. Inspect for excessive accumulation of carbon in combustion chamber or on piston tops. Clean and/or repair as necessary. *4. Check for connecting rods alignment. Correct as necessary. *5. Inspect for excessive clearance between rings and grooves. Repair or replace as necessary. *6. Check for broken piston rings. Replace as necessary.
Broken pistons and/or rings.	*1. Check for undersized pistons. Replace if necessary. *2. Check for wrong type and/or size of rings installed. Replace if necessary. *3. Check for tapered or eccentric cylinder bores. Correct as necessary. *4. Check connecting rod alignment. Correct as necessary. *5. Check for excessively worn ring grooves. Correct as necessary. *6. Check for improperly assembled piston pins. Replace as necessary. *7. Check for insufficient ring gap clearance. Correct as necessary. *8. Inspect for engine overheating. Correct as necessary. 9. Check for substandard fuel. Correct as necessary. 10. Check ignition timing. Correct as necessary.
Noisy connecting rods.	*1. Check connecting rods for improper alignment and correct as necessary. *2. Check for excessive bearing clearance and correct as necessary. *3. Check for eccentric or out-of-round crankshaft journals and correct as necessary. *4. Check for insufficient oil supply and correct as necessary. *5. Check for low oil pressure and correct as necessary. *6. Check for connecting rod bolts not tightened correctly and correct as necessary.

PROBLEM	CORRECTION
Noisy main bearings.	*1. Check low oil pressure and/or insufficient oil supply and correct as necessary. *2. Check for excessive bearing clearance and correct as necessary. *3. Check for excessive crankshaft end play and correct as necessary. *4. Check for eccentric or out-of-round crankshaft journals and correct as necessary.
Engine overheats	*1. See "loss of coolant" condition below. *2. Pressure check system. Correct leaks as needed. *3. Test coolant solution. Correct mix as needed. *4. Check belt tension; adjust if loose. 5. Set timing to specifications. *6. Clean away bugs, leaves, and the like, from radiator. *7. Flush system if restricted. Add coolant. *8. Relieve hose kinks by rerouting. Replace hose if necessary. *9. Check for lower radiator hose collapse. Check for hose spring position by squeezing lower end of hose. Replace as necessary. *10. Check fan clutch. Replace if necessary.
Loss of coolant	*1. Inspect system for leaks. Repair as needed.
Engine fails to reach normal operating temperature (cool air from heater).	*1. Install new thermostat of correct type and heat range. *2. Add coolant (50:50 coolant-water solution).

Diesel Engine Diagnosis

All of the mechanical engine problems that can occur on a gasoline engine can occur in the diesel engine as well. For diesel engine mechanical problems refer to the mechanical problems and corrections given in the gasoline engine diagnostic charts.

Other problems and corrections which apply to diesel engines are listed here.

Engine Will Not Start

1. *Glow Plug System.* If the engine is cold and hard to start, check the glow plugs. Since the diesel engine requires hot air to ignite the fuel, inoperative glow plugs will adversely affect engine starting.

2. *Insufficient Air.* If the air intake is restricted, the fuel will not ignite completely. The air pressure entering the manifold should be checked (past the filter) with a magnehelic gauge or equivalent.

3. *Insufficient Fuel.* If the supply tank has fuel, the fuel pressure out of the pump should be checked. If pressure is not to specifications, check the pressure into the injection pump. If this is not within specifications, check pressure into the filter. If all pressures are within specifications, remove the injectors and test on an injector test stand. Check and repair injection pump as necessary.

4. *Improper Fuel.* Check the type of fuel used. If the fuel contains water or air, or is the incorrect grade, the engine will not start properly.

5. *Check Timing.* Check the injection pump timing. Incorrect timing will result in the igniting of fuel at the wrong time. If the fuel is injected before the air is hot, or after the compression stroke, you will see heavy black smoke.

Intermittent Engine Operation

1. *Improper Fuel.* If the fuel contains water or air, or is the incorrect grade, the engine may stall.

2. *Restricted Fuel Filter.* If the fuel filter is restricted, this could cause the engine to stall at high speed from lack of fuel. Also check for restrictions at injection pump and at injectors.

3. *Insufficient Air.* If there is a restriction in the air inlet, the engine could have enough air to idle, but under full power it would stall.

Low Power

1. *Lack of Fuel.* If there is a restriction in the fuel line, the engine may not receive enough fuel to burn for proper power.

2. *Injection Pump Timing.* Check engine timing. If the fuel is being injected at the wrong time, the engine could lack power.

3. *Improper Fuel.* If the fuel is not the correct grade or contains water or air, the engine will lack power.

4. *Insufficient Air Supply.* If there is a restriction in the air intake, the engine will not receive enough air to ignite the fuel.

5. *Dirty or Clogged Injectors.* Check injectors for spray pattern. If the injectors are clogged, the engine will not receive enough fuel.

Fuel Knock

Fuel knock, also referred to as diesel knock, occurs when the combustible mixture of fuel vapor and air (formed during the period in which ignition lag has occurred at the beginning of fuel injection) has burnt at a time during the following period, thereby causing the abrupt rise in the pressure of gas. Where ignition lag is abnormally long, the quantity of fuel burning increases; this will cause the knocking that accompanies vibrations at the time of idling, or under some other conditions. As the number of rotations of the engine increases, the sound of knocking will be absorbed in the sound of the running engine; it cannot be heard clearly, but the knocking will add to various losses which naturally result in a fall of output. Knocking in diesel engines is apt to result from the following causes:

1. *Engine cooled too much.* Check the coolant temperature. If the temperature is lower than what is required for a normal running engine, locate and find the reason the temperature is too low.

2. *Injection timing too early.* Check engine timing and, if not set to specifications, time the engine in accordance with the service manual.

3. *Compression pressure too low.* Check the compression of the cylinders. Repair as required.

4. *Fuel will not ignite properly.* Inspect the fuel to see if water or air is present. There should be no air present in the fuel system. After inserting a clear tube between the water separator and the injection pump, watch for air bubbles. There should be none. Try running the vehicle from a source of known good fuel. If this stops the knocking, fuel was the problem.

Remember, diesel fuel is treated for the temperature conditions that it will be operating under. If the outside ambient temperature is high, and the diesel fuel was treated for cold temperatures, it may not vaporize correctly.

Excessive Smoke

Diesel engine exhaust can be classified into two categories according to visual appearance. The first category is blue-white smoke.

1. Blue-white smoke may be observed at engine start-up whether the engine is up to operating temperatures or not. This start-up smoke will be observed in warm as well as cold operation.

2. Blue-white smoke will continue to be seen at low idle speeds after a cold start-up, but this smoke will clear up soon after the vehicle is driven.

3. When ambient temperature is below 10°C (50°F), blue-white smoke can return after the engine warm-up period due to extended idling. This is because the combustion chambers cool down during periods of extended idling.

The second category of diesel engine exhaust smoke is black smoke. Black smoke is unburned fuel

which occurs whenever the engine is working hard. The engine works hard when it is going up a steep grade, pulling a trailer, carrying a heavy load, or accelerating. More black smoke will be observed at higher altitudes than at lower altitudes.

4. *Check Injector Pump Timing.* If timing is incorrect, the fuel will not be burned efficiently.

5. *Check Injectors.* If injectors are leaking, fuel will enter the combustion chamber at incorrect cycle.

Turbocharging Problems

If the *turbocharger* does not function properly, the engine can starve from lack of air. This can cause such symptoms as lack of power, poor performance, and bad fuel economy.

If there is oil leakage into the induction system via the turbocharger, engine oil consumption will be increased and blue exhaust smoke will be noticed.

PART 4   ENGINE REMOVAL AND DISASSEMBLY

The general procedures to follow for engine removal are similar in most cases. For special conditions and procedures, the manufacturer's service manual should be consulted.

1. Use fender covers.

2. Scribe mark around the hood hinges for reference when reinstalling hood.

3. Remove hood attaching bolts and have an assistant help you with removal. Avoid damage to car finish. Be especially careful when handling aluminum hoods.

4. Remove storage battery. Identify the battery and store it properly to avoid damage.

5. Drain engine coolant from radiator and engine block. Save coolant if it is to be used again; usually it is replaced because of contamination and deterioration.

6. Remove radiator, shroud, and fan. Disconnect transmission oil cooler lines first, if so equipped, and prevent fluid drainage from lines. If vehicle is equipped with air conditioning, do not disconnect AC condenser lines.

7. Remove air cleaner and emission-control lines.

8. Disconnect all electrical connections attached to engine assembly.

9. If vehicle is equipped with air conditioning, do not disconnect AC compressor lines. Remove compressor and place it in engine compartment so that it is out of the way for engine removal.

10. Do not disconnect power steering lines. Remove power steering pump and store in same manner as AC compressor.

11. Remove any other engine accessories that may interfere with engine removal (carburetor, starter, alternator, exhaust, fuel). Be sure to cap all diesel fuel lines to prevent entry of dirt.

12. Raise vehicle and place on safety jack stands just high enough to permit access under vehicle. (If raised too high, floor-type engine lift may not be able to raise engine high enough to clear engine compartment.)

13. Attach engine lift brackets to engine; attach one at the front and one at the rear. Use bolts of sufficient diameter and length to carry engine weight. Bolts used must tighten lift brackets firmly to engine. Connect lift and apply some tension.

14. Remove exhaust pipe to manifold bolts if not done previously.

15. Drain engine oil.

16. (a) If transmission is to be left in vehicle, it should be supported in its normal operating position. Be careful not to dent the automatic-transmission oil pan. Remove converter drive plate bolts since converter must stay with transmission to prevent front seal damage and fluid loss. Remove bell housing attaching bolts.

(b) If transmission is to be removed with engine, drain the transmission. Disconnect the transmission rear mount. Remove drive line (Tape U joints to cross.) Disconnect speedometer cable, vacuum and electrical connections, and control linkages. Remove cross member if necessary.

(c) On front-wheel-drive engines, engine and transaxle are sometimes removed as an assembly. In this case, drive axles must be disconnected from transaxle.

17. Remove motor mount attaching bolts.

18. Lift and tilt engine as required, being careful that engine does not bind or damage any engine compartment components during this procedure.

19. Lower engine close to floor to transport to desired location.

20. A good procedure to follow at this point is thorough cleaning of the engine's exterior and the engine compartment. A pressure-type cleaner usually is used for this. Avoid damaging car finish.

21. Mount engine safely in appropriate repair stand for disassembly.

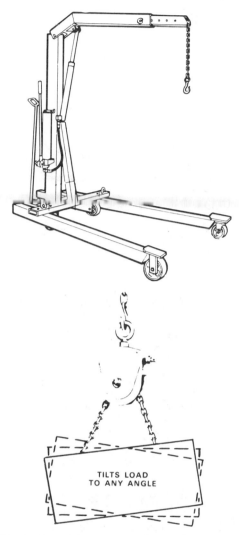

FIGURE 9-1. Portable crane and attachments used for engine removal. *(Courtesy of Owatonna Tool Company)*

Engine Disassembly Procedure

It is important that engine disassembly be done systematically and in proper sequence. A number of checks and measurements must be made during disassembly to determine the condition of engine components. All measurements taken during disassembly should be compared to manufacturer's specifications to determine serviceability of parts.

A thorough visual inspection of all parts should also accompany the disassembly procedure. The serviceability of parts is often determined by visual inspection when their condition is obvious. This eliminates cleaning and other service procedures on parts that require replacement.

The following general procedures apply in the majority of cases.

1. Remove transmission from engine if the two were removed from the vehicle as an assembly. (Re-

FIGURE 9-2. Position of floor crane for engine removal. *(Courtesy of Owatonna Tool Company)*

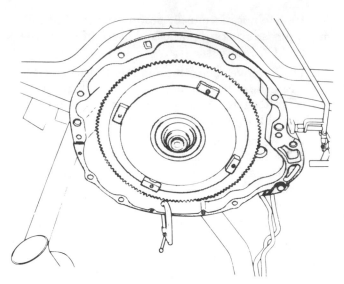

FIGURE 9-4. Torque converter must remain with transmission if engine is removed without transmission. Note that C clamp prevents converter from dropping out of bell housing. *(Courtesy of Chrysler Corporation)*

move clutch assembly on standard-transmission-equipped vehicle.)

2. Remove externally mounted parts: carburetor, starter, distributor, water pump, emission-control devices, injection pump and injectors.

FIGURE 9-3. Mounting engine in stand for overhaul procedures. *(Courtesy of Owatonna Tool Company)*

FIGURE 9-5. Engine in overhaul stand. Stand allows engine to be turned over for easy access. *(Courtesy of Owatonna Tool Company)*

FIGURE 9-6. Using portable crane to lower engine block into cleaning tank after all parts have been removed from block.

3. Remove intake and exhaust manifolds. (Identify right and left exhaust manifolds for proper assembly.) On in-line engines, intake and exhaust manifolds are often removed as an assembly and are not disconnected from each other unless a problem exists that would require disassembly.

4. Remove valve covers (cylinder head covers).

5. Remove necessary valve operating parts (rocker arms, pushrods, lifters). Keep these parts in order for proper reassembly. If lifters have varnish deposits, a slide hammer puller may have to be used for removal. Procedure will vary depending on engine design: in-block camshaft, overhead camshaft, horizontally opposed, and so on. Remove cylinder heads.

6. Remove harmonic balancer attaching bolt (if so equipped).

7. Remove harmonic balancer using special puller attached to balancer hub with two or three bolts. Be careful not to damage crankshaft with puller screw. Never use a two- or three-leg puller hooked over pulley or inertia ring for balancer removal. This could damage the balancer or the pulley.

8. Remove timing cover. *Caution:* This may require removal of the oil pan first on some models.

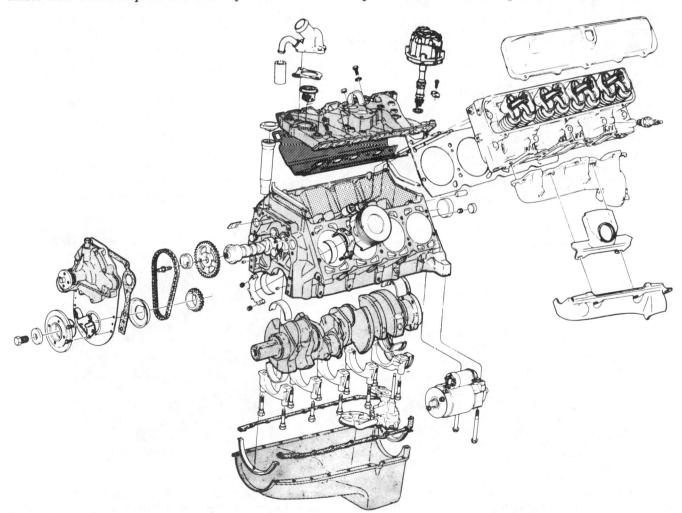

FIGURE 9-7. V8 engine parts relationship. *(Courtesy of General Motors Corporation)*

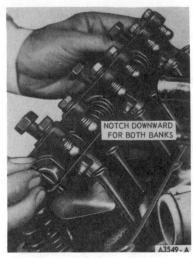

FIGURE 9-8. Rocker shaft removal or installation. *(Courtesy of Ford Motor Co. of Canada Ltd.)*

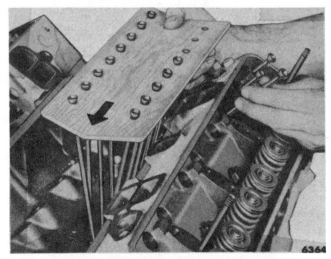

FIGURE 9-9. Pushrods must be kept in order for proper reassembly. *(Courtesy of Ford Motor Co. of Canada Ltd.)*

FIGURE 9-10. Valve lifters must also be kept in proper order during removal. Varnished lifters may require a slide-hammer type of puller for removal rather than the magnet shown here. *(Courtesy of Ford Motor Co. of Canada Ltd.)*

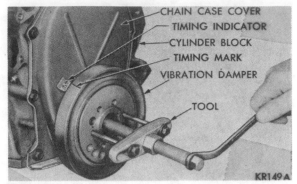

FIGURE 9-11. Special puller is used to remove harmonic balancer. *(Courtesy of Chrysler Corporation)*

9. Check camshaft drive condition to determine gear run-out, gear backlash, and camshaft end play (some models) on gear drives; chain deflection or backlash, sprocket wear and camshaft end play (some models) on chain drives; belt and sprocket condition and camshaft end play on belt drives.

10. Remove camshaft drive.

11. Remove camshaft (may require removal of thrust plate first on some models). Support camshaft during removal to avoid dragging lobes over bearing surfaces, which would damage bearings and lobes. Do not bump cam lobe edges, which can cause chipping.

12. Remove cylinder ridges; this requires the use of a special reamer. Various types of reamers are used. Follow tool manufacturer's instructions for use. Regardless of the type of ridge reamer used, the ridge should be removed completely. Avoid damaging the cylinder. Do not allow ridge reamer to cut into ring travel area. The ridge must be removed to

FIGURE 9-12. Chain and sprocket wear can be determined by checking amount of camshaft sprocket movement or chain deflection before disassembly. Compare results with manufacturer's specifications. *(Courtesy of Chrysler Corporation)*

FIGURE 9-13. Measure camshaft gear backlash (top) and run-out (bottom) on gear-driven camshaft before disassembly. Compare results with recommended wear limits. *(Courtesy of General Motors Corporation)*

FIGURE 9-14. Ridge reamer (top) must be used to remove ridge at top of worn cylinder before piston removal. Failure to do so will cause top ring to strike ridge and cause piston damage during piston removal. *(Courtesy of Hastings, Ltd., Toronto, Canada [top] and Ford Motor Co. of Canada Ltd. [bottom])*

avoid damaging the piston when pistons are removed.

13. Remove oil pan if not previously removed.

14. Remove oil pump assembly.

15. Make sure connecting rods and main bearing caps are properly identified for correct reassembly. All connecting rods should have numbers on both yokes and caps. Main bearing caps should be identified for location and position. If rods and main bearing caps do not have proper identification, they must be stamped with number stamps. The rods should be numbered in accordance with the engine cylinder numbering system on both yoke and cap on the same side of the rod. The main bearing caps and engine block should also be properly numbered.

16. Remove piston and rod assemblies as follows:

(a) Position crankshaft throw at the bottom of its stroke.

(b) Remove connecting rod nuts and cap. Tap cap lightly with soft hammer to aid in cap removal.

(c) Cover rod bolts to avoid damage to crankshaft journals.

(d) Carefully push out piston and rod assembly with wooden hammer handle or wooden drift and support piston by hand as it comes out of the cylinder. Be sure connecting rod does not damage cylinder during removal.

(e) With bearing inserts in rod and cap, replace cap (numbers on same side) and install nuts. (Store piston and rod assembly properly.) Repeat procedure for all other piston and rod assemblies.

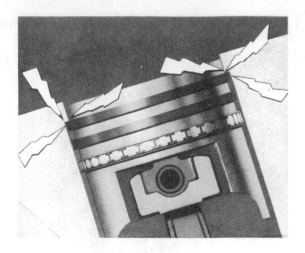

FIGURE 9-15. Piston damage can occur if cylinder ridge is not removed. *(Courtesy of Ford Motor Co. of Canada Ltd.)*

FIGURE 9-16. Use special tool to cover connecting rod bolts for piston removal. Short pieces of rubber hose or rubber spark-plug boots can be used in place of tool. This prevents damage to crankshaft journals. *(Courtesy of General Motors Corporation)*

FIGURE 9-17. Measuring flywheel ring gear run-out before disassembly. *(Courtesy of Ford Motor Co. of Canada Ltd.)*

FIGURE 9-18. Measuring torque converter drive plate (flex plate) run out. *(Courtesy of Ford Motor Co. of Canada Ltd.)*

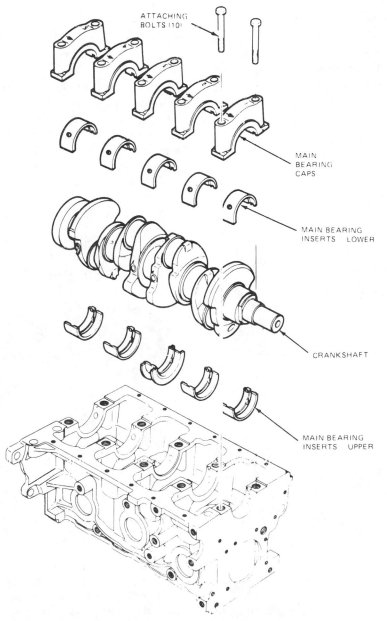

FIGURE 9-19. Removing bearing caps, crankshaft, and main bearings from engine block. *(Courtesy of Ford Motor Co. of Canada Ltd.)*

17. Check flywheel or converter drive plate run-out with dial indicator to determine whether replacement or reconditioning is required.

18. Remove flywheel or flex plate; scribe marking crankshaft and flywheel or plate aids in reassembly.

19. Remove main bearing cap bolts and main bearing cap.

20. Carefully remove crankshaft by lifting both ends equally to avoid binding and damage.

21. Store crankshaft in vertical position to avoid damage, or support in enough positions to avoid sag.

22. Remove main bearings from block and from main bearing caps. Remove rear main oil seal from block and from main bearing cap.

23. Install main bearing caps loosely in preparation for degreaser or hot tank cleaning.

24. Remove all core hole plugs in preparation for hot tank cleaning. This allows cleaning solution to clean all water jackets thoroughly.

25. Remove oil gallery plugs and cam bearing bore plug for cleaning.

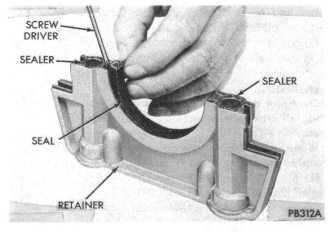

FIGURE 9-20. Split-type synthetic rubber rear main oil seal removal (above) and wick-type seal removal (below). *(Courtesy of Chrysler Corporation and General Motors Corporation)*

26. Carefully place engine block (and all other parts that are not subject to corrosion from the cleaning fluid being used) into the cleaning tank. Some cleaning solutions attack aluminum and other alloys. (Follow recommendations provided by cleaning fluid manufacturer.)

27. When thoroughly clean, remove engine block and other parts from cleaning tank. Thoroughly rinse cleaning fluid from all engine parts with water, giving particular attention to oil galleries, water jackets, and other passages.

28. Use compressed air to dry engine parts and remove water. Apply a light coat of engine oil to all machined surfaces to avoid rust.

PART 5 CYLINDER AND CYLINDER LINER SERVICE

If after thorough cleaning and visual inspection the cylinder block appears to be serviceable, it should be further inspected by various measurements to determine the type of servicing the block will require to restore it. If the block is not cracked and there is no apparent severe damage, the following procedures should be followed.

Measuring Cylinder Bore Size

An outside micrometer is set to the engine's standard bore diameter (as specified in the shop manual). The cylinder gauge is then set to the same

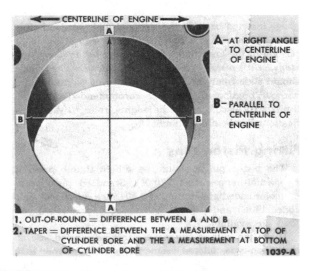

FIGURE 9-21. Measuring cylinder bore for out of round should be done at top, middle, and bottom of cylinder to determine worst condition. To measure taper, measure at bottom of cylinder and at a point just below ridge at top of cylinder. Difference between two measurements is amount of cylinder taper. Compare with specifications. *(Courtesy of Ford Motor Co. of Canada Ltd.)*

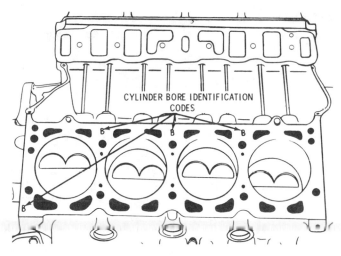

CYLINDER BORE IDENTIFICATION
CODES

BORE DIA.	CYL. BORE SELECTION	BORE SIZES	PISTON SELECTION	PISTON SIZE	PISTON DIA.	PISTON TO CYL. BORE CLEARANCE
4.056-4.058 STD.	A	4.0560-4.0565	A	4.0505 - 4.0510	4.0505 - 4.0525 STD.	.0050 to .0060
	B	4.0565-4.0570	B	4.0510 - 4.0515		
	C	4.0570-4.0575	C	4.0515 - 4.0520		
	D	4.0575-4.0580	D	4.0520 - 4.0525		
4.066-4.068 .010 O.S.	J	4.0660-4.0665	J	4.0605 - 4.0610	4.0605 - 4.0625 .010 O.S.	
	K	4.0665-4.0670	K	4.0610 - 4.0615		
	L	4.0670-4.0675	L	4.0615 - 4.0620		
	M	4.0675-4.0680	M	4.0620 - 4.0625		

FIGURE 9-22. Cylinder bore markings indicate bore size and piston size required for each cylinder to provide correct piston-to-cylinder clearance. *(Courtesy of General Motors Corporation)*

specification and the dial gauge is set at zero while positioned in the micrometer. The cylinder gauge is then inserted into the cylinder and pushed down to the area below ring travel. Since this area is not subject to wear, it will still be standard bore size if the engine has not been rebored. The cylinder gauge, when positioned exactly across the cylinder, should register zero (+ or −0.002 inch [or 0.0508 mm] for production tolerance) in this case. Gauge should be placed across cylinder (90° to crankshaft).

If the engine has been rebored to 0.030 of an inch (0.762 mm) oversize, the cylinder gauge will read 0.030 (0.762 mm) on the plus (+) side of the scale. This indicates the piston and the ring sizes required, if the cylinders are not to be rebored. This information also indicates whether cylinders that have been previously rebored, can be rebored again. Some engines can be rebored to a larger oversize than others. Cylinder measurements must be compared to manufacturer's maximum allowable rebore size to determine whether reboring is feasible.

FIGURE 9-23. Measuring cylinder with a special dial indicator type of cylinder gauge. *(Courtesy of General Motors Corporation)*

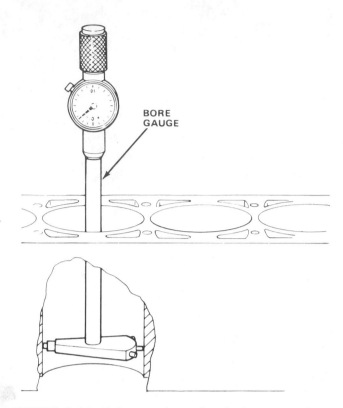

FIGURE 9-24. Cutaway view of cylinder measuring. *(Courtesy of American Motors Corporation)*

BORE GAUGE

Cylinder Taper

The difference in bore diameter at top of ring travel compared to bore diameter below ring travel is the amount of taper or wear. If excessive, cylinders should be rebored and fitted to new pistons. Most manufacturers allow a maximum of 0.005 to 0.010 inch (0.13 to 0.25 millimeter) before reboring is required. Some diesel engines may allow a maximum of only .001 inch (0.025 mm) taper.

Cylinder out of Round

Cylinders should be measured parallel to the piston pin and at right angles to the piston pin to determine cylinder out of round. This should be done at the top of ring travel, in the center of the cylinder, and at the bottom of ring travel. If out of round exceeds manufacturer's wear limits (approximately 0.002 to 0.005 inch or 0.05 to 0.13 milimeter), cylinder should be rebored and fitted to oversized piston.

Cylinder Waviness

Cylinder waviness can be detected by carefully moving the cylinder gauge the full length of ring travel in the cylinder and observing the dial. If waviness

is excessive, cylinders should be rebored and fitted to oversized pistons.

Deglazing Cylinder

If cylinders do not require reboring and if the instructions supplied by the piston ring manufacturer require it, the cylinders should be deglazed. This breaks up the glassy smooth cylinder wall surface. The honed surface promotes good cylinder and ring lubrication during engine break- in and ensures good ring seating. A 60° (included angle) crosshatch pattern of 25- to 30-microinch finish is desirable.

A flexible deglazing hone with stones of 180 to 200 grit is used for this purpose. The hone is driven at about 300 rpm with a slow-speed electric drill while being moved up and down in the cylinder. If the angle of the crosshatch pattern is not steep enough, the hone is not being stroked fast enough

FIGURE 9-25. Cylinder hones used to deglaze cylinders that are within wear limits. Hone must be operated at 500 rpm or less to achieve desired crosshatch pattern. Hone must be "stroked" (moved up and down) the entire length of the cylinder while in operation. Deglaze cylinders only if recommended by manufacturer of rings to be used. Bead type deglazer (top right) may also be used.

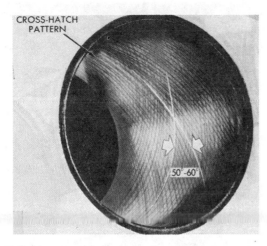

FIGURE 9-26. Cylinder after honing should have a visible 60° crosshatch pattern. Surface finish should have a pattern depth of 25 to 30 microinches. This requires a hone of 180 to 200 grit stones. *(Courtesy of Chrysler Corporation)*

or the drill speed is too fast. No excess material should be removed. Use solvent during honing to flush stones and keep them cutting.

Reboring Cylinders

Cylinders with excessive taper, out of round, or waviness are usually rebored and fitted to oversized pistons. Maximum oversize is limited by cylinder wall thickness and is usually stated in the manufacturer's shop manual. Cylinders that are badly scored or otherwise damaged but not cracked are also rebored.

Cylinders are rebored or rough honed to within approximately 0.003 inch (0.08 millimeter) of finished size. They are then individually finish honed to fit oversized pistons.

A cylinder block that cannot be replaced or rebored is usually machined and fitted with dry cylinder liners or sleeves. Sleeves are usually shrunk by freezing to allow easier installation. This provides an interference fit and good heat transfer.

Honing Cylinders to Remove Taper

If taper is not excessive, cylinders may be honed with a rigid hone to restore parallelism. Taper is honed out to fit pistons that have been expanded by a knurling process. This restores proper piston-to-cylinder clearance and reduces oil consumption when fitted with new piston rings.

This type of cylinder and piston service is usually done to extend the service life of an engine without the cost of purchasing new pistons and reboring the cylinders. The service life of this type of repair cannot be expected to be as long as that of an engine that has been rebored and fitted with new pistons. This type of repair is usually limited to cylinder taper of approximately 0.010 inch (0.25 millimeter) or less. This procedure also corrects most out-of-round or wavy cylinder conditions. Honing must be done with main bearing caps in place and bolts tightened to specified torque.

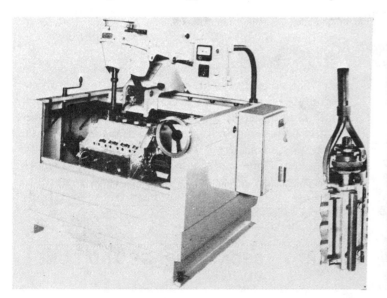

FIGURE 9-27. Cylinder resizing machine removes 0.008 inch (2 millimeters) per minute. Machine controls stock removal and size automatically and shuts off when preset cylinder size has been reached. This is normally done only in an engine rebuilding plant. Note cylinder crosshatch pattern. *(Courtesy of Sunnen Products Co. Ltd.)*

Cylinder Liner Inspection and Installation

Cylinder liners should be inspected for cracks, scoring, corrosion, flange irregularities, seal ring groove erosion, and in the case of dry liners, liner-to-block contact abnormalities. The outer circumference of dry cylinder liners must show evidence of good metal-to-metal contact to ensure good heat transfer to the water jackets. Liner-to-block bore clearance must be determined by measuring liner outside diameter and block bore diameter. The difference in these two measurements is the liner clearance. If this clearance is excessive, oversize outside diameter liners must be used. Follow the engine manufacturer's specifications.

Cylinder liners that show cracks, deep scoring, excessive corrosion, or flange irregularities must be replaced.

Liners must also be measured for inside diameter (cylinder bore size) to determine whether bore size is standard or oversize. Cylinder liner taper, out-of-round, and waviness must be measured to determine serviceability of the liner. Usually no more than a maximum of 0.001 inch (0.025 mm) of taper, out-of-round, or waviness is allowable. Liners with excessive taper, out-of-round, or waviness must be replaced or rebored if oversize pistons are available for the engine.

Install cylinder liners with new seals as outlined in the appropriate service manual. Be sure to observe all requirements regarding liner protrusion above block deck, as well as any indexing with the block (if required). Cylinder liners and pistons are matched units; be sure to install each numbered unit into the same number cylinder position in the block. Liners may have to be clamped in position to prevent them from being pushed out as the crankshaft is rotated during assembly.

PART 6   MAIN BEARING BORE SERVICE

Main bearing bores should be measured for alignment and out of round. The mating surfaces of main bearing caps and of the block should be cleaned and the caps installed without the bearings and tightened to specifications.

Each main bearing bore diameter is measured vertically and horizontally. The difference, if any, is the bore out of round. Maximum out of round allowable is approximately 0.002 inch or 0.05 millimeter. If excessive, line boring is required.

Bearing bore alignment is measured with a straight edge held against the inside of all the bear-

(a)

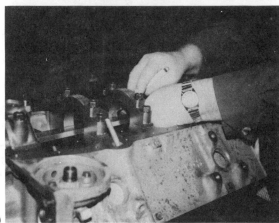

(b)

FIGURE 9–28. To measure (A) main bearing bore out of round and (B) alignment, main bearing caps must be in place and torqued to specifications without bearing inserts. If alignments or out of round exceed specifications, block must be line bored or honed.

ing bores. Both vertical and lateral alignments are checked.

A feeler gauge is used to measure between the straight edge and each bearing bore. If bore misalignment is excessive (over approximately 0.002 inch or 0.05 millimeter), line boring is required. Line boring is done by grinding several thousandths of an inch of material from the bearing cap mating surfaces, and then installing and tightening them to specifications. Bearing bores are then resized to original specifications by honing with a special full-length hone.

PART 7   DECK WARPAGE AND CORE PLUGS

Measuring Deck Warpage

The cylinder block deck should be smooth and clean to measure deck warpage. If excessive, machining may be required to true the surface and prevent head gasket leakage.

FIGURE 9-29. Line honing main bearing bores. This is usually done only in an engine rebuilding plant. *(Courtesy of Sunnen Products Co. Ltd.)*

Deck warpage is measured with a straight edge and feeler gauge. The straight edge is positioned lengthwise across the center of the deck. Check several points with the feeler gauge between straight edge and deck, particularly between cylinders. Deck is also checked with the straight edge across corners, and between each pair of cylinders (separately).

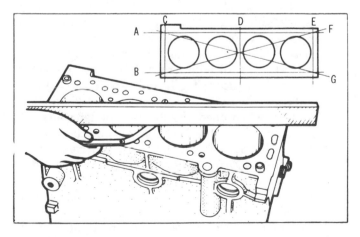

FIGURE 9-30. Measuring deck warpage with a straight edge and feeler gauge. *(Courtesy of Chrysler Corporation)*

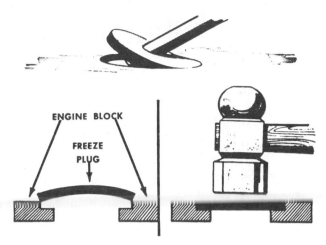

FIGURE 9-31. Removing and replacing dished type of core hole plug.

Maximum allowable limits before machining are usually .006″ (.15 mm) overall and .002″ (.05 mm) over any pair of cylinders.

Core Hole Plugs

New core hole plugs should be installed with the proper tool. Plugs should be coated with sealer and

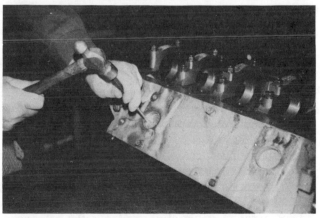

FIGURE 9-32. Removal of cup-type core hole plug.

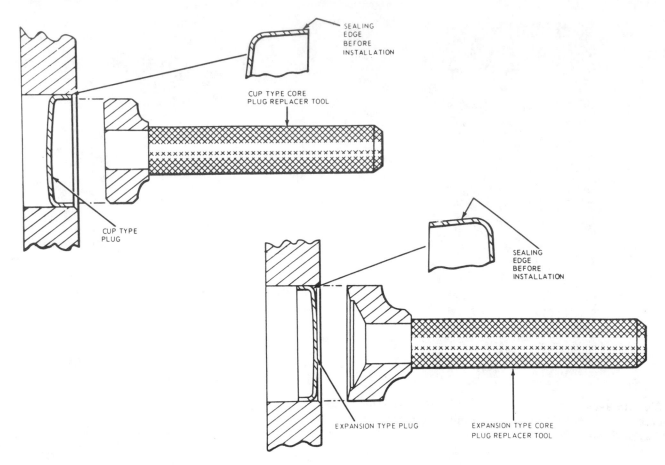

FIGURE 9-33. Two types of cup-type core hole plugs are used. Be sure to use the correct tool and method of installation and proper sealant. *(Courtesy of Ford Motor Co. of Canada Ltd.)*

then installed proper side out and to correct depth. Threaded plugs that are removed should also be sealed with sealer and installed.

PART 8   CAMSHAFT BEARING SERVICE

Camshaft bearings usually are replaced when the engine is overhauled. Bearings are removed and installed with a special tool. Some tools use a hammer to drive the bearings into place; others use a threaded puller.

Bearings are not always of equal size. It is important, therefore, to make sure that the correct bearing is installed in each of the bearing bores. Care must be exercised to avoid allowing the bearing to cock during installation, since this collapses the bearing and shaves metal from its outside circumference. Bearing oil holes must be properly aligned with oil holes in the block to ensure proper lubrication when installed. Hole alignment should be checked

again after installation. All bearings must also be installed to the correct depth.

The camshaft bearing bore plug can now be installed in the rear bearing bore. The plug should be coated with a good sealer to prevent oil leakage. The plug should also be installed with the proper tool to the correct depth to avoid contact with the rotating camshaft. See cylinder head service for overhead camshaft service.

The cylinder block should be thoroughly cleaned by first washing all cylinders with warm soapy water to remove all traces of grit and dirt. This cleaning should continue until a clean white cloth will not become dirty when used to rub the cylinder walls.

The rest of the block should also be thoroughly cleaned. All holes should be clean and clear of all dirt and fluids. Fluids (oil or water) in blind threaded holes can cause the block to crack when bolts are tightened due to the extreme hydraulic pressures produced.

All machined surfaces should be lightly oiled. The block should then be covered to prevent any dirt from entering prior to reassembly.

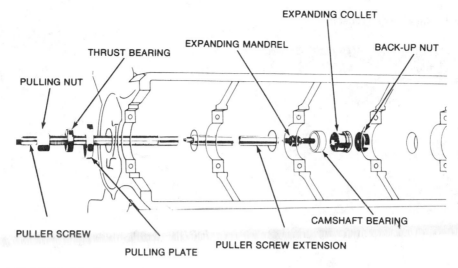

FIGURE 9-34. Camshaft bearing removing and installing tool (exploded view). *(Courtesy of Ford Motor Co. of Canada Ltd.)*

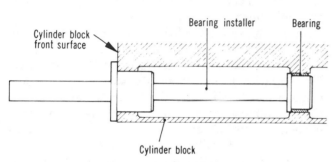

FIGURE 9-35. Camshaft bearing removal or installation with expanding collet tool. *(Courtesy of Chrysler Corporation)*

FIGURE 9-36. Oil holes in cam bearings must be properly aligned with oil holes in block when replacing camshaft bearings. *(Courtesy of Ford Motor Co. of Canada Ltd.)*

PART 9   CAMSHAFT ASSEMBLY SERVICE

The camshaft and camshaft drive assembly can be removed and replaced with the engine in the vehicle in most cases; however, this requires removal of the radiator and grill on in-block camshaft engines. Overhead camshaft replacement may require cylinder head removal.

Replacement of camshaft bearings on engines that have in-block camshafts is difficult without engine removal. The rear camshaft bearing and camshaft bearing bore plug are almost inaccessible while the engine is in the vehicle. Camshaft bearings should be replaced when the camshaft is being replaced. Valve lifters should also be replaced.

The in-block camshaft and camshaft bearings are easier to remove and replace on an engine that has been removed if this is done while the crankshaft is out. This provides better access to bearings and allows better support of the camshaft during removal and installation.

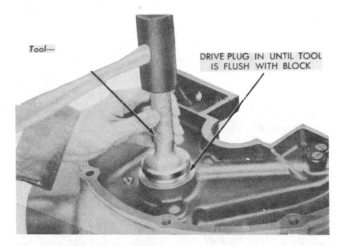

FIGURE 9-37. Cam bearing bore plug installation. Install to recommended depth. *(Courtesy of Ford Motor Co. of Canada Ltd.)*

207

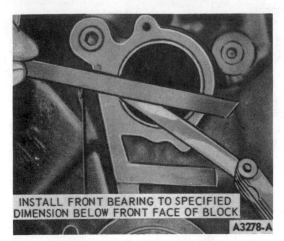

FIGURE 9-38. Front camshaft bearing must be installed to correct depth as specified by manufacturer. *(Courtesy of Ford Motor Co. of Canada Ltd.)*

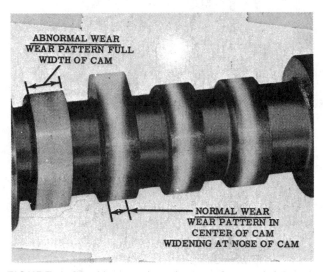

FIGURE 9-39. Abnormal and normal cam lobe wear patterns.

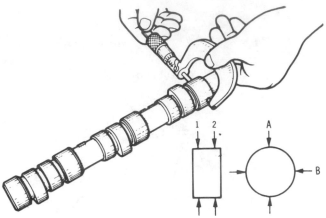

FIGURE 9-40. Measuring camshaft bearing journal taper and out of round. *(Courtesy of Chrysler Corporation)*

The camshaft should be inspected after cleaning in solvent for excessive wear, pitting, or chipped lobes. If the camshaft passes a thorough visual inspection, bearing journals should be measured for wear, out-of-round conditions, and taper. Camshaft lobes should be measured for wear and lobe lift.

If camshaft wear exceeds manufacturer's wear limits, it should be replaced with a new or rebuilt camshaft. A lobe lift loss of no more than 0.005 inch (0.13 millimeer) is generally accepted. Maximum camshaft bearing clearance allowable is usually 0.006 inch (0.15 millimeter).

Camshafts are rebuilt by grinding the bearing journals to an undersize of up to 0.015 inch (0.38 millimeter). Undersized bearings must be used with this type of camshaft. Cam lobes are reground to restore original lift if lobes are not worn excessively. Cam lobes are then acid etched, or *Parkerized*, to provide good oil retention ability and reduced wear, especially during initial starting and engine break-in.

Cam lobes should be coated with a good high

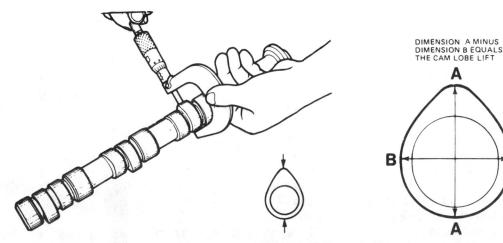

FIGURE 9-41. Measuring camshaft lobe lift and wear. Compare results with specifications. *(Courtesy of Ford Motor Co. of Canada Ltd.)*

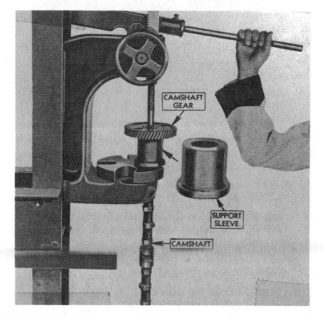

FIGURE 9-42. Using arbor press to replace camshaft gear. *(Courtesy of General Motors Corporation)*

pressure lubricant such as Lubriplate® before installation. Bearing journals and bearings should be lubricated with motor oil.

Camshafts that are held in place by a thrust plate or retainer must be checked for proper end play. If end play is incorrect, the thrust plate and gear or sprocket may have to be replaced. The rear cam bearing bore plug should be coated with a good sealer and installed to the correct depth to avoid contact with the end of the camshaft.

Damage to bearings during camshaft installation should be avoided by properly supporting the camshaft. Sharp edges of cam lobes may damage the bearings. A long bolt threaded into the drive end of the camshaft will allow the weight of the camshaft to be properly supported. The camshaft should be checked to see that it rotates freely without any binding after installation.

The camshaft drive should be installed and properly timed after the crankshaft is in place.

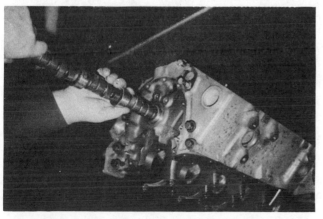

FIGURE 9-43. Removing or installing camshaft.

PART 10 CRANKSHAFT AND MAIN BEARING SERVICE

The crankshaft should be thoroughly inspected for damage to any machined surfaces. Main bearing journals, thrust surfaces, seal journal, and connecting rod bearing journals should appear smooth and polished without any nicks, burrs, grooves, ridges, scores, or cracks that could cause damage to bearings or shaft life. The keyway and other machined surfaces should also be in good condition. If the crankshaft passes a thorough visual inspection, it should be cleaned and measured.

Cleaning the crankshaft includes cleaning of the oil passages with a rifle-type brush, if necessary, and washing in solvent. Care must be taken during cleaning and measuring not to damage any machined surface. Blow out all oil passages and blow the crankshaft dry with compressed air.

The crankshaft should be measured to determine main and rod bearing journal size, taper, out of round, and run-out. These measurements must be compared to the manufacturer's specifications and wear limits. If wear limits are not exceeded, the crankshaft may be used again. Minor imperfections may be touched up by polishing with crocus cloth. If the crankshaft meets specifications, the pilot bushing (on standard transmission vehicles) should be inspected for wear and replaced if necessary.

Maximum wear limits are usually no more than 0.001 inch (0.025 millimeter) for journal taper and out of round. Maximum crankshaft run-out should generally not exceed 0.003 inch (0.080 millimeter).

If the crankshaft does not meet specified wear limits, it must be replaced. Rebuilt crankshafts are normally used for replacement.

Crankshafts are reground to an undersize in engine rebuilding shops to provide good bearing journal surfaces. Crankshafts are straightened if required.

Severely damaged journals are rebuilt by an automatic welding process and machined. Usually, crankshafts are not rebuilt if more than one journal requires buildup by welding.

During the grinding and polishing process, no more material is removed than is needed to produce a good journal. Journals are finished to normal undersizes of 0.010, 0.020, or 0.030 inch (0.25, 0.51, or 0.76 millimeter). All rod journals are reground to the same undersize. The main journals are also ground to the same undersize but may differ from the rod journal undersize.

Main bearings and bearing bores in the block and caps must be absolutely clean. Place correct size

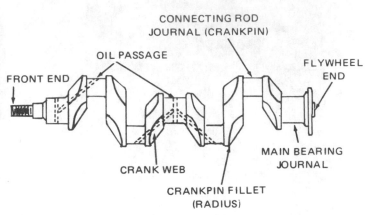

FIGURE 9-44. Crankshaft must be visually inspected for damage or cracks and then cleaned, including drilled oil passages, before measuring. (*Courtesy of Ford Motor Co. of Canada Ltd.*)

bearings in both block and main bearing caps. To do this, place bearing tang in notch and then press other side of bearing down into place. If upper and lower bearing halves are not identical, make sure that the upper half (with oil hole) is placed in the engine block. The flanged thrust bearing should be installed in the bore designed for this bearing.

Bearing Clearance

After all bearings are in place, carefully install crankshaft, but avoid crankshaft rotation to prevent scoring the bearings. Bearings and shaft must be free of oil during the procedure for checking bearing clearances. With crankshaft in place (no rear main seal at this point), place a piece of Plastigage® across each bearing journal. (If bearing clearances are being checked with engine in vehicle, Plastigage is placed across bearings in bearing caps, and the

A VS **B** = VERTICAL TAPER
C VS **D** = HORIZONTAL TAPER
A VS **C** AND **B** VS **D** = OUT OF ROUND
CHECK FOR OUT-OF-ROUND AT EACH END OF JOURNAL

FIGURE 9-45. Measuring crankshaft bearing journal size, taper, out of round, and wear. (*Courtesy of Federal Mogul [top] and Ford Motor Co. of Canada Ltd. [bottom]*)

FIGURE 9-46. With the crankshaft supported in the block by only the front and rear main bearings (all other bearings removed), crankshaft run-out can be measured with a dial indicator as shown here.

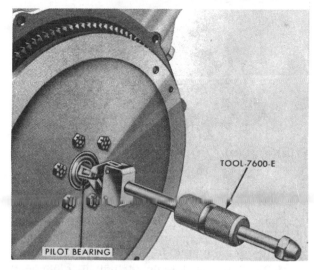

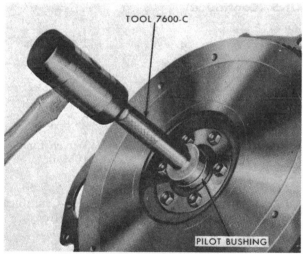

FIGURE 9-47. The crankshaft gear is normally not removed during engine overhaul unless it requires replacement. A puller is used for removal (above) and a special tool (below) is used for installation. *(Courtesy of Ford Motor Co. of Canada Ltd.)*

crankshaft is raised against the upper bearing during this procedure.)

Install bearing caps and tighten bolts to specified torque. Remove bearing caps and check clearance by measuring width of Plastigage® with scale provided on envelope. Compare with manufacturer's specifications. Clearances should be correct.

Remove Plastigage® carefully without scratching bearings or journals. Remove crankshaft and install rear main bearing oil seal.

FIGURE 9-49. Removing pilot bushing with a slide-hammer puller (above). Installing new bushing with a bushing driver (below).

FIGURE 9-48. Measuring pilot bushing wear. *(Courtesy of Ford Motor Co. of Canada Ltd.)*

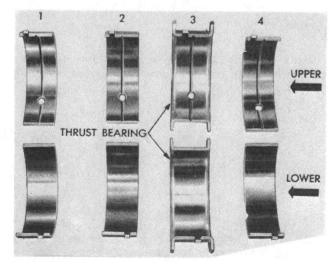

FIGURE 9-50. Crankshaft bearings must be properly installed without distorting the bearing. *(Courtesy of Chrysler Corporation)*

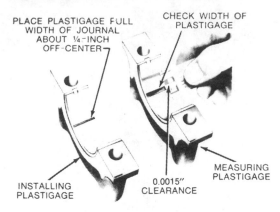

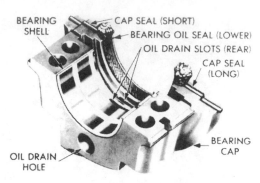

FIGURE 9-51. Using Plastigage to measure bearing clearance. Plastigage is placed across bearing when measuring clearance with engine in vehicle. To measure clearance with engine on bench, Plastigage is placed across journal. *(Courtesy of Ford Motor Co. of Canada Ltd.)*

FIGURE 9-53. Installing wick or rope type rear main bearing oil seal. *(Courtesy of Chrysler Corporation)*

Lip-type seal should be installed with lip toward oil. Wick-type seal should be thoroughly seated in groove with special tool and ends carefully trimmed to level of cap and block.

Thoroughly lubricate all bearings and seal with motor oil.

Install crankshaft and main bearing caps. Tighten main bearing caps one at a time, leaving the thrust bearing cap to the last.

Tighten main bearing cap bolts in three steps; first, to one-third of specified torque, then to two-thirds, and then to full specified torque.

Before tightening thrust main bearing cap, pry crankshaft back and forth to align thrust surfaces of flanged main bearing, and then tighten as specified above.

At this point, crankshaft end play should be checked. There should be sufficient end play to avoid bearing and crankshaft damage; refer to specifications.

Flywheel

The *flywheel* or *converter flex plate* should now be installed if in good condition. The starter ring gear and clutch friction surface should be in good condition and flywheel run-out within specifications. The drive bolt holes in the converter drive plate (flex plate) and starter ring gear (some models) should be in good condition and within run-out limits. All bolts

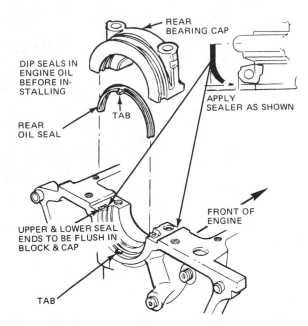

FIGURE 9-52. Installing rear main bearing oil seal (synthetic-rubber type). *(Courtesy of Ford Motor Co. of Canada Ltd.)*

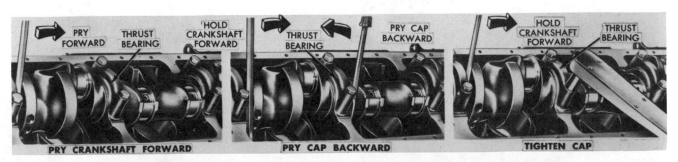

FIGURE 9-54. Aligning thrust surfaces of thrust bearing before tightening main bearing cap bolts to specifications. If this is not done, bearing failure may result. *(Courtesy of Ford Motor Co. of Canada Ltd.)*

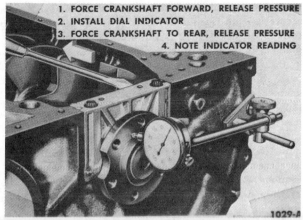

FIGURE 9-55. Measuring crankshaft end play with a dial indicator. End play should be within minimum and maximum limits specified by manufacturer. Excessive end play may require crankshaft replacement. *(Courtesy of Ford Motor Co. of Canada Ltd.)*

should be tightened to specified torque. If flywheel or flex plate is not in good condition, it should be replaced.

Crankshaft Gear

The *crankshaft gear* or *sprocket* should be replaced if teeth show signs of excessive wear. The camshaft drive gear, or sprocket and chain, should also be replaced if worn. Camshaft drive belt and sprockets should be inspected and replaced if damaged or worn. When installing camshaft drives, be sure to align all timing marks properly (camshaft gear or sprocket, crankshaft gear or sprocket, auxiliary shaft sprocket) to ensure correct camshaft-to-crankshaft timing (valve timing).

FIGURE 9-56. Installing camshaft sprocket and chain. Sprocket must be aligned with dowel pin or key in camshaft. *(Courtesy of Ford Motor Co. of Canada Ltd.)*

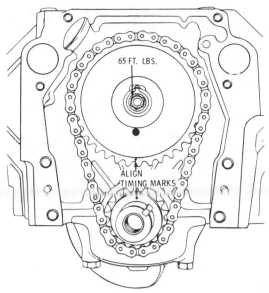

FIGURE 9-57. Timing marks on sprockets or gears must be properly aligned for correct camshaft and valve timing during assembly. *(Courtesy of General Motors Corporation)*

PART 11 PISTONS, RINGS AND CONNECTING ROD SERVICE

The pistons, pins, connecting rods, and connecting rod bearings may be replaced with the engine in the vehicle in most cases; however, a better job of cleaning and installation is possible if this is done with the engine removed.

Inspection and Cleaning

A good visual inspection of the pistons and rods will determine whether they warrant cleaning and further service. With piston rings removed, ring grooves can be checked for excessive damage. Piston skirts should not have any evidence of major scoring or cracks. If the connecting rod bearing has not turned in the big end of the rod, it is probably serviceable.

The piston head can be cleaned by using a scraper to remove most of the carbon. Aluminum pistons are easily damaged. Only careful cleaning will prevent piston damage. All cleaning tools must be used in a manner that will prevent scoring or gouging or removal of metal.

A *special ring groove cleaner* is used to remove all the carbon from the ring grooves. Oil drain back holes or slots in the oil ring groove must also be cleaned. These holes should not be enlarged during the cleaning process. The piston head and ring area may then be cleaned on the wire wheel of a bench

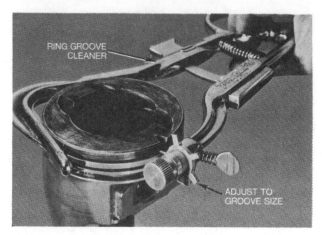

FIGURE 9-58. Cleaning piston ring grooves with a special scraper. All carbon must be removed without removing any metal from the piston. *(Courtesy of Ford Motor Co. of Canada Ltd.)*

grinder. Ring grooves and lands should not be rounded off during this process. Only light pressure of the piston against the wire wheel is used. The remainder of the piston can be cleaned with a soft, wire-bristle hand brush in solvent.

Piston and Pin Measuring

The piston should be measured at a point specified by the manufacturer's shop manual and the measurement should be compared to specifications.

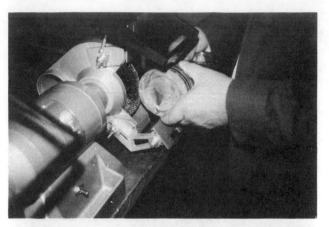

FIGURE 9-60. Cleaning pistons on a wire wheel. Care should be taken not to round off ring grooves. Piston skirts should not be cleaned in this manner.

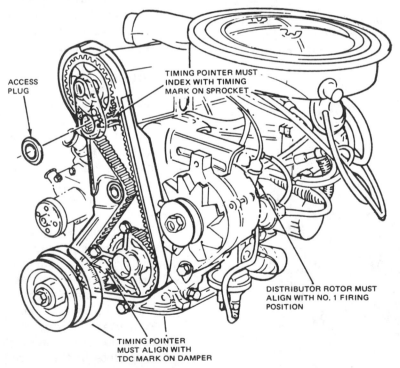

FIGURE 9-59. Overhead camshaft drive must be installed so that intermediate shaft and camshaft are properly timed to the crankshaft. *(Courtesy of Ford Motor Co. of Canada Ltd.)*

FIGURE 9-61. Cleaning piston skirt in solvent with a soft bristle brush to prevent damage to skirt surface. *(Courtesy of Ford Motor Co. of Canada Ltd.)*

FIGURE 9-63. Piston size should be measured at height specified in shop manual and at 90° to the piston pin. *(Courtesy of Ford Motor Co. of Canada Ltd.)*

Some manufacturers call for piston measurement across the thrust surfaces at pin height; others specify measurements to be taken just below the oil ring groove or at the bottom of the skirt. If the piston is collapsed, it should be replaced.

If there is any noticeable wear (looseness) of the piston pin in the piston, the piston and rod should be fitted with oversized piston pins during reassembly. Piston pins are available in a number of oversizes from 0.001 up to 0.005 inch in 0.001 inch increments from some manufacturers. Maximum allowable pin-to-piston clearance is usually 0.001 inch (0.03 millimeter).

Connecting Rod Measuring

With the bearing removed from the connecting rod and the rod cap mating surfaces clean, the rod is clamped in a special holding fixture. The rod cap is

then installed and the nuts tightened to specifications. The rod cap numbered side must be on the numbered side of the rod. The special holding fixture prevents the connecting rod from being twisted while the nuts are tightened or removed.

The big end of the connecting rod can now be measured for any out-of-round condition, as illustrated. Maximum allowable out of round is usually 0.001 inch (0.005 millimeter). If out-of-round limits are exceeded, the connecting rod can be resized (usually by a machine shop procedure). Several thousandths of an inch of material is ground from each side of the rod cap mating surface. The cap is installed and tightened to specifications. The big end is then honed to original size and roundness.

The connecting rod must also be checked for twist or bend. Connecting rod alignment can be

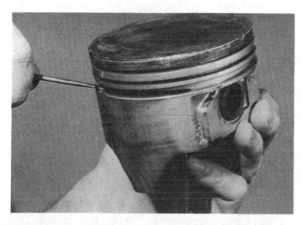

FIGURE 9-62. Cleaning oil drain back holes or grooves. *(Courtesy of Ford Motor Co. of Canada Ltd.)*

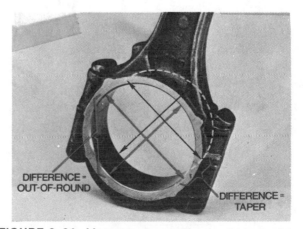

FIGURE 9-64. Measure connecting rod big end taper and out of round with bearing removed and cap torqued in place. *(Courtesy of Ford Motor Co. of Canada Ltd.)*

FIGURE 9-65. Special tool for checking connecting rod bend or twist. Attachments allow checking rod with piston attached or removed. Tapered rod is used to correct rod twist or bend with connecting rod clamped in special fixture or in vise with soft jaws. *(Courtesy of Sunnen Products Co. Ltd.)*

checked with the piston attached or removed on most alignment tools.

Twist or bend in the rod can be corrected by hand with the big end of the rod clamped in a vise with soft jaws. A long tapered rod specially made for this purpose is inserted in the hollow piston pin, and the rod is bent or twisted back to proper alignment and rechecked.

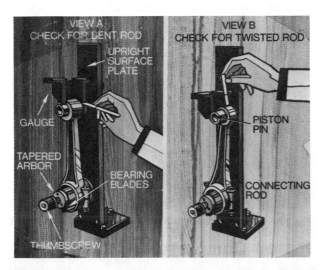

FIGURE 9-66. Connecting rod is checked for bend (left) or twist (right). *(Courtesy of Ford Motor Co. of Canada Ltd.)*

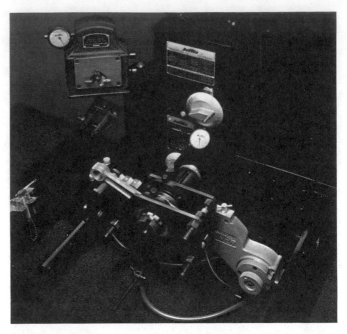

FIGURE 9-67. Honing connecting rod (after cap mating surface has been ground) to correct big end out of round. *(Courtesy of Sunnen Products Co. Ltd.)*

Installing Piston Pins and Rods

If piston pins are to be replaced, a special tool or press with special piston support adapters is used for the purpose. Great care must be taken to properly support the easily distorted aluminum piston, since it may require 2 to 3 tons of force to remove or install the piston pin when the piston pin is a press fit in the connecting rod.

During assembly, the correct piston-to-rod relationship must be maintained because of piston pin offset and oil spurt holes in the rod.

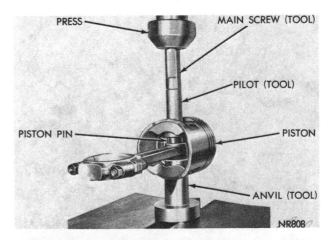

FIGURE 9-68. Removing piston pin with press and special adapters to properly support piston. Unless piston is properly supported, piston can easily be damaged. *(Courtesy of Ford Motor Co. of Canada Ltd.)*

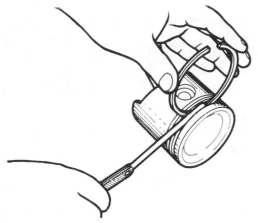

FIGURE 9-69. Checking ring side clearance in groove with feeler gauge and new piston ring. If clearance is excessive, ring grooves must be reconditioned. *(Courtesy of Chrysler Corporation)*

FIGURE 9-71. Pistons can be knurled as shown here to restore proper piston-to-cylinder clearance. Cylinders are honed to fit expanded (knurled) piston. *(Courtesy of Perfect Circle)*

Piston Rings

Piston ring groove wear, if excessive, can be corrected by machining the groove and installing a spacer above the ring to restore it to original width. *Piston ring side clearance* should be checked with new rings and a feeler gauge. Compression ring side clearance is usually from 0.002 to 0.004 inch (0.05 to 0.10 millimeter). Oil ring side clearance may be from 0.0002 to 0.0005 inch.

The *ring gap* should be measured by pushing the ring into the cylinder with an inverted piston to position the ring squarely in the cylinder. If the cylinders have not been rebored, and if there is any cylinder taper, the ring should be pushed to near the bottom of the cylinder to measure ring gap. Insufficient ring gap can cause ring ends to butt from expansion (owing to heat) and cause severe ring and cylinder damage.

If ring gap does not meet manufacturer's spec-

ifications, another ring set of the same size should be tried until the correct gap is achieved. In some cases, careful filing of ring ends has been done to achieve proper ring gap (if the gap is too small).

Piston rings should be installed according to ring manufacturer's instructions. Such specifications as placing the correct ring in its proper ring groove, right side up, and recommended ring gap positioning around the piston must be followed to ensure proper ring operation.

The oil ring spacer is installed first; then the top and bottom steel rails are spiraled into place. Oil rings of this type do not require special tools for installation. Compression rings must be installed next with a special ring expander to avoid distortion and breakage. Be careful not to expand the rings any more than necessary for installation. Compression rings must not be twisted.

Piston and Rod Installation

With the rod cap removed, the rings installed, and new bearing inserts properly installed (take note of

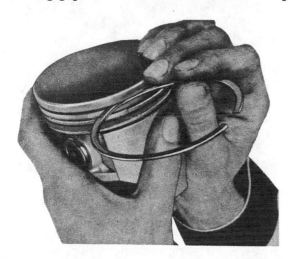

FIGURE 9-70. Rolling ring around piston ring groove to check for binding condition. *(Courtesy of General Motors Corporation)*

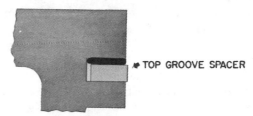

TOP GROOVE SPACER

FIGURE 9-72. Reconditioned piston ring groove with spacer in place. *(Courtesy of General Motors Corporation)*

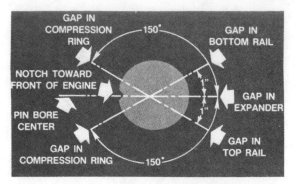

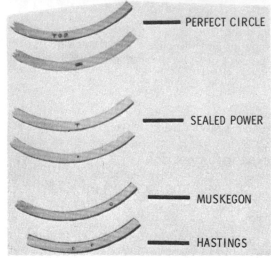

FIGURE 9-74. Ring manufacturer's instructions must be followed to properly install piston rings and stagger the gaps. *(Courtesy of Ford Motor Co. of Canada Ltd.* [top] *and General Motors Corporation* [bottom])

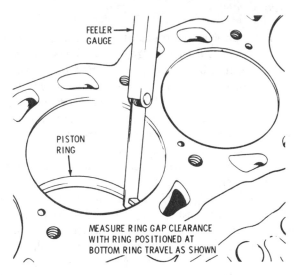

FIGURE 9-73. Using piston to push ring to bottom of ring travel in cylinder to measure ring gap. *(Courtesy of Ford Motor Co. of Canada Ltd.* [top] *and General Motors Corporation* [bottom])

oil hole alignment), the assembly is ready for installation.

Thoroughly lubricate the rings, piston and pin by dunking the piston in a can of SF motor oil. (Leave the bearing and journal dry for checking bearing clearance with Plastigage.) Install the ring compressor (notched side toward rod) down just far enough to cover all the rings, leaving enough piston uncovered to start it into the cylinder. Tighten compressor carefully and completely to compress all rings fully without changing the location of the ring gaps.

Cover the connecting rod bolts (to prevent

FIGURE 9-75. Installing sectional type of oil ring. With expander-spacer in groove, steel rails can be spiraled into place. Install top rail first. *(Courtesy of Ford Motor Co. of Canada Ltd.)*

FIGURE 9-76. Installing compression rings with a ring expander. Care must be exercised not to overexpand the rings. Rings are easily distorted or broken. *(Courtesy of Ford Motor Co. of Canada Ltd.)*

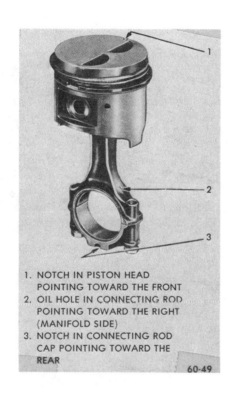

1. NOTCH IN PISTON HEAD POINTING TOWARD THE FRONT
2. OIL HOLE IN CONNECTING ROD POINTING TOWARD THE RIGHT (MANIFOLD SIDE)
3. NOTCH IN CONNECTING ROD CAP POINTING TOWARD THE REAR

60-49

FIGURE 9-77. Follow manufacturer's instructions to correctly assemble connecting rod to piston. Above is only one example of properly assembled piston and rod. *(Courtesy of General Motors Corporation)*

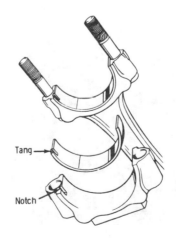

FIGURE 9-78. Bearing inserts must be installed in connecting rod and cap before installing piston. *(Courtesy of General Motors Corporation)*

219

FIGURE 9-79. Ring compressor must be used to compress piston rings for piston installation. *(Courtesy of Ford Motor Co. of Canada Ltd.)*

FIGURE 9-80. Tapping piston into cylinder with wooden hammer handle. *(Courtesy of Ford Motor Co. of Canada Ltd.)*

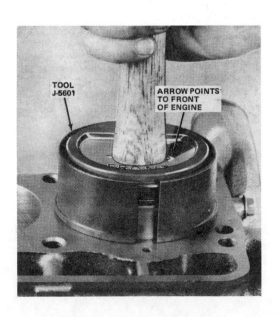

FIGURE 9-81. Using tapered sleeve type of ring compressor to install piston and rod assembly. Advantages of this type of ring compressor are that it is faster and the ring gap positioning is not disturbed during installation. *(Courtesy American Motors Corporation)*

FIGURE 9-82. To prevent connecting rod bolts from damaging the crankshaft journal during piston assembly installation, short pieces of hose can be used as shown here. *(Courtesy of General Motors Corporation)*

crankshaft damage) and install the assembly into the cylinder with the front of the piston toward the front of the engine. The crankpin for this cylinder should be at BDC for this operation. Carefully bump the piston into the cylinder with a wooden hammer handle while guiding the rod squarely over the crankshaft journal until fully seated. Do not allow the ring compressor to move away from the block during this operation. If it does, a piston ring may pop out, preventing further piston movement and possible ring and piston damage.

Measuring Bearing Clearance

Check bearing clearance with Plastigage in the same manner as the main bearings. If clearance is correct, carefully remove Plastigage, thoroughly lubricate

bearing journal with motor oil, and reassemble cap with new connecting rod bolt nuts tightened to specifications. New connecting rod nuts should be used, since they are usually of the self-locking type, and old nuts may become loose during engine operation.

Repeat this procedure for all piston and rod assemblies.

Measure connecting rod side clearance (connecting rod installed on crankspin, side-to-side movement) and compare to specifications. If excessive, connecting rods may have to be replaced.

It is good practice to turn the crankshaft to check for any excessive increase in effort required to turn the engine each time a piston and rod assembly is installed. If excessive effort is required to turn the crankshaft, the reason for this should be determined and corrected. This may require the removal and inspection of the last piston and rod assembly installed.

PART 12   OIL PUMP, OIL PAN AND TIMING COVER

The *engine oil pump* is normally replaced when the engine is overhauled. To check oil pump condition, refer to Lubrication System Service in Chapter 7.

The oil pump assembly and drive (where applicable) should now be installed. The oil pickup screen and tube, as well as the oil pump, should be absolutely clean. The oil pump should be primed (filled)

FIGURE 9-83. Measuring connecting rod side clearance. Clearance should be within minimum and maximum limits specified. If incorrect, connecting rods or crankshaft may have to be replaced.

FIGURE 9-84. Installing oil pump. (Refer to lubrication system service section for procedures required to check pump condition.) *(Courtesy of General Motors Corporation)*

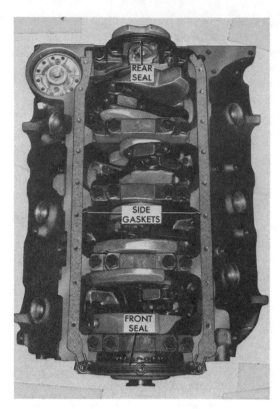

FIGURE 9-85. Oil pan gaskets and seals in place ready for oil pan installation on V8 engine. *(Courtesy of General Motors Corporation)*

with oil to ensure that the oil pump will function as soon as the engine is started.

The pickup tube and screen must be properly positioned and leak-free (no air leaks). This may re-

FIGURE 9-87. Installing timing cover seal. *(Courtesy of General Motors Corporation)*

quire a sealer on threaded pickup tubes or flange gaskets. Pickup tube positioning is critical to avoid oil pan interference and to ensure that the pickup is always submerged in oil during operation.

The *oil pan and timing cover* must be clean and the gasket flanges level for proper sealing. The timing cover seal should be replaced using the proper seal driver with the timing cover supported to avoid distortion. The seal should be installed with the lip toward the engine. New gaskets are used. Install oil slinger if used.

On engines that do not have dowel pins for timing cover alignment, the cover should be installed with the bolts installed loosely. The harmonic balancer (with the hub lubricated with Lubriplate®) is then installed far enough to center the timing cover

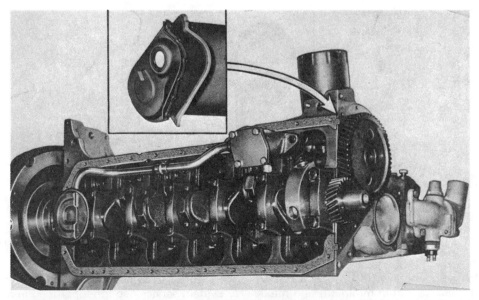

FIGURE 9-86. Oil pan gasket and timing cover gasket in place ready for installation for a six-cylinder engine. *(Courtesy of General Motors Corporation)*

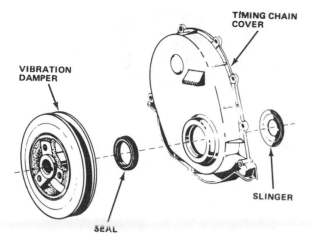

FIGURE 9-88. Details of oil slinger, timing cover, front seal, and vibration damper assembly. *(Courtesy of General Motors Corporation)*

over the crankshaft. The timing cover bolts are then tightened and harmonic balancer installation completed.

If the harmonic balancer hub has grooved wear where it runs on the oil seal, it should be replaced or repaired with a service sleeve available for this purpose. If the inertia ring has slipped or the elastomer insulator is excessively cracked, the balance should be replaced. If the retaining bolt is used, tighten it to specifications.

The oil pan should be installed with a new gasket and a new drain plug gasket. Tighten all bolts to manufacturer's specifications. Cork gaskets tend to "squish" out from between surfaces if they are oily or if a slow-drying sealer is used. They are better installed dry. If recommended, self-vulcanizing sealer may be used in place of gaskets.

Valve Lifter Installation

With the engine upright, the lifters can now be installed. *New hydraulic lifters* are normally installed when the engine is overhauled. If old lifters are to be used, they should be inspected for wear or damage and checked for correct leakdown rate. Due to the relatively low cost of lifters, and the amount of time required to service old lifters, it is not practical to do so.

Lifters should be primed (pumped up) manually and oiled externally before installation. Lifters that are not primed before installation may not pump up when the engine is started and may become scored internally, requiring replacement. In some cases, oversize-diameter lifters are used during engine manufacture. If this is the case, the correct oversize lifters should be used.

PART 13   CYLINDER HEAD AND VALVE SERVICE

Cleaning and Disassembly

Cylinder head and valve train services are often performed on engines without engine removal, if lower engine service is not required. Procedures for cylinder head removal, service, and installation are similar whether the engine has been removed or not.

Once the cylinder heads have been removed (see the section on engine disassembly), and if no obvious damage is apparent, the cylinder head assembly can be cleaned in the degreaser (hot tank), as was done with the engine block.

Preliminary cleaning can be done without the valves being removed. This protects the valve seats from damage when removing carbon deposits from the combustion chamber. Scrapers and a rotary wire brush are used for this purpose. Any deposits in the ports should also be removed.

Cylinder head disassembly includes removal of rocker arms and pivots, valves, springs, retainers, and locks. All parts should be kept in order for correct reassembly. A C-clamp type of valve spring compressor is used to compress the valve springs far enough to allow the locks to be removed. Sometimes the locks and retainer are stuck to the valve stem, and the spring cannot be compressed with the spring compressor. In this case, the spring retainer should be tapped with a soft-faced hammer while the spring compressor is applying some pressure to the spring. Tapping the retainer with the hammer will allow the locks and retainer to pop loose.

Care must be exercised when using the valve spring compressor to avoid slipping off the compressed spring. The compressed spring releases a powerful punch if it snaps out of place and can cause serious injury.

If the valve stem tips are mushroomed from rocker arm action, they should be dressed (filed to stem size) before valve removal to avoid damage to the valve guides. A fine hand file can be used for this purpose.

After disassembly the cleaning process can be completed. Any remaining deposits that were not accessible while the valves were in place must be removed.

Valve guides should be cleaned with a carbon scraper type valve guide cleaner, after which they should be cleaned with a rifle type brush.

On diesel engines, where applicable, carefully remove the glow plugs and fuel injectors. Fuel injectors may be held in place by a clamp or they may be of the screw-in type. Follow manufacturer's rec-

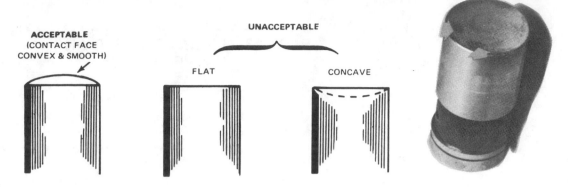

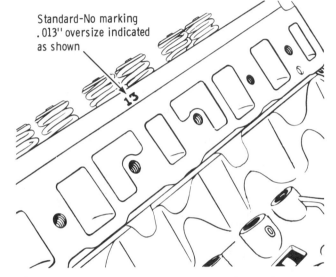

FIGURE 9-89. Inspect valve lifters for damage and wear as above. *(Courtesy of Ford Motor Co. of Canada Ltd.)*

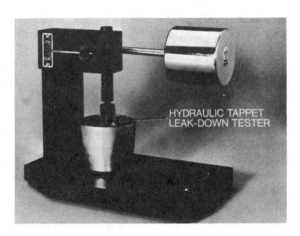

FIGURE 9-90. Hydraulic lifter leak-down tester. Tester uses special fluid to check lifter leak-down rate. This operation is usually not feasible due to the low cost of lifter replacement. *(Courtesy of Ford Motor Co. of Canada Ltd.)*

FIGURE 9-92. Some engines may have factory installed oversize stem valves and guides as indicated. *(Courtesy of General Motors Corporation)*

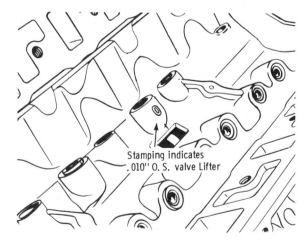

FIGURE 9-91. Some engines are equipped with oversize-diameter valve lifter during manufacture. When replacing lifters, this must be considered and the proper size of lifters installed. Both engine block and valve lifter are marked with a zero (as above) by one manufacturer to identify this condition. *(Courtesy of General Motors Corporation)*

FIGURE 9-93. Cleaning combustion chamber with rotary wire brush before valves are removed. This prevents damage to valve seats. *(Courtesy of Ford Motor Co. of Canada Ltd.)*

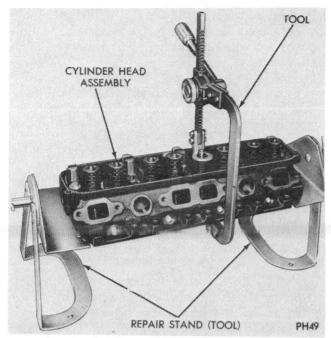

FIGURE 9-94. Using valve spring compressor for valve removal. *(Courtesy of Chrysler Corporation)*

ommendations for servicing these items including replacement of any injector gaskets, seals, or O rings. On some engines, the precombustion chambers may require servicing or replacement. Extreme

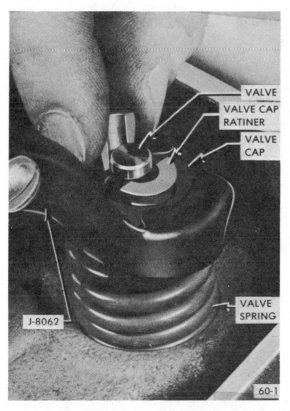

FIGURE 9-95. Removing valve retainer locks with spring compressed. *(Courtesy of General Motors Corporation)*

FIGURE 9-96. Valve guide cleaners: scraper (top), brush (bottom).

care must be exercised when handling any diesel fuel injection parts in order to prevent damage. Remove, clean, and install precombustion chambers as specified in the appropriate service manual.

Cylinder Head and Valve Measuring

Cylinder head warpage should be checked with a straight edge and feeler gauge and, if excessive, it should be corrected. A maximum of 0.006 inch (0.15 millimeter) overall and 0.002 inch (0.05 millimeter) over any six-inch area is generally accepted.

The valves should be cleaned on the wire wheel of the bench grinder (use face mask). The entire valve should be cleaned this way; however, damage to the valve face should be avoided. Any valves that are obviously damaged, burned, or cracked, or have

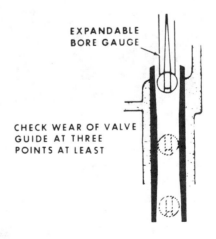

FIGURE 9-97. Measuring valve guide wear with small hole gauge and outside micrometer. Measurements are taken at three levels as indicated.

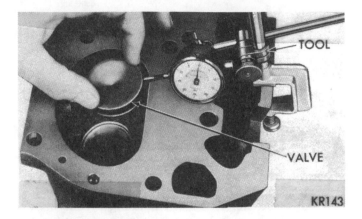

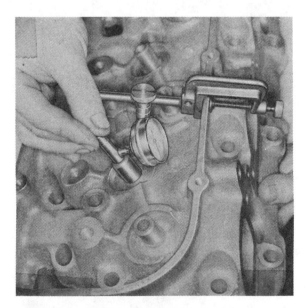

FIGURE 9-98. Different methods of checking valve stem-to-guide clearance. Follow procedure recommended by manufacturer. *(Courtesy of Chrysler Corporation* [top], *Ford Motor Co. of Canada Ltd.* [middle], *and General Motors Corporation* [bottom])

insufficient margin, should be replaced and do not require cleaning.

Valve stems should be measured for wear with an outside micrometer. Valves with stem wear in excess of 0.001 inch (0.03 millimeter) are usually replaced.

Caution: Do not damage sodium-filled valve stems. Sodium-filled valve stems are usually identifiable by their larger-diameter stems. The sodium in the valve stem explodes when exposed to atmosphere.

Valve stem-to-guide clearance can be measured in several different ways. Manufacturers differ in the method they recommend. The specifications given in the manufacturer's shop manual apply only when the method they recommend is followed.

A method that can be used on any make employs a dial indicator mounted on the cylinder head in such a way that valve stem side-to-side movement in the guide can be measured. The valve is inserted in the guide and the dial indicator is mounted so that the plunger contacts the valve stem as close to the guide as possible. With the valve off its seat about 1/4 inch, side-to-side movement of the valve stem is measured. If this measurement is excessive (over 0.005 inch or 0.13 millimeter), the valve guide should be reconditioned or replaced if not integral.

PART 14 VALVE GUIDE RECONDITIONING

When valve guide reconditioning or replacement is required, this must always be done before attempting to recondition the valve seats. This is necessary to maintain the correct relationship between the valve guides and seats.

Several methods of restoring correct valve stem-to-guide clearance are employed. On engines with re-

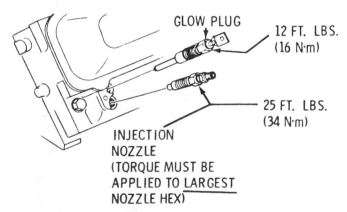

FIGURE 9-99. Glow plug and injector are both of the threaded type on this V8 GM diesel engine. *(Courtesy of General Motors Corporation)*

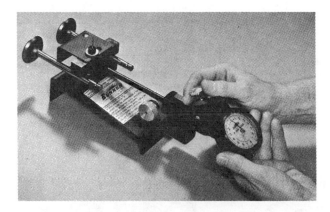

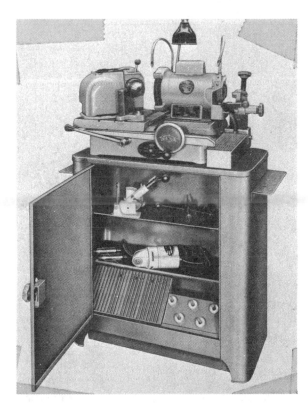

FIGURE 9-100. Direct reading dial indicator type of valve guide gauge. Gauge may be set to standard bore diameter with gauging device (top) or with outside micrometer. *(Courtesy of Sunnen Products Co. Ltd.)*

FIGURE 9-101. Valve and seat reconditioning equipment. *(Courtesy of Sioux Tools Inc.)*

placeable guides, guides are removed with a special press or driver and new guides installed to the correct depth. Valves with standard-diameter stems can then be used.

On cylinder heads with integral guides, the guides can be reamed to an oversize for which oversized stem valves are available. Another method is to machine the guides to allow new valve guide inserts of standard diameter to be installed.

A method known as *knurling* is also used to recondition valve guides. The appropriate knurling tool is inserted in the guide and turned. This causes it to spiral its way through the guide like the threads of a bolt. The knurling tool does not remove any metal, but rather displaces the metal to reduce valve guide diameter. After knurling, the guides are reamed to restore the guide to original diameter and provide proper valve stem-to-guide clearance. If proper valve stem-to-guide clearance is not restored, the valves will not seat properly and oil will get past the guides into the combustion chamber and exhaust system.

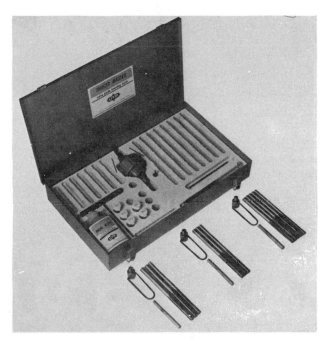

FIGURE 9-102. Valve guide knurling equipment. *(Courtesy of United Tool Processes)*

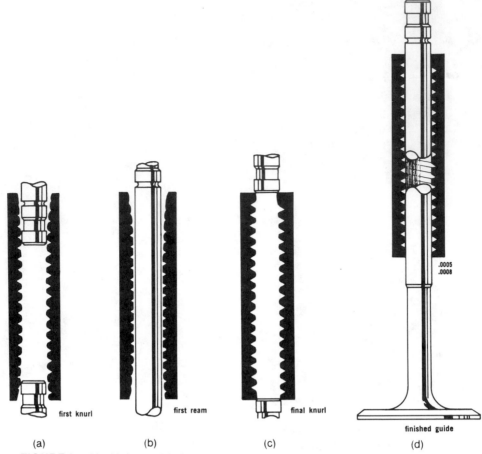

first knurl   first ream   final knurl

.0005
.0008

finished guide

(a)   (b)   (c)   (d)

FIGURE 9–103. Valve guide knurling procedures, (a) to (d). *(Courtesy of United Tool Processes)*

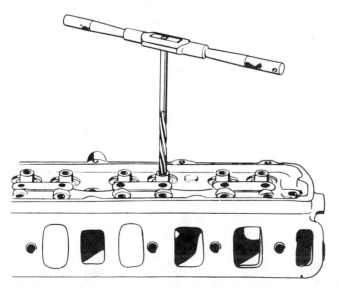

FIGURE 9–104. Reaming valve guide to oversize diameter. This procedure requires replacing valves with oversize stem valves. *(Courtesy of General Motors Corporation)*

PART 15   VALVE SEAT GRINDING AND REPLACEMENT

Seat reconditioning includes refacing the seat and correcting seat width in a manner that will provide proper seat-to-valve face contact as well as correct seat width.

Special equipment is required to correct valve seats. A high-speed driver (8000 to 12,000 rpm) is used to drive a grinding stone mounted on a pilot inserted tightly in the valve guide. Roughing stones, finishing stones, and special stones for induction hardened or stellite seats are available. When seats only require a little grinding, only the finishing stone is used. Seats that require more grinding may require the use of a roughing stone first, and then a finishing stone to complete the job. Seat grinding stones are available in a number of diameters and cutting angles to suit the various valve seat diameters and angles.

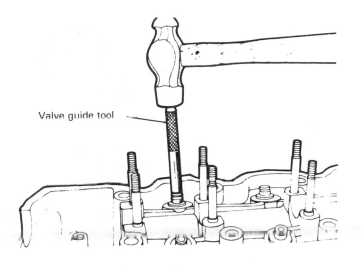

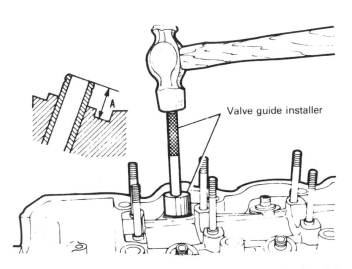

FIGURE 9-105. Replacing valve guides with special driver tool. Guides must be installed to specified depth. Typical example is shown at dimension A. *(Courtesy of Chrysler Corporation)*

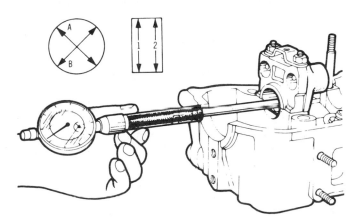

FIGURE 9-106. Measuring camshaft bearing bore taper and out of round on an overhead camshaft engine. Cam bearing caps are in place and tightened to specifications for this procedure. *(Courtesy of Chrysler Corporation)*

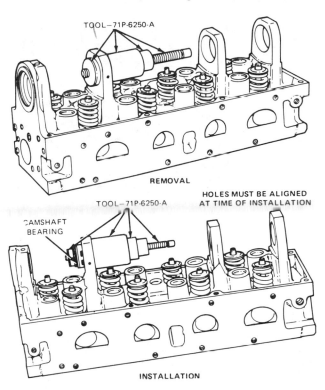

FIGURE 9-107. Replacing overhead camshaft bearings (typical). Many overhead camshaft designs do not have replaceable bearings. *(Courtesy of Ford Motor Co. of Canada Ltd.)*

Seat Replacement

Replaceable seats that are too badly damaged for correction by grinding can be replaced. Most integral seat heads can be machined and a new valve seat insert installed. Replacement valve seat inserts are slightly larger in diameter than the machined opening (counterbore) in the cylinder head. This provides an interference fit that assures good heat transfer and prevents the seat from becoming loose. This procedure usually requires cooling the seat insert sufficiently to cause it to shrink enough for easier installation. Normally, this type of work is done by specialty shops such as engine rebuilders or cylinder head rebuilders. After seat insert installation, seats must be ground to restore concentricity, squareness, correct seat width, and proper seat-to-valve face contact.

Seat Grinding

To grind the seats, select the proper diameter pilot and install it snugly in the valve guide. Select a seat grinding stone of the correct angle (same angle as the seat), usually 45° or 30°. The stone should be slightly larger in diameter than the valve head. Frequently dress the stone in the stone dressing fix-

FIGURE 9-108. Installing pilot in guide in preparation for grinding. (*Courtesy of Sioux Tools Inc.*)

ture, during the seat grinding procedure, to ensure a good seat finish.

It is a good idea to wipe the seats clean by using a piece of fine emery cloth between the stone and the seat and giving it a good hard rub. This avoids contaminating the seat grinding stone with any oil or carbon residue that may be on the valve seat. Seat grinding stones should be handled in a manner that will keep them clean. Stones will soak up oil like a blotter. This causes them to become glazed and in-effective for seat grinding. Remove only as much material from the seat as is required to provide a good finish of sufficient width all the way around the seat. Avoid any side pressure during the grind-ing process.

Grind the seat with short *bursts* only, checking frequently to inspect progress. Pressure of the stone

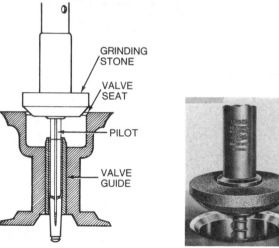

FIGURE 9-110. Grinding the valve seat. Do not remove any more material than necessary to produce a good valve seat surface. (*Courtesy of Sioux Tools Inc.*)

against the seat must be precisely controlled to avoid *chatter* and to provide a good seat finish. Ex-cessive pressure or chatter can destroy a valve seat very quickly. A drop of oil on the pilot and the star or hex drive can reduce the tendency to chatter. Avoid getting any oil on the seat or stone. *Note:* If the valve seat is too wide after grinding, it must be narrowed to specifications, usually 1/16 to 3/32 inch (1.6 mm to 2.3 millimeter), with the exhaust seat being the wider for better heat dissipation.

Seat Narrowing and Positioning

The objective in narrowing the valve seats is two-fold: (1) the seat should be the correct width, and (2) it should contact the center of the valve face. To de-termine whether overcutting or undercutting is re-

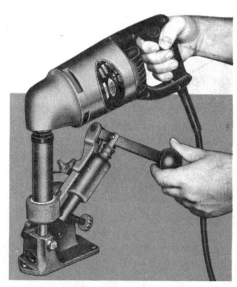

FIGURE 9-109. Dressing the seat grinding stone in preparation for seat grinding. (*Courtesy of Sioux Tools Inc.*)

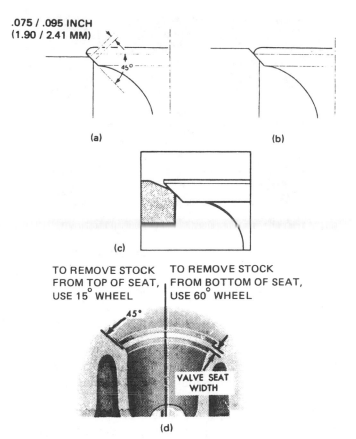

.075 / .095 INCH
(1.90 / 2.41 MM)

45°

(a)

(b)

(c)

TO REMOVE STOCK
FROM TOP OF SEAT,
USE 15° WHEEL

TO REMOVE STOCK
FROM BOTTOM OF SEAT,
USE 60° WHEEL

45°

VALVE SEAT
WIDTH

(d)

FIGURE 9–111. (a) Proper valve seat to face contact. (b) A seat that is too wide and requires overcutting to correct. (c) Corrected valve seat. (d) Method of valve seat narrowing. *(Courtesy of Sioux Tools Inc.* [a,b, and c] *and Ford Motor Co. of Canada Ltd.* [d]*)*

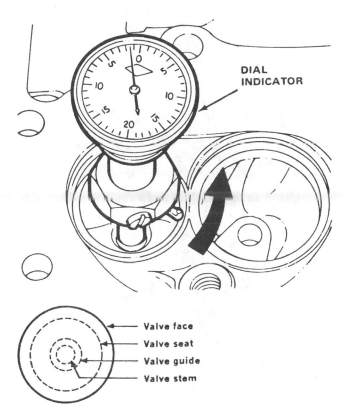

DIAL
INDICATOR

Valve face
Valve seat
Valve guide
Valve stem

FIGURE 9–112. Checking valve seat concentricity with special gauge. The gauge is turned in the direction of the arrow. As indicated, valve face, seat, guide, and stem must all be concentric. *(Courtesy of American Motors Corporation)*

quired to narrow the valve seat, a new or reconditioned valve must be used.

Overcutting is done in the same manner as seat grinding, except that a 15° stone is used for the purpose. This narrows the seat from the combustion chamber side and lowers the point of contact on the valve face (farther from the margin).

Undercutting is done similarly with a 60° stone, which narrows the seat from the port side.

To determine where the seat contacts the valve face, use the new or reconditioned valve. Mark the valve face with a series of pencil marks across the face of the valve all around the valve. Insert the valve in the guide, press down on the valve, and turn it one quarter-turn and back. Remove the valve and check the pencil marks. The pencil marks will be wiped out at the point where the seat contacts the valve. (Because of the interference angle, only the edge of the seat on the combustion chamber side will wipe out the pencil marks.) This should be about one-third of the way down on the face of the valve away from the margin to center the seat on the valve face. Turning the valve only one quarter-turn while in contact with the seat provides the means for check-

ing whether or not the seat is concentric. If the pencil marks are wiped out at one point all the way around the valve, seat concentricity is within limits. If the guide, seat, and valve have all been properly reconditioned, they will be concentric (centered in relation to each other). Concentricity is required to provide a good seal between the valve and seat.

PART 16   VALVE GRINDING

After the valves have been thoroughly cleaned and inspected, those that passed the inspection should be reconditioned. Some valve refacing equipment requires that valve reconditioning procedures follow a specific sequence. Valve refacers that support the valve tip in a coned shaft require the valve tip to be dressed and chamfered before it is refaced. If this is not done, the valve face will be ground off center. Equipment manufacturer's instructions for procedures and sequence should be followed.

To recondition a valve, the tip should be dressed and chamfered and the valve refaced. Remove only enough material to produce the desired results. If

FIGURE 9-113. Dressing a worn valve stem tip. *(Courtesy of Sioux Tools Inc.)*

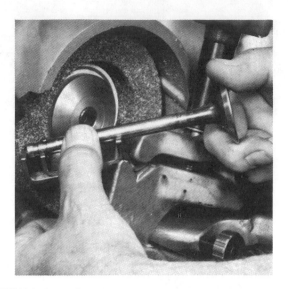

FIGURE 9-114. Chamfering a valve stem tip. *(Courtesy of Sioux Tools Inc.)*

too much material is removed from the valve tip, there may be interference between the rocker arm and spring retainer or valve rotator. Follow manufacturer's specifications for the allowable limits.

A bent or distorted valve will be easily noticed as the valve rotates in the machine. Valves damaged in this way should be replaced. Valves with insufficient (1/32 inch or 0.8 millimeter minimum) margin after refacing should also be replaced.

Valve stem length must be checked on some engines that have no provision for valve-train adjustment. Material removed from the valve face and valve seat increases the amount of valve stem length on the spring side of the cylinder head when the valve is seated. If excessive, this could cause the hydraulic lifter plunger to *bottom out* and prevent the valve from being fully seated when it is closed. A special tool is used to measure stem length on the

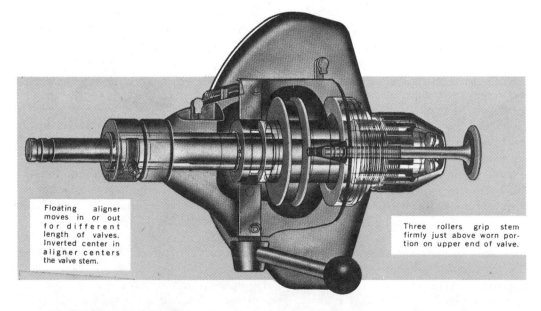

Floating aligner moves in or out for different length of valves. Inverted center in aligner centers the valve stem.

Three rollers grip stem firmly just above worn portion on upper end of valve.

FIGURE 9-115. Valve properly positioned in valve reface chuck. Chuck jaws must clamp valve on unworn machined surface of stem. Adjust floating shaft to support valve stem tip properly.

FIGURE 9-116. Refacing valve. Carriage lever is used to move valve across full width of stone during grinding. Valve must not be allowed to move off the edge of the stone during this operation. Both the valve face and the stone become rounded if this is allowed to happen. Valve must not be removed from chuck until grinding is completed. To inspect valve face, back stone away from valve, then move carriage and valve away from stone. *(Courtesy of Sioux Tools Inc.)*

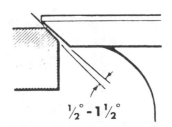

½° - 1½°

FIGURE 9-118. Grinding the valve at an angle of ½° to 1 ½° less than the seat produces an interference angle as shown. This provides a high pressure seal on the combustion chamber side of the valve and seat. *(Courtesy of Sioux Tools Inc.)*

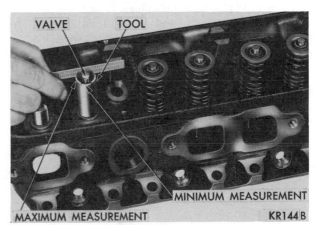

VALVE   TOOL

MINIMUM MEASUREMENT

MAXIMUM MEASUREMENT   KR144B

FIGURE 9-119. Some engines that do not have a valve lash adjustment require measuring the valve stem length. Grinding material from the stem tip corrects valve stem length and centers the hydraulic lifter plunger. Do not remove more material from the valve stem than the maximum allowed in the shop manual. Measurement must be done after valve and seat have been reconditioned. *(Courtesy of Chrysler Corporation)*

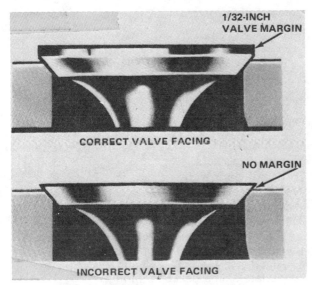

1/32-INCH VALVE MARGIN

CORRECT VALVE FACING

NO MARGIN

INCORRECT VALVE FACING

FIGURE 9-117. Reconditioned valve should have at least 1/32 inch of margin to prevent overheating and valve burning. *(Courtesy of American Motors Corporation)*

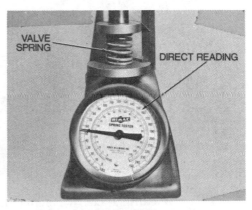

VALVE SPRING

DIRECT READING

FIGURE 9-120. Testing valve spring pressure. Springs are usually tested at two heights: the valve closed height and the valve open height. Pressures and heights should be within manufacturer's specifications. *(Courtesy of Ford Motor Co. of Canada Ltd.)*

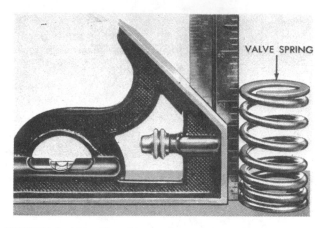

FIGURE 9-121. Checking valve springs for distortion. Spring should be checked at two locations 90° from each other. Maximum allowable distortion is usually no more than 1/16 inch. (*Courtesy of Chrysler Corporation*)

spring side of the head when the valve is held in its seated position.

Valve springs should be checked for acid etching, squareness, and pressures. Springs that do not meet manufacturer's specifications should be replaced. Valve spring installed height should be measured and corrected with shims if required.

Rocker arm studs that are damaged should be replaced. Some studs are threaded into the head; others are installed with an interference fit. A special tool is required to replace the interference fit stud. A stud remover can be used to replace threaded studs.

PART 17   ASSEMBLING THE CYLINDER HEAD

All cylinder head parts, valves springs, and the like should be absolutely clean for assembly. Valve stems and seats should be lubricated with engine oil during assembly. Make sure intake and exhaust valve springs are properly installed. Umbrella-type

FIGURE 9-122. Measuring the valve spring installed height. Material removed from valve face and seat can alter spring installed height and cause insufficient spring pressure. To correct, install appropriate shims between spring and head. Shims should not be used to correct springs that have failed the spring pressure test, Figure 9-120. (*Courtesy of Ford Motor Co. of Canada Ltd.*)

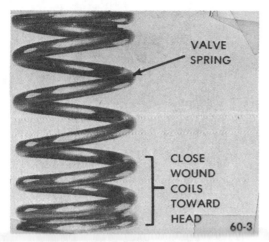

FIGURE 9-123. Correct method of spring assembly. *(Courtesy of General Motors Corporation)*

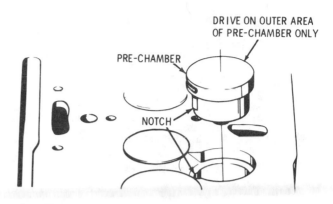

FIGURE 9-125. Prechamber on diesel engine head must be properly indexed with head during installation. *(Courtesy of General Motors Corporation)*

valve stem seals are installed on the valve stem before the spring is installed. Stem seals of the O-ring type that make the spring retainer act as an oil shedder are installed after the spring is compressed. The O ring is installed in the groove closest to the head; then the valve locks are installed.

Install valve rotators above or below the spring as specified by the manufacturer. Valve spring shims are installed between the spring and the head (if required). Variable-rate springs are usually installed with the closest spaced coils toward the cylinder head.

On engines with overhead camshafts, the valve operating mechanism and camshaft may require assembly before cylinder head installation and may require special tools. Follow the sequence specified by the manufacturer.

On diesel engines, install the precombustion chambers as required. Be sure to observe specifications regarding installation depth, protrusion, and indexing of prechambers. Install the injectors and

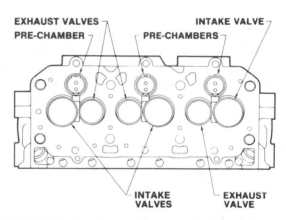

FIGURE 9-126. Prechambers correctly installed in V6 diesel engine head. *(Courtesy of General Motors Corporation)*

FIGURE 9-124. Umbrella-type valve stem seal is installed before spring and retainer are assembled. *(Courtesy of Ford Motor Co. of Canada Ltd.)*

FIGURE 9-127. Using guide studs assures gasket alignment, avoids gasket damage, and guides head into place. *(Courtesy of Ford Motor Co. of Canada Ltd.)*

FIGURE 9-128. Always tighten cylinder head bolts in proper sequence and in steps as specified in the appropriate shop manual for the engine being serviced. *(Courtesy of Chrysler Corporation)*

FIGURE 9-129. Rocker shaft assembly must be assembled and installed as specified in shop manual to ensure alignment of lubrication passages and correct location of special mounting bolts. Tighten mounting bolts down evenly, a little at a time, to prevent shaft distortion. Tighten to specified torque. *(Courtesy of Ford Motor Co. of Canada Ltd.)*

glow plugs. Follow all specifications regarding the use of new gaskets, seals, and O rings. Install injectors and glow plugs in the exact positions specified regarding indexing of fuel line fittings, and other connections. Torque glow plugs, injectors, clamping devices, and fuel line connections to specified torque.

Installing the Cylinder Head

Gasket surfaces, bolts, and bolt holes should be absolutely clean. Coat new gasket and cylinder bolt threads with recommended sealer (if specified by manufacturer) and position the head gasket on engine block. Make sure head gasket is installed right side up and correct end forward.

Carefully lower cylinder head into place without bumping or shifting the gasket. A slight nick in the gasket can cause gasket failure.

Install cylinder head bolts making sure bolts are in correct location if they are not of equal length. Tighten all bolts in the proper sequence in three steps and to specified torque to ensure good sealing.

If specified by manufacturer's shop manual, cylinder head bolts should be retorqued to specifications after the engine has been run and brought to operation temperature.

PART 18 VALVE MECHANISM SERVICE AND ADJUSTMENT

Pushrods should be inspected for wear and run-out. If pushrods are bent, they should be replaced. Make sure oil passages through pushrods are clear. Lubricate both ends of pushrods and install with proper end up and seated in lifters.

Rocker arms that are worn or damaged at the pushrod seat, the valve stem end, or the pivot area should be replaced. Oil passages should be clear and clean. Make sure the rocker arms are installed in the correct location. (Some rocker arms are offset.) The pivot area, the pushrod seat, and the valve tip end of the rocker arm should be lubricated during assembly.

The ball pivots, pedestal, or rocker shafts should be replaced if worn. If rocker stud nuts do not meet breakaway torque specifications, they should be replaced.

Procedure for Adjusting Valve Train

The objective in adjusting the mechanical lifter valve train is to provide sufficient valve lash (clearance) to allow for any expansion of parts due to heat and still ensure that valves will be fully seated when closed. At the same time, there must not be excessive lash, which would retard valve timing and cause rapid wear of valve-train parts.

The objective in adjusting the hydraulic lifter valve train is to center the plunger in the hydraulic lifter. This provides a zero lash in operation and allows the lifters to adjust automatically to compensate for wear or expansion and contraction of valve-train parts due to temperature changes.

The basic method for adjusting the valve train as described in Figure 9-130 is for a static valve adjustment. The static valve adjustment is required after an engine overhaul to ensure proper engine starting and prevent damage to the valves from pistons hitting the valves. Normally, if the static valves

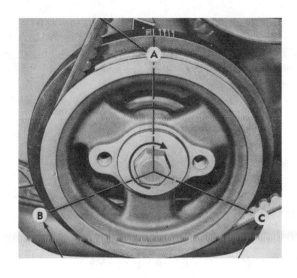

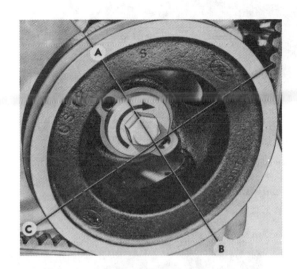

FIGURE 9-130. A static valve adjustment must be performed prior to starting an engine that has been overhauled. To adjust valves, proceed as follows:
(A) Put piston 1 in firing position (TDC at top of compression stroke).
(B) Adjust both valves for cylinder 1 to specifications.
(C) Turn crankshaft clockwise (as above) 120° for six-cylinder engines, 90° for eight-cylinder engines, 180° for four-cylinder engines. This places the next cylinder in the firing order sequence in position for valve adjustment.
(D) Adjust both valves for this cylinder.
(E) Repeat steps C and D until all valves for all cylinders have been adjusted.
(Courtesy of Ford Motor Co. of Canada Ltd.)

are adjusted accurately, no further valve adjustment is required, unless the cylinder heads are re-tightened.

Valve adjustment is sometimes done as a routine service procedure when there is no engine overhaul involved. This is often done with the engine running at a slow idle speed. When this is done, provision must be made to prevent oil from squirting and spraying over other engine parts. Also, when adjusting hydraulic lifter valve trains under these conditions, the adjusting screw or nut must be turned down slowly enough to allow for lifter leakdown and prevent the valve from being held open when it should be closed. Care must be taken not to overadjust and cause the lifters to bottom out and damage valve-train parts. Adjustment should only be made within the limits prescribed in the manufacturer's shop manual.

The *solid lifter valve train* usually has an adjusting screw of the self-locking type provided at the pushrod end of the rocker arm. Clearance or lash is measured between the valve stem and rocker arm

with a feeler gauge. Turning the adjusting screw will increase or decrease the amount of lash, depending on which direction the screw is being turned. Valves should be adjusted to specifications. A cold engine lash adjustment is usually 0.002 inch (0.05 millimeter) greater than the specifications for a hot engine.

The *hydraulic lifter valve train* may be of the adjustable or nonadjustable type. The adjustable type has an adjusting screw at the pushrod end of the rocker arm or an adjusting nut at the rocker arm stud; these are of the self-locking type.

Adjustment is normally made by backing off (loosening) the adjuster until zero lash is obtained, and then the adjusting screw or nut is turned down the specified number of turns. This completes the adjustment. Each cylinder is done in turn as shown in Figure 9-130.

The nonadjustable type of hydraulic lifter valve train may have selective-length pushrods available to center the lifter plunger, or correction may be made during the valve grinding procedure by cor-

FIGURE 9-131. Some engines have an adjusting screw on the rocker to adjust valve lash. *(Courtesy of Ford Motor Co. of Canada Ltd.)*

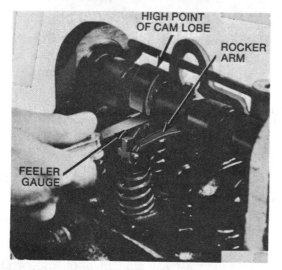

FIGURE 9-132. Measuring valve lash on overhead cam engine. *(Courtesy of Ford Motor Co. of Canada Ltd.)*

FIGURE 9-133. Intake manifold bolts must be tightened in sequence of steps specified in manufacturer's manual. *(Courtesy of Chrysler Corporation)*

recting valve stem length, as described earlier in this chapter. On engines using the selective-length pushrods, special tools are used to determine the correct length of pushrod to be used. Procedures and specifications as outlined in the appropriate shop manual must be followed to make the proper selection of pushrods.

Overhead camshaft valve-train adjustments also vary and include adjustable rocker arms, an adjustable lifter, an adjusting screw and wedge arrangement, and shims to provide the adjustment. Basic procedures are the same as for I-head valve trains described earlier.

PART 19 FINAL ASSEMBLY, INSTALLATION, AND START-UP PROCEDURE

Completing the engine assembly includes installing the intake and exhaust manifolds, carburetor, starter, distributor, water pump, emission-control devices, fuel pump, injectors, glow plugs, and motor mounts. If the transmission was removed after engine removal, it should now be installed. All bolts should be tightened to specifications and in the proper sequence as specified in the shop manual. Make sure torque converter drive bolts are properly aligned and tightened.

Normally, all these items should be inspected, cleaned, corrected, or replaced as needed before installation on a rebuilt engine.

The engine is installed into the previously cleaned engine compartment in a manner similar to that used to remove the engine. In general, the following procedure should be followed:

• Lower engine carefully into engine compartment with the engine at an angle which is lower at the rear.

• Carefully guide engine into place as it is being lowered, at the same time leveling the engine to its normal position.

• If engine and transmission are being installed as an assembly, carefully raise the rear of the assembly to allow cross-member installation.

• If transmission was left in the vehicle, avoid damage to clutch disc (standard transmission) or flex plate (automatic transmission) during alignment procedure.

• Connect bell housing to engine and tighten all attaching bolts to specifications (automatic transmission).

• Connect transmission to bell housing (standard transmission) and tighten all bolts to specifications.

- Align and connect torque converter; tighten converter drive bolts to specifications.

- Align motor mounts and tighten bolts to specifications.

- Remove engine lift attachment.

- Attach exhaust pipes with new gaskets.

- Make all electrical, fuel, and emission control connections; attach all linkages and install new oil filter.

- Install radiator and hoses.

- Fill cooling system with correct antifreeze solution (including reserve tank).

- Install specified amount of recommended engine oil, including allowance for oil filter.

- Install fully charged battery; make sure all connections are clean and tight.

- Make sure all connections are properly made and are tight before starting engine.

- Start engine and observe engine oil pressure to be sure system is operating normally.

- Set engine idle speed to approximately 1000 rpm.

- Observe oil pressure, coolant temperature indicator, and charge indicator to make sure all systems are operating properly.

- While the engine is running, carefully check for any oil or coolant leaks (correct if necessary); engine should be run until normal operating temperature is reached.

- If specified in shop manual, retorque cylinder heads after engine has reached operating temperature. (If heads are retorqued, valve adjustment may have to be corrected.).

- Install hood in accordance with scribe marks made when hood was removed.

- Correct coolant level if required.

PART 20 ENGINE BREAK-IN PROCEDURE

To assure proper seating of the rings, proper engine break-in procedures should be followed. The following procedure can be used to achieve good break-in. Road test the vehicle as follows:

- Select a section of road where the procedures can safely be followed.

- While driving at 30 mph (48 kmh), accelerate rapidly to 50 mph (80 kmh); then immediately decelerate to 30 mph (48 kmh) again.

- Repeat this procedure at least ten times.

This procedure heavily loads the rings on acceleration (high ring-to-cylinder wall pressure) and assures adequate lubrication of rings and cylinders on deceleration. This assures good seating of the rings. If proper ring seating is not achieved, an oil consumption problem may result.

After the break-in procedure, the vehicle should be returned to the shop and a thorough inspection made to ensure that there are no oil or coolant leaks and that fluid levels are correct.

The vehicle should now be prepared for customer acceptance by making sure that it is clean both inside and out.

The customer should be informed that it is good practice to change the engine oil and filter after the first 500 miles (800 kilometers) of driving. This removes any minor impurities and bits of metal that may have remained as a result of the overhaul. The vehicle can be driven normally after the break-in procedure.

PART 21 SELF-CHECK

1. It is important that engine disassembly be done _____ and in a proper _____.

2. Before the pistons can be removed, the cylinder _____ must be removed.

3. Main bearing caps and connecting rods are identified by _____.

4. Cylinders are measured to determine (a)_____,(b)_____,(c)_____.

5. Cylinder reconditioning requires that the cylinder wall finish have a _____pattern of _____ inch finish.

6. Cylinders with excessive taper are usually _____and fitted with _____pistons.

7. What is the purpose of align boring main bearing bores?

8. How is deck warpage measured?

9. Camshaft bearings are always the same size on any one engine. True or false?

10. A camshaft should be replaced if _____or _____ is excessive.

11. The crankshaft should be measured to determine main and rod bearing journal (a)_____, (b)_____, (c)_____, (d)_____.

12. The inside diameter of undersized main bearings is (larger) (smaller) than standard main bearings.

13. The most convenient way to measure bearing clearances is to use _____.

14. The connecting rod should be checked for _____ and _____.

15. A piston with a worn ring groove must be replaced. True of false?

16. It is not economically practical to spend much time on cleaning hydraulic lifters. True or false?

17. What are the generally accepted maximum limits allowed for cylinder head warpage?

18. To measure valve stem-to-guide clearance, a _____ is used.

19. Name three methods used to correct excessive valve stem-to-guide clearance.

20. To recondition the valve guide, the seat must be reconditioned first. True or false?

21. A properly reconditioned valve seat must meet at least three conditions. These are (a) _____, (b)_____, (c)_____.

22. A refaced valve must have at least _____ inch of margin to be serviceable.

23. Valve springs must be tested to assure (a)_____, (b)_____, (c)_____.

24. Gaskets should be examined, and if in reasonable condition, they should be used again. True or false?

25. A static valve adjustment is required after an engine overhaul to assure _____ and prevent _____.

PART 22   TEST QUESTIONS

1. Engine cylinders are measured to determine:
   (a) size, out of round, wear
   (b) clearance, size, out of round
   (c) out of round, stroke, wear
   (d) wear, clearance, out of round

2. Mechanic A says the cylinder ridge develops over a period of time as the result of combustion deposits. Mechanic B says the cylinder ridge develops as the result of metal removal by the rings. Who is right?
   (a) Mechanic A
   (b) Mechanic B
   (c) both are right
   (d) both are wrong

3. Excessive piston to cylinder clearance can cause:
   (a) piston slap
   (b) pin knock
   (c) ring slap
   (d) bearing knock

4. An undersized main bearing is one that has a:
   (a) smaller outside diameter and standard inside diameter
   (b) smaller inside diameter and standard outside diameter
   (c) smaller inside diameter and smaller outside diameter
   (d) larger bearing area but smaller outside diameter

5. Pistons should be measured to determine if they are worn:
   (a) across the thrust surfaces
   (b) in the ring grooves
   (c) in the pin bores
   (d) all of the above

6. Crankshaft measurements determine:
   (a) journal wear, thrust surface wear, and main journal alignment
   (b) rod journal alignment, end play, and thrust surface wear
   (c) end play, bearing clearance, and rod journal wear
   (d) rod and main journal size, taper, out of round, alignment, and thrust surface wear

7. Crankshaft main journal out of round should not exceed:
   (a) .001 inch (0.0254mm)
   (b) .0001 inch (0.00254mm)
   (c) .01 inch (0.254mm)
   (d) .10 inch (2.54mm)

8. The in-block camshaft for a V 6 engine has:
   (a) 3 lobes
   (b) 24 lobes
   (c) 6 lobes
   (d) 12 lobes

9. One camshaft of an overhead cam V 8 has:
   (a) 8 lobes
   (b) 16 lobes
   (c) 32 lobes
   (d) 4 lobes

10. Mechanic A says a four-cylinder engine will have 6000 power strokes in one minute at 3000 rpm. Mechanic B says each valve will open and close 3000 times in two minutes at 3000 rpm on a six-cylinder engine. Who is right?
    (a) Mechanic A

(b) Mechanic B

(c) both are right

(d) both are wrong

11. Mechanic A says cylinder head bolts should be tightened in sequence from front to back. Mechanic B says each cylinder head bolt should be tightened to full torque one after the other then retorqued. Who is right?

(a) Mechanic A

(b) Mechanic B

(c) both are right

(d) both are wrong

12. As bearing clearance increases, plastigauge becomes:

(a) narrower

(b) wide

(c) longer

(d) shorter

13. Connecting rod numbers on a V 8 engine are stamped:

(a) on the side of each rod

(b) on the front of each rod

(c) on the cap and rod on the side facing the camshaft

(d) on the cap and rod on the side opposite the camshaft

14. You are required to replace engine main bearings. Standard main bearing diameter is 2.080 inches. The crankshaft main journal measurement is 2.070 inches. What size bearings are required?

(a) standard size bearings

(b) .001 inch undersize

(c) .010 inch undersize

(d) .100 inch undersize

15. The rebuilder of an engine left out the oil pump pressure regulator valve spring. This would result in:

(a) no engine oil pressure

(b) very high engine oil pressure

(c) no by-pass oil when the filter is plugged

(d) filter drain back when the engine is stopped

16. Mechanic A says that taper-faced rings should be installed with the largest diameter to the top. Mechanic B says that scraper ring gaps on a three-piece oil ring should be installed with the gaps aligned with each other. Who is right?

(a) Mechanic A

(b) Mechanic B

(c) both are right

(d) both are wrong

17. Main bearing bore misalignment is corrected by:

(a) replacing main bearings

(b) replacing the crankshaft

(c) replacing the main bearing caps

(d) line boring

18. Oil pump wear is determined by measuring:

(a) gear backlash, gear to housing clearance

(b) rotor tip clearance, rotor to housing clearance

(c) gear to cover clearance, rotor to cover clearance

(d) all of the above

19. Cylinder deglazing is required to:

(a) assure proper clearances

(b) ensure proper ring seating

(c) ensure good piston fit

(d) none of the above

20. Valve, seat, and guide reconditioning should be done in the following order:

(a) valve first then the seat and guide

(b) seat first then the guide and valve

(c) seat first then the valve and guide

(d) guide first then the seat and valve

21. Excessive valve stem-to-guide clearance can be corrected by:

(a) reaming the guides and fitting oversize stem valves

(b) replacing the guides

(c) knurling the guides

(d) all of the above

22. Mechanic A says a good valve seat must be within specified width limits. Mechanic B says a good valve seat must contact the center of the valve face. Who is right?

(a) Mechanic A

(b) Mechanic B

(c) both are right

(d) both are wrong

23. Excessive oil consumption may be caused by:

(a) ring wear, cylinder wear, and valve stem wear

(b) cylinder wear and valve guide wear

(c) valve guide wear and valve stem wear

(d) all of the above

24. Noisy valve lifters may be caused by:

(a) low oil level

(b) worn valve guides

(c) worn camshaft

(d) all of the above

25. The cylinder ridge should be removed to:
    (a) facilitate new ring installation
    (b) prevent the piston from striking the ridge
    (c) ensure proper piston to cylinder clearance
    (d) prevent the top ring from striking the ridge

26. Noisy connecting rods may be caused by excessive bearing clearance. Noisy connecting rods may be caused by low oil pressure. Which statement is correct?
    (a) only the first one
    (b) only the second one
    (c) both are wrong
    (d) both are right

27. Detonation may damage the:
    (a) piston rings and valve stem seals
    (b) valve stem seals and pistons
    (c) pistons and spark plugs
    (d) spark plugs and valve stem seals

28. An oil level that is too high may cause:
    (a) oil consumption
    (b) noisy lifters
    (c) erratic oil pressure
    (d) all of the above

29. Noisy pistons may be caused by a collapsed piston. Piston slap may disappear when the engine reaches operating temperature. Which statement is correct?
    (a) the first one only
    (b) the second one only
    (c) both are wrong
    (d) both are right

30. Mechanic A says that valve float may be caused by weak valve springs. Mechanic B says that lifter pump up may be caused by valve float. Who is right?
    (a) Mechanic A
    (b) Mechanic B
    (c) both are right
    (d) both are wrong

Section 3

AIR, FUEL, AND EXHAUST SYSTEMS

The automotive air, fuel, and exhaust systems are designed to provide the correct amounts of air and fuel to the engine under all operating conditions and power demands. Fuel enrichment must be provided for starting cold engines. Adjustments to the air/fuel ratio must be made for high altitude operation and for hot engine idle conditions. This must all be achieved with minimal exhaust emissions as well as acceptable performance and economy. In addition, the exhaust system must provide the means for collecting the exhaust gases from each engine cylinder and directing them to a convenient location for release into the atmosphere. The exhaust system must dampen engine exhaust noise to an acceptable level without excessive restriction to exhaust flow. The exhaust system, in many cases, must also reduce the harmful emissions contained in exhaust gases before releasing them into the atmosphere.

A number of different types of each of these three systems currently in use are designed to achieve these results. Air supply systems include naturally aspirated systems and turbocharged systems. Fuel systems include: (1) the conventional car-buretor equipped system, many with electronically controlled fuel metering and altitude compensating devices; (2) the gasoline fuel injection system, some with port injection and others with throttle body injection, both electronically controlled; (3) the diesel fuel injection system; and (4) the propane (LPG or liquified petroleum gas) fuel system.

All of these systems are based on similar operating principles and are designed to achieve optimum results in performance, economy, and emissions standards. A compromise between these three objectives is, however, unavoidable in design considerations since it is not possible to achieve the optimum results in all three areas at the same time. For example, some degree of performance must be sacrificed to achieve acceptable economy and emissions, whereas the reverse is also true. Designers are faced with government regulations regarding emissions standards and fuel economy, and with consumer demands for performance, economy, and low emissions. This section of the text deals with the systems designed to achieve these results.

Chapter 10

Air Supply Systems

Performance Objectives

After thorough study of this chapter and sufficient practical experience on adequate training models, and with the appropriate shop manuals and equipment, you should be able to do the following:

1. Complete the self-check and test questions with at least 80 percent accuracy.
2. Follow the accepted general precautions outlined in this chapter.
3. Diagnose basic air supply system problems according to the diagnostic charts provided.
4. Safely remove, recondition, replace, and adjust any faulty air supply system components according to manufacturer's specifications.
5. Properly performance test the reconditioned system to determine the success of the repairs performed.
6. Prepare the vehicle for customer acceptance.

The air supply system must provide adequate air to each of the engine's cylinders for proper combustion during all phases of engine operation.

The air supply system includes all the components of the air cleaner assembly and the intake manifold on naturally aspirated engines. On turbocharged engines, it also includes the turbocharger and its control system, as well as that part of the exhaust system designed to operate the turbocharger.

On carbureted systems, the air flow portion of the carburetor forms an essential part of the air supply system. However, the carburetor will be discussed later in this section.

PART 1   AIR CLEANERS

The air cleaner is needed to protect the engine and fuel system from the harmful effects of dirt and abrasives present in air.

The air cleaner is not only an air filter, it is also an intake air temperature control system, an air silencer, and a flame arrestor (in case of engine backfire).

Depending on design and on the type of fuel system, the air cleaner may be mounted directly to a flange on the carburetor air horn, the fuel injection throttle body, or the intake manifold (on diesel engines). On any of these systems, it may also be mounted in a more remote location on the engine or engine compartment to reduce overall height. In this design, the air cleaner is connected to the carburetor, air horn, throttle body, or manifold by an air transfer duct.

All incoming air must pass through the filter element before entering the engine. This means that the air inlet system must be sealed to prevent unfiltered air (possibly containing abrasives) from bypassing the filter and entering the engine.

The air cleaner also provides filtered air to the positive crankcase ventilation system. Crankcase vapors may be directed to the air cleaner under heavy acceleration or heavy engine load conditions.

Filter Elements

Filter elements must be of precise dimension for any particular air cleaner to provide a seal at top and bottom to prevent any intake air from bypassing the filter. When installed with the air cleaner cover in place, the filter element is under slight compression to ensure sealing.

Filter elements usually consist of a special paper bellows between two sealing surfaces. An inside and an outside wire screen, or perforated metal screen, help support the paper element between the top and bottom seals. Element height, circumference, thickness, and spacing of bellows determine total available filter surface area. Filter element porosity is a factor in filtering effectiveness.

Some air cleaners use a synthetic foam pad around the outside of the paper element to increase filter effectiveness. This pad is moistened with oil in some instances to further increase its ability to entrap dirt.

Some carbureted engines are equipped with a carbon impregnated filter element which allows the air cleaner to act as a vapor storage area. This is used on some carburetors equipped with an open internal bowl vent. This type of filter element is quite dark in appearance and should not be mistaken for a dirty air filter.

Air Cleaner Capacity

The capacity of an air cleaner refers to its ability to deliver filtered air to the engine. This capacity is expressed in cubic feet (or cubic meters) of air flow per minute. The capacity of the air cleaner is specifically designed to meet the requirements of the particular engine on which it is used. Air cleaners are designed with sufficient overcapacity to allow for normal restriction caused by dirt between filter change intervals.

Air cleaner capacity must match engine displacement and operating speed ranges. Diesel engines require larger capacity air cleaners than do gasoline engines of the same size since diesel engines consume larger amounts of air. Some diesel engine air cleaners have a muffler in the snorkel tube to help reduce the noise of air rushing into the air cleaner.

PART 2 INTAKE AIR TEMPERATURE CONTROL SYSTEM

The temperature controlled air cleaner system provides heated intake air to the engine during warm up. Heated intake air improves engine performance during warm up, minimizes carburetor icing, and allows for leaner air/fuel mixtures that reduce hydrocarbon emissions.

The system supplies: (1) all heated air, (2) a mixture of heated air and ambient (outside) air, or (3) all ambient air. During high underhood temperature conditions or when ambient temperatures are high, no heated air is provided. This prevents excessively high temperature inlet air from entering the carburetor or engine. Excessively high intake air temperatures adversely affect both carburetor and engine operation.

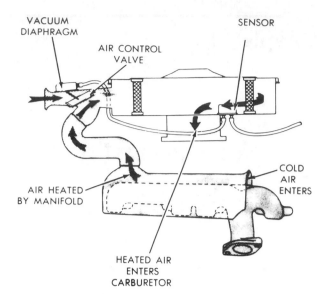

FIGURE 10-1. Carburetor inlet-air temperature control system. *(Courtesy of Chrysler Corporation)*

A typical air temperature control system uses a valve in the air cleaner inlet to control the source of inlet air. The position of this valve determines whether only heated air (a mixture of heated and ambient air) or only ambient air will be admitted to the engine. The valve is operated by a vacuum motor that acts against spring pressure.

A metal shroud surrounding the exhaust manifold collects manifold heat and directs it to the air cleaner through a connecting duct. Outside air is delivered to the air cleaner through connecting ducts. The control valve is positioned between these connections in the air cleaner snorkel in a position that allows closing of either passage or any position in between.

Vacuum to the vacuum diaphragm is controlled by a thermal vacuum switch located in the air cleaner. Intake air temperature acting on the thermal vacuum switch determines the degree of vacuum allowed to reach the vacuum diaphragm.

When the engine is cold, only heated air is allowed to reach the engine. As the engine warms up, an increasing amount of outside air mixes with the heated air. When intake air temperature is slightly above 100°F (38°C), the valve modulates heated and ambient air to maintain air temperature at about the 100°F (38°C) range. The result is a closely controlled intake air temperature which improves engine performance and reduces emissions.

When the engine is shut off, vacuum to the vacuum motor is no longer present. The spring in the vacuum motor causes the door in the snorkel to close the heated air opening and open the fresh air passage. As soon as the cold engine is started, the fresh air passage closes, and the heated air passage opens.

Under heavy acceleration (engine cold), intake

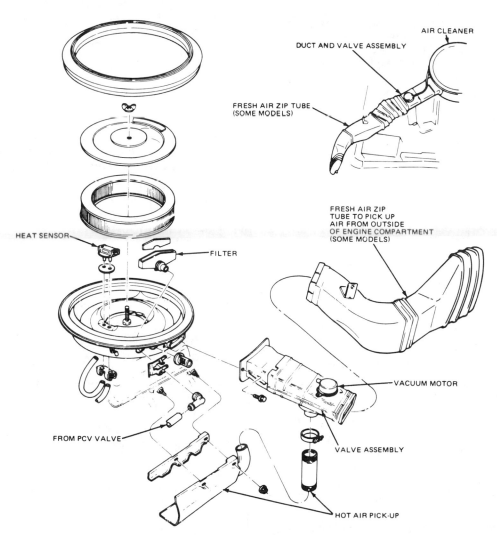

FIGURE 10-2. Exploded view of carburetor inlet-air temperature control system. Note fresh-air duct and tube that takes air in from outside the vehicle. *(Courtesy of Ford Motor Co. of Canada Ltd.)*

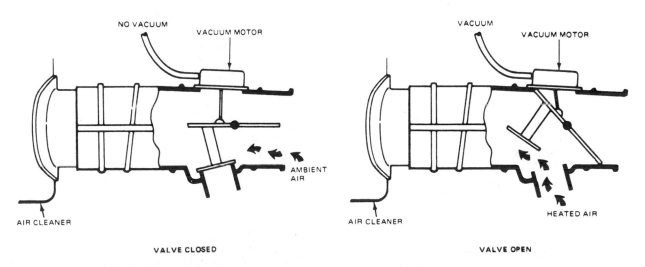

FIGURE 10-3. Vacuum motor operates air valve in air cleaner snorkel. *(Courtesy of Ford Motor Co. of Canada Ltd.)*

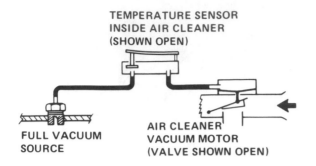

TEMPERATURE SENSOR
INSIDE AIR CLEANER
(SHOWN OPEN)

FULL VACUUM
SOURCE

AIR CLEANER
VACUUM MOTOR
(VALVE SHOWN OPEN)

FIGURE 10-4. Bimetal switch senses underhood air cleaner temperatures and controls vacuum-to-vacuum motor. *(Courtesy of Ford Motor Co. of Canada Ltd.)*

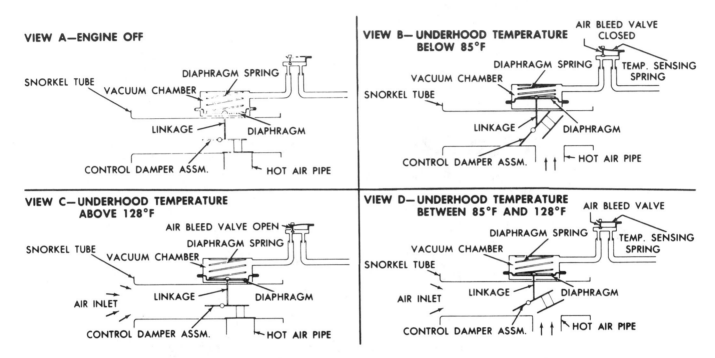

VIEW A—ENGINE OFF

SNORKEL TUBE
VACUUM CHAMBER
DIAPHRAGM SPRING
LINKAGE
DIAPHRAGM
CONTROL DAMPER ASSM.
HOT AIR PIPE

**VIEW B— UNDERHOOD TEMPERATURE
BELOW 85°F**

AIR BLEED VALVE
CLOSED
DIAPHRAGM SPRING
VACUUM CHAMBER
TEMP. SENSING
SPRING
SNORKEL TUBE
LINKAGE
DIAPHRAGM
CONTROL DAMPER ASSM.
HOT AIR PIPE

**VIEW C—UNDERHOOD TEMPERATURE
ABOVE 128°F**

AIR BLEED VALVE OPEN
DIAPHRAGM SPRING
SNORKEL TUBE
VACUUM CHAMBER
AIR INLET
LINKAGE
DIAPHRAGM
CONTROL DAMPER ASSM.
HOT AIR PIPE

**VIEW D—UNDERHOOD TEMPERATURE
BETWEEN 85°F AND 128°F**

AIR BLEED VALVE
DIAPHRAGM SPRING
VACUUM CHAMBER
TEMP. SENSING
SPRING
SNORKEL TUBE
AIR INLET
LINKAGE
DIAPHRAGM
CONTROL DAMPER ASSM.
HOT AIR PIPE

FIGURE 10-5. Schematic of air temperature control system under varying conditions. *(Courtesy of General Motors Corporation)*

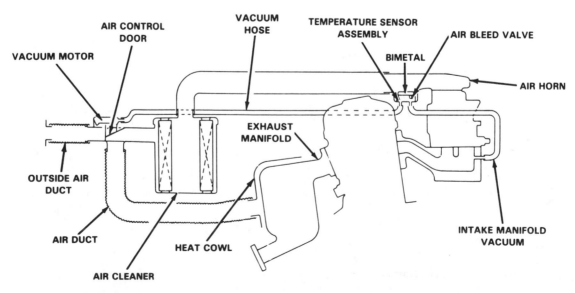

VACUUM MOTOR
AIR CONTROL
DOOR
VACUUM
HOSE
TEMPERATURE SENSOR
ASSEMBLY
AIR BLEED VALVE
BIMETAL
AIR HORN
EXHAUST
MANIFOLD
OUTSIDE AIR
DUCT
AIR DUCT
HEAT COWL
AIR CLEANER
INTAKE MANIFOLD
VACUUM

FIGURE 10-6. Typical remote-mounted air cleaner schematic diagram. *(Courtesy of Chrysler Corporation)*

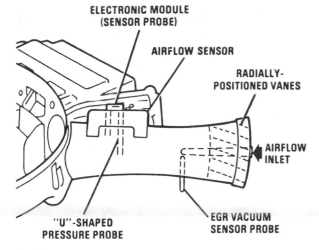

ELECTRONIC MODULE
(SENSOR PROBE)

AIRFLOW SENSOR

RADIALLY-
POSITIONED VANES

AIRFLOW
INLET

"U"-SHAPED
PRESSURE PROBE

EGR VACUUM
SENSOR PROBE

FIGURE 10-7. Air cleaner snorkel with radial vanes which create air turbulence and EGR vacuum sensor used with throttle body gasoline fuel injection system. *(Courtesy of Chrysler Corporation)*

manifold vacuum will drop, which allows spring pressure to open the temperature-control valve and allow denser cold air in to prevent hesitation. Some engines have an intake manifold vacuum controlled gulp valve in the air cleaner housing to allow extra air in under heavy acceleration.

Other Air Cleaner Features

Some vehicles are equipped with an air flow sensor in the air cleaner. This sensor produces an electrical signal, in proportion to air flow, and sends this information to the computer. To control the air/fuel ratio, the computer compares this information not only with other information sent by other engine sensors, but also with stored information in the computer. A stand pipe in the air flow sensor provides a vacuum signal to the exhaust gas recirculation system.

In some cases, the engine control computer is mounted directly to the outside of the air cleaner. Inlet air temperature is sensed by the computer which processes this information to aid in more closely controlling the air/fuel ratios.

In some systems a bimetal vacuum valve is used to regulate exhaust gas recirculation and air injection into the exhaust ports.

Some engines are equipped with a pulse air system to supply air to the exhaust system to help burn hydrocarbons remaining in the exhaust. Air for the pulse air system is taken from the air cleaner.

PART 3   INTAKE MANIFOLDS

The intake manifold is designed to deliver an equal amount of air, or air/fuel mixture, to each of the engine's cylinders. On diesel engines and port injected

engines, the manifold delivers air only. On carbureted systems and throttle body injection systems, the manifold delivers the air/fuel mixture.

In some cases the manifold may also have an air preheat, exhaust heat, coolant heat; an electric grid under the carburetor; or an electric heater in the manifold under the carburetor.

Intake manifolds are of cast iron or die cast aluminum construction. Aluminum manifolds reduce engine weight. Some are cast integrally with the cylinder head.

Manifold design varies greatly depending on engine type and type of fuel system used. Intake manifolds for V-type engines may have all runners on a single plane or they may be at different levels. A runnerless, box-type manifold is also used on some engines.

Ideally, the runners of the intake manifold should all be of the same length and shape. If they are of unequal length or different configuration, air and/or fuel delivery to the cylinders will not be quite

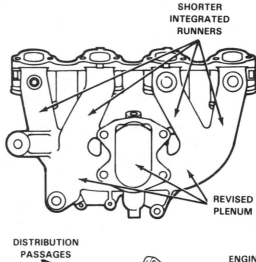

SHORTER
INTEGRATED
RUNNERS

REVISED
PLENUM

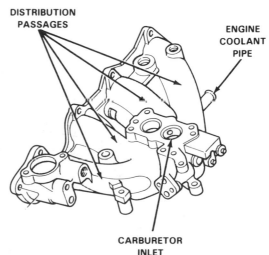

DISTRIBUTION
PASSAGES

ENGINE
COOLANT
PIPE

CARBURETOR
INLET

FIGURE 10-8. Typical four-cylinder engine intake manifold designs. *(Courtesy of Chrysler Corporation)*

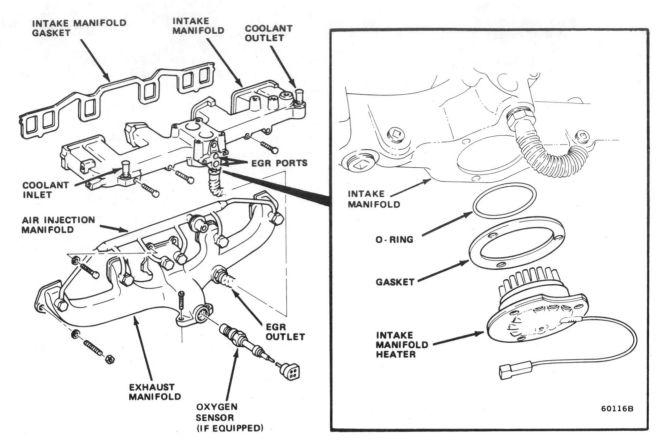

FIGURE 10-9. Intake and exhaust manifolds for an in-line six-cylinder engine with electric and coolant heated intake manifold. This system does not require a heat riser valve. (*Courtesy of American Motors Corporation*)

equal. This problem is overcome with the runnerless box-type manifold.

Some in-line, four-cylinder engines have four intake manifold runners of equal length; others have two runners that branch into four near the cylinder head. In-line, six-cylinder engines may have six separate runners or three runners branching off from a single main runner. In the three-runner system, each runner serves two cylinders. This is possible because the two cylinders do not use the intake runner at the same time. This design has siamesed ports in the cylinder head.

On V-type engines, each cylinder is served by a separate runner or by siamesed runners. Both open-

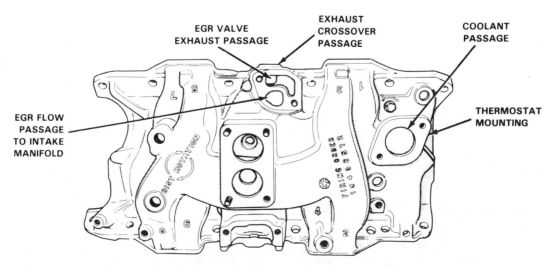

FIGURE 10-10. V8 engine intake manifold. (*Courtesy of Chrysler Corporation*)

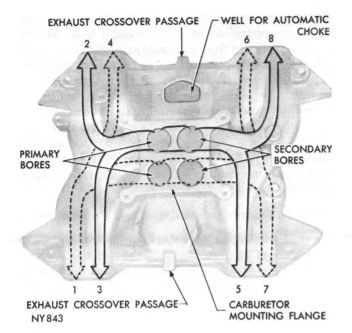

FIGURE 10-11. V8 engine intake manifold. Note how cylinders are fed from carburetor bores. Exhaust crossover passage provides heat for improved fuel vaporization and prevents carburetor icing. *(Courtesy of Chrysler Corporation)*

and closed-type manifolds have been used on V-type engines. The open type requires a separate lifter valley cover, whereas the closed type serves as the cover itself.

Intake manifolds for V-type engines may include coolant connecting passages between cylinder heads. Some include a provision for mounting the thermostat and thermostat housing.

Intake manifolds may be *wet* or *dry*. The wet intake manifold casting includes a coolant passage that connects the two cylinder head water jackets. The dry manifold has no coolant passage.

An exhaust crossover passage provides a path for exhaust gases to flow from one side to the other when the exhaust heat riser valve is closed. Exhaust gases are directed from one exhaust manifold through one cylinder head, then through the exhaust crossover passages in the intake manifold through the other cylinder head, and into its exhaust manifold.

The exhaust crossover provides heat to the base of the carburetor to improve the vaporization of fuel during engine warm-up and to reduce carburetor icing. On many engines, the exhaust crossover is also used to provide automatic choke heat. On four- and six-cylinder in-line engines the heat riser valve also directs heat to the base of the carburetor for the same reasons.

Connections to the intake manifold provide a vacuum source to operate power brakes, thermostatic air cleaners, exhaust gas recirculation valves, heater and air conditioning air flow control doors, automatic transmission vacuum modulators, and distributor vacuum advance units. Other devices include manifold absolute pressure sensors, manifold air temperature sensors, knock sensors, and exhaust gas recirculation passages.

Manifold gaskets may be of embossed steel, steel reinforced asbestos, or synthetic rubber design.

Intake manifolds must be leak proof. In other words, no outside air must be allowed to enter past any gaskets, fittings, and connections. Entry of air upsets the balance of air and fuel delivered and allows the entry of dirt or moisture.

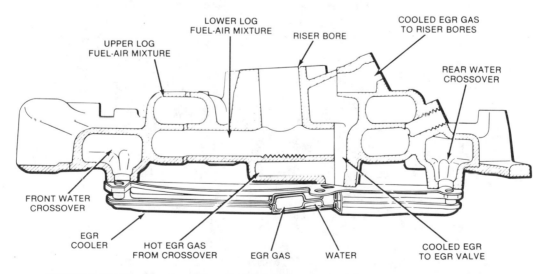

FIGURE 10-12. Cross-sectional view of intake manifold with EGR cooler. *(Courtesy of Ford Motor Co. of Canada Ltd.)*

PART 4 TURBOCHARGERS AND SUPERCHARGERS

The use of a turbocharger or supercharger will effectively increase the volumetric efficiency and therefore the performance of an engine for load and power demands. The effectiveness of the system remains, regardless of the altitude at which the vehicle is operated.

The difference between a turbocharger and a supercharger is the method used to drive the compressor (blower). The supercharger is mechanically driven, while the turbocharger is driven by the velocity of exhaust gases.

Many vehicles equipped with smaller engines and a turbocharger provide the performance of a larger engine and the economy of the smaller engine during normal operation.

The design capacity of the turbocharger is dependent on engine size and type, which is determined by the manufacturer. Control devices limit the degree of turbocharging to prevent detonation and engine damage.

Turbocharger Construction and Operation

The turbocharger consists of an exhaust-driven turbine (finned wheel), which in turn is connected to a compressor or blower by a shaft. Exhaust gases are directed over the turbine vanes, causing it to turn, depending on the velocity of the exhaust gases. The compressor, connected to the turbine by means of a shaft, turns at turbine speed. Extremely high speeds are reached by the turbine, requiring adequate pressure lubrication from the engine's lubrication system. A floating bearing lubricated inside and outside reduces the possibility of shaft seizure.

The compressor is situated in the induction system between the carburetor and the manifold. As the compressor turns, it increases the amount of air-fuel mixture (air only on diesel engines) delivered to the engine's cylinders.

An engine coolant controlled plenum is used to control plenum temperature and avoid overheating, or EGR gases may be cooled on some models. A detonation sensor located in the thermostat housing (or a manifold pressure sensor) sends a signal to the electronic spark control unit to retard spark timing and avoid detonation.

A spring-loaded diaphragm sensitive to intake manifold pressure regulates the wastegate. The wastegate causes exhaust gases to bypass the turbine when the predetermined manifold pressure is reached, thereby regulating manifold pressure at a safe level. Excessive turbocharging causes detonation and engine damage.

It may be necessary to let the engine idle for several minutes to allow the turbine to slow down before stopping the engine on some vehicles. If the

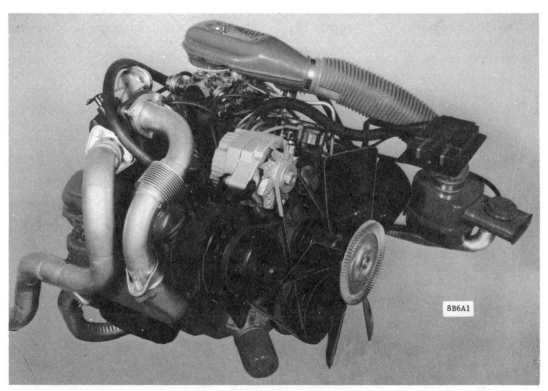

FIGURE 10–13. Turbocharged V6 engine. *(Courtesy of General Motors Corporation)*

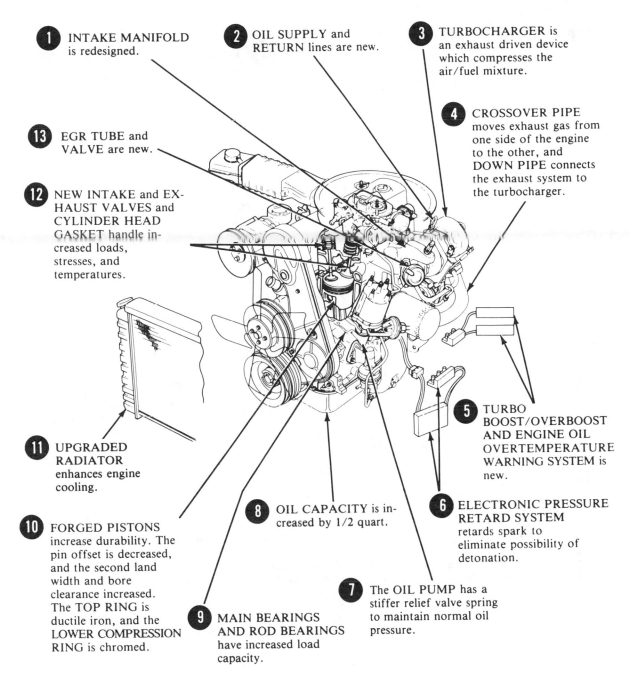

1 INTAKE MANIFOLD is redesigned.

2 OIL SUPPLY and RETURN lines are new.

3 TURBOCHARGER is an exhaust driven device which compresses the air/fuel mixture.

4 CROSSOVER PIPE moves exhaust gas from one side of the engine to the other, and DOWN PIPE connects the exhaust system to the turbocharger.

13 EGR TUBE and VALVE are new.

12 NEW INTAKE and EXHAUST VALVES and CYLINDER HEAD GASKET handle increased loads, stresses, and temperatures.

11 UPGRADED RADIATOR enhances engine cooling.

10 FORGED PISTONS increase durability. The pin offset is decreased, and the second land width and bore clearance increased. The TOP RING is ductile iron, and the LOWER COMPRESSION RING is chromed.

8 OIL CAPACITY is increased by 1/2 quart.

5 TURBO BOOST/OVERBOOST AND ENGINE OIL OVERTEMPERATURE WARNING SYSTEM is new.

6 ELECTRONIC PRESSURE RETARD SYSTEM retards spark to eliminate possibility of detonation.

7 The OIL PUMP has a stiffer relief valve spring to maintain normal oil pressure.

9 MAIN BEARINGS AND ROD BEARINGS have increased load capacity.

FIGURE 10-14. Typical turbocharger installation on four-cylinder gasoline engine. *(Courtesy of Ford Motor Co. of Canada Ltd.)*

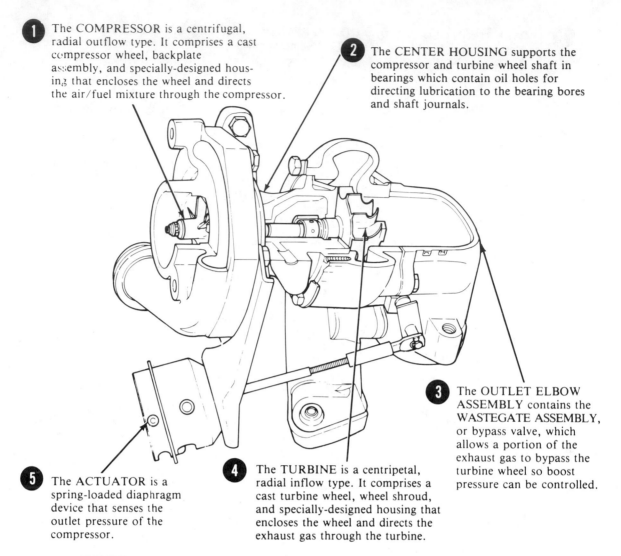

1 The COMPRESSOR is a centrifugal, radial outflow type. It comprises a cast compressor wheel, backplate assembly, and specially-designed housing that encloses the wheel and directs the air/fuel mixture through the compressor.

2 The CENTER HOUSING supports the compressor and turbine wheel shaft in bearings which contain oil holes for directing lubrication to the bearing bores and shaft journals.

3 The OUTLET ELBOW ASSEMBLY contains the WASTEGATE ASSEMBLY, or bypass valve, which allows a portion of the exhaust gas to bypass the turbine wheel so boost pressure can be controlled.

5 The ACTUATOR is a spring-loaded diaphragm device that senses the outlet pressure of the compressor.

4 The TURBINE is a centripetal, radial inflow type. It comprises a cast turbine wheel, wheel shroud, and specially-designed housing that encloses the wheel and directs the exhaust gas through the turbine.

FIGURE 10–15. Major components and their operation of a typical turbocharger. *(Courtesy of Ford Motor Co. of Canada Ltd.)*

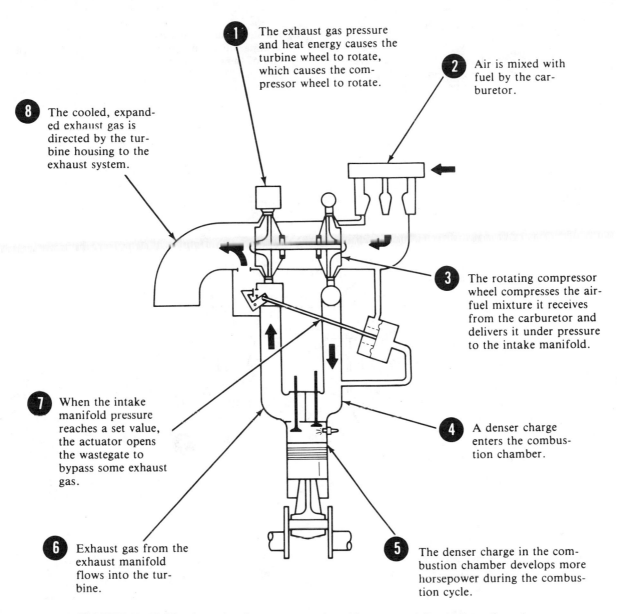

1. The exhaust gas pressure and heat energy causes the turbine wheel to rotate, which causes the compressor wheel to rotate.

2. Air is mixed with fuel by the carburetor.

3. The rotating compressor wheel compresses the air-fuel mixture it receives from the carburetor and delivers it under pressure to the intake manifold.

4. A denser charge enters the combustion chamber.

5. The denser charge in the combustion chamber develops more horsepower during the combustion cycle.

6. Exhaust gas from the exhaust manifold flows into the turbine.

7. When the intake manifold pressure reaches a set value, the actuator opens the wastegate to bypass some exhaust gas.

8. The cooled, expanded exhaust gas is directed by the turbine housing to the exhaust system.

FIGURE 10-16. Basic turbocharger operation. *(Courtesy of Ford Motor Co. of Canada Ltd.)*

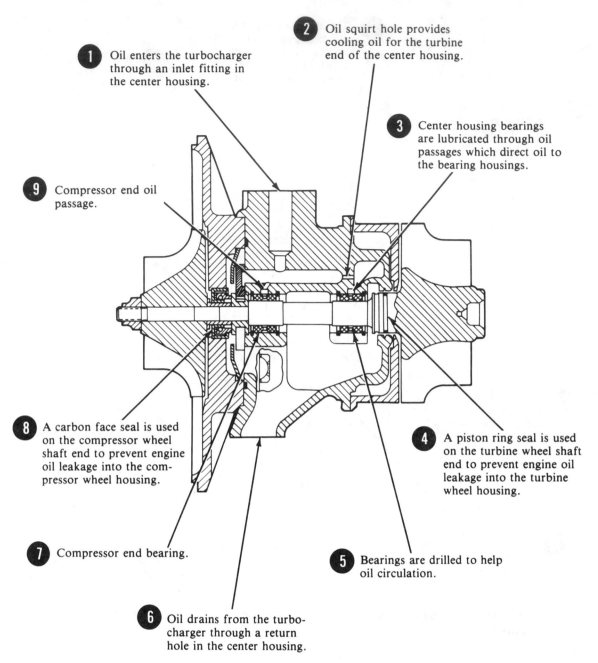

1 Oil enters the turbocharger through an inlet fitting in the center housing.

2 Oil squirt hole provides cooling oil for the turbine end of the center housing.

3 Center housing bearings are lubricated through oil passages which direct oil to the bearing housings.

9 Compressor end oil passage.

8 A carbon face seal is used on the compressor wheel shaft end to prevent engine oil leakage into the compressor wheel housing.

4 A piston ring seal is used on the turbine wheel shaft end to prevent engine oil leakage into the turbine wheel housing.

7 Compressor end bearing.

5 Bearings are drilled to help oil circulation.

6 Oil drains from the turbocharger through a return hole in the center housing.

FIGURE 10-17. Cross-sectional view of turbocharger lubrication. *(Courtesy of Ford Motor Co. of Canada Ltd.)*

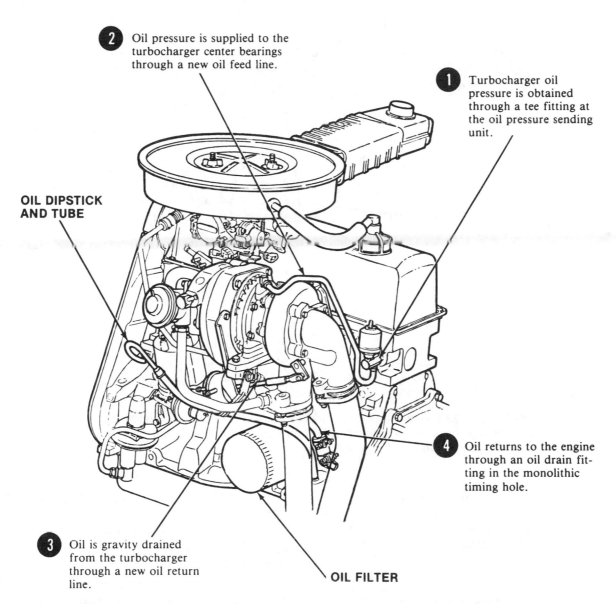

2 Oil pressure is supplied to the turbocharger center bearings through a new oil feed line.

1 Turbocharger oil pressure is obtained through a tee fitting at the oil pressure sending unit.

OIL DIPSTICK AND TUBE

4 Oil returns to the engine through an oil drain fitting in the monolithic timing hole.

3 Oil is gravity drained from the turbocharger through a new oil return line.

OIL FILTER

FIGURE 10–18. External components of turbocharger lubrication system. *(Courtesy of Ford Motor Co. of Canada Ltd.)*

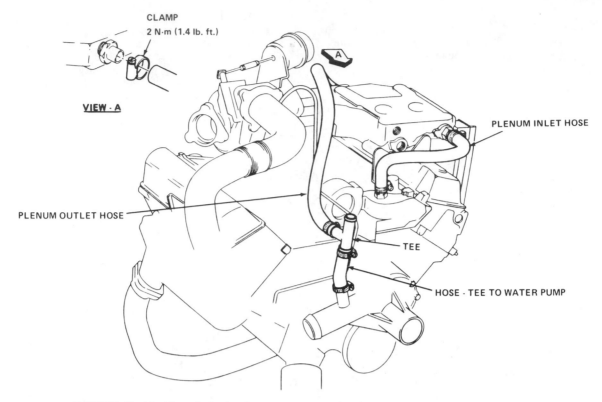

CLAMP
2 N·m (1.4 lb. ft.)

VIEW - A

A

PLENUM INLET HOSE

PLENUM OUTLET HOSE

TEE

HOSE - TEE TO WATER PUMP

FIGURE 10–19. The air-fuel mixture temperature is controlled by engine coolant flowing through the plenum (between carburetor and intake manifold). *(Courtesy of General Motors Corporation)*

engine is stopped when turbine speed is high, the turbine will continue running, and since lubrication pressure is no longer provided when the engine is stopped, turbine shaft and bearing damage may result.

PART 5 AIR SUPPLY SYSTEM DIAGNOSIS AND SERVICE

Air supply system service is performed as routine maintenance based on mileage and/or time intervals to maintain performance and emissions standards, and as part of the normal tune up procedure. The air cleaner should be serviced at regular intervals, as specified by the particular vehicle manufacturer, and more frequently (as often as required) when operating in dusty or dirty conditions.

General Precautions

The following precautions should be observed when servicing air supply systems.

1. Observe all normal personal and shop safety precautions. (See Chapter 1, Parts 1 and 2.)

2. During or after air cleaner removal, never allow anything to fall into the intake system whether the engine is running or not. (Dirt, rags, tools, parts, etc.).

3. If the engine is operated with air cleaner removed, beware of flame out of the carburetor if the engine backfires.

4. Do not use your hand to cover the air horn for choking purposes when starting the engine.

5. Do not pour raw fuel into the air horn to prime the engine; doing so could result in fire or explosion.

6. Do not place your hand (with or without a rag) over the intake of a diesel engine to attempt to

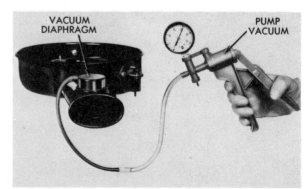

VACUUM DIAPHRAGM

PUMP VACUUM

FIGURE 10–20. Using a hand vacuum pump and gauge to test the vacuum motor on the air cleaner snorkel. *(Courtesy of Chrysler Corporation)*

stop the engine; doing so will cause injury to your hand and can digest the rag.

7. Follow all special regulations regarding service of propane fueled vehicles whether local, state, provincial, or federal.

Air Cleaner Diagnosis and Service

The air cleaner should be serviced when the carburetor is serviced, as well as at recommended service intervals. The air cleaner filter element (if not too dirty) can be cleaned by careful use of clean, dry compressed air to blow dirt from the surfaces. Care must be exercised not to rupture the paper element by holding the nozzle too close to the filter when cleaning.

If the element is too dirty to be cleaned or is oil or moisture contaminated, it should be replaced. If the air cleaner has a PCV filter, it too should be cleaned or replaced.

Checking Air Cleaner

1. Inspect system to be sure all hoses and ducts are connected.

2. If engine is too warm (above room temperature) remove air cleaner. Permit it to cool to room temperature.

3. Install cooled air cleaner with cold air intake hose disconnected.

4. Start engine. Watch damper valve in air cleaner snorkel.

5. When engine is first started, valve should be closed. As air cleaner warms up, valve should slowly open.

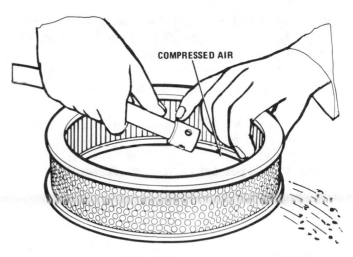

FIGURE 10-22. After tapping the filter as in Figure 10-21, low pressure shop air can be used to blow dirt from the element. Air pressure must be applied on the inner surface only since dirt has collected on the outer surface. This type of cleaning should be done when needed only between regular recommended filter change intervals. *(Courtesy of Chrysler Corporation)*

Note: In hot weather, the room temperature may be too hot for the snorkel valve to close when the engine is started. In this case, cool the temperature sensor in the air cleaner with a cool wet rag.

6. If valve doesn't close when the engine is started, check for vacuum at the diaphragm.

7. If vacuum is present, check for binding in the damper valve and operating link. If damper moves freely, replace diaphragm. (Failure of the diaphragm to close is more likely to result from mechanical bind

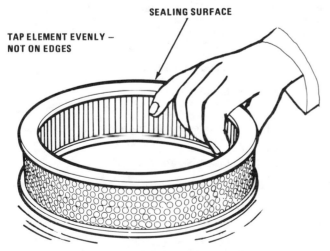

FIGURE 10-21. Some of the dirt on the air filter can be dislodged by tapping the element on a flat surface. Be sure to have the full circumference of the filter land flat on the surface each time to prevent damaging the filter. *(Courtesy of Chrysler Corporation)*

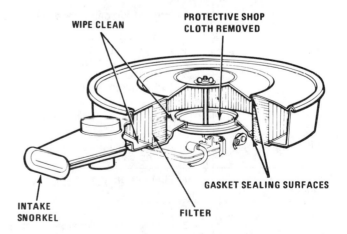

FIGURE 10-23. Before assembling the air cleaner, wipe all the surfaces clean. Be sure the correct size element is being used so that all sealing surfaces will effectively prevent entry of unfiltered air. *(Courtesy of Chrysler Corporation)*

due to a damaged or corroded snorkel assembly than from a failed diaphragm. This should be checked first, before replacing diaphragm.)

8. If no vacuum is present, check hoses for disconnects, cracks, or pinches. Repair or replace as necessary.

9. If hoses are OK, replace temperature sensor in the air cleaner.

Vacuum Motor and Damper Assembly

The vacuum motor should move the damper door from the full cold air position to the full hot air position when 5 to 7" Hg. vacuum is applied to the motor nipple.

Disconnect the vacuum hose that runs between the motor and the sensor at the motor nipple. Using an auxiliary hose, apply vacuum to the motor. (Use a hand vacuum pump or engine manifold vacuum.) The door should close.

Pinch the hose while the vacuum is still applied and remove the vacuum source. The door should remain closed. If it does not, it indicates a leak in the motor, and the motor assembly should be replaced.

Sensor Check (Quick Check)

1. Start test with engine cold; air cleaner at a temperature below 77°F (25°C). If the engine has been in recent use, allow it to cool. (Removing the air cleaner from the engine and placing it on the bench will aid in quickly cooling the sensor.) Momentarily disconnect vacuum hose at vacuum motor before proceeding with test.

2. Observe the damper door before starting the engine. It should be in the open snorkel position.

3. Start the engine and allow it to idle. Immediately after starting the engine, the damper door should be in the closed snorkel passage position.

4. As the engine warms up, the damper door should start to allow outside air and heated air to enter the carburetor inlet.

5. If the system is operating normally, as described above, and if the air cleaner fails to operate as above, replace the sensor.

PART 6   SELF-CHECK

1. List four functions of the air cleaner.
2. What is the purpose of heated intake air?
3. Describe the dry paper filter element and how it is mounted in the air cleaner.
4. Why are some air filter elements carbon impregnated?
5. List three factors that determine required air cleaner capacity.
6. What is the purpose of the intake manifold?
7. List four methods used to preheat intake air in intake manifolds.

DIAGNOSTIC CHART: TURBOCHARGER DIAGNOSIS AND SERVICE

PROBLEM	CAUSE	CORRECTION
Detonation	1. EGR system defect. 2. Actuator allows too much boost. 3. Internal turbocharger defect.	1. Diagnose and check as needed. 2. Check linkage and hoses. Defective waste-gate. 3. Refer to internal inspection of turbocharger.
Low power	1. Air inlet restriction. 2. Exhaust system restriction. 3. Heat riser valve defect. 4. Turbocharger defect.	1. Locate and correct. 2. Locate and correct. 3. Check and repair. 4. Check for exhaust leaks, collapsed plenum coolant hose, defective wastegate. Perform internal inspection of turbocharger.
Engine surges	1. Loose turbocharger bolts on compressor side.	1. Diagnose and correct.
Black exhaust smoke	1. Fuel system defect.	1. See fuel system section.
Engine noise	1. Loose exhaust system or leak. 2. Restricted turbocharger oil supply. 3. Internal turbocharger defect.	1. Correct as needed. 2. Locate and correct. 3. Inspect turbocharger.
Oil consumption	1. Leak at turbocharger oil inlet. 2. Turbocharger oil drain hose leaks or is stopped up. 3. Turbocharger defect, (internal).	1. Locate and correct. 2. Correct as needed. 3. Inspect turbocharger.

8. What is the effect of air leakage into the intake manifold on a carbureted engine? On a diesel engine?

9. Why is a turbocharger used on some engines?

10. List the six major components of the turbocharger.

PART 7   TEST QUESTIONS

1. Mechanic A says that the thermal sensor in the air cleaner determines the position of the inlet air control valve. Mechanic B says that this job is done by the vacuum motor. Who is right?
   - (a) Mechanic A
   - (b) Mechanic B
   - (c) both are right
   - (d) both are wrong

2. Heated air for air intake is taken from:
   - (a) the exhaust manifold shroud
   - (b) the exhaust crossover
   - (c) the heat riser valve
   - (d) all of the above

3. The position of the inlet air control valve is:
   - (a) in the cold air open position when the engine is shut off
   - (b) in a modulating position when the engine is running at operating temperature
   - (c) in the cold air closed position when the engine is running during warm up
   - (d) all of the above

4. How often should the air filter element be serviced?
   - (a) once a year
   - (b) twice a year
   - (c) once every 10,000 (16,000 km)
   - (d) whenever necessary

5. Mechanic A says that the vacuum motor should be tested with a hand-operated vacuum source. Mechanic B says that the air valve should retain its position if the vacuum line is pinched shut while vacuum is applied and the vacuum source removed. Who is right?
   - (a) Mechanic A
   - (b) Mechanic B
   - (c) both are right
   - (d) both are wrong

6. Low engine power may be caused by:
   - (a) restricted exhaust
   - (b) a stuck heat riser valve
   - (c) restricted air inlet
   - (d) all of the above

Chapter 11

Automotive Fuels

NAME OF PARAFFIN	USUAL FORM AT ROOM TEMPERATURE	APPROXIMATE BOILING POINT, °F (°C)	MAJOR USE
Methane	Gas	-259 (-218)	As gas for in- dustrial and domestic fuel; as a source of petrochem- ical com- pounds
Ethane	Gas	-128 (-89)	
Propane	Gas	-44 (-42)	
Butane	Gas	31 (-1)	In gas and gasoline
Pentane	Gas and liquid	97 (36)	Gasoline
Hexane	Liquid	156 (69)	Gasoline
Heptane	Liquid	209 (98)	Gasoline
Octane	Liquid	258 (126)	Gasoline
Nonane	Liquid	303 (151)	Gasoline
Decane	Liquid	345 (174)	Kerosene and gasoline

Performance Objectives

After thorough study of this chapter and the ap-propriate training aids, the student should be able to:

1. Complete the self-check and the test questions with at least 80 percent accuracy.
2. List six gasoline requirements for good perfor-mance and economy.
3. Define volatility, antiknock quality, deposit con-trol, and octane rating.
4. Define the cetane number of diesel fuel.
5. List the advantages and disadvantages of LP gas.

PART 1   SOURCE OF FUELS

Crude oil is a mixture of a vast number of chemicals made up of hydrogen and carbon, called hydrocar-bons. These hydrocarbons range from extremely light gases to semisolid materials like asphalt or wax. Gasoline is a blend of a number of these hy-drocarbons the liquid components of which have a boiling range of about $+80°$ to $+400°$F($27°$ to $204°$C).

Conventional diesel fuels are distillates with a boiling range of about $+300°$ to $+700°$F ($149°$ to $371°$C) obtained by the distillation of crude oil. They are predominantly straight-run fractions that con-tain the greatest amount of normal paraffins and naphthenes and the least amount of isoparaffins and aromatics. Normal paraffins and naphthenes have superior diesel ignition qualities, but they have the disadvantages of higher pour points than isoparaf-fins and aromatics.

PART 2   GASOLINE

Different types of hydrocarbons affect the charac-teristics of gasolines in which they occur. Practi-cally all petroleum hydrocarbons found in gasoline are members of four major groups as follows:

Paraffins. The general formula is C_nH_{2n+2}; they may exist as straight-chain molecules or as branched-chain molecules called isoparaffins.

Olefins. These compounds have the general for-mula C_nH_{2n}. They resemble paraffins except they have two less hydrogen atoms and contain one dou-ble bond between two carbon atoms.

Olefins have high octane values and are stable enough for gasoline. They are formed mainly in the cracking process. Diolefins are somewhat unstable and hence must be removed or stablized with suit-able additives, otherwise they would promote gum formation.

Naphthenes. These compounds also have the general formula C_nH_{2n}, but the carbon atoms are ar-ranged in a ring structure. They may also be called cycloparaffins. They occur in naphthas and higher-boiling fractions. In gasolines they have medium oc-tane numbers and high chemical stability.

Aromatics. Aromatics have the general for-mula C_nH_{2n-6}. The basic structure is a ring struc-

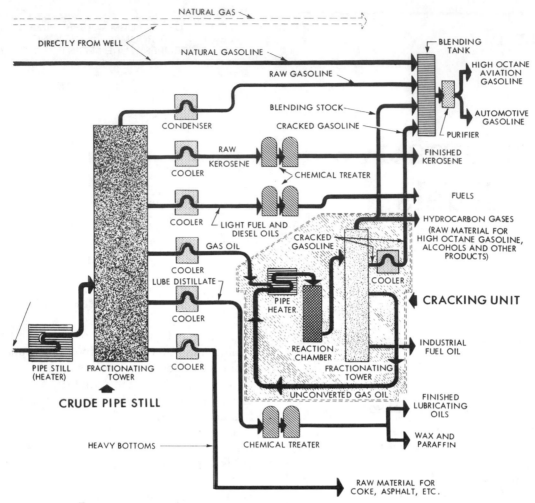

FIGURE 11-1. Basic schematic of crude oil refining process. About 44 gallons of gasoline can be produced from 100 gallons of crude oil.

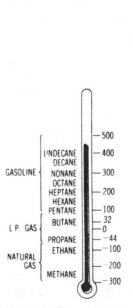

FIGURE 11-2. Boiling point or vaporization point of gasoline components as well as liquefied petroleum gas and natural gas.

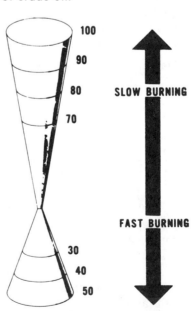

FIGURE 11-3. The octane rating of gasoline and cetane rating of diesel fuel. Note that the higher the octane rating number of the gasoline, the slower it burns, and the higher the cetane number of diesel, the faster it burns. *(Courtesy of Ford Motor Co. of Canada Ltd.)*

ture, but they are unsaturated. They are active chemically, and while the lower boiling compounds may be desirable in gasoline, the higher boiling fractions contribute to smoke and carbon formation.

PART 3   GASOLINE REQUIREMENTS

For top road performance and best fuel economy, a gasoline should provide the following:

- Good mileage under all driving conditions
- Fast starts
- Rapid warm-up
- Rapid acceleration
- Smooth performance
- Minimum engine maintenance

Three major factors that govern the performance characteristics of gasolines:

- Volatility
- Antiknock quality
- Deposit control

These factors are determined by the refiner's selection and processing of the hydrocarbons that comprise the gasoline base stock plus the use of additives to obtain desired properties.

Volatility

Volatility is a measure of the tendency of a gasoline to change from a liquid to a vapor. The distillation of a gasoline is an indication of its volatility and is obtained by a distillation test (ASTM D86). Another measure of gasoline volatility is its *Reid vapor pressure* (RVP), which is a measure of fuel vapor pressure at 100°F (38°C) under specified conditions (ASTM D323). It is largely a measure of the butane content of gasoline.

Performance characteristics controlled by volatility include the following:

- Cold starting
- Vapor lock (a pocket of vapor caused by overheated and boiling fuel)
- Carburetor icing
- Warm-up and acceleration
- Economy; short-trip and overall economy
- Combustion chamber deposits
- Crankcase dilution

Starting and Vapor Lock Protection

These properties are directly opposed, and it is necessary to strike a compromise in the interest of overall fuel performance. Starting ability is controlled by the Reid vapor pressure and the front end of the distillation curve, that is, the 10 to 20 to 30 percent temperatures or the percentage at 158°F (70°C). Fortunately, during the winter months when quick starting is important, it is possible to build in adequate front end volatility for starting without exceeding the desired vapor lock protection temperature. Conversely, during the summer months, vapor lock protection becomes all important, and the somewhat less volatile gasolines distributed in warm weather provide this protection without sacrificing starting ability. Spring and fall call for careful adjustment of front end volatility to make the best compromise.

It should be kept in mind that there is an exchange between RVP and front end distillation values and that vapor locking tendency should not be judged by RVP alone.

Carburetor Icing Protection

Although not as common an occurrence in current engines as in those of the past, carburetor icing is most likely to occur at ambient temperatures between 28° and 55°F (−2° and 13°C) when the relative humidity exceeds 65 percent. Moisture-laden air enters the carburetor and is mixed with fuel droplets. As the fuel evaporates, it removes heat from the air and from the surrounding metal parts and lowers their temperature. Within the range of conditions indicated, the throttle temperature is rapidly lowered to below 32°F (0°C), and condensing water vapor forms ice. The ice thus formed will cause stalling if the engine is idled during this phase.

The percentage evaporated at 212°F (100°C) is the significant factor in minimizing carburetor icing, since gasolines with higher mid-volatility (increasing percentage evaporated at 212°F or 100°C) create greater evaporative cooling.

Engine Warm-up and Acceleration

The effect of fuel volatility on engine performance is quite marked and is related to the 50 and 90 percent evaporated temperatures (or to the percentage at 212° and 320°F or 100° and 160°C). In general, the lower these temperatures are, the faster the engine will warm up. This is because once the engine starts, the temperature of its induction system must rise to a point where sufficient gasoline is vaporized to obtain good mixture distribution to all cylinders, and to permit full throttle acceleration without hesitation or "bucking" without choke. This is defined as warm-up time.

The trend has been toward lower 50 and 90 percent temperatures, since the motorist readily detects good warm-up and acceleration. Another advantage of a low 90 percent evaporated temperature is the reduced tendency for crankcase dilution.

Fuel Economy

The air-fuel carburetor setting has a major effect on gasoline consumption. If it is richer than necessary, the consumption will be high. The driver and driving conditions are important factors in fuel economy. Also, the usable BTU (British Thermal Unit) content of the fuel is significant. The higher boiling components have higher BTU contents per gallon; thus the back end of the distillation range is a measure of BTU content of the fuel. However, the higher boiling components contribute most to crankcase oil dilution and to some degree to combustion chamber deposits. Thus a compromise between economy, oil dilution, and deposits is necessary.

The less volatile fuel, or that which has a lesser percentage distilled at 212°F (100°C) and contains more BTUs (a wider back end), gives greater economy in a fully warmed up engine as in a vehicle on a long trip. But surveys show that about two thirds of all driving consists of trips of 6 miles (9.65 km) or less. For such short-trip driving, particularly in winter when engine temperature is lower, the more volatile fuel with a greater mid-fill volatility gives greater economy.

Antiknock Quality (Octane Number)

Increasing the pressure of the fuel mixture in the combustion chamber before ignition helps to increase the power of an engine. This is done by compressing the fuel mixture to a smaller volume. Higher compression ratios not only boost power but also give more efficient power. But as the compression ratio goes up, knocking tendency increases, and the antiknock value of the fuel becomes critical. All post-1971-model engine compression ratios have been reduced to an average of 8.2:1 to 10:1 to permit the use of lower-octane unleaded gasoline and to reduce combustion temperatures.

The octane number of a gasoline is a measure of its antiknock quality or ability to resist detonation during combustion. Detonation, sometimes referred to as *spark knock* or *ping,* can be defined as an uncontrolled explosion of the last portion of the burning fuel-air mixture due to excessive temperature and pressure conditions in the combustion chamber. Since detonation creates shock pressure waves, and hence audible knock, rather than smooth combustion and expansion of the fuel-air mixture, it results in loss of power, excessive localized temperatures, and engine damage if sufficiently severe.

There are two commonly used methods of determining the octane number of motor gasoline—the *motor method* and the *research method.* Both use the same type of laboratory single-cylinder engine, which is equipped with a variable head and a knock meter to indicate knock intensity. Using the test sample as fuel, the engine compression ratio and the air-fuel mixture are adjusted to develop a specified knock intensity. Two primary standard reference fuels, normal heptane and iso-octane, arbitrarily assigned 0 and 100 octane numbers, respectively, are then blended to produce the same knock intensity as the test sample. The percentage of iso-octane in the blend is considered the octane number of the test sample. Thus, if the matching reference blend is made up of 15 percent *n*-heptane and 85 percent iso-octane, the test sample is rated 85 motor or research octane number, according to the test method used.

The test conditions for the research method are less severe than for the motor method. Accordingly, commercial gasolines have a higher octane number by the research method than by the motor method.

Both ratings are required to predict the performance of the gasoline in actual road usage, but the relative importance depends on the type of engine and operating conditions. In truck and bus operation where the gasoline must perform at high temperatures and under maximum throttle, the motor octane number is more significant than the research octane number. Similarly, in passenger cars with automatic transmissions under full and part throttle, the motor octane number is more significant, particularly in engines of more recent manufacture. In passenger cars with manual transmissions at full throttle where the engine can be loaded at low engine speed, the research octane number is more significant than the motor octane number, whereas at part throttle the reverse is true.

Road octane number is the rating of the gasoline, in terms of reference fuels, by a test car under full throttle acceleration from 10 to 50 mph (16km to 81km). However, road octane tests are both inconvenient and expensive; they are usually avoided. An approximation may be made by calculation of the average of research and motor octane numbers: $(R + M)/2$.

A number of factors besides the compression ratio affect the octane requirement. Some of these are listed with their degrees of effect in Figure 11–4.

A final word on antiknock quality: Nothing is gained or lost by using gasoline of higher octane quality than required by the engine in the whole range of its operating conditions. The full value of higher-octane gasoline is only obtained when an engine is designed and adjusted to take advantage of it. Most post-1971-manufactured engines are satisfied by the *regular* grade gasoline and do not require the high-octane *premium* grade; but those that

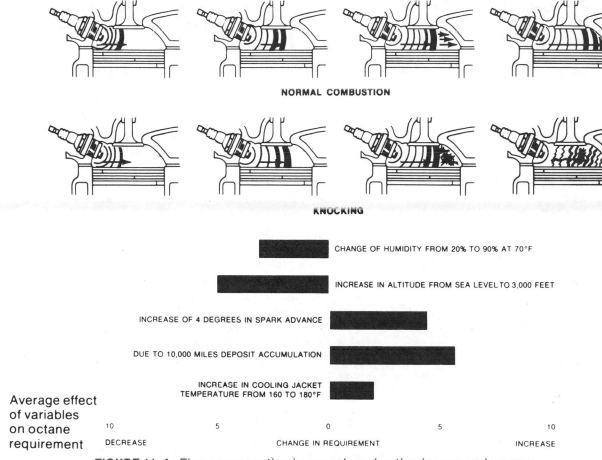

NORMAL COMBUSTION

KNOCKING

	CHANGE OF HUMIDITY FROM 20% TO 90% AT 70°F.
	INCREASE IN ALTITUDE FROM SEA LEVEL TO 3,000 FEET
INCREASE OF 4 DEGREES IN SPARK ADVANCE	
DUE TO 10,000 MILES DEPOSIT ACCUMULATION	
INCREASE IN COOLING JACKET TEMPERATURE FROM 160 TO 180°F	

Average effect of variables on octane requirement

10   5   0   5   10
DECREASE   CHANGE IN REQUIREMENT   INCREASE

FIGURE 11-4. Flame propagation in normal combustion is even and progressive. Too rapid burning of the fuel causes end gases to compress and heat to the point of self-ignition (detonation). This results in the two flame fronts colliding, which causes severe knocking. *(Courtesy of General Motors Corporation)*

are not satisfied will provide better fuel economy and performance (drivability) when converted to a higher-octane gasoline.

PART 4   GASOLINE ADDITIVES

The following is a list of gasoline additives with their properties and uses.

Oxidation Inhibitors. Gasoline stability is important, since gums formed during storage by the reaction of some gasoline components with each other and with oxygen may result in harmful deposits in the engine. Oxidation inhibitors are added to help in controlling gum and deposit formation.

Metal Deactivators. Reactions between the fuel and the metals in the fuel system may form abrasive and filter-plugging substances. Metal deactivator additives are used to inhibit such reactions.

Detergents. Detergent additives are used to keep carburetor parts clean and allow for the designed functioning of these engine components. All these additives have some degree of carburetor anti-icing capability.

Rust Inhibitors. Fuel system parts are protected by the addition of rust inhibitors.

Tetraethyl Lead. Tetraethyl lead (TEL) is used to improve the antiknock quality. Up to 3 grams of TEL added per gallon of gasoline will increase the octane rating by up to 15 numbers. The amount of TEL used is based on the response of the gasoline base stock to TEL and the economics of obtaining octane by refining processes versus the cost of TEL. Currently, TEL content is limited by federal regulation to 3.5 grams of lead per gallon. Scavengers are included with the TEL additive. These promote the removal of lead salts formed in the combustion chamber after combustion.

Unleaded Gasoline

The extensive use of catalytic converters in the post-1974 models (used to meet the regulatory tailpipe emissions standards) has imposed a requirement for

PROPERTIES OF EXXON® GASOLINES

	EXXON 2000 (UNLEADED)	EXXON (LEADED)	EXXON EXTRA UNLEADED
Research octane number[a]	93	94	97
Motor octane number[a]	84	84	87
TEL content	Nil[b]	Approx. 2 grams/gal	Nil[b]
Approximate compression ratio served	8.2:1	8.2:1	8.2:1 and higher
Carburetor icing control		Adequate	
Volatility adjustments		Continually with season for each market area	
Detergent		For required carburetor deposit control	

[a]Lower for higher-altitude market areas.
[b]Trace lead contents are due to pickup in the distribution system.

unleaded gasolines for these cars. These gasolines are limited to 0.06 gram per gallon (.013 grams per liter) of lead content due to the deactivating or poisioning effect lead has on the catalyst. Therefore, TEL is not added to unleaded gasolines. The required antiknock quality is obtained by blending components of the required octane quality. Methylcyclopentadienyl manganese tricarbonyl (MMT), a catalyst-compatible octane improver, may also be used to further improve the antiknock quality of unleaded gasolines. Other additives, referred to previously, are also usually used in unleaded gasoline.

Gasohol

Gasohol is a mixture of unleaded gasoline and grain alcohol (ethanol). Approximately 90 percent unleaded gasoline and 10 percent ethanol form the mixture. It may be used in vehicles where unleaded gasoline is normally recommended. If driveability or performance problems are experienced as a result of using gasohol, its use should be discontinued and only 100 percent unleaded fuel should be used.

PART 5   DIESEL FUELS

Cetane Number

Cetane number is a measure of the autoignition quality of a diesel fuel. The shorter the interval between the time the fuel is injected and the time it begins to burn (called the *ignition delay period*), the higher the cetane number. It is a measure of the ease with which the fuel can be ignited and is most significant in low-temperature starting, warm-up, and smooth, even combustion (Figure 11–5).

Some hydrocarbons ignite more readily than others and are desirable because of this short ignition delay. The preferred hydrocarbons, in order of their decreasing cetane numbers, are normal paraffins, olefins, naphthenes, isoparaffins, and aromatics.

This is the reverse order of their antiknock quality. Cetane number is measured in a single cylinder test engine with a variable compression ratio. The reference fuels used are mixtures of cetane, which has a very short ignition delay, and α-methyl naphthalene, which has a long ignition delay. The percentage of cetane in the reference fuel that gives the same ignition delay as the test fuel, is defined as the cetane number of the test fuel.

Diesel engines whose rated speeds are below 500 rpm are classed as slow-speed engines, from 500 to 1200 rpm as medium speed, and over 1200 rpm as

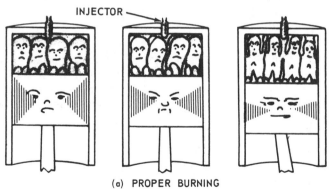

INJECTOR

(a)   PROPER BURNING

(Fuel Charge Ignites Early and Burns Evenly To Overcome Knocking)

(b)   POOR IGNITION

(Ignition Of Fuel Charge Is Delayed, Followed By A Small Explosion)

FIGURE 11–5. Knock in diesel engines. In diesel engines, knock is due to the fuel igniting too slowly. It should start to burn almost as soon as it is injected (A). If there is much delay, a fuel buildup results, which burns with explosive force (B) and causes knocking.

high speed. The cetane numbers of readily available fuels range from 40 to 55 with values of 40 to 50 most common. These cetane values are satisfactory for medium- and high-speed engines; low-speed engines may use fuels in the 25 to 35 cetane number range.

Addition of certain compounds such as ethyl nitrate, acetone peroxide, and amyl nitrate will improve cetane number. Amyl nitrate is available commercially for this purpose.

Volatility

The distillation characteristics of the fuel describe its volatility. A properly designed fuel has the optimum proportion of low boiling components for easy cold starting and fast warm-up and heavier components that provide power and fuel economy when the engine reaches operating temperature. Either too high or too low volatility may promote smoking, carbon deposits, and oil dilution due to the effect of fuel injection and vaporization in the combustion chamber. The 10, 50, and 90 percent points and the final boiling point are the principal volatility controls. Diesel engines in automotive, agricultural, and construction service use fuels with a final boiling point approaching 700°F (371°C). Urban buses generally use a fuel with a lower final boiling point to minimize exhaust smoke and odor. Detroit Diesel® specifies a 550°F (288°C) maximum end point for their engines in city bus service.

Viscosity

The viscosity of the fuel affects atomization and fuel delivery rate. The viscosity of diesel fuel is normally specified at 100°F (38°C). Fuels for medium- and high-speed engines generally lie in the range from 1.4 to 4.3 centistokes viscosity at 100°F (38°C). The lubricating properties of some low-viscosity, low-pour winter fuels can be improved by addition of 1 percent crankcase oils or lubricity additives. This is important where injection pumps and injectors depend on fuel oil for lubrication, and the fuel oil viscosity is below 1.3 centistokes at 100°F (38°C).

Pour Points and Cloud Points

Before the pour point of a fuel is reached, the fuel will become cloudy due to the formation of wax crystals. This usually occurs some 10° to 15°F (5° to 8°C) above the pour point and is referred to as the cloud point. Wax crystals may begin to plug the fuel filters when the fuel temperature drops to the cloud point. How critical this is in winter operation depends on the design of the fuel system with regard to fuel line bore, freedom from bends, size and location of filters, and degree of warm fuel recirculation, as well as the amount and kind of wax crystals.

Additives known as *flow improvers* are being used successfully to improve the fuel fluidity at low temperatures. Flow improvers modify wax crystal growth so that the wax which forms at low temperatures will pass through the fine (typically 10 to 20 microns) fuel filter screens. The addition of typically 0.1 percent flow improver can result in satisfactory fuel flow at 15°F (9°C) colder temperatures than is possible with untreated fuel.

Flash Points

Flash point is determined by heating the fuel in a small enclosed chamber until the vapors ignite when a small flame is passed over the surface of the liquid. The temperature of the fuel at this point is the flash point. The flash point of a diesel fuel has no relation to its performance in an engine nor to its autoignition qualities. It does provide a useful check on suspected contaminants such as gasoline, since as little as 0.5 percent of gasoline present can lower the flash point of the fuel very markedly.

Sulfur Content

Sulfur in diesel fuel can cause combustion chamber deposits, exhaust system corrosion, and wear on pistons, rings, and cylinders, particularly at low water-jacket temperatures. Sulfur tolerance by an engine is dependent on the type of engine and the type of service.

A fuel sulfur content above 0.4 percent is generally considered as medium or high, whereas fuel with a sulfur content below 0.4 percent is considered low. Summer grades of commercially available diesel fuel are commonly in the 0.2 to 0.5 percent sulfur range. Winter grades often have less than 0.2 percent sulfur. Some slow medium-speed engines in stationary service are designed to operate on heavy fuels that have sulfur contents up to 1.25 percent or even higher.

Diesel engine crankcase oils are formulated to combat various levels of fuel sulfur content, and it is important to use the engine builder's recommended crankcase oil quality and oil change intervals, which often relate to the sulfur level of the fuel as well as to other service conditions.

Most diesel fuels are low in sulfur content, and by using the engine builder's recommended crankcase oil quality and oil change intervals, there should be no concern with the effects of fuel sulfur.

Diesel Fuel Classification

The American Society for Testing Materials (ASTM) has set minimum quality standards for diesel fuel grades as a guide for engine operators. These are grades 1-D, which specifies winter fuel, and 2-D, which defines summer fuel. These definitions are very broad, and the diesel fuels marketed will meet one of these definitions. The Canadian government 3-GP-6d diesel fuel specification recognizes five categories of diesel fuels with more restrictive standards than ASTM.

Quality requirements such as sulfur, ash, water, sediments, and corrosion rating are met by diesel fuel that is blended on a seasonal and geographical basis to satisfy anticipated temperature conditions.

PART 6 DIESEL OPERATING PROBLEMS

Why Diesels Smoke

White smoke is caused by tiny droplets of unburned fuel. It is usually caused by low engine temperatures and disappears when the engine warms up.

Black smoke is caused by a mechanical defect such as a faulty injector or by overloading and/or overfueling the engine. Blue-gray smoke is the result of burning lube oil. It indicates a mechanical defect.

Diesel engines producing smoke also tend to produce objectionable odors.

Why Diesels Knock

In diesel engines, knock is due to the fuel igniting too slowly. It should start to burn almost as soon as it is injected. If there is much delay, a fuel buildup results, which burns with explosive force and causes knocking.

Dirt and Water (Ice)

Diesel fuel line filters and injector filters are in the 2- to 10-micron range. Fuel tanktops, hoses, and nozzles must be kept clean, and water must be minimal to prevent plugging of these filters with dirt or emulsions.

Ice and water are usually formed from condensation or from dissolved water that forms cloud ice at prolonged low temperatures and may cause filter plugging. Small quantities of alcohol can be used to alleviate fuel line or filter ice plugging.

Diesel Fuel Handling

One of the most critical parts of the diesel engine is the fuel-injection system. Many of the components of this system are highly finished and operate with clearances as small as 0.0001 inch (0.00254 mm). Since any foreign material that finds its way into the system can damage these parts and seriously impair engine performance, clean fuel is essential to the proper operation of the engine.

PART 7 PROPANE (LIQUIFIED PETROLEUM GAS, LPG)

LP gas or propane is a by-product of the crude oil refining process in the production of gasoline. It is also obtained as a by-product of natural gas.

LPG is a mixture of propane and butane. It is a vapor in its natural state but it is stored highly compressed; this changes it into a liquid. As a liquid it is much easier to handle, store, and transport. It is stored in very strong tanks (to withstand the pressure) and is converted to vapor before it enters the engine's cylinders.

LP gas consists of a higher proportion of propane and a smaller amount of butane. The actual mixture is varied for use in summer and winter as is the case with gasoline. Propane has a lower boiling point (vaporizes more readily) than butane which makes it easier to ignite. The propane content is, therefore, higher for winter fuel than it is for summer. The lower percentage of propane for summer fuel also helps reduce maximum fuel tank pressures in warm weather caused by higher tank and fuel temperatures.

The effects of temperature on pressure of propane, butane, and propanebutane mixtures are illustrated. The heat energy of propane and butane is less than that of gasoline. The octane rating of LP gas, however, is higher than that of gasoline but it

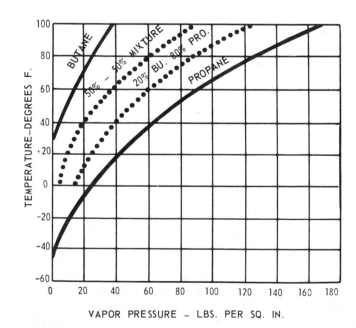

FIGURE 11-6. Effect of temperature on butane, propane, and butane-propane mixtures.

	Propane	Butane
Boiling Point	—44°F.	+32°F.
Heat Needed to Vaporize One Pound Of Liquid	185 BTU	165 BTU
Vapor Pressure At 100°F.	172 Psi	38 Psi
Heat Value Per Gallon	91,960 BTU	103,500 BTU
Octane Rating	125	91

FIGURE 11-7.

burns slower. For this reason, engine compression ratios can be slightly higher in propane fueled engines, and ignition timing may be advanced.

Some of the advantages of using LP gas include the following:

- Less engine wear
- Less oil consumption
- Fewer emissions
- Longer engine life
- Lower maintenance costs

These advantages are offset to some degree by some disadvantages of using LP gas, such as these:

- Fewer refueling stations
- Harder to start in cold weather
- Higher cost of fuel system components
- Higher cost of fuel storage and handling of equipment

The advisability of using LP gas depends on the relative cost and availability of LP gas as compared to other fuels in any particular locality.

The use and handling of LP gas is quite safe if all proper procedures are followed and only recommended equipment is used. Anyone using or servicing LP gas or LP gas vehicles should do so only if fully qualified regarding its use and servicing of LP gas equipment. All local, state, or provincial and federal regulations regarding the use of LP gas and the servicing of LP gas vehicles must be followed.

Compressed Natural Gas (CNG) System

The CNG system is similar in many ways to the LPG system described above. A major difference is that fuel is stored under much higher pressure, which requires stronger fuel tanks.

Aluminum alloy tanks of special construction allow sufficient fuel to be carried for automotive applications without the prohibitive weight problem of equivalent capacity steel tanks. Aluminum's interior surfaces also prevent rust and corrosion from moisture sometimes found in natural gas.

PART 8 SELF-CHECK

1. Crude oil is a mixture of hydrogen and carbon. True or false.
2. List five requirements of gasoline for good performance and fuel economy.
3. The tendency of gasoline to change from a liquid to a vapor is a measure of its _____.
4. The antiknock quality of a gasoline is its _____ number.
5. List four common additives used in gasoline manufacturing.
6. Define the cetane number of diesel fuel.
7. Why do diesel engines smoke?
8. LPG is a mixture of _____ and _____.

PART 9 TEST QUESTIONS

1. Mechanic A says crude oil is a mixture of hydrogen and carbon. Mechanic B says hydrocarbons range from light gases to semi-solid materials. Who is right?
   (a) Mechanic A
   (b) Mechanic B
   (c) both are right
   (d) both are wrong

2. Three factors that govern the performance characteristics of gasoline are:
   (a) volatility, antiknock quality, and cetane rating
   (b) cetane rating, octane rating, and volatility
   (c) volatility, paraffinity, and antiknock quality
   (d) deposit control, antiknock quality, and volatility

3. Mechanic A says leaded gasoline can be used in all vehicles. Mechanic B says unleaded fuel can be used in all vehicles. Who is right?
   (a) Mechanic A
   (b) Mechanic B
   (c) both are right
   (d) both are wrong

4. The cetane rating of diesel fuel is:
    (a) the same as the octane rating of gasoline
    (b) a measure of its auto-ignition quality
    (c) a measure of its heat value
    (d) the same as the Reid vapor pressure of gasoline

5. Some of the advantages of LP gas are:

    (a) less engine wear, fewer refueling stations, and lower maintenance costs
    (b) lower maintenance costs, less engine wear, and longer engine life
    (c) longer engine life, easier starting in cold weather, less engine wear
    (d) less engine wear, lower cost of handling, and lower maintenance costs

Chapter 12

Fuel Supply Systems

Performance Objectives

After thorough study of this chapter and sufficient practical experience on adequate training models, and with the appropriate shop manuals and equipment, you should be able to do the following:

1. Complete the self-check and test questions with at least 80 percent accuracy.
2. Follow the accepted general precautions outlined in this chapter.
3. Describe the purpose, construction, and operation of each of the fuel supply systems and their components.
4. Diagnose basic fuel supply system problems according to the diagnostic charts provided.
5. Safely remove, recondition, replace, and adjust any faulty fuel supply system components according to manufacturer's specifications.
6. Properly performance test the reconditioned system to determine the success of the repairs performed.
7. Prepare the vehicle for customer acceptance.

The fuel supply system is designed to provide a continuous and adequate supply of fuel under sufficient pressure for all operating conditions. The evaporative emission control system prevents the escape of raw fuel vapors from the fuel system to the atmosphere.

PART 1   GASOLINE FUEL SUPPLY SYSTEM

Fuel Tanks

The fuel tank contains a supply of fuel to allow the vehicle to drive a considerable distance without refueling. The tank is so designed that about 10 percent of the tank volume will not fill up with fuel. Air in this area allows fuel to expand without loss of fuel. This expansion area is connected by means of tubing to the charcoal canister.

The tank is provided with a filler tube and cap. Vehicles designed for unleaded fuel use have a restrictor in the filler tube that prevents the entry of the larger leaded-fuel delivery nozzle at the gas pumps.

The tank cap has two valves. A pressure relief valve, which is normally closed, prevents the escape of fuel vapors. Vacuum valves allow atmospheric pressure into the tank as fuel is consumed. With no provision for entry of air, very little fuel could be removed from the tank or the tank would collapse, or both.

The fuel tank unit includes a fuel pick-up tube and screen or filter and a float-operated fuel gauge sending unit. A vapor separator and roll-over valve are located at the top of the tank or somewhere in the line between the tank and the charcoal canister. The fuel tank pickup tube is connected to the fuel pump by means of steel tubing and flexible lines.

Fuel Pumps

The fuel pump delivers a sufficient volume of fuel under adequate pressure to the carburetor for all operating conditions. Two types of fuel pumps are commonly used: the mechanical fuel pump and the electrical fuel pump. The electrical fuel pump may be located inside or outside the fuel tank.

The mechanically operated fuel pump consists of a lever-operated spring-loaded diaphragm, an inlet valve, and an outlet valve. The lever is operated from an eccentric on the camshaft or auxiliary shaft. A pushrod may be used between the eccentric and the lever. The lever pivots on a pin to provide rocker arm action. The other end of the lever is connected to the diaphragm link with a sliding or slotted connection. This allows the diaphragm to be pulled by the lever.

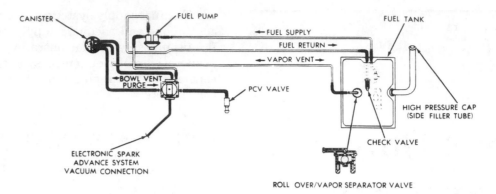

CANISTER   FUEL PUMP   FUEL TANK

← FUEL SUPPLY
FUEL RETURN →
← VAPOR VENT

BOWL VENT
PURGE   PCV VALVE   HIGH PRESSURE CAP
(SIDE FILLER TUBE)

CHECK VALVE

ELECTRONIC SPARK
ADVANCE SYSTEM
VACUUM CONNECTION

ROLL OVER/VAPOR SEPARATOR VALVE

FIGURE 12-1. Fuel system and evaporative emission control system schematic and component identification. *(Courtesy of Chrysler Corporation)*

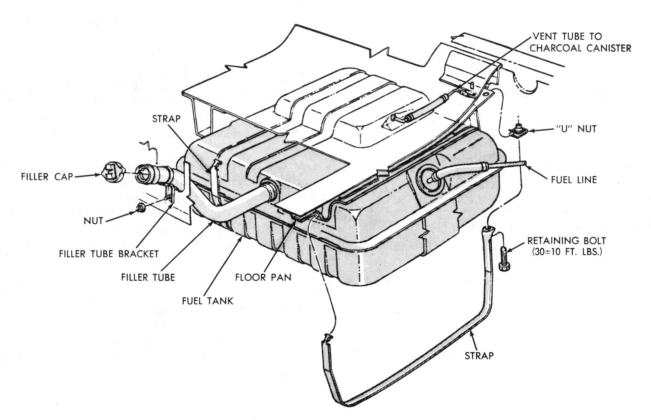

VENT TUBE TO
CHARCOAL CANISTER

STRAP

"U" NUT

FILLER CAP

FUEL LINE

NUT

FILLER TUBE BRACKET

RETAINING BOLT
(30±10 FT. LBS.)

FILLER TUBE   FLOOR PAN

FUEL TANK

STRAP

FIGURE 12-2. Fuel tank and mounting components. Note expansion tank (raised portion of tank). *(Courtesy of Chrysler Corporation)*

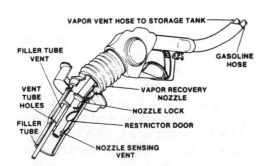

VAPOR VENT HOSE TO STORAGE TANK

FILLER TUBE
VENT

GASOLINE
HOSE

VENT
TUBE
HOLES

VAPOR RECOVERY
NOZZLE

FILLER
TUBE

NOZZLE LOCK

RESTRICTOR DOOR

NOZZLE SENSING
VENT

FIGURE 12-3. Note fuel restrictor in fill pipe. Restrictor allows only smaller unleaded fuel filler nozzle to enter fill pipe. Note vapor recovery type of fill nozzle. *(Courtesy of Chrysler Corporation)*

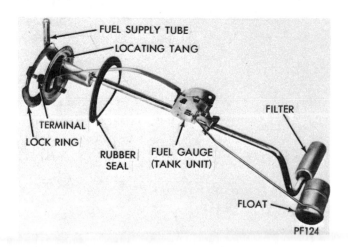

FIGURE 12-4. Fuel pickup tube, filter, and gauge sending unit. This assembly is located in the fuel tank. *(Courtesy of Chrysler Corporation)*

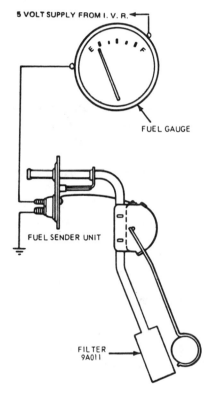

FIGURE 12-5. Hinged float on tank unit operates variable resistor sending unit. An electrical signal sent to the fuel gauge varies with the level of fuel in the tank. Gauge reading shows level of fuel in tank. *(Courtesy of Ford Motor Co. of Canada Ltd.)*

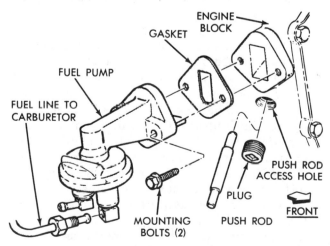

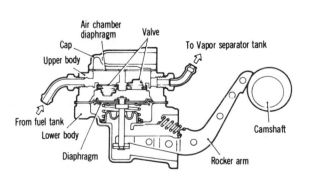

FIGURE 12-6. Mechanical fuel pump is operated by an eccentric on the camshaft or accessory shaft. Note fuel vapor return line, fuel inlet, and outlet. *(Courtesy of Chrysler Corporation)*

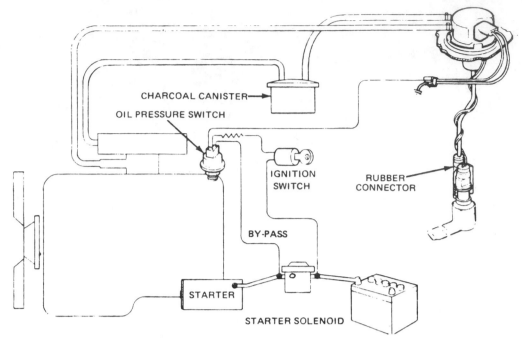

FIGURE 12-7. Schematic of an in-tank electric fuel pump system. *(Courtesy of Ford Motor Co. of Canada Ltd.)*

When the diaphragm is lifted, it creates a low pressure area in the pump. Atmospheric pressure on the fuel in the tank causes fuel to be forced into the low-pressure area in the pump past the one-way inlet valve. Spring pressure keeps the outlet valve closed during the pump intake stroke.

When the lever moves down, the diaphragm spring forces the diaphragm down and pressurizes the fuel. This pressure closes the inlet valve and opens the outlet valve.

Spring pressure forces the diaphragm down far enough to supply the carburetor with enough fuel to maintain the correct fuel level in the carburetor. Fuel pressure is dependent on diaphragm spring pressure. Normal fuel pump pressure ranges from approximately 3 to 8 psi (20.7 to 55 kilopascals), for carburetor systems. Gasoline fuel injection supply pumps operate at pressures up to about 60 psi (415 kPa) in some cases, using electric fuel pumps.

Electrical fuel pumps may be of the rotary-vane type or the diaphragm type. The in-tank electric pump is the rotary type. The rotary type is a self-contained unit with a small electric motor. The diaphragm type of pump is operated by an electric solenoid. Seamless steel tubing and flexible synthetic rubber lines are used for fuel lines and vapor recovery systems.

Filters

A second fuel filter in addition to the in-tank filter is used in the gasoline fuel system. This filter may be an in-line filter located in the fuel line between the pump and the carburetor, or it may be a filter in the carburetor at the fuel inlet.

In-line filters are usually an accordion type of paper element. In-carburetor filters may be of the paper-element type or they may be sintered bronze elements. Some vehicles have the fuel filter incorporated in the fuel pump assembly.

PART 2   EVAPORATIVE EMISSION CONTROL

The evaporative emission control system is designed to prevent the escape of raw fuel vapors (hydrocarbons) from the vehicle into the atmosphere. Components of this system include the expansion tank or chamber (inside the fuel tank), a vapor separator, a vapor line from the vapor separator to a charcoal canister, a vapor return line from either the fuel pump or fuel filter, a carburetor bowl vent valve and vapor line connecting it to the carbon canister, and a purge line from the canister to the intake manifold carburetor base. Although not involved with evaporative emission control, a roll-over valve is included in this system to prevent the escape of raw fuel in case of accidental vehicle upset.

When the temperature of the fuel in the fuel tank increases, the fuel expands. This increaes fuel tank pressure, which forces vapors from the expansion tank through the vapor separator orifice and through the vapor line to the carbon canister in the engine compartment. During periods of engine op-

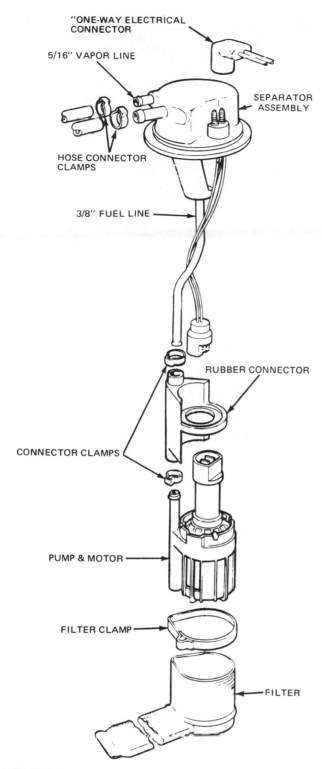

FIGURE 12-8. Detailed view of electric fuel pump components. *(Courtesy of Ford Motor Co. of Canada Ltd.)*

eration when sufficient fuel is being consumed, this action would not take place. Most carburetors have a bowl vent connected to the carbon canister by a vapor line. At engine idle or when the engine is stopped, the bowl vent is open, allowing bowl vapors to escape to the canister where they are stored until purging takes place.

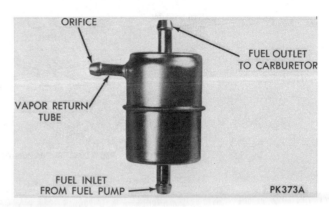

FIGURE 12-9. In-line type of gasoline fuel filter used on many vehicles. A metered opening (orifice) allows fuel vapors to return to the fuel tank. *(Courtesy of Chrysler Corporation)*

The fuel pump or fuel filter on many vehicles is equipped with a metered orifice on the pressure side, which is connected to a return line to the fuel tank. This allows hot fuel and vapor to return to the fuel tank under all conditions. With the engine running, this assures a continuous supply of cool fuel in the fuel delivery system to prevent vapor lock. With the engine stopped, it relieves fuel pressure between the carburetor and fuel pump to improve hot starting.

The carbon canister is a steel or plastic container filled with tightly packed activated carbon (approximately 700 grams). This carbon has the ability to store many times its weight in fuel vapors. Storing and purging (cleaning) of the carbon can continue repeatedly and indefinitely. A filtered fresh-air inlet allows entry of clean, fresh air during purging.

A purge line is connected from the canister to the induction system. Engine intake manifold vac-

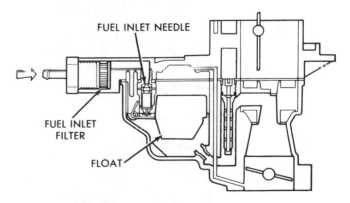

FIGURE 12-10. Fuel filter mounted at inlet fitting in carburetor. Both bellows-type paper elements (shown here) and sintered-bronze filter elements are used. *(Courtesy of Chrysler Corporation)*

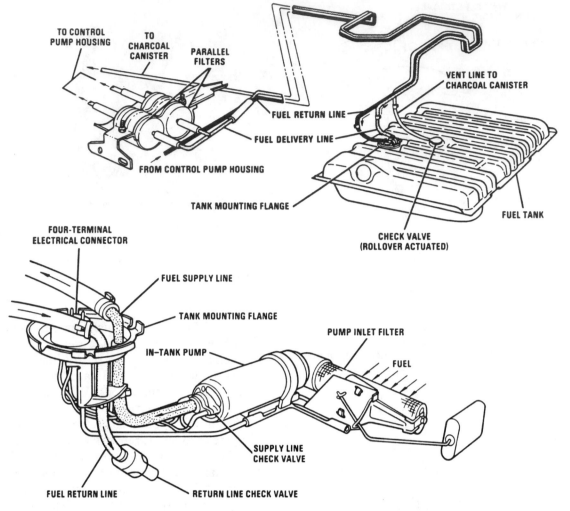

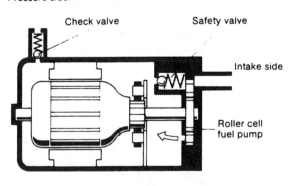

FIGURE 12–11. Fuel supply system components for Chrysler's throttle body gasoline fuel injection system. *(Courtesy of Chrysler Corporation)*

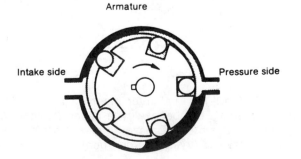

FIGURE 12–12. Wet type of electric fuel pump is used in continuous injection system. This pump is submerged in fuel and the brushes armature and bearings operate in fuel. Since there is never a combustible mixture present, there is no danger of igniting the gasoline. The fuel lubricates and cools the pump motor. Note centrifugal roller pumping element. *(Courtesy of Robert Bosch Canada Ltd.)*

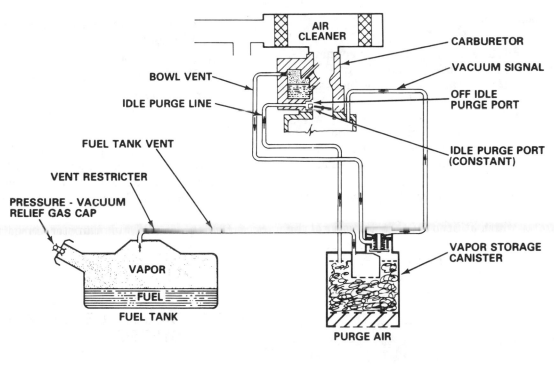

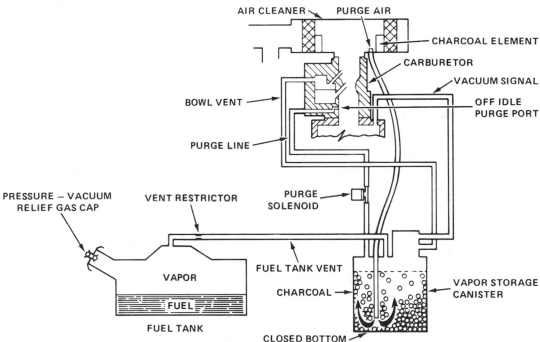

FIGURE 12-13. Open canister (top) and closed canister (bottom) evaporative emission control system schematics. *(Courtesy of General Motors Corporation)*

uum causes fresh air to pass over the carbon in the canister. This air flow carries the fuel vapors into the induction system during engine operation. On some vehicles, purging takes place only when engine speed is above idle speed. A vacuum or solenoid actuated purge valve is used to control purging on some systems.

Dual Canister Systems

A dual canister evaporation control system is used on some vehicles. When fuel evaporates in the carburetor float chamber, the vapors pass through vent hoses or tubes to the primary canister, where they are temporarily held until they can be drawn into the intake manifold when the engine is running. A vacuum port located in the base of the carburetor governs vapor flow to the engine. The fuel tank is vented through a vapor vent tube assembly. A tube from the vent tube assembly leads to the secondary charcoal canister where evaporated fuel vapors from the fuel tank are temporarily held until they can be drawn into the intake manifold when the engine is running.

Fuel vapors are purged from the primary canister through the use of a vacuum connection on the carburetor which utilizes the throttle valve of the carburetor as a purge valve. Fuel vapors from the secondary canister are purged through the PCV hose to the carburetor utilizing a vacuum signal from the distributor vacuum hose to open the canister purge system.

Another dual canister system uses a second canister as an overload for increased storage capacity. The two canisters are interconnected by a vapor line.

Computer Controlled Canister Purge

This is accomplished with an electrically operated solenoid valve that is controlled by the ECM.

- When the solenoid is electrically energized, it will not allow purge.

- When the solenoid is not electrically energized, it allows purge.

- Purge is enabled approximately 10 seconds after engine coolant temperature reaches 120 degrees.

At this time, fuel vapors move from the vapor canister through the purge solenoid to the throttle body. At closed throttle, the vapors enter the intake manifold through a .030 inch (0.762 mm) drilling below the throttle valves.

During off idle, full canister purge is allowed through additional ports uncovered by the throttle valves.

PART 3   DIESEL FUEL SUPPLY SYSTEM

The typical fuel supply system consists of the following components:

- Fuel tank
- In-tank fuel filter and pick-up tube

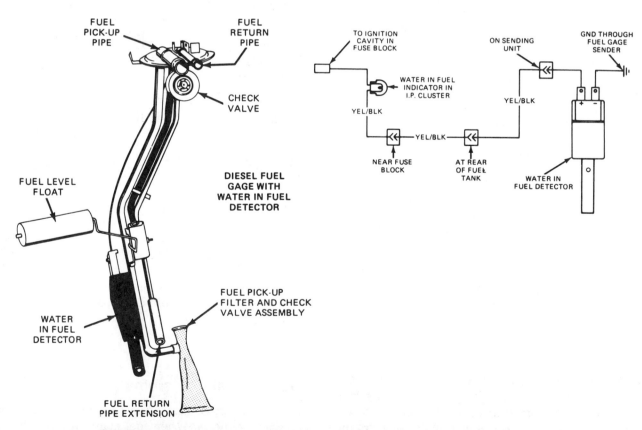

FIGURE 12–14. In-tank unit of GM diesel engine fuel supply system (left) and electrical circuit (right) of water in fuel detector. Note fuel pickup filter, fuel gauge sending unit, and fuel return line. *(Courtesy of General Motors Corporation)*

- Fuel gauge sending unit (in tank)
- Water detector (in tank)
- Fuel supply lines and return lines
- Fuel filters and water separators

These components are all very similar to those described for the gasoline fuel supply system in Part 1 of this chapter with the exception of the water separator and the water in fuel detector and will, therefore, not be described again.

Since the diesel injection system (injection pump and fuel injectors) is extremely sensitive to the presence of any water in the fuel it is critical to the proper operation of the system that water does not reach these components. Clearances between operating parts are extremely small; therefore, any contamination resulting from water, rust, or dirt will cause these parts to fail. The fuel supply system must be kept as free from dirt and moisture as possible, and the water separator and fuel filters must be properly maintained.

In addition to the components listed above, there is also a fuel transfer pump usually attached to or part of the fuel injection pump. This pump supplies fuel under fairly high pressure (around the 60 psi (415 kPa) range) to the injection pump. These pumps are described in the section on diesel fuel injection, Chapter 15.

PART 4   PROPANE FUEL SUPPLY SYSTEM

The propane fuel system is a completely closed system which contains a supply of pressurized liquid propane fuel. The liquid propane is delivered by specially approved fuel lines to a fuel lock and a converter/regulator. The converter/regulator changes the pressurized liquid to a low-pressure vapor and meters fuel vapor delivery to a simple carburetor. The carburetor, responding to engine vacuum, mixes fuel vapor with air in the venturi and regulates air/fuel delivery to the engine.

It is the nature of propane fuel to vaporize at normal atmospheric pressures and temperatures above $-44°F$ ($-42°C$). Since the engine needs vaporized fuel for combustion, the job of the propane fuel system is simply to meter the quantity of vapor delivered.

The propane fuel system consists of four major components:

- Fuel tank assembly
- Fuel lock and filter
- Converter/regulator with electric primer
- Carburetor

Fuel Tank Assembly

The fuel tank assembly is composed of specially approved materials that meet design standards and specifications for a pressurized propane fuel system.

The fuel tanks store the liquid fuel supply. Two equalizing tubes connect the tanks. An excess flow valve inside the tank will shut off fuel flow automatically in the event of a major fuel line leak. A mechanical float rides on the liquid fuel and operates a magnet in the mounting flange of the sending unit. The magnet in turn moves another magnet in the fuel gauge sending unit to change electrical resistance to the fuel gauge.

Outside the fuel tank are several safety valves: The manual shut-off valve, the hydrostatic relief valve, the fill valve, the 80 percent stop-fill valve, and the pressure relief valve. The basic valve functions are as follows:

- *Fill valve*—double back-seat fuel inlet valve used to fill tanks with fuel
- *80 percent Stop-Fill Valve*—vent for limited maximum safe fuel supply (also called "fixed liquid level gauge")
- *Manual Shut-Off Valve*—to close off liquid fuel flow from tank during service (attached to tank—looks like a water spigot)
- *Hydrostatic Relief Valve*—for relieving liquid fuel pressure during excessive ambient temperature (next to shut-off valve)
- *Pressure Relief Valve*—for relieving excess vapor tank pressure during excessive ambient temperature (right gear quarter outlet)
- *Excess Flow Valve*—stops fuel flow in the event of a major leak (inside tanks)

Fuel Lock and Filter

The fuel lock, inside the engine compartment, shuts off liquid fuel supply when the engine is not running.

Liquid fuel under pressure enters the fuel lock through a filter element. A check valve blocks the fuel until engine vacuum opens the valve.

Converter/Regulator

The converter/regulator receives liquid fuel under pressure from the fuel lock with the engine cranking or running. The converter/regulator contains a diaphragm chamber that allows liquid propane to expand under low pressure. The regulator contains metering components to control vapor flow.

Engine coolant circulates through a passage in

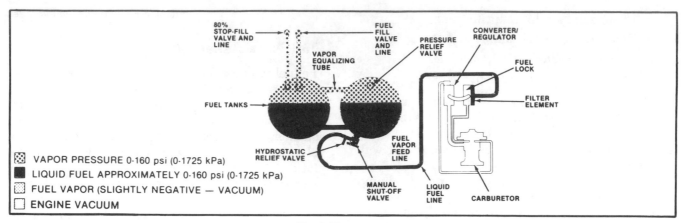

Fuel Flow — Engine Off

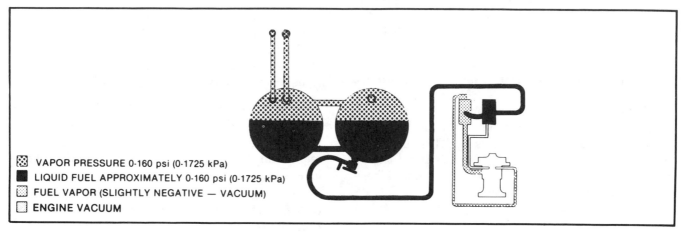

Fuel Flow — Engine Running

FIGURE 12–15. Propane fuel supply system schematic with dual tanks connected by equalizing tubes. *(Courtesy of Ford Motor Co. of Canada Ltd.)*

the converter/regulator to warm the unit and prevent freezing. The coolant flows from the heater core to the converter/regulator and back to the engine.

Carburetors

The LP-gas carburetor must mix fuel vapor with air in the proper ratio for each speed and load of the engine.

The LP-gas carburetor does much the same job as gasoline carburetor models. The main difference is that, when fuel enters the LP-gas model, it is a vapor, while in the gasoline, it is a liquid.

Since the fuel is already a vapor, the LP-gas carburetor does not need a fuel bowl system built in. It does not need a venturi to vaporize fuel, although some models based on gasoline principles do have one.

The metering valve varies the amount of fuel vapor entering the carburetor.

The spray bar takes the fuel vapor and mixes it with air flow coming in from the air cleaner.

The throttle plate contains the incoming air and works with the metering valve to get the best fuel/air mixture for each load and speed.

PART 5   FUEL SUPPLY SYSTEM DIAGNOSIS AND SERVICE

Performance, economy, and emissions problems can result from fuel supply system problems. However, it must be remembered that similar symptoms may be caused by other systems such as air cleaners, carburetors, fuel injection equipment, electrical, exhaust, cooling, lubrication, and engine mechanical problems. A complete understanding of all systems must be acquired in order to intelligently diagnose problems in a manner which will identify the problem system and isolate the problem component in the faulty system. It is with this approach that the following diagnostic charts are here presented after the general precautions.

PART 6 GENERAL PRECAUTIONS

Servicing fuel systems requires fully recognizing all the potential hazards of handling highly volatile and explosive fuels and dangerously poisonous carbon monoxide exhaust gases. Serious personal injury and property damage may result from a careless at-

FIGURE 12–16. When servicing fuel tanks, proper equipment should be used to safely handle and store highly flammable and explosive gasoline. This unit is used to remove fuel from fuel tank and is used to fill tank after repairs. *(Courtesy of Chrysler Corporation)*

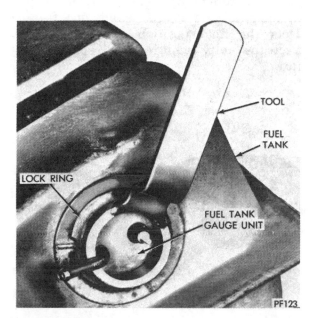

FIGURE 12–17. Special tool used to remove retaining ring holding fuel tank sending unit. *(Courtesy of Chrysler Corporation)*

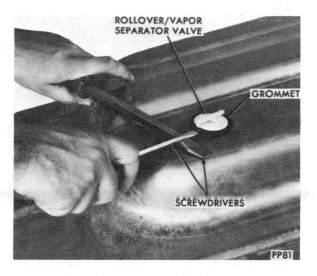

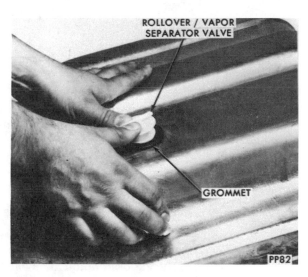

FIGURE 12–18. Removing and installing one type of rollover-vapor separator valve. *(Courtesy of Chrysler Corporation)*

titude toward safe service procedures. Precautions that must be observed are as follows:

• Observe all precautions listed in Chapter 1, Parts 1 & 2.

• Do not disassemble any fuel system components without due consideration of the consequences (spilling fuel, pressurized lines, and so on).

• Carburetor and vehicle must be properly identified to obtain correct parts and specifications.

• Disconnect negative battery cable before disconnecting any fuel lines.

• Always follow manufacturer's recommended specifications and torque values.

• Make sure there are no fuel or exhaust leaks after working on these systems.

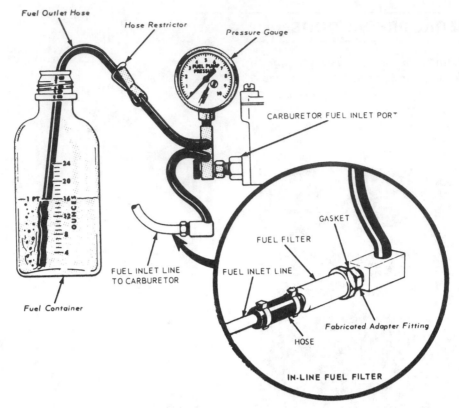

FIGURE 12-19. Arrangement and equipment used to test fuel pump pressure and volume. *(Courtesy of Ford Motor Co. of Canada Ltd.)*

• Handle carburetor cleaning fluids with care; skin contact or inhaling vapors should be avoided as much as possible.

• Cleaning fluid should be kept covered to avoid evaporation and contamination.

• Fuel tanks should be sent for repair to a shop equipped to safely handle this work. Welding should not be attempted.

• Welding of any kind under the vehicle or in the engine compartment requires due consideration of the explosive nature of fuels and the fire hazard of oil and wiring.

• Vehicle must have parking brake applied and transmission in park position (automatic transmission) or neutral to prevent accidental vehicle movement when running engine.

• Exhaust gases must be properly vented to outside of service area.

• Observe safe procedures when handling or storing fuel removed from fuel system components.

• Observe all local, state, and federal law pre-

cautions regarding propane fuel system service. Do not attempt this service unless fully qualified to do so.

• Abide by local laws for the disposal of contaminated fuels.

The following problems are dealt with in the charts:

1. Engine cranks normally. Will not start.
2. Engine starts and stalls.
3. Engine starts hard.
4. Engine idles abnormally and/or stalls; inconsistent engine idle speeds.
5. Engine diesels (after-run) upon shut-off.
6. Engine hesitates on acceleration.
7. Engine has less than normal power at low speeds.
8. Engine has less than normal power on heavy acceleration or at high speed.
9. Engine surges.
10. Poor gas mileage.

PROBLEM	CAUSE	CORRECTION
Engine cranks normally, but will not start.	Improper starting procedure used.	Check with the customer to determine if proper starting procedure is used, as outlined in the owner's manual.
	Choke valve not operating properly.	Adjust the choke thermostatic coil to specification. Check the choke valve and/or linkage as necessary. Replace parts if defective. If caused by foreign material and gum, clean with suitable non-oil-base solvent. *Note:* After any choke system work, check choke vacuum break settings and correct as necessary.
	No fuel in carburetor.	Remove fuel line at carburetor. Connect hose to fuel line and run into metal container. Remove the wire from the "bat" terminal of the distributor. Crank over engine, If there is no fuel discharge from the fuel line, test fuel pump. If fuel supply is okay, check the following:
		a. Inspect fuel inlet filter. If plugged, replace.
		b. If fuel filter is okay, remove air horn and check for a bind in the float mechanism or a sticking inlet needle. If okay, adjust float as specified.
	Engine flooded. To check for flooding, remove the air cleaner with the engine immediately shut off and look into the carburetor bores. Fuel will be dripping off nozzles.	Remove the air horn. Check fuel inlet needle and seat for proper seal. If the needle is leaking, replace. Check float for free movement, bent float hanger, or binds in the float arm. If foreign material is in fuel system, clean the system and replace fuel filters as necessary. If excessive foreign material is found, completely disassemble and clean.
Engine starts but will not keep running.	Fuel pump.	Check fuel pump pressure and volume; replace if necessary.
	Idle speed.	Adjust idle to specifications.
	Choke heater system malfunctioning (may cause loading).	Check vacuum supply at hot-air inlet to choke housing. Check for plugged, restricted, or broken heat tubes. Check routing of all hot-air parts.
	Loose, broken, or incorrect vacuum hose routing.	Check condition and routing of all vacuum hoses; correct as necessary. Check for free movement of fast-idle cam. Clean and/or realign as necessary.
	Choke vacuum break units are not adjusted to specification or are defective.	Adjust both vacuum break assemblies to specification. If adjusted okay, check the vacuum break units for proper operation. Always check the fast-idle cam adjustment when adjusting vacuum break units.
	Choke valve sticking and/or binding.	Clean and align linkage or replace if necessary. Readjust all choke settings.
	Insufficient fuel in carburetor.	Check fuel pump pressure and volume. Check for partially plugged fuel inlet filter. Replace if contaminated. Check the float level adjustment for binding condition. Adjust as specified.
Engine starts hard (cranks normally).	Loose, broken, or incorrect vacuum hose routing.	Check condition and routing of all vacuum hoses; correct as necessary.
	Incorrect starting procedures.	Check to be sure customer is using the starting procedure outlined in owner's manual.
	Malfunction in accelerator pump system.	Check accelerator pump adjustment and operation. Check pump discharge ball for sticking or leakage.
	Choke valve not closing.	Adjust choke thermostatic coil. Check choke valve and linkage for binds and alignment. Clean and repair or replace as necessary.
	Vacuum breaks misadjusted or malfunctioning.	Check for adjustment and function of vacuum breaks. Correct as necessary.
	Insufficient fuel in bowl.	Check fuel pump pressure and volume. Check for partially plugged fuel inlet filter. Replace if dirty. Check float mechanism. Adjust as specified.

PROBLEM	CAUSE	CORRECTION
	Flooding.	Check float and needle and seat for proper operation.
	Where used, check to see if vent valve is inoperative or misadjusted.	Check for operation and adjustment of vent valve (if used).
	Slow engine cranking speed.	Refer to starting circuit diagnosis.
Engine idles abnormally (too fast or too slow).	Incorrect idle speed.	Reset idle speed per instruction on underhood label.
	Air leaks into carburetor bores beneath throttle valves, manifold leaks, or vacuum hoses disconnected or installed improperly.	Check all vacuum hoses and restrictors leading into the manifold or carburetor base for leaks or being disconnected. Install or replace as necessary.
		Torque carburetor to manifold bolts. Using a pressure oil can, spray light oil or kerosene around manifold to head surfaces and carburetor throttle body. *Note:* Do not spray at throttle shaft ends. If engine rpm changes, tighten or replace the carburetor or manifold gaskets as necessary.
	Clogged or malfunctioning PCV system.	Check PCV system. Clean and/or replace as necessary.
	Carburetor flooding.	Remove air horn and check float adjustments.
	Check by using procedure outlined under "Engine Flooded."	Check float needle and seat for proper seal. If a needle and seat tester is not available, apply vacuum to the needle seat with needle installed. If the needle is leaking or damaged, replace.
		Check float for free movement.
		Check for bent float hanger or binds in the float arm.
		If foreign material is found in the carburetor, clean the fuel system and carburetor. Replace fuel filters as necessary.
	Restricted air cleaner element.	Replace as necessary.
	Idle system plugged or restricted.	Clean carburetor.
	Incorrect idle mixture adjustment.	Readjust per specified procedure.
	Defective idle stop solenoid, idle speed-up solenoid, or wiring.	Check solenoid and wiring.
	Throttle blades or linkage sticking and/or binding.	Check throttle linkage and throttle blades (primary and secondary) for smooth and free operation. Correct problem areas.
Engine diesels (after-run) upon shut off.	Loose, broken, or improperly routed vacuum hoses.	Check condition and routing of all vacuum hoses. Correct as necessary.
	Incorrect idle speed.	Reset idle speed per instructions on label in engine compartment.
	Malfunction of idle stop solenoid, idle speed-up solenoid, or dashpot.	Check for correct operation of idle solenoid. Check for sticky or binding solenoid.
	Fast-idle cam not fully off.	Check fast-idle cam for freedom of operation. Clean, repair, or adjust as required. Check choke heated air tubes for routing, fittings being tight, or tubes plugged. Check choke linkage for binding. Clean and correct as necessary.
	Excessively lean condition caused by maladjusted carburetor idle mixture.	Adjust carburetor idle mixture.
	Ignition timing retarded.	Set to specifications.
Engine hesitates on acceleration.	Loose, broken, or incorrect vacuum hose routing.	Check condition and routing of all vacuum hoses; correct or replace.
	Accelerator pump not adjusted to specification or inoperative.	Adjust accelerator pump or replace.
	Inoperative accelerator pump system.	Remove air horn and check pump cup. If cracked, scored, or distorted, replace the pump plunger.
	Note: A quick check of the pump system can be made as follows: With the engine off, look into the carburetor bores and observe pump nozzles while quickly opening throttle lever. A full stream of fuel should emit from each pump nozzle.	Check the pump discharge ball for proper seating and location.
	Foreign matter in pump passages.	Clean and blow out with compressed air.
	Float level too low.	Check and reset float level to specification.
	Front vacuum break diaphragm not functioning properly.	Check adjustment and operation of vacuum break diaphragm.

PROBLEM	CAUSE	CORRECTION
	Air valve malfunction.	Check operation of secondary air valve. Check spring tension adjustment.
	Power-enrichment system not operating correctly.	Check for binding or stuck power piston(s); correct as necessary.
	Inoperative air cleaner heated air control.	Check operation of thermostatic air cleaner system.
	Fuel filter dirty or plugged.	Replace filter and clean fuel system as necessary.
	Distributor vacuum or mechanical advance malfunctioning.	Check for proper operation.
	Timing not to specifications.	Adjust to specifications.
	Choke coil misadjusted (cold operation).	Adjust to specifications.
	EGR valve stuck open.	Inspect and clean EGR valve.
Engine has less then normal power at normal accelerations.	Loose, broken, or incorrect vacuum hose routing.	Check condition and routing of all vacuum hoses.
	Clogged or defective PCV system.	Clean or replace as necessary.
	Choke sticking.	Check complete choke system for sticking or binding. Clean and realign as necessary. Check adjustment of choke thermostatic coil. Check connections and operation of choke hot-air system. Check jets and channels for plugging; clean and blow out passages.
	Clogged or inoperative power system.	Remove air horn and check for free operation of power pistons.
	Air cleaner temperature regulation improper.	Check regulation and operation of air cleaner system.
	Transmission malfunction.	Refer to transmission diagnosis.
	Ignition system malfunction.	Check ignition system.
	Exhaust system.	Check for restrictions. Correct as required.
Less than normal power on heavy acceleration or at high speed.	Carburetor throttle valves not going wide open. Turn off engine and check by pushing accelerator pedal to floor.	Correct throttle linkage to obtain wide open throttle in carburetor.
	Secondary throttle lockout not allowing secondaries to open.	Check for binding or sticking lockout lever. Check for free movement of fast-idle cam. Check choke heated air system for proper and tight connections plus flow through system. Check adjustment of choke thermostatic coil. Make necessary corrections and adjustments.
	Spark plugs fouled, incorrect gap.	Clean, regap, or replace plugs.
	Plugged air cleaner element.	Replace element.
	Air valve malfunction (where applicable).	Check for free operation of air valve. Check spring tension adjustment. Make necessary adjustments and corrections.
	Plugged fuel inlet filter.	Replace with a new filter element.
	Insufficient fuel to carburetor.	Check fuel pump and system; run pressure and volume test.
	Power-enrichment system not operating correctly.	Remove the air horn and check for free operation of power piston(s); clean and correct as necessary.
	Choke closed or partially closed.	Free choke valve or linkage.
	Float level too low.	Check and reset float level to specification.
	Transmission malfunction.	Refer to transmission diagnosis.
	Ignition system malfunction.	Check ignition system.
	Fuel metering jets restricted.	If the fuel metering jets are restricted and an excessive amount of foreign material is found in the fuel bowl, the carburetor should be completely disassembled and cleaned.
	Fuel pump.	Check fuel pump pressure and volume; inspect lines for leaks and restrictions.
	Exhaust system.	Check for restrictions. Correct as required.
	Loose, broken, or incorrect vacuum hose routing.	Check condition and routing of all vacuum hoses. Correct as necessary.
	PCV system clogged or malfunctioning.	Check PCV system. Clean or replace as necessary.
	Loose carburetor, EGR, or intake manifold bolts and/or leaking gaskets.	Torque carburetor to manifold bolts. Using a pressure oil can, spray light oil or kerosene around manifold to head mounting surface and carburetor base. If engine rpm changes, tighten or replace the carburetor or manifold gaskets as necessary. Check EGR mounting bolt torque.
	Low or erratic fuel pump pressure.	Check fuel delivery and pressure.

PROBLEM	CAUSE	CORRECTION
	Contaminated fuel.	Check for contaminants in fuel. Clean system if necessary.
	Fuel filter plugged.	Check and replace as necessary.
	Float level too low.	Check and reset float level to specification.
	Malfunctioning float and/or needle and seat.	Check operation of system. Repair or replace as necessary.
	Power piston stuck or binding.	Check for free movement of power piston(s). Clean and correct as necessary.
	Fuel jets or passage plugged or restricted.	Clean and blow out with compressed air.
	Ignition system malfunction.	Check ignition system.
	Exhaust system.	Check for restrictions. Correct as necessary.
Poor gas mileage.	Customer driving habits.	Run mileage test with customer driving if possible. Make sure car has 2000 to 3000 miles for the break-in period.
	Loose, broken, or improperly routed vacuum hoses.	Check condition of all vacuum hose routings. Correct as necessary.
	Engine in need of service.	Check engine compression, examine spark plugs; if fouled or improperly gapped, clean and regap or replace. Check ignition wire condition and check and reset ignition timing. Replace air cleaner element if dirty. Check for restricted exhaust system and intake manifold for leakage. Check carburetor mounting bolt torque. Check vacuum and mechanical advance.
	Fuel leaks.	Check fuel tank, fuel lines, and fuel pump for any fuel leakage.
	High fuel level in carburetor.	Check fuel inlet needle and seat for proper seal. Test, using suction from a vacuum source. If needle is leaking, replace. Check for loaded float. Reset float level to specification. If excessive foreign material is present in the carburetor bowl, the carburetor should be cleaned.
	Power system in carburetor not functioning properly. Power piston(s) sticking or metering rods out of jets.	Remove air horn and check for free movement of power piston(s). Clean and correct as necessary.
Engine starts but will not continue to run or will run but surges and backfires.	Faulty fuel pump.	Perform fuel pump test. Remove and replace fuel pump as required.
Engine will not start.	Faulty fuel pump.	Perform diagnostic tests on the fuel pump. Remove and replace fuel pump as required.
Gasoline odor.	Tank overfilled.	Do not "pack" tank. Fill to automatic shut off.
	Fuel feed or vapor return line leaking.	Correct as required.
	Leak in fuel tank.	Purge tank and repair or replace tank as required.
	Disconnected fuel tank vent lines or hoses.	Connect lines or hoses as required.
	Purge lines not connected, improperly routed, plugged, or pinched.	Check, connect, and open lines as required.
	Faulty fill cap.	Install new cap.
Collapsed fuel tank.	Plugged or pinched vent lines or hoses, and defective cap.	Check all lines from tank to canister and replace cap.
Fuel tank rattles.	Mounting straps loose.	Tighten straps to specifications.
	Baffle loose.	Replace fuel tank.
	Foreign material in tank.	Remove tank and clean.
	Felt strips improperly located.	Install strips.

PROBLEM	CAUSE	CORRECTION
Fuel starvation.	Tank gauge unit filter plugged. Fuel line pinched, plugged, or misrouted. Fuel pump not operating. Choke system.	Replace filter. Check, open, or reroute as required. See fuel pump test. Check choke heated air tubes for routing and/or plugging that would restrict hot air flow to choke housing. Check choke linkage for binding. Clean or repair as required. Check adjustment of thermostatic coil. Readjust to specification as required.
	Plugged air cleaner element. Exhaust system. Low tire pressure or incorrect tire size. Transmission malfunction.	Replace element. Check for restrictions. Correct as required. Inflate tires to specifications and use correct tire sizes. Refer to transmission diagnosis.
Car feels like it is running out of gas; surging occurs in mid-speed range.	Plugged fuel filters. Faulty fuel pump Foreign material in fuel system or kinked fuel pipes or hoses.	Remove and replace filters. Perform fuel pump test. Remove and replace fuel pump as required. Inspect pipes and hoses for kinks and bends; blow out to check for plugging. Remove and replace as required.

PART 8   DIESEL FUEL SYSTEM DIAGNOSIS AND SERVICE PROCEDURE

PROBLEM	CAUSE	CORRECTION
Engine will not crank or cranks slowly.	1. Loose or corroded battery cables. 2. Discharged batteries. 3. Starter inoperative. 4. Wrong engine oil.	1. Check connections at batteries, engine block, and starter solenoid. 2. Check generator output and generator belt adjustment. 3. Check voltage to starter and starter solenoid. If OK, remove starter for repair. 4. Drain and refill with oil of recommended viscosity.
Engine cranks normally; will not start.	1. Incorrect starting procedure. 2. No voltage to fuel solenoid. 3. Glow plugs inoperative. 4. No fuel to nozzles. 5. No fuel to injection pump. 6. Restricted fuel tank filter. 7. Incorrect or contaminated fuel.	1. Use recommended starting procedure. 2. Connect a 12-volt test lamp from wire at injection pump solenoid to ground. Turn ignition to *on*. Lamp should light. Correct as required. 3. Check glow plugs and replace if needed. Check electrical feed to glow plugs and correct as needed. 4. Loosen injection line at a nozzle. Do not disconnect. Use care to direct fuel away from sources of ignition. Wipe connection to be sure it is dry. Crank 5 seconds. Fuel should flow from injection line. Tighten connection. 5. Remove line at inlet to injection pump fuel filter. Connect hose from line to metal container. Crank engine. If no fuel is discharged, test the engine fuel pump. If the fuel pump is OK, check the injection pump fuel filter and, if plugged, replace it. If fuel filter and line to injection pump are OK, remove injection pump for repair. 6. Remove and check filter. 7. Flush fuel system and install correct fuel.

PROBLEM	CAUSE	CORRECTION
	8. Pump timing incorrect.	8. Make certain that pump timing mark is aligned with mark on adapter.
	9. Low compression.	9. Check compression to determine cause.
Engine starts but will not continue to run at idle.	1. Slow idle incorrectly adjusted.	1. Adjust idle screw to specification.
	2. Fast-idle solenoid inoperative.	2. With engine cold, start engine; solenoid should move to hold injection pump lever in fast-idle position. If solenoid does not move, correct as needed.
	3. Restricted fuel return system.	3. Disconnect fuel return line at injection pump and route hose to a metal container. Connect a hose to the injection pump connection; route it to the metal container. Crank the engine and allow it to idle. If engine idles normally, correct restriction in fuel return lines.
	4. Pump timing incorrect.	4. Make certain that timing mark on injection pump is aligned with mark on adapter.
	5. Limited fuel to injection pump.	5. Test the engine fuel pump; check fuel lines. Replace as necessary.
	6. Air in injection lines to nozzles.	6. Loosen injection line at nozzle(s) and bleed air. Use care to direct fuel away from sources of ignition.
	7. Incorrect or contaminated fuel.	7. Flush fuel system and install correct fuel.
	8. Injection pump malfunction.	8. Remove injection pump for repair.
	9. Fuel solenoid closes in run position.	9. Ignition switch out of adjustment.
Engine starts, idles rough, without abnormal noise or smoke.	1. Slow idle incorrectly adjusted.	1. Adjust slow-idle screw to specification.
	2. Injection line leaks.	2. Wipe off injection lines and connections. Run engine and check for leaks. Correct leaks.
	3. Air in injection lines to nozzles.	3. Loosen injection line at nozzle(s) and bleed air. Use care to direct fuel away from sources of ignition.
	4. Nozzle(s) malfunction.	4. With engine running, loosen injection line fitting at each nozzle in turn. Use care to direct fuel away from sources of ignition. Each good nozzle should change engine idle quality when fuel is allowed to leak. If nozzle is found that does not change idle quality, it should be replaced.
	5. Incorrect or contaminated fuel.	5. Flush fuel system and install correct fuel.
Engine starts and idles rough with excessive noise and/or smoke.	1. Injection pump timing incorrect.	1. Be sure timing mark on injection pump is aligned with mark on adapter.
	2. Air in injection lines to nozzles.	2. Loosen injection line at nozzle(s) and bleed air. Use care to direct fuel away from sources of ignition.
	3. Nozzle(s) malfunction.	3. With engine running, loosen injection line at each nozzle, one at a time. Use care to direct fuel away from sources of ignition. Each good nozzle should change engine idle quality when fuel is allowed to leak. If a nozzle is found that does not affect idle quality or changes noise and/or smoke, it should be replaced.
	4. High-pressure lines incorrectly installed.	4. Check routing of each line; correct as required.
Engine misfires above idle but idles correctly.	1. Plugged fuel filter.	1. Replace filter.
	2. Incorrect injection pump timing.	2. Be sure that timing mark on injection pump and adapter are aligned.
	3. Incorrect or contaminated fuel.	3. Flush fuel system and install correct fuel.
Engine will not return to idle.	1. External linkage binding or misadjusted.	1. Free up linkage. Adjust or replace as required.
	2. Internal injection pump malfunction.	2. Remove injection pump for repair.
Fuel leaks.	1. Loose or broken fuel line or connection.	1. Examine complete fuel system, including tank, lines, injection, and fuel return lines. Determine source and cause of leak and repair.
	2. Injection pump internal seal leak.	2. Remove injection pump for repair.

PROBLEM	CAUSE	CORRECTION
Noticeable loss of power.	1. Restricted air intake. 2. Restricted or damaged exhaust system. 3. Plugged fuel filter. 4. Plugged fuel tank vacuum vent in fuel cap. 5. Pinched or otherwise restricted return system. 6. Restricted fuel supply from fuel tank to injection pump. 7. Incorrect or contaminated fuel. 8. Restricted fuel tank filter. 9. Plugged nozzle(s). 10. Low compression.	1. Check air cleaner element. 2. Check system and replace as necessary. 3. Replace filter. 4. Replace cap. 5. Examine system for restriction and correct as required. 6. Examine fuel supply system to determine cause of restriction. Repair as required. 7. Flush fuel system and install correct fuel. 8. Remove fuel tank and check filter. 9. Remove nozzles. Have them checked for plugging and repair or replace. 10. Check compression to determine cause.
Noise; "rap" from one or more cylinders (sounds like rod bearing knock).	1. Air in fuel system. 2. Air in high-pressure line(s). 3. Nozzle(s) sticking open or with very low nozzle opening pressure.	1. Check for air leaks in fuel line and correct. 2. Loosen injection line at nozzle(s) and bleed air at each cylinder determined to be causing noise. Use care to direct fuel away from sources of ignition. 3. Loosen injection lines at nozzles one at a time. Noise will stop or change when line is loosened at bad nozzle. Remove nozzle for repair.
Engine will not shut off with key.	1. Injection pump fuel solenoid does not return fuel valve to *off* position.	1. Check electrical circuit and correct as needed.

PART 9 EVAPORATIVE SYSTEM DIAGNOSIS AND SERVICE

The fuel vapor recovery system should be free of any leaks in order to contain any hydrocarbon vapors. Determining whether there are any leaks in the system may require performing an evaporative system pressure test. This test must only be performed at recommended pressures in order to prevent damage to the system.

Visual inspection of all lines and hoses without pressurizing the system will, in most cases, identify problems such as damaged, kinked, flattened, swollen, or leaking lines or connections. Faulty lines, connectors, and clamps must be replaced. Cracked or damaged vapor canisters must also be replaced. Fuel tank caps must meet vacuum valve and pressure relief valve opening specifications. Faulty caps must be replaced.

The following chart lists typical problems and corrections.

PROBLEM	POSSIBLE CAUSES	CORRECTION
Loss of fuel or vapor odor in filler cap or fuel tank area. Perform Evaporative System Pressure Test to determine possible causes.	1. Leaking or plugged fuel or evaporative hoses. 2. Fuel cap leaking. 3. Fuel filler neck leaking. 4. Sending unit or gasket leaking.	1. Repair or replace hoses as necessary. 2. Repair or replace cap as necessary. 3. Repair or replace as necessary. 4. Repair or replace as necessary.

PROBLEM	POSSIBLE CAUSES	CORRECTION
Fuel loss or vapor odor in underhood area—Perform Evaporative System Pressure Test to determine possible causes	1. Liquid fuel leaking from fuel lines, fuel pump, or carburetor. 2. Canister cracked or damaged. 3. Malfunctioning canister control valve or hoses. 4. Disconnected, misrouted, kinked, deteriorated, or damaged vapor lines. 5. Bowl vent hose misrouted. 6. Air cleaner or air cleaner gasket improperly installed.	1. Tighten connections or repair or replace as necessary. 2. Replace canister. 3. Repair or replace canister control valve or hoses. 4. Check for proper connections, routings, and condition. Repair or replace as necessary. 5. Route hose properly, with no low spots. 6. Install air cleaner properly, replacing gasket if necessary.
Poor idle or poor driveability	1. Inoperative purge valve. 2. Inoperative bowl vent valve.	1. Repair or replace hoses, purge valve, and canister. 2. Repair or replace hoses or correct vent valve.
Collapsed or expanded fuel tank	1. Plugged or pinched vapor pipe, hoses, or defective fuel cap. 2. Canister filter plugged.	1. Inspect all lines from tank to canister. Repair or replace as necessary. Replace fuel cap. 2. Replace filter.

Servicing propane fuel supply systems is beyond the scope of this text since specialized training and equipment are required by law.

PART 10   SELF-CHECK

1. Name the major components of the gasoline fuel supply system.
2. What is the purpose of the two valves in the fuel tank cap?
3. Describe the operation of the mechanically operated diaphragm type fuel pump.
4. Some electric fuel pumps operate submerged in gasoline. True or false.
5. Describe the operation of the vapor canister.
6. Describe the difference between the open canister and closed canister vapor control systems.
7. Why is a water separator required in a diesel fuel supply system?
8. Why is a fuel supply pump not required in LP fuel systems?
9. List as many gasoline fuel supply system problems as you can that would prevent starting.

PART 11   TEST QUESTIONS

1. The roll over valve is required to:
   (a) control vapors to the canister
   (b) control EGR operation
   (c) control fuel return to the tank
   (d) prevent fuel spill in case of vehicle upset

2. Output pressure of a diaphragm type fuel pump is determined by:
   (a) distance of the stroke
   (b) length of operating arm
   (c) diaphragm spring pressure
   (d) float level in carburetor

3. Mechanic A says fresh air enters the vapor canister through a canister filter. Mechanic B says fresh air for the vapor canister comes from the air cleaner. Who is right?
   (a) Mechanic A
   (b) Mechanic B
   (c) both are right
   (d) both are wrong

4. Propane fuel temperature in the converter-regulator is controlled by:
   (a) exhaust gas heat
   (b) an electric heater
   (c) heated intake air
   (d) engine coolant

5. Mechanic A says fuel pumps should be tested for output pressure only. Mechanic B says fuel pumps should be tested for fuel output volume only. Who is right?
   (a) Mechanic A
   (b) Mechanic B
   (c) both are right
   (d) both are wrong

6. Raw fuel odor could be caused by:
   (a) fuel cap leaking
   (b) a cracked canister
   (c) low spots in bowl vent hose
   (d) all of the above

Chapter 13

Carburetors

The automotive carburetor is situated between the air cleaner and the intake manifold. The carburetor must meter the proper amounts of air and fuel for all operating conditions and driver demands. The correct air/fuel ratio for each condition must be produced by the carburetor. In addition, the fuel must be adequately vaporized and mixed with the air to provide good engine operation.

The carburetor is designed to take advantage of the principles of pressure difference and venturi action to achieve these results. Most carburetors use the common basic systems (idle and low speed, main metering, power, accelerator, and choke systems) with many additional features and design variations to satisfy performance and economy requirements as well as emissions standards.

PART 1 CARBURETOR PRINCIPLES

As the engine is being cranked by the starting system, the pistons moving down on the intake stroke create a low-pressure area in the intake manifold below the carburetor throttle plate. Since this pressure is less than atmospheric pressure, air flow will be created through the carburetor into the manifold and cylinders.

The degree of pressure difference above and below the carburetor throttle plate is dependent on atmospheric pressure (which varies with altitude; see Figure 13-1) and amount of throttle plate opening. Since both liquids and vapors will flow from a high- to a low-pressure area in an attempt to equalize the pressures, both fuel and air will begin to flow into the manifold and cylinders.

Any pressure value less than atmospheric pressure is commonly called *vacuum*. Intake manifold vacuum is measured with a vacuum gauge and expressed in inches of vacuum (inches of mercury) or kilopascals. Average intake manifold vacuum at engine idle speed (throttle plate nearly closed) is approximately 18 to 20 inches of mercury at sea level or 61 to 68 kilopascals (about 10 psi). As the throttle plate (at carburetor base) is opened further, more atmospheric pressure is allowed to enter the manifold, reducing the pressure difference. At wide open throttle, manifold vacuum is almost zero (almost at atmospheric pressure). The volume of flow, however, is greatly increased even though the pressure difference is considerably less than at closed throttle.

The Venturi Principle

The venturi principle is used to create fuel flow from the float bowl to the main discharge nozzle in the venturi (main metering system). Opening the throt-

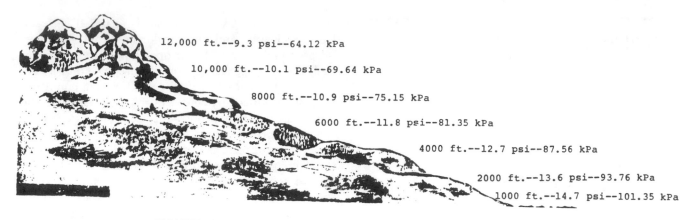

12,000 ft.--9.3 psi--64.12 kPa

10,000 ft.--10.1 psi--69.64 kPa

8000 ft.--10.9 psi--75.15 kPa

6000 ft.--11.8 psi--81.35 kPa

4000 ft.--12.7 psi--87.56 kPa

2000 ft.--13.6 psi--93.76 kPa

1000 ft.--14.7 psi--101.35 kPa

FIGURE 13-1. The effects of altitude on atmospheric pressure.

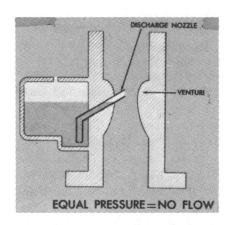

FIGURE 13-2. If pressures above and below the carburetor venturi are the same, there will be no air flow. At the same time, if atmospheric pressure in the fuel bowl is the same as pressure in the venturi (fuel level being below the discharge nozzle), there will also be no fuel flow. *(Courtesy of General Motors Corporation)*

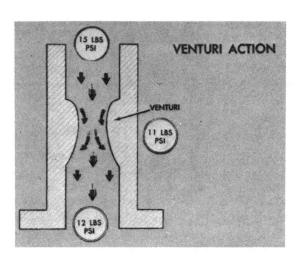

FIGURE 13-4. As the piston in the engine moves down on the intake stroke, a low-pressure area is created below the venturi. This causes air velocity past the venturi to increase, lowering venturi pressure. *(Courtesy of General Motors Corporation)*

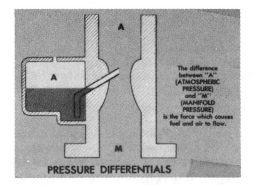

FIGURE 13-3. Carburetor operation relies on pressure differentials as shown here. *(Courtesy of General Motors Corporation)*

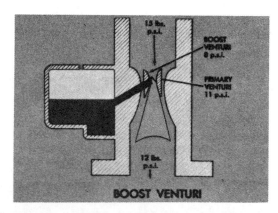

FIGURE 13-5. A second venturi increases air velocity and further lowers venturi pressure. *(Courtesy of General Motors Corporation)*

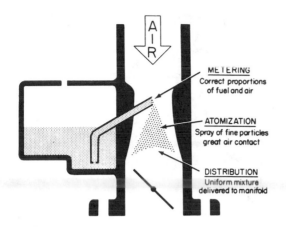

FIGURE 13-6. The main discharge nozzle of the carburetor is located in the low-pressure area of the venturi. The fuel level in the carburetor bowl is maintained at a level below the discharge nozzle. Atmospheric pressure acting on the fuel in the bowl will cause fuel to flow from the discharge nozzle whenever venturi pressure is below atmospheric pressure. Air flow carries the fuel-air mixture to the manifold for distribution. *(Courtesy of General Motors Corporation)*

tle plate increases air flow through the carburetor. A restriction built into the carburetor air horn (venturi) causes the velocity (speed) of the air to increase at this point. The increased velocity of air flow results from the same volume of air passing through the restriction as passes through the larger portion of the air horn.

The velocity of air flow past the restriction or venturi creates a low-pressure area in the venturi (Figure 13–4) at its narrowest point. The main discharge nozzle is located in this low-pressure area. Atmospheric pressure on the fuel in the fuel bowl causes fuel to flow through the discharge nozzle, where it breaks up and is vaporized and mixed with incoming air. Some carburetors use two or three venturis to achieve the desired fuel flow.

Air-Fuel Ratio

Operating and starting conditions and performance and emission requirements determine the required air-fuel ratio. A rich air-fuel mixture of about 8:1 to 10:1 is required for starting. For idle and low speed, a mixture of approximately 14:1 to 16:1 is required. Cruising speed ratios can be as lean as 18:1. Acceleration and full-power operation require richer mixtures to produce the power required.

Air-fuel ratios are stated in terms of weight. For example, an air-fuel ratio of 15:1 would mean that 15 pounds of air is used to burn 1 pound of fuel (15 kilograms of air to 1 kilogram of fuel). If measured

by volume, the oxygen from approximately 9000 gallons of air is required to burn 1 gallon of gasoline (or 9000 liters of air to 1 liter of fuel). Air is approximately 20 percent oxygen and the other 80 percent is mostly nitrogen.

PART 2 CARBURETOR CIRCUITS

Float Circuit

The float circuit includes: a fuel bowl that contains a supply of fuel; a float, and a float-operated valve, to control the level of fuel in the bowl; the bowl vents to maintain correct fuel bowl pressure; and vent bowl vapors to the carbon canister.

As fuel from the bowl is consumed, the fuel level in the bowl drops. This allows the float to drop, which opens the needle valve to allow additional fuel into the float bowl. When sufficient fuel has entered the bowl, the float again rises and closes the float valve (needle valve) to shut off further entry of fuel. While the engine is running, this action continues to maintain the proper level of fuel in the carburetor bowl.

Idle and Low-Speed Circuit

The idle and low-speed circuit provides the proper air-fuel mixture for idle and low-speed operation. It consists of an idle tube located in a well and connected to the fuel bowl, a metered fuel orifice, a metered air bleed, and a passage through the carburetor body to a position just below the nearly closed throttle plate. At this point, a small orifice (hole) allows the air-fuel mixture to enter the throttle bore for idle operation. The amount of air-fuel mixture allowed through this orifice is controlled by a tapered air-fuel mixture screw. One or two additional metered openings connected to the same passage are located just above the nearly closed throttle plate (Figure 13–9). Progressively more air-fuel mixture is allowed to flow as the throttle plate is opened to provide for low-speed operation.

With the throttle plate at idle position, only the idle port is exposed to vacuum. Atmospheric pressure in the fuel bowl causes fuel to flow through the idle passage. Air is added through the idle air bleed. This air breaks up the fuel partially, and further vaporization takes place as it is discharged from the idle port. The idle air bleed also prevents siphoning of fuel through the idle system when the engine is stopped.

As the throttle plates are opened, the off-idle or low-speed ports are also exposed to low pressure, and additional air-fuel mixture is supplied through

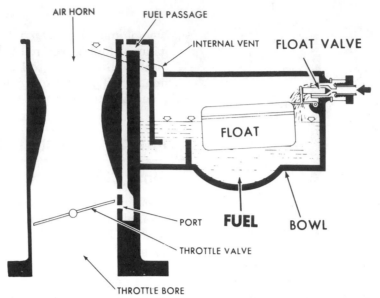

FIGURE 13-7. The float system controls the level of fuel in the carburetor float bowl.

these ports for low-speed operation. As soon as the throttle plate is opened sufficiently, the air velocity past the main discharge nozzle will start fuel flow from the main metering system.

Main Metering System

The main metering system provides fuel flow for cruising speeds. It includes a main metering jet (calibrated orifice) located between the fuel bowl and the main well, the main discharge nozzle that connects the main well to the narrow point in the venturi, and air bleeds.

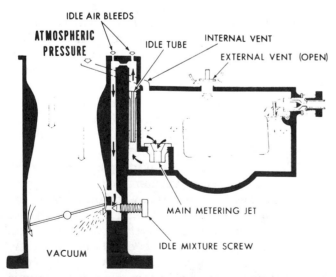

FIGURE 13-8. Both internal and external bowl venting are used in carburetors to maintain proper fuel bowl pressure and to allow escape of fuel vapors. The idle discharge port is located below the almost closed throttle plate.

The main metering jet meters the amount of fuel flow in direct proportion to air velocity in the venturi. Fuel flow in this system is caused by the venturi effect explained earlier. Increasing the throttle opening increases venturi air velocity and therefore increases fuel flow.

Power-Enrichment System

The power-enrichment system adds fuel to the main well for high-power demands. Several different types of power-enrichment devices are used. Mechanically or vacuum-operated metering rods located in the main metering jets, and mechanically or vacuum-operated power valves (sometimes called economizer valves) are examples.

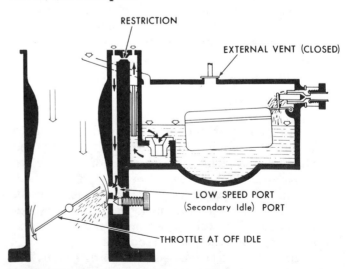

FIGURE 13-9. The off idle ports for low-speed operation allow progressively more air-fuel mixture to flow with increased throttle opening.

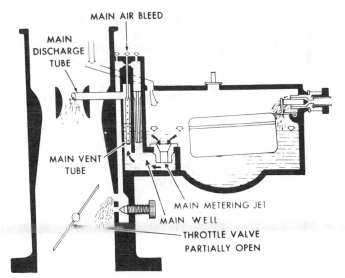

FIGURE 13-10. The main metering system components provide fuel flow for all speeds above off-idle operation.

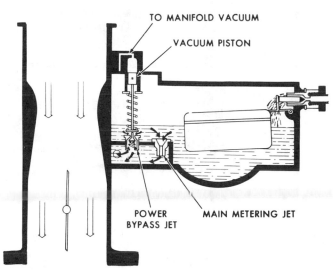

FIGURE 13-12. A vacuum- and spring-operated power valve is used on some carburetors to provide power enrichment instead of a metering rod.

Mechanically operated metering rods are raised higher in the main jet (tapered or stepped rods) or lifted out of the main jet completely (rods that are not tapered or stepped) when the throttle plate is at or near the wide open position. Other carburetors use vacuum-operated metering rods of the same types that are connected to a vacuum piston or diaphragm. High vacuum (during low-power demands) keeps the piston and metering rods down in the metering jets against spring pressure. When the throttle is opened to reduce vacuum sufficiently, spring pressure forces the piston or diaphragm up, which raises the metering rods in the jets and allows increased fuel flow.

Some carburetors use a separate power valve (sometimes called an *economizer*) that allows fuel to enter the main well in addition to the fuel from the main metering jet. These valves are operated similarly to the metering rods described above by a vacuum piston, diaphragm, or mechanical means.

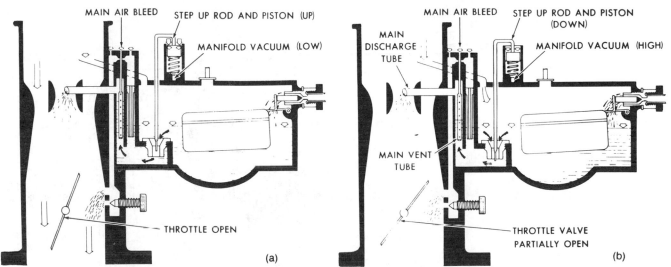

FIGURE 13-11. (A) The power-enrichment system provides additional fuel flow through the main metering system when power demands are high. High power demand drops intake manifold vacuum, which allows spring pressure to raise the metering rod higher in the main jet for increased fuel flow. (B) During low power demands and high vacuum, the piston and metering rod are pulled down to restrict fuel flow at the main jet.

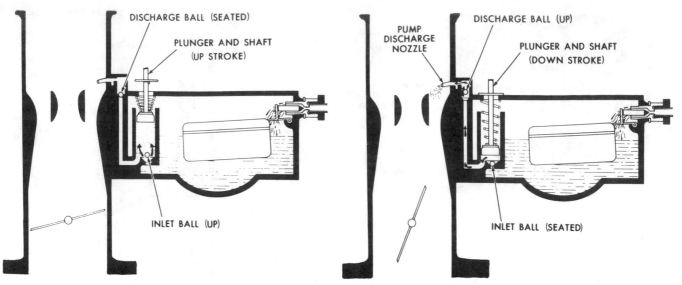

FIGURE 13-13. An accelerator pump (accelerator linkage operated) provides additional fuel for acceleration through a separate pump discharge passage and nozzle. Note intake and discharge check balls.

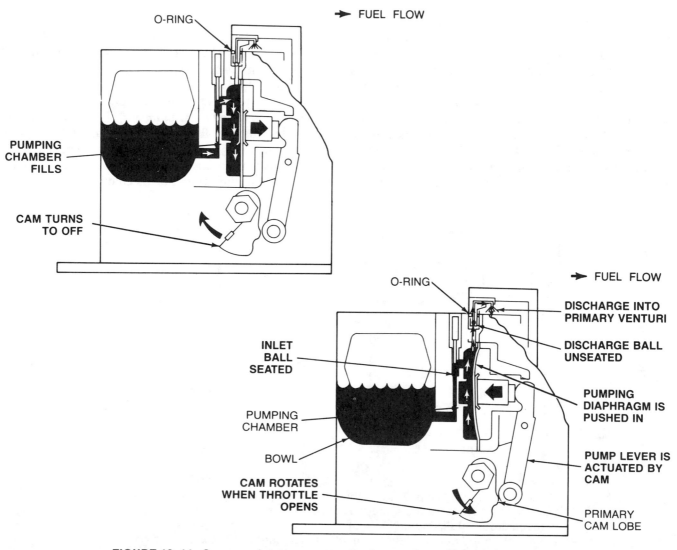

FIGURE 13-14. Some carburetors use a diaphragm type of accelerator pump as shown here.

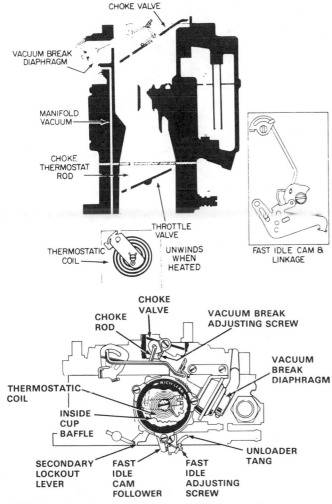

FIGURE 13-15. The choke system is required to provide fuel enrichment for cold engine starting. A fast-idle link can prevent cold engine stalling. Note the location of the thermostatic coils, the vacuum choke break, and the choke unloader tang. *(Courtesy of General Motors Corporation)*

Accelerator Pump System

An accelerator pump is needed in the carburetor to provide momentary fuel enrichment during acceleration. When the throttle is opened, air suddenly rushes in; however, a time lag because of the inertia of the fuel causes a momentary lean condition. The accelerator pump provides fuel enrichment to overcome this condition by forcing fuel into the venturi through the pump discharge nozzles.

At closed throttle, the accelerator pump plunger (or diaphragm), which is connected to the throttle linkage, is raised to the top of the intake stroke. As the plunger is raised, the discharge check valve seats to prevent entry of air, and the inlet check valve opens to allow fuel to enter and fill the pump well below the plunger. When the accelerator pedal is depressed, the slotted or sliding connection to the accelerator pump plunger allows the linkage to move without forcing the plunger down. A duration spring mounted between the plunger and linkage forces the plunger down at a rate determined by spring pressure and pump discharge nozzle size.

If the accelerator pump does not work effectively, the vehicle will hesitate or "stumble" when accelerated. Reasons for accelerator pump failure include a restricted discharge passage, missing check balls or valves, a leaking diaphragm, a damaged pump plunger cup, a broken duration spring, and incorrect linkage adjustment.

Choke System

A choke valve is needed to provide full enrichment for starting a cold engine. The choke valve is located in the carburetor air horn. The choke shaft is often

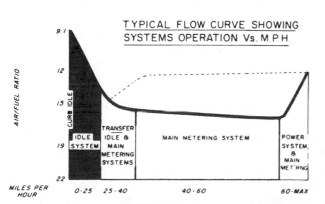

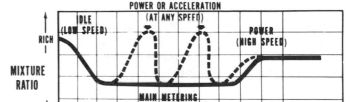

FIGURE 13-16. Approximate speed ranges at which the different carburetor systems operate and the approximate air-fuel ratios for each speed range. *(Courtesy of General Motors Corporation)*

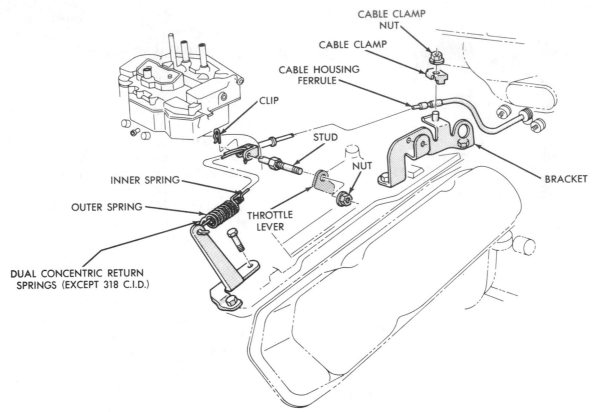

FIGURE 13-17. Typical carburetor throttle linkage arrangement that connects the throttle shaft to the accelerator pedal. *(Courtesy of Chrysler Corporation)*

located off center on the choke plate to allow partial choke opening as soon as the engine is cranked or started. The difference in surface area of the choke plate on each side of the shaft causes the wide side of the plate to move down to allow air entry. The choke valve or plate is operated manually by a dashboard-mounted cable or automatically by a bimetal spring and electric heating device.

When the choke plate is closed, air flow into the carburetor is restricted. This increases the vacuum at the idle and low-speed ports and at the main discharge nozzle. Increased fuel flow from the idle circuit, as well as fuel flow from the main discharge nozzle, provides the enriched mixture required for starting. Since a smaller amount of the fuel is vaporized when the engine is cold started, additional fuel is required so that sufficient fuel will be vaporized to support combustion.

Automatic Choke Control

Most vehicles today are equipped with an automatic choke. This type of choke uses a flat-wound bimetal spring to close the choke when the engine is cold and the throttle is opened. (Unless the throttle is opened the fast idle cam and linkage will not allow the choke to close.)

As soon as the engine starts, air velocity partially opens the offset choke valve to lean out the mixture. A vacuum piston or one or two vacuum diaphragms are used on many carburetors to further increase the choke opening. The vacuum piston (or diaphragm) is connected to the choke shaft. As soon as the engine starts, intake manifold vacuum pulls the piston or diaphragm back, which opens the choke slightly to prevent stalling.

As the engine warms up, exhaust manifold heat applied to the flat-wound bimetal choke spring causes the spring to unwind and open the choke even further. Continued engine operation will cause the choke to open fully at operating temperature. Many vehicles use an electric heating device to help heat the bimetal spring. This reduces choke *on* time and reduces exhaust emissions.

Fast-Idle Cam

The fast-idle cam pivots on a carburetor-mounted screw and is connected to the choke shaft by a rod. The cam is located in a manner that will prevent the throttle from returning to normal idle position when the choke is on. Several steps on the cam provide different fast-idle throttle positions for various choke plate openings. As a result, the fast-idle speed is reduced as the choke opens further. A fast idle is needed during engine warm-up to provide enough throttle opening to prevent stalling.

Choke Unloader

The choke unloader is a device connected to the accelerator linkage to partially open the choke at wide open throttle. To be able to start a cold engine that has been flooded with gasoline, the choke unloader is required. At wide open throttle the partially opened choke allows additional air to lean out the mixture and reduce fuel flow. The choke unloader is throttle linkage actuated.

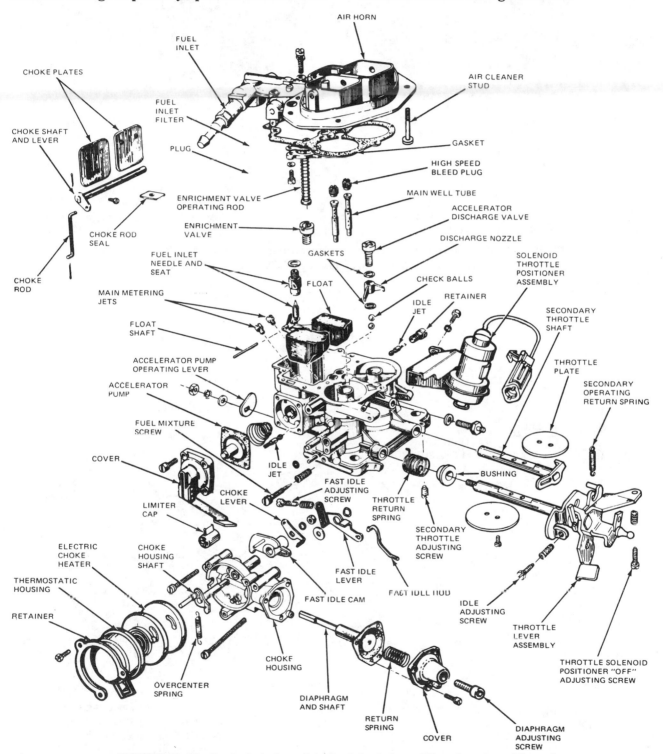

FIGURE 13-18. Exploded view of typical dual-stage 2V carburetor with parts identified. *(Courtesy of Ford Motor Co. of Canada Ltd.)*

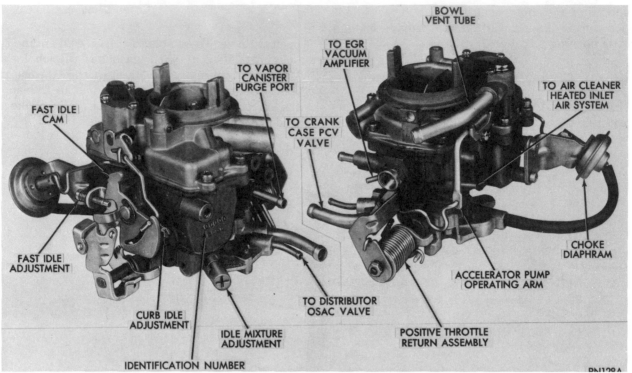

FIGURE 13–19. External view of single-barrel carburetor showing various connections and external adjustments. *(Courtesy of Chrysler Corporation)*

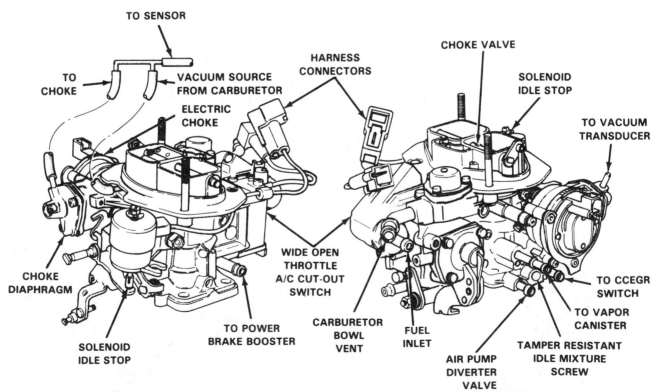

FIGURE 13–20. External view of two-stage Holley 2V carburetor showing external connections. *(Courtesy of Chrysler Corporation)*

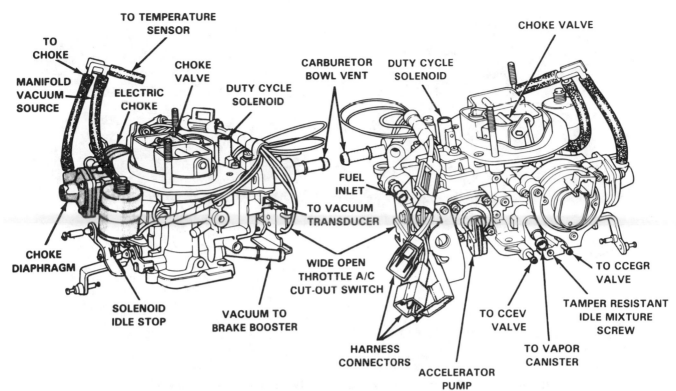

FIGURE 13-21. External views of Holley 6520 2V two-stage electronic feedback carburetor. (*Courtesy of Chrysler Corporation*)

PART 3   CARBURETOR TYPES

Carburetor types include single-barrel (1V), two-barrel (2V), and four-barrel (4V) designs. Single-barrel carburetors are used on many four-cylinder engines and on in-line six-cylinder engines. Two-barrel carburetors are used on four, six, and eight-cylinder engines.

Two types of two-barrel carburetors are in use. The single-stage carburetor has two barrels that operate like two-single-barrel carburetors with a common float bowl. Each barrel provides the air-fuel mixture for one half of the engine's cylinders.

The two stage, two-barrel carburetor uses a primary barrel and a secondary barrel. In this design the primary barrel supplies all the air-fuel requirements for idle, cruising, and normal power demands. The secondary barrel provides additional air-fuel requirements for high-speed and high-power demands. The secondary system does not function until about 60 to 70 percent throttle opening.

The four-barrel carburetor is commonly used on V-8 engines. This carburetor consists of a two-barrel primary system that supplies all the air-fuel requirements for idle, cruising, and normal power demands and a two-barrel secondary system that provides additional air-fuel supply for high-speed and high-power demands.

Each primary barrel feeds four cylinders and each secondary barrel also feeds four cylinders. The secondary system is not in operation until approximately 60 to 70 percent throttle opening has been reached. Secondary throttle valves may either be vacuum or mechanically operated, depending on design. Secondary air valves are used in the air horn to provide venturi action and to control air flow.

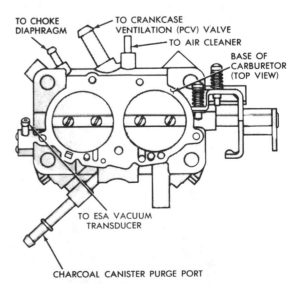

FIGURE 13-22. Bottom view of two-barrel carburetor throttle body. (*Courtesy of Chrysler Corporation*)

303

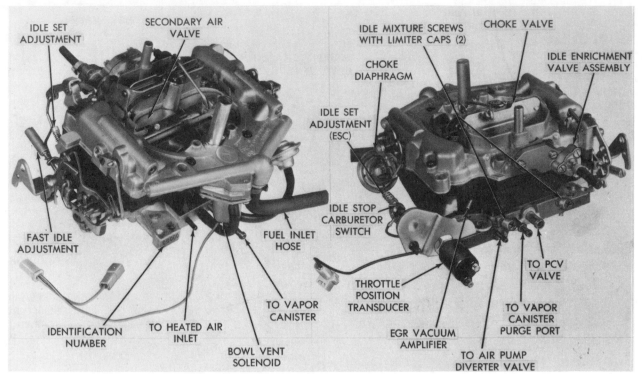

FIGURE 13-23. External view of four-barrel 4V carburetor. *(Courtesy of Chrysler Corporation)*

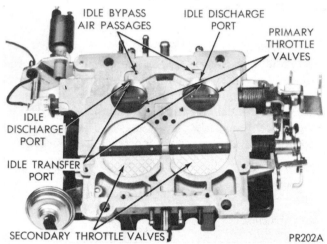

FIGURE 13-24. Bottom view of four-barrel carburetor showing primary and secondary throttle plates. *(Courtesy of Chrysler Corporation)*

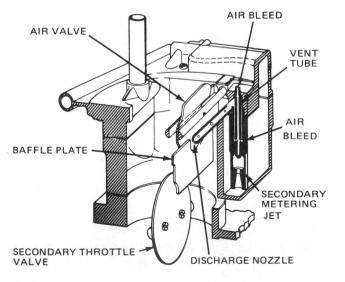

FIGURE 13-25. Secondary metering system on a Carter four-barrel carburetor. *(Courtesy of General Motors Corporation)*

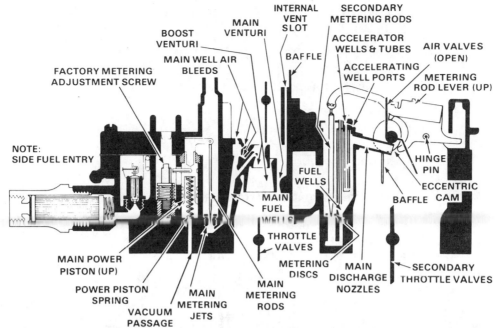

FIGURE 13-26. Cross-sectional view of nonfeedback four-barrel carburetor. Note primary and secondary throttle valves, air valves, and secondary metering system. *(Courtesy of General Motors Corporation)*

PART 4   OTHER CARBURETOR FEATURES

A number of different devices not yet mentioned are used on many carburetors. The most common include mechanically and electrically operated bowl vents, idle limiter caps, idle restrictors, carburetors with no external idle mixture adjustment, antistall dashpot, antidieseling solenoid, sol-a-dash, hot idle compensator, idle enrichment system, electronic fuel-control devices, decel valve, antipercolator vent or valve, altitude-compensator devices, choke-control devices, and a variable venturi carburetor.

PART 5   ELECTRONIC FEEDBACK CONTROLLED CARBURETORS

The electronic feedback controlled carburetor system provides better combustion by control of the air/fuel mixture. Better combustion reduces exhaust emissions while still providing the required performance and economy.

The system is designed to maintain control of the air/fuel mixture over a narrow band or window on each side of the ideal or stoichiometric mixture of about 14.7 to 1.

A number of engine sensors provide information to a pre-programmed computer which, in turn, provides an electrical output signal to operate the mixture control solenoid on the carburetor. The solenoid pulsates or cycles ten times a second to control the position of the metering valve in the fuel bowl of the carburetor. This cycle rate is fast enough to provide almost instantaneous response to computer commands. The valve cycles between open and closed positions. Enriching or leaning out the mixture occurs when the solenoid and valve are in the rich or lean mode more than 50 percent of the time during each second.

Some designs use the solenoid to control a vacuum signal to one or two diaphragms in the carburetor which in turn control the air/fuel metering. Another design uses a *stepper* motor instead of a solenoid to achieve the same results. The stepper motor is an electric motor which turns in either direction only a small part of a revolution at each command from the computer. This turns a threaded metering device in or out depending on lean or rich commands.

System Operation

System operation is described as being in one of two operating modes: open loop or closed loop. Typical operation is as follows.

Open Loop Operation

During this mode of operation the air/fuel ratio is a result of information already stored in the computer and information received by the computer from engine sensors other than the exhaust oxygen sensor.

305

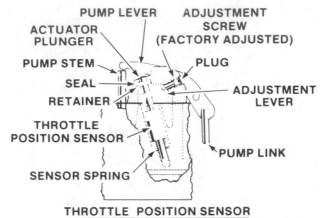

THROTTLE POSITION SENSOR

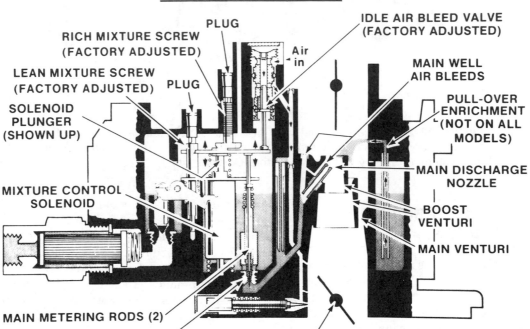

FIGURE 13-27. Cutaway view of E2MC General Motors single-stage 2V electronic feedback carburetor and detail of throttle position sensor. *(Courtesy of General Motors Corporation)*

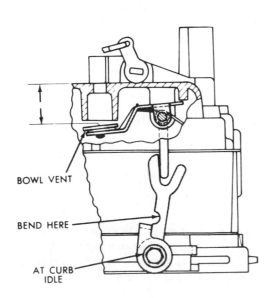

FIGURE 13-28. Mechanically operated bowl vent valve allows vapor from bowl to pass to carbon canister at closed throttle. Bowl vent is accelerator linkage actuated. *(Courtesy of Chrysler Corporation)*

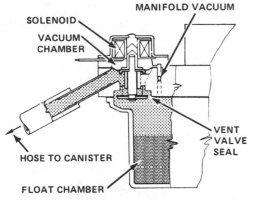

FIGURE 13-29. A solenoid-assisted vacuum-operated bowl vent valve is used on some carburetors. When the engine is not running, bowl vapors are vented to the canister. *(Courtesy of General Motors Corporation)*

Conditions which cause open loop operation are:

- Engine start-up
- Coolant temperature too low
- Exhaust gas temperature and oxygen sensor temperature too low
- Engine at idle speed
- Wide open throttle operation

Closed Loop Operation

During this mode of operation the air/fuel ratio is a result of information already in the computer and information received by the various engine sensors including the exhaust gas oxygen sensor.

Conditions which result in closed loop operation are:

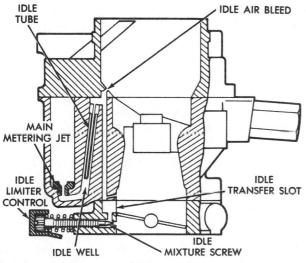

FIGURE 13-30. Idle limiter caps limit the amount of idle mixture screw adjustment to prevent overenriched idle mixtures for emission control. *(Courtesy of Chrysler Corporation)*

- Coolant at operating temperature
- Exhaust gas and oxygen sensor at operating temperature
- Engine above idle speed
- Operation at less than wide open throttle

Sensors Providing Input to the Computer

Oxygen Sensor

The oxygen sensor is located in the exhaust manifold. The sensor will tell the computer how much oxygen is present in the exhaust gases. Since this amount is proportional to rich and lean mixtures, the computer will adjust the duty cycle lower if exhaust gas is too lean or higher if too rich.

The oxygen sensor is essentially a battery containing a cylinder of electrolyte (zirconium dioxide),

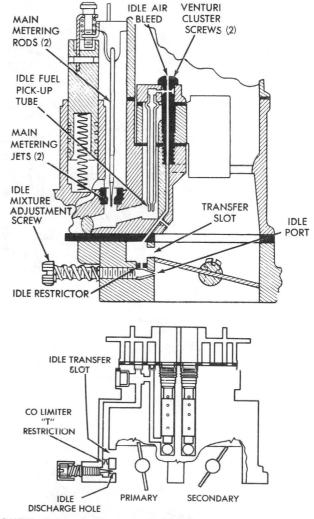

FIGURE 13-31. Additional methods of limiting idle mixture enrichment include idle restrictors as shown here. *(Courtesy of Chrysler Corporation)*

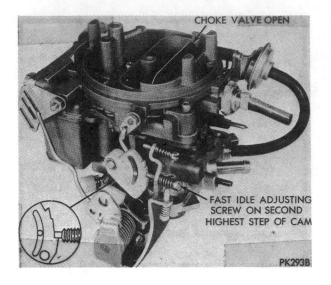

CHOKE VALVE OPEN

FAST IDLE ADJUSTING
SCREW ON SECOND
HIGHEST STEP OF CAM

PK293B

FIGURE 13–32. The fast-idle link connects the choke valve to the fast-idle cam. A fast idle during cold engine operation and during engine warm-up prevents stalling. The fast-idle screw is attached to a bracket, which is connected to the throttle shaft. *(Courtesy of Chrysler Corporation)*

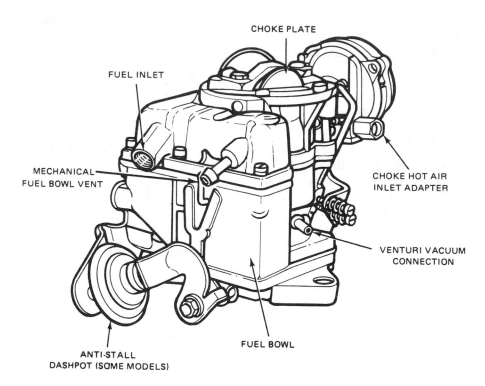

CHOKE PLATE

FUEL INLET

MECHANICAL
FUEL BOWL VENT

CHOKE HOT AIR
INLET ADAPTER

VENTURI VACUUM
CONNECTION

FUEL BOWL

ANTI-STALL
DASHPOT (SOME MODELS)

FIGURE 13–33. An antistall dashpot prevents fast closing of the throttle when the accelerator pedal is suddenly released. This prevents engine stalling under this condition. *(Courtesy of Ford Motor Co. of Canada Ltd.)*

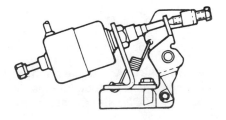

FIGURE 13–34. The antidieseling solenoid provides a normal idle speed throttle stop when the engine is running. When the engine is shut off, the solenoid is de-energized, allowing the solenoid plunger to retract and the throttle plates to close completely. This cuts off the air-fuel supply to the engine and prevents dieseling (after running). *(Courtesy of Ford Motor Co. of Canada Ltd.)*

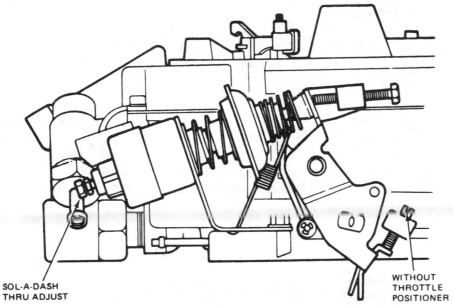

SOL-A-DASH
THRU ADJUST

WITHOUT
THROTTLE
POSITIONER

FIGURE 13-35. A combination dashpot and solenoid is used on Ford's variable venturi carburetor. *(Courtesy of Ford Motor Co. of Canada Ltd.)*

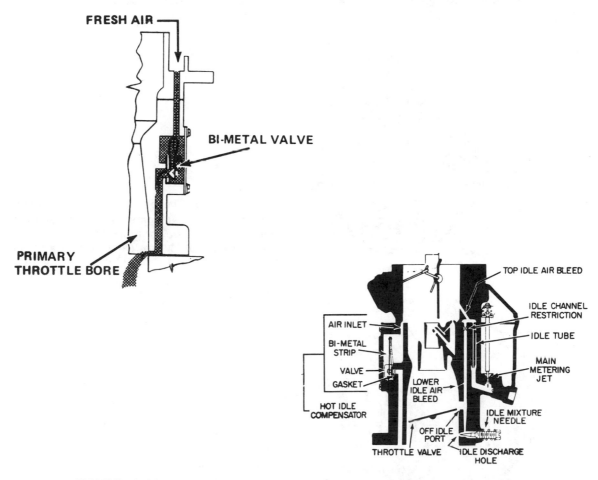

FRESH AIR

BI-METAL VALVE

PRIMARY
THROTTLE BORE

TOP IDLE AIR BLEED

IDLE CHANNEL
RESTRICTION

AIR INLET

BI-METAL
STRIP

IDLE TUBE

VALVE

MAIN
METERING
JET

GASKET

LOWER
IDLE AIR
BLEED

HOT IDLE
COMPENSATOR

IDLE MIXTURE
NEEDLE

OFF IDLE
PORT

THROTTLE VALVE

IDLE DISCHARGE
HOLE

FIGURE 13-36. A hot-idle compensator valve is used to allow additional air to enter the carburetor below the throttle plate to prevent hot-idle stalling. A hot engine can cause fuel in the carburetor to boil and overenrich the idle mixture. The hot-idle compensator compensates for this condition. *(Courtesy of General Motors Corporation)*

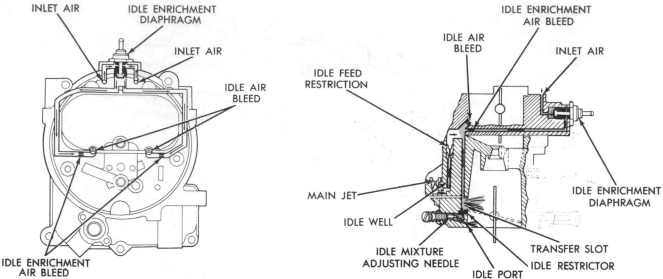

FIGURE 13-37. An idle-enrichment system is used on some carburetors to provide fuel enrichment for cold engine operation and prevent stalling. A thermal switch in contact with engine coolant cuts the system out when the engine is warm. Other systems use a solenoid valve operated by an electric timer allowing approximately 35 seconds of enrichment when the engine is cold each time the ignition key is turned on. *(Courtesy of Chrysler Corporation)*

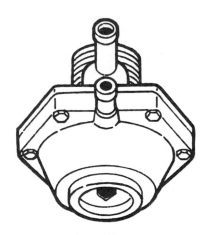

FIGURE 13-38. The deceleration valve shown here is used with some vehicles to provide enriched air-fuel during deceleration for more complete burning of fuel. *(Courtesy of Ford Motor Co. of Canada Ltd.)*

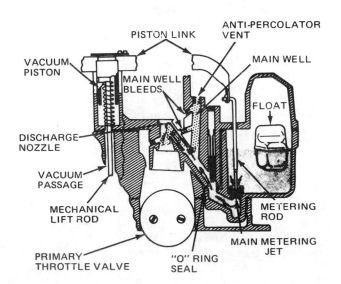

FIGURE 13-39. An antipercolator vent or valve is used on some carburetors. A hot engine can cause fuel in the main well to boil, causing too rich a fuel mixture, stalling, and hard starting of a hot engine. The antipercolator vent allows fuel vapors to escape from the main well. *(Courtesy of General Motors Corporation)*

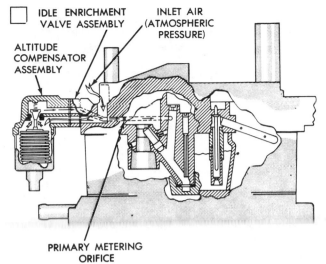

IDLE ENRICHMENT VALVE ASSEMBLY

INLET AIR (ATMOSPHERIC PRESSURE)

ALTITUDE COMPENSATOR ASSEMBLY

PRIMARY METERING ORIFICE

FIGURE 13-40. A pressure-sensitive (aneroid) bellows operates an air valve to increase the amount of air flow at high-altitude operation. Without the altitude compensator, the air-fuel ratio would be too rich for high-altitude operation. *(Courtesy of Chrysler Corporation)*

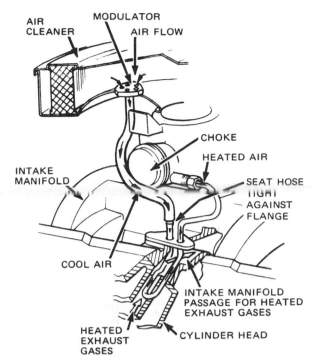

AIR CLEANER

MODULATOR AIR FLOW

CHOKE
HEATED AIR

INTAKE MANIFOLD

SEAT HOSE TIGHT AGAINST FLANGE

COOL AIR

INTAKE MANIFOLD PASSAGE FOR HEATED EXHAUST GASES

HEATED EXHAUST GASES

CYLINDER HEAD

FIGURE 13-41. One method of providing exhaust manifold heated air to the bimetal spring for automatic choke control. *(Courtesy of General Motors Corporation)*

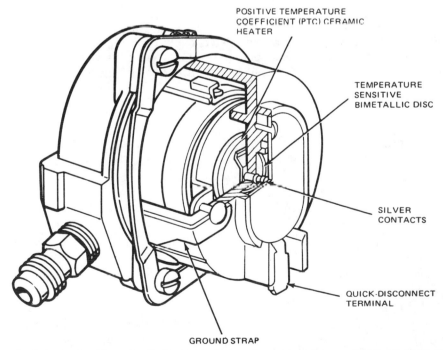

POSITIVE TEMPERATURE COEFFICIENT (PTC) CERAMIC HEATER

TEMPERATURE SENSITIVE BIMETALLIC DISC

SILVER CONTACTS

QUICK-DISCONNECT TERMINAL

GROUND STRAP

FIGURE 13-42. Electrically heated choke element reduces choke on time to provide better emission control. *(Courtesy of Ford Motor Co. of Canada Ltd.)*

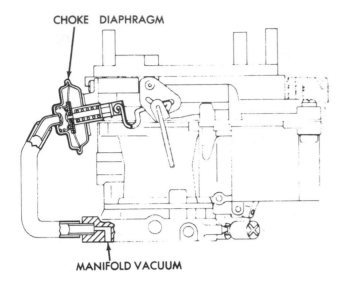

CHOKE DIAPHRAGM

MANIFOLD VACUUM

FIGURE 13–43. The choke diaphragm opens the choke partially as soon as the engine starts. This allows extra air in to prevent stalling while the choke bimetal is still cold. *(Courtesy of Chrysler Corporation)*

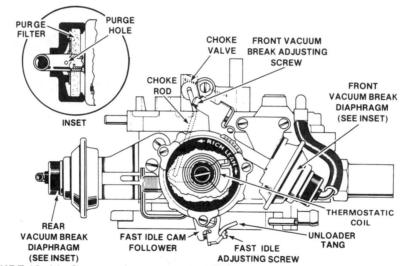

PURGE FILTER

PURGE HOLE

INSET

CHOKE ROD

CHOKE VALVE

FRONT VACUUM BREAK ADJUSTING SCREW

FRONT VACUUM BREAK DIAPHRAGM (SEE INSET)

THERMOSTATIC COIL

UNLOADER TANG

FAST IDLE ADJUSTING SCREW

FAST IDLE CAM FOLLOWER

REAR VACUUM BREAK DIAPHRAGM (SEE INSET)

FIGURE 13–44. Some carburetors use two choke diaphragms, as shown here. At wide-open throttle, the unloader tang partially opens the choke. This allows easier starting of a flooded cold engine. *(Courtesy of General Motors Corporation)*

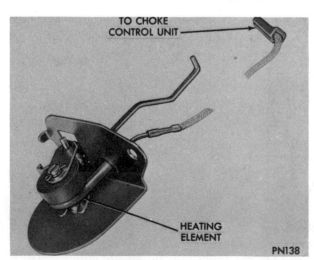

TO CHOKE CONTROL UNIT

HEATING ELEMENT

PN138

FIGURE 13–45. This type of electric choke heater is used on engines that have the bimetal spring located in the exhaust crossover or the exhaust manifold. *(Courtesy of Chrysler Corporation)*

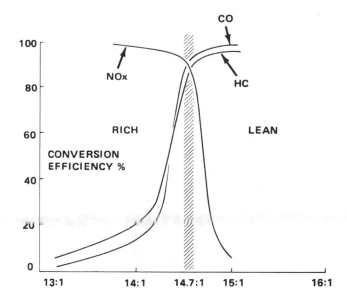

FIGURE 13-46. Typical stoichiometric mixture "window" required for high catalytic converter efficiency. (*Courtesy of American Motors Corporation*)

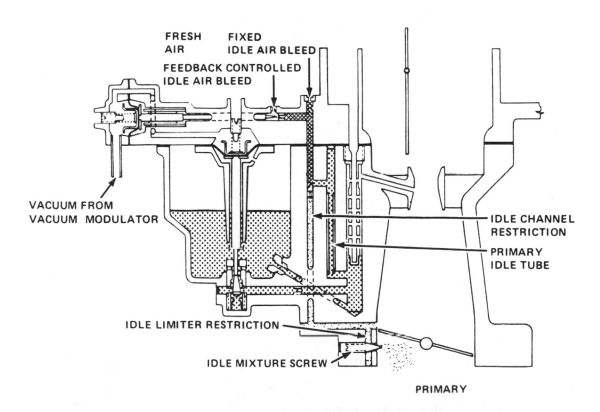

FIGURE 13-47. This carburetor incorporates electronic control of the air-fuel ratio in the idle and main metering systems. Signals from an oxygen sensor in the exhaust pipe or manifold, a manifold vacuum switch, and a coolant temperature switch are fed to the electronic control unit. The ECU tells the vacuum modulator how much vacuum to feed to the vacuum diaphragms in the carburetor idle and main metering systems. This provides precise control of the air-fuel ratio for good emission control. (*Courtesy of General Motors Corporation*)

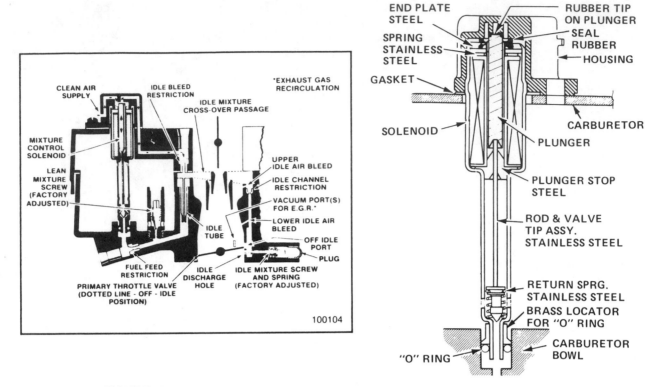

FIGURE 13-48. Details of mixture solenoid controlled by electronic feedback control system on E2SE, 2V General Motors two-stage carburetor. *(Courtesy of General Motors Corporation)*

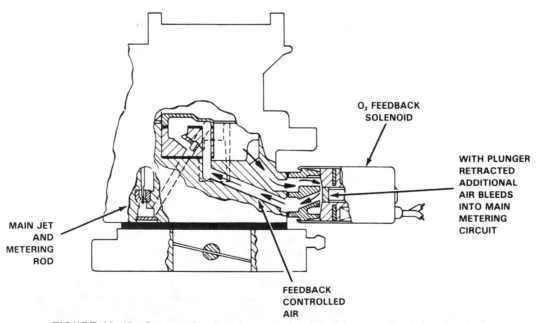

FIGURE 13-49. Oxygen feedback control solenoid controls air in circuit for mixture control. *(Courtesy of Chrysler Corporation)*

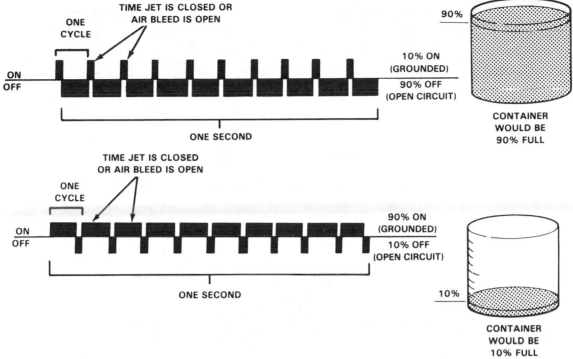

FIGURE 13-50. Electronic carburetor feedback rich and lean cycling modes. *(Courtesy of Chrysler Corporation)*

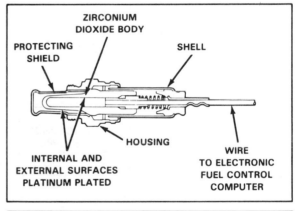

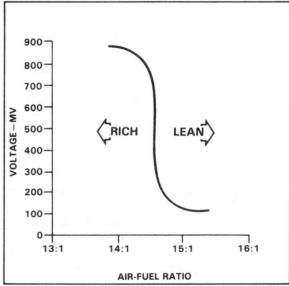

FIGURE 13-51. Oxygen sensor cutaway view (top) and typical output voltage curve. *(Courtesy of Chrysler Corporation)*

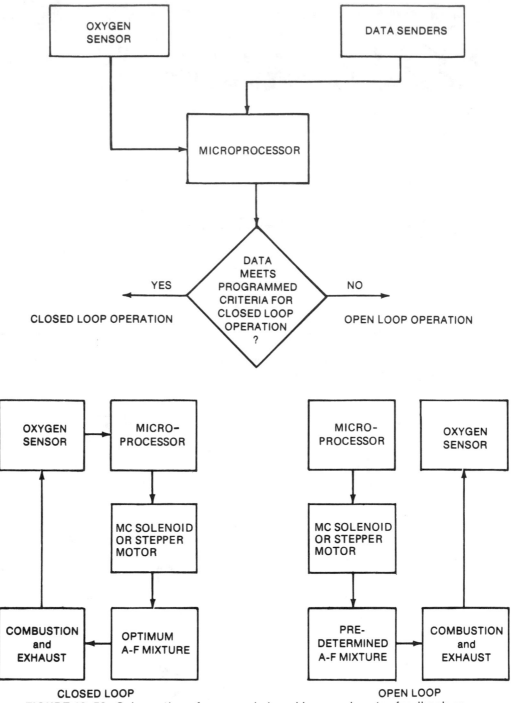

FIGURE 13-52. Schematics of open and closed loop carburetor feedback operation. *(Courtesy of American Motors Corporation)*

which is coated inside and out with platinum. The outer platinum electrode is exposed to the hot exhaust gases while the inner platinum electrode is exposed to the atmosphere. A porous ceramic coating protects the fragile platinum against damage.

Voltage is generated when the tip of the sensor is heated to operating temperature by the flow of oxygen and hot exhaust gases over it. When the oxygen content is high (lean mixture), it puts out a low voltage. When the oxygen output is low (rich mixture), the voltage output is high. The sensor output voltage is used by the computer to calculate and adjust the air/fuel mixture. As the engine returns to idle, the oxygen sensor will cool down to below closed loop operating temperature and put the system into open loop operation.

Vacuum Sensor (Manifold Absolute Pressure, MAP)

Vacuum sensors or MAP sensors are used to provide an electrical signal to the computer which may provide information concerning throttle position, engine load, engine speed, and barometric (atmospheric) pressure as well as the altitude at which the vehicle is operating.

Variations in these conditions require adjustment to the air/fuel ratio by commands from the computer to the mixture control device on the carburetor.

Coolant Temperature Sensor

The coolant temperature sensor tells the computer whether the engine coolant is below or at operating temperature. If coolant temperature is too low, the system operates in open loop.

PART 6 CARBURETOR SERVICE

General Precautions

Be sure to follow all normal personal and shop safety practices as outlined in Chapter 1, Parts 1 and 2, as well as those in Chapter 10, Part 4, and Chapter 12, Part 6, of this text. Some additional precautions are given in this section as well.

Tamper Proof Feature Precautions

Many carburetor adjustment points either have been permanently sealed and/or made inaccessible to prevent indiscriminate adjustment in the field. These settings have been made at the factory to meet federal and state emissions standards required by law. It is, therefore, essential that the factory procedure, as outlined in the appropriate manufacturer's service manual, be strictly followed for the temporary removal of plugs, caps, rivets, and other tamper proof devices. Servicing of the carburetor must be performed in a manner which will restore its function and its tamper proof devices to the original intent of the carburetor design.

Depending on the make, year, and model of the carburetor, tamper proofing may include such items as lean mixture screws, rich mixture screws, idle mixture needle, riveted choke cover, idle speed control, dashpot, choke break, idle load compensator, idle air bleed, power enrichment, and the like.

Caution: The practice of priming an engine by pouring gasoline into the carburetor air horn for starting before or after servicing the fuel system should be strictly avoided. Cranking the engine and then priming by depressing the accelerator pedal several times should be adequate.

Diagnosing carburetor complaints may require that the engine be started and run with the air cleaner removed.

Caution: While running the engine in this mode, it is possible that the engine could backfire. A backfiring situation is likely to occur if the carburetor is

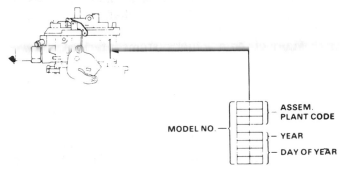

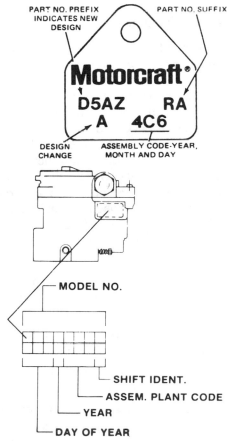

FIGURE 13-53. Carburetor identification, including make, model, and year, is important information required for servicing carburetors and ordering parts. Some methods used for carburetor identification are shown here. *(Courtesy of General Motors Corporation* [top and bottom] *and Ford Motor Co. of Canada Ltd.* [middle]*)*

malfunctioning, but removal of the air cleaner alone can lean the air/fuel ratio in the carburetor to the point of producing an engine backfire. All necessary precautions should be observed to prevent accident or injury resulting from backfire.

Problem Diagnosis

For carburetor problem diagnosis and diagnosis of fuel supply systems refer to the diagnostic charts in Chapter 12, Part 6, of this text.

Many of today's fuel systems interface with exhaust and emission control systems and on-board electronic diagnostic systems. The appropriate manufacturer's service repair manual should be consulted for diagnosis and repair procedures. Some of these systems require very precise precautions and diagnostic procedures performed in a specific sequence to isolate the problem area. The variety and complexity of these systems prohibits covering them in this text.

Service Procedure

A thorough road test and check of minor carburetor adjustments should precede major carburetor service. Specifications for some adjustments are listed on the vehicle emission control information label found in each engine compartment.

Many performance complaints are incorrectly directed at the carburetor. Some of these are a result of loose, maladjusted, or malfunctioning engine or electrical components. Others develop when vacuum hoses become disconnected or are improperly routed. The proper approach to analyzing carburetor complaints should include a routing check of such areas as the following and correct as needed.

1. Inspect all vacuum hoses and actuators for leaks. Refer to the vacuum hose routing diagram label located under the hood in the engine compartment for proper hose routing.

2. Tighten intake manifold bolts and carburetor mounting bolts to specifications.

3. Perform cylinder compression test.

4. Clean or replace spark plugs.

5. Test resistance of spark plug cables.

6. Inspect ignition primary wire and vacuum advance operation. Test coil output voltage, primary, and secondary resistance.

7. Reset ignition timing.

8. Check carburetor idle mixture and speed adjustment. Adjust throttle stop screw to specifications.

9. Test fuel pump for pressure and vacuum.

10. Inspect manifold heat control valve in exhaust manifold for proper operation.

11. Remove carburetor air filter element and blow out dirt gently with an air hose. Install a new recommended filter element if necessary. Replace fuel filter.

12. Inspect crankcase ventilation system.

13. Road test vehicle as a final test.

14. If the problem is not corrected, proceed with carburetor removal and repair.

Carburetor Removal

Caution: Do not attempt to remove the carburetor from the engine of a vehicle that has just been road tested. Allow the engine to sufficiently cool to prevent accidental fuel ignition or personal injury.

1. Disconnect battery ground cable.

2. Remove air cleaner.

3. Remove fuel tank pressure vacuum filler cap. The fuel tank should be under a small pressure.

4. Place a container under fuel inlet fitting to catch any fuel that may be trapped in fuel line.

5. Disconnect fuel inlet line using two wrenches to avoid twisting the line.

6. Disconnect throttle linkage, choke linkage, all vacuum hoses, and electrical connections.

7. Remove carburetor mounting bolts or nuts and carefully remove carburetor from engine compartment. Hold carburetor level to avoid spilling fuel from fuel bowl. Drain fuel from carburetor and dispose of fuel in recommended manner. Disassemble carburetor as recommended in service manual.

Cleaning Carburetor Parts

There are many commercial carburetor cleaning solvents available that can be used with good results.

The choke diaphragm, choke heater, and some plastic parts of the carburetor can be damaged by solvents. Many carburetors use shafts and linkage treated with a special coating to reduce friction and binding. Avoid placing these parts in any liquid. Clean the external surfaces of these parts with a clean cloth or a soft brush. Shake dirt or other foreign material from the stem (plunger) side of the diaphragm. Compressed air can be used to remove loose dirt but should not be connected to the vacuum diaphragm fitting.

If the commercial solvent or cleaner recommends the use of water as a rinse, *hot* water will produce better results. After rinsing, *all* water must

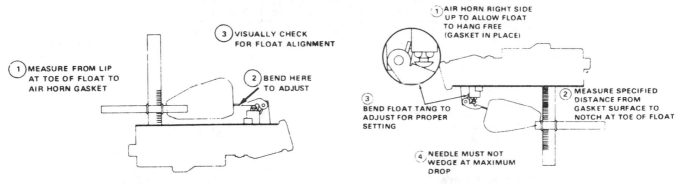

FLOAT LEVEL ADJUSTMENT   FLOAT DROP ADJUSTMENT

FIGURE 13-54. Common method of measuring and correcting float level and float drop. Float adjustment is critical to proper fuel level control in the carburetor. Incorrect float level affects performance and economy. (*Courtesy of General Motors Corporation*)

be blown from the passages with air pressure. *Never clean jets with a wire, drill, or other mechanical means* because the orifices may become damaged, causing improper performance.

Carburetor Assembly

When checking parts removed from the carburetor, it is recommended that new parts be installed whenever the old parts are questionable.

Assemble the carburetor in the recommended sequence making sure no parts are left out, and during assembly making any required adjustments to manufacturer's specifications. A new carburetor kit

must be used during assembly. The kit normally includes such items as gaskets, seals, retaining clips, check balls or valves, needle and seat, accelerator pump, and the necessary tamper proofing plugs and rivets.

Some kits contain parts for several different models of the same carburetor; in this case, some of the kit parts may not be needed. Careful examination is required to ensure that all the correct kit parts are used. It is good practice to replace the float assembly during carburetor overhaul.

A leaking metal float or a saturated composition float will continue to cause carburetor operating problems.

Evenly tighten all attaching screws in the right sequence and to specifications. Overtightening will strip threads. Make all required external adjustments before carburetor installation. Some adjustments, of course, are made after installation. Many

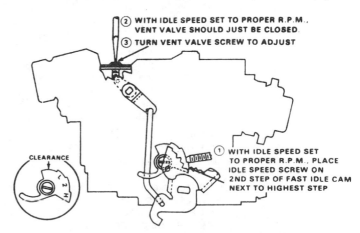

FIGURE 13-55. Accelerating pump adjustment on one type of carburetor. Correct pump adjustment is essential for good performance. (*Courtesy of General Motors Corporation*)

FIGURE 13-56. Bowl vent valve must be open when throttle is closed to allow bowl vapors to escape to canister. Vent valve must close at slight throttle opening to allow internal vent to provide balanced carburetion. (*Courtesy of General Motors Corporation*)

319

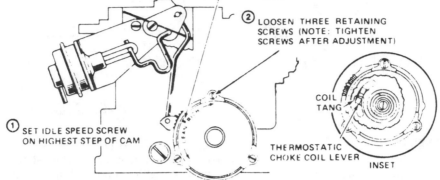

③ WITH CHOKE VALVE WIDE OPEN (ENGINE COLD) ROTATE COVER AGAINST COIL TENSION UNTIL CHOKE VALVE CLOSES. SET MARK ON COVER TO SPECIFIED POINT ON CHOKE HOUSING. NOTE: ON MODELS WITH SLOTTED COIL PICK-UP LEVER, MAKE SURE COIL TANG IS INSTALLED IN SLOT IN LEVER (SEE INSET).

② LOOSEN THREE RETAINING SCREWS (NOTE: TIGHTEN SCREWS AFTER ADJUSTMENT)

COIL TANG

① SET IDLE SPEED SCREW ON HIGHEST STEP OF CAM

THERMOSTATIC CHOKE COIL LEVER

INSET

FIGURE 13–57. Automatic choke adjustment must be correct to provide easy starting, good performance during warm-up, and to avoid an overrich fuel mixture. *(Courtesy of General Motors Corporation)*

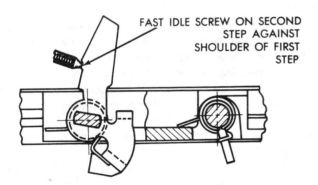

FAST IDLE SCREW ON SECOND STEP AGAINST SHOULDER OF FIRST STEP

FIGURE 13–58. Fast-idle cam adjustment provides additional throttle opening at idle during engine warm-up to prevent stalling. *(Courtesy of Chrysler Corporation)*

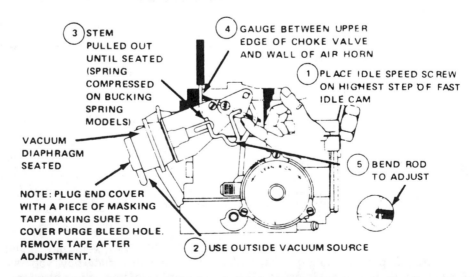

③ STEM PULLED OUT UNTIL SEATED (SPRING COMPRESSED ON BUCKING SPRING MODELS)

④ GAUGE BETWEEN UPPER EDGE OF CHOKE VALVE AND WALL OF AIR HORN

① PLACE IDLE SPEED SCREW ON HIGHEST STEP OF FAST IDLE CAM

VACUUM DIAPHRAGM SEATED

NOTE: PLUG END COVER WITH A PIECE OF MASKING TAPE MAKING SURE TO COVER PURGE BLEED HOLE. REMOVE TAPE AFTER ADJUSTMENT.

⑤ BEND ROD TO ADJUST

② USE OUTSIDE VACUUM SOURCE

FIGURE 13–59. Vacuum choke break must be adjusted to specifications to partially open the choke after the engine starts. If the choke were to remain closed, the engine would stall. *(Courtesy of General Motors Corporation)*

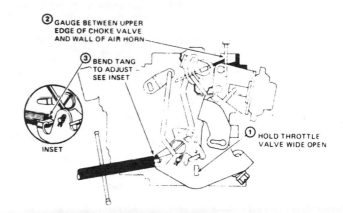

FIGURE 13-60. Choke unloader should open choke the specified amount at wide-open throttle to assist in starting a flooded engine. *(Courtesy of General Motors Corporation)*

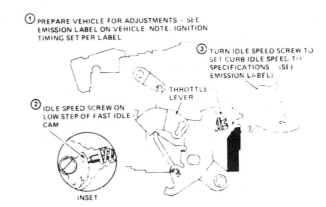

FIGURE 13-61. Idle speed adjustment without solenoid. *(Courtesy of General Motors Corporation)*

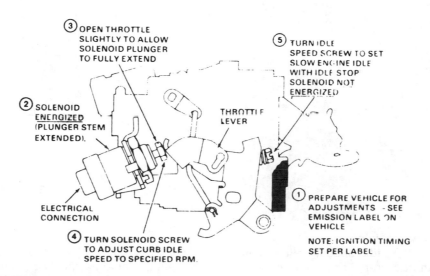

FIGURE 13-62. Idle speed adjustment with solenoid. *(Courtesy of General Motors Corporation)*

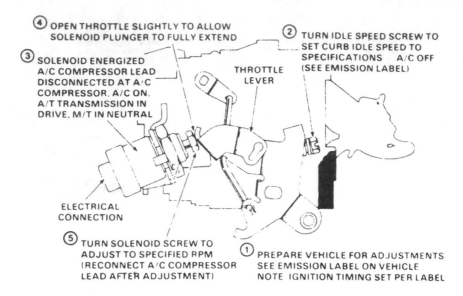

④ OPEN THROTTLE SLIGHTLY TO ALLOW SOLENOID PLUNGER TO FULLY EXTEND

③ SOLENOID ENERGIZED A/C COMPRESSOR LEAD DISCONNECTED AT A/C COMPRESSOR, A/C ON, A/T TRANSMISSION IN DRIVE, M/T IN NEUTRAL

② TURN IDLE SPEED SCREW TO SET CURB IDLE SPEED TO SPECIFICATIONS A/C OFF (SEE EMISSION LABEL)

THROTTLE LEVER

ELECTRICAL CONNECTION

⑤ TURN SOLENOID SCREW TO ADJUST TO SPECIFIED RPM (RECONNECT A/C COMPRESSOR LEAD AFTER ADJUSTMENT)

① PREPARE VEHICLE FOR ADJUSTMENTS SEE EMISSION LABEL ON VEHICLE NOTE IGNITION TIMING SET PER LABEL

FIGURE 13-63. Idle speed adjustment on one type of vehicle equipped with air conditioning. *(Courtesy of General Motors Corporation)*

of the more common adjustments are illustrated in this section.

Carburetor Installation

Inspect the mating surfaces of carburetor and intake manifold. Be sure both surfaces are clean and free of nicks, burrs, or other damage.

Place a new flange gasket on the manifold surface.

Some flange gaskets can be installed upside down or backwards. To prevent this, match holes in the flange gasket to holes on bottom of carburetor; then place gasket properly on intake manifold surface.

1. Carefully place carburetor on manifold without trapping choke rod under carburetor linkage.

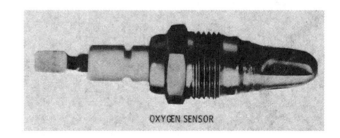

OXYGEN SENSOR

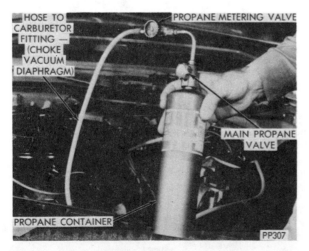

HOSE TO CARBURETOR FITTING — (CHOKE VACUUM DIAPHRAGM)

PROPANE METERING VALVE

MAIN PROPANE VALVE

PROPANE CONTAINER

PP307

FIGURE 13-64. Many vehicles use the propane-enriched method of setting idle speed. Follow vehicle and equipment manufacturer's specifications. Idle speed should increase specified amount when enriched with propane. *(Courtesy of Chrysler Corporation)*

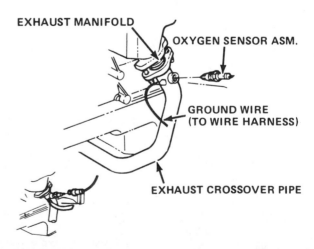

EXHAUST MANIFOLD

OXYGEN SENSOR ASM.

GROUND WIRE (TO WIRE HARNESS)

EXHAUST CROSSOVER PIPE

FIGURE 13-65. Vehicles equipped with electronic fuel metering should be checked to make sure that sensors and control units are functioning properly. *(Courtesy of General Motors Canada Ltd.)*

2. Install carburetor mounting bolts or nuts and tighten alternately, a little at a time, to compress flange gasket evenly. The nuts or bolts must be drawn down tightly to prevent vacuum leakage between carburetor and intake manifold.

3. Connect throttle and choke linkage, fuel inlet line, and all vacuum and electrical connections to the carburetor.

4. Check carefully for worn or loose vacuum hose connections. Refer to the vacuum hose routing diagram label located under the hood in the engine compartment.

5. Check to be sure the choke plate opens and closes fully when operated.

6. Check to see that full throttle travel is obtained.

7. Install air cleaner. The air cleaner should be cleaned or replaced at this time to insure proper carburetor performance.

8. Connect battery cable.

9. Check carburetor idle mixture adjustment. Refer to emission control label in engine compartment and perform all adjustments in the required sequence and to specifications.

10. Perform the required tests for satisfactory performance and emission levels.

PART 7   SELF-CHECK

1. The carburetor operates on the principle of _____.

2. The ratio of air to fuel is measured by volume. True or false?

3. List the six major carburetor circuits.

4. What effect does altitude have on carburetor air/fuel ratios?

5. What is the purpose of the carburetor throttle solenoid?

6. What is the purpose of carburetor air bleeds?

7. The electric choke closes the choke as soon as the ignition switch is turned on. True or false?

8. What effect does a high carburetor float level have on fuel consumption?

9. List three methods used to preheat the air/fuel mixture and prevent icing.

10. Describe carburetor venturi action.

11. List four methods of power enrichment used on carburetors.

12. State four factors that cause the choke valve to open.

13. What is the purpose of the following carburetor devices:
   (a) fast idle cam
   (b) choke unloader
   (c) solenoid idle stop
   (d) altitude compensator
   (e) mixture control solenoid
   (f) two-way bowl vent
   (g) idle fuel shut-off solenoid
   (h) dashpot

14. What is the purpose of the oxygen sensor?

15. All carburetor parts should be cleaned with carburetor cleaner. True or false?

16. What is the reason for proper float level adjustment?

17. What effect would a ruptured choke diaphragm have on choke operation?

PART 8   TEST QUESTIONS

1. The stoichiometric air/fuel ratio is:
   (a) 10.7 to 1
   (b) 14.7 to 1
   (c) 12.7 to 1
   (d) 15.7 to 1

2. Six main carburetor circuits are the following:
   (a) float, idle, main metering, power, choke, accelerator
   (b) air bleed, idle, solenoid, throttle, accelerator, pump
   (c) pump, idle, throttle, choke, main metering, power
   (d) throttle, bypass, main metering, power, choke, float

3. Carburetors are classified as:
   (a) single stage and two stage
   (b) 1V, 2V, and 4V
   (c) feedback controlled and variable venturi
   (d) all of the above

4. Feedback controlled carburetors operate in either of two modes:
   (a) feedback and feed forward
   (b) bypass and non-bypass
   (c) open loop and closed loop
   (d) suction throttling and non-suction throttling

5. The carburetor operates on the principle of:

(a) equal pressures in the venturi

(b) vacuum and heat

(c) heat and pressure

(d) differences in pressure

6. The air/fuel ratio is based on:

(a) weight of fuel and volume of air

(b) weight of fuel and air

(c) volume of fuel and air

(d) volume of fuel and weight of air

7. The power enrichment system adds fuel to the:

(a) low speed circuit

(b) accelerator pump circuit

(c) main metering circuit

(d) float circuit

8. The automatic choke is closed by:

(a) vacuum

(b) a bimetal spring

(c) atmospheric pressure

(d) accelerator linkage

9. The anti-dieseling solenoid plunger is extended when the:

(a) ignition key is on

(b) ignition key is off

(c) choke is on

(d) choke is off

10. Tamper proof devices on carburetors prevent:

(a) indiscriminate adjustment of carburetor

(b) carburetor service

(c) carburetor overhaul

(d) carburetor theft

Chapter 14

Gasoline Fuel Injection Systems

Performance Objectives

After thorough study of this chapter and sufficient practical experience on adequate training models, and with the appropriate shop manuals and equipment, you should be able to do the following:

1. Complete the self-check and test questions with at least 80 percent accuracy.

2. Follow the accepted general precautions outlined in this chapter.

3. Describe the purpose, construction, and operation of each of the fuel systems and their components.

4. Diagnose basic fuel system problems according to manufacturer's manuals.

5. Safely remove, recondition, replace, and adjust any faulty fuel system components according to manufacturer's specifications.

6. Properly performance test the reconditioned fuel system to determine the success of the repairs performed.

7. Prepare the vehicle for customer acceptance.

Gasoline fuel injection systems have been used for many years. Advantages of gasoline fuel injection over carbureted systems include more precise control over fuel metering resulting in better performance, improved economy, and lower exhaust emissions.

Gasoline fuel injection systems are mechanically or electronically controlled. Electronic systems use a number of engine sensors to feed information to the *electronic control unit* or *computer*. The computer processes the information based on stored information already in the computer, processes the information, and then tells the fuel injectors how much fuel to inject.

PART 1   TYPES OF FUEL INJECTION SYSTEMS

Several types of fuel injection systems are in use. They can be classified as follows:

- Port injection
- Throttle body injection
- Continuous injection
- Pulse timed injection

Port injection systems inject the fuel into the intake port very close to the intake valve. Port injection may be either continuous injection or pulse timed injection.

Throttle body injection injects the fuel into a throttle body which regulates air flow to the engine. Throttle body injection may also be either continuous or pulse timed.

Continuous injection means that fuel is sprayed continuously into the intake system. Continuous injection systems may be either port injection or throttle body injection systems.

Pulse timed injection means that fuel is injected into the intake system by injectors that spray fuel in short bursts. Pulse timed injection may be either port injection or throttle body injection.

PART 2   BOSCH CONTINUOUS INJECTION SYSTEM (CIS)

The Bosch CIS system is a mechanically operated injection system. This system uses the following components to provide precise air/fuel mixture control.

1. Fuel tank
2. Electric fuel pump
3. Fuel accumulator
4. Fuel filter

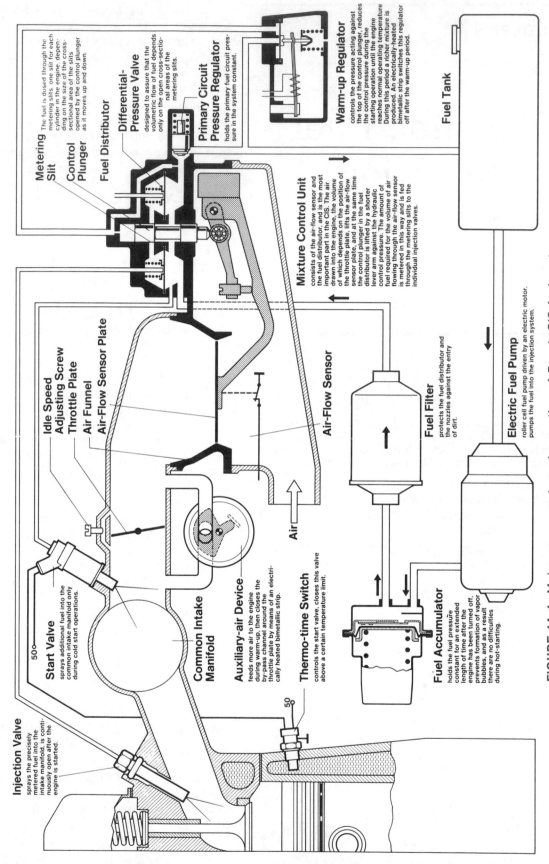

Injection Valve

sprays the precisely metered fuel into the intake manifold. is continuously open after the engine is started.

Start Valve

sprays additional fuel into the common intake manifold only during cold start operations.

Idle Speed Adjusting Screw
Throttle Plate
Air Funnel
Air-Flow Sensor Plate

Common Intake Manifold

Auxiliary-air Device

feeds more air to the engine during warm-up, then closes the by-pass channel around the throttle plate by means of an electrically heated bimetallic strip.

Thermo-time Switch

controls the start valve, closes this valve above a certain temperature limit.

Air-Flow Sensor

Air

Fuel Filter

protects the fuel distributor and the nozzles against the entry of dirt.

Fuel Accumulator

holds the fuel pressure constant for an extended length of time after the engine has been turned off, prevents formation of vapor bubbles, and as a result there are no difficulties during hot-starting.

Metering Slit

The fuel is dosed through the metering slits one slit for each cylinder in the engine. depending on the size of the cross-sectional area of the slits opened by the control plunger as it moves up and down.

Control Plunger

Fuel Distributor

Differential-Pressure Valve

designed to assure that the volumetric flow of fuel depends only on the open cross-sectional areas of the metering slits.

Primary Circuit Pressure Regulator

holds the primary fuel circuit pressure in the system constant.

Warm-up Regulator

controls the pressure acting against the top of the control plunger, reduces the control pressure during the starting operation until the engine reaches normal operating temperature During this period a richer mixture is produced. An electrically-heated bimetallic strip switches this regulator off after the warm-up period.

Mixture Control Unit

consists of the air-flow sensor and the fuel distributor, and is the most important part in the CIS. The air drawn into the engine, the volume of which depends on the position of the throttle plate, lifts the air-flow sensor plate, and at the same time the control plunger in the fuel distributor is lifted by a shorter lever arm against the hydraulic control pressure. The amount of fuel required for the volume of air flowing through the air-flow sensor is metered in this way and is fed through the metering slits to the individual injection valves.

Fuel Tank

Electric Fuel Pump

roller cell fuel pump driven by an electric motor. pumps the fuel into the injection system.

FIGURE 14-1. Major components and operation of Bosch CIS fuel system. *(Courtesy of Robert Bosch Canada Ltd.)*

5. Mixture control unit components

   (a) Fuel distributor

   (b) Air-flow sensor

   (c) Primary circuit pressure regulator

   (d) Idle mixture adjusting screw

   (e) Air-flow sensor contact

6. Warm-up regulator

7. Injection valve

8. Start valve

9. Common intake manifold

10. Auxiliary-air device

11. Thermo-time switch

12. Throttle plate

13. Idle speed adjusting screw

Bosch CIS Operation

A roller type fuel pump driven by an electric motor pumps the fuel.

The quantity of fuel fed to the engine is metered in proportion to the volume of air drawn through the mixture control unit.

The fuel is continuously sprayed by injection valves into the intake manifolds of the individual engine cylinders. From there, it is drawn into the cylinder together with the air during the inlet stroke.

The mixture control unit consists of the air-flow sensor and the fuel distributor.

The air-flow sensor is suspended in front of the throttle plate. It consists of a round plate mounted on a lever and suspended in an air funnel in such a way that it is deflected upward a distance proportional to the volume of air drawn into the engine through the funnel.

The function of the fuel distributor is to feed fuel to the engine proportional to air-flow sensor plate travel. By means of a control plunger, narrow rectangular slits (one for each of the cylinders in the engine) are opened or closed varying amounts. These metering slits are made larger or smaller in terms of open cross-section. The control plunger is supported on a lever in the air-flow sensor and, therefore, follows the movements of the air-flow sensor plate. As a result, the amount the control plunger rises is proportional to the amount of fuel fed to the engine.

The components responsible for this are the differential-pressure valves, one of which follows each metering slit. As a result of these differential-pressure valves, a constant pressure differential prevails at each metering slit. As long as this pressure differential exists, the quantity of fuel fed to the engine is proportional to the open cross-sectional area of the metering slit.

The position of the control plunger is influenced by the control pressure applied to it. After the engine has reached the normal operating temperature, this control pressure is about 50 psi (345 kPa). At such time, the force applied to the control plunger is much less than when the engine is warm. As a result, the air-flow sensor plate in the air-flow sensor is raised a greater distance for the same volumetric rate of air flow, and a larger amount of fuel is fed to the engine.

The function of the warm-up regulator is to increase the control pressure after the engine has warmed up. This is accomplished by a bimetallic strip in the cold condition acting against the delivery valve spring, which determines control pressure. When the engine is turned on, however, this bimetallic strip is electrically heated, and as it becomes warmer, the delivery valve spring becomes more and more effective, increasing control pressure.

Compensation for the greater frictional load (frictional resistance) during the warm-up period is made by increasing the volumetric efficiency of cylinder filling by means of an auxiliary-air device installed in a line bypassing the throttle plate. The amount of air which passes through the auxiliary-air device is controlled by a sliding plate in which a specially shaped hole is drilled. The position of this plate, and the degree to which the hole opens the auxiliary-air channel, is controlled by an electrically heated bimetallic strip.

The start valve, controlled by the thermo-time switch, sprays additional fuel into the common intake manifold during engine starting.

The engine idle speed is adjusted with the idle speed adjusting screw on the throttle plate fitting.

The idle mixture adjusting screw, accessible from outside on the mixture control unit, is provided for adjustment of the idle air/fuel mixture.

Injectors

CIS injectors open at a pre-set pressure and continually spray atomized fuel into the intake port near each intake valve. The injectors are push-fit into plastic bushings in the cylinder head. Clamps hold injectors in place. A vibrator pin inside the injector helps to break up and atomize the fuel droplets. Each injector also has its own fuel filter to catch any dirt that might enter the system after the main filter. The pin and spring seal residual fuel pressure in the line between the injector and the fuel distributor to ensure quick starting. The hexagonal section on the injector is provided to hold the valve stationary while the fuel line is attached.

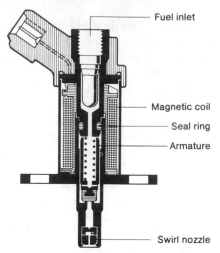

FIGURE 14-2. Cross-sectional view of typical Bosch fuel injector. *(Courtesy of Robert Bosch Canada Ltd.)*

Electrical Circuit Operation (Figure 14-3)

The air-flow sensor plate activates a switch which is closed when the engine is turned off. When the air-flow sensor plate rises from its seat, however, the ground line from Relay 1 is opened.

When the ignition is switched on (Terminal 15), Relay I is energized. Relay II remains at rest, how-

ever, and the electric fuel pump remains switched off.

When the engine is started (Terminal 50), the control current for Relay II flows through the working contact of Relay I, and the electric fuel pump is switched on through the working contact of Relay II. At the same time, current starts to flow to the warm-up regulator and to the auxiliary-air device. The start valve is also switched on at this time through a thermo-time switch. As soon as the engine draws in air, the air-flow sensor plate in the air-flow sensor rises from its seat and opens the ground line from Relay I. Relay I is then de-energized and returns to its off position. Relay II remains energized, however, and the electric fuel pump continues to operate.

If the engine comes to a stop as a result of exceptional conditions, the electric fuel pump is also automatically stopped even though the ignition is still turned on. This results from the switch at the air-flow sensor closing. This switches Relay I to the working position and interrupts the control line leading to Relay II. At this point, there is no longer a connection from Terminal 30 to the electric fuel pump.

Some versions of the CIS system use an exhaust gas oxygen sensor and electronic control unit to more closely control the air/fuel mixture.

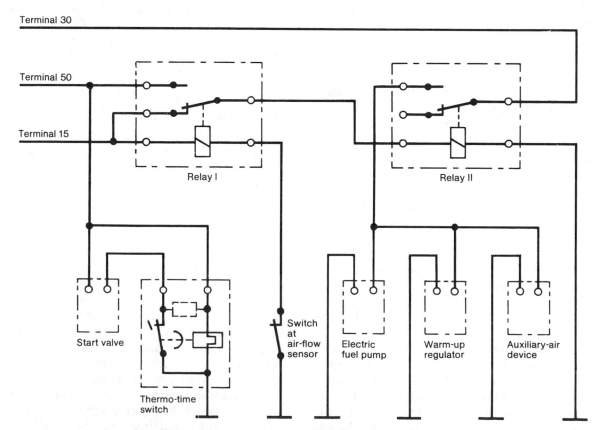

FIGURE 14-3. Bosch CIS electrical system circuit without O₂ feedback system. *(Courtesy of Robert Bosch Canada Ltd.)*

PART 3 BOSCH ELECTRONIC FUEL INJECTION SYSTEMS

The Bosch Electronic Fuel Injection systems are port injection types. Two similar systems are used, the major difference being the major controlling factor in the system. One system is responsive to manifold pressure, whereas the other is controlled by intake air flow. Both types are pulse timed systems. Both systems use a roller type electrically driven submerged fuel pump, a fuel pressure regulator, a cold start valve controlled by a thermal switch or a thermal time switch, an engine temperature sensor, an auxiliary-air device, a throttle position switch, an engine speed sensor or trigger contacts in the distributor, an electronic control unit, and fuel injectors. Some systems are equipped with an exhaust gas oxygen sensor to provide close monitoring of exhaust gases. The oxygen sensor provides a voltage signal to the electronic control unit. All input signals to the electronic control unit are processed, and fuel is injected to provide the best possible air/fuel ratio based on the input signals provided. The result is good emission control, performance, and economy.

System Operation

The principal difference between the intake system in the EFI-L and the intake system in the EFI-D lies in the air-flow sensor in the EFI-L.

The function of the air-flow sensor is to generate a voltage signal proportional to the amount of air drawn into the engine. This signal and the information on the engine speed are the main inputs used

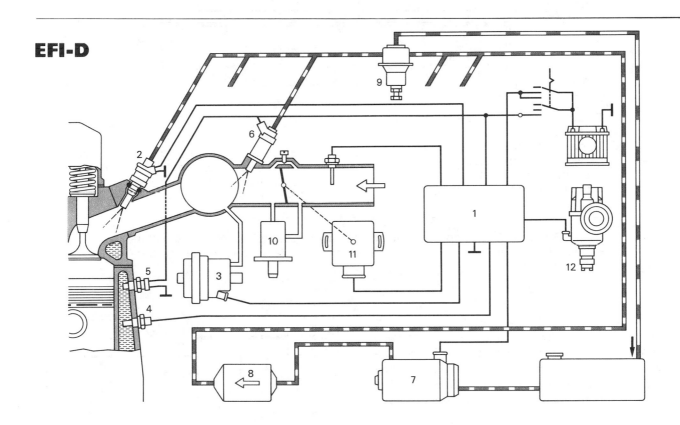

1. Electronic control unit
2. Injection valve
3. Pressure sensor
4. Temperature sensor
5. Thermal switch or thermal time sensor
6. Start valve
7. Electronic fuel pump
8. Fuel filter
9. Fuel pressure regulator
10. Auxiliary air device
11. Throttle valve switch
12. Trigger contacts

FIGURE 14-4. Components and schematic of Bosch EFI-D electronic fuel injection system using manifold pressure sensor. *(Courtesy of Robert Bosch Canada Ltd.)*

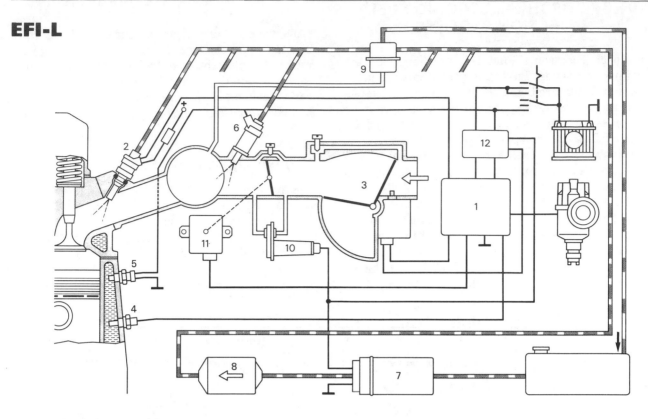

1. Electronic control unit
2. Injection valve
3. Pressure sensor
4. Temperature sensor
5. Thermal time switch
6. Start valve

7. Electronic fuel pump
8. Fuel filter
9. Fuel pressure regulator
10. Auxiliary air device
11. Throttle valve switch
12. Relay set

FIGURE 14-5. Components and schematic of Bosch EFI-L electronic fuel injection system using intake air flow sensor. *(Courtesy of Robert Bosch Canada Ltd.)*

to determine the duration of injection. In the air-flow sensor, the air drawn in by the engine exerts a force on a movable air-flow sensor flap. Depending on the air flow and the effective opposing restoring force of a spring, the air-flow sensor flap is held in a certain angular position which is sensed by a potentiometer.

A compensation flap attached to the air-flow sensor flap compensates for possible back-pressure oscillations because it has the same effective surface area as the sensor flap, so these oscillations have no effect on the air-flow sensing function. At the same time, the compensation flap, together with a damping chamber, reduces oscillations in the measurement system.

The air-flow sensor flap is also fitted with a non-return valve designed to protect the air-flow sensor against damage in event of back-pressure surges.

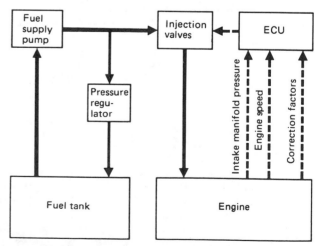

FIGURE 14-6. Schematic of EFI input and output of electronic control unit (ECU) of Bosch fuel injection system. *(Courtesy of Robert Bosch Canada Ltd.)*

• The injection system employing air-flow sensing automatically takes into account all changes in the engine that can occur during the service life of the vehicle (abrasion, deposits in the combustion chamber, change in valve adjustment, etc.). Uniform good quality of exhaust gas is, therefore, assured.

• In the EFI-L, part of the exhaust gas can be recirculated to lower the temperature in the combustion chamber. The air-flow sensor measures only the fresh air drawn into the engine, and the control unit meters the quantity of fuel required for only the amount of fresh air.

• A supplementary mechanism for mixture enrichment during acceleration is not required because the signal transmitted by the air-flow sensor precedes charging of the cylinders. In addition, idle stability is improved.

PART 4 GM PORT INJECTION

The electronic gasoline fuel-injection system provides the means for very precise control of the air-fuel ratio to the engine and delivers an equal amount

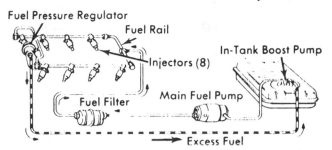

FIGURE 14-8. Fuel flow diagram for electronic gasoline fuel injection. (*Courtesy of General Motors Corporation*)

to each cylinder. In the conventional carburetor-manifold system, this is not possible.

The components of a typical system are shown in Figure 14-11. Five sensors transmit information to a preprogrammed analog computer called the *electronic control unit* (ECU). The ECU computes this information continuously and directs the resulting appropriate commands to the EGR solenoid, fuel pump, fast-idle valve, and the two groups of injector valves (see Figure 14-7).

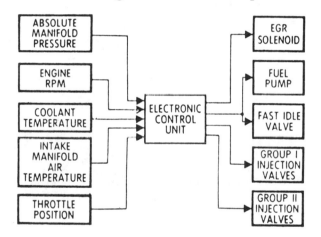

FIGURE 14-7. Schematic showing sensor signals to electronic control unit. ECU controls devices on right according to signals received from devices on left. (*Courtesy of General Motors Corporation*)

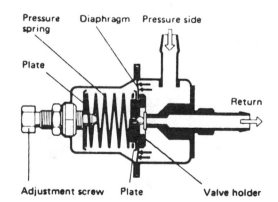

FIGURE 14-9. Fuel pressure regulator. Excess fuel pressure is vented through the return line back to the fuel tank. (*Courtesy of General Motors Corporation*)

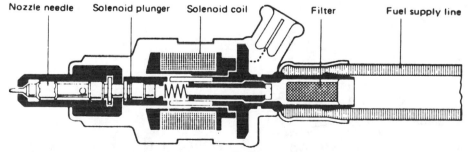

FIGURE 14-10. Electronic gasoline fuel injector components (cross-sectional view). (*Courtesy of General Motors Corporation*)

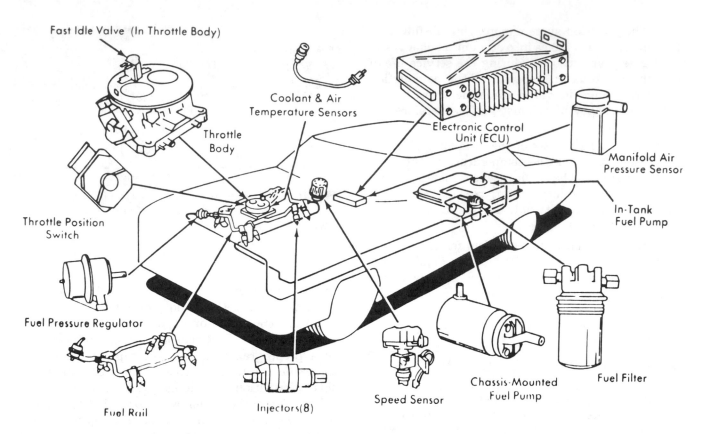

Fast Idle Valve (In Throttle Body)

Throttle Body

Coolant & Air Temperature Sensors

Electronic Control Unit (ECU)

Manifold Air Pressure Sensor

Throttle Position Switch

In-Tank Fuel Pump

Fuel Pressure Regulator

Fuel Rail

Injectors(8)

Speed Sensor

Chassis-Mounted Fuel Pump

Fuel Filter

FIGURE 14-11. Electronic fuel-injection system components for gasoline injection. *(Courtesy of General Motors Corporation)*

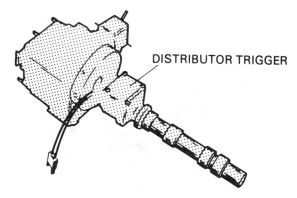

DISTRIBUTOR TRIGGER

FIGURE 14-12. Distributor trigger senses engine speed and sends this information to the electronic control unit. *(Courtesy of General Motors Corporation)*

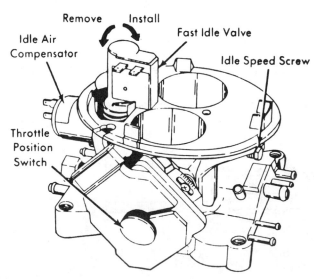

Idle Air Compensator

Remove   Install

Fast Idle Valve

Idle Speed Screw

Throttle Position Switch

FIGURE 14-13. Electronic fuel-injection throttle assembly controls air flow only. *(Courtesy of General Motors Corporation)*

The ECU is designed and programmed to provide the correct air-fuel ratio for all operating conditions. Fuel delivery pressure is kept at a constant pressure of approximately 38 to 40 psi (262 to 276 kilopascals). The amount of fuel delivered to the cylinders is varied by the amount of time (duration) the injectors are open. Fuel is injected into the intake ports just ahead of the intake valves.

PART 5 GENERAL MOTORS ELECTRONIC FUEL INJECTION (EFI)

EFI is a fuel metering system where the amount of fuel delivered by the injector is determined by an electronic signal supplied by the electronic control module (ECM).

With EFI, the carburetor is removed from the system. The float bowl and its mechanisms, the idle circuit, off-idle fuel enrichment, accelerator pump, choke system, multiple venturies, etc., are all eliminated. In essence, only the relatively small lower portion, or throttle body, is retained and a simple solenoid-operated fuel injector is added. Total control of the air/fuel ratio is accomplished.

The throttle body injector is a device that does not control, but rather is controlled by, the ECM.

The ECM monitors various engine and vehicle conditions needed to calculate the fuel delivery of the injector.

Fuel is supplied to the system from an in-tank, dual-turbine fuel pump which supplies fuel through an in-line fuel filter to the throttle body. Fuel is made

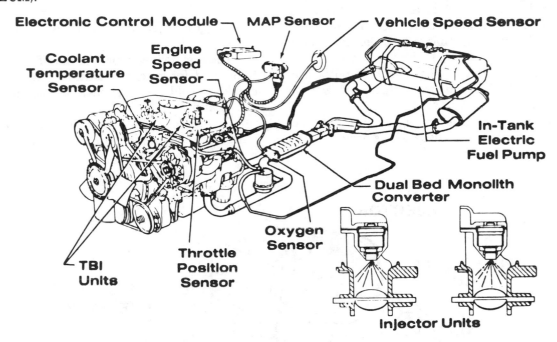

FIGURE 14-14. Component layout of electronic throttle body fuel injection system by General Motors. *(Courtesy of General Motors Corporation)*

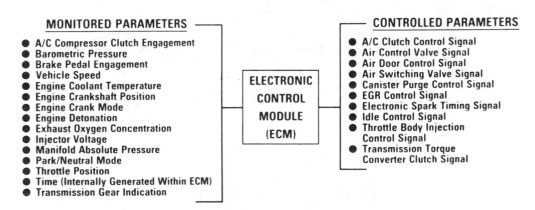

FIGURE 14-15. Input and output factors of electronic control module of system shown in Figure 14-14. *(Courtesy of General Motors Corporation)*

available via internal passages to the injector unit. Finally, the fuel pressure regulator, which maintains a constant pressure of 10 to 11 psi, returns excess fuel to the fuel tank through the fuel return line.

The fuel injector mounted at the top of the throttle body is an electromagnetic fuel nozzle. The injector is *pulsed* on to allow fuel to flow.

The electronic control module (ECM) is the control center of the throttle body injection system. The ECM controls the exhaust emissions by modifying fuel delivery to achieve as near as possible an air/fuel ratio of 14.7 to 1.

The injector *on* time is determined by various inputs or "monitored parameters."

The ECM receives this constantly monitored input information, processes it, and generates output commands to the various "controlled parameters," which are the systems that affect vehicle performance.

The ECM determines the length of pulse necessary for a sufficient amount of fuel to flow from the injector.

By increasing the injector pulse time, more fuel is delivered; thus, the air/fuel ratio is enriched. De-

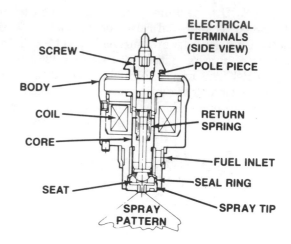

FIGURE 14-17. Fuel injector for GM, EFI, TBI system. *(Courtesy of General Motors Corporation)*

creasing the injector pulse time leans the air/fuel ratio.

The fuel delivery may be modified by the ECM to account for special operating conditions such as cranking, cold starting, altitude, acceleration, and deceleration.

One feature that throttle body injection provides is its ease of start-up. No longer is it necessary

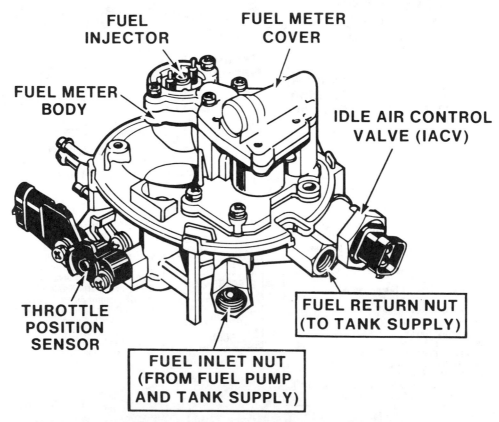

FIGURE 14-16. Throttle body injection assembly for General Motors electronic fuel injection. *(Courtesy of General Motors Corporation)*

to "pump" the accelerator to set the choke on a cold engine.

The ECM contains an engine calibration unit called a PROM (Programmable Read Only Memory), which provides specific programmed calibration instructions that tailor the ECM to the specific engine/vehicle combination for which it is intended.

The ECM performs the diagnostic function of the system, recognizing operational problems, alerting the driver through the "check engine" light, and storing a code or codes that identify the problem areas to aid the technician in making repairs.

PART 6 GENERAL MOTORS DIGITAL FUEL INJECTION (DFI)

The GM Digital Fuel Injection system (DFI) is a pulse timed, speed and air density system that injects fuel into a throttle body above the throttle blade. Fuel is metered into the engine via two electronically controlled fuel injectors. The DFI system also includes a variety of sensors that continually

monitor a wide range of variables, feeding this information to an electronic control module (ECM). The ECM then performs high speed digital computations for the correct air/fuel mixture ratio necessary to achieve desired performance and emission standards.

The basic DFI systems include:

- Fuel delivery
- Air induction
- Data sensors and switch signals
- Electronic controls and interface
- Electronic spark timing
- Idle speed control
- Emission systems
- Transmission converter clutch
- Cruise control
- Fuel data panel
- System diagnosis

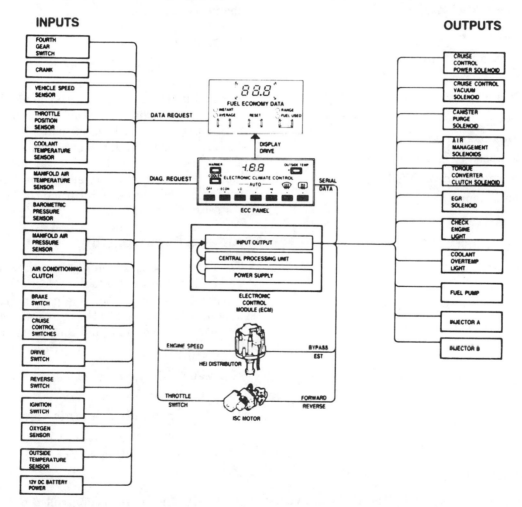

FIGURE 14-18. General Motors TBI digital fuel injection system inputs and outputs. *(Courtesy of General Motors Corporation)*

Fuel Delivery System

The fuel delivery system consists of a manifold-mounted throttle body assembly that incorporates two integrally mounted injectors and a fuel pressure regulator.

Fuel is fed to this assembly at a relatively low pressure—10 pounds per square inch—from a twin turbine in-tank fuel pump. There is an in-line 10-micron fuel filter.

The electric-motor-driven twin turbine type pump is integral with the fuel tank float unit and provides fuel at a positive pressure to the throttle body.

The fuel tank is specifically designed for digital fuel injection and contains a special bathtub-type reservoir that is used to supply fuel to the fuel pump pickup.

Two injector valves are electronically actuated and serve to meter and direct the atomized fuel into the throttle body above the throttle blade.

Data Sensors and Switch Signals

Data Sensors:

- Coolant temperature sensor (CTS)
- Manifold air temperature (MAT)
- Manifold absolute pressure (MAP)
- Barometric absolute pressure (BARO)
- Throttle position sensor (TPS)
- Engine speed (distributor)
- Vehicle speed sensor (VSS)
- Oxygen sensor (O_2)

Switch Signals:

- Ignition switch
- Crank signal (Ign. Sw.)
- Brake switch
- Drive signal (ADL/park/neutral sw.)
- Reverse signal (ADL/park/neutral sw.)
- 4th gear switch
- A/C clutch signal
- Cruise enable switch
- Cruise set switch
- Cruise resume/accel. switch
- Throttle switch (ISC)

Electronic Controls

Many of the inputs received by the ECM are variable signals and are continually changing.

It is the function of the electronic control module to interpret these sensor signals, as well as switched inputs, and process them to control the:

- Fuel delivery system
- Ignition timing
- Idle speed control (ISC)
- Exhaust gas recirculation (EGR)
- Air management
- Canister purge
- Diagnostics
- Transmission converter clutch

PART 7 FORD ELECTRONIC FUEL INJECTION

The Ford Electronic Fuel Injection System is a single-point, throttle body, pulse timed modulated injection system. Fuel is metered into the intake air stream, according to engine demands, by two solenoid injection valves mounted in a throttle body on the intake manifold.

Operation

Fuel is supplied from the fuel tank by a high pressure, electric fuel pump mounted in the fuel tank. The fuel is filtered and sent to the air throttle body where a regulator keeps the fuel delivery pressure at a constant 269.0 kPa (39 psi). Two injector nozzles are vertically mounted above the throttle plates and connected in parallel with the fuel pressure regulator. Excess fuel supplied by the pump, but not needed by the engine, is returned to the fuel tank by a steel fuel return line.

Air and Fuel Control

The throttle body assembly is comprised of six individual components which perform the fuel and air metering function in the engine. The throttle body assembly is mounted to the conventional carburetor pad of the intake manifold and consists of:

- Air control
- Fuel injector nozzles
- Fuel pressure regulator
- Fuel pressure diagnostic valve
- Cold engine speed control
- Throttle position sensor

Air Control

Air flow to the engine is controlled by two butterfly valves mounted in a two-piece, die cast aluminum housing called the throttle body. The butterfly valves

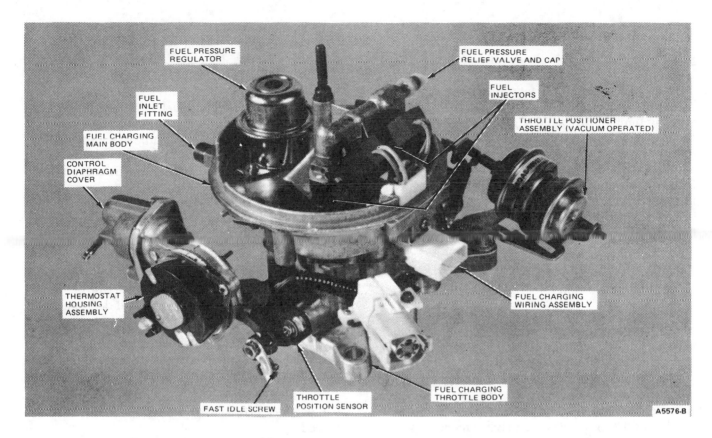

FIGURE 14-19. Ford TBI electronic fuel injection throttle body injection assembly. (*Courtesy of Ford Motor Co. of Canada Ltd.*)

are identical in configuration to the throttle plates of a conventional carburetor and are actuated by a similar linkage and pedal cable arrangement.

Fuel Injector Nozzles

The fuel injector nozzles are mounted vertically above the throttle plates and are electromechanical devices which meter and atomize the fuel delivered to the engine. The injector valve bodies consist of a solenoid-actuated pintle and needle valve assembly. An electrical control signal from the electronic processor activates the solenoid, causing the pintle to move inward off its seat to allow fuel to flow. The injector flow orifice is fixed, and the fuel supply pressure is constant; therefore, fuel flow to the engine is controlled by how long the solenoid is energized.

Fuel Pressure Regulator

The pressure regulator mounts to the fuel charging main body near the rear of the air horn surface. The regulator is located so as to nullify the effects if the supply line pressure drops. Its design is such that it is not sensitive to back pressure in the return line to the tank.

A second function of the pressure regulator is to maintain fuel supply pressure upon engine and fuel pump shutdown. The regulator functions as a downstream check valve and traps the fuel between itself and the fuel pump. The maintenance of fuel pressure upon engine shutdown prevents fuel line vapor formation and allows for rapid restarts and stable idle operation immediately thereafter. It regulates the fuel pressure to the injector nozzles at a constant nominal value of 269.0 kPa (39 psi).

Fuel Pressure Diagnostic Valve

The diagnostic pressure valve (Schrader style) is located at the top of the EFI fuel metering body. This valve provides a convenient point for service personnel to monitor fuel pressure, to bleed down the system pressure prior to maintenance, and to bleed out air which may have been introduced at assembly plant start-up or filter servicing.

Cold Engine Speed Control

The additional engine speed required during cold idle is accomplished by a throttle stop cam positioner similar to that used on conventional carburetors. The cam is positioned by a bimetal spring and an electric temperature heating element. The electrical source for the heating element is from the alternator stator, which provides voltage only when the engine is running.

The heating element is designed to provide the necessary warm-up profile in accordance with the starting temperature (cold engine prior to crank) and the length of time after starting. Multiple positions on the cam profile allow for a decreasing cold engine speed to curb idle speed during warm-up. A second feature of the cold engine speed control is automatic kickdown from high cam (fast idle) engine speed to some intermediate speed. This is accomplished by the computer vacuum to the automatic kickdown motor which physically moves the high speed cam a predetermined time after the engine starts.

Throttle Position Sensor

This sensor is mounted to the throttle shaft on the choke side of the fuel charging assembly and is used to supply a voltage output proportional to the change in the throttle plate position. The TP sensor is used by the computer to determine the operation mode (closed throttle, part throttle, and wide open throttle) for selection of the proper fuel mixture, spark, and EGR at selected driving modes.

PART 8   CHRYSLER ELECTRONIC FUEL INJECTION (CONTINUOUS FLOW)

The Chrysler Electronic Fuel Injection (EFI) system is a continuous flow, single-point, throttle body, electronically controlled system. A single system monitors the ratio of air to fuel electronically, compares it to an ideal ratio, and adjusts it automatically to changing environmental and engine conditions.

Specifically, the Chrysler EFI system:

• Provides an integrated and pre-programmed computer that commands ignition timing, air/fuel ratio, and emission control systems

• Employs an unusually wide variety of sensor inputs on which to base its command decisions and insure more precise control

• Has the ability to update and revise its programming to better suit current ambient and engine operating conditions

• Can function with a high degree of precision, even when certain sensor inputs are inoperative or misleading

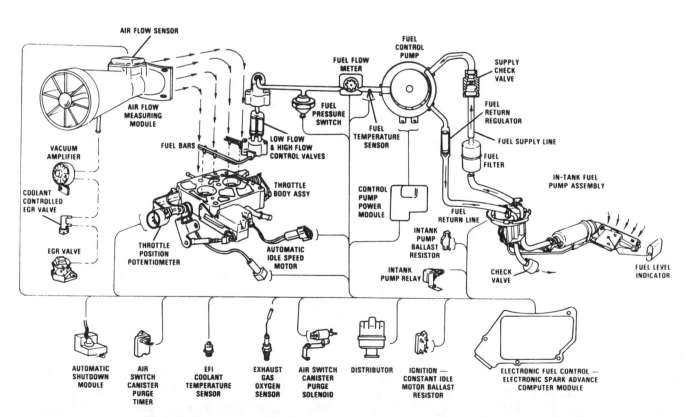

FIGURE 14-20. Component layout of Chrysler's TBI electronic fuel injection system. This is a continuous injection system using an air flow sensor. *(Courtesy of Chrysler Corporation)*

Since EFI's fuel metering is electronically commanded, it is not subject to low airflow errors of venturi-controlled metering used by carburetors. Also, since fuel is delivered under positive pressure through injection nozzles, excellent fuel atomization is assured, even at low airflow rates. This improves air/fuel mixing and minimizes variations in air/fuel ratio delivered to each cylinder.

Fuel Supply Subsystem

The EFI fuel supply subsystem is the link between the fuel tank and the EFI fuel control subsystem. The link is composed of two separate circuits which form a closed loop. The first portion of the loop (the fuel delivery circuit) delivers a constant flow of fuel under pressure from the tank to the fuel control subsystem. Since the fuel control subsystem uses only a small portion of the delivered fuel, the remainder of the fuel is returned to the fuel tank through the second portion of the loop (the fuel return circuit).

Although the closed loop arrangement is more complex than the usual single-line type, it does provide two important advantages. First, the delivery circuit is pressurized. There is less likelihood of vapor bubbles forming, and those that may form are readily purged through the return circuit.

Second, there is a generous oversupply of fuel provided; thus, varying demands by the fuel control subsystem encounter little or no inlet pressure variation, and more precise and predictable fuel metering is assured.

Fuel Delivery Circuit

The parts and functioning of the fuel delivery circuit are relatively simple and straightforward. An in-tank pump picks up fuel from the fuel tank and delivers it forward through the fuel delivery line and a pair of filters to the control pump housing. Two fuel filters mounted in parallel in the delivery line remove sediment. A pair of check valves (delivery line check valve, control pump housing check valve) help keep the delivery line and control pump housing filled with fuel when the in-tank pump is shut down.

Fuel Return Circuit

The essential parts of the return circuit of the closed fuel supply loop include the control pump housing, pressure regulator and by-pass orifice, fuel return line, and the fuel return line check valve.

The Fuel Control Subsystem

The EFI fuel control subsystem is the control link between the fuel supply subsystem and the point where fuel is finally injected for mixing with the incoming airstream. Located in the engine compartment, the entire subsystem is mounted on the hydraulic support plate assembly under the air cleaner assembly and atop the throttle body, spacer, and intake manifold of the engine. The heart of the sub-

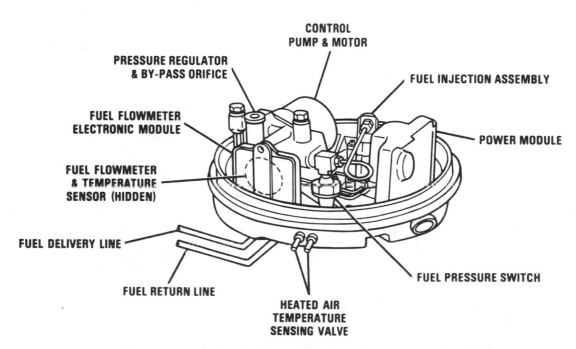

FIGURE 14-21. Chrysler EFI, TBI throttle body fuel control assembly. *(Courtesy of Chrysler Corporation)*

system is the control pump, which picks up constant-pressure supply fuel and boosts it to the desired metering pressure. This is the point at which the amount of fuel fed to the engine is actually controlled. From the control pump outlet, the metered fuel passes through a fuel flowmeter and temperature sensor assembly (integral with the fuel flowmeter), past a fuel pressure switch and, finally, to the fuel injection assembly. Also mounted on the hydraulic support plate are the power module (which supplies electric power to the control pump) and the inlet air temperature sensing valve (part of the heated air system).

Control Pump

The control pump consists of a positive-displacement, slipper-type pump driven by a variable-speed direct current motor. The total characteristics of the control subsystem are such that the outlet (metering) pressure boost, over the constant inlet supply pressure, is in proportion to the power supplied to the control pump motor. This is an important asset in achieving relatively precise control pump metering response to everchanging engine conditions.

Fuel Flowmeter and Temperature Sensor

The fuel flowmeter consists of a cylindrical cavity containing a free-turning wheel shaped somewhat like a gear, except that the "teeth" are actually small, curved vanes.

Fuel enters the cavity at an angle and moves the vanes. This causes the wheel to spin at a rate proportional to fuel flow. As the wheel spins, the vanes interrupt the light path between a light-emitting diode (LED) and a phototransistor. The phototransistor *sees* pulses of light. The frequency of the pulses is proportional to the rate of fuel flow and is interpreted as flow rate by the fuel flowmeter module.

The fuel flow is also in contact with a silicon thermistor whose electrical conductivity is a function of fuel temperature (and is so read by the electronic module). These two sensor outputs—fuel flow and fuel temperature—are circuited to the combustion control computer. They serve as part of the information evaluated to precisely control the speed of the control pump motor.

Fuel Pressure Switch

The fuel pressure switch is positioned in the fuel control circuit between the fuel flowmeter and the fuel injection assembly. It is normally open when there is insufficient metering pressure in the circuit to start or run the engine and is closed when there is insufficient metering pressure. When closed (with the ignition key in the *START* position), the fuel pressure switch completes a by-pass circuit that drives the control pump at full speed. This condition causes the pump to flush, prime, and pressurize the fuel control circuit and to help ensure a prompt engine start.

Fuel Injection Assembly

Metered fuel entering the fuel injection assembly is directed to two pressure-regulating valves. Each

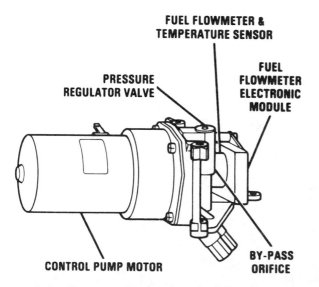

FIGURE 14–22. Fuel pump and pressure regulator for Chrysler EFI, TBI system. *(Courtesy of Chrysler Corporation)*

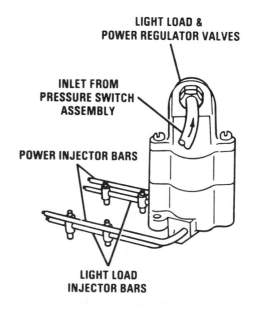

FIGURE 14–23. Power regulator valve and fuel spray bar assembly for Chrysler EFI, TBI system. *(Courtesy of Chrysler Corporation)*

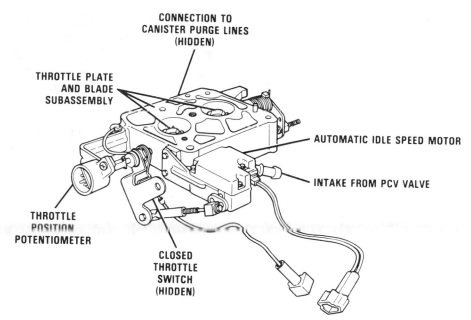

FIGURE 14-24. Throttle body assembly for Chrysler EFI, TBI system. *(Courtesy of Chrysler Corporation)*

valve feeds into its own U-shaped fuel injection bar, located over the throttle body assembly.

The light load regulator valve opens when metered fuel pressure reaches or exceeds 21 psi and delivers fuel to the light load injector bar. Four tiny holes in the lower surface of the injector bar spray fuel onto crescent-shaped ridges at the edges of the throttle plates, where the actual fuel-air mixing occurs. Airfoil-shaped light load injector nozzles around the injector holes help refine the fuel spray patterns. The light load circuit supplies all of the engine's fuel requirements when metering fuel pressure is between 21 and 34 psi and some of the requirements beyond these pressures.

When metered fuel pressures reach or exceed 34 psi (as in the case of heavy loads or for starting), the power regulator valve opens. The power fuel injector bar then adds its spray pattern to the fuel-air mixing process. However, the power injector bar neither has nor needs the airfoil-shaped nozzles to produce a proper fuel spray pattern.

Sensors

Sensors providing information to the combustion control computer for air/fuel mixture control include the following:

1. Air flow sensor—in air cleaner snorkel

2. Throttle position potentiometer—at throttle body

3. Air temperature sensor—in computer

4. Fuel flowmeter—at throttle body support plate

5. Fuel temperature sensor—in fuel flowmeter cavity

6. Fuel pressure switch—on throttle body support plate

7. Coolant temperature sensor—in intake manifold coolant crossover passage

8. Oxygen sensor—in exhaust manifold

9. Ignition switch—in steering column

10. Engine speed sensor—at distributor

11. Air conditioner *on* sensor

12. Time sensor—in computer

All the information from these sensors is analyzed by the computer to determine the air/fuel ratio best suited for the operating conditions. This information also determines whether the oxygen sensor system will operate in open or closed loop.

PART 9 CHRYSLER PULSE TIMED ELECTRONIC FUEL INJECTION

This system uses a single pulse timed injector in the throttle body which pulses once for each intake stroke. The operation of the injector is controlled by a number of sensors, which feed information to a digital electronic logic module and a power module.

System Operation

When the ignition key is turned *on*, the power module then supplies eight volts to the logic module and the distributor pickup. The logic module sends five

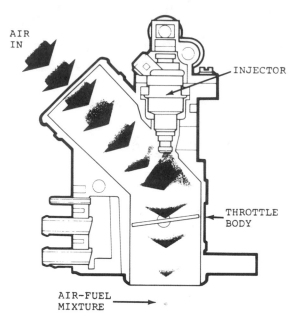

FIGURE 14-25. Chrysler's TBI pulse-time throttle body and fuel injector. For each cylinder intake stroke, the fuel injector pulses once and sends a spray of fuel into the airstream within the throttle body. *(Courtesy of Chrysler Corporation)*

volts to the charge temperature sensor, the throttle position sensor, the manifold absolute pressure (MAP) sensor, and the coolant sensor.

Finally, the power module supplies voltage to the auto-shutdown relay and the logic module.

The automatic shutdown (ASD) relay, which is normally open, closes at this point. It stays closed for about a half a second and then opens again unless the engine is cranked. When the relay is closed, the logic module commands the power module to send a single "prime shot" of fuel to the engine.

Engine Cranking

When the engine is cranked by the starter, the distributor sends pulses to the logic and power modules.

If the power module does not sense battery voltage and distributor pulses at a rate of 60 rpm within a half-second after the first distributor pulse, the automatic shutdown relay will not stay closed, and the engine will not start. This fast shutdown is a safety feature in the event of an accident.

If the proper signals are received by the power module, it will close the automatic shutdown relay and provide battery voltage to the electric in-tank fuel pump, the logic module, the ignition coil, through the power module itself, and the fuel injector.

During cranking, the logic module continues to receive information from the coolant temperature sensor, the throttle position sensor, the MAP sensor, and the distributor pickup that senses rpm.

The logic module makes calculations based on all these inputs and supplies power to the automatic idle speed motor, opening it for proper starting. The logic module also sends information to the power module to control ignition coil and fuel injector operation.

Engine Running

Once the engine is running, the logic module constantly monitors the various inputs and makes calculations that control spark advance, fuel delivery, and automatic idle speed.

For example, a low signal from the O_2 sensor indicates that the fuel mixture is too lean. The logic module commands the power module to increase the fuel pulse duration at the fuel injector.

It is important to remember that the logic module constantly evaluates all inputs and adjusts the output signals accordingly. Therefore, there are no simple relationships between a single input and a single output.

Limp-In Mode

Another important feature is the limp-in mode. It is activated whenever one of three crucial systems fails:

- MAP sensor
- Throttle position sensor
- Coolant temperature sensor

If the logic module detects a questionable input from any of these three systems, it goes into the limp-in mode rather than shutting down the engine.

In any limp-in mode, the logic module replaces the questionable signal with nominal values that allow the car to be driven without damage to the engine. It does this by using other inputs to approximate a value for the questionable input. For example, a bad MAP signal would be replaced by the throttle position signal, and the logic module would drive the AIS motor to minimum idle speed.

PART 10   GASOLINE FUEL INJECTION DIAGNOSIS AND SERVICE

General Precautions

All the normal personal and shop safety precautions should be observed when servicing fuel injection systems as well as those precautions outlined in Chapter 13, Part 6.

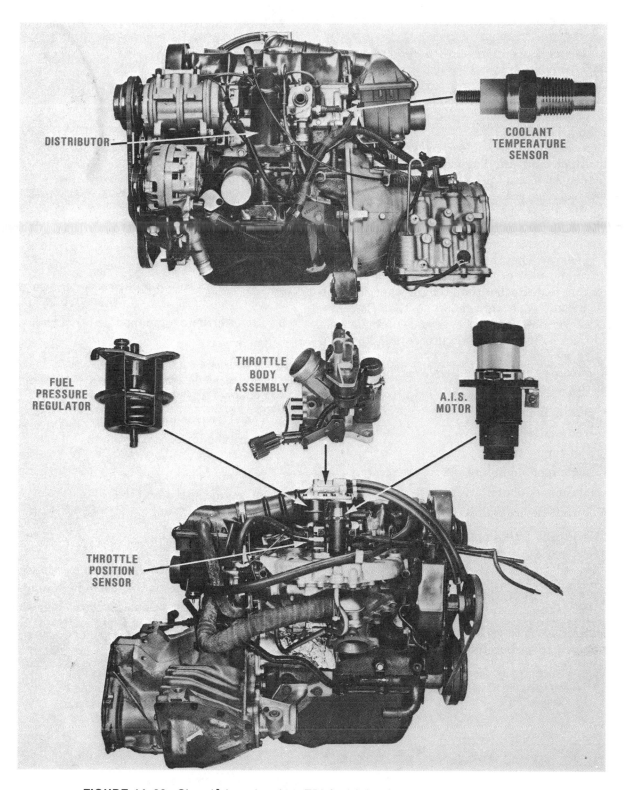

FIGURE 14-26. Chrysler's pulse-time TBI fuel injection system and component location on engine. *(Courtesy of Chrysler Corporation)*

In addition, it should be emphasized that gasoline fuel injection systems may operate under pressure as high as 100 psi (690 kPa). Extreme care must be exercised when loosening fuel line fittings to properly control and contain the fuel which will escape under very high pressure. Some fuel systems provide a service valve which allows depressurizing the system before any lines are disconnected. However, proper containment of the fuel is required in all cases.

The wide variety and complexity of designs, including the varying levels of the use of electronic

343

control devices, does not allow a common general approach to diagnosis and service procedures. It is essential, therefore, that the technician be thoroughly familiar with the components and operation of the system before any attempt is made at servicing and diagnosis.

Many electronic fuel injection systems are interfaced with an on-board diagnostic system. Very precise precautions and special procedures performed in exact sequence are required to isolate the problem area in these systems.

The fault codes displayed by the logic module are excellent for diagnosis of an EFI-equipped vehicle. However, they must be used properly; they only give you part of the information you need for an accurate test. Rather than telling what the problem is, a fault code only tells you that there is a problem. To determine the actual problem, you should refer to the diagnostic procedures in the appropriate service manual.

Remember that any fault code can be caused by any of the following:

- Sensor failure
- Harness failure
- Bad connection
- Logic module failure
- Power module failure
- Output device failure

This is why it is important to understand the diagnostic system to correct a problem.

PART 11   SELF-CHECK

1. List four advantages of gasoline fuel injection as compared to carbureted systems.

2. Name the four general types of gasoline fuel injection systems.

3. Give a brief definition of each of the four systems in question 2.

4. List at least six sensors used in electronic fuel injection systems.

PART 12   TEST QUESTIONS

1. The throttle body replaces the:
   (a) fuel pump
   (b) electronic computer
   (c) power module
   (d) carburetor

2. There is no single input sensor in control of the EFI system at any one time. True or false.

3. The electronic logic module is controlled by the:
   (a) driver
   (b) sensors
   (c) operating conditions
   (d) all of the above

4. The O_2 sensor monitors:
   (a) intake air oxygen content
   (b) exhaust oxygen content
   (c) intake air temperature
   (d) engine speed and load

5. The purpose of the limp-in mode is to:
   (a) allow engine operation in spite of certain sensor failures
   (b) allow engine to operate in extreme cold
   (c) allow engine to operate in high temperatures
   (d) allow engine to operate with clogged air filter

Chapter 15

Diesel Fuel Systems

Performance Objectives

After thorough study of this chapter and sufficient practical experience on adequate training models, and with the appropriate shop manuals and equipment, you should be able to do the following:

1. Complete the self-check and test questions with at least 80 percent accuracy.
2. Follow the accepted general precautions outlined in this chapter.
3. Describe the purpose, construction, and operation of each of the fuel systems and their components.
4. Diagnose basic fuel system problems according to manufacturer's manuals.
5. Safely remove, recondition, replace, and adjust any faulty fuel system components according to manufacturer's specifications.
6. Properly performance test the reconditioned fuel system to determine the success of the repairs performed.
7. Prepare the vehicle for customer acceptance.

PART 1   GENERAL PRINCIPLES

The diesel fuel system is designed to perform the following functions:

- Store a supply of fuel
- Filter dirt and water out of the fuel
- Deliver (pump) the fuel from the tank to the injection pump
- Inject the fuel into the cylinders
- Atomize the fuel in a precise spray pattern to provide good fuel vaporization
- Meter the amount of fuel injected
- Advance and retard the timing of fuel injection
- Control engine speed by governing minimum and maximum engine speeds

It should be remembered that diesel engines

1. are similar to gasoline engines in that power is developed by expanding gases
2. are more efficient in converting fuel into heat energy and mechanical energy due to a higher rate of expansion of gases and slower vaporization of fuel
3. do not have throttle valves in the air intake system as do gasoline engines
4. compress air only during the compression stroke and have a much higher compression ratio
5. inject fuel into the combustion chamber at a precise time in relation to piston position and stroke
6. inject fuel at extremely high pressures—up to 15,000 psi (103,425 kPa) or higher
7. do not have an ignition system—fuel is ignited by the heat of the compressed air in the cylinder
8. precisely control the amount of fuel injected and the duration of injection to control engine speed and power
9. have a higher air to fuel ratio than gasoline engines—up to 60 to 1 as compared to a maximum of about 18 to 1 for gasoline engines
10. are normally noisier than gasoline engines

The diesel engine requires a fuel supply system, fuel filters, fuel injection pump, fuel injectors, and connecting fuel lines.

For a description of diesel fuel, cetane number, fuel characteristics and smoke problems see Chapter 11, "Source of Fuels," and Part 2 "Diesel Fuels." The fuel supply system is similar to the gasoline fuel supply system components described in Chapter 12.

345

See Chapter 12, Part 2, for diesel fuel supply systems.

Since the diesel engine has no ignition system and since ignition begins at the moment when fuel is injected into the cylinder, the fuel injection pump must operate in a manner which will inject the fuel at the precise instant when the piston is at the correct position on the compression stroke. Factors that determine when this should occur include the ignition lag time of the fuel, engine temperature, speed and load and exhaust emission considerations.

Diesel injection pumps are driven from the engine crankshaft by means of gears or by a positive drive type of toothed timing belt. Injection pumps incorporate a governor which is required to control engine speed in addition to the accelerator system. The accelerator linkage acts on the governor spring to determine engine speed. Without the governor, diesel engines that do not have air throttling systems would not idle at proper speeds and could increase in speed to the point of destruction of the engine.

Diesel Injection Pumps

There are four general types of diesel fuel systems in use. These are:

- The common rail system
- The pump controlled system
- The unit injection system
- The distributor pump system

Only the distributor pump system common to automobiles and light trucks will be discussed in more detail here.

The Common Rail System

This sytem uses a high pressure pump to deliver fuel to a common rail. The injectors are connected to the rail (which is full of high pressure fuel) by high pressure fuel lines. Injectors are actuated by a cam, push rod, and rocker arm mechanism. The duration of injection (injector open time) determines the amount of fuel delivery by varying the effective length of the push rod system. A control wedge mechanism is used to maintain this control.

The Pump Controlled System

This system uses a high pressure pump plunger and metering unit for each cylinder. The plungers are helix grooved to provide metering of fuel quantity. Plungers are cam operated to deliver fuel under high pressure through high pressure fuel lines to each injector at the correct time in relation to piston position and stroke. Rotating the plunger in its barrel changes the effective stroke of the pump for fuel metering.

The Unit Injection System

This system uses one injector for each cylinder. The high pressure pumping and metering unit forms part of the injector. Injectors are cam operated. Rotating the plungers in their barrels controls the quantity of fuel delivered at each pumping stroke.

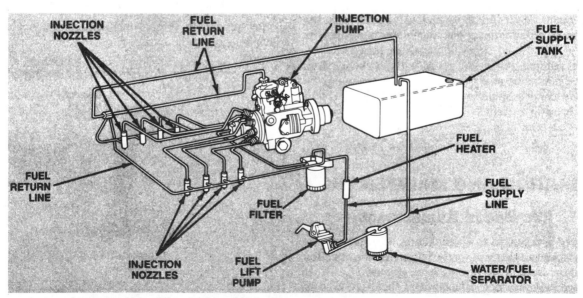

FIGURE 15-1. Diesel fuel-injection system. *(Courtesy of Ford Motor Co. of Canada Ltd.)*

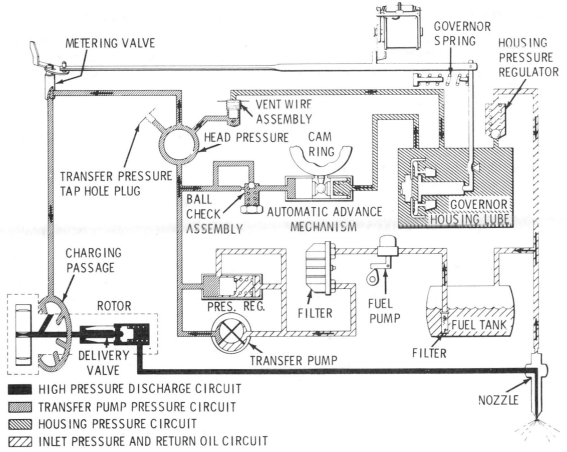

FIGURE 15-2. Diesel fuel system schematic of Stanadyne system. *(Courtesy of General Motors Corporation)*

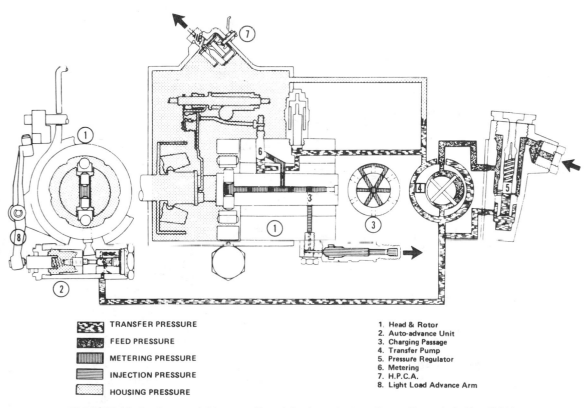

TRANSFER PRESSURE
FEED PRESSURE
METERING PRESSURE
INJECTION PRESSURE
HOUSING PRESSURE

1. Head & Rotor
2. Auto-advance Unit
3. Charging Passage
4. Transfer Pump
5. Pressure Regulator
6. Metering
7. H.P.C.A.
8. Light Load Advance Arm

FIGURE 15-3. General Motors diesel fuel system schematic using the CAV injection pump. *(Courtesy of General Motors Corporation)*

The Distributor Pump System

Several types of distributor pumps are used in automotive diesel fuel injection systems. The more common types include the Bosch VE4F distributor pump, the Diesel Kiki pump, which is very similar to the Bosch pump, the Stanadyne (Roosa Master) pump and the CAV pump. The CAV pump resembles the Stanadyne pump in many respects.

PART 2   STANADYNE DB2 DISTRIBUTOR PUMP SYSTEM

The following description applies to the diesel fuel system as used by Ford on their 6.9-liter diesel engine using a Stanadyne DB2 distributor type pump.

Diaphragm Fuel Pump

The fuel pump is similar to the type used on gasoline engines. It is operated by a lever that runs on the fuel pump eccentric located on the camshaft.

Fuel Supply and Return Lines

The lift pump draws the fuel through the water/fuel separator from the supply tank. The fuel is then pumped through both the fuel heater and the fuel filter to the injection pump inlet. The injection pump then distributes the fuel to the injection nozzles.

Fuel is returned to the fuel tank by way of fuel return lines. A line runs off the fuel filter (fuel is metered through a .040″ [1.016mm] orifice) that connects to the right bank of injection nozzles. This line connects at the rear left of the engine to the fuel return lines from the injection pump and left bank

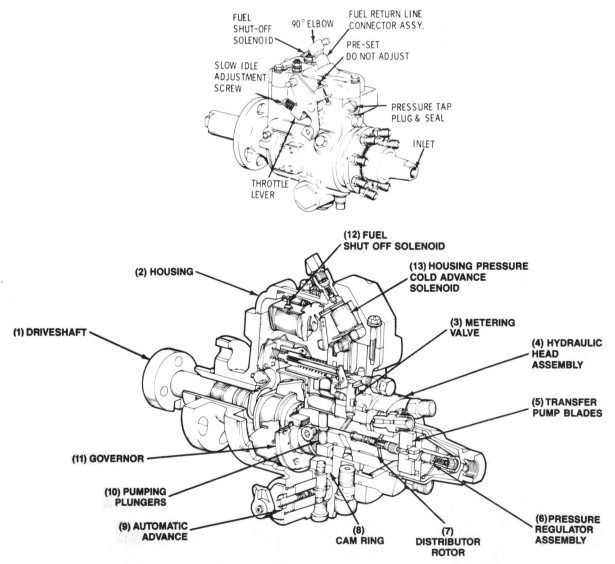

FIGURE 15–4. External and cutaway view of distributor type of diesel fuel-injection pump. *(Courtesy of Ford Motor Co. of Canada Ltd.)*

of injection nozzles. Fuel is then returned to the fuel supply tank.

Water/Fuel Separator

The water/fuel separator works on two principles: first, that water is heavier than diesel fuel and will sink to the bottom of the separator, and second, that a *sock* attached to the inside of the separator at the fuel inlet will assist in the separation of water from the fuel. The water tends to cling to the inside of the sock, which in turn hangs down into the lower part of the separator.

If the separator becomes approximately 1/3 full with water, a warning indicator lamp will light on the instrument panel. Also, the lamp comes on when the ignition key is switched to "START" to prove out the lamp and water level sensor circuit. Should the lamp stay "ON" after the engine is started, drain the water from the separator.

Injection Lines

The injection lines are precisely cut and bent to specification so as to deliver a specified amount of fuel to the injection nozzles.

Caution: Under no circumstances are the injection lines to be bent or crimped. Doing so could impede the flow of fuel to the injection nozzles, which could cause the engine to run rough.

Distributor Injection Pump

Figure 15–4 shows a cutaway view of the pump. The main components are: (1) driveshaft, (2) housing, (3) metering valve, (4) hydraulic head assembly, (5) transfer pump blades, (6) pressure regulator assembly, (7) distributor rotor, (8) cam ring, (9) automatic advance, (10) pumping plungers, and (11) governor. The main rotating components are (1) the driveshaft, (5) transfer pump blades, (7) distributor rotor, and (11) governor. The driveshaft engages the distributor rotor in the hydraulic head. The drive end of the pump rotor incorporates two pumping plungers. The plungers are actuated toward each other simultaneously by an internal cam ring through rollers and shoes that are carried in slots at the drive end of the rotor. The number of cam lobes normally equals the number of engine cylinders.

Located on the top of the injection pump housing are two electrical connections. The front connection controls the fuel shut-off solenoid (12), which is wired directly to the ignition switch. This shuts off the fuel supply when the ignition switch is turned off. The rear connection controls the housing pressure cold advance solenoid (13), which is wired to a coolant temperature switch. This switch turns off current to the solenoid when the coolant temperature reaches 112°F. This cold advance solenoid is used to reduce white smoke while the engine is cold.

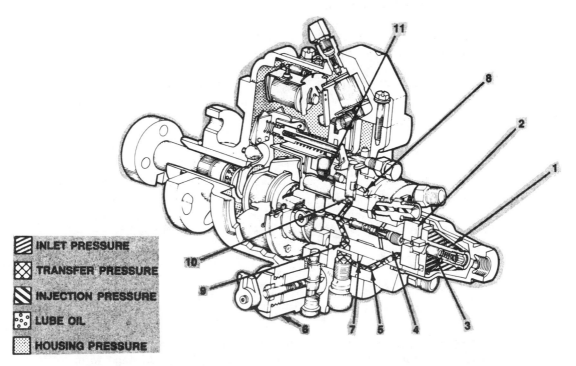

FIGURE 15–5. Stanadayne DB2 injection pump fuel flow. *(Courtesy of Ford Motor Co. of Canada Ltd.)*

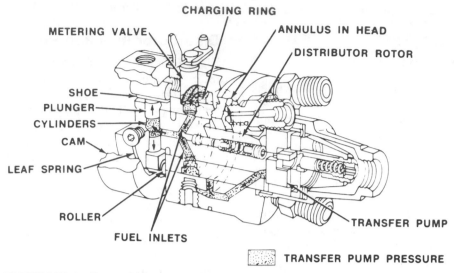

FIGURE 15-6. Roosa Master pump metering is achieved by three controlling factors: (1) transfer pump fuel pressure, (2) metering valve position, and (3) leaf spring tension keeping the pumping plungers together. *(Courtesy of Diesel Systems Group—Stanadyne, Inc.)*

The operating principles of the pump can be understood more readily by following the fuel circuit during a complete pump cycle. Fuel flows into the pump inlet (Figure 15-5) through the inlet filter screen (1), and by the vane type fuel transfer pump (2). Some fuel is bypassed through the pressure regulator assembly (3) to the suction side. Fuel under transfer pump pressure flows through the center of the transfer pump rotor, past the transfer pump pressure port and the rotor retainers (4) into a circular groove on the rotor. It then flows through a connecting passage (5) in the head to the automatic advance (6) and up through a radial passage (8) to the metering valve. The radial position of the me-

tering valve, controlled by the governor, regulates flow of the fuel into the radial charging passage (9), which incorporates the head charging ports. As the rotor revolves, the two rotor inlet passages (10) register with the charging ports in the hydraulic head, allowing fuel to flow into the pumping chamber. With further rotation, the inlet passages move out of registry and the discharge port of the rotor registers with one of the head outlets. While the discharge port is opened, the rollers (11) contact the cam lobes forcing the plungers together. Fuel trapped between the plungers is then pressurized and delivered by the nozzle to the combustion chamber.

Self-lubrication of the pump is a built-in feature

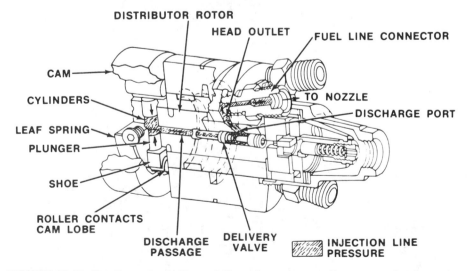

FIGURE 15-7. Continued rotation of the rotor causes plungers to be forced closer together, forcing fuel out of high-pressure discharge passage to injector. Inlet passage is closed when rotor is in this position. *(Courtesy of Diesel Systems Group—Stanadyne, Inc.)*

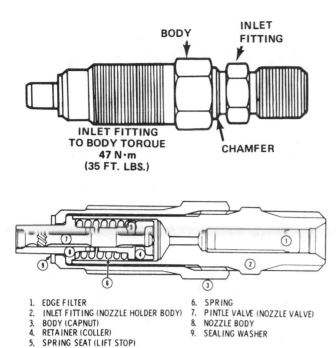

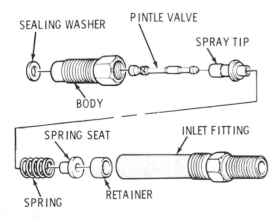

1. EDGE FILTER
2. INLET FITTING (NOZZLE HOLDER BODY)
3. BODY (CAPNUT)
4. RETAINER (COLLER)
5. SPRING SEAT (LIFT STOP)
6. SPRING
7. PINTLE VALVE (NOZZLE VALVE)
8. NOZZLE BODY
9. SEALING WASHER

FIGURE 15-8. Fuel injector components of General Motors diesel engine used in cars and light trucks. *(Courtesy of General Motors Corporation)*

of the design for this injection pump. As fuel at transfer pump pressure reaches the charging ports, slots on the rotor shank allow fuel and any entrapped air to flow into the pump housing cavity. In addition, an air vent passage in the hydraulic head connects the outlet side of the transfer pump with the pump housing. This allows air and some fuel to be bled back to the fuel tank via the return line. The bypassed fuel fills the housing, lubricates the internal components, and cools and carries off any small air bubbles. The pump operates with the housing completely full of fuel. There are no dead air spaces within the pump.

FIGURE 15-9. Injector components of General Motors car and light truck engine. *(Courtesy of General Motors Corporation)*

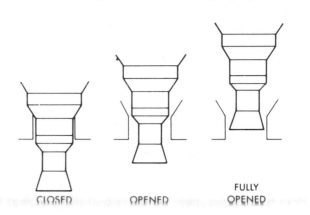

FIGURE 15-10. Details of injector pintle-type nozzle. *(Courtesy of Chrysler Corporation)*

Fuel Injection Nozzles

The injection nozzles have an inward opening, differential hydraulically operated, spray hole. Their function is to direct a metered amount of fuel, under high pressure from the fuel injection pump, into the engine combustion chamber.

The injection nozzle assembly consists of two principal sub-assemblies—the nozzle and the nozzle holder.

The nozzle holder is used to hold the nozzle in its correct position in the cylinder head and to provide channels for conducting fuel oil to the nozzle. The holder also contains the spring retainer (intermediate plate) spring, and shims for adjusting the

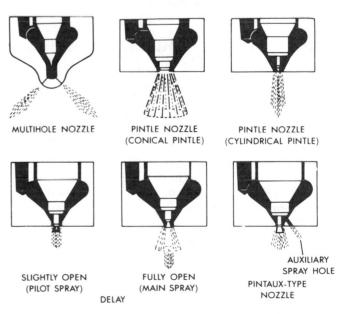

FIGURE 15-11. Various injector design types and resulting spray patterns. Injector type used is determined by engine combustion chamber design. *(Courtesy of Chrysler Corporation)*

opening pressure of the nozzle valve. The lower end of the holder has an accurately ground and lapped surface which makes a leakproof and pressure tight seal with the corresponding lapped surface at the upper end of the spring retainer (intermediate plate). The intermediate plate mates with the lapped surface of the upper end of the nozzle. The nozzle and intermediate plate are held in alignment by dowel pins and are secured to the nozzle holder by the nozzle retainer nut.

Nozzle parts are lapped to form an extremely close fitting matched set. Body and valve cannot be exchanged singly and must be replaced as an assembly. The spray hole is sized to provide a spray pattern of finely atomized fuel to produce the most efficient combustion and engine performance. Operation of the injection nozzle assembly is simple and positive. The metered quantity of fuel from the injection pump enters the nozzle holder through the inlet fitting and passes through connection ducts to the pressure chamber, just above the nozzle valve seat. At the instant the pressure of fuel acting on the differential area of the valve exceeds a predetermined spring load, it lifts the valve from its seat and fuel flows from the nozzle until delivery from the injection pump ceases. Then a positive cut-off of fuel occurs as the valve is seated by the nozzle spring. A certain amount of fuel seepage between lapped surfaces of the nozzle valve and body is necessary for lubrication. This leakage oil accumulates in the spring cavity and drains through to the leak-off provided for this purpose.

PART 3 DIESEL KIKI AND BOSCH VE4F DISTRIBUTOR PUMP

This pump is used by General Motors, Isuzu, Chrysler, and others. Volkswagen uses a similar pump manufactured by Robert Bosch. Diesel Kiki manufactures pumps under license from Bosch. This explains the design similarity. This discussion is based on the Diesel Kiki distributor pump.

The Diesel Kiki pump is driven by a timing cog belt from the engine crankshaft.

The feed pump contained in the injection pump draws the fuel from the fuel tank through the fuel filter (in which the fuel/water separator is contained) into the injection pump. The fuel, pressurized by the feed pump, flows into the pump housing. The fuel pressure in the pump housing is controlled. The excess fuel in the pump housing returns to the fuel tank through the overflow tube. Thus, the fuel circulation enables the cooling and the lubrication of the injection pump. The overflow fuel in the nozzle

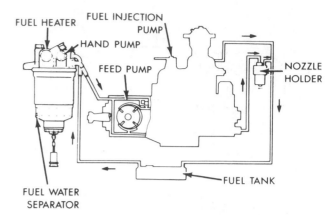

FIGURE 15–12. Basic schematic of Diesel Kiki fuel system. *(Courtesy of Chrysler Corporation)*

holder returns from the overflow tube through the union of the injection pump to the fuel tank.

The injection pump is lubricated by the fuel in the pump. The fuel injection pump is driven by a driveshaft which simultaneously drives the fuel-supply pump, cam disc, and plunger.

The cam plate has four cam faces. Cam projections face in the axial direction so that when the cam plate rotates, the movement of the roller causes the plunger to reciprocate as it rotates.

The governor contained in the upper injection pump housing is mounted on the governor shaft with the flyweight in its holder. The governor shaft

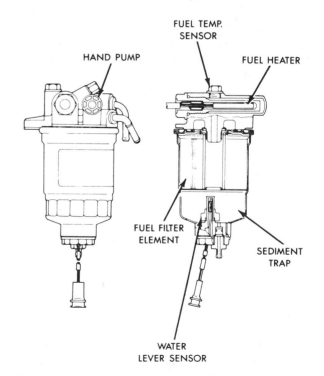

FIGURE 15–13. Fuel filter, water separator, fuel heater, fuel temperature sensor, sediment trap, and hand priming pump are all contained in this filter assembly. *(Courtesy of Chrysler Corporation)*

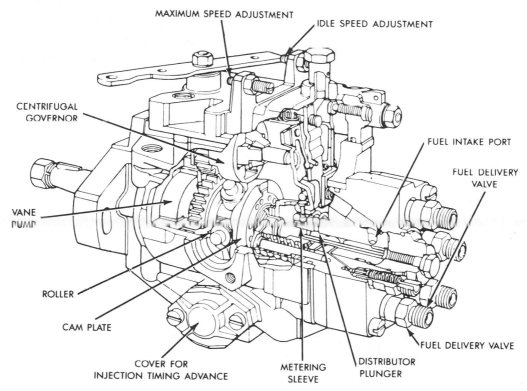

FIGURE 15-14. Bosch VE4F single-plunger distributor type of fuel injection pump. Diesel Kiki distributor pump is very similar. *(Courtesy of Chrysler Corporation)*

is mounted to enable the governor sleeve to slide. The governor is driven by a gear on the driveshaft through a rubber damper.

The timer contained in the lower injection pump is operated by the fuel pressure in the pump housing, which is controlled by the regulating valve.

Vane Pump

The rotary vane pump inside the injection pump draws fuel through the filter from the tank and supplies it to the distributor plunger.

The vane pump rotor is driven by the engine camshaft spur belt. As the rotor spins, centrifugal force holds the vanes against the walls of the pressure chamber—the off-center layout of the rotor and pressure chamber *"squeezes"* fuel trapped between the vanes and forces it out the delivery port.

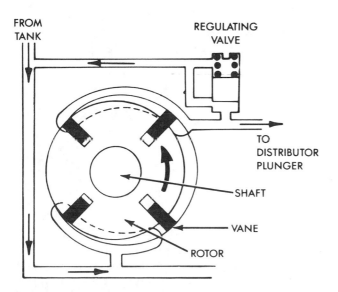

FIGURE 15-15. Vane type of supply pump and pressure regulation as used in Bosch VE4F and Diesel Kiki fuel injection pumps. *(Courtesy of Chrysler Corporation)*

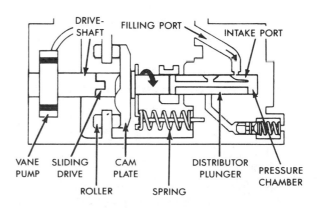

FIGURE 15-16. Details of high pressure pumping and distributing section of Bosch VE4F and Diesel Kiki injection pumps. *(Courtesy of Chrysler Corporation)*

353

Vane pump delivery pressure is between 303–689 kPa (44–100 psi) depending on engine speed and is controlled by the regulating valve.

Regulating Valve

Fuel quantity transferred by feed pump is several times that required for injection, and surplus fuel is returned to the intake side of the feed pump by way of a regulating valve.

Pressure characteristics of feed fuel against the rotating speed of feed pump are controlled by the spring of the regulating valve.

Injection and Distribution

The injection pump driveshaft turns the vane pump, distributor plunger, and cam plate as a unit.

Springs hold the cam plate and distributor plunger against stationary rollers. In this way, the plunger also moves back and forth as it turns.

Whenever an intake port in the plunger is in line with the filling port in the pump body, fuel from the vane pump fills the pressure chamber.

As the plunger turns, the intake port is covered up so that fuel is trapped in the pressure chamber. Now the cam plate and rollers push the plunger and pressurize the fuel to about 12,411 kPa (1,800 psi).

As the plunger continues to turn, the outlet port in the plunger lines up with the injection passage in the pump body, opening the check valve and supplying high-pressure fuel to the injector.

The injection ports in the pump are arranged so the injectors receive fuel in the cylinder firing sequence.

Fuel Delivery Valves

The fuel delivery valves on the injection pump help ensure that the injector will close quickly at the end of each injection. The injectors must close quickly in order to prevent fuel "dribble" which can cause pre-ignition and high exhaust emissions.

At the start of injection, the delivery valve is lifted off its seat, and pressurized fuel flows to the injector.

At the end of injection, the delivery valve moves to the closed position. A column of fuel is now trapped in the injection line.

The force of the spring will push the valve back further onto its seat and the trapped column of fuel now expands. The sudden drop in pressure, caused by the expanding fuel, allows the injector to snap shut and eliminate any fuel "dribble."

Metering Fuel—Governor

The amount of fuel injected is controlled by changing the injection cut-off point according to engine speed and load conditions.

The injection cut-off point is controlled by the position of a metering sleeve on the distributor plunger. The metering sleeve usually covers a relief port in the plunger. Uncovering the relief port stops injection by depressurizing the fuel.

The position of the metering sleeve is controlled by a balance of two opposing forces: spring pressure exerted through accelerator pedal linkage vs. governor spring pressure created by injection pump rpm.

Starting

When the engine is not running, the leaf spring presses the starting lever to the left so that the metering sleeve moves to the right.

The distributor plunger must move further before the relief port is exposed. In this way, injection lasts longer so that more fuel is supplied during starting. The greatest amount of fuel per pump stroke is injected during starting and engine warm-up.

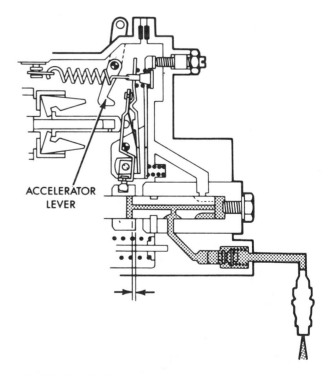

ACCELERATOR LEVER

FIGURE 15-17. Fuel metering is determined by position of metering sleeve, which controls effective stroke of pumping plunger. Metering sleeve position is determined by a combination of throttle position and governor action. This shows components in idle position. *(Courtesy of Chrysler Corporation)*

Idle

At idle speed, the weights in the centrifugal governor (rpm controlled) are partly extended so that the governor sleeve moves to the right. The starting lever is pushed against the control lever so that the metering sleeve moves to the left.

The distributor plunger now moves a short distance before the relief port is uncovered. Under this condition, injection lasts a short time so that a small amount of fuel is supplied at idle—just enough to keep the engine running.

The injection pump automatically compensates for effects of temperature and load changes at idle. When idle speed begins to drop, the centrifugal governor weights and the governor sleeve retract; the idle spring then pushes the metering sleeve to the right, increasing the amount of fuel to correct the idle speed.

Acceleration

During acceleration, this action of the control lever is pulled to the left by linkage from the accelerator pedal.

The metering sleeve moves to the right, so that more fuel is injected before the relief port is uncovered—engine speed increases until the movement of the governor "neutralizes" the effect of the pedal linkage.

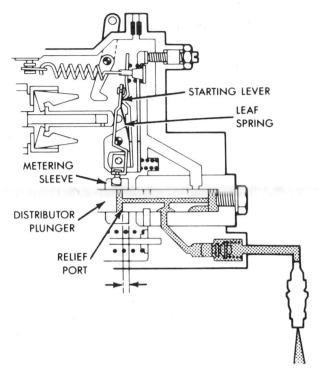

FIGURE 15-19. Governor operation during acceleration or power demand. *(Courtesy of Chrysler Corporation)*

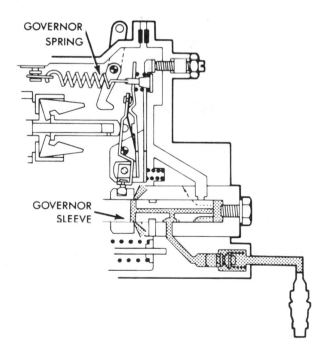

FIGURE 15-18. Governor and metering sleeve position at part throttle on Bosch VE4F or Diesel Kiki pump. *(Courtesy of Chrysler Corporation)*

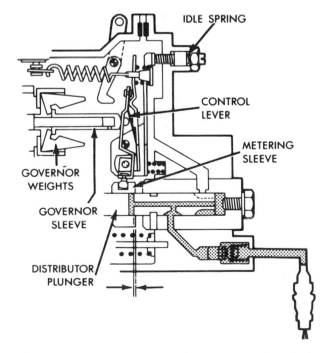

FIGURE 15-20. Governor action and metering during wide-open throttle operation. *(Courtesy of Chrysler Corporation)*

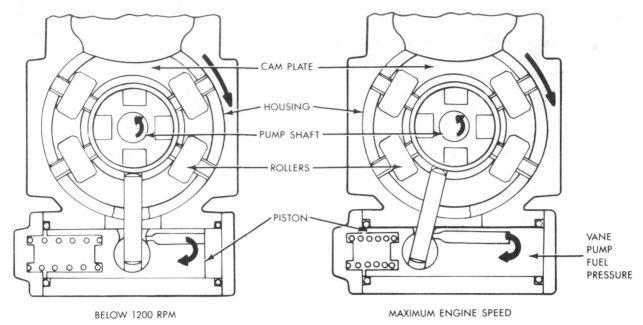

BELOW 1200 RPM

MAXIMUM ENGINE SPEED

FIGURE 15–21. Injection timing is controlled by vane pump pressure acting on a piston opposed by spring pressure. As engine speed increases, vane pump pressure increases to advance injection timing. *(Courtesy of Chrysler Corporation)*

Maximum Speed

With pedal linkage at "full load," engine speed increases. At this point, the governor is spinning with enough centrifugal force for the governor sleeve to "stretch" the governor spring and force the control lever to the right.

The metering sleeve moves far enough to the left to uncover the relief port at the beginning of the distribution plunger stroke. There is no pressure for injection until engine speed drops and the metering sleeve moves to the right again.

This provision acts as a speed limiter and is designed to react slowly enough so that engine performance simply "flattens out" at the top limit.

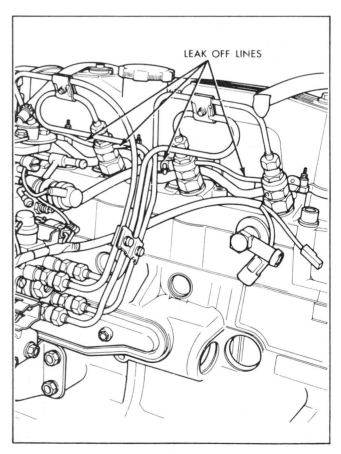

FIGURE 15–23. Injector leak-off (or fuel return) lines return excess fuel from injectors to pump or tank depending on system design. *(Courtesy of Chrysler Corporation)*

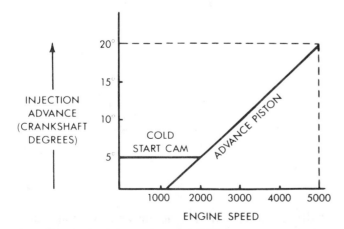

FIGURE 15–22. Typical action of injection timing advance in relation to engine speed. *(Courtesy of Chrysler Corporation)*

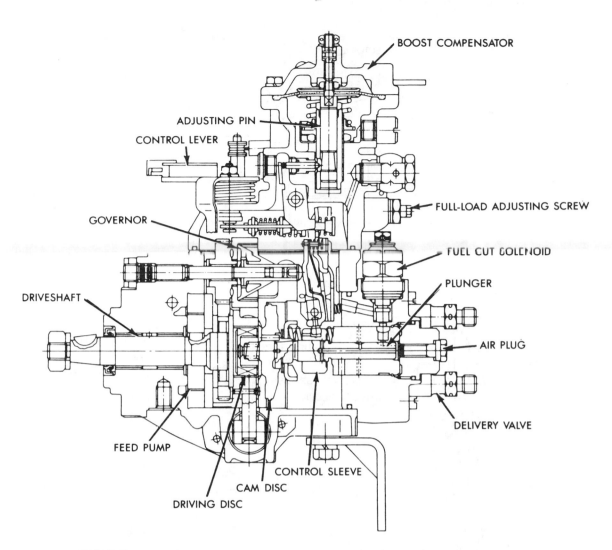

FIGURE 15-24. Boost compensator reacts to turbocharger boost pressure to help regulate fuel delivery. *(Courtesy of Chrysler Corporation)*

Injection Timing Advance

Near the end of each compression stroke, diesel fuel is injected directly into the combustion chamber. Injection must continue well past piston TDC in order to burn the necessary amount of fuel to provide engine power.

As engine speed increases, stroke time becomes shorter and injection time becomes longer. Burning must begin sooner to ensure that peak combustion pressures still occur at the most efficient point near TDC.

Diesel injection timing is advanced by a hydraulic piston in this injection pump.

As engine speed increases, fuel pressure from the vane pump also increases. Vane pump pressure pushes the injection advance piston to the left against the spring so that the roller housing turns slightly.

Since the cam plate is turning in the opposite direction, the *ramps* on the cam plate engage the roller sooner, whenever the injection advance piston moves to the left. This means that the distributor plunger begins injection sooner.

The injection timing advance piston is located in the bottom of the injection pump body.

One type of cold start assistance device used with smaller engines is a control on the pump which advances injection timing at idle and during low speed running.

A lever turns a cam which pushes the hydraulic piston to the left. This advances injection timing about 5°.

This injection advance provides more time for the fuel to burn, which improves performance and prevents smoking during cold starts and warm-up.

The cold start cam does not advance the com-

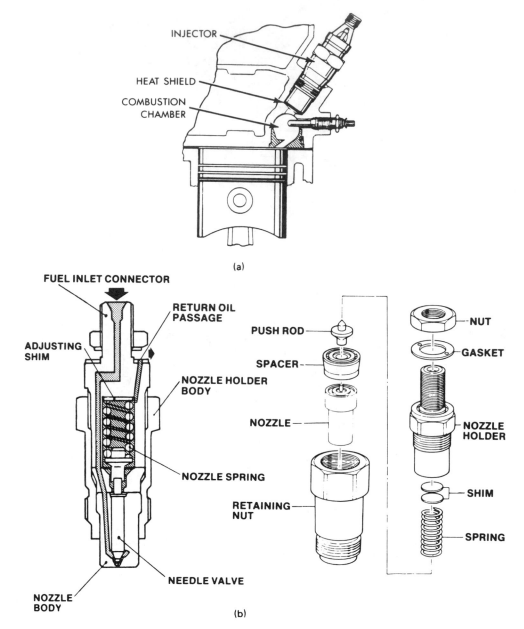

FIGURE 15-25. (A) Details of Diesel Kiki injector and glow plug location. *(Courtesy of Chrysler Corporation)* (B) Components of screw-in type fuel injector. *(Courtesy of General Motors Corporation)*

plete range of injection timing. Above a preset value, the piston operates normally and does not contact the cam.

For decreasing the exhaust gas (NO$_x$) level and the noise, injection advance is delayed during normal running conditions. The timer piston, during normal running, is on the retarded side as fuel is returned from the retard orifice to decrease the fuel pressure in the pump. During high-load conditions (over 65° of full throttle), the accelerator lever turns the accelerator switch *ON*, and as the piston in the solenoid valve closes the orifice, fuel pressure is raised to move the timing piston to an advance position.

Fuel Injectors

The main purpose of the fuel injection nozzle is to direct and atomize the metered fuel into the combustion chamber. The combustion chamber design dictates the type of nozzle, the droplet size, and the spray required to achieve complete combustion within a given time and space.

Fuel from the injection pump enters and pressurizes the fuel in the supply passage and pressure chamber. When the force on the lift area is greater than the set spring force on the spindle, the needle valve lifts off its seat and comes to rest with its upper shoulder against the face of the holder. Fuel is forced out into the combustion chamber in a spray pattern, which depends on the type of nozzle used.

The throttle type nozzle has a relatively large injection hole. The end of the needle valve takes the form of a thin conical pin that is slightly smaller than the size of the injection hole of the nozzle; its end is a little protruded from the end of the injection hole.

When the fuel pressure sent by injection pump has reached the pressure required for the start of injection, the needle valve starts to be lifted by the force of fuel pressure, and subsequently the fuel injection through the injection hole starts.

Since fuel is injected through the injection hole, and the circular gap at the end of the needle valve, at the beginning of injection stroke the area of the injection hole is throttled so that only a small quantity of fuel is injected. As the needle valve is pushed up, the area of the injection hole increases so that the main injection of fuel can occur. To accomplish this, the nozzle is designed to keep injection quantity small during the ignition delay interval (from the start of injection to ignition) so that the knocking inherent to diesel engines can be reduced.

PART 4 STARTING AIDS

Since diesel fuel does not vaporize or ignite as readily as gasoline, starting aids are required. These include glow plugs, fuel heaters, and engine block heaters. The glow plugs located in the combustion chamber pre-heat the air and fuel during cranking and/or prior to cranking depending on system design. Engine block heaters are used in colder climates to heat engine coolant, which in turn keeps the cylinder block and head at temperatures where starting is made possible. The fuel heater electrically preheats the fuel before it reaches the filter. Some injection pumps are equipped with a mechanical advance mechanism to provide injection timing advance for cold starts.

General Motors Type Fuel Preheater

The diesel fuel heater is a thermostatically controlled electrical resistance type heater designed to heat the fuel before it enters the engine mounted fuel filter to reduce the possibility of wax plugging the filter when the fuel temperature is 20°F or lower.

Twelve volts are directed to the heater whenever the ignition is in the run position. The heater consists of a strip spiral wound around the fuel pipe. A bimetal thermal switch senses the fuel temperature and closes and electrical circuit when the fuel temperature is about 22°F to 41°F. The circuit opens at 54°F to 72°F.

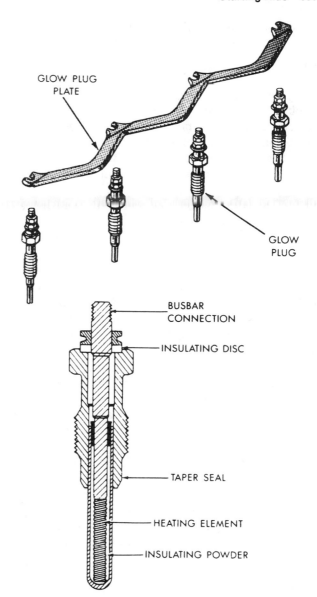

FIGURE 15-26. Glow plug electrical connector plate and cross section of glow plug. *(Courtesy of Chrysler Corporation)*

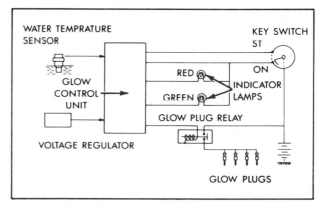

FIGURE 15-27. Electrical schematic of glow plug system. *(Courtesy of Chrysler Corporation)*

Other examples of fuel heaters used in other diesel fuel systems are illustrated.

Glow Plug System

The glow plugs are designed to improve starting conditions for diesel engines. They are low voltage (usually 12V or 6V) heating elements inserted into the combustion chamber or into the intake manifold. They are controlled by the ignition switch or a separate switch mounted on the instrument panel. The glow plugs are used only briefly to heat the air within the combustion chamber. This heat helps to maintain temperature and pressure inside the combustion chamber at a level conducive to ignition at start-up.

Since glow plugs are used to heat the air, the time they are on depends on two factors: (1) the ambient temperature within the combustion chamber and (2) how quickly the glow plugs heat up (which depends on the voltage required to heat the element).

The operation of the system is controlled by a controller module, which will shut off the system when the air is heated sufficiently and/or the engine is started. This controller is usually threaded into the engine block with a temperature-sensitive probe inserted into a coolant passage. This allows the controller to determine how long the glow plugs will be on.

Another system uses a cycling relay which pulses the on/off time of the glow plugs. In this system, if the key is left on without starting the engine, the glow plugs will cycle on and off until the batteries are dead (in about four hours).

Mechanical Advance for Starting

Some injection pumps use a cam and lever mechanism to provide some measure of injection timing advance for cold engine starting. The system acts mechanically on the hydraulic advance piston. When the engine is running, the piston operates normally above a preset advance level.

PART 5   GENERAL SERVICE
           PRECAUTIONS

Be sure to follow all normal personal and shop safety practice as outlined in Chapter 1, Parts 1 and 2, Chapter 10, Part 4, and Chapter 12, Part 6.

In addition, some special precautions should be observed regarding diesel fuel systems service including the following:

1. Never disconnect any fuel lines while the engine is running.

2. Be sure to properly cap all disconnected fuel lines and fittings.

3. Always use two wrenches whenever disconnecting a fuel line fitting from any double nut connection to prevent line twisting.

4. Never bend or damage injection lines in any way.

5. Fuel system components have many precision machined surfaces; handle them with extreme care to avoid damage.

6. Observe cleanliness of all parts and the entire area; this is essential during assembly. A very small piece of dirt can cause complete failure. Abrasives damage friction surfaces severely. Extremely close tolerances are destroyed by small particles of dirt or foreign material.

7. Use only filtered compressed shop air for cleaning fuel systems parts after washing.

8. Use only filtered and temperature-controlled testing fluids for injector and injection pump service.

9. Perform all injector and injection pump service in a controlled environment—a lab with controlled temperature and filtered air.

10. Very high fuel injection pressures (15,000 psi, 103,425 kPa) will penetrate skin easily and cause serious damage and infection; avoid all contact with fuel under injection pressure.

11. Avoid inhaling fuel and test fluid vapors. Use a face mask and filter.

12. Have all test equipment accurately calibrated for test results to be valid.

13. Be absolutely sure that the correct specifications are being used for any given make or model of fuel system and fuel system components. Refer to the appropriate service manual for specifications.

14. Be sure to follow the specifications in the appropriate shop service manual for installation, alignment, and timing of injectors and injection pumps.

PART 6   DIESEL FUEL INJECTION DIAGNOSIS AND SERVICE PROCEDURE

DIAGNOSTIC CHART

PROBLEM	CAUSE	CORRECTION
Engine will not crank or cranks slowly.	1. Loose or corroded battery cables.	1. Check connections at batteries, engine block, and starter solenoid.
	2. Discharged batteries.	2. Check generator output and generator belt adjustment.
	3. Starter inoperative.	3. Check voltage to starter and starter solenoid. If OK, remove starter for repair.
	4. Wrong engine oil.	4. Drain and refill with oil of recommended viscosity.
Engine cranks normally; will not start	1. Incorrect starting procedure.	1. Use recommended starting procedure.
	2. No voltage to fuel solenoid.	2. Connect a 12 volt test lamp from wire at injection pump solenoid to ground. Turn ignition to *on*. Lamp should light. Correct as required.
	3. Glow plugs inoperative.	3. Check glow plugs and replace if needed. Check electrical feed to glow plugs and correct as needed.
	4. No fuel to nozzles.	4. Loosen injection line at a nozzle. Do not disconnect. Use care to direct fuel away from sources of ignition. Wipe connection to be sure it is dry. Crank 5 seconds. Fuel should flow from injection line. Tighten connection.
	5. No fuel to injection pump.	5. Remove line at inlet to injection pump fuel filter. Connect hose from line to metal container. Crank engine. If no fuel is discharged, test the engine fuel pump. If the fuel pump is OK, check the injection pump fuel filter and, if plugged, replace it. If fuel filter and line to injection pump are OK, remove injection pump for repair.
	6. Restricted fuel tank filter.	6. Remove and check filter.
	7. Incorrect or contaminated fuel.	7. Flush fuel system and install correct fuel.
	8. Pump timing incorrect.	8. Make certain that pump timing mark is aligned with mark on adapter.
	9. Low compression.	9. Check compression to determine cause.
Engine starts but will not continue to run at idle.	1. Slow idle incorrectly adjusted.	1. Adjust idle screw to specification.
	2. Fast-idle solenoid inoperative.	2. With engine cold, start engine; solenoid should move to hold injection pump lever in fast-idle position. If solenoid does not move, correct as needed.
	3. Restricted fuel return system.	3. Disconnect fuel return line at injection pump and route hose to a metal container. Connect a hose to the injection pump connection; route it to the metal container. Crank the engine and allow it to idle. If engine idles normally, correct restriction in fuel return lines.
	4. Pump timing incorrect.	4. Make certain that timing mark on injection pump is aligned with mark on adapter.
	5. Limited fuel to injection pump.	5. Test the engine fuel pump; check fuel lines. Replace as necessary.
	6. Air in injection lines to nozzles.	6. Loosen injection line at nozzle(s) and bleed air. Use care to direct fuel away from sources of ignition.
	7. Incorrect or contaminated fuel.	7. Flush fuel system and install correct fuel.
	8. Injection pump malfunction.	8. Remove injection pump for repair.
	9. Fuel solenoid closes in run position.	9. Ignition switch out of adjustment.
Engine starts, idles rough, without abnormal noise or smoke.	1. Slow idle incorrectly adjusted.	1. Adjust slow-idle screw to specification.
	2. Injection line leaks.	2. Wipe off injection lines and connections. Run engine and check for leaks. Correct leaks.
	3. Air in injection lines to nozzles.	3. Loosen injection line at nozzle(s) and bleed air. Use care to direct fuel away from sources of ignition.

PROBLEM	CAUSE	CORRECTION
	4. Nozzle(s) malfunction.	4. With engine running, loosen injection line fitting at each nozzle in turn. Use care to direct fuel away from sources of ignition. Each good nozzle should change engine idle quality when fuel is allowed to leak. If nozzle is found that does not change idle quality, it should be replaced.
	5. Incorrect or contaminated fuel.	5. Flush fuel system and install correct fuel.
Engine starts and idles rough with excessive noise and/or smoke.	1. Injection pump timing incorrect.	1. Be sure timing mark on injection pump is aligned with mark on adapter.
	2. Air in injection lines to nozzles.	2. Loosen injection line at nozzle(s) and bleed air. Use care to direct fuel away from sources of ignition.
	3. Nozzle(s) malfunction.	3. With engine running, loosen injection line at each nozzle, one at a time. Use care to direct fuel away from sources of ignition. Each good nozzle should change engine idle quality when fuel is allowed to leak. If a nozzle is found that does not affect idle quality or changes noise and/or smoke, it should be replaced.
	4. High-pressure lines incorrectly installed.	4. Check routing of each line; correct as required.
Engine misfires above idle but idles correctly.	1. Plugged fuel filter.	1. Replace filter.
	2. Incorrect injection pump timing.	2. Be sure that timing mark on injection pump and adapter are aligned.
	3. Incorrect or contaminated fuel.	3. Flush fuel system and install correct fuel.
Engine will not return to idle.	1. External linkage binding or misadjusted.	1. Free up linkage. Adjust or replace as required.
	2. Internal injection pump malfunction.	2. Remove injection pump for repair.
Fuel leaks.	1. Loose or broken fuel line or connection.	1. Examine complete fuel system, including tank, lines, injection, and fuel return lines. Determine source and cause of leak and repair.
	2. Injection pump internal seal leak.	2. Remove injection pump for repair.
Noticeable loss of power.	1. Restricted air intake.	1. Check air cleaner element.
	2. Restricted or damaged exhaust system.	2. Check system and replace as necessary.
	3. Plugged fuel filter.	3. Replace filter.
	4. Plugged fuel tank vacuum vent in fuel cap.	4. Replace cap.
	5. Pinched or otherwise restricted return system.	5. Examine system for restriction and correct as required.
	6. Restricted fuel supply from fuel tank to injection pump.	6. Examine fuel supply system to determine cause of restriction. Repair as required.
	7. Incorrect or contaminated fuel.	7. Flush fuel system and install correct fuel.
	8. Restricted fuel tank filter.	8. Remove fuel tank and check filter.
	9. Plugged nozzle(s).	9. Remove nozzles. Have them checked for plugging and repair or replace.
	10. Low compression.	10. Check compression to determine cause.
Noise; "rap" from one or more cylinders (sounds like rod bearing knock).	1. Air in fuel system.	1. Check for air leaks in fuel line and correct.
	2. Air in high-pressure line(s).	2. Loosen injection line at nozzle(s) and bleed air at each cylinder determined to be causing noise. Use care to direct fuel away from sources of ignition.
	3. Nozzle(s) sticking open or with very low nozzle opening pressure.	3. Loosen injection lines at nozzles one at a time. Noise will stop or change when line is loosened at bad nozzle. Remove nozzle for repair.
Engine will not shut off with key.	1. Injection pump fuel solenoid does not return fuel valve to *off* position.	1. Check electrical circuit and correct as needed.

PART 7   INJECTOR SERVICE

Injector service varies, depending on the particular make and model. All removal, disassembly, inspection, overhaul, reassembly, testing, adjusting, and installation procedures for any given make and model should be followed as recommended in the appropriate manufacturer's shop service manual.

It is critical to good engine performance that all injectors for any engine be of the same type and size. Never mix mated and lapped injector parts.

Some injectors are not repairable and must be

replaced if defective. Others can be overhauled and adjusted.

While many service shops are equipped to provide injector rebuilding, other shops rely on replacing injectors with rebuilt or new injectors.

The following service procedures apply in general to most injectors for automotive applications. In addition, the appropriate service manual must be used for all special procedures and all service data.

General Procedure for Injector Service

1. Clean the area around the injectors before removal in order to prevent dirt and other foreign matter from entering the fuel system.

2. Disconnect all fuel lines from injectors. Cap all openings.

3. Remove the injector. Follow service manual procedures.

4. If the problem diagnosis procedure has established that an engine compression test is required, this should be done when the injectors are removed. Record the results of the compression test. If an engine compression problem is indicated, repair the engine as necessary.

5. Disassemble and clean the injectors according to the appropriate manufacturer's service manual. Do not mix parts from one injector with those of another injector.

6. Inspect carefully all injector parts and compare wear and damage to service limits indicated in the appropriate manufacturer's service manual. Inspection may require the use of a magnifying glass due to the extremely close tolerances and finely honed surfaces of injector parts. Some injector parts are not available separately. Mating parts such as nozzles must be purchased as an assembly due to the very close tolerances of these parts.

7. Assemble the injector according to the procedures given in the appropriate service manual.

FIGURE 15-29. Using a soft brass bristle brush to clean injector nozzle tip. (*Courtesy of Diesel Systems Group—Stanadyne, Inc.*)

Never apply undue pressure or force. All parts must be at normal room temperature and be properly lubricated with the specified fuel oil. If parts are not at equal temperatures, it may be impossible to assemble them.

8. Mount the injector on the specified test stand and, using the specified test fluid, which should be at the proper testing temperature, proceed with injector testing and adjustment.

9. Testing and adjusting must be done to

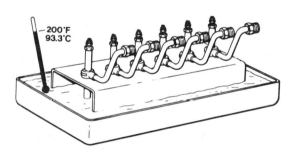

FIGURE 15-30. Injectors in rack with nozzles immersed in special cleaning fluid at controlled temperature to help loosen deposits. (*Courtesy of Diesel Systems Group—Stanadyne, Inc.*)

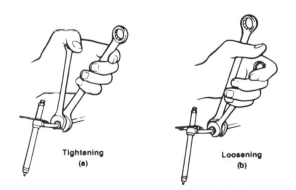

FIGURE 15-28. Always use two wrenches on fuel line fittings to prevent damage to lines. (*Courtesy of Diesel Systems Group—Stanadyne, Inc.*)

FIGURE 15-31. Nozzle testing and cleaning pump with protective transparent plastic spray containing cone. (*Courtesy of Diesel Systems Group—Stanadyne, Inc.*)

FIGURE 15-32. Adjusting nozzle opening pressure screw on one type of injector. Some injectors use shims to adjust opening pressure. *(Courtesy of Diesel Systems Group—Stanadyne, Inc.)*

achieve the following (depending on make and model of injector):

(a) specified nozzle-opening pressure

(b) correct spray pattern

(c) proper chatter

(d) no nozzle drip at specified fuel pressure

10. Prepare cylinder head, injector openings, precombustion chamber, and air cells (as required) for injector installation. This includes making sure that there is no gasket left in the injector mounting

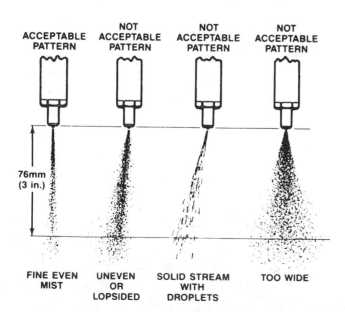

FIGURE 15-33. Typical injector spray patterns. Nonacceptable patterns may be caused by deposits, injector damage, or incorrect opening pressure. *(Courtesy of Ford Motor Co. of Canada Ltd.)*

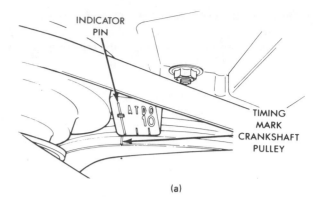

(a)

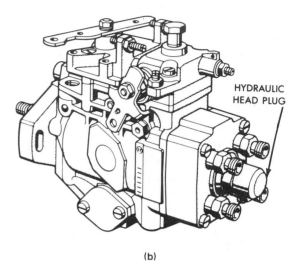

(b)

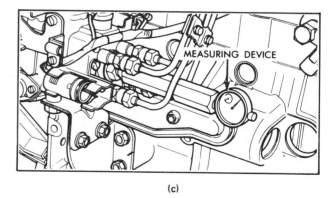

(c)

FIGURE 15-34. Typical injection pump timing setting sequence on Diesel Kiki and Bosch VE4F injection pump: (A) Position crankshaft as specified; (B) Remove hydraulic head plug; (C) Insert special dial type measuring tool. Then position and tighten the pump mounting to achieve the specified pump plunger timing position. *(Courtesy of Chrysler Corporation)*

hole, cleaning carbon from the injector opening and precombustion chamber, removing of old O-rings and installing of new O-rings and gaskets. Follow the appropriate shop manual to ensure a positive seal around the injector.

11. Position injectors into cylinder heads as required to achieve proper fuel line connections and

injector-operating mechanism connections. Tighten the injector to specified torque, following the proper sequence in proper increments as specified in the appropriate service manual.

12. Connect all fuel lines and tighten to specifications.

13. Bleed all air from fuel system (some models only).

14. Start the engine and inspect for fuel leaks.

PART 8   SELF-CHECK

1. List eight functions performed by the diesel fuel system.

2. List six ways in which diesel engines and fuel systems are different from gasoline engines.

3. How is the diesel injection pump driven?

4. What are the four general types of diesel fuel systems?

5. The high pressure pumping element in the DB2 Stanadyne pump consists of _____ and _____ operated _____.

6. Fuel metering in the Diesel Kiki injection pump is achieved by a _____ _____ controlling a _____ port.

7. What is the purpose of the fuel injector?

PART 9   TEST QUESTIONS

1. The water fuel separator works on the following principles:
   (a) relative weight difference and water filtering
   (b) water filtering and trapping water
   (c) water is heavier than fuel and fuel penetrates filters more easily
   (d) all of the above

2. The Stanadyne DB2 pump is lubricated by:
   (a) the engine lubrication system
   (b) its own oil sump
   (c) grease
   (d) diesel fuel

3. When a Stanadyne DB2 pump is equipped with eight cam lobes: Mechanic A says the pump is for a four-cylinder engine. Mechanic B says it is for an eight-cylinder engine. Who is right?
   (a) Mechanic A
   (b) Mechanic B
   (c) both are right
   (d) both are wrong

4. The injector assembly consists of two principal sub-assemblies:
   (a) the nozzle and nozzle holder
   (b) the nozzle holder and the pintle
   (c) the pintle and the nozzle
   (d) the pintle and the barrel

5. The Diesel Kiki injection pump is driven by a:
   (a) gear
   (b) V belt
   (c) chain
   (d) cog belt

6. The purpose of the governor is to control:
   (a) the fuel metering device
   (b) injection timing
   (c) injection timing advance
   (d) all of the above

7. Positive cut off of fuel injection is assured by the use of:
   (a) a governor
   (b) a fuel delivery valve
   (c) injector nozzle size controls
   (d) a drain back valve

Chapter 16

Exhaust Systems

Performance Objectives

After adequate study of this chapter and sufficient practical experience on appropriate training models and with proper tools, equipment, and shop manuals, you should be able to do the following:

1. Complete the self-check and test questions with at least 80 percent accuracy.

2. Describe the purpose, construction, and operation of the exhaust system.

3. Diagnose exhaust system problems according to manufacturer's diagnostic procedures.

4. Recondition and replace faulty components as required to restored system efficiency.

5. Correctly adjust system components according to manufacturer's specifications.

6. Test the systems to determine the success of the service performed.

7. Prepare the vehicle for customer acceptance.

PART 1   PURPOSE AND FUNCTION

The purpose of the exhaust system is to collect the exhaust gases from the engine and deliver them to a point at the rear of the vehicle where they are dispersed to atmosphere. The exhaust system is also designed to reduce exhaust noise and exhaust emissions, and to provide the back pressure required for combustion chamber temperature control under a wide range of operating conditions.

Heat is provided by the exhaust system to preheat the air for the induction system, to preheat the air-fuel mixture, to improve fuel vaporization, and for automatic choke operation.

Exhaust system components must be of sufficient capacity to effectively remove the exhaust gases produced by the engine at all operating speeds and loads. Any restriction in the exhaust system, caused by external damage or by internal deterioration, will affect the engine's performance.

The exhaust system must be properly alligned to prevent stress, leakage, and body contact. If the system contacts any suspension, body, or drive train parts, it may amplify objectionable noises originating from the engine or body, or may in fact create new noises. Loose, broken, misaligned clamps, hangers, brackets, shields, or pipes may cause these conditions.

PART 2   EXHAUST MANIFOLD AND GASKETS

Four-cylinder in-line engines have either three- or four-runner exhaust manifolds. On the three-runner manifold the center runner collects exhaust gases from the two center cylinders.

Six-cylinder in-line engines have either a six- or a four-runner manifold. On the four-runner exhaust manifold the two middle runners each collect exhaust gases from two cylinders.

The V-6 engine has two exhaust manifolds each with three runners. The V-8 engine has two exhaust manifolds. Each manifold has either three or four runners. The three-runner manifold has the center runner collecting exhaust gases from the center two cylinders on each side.

Exhaust manifolds are of one-piece, cast-iron or steel construction. Extreme temperature variations are encountered by exhaust manifolds. A hot exhaust manifold is often splashed with cold water when driving through puddles on the road. Manifolds expand and contract considerably owing to temperature change, and cracking can result. Some manifolds use reinforcing ribs to reduce distortion and the possibility of cracking.

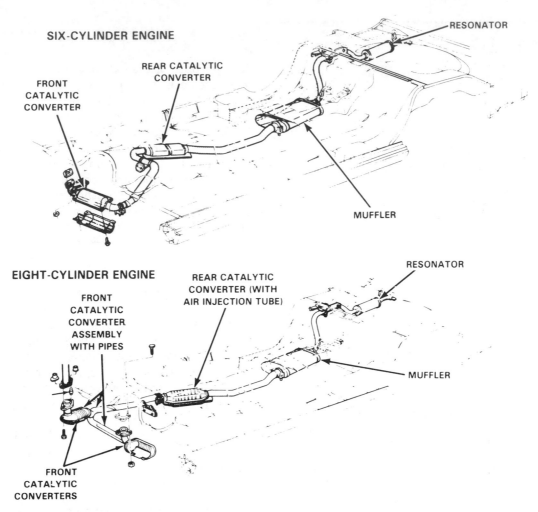

FIGURE 16-1. Typical exhaust system layouts for six- and eight-cylinder vehicles. Many variations of converter and muffler positions and pipe routing are used on different makes and models of vehicles.

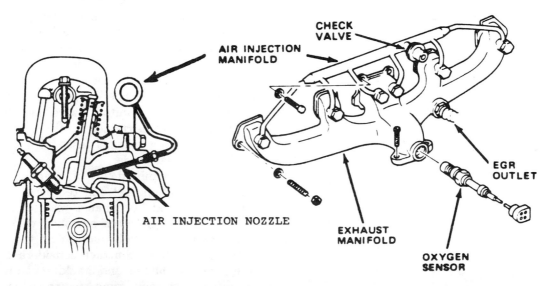

FIGURE 16-2. Six-cylinder exhaust manifold with air injection manifold and nozzles as well as oxygen sensor. *(Courtesy of American Motors Corporation)*

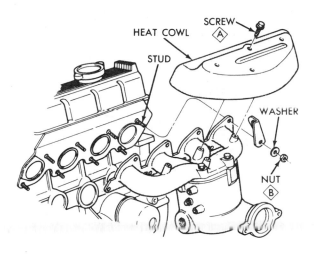

FIGURE 16-3. Four-cylinder exhaust manifold with close coupled catalytic converter and heat cowl. *(Courtesy of Chrysler Corporation)*

The exhaust manifold is connected to the exhaust pipe by a flanged connection with a gasket in between, or by a ball joint type of connection. The ball joint connection has a graphite impregnated seal and may be spring loaded in order to allow engine movement resulting from torque reaction. This is particularly important for transverse engine exhaust systems since engine movement is forward and backward, rather than side to side (as is the case with longitudinally mounted engines).

The exhaust manifold is attached to the cylinder head with studs and nuts or with cap screws. Gaskets may or may not be used between the head and manifold. When used, gaskets are either the em-

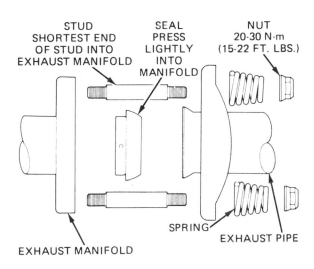

FIGURE 16-4. Typical ball joint exhaust pipe to exhaust manifold connection. Movement of engine relative to exhaust system is accommodated by this type of coupling. Transverse mounted engine torque reaction has a greater effect on exhaust system than that of longitudinally mounted engines. *(Courtesy of General Motors Corporation)*

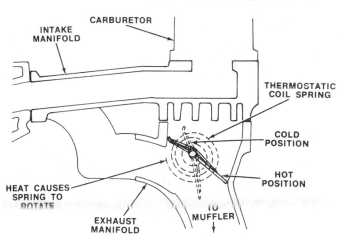

FIGURE 16-5. Cross section of typical heat riser valve in cold and hot positions.

bossed steel type or the steel-reinforced asbestos type.

Many exhaust manifolds are equipped with fittings and passages for air injection into the exhaust gases. See Chapter 17, Part 11, for details.

Heat Riser Valve

Most exhaust systems use a heat riser valve to direct exhaust heat to the base of the carburetor to improve vaporization during engine warm-up and to prevent carburetor icing. The heat riser valve is controlled by a flat-wound temperature-sensitive spring that unwinds and opens the valve when the engine

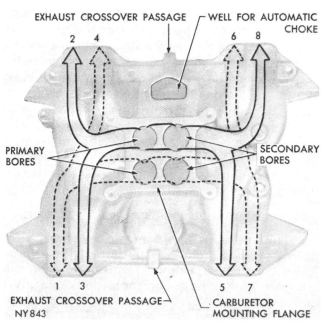

FIGURE 16-6. V8 engine intake manifold. Exhaust crossover passage provides heat for improved fuel vaporization and prevents carburetor icing. *(Courtesy of Chrysler Corporation)*

warms up, or by a vacuum motor controlled by a coolant temperature-sensitive vacuum switch. As soon as the engine starts, intake manifold vacuum is directed to the vacuum motor through the coolant switch to close the heat riser valve. As the engine warms up, the coolant vacuum switch cuts off vacuum to the heat riser valve vacuum motor, which allows the spring to open the valve.

The thermostatically controlled valve directs heated exhaust gases to the heat chamber in the intake manifold beneath the carburetor to help vaporize the fuel mixture during engine warm-up period. On all V-type engines, when the valve is closed, the exhaust gases are directed to the heat chamber through one side of the exhaust cross-over passage; after circulating through the heat chamber, the gases are directed to the exhaust manifold through the other side of the passage.

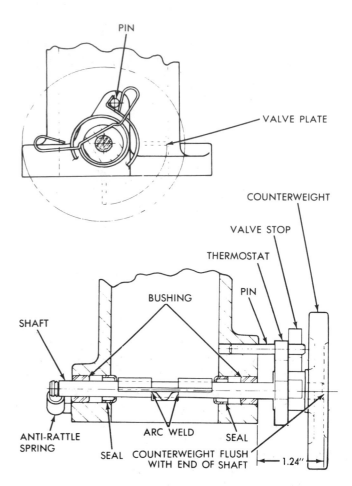

FIGURE 16-7. Exhaust heat riser valve directs heat to the area just below the carburetor to improve fuel vaporization and warm-up performance. A thermostatic spring opens the valve when the engine is warmed up. *(Courtesy of Chrysler Corporation)*

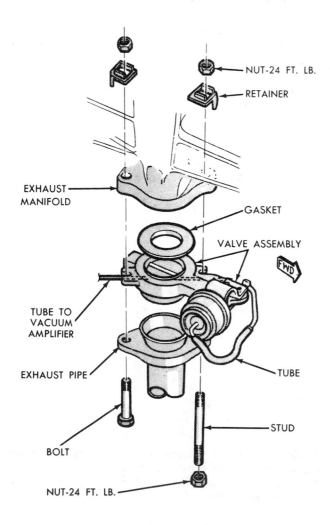

FIGURE 16-8. Some vehicles use a manifold vacuum controlled heat riser valve as shown here. Vacuum control ensures positive closing of the valve when the engine is cold. A coolant-sensitive thermal switch cuts off vacuum supply when the engine has reached a specified temperature. *(Courtesy of Chrysler Corporation)*

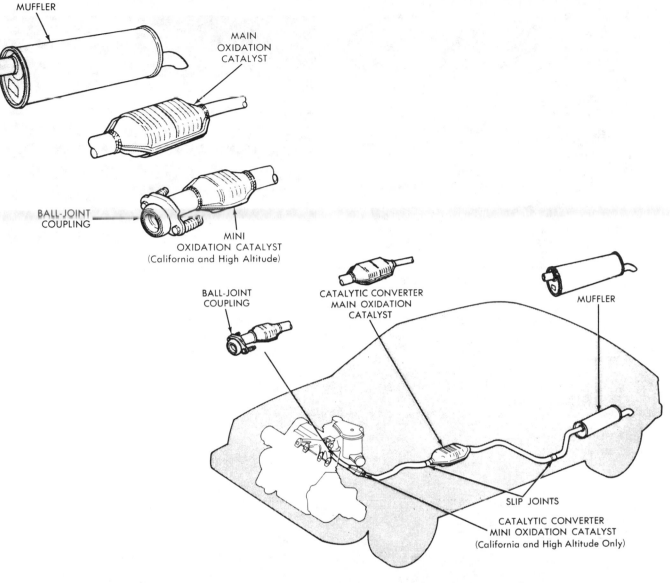

MUFFLER

MAIN OXIDATION CATALYST

BALL-JOINT COUPLING

MINI OXIDATION CATALYST
(California and High Altitude)

BALL-JOINT COUPLING

CATALYTIC CONVERTER MAIN OXIDATION CATALYST

MUFFLER

SLIP JOINTS

CATALYTIC CONVERTER MINI OXIDATION CATALYST
(California and High Altitude Only)

FIGURE 16-9. Typical transverse engine exhaust system components. An exhaust pipe connects the exhaust manifold to the converters and muffler. The tail pipe directs exhaust out of the muffler. The entire system is supported by a series of brackets and hangers to the vehicle body or frame. *(Courtesy of Chrysler Corporation)*

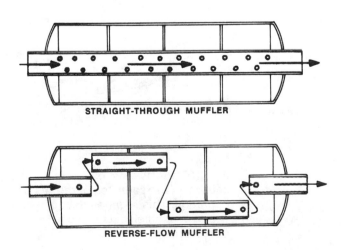

STRAIGHT-THROUGH MUFFLER

REVERSE-FLOW MUFFLER

FIGURE 16-10. Basic muffler design cross section. Straight through flow type (above) and reverse flow (bottom).

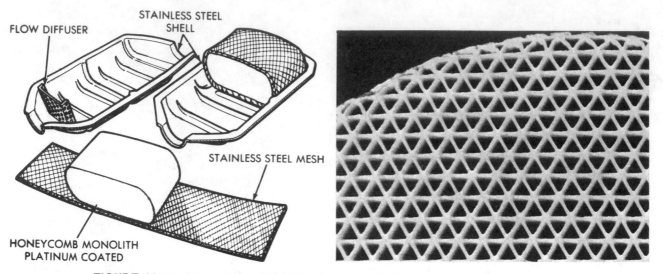

FLOW DIFFUSER

STAINLESS STEEL SHELL

STAINLESS STEEL MESH

HONEYCOMB MONOLITH PLATINUM COATED

FIGURE 16-11. Biscuit type of catalytic converter showing monolithic cellular construction. *(Courtesy of Chrysler Corporation)*

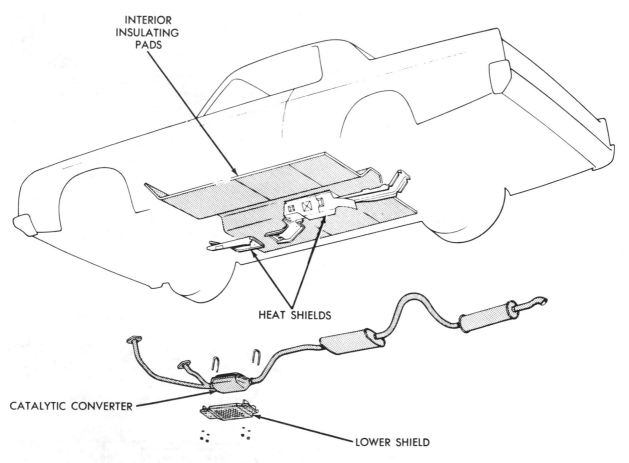

INTERIOR INSULATING PADS

HEAT SHIELDS

CATALYTIC CONVERTER

LOWER SHIELD

FIGURE 16-12. The oxidation (burning) that takes place in the converter causes it to reach temperatures as high as 1500°F (760°C) under normal operation. This requires adequate passenger compartment protection by the use of heat shields. Lower shield decreases fire hazard. *(Courtesy of Chrysler Corporation)*

PART 3   MUFFLERS AND RESONATORS

Mufflers and resonators are used to reduce the noise level of the exhaust. An exhaust pipe connects the manifold to the converters and mufflers. A tail pipe conducts exhaust gases from the muffler to the rear of the vehicle. The entire system is supported by a series of hangers that allow sufficient flexing to accommodate engine movement resulting from acceleration and deceleration. U-type clamps are often used to connect the pipes to the muffler, converter, or resonator. Rust and corrosion resistant material, such as aluminized steel, is usually used for all of these components.

Single and Dual Exhaust Systems

A vehicle may be equipped with either a single or a dual exhaust system. Most four- and six-cylinder engines use a single exhaust system.

Many V-type engines use a dual exhaust system for increased power, performance, and volumetric efficiency. A dual exhaust system has a separate system of pipes, mufflers, and converters for each bank of cylinders.

PART 4   CATALYTIC CONVERTERS

The use and location of catalytic converters vary with year and model.

The catalytic converter, unlike other emission control devices, does not control the formation of emissions. It has no moving parts, and it doesn't depend on engine vacuum or pressure or other mechanical functions. The catalytic converter is a simple, effective device designed to reduce emissions from unacceptable to acceptable levels.

The converter contains an element coated with a catalyst. A catalyst is something that causes a chemical reaction that normally cannot happen. There are three basic catalysts used in the converter: platinum, palladium, and rhodium.

The catalytic converter contains one or two monolithic or pellet type ceramic elements. The surfaces are coated with catalyst material. A stainless steel mesh also protects the elements from shock, and a stainless steel shell encloses the entire assembly.

Heat shields protect the car from high temperature damage. The shield encloses an air space around the converter shell. Air is a poor heat conductor, so the high temperature localizes at the converter. It is very important that heat shields and exhaust components are correctly installed.

The presence of platinum or palladium with heat

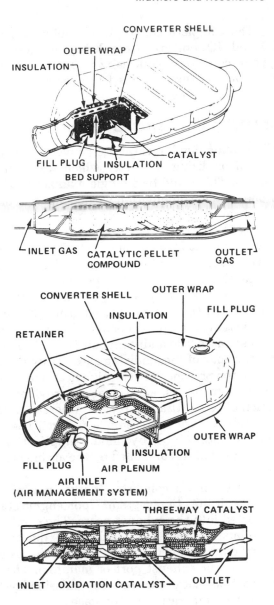

FIGURE 16-13. Catalytic converter designs. Two-way oxidizing catalyst (top) and three-way oxidizing reducing catalyst (bottom). *(Courtesy of General Motors Corporation)*

and unburned fuel (HC, CO) adds oxygen to the reaction. This is called oxidizing. The oxidation of HC and CO produces H_2O and CO_2 (water and carbon dioxide).

Vehicles with more stringent government requirements for controlling NO_x, require a combination *oxidizing-reducing* catalyst. The oxidizing portion uses platinum or palladium as described above. The reducing portion uses rhodium as a catalyst.

Rhodium in the presence of heat and NO_x removes oxygen from the compounds. This removal is called "reducing" because it reduces the amount of oxygen remaining in the compound.

The complete converter assembly lowers HC, CO, and NO_x and is called a three-way catalyst. This type of converter requires very precise engine control, such as that provided by electronic feedback carburetor systems.

Catalytic Converter Operation

All systems (having catalytic converters) use some form of oxidizing converter which treats only HC and CO. This could be a single oxidizing converter, or one used in combination with some form of three-way catalyst.

Two types of three-way converters are used, but they each treat HC, CO, and NO_x. The smaller type contains a mixture of oxidizing catalyst with reducing catalyst. The larger type contains two elements—an oxidizing catalyst and a three-way catalyst. On the latter type, air from the air injection system is supplied between the two elements. In most cases, the additional air is used to improve the efficiency of the oxidizing catalyst by adding oxygen in the presence of very high heat and unburned fuel. In some cases, additional air provides the formation of NO_x. (It adds oxygen, whereas the reducing catalyst is trying to remove oxygen.) The system type is determined by model application. The switching of air is controlled by the air injection system.

The catalytic converter works in conjunction with the air injection system. Upon engine start, air is injected into the exhaust ports. The combination of combustion heat, unburned vapors due to choke-rich mixtures, and fresh air, begins the oxidation process in the exhaust port or manifold. The chemical reaction that occurs reduces emission levels and raises the temperature of the gases.

When this hot, oxidizing mixture enters the converter, the gases flow through the honeycomb openings. The catalyst increases the reaction; much of the HC and CO convert to H_2O, and CO_2 (water

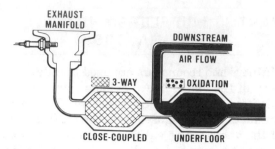

FIGURE 16–15. Three-way close coupled and two-way underfloor converter arrangement with air injection between the two. *(Courtesy of Chrysler Corporation)*

and carbon dioxide). In the three-way converter, the rhodium catalyst also reacts; it removes oxygen from the various oxides of nitrogen (NO_x) compounds formed during combustion.

On engines with air injection switching, the switch valve is calibrated to redirect air at specified engine temperature. When this occurs, air is injected into the converter assembly. This heightens the chemical reaction because the converter is very hot. The additional oxygen improves the oxidizing efficiency of the converter.

In all systems, basic catalytic converter operation is the same: HC, CO, and NO_x gases enter the converter; oxidizing catalysts change HC and CO and yield H_2O and CO_2 plus lower levels of HC and CO, and the same level of NO_x; oxidizing-reducing catalysts convert HC and CO to H_2O and CO_2, convert NO_x to other nitrogen compounds, and yield lower levels of HC and CO plus H_2O and CO_2. The tailpipe emits these compounds along with soot and various other gases.

The converters cannot regulate oxidation or reduction. The process depends on how much air and fuel are available. The more efficient the other systems control emissions coming out of the engine, the better and longer the converter operation.

Rich mixtures during acceleration, heavy load, and wide-open throttle (WOT) cause more unburned HC to enter the catalytic converter. The higher HC exhaust provides more fuel for the catalyst. If

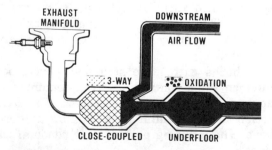

FIGURE 16–14. Typical arrangement of three-way-two-way close coupled and two-way under-floor converter arrangement with air injection behind three-way portion of close coupled converter. *(Courtesy of Chrysler Corporation)*

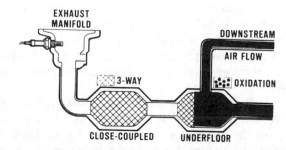

FIGURE 16–16. Three-way close coupled and three-way-two-way underfloor converter arrangement with air injection in the middle of the underfloor converter. *(Courtesy of Chrysler Corporation)*

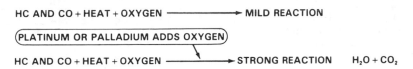

- OXIDIZING CATALYST

HC AND CO + HEAT + OXYGEN ──────→ MILD REACTION

(PLATINUM OR PALLADIUM ADDS OXYGEN)

HC AND CO + HEAT + OXYGEN ──────→ STRONG REACTION $H_2O + CO_2$

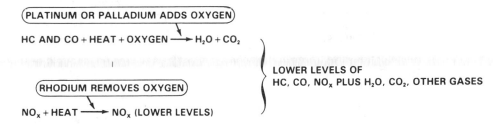

- OXIDIZING-REDUCING CATALYST

(PLATINUM OR PALLADIUM ADDS OXYGEN)

HC AND CO + HEAT + OXYGEN ──→ $H_2O + CO_2$

(RHODIUM REMOVES OXYGEN)

NO_x + HEAT ──→ NO_x (LOWER LEVELS)

LOWER LEVELS OF
HC, CO, NO_x PLUS H_2O, CO_2, OTHER GASES

FIGURE 16–17. Effects of oxidizing (two-way) catalyst (top) and three-way oxidizing reducing catalyst (bottom) on exhaust gases. *(Courtesy of Chrysler Corporation)*

enough air is available, the catalyst will produce hotter reactions; the leaner mixtures of normal driving produce less heat in the converter.

Unfortunately, converter reaction also occurs during malfunctions such as engine misfires, overrich carburetor, and faulty ignition timing.

Caution: Overrich mixtures and malfunctions can overheat the converter and cause heat damage to vehicle components. These mixtures can result in hotter reaction in the catalyst. Repair all engine malfunctions promptly. Avoid running an engine that misfires or has overrich mixtures. If engine misfiring occurs, avoid prolonged engine idling (hot or cold). Do not disconnect or short spark plug wires during diagnosis. Any of these events can cause converter overheating and possible damage.

Overheating and Blockage

Overheating from overrich mixtures, late timing, or misfiring can melt the catalyst element. This will reduce the effectiveness of the converter by cutting off exhaust exposure to the catalyst. Extreme melting will produce a "lump" that blocks the exhaust flow out of the system. This will produce major engine problems, such as backfire, low power, and overheating.

Lead Fouling

Catalytic converters require engine fuel without lead additives. Lead deposits will coat the catalyst and stop the reaction—called lead fouling. The fuel filler neck restriction prevents entry of leaded fuel to a vehicle marked *UNLEADED FUEL ONLY*. A federal law also prohibits putting leaded fuel in a no-lead vehicle. If a vehicle fails an emission inspection as a result of a lead fouling, a new catalytic converter(s) must be installed. The lead cannot be removed.

PART 5 EXHAUST SYSTEM DIAGNOSIS AND SERVICE

General Precautions

Follow all the normal personal and shop safety precautions.

Remember: The normal operating temperature of the exhaust system is very high. Never work around or attempt to service any part of the exhaust system until it has cooled. Use special care when working around the catalytic converter. These units heat to a high temperature after only a short period of engine operation.

- Don't park the vehicle over combustible material like tall grass or piles of leaves.

- Don't apply body undercoating to heat shields or exhaust components. It will reduce heat shielding and cause odors.

- Don't short out or disconnect spark plug wires for diagnosis.

PROBLEM	CAUSE	CORRECTION
Excessive exhaust noise	1. Leaks at pipe joints. 2. Burned or blown out muffler. 3. Burned or rusted out exhaust pipe. 4. Exhaust pipe leaking at manifold flange. 5. Exhaust manifold cracked or broken. 6. Leak between manifold and cylinder head. 7. Restriction in muffler or tailpipe.	1. Tighten clamps at leaking joints. 2. Replace muffler assembly. 3. Replace exhaust pipe. 4. Tighten joint connection attaching bolt nuts. 5. Replace manifold. 6. Tighten manifold to cylinder head stud nuts or bolts to specifications. 7. Remove restriction if possible or replace as necessary.
Leaking exhaust gases	1. Leaks at pipe joints. 2. Damaged or improperly installed gaskets.	1. Tighten U-bolt nuts at leaking joints. 2. Replace gaskets as necessary.
Engine hard to warm-up or will not return to normal idle	1. Heat control valve frozen in the open position. 2. Blocked crossover passage in intake manifold.	1. Free up manifold heat control valve using a suitable solvent. 2. Remove restriction or replace intake manifold.
Heat control valve noisy	1. Thermostat broken. 2. Broken, weak, or missing anti-rattle spring.	1. Replace thermostat. 2. Replace spring.

Exhaust system service is required if any of the following occurs:

- The heat riser valve is not functioning properly.
  - There is exhaust leakage.
  - There is an exhaust restriction.
  - There is abnormal exhaust noise.

Heat Riser Valve Service

To function properly, the heat riser valve must operate freely without sticking. If it is stuck or sticky, use penetrating oil and work it back and forth until it operates freely or replace it.

The heat riser valve control (bimetal spring or vacuum motor) must close the heat riser valve when the engine is cold and open it when the engine is at specified operating temperature. If it does not do this, it should be replaced; or in the case of the vacuum motor type, the source and supply lines of vacuum should be checked and corrected if required.

The temperature control sensor and vacuum motor should be tested for proper operation. Make sure that vacuum and temperature specifications for these units are met. If faulty, they should be replaced.

For proper inlet-air temperature control, the entire induction system should be free of leaks.

Exhaust Leakage

The entire exhaust system, exhaust manifolds, pipes, mufflers, resonators, and catalytic converters should be free of leaks. In most cases component replacement is required.

Deterioration due to rust and corrosion requires replacement of the faulty unit. Clamped connections may allow leakage if installed incorrectly. Where this is the case, the connections and clamps should be checked for correct size and positioning and any errors corrected. Many tail pipes and mufflers have small moisture drain holes, which should not be considered as exhaust leaks requiring repairs.

Exhaust Restriction

Any external damage such as dents may cause an exhaust restriction. Damaged components should be replaced.

Internal restrictions are not as easily detected but can be the cause of lack of engine power. Top speed and power are reduced by exhaust restrictions. A catalytic converter, contaminated as a result of using leaded fuel, will cause the exhaust to be restricted. The contaminated converter may require replacement of the entire unit or (on some

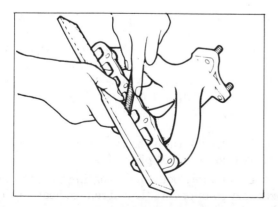

FIGURE 16-18. Checking gasket surface alignment of exhaust manifold with straight edge and feeler gauge. (Courtesy of Chrysler Corporation)

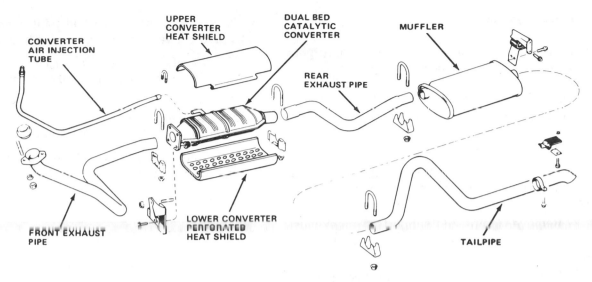

FIGURE 16-19. Typical exhaust system components. *(Courtesy of American Motors Corporation)*

models) replacement of the pellets in the converter. A muffler or resonator that is corroded or rusted on the inside may also cause a restricted exhaust. Faulty units should be replaced.

A partially restricted or blocked exhaust system usually results in loss of power or backfire up through the carburetor. Verify that the condition is not caused by ignition or fuel system problems, then perform a visual inspection of the exhaust system. If the restriction cannot be located by visual inspection, perform the following procedure.

- Attach vacuum gauge to intake manifold.

- Connect tachometer.

- Start engine and observe vacuum gauge. Gauge should indicate a vacuum of 16 to 21 in. Hg (53.88 to 70.73 kPa).

- Increase engine speed to 2000 rpm and observe vacuum gauge. Vacuum will decrease when speed is increased rapidly, but it should stabilize at 16 to 21 in. Hg (53.88 to 70.73 kPa) and remain constant. If vacuum remains below 16 in. Hg (53.88 kPa), exhaust system is restricted or blocked.

Exhaust Noise (Abnormal)

Exhaust noise may be the result of exhaust leakage, misalignment of the system (causing a rattle), or the muffler or resonator may have a loose internal baffle that causes a rattle. The faulty units should be replaced and the entire system aligned properly to

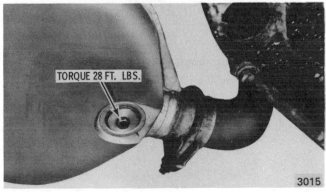

FIGURE 16-20. Replacing catalyst pellets in General Motors type of catalytic converter. Converter must be replaced on other types when catalyst has become ineffective. *(Courtesy of General Motors Corporation)*

provide adequate clearance at all suspension heights and when accelerating or decelerating.

Exhaust Pipe, Muffler, Converter, and Tailpipe Replacement (General)

Removal

1. Raise vehicle on hoist and apply penetrating oil to clamp bolts and nuts of component being removed.

2. Remove clamps and supports from exhaust system to permit alignment of parts during assembly.

3. Clean ends of pipes and/or muffler to ensure mating of all parts. Discard broken or worn insulators, rusted clamps, supports, and attaching parts.

When replacement is required on any component of the exhaust system, it is most important that original equipment parts (or their equivalent) be used to ensure proper alignment with other parts in the system and to provide acceptable exhaust noise levels.

Installation

1. Assemble pipes, muffler, converter, shields, supports, and clamps loosely to permit proper alignment of all parts.

2. Be sure pipes are positioned to proper depth in muffler, converter, or resonator while tightening clamps.

3. Beginning at front of system, align and clamp each component to maintain position and proper clearance with underbody parts.

4. On models using ball-type connections, alternately tighten bolts to ensure flanges are even and parallel.

5. Tighten all clamps and supports to the proper torques.

PART 6   SELF-CHECK

1. What is the purpose of the exhaust system?
2. List eight components of the exhaust system?
3. Why is a heat riser valve used?

4. Why is a spring-loaded ball joint connection required between the exhaust pipe and manifold?

5. What kinds of catalysts are used in an oxidizing converter and what pollutants do they control?

6. The oxidizing-reducing catalyst uses three catalysts to control three pollutants. Name the three catalysts and the three pollutants.

7. Why must unleaded fuel be used in catalyst equipped vehicles?

PART 7   TEST QUESTIONS

1. Exhaust manifolds are made of:
   (a) aluminum or steel
   (b) steel or cast iron
   (c) cast iron or aluminum
   (d) aluminum or platinum

2. Catalysts used in catalytic converters include:
   (a) platinum, palladium, rhodium, and aluminum
   (b) aluminum, irridium, valium, and palladium
   (c) plutonium, uranium, palladium, aluminum
   (d) rhodium, platinum, and palladium

3. A blocked exhaust crossover passage in the intake manifold of a V-type engine causes:
   (a) faster engine warm-up
   (b) less fuel to be used
   (c) poor fuel vaporization during warm-up
   (d) excessive fuel vaporization during warm-up

4. The catalytic converter:
   (a) promotes oxidation of exhaust gases to reduce emissions
   (b) provides quieter operation of exhaust only
   (c) controls exhaust back pressure
   (d) removes condensation and particulates
   (e) reduces exhaust back pressure

5. Exhaust noise may be caused by:
   (a) leaks at pipe joints
   (b) burned or blown out muffler
   (c) burned or rusted out exhaust pipe
   (d) exhaust pipe leaking at manifold flange
   (e) all of the above

Chapter 17

Emission Controls

Performance Objectives

After adequate study of this chapter and sufficient practical experience on appropriate training models, and with proper tools, equipment, and shop manuals, you should be able to do the following:

1. Complete the self-check and test questions with at least 80 percent accuracy.

2. Describe the purpose, construction and operation of (a) the PCV system, (b) the evaporative control system, and (c) the exhaust emission control systems.

3. Diagnose emission-control systems problems according to manufacturer's diagnostic procedures.

4. Recondition and replace faulty components as required to restore system efficiency.

5. Correctly adjust system components according to manufacturer's specifications.

6. Test the systems to determine the success of the service performed.

7. Prepare the vehicle for customer acceptance.

PART 1   AIR POLLUTION

Ingredients necessary to form photochemical smog are hydrocarbons (HC) and nitrogen oxides (NO_x) in the presence of continued sunlight. Both of these gases exist in many forms and come from a variety of sources. One major source of NO_x and hydrocarbons is automobiles.

The requirements for smog formation are sunshine and relatively still air. When the concentration of HC in the atmosphere becomes sufficiently high and NO_x is present in the correct ratio, the ac-

FIGURE 17-1. Smog over heavily populated area. Much of this smog is caused by automotive emissions. *(Courtesy of Ford Motor Co. of Canada Ltd.)*

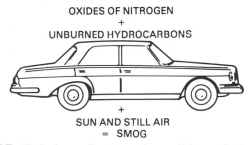

FIGURE 17-2. Ingredients and conditions that create smog.

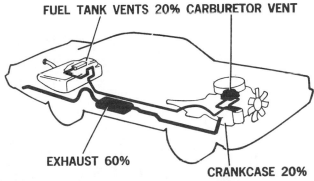

FIGURE 17-3. Sources of vehicle emissions. *(Courtesy of Chrysler Corporation)*

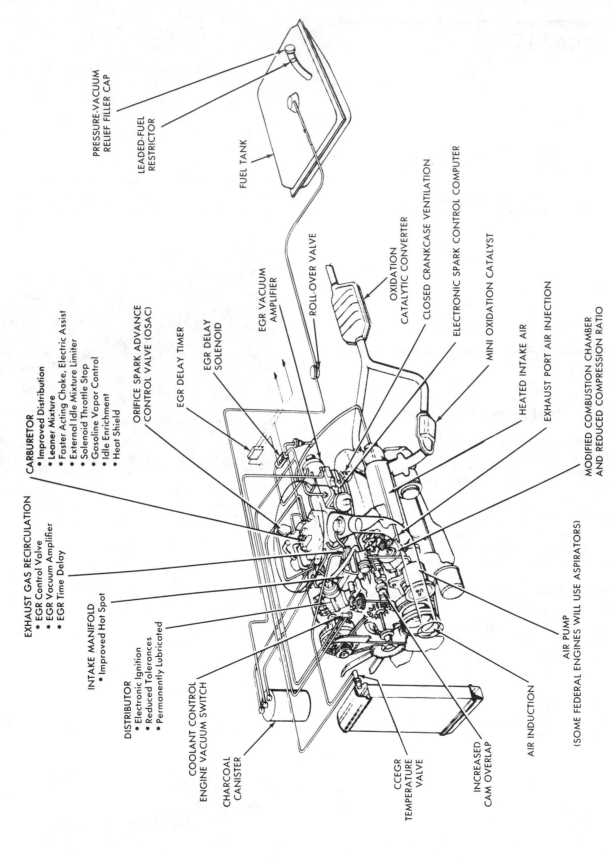

EXHAUST GAS RECIRCULATION
• EGR Control Valve
• EGR Vacuum Amplifier
• EGR Time Delay

INTAKE MANIFOLD
• Improved Hot Spot

DISTRIBUTOR
• Electronic Ignition
• Reduced Tolerances
• Permanently Lubricated

COOLANT CONTROL
ENGINE VACUUM SWITCH

CHARCOAL
CANISTER

CCEGR
TEMPERATURE
VALVE

INCREASED
CAM OVERLAP

AIR INDUCTION

AIR PUMP
(SOME FEDERAL ENGINES WILL USE ASPIRATORS)

CARBURETOR
• Improved Distribution
• Leaner Mixture
• Faster Acting Choke, Electric Assist
• External Idle Mixture Limiter
• Solenoid Throttle Stop
• Gasoline Vapor Control
• Idle Enrichment
• Heat Shield

ORIFICE SPARK ADVANCE
CONTROL VALVE (OSAC)

EGR DELAY TIMER

EGR DELAY
SOLENOID

EGR VACUUM
AMPLIFIER

ROLL-OVER VALVE

OXIDATION
CATALYTIC CONVERTER

CLOSED CRANKCASE VENTILATION

ELECTRONIC SPARK CONTROL COMPUTER

MINI OXIDATION CATALYST

HEATED INTAKE AIR

EXHAUST PORT AIR INJECTION

MODIFIED COMBUSTION CHAMBER
AND REDUCED COMPRESSION RATIO

PRESSURE-VACUUM
RELIEF FILLER CAP

LEADED-FUEL
RESTRICTOR

FUEL TANK

FIGURE 17-4. Emission-control systems and devices. *(Courtesy of Chrysler Corporation)*

tion of sunshine causes them to react chemically, forming photochemical smog.

With a thermal inversion (where warmer air above prevents upward movement of cooler air near the ground), smog can accumulate under this lid all the way down to the ground within a few hours. The first effect of a smog buildup is reduced visibility and the blotting out of scenery in the distance; then, as the buildup of smog approaches ground level, its irritating effects on eyes, nose, and throat are sensed.

Vehicle emissions come from three different sources: exhaust, crankcase, and fuel evaporation. Numerous changes have been made to engines to meet emission standards. Emission-control requirements for the state of California vary from those of other states or provinces owing to its unique climate and location; therefore, some of the emission controls described apply specifically to California.

Control of exhaust emissions (hydrocarbons, carbon monoxide, and oxides of nitrogen) is accomplished by a combination of engine modification and the addition of special engine control components. *Modifications to the combustion chamber, intake manifold, camshaft, carburetor and distributor, along with heated intake air and fresh air induction, form the basic control system.*

Additional engine control devices include an *exhaust gas recirculation system* (EGR) to reduce oxides of nitrogen emissions, *electric assist choke, spark advance controls, power heat control valve, an air pump* and *a catalytic converter*. Effectiveness of the system depends on proper adjustments, such as engine idle speed, ignition timing, and carburetor idle mixture being set according to the specifications shown on the label under the hood.

Hydrocarbons (HC). Hydrocarbon emissions are the result of incomplete combustion. They are excess fuel left unburned, or partially burned, in the combustion chamber after ignition has occurred.

Carbon Monoxide (CO). Carbon monoxide is the result of incomplete combustion of the fuel mixture due to an insufficient amount of oxygen in the air-fuel mixture.

Oxides of Nitrogen (NO_x). Nitrogen oxides are found when combustion temperatures reach high levels. The chemical nature of nitrogen and oxygen requires very high temperatures in order to combine both elements in any form. The x in NO_x means that an oxide of nitrogen is formed when one molecule of nitrogen combines with any number of molecules of oxygen.

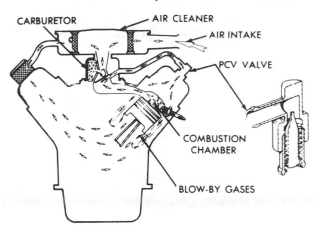

FIGURE 17-5. Crankcase ventilation system. *(Courtesy of Chrysler Corporation)*

PART 2 POSITIVE CRANKCASE VENTILATION (PCV) SYSTEM

The crankcase ventilation system is designed to eliminate emission of fumes, vapors, and blowby gases from the crankcase by directing these fumes back through the combustion chamber. When the engine is running part throttle, or at idle, gases flow from the cylinder head cover, through the PCV valve, through the carburetor base, or directly into the intake manifold. At wide-open throttle, there is little or no vacuum at the valve. Flow reverses and goes through the molded hose, into the air cleaner, through the carburetor, and into the intake manifold, preventing any crankcase vapors from escaping to the atmosphere. See Chapter 7, Parts 5 and 8 for more on PCV systems.

PART 3 EVAPORATIVE EMISSION CONTROLS

The purpose of the evaporative control system is to prevent the emissions of gasoline vapors from the fuel tank and carburetor into the atmosphere. When fuel evaporates in the carburetor float chamber or fuel tank, the vapors pass through vent hoses or tubes to a charcoal canister where they are temporarily held until they can be drawn into the intake manifold when the engine is running. The charcoal canister is for the storage of fuel vapors from the fuel tank and carburetor fuel bowl. For additional information, see Chapter 12, Parts 2 and 9.

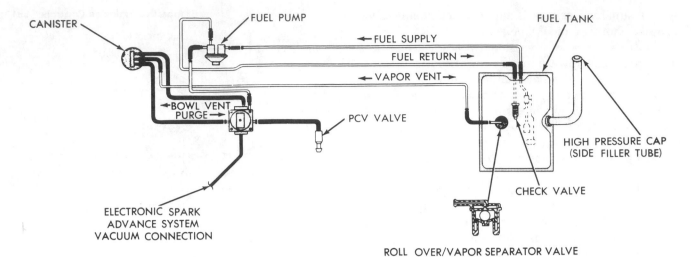

FIGURE 17-6. Typical evaporative emission control system. *(Courtesy of Chrysler Corporation)*

PART 4   ENGINE DESIGN MODIFICATIONS

Combustion Chamber Design

Combustion chambers have been modified in shape to reduce exhaust emissions. These changes have been made to eliminate close clearance spaces that have a tendency to quench the flame before all the fuel-air mixture is burned. Quench heights have been modified, and this permits more complete burning of fuel-air mixture in these areas. A substantial reduction of HC has been achieved as a result of the changes in quench height.

Lower Compression Ratios

Compression ratios were reduced. The change in ratios has been achieved by various modifications in quench height and in the piston head design. This type of change has resulted in slightly lower HC and NO_x levels.

Camshaft Valve Overlap Increased

Greater valve overlap causes some dilution of the intake mixture to lower peak combustion temperatures and reduces nitrous oxide emissions.

Induction Hardened Exhaust Valve Seats

This feature allows satisfactory operation on lead-free fuel, without harming the valves and valve seats. During engine production, exhaust valve seats in the cylinder heads are heated by induction

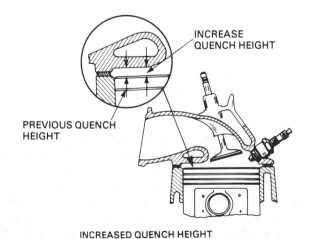

INCREASED QUENCH HEIGHT

FIGURE 17-7. Increased quench height allows fuel to be more completely burned in the quench area of the combustion chamber. This reduces hydrocarbon emissions.

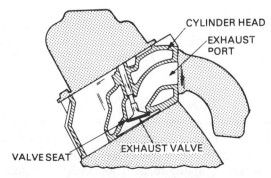

INDUCTION HARDENED EXHAUST VALVE SEAT

FIGURE 17-8. Better valves and induction hardened valve seats are required to improve valve and seat life when using unleaded fuels.

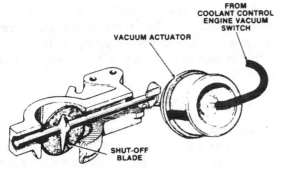

FROM
COOLANT CONTROL
ENGINE VACUUM
SWITCH

VACUUM ACTUATOR

SHUT-OFF
BLADE

FIGURE 17-9. Vacuum-operated exhaust heat riser valve improves fuel vaporization during engine warm-up. *(Courtesy of Chrysler Corporation)*

coils to a temperature of 1700°F (926.67°C) and then allowed to cool. This process hardens the seats to a depth of 0.05 to 0.08 inch (1.27 mm to 2.032 mm), giving greater resistance to wear.

Intake Manifold

Intake manifolds have been modified to ensure more rapid vaporization of fuel during engine warm-up. The exhaust crossover floor of the intake manifold between the inlet gases and exhaust gases has been thinned out, thereby reducing the time required to get the heat from the exhaust gases into the inlet gases.

Vacuum-Operated Heat Riser Valve

The power heat control valve accomplishes two things: (1) the incoming air-fuel mixture is pre-heated for better vaporization, and (2) the "mini"-converter heats up faster owing to increased exhaust gas flow and heat. This only applies to some models.

A coolant-controlled switch controls vacuum to the heat control valve vacuum actuator. Below, specified coolant temperature manifold vacuum is applied to the actuator, closing the heat riser valve. When engine temperatures rise above this specified point, manifold vacuum to the heat control valve is shut off at the vacuum control valve, opening the right-side exhaust manifold and allowing exhaust gases to flow through both manifolds in the normal fashion. See Chapter 16, Part 2, for more on heat riser valves.

PART 5   FUEL SYSTEM MODIFICATIONS

A number of modifications to the fuel system have come about in order to provide better emission control. These modifications are included in Section 3 and are not dealt with here. However, a list of the more common fuel system modifications used for better emission control are given here.

- No-lead fuel (to prevent damage to catalytic converters)
- Controlled inlet-air temperature
- Evaporative control system
- Electric choke
- Idle mixture limiters and restrictors
- Idle enrichment system
- Deceleration valve
- Electronic fuel metering
- Altitude compensating system
- Variable venturi carburetor
- Electronic fuel injection

Refer to Section 3 of this text and to manufacturer's manuals for specific details of units used on any particular vehicle.

PART 6   IGNITION SYSTEM MODIFICATIONS

A number of ignition system modifications have resulted from efforts to reduce harmful exhaust emissions. Included among these are the following:

- Dual diaphragm vacuum advance and retard distributor timing control
- Solenoid controlled vacuum advance
- Electronic ignition
- Computer controlled timing

A number of minor changes to spark plugs, high-tension wires, and other ignition system components have also taken place. Refer to Chapter 24 in this text for further details and to manufacturer's manuals.

PART 7   EXHAUST SYSTEM MODIFICATIONS

A vacuum-motor-operated heat riser valve regulated by a coolant temperature vacuum switch is used to promote better fuel vaporization during engine warm-up. See Chapter 16 for details. Chapter 16 also covers details of catalytic converter operation.

Catalytic converters have been added to the exhaust system to reduce the levels of HC, CO, and NO_x. Exhaust gases are directed through the catalyst coated material in the converter which increases the rate of oxidation of HC and CO in the platinum-palladium converter. The level of NO_x is reduced by the use of rhodium as a catalyst. An oxygen sensor senses oxygen content in the exhaust gases and sends an electrical signal to a computer which then adjusts the air/fuel ratio accordingly. See Chapter 13, Part 5, for details.

PART 8 EXHAUST GAS RECIRCULATION

The purpose of an exhaust gas recirculation system is to reduce oxides of nitrogen in the vehicle exhaust. This system recirculates a portion of the engine exhaust gas back into the induction system. This reduces combustion temperatures to reduce NO_x emissions since exhaust gases are inert.

Control of exhaust gas recirculation rate is accomplished by two methods within the basic EGR system. These methods are ported vacuum control with an EGR valve and venturi vacuum control with an EGR valve. Each of these two systems utilizes exhaust gas recirculation flow control valves, dif-

fering primarily in the method of vacuum control. The valve is a vacuum diaphragm actuated, poppet-type unit used to modulate exhaust gas flow to the induction passage in response to a varying vacuum signal.

Ported Vacuum Control System

The ported vacuum control system utilizes a slot-type port in the carburetor throttle body, which is progressively exposed to an increasing percentage of manifold vacuum as the throttle blades open. This throttle bore port is connected to the EGR valve by means of a hose. The flow rate is dependent on manifold vacuum, throttle position, and exhaust gas back pressure.

Venturi Vacuum Control System

The venturi vacuum control system uses a vacuum tap at the throat of the carburetor venturi to provide a control signal. Because of the low value of this signal, it is necessary to use a vacuum control unit (amplifier) to increase the signal strength to the level required to operate the valve. The amplifier uses manifold vacuum to provide the source of amplification. Elimination of EGR at wide open throttle operation (WOT) is accomplished by a dump

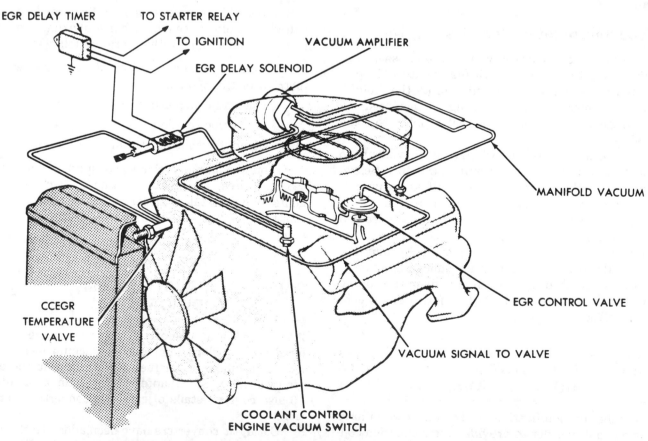

FIGURE 17–10. Typical exhaust gas recirculation system. *(Courtesy of Chrysler Corporation)*

DON'T WANT EGR @		BECAUSE
Idle	. . . .	Causes roughness
WOT	. . . .	Reduces maximum power
Cold Start	. . . .	Engine not hot enough to produce much NO_x; causes hard starting, roughness, hesitation, stalls

ENGINE CONDITION		HOW MUCH EGR
Off Idle Light Throttle	} Minimum air/fuel mixture, low combustion temperatures	Very little off idle Small amount at light throttle
Medium Throttle —	Moderate air/fuel mixture and combustion temperatures	Moderate amount proportional to air/fuel flow
Heavy Throttle (Not WOT) —	Rich mixtures, high power, high combustion temperatures	Maximum flow
Acceleration —	Need smooth engine performance and rich mixtures	Very little until speed stabilizes

FIGURE 17-11. Vehicle requirements for exhaust gas recirculation. *(Courtesy of Chrysler Corporation)*

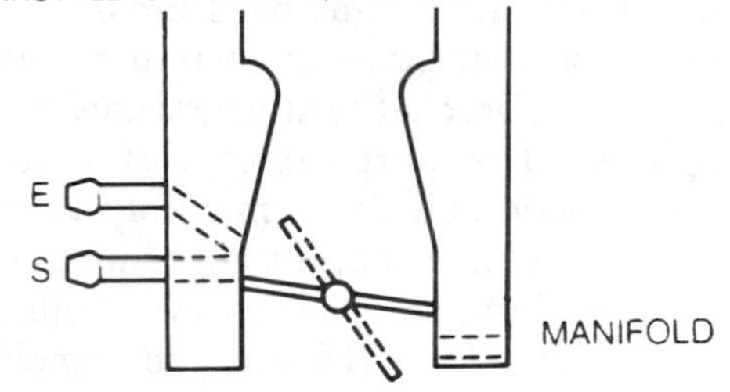

MANIFOLD VACUUM IS STRONG AT CLOSED THROTTLE; OTHERS ARE ZERO AT CLOSED THROTTLE. "S" VACUUM COMES ON FIRST WHEN THROTTLE IS CRACKED; THEN "E."

E

S

MANIFOLD

FIGURE 17-12. Vacuum sources at carburetor. S = Spark port vacuum. E = EGR vacuum port. *(Courtesy o Ford Motor Co. of Canada Ltd.)*

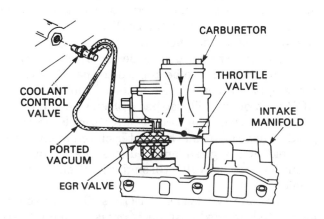

PORTED VACUUM-EXHAUST GAS RECIRCULATION

VENTURI VACUUM EXHAUST GAS RECIRCULATION

FIGURE 17-13. EGR system control vacuum sources.

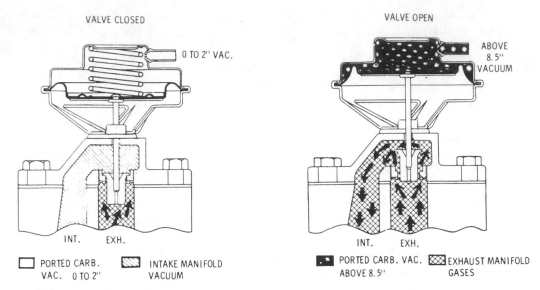

FIGURE 17-14. Ported vacuum-operated EGR valve. *(Courtesy of General Motors Corporation)*

diaphragm that compares venturi and manifold vacuum to determine when WOT is achieved. At WOT, vacuum is dumped, limiting output to the EGR valve to manifold vacuum, which is at or near zero. As in the ported control system, the valve opening is set above the manifold vacuum available at WOT, permitting the valve to be closed at WOT. This system is dependent on engine intake airflow as indicated by the venturi signal, and is also affected by intake vacuum and exhaust gas back pressure.

On some engines, an external vacuum reservoir tank is mounted on a bracket that is attached to the vacuum amplifier. The purpose of this external reservoir is to provide additional manifold vacuum as the source for amplification, if the vacuum in the amplifier has been dumped. The reservoir will provide manifold vacuum for EGR until the amplifier vacuum supply can be replenished.

Coolant Control Valve

Both the ported vacuum and venturi vacuum EGR control systems utilize an engine coolant controlled exhaust gas recirculation control feature. The coolant control valve opens so that vacuum is applied to the EGR valve, allowing exhaust gas to recirculate in the normal manner when specified coolant temperature is reached.

EGR Delay System. Some vehicles are equipped with an EGR delay system having an electrical timer mounted on the fire wall in the engine compartment, which controls an engine-mounted solenoid. The solenoid is connected by "tees" between the manifold vacuum source and the vacuum amplifier. The purpose of this system is to prevent exhaust gas recirculation for approximately 35 seconds after the ignition is turned on.

EGR Valve Operation

The exhaust gas recirculation system is used on engines to meter exhaust gas into the engine induction system through passages cast into the intake manifold or carburetor to intake-manifold spacer.

The introduction of exhaust gas into the air/fuel mixture lowers the combustion temperature, thereby reducing the amount of oxides of nitrogen (NO_x) formed. The amount of exhaust gas admitted is regulated by a vacuum controlled valve (EGR valve) in response to engine operating condition. The ECM controls the ported vacuum to the EGR valve with a solenoid valve. When the engine is cold, within a specified load range and above a specified rpm, the solenoid valve is energized and blocks vacuum to the EGR valve. When the engine is warm, the solenoid valve is de-energized and EGR is allowed. A second EGR system uses a bleed solenoid on the EGR line. In this case, the solenoid is energized when it is cold and bleeds some of the vacuum off of the system so that the EGR will operate when cold but at about half normal vacuum. When the engine is warm, the solenoid is de-engerized, allowing full ported vacuum to be applied to the EGR valve. Some applications will use a normal on/off type of EGR control but will also use a bleed solenoid which is operated when the torque converter clutch is applied. When the torque converter clutch applies, the solenoid is energized and reduces the vacuum to about half normal value through the bleed in the solenoid.

There are two types of EGR systems: vacuum modulated and exhaust back pressure modulated. The major difference between the valves is the method used to control how far each valve opens.

With vacuum modulated EGR, the amount of

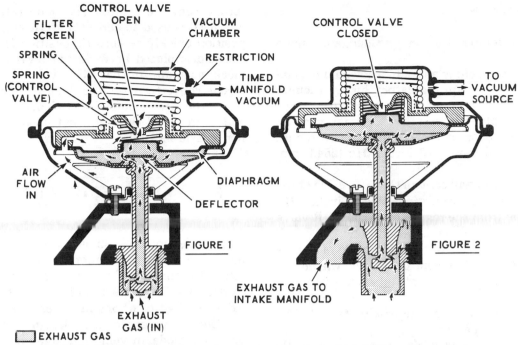

FIGURE 17-15. Exhaust gas back-pressure-controlled EGR valve operation. *(Courtesy of General Motors Corporation)*

exhaust gas admitted to the intake manifold depends on a vacuum signal (ported vacuum) which is controlled by throttle position. When the throttle is closed (idle or deceleration) there is no vacuum signal to the EGR valve because the EGR vacuum port is above the closed throttle valve. As the throttle valve is opened, a ported vacuum signal is supplied to the EGR valve, admitting exhaust gas to the intake manifold.

The exhaust back pressure modulated EGR uses a transducer located inside the EGR valve to control the operating vacuum signal. The vacuum signal is generated in the same manner as for the vacuum modulated EGR system. The integral transducer uses exhaust gas pressure to control an air bleed within the valve to modify the vacuum signal from the carburetor.

Computer Controlled EGR (GM)

A pulse width modulated solenoid is utilized to control EGR supply vacuum. The duty cycle of the solenoid is controlled by the ECM in response to

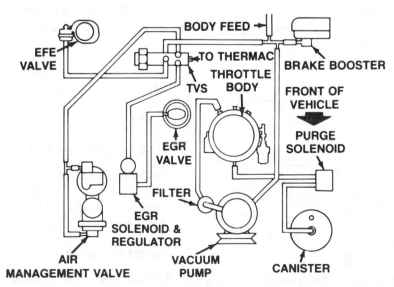

FIGURE 17-16. Computer controlled EGR vacuum diagram. Other vacuum lines are also shown. Note EGR solenoid and vacuum regulator. *(Courtesy of General Motors Corporation)*

engine coolant temperature, engine load, and engine rpm.

The EGR solenoid is actually a solenoid in combination with a vacuum regulator. Supply vacuum is first available to the regulator portion of the solenoid assembly through the thermal vacuum switch. The purpose of the regulator is to reduce supply vacuum down to 10 inches Hg (254.0 mm Hg).

Next, the ECM will control the duty cycle of the EGR solenoid which proportions this 10 inches. Hg vacuum signal from the regulator to the EGR valve in response to various engine conditions.

The ECM will control the duty cycle of the solenoid such that a 10 percent duty cycle will enable EGR full on, and a 90 percent duty cycle will turn EGR full off.

EGR is *activated* at approximately 120°F (50°C) coolant temperature.

EGR is *deactivated* during wide open throttle and idle operation.

Diesel EGR Operation (Typical GM)

Vacuum from the vacuum pump is modulated by the vacuum regulator valve (VRV) mounted on the injection pump. Vacuum is highest at idle and decreases to zero at wide open throttle. The EGR valve is open to its maximum at idle and closed at wide open throttle. The amount of EGR valve opening is further modulated by a vacuum modulator valve (VMV). The VMV allows for an increase in vacuum to the EGR valve as the throttle is closed (up to the switching point of the VMV). A response vacuum reducer (RVR) valve is used between the VRV and

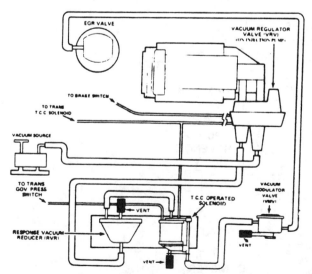

FIGURE 17-17. Diesel engine EGR system as used on GM V6 diesel engine. Vacuum regulator valve is mounted on diesel injection pump. *(Courtesy of General Motors Corporation)*

torque converter clutch (TCC) operated solenoid. The RVR is used to allow the EGR valve to change position quickly as throttle position is changed. A solenoid is placed between the RVR and VMV to block vacuum to the EGR valve whenever the torque converter clutch is applied. The solenoid is fed 12 volts from the TCC switch portion of the VRV and is grounded through the transmission's governor pressure switch.

PART 9   AIR-INJECTION SYSTEM (NON-COMPUTER)

An air-injection system is used to reduce carbon monoxide and hydrocarbons. The system adds a controlled amount of air to exhaust gases, causing oxidation of the gases and reduction of carbon monoxide and hydrocarbons in the exhaust stream.

Depending on system design and the make, year, and model of vehicle, air may be injected into one or more of the following locations:

1. Exhaust ports in the cylinder head
2. Exhaust manifold ports
3. Exhaust pipe
4. Catalytic converter
5. Pipe between two converters

Air from the air injection system is used to pressure purge the charcoal canister in some systems.

Air may be diverted from being injected into the exhaust gases by diverting it to one of the following:

1. The atmosphere
2. The intake manifold
3. The air cleaner

The air-injection system consists of a belt-driven air pump, a combination diverter-pressure relief valve, rubber hoses, a check valve to protect the hoses and other components from hot gases, and an injection tube.

Air-Injection Pump

The belt-driven air pump is mounted on the front of the engine. This vane-type pump is driven from the crankshaft pulley and supplies a high volume of air at low pressure to the exhaust system.

Diverter Valve

The purpose of the diverter valve is to prevent backfire in the exhaust system during sudden deceleration. Sudden throttle closure at the beginning of deceleration temporarily creates an air-fuel mixture

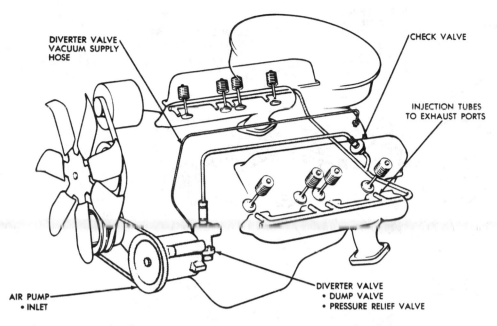

FIGURE 17-18. Air injection system injects air (oxygen) to exhaust gases to assist in burning any unburned hydrocarbons in the exhaust system. *(Courtesy of Chrysler Corporation)*

too rich to burn. This mixture becomes burnable when it reaches the exhaust area and combines with injector air. The next firing of the engine will ignite this air-fuel mixture. The diverter valve senses the sudden increase in intake manifold vacuum, causing the valve to open and allowing air from the air pump to divert through the valve.

A pressure relief valve, incorporated in the same housing as the diverter valve, controls pressure within the system by diverting excessive pump output at higher engine speeds to the atmosphere through the silencer.

Check Valve

A one-way check valve is located in the injection tube assembly. This valve prevents hot exhaust gases from backing up into the hose and pump. This valve will protect the system in the event of pump belt failure, abnormally high exhaust system pressure, or air hose ruptures.

Aspirator Air System

Some engines have an aspirator system. This valve utilizes exhaust pressure pulsation to draw air into

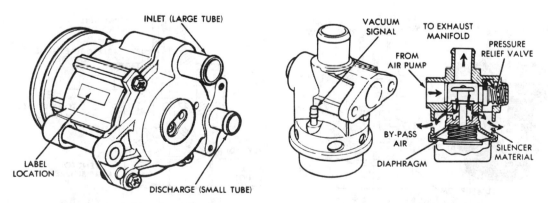

FIGURE 17-19. Typical air pump and diverter valve used with system shown in Figure 17-18. Diverter valve diverts air from exhaust system to prevent explosions in the exhaust system during high intake manifold vacuum conditions such as deceleration. *(Courtesy of Chrysler Corporation)*

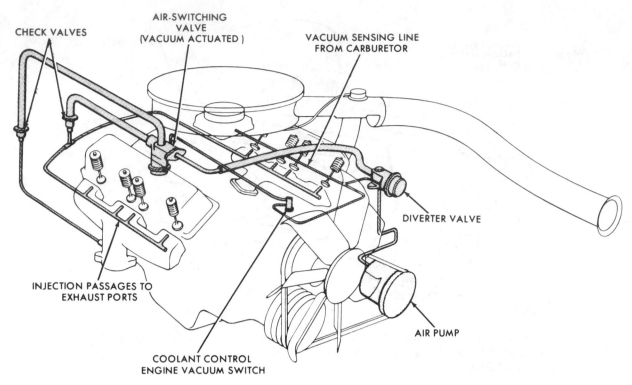

FIGURE 17-20. Air injection system with air switching valve. Switching valve directs air to exhaust ports or to manifold. *(Courtesy of Chrysler Corporation)*

the exhaust system, reducing carbon monoxide (CO) and, to a lesser degree, hydrocarbon (HC) emissions. It draws fresh air from the "clean" side of the air cleaner past a one-way valve.

The valve opens to allow fresh air to mix with the exhaust gases during negative pressure (vacuum) pulses that occur in the exhaust ports and manifold passages. If the pressure is positive, the valve closes, and no exhaust gas is allowed to flow past the valve and into the "clean" side of the air cleaner. The aspirator valve works most efficiently at idle and slightly off idle, where the negative pulses are maximum. At higher engine speeds, the aspirator valve remains closed.

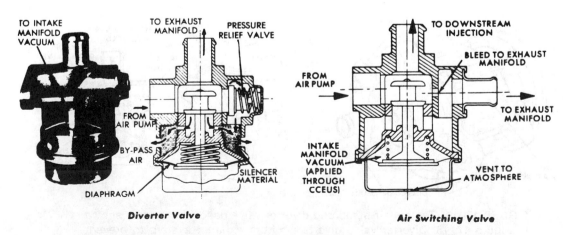

FIGURE 17-21. Diverter valve and air switching valve. Details for system shown in Figure 17-20. *(Courtesy of Chrysler Corporation)*

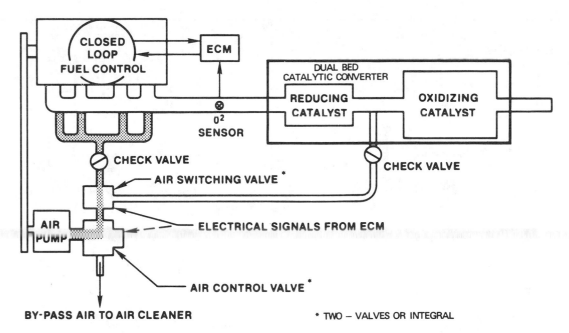

FIGURE 17-22. Typical air injection system in closed loop operation. Shaded areas show air flow. *(Courtesy of General Motors Corporation)*

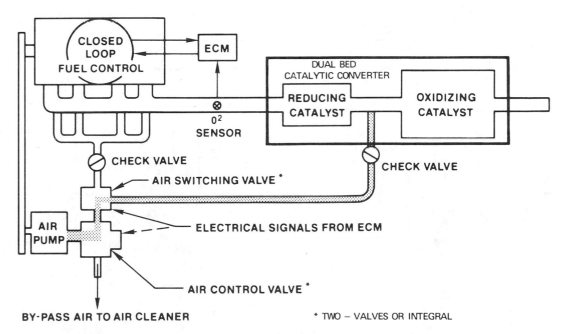

FIGURE 17-23. Air injection system in open loop operation. Note air flow directed between catalysts. *(Courtesy of General Motors Corporation)*

PART 10 COMPUTER CONTROLLED AIR INJECTION SYSTEM (TYPICAL)

An air injection (AIR) system is used to provide additional oxygen to continue the combustion process after the exhaust gases leave the combustion chamber. The AIR system uses an engine-driven pump to inject air into the exhaust port of the cylinder head, exhaust manifold, or the catalytic converter. The AIR system operates at all times and will by-pass air during high speeds and loads on ECM command. The air management valve performs the bypass or divert function, and the check valve protects the air pump from damage by preventing a backflow of exhaust gas.

The AIR system helps reduce hydrocarbons

391

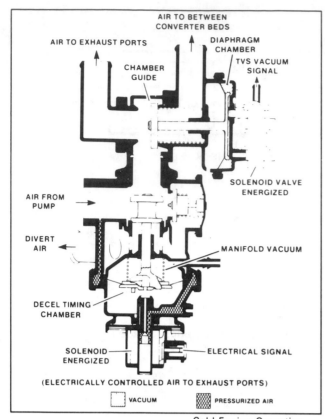

Cold Engine Operation

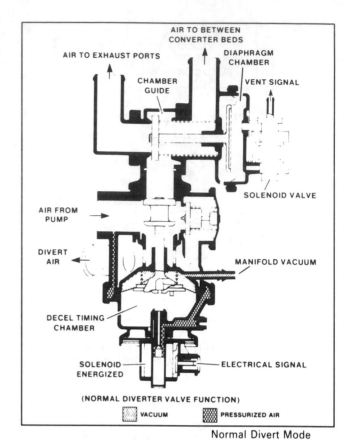

Normal Divert Mode

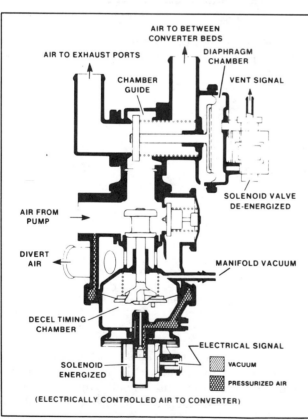

Warm Engine Operation

Electric Divert Mode

FIGURE 17-24. Combination diverter valve and air switching valve used with computer controlled air management system. *(Courtesy of General Motors Corporation)*

(HC) and carbon monoxide (CO) contained in the exhaust gases. It does this by injecting air into the exhaust during cold engine operation. This air injection helps the catalytic converter quickly reach proper operating temperature during warm-up. When the engine is warm or is in "closed loop mode," the AIR system injects air between the beds of a dual-bed catalytic converter and diverts air on three-way converter to lower the HC and CO in the exhaust.

The AIR systems utilize the following components:

1. Engine-driven AIR pump
2. AIR management valves (air control, air switching, three-way air divert)
3. Pulsair (instead of 1, 2, and 5)
4. AIR flow and control hoses
5. Check valves
6. Dual-bed catalytic converter
7. Single-bed catalytic converter

The belt-driven vane type air pump located at the front of the engine supplies clean air to the AIR system. The AIR system uses air from the air pump to cause further oxidation (burning) of hydrocarbons (HC) and carbon monoxide (CO) before they are discharged from the tailpipe.

When the engine is cold, the ECM energizes an AIR control solenoid. This allows air to flow to an AIR switching valve. The AIR switching valve is energized to direct air to the exhaust ports.

On a warm engine or when in "closed loop," the

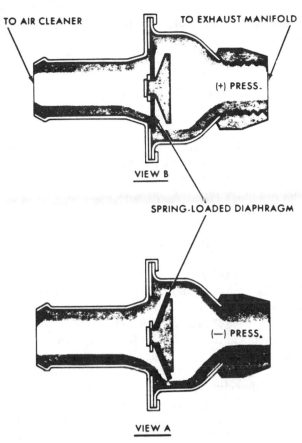

FIGURE 17-26. Aspirator valve operates in response to positive and negative exhaust gas pressures. *(Courtesy of Chrysler Corporation)*

ECM de-energizes the AIR switching valve, directing air between the beds of the catalytic converter or to the atmosphere on three-way catalysts. This provides additional oxygen for the oxidizing catalyst to decrease the carbon monoxide (CO) and hydrocarbon (HC) levels, while at the same time keeping oxygen levels low in the first bed of the converter. This enables the reducing catalyst to effectively decrease the levels of oxides of nitrogen (NO_x).

Under certain operating modes (wide open throttle, warmed up engine with single bed three way, etc.), or if the ECM self-diagnostic system detects any problem in the "System," air is diverted (divert mode) to the air cleaner or directly to atmosphere.

The air-flow and control hoses transmit pressurized air to the catalytic converter, or to the exhaust ports via internal (intake manifold) passages or external piping.

The check valves prevent backflow of exhaust gas into the air distribution system. The valve prevents backflow when the air pump bypasses at high

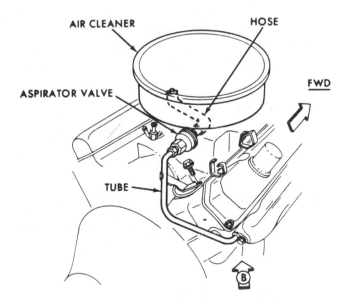

FIGURE 17-25. Some vehicles use an aspirator system to promote reduction of HC in the exhaust. This system does not have an air pump. *(Courtesy of Chrysler Corporation)*

speed and loads, or in case the air pump malfunctions.

PART 11 EMISSION CONTROL SYSTEM DIAGNOSIS AND SERVICE

The emission-control systems warranty is stated in the operator's or owner's manual—a publication given to new car purchasers at the time of purchase. This warranty information stipulates that the owner must maintain and use the car in accordance with written instructions to assure proper functioning of emission-control devices and systems on the vehicle.

The emission-control system requires essentially the same maintenance that is recommended for normal car care. Periodic inspection and servicing of various items is essential, however, to assure continued validation of the warranty and to assure that the system is functioning properly. Emission devices and systems to be serviced and the frequency of service are identified in the owner's manual and in the appropriate shop manual.

Emission control systems and devices are often part of other systems and therefore are not serviced in isolation. All systems involved with emission control and control devices should be considered when diagnosing and servicing these items.

For information on emission control system diagnosis and service, refer to the following sections of this text:

- PCV System Service—Chapter 7, Part 8
- Evaporative Emission Control Service—Chapter 12, Part 9
- Engine Service—Chapter 9
- Fuel Supply System Service—Chapter 12, Part 5
- Carburetor Service—Chapter 13, Part 6
- Gasoline Fuel Injection Service—Chapter 14, Part 9
- Diesel Fuel System Service—Chapter 15, Part 6
- Ignition System Service—Chapter 24, Part 4
- Exhaust System Service—Chapter 16, Part 5
- Diagnosis and Performance Testing—Chapter 26
- EGR Service—Chapter 17, Part 12
- Air Injection System Service—Chapter 17, Part 13

General Precautions

All the normal personal and shop safety precautions and procedures should be followed as outlined in Chapter 1, Parts 1 and 2.

General Diagnosis Sequence

1. *Verify the customer complaint.* It is very important that you get an accurate description of the problem. Verify (when possible) the complaint. Road testing is the only recommended way to do this.

2. *Perform visual checks.* Experience has shown that many problems are caused by loose connectors, frayed insulation, loose hose clamps, and leaks in vacuum or fuel lines. A short visual check will help you spot these most common faults and save a lot of unnecessary test and diagnostic time. If there are no obvious faults that can be identified visually, proceed with the test sequence.

3. *Perform diagnostic procedure.* The procedure should be broken down into four categories: visual inspection, no start, cold driveability, and warm driveability. The customer can tell you the mode in which the problem occurs. Use *only* that procedure. There is no need to go through the no start test when the complaint is warm driveability.

Problems

Vacuum leaks will cause the system to operate richer than normal, and the owner may complain about poor fuel economy. This may be indicated in the warm driveability test procedure.

Fuel contamination of the crankcase will cause the oxygen feedback system to operate the engine leaner than normal. The owner complaint will be a surging condition. The warm driveability test procedure should be followed after the visual inspection. Fuel contamination of the crankcase can be suspected and/or extremely rich carburetion.

In order for the ignition and fuel systems to function properly, all electrical, vacuum, or air hose connections must be tight. Before proceeding with the diagnostic procedure, the following must be checked.

Electrical Connections

Terminals in connectors must lock together. Look for connectors that are not fully plugged into each other or terminals that are not fully plugged into the insulator.

1. *Ignition System Connections*
   (a) Connectors at computer
   (b) Pickup coil connector at distributor

(c) Spark plug wires

(d) Coil wire (cap and coil connections)

(e) Connectors at coil

(f) Starter relay

2. *Fuel Control System*

(a) Connector at vacuum delay switch (where applicable)

(b) Connector at coolant switch

(c) Connector at oil pressure switch

(d) Connector at choke

(e) Connectors at carburetor harness

(f) Carburetor ground

(g) Carburetor ground switch

(h) Engine harness to main harness connector

(i) Battery cables

(j) Battery ground on engine

(k) Engine to firewall ground strap

(l) O_2 sensor connector

Hose Connections

All hoses must be fully and firmly fitted to their connections. Also, they cannot be pinched anywhere along their routing. Look for hoses that are not fully plugged in or are pinched or cut.

1. *PCV System*

(a) Hose between intake manifold and PCV valve

(b) PCV valve plugged in

(c) Correct PCV valve

2. *Computer*

(a) Hose between vacuum transducer and carburetor

(b) Hose at vacuum delay switch (where applicable)

(c) Air intake hose

3. *EGR System*

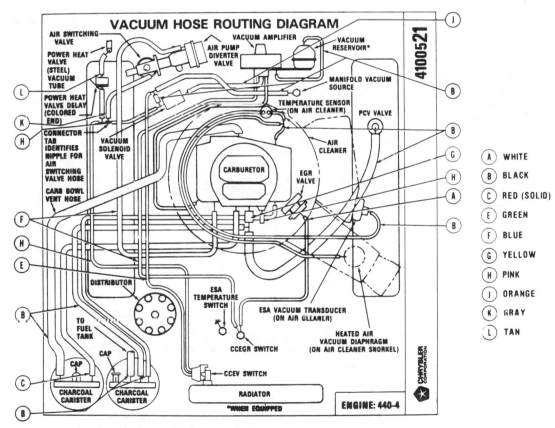

FIGURE 17-27. A vacuum hose routing diagram label is located in the engine compartment in the area near or next to the emission-control label. This label shows the location of all the components in the emission-control system. *(Courtesy of Chrysler Corporation)*

(a) Hose between carburetor and coolant vacuum valve

(b) Hose between coolant vacuum valve and EGR valve

4. *Air Switching System*

(a) Hose between carburetor and coolant vacuum valve

(b) Hose between coolant vacuum valve and air switching/relief valve

(c) Hose between air pump and air switching/relief valve

(d) Hose between air switching/relief valve and exhaust manifold

(e) Hose between air switching/relief valve and plumbing to catalyst

5. *Evaporative Control System*

(a) Hose between carburetor and external bowl vent valve

(b) Hose between external bowl vent valve and canister

(c) Hose between external bowl vent valve and air switching/relief valve

(d) Hose between canister and carburetor

(e) Hose between canister and fuel tank line

6. *Choke System*

(a) Hose between carburetor and connectors

(b) Hoses to:
(1) choke pull off diaphragm
(2) heated air door sensor

7. *Heated Air Door System*

(a) Hose between air sensor and delay valve

(b) Hose between delay valve and door diaphragm

(c) Hose between air cleaner and exhaust manifold heat stove

8. *Power Brakes and/or Speed Control (Where Applicable)*

(a) Hose between manifold and power brake booster

(b) Hose between power brake booster and speed control servo, or intake manifold and speed control servo

9. *Heater/AC System*

(a) Vacuum hose at water valve

(b) Vacuum supply hose to instrument panel control

| FORD | FORD MOTOR COMPANY | SHIFT SCHED. | MAINT. SCHED. | B |
| | VEHICLE EMISSION CONTROL INFORMATION | | | |

ENGINE FAMILY 302 'D'' (1CVS) EGR/CATALYST/PCV*

ENGINE DISPLACEMENT 302 CID

SPARK PLUG ARF 52 GAP .048 .052

VALVE LASH	HYD – NOT ADJ			
TRANSMISSION/GEAR		AUTO/NEUT	AUTO/DRIVE	MAN/NEUT
IGNITION TIMING		6° BTDC		
TIMING RPM		500		
CHOKE SETTING		INDEX		
FAST IDLE RPM	HIGH CAM	2100		
	KICKDOWN			
CURB IDLE RPM	A/C		650	
	NON-A/C		650	
TSP OFF RPM	A/C			
	NON-A/C			
IDLE MIXTURE ARTIFICIAL ENRICHMENT RPM				
STD. FLOW PCV VALVE	GAIN	30-110		
	RESET	40-80		
HIGH FLOW PCV VALVE	GAIN	80-180		
	RESET	80-120		

MAKE ALL ADJUSTMENTS WITH ENGINE AT NORMAL OPERATING TEMPERATURE. A/C AND HEADLIGHTS OFF. CONSULT SERVICE PUBLICATIONS FOR ADDITIONAL INSTRUCTIONS ON THE FOLLOWING PROCEDURES.

IGNITION TIMING – ADJUST WITH HOSES DISCONNECTED AND PLUGGED AT THE DISTRIBUTOR; AND AT THE VACUUM SWITCH, IF EQUIPPED WITH CCT SYSTEM.

CURB IDLE – ADJUST WITH ALL VACUUM HOSES CONNECTED. AIR CLEANER IN POSITION AND THROTTLE SOLENOID POSITIONER ENERGIZED (IS SO EQUIPPED).

IDLE MIXTURE – PRESET AT THE FACTORY. DO NOT REMOVE THE LIMITER CAP(S). EXCEPT IN ACCORDANCE WITH SERVICE PUBLICATIONS.

*REPLACE PCV WITH HIGH FLOW VALVE NO. EV 93 AT AND AFTER 30,000 MILES.

CATALYST

D7BE-9C485-MA   7-025

FIGURE 17–28. The emissions information label is located in the engine compartment. Such labels are required by law, and each vehicle has a label containing information applicable to the engine in that vehicle. The following items are included on each label: engine displacement and engine family identification; model year; curb idle speed settings: timing, rpm, mixture for altitudes below 4000 feet; statement that the vehicle conforms to either California or U.S. Environmental Protection Agency requirements, or both. *(Courtesy of Ford Motor Co. of Canada Ltd.)*

PART 12 EGR SYSTEM DIAGNOSIS AND SERVICE

Sometimes EGR can cause problems that appear to be malfunctions in other systems and vice versa. Usually, if not always, EGR will cause roughness if it operates when it should not: idle, WOT, cold starts, and warm-up. Or EGR could cause spark knock if it fails to operate when hot.

EGR System Inspection

Inspect all hose connections between carburetor, intake manifold, coolant control valve, and EGR valve. Replace or repair any leaking connections or hoses that are hardened or cracked.

Check the EGR valve operation with the engine warm and running. Idle the engine for 70 seconds with the carburetor throttle closed (and the transmission in neutral and wheels blocked). Snap open the throttle to reach an engine speed of at least 2000 rpm but not more than 3000 rpm. Observe the valve stem groove for movement relative to the mounting block. Repeat the procedure several times. Movement indicates proper operation. Faulty operation should be detected by following the diagnosis tests.

EGR Diagnosis

- If the EGR valve stem does not move, apply vacuum (at least 10 inches Hg [254.0 mm Hg]) to the valve. Replace the valve if it fails to open. Clamp the vacuum supply hose. The valve should be replaced if it does not stay open for at least 30 seconds.

- If the EGR valve checks out (as above) but does not open during engine operation, bypass the coolant control valve with a separate vacuum hose. If EGR valve stem movement is restored, replace the coolant control valve or repair the vacuum supply hose.

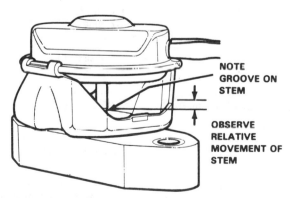

NOTE GROOVE ON STEM

OBSERVE RELATIVE MOVEMENT OF STEM

FIGURE 17–29. EGR valve action may be checked by observing valve stem movement as engine is accelerated from idle to 2000 rpm. (Courtesy of Chrysler Corporation)

- If engine idle is rough, disconnect the EGR valve vacuum hose. If rough idle continues, remove the valve for inspection and clean or replace as necessary. If disconnecting the hose restores smooth idle, take a vacuum reading at the supply hose. If the vacuum exceeds 1 inch Hg (25.4 mm Hg) on the gauge, check carburetor idle adjustment, or check for throttle plates binding in the carburetor bore(s).

EGR Valve Service

An open EGR valve, whether stuck from deposits, incorrect hose routing, or a faulty coolant vacuum switch cold closed valve, will cause rough idle and low-speed performance. For engines using fuel containing lead, the EGR valve must be cleaned according to the recommended maintenance interval and procedure. Otherwise, maintenance is limited to inspection.

PART 13 AIR INJECTION SYSTEM DIAGNOSIS AND SERVICE

Air Pump System

For satisfactory emission control and engine durability, it is important that the air pump be operating at all times (except when performing tests). For proper operation of the air pump, it is necessary that the air pump drive belt be in good condition and adjusted to the specified tension. Check the condition of the air pump belt and adjust the tension according to specifications at least every oil change.

The air pump is not a serviceable item. When necessary, replace it with a new pump. Do not disassemble the pump for any reason. Do not clamp the pump in a vise or use a hammer or pry bar on pump housing.

Cover the air pump centrifugal filter fan when pressure-washing or steam cleaning the engine to prevent liquids from entering the pump. The pump does not require lubrication. Wipe clean any oil on the pump housing. Oil can deteriorate the pump mechanism.

Air System

1. If the pump is excessively noisy, check the belt tension and condition and repair if necessary. If the noise continues, disconnect the drive belt temporarily, and run the engine. If the noise stops, examine the pump for cause. Replace if necessary.

2. If the system emits "air-leaking" noises, inspect each of the hoses, connections, and mounting locations for leaks.

3. If the switch/relief or diverter valve does not change air direction, apply a vacuum pump to the valve port and check for proper operation.

4. A hissing noise may indicate a defective pulse air valve or improper torque at manifold. Inspect the pulse air valve.

5. If one or more check valves have failed, exhaust gas will enter the carburetor through the air cleaner and cause poor driveability indicated by a surge or poor performance. Check the pulse air valve.

6. If exhaust gases pass through the pulse air valve, excessive heat is transmitted to the valve body, indicated by burned off paint. Also, rubber hose will deteriorate. Failure will be indicated by a hissing noise. Replace the air valve as required.

7. If the rubber hose to the air cleaner deteriorates, particles may enter the carburetor causing poor driveability. It will be necessary to clean the carburetor and replace the pulse air valve.

Exhaust Gas Analysis

To determine the levels of HC and CO present in the exhaust gases, an infrared analyzer is used. The analyzer is equipped with a probe which is inserted in the tailpipe of the vehicle or in the exhaust system ahead of the catalyst. A sample of exhaust gases is picked up by the probe and delivered to the analyzer. Two dials on the face of the analyzer indicate the HC and CO levels present in the exhaust. The HC meter indicates the amount in parts per million (ppm). The CO meter indicates the amount in percentage. Many emissions charts indicate maximum allowable levels in grams per mile (gpm). A conversion chart must be used to convert ppm of HC and percentage of CO to grams per mile. Conversion charts must be obtained from the equipment manufacturer or the federal or state regulating authorities.

It is important to remember when using the infrared analyzer that probing the exhaust downstream from the converter is not an accurate method of analyzing pollution levels produced by the en-

THE INFRARED EXHAUST EMISSION SYSTEM DIAGNOSIS CHART

	IDLE	1000 RPM	2000 RPM	TEST RESULTS	TYPICAL MALFUNCTIONS	RECOMMENDATIONS
CO 1				Normal	Poor point action. Open plug wire or fouled plug.	Recheck with scope.
HC	High	High	High	High all speeds		
CO 2				Normal	Vacuum leak affecting one cylinder.	Check for vacuum leak.
HC	High	High	High	Unsteady		
CO 3	Low	Low	Low	Low	General vacuum leak.	Check for general vacuum leak.
HC	High	High		High at low rpm	Should decrease at higher rpm.	
CO 4	High			High at idle	PCV valve restricted or carburetor idle mixture misadjusted.	Check the PCV valve or adjust the carburetor.
HC				Above normal		
CO 5	High	High	High	High at all rpm	Dirty air cleaner choke malfunction or carburetor malfunction.	Replace the air cleaner, service the choke, overhaul carburetor.
HC				Above normal		
CO 6	High	High		High at low speeds	Rich carburetor adjustment.	Adjust the carburetor to specification.
HC	High			High at idle		
CO 7				Normal	Ignition misfire at high speed or floating exhaust valves.	Recheck with scope.
HC			High	High at high rpm		
CO 8				Normal	Compression loss or vacuum leak.	Check compression and manifold vacuum.
HC	High			High at idle only		
CO 9	Low			Very low at idle only	Lean carburetor adjustment.	Adjust carburetor to specification.
HC	High			High at idle only		

APPROX. SPEED

FIGURE 17-30. Typical test sequence and problem diagnosis using the Infrared Exhaust Analyzer.

gine. The catalyst may in fact be overworked and overheated in attempting to reduce excessive emissions produced by the engine. Some vehicles are equipped with exhaust analysis probing access plugs ahead of the catalyst. Be sure to follow equipment and vehicle manufacturer's recommendations as well as federal and state regulations regarding procedures and emission levels, pages 579 to 588.

PART 14 SELF-CHECK

1. List the three major pollutants and describe each one briefly.

2. The three areas in the automobile that are responsible for emissions are as follows:
   (a) _____ for about _____ percent.
   (b) _____ for about _____ percent.
   (c) _____ for about _____ percent.

3. How does the PCV system work?

4. What is the purpose of the charcoal canister?

5. List five engine design modifications used to help control emissions.

6. Why is a vacuum control used on some heat riser valves?

7. List six fuel system design features used to control emissions.

8. Describe the engine operating conditions during which EGR is:
   (a) required
   (b) not required

9. Computer controlled EGR is regulated by a _____ solenoid.

10. Air injection system air may be diverted to:
    (a) _____
    (b) _____
    (c) _____

11. What is the purpose of the pulse air system?

PART 15 TEST QUESTIONS

1. The requirements to produce smog are:
   (a) oxides of nitrogen
   (b) unburned hydrocarbons
   (c) sunshine and still air
   (d) all of the above

2. The positive crankcase ventilation system controls approximately what percentage of automotive emissions?
   (a) 50 percent
   (b) 40 percent
   (c) 60 percent
   (d) 20 percent

3. The charcoal canister stores gasoline vapors when:
   (a) engine is running
   (b) engine is running at low speed
   (c) engine is running at high speed
   (d) engine is not running

4. Exhaust emissions constitute what percentage of total vehicle emissions?
   (a) 80 percent
   (b) 20 percent
   (c) 60 percent
   (d) 40 percent

5. The EGR valve may be controlled by:
   (a) ported vacuum
   (b) venturi vacuum
   (c) exhaust back pressure
   (d) any of the above

6. The diverter valve is used in the:
   (a) catalytic converter
   (b) EGR system
   (c) air injection system
   (d) fuel supply system

7. The air injection system is pumping air downstream into the exhaust between the two catalysts. Mechanic A says the system is in open loop operation. Mechanic B says the system is in closed loop operation. Who is right?
   (a) Mechanic A
   (b) Mechanic B
   (c) both are right
   (d) both are wrong

8. If the EGR valve stem does not move under any engine operating condition the cause could be:
   (a) a faulty vacuum line
   (b) a faulty coolant switch
   (c) a seized EGR valve
   (d) any of the above

9. A noisy air injection pump could be caused by:
   (a) incorrect belt tension or a faulty belt
   (b) an air leak
   (c) a worn air pump
   (d) any of the above

10. A high CO level at all engine speeds could be caused by:
    (a) a dirty air cleaner
    (b) a faulty choke
    (c) a high float level
    (d) any of the above

Section 4

ELECTRICAL AND ELECTRONIC SYSTEMS

The use of electricity in automobiles has steadily increased over the years. Electricity is used by such systems and components as follows:

- Ignition system
- Starting system
- Charging system
- Lighting system
- Horns
- Wipers and washers
- Heating
- Air conditioning
- Power seats
- Power windows
- Power door locks
- Speed control
- Instrumentation
- Computers
- Emission-control systems

A thorough understanding of how electricity acts is necessary for the automotive technician to be able to intelligently diagnose and service each system and its components.

Chapter 18

Batteries

Performance Objectives

After thorough study of this chapter and the appropriate training models and test equipment you should be able to:

1. Complete the self-check and the test questions with at least 80 percent accuracy.
2. State the purpose of the lead acid storage battery.
3. Describe the basic construction features of the battery.
4. Describe the basic operation of the battery during charging and discharging cycles.
5. Clean and test any automotive battery and interpret the test results to determine whether the battery is serviceable.
6. Diagnose basic battery problems.
7. Charge any automotive battery needing a charge.
8. Replace a battery as required.
9. Prepare the vehicle for customer acceptance.

PART 1   PURPOSE AND CONSTRUCTION

The purpose of the lead-acid battery in the automobile is to provide electrical energy to the following:

• The starting system, whenever needed; and the ignition system

• The lighting system

• The accessories (all power equipment, heating, air conditioning, radios, and tape players—whenever the charging system is not able to perform these functions)

The battery is also a sort of electrical shock absorber or voltage stabilizer for any abnormal stray voltages created by any of the automobile's various electrical systems.

Battery Cell

Each cell in the battery is made up of a number of positive plates and a number of negative plates separated by insulating separator plates. Negative and positive plates are arranged alternately in each cell. All the negative plates are connected to each other and so are the positive plates. This arrangement provides a positive cell connection and a negative cell connection. This assembly is submerged in a cell case full of battery electrolyte, which is 64 percent water and 36 percent sulfuric acid.

Each battery cell produces approximately 2 volts, regardless of the number or size of plates per cell. Six of these 2-volt cells arranged in a single battery case form a 12-volt battery. The battery case is usually made of polypropylene. The case has built-in cell dividers and sediment traps. The six battery

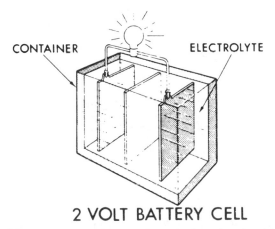

CONTAINER   ELECTROLYTE

2 VOLT BATTERY CELL

FIGURE 18-1. A wet battery is a device that is able to convert chemical energy to electrical energy. The chemical action can be reversed to recharge the battery. *(Courtesy of Ford Motor Co. of Canada Ltd.)*

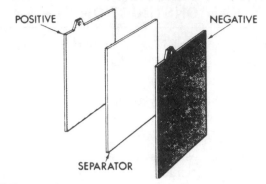

FIGURE 18-2. The basic components required in a battery cell. *(Courtesy of Ford Motor Co. of Canada Ltd.)*

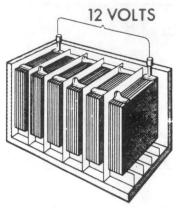

FIGURE 18-4. Assembling six 2-volt cells and connecting them in series inside a single battery case creates a 12-volt battery. *(Courtesy of Ford Motor Co. of Canada Ltd.)*

cells are connected in series. This means that the positive side of a cell is connected to the negative side of the next cell throughout all six cells. If the cells were connected in parallel (positive to positive and negative to negative), the battery would have only a 2-volt potential.

Battery Polarity

The positive plate group in one end cell of a battery is connected to the positive battery external terminal. This terminal is identified in one of the following ways: POS, +sign, or red-colored terminal. The tapered positive post is also larger in diameter than the negative post.

The negative plate group at the other end of the battery is connected to the external negative battery terminal. It can be identified as follows: NEG or −sign on terminal. The tapered negative post is

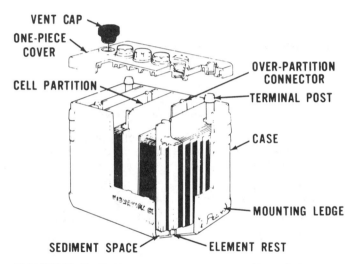

FIGURE 18-5. Battery case components. Note that partitions separate the cells from each other. *(Courtesy of Ford Motor Co. of Canada Ltd.)*

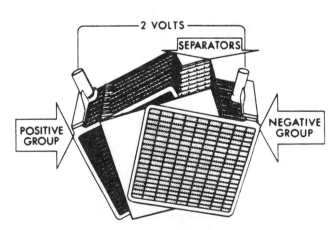

FIGURE 18-3. Automotive battery cells have a number of positive and negative plates insulated from each other by separator plates. Increasing the number of plates increases the surface area exposed to chemical action, thereby increasing capacity. Regardless of the number of plates per cell, each cell is capable of producing only approximately 2 volts. *(Courtesy of Ford Motor Co. of Canada Ltd.)*

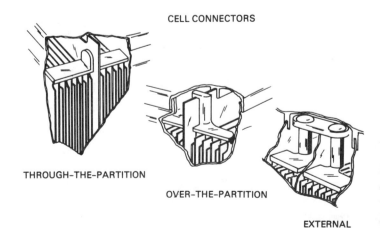

FIGURE 18-6. Different types of cell connectors. Sealed top batteries use the internal type of cell connectors. *(Courtesy of Ford Motor Co. of Canada Ltd.)*

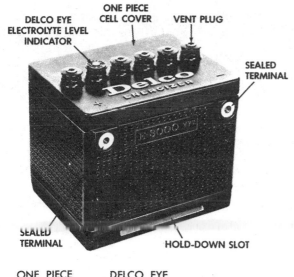

FIGURE 18-7. Battery manufacturers do not always use the same types of battery terminals or terminal locations. *(Courtesy of General Motors Corporation)*

end. Connections must be clean and tight to prevent arcing, corrosion, and high resistance.

PART 2 BATTERY TYPES

Wet and Dry Charged Batteries

Batteries are generally shipped without any electrolyte. These batteries are charged wet at the factory. The electrolyte is then removed and the cell plates dried out before shipment. Dry charged batteries can be stored longer than wet batteries. When a dry charged battery is put in use, it is filled to the correct level with electrolyte and activated by a short period of charging before installation.

Battery sales outlets may store wet batteries rather than dry batteries if their sales volume is high enough whereby batteries are not in storage for any significant length of time.

Maintenance-Free Batteries

The maintenance-free battery has cell plates made of a slightly different compound. This reduces the amount of vaporization that takes place during normal operation. This type of battery is also not as easily overcharged.

The battery is completely sealed except for a small vent so that acid and vapors cannot escape. An expansion chamber allows internal expansion and contraction to take place. Since vapors cannot escape from this battery, it is not necessary to periodically add water to the battery. This also reduces the possibility of corrosion and surface

smaller in diameter than the positive post. Proper battery polarity must always be adhered to when working with automotive electrical systems. With the exception of some older European and Asian models prior to 1971 as well as North American cars prior to the mid 1950s, all cars are 12-volt negative-grounded systems.

Battery Cables

Battery cables must be of sufficient current-carrying capacity to meet all electrical loads. Normal 12-volt cable size usually is 4 gauge (19 mm²) or 6 gauge (13 mm²). Various cable clamps and terminals are used to provide a good electrical connection at each

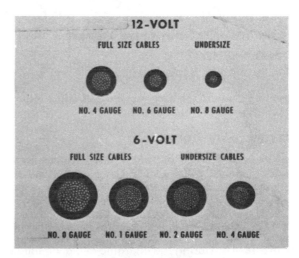

FIGURE 18-8. Comparison of battery cable diameters. *(Courtesy of Chrysler Corporation)*

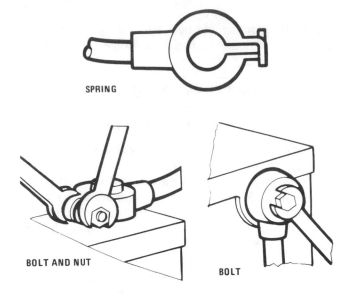

SPRING

BOLT AND NUT

BOLT

FIGURE 18-9. Three types of battery cable connectors. *(Courtesy of Chrysler Corporation)*

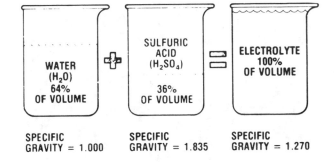

WATER (H₂0) 64% OF VOLUME

SULFURIC ACID (H₂SO₄) 36% OF VOLUME

ELECTROLYTE 100% OF VOLUME

SPECIFIC GRAVITY = 1.000

SPECIFIC GRAVITY = 1.835

SPECIFIC GRAVITY = 1.270

FIGURE 18-10. Composition and specific gravity of battery electrolyte. *(Courtesy of Chrysler Corporation)*

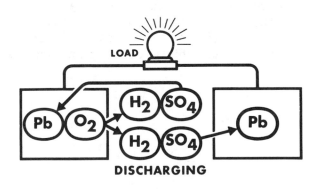

FIGURE 18-11. Chemical action inside battery as current is being used and battery is discharging. P_B is sponge lead, O_2 is oxygen; therefore, P_BO_2 is a lead oxide. H_2 is hydrogen, SO_4 is sulfate; therefore H_2SO_4 is sulfuric acid.

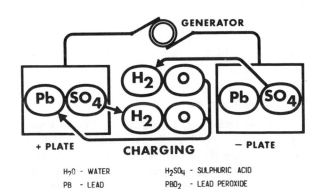

H_2O - WATER H_2SO_4 - SULPHURIC ACID

PB - LEAD PBO_2 - LEAD PEROXIDE

FIGURE 18-12. During the charging cycle, chemical action inside the battery is the reverse of that shown in Figure 18-11.

AH Rating	Cranking Power at 0°F
48	325A
59	375A
70	440A
85	500A

FIGURE 18-13. Battery rating comparisons. Ampere hour rating is determined as follows: discharge the battery at 1.20 × AH rating of battery for 20 hours at 80°F (26.6°C). The battery voltage should not drop below 1.75 volts per cell under these conditions. Cranking power at 0°F is defined as follows: cranking load in amperes that a battery is able to deliver for 30 seconds at 0°F without falling below 7.2 volts for a 12-volt battery.

discharge due to electrolyte on the surface of the battery.

Some maintenance-free batteries have a built-in hydrometer indicating the state of charge of the battery. Others cannot be tested with a hydrometer since they are sealed.

PART 3 CHEMICAL ACTION

Charging and Discharging

In operation, the battery is normally being partially discharged and recharged. This is actually a constant reversing of the chemical action taking place in the battery. The continual cycling of the charge and discharge modes slowly wears away the active materials on the battery cell plates. This eventually causes the battery positive plates to oxidize. When this oxidizing has reached the point of insufficient active plate area to charge the battery, the battery is worn out and must be replaced.

PART 4 BATTERY RATINGS

Battery capacity ratings are established by the Battery Council International (BCI) and the Society of Automotive Engineers. Commonly used ratings are as follows:

- Cold cranking
- Reserve capacity

Battery Freezing Temperatures			
Specific Gravity	Freezing Temp.	Specific Gravity	Freezing Temp.
1.280	−90°F	1.150	+ 5°F
1.250	−62°F	1.100	+19°F
1.200	−16°F	1.050	+27°F

FIGURE 18-14. Specific gravity of battery electrolyte at which electrolyte will freeze is shown. *(Courtesy of Ford Motor Co. of Canada Ltd.)*

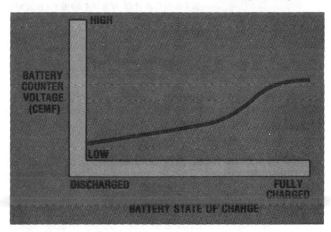

FIGURE 18-15. As the battery becomes fully charged, the battery's resistance to charging system output increases. Very little current is required to keep a battery in a fully charged condition if no current is being consumed. *(Courtesy of Chrysler Corporation)*

- Ampere-hour
- Watt-hour

Cold Cranking. The load in amperes a battery is able to deliver for 30 seconds at 0°F (−17.7°C) without falling below 7.2 volts for a 12-volt battery.

Reserve Capacity. The length of time in minutes a battery can be discharged under a specified load at 80°F (26.6°C) before battery cell voltage drops below 1.75 volts per cell.

Ampere Hour. Discharge the battery at one twentieth times the ampere hour rating for 20 hours

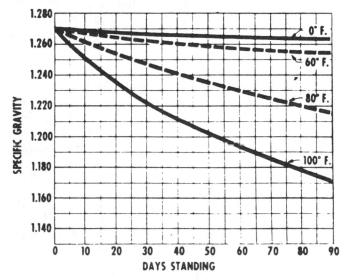

FIGURE 18-16. Self discharge rates of batteries in storage at various temperatures and time periods. The least discharge occurs at the lower temperatures. *(Courtesy of Battery Council International)*

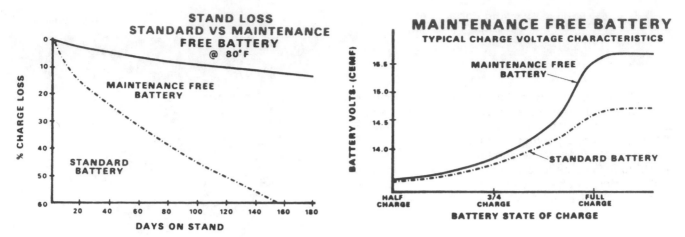

FIGURE 18-17. Comparison of resistance to charging (CEMF—Counter electromotive force) (above) and percentage of charge loss over a given time period (below) between standard battery and maintenance-free battery. *(Courtesy of Battery Council International)*

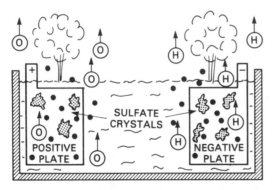

FIGURE 18-18. A battery becomes sulfated due to a discharged condition. Hardened sulfate crystals penetrate the pores of the plates. These crystals become insoluble. Prolonged charging at a low rate is required to restore it. Charging a sulfated battery at too high a rate can buckle the plates and destroy the battery. A battery that has been sulfated for too long cannot be restored.

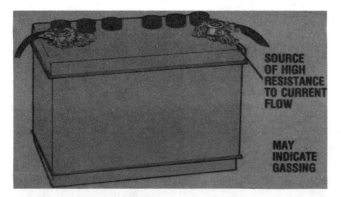

FIGURE 18-19. A charging rate that is too high will cause gassing and will result in sulfate deposits at the battery terminals. Electrolyte on the terminals can also cause the creation of deposits. *(Courtesy of Chrysler Corporation)*

at 80°F (26.6°C) without cell voltage falling below 1.75 volts per cell. This term was used for many years in the rating of storage batteries. The term and the method have been replaced by Cold Cranking and Reserve Capacity ratings described above.

Watt Hour. Ampere hours times battery voltage yields the watt-hour rating.

Factors that determine the battery rating required for a vehicle include engine size and type and climatic conditions under which it must operate. Battery power drops drastically as temperatures drop below freezing. As the temperature drops much below freezing, the engine is harder to crank owing to increased friction resulting from oil thickening.

The correct shape, physical size, post location, and battery rating requirements must all be considered when replacing a battery.

It takes one ampere of cold cranking power per cubic inch of engine displacement. Therefore, a 200 CID engine should have a battery with a cold cranking capacity of 200 amperes. In metric terms, it takes 1 ampere of cold cranking capacity for every 16 cubic centimeters of engine displacement. A 1.6 liter engine (1600 cm³) should have a battery with a cold cranking capacity of 100 amperes.

PART 5 BATTERY DIAGNOSIS AND SERVICE

The battery is the heart of the various electrical systems in the automobile. Since this is so, it is important not to overlook the battery when servicing the electrical system.

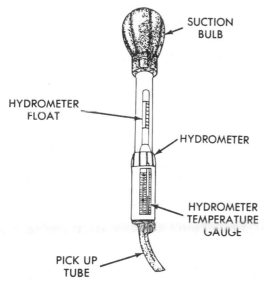

FIGURE 18-20. Components of a typical battery hydrometer used to check the specific gravity of battery electrolyte to determine the battery state of charge. *(Courtesy of Chrysler Corporation)*

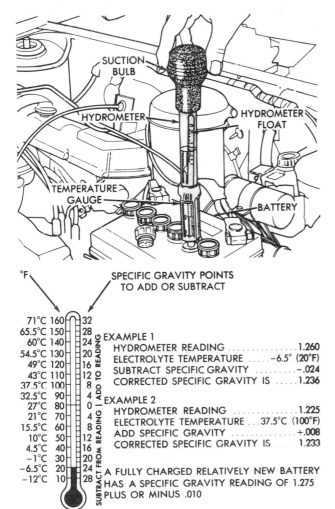

FIGURE 18-21. To accurately determine the state of charge of a battery, the reading must be temperature corrected as shown here. *(Courtesy of Chrysler Corporation)*

EXAMPLE 1
HYDROMETER READING 1.260
ELECTROLYTE TEMPERATURE . . . . .–6.5° (20°F)
SUBTRACT SPECIFIC GRAVITY . . . .–.024
CORRECTED SPECIFIC GRAVITY IS 1.236

EXAMPLE 2
HYDROMETER READING 1.225
ELECTROLYTE TEMPERATURE . . .37.5°C (100°F)
ADD SPECIFIC GRAVITY . . . .+.008
CORRECTED SPECIFIC GRAVITY IS 1.233

A FULLY CHARGED RELATIVELY NEW BATTERY HAS A SPECIFIC GRAVITY READING OF 1.275 PLUS OR MINUS .010

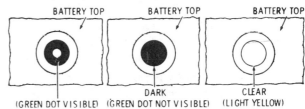

FIGURE 18-22. Maintenance-free battery with built-in, color-coded hydrometer readings. Green = charged; dark, no dot = discharged; clear = replace battery. *(Courtesy of General Motors Corporation)*

General Precautions

To avoid personal injury and property damage, it is important to observe safe procedures when servicing or replacing lead-acid batteries. The following precautions, if observed properly, can prevent accidental injury or damage.

1. Battery acid is extremely corrosive. Avoid contact with skin, eyes, and clothing. If battery acid should accidentally get into your eyes, rinse thoroughly with clean water and see your doctor. Contacted skin should be thoroughly washed with clean water; some baking soda with the wash will neutralize the action of the acid. Painted surfaces and metal parts are also easily attacked by acid, and contact should be avoided.

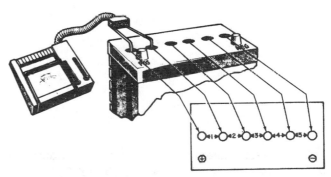

FIGURE 18-23. Individual battery cell voltage tester. *(Courtesy of Chrysler Corporation)*

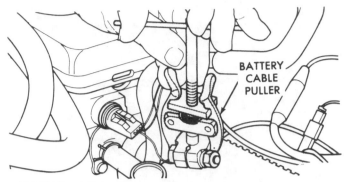

FIGURE 18-24. Since it is easy to damage battery posts, the correct tools should be used to remove battery cables. *(Courtesy of Chrysler Corporation)*

2. When making connections to a battery in or out of the vehicle, always observe proper battery polarity: positive to positive and negative to negative.

3. Avoid any arcing (sparks) or open flame near battery. The battery produces highly explosive vapors that can cause serious damage if accidentally ignited.

4. When disconnecting battery cables always remove ground cable first; and when connecting cables, always connect ground cable last. This helps to avoid accidental arcing.

5. Observe equipment manufacturer's instructions when charging batteries. Never allow battery temperature to exceed 125°F (51.6°C).

6. Some battery manufacturers place restrictions on the use of a booster battery to jump start. Follow battery manufacturer's recommendations. One manufacturer says, "Do not charge, test, or jump start this battery when the built-in hydrometer is clear or yellow: battery must be replaced."

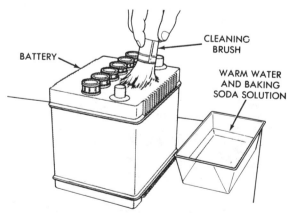

FIGURE 18-25. Cleaning the battery with a water and baking soda solution neutralizes battery electrolyte. Solution should not be allowed to enter battery. *(Courtesy of Chrysler Corporation)*

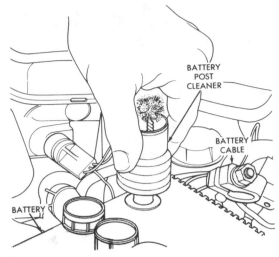

FIGURE 18-26. Battery post cleaner has internal wire brush. *(Courtesy of Chrysler Corporation)*

7. Use proper battery carrier to handle the battery; this avoids injury and possible battery damage.

8. Use proper protective clothing (apron, gloves, and face shield) when handling batteries to ensure safety.

9. Do not weld or smoke near a battery charging or storage area.

Emergency Jump Starting with Auxiliary (Booster) Battery

Notice: Do not push or tow the vehicle to start. Damage to the emission system and/or other parts of the vehicle may result. Do not jump start the ve-

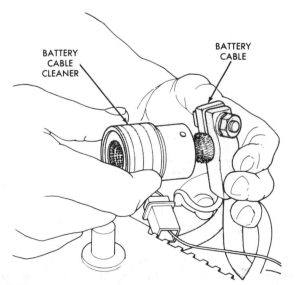

FIGURE 18-27. Cleaning battery cable clamp. *(Courtesy of Chrysler Corporation)*

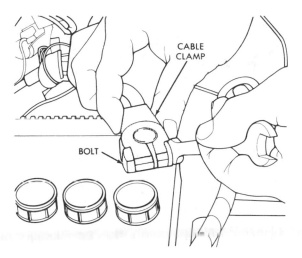

FIGURE 18-28. Battery connections must be clean and tight. Do not overtighten or break post loose. *(Courtesy of Chrysler Corporation)*

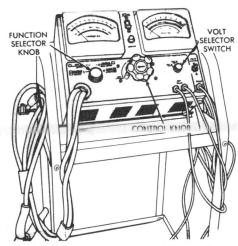

FIGURE 18-29. Equipment used to load test a battery. Unit includes voltmeter, ammeter, a variable resistor operated by the control knob, a function selector knob, a volt selector switch, and the required leads and connectors. *(Courtesy of Chrysler Corporation)*

hicle unless the manufacturer of the battery or the vehicle with a dead battery allows this procedure.

Both the booster and discharged battery should be treated carefully when using jumper cables. Follow the procedure outlined below, being careful not to cause sparks.

Caution: Departure from these conditions or the procedure below could result in (1) serious personal injury (particularly to eyes) or property damage from such causes as battery explosion, battery acid, or electrical burns; and/or (2) damage to electronic components of either vehicle.

Never expose a battery to an open flame or electric spark—batteries generate a gas that is flammable and explosive.

Remove rings, watches, and other jewelry. Wear

approved eye protection. No smoking. Do not jump start a battery with a frozen electrolyte.

Do not allow battery fluid to contact eyes, skin, fabrics, or painted surfaces—its fluid is a corrosive acid. Flush any contacted area with water immediately and thoroughly. Be careful that metal tools or jumper cables do not contact the positive battery terminal (or metal in contact with it) or any other metal on the car because a short circuit could

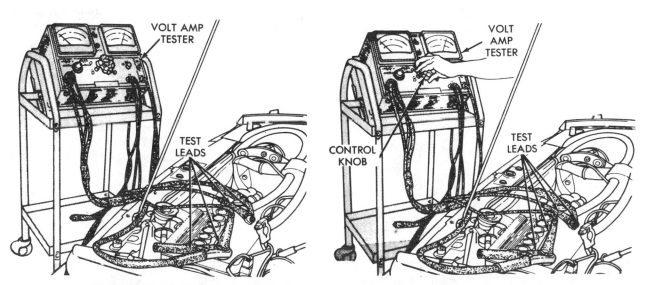

FIGURE 18-30. Battery capacity (load) tester connections and load being applied to battery. Follow procedure in text. *(Courtesy of Chrysler Corporation)*

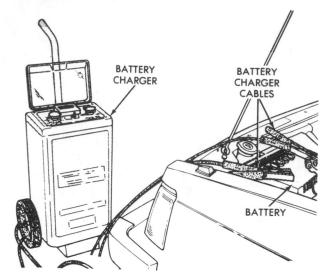

FIGURE 18-31. Charging battery in vehicles. Battery cables should be removed from battery posts for charging to prevent damage to vehicle electrical system. *(Courtesy of Chrysler Corporation)*

occur. Batteries should always be kept out of the reach of children.

1. Set the parking brake and place automatic transmission in *PARK* (*NEUTRAL* for manual transmission). Turn off the ignition, lights, and all other electrical loads.

2. Check the built-in hydrometer. If it is clear or light yellow, replace the battery.

3. Only 12-volt batteries can be used to start the engine. For systems other than 12-volt, or other

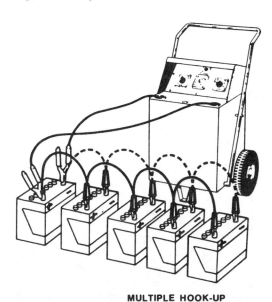

MULTIPLE HOOK-UP

FIGURE 18-32. Charging a number of batteries at the same time. Batteries are connected in parallel so combined battery voltage remains at 12 volts. *(Courtesy of Ford Motor Co. of Canada Ltd.)*

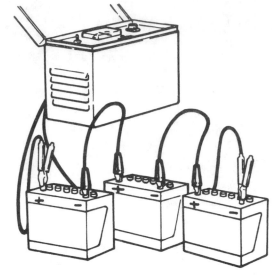

CONSTANT-CURRENT SLOW CHARGING

FIGURE 18-33. Many types of battery slow chargers are available. Always follow equipment manufacturer's instructions for hook up and charging rates. These batteries are connected in series. *(Courtesy of Ford Motor Co. of Canada Ltd.)*

than negative ground, consult the appropriate service manual.

Notice: When jump starting a vehicle with special high rate charging equipment, be sure charging equipment is 12-volt negative ground. *DO NOT* use 24-volt charging equipment. Using such equipment can cause serious damage to the electrical system.

4. Attach the end of one jumper cable to the positive terminal of the booster battery and the other end of the cable to the positive terminal of the discharged battery. Do not permit vehicles to touch each other because this could cause a ground connection and counteract the benefits of the procedure.

5. Attach one end of the remaining negative cable to the negative terminal of the booster battery, and the other end to a solid engine ground (such as A/C compressor bracket or generator mounting bracket) at least 18 inches from the battery of the vehicle started. (*DO NOT CONNECT DIRECTLY TO THE NEGATIVE TERMINAL OF THE DEAD BATTERY*).

6. Start the engine of the vehicle that is providing the jump start and turn off electrical accessories. Then start the engine in the car with the discharged battery.

7. Reverse these directions exactly when removing the jumper cables. The negative cable must be disconnected from the engine that was jump started first.

Standard Battery Service

Proper battery service includes the following:

• Visual inspection of battery, battery cables, battery stand, and hold down for leakage, corrosion, and dirt.

• Check electrolyte level and specific gravity. If electrolyte is too low, add sufficient distilled water to raise electrolyte to correct level. After adding water, battery must be charged before a valid specific gravity test can be performed.

Determine battery state of charge with hydrometer or with expanded scale voltmeter. The battery must be stabilized (surface charge removed) before checking state of charge.

To stabilize a battery after charging, apply 15-ampere load for 15 seconds by turning the headlights on bright beam for 15 seconds; then proceed with testing. The following open circuit voltage figures are for batteries at 80°F (26.7°C).

Open Circuit Volts	Percent Charge
11.7 or less	0%
12.0	25%
12.2	50%
12.4	75%
12.6 or more	100%

Charging the Battery

Standard Battery Charging Guide (12-Volt and 6-Volt Batteries)

Caution: Do not use for maintenance-free batteries. Recommended rate and time for fully discharged condition.

RATED BATTERY CAPACITY (RESERVE MINUTES)	SLOW CHARGE	FAST CHARGE
80 minutes or less	14 hours @ 5 amperes 7 hours @ 10 amperes	1-¾ hours @ 40 amperes 1 hours @ 60 amperes
Above 80 to 125 minutes	20 hours @ 5 amperes 10 hours @ 10 amperes	2-½ hours @ 40 amperes 1-¾ hours @ 60 amperes
Above 125 to 170 minutes	28 hours @ 5 amperes 14 hours @ 10 amperes	3-½ hours @ 40 amperes 2-½ hours @ 60 amperes
Above 170 to 250 minutes	42 hours @ 5 amperes 21 hours @ 10 amperes	5 hours @ 40 amperes 3-½ hours @ 60 amperes
Above 250 minutes	33 hours @ 10 amperes	8 hours @ 40 amperes 5-½ hours @ 60 amperes

If a battery is to be left on charge overnight, use only the slow charge rate. Charge maintenance-free batteries at rates given in Step 2, below. After charging, stabilize the battery before repeating state of charge tests.

If time is available, the lower charging rates in amperes are recommended; they must be used when a battery may have a problem (i.e., if it is sulfated or has a temperature below 15°F (−26.1°C).

• Check individual cell voltage on batteries where this applies. Minimum cell voltage should not vary more than 1/10 volt between cells. If it does, replace battery.

• Clean battery, cables, and battery carrier of vehicle. The cable terminals should be cleaned before connecting them to the battery. After the connections have been made, apply a thin coating of petroleum jelly on the post and cable terminals to retard corrosion. Never hammer cable terminals onto battery posts. The covers, undercover post connections, or post-to-cover connections could be severely damaged. Do not over-torque the terminal bolts of side terminal batteries. The threads may strip or the battery could be damaged.

Common Torque Valves

Tapered terminal posts (SAE): 50–70 lb. in.
  Side terminals 70 lb. in.
Use a baking soda and water solution after removing the battery. Clean the battery, battery stand, and battery cables with this solution. Do not allow solution to enter battery. Rinse with clear water.

• Battery load test.
Follow the procedure in Step 3, below.

Maintenance-Free Battery Service

Step 1 Inspection.
Visually inspect the battery and service the cables and battery carrier as in standard battery service above.

Step 2 Electrolyte Levels and State of Charge.
Check the electrolyte level in the cells if possible. The level can be seen through translucent plastic cases. It can also be checked in batteries that are not sealed. If the electrolyte level is below the tops of the plates in any cell, add water if the vents are removable. If the battery is sealed and water cannot be added to it, replace the battery and check the charging system for a malfunction, such as a high voltage regulator setting. Follow instructions of

BATTERY CAPACITY (RESERVE MINUTES)	SLOW CHARGE
80 minutes or less	10 hours @ 5 amps 5 hours @ 10 amps
Above 80 to 125 minutes	15 hours @ 5 amps 7-½ hours @ 10 amps
Above 125 to 170 minutes	20 hours @ 5 amps 10 hours @ 10 amps
Above 170 to 250 minutes	30 hours @ 5 amps 15 hours @ 10 amps
Above 250 minutes	20 hours @ 10 amps

manufacturer if the battery has a special indicating device.

If the level is O.K. and the stabilized open circuit voltage is below 12.4 volts, charge the battery using a constant potential taper charger. The initial charge rate should not exceed 30 amperes and should taper down to rates given here.

General Motors Delco Sealed Batteries

When it is necessary to charge the battery, the following basic rules must be followed:

1. Do not charge battery if hydrometer is clear or light yellow. Replace battery.

2. If the battery feels hot 125°F (52°C), or if violent gassing or spewing of electrolyte through the vent holes occurs, discontinue charging or reduce charging rate.

Charge the battery until the green ball appears. Tipping or shaking the battery may be necessary to make the green ball appear. Temperature of the battery will affect the charging rate, and most charging equipment will not charge at a constant rate. For example, if the charger starts at 30 amperes and drops off to 10 amperes after 1 hour, the average current for that hour was 20 amperes. The actual boost charge was 20 ampere-hours. The sealed battery can be fast charged or slow charged with ordinary chargers in the same manner as conventional batteries. Either method will restore the battery to full charge.

Many chargers have special settings for sealed batteries. These settings reduce the charge voltage and limit the current. It is not necessary to use these settings with these sealed batteries.

Step 3 Load Test Procedure.
The load test procedure is conducted to determine if the battery requires recharging or replacement. Test each battery separately.

1. Disconnect the battery cables (ground connection first) and connect the voltmeter and load test leads to the battery terminals, making sure the load switch on the tester is in the *OFF* position.

2. Apply a test load equal to 1/2 the cold cranking amperes rating @ 0°F (−18°C) of the battery for 15 seconds; for example, if a battery has a cold cranking rating @ 0°C of 350 amperes, use a test load of 175 amperes.

3. Read the voltage at 15 seconds and remove the load. If the voltage is less than the minimum specified below, replace the battery.

MINIMUM VOLTS	ESTIMATED ELECTROLYTE TEMPERATURE	
9.6	70° F	(21° C) and above
9.5	60° F	(16° C)
9.4	50° F	(10° C)
9.3	40° F	(4° C)
9.1	30° F	(− 1° C)
8.9	20° F	(− 7° C)
8.7	10° F	(− 12° C)
8.5	0° F	(− 18° C)

If the voltage meets or exceeds the specified minimum, clean the battery and return it to service.

If the battery tests well but fails, for no apparent reason, to perform satisfactorily in service, the following are some of the more important factors that may point to the cause of trouble:

1. Vehicle accessories left on overnight

2. Slow average driving speeds for short periods

3. The electrical load is more than the generator output, particularly with the addition of after market equipment

4. Defects in the charging system, such as electrical shorts, slipping fan belt, faulty generator, or voltage regulator

5. Battery abuse, including failure to keep the battery cable terminals clean and tight or loose battery hold-down

6. Mechanical problems in the electrical system, such as shorted or pinched wires

PART 6 SELF-CHECK

1. What is the purpose of the automotive battery?

2. Battery electrolyte consists of _____ percent water and _____ percent sulfuric acid.

3. What is the specific gravity of pure water?

4. Battery voltage increases as the number of plates per cell is increased. True or false?

5. The two battery ratings in present use are _____ _____ and _____.

6. The state of charge of a battery can be checked by using either a _____ or a _____.

7. Describe how to perform a battery load test.

8. Battery vapors are highly explosive. True or false?

PART 7   TEST QUESTIONS

1. Battery electrolyte consists of approximately:
   - (a) 35 percent sulfuric acid and 65 percent water
   - (b) 65 percent sulfuric acid and 35 percent water
   - (c) 35 percent muriatic acid and 65 percent water
   - (d) 65 percent muriatic acid and 35 percent water

2. A battery cell consists of:
   - (a) positive plates, negative plates, sponge plates, lead plates
   - (b) insulator plates, positive plates, negative plates, electrolyte
   - (c) sulfuric acid, electrolyte positive plates, negative plates
   - (d) sponge plates, lead plates, antimony plates, cadmium plates

3. Battery cells are connected in:
   - (a) series
   - (b) parallel
   - (c) series-parallel
   - (d) none of the above

4. A car is brought into the shop with a dead battery. What should be done?
   - (a) replace the battery
   - (b) test the battery and charge it
   - (c) charge the battery and test it
   - (d) jump start the car

5. The following should be considered when replacing a battery.
   - (a) physical size and post location
   - (b) cold cranking capacity and reserve capacity
   - (c) engine size and climatic conditions
   - (d) all of the above

Chapter 19

Electrical Principles

A remarkable electric system is housed under the hood of automobiles; it produces electrical energy, stores it in chemical form, and delivers it on demand to any of the auto's electrical systems—from low voltages (12 volts or less) to high voltage surges of upwards of 30,000 volts.

Many components and accessories are operated by electricity: the starter motor that cranks your engine, the ignition system that keeps your car running once started, the headlight and signal light systems that light the road and signal your intentions to other vehicles, the heater and the defroster, the radio, the gauges, and the air conditioning.

These are but a few applications of electricity in the automobile.

A thorough understanding of how electricity acts is necessary for the automotive technician to be able to intelligently diagnose and service each system and its components.

PART 1   ELECTRICITY

Electricity behaves according to definite rules that produce predictable results and effects. The rules of electricity can best be explained by looking at the structure of an atom. An atom is composed of a complex arrangement of negatively charged electrons in orbit around a positively charged nucleus—much like our moon revolves around the earth. The nucleus consists of protons (positively charged particles) and neutrons (particles with no charge) tightly bound together. The nucleus exerts an attractive force on the electrons (due to its positive charge) holding them within fixed orbits around the nucleus.

The electrons are free to move within their orbits at fixed distances around the nucleus. When two electrons approach each other, they repel each other because they are negatively charged. The electrons try to stay as far away from each other as they can get without leaving their orbits.

Any substance composed of identical atoms (atoms all having the same number of electrons, protons, and neutrons) is called an element. When a substance is made of more than one element, each bound chemically together, it is called a compound. Electrically speaking, there are three types of substances: conductors, insulators, and semi-conductors. A conductor is capable of supporting the flow of electricity through it and an insulator is not. The difference is that the outermost electrons in a conductor's atoms are loosely held by the nucleus, whereas an insulator's atoms hold its outermost electrons very tightly. The electrons in the atoms of a conductor can be freed from their outer orbits by

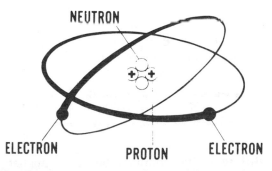

FIGURE 19-1. The principle of electricity can best be explained when the structure of an atom is understood. *(Courtesy of Chrysler Corporation)*

BALANCED

FIGURE 19-2. The electrons in an electrical conductor remain balanced (no electrical flow) until a force is applied that will knock some of the electrons out of their orbit. *(Courtesy of Chrysler Corporation)*

forces such as heat, light, pressure, friction, and magnetism. When electrons are knocked out of orbit, they can form an electrical current—under the proper conditions. When electrons in the atoms of a conductor are affected by a force, an unbalanced condition will occur in the atom between the negative charges of the electrons and the positive charges of the nucleus. The force tries to push the electron from its orbit. If an electron is freed from its orbit, the atom acquires a positive charge because it now has one more proton than electrons. The atom wants to return to an electrically balanced state. These unbalanced atoms attract electrons from the orbit of other balanced atoms to fill their empty orbit. This sets up a chain reaction of capturing and releasing electrons from one atom to another. These freed electrons try to move away from the force by transferring from one atom to the next through the conductor.

A stream of free electrons forms and an electrical current is born. The strength of the current depends on the strength of the affecting force.

An electrical current will continue to flow through the conductor as long as the electromotive force (EMF) is acting on the conductor's atoms and electrons. Stated in another way, current will continue to flow as long as a potential exists in the conductor, as long as there is a build up of excess electrons at the end of the conductor farthest from EMF, and as long as there is a lack of electrons at

FIGURE 19-3. The continuation of an applied force causing electrons to be knocked out of their orbit results in a flow of electrons. *(Courtesy of Chrysler Corporation)*

the EMF end. This is called a voltage difference or *potential.*

Producing Electricity

An electrical current can be formed under certain conditions by the following forces: friction, chemical, heat (thermal), pressure (piezo-electric), and magnetism (induction).

Friction

When two materials are rubbed together, frictional contact between them will actually rub some of the electrons from their orbits. This causes a transfer of electrons to one of the materials and a lack of electrons in the other material. This gives a *static negative charge* to one material and a *static positive charge* to the other. When these materials are brought close to a grounded object, a spark will jump between the materials and the grounded object. A negatively charged object has a surplus of electrons. A positively charged object has a lack of electrons.

This accounts for the behavior of like charges repelling each other and unlike charges attracting each other.

Pressure

Perhaps the best known use of electricity produced by pressure is the crystal in the arm of a record player or in the diaphragm of a crystal microphone. Crystals of certain materials, such as quartz or Rochelle salt, develop a small electric charge when pressure is applied to them. When sound waves strike the diaphragm of a microphone, mechanical pressure is transferred to the crystal. This causes the crystal to flex and bend, producing a small voltage at its surface. This voltage is of the same frequency and amplitude as the incoming sound. This current is then amplified. This is called a piezo-electric effect.

Heat

A direct conversion of heat to electricity can be accomplished by heating a bimetallic junction of twisted wires made from two dissimilar metals like copper and iron. This type of junction is called a thermocouple.

Producing electricity in this manner is called *thermal conduction.* Since thermocouples cannot produce large amounts of electrical current, they are used as heat-sensing units. The amount of electrical current generated is dependent on the difference in temperature between the bimetallic junction of the thermocouple and the opposite ends of the wire. The greater the temperature difference, the greater the flow of current and voltage produced. An example of this in the automobile is the oxygen (O_2) sensor.

PART 2 MAGNETS AND MAGNETISM

Magnetism produces nearly all the electricity used in our homes, offices, and industries. The alternator in your car uses magnetism to produce the electrical current to run electrical systems and keep the battery fully charged.

There are two kinds of magnets—natural and artificial. All magnets have *polarity*—like the earth, they have a north and a south pole. *Like poles* (N-N, S-S) repel, while *unlike* or *opposite poles* (N-S) attract each other.

Natural magnets are found in the earth in the form of a black iron ore called *magnetite,* which will attract pieces of iron and steel. If you suspend these materials on a string, they will align themselves with the earth's magnetic north pole.

Artificial magnets can be produced by putting pieces of iron, steel, or certain alloys of aluminum and nickel (called *ALNICO*) in an intense magnetic field. These substances will acquire all the magnetic properties of magnetite, only stronger. The softer metal magnets (iron magnets) eventually lose their magnetic properties. The harder magnets made of steel and alnico tend to retain their magnetic properties indefinitely.

An electromagnet is made by wrapping a soft iron or steel core with a coil of insulated wire. When the ends of the wire are connected to an electric current, the steel or iron core acquires all the properties of a natural magnet but many times stronger. The iron core serves to concentrate the magnetism in an area surrounding the electromagnet.

Magnetic force is invisible. The only way we know it exists is by the effect it produces. A magnet's action can best be explained as having invisible lines of force (a *magnetic field*) leaving the magnet at one end or pole and reentering the magnet at the other end. These invisible lines of force are called *flux lines.* The shape and space they occupy is called a *flux pattern.* The number of lines of flux per inch is called the *flux density.* Flux lines are continuous and unbroken; they do not cross each other. The strength of the magnetic field is dependent on the flux density. The stronger the magnetic field, the greater the flux density.

Electricity and magnetism are very closely related. Magnetism can be used to produce electricity, and electricity can be used to produce magnetism. This is why generators and alternators produce electricity and motors use magnetism to produce mechanical energy. Whenever a magnetic field is passed through a conductor, a voltage is produced

in that conductor—current begins to flow. When a lamp is connected to the ends of a conductor, a current will flow, lighting the lamp. This is called *electromagnetic induction.* This is the principle behind all generators and alternators.

Two types of magnets are used in the automobile's electrical system—the permanent magnet and the electromagnet. Invisible lines of force (magnetic field) are present between the north and south poles of magnets. These lines of force have direction; in other words, they exert a force from the north pole to the south pole by convection. This force is utilized to induce an electrical current in a generator to produce electricity. It is also used in a starting motor to "push" a group of rotating conductors (armature) to start the engine, as well as for many other functions.

PART 3 HOW ELECTRICITY FLOWS THROUGH A CONDUCTOR

Keep in mind these six rules of electrical behavior:

1. All electrons repel each other.

2. All like charges repel each other. (Negatively charged objects repel other negatively charged objects; positively charged objects repel other positively charged objects.)

3. Unlike charges attract each other. (Positively charged objects attract negatively charged objects and vice versa.)

4. Electrons flow in a conductor only when affected by an electromagnetic force (EMF).

5. A voltage difference is created in the conductor when an EMF is acting on the conductor. Electrons flow only when a voltage difference exists between the two points in a conductor.

6. Current tends to flow to *ground* in an electrical circuit. Ground is defined as the area of lowest voltage. Electrical current moves through a conductor to ground in an attempt to reach a balance or equilibrium with the ground voltage (which is zero).

When electrons are set into motion, they display a variety of behaviors. The behavior of electrons moving through a conductor accounts for the many things electricity can do for you. By understanding how electricity behaves, you will be able to understand the function and operation of the various automotive electrical systems. This will aid you in diagnosing automotive electrical problems.

Let us turn our attention to a single copper atom in a conductor. The copper atom has a single electron in its outermost orbit. This electron is not tightly held by the nucleus, and it can easily be freed by an electromotive force (EMF).

Once an electron escapes from its orbit, it is free to move—possibly colliding with other atoms in the conductor. As the free electron approaches the outer orbit of another copper atom, its electrostatic force starts to interact with the electron in orbit, repelling it. At the same time it is repelling this electron, the nucleus of that atom is attracting the free electron into its orbit. The free electron now enters the copper atom's orbit, replacing the ejected electron. As more and more electrons collide with other atoms in the conductor, an electrical current begins.

Once EMF is applied, it causes electrons to be freed from their orbits. This starts a chain reaction between the electrons and atoms in the conductor, causing the freed electrons to move away from the electromotive force. This effect is called *electron drift* and accounts for how electrons flow through a conductor. Whenever electrons flow or drift in mass, an electrical current is formed.

Voltage

Voltage can be described as an electrical pressure. In the automobile the battery or generator is used to apply this pressure. The amount of pressure applied to a circuit is stated in the number of volts. Another term for voltage is *electromotive force*. The symbol for electromotive force is E. The symbol for volts is V.

Current

Current can be described as the rate of electron flow. Current is measured in amperes. Current will in-

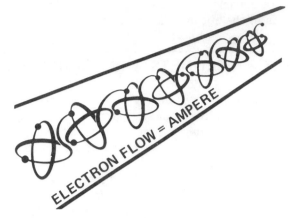

FIGURE 19-5. Current resulting from the pressure difference is measured in amperes. *(Courtesy of Chrysler Corporation)*

crease as pressure or voltage is increased—provided that circuit resistance remains constant.

Another term for amperes is intensity of current. The symbol for current intensity is I. The symbol for amperes is A.

Resistance

Resistance in an electrical circuit is measured in ohms. The ohm is the unit of resistance (and of impedance) in the International System of Units (SI). The ohm is the resistance of a conductor such that a constant current of one ampere in it produces a voltage of one volt between its ends. The size and type of material used as a conductor, as well as its length and temperature, will determine the resistance of the conductor. The symbol for ohms is the Greek letter omega, Ω.

Conductors and Insulators

Conductors or wires of heavier cross-section are required for high-amperage current; smaller conductors can be used for low-amperage current. If too light a conductor is used, the conductor will overheat and actually melt the wire. Low-voltage conductors do not require heavy insulation. High-

FIGURE 19-4. The rate of current is dependent on the strength of the applied force or voltage (pressure) and the resistance to electron flow. *(Courtesy of Chrysler Corporation)*

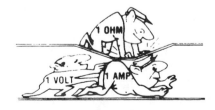

FIGURE 19-6. The flow of electrons encounters resistance in the form of lamp filaments, motor windings, resistors, and the conductors themselves. Resistance is measured in ohms. *(Courtesy of Chrysler Corporation)*

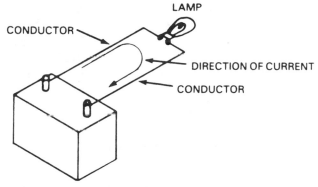

FIGURE 19-7. The lamp is brightly lit due to the current passing through it.

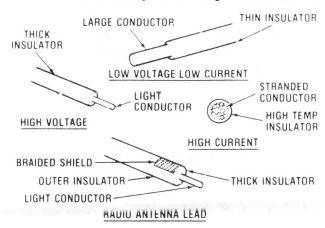

RADIO ANTENNA LEAD

FIGURE 19-9. Different types of insulators and conductors are used in the automobile to carry the flow of electricity. Large-diameter conductors are required for high-amperage flow. Heavily insulated smaller-diameter conductors are used for low-amperage, high-voltage flow. *(Courtesy of Chrysler Corporation)*

voltage conductors such as sparkplug wires require a heavy insulator to prevent current from jumping through the insulator to ground.

Ohm's Law

Ohm's law states that the current in an electric circuit is inversely proportional to the resistance of the circuit, and is directly proportional to the electromotive force (emf) in the circuit. Ohm's law applies only to linear constant-current circuits.

An electric circuit has a resistance of one ohm when an applied voltage (emf) of one volt causes current at the rate of one ampere. The equivalent equation would be:

$$R = \frac{E}{I}, \text{ or } R = \frac{V}{I},$$

where R is resistance, in ohms; E is the applied emf, in volts; V is the voltage drop across the resistance, in volts; and I is the resulting current through the resistance, in amperes. The use of E or V for voltage is determined by the circuit. E represents a voltage (emf or potential rise) of a power source such as a battery, a generator, or a battery charger. V represents the voltage drop (or potential fall) that occurs in the electric circuit connected to the power source. For normal operation, E (of the source) $= V$ (of the circuit).

$I = E/R$ or $I = V/R$ with the same symbolic meanings as before. A further rearrangement of this formula allows one to find the voltage drop across a resistance; thus, $V = IR$.

To summarize:

voltage, V (in volts) $= I$ (in amperes) $\times R$ (in ohms)

$$\text{current, } I \text{ (in amperes)} = \frac{E \text{ (in volts)}}{R \text{ (in ohms)}} \quad \text{or}$$

$$I \text{ (in amperes)} = \frac{V \text{ (in volts)}}{R \text{ (in ohms)}}$$

$$\text{resistance, } R \text{ (in ohms)} = \frac{E \text{ (in volts)}}{I \text{ (in amperes)}} \quad \text{or}$$

$$R \text{ (in ohms)} = \frac{V \text{ (in volts)}}{I \text{ (in amperes)}}$$

OHM'S LAW

$$\text{AMPERES} = \frac{\text{VOLTS}}{\text{OHMS}}$$

$$\text{OHMS} = \frac{\text{VOLTS}}{\text{AMPERES}}$$

$$\text{VOLTS} = \text{AMPERES} \times \text{OHMS}$$

FIGURE 19-10. There is a definite relationship between volts, amperes, and ohms. Ohm's law can be used to calculate any one unknown factor when the other two are known. *(Courtesy of Chrysler Corporation)*

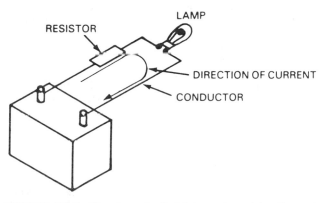

FIGURE 19-8. The lamp's light is reduced by the addition of a resistor (resistance) in the current path.

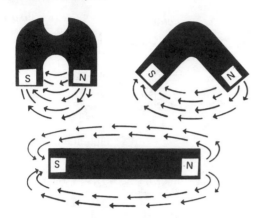

FIGURE 19-11. Permanent magnets have a north pole and a south pole regardless of physical shape. Invisible magnetic lines of force are present between the two poles. The direction of these lines of force is always from the north magnetic pole to the south magnetic pole.

In shorter form (without unit specifications), $V = IR$, $I = E/R$, or $I = V/R$, $R = E/I$, or $R = V/I$.

Here is an example of the application of one of the above equations. A vehicle with a 12-volt battery has a starting system in which the starting motor draws 150 amperes (A) of current. The resistance (R) of the starting motor circuit could be found by use of the equation:

$$R = \frac{E}{I}. \text{ Therefore } R = \frac{12\ (V)}{150\ (A)} = 0.08\ \Omega$$

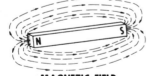

MAGNETISM & PERMANENT MAGNETS

MAGNETIC FIELD

UNLIKE POLES ATTRACT

LIKE POLES REPEL

FIGURE 19-12. Due to the direction of the magnetic lines of force, the opposite poles of two magnets will attract each other, while like poles of two magnets will repel each other.

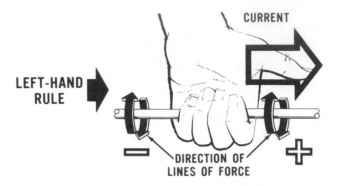

FIGURE 19-13. In the electron theory, current is from negative to positive. In this case, the left hand can be used with the thumb pointing in the direction of current. The fingers then point in the direction of the magnetic field. *(Courtesy of Chrysler Corporation)*

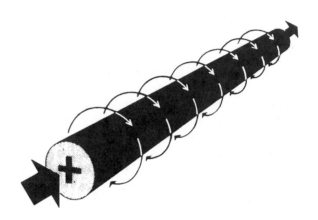

FIGURE 19-14. Magnetic lines of force (magnetic field) exist around a current-carrying conductor. In the conventional theory of current direction, current is said to be from positive to negative. Using the right hand as shown here, with the thumb pointing in the direction of current, the fingers indicate the direction of the magnetic field.

The large battery cables and heavy starter windings offer little resistance to current, as shown by this example.

PART 4   ELECTRICAL POWER

Electricity is a medium for conveying energy, and the rate of work done by electricity is called *power*. In terms of other electrical units, power (P) = voltage

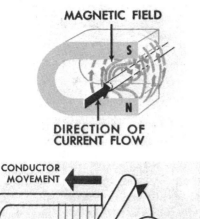

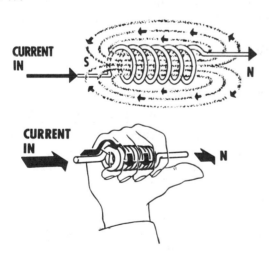

FIGURE 19-15. As a conductor is passed through a magnetic field, a current will be induced in the conductor. This principle is used to produce electricity in generators and alternators. *(Courtesy of General Motors Corporation)*

FIGURE 19-16. When a current-carrying conductor is wound in the form of a coil, the magnetic lines of force will be inside the coil and will be concentrated, making a stronger magnetic field. The polarity (direction) of these magnetic lines of force can be established by using the right hand with the fingers pointing in the direction of current in the coil winding. The thumb then points to the north pole. *(Courtesy of General Motors Corporation)*

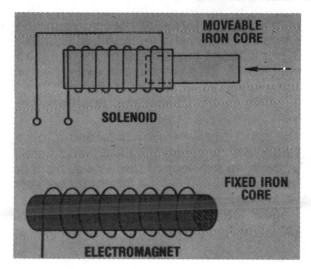

FIGURE 19-17. The magnetic lines of force can be further concentrated by the use of a soft iron core inside the coil. The soft iron core readily loses the induced magnetism when current in the coil is stopped. Examples of the use of this principle are the starter solenoid (movable iron core) and the ignition coil (fixed iron core). *(Courtesy of Chrysler Corporation)*

(E or V) × current (I), or $P=EI$. Also $P=VI$, where P is power in watts (W), E is an applied emf in volts, I is the current in amperes from the power source, and V is the voltage drop in volts, across the circuit resistance. Using the previous example of a 12-volt starting motor drawing 150 amperes, the power used by the motor would be: $P=EI=12$ $(V) \times 150$ $(A)=$ 1800 W.

Another example would be the calculation of the current drawn by a 12-volt, 60-watt headlight. Rearranging the power equation $P=VI$ gives $I=P/V$. Therefore the headlight current is:

$$I = \frac{P}{V} = \frac{60\ (W)}{12\ (V)} = 5\ A.$$

Horsepower ratings may be converted to electrical power ratings by use of the conversion factor: 1 horsepower (hp) = 746 watts (W) or 1 hp = 746 W.

PART 5   ELECTRICAL CIRCUITS

Every electrical system requires a *complete circuit* for it to function. A complete circuit is simply an uninterrupted path for electricity to flow from its source through all circuit components and back to the electrical source. Whenever the circuit is broken (interrupted), electricity will not flow. This interruption of current can be the result of a switch in the *off* position, a blown fuse, or an *open* (broken) wire.

There are basically three different types of electrical circuits: the series circuit, the parallel circuit, and the series-parallel circuit. An electrical system,

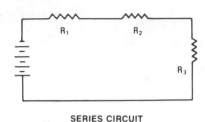

SERIES CIRCUIT

FIGURE 19-18. Three resistances (loads) are connected in series. *(Courtesy of Chrysler Corporation)*

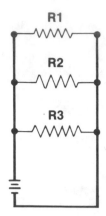

FIGURE 19-19. Parallel circuit showing three resistances (loads) connected in parallel. *(Courtesy of Chrysler Corporation)*

however, may have one or more or a combination of these circuits in the automobile.

Series Circuit

The series circuit provides only a single path for current from the electrical source through all the circuit's components and back to the electrical source. If any one component fails, the entire circuit will not function.

The total resistance in a series circuit is simply the sum of all the resistances in the circuit. For example, a series circuit (a light and two switches), would have a total resistance of 4 ohms if the light had a resistance of 2 ohms and the switches a resistance of 1 ohm each.

$$R = 2\,\Omega + 1\,\Omega + 1\,\Omega = 4\,\Omega$$

Parallel Circuit

A parallel circuit provides two or more paths for electricity to flow. Each path has separate resistances (or loads) and operates independently or in conjunction with the other paths in the circuit, depending on design. In this type of circuit, if one parallel path does not function, the other parallel sections of the circuit are not affected. An example of this is the headlight circuit; if one headlight is burned out the other headlight will still operate.

To calculate the total resistance in a parallel circuit, the following method must be used.

$$R = \frac{1}{\frac{1}{R1} + \frac{1}{R2} + \frac{1}{R3}} \text{ or } \frac{1}{R} = \frac{1}{R_1} + \frac{1}{R_2} + \frac{1}{R_3}$$

depending on the number of resistances and so on, that are in parallel.

If $R1$, $R2$, and $R3$ are 4, 6, and 8 ohms, respectively, total resistance would be calculated as follows:

$$R = \frac{1}{\frac{1}{4} + \frac{1}{6} + \frac{1}{8}}$$

$$= \frac{1}{\frac{6}{24} + \frac{4}{24} + \frac{3}{24}}$$

$$= \frac{1}{\frac{13}{24}} \text{ or } 1 \div \frac{13}{24}$$

$$= 1 \times \frac{24}{13} \text{ or } 1.85\,\Omega$$

In a parallel circuit the total resistance in the circuit will always be less than the lowest single device or resistance. The reason for this is that electricity has more than one path to follow.

Series-Parallel Circuits

A series-parallel circuit combines the series and the parallel circuits. To calculate total resistance in a series-parallel circuit, calculate the series portion of the circuit as stated above. Then calculate the parallel portion of the circuit and add to the series resistance.

Examples of a series-parallel circuit are shown in Figure 19-21 and 19-22. In Figure 19-21 the headlight and dimmer switches are in series, while the headlights are in parallel with each other.

Voltage Drop

As current passes through a resistance, circuit voltage across it will drop. Total voltage drop in an electrical circuit will always equal available voltage at the source of electrical pressure.

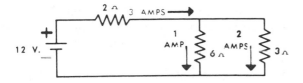

FIGURE 19-20. Series-parallel circuit. *(Courtesy of General Motors Corporation)*

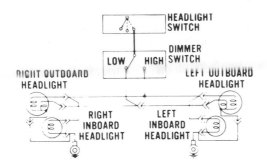

FIGURE 19-21. Headlamp circuit is an example of series-parallel circuit. *(Courtesy of Ford Motor Co. of Canada Ltd.)*

Circuit resistance, if excessive at any point, will result in excessive voltage drop across that portion of the circuit. The voltage drop method is commonly used to determine circuit resistance. The voltage

drop across a battery cable, for example, should not exceed 2/10 volt per 100 amps at 68°F (20°C).

The voltage drop method is the SAE recommended method for checking cable resistance. When checking voltage drop, the voltmeter is connected in parallel over the portion of the circuit being tested, and the results are compared to specifications.

Voltage drop can only be measured in a circuit when there is a flow of electricity present. With no electrical flow, the voltage (potential difference or pressure) remains the same anywhere in the circuit. Shop voltmeters are designed to indicate positive voltage potential on the upscale side of zero.

PART 6 OPENS, SHORTS, AND GROUNDS

Electrical systems may develop an *open* circuit, a *shorted* circuit, or a *grounded* circuit. Each of these conditions will render the circuit more or less ineffective.

Opens

An *open circuit* is a circuit in which there is a break in continuity. As stated earlier, for electricity to be able to flow there must be a complete and continu-

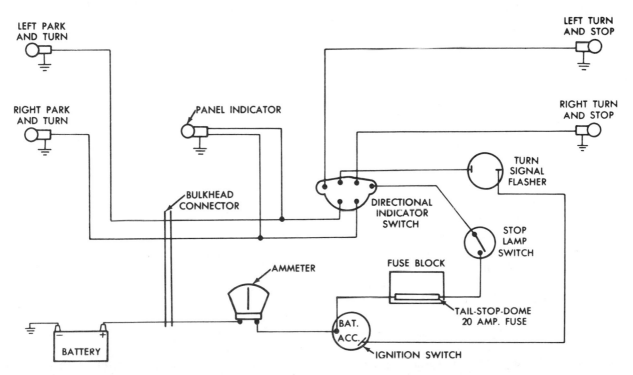

FIGURE 19-22. Turn signal circuit is another example of a series-parallel circuit. *(Courtesy of Chrysler Corporation)*

ous path from the electrical source through the circuit back to the electrical source. If this path is broken, the condition is referred to as an open circuit. An open circuit, therefore, is no longer operational and acts the same as if it were switched off.

Shorts

A *shorted circuit* is a circuit that allows current to bypass part of the normal path. An example of this would be a shorted coil. Coil windings are normally insulated from each other; however, if this insulation breaks down and allows copper-to-copper contact between turns, part of the coil windings will be bypassed. In an ignition coil primary winding, this condition would reduce the number of windings through which electricity will flow. If the short caused 50 windings of approximately 200 windings to be bypassed, this would reduce coil capacity by 25 percent.

Grounds

A *grounded circuit* is a condition that allows current to return to ground before it has reached its intended destination. An example of this would be a grounded tail light circuit. If the wire leading to the tail light has an insulation breakdown allowing the wire to touch the frame or body of the vehicle, electricity will flow to ground at this point and return directly to the battery without reaching the tail light.

PART 7 ELECTRICAL CIRCUIT DIAGNOSIS AND SERVICE PROCEDURE

A number of common tools and instruments are used to diagnose automotive electrical circuits. The most common are the test light, the jumper wire, the voltmeter, the ammeter, and the ohmmeter. The ammeter and voltmeter are often combined in a single piece of test equipment, which also may include a carbon pile resistor capable of applying varying loads to electrical circuits. The ohmmeter is often included in the multimeter, which is able to measure small amounts of current and voltage, as well as resistance.

Variations of equipment combinations are available from different manufacturers. Some of these types of multiuse test equipment will be dealt with

in the appropriate sections of this text. Examples include charging system testers, ignition system testers, and starting system testers, as well as oscilloscopes.

In every case both the test equipment manufacturer's instructions and the vehicle manufacturers instructions should be followed for proper and accurate diagnosis. Test sequences given by vehicle manufacturers should be followed for systematic problem identification. Test results must be compared to vehicle manufacturer's specifications and recommended repair procedures followed. In many cases, component replacement is recommended rather than component repair particularly when solid-state components are involved.

Figures 19–23 to 19–36 illustrate the use of the basic equipment required for testing electrical circuits.

Basic circuit testing and the use of basic test equipment follows here.

Jumper Wire

The simplest electrical troubleshooting tool is also one of the most important—a jumper wire. Make it at least a meter in length and use alligator clips on the ends.

Connect one end to battery positive and you have an excellent 12-volt power supply. Use it to check lamp bulbs, motors, or as a power feed to any 12-volt component. But be careful and don't drop the other end; any place you touch on the engine or body is *ground*—battery negative—big sparks and high current will result, possibly "cooking" the jumper wire!

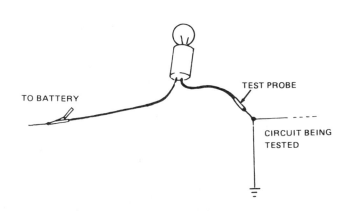

FIGURE 19-23. Using a jumper wire to bypass a switch that is suspected of being defective. *(Courtesy of Chrysler Corporation)*

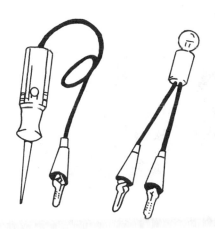

FIGURE 19-24. Two types of test lights for checking electrical circuits. *(Courtesy of Chrysler Corporation)*

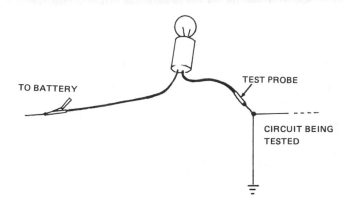

TO BATTERY

TEST PROBE

CIRCUIT BEING
TESTED

FIGURE 19-25. Testing continuity in a portion of a ground circuit. *(Courtesy of Chrysler Corporation)*

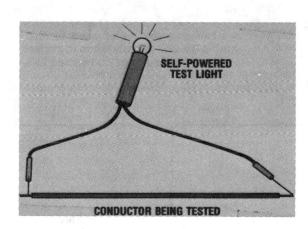

SELF-POWERED
TEST LIGHT

CONDUCTOR BEING TESTED

FIGURE 19-26. Battery-powered test light used to determine continuity in an electrical conductor. *(Courtesy of Chrysler Corporation)*

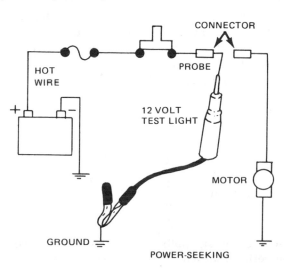

CONNECTOR

HOT
WIRE

PROBE

12 VOLT
TEST LIGHT

MOTOR

GROUND

POWER-SEEKING

FIGURE 19-27. Isolating portions of a circuit to determine faulty section of the circuit. *(Courtesy of Chrysler Corporation)*

FIGURE 19-28. Using a circuit-breaker type of tester across a blown fuse allows the circuit being tested to remain live in order to locate faulty portion of circuit with other test equipment. *(Courtesy of Chrysler Corporation)*

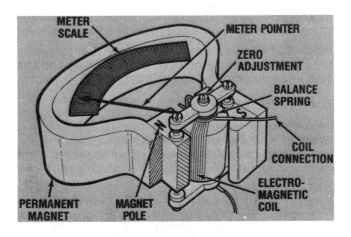

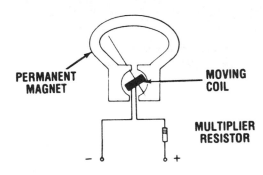

FIGURE 19-29. Typical voltmeter construction. The meter pointer is attached to a movable coil and is held at the 0 point on the scale by a coiled balance spring. As voltage is applied to the movable coil winding, it creates a magnetic field with opposite polarity to the permanent magnetic poles. Since opposite poles attract, the meter pointer will move up scale in direct proportion to the voltage applied. The voltmeter is used to test circuit voltage and voltage drop (resistance). The resistor determines the range of voltage that the voltmeter is able to measure. *(Courtesy of Chrysler Corporation)*

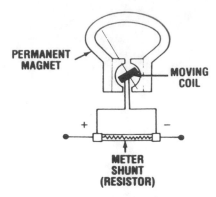

FIGURE 19-30. Ammeter construction is similar to voltmeter construction. The resistor here is connected in parallel, whereas in the voltmeter it is connected in series. The ammeter is used to measure the amount of current in a circuit and must always be connected into the circuit in series. Always connect voltmeter and ammeter leads to a circuit by connecting positive leads to positive side of circuit and negative leads to negative side of circuit. *(Courtesy of Chrysler Corporation)*

Test Lamp

Sometimes you want to *look* for power, rather than *supply* it. That's when a *test lamp* is perfect. Just ground one side and you can go to most "hot" 12-volt points in the car and the lamp will light. But sometimes it won't light up fully with a hot circuit. For example, if you test the circuit *after* the voltage has "dropped" over a load. Try it at the ballast resistor. The battery side will light the lamp, but the lowered voltage *after* the resistor will only cause the lamp to glow dimly.

Circuit Breaker

A circuit breaker reacts to excess current by heating, opening up, and cutting off the excess current. With no current flowing, the heating stops, and the breaker closes again and restores the circuit. If the high-current cause is still in the circuit, the breaker will open again. This cycling on and off will continue as long as the circuit is overloaded.

You can use a cycling breaker fitted with alligator clips in place of a fuse which keeps blowing. The circuit breaker will keep the circuit "alive" while you check the circuit for the cause of high current draw—usually a short.

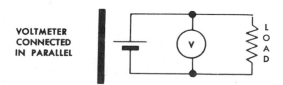

FIGURE 19-31. Method used to connect voltmeter properly. *(Courtesy of General Motors Corporation)*

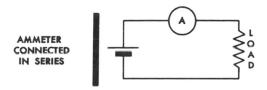

FIGURE 19-32. Proper method of connecting ammeter into circuit. *(Courtesy of General Motors Corporation)*

Voltmeter

A voltmeter is connected in parallel with a circuit—it reads directly in volts. In parallel the meter draws only a small current—just enough to sample the voltage. That's why you can "short" right across the battery terminals with a voltmeter without damaging it.

However, never try to check voltage by putting the meter in *series*. The voltmeter hookup should always parallel the circuit being measured because you don't want the high resistance meter disrupting the circuit in a series connection.

Closed Circuit Voltage. In Figure 19-36 the voltage at *A* is 12 volts positive. There is a drop of six volts over the 1.0-ohm resistor and the reading is 6 volts positive at *B*. The remaining voltage drops in the fan load and the voltmeter reads zero (12 volts negative) at *C* indicating normal motor circuit operation.

Open Circuit Voltage. Now we read the voltage in the same circuit as above but with *no* electricity flowing because there is an open circuit (broken wire or poor ground) at point *X*. The voltage at *A, B,* and *C* will be 12 volts positive indicating circuit continuity up to, but not through, point *X*. Remember, there is no voltage drop across a resistor or load if there is no electrical flow.

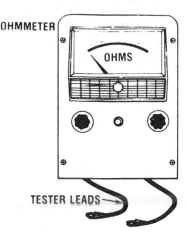

FIGURE 19-34. Typical ohmmeter used to test resistance and continuity in various electrical components. *(Courtesy of Chrysler Corporation)*

Ohmmeter

Another useful meter measures resistance. The ohmmeter is an excellent *continuity* checker, too. If you want to see if a wire is *continuous* or open inside a harness, clipping the ohmmeter leads to each end will show zero ohms (if the wire is good).

Just remember *never* to use an ohmmeter in a hot circuit. Always be sure there is no power (voltage or current) in the circuit when using an ohmmeter to avoid damaging it.

Ohmmeters have batteries for their power supply. For that reason, don't leave the ohmmeter connected for longer than necessary to read the scale or the batteries will run down.

FIGURE 19-33. Typical volts amps tester.

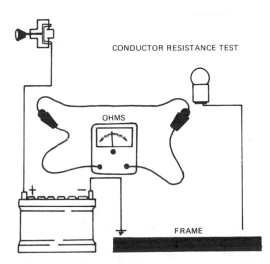

FIGURE 19-35. The ohmmeter is self-powered and should never be connected into a live circuit. Conductor has been removed from circuit to test resistance as shown here. *(Courtesy of Chrysler Corporation)*

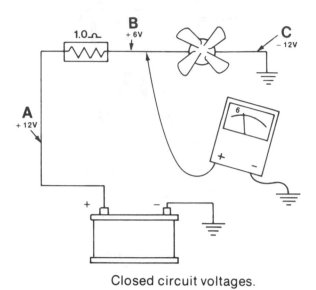

Closed circuit voltages.

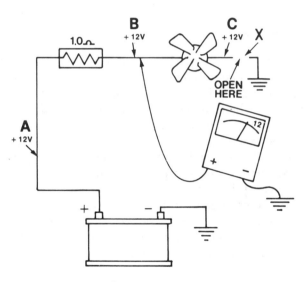

Open circuit voltages.

FIGURE 19-36. Using a voltmeter to isolate a problem in a motor circuit.

Ammeter

You measure current draw with an ammeter. But unlike the parallel voltmeter, you must put the ammeter *in series* with the load to read the current draw. That means disconnecting the load and reconnecting with all the current going through the meter. Polarity must be followed—the red lead going to the positive side. Be sure to use only the induction type of ammeter with the clamp type of induction pickup on computer equipped cars.

Always use an ammeter that can handle the expected current since excessive current can damage a meter. Also, never connect an ammeter across a

circuit (parallel) or you may damage the meter or the circuit.

WIRING TEST CHART

TYPE OF FAILURE	TEST UNIT AND EXPECTED RESULTS IF WIRING FAILED	
Open (Broken wire)	Ohmmeter —	Infinite resistance at other end of wire. Infinite to adjacent wire. Infinite to ground.
	Voltmeter —	Zero volts at other end of wire
Ground (bare wire touching frame)	Ohmmeter —	Zero resistance to ground. Infinite to adjacent wire. May or may not be infinite to other end of wire.
	Voltmeter —	Instead of testing, normally look for blown fuse or tripped circuit breaker.
Short (rubbing of two bare wires)	Ohmmeter —	Zero resistance to adjacent wire Infinite to ground. Zero to other end of wire.
	Voltmeter —	Voltage will be read on both wires.

PART 8   SELF-CHECK

1. Electron flow is caused by _____.
2. State Ohm's law.
3. What are the three common types of electrical circuits?
4. Like magnetic poles _____ and unlike poles _____.
5. All current-carrying conductors have a _____ surrounding the conductor.
6. Forming a conductor into a coil strengthens the _____ when the conductor carries current.
7. What causes voltage drop?
8. List four methods by which electricity can be produced.
9. What causes electron flow?
10. Define electrical opens, shorts, and grounds.

PART 9   TEST QUESTIONS

1. An atom consists of:
   (a) electrons, neutrons, and protons
   (b) positive, negative, and neutral electrons
   (c) positive electrons, negative protons, and neutrons
   (d) positive protons, negative neutrons, and electrons

2. Mechanic A says that all electrons repel each other. Mechanic B says unlike charges attract each other. Who is right?
   (a) Mechanic A
   (b) Mechanic B
   (c) both are right
   (d) both are wrong

3. Mechanic A says that $R = V \times I$. Mechanic B says that $I = E \times R$. Who is right?
   (a) Mechanic A
   (b) Mechanic B
   (c) both are right
   (d) both are wrong

4. Electrical power can be calculated as follows:
   (a) $P = IR$
   (b) $P = E \div R$
   (c) $P = E \div I$
   (d) $P = EI$

5. Total resistance in a circuit with three parallel resistances of 3 ohms, 4 ohms, and 6 ohms each is:
   (a) 7.5 ohms
   (b) 0.75 ohms
   (c) 75 ohms
   (d) .75 ohms

6. An automotive lighting circuit consists of components connected in:
   (a) series
   (b) parallel
   (c) series-parallel
   (d) all of the above

7. A switch suspected of being faulty may be checked with:
   (a) a jumper wire
   (b) a test light
   (c) an ohmmeter
   (d) any of the above

8. Circuit resistance can be tested with:
   (a) a jumper wire
   (b) a test light
   (c) an ohmmeter
   (d) any of the above

Chapter 20

Electrical and Electronic Devices

─── Performance Objectives ───

After sufficient study of this chapter, the appropriate training models, and shop manuals, you should be able to:

1. Complete the self-check and test questions with at least 80 percent accuracy.

2. Identify, on a vehicle specified by your instructor, any of the components covered in this chapter and describe their operations.

The automobile uses a wide variety of electric and electronic devices. These range from a very simple on-off switch to a computer capable of doing a multitude of jobs. The automotive technician should have a good basic understanding of how these devices operate in the automobile in order to successfully diagnose and correct electrical system problems.

The basic operation of these devices is described here, and examples of their use in an automobile are given as well.

PART 1   ELECTRICAL WIRING

Electrical wires may be one solid single strand, or a number of smaller wires twisted together to form a stranded wire. Wires are usually stranded for more flexibility in automotive wiring.

Wire diameter is specified in gauge sizes or in millimeters (mm²). Gauge sizes use numbers to indicate size. The smaller the gauge number is, the larger the wire diameter. The larger the metric number designation, the larger the wire cross section.

Large-diameter wires are required for circuits subject to high-current (amperes). Smaller-diameter wires are used for low current.

Heavy insulation is required for high-voltage wires (e.g., spark plug wires) and lighter insulation is used for low-voltage circuits. The uninsulated side of automobile electrical circuits uses the car frame and body for a return path. The insulated side of the circuit is sometimes called the live side.

General Motors Computer Command Control (CCC) wiring contains many special design features not found in standard vehicle wiring. Environmental protection is used extensively to protect electrical contacts. Special twisted and twisted/shielded cable is essential to system performance. Additionally, special high density connections are used in many of the wiring harnesses.

The current and voltage levels in the CCC system are very low. There are three types of cable construction used: straight wire, twisted wires, and twisted/shielded wires. Unwanted induced voltages are prevented from interfering with computer operation. Environmental deterioration by moisture, rust, and corrosion is prevented for the same reason.

Wire terminals and connectors include a great variety of types and sizes. Terminals and connectors are attached to wires by crimping, soldering the connection, or both. Terminals may be of the flat round hole, round male and female, flat male and

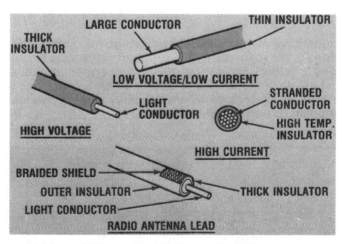

FIGURE 20–1. Different types of insulators and conductors are used in the automobile to carry the flow of electricity. Large-diameter conductors are required for high amperage. Heavily insulated smaller-diameter conductors are used for low amperage, high voltage. *(Courtesy of Chrysler Corporation)*

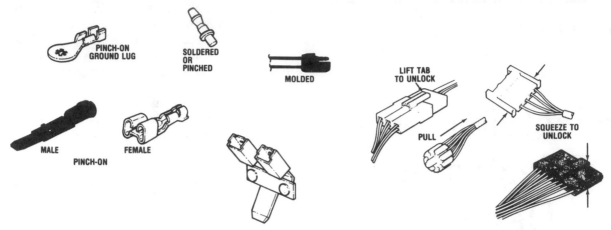

FIGURE 20-2. Common types of wiring terminals and connectors. *(Courtesy of Chrysler Corporation)*

female single, or multiple designs. Bulkhead or multi-connectors group two or more wires together in a two-piece plastic connector. Many of these use a locking device to prevent the connector from separating due to vibration and the like. Various locking methods are used. The locking may be of the squeeze-to-unlock, or the lift-tab-to-unlock type. Be sure to unlock the connection before attempting to pull it apart, and be sure the connection is locked after completing the connection.

CABLE CONVERSION CHART	
METRIC SIZE	**CURRENT GAGE**
.5mm²	20 GA.
.8mm²	18 GA.
1.0mm²	16 GA.
2.0mm²	14 GA.
3.0mm²	12 GA.
5.0mm²	10 GA.
8.0mm²	8 GA.
13.0mm²	6 GA.
19.0mm²	4 GA.

FIGURE 20-3. Wire size comparison chart. *(Courtesy of General Motors Corporation)*

Symbol	Meaning
	NORMALLY OPEN CONTACT
	NORMALLY CLOSED CONTACT
	THERMAL ELEMENT (BI-METAL STRIP)
	CIRCUIT BREAKER
	COIL
	LAMP
	FUSE
	THERMISTOR
Ω	OHMS
	SPLICE
	DENOTES WIRE GOES THROUGH MAIN GROMMET TO BODY COMPARTMENT H-N-P-D-C MODELS
	RESISTOR
	VARIABLE RESISTOR
	DIODE
	GROUND
	SWITCH NORMALLY CLOSED
	SWITCH NORMALLY OPEN
	SWITCH (GANGED) NORMALLY CLOSED
	CONNECTOR
	MULTIPLE CONNECTOR
	MALE CONNECTOR
	FEMALE CONNECTOR

FIGURE 20-4. Commonly used electrical wiring diagram symbols. *(Courtesy of Chrysler Corporation)*

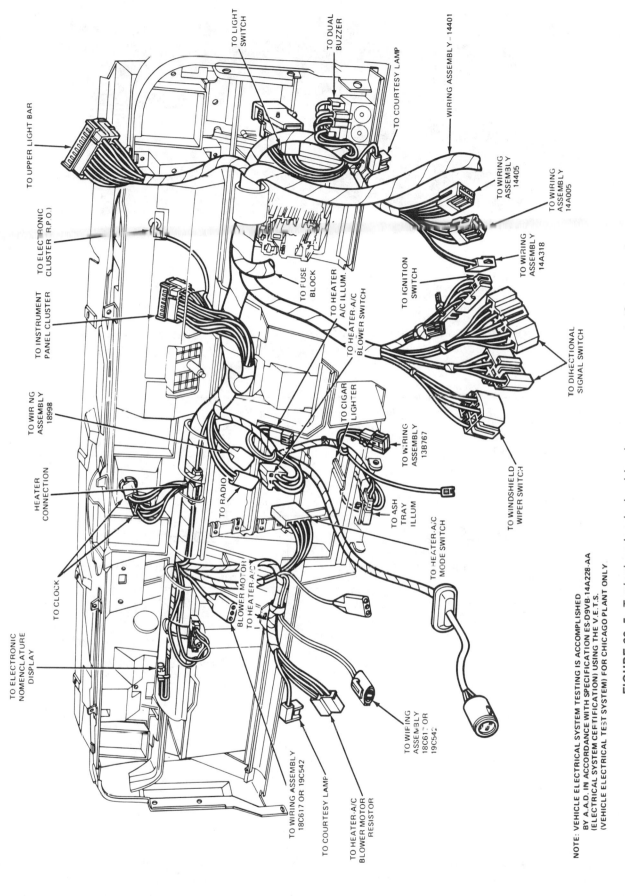

TO UPPER LIGHT BAR

TO LIGHT SWITCH

TO DUAL BUZZER

TO COURTESY LAMP

WIRING ASSEMBLY - 14401

TO ELECTRONIC CLUSTER (R.P.O.)

TO WIRING ASSEMBLY 14405

TO WIRING ASSEMBLY 14A005

TO INSTRUMENT PANEL CLUSTER

TO FUSE BLOCK

TO HEATER A/C ILLUM.

TO WIRING ASSEMBLY 14A318

TO HEATER A/C BLOWER SWITCH

TO IGNITION SWITCH

TO WIRING ASSEMBLY 18998

TO CIGAR LIGHTER

TO DIRECTIONAL SIGNAL SWITCH

HEATER CONNECTION

TO RADIO

TO WIRING ASSEMBLY 13B767

TO WINDSHIELD WIPER SWITCH

TO CLOCK

TO ASH TRAY ILLUM.

TO ELECTRONIC NOMENCLATURE DISPLAY

TO HEATER A/C MODE SWITCH

BLOWER MOTOR

TO HEATER A/C

TO WIRING ASSEMBLY 18C617 OR 19C542

TO COURTESY LAMP

TO HEATER A/C BLOWER MOTOR RESISTOR

TO WIRING ASSEMBLY 18C617 OR 19C542

NOTE: VEHICLE ELECTRICAL SYSTEM TESTING IS ACCOMPLISHED BY A.A.D. IN ACCORDANCE WITH SPECIFICATION ES-D9VB-14A228-AA (ELECTRICAL SYSTEM CERTIFICATION) USING THE V.E.T.S. (VEHICLE ELECTRICAL TEST SYSTEM) FOR CHICAGO PLANT ONLY.

FIGURE 20-5. Typical under dash wiring harness arrangement. *(Courtesy of Ford Motor Co. of Canada Ltd.)*

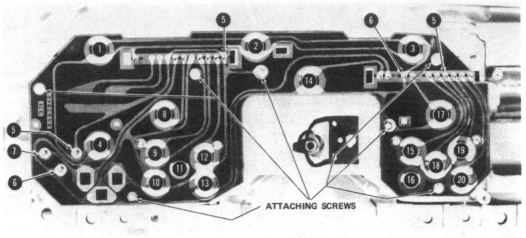

1-2-3-4 - PANEL LIGHTS
5 - 12V (IGN)
6 - GROUND
7 - FUEL GAGE TANK UNIT
8 - RT. TURN INDICATOR
9 - SEAT BELTS

10 - LOW COOLANT (OPT.)
11 - LOW FUEL (OPT.)
12 - HOT
13 - EXT. LAMP (OPT.)
14 - HI BEAM INDICATOR

15 - OIL PRESSURE
16 - LIGHTS ON (OPT.)
17 - LEFT TURN INDICATOR
18 - BRAKE
19 - GENERATOR
20 - CHECK IGNITION

FIGURE 20-6. Printed instrument panel circuit reduces number of wires required. *(Courtesy of General Motors Corporation)*

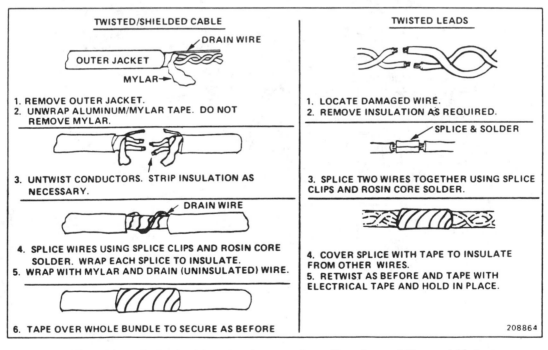

FIGURE 20-7. Typical wiring repair procedure. *(Courtesy of General Motors Corporation)*

PART 2   SWITCHES

Electrical switches are used to open and close electrical circuits. Some of these are operated manually, whereas others operate automatically. Manually operated switches include the following types: push-pull, toggle, turn, and slider. Manually operated switches are used to operate: headlamps, radios, tape players, speakers, heaters, air conditioners, rear window defoggers, windshield wipers, speed control, power seats, power door locks, power trunk locks, power gas fill locks, glow plugs, the ignition system, the starting system, trip and fuel calculators, and the like.

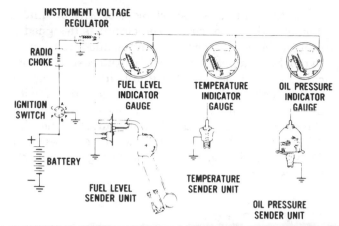

FIGURE 20-0. Typical instrument circuit. *(Courtesy of Ford Motor Co. of Canada Ltd.)*

Some of these are switched on manually but switch off automatically; others must be switched on and off manually.

Automatic switches include those controlled by heat, pressure, vacuum, solenoids, and relays. Heat sensitive switches are used for coolant temperature indicators controlled by a thermal sending unit in contact with engine coolant. They may control cold engine temperature indicator lights as well as hot engine indicators. An example of a pressure sensi-

tive switch is the oil pressure indicator sending unit or switch screwed into a main engine oil gallery. With the engine off, there is no oil pressure: the switch is closed. When the ignition switch is turned on, the oil pressure indicator light goes on. When the engine is started and engine oil pressure rises above approximately 8 to 12 psi (55 to 82 kPa), the switch contacts separate, opening the circuit; then the dash indicator light goes out.

A vacuum-operated switch screwed into the intake manifold sends an electrical signal to the engine control computer which, in turn, adjusts the air/fuel ratio and ignition timing to suit engine speed and load. Intake manifold vacuum is an accurate indicator of engine load.

A relay is a switch that opens and closes an electrical circuit conducting relatively high current controlled by a circuit of relatively low current value. This reduces the need for long, heavy electrical wiring in many cases since only light wire is used to connect the relay to the actuating device or switch. Horn relays and starter relays are good examples of the relay type of switch. When the control circuit switch is closed, the relay coil winding becomes an electromagnet which causes the armature of the relay to be drawn toward the coil, closing the relay points or contacts. One of the relay contacts is connected to the power source and the other to the device to be operated. Closing the relay points actuates the device such as the horn or starting motor.

Many vehicles use a multifunction switch mounted on the steering column sometimes called a "smart" switch. This switch controls such items as windshield wipers and washers, signal lights, headlight dimmer, speed control, and hazard warning lights.

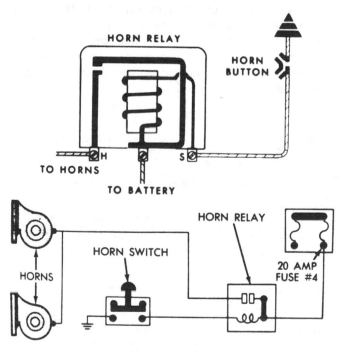

FIGURE 20-9. Horn relay schematic (top). Example of relay use is shown below. Small amount of current from battery makes electromagnet out of coiled wire and core when horn switch completes circuit to ground. Magnetism pulls upper contact against lower contact to complete circuit from battery to horns. *(Courtesy of General Motors Corporation [top] and Chrysler Corporation [bottom])*

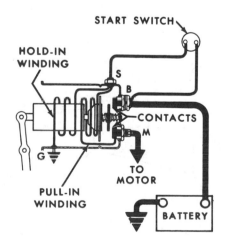

FIGURE 20-10. The starter solenoid is used to engage the starter pinion gear with the flywheel ring gear. *(Courtesy of General Motors Corporation)*

PART 3   CIRCUIT PROTECTION

Fuses and Fusible Links

A chain is only as strong as its weakest link; when a load is applied the weakest link will break.

In the same way, a fuse or a fusible link is the weakest point electrically in an electric circuit. It is needed in order to protect wiring and other components in the circuit from damage due to overloading of the circuit. Circuit overload can occur due to mechanical overload of the electrical device (i.e., windshield wiper motor, heater motor) or to shorts or grounds in the circuit.

Because of their lower current capacity, fuses and fusible links are designed to "blow" or "burn out" at a predetermined value, depending on the circuit capacity they are designed to protect. One type of fuse is the cylindrical glass type with the fusible link visible in the glass and connected at each end to a metal cap. The metal capped ends snap into place between two spring clip connectors in the fuse holder. Another type is enclosed in transparent plastic and has two blade terminals that plug into corresponding connectors in the fuse holder. Fuse capacity ranges anywhere from about 3 to 30 amperes. A failed fuse is easily identified by the gap in the wire visible in the fuse. The cause for fuse failure should be determined and corrected before fuse replacement. Replacement fuses should never exceed original fuse capacity.

A fusible link is a short piece of wire of smaller diameter than the wire in the circuit is designed to protect. When the circuit is overloaded, it burns in two before damage can occur to the rest of the circuit. Fusible links are identifiable in the wiring harness by color code or by a tag attached to it. Fusible links are insulated in the same way as the rest of the circuit. A failed fusible link can often be identified by heat-damaged insulation or exposed wire. They are used in such circuits as charging and lighting systems.

Circuit Breakers

Circuit breakers are designed for circuit protection as are the fuse and the fusible link. The circuit breaker is more costly but has the advantage of opening and closing the circuit intermittently. In a headlight circuit, for example, the circuit breaker allows headlights to go on and off, which allows the driver to safely pull over to the side and stop. A fuse or fusible link failure, in this circuit, would cause the lights to go out completely, leaving the driver in the dark.

A circuit breaker has a pair of contact points, one of which is attached to a bimetal arm. The arm and contacts are connected in series in the circuit.

When circuit overload current heats the bimetal arm, the arm bends to open the contacts, stopping electrical flow in the circuit. When the arm cools, the contacts close again, energizing the circuit once more. This action continues until the circuit is switched off or repaired.

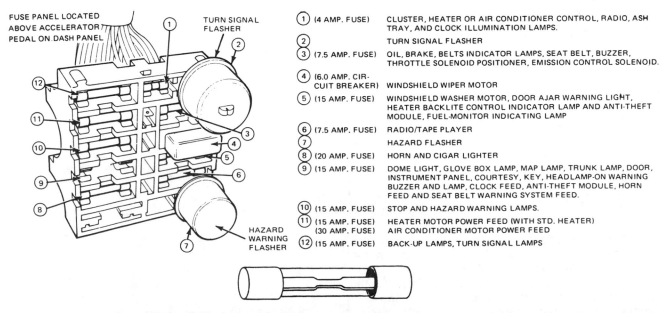

FIGURE 20–11. Individual circuit overload protection is provided by fuses or circuit breakers as shown in this fuse block. *(Courtesy of Ford Motor Co. of Canada Ltd.)*

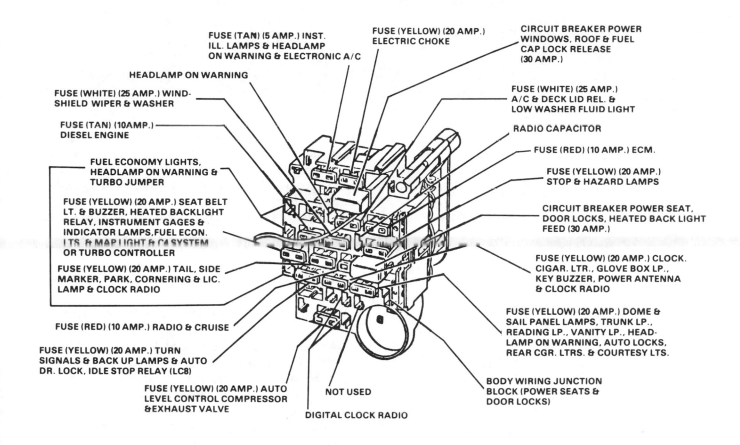

FUSE (TAN) (5 AMP.) INST. ILL. LAMPS & HEADLAMP ON WARNING & ELECTRONIC A/C

FUSE (YELLOW) (20 AMP.) ELECTRIC CHOKE

CIRCUIT BREAKER POWER WINDOWS, ROOF & FUEL CAP LOCK RELEASE (30 AMP.)

HEADLAMP ON WARNING

FUSE (WHITE) (25 AMP.) WIND-SHIELD WIPER & WASHER

FUSE (TAN) (10AMP.) DIESEL ENGINE

FUSE (WHITE) (25 AMP.) A/C & DECK LID REL. & LOW WASHER FLUID LIGHT

RADIO CAPACITOR

FUSE (RED) (10 AMP.) ECM.

FUEL ECONOMY LIGHTS, HEADLAMP ON WARNING & TURBO JUMPER

FUSE (YELLOW) (20 AMP.) STOP & HAZARD LAMPS

FUSE (YELLOW) (20 AMP.) SEAT BELT LT. & BUZZER, HEATED BACKLIGHT RELAY, INSTRUMENT GAGES & INDICATOR LAMPS, FUEL ECON. LTS. & MAP LIGHT & C4 SYSTEM OR TURBO CONTROLLER

CIRCUIT BREAKER POWER SEAT, DOOR LOCKS, HEATED BACK LIGHT FEED (30 AMP.)

FUSE (YELLOW) (20 AMP.) TAIL, SIDE MARKER, PARK, CORNERING & LIC. LAMP & CLOCK RADIO

FUSE (YELLOW) (20 AMP.) CLOCK. CIGAR. LTR., GLOVE BOX LP., KEY BUZZER, POWER ANTENNA & CLOCK RADIO

FUSE (RED) (10 AMP.) RADIO & CRUISE

FUSE (YELLOW) (20 AMP.) DOME & SAIL PANEL LAMPS, TRUNK LP., READING LP., VANITY LP., HEAD-LAMP ON WARNING, AUTO LOCKS, REAR CGR. LTRS. & COURTESY LTS.

FUSE (YELLOW) (20 AMP.) TURN SIGNALS & BACK UP LAMPS & AUTO DR. LOCK, IDLE STOP RELAY (LC8)

FUSE (YELLOW) (20 AMP.) AUTO LEVEL CONTROL COMPRESSOR & EXHAUST VALVE

NOT USED

DIGITAL CLOCK RADIO

BODY WIRING JUNCTION BLOCK (POWER SEATS & DOOR LOCKS)

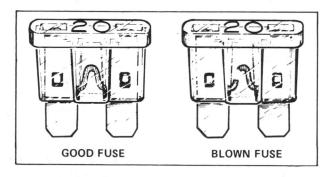

GOOD FUSE   BLOWN FUSE

FIGURE 20-12. Typical mini-fuse panel. Note difference between good fuse and blown fuse. (*Courtesy of General Motors Corporation*)

Voltage Limiter

The instrument voltage regulator is designed to limit voltage to the instrument panel gauges. Power to the voltage limiter is supplied when the ignition switch is in the "on" or "acc." position. Voltage is limited to approximately five volts at the instrument gauges.

The voltage limiter consists of a bimetal arm, a heating coil, and a set of contact points enclosed in a housing. Two terminals provide connections in series into the circuit. When the ignition switch is turned on, the heating coil heats the bimetal arm causing it to bend and open the contacts. This disconnects the voltage supply from the heating coil as well as from the circuit. When the bimetal arm cools sufficiently, the contacts close and the cycle repeats itself. The rapid opening and closing of the contacts results in a pulsating voltage at the output terminal averaging approximately five volts.

The voltage limiter protects the instrument gauges against high voltage surges and prevents erroneous gauge readings caused by voltage fluctuations.

439

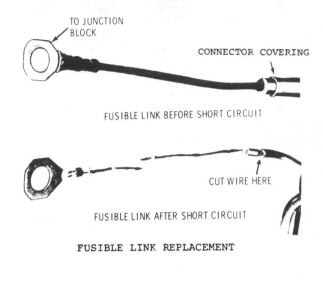

FUSIBLE LINK BEFORE SHORT CIRCUIT

FUSIBLE LINK AFTER SHORT CIRCUIT

FUSIBLE LINK REPLACEMENT

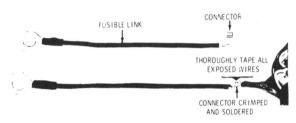

FUSIBLE LINK REPAIR

FIGURE 20-13. Typical fuse links and fuse link repair. *(Courtesy of General Motors Corporation)*

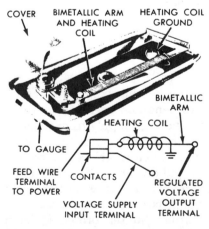

FIGURE 20-14. Typical instrument panel voltage limiter, components, and schematic. *(Courtesy of Ford Motor Co. of Canada Ltd.)*

PART 4 RESISTORS

Resistors are devices used in electrical circuits to reduce current and voltage levels from those supplied by the power source. Resistors are usually made from wire. They are used to protect devices or circuits designed to operate at lower current levels than that supplied by the battery or charging system. They are also used to control current and voltage levels produced by charging systems and to control light intensity.

Resistors provide opposition to electron flow. This opposition causes the electrons to work harder to try to get through. The increased electron activity generates heat. Since some of the electrical energy is used up to produce heat, the voltage through the resistor is at a reduced level.

Several types of resistors are used in the automobile. These include fixed value resistors, variable resistors, ballast resistors, and thermistors.

The fixed resistors (for example, in a spark plug) maintain a constant resistance value once operating temperature has been reached. A manually operated rheostat or variable resistor (as in the dash light control switch incorporated in the headlamp switch) inserts more or less resistance into the circuit to dim or brighten the dash lights as the switch knob is turned. A ballast resistor is a wire coil housed in a ceramic block to regulate temperature changes. The resistance of a ballast resistor increases with increased current and decreases with decreased current. Increased current causes the resistor to heat up which, in turn, increases resistance. Ballast resistors are used in point-type ignition systems to protect the ignition points and the coil. A bypass circuit allows battery voltage to the coil during cranking to improve starting.

The resistance value of a thermistor (a type of resistor) varies with temperature. As the temperature of the thermistor increases, its resistance decreases. It is used in charging systems to vary charge voltage with temperature.

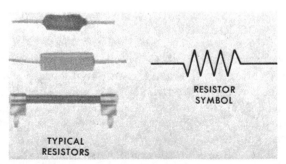

FIGURE 20-15. Some typical types of resistors used to control current and voltage values in the electrical system. Note resistor symbol used in wiring diagrams.

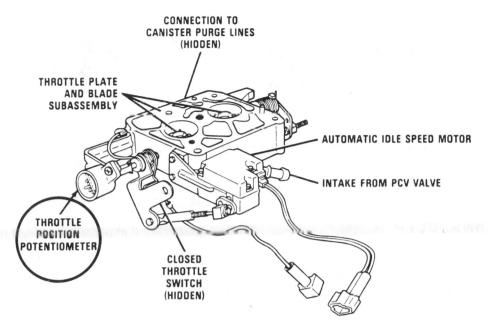

CONNECTION TO
CANISTER PURGE LINES
(HIDDEN)

THROTTLE PLATE
AND BLADE
SUBASSEMBLY

AUTOMATIC IDLE SPEED MOTOR

INTAKE FROM PCV VALVE

THROTTLE
POSITION
POTENTIOMETER

CLOSED
THROTTLE
SWITCH
(HIDDEN)

FIGURE 20-16. Location of typical throttle position potentiometer on fuel injection throttle body. Variable voltage signal produced by this unit is provided to computer to help control amount of fuel injected. *(Courtesy of Chrysler Corporation)*

Potentiometer

A potentiometer is a rheostat or resistor with one or more sliding contacts used to produce a varying voltage signal. A typical example of its use is the throttle position potentiometer used in the gasoline fuel injection system. The amount of fuel injected increases or decreases as a result of throttle position. Throttle position determines the voltage signal to the computer which in turn controls the fuel injectors in proportion to the voltage signal produced by the throttle position switch.

PART 5 CAPACITORS (CONDENSERS)

A capacitor is a device that is used in an electrical circuit to temporarily store an electrical charge until it is needed to perform its job or until it can be safely dissipated if it is not to be used.

The typical condenser consists of several thin layers of electrically conductive material, such as metal foil, separated by thin insulating material known as dielectric material. Alternate layers of foil are connected to one terminal of the condenser. The other layers of foil are connected to ground. The entire assembly is rolled up tightly and enclosed in a metal cylinder. The unit is completely sealed and moisture proof. The metal container is the ground connection, and a pigtail lead provides the other connection. In the point ignition system, the condenser is connected in parallel with the ignition points. When the points open, the surge of current (excess electrons) enters the condenser and is stored on the condenser plates. The condenser prevents arcing of current across the points as they separate, thereby prolonging point life.

In a capacitor discharge ignition system, a condenser is used to store the electrical charge used to fire the spark plugs. In this system, electrical energy is stored in the capacitor and discharged at the precise instant when the plug should be fired. The capacitor is then recharged and discharged repeatedly and as rapidly as required, depending on engine speed.

Capacitors of various types and sizes are used in electrical circuits to collect and dissipate stray or unwanted current. This prevents the unwanted cur-

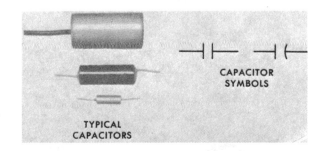

CAPACITOR
SYMBOLS

TYPICAL
CAPACITORS

FIGURE 20-17. Typical capacitors used to prevent arcing, control radio interference, and provide circuit protection. Wiring diagram symbols used are also shown. Capacitors (condensers) are used to store undesirable electrical surges and eddy currents temporarily until they can be safely dissipated.

441

rent from interfering with other electrical functions. A radio-suppressor type of capacitor is a typical example. The capacity or capacitance of a condenser is measured in units called *farads*. A farad is a charge of one ampere for one second producing a one-volt potential difference. A microfarad is 0.000001 (1/1,000,000) farad. Automotive point ignition condensers have an approximate capacitance of .15 to .28 microfarad.

PART 6   TRANSDUCER

A transducer is a device that converts another form of energy to an electrical signal. Vacuum transducers or MAP (manifold absolute pressure) sensors are used to provide a varying voltage signal depending on intake manifold pressure to the computer which controls ignition timing, air/fuel ratio, and the turbocharger waste gate.

A throttle position switch or transducer is used to send a varying voltage signal, dependent on throttle position, to the electronic control unit or computer. The computer uses this information to increase or decrease fuel delivery accordingly.

PART 7   SEMICONDUCTORS, DIODES, AND TRANSISTORS

Semiconductors are neither good conductors nor good insulators. Semiconductor materials, such as silicon, are used in diodes and transistors. Silicon is an ingredient commonly found in beach sand. The capability of the silicon wafer *chip*, as used in computers, is astounding.

A tiny silicon wafer one quarter the size of a man's fingernail can be manufactured to accommodate a million or more electronic components,

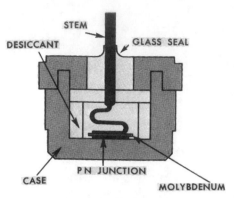

FIGURE 20-19. Cross-sectional view of diode construction. Materials used vary somewhat in different diodes. Both positive and negative diodes are used. A positive diode will allow current in one direction only from the stem, through the diode material (*pn* junction), to the diode case. A negative diode allows current in the opposite direction only. *(Courtesy of General Motors Corporation)*

diodes, and transistors, all interconnected with extremely thin films of metal. The silicon chip also has the ability to make decisions (logic) and to recall stored information (memory).

The amazing qualities of this material have revolutionized the electronics industry and have heavily impacted on the automotive industry—both in the factory through robotics, and in the automobile through computers. Computers in the automobile now control ignition, ignition timing, air/fuel ratios, emission control systems, transmission shifting, torque converter clutches, braking ratios front to rear, lighting systems, instrument panels, on-board diagnostic systems, and other items.

It is not necessary for the automotive techni-

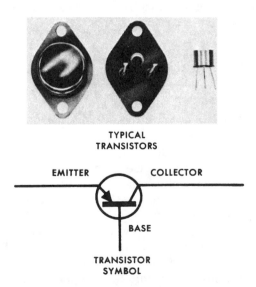

FIGURE 20-20. Typical transistor and transistor symbol. A small base current turns the transistor on, allowing a larger current from emitter to collector. *(Courtesy of General Motors Corporation)*

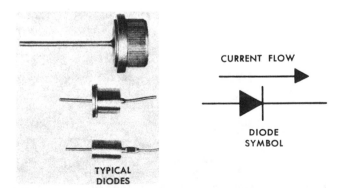

FIGURE 20-18. Typical diodes and diode symbol showing direction of current. *(Courtesy of General Motors Corporation)*

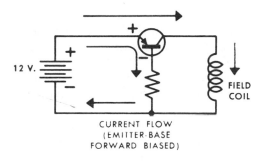

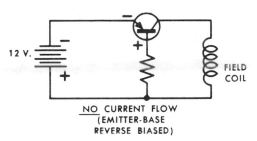

CURRENT FLOW
(EMITTER-BASE
FORWARD BIASED)

NO CURRENT FLOW
(EMITTER-BASE
REVERSE BIASED)

FIGURE 20-21. Diagrams showing transistor operation. *(Courtesy of General Motors Corporation)*

cian to fully understand the intricacies of the computer in order to diagnose and service automotive electronic systems, since these components are not serviced in the automotive shop. However, a basic understanding of the operating principles of these devices is needed to properly diagnose and repair these systems.

Diodes

A diode is a solid state (completely static) device that allows current to pass through itself in one direction only (within its rated capacity). Acting as a one-way electrical check valve, it allows current to pass in one direction and blocks it in the other direction.

The silicon wafer is chemically treated to produce either a positive or negative diode. Diodes may be encased in non-corrosive heat conductive metal with the case acting as one lead and a metal wire connected to the opposite side of the wafer as the other lead. The unit is hermetically sealed to prevent the entry of moisture. This type of diode is used

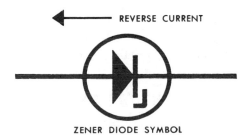

REVERSE CURRENT

ZENER DIODE SYMBOL

FIGURE 20-22. The Zener diode will allow current in the reverse direction when specified voltage is imposed. *(Courtesy of General Motors Corporation)*

in some AC charging system alternators. A minimum of six diodes is used—three positive diodes and three negative diodes to provide full wave rectification (changing alternating current to direct current). Many charging systems use more than six diodes.

Other diodes used in electronic systems are much smaller and may be sealed in epoxy resins with two leads for connection into the circuit. Diodes in computers may be very tiny in comparison to the more visible charging system diode.

Negative diodes are identified by a black paint mark, a part number in black, or a black negative sign. Positive diodes are similarly identified in red or with a red positive sign.

The manner in which the metallic disc is installed in the diode assembly determines whether the diode is negative or positive. (Inverting the disc in a positive diode would make it a negative assembly.) This disc is only .008" to .010" thick and approximately one-eighth of an inch square, depending upon current rating.

Some rectifier assemblies contain diodes that are exposed, while others have them built in. Those with built-in diodes contain only the wafer portion of the diode.

The silicon crystal material for diodes and transistors is processed or "doped" by adding other material to it. Phosphorus or antimony may be used to produce a negative or N type material. These materials have five electrons in the outer ring of their atoms. This results in the atoms of the N material having one extra or free electron. The free electron can be easily made to move through the material when voltage is applied. Electrons are considered to be negative current carriers.

Boron or indium may be used to treat silicon crystal to produce a positive or P type material. These elements have only three electrons in the outer ring of their atoms. This leaves a shortage of one electron in the atoms of P type material. This shortage or vacancy is called a *hole*. Holes are considered to be positive current carriers.

A diode consists of a very thin slice of each material, P type and N type placed together. The area where the two materials meet is called the *junction*. When the N material side of the diode is connected to a negative current supply, such as the battery negative terminal, and the P material side is connected to the positive battery terminal, the diode will conduct current. This happens because the negative battery terminal has an excess of electrons that repel the electrons in the diode toward the positive side. At the same time, the positive holes in the P material move toward the N side. This interchange of electrons and holes occurs at the junction of the N and P material in the diode. Connecting a diode in this manner is called *forward bias*.

When a diode is connected in the opposite manner (reverse bias) it will not conduct current. It cannot do so since the N material side of the diode is connected to the positive battery terminal and the P material side to the negative battery terminal. The electrons in the N material are attracted to the positive battery terminal side away from the diode junction. At the same time, the holes in the positive diode material are attracted to the negative battery terminal side of the diode away from the junction area. This in effect creates an open circuit which cannot conduct current.

Of course, these conditions apply only if normal diode design voltage is not exceeded. When applied in reverse bias, excessive current will cause the bond structure to break down and allow reverse current, which causes the diode to be damaged. Diodes are designed with the necessary current and voltage capacity for the circuit in which they are to be used.

Excessive reverse current will destroy a diode due to excessive heat. A "blown" diode will not conduct current, resulting in an open circuit. Blown diodes must be replaced. A shorted diode will conduct current in both directions and must be replaced.

Light emitting diodes (LED) may be used for digital display of instrument panel gauges on some vehicles.

Zener Diode

The zener diode is a specially designed diode that conducts current like a normal diode but will also safely conduct current in a reverse direction when reverse current reaches the specified design voltage. A zener diode can prevent reverse current if it is below design voltage, but when reverse current reaches and exceeds design voltage, the zener diode will conduct reverse current. This type of diode is used in control circuits such as in the field current in an alternator.

Transistors

A transistor is a solid state switching device used to control current in a circuit. It operates like a relay except that it has no moving parts. A relatively small current is used to control a larger current. The transistor either allows current to pass or stops it.

Transistors used in automotive applications are usually of the PNP type. This means that they are designed with a thin slice of N material sandwiched between two pieces of P material. The P material on one side is called the *emitter*, the N material in the

middle is called the *base*, and the other P material is called the *collector*. NPN transistors are also produced but are not commonly used in automotive applications.

The very thin slice of N type base material is attached to a surrounding metallic ring which provides the means for circuit connection. The emitter and collector material are also provided with circuit connections. The physical arrangement of the three pieces of material is such that the distance between the emitter and the collector is shorter than the distance between the emitter and the base. This feature results in the unique manner in which the transistor controls current.

A transistor is connected into a circuit in a manner that allows a low base-emitter current to control a larger collector-emitter current. A typical example of this is in the control module of an electronic ignition system.

When the base circuit is energized (by closing the ignition switch for example), a small base current is applied to the transistor emitter-base. This causes the electrons and holes in the emitter-base to act in a similar manner as in a diode described earlier. However, since the emitter is closer to the collector than it is to the base, most of the current is conducted by the emitter-collector section of the transistor. This is caused by the fact that electricity normally follows the path of least resistance.

The control current is called base current. The base circuit or current controls the emitter-collector current.

The same type of semiconductor material used in diodes is also used in transistors. The transistor, however, uses a second section of this material resulting in three terminals instead of two (as in the diode). If, for example, the base circuit of a transistor is energized with five amperes of current, the transistor divides this current into base current and emitter-collector current. This is known as the *current gain factor*. This factor varies with transistor design. The emitter-collector current may be 24 times that of the base current. In this example, therefore, base current would be 0.2 ampere and emitter-collector current would be 4.8 amperes.

Transistors are used in electronic voltage regulators to control charging system voltage, in electronic ignition systems to control ignition coil primary current, and in computers.

PART 8   COMPUTERS AND MICROPROCESSORS

The computer has become a valuable component of the automobile. The silicon chip and integrated circuitry are being used to control automobile operation resulting in better performance, lower fuel consumption, and fewer emissions. It is also used to provide comprehensive on-board systems diagnosis. The computer may even provide a correction factor for deviations from normal air/fuel ratios caused by production tolerances in the engine, the sensors, and the electronic interface with the fuel system, as well as drift from the norm, caused by system component aging.

Actually, the computer has taken over many of the functions formerly performed by vacuum mechanical, electromechanical, or mechanical devices. Among these are distributor vacuum advance, centrifugal advance, carburetor power enrichment, idle speed control, exhaust gas recirculation, air injection, canister purging, instrument panel gauges, torque converter clutch, automatic transmission shifting, and system monitoring and diagnosis. It must be pointed out that many different models of vehicles may employ only a few of these functions, whereas others may have computerized control of most or all of these functions.

While it is not within the scope of this text to explain the electronic operation of the computer, it is worthwhile to consider its basic function. The computer consists of a power supply, a central processing unit (including the memory system), and an input and output system. The input signals received by the computer are processed in conjunction with stored information in the memory system. Based on input signal information and stored memory information, the computer makes the appropriate decision to provide the output signals needed to adjust or operate the various output devices.

Computer systems may include both RAM and ROM memory capability. Random access memory (RAM) temporarily stores bits of information from the various input signals before being acted upon by the program. Output data to be sent to output devices are also stored by RAM. The computer must compute this information and produce output signals based on input signals. The information stored in this manner is lost on some vehicles when the ignition key is turned off. This is why diagnostic procedures should be performed before the ignition is turned off; otherwise, before diagnostic information is valid, the engine must be started and operated until all systems have again become normalized. This is, of course, time consuming.

Another type of memory called ROM (read only memory) is permanent. This information need not be computed; it need only be consulted or looked up by the computer. The information remains in the system even when the ignition switch is turned off. An example of this type of data storage is ignition distributor advance that can be precomputed for an engine and the data stored in ROM.

Each memory location in the computer can store eight bits of information. Eight bits equal one *byte* according to computer programmers. Computer memory capacity is stated in Ks. One K stands for 1024 bits of information. A 64K RAM is, therefore, able to store 65,536 bits of information. New chips have been developed with four times this capacity—vastly in excess of what is needed for automotive applications but required for high technology industrial applications.

The automotive technician must be acquainted with electronics terminology which includes such terms as: diodes, transistors, capacitors, zener di-

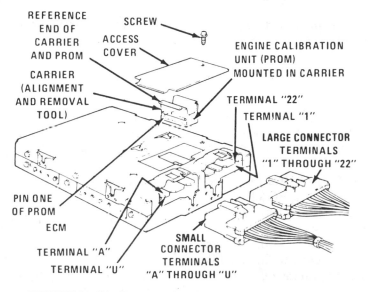

FIGURE 20–23. Details of typical PROM unit in relation to computer. *(Courtesy of General Motors Corporation)*

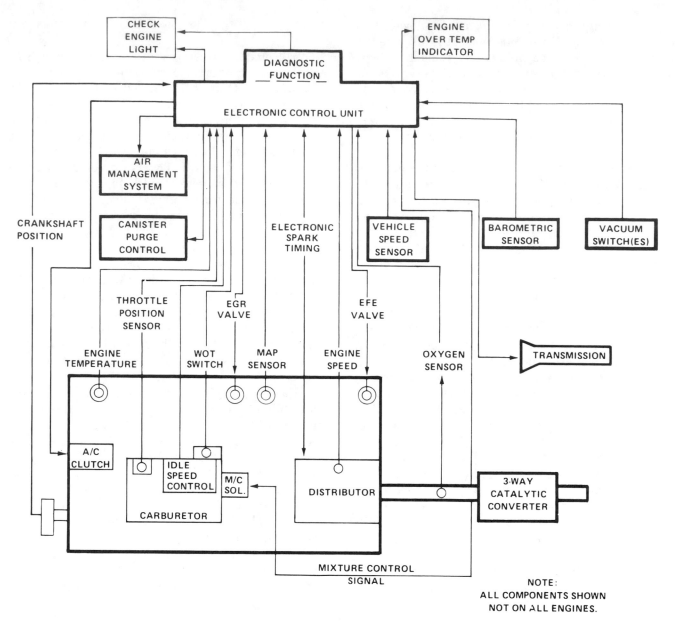

FIGURE 20-24. Input and output factors of computer-controlled engine system. (*Courtesy of General Motors Corporation*)

odes, transducers, semiconductors, ECU (electronic control unit), ECM (electronic control module), CPU (central processing unit), microprocessor, computer, digital computer, DFI (digital fuel injection), EFI (electronic fuel injection), ESC (electronic spark control), EST (electronic spark timing), electronic ignition, electronic voltage regulator, data panel, digital display panel, MCU (microprocessor control unit), LED display or readout (light emitting diode), and others depending on make, year, and model of vehicle.

PART 9   SELF-CHECK

1. Why are most automotive wires of the stranded type?

2. Wire size is specified by _____ or by _____ .

3. Why do some wires require heavy insulation?

4. State the basic purpose of the following devices in electrical circuits.

(a) switch

(b) fuse

(c) circuit breaker

(d) voltage limiter

(e) fusible link

(f) resistor

(g) capacitor

(h) diode

(i) transistor

5. What is the basic difference in function between RAM and ROM memory systems in a computer?

PART 10   TEST QUESTIONS

1. Automotive wiring systems may include:

(a) stranded wire

(b) single strand wire

(c) insulated and non-insulated wire

(d) any of the above

2. The current carrying capacity of a wire is determined by its:

(a) length

(b) cross-sectional size

(c) temperature

(d) all of the above

3. Mechanic A says that a fusible link is slightly smaller in diameter than the wire it is to protect. Mechanic B says the fusible link is the weakest link in the electrical circuit. Who is right?

(a) Mechanic A

(b) Mechanic B

(c) both are right

(d) both are wrong

4. Wire connectors include:

(a) blade terminals

(b) bulkhead connectors

(c) round hole terminals

(d) all of the above

5. Diode polarity results from the:

(a) method in which it is manufactured

(b) the way it is connected in the circuit

(c) battery polarity

(d) generator polarity

6. A relay is used to:

(a) control a large current with a small current

(b) operate a horn

(c) reduce total vehicle cost

(d) all of the above

7. A resistor is used to:

(a) store electrical energy temporarily

(b) increase circuit voltage

(c) both (a) and (b)

(d) none of the above

Chapter 21

Cranking Systems

Performance Objectives

After studying this chapter thoroughly and sufficient practical experience on adequate training models, and with the appropriate shop manuals, tools, and equipment, you should be able to do the following:

1. Complete the self-check and test questions with at least 80 percent accuracy.
2. Follow the accepted general precautions outlined in this chapter.
3. Describe the purpose, construction, and operation of the cranking system and each of its components.
4. Diagnose basic cranking system problems according to the diagnostic chart provided.
5. Safely remove, recondition, adjust, and replace any faulty cranking system components in accordance with manufacturer's specifications.
6. Properly performance test the reconditioned cranking system to determine the success of the repairs performed.
7. Prepare the vehicle for customer acceptance.

The cranking system is designed to change the electrical energy of the battery to mechanical energy through the use of the cranking motor (starter). The system must crank the engine over at sufficient speed to allow the engine to run when the cylinders begin to fire.

The cranking system for automotive vehicles consists of the following units:

- Storage battery and cables
- Cranking motor and solenoid switch
- Engine drive unit
- Control circuit

PART 1 CRANKING MOTORS AND CIRCUITS

Cranking systems are much the same in general design and operation. The motor consists of the drive mechanism, the frame, armature, brushes, and field windings. Some cranking motors also have a magnetically operated switch that closes and opens the circuit between the battery and cranking motor. The magnetically operated switch is referred to as a *relay* or *solenoid switch*. In addition to closing and opening the circuit, the solenoid switch also shifts the drive pinion of the cranking motor into mesh with the teeth on the engine flywheel so the engine can be cranked.

The *armature* is supported on bearings so that it can rotate freely. Current enters the motor through the field windings and then goes to the brushes, which ride the armature commutator. Current then passes through the armature windings, creating two strong magnetic fields. These fields oppose each other in such a way that the armature is forced to rotate. The armature may drive the drive pinion directly or through a gear reduction.

Rotation of the armature causes the cranking motor drive pinion to rotate. When the drive pinion is meshed with the teeth of the flywheel ring gear, cranking of the engine takes place.

The cranking motor is designed to operate under great overload and to produce a high power for its size. It can do this for a short period of time only since, to produce such power, a high current must be used. If the cranking motor operation is continued for any length of time, heat will cause serious damage. For this reason, the cranking motor must never be used for more than 30 seconds at any one time, and cranking should not be repeated without a pause of at least 2 minutes to permit the heat to escape.

The *drive mechanism* is a vital part of the

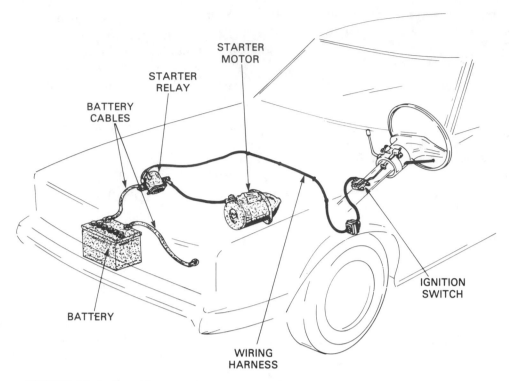

FIGURE 21-1. Cranking system component location (typical). *(Courtesy of Ford Motor Co. of Canada Ltd.)*

cranking motor, since it is through the drive that power is transmitted to the engine, cranking it as the cranking motor armature rotates. The drive mechanism has two functions. The first is to transmit the cranking torque to the engine flywheel when the cranking motor is operated and to disconnect the cranking motor from the flywheel after the engine has started. The second is to provide a gear reduction between the cranking motor and the engine so there will be sufficient torque to turn the engine over at cranking speed. There are approximately 15 teeth on the flywheel for every tooth on the drive pinion. This means that the cranking motor armature will rotate about 15 times for every engine revolution on a direct drive starter.

If the cranking motor drive pinion remained meshed with the flywheel ring gear at engine speeds above 1000 rpm, and the pinion transmitted its rotation to the cranking motor armature, the armature would be spun at high speeds. Such speeds, approaching 15,000 rpm, would cause the armature windings to be thrown from the armature slots and the segments to be thrown from the commutator. To avoid this, the drive mechanism must disengage the pinion from the flywheel ring gear as soon as the engine begins to operate.

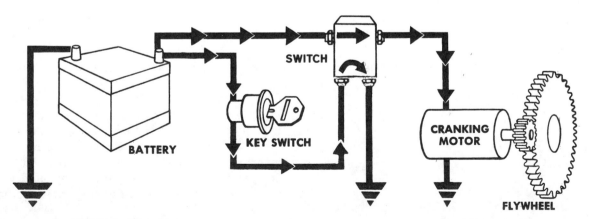

FIGURE 21-2. Cranking system schematic and gear reduction. *(Courtesy of General Motors Corporation)*

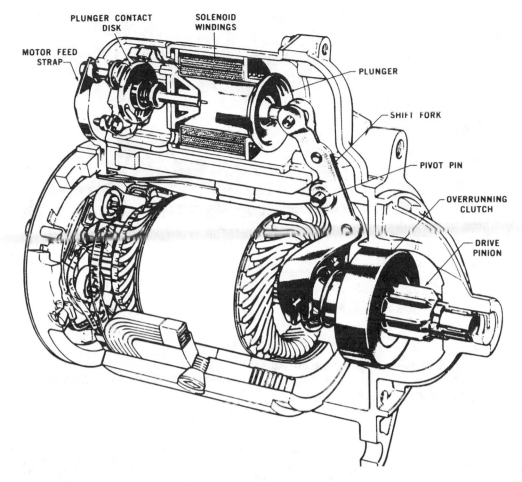

FIGURE 21-3. Cross-sectional view of typical solenoid type of cranking motor. *(Courtesy of Ford Motor Co. of Canada Ltd.)*

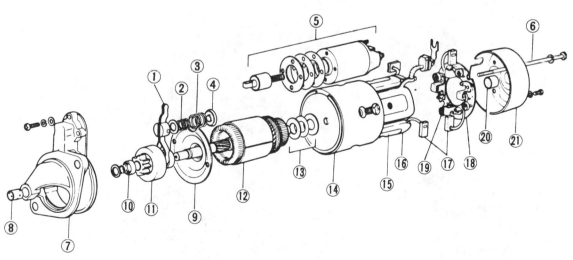

(1) Lever assembly
(2) Lever spring (A)
(3) Lever spring (B)
(4) Spring retainer
(5) Magnetic switch
(6) Through bolt
(7) Front bracket

(8) Front bracket bearing
(9) Center bracket
(10) Stop ring
(11) Overrunning clutch
(12) Armature
(13) Washer
(14) Yoke assembly

(15) Pole piece
(16) Field coil
(17) Brush
(18) Brush holder
(19) Brush spring
(20) Rear bracket bearing
(21) Rear bracket

FIGURE 21-4. Exploded view of solenoid type of cranking motor with components identified. *(Courtesy of Chrysler Corporation)*

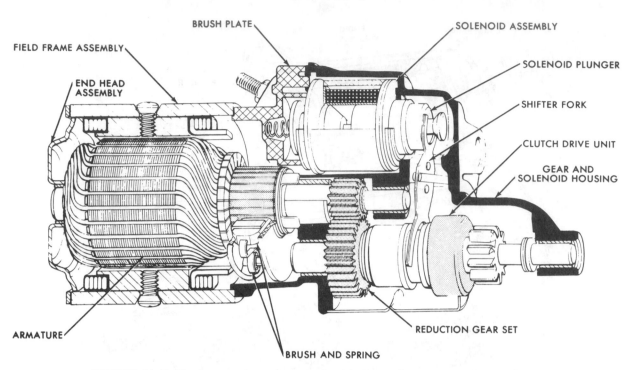

FIELD FRAME ASSEMBLY

BRUSH PLATE

SOLENOID ASSEMBLY

SOLENOID PLUNGER

END HEAD ASSEMBLY

SHIFTER FORK

CLUTCH DRIVE UNIT

GEAR AND SOLENOID HOUSING

ARMATURE

BRUSH AND SPRING

REDUCTION GEAR SET

FIGURE 21-5. Faster running armature in this type of starter requires reduction between armature shaft and starter drive pinion. *(Courtesy of Chrysler Corporation)*

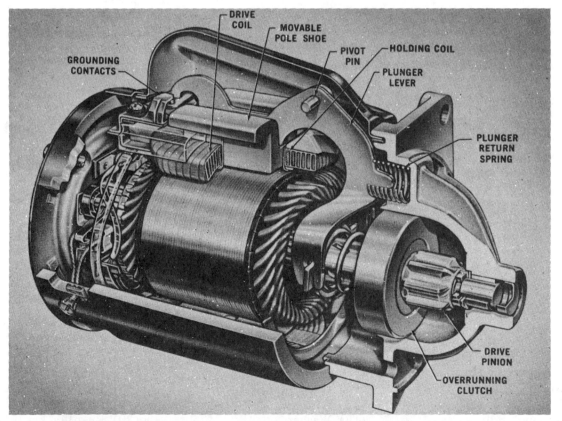

GROUNDING CONTACTS

DRIVE COIL

MOVABLE POLE SHOE

PIVOT PIN

HOLDING COIL

PLUNGER LEVER

PLUNGER RETURN SPRING

DRIVE PINION

OVERRUNNING CLUTCH

FIGURE 21-6. Positive engagement type of cranking motor. This type uses a separate starter relay switch. Grounding contacts short out pull in winding when starter is engaged. Movable pole shoe is down when starter is engaged and up when disengaged. *(Courtesy of Ford Motor Co. of Canada Ltd.)*

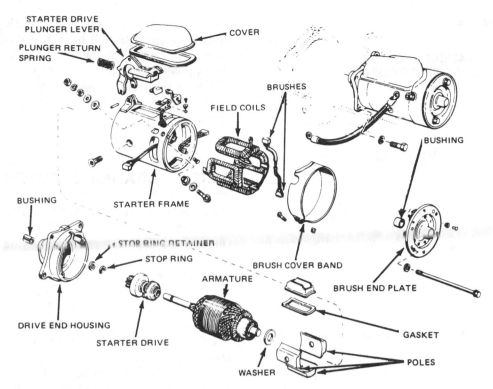

FIGURE 21-7. Exploded view of positive engagement type of starting motor. *(Courtesy of Ford Motor Co. of Canada Ltd.)*

PART 2   MOTOR PRINCIPLES

Magnetically, the cranking motor is made up of two parts: the armature and the field winding assembly. The armature consists of a number of low-resistance conductors placed in insulated slots around a soft iron core assembled onto the armature shaft. The commutator consists of a number of copper segments insulated from each other and from the armature shaft. The conductors are so connected to each other and to the commutator that electricity will flow through all the armature conductors when brushes are placed on the commutator and a source of current is connected to the brushes. This creates magnetic fields around each conductor. Current through the field windings creates a powerful magnetic field. In Figures 21-8 and 21-9, looking end-on at the conductor, it will be noted that to the right of the conductor the magnetic field from the magnet and the circular magnetic field around the conductor oppose each other. To the left of the conductor they are in the same direction. When a current-carrying conductor is located in a magnetic field, the field of force is distorted, creating a strong field on one side of the conductor and a weak field on the opposite side. The conductor will be forced to move in the direction of the weak field; therefore, in this instance, the conductor will be pushed to the

right. The more current through the conductor, the stronger is the force exerted on the conductors.

The application of this principle is shown in Figure 21-10, which shows a simple, one-turn armature electric motor. The magnetic field is created by means of current through the field coil windings, which are assembled around the two poles. The direction of current tends to increase the magnetic field between the two poles. The U-shaped armature winding that is placed between the two poles is connected to a two-segment commutator. In the posi-

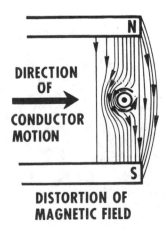

FIGURE 21-8. Strong magnetic field at left of current-carrying conductor forces conductor to move toward weak magnetic field at right of conductor.

MAGNETIC FORCE ON A CURRENT-CARRYING CONDUCTOR

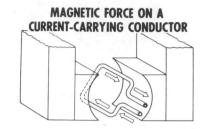

FIGURE 21–9. Action of magnetic fields causes looped conductor to rotate.

tion shown, current direction is from the battery through the right-hand brush, through the right-hand segment of the commutator, into the armature winding, past the south pole and then, past the north pole. Then, on into the left-hand commutator segment, left-hand brush, through the north pole field winding, south pole field winding, and back to the battery. The magnetic fields around the conductor will be in the two directions shown by the circular arrows. It can be seen that the left-hand side of the armature winding will be pushed upward while the right-hand side will be pushed downward, thus imparting a clockwise rotation.

Since the armature winding and commutator are assembled together and must rotate together, movement of the winding also causes the commutator to turn. By the time the left-hand side of the winding

has swung around toward the south pole, the commutator segments will have reversed their connections with respect to the brushes. Current is then in the opposite direction with respect to the winding; but since the winding has turned 180°, the force exerted on it will still tend to rotate it in a clockwise direction.

PART 3   CRANKING MOTOR CIRCUITS

Normally in cranking motors, the field windings and the armature are connected in such a way that all the current that enters the cranking motor passes through both field windings and the armature. In other words, the motor is series wound—the fields and armature are connected in series. All conductors are heavy ribbon-copper types that have a very low resistance and permit a high current. The more current, the higher is the power developed by the cranking motor.

Some cranking motors are four-pole units, but have only two field windings, thus keeping resistance low. Notice the path of the current through this cranking motor (Figure 21–11). It will be noted that in operation the poles with field coil windings have a north polarity at the pole shoe face. The lines of force pass through the armature, enter the plain pole shoes, and pass through the frame and back to the original north shoe to complete the magnetic circuit. In all cranking motors the adjacent pole shoes must be of opposite polarity so that, in a four-pole motor, there is a N, S, N, S sequence around the frame.

Other cranking motors are four-pole, four-field winding, four-brush units. Here, the field windings are paired off so that half the current is through one set of field windings to one of the insulated brushes, whereas the other half of the current is through the other set of field windings to the other insulated

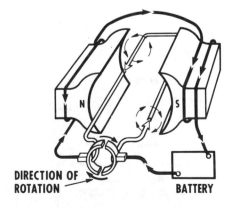

FIGURE 21–10. Armature loop and field windings are connected in series through brushes and commutator to create magnetic fields that cause armature to rotate.

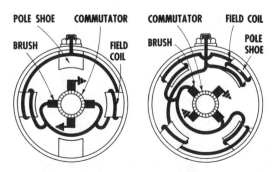

FIGURE 21–11. Schematic wiring diagram of two-field, four-pole, four-brush, series-wound cranking motor (at left). Schematic wiring diagram of four-brush, four-field, four-pole, series-wound cranking motor (at right). *(Courtesy of General Motors Corporation)*

brush. With four field coil windings, it is possible to create more ampere turns and consequently stronger magnetic fields, thus producing cranking motors with greater torque or cranking ability. By tracing the current from the terminal, it will again be noted that the poles alternate S, N, S, N, providing four magnetic paths through the armature core.

The Compound Motor

A compound motor has both series field coils and shunt windings. As a result, it has characteristics between the series and the shunt-type motor, combining good starting torque with fairly constant operating speed. The compound motor is particularly useful for applications where heavy loads are suddenly applied. In automotive starter applications, a shunt coil may be used to limit the maximum free speed at which the starter can operate. The compound-type motor has been frequently used for automotive starters.

The cranking motor designed for heavy-duty service uses six poles and six brushes. Here, the current is split in three ways—one third through each pair of field windings to one of the three insulated brushes.

Increasing the number of circuits through the cranking motor helps to keep the resistance low so that a high current and a high power can be developed.

As a rule, all the insulated brushes are connected together by means of jumper leads or bars so that the voltage is equalized at all brushes. Without these equalizing bars there may be conditions that cause arcing and burning of commutator bars, eventually insulating the brush contact and preventing cranking.

PART 4   CRANKING MOTOR SOLENOID CIRCUITS

The starting system actually consists of two separate but related circuits: the starter control circuit, and the motor feed or power supply circuit. The control circuit includes: the starting portion of the ignition switch, the neutral start switch (if equipped) and the light gauge wire (included in the wiring harness) that connects these components to the relay or solenoid. The motor feed circuit consists of heavy gauge cable from battery to relay to starter or directly from battery to solenoid (for solenoid-operated starters). The heavy cable carries the high current required to operate the starter motor with minimal losses due to internal resistance.

The solenoid switch on a cranking motor not only closes the circuit between the battery and the cranking motor, but also shifts the cranking motor pinion into mesh with the engine flywheel ring gear. This is accomplished by means of a linkage between the solenoid plunger and the shift lever on the cranking motor. Solenoids are energized directly from the battery through the switch or in conjunction with a solenoid relay.

When the circuit is completed to the solenoid, current from the battery is through two separate windings, designated as the *pull-in* and the *hold-in* windings. These windings produce a combined magnetic field that pulls in the plunger, so the drive pinion is shifted into mesh and the main contacts in the solenoid switch are closed, completing the cranking motor circuit.

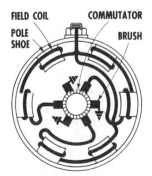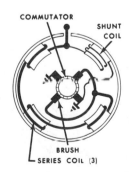

FIGURE 21–12. Schematic wiring diagram of a six-field, six-pole, six-brush, series-wound cranking motor (at left). Shunt coil controls excessive armature speed at light load, allowing heavier field coil winding for more torque (at right). *(Courtesy of General Motors Corporation)*

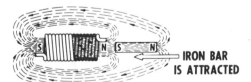

THE EFFECT ON THE FIELD OF FORCE CAUSED BY THE PRESENCE OF AN IRON BAR. THE BAR WILL BE DRAWN TO THE CENTER OF THE COIL.

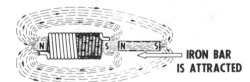

REVERSAL OF CURRENT FLOW CAUSES CHANGE OF POLARITY. THE BAR WILL BE DRAWN TO THE CENTER OF THE COIL WITH THE SAME FORCE.

FIGURE 21–13.

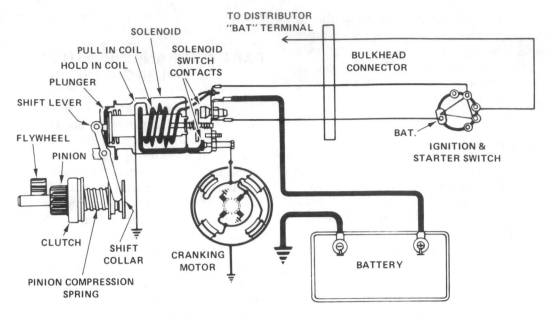

FIGURE 21-14. Solenoid wiring schematic showing pull-in and hold-in winding. Pull-in winding is shorted out when solenoid is engaged. *(Courtesy of General Motors Corporation)*

Closing the main contacts in the solenoid switch at the same time shorts out the pull-in winding, since it is connected across the main contacts. The heavy current through the pull-in winding occurs only during the movement of the plunger.

When the control circuit is broken after the engine is started, current no longer reaches the hold-in winding. Tension of the return spring then causes the plunger to return to the at-rest position. Low system voltage or an open circuit in the hold-in winding will cause an oscillating action of the plunger. The pull-in winding has sufficient magnetic strength to close the main contacts, but when they are closed the pull-in winding is shorted out, and there is no magnetic force to keep the contacts closed. Check for a complete circuit of the hold-in

winding as well as the condition of the battery whenever chattering of the switch occurs.

Whenever a solenoid is replaced on a cranking motor, it is necessary to adjust the pinion travel. (The exact clearance and the method of adjustment varies among different motor designs.)

Starter Relay

The starter relay is a magnetic switch that connects the starter to the battery through the heavy battery cables for the brief period that the engine is being cranked. The relay is mounted near the battery or the starter to keep the cables as short as possible. When the relay coil is activated by the ignition switch, the movable core or plunger is drawn into contact with the internal contacts of the battery and

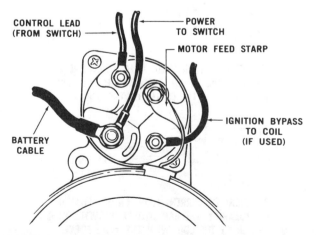

FIGURE 21-15. Wiring connections at starter solenoid (typical). *(Courtesy of Ford Motor Co. of Canada Ltd.)*

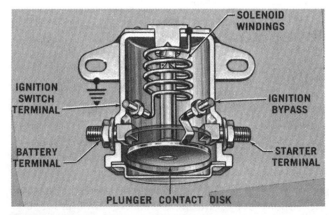

FIGURE 21-16. Cross-sectional view of starter relay used with positive engagement and Bendix drive cranking motors. *(Courtesy of Ford Motor Co. of Canada Ltd.)*

starter terminals. This provides full battery current to the starting motor. A secondary relay function is to initiate the alternate electrical path to the ignition coil, bypassing the resistance wire (or ballast resistor). This is accomplished by an internal connection which is energized by the relay plunger disk when it completes the circuit between the battery and starter internal contacts.

Both relays and solenoid switches are electromagnets used to control the switching of circuits, but the relay opens and closes circuits by means of a pivoted contact arm, while the solenoid switch uses the movable core principle.

Neutral Start Switch

Vehicles equipped with automatic transmissions (and some manual transmission vehicles) require a means of preventing the engine from being started in gear. If not, when the engine starts, the car would tend to lunge forward (or backward), possibly causing an accident. Most automobile manufacturers include a switch in the starting circuit that is mechanically opened by the shift lever when moved to any position other than *NEUTRAL* or *PARK*. The neutral switch may be located at the transmission or in the steering column.

PART 5   CRANKING MOTOR DRIVES

There are two common types of cranking motor drive now in general automotive use—the overrunning clutch and the Bendix drive.

Overrunning Clutch

The overrunning clutch is the device that has made the solenoid-actuated type of starter feasible. It is a roller-type clutch that transmits torque in only one direction, turning freely in the other. In this way, torque can be transmitted from the starting motor to the flywheel, but not from the flywheel to the starting motor.

A typical overrunning clutch is shown in Figure 21–17. The clutch housing is internally splined to the starting motor armature shaft. The drive pinion turns freely on the armature shaft within the clutch housing. When the clutch housing is driven by the armature, the spring-loaded rollers are forced into the small ends of their tapered slots and wedge tightly against the pinion barrel. This locks the pinion and clutch housing solidly together, permitting the pinion to turn the flywheel and thus crank the engine.

When the engine starts, the ring gear begins to drive the pinion faster than the starter motor be-

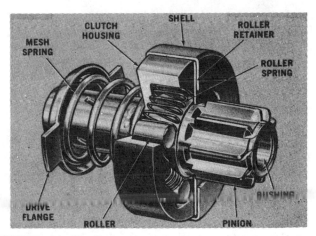

FIGURE 21–17. Cross-sectional view of overrunning clutch type of starter drive. *(Courtesy of Ford Motor Co. of Canada Ltd.)*

cause of the pinion-to-ring gear reduction ratio. This action unloads and releases the clutch rollers, permitting the pinion to rotate freely around the armature shaft without stressing the starter motor.

The operator should always be careful not to reengage the cranking motor drive too soon after a false start. It is advisable to wait at least 5 seconds between attempts to crank. Burred teeth on the flywheel ring gear are an indication of attempted engagement while the engine is running.

Bendix Drive

The Bendix drive depends on inertia to provide meshing of the drive pinion with the engine flywheel ring gear. Illustrated in Figure 21–18 is a cranking motor drive housing with a Bendix drive.

The Bendix drive consists of a drive pinion, sleeve, spring, and spring fastening screws. The drive pinion is normally unbalanced by a counterbalance on one side. It has screw threads on its inner bore. The Bendix sleeve, which is hollow, has screw threads cut on its outer diameter that match the screw threads of the pinion. The sleeve fits loosely

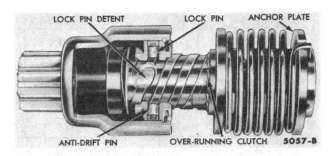

FIGURE 21–18. Bendix type of starter drive.

on the armature shaft and is connected through the Bendix drive spring to the Bendix drive head, which is keyed to the armature shaft. Thus, the Bendix sleeve is free to turn on the armature shaft within the limits permitted by the flexing of the spring.

When the cranking motor switch is closed, the armature begins to revolve. The rotation is transmitted through the drive head and the spring to the sleeve, so that all these parts pick up speed with the armature. The pinion, however, being a loose fit on the sleeve screw thread, does not pick up speed along with the sleeve. In other words, the increased inertia of the drive pinion due to the effect of the counterbalance prevents it from rotating. The result is that the sleeve rotates within the pinion. This forces the drive pinion endwise along the armature shaft so that it goes into mesh with the flywheel teeth. As soon as the pinion reaches the pinion stop, it begins to rotate along with the sleeve and armature. This rotation is transmitted to the flywheel. The Bendix spring takes up the shock of meshing.

When the engine begins to operate, it spins the pinion at a higher speed than that of the cranking motor armature. This causes the pinion to rotate relative to the sleeve, so that the pinion is driven back out of mesh from the flywheel teeth. Thus, the Bendix drive automatically meshes the pinion with the flywheel ring gear to provide cranking, and automatically demeshes the pinion from the flywheel ring gear as soon as the engine starts. The spring-loaded anti-drift pins prevent disengagement until the engine speed reaches approximately 350 rpm.

PART 6 CRANKING SYSTEM DIAGNOSIS AND SERVICE PROCEDURE

In general, cranking system diagnosis and service includes checking the following:

1. Engine mechanical condition.
2. Battery and battery cables.
3. Starting control circuit.
4. Cranking motor current draw.
5. Cranking motor removal, cleaning, inspection, testing, overhaul, and installation, or replacing cranking motor with a new or rebuilt unit.

The current trend is increasingly toward diagnosing the system and replacing the faulty unit with a new or rebuilt unit. This reduces the "down time" of a vehicle requiring repairs.

General Precautions

When servicing the starting system the same general precautions should be followed as are outlined in Chapter 18. In addition, several other precautions should be observed.

• Always disconnect battery ground cable before disconnecting wiring from starting motor or removing starting motor.

• Always have vehicle properly positioned on hoist or safely supported on jack stands for any work underneath vehicle.

• For any cranking tests, make sure transmission is in neutral or park with the parking brake applied. Follow directions to disconnect ignition system to prevent engine starting.

• Be sure all tester leads are free and clear of rotating engine parts.

• Do not wash or immerse electrical components in solvent; clean with compressed air only.

Preliminary Inspection

Always begin with a quick visual check of the supply circuit parts to note any obvious trouble sources such as corroded or loose connections. The supply circuit consists of the battery, battery cables, clamps, and connectors.

Many slow-turning starters have been corrected by simply cleaning the battery terminal posts and cable clamps. Inspect starter and ground cables for corrosion or damage. In checking the supply circuit, always begin with a visual inspection of the battery post and cable clamps.

Test the battery to make sure it is in good condition and has a minimum specific gravity reading of 1.220, temperature corrected, and see that the battery passes the High Rate Discharge Test shown in Chapter 18.

Engine Won't Crank Properly

There are several possible causes for this condition. Assuming that the battery checks out and has been eliminated as a possible cause, either battery power is being prevented from reaching the starter motor or the motor is defective and must be repaired or replaced. First perform the starting control circuit test.

Starting Control Circuit Test

The purpose of this test is to determine whether failure to crank is due to open circuits, defective wiring, or poor connections causing excessive resistance in the starter control circuit. Make sure the ignition switch is *off,* and disconnect the ignition bypass lead

DIAGNOSTIC CHART

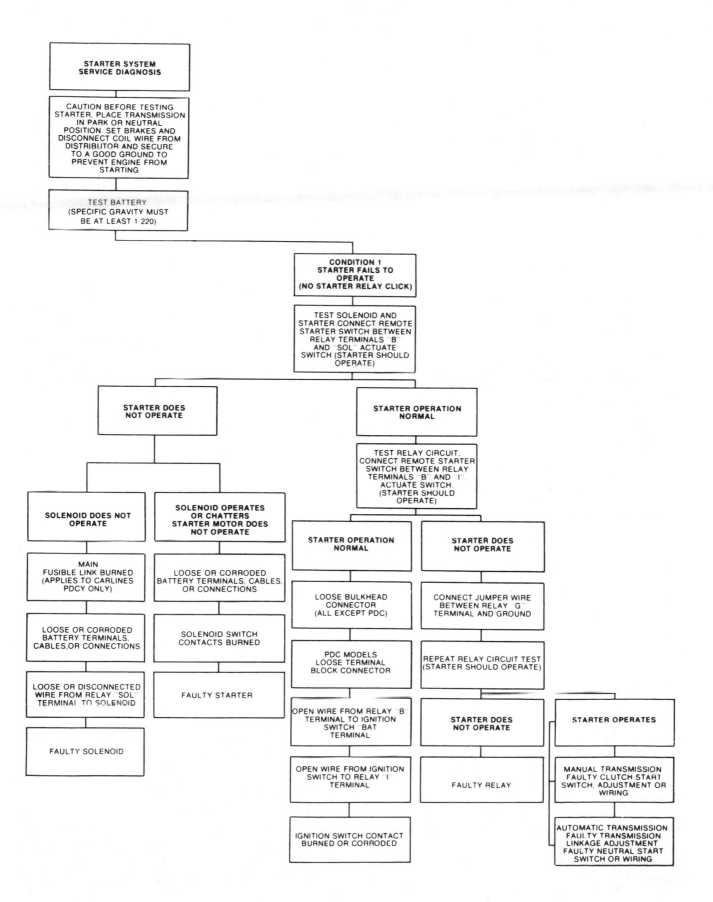

STARTER SYSTEM
SERVICE DIAGNOSIS

CAUTION BEFORE TESTING
STARTER, PLACE TRANSMISSION
IN PARK OR NEUTRAL
POSITION. SET BRAKES AND
DISCONNECT COIL WIRE FROM
DISTRIBUTOR AND SECURE
TO A GOOD GROUND TO
PREVENT ENGINE FROM
STARTING

TEST BATTERY.
(SPECIFIC GRAVITY MUST
BE AT LEAST 1.220)

CONDITION 1
STARTER FAILS TO
OPERATE
(NO STARTER RELAY CLICK)

TEST SOLENOID AND
STARTER CONNECT REMOTE
STARTER SWITCH BETWEEN
RELAY TERMINALS "B"
AND "SOL". ACTUATE
SWITCH (STARTER SHOULD
OPERATE)

STARTER DOES
NOT OPERATE

STARTER OPERATION
NORMAL

TEST RELAY CIRCUIT.
CONNECT REMOTE STARTER
SWITCH BETWEEN RELAY
TERMINALS "B" AND "I".
ACTUATE SWITCH.
(STARTER SHOULD
OPERATE)

SOLENOID DOES NOT
OPERATE

SOLENOID OPERATES
OR CHATTERS
STARTER MOTOR DOES
NOT OPERATE

STARTER OPERATION
NORMAL

STARTER DOES
NOT OPERATE

MAIN
FUSIBLE LINK BURNED
(APPLIES TO CARLINES
PDCY ONLY)

LOOSE OR CORRODED
BATTERY TERMINALS, CABLES,
OR CONNECTIONS

LOOSE BULKHEAD
CONNECTOR
(ALL EXCEPT PDC)

CONNECT JUMPER WIRE
BETWEEN RELAY "G"
TERMINAL AND GROUND

LOOSE OR CORRODED
BATTERY TERMINALS,
CABLES,OR CONNECTIONS

SOLENOID SWITCH
CONTACTS BURNED

PDC MODELS
LOOSE TERMINAL
BLOCK CONNECTOR

REPEAT RELAY CIRCUIT TEST
(STARTER SHOULD OPERATE)

LOOSE OR DISCONNECTED
WIRE FROM RELAY "SOL"
TERMINAL TO SOLENOID

FAULTY STARTER

OPEN WIRE FROM RELAY "B"
TERMINAL TO IGNITION
SWITCH "BAT"
TERMINAL

STARTER DOES
NOT OPERATE

STARTER OPERATES

FAULTY SOLENOID

OPEN WIRE FROM IGNITION
SWITCH TO RELAY "I"
TERMINAL

FAULTY RELAY

MANUAL TRANSMISSION
FAULTY CLUTCH START
SWITCH, ADJUSTMENT OR
WIRING

IGNITION SWITCH CONTACT
BURNED OR CORRODED

AUTOMATIC TRANSMISSION
FAULTY TRANSMISSION
LINKAGE ADJUSTMENT
FAULTY NEUTRAL START
SWITCH OR WIRING

459

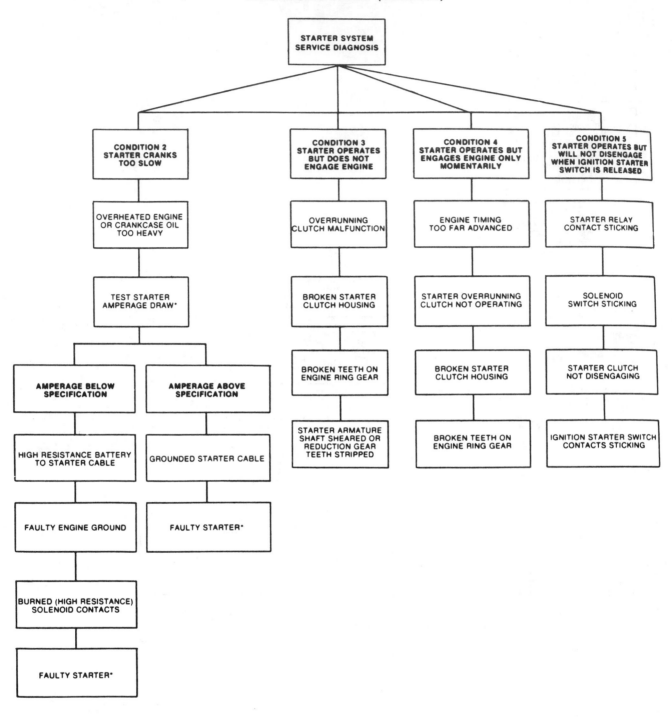

at the relay (or solenoid) to prevent the engine from starting.

Connect a jumper wire from the battery positive terminal to the starter relay S (or solenoid switch) terminal. Observe whether the engine cranks now. If the engine won't crank, check the starter (ignition) switch circuit and the neutral start switch circuit (if so equipped). Clean and tighten the connections, and repair or replace any defective components.

The next step is to check out the starter relay (or solenoid).

Relay Bypass Test (Positive Engagement Starter)

The purpose of this test is to determine if the starter relay is defective. Remove the ignition bypass lead at the relay and make sure the ignition switch is *off* to prevent starting the engine. Connect a heavy

FIGURE 21-19.

jumper cable from the battery positive terminal and hold it against the starter relay "starter" terminal. Observe whether the engine cranks with the jumper connected. If the engine cranks now, the starter relay is defective and should be replaced.

Starter Solenoid Test (Solenoid-Actuated Starter)

Disconnect the distributor pigtail connector to prevent starting. Connect the voltmeter leads between the solenoid "switch" terminal and ground. Observe the voltage while cranking with the switch *on*. If the reading exceeds 10 volts, replace the solenoid.

Starting Motor Load Test

Refer to Figure 21-20 for the positive engagement starter and Figure 21-21 for the solenoid-actuated starter. Make sure the load control knob of the battery-starter tester is turned *off*. Leaving the battery cables in place, connect the ammeter test leads to the battery terminals. Connect the voltmeter test

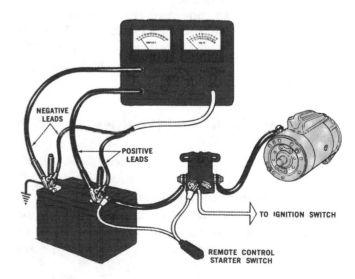

FIGURE 21-20. Starting motor load test (positive engagement Ford starters). *(Courtesy of Ford Motor Co. of Canada Ltd.)*

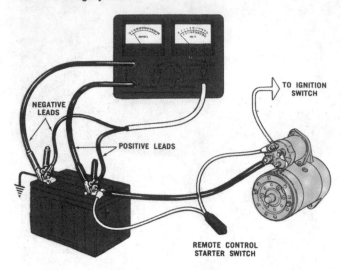

FIGURE 21-21. Starting motor load test (solenoid-actuated starter). *(Courtesy of Ford Motor Co. of Canada Ltd.)*

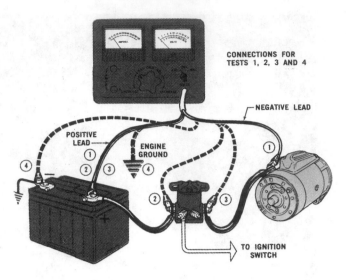

FIGURE 21-22. Cranking circuit test (Ford positive engagement type starter). *(Courtesy of Ford Motor Co. of Canada Ltd.)*

leads to the battery terminals. Disconnect the ignition bypass lead at the relay (or solenoid) terminal to prevent starting. Install a remote control starter switch between the battery positive terminal and the starter relay (or solenoid) *switch* terminal. With the ignition switch *off*, crank the starter and carefully read the voltmeter. Stop cranking and adjust the load control knob until the voltmeter reads exactly the same as when the engine was being cranked. Now, read the ammeter. This reading is the current draw for the starter when cranking under load.

If the current draw is within specifications, the starter is all right. If the current draw is above specifications, the problem may be caused by excessive engine drag due to congealed engine oil or a major mechanical problem, such as a cracked head or block causing coolant to leak into the cylinders or seized piston rings or bearings. Check for these conditions before removing the starter.

Cranking Circuit Test (Positive Engagement)

Preliminary Steps

1. Disconnect the ignition bypass lead at the relay to prevent starting (see Figure 21-22).

2. Connect a remote-control starter switch between the relay *Bat* and relay *S* terminals to crank the engine.

3. Connect the voltmeter leads as indicated to each test below and read the voltage drop while cranking the engine (ignition switch *off*).

Tests

1. Positive lead to battery + terminal; negative lead to starter *Bat* terminal. Reading should be no more than 0.5 volts.

2. Positive lead to battery + terminal; negative lead to relay *Bat* terminal. Reading should be no more than 0.1 volt.

3. Positive lead to battery + terminal; negative lead to relay *Starter* terminal. Reading should be no more than 0.3 volts.

4. Negative lead to battery − terminal; positive lead to engine ground. Reading should be no more than 0.1 volt.

Cranking Circuit Test (Solenoid-Actuated Starter)

Preliminary Steps

1. Disconnect the ignition bypass lead at the solenoid to prevent starting (see Figure 21-23).

2. Connect a remote-control starting switch between the solenoid *Bat* terminal and the solenoid *Switch* terminal.

3. Connect the voltmeter leads as indicated for each test below and read the voltage drop while cranking the engine (ignition switch *off*).

Tests

1. Positive lead to battery + terminal; negative lead to solenoid *Starter* terminal. Reading should be no more than 0.5 volts.

2. Positive lead to solenoid *Bat* terminal; neg-

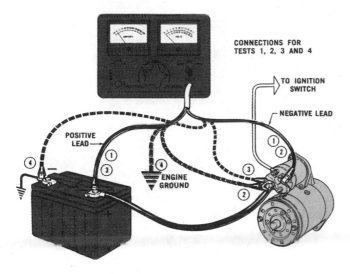

FIGURE 21–23. Cranking circuit test (solenoid-actuated starter). *(Courtesy of Ford Motor Co. of Canada Ltd.)*

ative lead to solenoid *Starter* terminal. Reading should be no more than 0.3 volts.

3. Positive lead to battery + terminal; negative lead to solenoid *Bat* terminal. Reading should be no more than 0.2 volts.

4. Negative lead to battery – terminal; positive lead to engine ground. Reading should be no more than 0.1 volt.

If the preceding tests have not isolated the cause of the problem, remove the starter from the vehicle and perform the starter no-load test.

Starter No-Load Test

The starter no-load test (Figure 21–24) will uncover such faults as open or shorted windings, rubbing armature, and bent armature shaft. The starter can be tested, at no load, on the test bench only. *Note:* It

is advisable to mount the starter securely in a vise while performing this test.

Make the test connections as shown at left in Figure 21–24 for the positive engagement starter and at right for the solenoid starter. The starter will run without load. Be sure that there is no current through the ammeter. Determine the exact reading on the voltmeter.

Disconnect the starter from the battery, and adjust the resistance of the rheostat until the voltmeter indicates the same reading as that obtained while the starter was running. The ammeter will indicate the starter no-load current draw.

This test eliminates a possible hard-to-crank engine from the testing procedure. The no-load test will reveal whether a defect exists within the starter motor. If the test readings are not within specifications, the motor should be disassembled, cleaned, inspected, and tested in accordance with the following bench test procedures.

Armature Open-Circuit Test

An open circuit armature may be detected by examining the commutator for evidence of burning (Figure 21–25). A spot burned on the commutator is caused by an arc formed every time the commutator segment, connected to the open circuit winding, passes under a brush.

Armature and Field Grounded Circuit Test

This test will determine if the winding insulation has failed, permitting a conductor to touch the frame or armature core. To determine if the armature windings are grounded, make the connections as shown

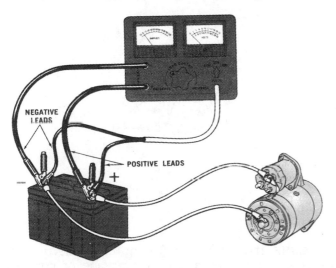
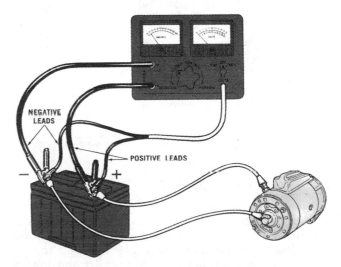

FIGURE 21–24. Starter no-load test. *(Courtesy of Ford Motor Co. of Canada Ltd.)*

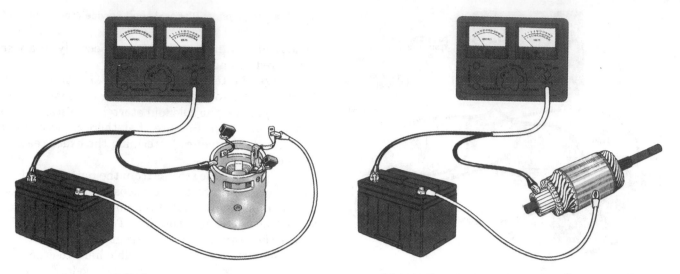

FIGURE 21-25. Armature open circuit and field coil test. *(Courtesy of Ford Motor Co. of Canada Ltd.)*

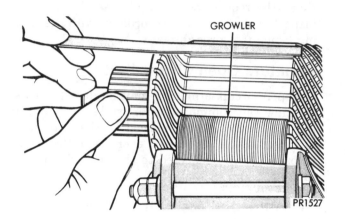

GROWLER

FIGURE 21-26. Short circuits in the armature are located by use of a growler. When the armature is revolved in the growler with a steel strip such as a hacksaw blade held above it, the blade will vibrate above the area of the armature core in which the short circuit is located. Shorts between bars are sometimes produced by brush dust or copper between the bars. These shorts can be eliminated by cleaning out the slots. *(Courtesy of Chrysler Corporation)*

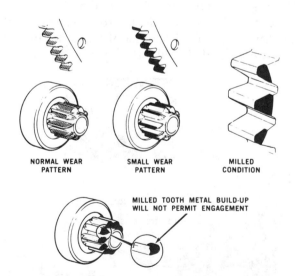

NORMAL WEAR PATTERN   SMALL WEAR PATTERN   MILLED CONDITION

MILLED TOOTH METAL BUILD-UP WILL NOT PERMIT ENGAGEMENT

FIGURE 21-27. Small wear pattern indicates incorrect starter alignment and shallow mesh of drive teeth with ring gear teeth. Milled teeth or teeth battered from butting during engagement may require drive and ring gear replacement. *(Courtesy of Ford Motor Co. of Canada Ltd.)*

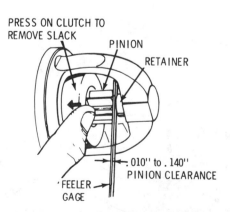

PRESS ON CLUTCH TO REMOVE SLACK

PINION

RETAINER

.010'' to .140'' PINION CLEARANCE

FEELER GAGE

FIGURE 21-28. Starter drive end clearance must be correct to prevent gear housing breakage. Approximate clearances are shown. *(Courtesy of Chrysler Corporation)*

at left in Figure 21–25. If the voltmeter indicates any voltage, the armature windings are grounded. Grounded field windings can be detected by making the connections as shown at right. If the voltmeter indicates any voltage, the field windings are grounded.

Open Field Circuit

Connect leads to each end of field coil to test for opens. If field coil has an open circuit, voltmeter will not register any reading. Grounded field coils must be disconnected before testing.

PART 7 SELF-CHECK

1. A solenoid switch is only used with a Bendix drive. True or false?

2. The drive pinion has about 15 teeth for every tooth on the engine flywheel. True or false?

3. An overrunning clutch only provides for demeshing of the drive pinion. True or false?

4. Increasing the number of circuits in a cranking motor increases the resistance. True or false?

5. The ideal battery cable should be short and of heavy gauge. True or false?

6. Excessive heat is generated when a cranking motor is operated more than 30 seconds. True or false?

7. The armature core is made of iron to complete the magnetic circuit. True or false?

8. The Bendix drive is an inertia type of cranking motor drive. True or false?

9. Cranking motor test specifications are given at high voltage to show errors more clearly. True or false?

10. The overrunning clutch uses a shift lever to actuate the drive pinion. True or false?

11. The armature windings and commutator rotate together. True or false?

12. All the electricity through the field coils also flows through the armature. True or false?

13. A high-voltage drop is desirable in the cranking circuit. True or false?

PART 8 TEST QUESTIONS

1. In a series wound cranking motor, current flows through the:
   (a) field windings and pole shoes
   (b) pole shoes and armature
   (c) starter frame and field windings
   (d) armature and field windings

2. The starting motor should not be operated continuously for more than:
   (a) 30 seconds
   (b) 3 minutes
   (c) 3 seconds
   (d) 30 minutes

3. An overrunning clutch is used in the:
   (a) Bendix starter drive
   (b) inertia starter drive
   (c) positive shift starter drive
   (d) none of the above

4. A starter solenoid that clicks rapidly when the key is turned to the start position indicates a faulty:
   (a) battery
   (b) solenoid switch
   (c) cable connection
   (d) any of the above

5. When diagnosing starting system problems the procedure is to first test the:
   (a) field current draw
   (b) battery and battery cables
   (c) starting motor current flow
   (d) solenoid hold-in winding

Chapter 22

AC Charging Systems

Performance Objectives

After thorough study of this chapter, sufficient practice on adequate training models, and with the necessary tools, equipment, and manuals, you should be able to do the following:

1. Complete the self-check and test questions with at least 80 percent accuracy.
2. Observe the accepted general precautions outlined in this chapter.
3. Describe the purpose, construction, and operation of AC charging systems and their components.
4. Accurately diagnose charging system faults.
5. Safely remove, test, recondition, replace, and adjust faulty charging system components according to manufacturer's specifications.
6. Properly performance test the reconditioned components and the entire charging system to determine the success of the repairs performed.
7. Prepare vehicle for customer acceptance.

PART 1 ALTERNATING CURRENT (AC) GENERATORS

The AC generator charging system produces electrical energy. This energy is used to maintain the proper state of charge in the battery and supply current to all electrically powered equipment in the car. It does this by converting mechanical energy into electricity.

In an AC generator an electromagnet is rotated inside a stationary conductor so that lines of force cut across the conductor. The magnet is called the *rotor* and the conductor is called a *stator*.

The rotor core is wound with wire and connected to an external source of current through two slip rings and brushes. This represents a simple form of externally excited field used in most alternators.

The conductor, represented by the single loop of wire, forms the stator part of the alternator. Because the rotor is externally excited by direct current, one pole will always be north and the other south. Current through the stator will reverse directions constantly.

Rotor Assembly

Actually, the alternator rotor has more than two poles. A commonly used rotor has 12 poles. The rotor consists of a core, coil, two pole pieces, and two slip rings. An external direct current is supplied to the rotor coil through slip rings and brushes. The field coil is located inside two interlocking pole pieces. Each of these pole pieces has six poles, providing a total of twelve poles for the complete rotor assembly.

Voltage Output

The following factors affect the magnitude of voltage generated:

1. Voltage will increase as the speed of rotor is increased.

2. Voltage will increase as the strength of the rotor magnetic field is increased.

3. The strength of the rotor magnetic field may be increased by the following:

(a) The number of turns and type of wire used in the rotor.

(b) The air gap between the rotor poles and stator. Reducing the air gap increases the strength of the field.

(c) The voltage applied to the rotor through the slip rings and brushes.

4. Voltage will increase as the number of turns of wire in the stator winding is increased. This is

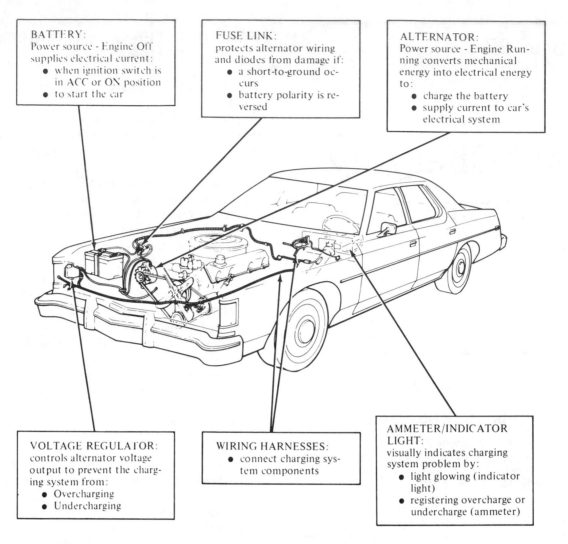

BATTERY:
Power source - Engine Off supplies electrical current:
- when ignition switch is in ACC or ON position
- to start the car

FUSE LINK:
protects alternator wiring and diodes from damage if:
- a short-to-ground occurs
- battery polarity is reversed

ALTERNATOR:
Power source - Engine Running converts mechanical energy into electrical energy to:
- charge the battery
- supply current to car's electrical system

VOLTAGE REGULATOR:
controls alternator voltage output to prevent the charging system from:
- Overcharging
- Undercharging

WIRING HARNESSES:
- connect charging system components

AMMETER/INDICATOR LIGHT:
visually indicates charging system problem by:
- light glowing (indicator light)
- registering overcharge or undercharge (ammeter)

FIGURE 22-1. Location of AC charging system components on typical automobile. *(Courtesy of Ford Motor Co. of Canada Ltd.)*

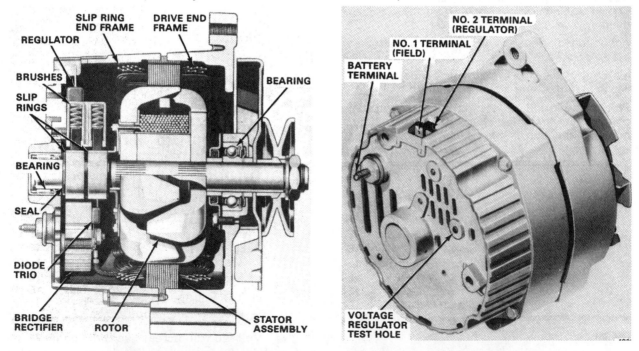

FIGURE 22-2. AC generator terminals on one type of AC generator (typical) and cross-sectional view. *(Courtesy of General Motors Corporation)*

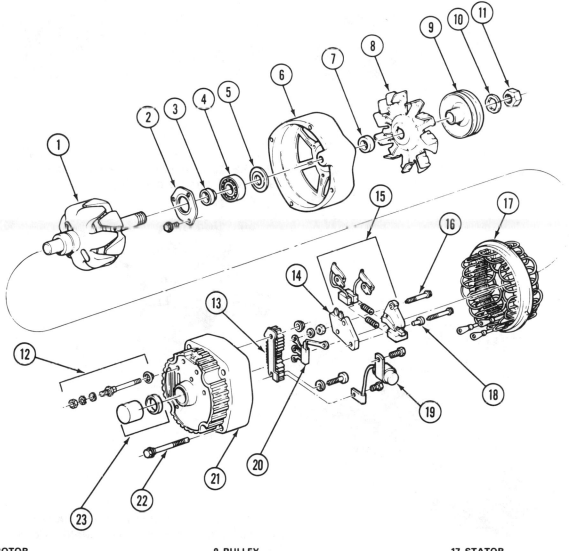

1. ROTOR	9. PULLEY	17. STATOR
2. FRONT BEARING RETAINER PLATE	10. LOCKWASHER	18. INSULATING WASHER
3. COLLAR (INNER)	11. PULLEY NUT	19. CAPACITOR
4. BEARING	12. TERMINAL ASSEMBLY	20. DIODE TRIO
5. SLINGER	13. BRIDGE RECTIFIER	21. REAR HOUSING
6. FRONT HOUSING	14. REGULATOR	22. THROUGH-BOLT
7. COLLAR (OUTER)	15. BRUSH ASSEMBLY	23. BEARING AND
8. FAN	16. SCREW	SEAL ASSEMBLY

FIGURE 22-3. Exploded view of AC generator with component identification. *(Courtesy of General Motors Corporation)*

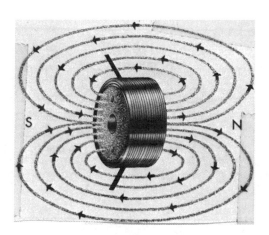

FIGURE 22-4. Magnetic field surrounding AC generator rotor field windings. *(Courtesy of General Motors Corporation)*

469

FIGURE 22-5. Exploded view of rotor. *(Courtesy of General Motors Corporation)*

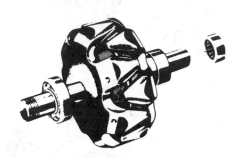

FIGURE 22-6. Assembled rotor and bearings. *(Courtesy of General Motors Corporation)*

FIGURE 22-7. Method used to energize rotor field windings. *(Courtesy of General Motors Corporation)*

FIGURE 22-8. Magnetic field surrounding alternating N and S pole fingers of rotor. *(Courtesy of General Motors Corporation)*

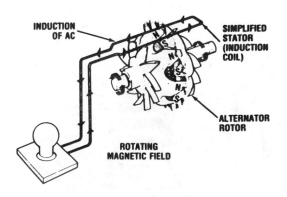

INDUCTION OF AC

SIMPLIFIED STATOR (INDUCTION COIL)

ALTERNATOR ROTOR

ROTATING MAGNETIC FIELD

FIGURE 22-9. Rotating magnetic field induces current in stationary stator winding. *(Courtesy of Chrysler Corporation)*

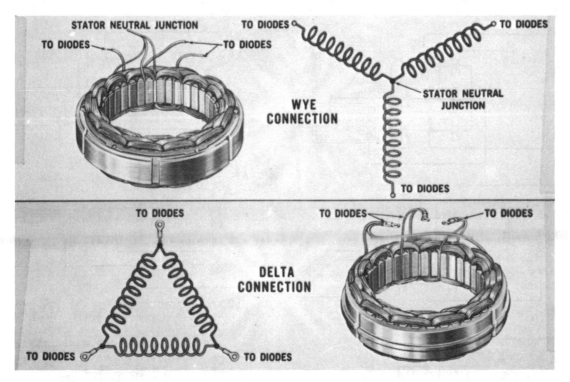

FIGURE 22-10. Automotive AC generators have a stator assembly with three sets of field windings (three phases) connected either in a Y (wye) arrangement or a delta arrangement. *(Courtesy of Ford Motor Co. of Canada Ltd.)*

because more conductors will be cut by the lines of force from the rotor.

Single-Phase Stator

A simple alternator having a single loop of wire to represent the stator winding serves to illustrate how an alternating current is produced. An alternator of this type is called a single-phase alternator, regardless of the number of turns of wire in the stator winding. When all the windings in the stator are connected in *series* to form one continuous circuit, the term *single-phase* applies.

Three-Phase Stator

The stator assembly in the alternator has three sets of windings. Each winding has one terminal or end that is independent of the others. They are shown as 1, 2, and 3. The other end of each winding is connected to form an insulated junction called a Y connection. See Figure 22-11.

The single-phase AC voltage is produced between any two of the open terminals. Combining these three single phases forms the three-phase connected stator. This means that it produces three overlapping sets of current. Some alternators use a *delta* connection of the three phases. See Figure 22-12.

Six Diodes Used

Six silicone-diode rectifiers are used to rectify the AC output of the three-phase connected alternator to direct current. Three of these positive diodes are mounted on a heat sink that is called a *positive rectifier assembly*. This rectifier assembly is insulated from the alternator end shield and connected to the alternator output BATT terminal of the alternator.

The other three diodes have negative polarity and are mounted on a heat sink and are called a *negative rectifier assembly*. This rectifier assembly is mounted directly to the alternator end shield, which is a ground.

Both rectifier assemblies are mounted in the air stream to provide adequate cooling of the diodes.

Rectifier Circuit

The diodes are connected into the alternator circuit between the stator winding and the battery and the vehicle electrical load. This arrangement provides a smooth direct current. The diodes also provide a blocking action to prevent the battery from discharging through the alternator. There are two diodes in each phase; one diode allows current in one direction, and the other diode in the same phase allows current in the opposite direction.

A capacitor is connected from the output BATT

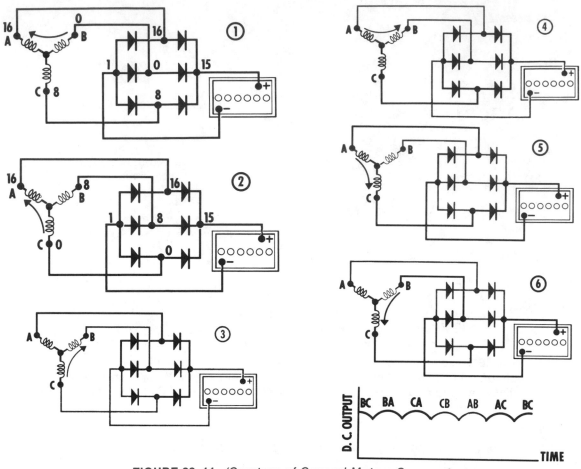

FIGURE 22-11. (Courtesy of General Motors Corporation)

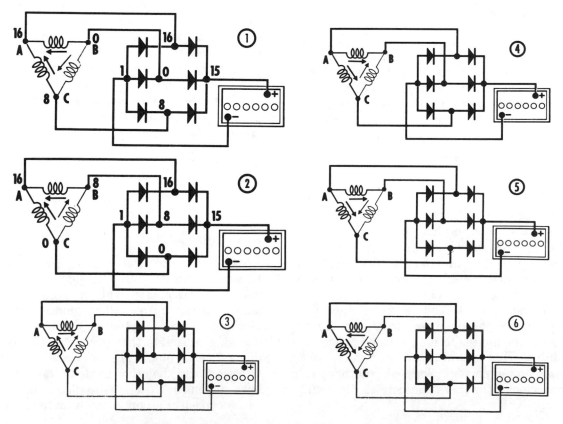

FIGURE 22-12. (Courtesy of General Motors Corporation)

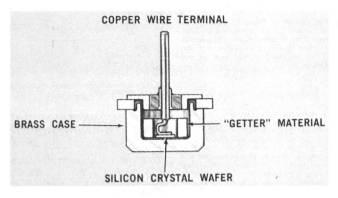

FIGURE 22-13. Cross-sectional view of diode as used in AC generators. (*Courtesy of Ford Motor Co. of Canada Ltd.*)

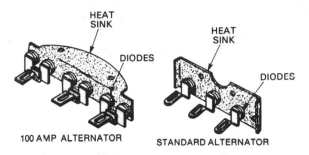

FIGURE 22-14. Comparison of heat sinks and diodes of high-output alternator on left and standard alternator on right. (*Courtesy of Chrysler Corporation*)

to ground. It is used to absorb any peak voltages and thus protects the rectifiers and helps reduce radio interference.

Full-Wave Rectification

Alternators are full-wave rectification. Full-wave rectification of the stator output utilizes the total potential by redirecting the current from the stator windings so that all current is in one direction. All current delivered to the output terminal is direct current.

Alternator Operation

This discussion of alternator operation follows the principle of positive voltage output. If desired, the electron theory of negative voltage output may be applied to the diagrams (Figures 22–11 and 22–12) and the discussion by reversing the direction of the arrows in the diagrams and by reversing the direction of current in the discussion.

For convenience, the three AC voltage curves provided by the "Y"- *connected stator* for each revolution of the rotor have been divided into six periods, 1 through 6. Each period represents one-sixth of a rotor revolution, or 60 degrees.

An inspection of the voltage curves during period 1 reveals that the maximum voltage being produced appears across stator terminals *BA*. This means that the current will be from *B* to *A* in the stator winding during this period and through the diodes as illustrated.

In order to more clearly see why the current during period 1 is as illustrated, assume that the peak phase voltage developed from *B* to *A* is 16 volts. This means that the potential at *B* is zero volts, and the potential at *A* is 16 volts.

Between periods 1 and 2, the maximum voltage being impressed across the diodes changes or switches from phase *BA* to phase *CA*.

Taking the instant of time at which this voltage is 16 volts, the potential at *A* is 16 and at *C* is zero. Following the same procedure for periods 3–6, the

current conditions can be determined, and they are shown in the illustrations. These are the six major current conditions for a three-phase "Y"- connected stator and rectifier combination.

The voltage obtained from the stator-rectifier combination when connected to a battery is not perfectly flat, but is so smooth that, for all practical purposes, the output may be considered to be a nonvarying DC voltage. The voltage, of course, is obtained from the phase voltage curves and can be pictured as illustrated (Figure 22–11).

A delta-connected stator wound to provide the same output as a "Y"-connected stator also will provide a smooth voltage and current ouput when connected to a six-diode rectifier. For convenience, the three-phase AC voltage curves obtained from the basic delta connection for one rotor revolution are reproduced here and have been divided into six periods (Figure 22–12).

During period 1, the maximum voltage being developed in the stator is in phase *BA*. To determine the direction of current, consider the instant at which the voltage during period 1 is at maximum, and assume this voltage to be 16 volts. The potential at *B* is zero and at *A* is 16.

An inspection of the delta stator, however, reveals a major difference from the "Y" stator. Whereas the "Y" stator conducts current through only two windings throughout period 1, the delta stator conducts current through all three. The reason for this is apparent, since phase *BA* is in parallel with phase *BC* plus *CA*. Note that, since the voltage from *B* to *A* is 16, the voltage from *B* to *C* to *A* must also be 16. This is true since 8 volts is developed in each of these two phases.

During period 2, the maximum voltage developed is in phase *CA*, and the voltage potentials are shown on the illustration (Figure 22–12) at the instant the voltage is maximum. Also shown are the other phase voltages, and again, the current through the rectifier is identical to that for a "Y" stator, since the voltages across the diodes are the same.

However, as during period 1, all three delta phases conduct current as illustrated (Figure 22-12).

Following the same procedure for periods 3-6, the current directions are shown. These are the six major current conditions for a delta stator.

Open Rectifiers (Diode)

If the positive or negative diode is open circuited, there is no current in either direction. An open diode results in loss of current and an ouput less than normal.

Shorted Rectifiers (Diode)

When the positive or negative rectifier is shorted, (diode) current is allowed in either direction. When the positive diode is shorted, it may also drain the battery. When there is current through the heat sink, it can reverse through the shorted diode instead of to the battery. A shorted diode will reduce alternator current output.

Battery Polarity

If a battery were installed and connected with polarity reversed, a short circuit would be created through the diodes. Current would then be from the positive and negative diodes and into the heat sink. From the heat sink, a completed circuit would exist back to the negative battery terminal. Full battery voltage would be impressed on the diodes. The resulting high-current would damage the diodes and/or damage the wiring harness. Some automobiles have a fusible link to protect the system in case of accidental reverse polarity.

Reverse Current Prevention

The positive post of the battery is connected to the alternator output terminal and the positive heat sink. However, the positive diode will not allow current into the stator windings. The diodes eliminate the need for a cutout relay used with DC generators.

Grounded-Brush Alternator

This unit has a single field terminal connected to a brush. The other brush is mounted to the alternator housing. In this system, the field circuit is grounded at the alternator through the brush mounted to the alternator housing.

Insulated-Brush Alternator

This unit has both field brushes insulated from the alternator housing. The single terminal is connected to a brush; the other brush is connected to the heat sink instead of ground.

Isolated-Field Alternator

This unit has two insulated brushes, with each brush having a field terminal. Neither brush has a direct ground to the alternator housing or the heat sink. This means the internal field circuit of the alternator is isolated.

Grounding

The grounded-brush alternator's field circuit is grounded at the alternator housing. The insulated-

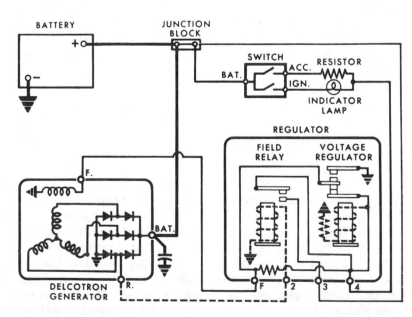

FIGURE 22-15. This system uses a field relay to energize the field in the rotor. *(Courtesy of General Motors Corporation)*

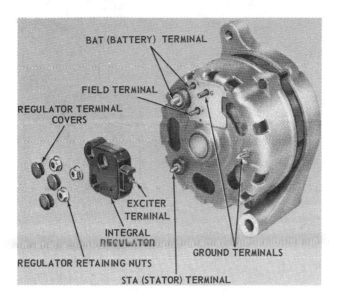

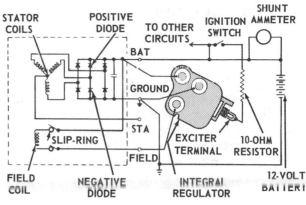

FIGURE 22-16. Integral voltage regulator as used on some charging systems. *(Courtesy of Ford Motor Co. of Canada Ltd.)*

brush and isolated-field alternator's field circuits are grounded in the electronic voltage regulator.

Summary

1. An alternator has two component circuits: one, the field circuit, is being fed current from a power source, the other is in the stator windings and terminal components.

2. The transfer of energy between the two circuits is effected by induction as the moving north and south rotor fingers alternately pass the stator windings. (The design gap between fingers collapses the magnetic field for each winding as rotation continues. This means that the magnetic fields build and collapse in typical alternating current cycles even though the phases overlap.)

3. The voltage induced by the field applies its current-driving force to the pair of stator wind-

ings being most strongly energized. Accordingly, it pushes current to the diodes.

4. The positive diodes pass current to the alternator output terminal. The negative diodes pass current returning through the ground circuit. (Each type of diode blocks current of opposite polarity.)

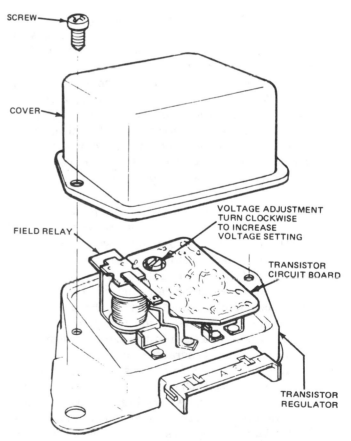

FIGURE 22-18. Field relay and electronic voltage regulator unit. *(Courtesy of Ford Motor Co. of Canada Ltd.)*

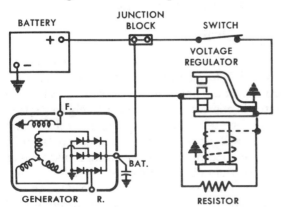

FIGURE 22-17. This system uses a special ignition switch to carry field current to alternator. An electromechanical voltage regulator controls system voltage. *(Courtesy of General Motors Corporation)*

PART 2   AC GENERATOR REGULATORS

Current Control

The AC generator is "self limiting" in its maximum output. This occurs as the magnetic field produced by the current in the stator windings opposes in polarity and approaches in value the magnetic field provided by the rotor as the generator output increases. This causes the generator to limit its own output to a maximum value.

Voltage Regulator

The voltage delivered by an alternator must be regulated to protect the charging circuit. Circumstances or preference determine whether this is accomplished with a vibrating-type electromechanical regulator, with a transistorized regulator, or with an integral electronic regulator that incorporates transistors, diodes, and resistors in an arrangement which accomplishes the same end.

Electromechanical Regulator

Operation of the electromechanical regulator is basically the same as the voltage regulator used with DC generators. However, when used with an alternator, the regulator need only provide one basic function, that is, to maintain the charging system voltage at a constant level. To accomplish this, we use a two-stage *voltage limiter*. A current limiter is not used, since an alternator is self-limiting in its production of current. The field relay acts as a means for connecting the voltage limiter to the charging system on some systems.

When the ignition switch is turned on, battery current is through the ignition switch, through the alternator indicator lamp and resistor to the voltage regulator I terminal. From there we can trace the current to the voltage limiter upper contacts, via internal connections, and out through the voltage regulator F terminal to the alternator FLD terminal (rotor coil). There is enough current through the circuit to prime the alternator so that when the engine is started the magnetism in the field will cause the alternator to start generating voltage.

While engine rpm is increasing from cranking speed to idle speed, the alternator develops sufficient voltage at its STA terminal to close the field relay contacts. This action turns out the alternator indicator lamp and applies battery voltage to the alternator field via the voltage regulator A terminal,

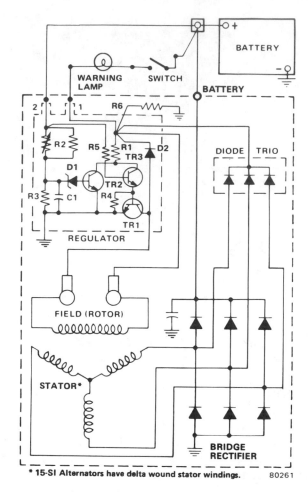

FIGURE 22–19. Initial field current in this diagram is provided through the ignition switch and indicator light circuit. When the alternator starts to produce current, additional current is provided to the field by the diode trio from the alternator stator output. *(Courtesy of General Motors Corporation)*

the field relay contacts, and the voltage limiter upper contacts. Some units provide added field current through a diode trio (see Figure 22–19).

Voltage Limiter

The voltage limiter is a two-stage device. It is used to control field current and to extend the range of alternator rpm that can be controlled. When the alternator is operating at comparatively low speeds or when the system load is heavy, the voltage limiter armature will vibrate on the lower contacts and limit voltage by intermittently inserting resistance in the alternator field circuit. Regulation will continue on the lower contacts until the voltage rises to a value at which the resistor will no longer provide control.

At high alternator speeds, or when the battery is fully charged and the electrical load is light, the voltage attempts to rise; in so doing, the armature

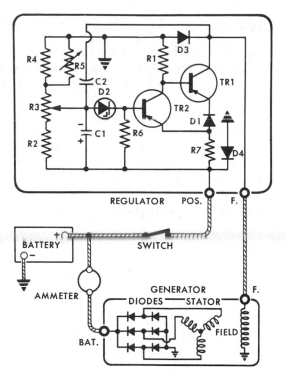

FIGURE 22-20. Schematic of an electronic voltage regulator. *(Courtesy of General Motors Corporation)*

is pulled down and starts vibrating on the upper contacts. This provides additional control by intermittently inserting the resistance or bypassing the field to ground. When the contacts are closed, the current in the field circuit drops as the magnetic

field in the rotor collapses. The result is a drop in alternator output voltage. When the voltage drops below the lower stage calibration point, the upper contacts open. This vibrating action takes place many times per second. Changes in the system load or changes in speed may cause the above sequence of operations to vary.

To summarize, the voltage limiter may be found to be operating on either set of contacts (upper or lower) depending on load and speed conditions at the time, but never on both.

Electronic Voltage Regulator

The electronic voltage regulator is a solid-state unit with no moving parts or adjustment. It is serviced only by replacement. This regulator governs the electrical system voltage by limiting the output voltage that is generated by the alternator. This is accomplished by controlling the value of field current that is allowed to pass through the field windings. Basically, the electronic regulator operates as a voltage-sensitive switch.

The electronic regulator contains several transistors, diodes, resistors, and a capacitor. A large transistor is placed in series with the alternator field winding and a control circuit that senses the system voltage. This control unit turns the transistor on and off many times a second to keep the field current and alternator output voltage at a proper level.

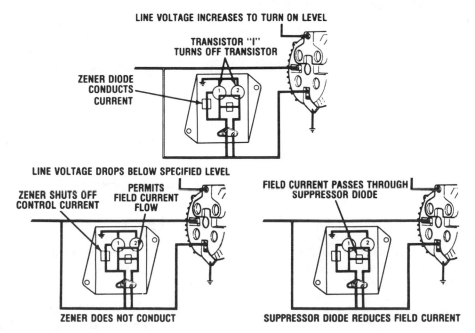

FIGURE 22-21. Electronic voltage regulator operation. *(Courtesy of Chrysler Corporation)*

PART 3 AC GENERATOR CHARGING SYSTEM DIAGNOSIS AND SERVICE PROCEDURE

Alternating-current generator charging system service includes a general overall visual inspection, system and component diagnosis, and component replacement or repair. A thorough understanding of the principles of operation is essential for accurate diagnosis and service. Continuing variations in design and application can be readily dealt with if operating principles are understood.

General practice is increasingly toward replacement of faulty components rather than repair. A good multiscale voltmeter, an ammeter, and an ohmmeter or test light are essential equipment for diagnosing AC charging systems. As with other electrical system service, battery inspection and testing as described in Chapter 18 should be included in charging system service.

General Precautions

Refer to Chapter 18 for general precautions regarding battery service. In addition, the following precautions should be observed:

1. Follow test equipment manufacturer's instructions for testing.

2. Disconnect battery ground cable before removing alternator for service.

3. Always observe proper battery polarity.

4. Observe vehicle manufacturer's procedures and specifications.

5. Do not attempt to polarize the alternator.

6. Do not accidentally ground any alternator terminals.

7. Do not operate alternator on an open circuit.

8. Use only the induction pickup-type of ammeter on computer equipped cars — never the series connected ammeter.

The normal sequence of operations for servicing the AC charging system will depend on the nature of the problem. Charging system problems can be classified as follows:

1. Noisy alternator
2. Overcharging
3. Undercharging

Noisy Alternator

A noisy water pump, power steering pump, fan, or other drive belt noise should not be confused with alternator noise. Once it has definitely been established that it is the alternator which is the source of the noise, follow the diagnostic chart to identify the possible reasons for alternator noise. Some of the problems listed can be corrected without alternator removal; others require alternator removal and repair or replacement.

Overcharging or Undercharging

Battery condition is a good indicator of charging system operation. Excessive gassing and the need for repeatedly adding water to the battery indicate that the charging system voltage may be too high. A weak battery (poor cranking and low voltage) may indicate insufficient charging or a faulty battery. To determine whether the battery or the charging system is at fault, follow the diagnostic chart in this section.

Figures 22-22 to 22-25 show typical tests required to determine whether the alternator, the regulator, or connecting wiring are at fault. Faulty regulators are replaced. Faulty wiring is repaired, replaced, or disassembled, tested, and repaired. Typical testing and repair procedures are shown in Figures 22-26 to 22-38. After repairs or replacement have been completed, the system should again be tested for proper output.

AC Generator Removal

1. Disconnect negative battery cable at battery. Caution: Failure to observe this step may result in an injury from hot battery lead at generator.

2. Disconnect wiring leads from generator.

3. Loosen adjusting bolts and move generator to provide slack in belt.

4. Remove generator drive belt.

5. Remove thru bolts which retain generator.

6. Remove generator from car.

Installation

1. If removed from car, install generator to mounting bracket with bolts, washers, and nuts. Do not tighten.

2. Install generator drive belt.

3. Tighten belt to the specified belt tension. See the engine cooling section for proper belt tensioning procedures.

AC GENERATOR CHARGING SYSTEM DIAGNOSTIC CHART

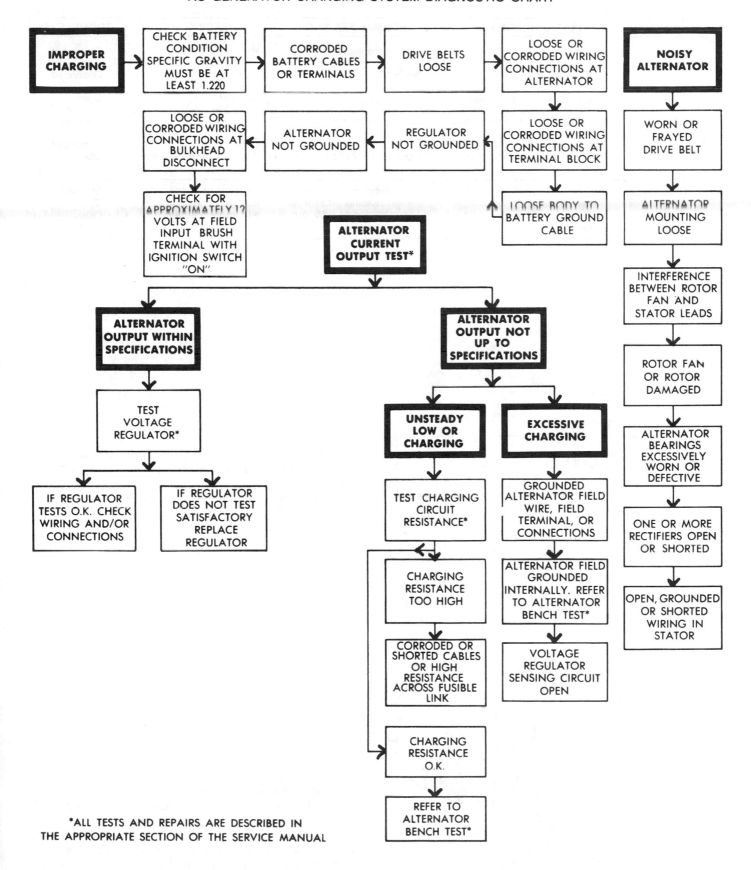

IMPROPER CHARGING → CHECK BATTERY CONDITION SPECIFIC GRAVITY MUST BE AT LEAST 1.220 → CORRODED BATTERY CABLES OR TERMINALS → DRIVE BELTS LOOSE → LOOSE OR CORRODED WIRING CONNECTIONS AT ALTERNATOR

NOISY ALTERNATOR

LOOSE OR CORRODED WIRING CONNECTIONS AT BULKHEAD DISCONNECT ← ALTERNATOR NOT GROUNDED ← REGULATOR NOT GROUNDED ← LOOSE OR CORRODED WIRING CONNECTIONS AT TERMINAL BLOCK

WORN OR FRAYED DRIVE BELT

CHECK FOR APPROXIMATELY 12 VOLTS AT FIELD INPUT BRUSH TERMINAL WITH IGNITION SWITCH "ON"

LOOSE BODY TO BATTERY GROUND CABLE

ALTERNATOR MOUNTING LOOSE

ALTERNATOR CURRENT OUTPUT TEST*

INTERFERENCE BETWEEN ROTOR FAN AND STATOR LEADS

ALTERNATOR OUTPUT WITHIN SPECIFICATIONS

ALTERNATOR OUTPUT NOT UP TO SPECIFICATIONS

ROTOR FAN OR ROTOR DAMAGED

TEST VOLTAGE REGULATOR*

UNSTEADY LOW OR CHARGING

EXCESSIVE CHARGING

ALTERNATOR BEARINGS EXCESSIVELY WORN OR DEFECTIVE

IF REGULATOR TESTS O.K. CHECK WIRING AND/OR CONNECTIONS

IF REGULATOR DOES NOT TEST SATISFACTORY REPLACE REGULATOR

TEST CHARGING CIRCUIT RESISTANCE*

GROUNDED ALTERNATOR FIELD WIRE, FIELD TERMINAL, OR CONNECTIONS

ONE OR MORE RECTIFIERS OPEN OR SHORTED

CHARGING RESISTANCE TOO HIGH

ALTERNATOR FIELD GROUNDED INTERNALLY. REFER TO ALTERNATOR BENCH TEST*

OPEN, GROUNDED OR SHORTED WIRING IN STATOR

CORRODED OR SHORTED CABLES OR HIGH RESISTANCE ACROSS FUSIBLE LINK

VOLTAGE REGULATOR SENSING CIRCUIT OPEN

CHARGING RESISTANCE O.K.

REFER TO ALTERNATOR BENCH TEST*

*ALL TESTS AND REPAIRS ARE DESCRIBED IN THE APPROPRIATE SECTION OF THE SERVICE MANUAL

AC GENERATOR BENCH TESTS

COMPONENT	TEST CONNECTION	NORMAL READING	IF READING WAS:	TROUBLE IS:
Rotor	Ohmmeter from slip ring to rotor shaft	Infinite resistance	Very low	Grounded
	Test lamp from slip ring to shaft	No light	Lamp lights	Grounded
	Test lamp across slip rings	Lamp lights	No light	Open
Stator	Ohmmeter from any stator lead to frame	Infinite resistance	Very low	Grounded
	Test lamp from lead to frame	No light	Lamp lights	Grounded
	Ohmmeter across any pair of leads	Less than 1/2 ohm	Any very high reading	Open
Diodes	Ohmmeter across diode, then reverse leads	Low reading one way; high reading other way	Both readings low / Both readings high	Shorted / Open
	12-V test lamp across diode then reverse leads	Lamp lights one way, but not other way	No light either way / Lamp lights both ways	Open / Shorted

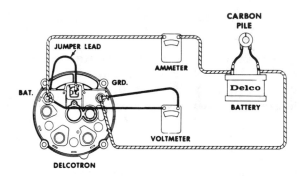

FIGURE 22-22. Testing alternator output on internally grounded unit. Note jumper wire from battery to field terminal for full field energization and maximum output (B-type system). *(Courtesy of General Motors Corporation)*

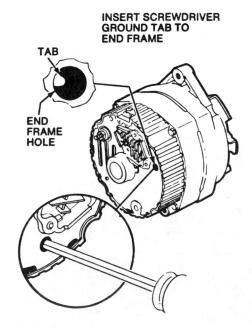

FIGURE 22-23. Some Delco alternators are provided with access to the ground brush in the alternator through a D-shaped or round hole. A screwdrive is inserted to touch both the ground tab and the generator frame. This causes maximum field current and maximum alternator output. If output is within 10 amps of rated output, alternator is not at fault. Problem could be regulator. *(Courtesy of General Motors Corporation)*

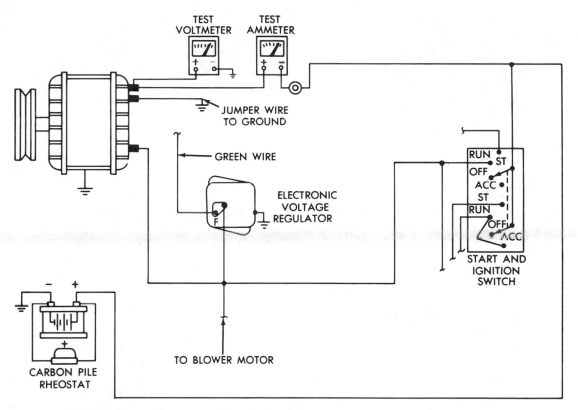

FIGURE 22–24. Method of testing alternator output on externally grounded system. Note disconnected field lead from regulator and grounded alternator field terminal for maximum output (A type system). *(Courtesy of Chrysler Corporation)*

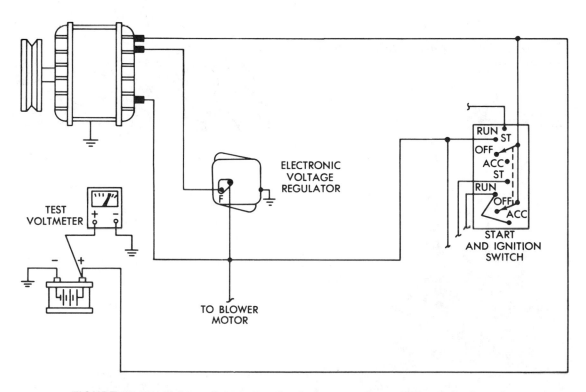

FIGURE 22–25. Using voltmeter to check system voltage. This method can be used on all systems. *(Courtesy of Chrysler Corporation)*

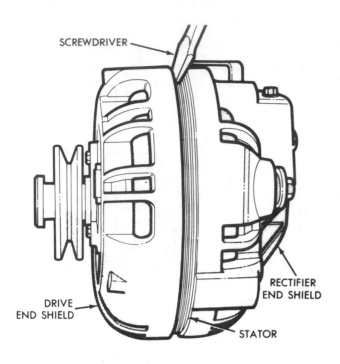

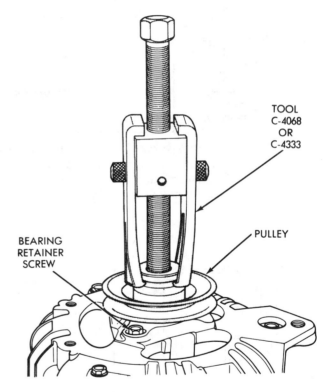

FIGURE 22-26. After through bolts have been removed, alternator frame can be separated as shown here. *(Courtesy of Chrysler Corporation)*

FIGURE 22-27. Drive pulley removal (typical). *(Courtesy of Chrysler Corporation)*

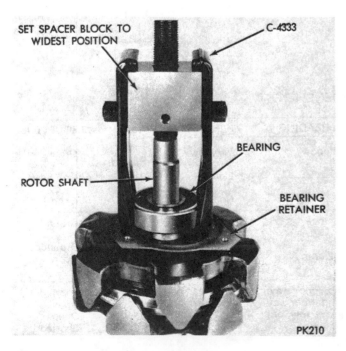

FIGURE 22-28. Removing drive end bearing from rotor shaft with puller. *(Courtesy of Chrysler Corporation)*

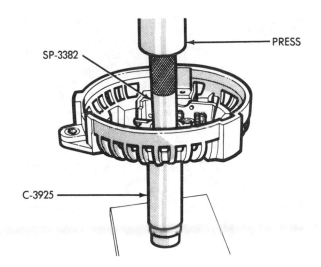

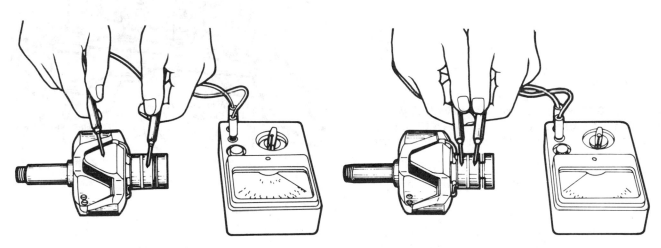

FIGURE 22-29. Removing bearing from rectifier end frame with special adapters and press. *(Courtesy of Chrysler Corporation)*

FIGURE 22-30. Testing rotor with ohmmeter. *(Courtesy of Chrysler Corporation)*

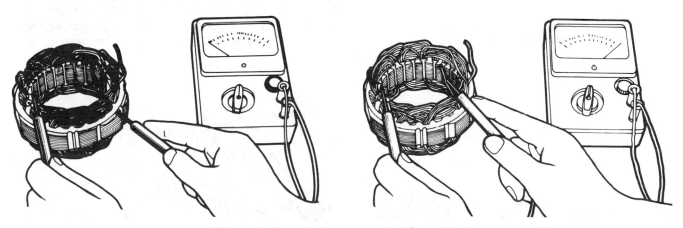

FIGURE 22-31. Testing stator with ohmmeter. *(Courtesy of Chrysler Corporation)*

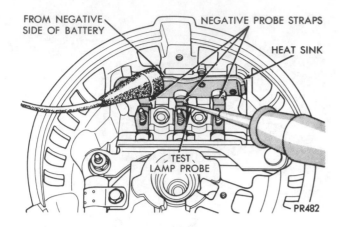

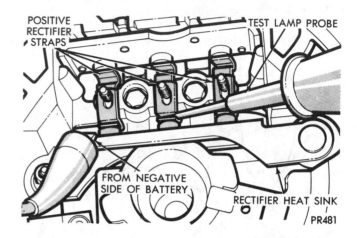

FIGURE 22-32. Testing negative diodes with 12-volt test lamp. Ohmmeter can also be used. See AC generator bench test chart. *(Courtesy of Chrysler Corporation)*

FIGURE 22-33. Testing positive diodes with 12-volt test lamp. Ohmmeter can also be used. See AC generator bench test chart. *(Courtesy of Chrysler Corporation)*

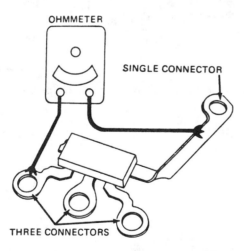

FIGURE 22-34. To check diode trio, connect ohmmeter as shown, then reverse lead connections. Should read high and low. If not, replace diode trio. Repeat same test between single connector and each of other connectors. *(Courtesy of General Motors Corporation)*

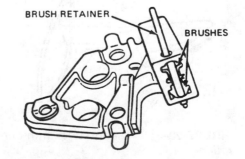

FIGURE 22-35. Retaining pin may be used to hold brushes back against spring pressure to aid in alternator assembly. *(Courtesy of General Motors Corporation)*

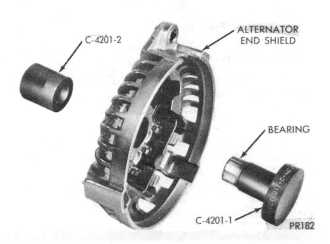

FIGURE 22-36. Special adapters are used to install rectifier end frame bearing (typical). *(Courtesy of Chrysler Corporation)*

FIGURE 22-37. Installing bearing and drive end frame on rotor shaft with press. *(Courtesy of Chrysler Corporation)*

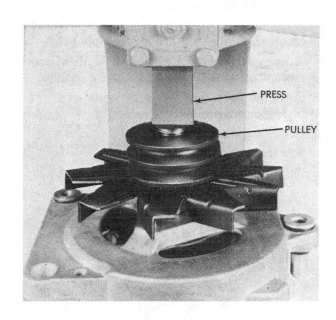

FIGURE 22-38. Installing drive pulley with press before rectifier end frame is installed. *(Courtesy of Chrysler Corporation)*

4. Tighten bolts.

5. Install generator terminal plug and battery leads to generator.

6. Connect negative battery cable.

PART 4   SELF-CHECK

1. The major parts of the AC generator are the _____.

2. How is the magnetic field in an AC generator increased?

3. The AC generator has a rotating electromagnet. True or false?

4. Without energizing the field, the AC generator will not produce current. True or false?

5. The AC generator brushes carry total generator output. True or false?

6. The AC generator requires three diodes for full-wave rectification. True or false?

7. Stator windings are connected to each other by the _____ or the _____ method.

8. Current in the AC generator stator windings is always in the same direction. True or false?

9. The alternator diode is a two-way electrical check valve. True or false?

10. What effect does a shorted diode have on an alternator output?

11. What is the purpose of the fusible link between the battery and the diodes on some AC charging systems?

12. The AC charging system regulator controls current and voltage output. True or false?

13. What four pieces of test equipment are used to check charging systems and components?

14. A noisy alternator may be the result of one or more shorted or open diodes. True or false?

15. Corroded battery posts or terminals can cause improper charging. True or false?

16. How should a diode be tested?

17. The rotor should be tested for
(a) _____ ,

(b) _____ ,

(c) _____ .

18. The stator should be tested for (a) _____ ,
(b) _____ .

PART 5   TEST QUESTIONS

1. The AC generator's current producing winding is a:
   (a) rotating single-phase winding
   (b) rotating three-phase winding
   (c) stationary three-phase winding
   (d) stationary single-phase winding

2. AC generator current is changed to DC current by the:
   (a) slip rings
   (b) commutator
   (c) transistor
   (d) diodes

3. The AC generator regulator controls:
   (a) current only
   (b) voltage only
   (c) current and voltage
   (d) current, voltage, and battery reverse current flow

4. The AC generator rotor should be checked for:
   (a) opens
   (b) shorts
   (c) grounds
   (d) all of the above

5. Diodes should be checked for:
   (a) shorts
   (b) opens
   (c) grounds
   (d) all of the above

6. Checking the charging system should include checking the:
   (a) battery and cables
   (b) generator belt
   (c) wiring connections
   (d) all of the above

Chapter 23

DC Charging Systems

Performance Objectives

After thorough study of this chapter, sufficient practice on adequate training models, and with the necessary tools, equipment, and manuals, you should be able to do the following:

1. Complete the self-check and test questions with at least 80 percent accuracy.

2. Observe the accepted general precautions outlined in this chapter.

3. Describe the purpose, construction, and operation of DC charging systems and their components.

4. Accurately diagnose charging system faults.

5. Safely remove, test, recondition, replace, and adjust faulty charging system components according to manufacturer's specifications.

6. Properly performance test the reconditioned components and the entire charging system to determine the success of the repairs performed.

7. Prepare vehicle for customer acceptance.

DC Generator Principles

There is a great deal of similarity between a cranking motor and a generator. The cranking motor converts electrical energy into mechanical energy, whereas the generator converts mechanical energy into electrical energy.

The generator functions on the principle that any conductor connected into a completed circuit will have a current induced in it when it is moved through a magnetic field. Residual magnetism in the pole shoes provides enough field strength (magnetic lines of force) for the generator to start charging. The generator is made up of two major parts, the armature and the field winding assembly. The armature consists of a number of conductors placed in insulated slots around a soft iron core, which is assembled onto the armature shaft. The conductors are connected to each other and to the commutator. When brushes are placed on the commutator, any current induced in the conductors is carried away from the armature through the brushes. Part of this current is shunted through the field windings so that the magnetic field in which the conductors are moved is strengthened. This tends to produce a greater amount of current in the conductors.

Figure 23–2 shows a simple one-turn armature generator. If the armature loop is rotated in a clockwise direction, as indicated, current will be induced in the left-hand side of the loop away from the reader and in the right-hand side of the loop toward the reader. Use the right-hand rule to check the directions of current in the two sides of the loop. The current that is induced is to the right-hand segment of the commutator and through the right-hand brush. From there most of it is through the external circuit and the connected electrical load. Then it is to the left-hand brush and left-hand segment of the commutator and back into the loop. The remainder of the induced current is through the two field windings, which are assembled around the two magnetic pole shoes. This current is in the right direction to strengthen the magnetic field between the two pole shoes. In the complete generator assembly the pole shoes would be fastened into a field frame, and the field frame would form the return magnetic circuit for the lines of force from the north pole to the south pole. The magnetic lines of force pass from the magnetic north to the magnetic south pole through the external magnetic circuit.

The use of a commutator with segments keeps the current in the external electrical circuit in the same direction, regardless of the relative positions of the two sides of the loop with respect to the north

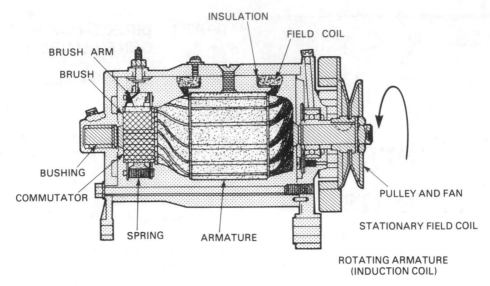

FIGURE 23-1. Direct current (DC) generator cross section.

and south magnetic poles. For instance, when the left-hand side of the loop has rotated 180°, it will be moving in the opposite direction with respect to the magnetic field. However, since the commutator segment to which it is connected also has rotated 180°, this current will be fed to the right-hand brush. As far as the external circuit is concerned, the current still continues in the same direction.

When the conductor is halfway between the two poles, it is in the neutral position where no current is generated and where the direction of current in the conductor reverses. This is also the position where the brush changes connections with the commutator bars. Actually, AC current is generated, but the commutator acts as a rectifier or rotating reversing switch that maintains DC current in the external circuit.

Generator Circuits

Generators are connected internally in two different ways, depending on the type of generator regulator used. The two methods of connection are shown in Figure 23-3. It is important to bear these differences in mind in any check or adjustment of the generator since different checks are required for each type.

All shunt generators must have some form of external regulation. Regulation is normally provided by the use of spring-loaded contacts and a resistance. The contacts are opened magnetically by means of a winding or windings. When the points are opened, the resistance is inserted into the generator field circuit, so that the amount of field current is cut down. This reduces the strength of the generator magnetic field and lowers the generator

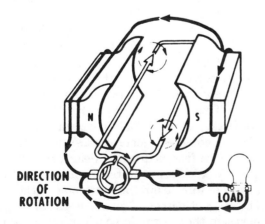

FIGURE 23-2. Simple DC generator with a single-loop armature and a two segment commutator. Commutator rectifies generator current from AC to DC. Residual magnetism in the pole shoes provides sufficient magnetic field strength for the generator to start charging.

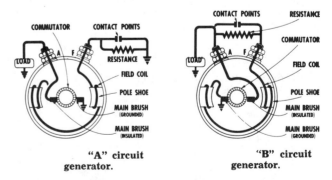

"A" circuit generator.

"B" circuit generator.

FIGURE 23-3. Two most common DC generator circuits. "A" circuit generator has shunt-wound field coils which are grounded externally through the regulator. "B" circuit generator also has shunt-wound field coils (through regulator), but field coils are grounded inside the generator through the grounded brush. *(Courtesy of General Motors Corporation)*

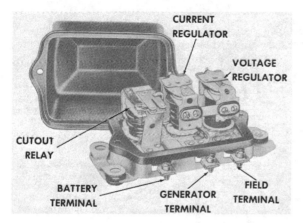

FIGURE 23-4. Three-unit DC charging system generator regulator controls current and voltage. Cutout relay disconnects battery from generator when ignition switch is turned off. *(Courtesy of General Motors Corporation)*

output. When the contacts are closed, the resistance is removed, field current increases, and generator output rises.

The difference between the two types of generator circuits lies mainly in that part of the field circuit in which the resistance is inserted. In the B circuit the generator regulator inserts resistance between the insulated side of the circuit and the field. In the A circuit system the resistance is inserted between the field and ground.

There is no particular advantage to either circuit, but because of the difference in the method of connecting the regulator into the field circuit, the regulators must not be interchanged.

Bucking Field

Some generators have additional turns on the armature to produce the necessary voltage to obtain a charging rate at very low speeds. When the range of operating speeds is great, voltage regulation at the higher speeds becomes a very important problem. As stated earlier, the voltage produced in a generator depends upon the strength of the magnetic field, the number of the armature conductors in series, and the speed of armature rotation. When the number of conductors and the speed are both great, then only a very weak field is required to produce the required voltage. On some generators, operating at very high speeds, it is possible to produce more than the required voltage even with an open-circuited field. The residual magnetism of the pole shoes supplies enough magnetic field to produce the voltage, but this voltage cannot be controlled. Even though the voltage winding of the regulator opens the contacts and inserts a resistance in the field circuit, the voltage will continue to climb.

To control the voltage on this type of unit, it is necessary to use what is known as a bucking field. It is a shunt coil wound on one pole shoe and connected directly across the brushes of the armature. The winding is in the reverse direction from the normal field winding and has an opposing magnetic effect. At low speeds, when the normal field is strong, the opposing effect is not great, but at higher speeds, when the current in the regular field circuit is reduced by the voltage regulator, the opposing effect is greater than the residual magnetic field. Thus,

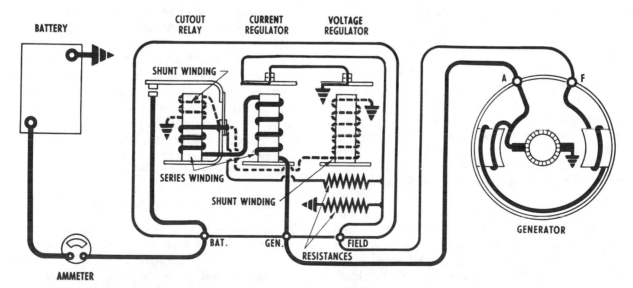

FIGURE 23-5. Schematic diagram of "A" circuit generator and three-unit regulator. *(Courtesy of General Motors Corporation)*

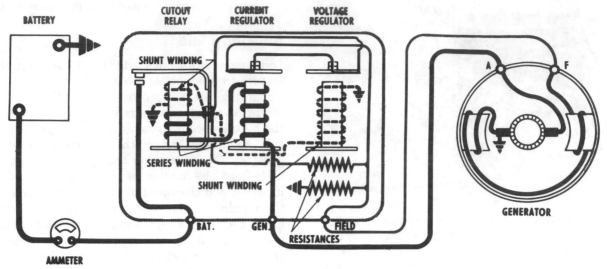

FIGURE 23-6. Schematic diagram of "B" circuit generator and three-unit regulator. *(Courtesy of General Motors Corporation)*

the current through the regular field coils can be controlled by the regulator and a normal voltage maintained.

PART 2 DC GENERATOR REGULATORS

For the generating system to operate, the armature wire from the generator must be connected to the generator (GEN) terminal of the regulator, the field terminal of the generator connected to the field (F) terminal of the regulator, and the wire from the battery through the ammeter to the battery (BAT) terminal of the regulator.

Circuit Breaker (Cutout Relay)

When the generator voltage builds up to a value great enough to charge the battery, the magnetism induced by the current through the shunt winding is sufficient to overcome the armature spring tension and pull the armature toward the core so that the contact points close. This completes the circuit between the generator and battery. The current from the generator to the battery passes through the series winding in the proper direction to add to the magnetism, holding the armature down and the points closed.

When the generator slows down or stops, current reverses from the battery to the generator. This reverse direction of current flows through the series winding, thus causing a reversal of the series winding magnetic field. The magnetic field of the shunt winding does not reverse. Therefore, instead of helping each other, the two windings now magnetically

oppose each other so that the resultant magnetic field becomes insufficient to hold the armature down. The flat spring pulls the armature away from the core so that the points separate; this opens the circuit between the generator and battery.

Voltage Regulator

When the generator voltage reaches the value for which the voltage regulator is adjusted, the magnetic field produced by the winding overcomes the armature spring tension and pulls the armature down so that the contact points separate. This inserts resistance into the generator field circuit so that the generator field current and voltage are reduced. Reduction of the generator voltage opens the regulator series winding circuit so that its magnetic field collapses completely. This allows the spiral spring to pull the armature away from the core so that the contact points again close. This directly grounds the generator field circuit so that the generator voltage and output increase. The above cycle of action again takes place, and the cycle continues at a rate of 150 to 250 times a second, regulating the voltage to a constant value. By thus maintaining a constant voltage, the generator supplies varying amounts of current to meet the varying states of battery charge and electrical load.

Temperature Compensation

The voltage regulator is compensated for temperature by means of a bimetal thermostatic hinge on the armature. This causes the regulator to regulate for a higher voltage when cold, which partly compensates for the fact that a higher voltage is required to charge a cold battery.

490

Current Regulator

When electrical devices are turned on and the battery is in a discharged condition, the voltage may not increase to a value sufficient to cause the voltage regulator to operate. Consequently, generator output will continue to increase until the generator reaches its rated maximum output. This is the current value for which the current regulator is set. Therefore, when the generator reaches its rated output, this output through the current regulator winding creates sufficient magnetism to pull the current regulator armature down and open the contact points. With the points open, resistance is inserted into the generator field circuit so that the generator output is reduced.

As generator output starts to fall, the magnetic field of the current regulator winding is reduced, the spiral spring tension pulls the armature up, and the contact points close, removing the resistance from the field circuit. Output increases and the above cycle is repeated. The cycle continues to take place while the current regulator is in operation 150 to 250 times a second, preventing the generator from exceeding its rated maximum.

When the electrical load is reduced, electrical devices are turned off, or battery comes up to charge, the voltage increases so that the voltage regulator begins to operate and tapers the generator output down. This prevents the current regulator from operating. Either the voltage regulator or the current regulator controls the generator at any one time; the two never operate at the same time.

Resistances

The current and voltage regulator circuits use a common resistance, which is inserted in the field circuit when either the current or voltage regulator operates. A second resistance is connected between the regulator field terminal and the relay frame, which places it in parallel with the generator field coils. The sudden reduction in field current occurring when either the current or voltage regulator contact points open is accompanied by a surge of induced voltage in the field coils as the strength of the magnetic field changes. These surges are partially dissipated by arcing at the contact points.

The cutout relay disconnects the battery from the charging system any time the engine is shut off. If the cutout points stick, the battery current will try to drive the generator. This will discharge the battery very quickly.

The voltage regulator controls maximum voltage output in order to prevent the battery from being overcharged and to protect the electrical components in the vehicle. Excessive voltage can cause

lights to flare and to burn out prematurely and reduce the life of other electrical components.

The current regulator controls the maximum current output of the generator to prevent the generator from overheating and being burned out.

PART 3   DC GENERATOR CHARGING SYSTEM DIAGNOSIS AND SERVICE PROCEDURE

Direct-current generator charging systems have not been commonly used on automobiles for many years. However, there are still some older units around equipped with this system.

In general, the practice has been to diagnose the system to determine whether the battery, generator, regulator, or related wiring are at fault, and then to replace or repair the faulty components. The following procedures will quickly lead to the source of the problem. The equipment required is the voltmeter and the ammeter. As with any other electrical problem, the battery must be properly checked as outlined in Chapter 18, Part 5. Follow the same General Precautions given in Chapter 22 when servicing DC charging systems.

DC Charging System Checks

In analyzing complaints of generator-regulator operation, any of several basic conditions may be found.

Fully Charged Battery and Low Charging Rate. This indicates normal generator-regulator operation.

Fully Charged Battery and a High Charging Rate. This usually indicates that the voltage regulator unit either is not limiting the generator voltage as it should or is set too high. A high charging rate to a fully charged battery will damage the battery, and the accompanying high voltage is very injurious to all electrical units. This operating condition may result from the following:

1. Improper voltage regulator setting.

2. Defective voltage regulator unit.

3. Grounded generator field circuit in either generator, regulator, or wiring; may be trouble in A circuit.

Low Battery and High Charging Rate. This is normal generator-regulation action.

Low Battery and Low or No Charging Rate. This condition could be due to the following:

1. Loose generator belt.

2. Loose connections, or damaged external wiring.

3. Defective battery.

4. High circuit resistance.

5. Low regulator setting.

6. Oxidized regulator contact points.

7. Defects within the generator.

8. Cutout relay not closing.

9. Open series circuit within regulator.

10. Generator not properly polarized.

If the condition is not caused by loose connections or damaged wires, proceed as follows to locate cause of trouble.

A Circuit

To determine whether the generator or regulator is at fault, momentarily ground the F terminal of the regulator and increase generator speed. If output does not increase, the generator is probably at fault and it should be checked. Other causes for the output not increasing may be the relay not closing or an open series winding in the regulator. If the generator output increases, the trouble is due to the following:

1. A low voltage (or current) regulator setting.

2. Oxidized regulator contact points that insert excessive resistance into the generator field circuit so that output remains low.

3. Generator field circuit open within the regulator.

B Circuit

To determine whether the generator or regulator is at fault, momentarily place a jumper lead between the GEN and FLD terminals of the regulator and increase generator speed. If output does not increase, the generator is probably at fault and it should be checked. Other causes for the output not increasing may be the relay not closing or an open series winding in the regulator. If the generator output increases, the trouble is due to the following:

1. A low voltage (or current) regulator setting.

2. Oxidized regulator contact points that insert excessive resistance into the generator field circuit so that output remains low.

3. Generator field circuit open within the regulator.

Burned Resistances, Windings, or Contacts. These result from open circuit operation, open resistance units, or loose or intermittent connections in the charging circuit. Where burned resistances, windings, or contacts are found, always check car wiring before installing a new regulator. Otherwise, the new regulator may also fail in the same way.

Burned Relay Contact Points. This may be due to reversed generator polarity. Generator polarity must be corrected after any checks of the regulator or generator or after disconnecting and reconnecting leads.

Polarizing Generator: A Circuit. After reconnecting leads, momentarily connect a jumper lead between the GEN and BAT terminals of the regulator. This allows a momentary surge of current through the generator, which correctly polarizes it. Failure to do this may result in severe damage to the equipment, since reversed polarity causes vibration, arcing, and burning of the relay contact points.

Polarizing Generator: B Circuit. To polarize circuit B generators, disconnect the lead from the FLD terminal of the regulator and momentarily touch this lead to the BAT terminal of the regulator. This allows a momentary surge of current through the

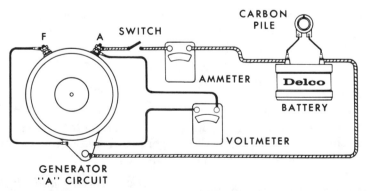

FIGURE 23-7. Method used to check "A" circuit type of charging system output. Note jumper wire from generator field terminal to ground. This causes maximum field energization and therefore maximum generator output. *(Courtesy of General Motors Corporation)*

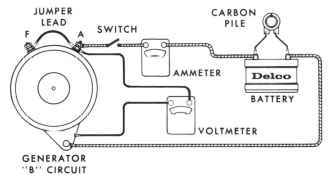

JUMPER LEAD   SWITCH   CARBON PILE

F   A

AMMETER

Delco

BATTERY

VOLTMETER

GENERATOR "B" CIRCUIT

FIGURE 23-8. Method used to check "B" circuit. type of charging system output. Note jumper wire from generator armature terminal to field terminal for maximum generator output. *(Courtesy of General Motors Corporation)*

generator, which correctly polarizes it. Failure to do this may result in severe damage to the equipment, since reversed polarity causes vibration, arcing, and burning of the relay contact points.

PART 4   SELF-CHECK

1. Name all the major components of a DC generator.

2. The DC generator operates on the principle of moving a _____ through a _____ to induce current.

3. The initial magnetic field in the DC generator is the result of residual magnetism. True or false?

4. What is the purpose of the commutator and brush assembly?

5. Explain the basic difference between A circuit and B circuit DC generators.

6. The DC regulator consists of *what* three major components?

7. What prevents battery current from reaching the generator when the engine is shut off?

8. What could cause battery overcharging?

9. List six causes of battery undercharging.

PART 5   TEST QUESTIONS

1. To determine whether the generator or regulator is at fault in an A circuit system:
   (a) momentarily ground the armature terminal
   (b) momentarily ground the battery terminal
   (c) momentarily ground the field terminal
   (d) any of the above

2. If the voltage regulator is at fault it could be:
   (a) a low voltage regulator setting
   (b) oxidized regulator points
   (c) an open field circuit in the regulator
   (d) any of the above

3. To polarize an A circuit generator, you should momentarily connect:
   (a) the generator and battery terminals
   (b) the generator and field terminals
   (c) the field and battery terminals
   (d) any of the above

4. To polarize a B circuit generator, you should momentarily connect:
   (a) the disconnected field lead to the regulator battery terminal
   (b) the disconnected armature terminal to the regulator battery terminal
   (c) the field to the armature
   (d) any of the above

5. To determine if the generator or regulator is at fault in a B circuit system:
   (a) momentarily place a jumper lead between the generator and field terminals of the regulator
   (b) momentarily ground the field
   (c) momentarily ground the armature
   (d) any of the above

Chapter 24

Ignition Systems

Performance Objectives

After adequate study of this chapter and sufficient practical work on the appropriate components, and with the necessary shop manuals, tools, and equipment, you should be able to do the following:

1. Complete the self-check and test questions with at least 80 percent accuracy.

2. Describe the purpose, construction, and operation of (a) the electronic ignition system and its components, and (b) the contact point ignition system and its components.

3. Diagnose ignition system problems according to the diagnostic chart and procedures provided.

4. Recondition or replace faulty components as required.

5. Correctly adjust components as required.

6. Test the system to determine the success of the service performed.

7. Prepare the vehicle for customer acceptance.

The purpose of the ignition system is to ignite the air/fuel mixture in each cylinder at the right time and in the order which corresponds to the engine's firing order. Two basic circuits, the primary (low-voltage) circuit and the secondary (high-voltage) circuit, are contained in the ignition system.

The purpose of the primary circuit is to build up a strong magnetic field in and about the coil secondary windings and to cause this field to collapse when required.

The purpose of the secondary circuit is to transform the collapsing primary field into a high voltage necessary to provide a spark at the spark plug gap. Only enough voltage is produced to jump the gap (approximately 7000 to 9000 volts) at normal idle speed. At higher engine loads and speeds, increased voltage is required to overcome increased internal resistance.

When the ignition switch is turned on, battery or generator electricity flows through the closed ignition switch, through the ignition resistor assembly and coil primary windings, the switching transistor (or distributor contact points on non-electronic ignition), and back to the battery through ground, thereby completing the primary ignition circuit and causing the current in the coil primary windings to provide a strong magnetic field. This is the primary circuit "on" time (or dwell period).

When the switching transistor (or contact points) interrupts current in the primary circuit, the magnetic field built up around the coil secondary windings is caused to collapse quickly across the secondary windings. This sudden collapse of the magnetic field induces a high voltage in the secondary windings.

Secondary voltage potential can reach 40,000 volts; however, only the voltage required to jump the spark plug gap is produced. The high secondary voltage potential is required to overcome resistance in the secondary circuit due to speed, load, air/fuel ratio, and secondary system deterioration.

Therefore, the high voltage (secondary voltage) that is necessary to force the spark across the spark plug gap is produced whenever current in the primary circuit is interrupted.

The secondary voltage induced in the coil flows through the coil secondary lead (coil tower) to the center terminal of the distributor cap and is conducted across the revolving distributor rotor to the correct distributor cap terminal in accordance with the firing order of the engine. The current then travels through the spark plug wire to the center electrode of the spark plug. As the spark jumps the gap between the insulated center electrode to the grounded outer electrode, the remaining energy in the coil is drained from the coil through the secondary circuit and thereby sustains the spark at the gap for a fraction of a second.

PART 1   ELECTRONIC IGNITION

The electronic ignition system uses a switching transistor to interrupt primary current. The switching transistor is part of the electronic control module. This transistor is controlled by a pulse generator in the distributor.

With the engine running, primary current passes through the ignition switch through a resistor (some models only), through the primary coil winding, through the transistor in the control module to ground. As soon as the pulse generator sends a zero or negative voltage signal (depending on model) to the control module, this primary current is interrupted. Interruption of primary current causes the magnetic field in the ignition coil to collapse, which induces a high voltage in the secondary to fire the appropriate spark plug. (For transistor operation refer to Chapter 20, Part 7.)

Vacuum advance and centrifugal advance units are used with electronic ignition systems that do not have electronic timing controls. Electronic ignition systems require little maintenance and are much more efficient than the older contact ignition systems. There is less misfiring and consequently better performance and emissions control.

PART 2   IGNITION COIL (Figures 24–11 and 24–12)

An ignition coil is a pulse transformer that steps up the low voltage from the battery or generator to a voltage high enough to ionize (electrically charge) the spark plug gap and ignite the air/fuel mixture in the cylinder. A typical coil is made up of a primary winding consisting of a few hundred turns of relatively large wire and a secondary winding consisting of many thousand turns of very small wire. These windings are insulated and assembled over a soft iron core and are enclosed by a soft iron shell. This assembly is inserted into a one-piece steel or die cast aluminum coil case, which is filled with oil and hermetically sealed by a coil cap made of molded insulating material. The cap contains the primary and secondary high voltage terminals.

Ignition coils are hermetically sealed to prevent the entrance of moisture, which would cause coil failure. During manufacture, the coil case is filled with oil at a high temperature. As the oil temperature decreases to more nearly match the temperature of the surrounding air, the oil contracts to occupy less volume, thus allowing room for expansion when the coil heats up during normal operation. The oil acts as an insulator to prevent high voltage arc-over within the coil.

Some coil designs are not encased in a metal housing. Instead of being filled with oil, this type is potted in plastic and has external laminations much like a transformer. The coil has the usual two pri-

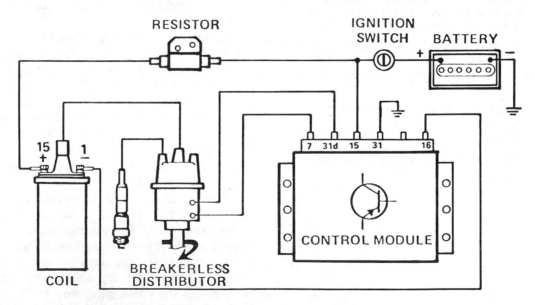

FIGURE 24–1. Basic electronic ignition circuit. Primary circuit is controlled by the pulse distributor and transistor. The pulse distributor signals the transistor to interrupt the primary circuit, which causes a high voltage to be induced in the secondary, and then completes the primary circuit again. This action is repeated each time a spark plug is fired.

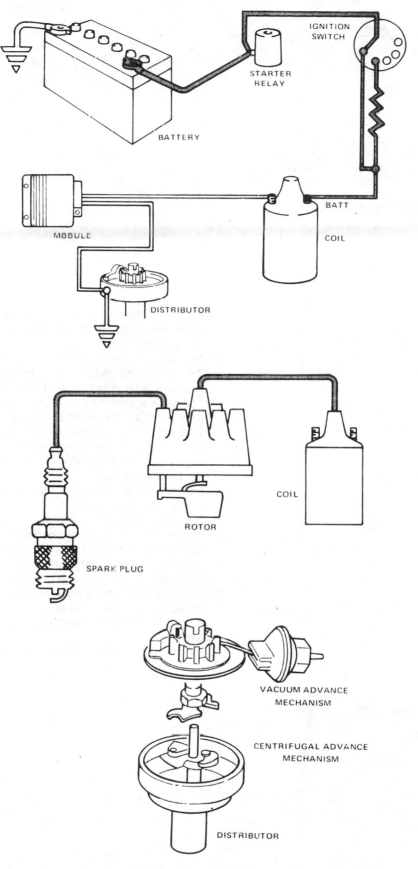

FIGURE 24–2. Ford's solid-state ignition system components. *(Courtesy of Ford Motor Co. of Canada Ltd.)*

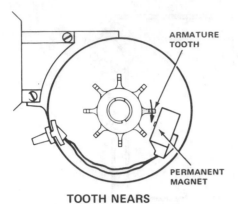

**TOOTH NEARS
PERMANENT MAGNET**

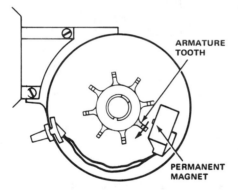

ALIGNED

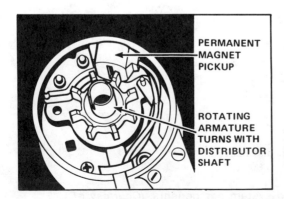

**TOOTH AWAY FROM
PERMANENT MAGNET**

A. As each tooth (pole) of the armature nears the permanent magnet, an electrical signal is generated in the pickup coil.
B. As each tooth (pole) of the armature goes away from the permanent magnet, an electrical signal of opposite polarity is generated in the pickup coil.
C. The signals generated go from positive to negative and back again as the distributor rotates.
D. This signal tells the module to turn off, producing the same effect in the primary circuit as the opening of the contacts in a conventional ignition system; it breaks the primary circuit.
E. The sudden stoppage of current to the ignition coil primary winding causes its magnetic field to collapse, inducing a high voltage in the secondary winding.
F. This high voltage surge is delivered to the correct spark plug, the one ready to fire, by the distributor rotor, cap, and secondary wiring, exactly as it happens in the distributor with contact points.
G. A timing circuit in the module turns the primary circuit on again to engage the coil for the next spark cycle. This can be compared to the conventional ignition system dwell.

(Courtesy of Ford Motor Co. of Canada Ltd.)

FIGURE 24-3. Ford's solid-state ignition distributor showing pulse generator. *(Courtesy of Ford Motor Co. of Canada Ltd.)*

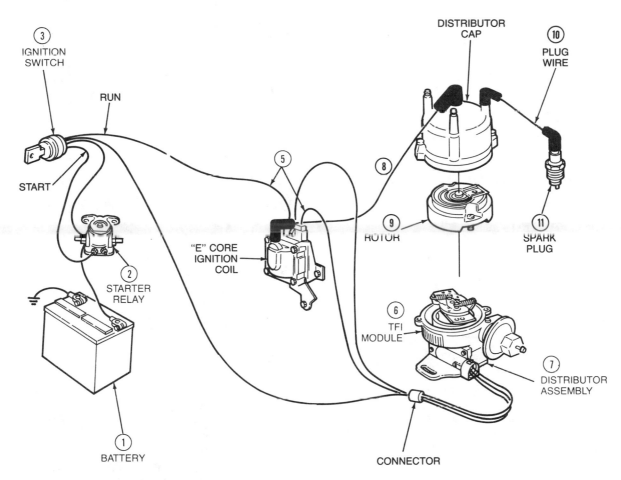

FIGURE 24-4. Ford Thick Film Integrated (TFI) ignition system components. *(Courtesy of Ford Motor Co. of Canada Ltd.)*

mary connections (labeled + and −) and one secondary connection which has a male terminal similar to the distributor cap terminals. This coil has a very low primary resistance and is used without a ballast resistor.

A "current control" circuit was added to the ignition module which eliminated the need for ballast resistors.

The ignition coil is connected in series between the resistor and distributor assemblies. The function of the coil is to induce in its secondary windings the voltage required to cause a spark at the spark plug gap. The primary terminal posts of the coil are marked *BAT.* and *DIST.* or positive (battery) and negative (distributor), + or −. This ensures correct plug polarity (center electrode negative). Negative plug polarity requires less voltage to jump the spark plug gap. Electricity will jump from the hot center electrode to the cooler ground electrode more easily than it will the opposite way. If primary ignition wires are incorrectly hooked up to the coil,

the coil will have reverse polarity, resulting in poor performance and a high-speed miss.

Secondary Voltage Requirements

Voltage in the coil secondary increases until the voltage at the spark plug becomes so high that the plug gap breaks down and is ionized, and part of the secondary energy is dissipated in the form of an arc which ignites the air/fuel mixture.

The voltage required to fire a spark plug depends on many factors such as engine compression ratio, engine speeds, fuel mixture ratios, spark plug temperatures, the width and shape of spark plug gaps, and many other factors. Actual voltage produced by the secondary system is determined by the requirement of the spark plug.

Used plugs may require as much as 5000 volts more to fire than new plugs, due to the increase in plug gap and the rounding of the center electrode that occurs with usage. Cleaning the plug, filing the

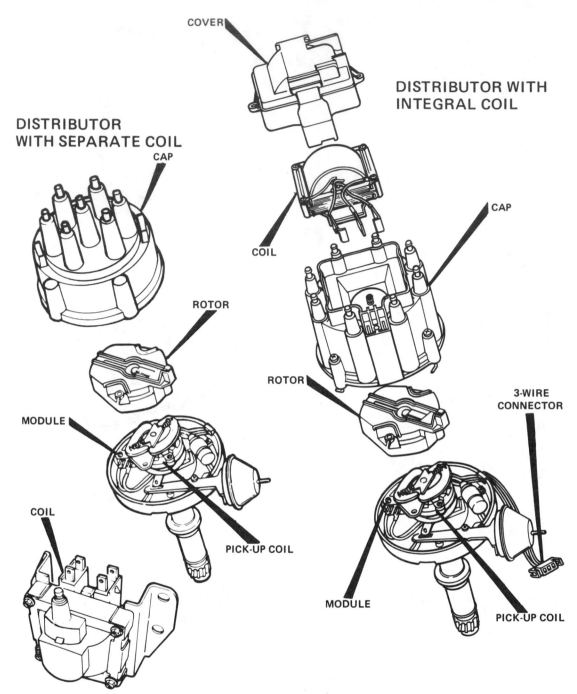

DISTRIBUTOR WITH SEPARATE COIL

COVER

CAP

ROTOR

MODULE

COIL

PICK-UP COIL

DISTRIBUTOR WITH INTEGRAL COIL

COIL

CAP

ROTOR

3-WIRE CONNECTOR

MODULE

PICK-UP COIL

FIGURE 24-5. High-energy ignition system components. Note unitized and separate coil types. *(Courtesy of General Motors Corporation)*

electrodes flat, and readjusting the gap will lower the voltage requirement to approximately that of a new plug, as long as the plug is not otherwise defective.

The maximum voltage requirement occurs at acceleration at low speeds. A "missing" condition is usually first noticed under these conditions, where the voltage requirement first exceeds the maximum available voltage.

The margin of voltage which can be produced above that required to fire the spark plugs repre-

sents the electrical reserve built into the ignition system.

Since electrons flow more readily from a hot surface than a cold one, the spark gap ionizes more readily from the center electrode, which is the hottest part of the spark plug. Thus, a spark plug with a negative polarity at the center electrode requires much less voltage to fire than one with a positive polarity at the center electrode.

The coil is wound to provide a negative polarity voltage at the spark plug center electrode when it

500

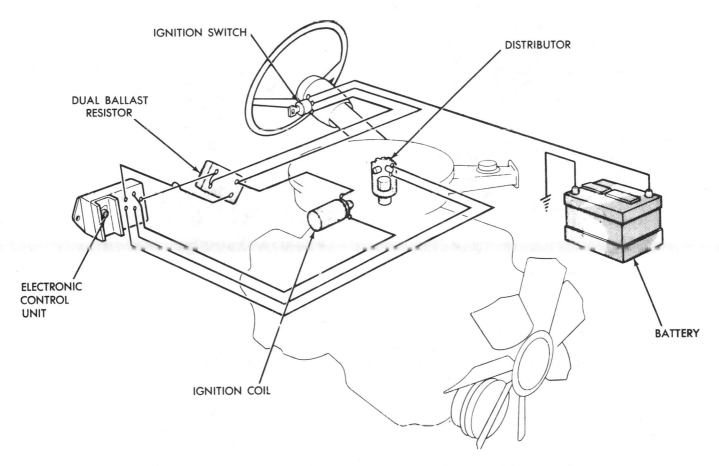

FIGURE 24-6. Chrysler's electronic ignition system. Some models use a single ballast resistor. *(Courtesy of Chrysler Corporation)*

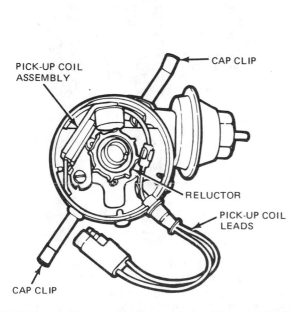

FIGURE 24-7. Chrysler's electronic ignition distributor showing pulse generator components. Some models use two pick-up coils—a start pick-up and a run pick-up. *(Courtesy of Chrysler Corporation)*

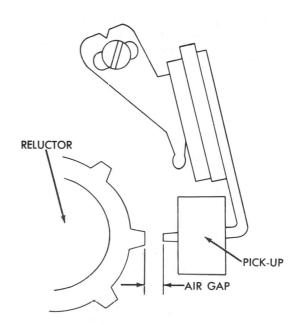

FIGURE 24-8. Chrysler's electronic ignition distributor requires precise adjustment of air gap as shown. This adjustment has no effect on dwell, which is controlled entirely by the control module in all types of electronic ignitions. *(Courtesy of Chrysler Corporation)*

501

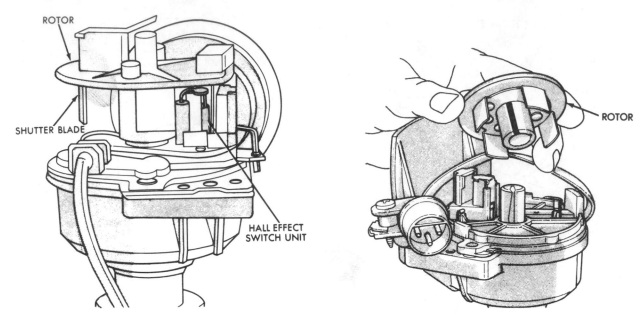

FIGURE 24-9. Hall effect type of distributor pulse generator. Maximum pulse voltage is produced when shutter blade passes between magnet and pole piece. Pulse voltage turns off switching transistor in control module. *(Courtesy of Chrysler Corporation)*

is properly connected, regardless of battery ground polarity.

PART 3   DISTRIBUTOR (Figures 24-13 to 24-25)

The distributor consists basically of a housing, shaft, drive connection, subplate and advance plate, centrifugal advance, vacuum advance, control module, distributor cap, and rotor. In unitized ignition

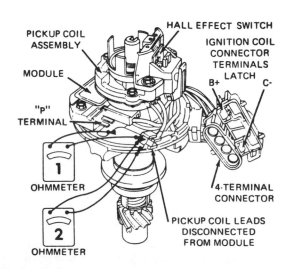

FIGURE 24-10. Checking pick-up coil on HEI distributor with Hall effect switch. *(Courtesy of General Motors Corporation)*

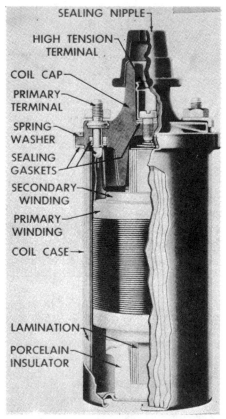

FIGURE 24-11. Ignition coil construction. Coil is oil filled to prevent entry of moisture and to protect insulation. The primary winding has about 200 turns of wire. The secondary winding has about 20,000 turns of very fine wire. Coil construction varies somewhat depending on the type of ignition system for which it was designed. *(Courtesy of General Motors Corporation)*

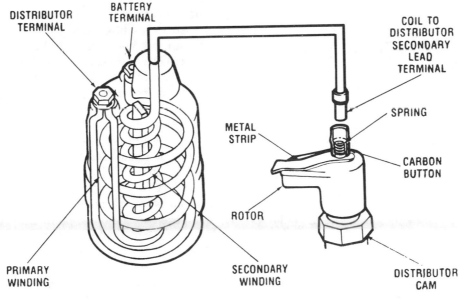

FIGURE 24-12. Primary and secondary coil winding schematic showing secondary connection to distributor rotor. (There are actually many more coil windings than are shown here; see Figure 24-11.)

systems, the distributor also contains the ignition coil and control module. The distributor is driven at engine camshaft speed. On overhead cam engines, the distributor is driven from the camshaft or from an auxiliary shaft. On in-block cam engines, the distributor and engine oil pump are usually driven by the same drive gear on the camshaft. The driven gear may be on the distributor shaft or the oil pump drive. A drive connection between the distributor shaft and oil pump allows both units to be driven from the same gear on the camshaft. This drive arrangement is also used on some overhead cam engines where an auxiliary shaft is used to perform this task. A slot and blade connection, hex drive connection, or slot and pin connection may be used between the distributor and the oil pump.

The rotor is mounted on the top of the distributor shaft by a positive drive connection (flat section or notch and drive lug).

The distributor cap is positioned on the housing by means of a notch and lug to keep the cap in alignment with the housing. The cap is held firmly in place by screws or by spring-type retaining clips. The distributor housing is held in place in the engine block or cylinder head by a cap screw and retainer plate or washer. This assures that the housing will not move. A gasket or seal is used between the housing and engine.

The distributor is installed on the engine so that the drive connection will align the rotor tip with the distributor cap terminal for number one cylinder when the piston is at the top of the compression stroke. This provides initial timing for start up after which ignition timing is set to specifications located on the vehicle emissions label or in the service manual. Spark plug wires are connected to the distributor cap in the order corresponding to the firing order of the engine and the direction of distributor shaft rotation. Some shafts turn clockwise, while others turn counterclockwise when viewed from the rotor end.

A metal trigger wheel (also called reluctor, timer core, or armature), having the same number of teeth as there are engine cylinders, is attached to the upper part of the distributor shaft. As each tooth lines up with the permanent magnet of the pickup coil, a change occurs in the voltage produced in the pickup module. This voltage signal is sent to the control module switching transistor, which interrupts primary current in the coil. This, in turn, causes the high voltage secondary required to fire the spark plug. This happens once each time a tooth lines up with the magnet of the pickup coil. The control module completes the primary circuit again each time a plug has fired. The primary current "on time" (or dwell period) is a function of the control module and cannot be changed. On some systems, the dwell period remains constant regardless of engine speed. On other systems, the dwell period changes with engine speed.

The pickup module is shifted by the vacuum advance unit to provide vacuum advance. The trigger wheel is shifted by the centrifugal advance unit to provide mechanical advance.

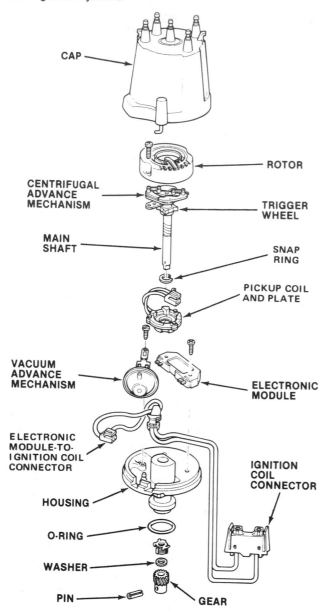

CAP

ROTOR

CENTRIFUGAL ADVANCE MECHANISM

TRIGGER WHEEL

MAIN SHAFT

SNAP RING

PICKUP COIL AND PLATE

VACUUM ADVANCE MECHANISM

ELECTRONIC MODULE

ELECTRONIC MODULE-TO-IGNITION COIL CONNECTOR

IGNITION COIL CONNECTOR

HOUSING

O-RING

WASHER

PIN

GEAR

FIGURE 24-13. Typical HEI electronic ignition distributor components—nonintegral coil type. *(Courtesy of American Motors Corporation)*

Ignition Timing (Figure 24-16)

The combustion or burning of the fuel/air mixture requires a given time interval. During high-speed engine operation, due to the increase in engine speed the spark must occur earlier in the compression stroke if the full power of combustion is to be obtained at the proper time. A mechanical centrifugal advance mechanism is used to provide the desired advance.

Ignition timing must be adjusted to suit other engine operating factors as well. Under light load and high intake manifold vacuum conditions, addi-tional advance is needed since cylinder compression pressures are lower and combustion takes longer. A vacuum advance unit on the distributor is used to achieve the desired advance. Computer control of ignition timing includes sensors for engine coolant temperature, engine speed, manifold absolute pressure, exhaust temperature, barometric pressure, and throttle position.

Many ignition systems use an ignition distributor which provides vacuum advance and centrifugal advance.

Electronic ignition systems retain ignition timing characteristics over a much longer period of time compared to the older point ignition. Contact point deterioration, rubbing block wear, and distributor cam wear cause contact point ignition timing to change, requiring more frequent service than electronic ignition systems. Wear on camshaft drives, auxiliary shaft drives, distributor drives, and centrifugal advance units still affect ignition timing. Decreased manifold vacuum due to engine wear will also affect ignition timing.

Vacuum Advance (Figure 24-17)

A stationary plate is supported in the distributor housing around the perimeter. A pivot feature provides movable plate response to the advance and retard action of the vacuum spark control diaphragm, which is linked directly to the vacuum advance plate.

A magnetic coil and magnet assembly is mounted on the plate in electronic ignition systems. In contact point ignition, a set of contact points and a condenser are mounted on the plate.

When the engine is operating under part-throttle light load, the combustion process is slower. Because the part-throttle mixture is less highly compressed, the combustion process requires more time, and additional spark advance is required for maximum power and economy. Since engine manifold vacuum varies with engine load, it is used to control movement of the advance plate and provide the required advance.

The vacuum port in the carburetor throttle bore is located above the closed position of the throttle plate to prevent spark advance at idle. Therefore, as the throttle plates are closing from part-throttle to idle speed, the vacuum source to the diaphragm is cut off; the spring in the diaphragm housing, acting on the diaphragm, causes the advance plate to return to its full retarded position.

When the engine is being operated under a steady part-throttle cruising condition, such as on a level road at 40 miles (64 kilometers) per hour, both the vacuum advance and the centrifugal weights advance the spark in correct proportion to engine load

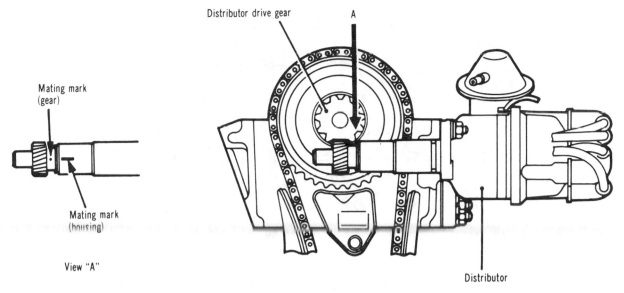

FIGURE 24-14. Distributor driven directly from overhead camshaft. *(Courtesy of Chrysler Corporation)*

and engine speed, respectively. If the throttle is suddenly opened to wide open position, engine vacuum decreases proportionately to throttle opening, and the diaphragm spring quickly forces the advance plate to its normal retard position.

As the carburetor primary throttle plates are opening from slow idle to a part-throttle position, a vacuum port in the primary throttle bore is exposed to manifold vacuum. The vacuum port is connected to the vacuum diaphragm housing attached to the distributor assembly. The diaphragm is linked directly to the distributor advance plate. The vacuum acting on the diaphragm causes plate rotation in a direction opposite to distributor shaft rotation. This causes the primary circuit to be interrupted earlier during the compression stroke, thereby advancing the spark.

A defective vacuum advance unit will impede acceleration and part-throttle performance in addition to increasing fuel consumption and exhaust emissions.

Centrifugal Advance (Figures 24-18 and 24-19)

To obtain a high-speed spark advance in correct proportion to engine speed, the distributor assembly contains a mechanical advance that consists of two

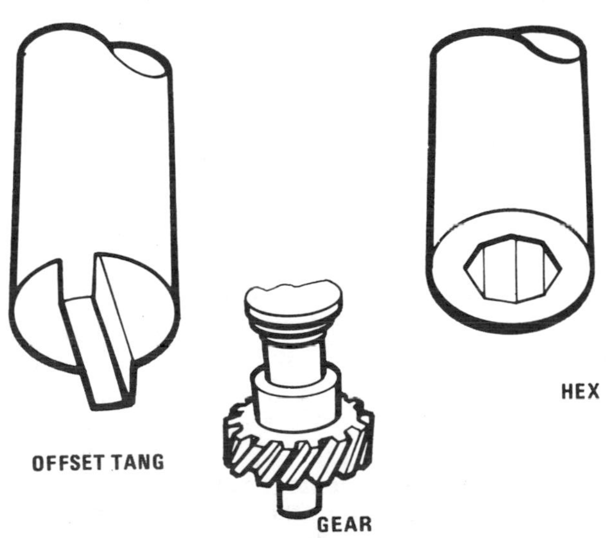

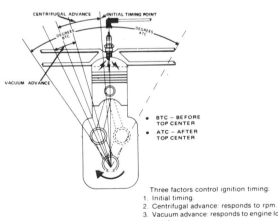

Three factors control ignition timing:
1. Initial timing.
2. Centrifugal advance: responds to rpm.
3. Vacuum advance: responds to engine load and throttle opening.
(Courtesy of Ford Motor Co. of Canada Ltd.)

Centrifugal spark advance varies with rpm and is controlled by centrifugal advance mechanism. Conditions that require *more* spark advance are as follows:
1. Higher engine speeds.
2. Low engine loads: (a) cruise, (b) light vehicle weight.

Vacuum spark advance varies with load and is controlled by vacuum advance mechanism. Conditions that require *less* spark advance are as follows:
1. Lower engine speeds.
2. Higher engine loads: (a) acceleration, (b) high vehicle speed, (c) heavy vehicle weight.

FIGURE 24-15. Several different distributor drive designs. *(Courtesy of Chrysler Corporation)*

FIGURE 24-16. Spark timing requirements. *(Courtesy of Ford Motor Co. of Canada Ltd.)*

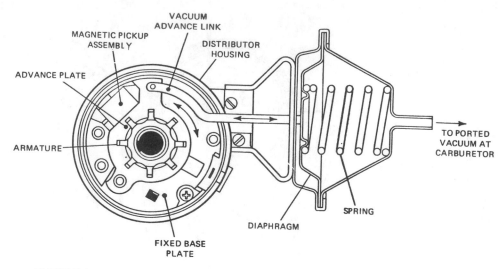

FIGURE 24-17. Distributor vacuum advance unit and vacuum connection to carburetor. *(Courtesy of General Motors Corporation)*

spring-controlled centrifugal-type governor weights attached to a mounting flange on the distributor shaft directly below or above the advance plate. The distributor cam (point ignition) or armature (electronic ignition) is positioned on the distributor shaft so that it is centered between the two weights.

As the speed of rotation of the distributor shaft increases, the centrifugal force of distributor shaft rotation causes the weights to be thrown outward. The outward motion of the weights rotates the cam assembly ahead of distributor shaft rotation. By positioning the cam or armature ahead of distributor shaft rotation, the distributor causes the primary circuit to be interrupted earlier in the compression stroke, thereby advancing the spark.

A control spring is connected between each weight and its tab, which is integral with the mounting flange. These springs control the rate of centrifugal spark advance.

Computer Controlled Advance (Figures 24-25 to 24-31)

Vehicles equipped with computer controlled timing may or may not have vacuum and centrifugal advance mechanisms. The computer adjusts ignition timing as a result of various input signals from the engine. The distributor centrifugal advance unit is not required when an engine speed sensor input is provided to the computer. The vacuum advance unit

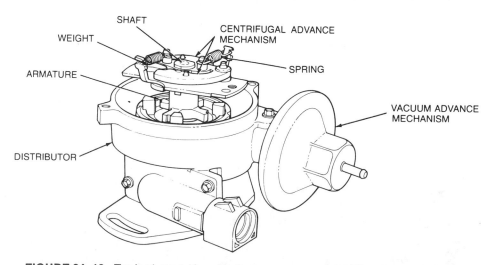

FIGURE 24-18. Typical centrifugal advance components. The distributor shaft drives the armature through the centrifugal advance mechanism of the distributor. As speed increases, the advance weights move out by centrifugal force, against the forces of calibration springs. This advances the armature so that the spark occurs sooner.

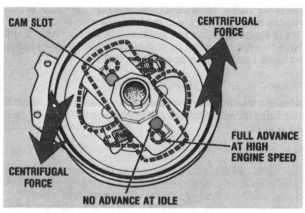

FIGURE 24-19. Two common types of distributor centrifugal advance mechanisms. *(Courtesy of Chrysler Corporation [top] and Ford Motor Co. of Canada Ltd. [bottom])*

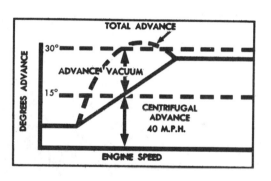

FIGURE 24-20. Normal centrifugal and vacuum ignition advance curves at various engine speeds. *(Courtesy of General Motors Corporation)*

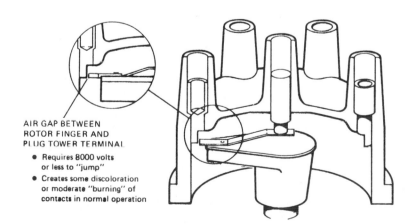

AIR GAP BETWEEN ROTOR FINGER AND PLUG TOWER TERMINAL

- Requires 8000 volts or less to "jump"
- Creates some discoloration or moderate "burning" of contacts in normal operation

FIGURE 24-21. Cap and rotor relationship.

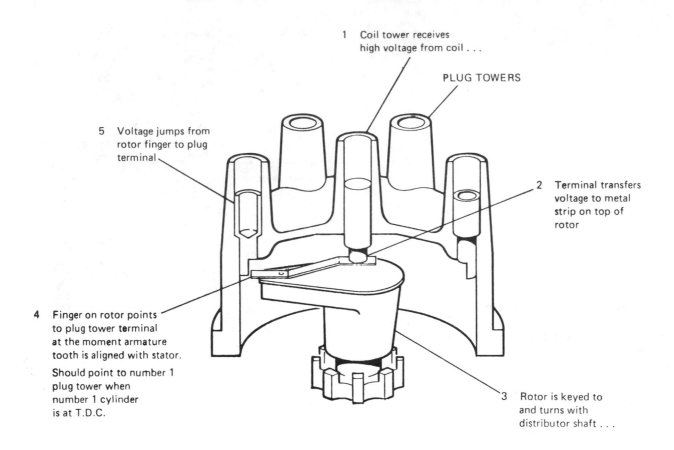

1 Coil tower receives high voltage from coil . . .

PLUG TOWERS

5 Voltage jumps from rotor finger to plug terminal

2 Terminal transfers voltage to metal strip on top of rotor

4 Finger on rotor points to plug tower terminal at the moment armature tooth is aligned with stator.

Should point to number 1 plug tower when number 1 cylinder is at T.D.C.

3 Rotor is keyed to and turns with distributor shaft . . .

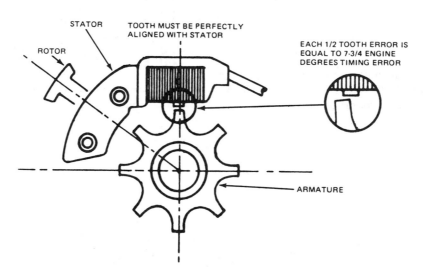

STATOR

ROTOR

TOOTH MUST BE PERFECTLY ALIGNED WITH STATOR

EACH 1/2 TOOTH ERROR IS EQUAL TO 7-3/4 ENGINE DEGREES TIMING ERROR

ARMATURE

FIGURE 24-22. Cutaway view of distributor cap and rotor relationship.

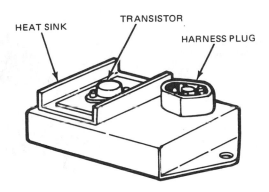

FIGURE 24-23. Electronic ignition control module. *(Courtesy of Chrysler Corporation)*

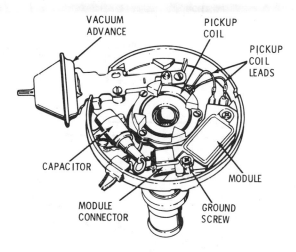

FIGURE 24-24. HEI distributor showing pulse generator and control module *(Courtesy of General Motors Corporation)*

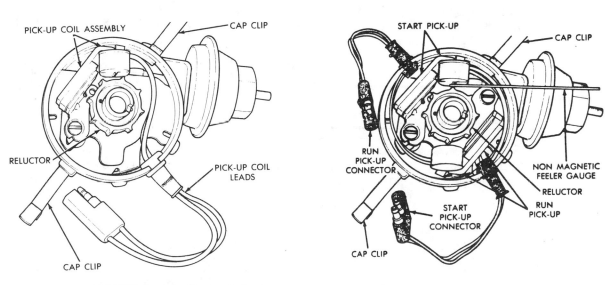

FIGURE 24-25. Single (left) and dual (right) pickup distributors for Chrysler computer-controlled ignition systems. *(Courtesy of Chrysler Corporation)*

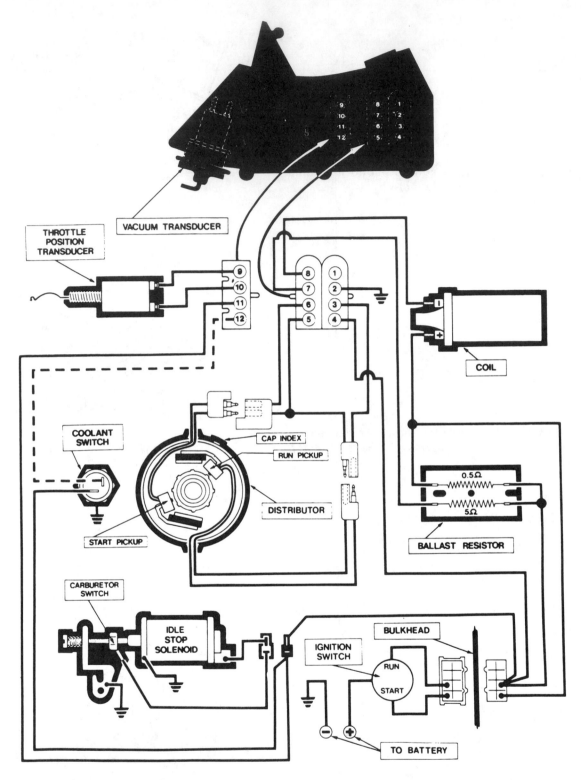

FIGURE 24-26. Spark control computer wiring diagram. *(Courtesy of Chrysler Corporation)*

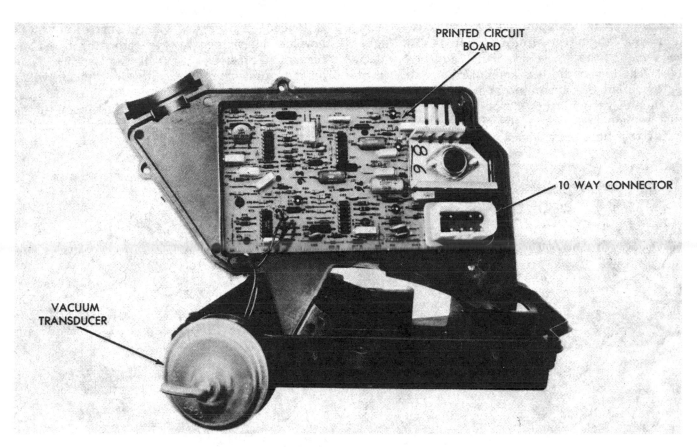

FIGURE 24-27. Spark control computer internal circuitry (Courtesy of Chrysler Corporation)

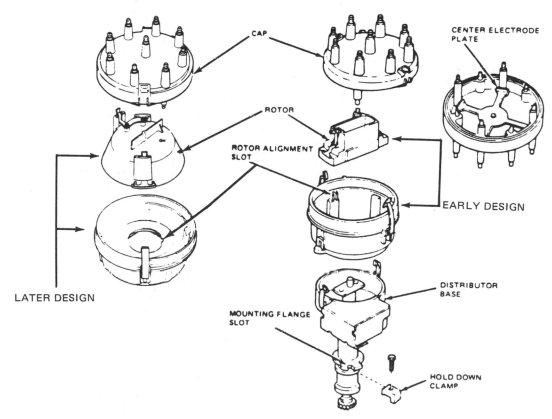

FIGURE 24-28. Ford's electronic engine control system uses unique distributor shown here. The only function of this distributor is to distribute secondary voltage to the spark plugs.

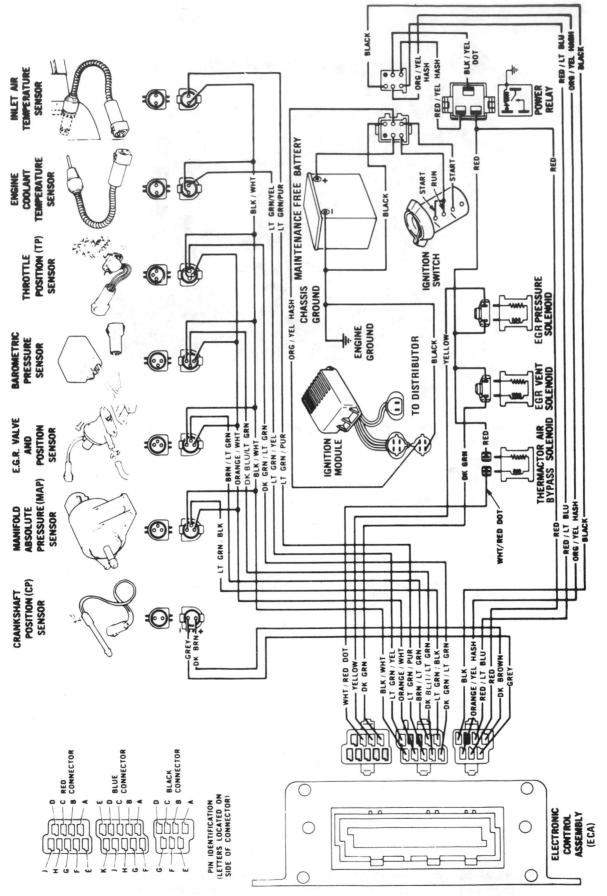

FIGURE 24-29. Ford's electronic engine control wiring diagram. (Courtesy of Ford Motor Co. of Canada Ltd.)

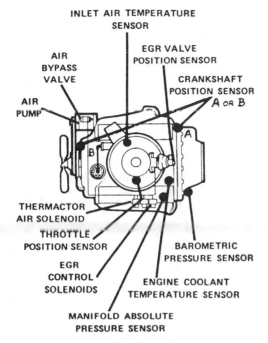

INLET AIR TEMPERATURE
SENSOR

EGR VALVE
POSITION SENSOR

AIR
BYPASS
VALVE

CRANKSHAFT
POSITION SENSOR
A or *B*

AIR
PUMP

THERMACTOR
AIR SOLENOID

THROTTLE
POSITION SENSOR

BAROMETRIC
PRESSURE SENSOR

EGR
CONTROL
SOLENOIDS

ENGINE COOLANT
TEMPERATURE SENSOR

MANIFOLD ABSOLUTE
PRESSURE SENSOR

FIGURE 24-30. Ford's electronic engine control system showing sensor location. *(Courtesy of Ford Motor Co. of Canada Ltd.)*

is not required if a manifold absolute pressure sensor or vacuum sensor input is provided to the computer. The computer adjusts ignition timing much more precisely for better emission control, fuel economy, and performance.

PART 4   HIGH-TENSION WIRES

High-voltage or high-tension coil and spark-plug wires are heavily insulated to prevent high-voltage leaks to ground or to other high-tension wires (cross firing). Secondary suppression is required to prevent radio and television communications interference. Television and radio suppression (TVRS) high-tension wires are used for this purpose.

This type of wiring must be handled with care to avoid damage and high resistance, especially when removing wires from distributors and spark plugs. Heavy synthetic rubber insulators at both ends of the wire help prevent moisture from causing high-voltage shorts.

Insulation on high tension wires deteriorates over a period of time from the action of oil, heat, moisture, and the effects of corona. Insulation breakdown or excessive resistance requires wire replacement.

Resistance values for high-tension wires vary considerably depending on make, year, and model of vehicle. Total resistance for any one wire should not exceed manufacturer's specifications. Resistance values should not vary excessively between wires on any set.

High-tension wires and spark plugs operate as a team. Therefore, it is important that high-tension

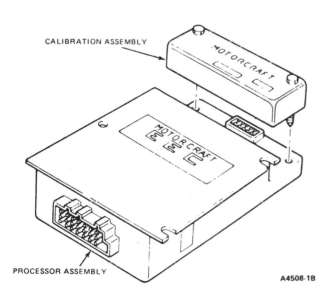

CALIBRATION ASSEMBLY

PROCESSOR ASSEMBLY

A4508-1B

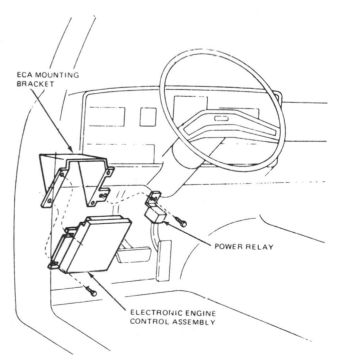

ECA MOUNTING
BRACKET

POWER RELAY

ELECTRONIC ENGINE
CONTROL ASSEMBLY

FIGURE 24-31. Ford's electronic engine control uses a control module with a ROM calibration unit located as shown here. *(Courtesy of Ford Motor Co. of Canada Ltd.)*

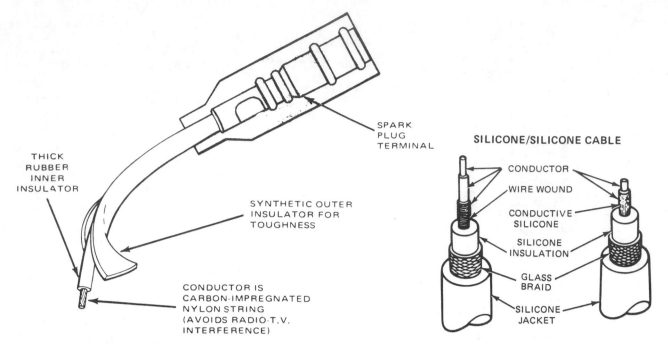

THICK RUBBER INNER INSULATOR

SPARK PLUG TERMINAL

SYNTHETIC OUTER INSULATOR FOR TOUGHNESS

CONDUCTOR IS CARBON-IMPREGNATED NYLON STRING (AVOIDS RADIO-T.V. INTERFERENCE)

SILICONE/SILICONE CABLE

CONDUCTOR

WIRE WOUND

CONDUCTIVE SILICONE

SILICONE INSULATION

GLASS BRAID

SILICONE JACKET

FIGURE 24-32. TVRS high-tension spark-plug wire construction. *(Courtesy of Ford Motor Co. of Canada Ltd.)*

wire types and spark plug types be used that are designed to work together to provide the total resistance required.

High-tension wires have male or female metal terminal connectors which plug into the distributor cap to provide a positive electrical connection in spite of vibration. Some types lock into place with locks inside the distributor cap. These cannot be pulled from the cap without first removing the cap and releasing the locking device from the inside. The other end of the wire has a metal terminal that attaches to the spark plug terminal.

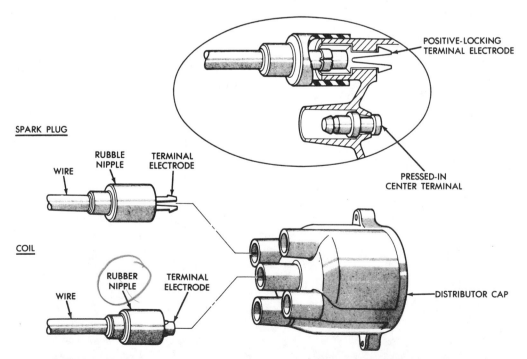

POSITIVE-LOCKING TERMINAL ELECTRODE

PRESSED-IN CENTER TERMINAL

SPARK PLUG

WIRE

RUBBLE NIPPLE

TERMINAL ELECTRODE

COIL

WIRE

RUBBER NIPPLE

TERMINAL ELECTRODE

DISTRIBUTOR CAP

FIGURE 24-33. High-tension wiring with locking device snaps into lock position inside distributor cap. Locking device must be released before attempting to remove wires from cap. *(Courtesy of Chrysler Corporation)*

PART 5 SPARK PLUGS

The purpose of the spark plug is to provide a proper gap in the combustion chamber across which a spark can be made to jump and ignite the fuel/air mixture under all speed and load conditions.

Although it has no moving parts, the spark plug is exposed to more severe stress than any other part of the engine. It must deliver a high voltage spark, with split second timing, thousands of times a minute—and under widely varying, always hostile, operating conditions.

To form a perfect seal in the combustion chamber, each spark plug must exactly match the dimensional characteristics of the cylinder head it is designed to fit in three important ways: (1) thread diameter, (2) reach, and (3) sealing method.

1. *Thread Diameter*

Spark plugs are made in 10, 12, 14, and 18 mm thread diameters. These thread dimensions have been standardized by the Society of Automotive Engineers (SAE) and are used by all spark plug manufacturers.

2. *Reach*

Dimensional match is critical since it determines the position of the spark gap inside the combustion chamber. If the reach is too short:

- Shrouded gap may misfire.
- Exposed cylinder threads will collect combustion deposits and could cause pre-ignition.

If the reach is too long:

- Pre-ignition may result from overheating exposed plug threads.
- Carbon deposits on exposed plug threads can cause damage to threads in cylinder head when plug removal is attempted.
- Severe engine damage may result (piston can hit the plug).

3. *Sealing Method*

Two methods of sealing the spark plug against the cylinder head are used. One method uses a tapered seat which provides a wedge type seal against the cylinder head. The other method uses a flat surface sealed with a compressible gasket.

Heat Range

The heat range of a spark plug refers to the heat dissipation properties of the plug or the temperature limits within which a particular plug operates most efficiently, depending upon its ability to dissipate the heat of combustion. A spark plug will retain part of the heat of combustion to burn away the carbon and oil deposits that form on the plug electrodes as a result of combustion. If the electrodes do not sustain a sufficiently high temperature, these deposits would accumulate to the extent of fouling the plug. If excessive heat is retained by the plug,

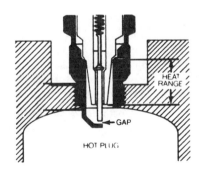

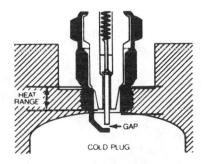

FIGURE 24-35. Spark-plug heat range. Hot plug: longer heat path from tip to shell, and much insulator exposed heat flows slowly; cold plug: shorter heat path from tip to shell, and little insulator heat flows quickly. *(Courtesy of Ford Motor Co. of Canada Ltd.)*

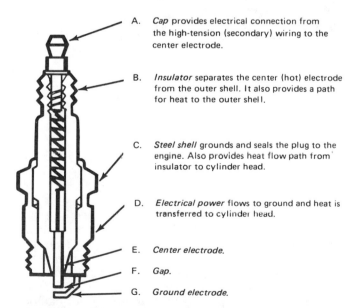

A. *Cap* provides electrical connection from the high-tension (secondary) wiring to the center electrode.

B. *Insulator* separates the center (hot) electrode from the outer shell. It also provides a path for heat to the outer shell.

C. *Steel shell* grounds and seals the plug to the engine. Also provides heat flow path from insulator to cylinder head.

D. *Electrical power* flows to ground and heat is transferred to cylinder head.

E. *Center electrode.*

F. *Gap.*

G. *Ground electrode.*

FIGURE 24-34. *(Courtesy of Ford Motor Co. of Canada Ltd.)*

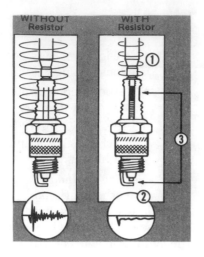

FIGURE 24-36. Resistor plugs are very effective in suppressing ignition interference for three important reasons: (1) Radiation from ignition cables is greatly reduced in strength; (2) the high-frequency part of the spark is virtually eliminated; (3) the suppressor element is near the spark-plug gap for maximum effectiveness. *(Courtesy of Champion Spark Plug Company of Canada, Limited)*

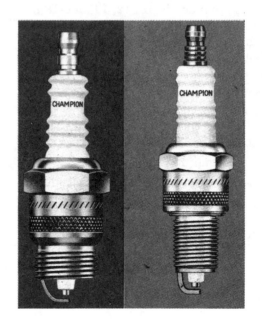

FIGURE 24-37. Plug on left has tapered seat which requires no gasket and has short thread reach. Plug on right has longer reach and requires gasket for sealing. *(Courtesy of Champion Spark Plug Company of Canada, Limited)*

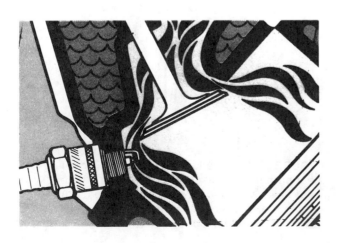

FIGURE 24-38. The turboaction design benefits from an effect called charge cooling at higher engine speeds, whereby the cool, incoming, air-fuel charges lower the temperature of the firing tip. By providing more protection against overheating at high speed, the plug can be designed to operate at a higher temperature level at low speeds, and at idle, to combat the effects of carbon fouling. *(Courtesy of Champion Spark Plug Company of Canada, Limited)*

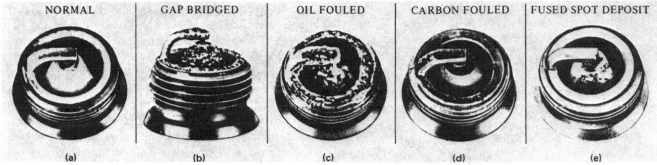

NORMAL	GAP BRIDGED	OIL FOULED	CARBON FOULED	FUSED SPOT DEPOSIT
(a)	(b)	(c)	(d)	(e)

FIGURE 24–39. Clean and gap spark plugs that are (A) identified by light tan or gray deposits on the firing tip; (B) identified by deposit buildup closing gap between electrodes; caused by oil or carbon fouling; (C) identified by the wet black deposits on the insulator shell or electrodes; caused by excessive oil entering combustion chamber through worn rings and piston, excessive clearance between valve guides and stems; (D) identified by black, dry fluffy carbon deposits on insulator tips, exposed steel surfaces and electrodes; caused by too cold a plug, weak ignition, dirty air cleaner, defective fuel pump, too rich a fuel mixture, improperly operating heat riser or excessive idling; (E) identified by melted or spotty deposits resembling bubbles or blister; caused by sudden acceleration. *(Courtesy of Ford Motor Co. of Canada Ltd.)*

the insulator tip will become heated to the point of glowing and cause preignition. This is premature ignition of the mixture by the glowing plug rather than by the correctly timed spark jumping the gap.

A *cold*-type plug is used in engines where a greater amount of heat must be dissipated to prevent overheating of the spark plug and possible preignition. A *hot*-type plug is designed for use in engines operating in a low average temperature, such as might be encountered in consistent low-speed driving. The swirling action of the gases min-

imizes the formation of carbon deposits at low speed by cleaning the inside of the plugs. The net result is a spark plug that resists low-speed fouling, will not cause deterioration, and renders improved service life.

The spark-plug gap must be large enough to provide an ample spark for idle and low-speed operation but not so large as to prevent a spark at high speed and heavy-load conditions. Spark-plug gaps range from approximately 0.035 to 0.050 inch (0.87 to 1.28 millimeters) on most engines.

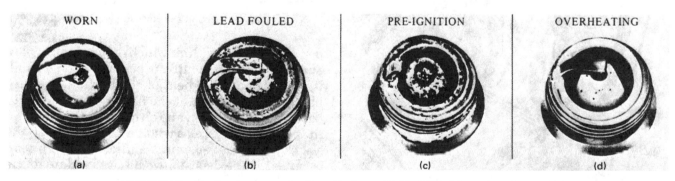

WORN	LEAD FOULED	PRE-IGNITION	OVERHEATING
(a)	(b)	(c)	(d)

FIGURE 24–40. Replace spark plugs that are (A) identified by severely eroded or worn electrodes; caused by normal wear; (B) identified by dark gray, black, yellow, or tan deposits or a fused, glazed coating on the insulator tip; caused by highly leaded gasoline; (C) identified by melted electrodes and possibly blistered insulator; metallic deposits on insulator indicate engine damage; caused by wrong type of fuel, incorrect ignition timing or advance, too hot a plug, burnt valves, or engine overheating; (D) identified by a white or light gray insulator with small black or gray-brown spots and with a bluish-burnt appearance of electrodes; caused by engine overheating, wrong type of fuel, loose spark plug, too hot a plug, low fuel pump pressure, or incorrect ignition timing. *(Courtesy of Ford Motor Co. of Canada Ltd.)*

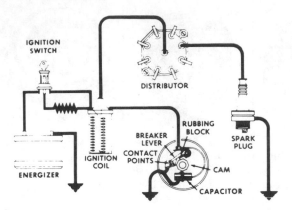

FIGURE 24-41. Typical contact point ignition system schematic. *(Courtesy of General Motors Corporation)*

PART 6   CONTACT POINT IGNITION

In contact point ignition, a mechanical switch (contact points) and a condenser are used to control primary current to the ignition coil.

When the ignition switch is turned on, battery or generator electricity flows through the closed ignition switch, through the ignition resistor assembly and coil primary windings, to the distributor contact points. When the distributor contact points are closed, electricity flows back to the battery through ground, thereby completing the primary ignition circuit and causing the current in the coil primary windings to provide a strong magnetic field. This is the points closed or dwell period. (See Figure 24-42.)

When the distributor contact points are opened by the revolving distributor cam, the primary circuit is broken, and the magnetic field built up around the coil secondary windings quickly collapses across the secondary windings. This sudden collapse of the magnetic field induces a high voltage in the secondary windings.

Ignition Resistor

The ignition resistor assembly is connected in series between the ignition switch and the primary positive terminal of the coil—when the ignition switch is in the *run* position. The function of the ignition resistor is to protect the distributor breaker points during low-speed operation when the breaker points are closed for longer intervals and there is a possibility of excessive current burning the breaker points. Since current is present for shorter intervals at higher speeds, the resistor runs cooler, allowing more current through the primary circuit. The shorter current intervals require higher current in the primary to be able to produce adequate secondary voltage.

The resistor assembly is bypassed from the ignition primary circuit during cranking of the engine to provide increased voltage to the coil while the starting motor is draining voltage from the battery.

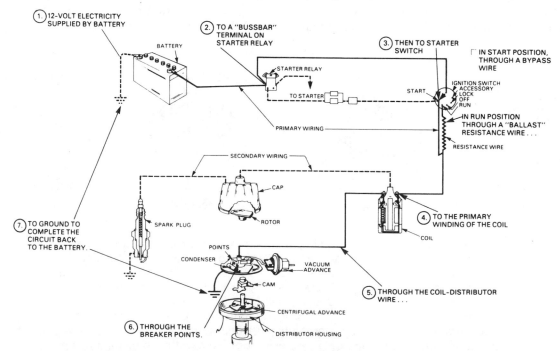

FIGURE 24-42. The low-voltage primary circuit supplies current to the coil primary to charge the coil when the distributor points are closed. *(Courtesy of Ford Motor Co. of Canada Ltd.)*

Condenser (Capacitor)

Contact point ignition distributors use a condenser connected electrically in parallel with the contact points. The condenser is normally mounted on the breaker plate.

As the points begin to open and the primary circuit is broken, the condenser absorbs the primary current, which tends to arc across the opening points due to its inertia. The condenser, through its absorption of the surging primary current, reduces arcing at the distributor points. Self-induction caused by the collapsing magnetic field may cause current in the primary to reach 350 volts. When the condenser has reached maximum voltage, it is discharged back into the primary circuit. The condenser is charged and discharged several times, with decreasing voltage oscillations, until all the current has dissipated. Without the condenser, the engine would not run since arcing at the points would prevent a clean cut off of primary current and, therefore, prevent the necessary collapse of the magnetic field, which is needed to produce the induced secondary voltage to fire the plugs.

PART 7   IGNITION SYSTEM DIAGNOSIS AND SERVICE PROCEDURE

General Precautions

Follow all the normal personal and shop safety procedures as well as those in Chapter 18, Part 5, and Chapter 21, Part 6.

A quick and effective method of testing the entire ignition system is by the use of an automotive oscilloscope. This equipment will provide all the testing and diagnostic capability required. See Chapter 26 for this procedure.

Servicing the electronic ignition system includes the following basic procedures:

1. Determine whether adequate secondary voltage is being delivered to the spark plugs.

2. Determine whether adequate secondary voltage output is available at the coil.

3. Determine primary circuit system current supply.

4. Determine primary circuit control system operation.

5. Determine operation of electronic ignition timing control sensors and module.

To check the system without the scope, proceed as follows.

Secondary Voltage at Spark Plugs

Carefully remove one spark-plug wire from the plug and hold it about 1/4 inch away from a good ground or use special test spark plug designed for this purpose. (Use ignition pliers to hold wire.) Crank engine and observe spark at wire being held. There should be a strong spark and evidence of a snapping sound indicating sufficient secondary voltage potential. If this spark is present in all spark-plug wires, the trouble is in the spark plugs or in some part of the vehicle other than the ignition system. If spark is not present, proceed as follows.

Secondary Voltage at Coil

Remove high-tension coil lead from distributor cap and hold 1/4 inch from a good ground. Crank engine and observe spark. Spark should be of high intensity and have an audible snapping sound. If spark is present, trouble is in secondary distribution system, cap, rotor, high-tension wires, or spark plugs.

If good spark is not present, proceed as follows.

Coil Primary Input Voltage

Check voltage with voltmeter at coil positive terminal (1) with key in start position (engine cranking) and (2) with key in run position. Compare results with manufacturer's specifications.

If voltage is incorrect, check primary circuit components resistance and correct as needed. Loose or corroded connections, open circuit, and poor ignition switch or resistor are some of the possible causes.

If coil input voltage is correct, test ignition coil and compare to manufacturer's specifications. If faulty, replace coil. If coil tests prove coil to be good, proceed as follows.

Coil Test

1. Connect ohmmeter leads to primary terminals on coil.

2. Read ohmmeter scale.

    (a) An infinite reading indicates an open primary winding (replace coil).

    (b) Ohmmeter reading should meet specifications.

3. Connect ohmmeter to coil primary positive terminal and to high-tension terminal.

    (a) An infinite reading indicates an open secondary winding (replace coil).

    (b) Ohmmeter resistance reading should meet specifications. (A reading that is too low indicates a shorted secondary winding; replace coil.)

DIAGNOSTIC CHART

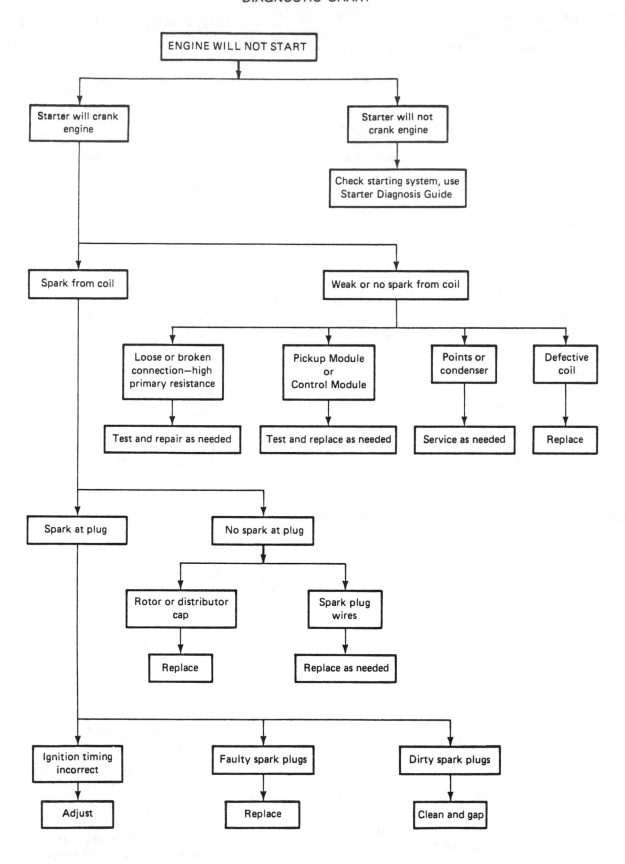

ENGINE WILL NOT START

- Starter will crank engine
- Starter will not crank engine
  - Check starting system, use Starter Diagnosis Guide

Spark from coil

Weak or no spark from coil
- Loose or broken connection—high primary resistance
  - Test and repair as needed
- Pickup Module or Control Module
  - Test and replace as needed
- Points or condenser
  - Service as needed
- Defective coil
  - Replace

Spark at plug

No spark at plug
- Rotor or distributor cap
  - Replace
- Spark plug wires
  - Replace as needed

- Ignition timing incorrect
  - Adjust
- Faulty spark plugs
  - Replace
- Dirty spark plugs
  - Clean and gap

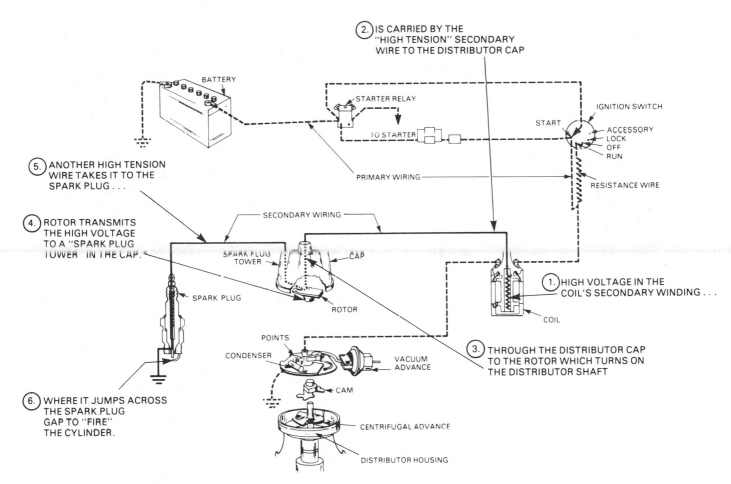

FIGURE 24–43. The coil secondary produces the high voltage required to fire the correct spark plug at the appropriate time. *(Courtesy of Ford Motor Co. of Canada Ltd.)*

Distributor Tests

Every electronic ignition system (if not computerized) has a pickup module in the distributor which should be tested with an ohmmeter. Connect the ohmmeter to the disconnected leads from the pickup module. The resistance through the pickup coil windings should be as specified in the shop manual for the unit being serviced. On many Chrysler systems resistance should be between 150 to 900 ohms. On many Ford Dura Spark systems resistance should be between 400 and 1000 ohms. Many HEI systems should have a resistance between 500 and 1500 ohms.

On some systems (Chrysler and BID) the air gap between the pickup and the reluctor or armature is adjustable. This clearance must be measured with a non-magnetic-type feeler gauge and adjusted to specifications.

On systems where this clearance is not adjustable, but the original clearance has been altered, the pickup coil or armature or both must be replaced, since they have been damaged.

Distributor Advance Testing

This test can be done on the car or in a distributor testing machine. Follow equipment manufacturer's instructions for using testers.

1. Vacuum advance should be checked at several specified vacuum values. Amount of vacuum

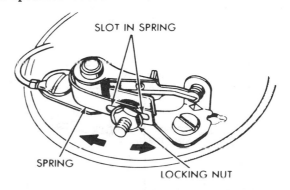

FIGURE 24–44. Typical distributor breaker points (contact points). Note adjustment screw for adjusting point gap and slotted spring for adjusting spring tension. *(Courtesy of Ford Motor Co. of Canada Ltd.)*

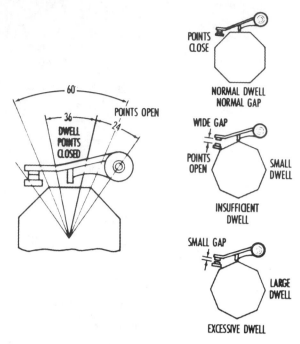

FIGURE 24-45. Dwell is the term used to describe the time during which the points are closed. This dwell period is stated in degrees of distributor shaft rotation. Increased dwell retards ignition timing; reduced dwell advances timing. *(Courtesy of Ford Motor Co. of Canada Ltd.)*

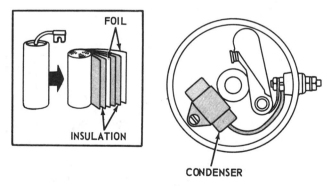

FIGURE 24-46. Distributor condenser construction with alternate layers of foil and insulation.

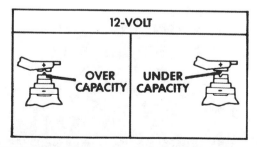

FIGURE 24-47. Effects of condenser capacity on ignition points. Metal transfers from one contact to the other. *(Courtesy of Ford Motor Co. of Canada Ltd.)*

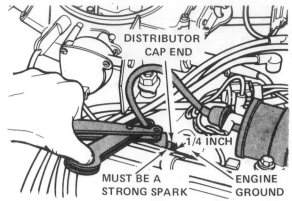

FIGURE 24-48. Checking coil secondary output. *(Courtesy of Ford Motor Co. of Canada Ltd.)*

advance should meet vehicle manufacturer's specifications at specified vacuum for good performance and fuel economy. Replace a faulty vacuum advance unit.

2. Centrifugal advance must be checked at speeds specified by vehicle manufacturer. Amount of centrifugal advance must meet manufacturer's specifications at specified speeds. Tests must be performed with vacuum supply to vacuum advance unit disconnected.

Secondary Circuit Testing

The rotor and distributor cap should be carefully inspected for corrosion and damage such as cracks or burned terminals, corroded high-tension terminals, and so on. Faulty parts should be replaced. A good distributor cap should be cleaned in hot soapy water, rinsed, and dried.

Rotor gap clearance can only be checked with an oscilloscope. (See Chapter 26.)

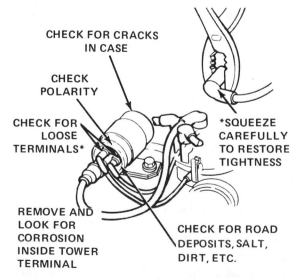

FIGURE 24-49. Checks to be made at coil (nonunitized ignition coil). *(Courtesy of Ford Motor Co. of Canada Ltd.)*

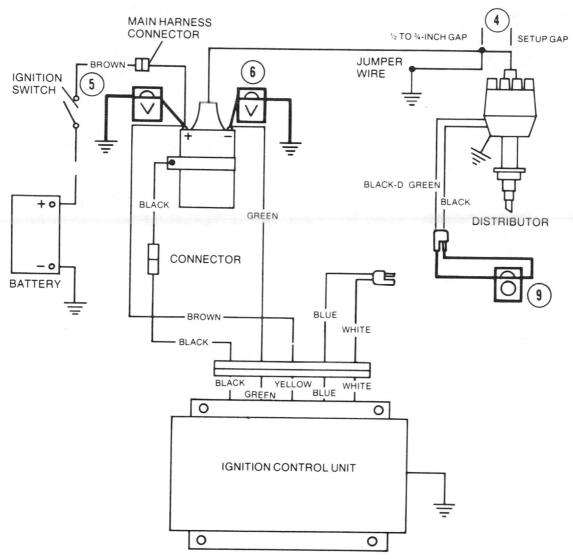

FIGURE 24-50. Checking coil secondary output at (4); available primary voltage at coil (5); coil primary winding voltage at (6); and checking pickup coil resistance with ohmmeter at (9).

Distributor Removal and Installation

If the distributor is to be removed, the following general procedure may be followed.

Removal

1. Disconnect all high tension wires at distributor. Procedure varies and requires removal of distributor cap in some cases to unlock HT wires.

2. Disconnect remaining electrical and vacuum connections at distributors.

3. Remove distributor "hold down device."

4. Lift out distributor.

Installation

1. Position engine crankshaft so that No. 1 piston is at TDC position of compression stroke and ignition timing indicator is at zero degrees.

2. Position the distributor shaft prior to installation to achieve the following results when the distributor is in the fully installed position:

- armature tooth and pickup pole piece properly aligned.
- rotor tip aligned with No. 1 high-tension terminal in cap.
- oil pump drive fully engaged (some models only).

Do not attempt to force the distributor into place with the clamping device—this will cause breakage.

The procedure will vary somewhat with the design of the distributor and oil pump drive as well as the direction of distributor shaft rotation.

On contact point distributors, the procedure is the same except that in item 2 above, instead of

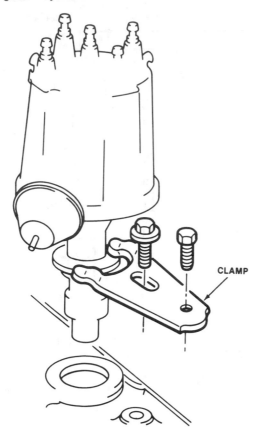

FIGURE 24-51. Typical distributor hold down clamp. *(Courtesy of American Motors Corporation)*

aligning the armature tooth, the shaft should be positioned so that the contact points just barely begin to open when the rotor is aligned as above.

This procedure provides initial ignition timing which will allow the engine to be started. Timing should be further adjusted as described later.

Fully Computerized Systems

Computer controlled systems are provided with a diagnostic connector in the engine compartment or under the dash depending on make and model.

The system provides for on-board diagnostic procedures which provide trouble codes through the instrument panel display. When checking a computer controlled system, be sure to follow the on-board diagnostic procedures first, as outlined in the appropriate service manual. If this procedure does not isolate the problem, additional tests must be made utilizing the diagnostic connector, the appropriate test equipment (usually a voltmeter and ohmmeter or special tester with digital readout capability), and the procedure outlined in the appropriate service manual. As many as 50 trouble codes may be involved.

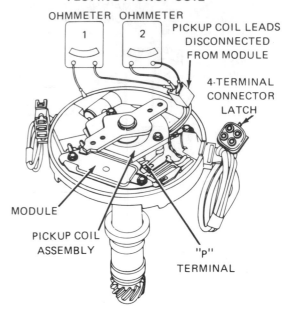

TESTING PICKUP COIL

FIGURE 24-52. On all distributors, remove rotor and pickup coil leads from module. Connect ohmmeter Test 1 and then Test 2. If vacuum unit is used, connect vacuum source to vacuum unit. Replace unit if inoperative. Observe ohmmeter throughout vacuum range; flex leads by hand without vacuum to check for intermittent opens.

Test 1—should read infinite at all times.
Test 2—should read steady at one value within 500–1500 ohm range.
Note: Ohmmeter may deflect if operating vacuum unit causes teeth to align. This is not a defect. If pickup coil is defective, replace.
(Courtesy of General Motors Corporation)

What it all comes down to is that the problem is in one of four areas:

- The computer
- The input sensors
- The output devices
- The connecting wiring

High-Tension Wires and Spark Plugs

High-tension wires should be inspected for insulation deterioration, and if good, they should be tested with an ohmmeter to determine resistance values. If resistance does not meet specifications, wires should be replaced. Resistance values vary depending on the make and model of the vehicle being serviced.

Spark plugs should be removed, cleaned, filed, properly gapped, and tested to determine serviceability. Only plugs of the proper heat range, reach, size, and type should be used. Failure to follow vehicle manufacturer's specifications may re-

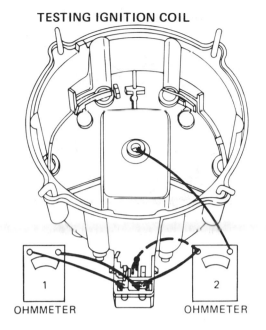

FIGURE 24-53. Connect ohmmeter, Test 1. Reading should be zero, or nearly zero. If not, replace coil. Connect ohmmeter both ways, Test 2. Use high scale. Replace coil *only* if *both* readings are *infinite. (Courtesy of General Motors Corporation)*

PICKUP COIL REMOVED AND DISASSEMBLED

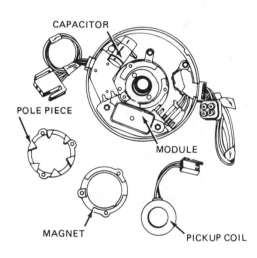

FIGURE 24-54. Remove retaining ring and remove pickup coil, magnet, and pole piece. *(Courtesy of General Motors Corporation)*

FIGURE 24-55. Remove two module attaching screws and capacitor attaching screw. Lift module, capacitor, and harness assembly from base. Disconnect wiring harness from module. Check module with an approved module tester. Install module, wiring harness, and capacitor assembly. Use silicone lubricant on housing under module. *(Courtesy of General Motors Corporation)*

MODULE REMOVED

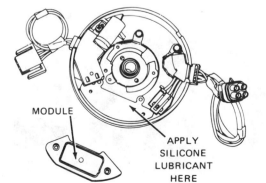

525

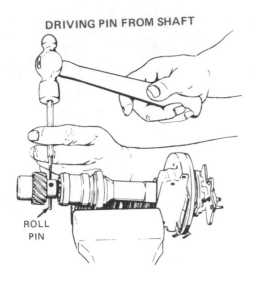

DRIVING PIN FROM SHAFT

ROLL PIN

FIGURE 24-56. Mark distributor shaft and gear so they can be reassembled in same position. Drive out roll pin. *(Courtesy of General Motors Corporation)*

SHAFT ASSEMBLY REMOVED

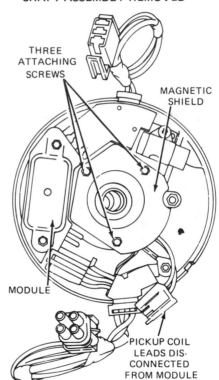

THREE ATTACHING SCREWS

MAGNETIC SHIELD

MODULE

PICKUP COIL LEADS DIS- CONNECTED FROM MODULE

FIGURE 24-57. Remove gear and pull shaft assembly from distributor. *(Courtesy of General Motors Corporation)*

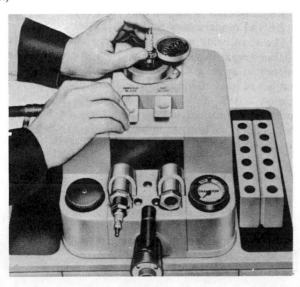

FIGURE 24-58. Using sand-blast type of spark-plug cleaner. *(Courtesy of Champion Spark Plug Company of Canada, Limited)*

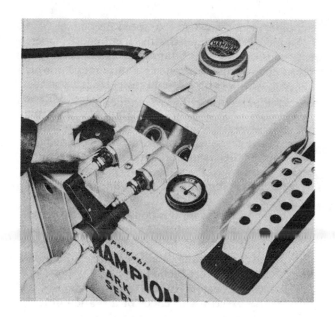

FIGURE 24-59. After cleaning, filing, and gapping, spark plugs are tested on the same machine under regulated pressure. *(Courtesy of Champion Spark Plug Company of Canada, Limited)*

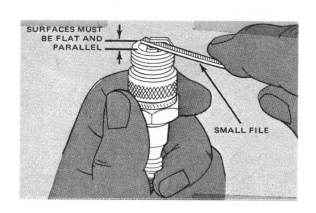

FIGURE 24-60. After cleaning, spark plugs must be filed as shown here. *(Courtesy of Ford Motor Co. of Canada Ltd.)*

FIGURE 24-61. Adjusting plug gap is done by careful bending of the ground electrode. Excessive plug gap requires excessive voltage to fire the plug. Insufficient gap may result in too weak a spark to ignite the air-fuel mixture. Adjust to recommended specifications only. *(Courtesy of Ford Motor Co. of Canada Ltd.)*

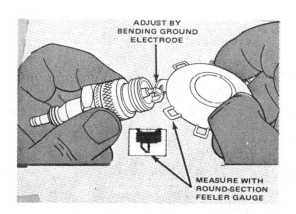

sult in serious engine damage, as well as poor performance and economy.

If a compression test or cylinder leak down test is to be performed, it should be done when the plugs are out. See Chapter 26 for the procedure.

Ignition Timing

Ignition timing should be set at the vehicle manufacturer's specifications using a timing light. Ignition timing marks are usually located at the crankshaft pulley. The timing light is connected to the battery and to the number 1 spark plug. The engine is then started and run at idle. Follow the vehicle manufacturer's directions for checking timing, which may require disconnecting the vacuum supply to the distributor vacuum advance unit.

To adjust timing, loosen the distributor hold-down bolt and turn the distributor housing in the same direction as shaft rotation to retard timing, and turn against shaft rotation to advance timing. (Direction of distributor shaft rotation can easily be determined by looking at the vacuum advance connecting link to the breaker plate. The link points in the direction of shaft rotation.) After adjusting timing, tighten the hold-down bolt and recheck timing to ensure that it has not changed while tightening the bolt.

Correct ignition timing is critical to good performance and economy. Timing that is advanced too far causes pinging and may even cause serious engine damage. Timing that is retarded too far can cause poor performance and overheating.

Typical Firing Orders and Cylinder Numbering

The following list represents the cylinder numbering systems and firing orders used in recent years by the various vehicle manufacturers listed. The letters following each vehicle make are coded to Figure 24-66.

1. AMC - D O U
   - Jeep - DOU
   - Renault - DE
2. Chrysler - Dodge - Plymouth - H O U
   - Arrow - Champ - Colt - Cricket - Sapporo - FD
3. Ford - C D H O R W X
   - Courier - DG
4. GM - D H O Q S U V X
   - Opel - Isuzu - D
5. Datsun - D F O
6. Honda - F
7. Mazda - A D
8. Subaru - J
9. Toyota - D O
10. VW - D H K

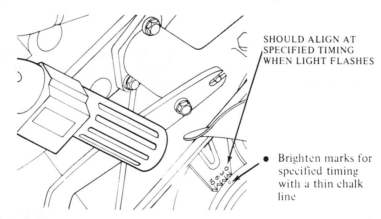

SHOULD ALIGN AT SPECIFIED TIMING WHEN LIGHT FLASHES

Brighten marks for specified timing with a thin chalk line

FIGURE 24-62. Method of adjusting ignition timing:
A. Dwell must be set to specifications *before* checking timing.
B. Vacuum lines disconnected from distributor diaphragm and plugged (if specified).
C. Engine operating at recommended speed.
D. Adjust to specifications on decal.
E. If timing is not to specifications:
   1. Loosen distributor mount.
   2. Turn distributor housing to align marks.
   3. Tighten mount.
   4. Recheck timing.
(Courtesy of Ford Motor Co. of Canada Ltd.)

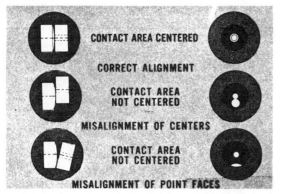

FIGURE 24-63. Correct contact point alignment is essential to good performance and long contact point life. (Courtesy of Ford Motor Co. of Canada Ltd.)

Contact Point Ignition System Testing

Coil Input Voltage

This test will determine whether the primary circuit voltage supply system to the coil has excessive resistance.

1. Connect voltmeter positive lead to positive primary terminal of coil and attach other lead to a good ground.

2. Set voltmeter to proper scale.

3. Disconnect and ground coil high-tension lead from distributor cap to prevent engine from starting.

4. Turn ignition switch to starting position and observe voltage while cranking. Voltage should not be below specifications (usually not less than 9.5 volts).

5. If voltage is too low the reason could be one or more of the following:

(a) Battery condition.

(b) Excessive starter current draw.

(c) Excessive resistance in ignition resistor bypass circuit.

6. With voltmeter connected as in step 1 and with ignition switch in run position (engine off), the voltmeter should read specified voltage (usually approximately 7.5 volts).

7. If voltage is below specifications, the reason could be one or more of the following:

(a) Battery condition.

(b) Ignition switch resistance.

(c) Excessive resistance in ignition ballast resistor or resistor wiring.

If these tests meet specifications, test the coil as outlined earlier.

Distributor Testing

Visual inspection of the distributor will determine the condition of the points, rotor, distributor cap, cam, and shaft and bushing wear. The distributor can be tested on or off the car depending on the equipment available.

Burned, pitted, or blued points should be replaced without testing. However, the reason for points failure should also be corrected. Pitted points can be caused by a condenser of incorrect capacity. Replace condenser. Too high a charging rate can cause burned or blued points. Correct the charging system problem. The points and condenser are usually replaced as routine procedure when servicing the distributor.

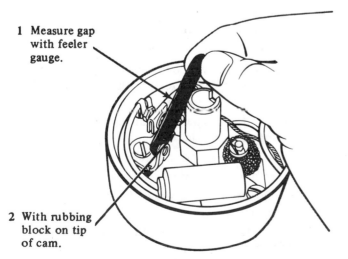
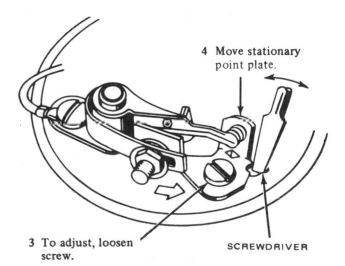

FIGURE 24-64. Initial point gap adjustment is made with rubbing block on high point of cam. (Courtesy of Ford Motor Co. of Canada Ltd.)

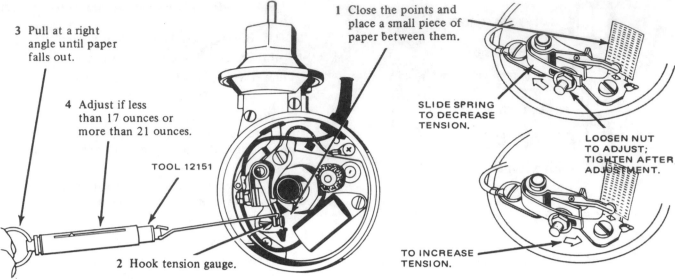

3 Pull at a right angle until paper falls out.

4 Adjust if less than 17 ounces or more than 21 ounces.

TOOL 12151

2 Hook tension gauge.

1 Close the points and place a small piece of paper between them.

SLIDE SPRING TO DECREASE TENSION.

LOOSEN NUT TO ADJUST; TIGHTEN AFTER ADJUSTMENT.

TO INCREASE TENSION.

FIGURE 24-65. Correct point spring tension is required to prevent point bounce (insufficient tension) or rapid wear (excessive tension). *(Courtesy of Ford Motor Co. of Canada Ltd.)*

Point Dwell Testing

On or off the car, the initial point gap can be adjusted and checked with a feeler gauge when the rubbing block is on the high point of the cam.

1. Connect dwell meter negative lead to a good ground and the positive lead to the coil negative primary terminal.

2. Select proper scale on dwell meter (four, six, or eight cyl.) and read dwell with engine running.

3. If dwell is incorrect, adjust point gap. Insufficient dwell means point gap is too wide, and excessive dwell means too little point gap.

4. If dwell reading is irregular, the reason could be a worn distributor cam or worn distributor shaft and bushings. Dwell readings should meet specifications.

Distributor Advance Testing

This test can be done on the car or in a distributor testing machine. Follow instructions outlined earlier.

PART 8 SELF-CHECK

1. The three electronic ignition circuits are
   (a) _____
   (b) _____
   (c) _____

2. In electronic ignition the primary circuit is broken when the _____ receives a signal from the _____.

3. What are the advantages of electronic ignition as opposed to point ignition?

4. Dwell is adjusted in the distributor on electronic ignition systems. True or false?

5. What are the advantages of electronic control of ignition timing?

6. What are the four major steps required to determine electronic ignition system faults?

7. Coil input voltage should be at least _____ during cranking.

8. Low resistance in the coil secondary indicates _____.

9. After cleaning spark plugs, they should be
   (a) _____
   (b) _____
   (c) _____

10. How is ignition timing adjusted?

11. Why is vacuum advance needed?

12. Centrifugal advance causes the distributor cam to rotate slightly ahead of distributor shaft rotation. True or false?

13. The ignition bypass circuit bypasses the _____ during engine starting.

14. What is the effect of incorrect coil polarity?

15. What are TVRS spark plug wires?

16. Spark plugs are classified in three major ways. What are they?

17. What effect does changing point gap have on dwell?

18. What effect does dwell change have on ignition timing?

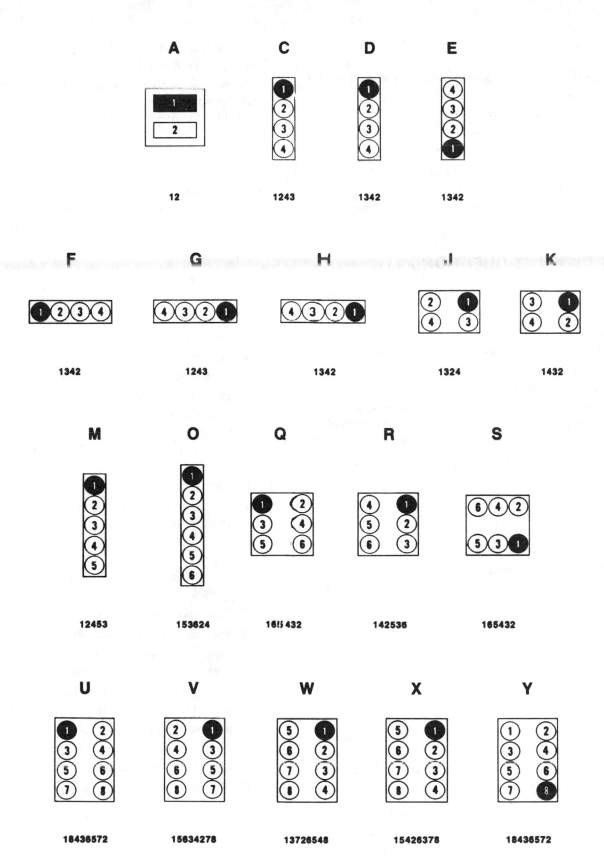

FIGURE 24–66. Common cylinder numbering methods and firing orders. See text for further explanation. *(Courtesy of Ford Motor Co. of Canada Ltd.)*

19. In the contact type of ignition system, list the components of
    (a) the primary circuit
    (b) the secondary circuit

20. Define *distributor point dwell.*

21. When the points close, a high secondary voltage is induced. True or false?

22. What is the purpose of the condenser in contact point ignition?

PART 9   TEST QUESTIONS

1. The electronic ignition system has the following advantages over older point ignitions:
   (a) less pollution
   (b) higher potential secondary voltage
   (c) reduced misfiring
   (d) all of the above

2. Which three components in the solid state ignition system replace the actions of the breaker cam, contact point, and condenser in the conventional system?
   (a) ignition coil
   (b) armature
   (c) magnetic pickup assembly
   (d) control module
   (e) rotor

3. Which component in the solid state ignition system transmits signals to the control module?
   (a) armature
   (b) ignition coil
   (c) rotor
   (d) magnetic pickup assembly

4. What is the main function of the control module?
   (a) it allows battery current to flow to the coil primary winding
   (b) it interrupts the flow of current on signal from the distributor

   (c) both A and B
   (d) neither A nor B

5. Each time a tooth (or pole) on the armature aligns with the magnetic core in the pickup assembly, a pulse of current is sent to the control module. The effect is to:
   (a) turn the primary ignition current off
   (b) turn the primary ignition current on
   (c) turn the secondary ignition current on
   (d) turn the secondary ignition current off

6. One circuit operates the same way in both the contact point and solid state ignition systems. Which one?
   (a) primary
   (b) secondary
   (c) base
   (d) all of the above

7. Spark plugs are classified by:
   (a) heat range, reach, gap, thread diameter
   (b) gap, reach, heat range, fouling protection
   (c) thread diameter, heat range, reach, electrode design
   (d) electrode design, gap, heat range, fouling protection

8. The contact point ignition system includes:
   (a) the primary circuit and secondary circuit
   (b) the low-speed circuit and high-speed circuit
   (c) the primary circuit and the low-voltage circuit
   (d) the secondary circuit and the high-voltage circuit

9. The ignition coil changes:
   (a) low amperage to high amperage
   (b) low voltage to high voltage
   (c) high voltage to low voltage
   (d) high amperage to low voltage

10. Rubbing block wear increases point dwell and:
    (a) advances ignition timing
    (b) does not affect ignition timing
    (c) retards ignition timing
    (d) none of the above

Chapter 25

Instruments and Accessories

Performance Objectives

After sufficient study of this chapter and adequate practice on the appropriate training models, and with the necessary tools, equipment, and shop manuals, you should be able to do the following:

1. Complete the self-check and test questions with at least 80 percent accuracy.

2. State the purpose of, and describe the basic construction and operation of, common lighting systems, instruments, accessories, and their components.

3. Properly diagnose, test, and correct specified lighting systems, instruments, and accessories, as required by vehicle manufacturer's specifications.

4. Test the repaired system or unit to determine the success of the service performed.

5. Prepare the vehicle for customer acceptance.

Every automobile is equipped with several lighting systems and a number of instruments and accessories. The number and types of systems and components vary considerably among the different makes and models. Lighting systems include headlights, tail lights, park lights, brake lights, turn signal lights, cornering lights, side marker lights, hazard warning lights, back-up lights, interior lights, dash or instrument lights, and other convenience lights.

Instruments include indicator lights or gauges mounted in the instrument panel or dashboard to inform the driver about engine and vehicle systems operation. Some of these instruments and accessories are covered in the appropriate chapters elsewhere in this text. This includes engine temperature, engine oil pressure, charging system, and fuel level indicators. Other items covered in this chapter are speedometers and odometers.

Safety and warning devices include horns, windshield wipers, washers, message displays on the dash, buzzers, tone generators, and theft deterrent systems.

Accessory devices that make driving easier and more pleasant include speed control, clocks, radios, tape players, power seats, power windows, power door locks, power trunk release, and heated rear windows. Heating and air conditioning systems are covered in Chapter 40.

PART 1 LIGHTING SYSTEMS

Headlamp System

A typical lighting system is shown in Figures 25–1 and 25–2.

The headlamp system consists of two or four headlamps. Headlamps may be round or rectangular. Round headlamps come in two sizes as do rectangular headlamps. On the two-headlamp system, each headlamp has two filaments, a high beam, and a low beam. On the four-headlamp system, the two outer headlamps are of the two-filament type, and the two inner headlamps have only one high-beam filament. In the vertical arrangement, the two upper lights are double filament.

The headlamp system is controlled by two switches—the headlamp switch and the dimmer switch. The headlamp switch usually has two positions. The first position turns on the parking, side marker, tail, license, and instrument lights. The second position turns on all of these plus the headlamps. Rotating the switch knob operates a rheostat which dims or brightens dash lights. Turning the switch to its extreme counterclockwise position also turns on the interior light. The dimmer switch is a two-position

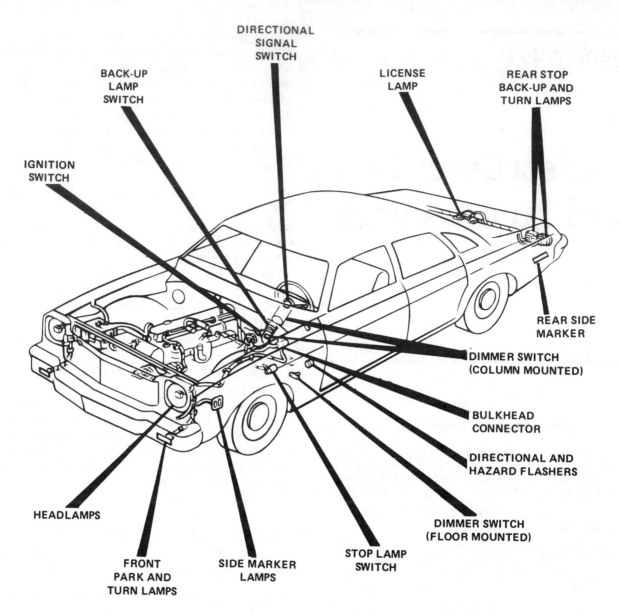

FIGURE 25-1. Typical lighting system component location. *(Courtesy of General Motors Corporation)*

switch either foot operated and floor mounted, or hand operated and steering column mounted. In one position, the dimmer switch will be in the high-beam position, but the other position is for low beam. A high-beam indicator light on the dash is also usually provided. The headlamp circuit is normally protected by a circuit breaker, while other lights are usually provided with fuse protection.

Headlamps are normally of the sealed beam unit design except for some European models. Two types of headlamps are used—the conventional type of

about 75,000 candlepower (CP) and the halogen type with up to twice the candlepower, 150,000 CP. Maximum headlamp power is limited by law and varies somewhat between countries. In Europe, for example, some countries allow up to 225,000 candlepower.

Two-filament headlamps have a three-prong connector—one for each filament and one for the ground connection. Single-filament headlamps have a two-prong connector—one for the live wire and one for the ground connection.

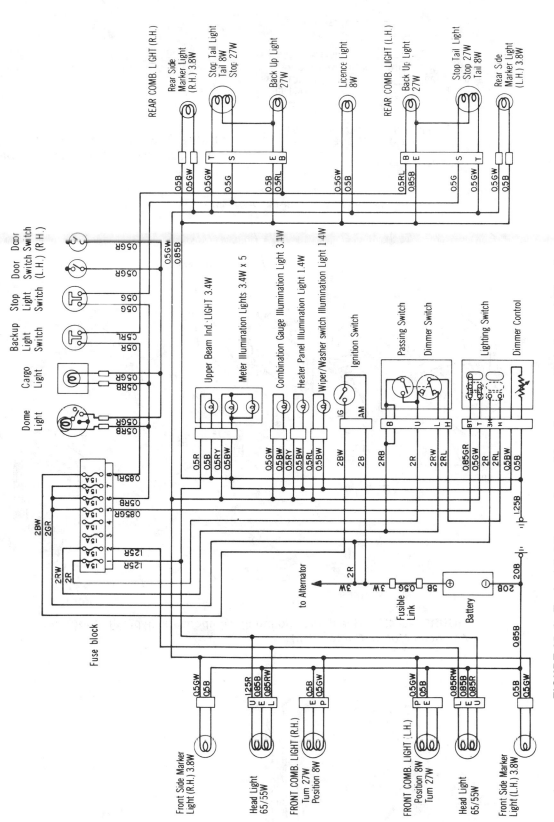

FIGURE 25-2. Typical lighting system wiring diagram. *(Courtesy of Chrysler Corporation)*

535

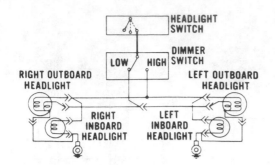

FIGURE 25-3. Typical four-headlamp system electrical circuit. *(Courtesy of Ford Motor Co. of Canada Ltd.)*

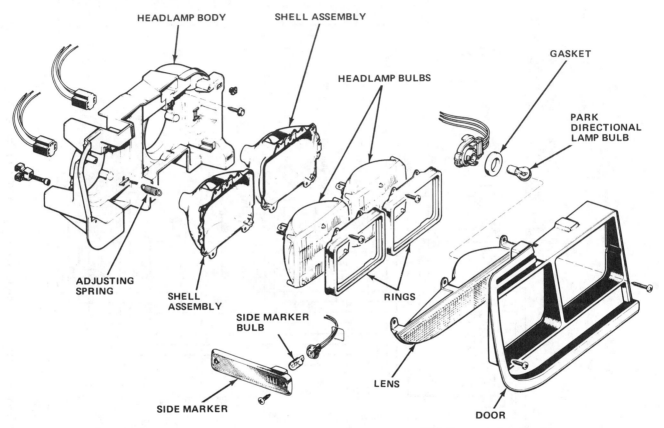

FIGURE 25-4(A). Headlamp mounting components (typical). *(Courtesy of American Motors Corporation)*

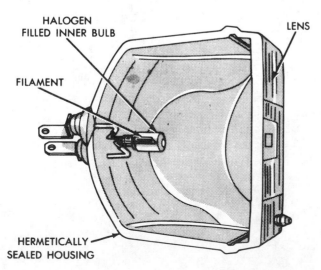

FIGURE 25-4(B). Halogen sealed beam headlamp. *(Courtesy of Chrysler Corporation)*

Halogen Headlamp System

The optional halogen headlamp system includes both two-lamp and four-lamp systems, with all lamps having a halogen inner bulb. These systems have increased high beam lamp output compared to a standard sealed beam system, but require no increase in electrical power. The halogen light is "whiter" than the sealed beam light.

The halogen high beam lamp consists of a hermetically sealed glass housing that protects the reflecting surface and contains a halogen inner bulb. This small inner bulb is made of a high temperature-resistant glass. The bulb encloses the tungsten filament and contains a small amount of halogen vapor—typically an iodine or similar vapor. The high temperature operation of the tungsten filament results in the high light output and maintains the "cycling" of the halogen vapor. In this cycling process, the vapor combines with particles of tungsten that are evaporated from the high temperature filament and redeposits these particles back into the hot filament—instead of on the bulb wall.

The cycling process results in long-lasting filaments, virtually eliminates bulb blackening, and insures continuing brightness.

Headlight Aiming (Figures 25–5 and 25–6)

The headlights must be properly aimed in order to obtain maximum road illumination and safety that has been built into the headlight system. Proper aiming is most important because the increased range and power of lights make even slight variations from recommended aim hazardous to approaching motorists. The headlights must be checked for proper aim whenever a sealed beam unit is replaced and after any adjustment or repair of front end sheet metal or change in suspension height.

Regardless of the method used for checking headlight aim, the car must be at normal weight—with gas, oil, water, and spare tire. Tires must be uniformly inflated to specified pressure. If the car will regularly carry an unusual load in its rear compartment, or will pull a trailer, these loads should be on the car when the headlights are checked. Some states have special requirements for headlight aiming adjustment, and these requirements should be known and observed.

Horizontal and vertical aiming of each sealed beam unit is provided by two adjusting screws which move the mounting ring in the body against the tension of the coil spring. There is no adjustment for focus, since the sealed beam unit is set for proper focus during manufacturing. Access to ad-

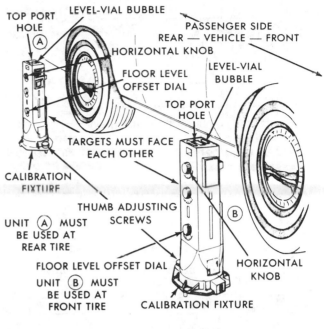

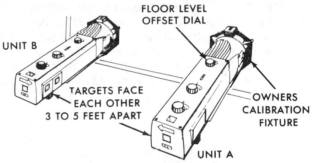

FIGURE 25–5. Calibrating headlamp aiming equipment to take into account any deviation from level of the shop floor—front to back (top) and side to side (bottom). Procedure varies depending on type of equipment used. *(Courtesy of Chrysler Corporation)*

justing screws requires trim removal on many vehicles.

Headlight aiming equipment should accommodate all sealed beam headlights in any standard shape or size and in any configuration. Different light shapes and sizes are accommodated through the use of adapters provided in a kit. Regardless of configuration, headlights are always aimed in pairs as follows: the two upper and the two lower; the two inner and the two outer. Follow equipment and vehicle manufacturer's specifications as well as federal, state, and local regulations governing headlamp aiming. Damage to light-sensor-type headlight aiming equipment may occur if filters are not used when aiming halogen headlamps.

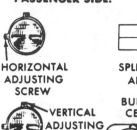

LEVEL BUBBLE
VERTICAL DIAL
HORIZONTAL DIAL
VIEWING PORT

LEVEL BUBBLE
VERTICAL DIAL
HORIZONTAL DIAL
VIEWING PORT

SIGHT OPENINGS
(MUST FACE EACH OTHER)

UNIT B
MUST BE USED ON
PASSENGER SIDE.

UNIT A
MUST BE USED ON
DRIVERS SIDE.

HORIZONTAL
ADJUSTING
SCREW

SPLIT IMAGE
ALIGNED

SPLIT IMAGE
NOT ALIGNED

VERTICAL
ADJUSTING
SCREW

BUBBLE NOT
CENTERED

BUBBLE
CENTERED

FIGURE 25-6. Headlights are adjusted vertically and horizontally to specifications prescribed by law. Horizontal adjustment is achieved by aligning split image in viewer on each unit. Vertical adjustment is achieved by centering level bubble on each unit. Procedure varies with type of equipment used. *(Courtesy of Chrysler Corporation)*

Tail, Park, and Brake Lights (Figure 25-7)

Tail lamp bulbs are usually double filament types— one filament for the tail lamp function and the other for the turn signal and brake light function. Front park lamp bulbs are also usually of the double-filament type serving both park and signal functions. License lamp and side marker bulbs are normally single-filament types. Single-filament bulbs may be single- or double-contact types. Single-contact types are grounded through the bulb base, while double-contact, single-filament types have two wires—one live and the other a ground. Double-filament bulbs have two contacts and two wire connections to it if grounded through the base. If not grounded through the base of the bulb, a two-filament bulb has three contacts and three wires connected to it. Bulb sockets are spring loaded to provide good electrical contact with bulb contacts. A typical side marker and cornering light circuit is illustrated in Figure 25-7.

Directional Signal Lights (Figure 25-7 and 25-8)

When the ignition switch is in the *on* position, and the signal light switch mounted on the steering column is operated, the front and rear signal lights on the same side flash *on* and *off* to indicate the intention to turn. If so equipped, the side marker lamps will also flash *on* and *off* and the cornering light on the same side will be in the *on* mode. When the signal light switch is moved to the opposite position, the lights on the opposite side of the vehicle will operate similarly. A signal indicator light on the instrument panel also flashes.

The turn signal switch is mounted in a housing at the upper end of the steering column below the steering wheel. A turn signal actuating plate is mounted to a pivot and contacts the turn signal switch. This switch is integral with a wire harness and a multiple connector.

A cancelling cam assembly fits over the steering shaft and the cam turns with the steering wheel.

When the signal lever is in either turn position, a projection on the cancelling cam contacts a spring on the actuating plate once per revolution of the steering wheel. Rotation of the steering wheel and cam in one direction does not move the actuating plate; rotation in the other direction causes the actuating plate to be pushed back to neutral position, thereby providing automatic cancelling after a turn.

Hazard Warning Lights

The hazard warning system, when turned on, causes all turn signal lights to flash simultaneously. This system makes use of the regular turn signal wiring and light bulbs but has a separate supply wire, flasher unit, and off-on switch. This makes it possible to operate the system even though the ignition switch and doors are locked. The system is activated by pushing in on the switch knob usually located just below the steering wheel on the right side of the steering column. The hazard flasher system should be turned off before the car is driven.

Flasher Operation

A simple light duty flasher consists of a bimetal strip with a heating coil and a contact point plus a stationary contact point. The contact points are normally in a closed position. When the turn signal switch is turned on, electricity heats up the bimetal strip by means of the heating coil. The heated bimetal strip bends, opening the contact points which interrupts current to the signal lights. The lack of current allows the bimetal strip to cool and straighten, which closes the contact points to com-

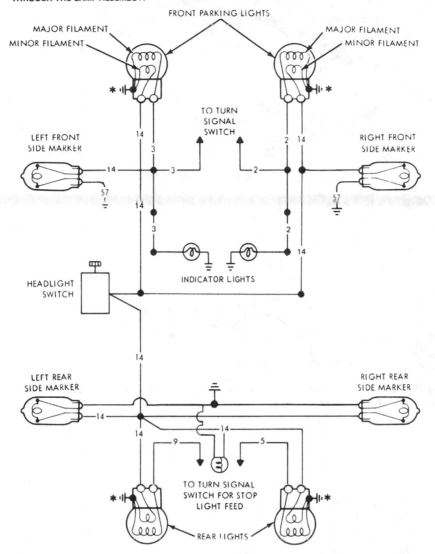

FIGURE 25-7. Turn signal light system wiring diagram. *(Courtesy of Ford Motor Co. of Canada Ltd.)*

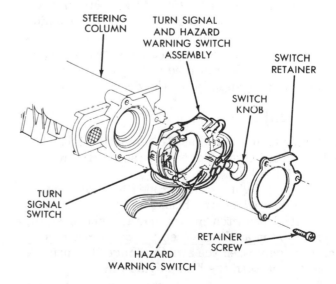

FIGURE 25-8. Typical turn signal switch and wiring harness mounted in steering column. *(Courtesy of Chrysler Corporation)*

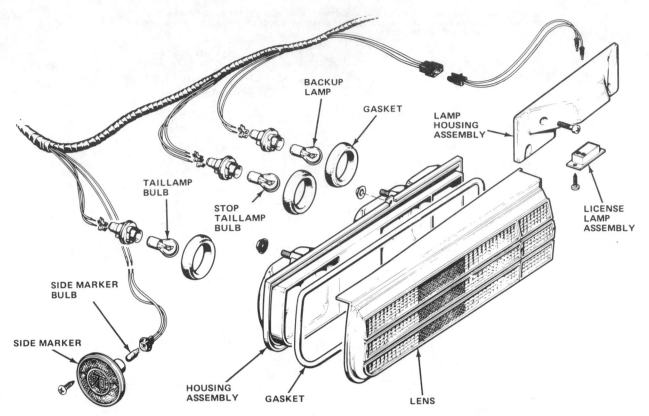

FIGURE 25-9. Rear lamp and side marker lamp mounting detail (typical). *(Courtesy of American Motors Corporation)*

plete the circuit to the signal lights. This sequence is rapidly repeated causing the lights to flash.

A heavy duty flasher normally uses an electromagnet to operate one or more sets of contacts to cause front and side signal lights to flash alternately in some cases. The normally open contact points are closed by the action of the electromagnet. Closing the contacts energizes a second winding which is reverse wound, causing the electromagnet to operate in reverse and open the points once again. The cycle is rapidly repeated as long as the primary current is being supplied to the flasher.

Stop Lights

Each rear lamp is used as a combination tail, stop, and direction signal light. The tail lights are controlled by the light switch.

The stop lights are controlled by a mechanical switch mounted on the brake pedal bracket. This spring loaded switch makes contact whenever the brake pedal is applied. When the brake pedal is released, it depresses the switch plunger to open the contacts and turn the brake lights off.

The direction signal switch is in the circuit, so the stop lights may be flashing or constant, depending on the position of the switch.

Brake Warning Light

The brake warning light will light with the ignition in the *on* position, when the parking brake is depressed or when there is a difference in pressure between the two hydraulic brake circuits. The light will also light, serving as a bulb check, when the key is turned to the *start* position.

Back-Up Lights

Most cars are equipped with two single-filament lamp back-up light assemblies. The lights are actuated when the ignition switch is in the *on* position and only when the transmission selector lever is positioned in reverse. A back-up light switch is actuated either by shift linkage on the steering column or by the shift mechanism in the transmission, depending on design.

PROBLEM	CAUSE	CORRECTION
Headlamps All exterior lamps do not light.	1. Loose wiring connections. 2. Open wiring. Bad ground. 3. Damaged headlamp switch.	1. Check and secure connection at headlamps switch and dash panel connector. 2. Check power to and from headlamp switch. Check ground at bulbs. Service as necessary. 3. Replace headlamp switch.
One headlamp does not work.	1. Loose connection. Bad ground. 2. Bulb burnt out. 3. Corroded or damaged connector.	1. Secure connection at headlamp Check ground at headlamp. 2. Replace sealed beam. 3. Replace as required.
Both low-beam or both high-beam head-lamps do not work.	1. Loose connections. 2. Damaged dimmer switch. 3. Open wiring.	1. Check and secure connections at dimmer switch and headlamp switch. 2. Check dimmer switch operation. Replace if necessary. 3. Service as necessary.
All headlamps out. Park and tail lamps O.K.	1. Loose connections. 2. Damaged dimmer switch. 3. Damaged headlamp switch. 4. Open wiring or poor ground.	1. Check and secure connections at dimmer switch and headlamp switch. 2. Check dimmer switch operation. Replace if necessary. 3. Replace if necessary. 4. Service as necessary.
Tail lamps One tail lamp out.	1. Bulb burnt out. 2. Open wiring or poor ground. 3. Corroded bulb socket. 4. Blown fuse in fuse panel.	1. Replace bulb. 2. Service as necessary. 3. Service or replace socket. 4. Service as necessary.
All tail lamps, park lamps, and instrument lamps O.K., but lamps do not function.	1. Loose connections. 2. Open wiring or poor ground. 3. Damaged headlamp switch.	1. Secure wiring connections where accessible. 2. Service as necessary. 3. Service headlamps switch.
Back-up-lamps One light does not function.	1. Check fuse in panel. 2. Bulb burnt out. 3. Loose connection. 4. Open wiring.	1. Replace fuse. 2. Replace bulb. 3. Tighten connectors. 4. Service as necessary. 5. Check a circuit that shares the same fuse. Replace fuse.
Both lamps do not function	1. Fuse burnt out 2. Back-up lamp switch out of adjustment. 3. Damaged back-up lamp switch. 4. Loose connections. 5. Open wiring or poor ground.	1. Adjust switch. 2. Replace switch. 3. Tighten connectors. 4. Service as required.
Parking lamps One parking lamp does not light.	1. Loose connections. 2. Bulb burnt out. 3. Open wiring or poor ground.	1. Tighten connections. 2. Replace bulb. 3. Check for corroded socket. Service as required.
Both parking lamps do not light.	1. Loose connections. 2. Open wiring or poor ground. 3. Bulbs burnt out.	1. Tighten connections. 2. Check for corroded socket. Service as required. 3. Replace bulbs.
Front side marker lamps Front side marker lamp does not light — park and tail lamps OK	1. Loose connections. 2. Bulb burnt out. 3. Open wiring or poor ground.	1. Tighten connections. 2. Replace bulb. 3. Check socket for corrosion and good ground. Service as required.
Cornering lamps	1. Cornering lamp relay. 2. Bulb burnt out. 3. Loose connections. 4. Open wiring or poor ground.	1. Replace relay. 2. Replace bulb. 3. Tighten connectors. 4. Service as necessary.
One lamp will not operate. Turn signals OK	1. Inoperative relay and/or poor ground.	1. Service bad ground or replace damaged relay as required.

541

PROBLEM	CAUSE	CORRECTION
Both lamps will not operate. Turn signals OK	1. Fuse burnt out.	1. Replace fuse. If fuse blows again, check for short circuit.
	2. Loose connections.	2. Tighten connections.
	3. Poor relay grounds.	3. Service ground.
	4. Open wiring.	4. Service as required.
Stop lamps Stop lamps do not light.	1. Fuse burned out.	1. Replace fuse or CB If device blows again, check for short circuit.
	2. Problem in turn signal circuit or switch.	2. Service turn signal circuit or replace turn signal.
	3. Loose connections.	3. Secure connections at stop lamp switch.
	4. Stop lamp switch inoperative.	4. Replace stop lamp switch.
	5. Open wiring.	5. Service as required.
Turn signal lamps One or more inoperative	1. Bulb burned out.	1. Replace bulb.
	2. Loose connections.	2. Secure connections.
	3. Open wiring or poor ground.	3. Service as required.
	4. Turn signal switch inoperative.	4. Replace turn signal switch.
All lamps inoperative	1. Fuse burned out.	1. Replace fuse or CB If device blows again, check for short circuit.
	2. Turn signal flasher.	2. Substitute a known good flasher.
	3. Loose connections.	3. Tighten connections.
	4. Open wiring or poor ground.	4. Service as required.
	5. Turn signal switch inoperative.	5. Replace turn signal switch.
Hazard flasher lamps Lamps do not flash	1. Turn signal operation improper.	1. Service turn signal system.
	2. Fuse burned out.	2. Replace fuse. If fuse blows again, check for a short circuit.
	3. Hazard flasher inoperative.	3. Substitute a known good flasher.
	4. Open wiring.	4. Service as required.
	5. Hazard flasher switch inoperative.	5. Service or replace the turn signal switch assembly which includes the hazard flasher switch.

PART 2   INSTRUMENTS

Instrument panel gauges, lights, and meters are provided to monitor the operation of most of the systems on the automobile. Gauges or indicator lights monitor such items as fuel level, engine coolant temperatures, engine oil pressure, and intake manifold vacuum. Indicator lights are used to warn of low fluid levels, brake failure, and light failure. The advantage of indicator lights is that they are more readily noticed than gauge readings. Vehicle speed is indicated by a gauge or by a digital display. Power for all instrument is supplied through the ignition switch.

Bimetal or Thermal Gauges

The bimetal gauge operates on the principle of the difference in expansion of two dissimilar metals in a flat bar with a heating coil wound around it. The heating coil is connected electrically, through a variable resistance sending unit, to ground. As a change in heat or pressure changes the resistance value of the sending unit, a varying level of current is applied to the heating coil around the bimetal strip in the gauge. The free end of the bimetal strip is linked

to a gauge pointer. As the bimetal strip bends with the increased or decreased heat, the indicator moves up scale or down. This type of gauge is often used with a bimetallic constant voltage regulator which maintains gauge voltage at approximately 5 volts. Full battery voltage should never be applied to gauges using the voltage regulator.

Balanced Coil or Magnetic Gauges

The balanced coil or magnetic gauge operates on the principle of magnetism. Two magnetic coils, with a pivoting-needle-type indicator mounted between the coils, are the major parts of this gauge. One coil winding is calibrated to provide a fixed resistance and, therefore, a fixed magnetic force acting on the needle. The other coil is connected in series with a variable resistance to ground. The variable resistance causes the magnetic strength of the other coil to vary with the resistance of the sending unit. The difference in magnetic strength between the two coils determines the position of the needle on the gauge.

Indicator Lights

Indicator lights are connected in series, through a switch or variable-resistance-type sending unit or sensor, to ground. When the switch or resistance

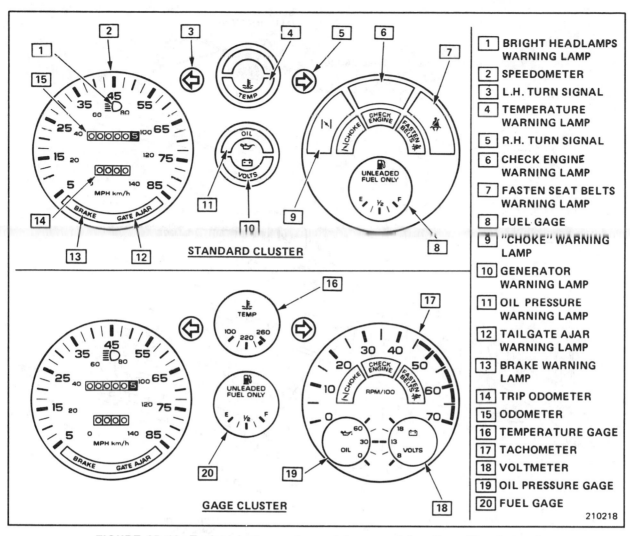

FIGURE 25-10. Typical instrument panel types and function. *(Courtesy of General Motors Corporation)*

value in the sending unit allows the circuit to be completed to ground, the indicator light goes on. Coolant temperature, low charge rate, low fuel level, low oil pressure, and the like use indicator lamp systems on many vehicles.

Ammeter

The ammeter is used to indicate current to, or out of, the battery. When more current is being used than the charging system is able to provide, the extra current is provided by the battery, and the ammeter needle will read on the minus (−) side. Whenever the battery is not fully charged and the charging system produces more current than is required for vehicle operation, the battery is being charged and the ammeter will read on the plus (+) side. If the battery is fully charged and the charging system is able to provide current to charge the bat-

tery, the voltage regulator reduces charging system output, and the ammeter indicator points to zero or mid-scale (no charge and no discharge).

A conventional ammeter must be connected in series between the battery and alternator to indicate the rate of current into and out of the battery. Since the ammeter must be mounted in the instrument panel, this would require heavy wiring to and from the ammeter. To avoid this problem, a specially calibrated voltmeter is used instead to indicate charge and discharge. Since the voltmeter is connected in parallel, it can be used to indicate the voltage drop across a special resistance wire connected between the battery and alternator. When voltage is higher at the alternator end, the ammeter pointer indicates charge (+). When voltage is higher at the battery end of the resistance wire, the ammeter indicates discharge (−). With equal voltage at both ends of the wire, the ammeter reads zero.

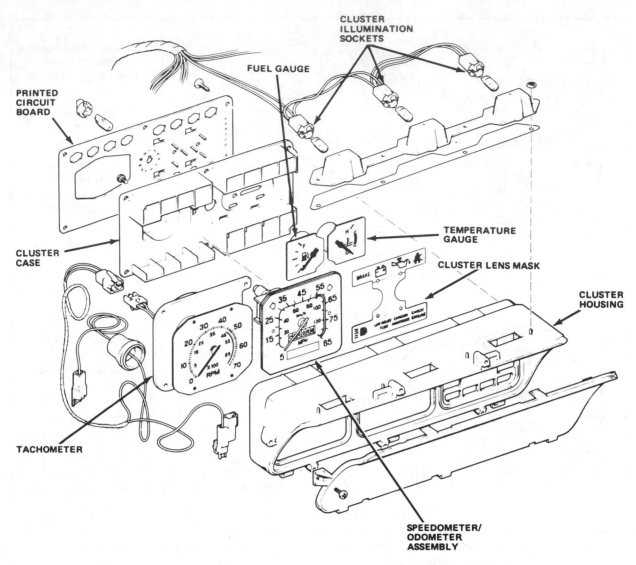

FIGURE 25-11. Typical instrument cluster mounting detail. *(Courtesy of American Motors Corporation)*

Speedometer and Odometer

The speedometer incorporates both a speed indicating mechanism and an odometer to record total mileage. A flexible cable, which enters the speedometer driven gear in the front drive wheel, or the transmission on one end and the speedometer head at the other, rotates both mechanisms whenever the transmission main shaft, propeller shaft, and wheels rotate. For cruise-control-equipped cars, there are two cables: one from the transmission to the cruise control regulator, and the other from the regulator to the speedometer head.

The odometer is driven by a series of gears from a worm gear cut on the magnet shaft. The odometer discs are so geared that, as any one disc finishes a complete revolution, the next disc to left is turned one-tenth of a revolution.

The speedometer head has a needle indicator mounted on a small shaft with a coiled hair spring connected to the needle to hold it at zero when the car is stopped. A small drum, also attached to the indicator needle shaft, reacts to a magnet rotating inside the drum when driven by the speedometer cable. The faster the magnet spins, the farther the drum moves in response to the magnetism produced and against spring tension. Speedometers are calibrated to accurately indicate road speed when matched with proper wheel and tire size, as well as speedometer drive gear size. Federal, state, and local laws require speedometer accuracy standards to be met.

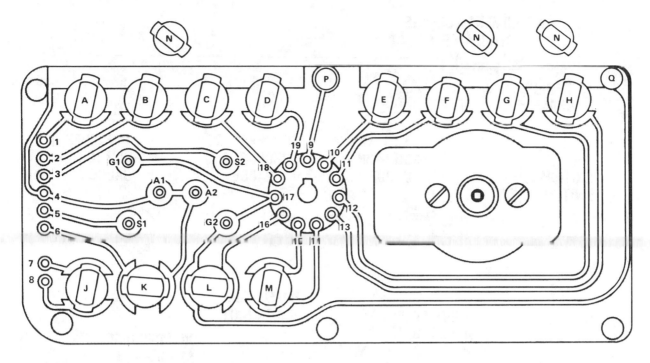

PIN TERMINALS

1. FASTEN BELTS
2. OIL PRESSURE WARNING
3. FUEL GAUGE
4. CLUSTER IGNITION FEED
5. TEMPERATURE GAUGE
*6. EMISSION MAINTENANCE
7. NOT USED
8. NOT USED
9. CLOCK
10. RIGHT TURN
11. NOT USED
12. NOT USED
13. LEFT TURN
14. HIGH BEAM
15. HIGH BEAM GROUND
16. LOW WASHER FLUID
17. GROUND
18. ALTERNATOR WARNING
19. BRAKE

LAMPS

A FASTEN BELT
B OIL PRESSURE WARNING
C ALTERNATOR WARNING
D BRAKE
E RIGHT TURN
F NOT USED
G NOT USED
H LEFT TURN
J NOT USED
*K EMISSION MAINTENANCE
L LOW WASHER FLUID
M HIGH BEAM
N ILLUMINATION

OTHER

S1 TEMPERATURE GAUGE SENDER TERMINAL
A1 TEMPERATURE GAUGE IGNITION FEED TEMINAL
G1 TEMPERATURE GAUGE GROUND TERMINAL
S2 FUEL GAUGE SENDER TERMINAL
A2 FUEL GAUGE IGNITION FEED TERMINAL
G2 FUEL GAUGE GROUND TERMINAL
P CLOCK FEED
Q CLOCK GROUND

* EMISSION MAINTENANCE USED ONLY ON CERTAIN FOUR-CYLINDER ENGINE MODELS

FIGURE 25–12. Rear view of printed circuit board instrument panel with electrical components identified. *(Courtesy of American Motors Corporation)*

Federal law requires that the odometer, in any replacement speedometer, must register the same mileage as that registered in the removed speedometer.

Most speedometer problems—noise and erratic operation—result from lack of lubrication or from cable and housing distortion. Sharp bends or kinks in housing or cable usually require cable and housing replacement. If a cable is broken, the cause (usually a damaged, kinked, or misrouted housing) should be determined and corrected. Both cable and housing should be replaced. Only the recommended lubricant (such as white lube) should be used on speedometer cables.

Electronic Instrument System

The major difference between the electronic instrument panel and the conventional instrument panel is the manner in which information is displayed. The same types of sending units or sensors are used in both systems. The speedometer cable is also the same except that, instead of turning a magnet, the cable turns an optical sensor.

Instrument displays consist of a system of light bars, graphs, or digital gauges. The instrument panel portion of the system normally operates trouble free. Problems with sending units and wiring connections are usually the cause of malfunctions.

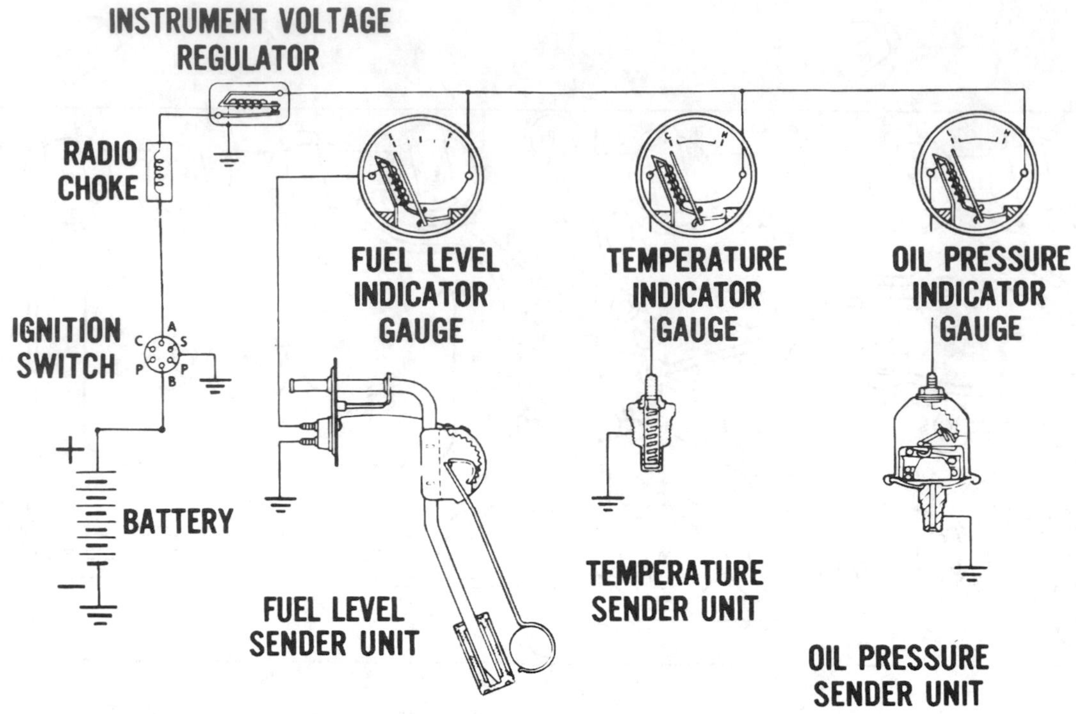

INSTRUMENT VOLTAGE REGULATOR

RADIO CHOKE

IGNITION SWITCH

C A S
P B P

BATTERY

FUEL LEVEL INDICATOR GAUGE

TEMPERATURE INDICATOR GAUGE

OIL PRESSURE INDICATOR GAUGE

FUEL LEVEL SENDER UNIT

TEMPERATURE SENDER UNIT

OIL PRESSURE SENDER UNIT

FIGURE 25-13. Typical bimetal-type gauge system. *(Courtesy of Ford Motor Co. of Canada Ltd.)*

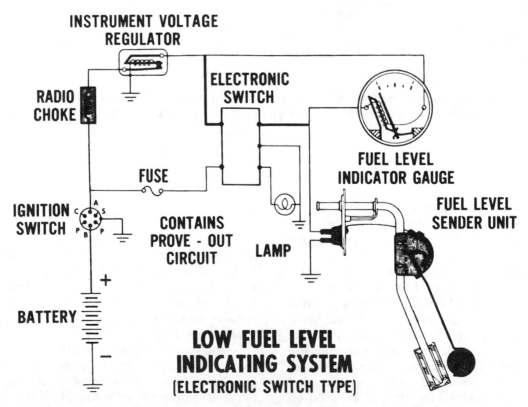

INSTRUMENT VOLTAGE REGULATOR

RADIO CHOKE

ELECTRONIC SWITCH

FUEL LEVEL INDICATOR GAUGE

FUSE

IGNITION SWITCH

C A S
P B P

CONTAINS PROVE - OUT CIRCUIT

LAMP

FUEL LEVEL SENDER UNIT

BATTERY

LOW FUEL LEVEL INDICATING SYSTEM
(ELECTRONIC SWITCH TYPE)

FIGURE 25-14. Low fuel level indicating system (electronic switch type). *(Courtesy of Ford Motor Co. of Canada Ltd.)*

546

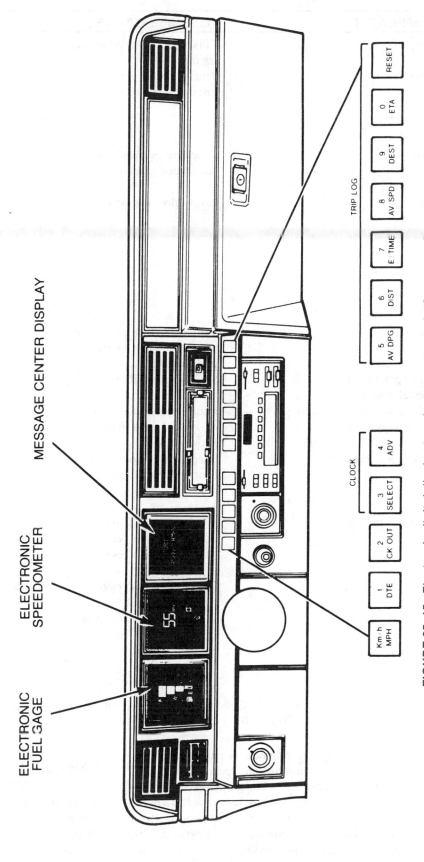

FIGURE 25-15. Electronic digital-display type instrument panel. (*Courtesy of Ford Motor Co. of Canada Ltd.*)

MESSAGE CENTER DISPLAY

ELECTRONIC SPEEDOMETER

ELECTRONIC FUEL GAGE

COMPLAINT	POSSIBLE CAUSE	PROCEDURE
Noisy	Kinked, pinched or burned casings.	Replace both the cable and casing. Recheck for noise.
Noisy	Bent or improper length cable tips.	Replace both the cable and casing. Recheck for noise. If cable is too long, carefully clip a short length, then check for noise.
Noisy	Improper or insufficient lubrication of cable.	Lubricate cable with P/N 6478535 lubricant or equivalent. Pack ferrule with lubricant.
Noisy	Faulty driven gear or rough drive gear.	Remove driven gear assembly from transmission. Check for free rotation of gear in sleeve. Check for burrs, flash or unusual worn spots. If gears appear faulty, replace and recheck for noise.
Whine	Oversize driven gear stem in transmission binds with adapter.	Replace driven gear and stem.
Buzzing sound with manual transmission.	Shift linkage vibration.	Adjust transmission shift linkage.
Ticking or ringing sound with jumpy pointer between 0 and 30 MPH.	Faulty speedometer head, or kinked cable (see above).	Remove speedometer head for repair.
Sticky speedometer pointer.	Speedometer pointer is bent and rubs.	Remove speedometer cluster or lens and straighten pointer. Recheck speedometer operation.
Incorrect calibration.	Wrong transmission adapter, driven gear, drive gear, or sleeve.	Check speedometer gear reference for correct application and replace if necessary.
Incorrect calibration.	Oversize or undersize tires.	Check calibration using correct tire size.
Incorrect calibration.	Faulty speedometer head (if odometer is correct).	Remove speedometer for repair.
Incorrect calibration.	Wrong axle ratio.	Check for proper axle ratio and repair as necessary.

FIGURE 25-16. Speedometer trouble diagnosis chart. *(Courtesy of General Motors Corporation)*

A great variety of convenience features are provided with electronic instrument panels. Some of these features include fuel consumption rate indicators, distance vehicle is able to travel with remaining fuel indicators, monitors of various fluid levels in the vehicle, light out warning systems, and many others depending on design.

Replacement of any gauges or instruments normally requires removal of the entire instrument cluster or panel before access to individual gauges is possible.

PART 3   ACCESSORIES

Many automobile accessories are power operated to reduce the effort required to operate the device. Power is supplied by the vehicle electrical system through an operating switch to one or more electric motors. Some of the more common of these power accessories will be discussed here. Most of them rely on the operation of the permanent magnet type of electric motor.

Permanent Magnet Motors

Many of the small motors used in automotive applications use permanent magnets, rather than electromagnets, to provide the stationary magnetic field. Since the field strength is constant, like that of the shunt-type motor, permanent magnet motors have similar operating characteristics. These motors, because of their constant-speed operation, are used for such applications as windshield wipers, blower motors, window regulators, and seat positioners. Motor operation is very similar to starting motor operation description in Chapter 21.

The major differences are:

• permanent magnet fields are used
• motors carry much less current than starters since they carry much lighter loads
• motors are much smaller than starter motors.

Under normal operating conditions, motors are generally designed to last the life of the vehicle. Problems are usually the result of poor connections, poor ground, faulty switches or wiring, and the like. Faulty motors are normally replaced, not repaired.

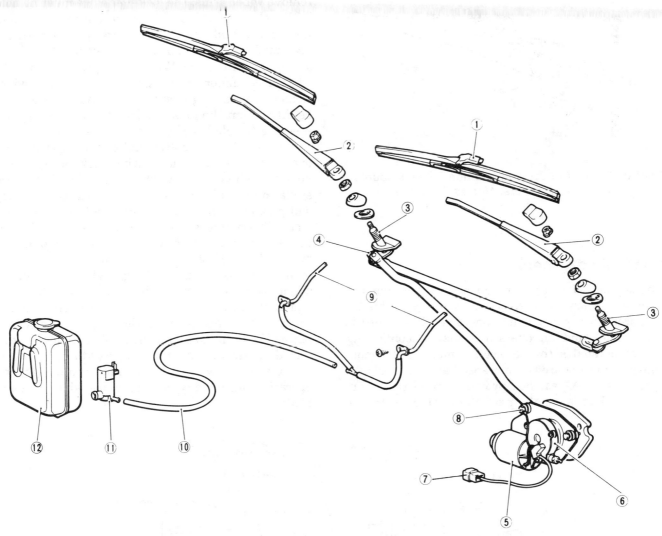

(1) Wiper blade
(2) Wiper arm
(3) Pivot shaft
(4) Wiper linkage
(5) Wiper motor
(6) Motor gear box
(7) Motor wire connector
(8) Wiper motor assembly grounding point
(9) Washer nozzle
(10) Washer tube
(11) Washer motor assembly
(12) Washer liquid tank

FIGURE 25-17. Windshield wiper and washer components. *(Courtesy of Chrysler Corporation)*

MULTI-FUNCTION LEVER

A. PUSH LEVER UP FOR RIGHT TURN.
B. PUSH LEVER DOWN FOR LEFT TURN.
C. PULL LEVER TOWARD DRIVER TO SELECT
   HEADLIGHT BEAMS.
D. PUSH SWITCH TO "ON" TO ENGAGE CRUISE SYSTEM.*
E. PUSH CRUISE "SET" BUTTON IN AT DESIRED SPEED.*
F. TURN BAND TO CONTROL STANDARD OR "PULSE"*
   WINDSHIELD WIPERS.
G. PUSH PADDLE TO SPRAY WASHER FLUID AND
   ACTIVATE LOW-SPEED WIPERS.

*OPTIONAL EQUIPMENT

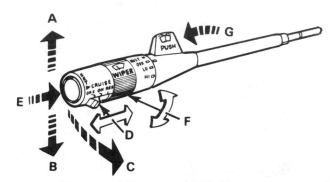

FIGURE 25–18. Typical multifunction column-mounted switch. *(Courtesy of General Motors Corporation)*

Windshield Wipers

The typical wiper system consists of a permanent magnet rotary motor, wiper arms and blades mounted on a pivot shaft—one at each side of the windshield—and an operating linkage connecting the pivot shafts to the electric motor. The most common motors are the two-speed and the variable-speed types. A gear box provides speed reduction. The gear box is usually part of, or attached to, the

motor housing. A two-speed or variable-speed switch provides operator control. A windshield-washer switch is also usually incorporated into the wiper switch. Some switches are provided with an intermittent switch function providing wipe-pause-wipe intervals. Frequency of wipe-pause intervals can also be controlled by switch position which operates a rheostat.

Wiper blade arms are usually attached through a snap lock device to splined pivot shafts. Wiper arms must be properly positioned on splined pivot shafts to ensure a proper wiping pattern on the windshield as well as correct parking position. To remove wiper arms, the locking device must be held in the release position while the arm is removed from the shaft. Installation only requires proper positioning—pushing the arm onto the pivot shaft until the lock snaps into place. Wiper arms pivot against the windshield under spring pressure to ensure wiper element pressure against the glass. Wiper blades can be lifted from the glass surface against this spring pressure for blade or element replacement.

Wiper blades are attached to the wiper arm by one of several different spring lock designs. Removal requires releasing the spring lock device. Installation usually requires only engaging the blade and pushing it into place until the lock snaps into place. The rubber wiping element has a metal backing strip and is held in place in the wiper blade by means of metal hooks and a locking device. Removal requires release of the locking device which allows sliding the wiper element from the wiper blade. Installation requires only sliding the element between the retaining hooks until the element locks into place. Wiper blades and arms should not be distorted in any way during this procedure.

Rear window wipers are similar in design and operation but usually have only one wiper arm and blade.

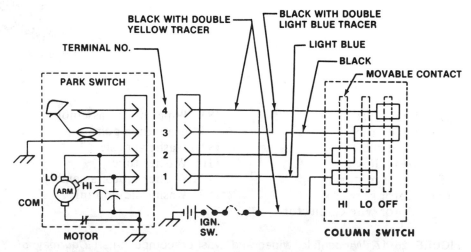

FIGURE 25–19. Typical two-speed wiper wiring diagram.

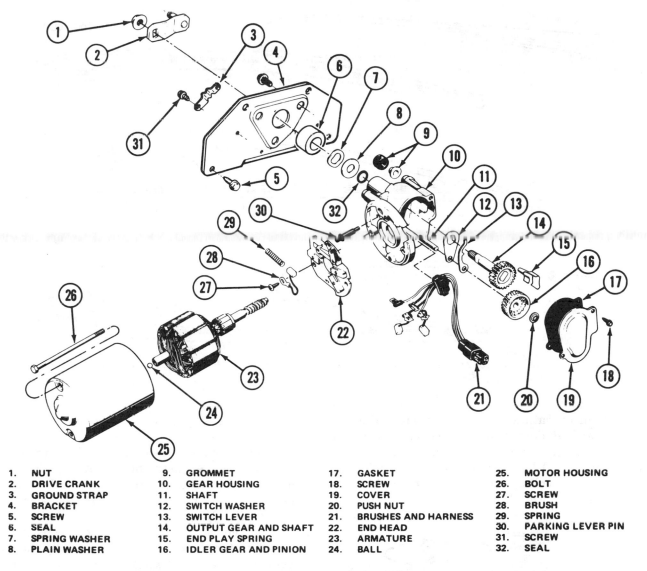

1.	NUT	9.	GROMMET	17.	GASKET	25.	MOTOR HOUSING
2.	DRIVE CRANK	10.	GEAR HOUSING	18.	SCREW	26.	BOLT
3.	GROUND STRAP	11.	SHAFT	19.	COVER	27.	SCREW
4.	BRACKET	12.	SWITCH WASHER	20.	PUSH NUT	28.	BRUSH
5.	SCREW	13.	SWITCH LEVER	21.	BRUSHES AND HARNESS	29.	SPRING
6.	SEAL	14.	OUTPUT GEAR AND SHAFT	22.	END HEAD	30.	PARKING LEVER PIN
7.	SPRING WASHER	15.	END PLAY SPRING	23.	ARMATURE	31.	SCREW
8.	PLAIN WASHER	16.	IDLER GEAR AND PINION	24.	BALL	32.	SEAL

FIGURE 25–20. Wiper motor components. *(Courtesy of American Motors Corporation)*

Windshield Washer

This system consists of a fluid reservoir, fluid hoses and nozzles, an electric-motor-driven pump, and a control switch. Washer systems are used on both front and rear windows. Each system operates independently from the other.

When the switch is turned on, the electric pump forces fluid through the hoses and nozzles onto the window glass. Nozzles are aimed to provide precise spray patterns for maximum effectiveness. Nozzles are usually adjustable to allow aiming. System operation relies on the use of clean fluid to prevent clogging of nozzles. Special washer fluid with non-smear detergent should be used rather than water. In freezing weather, windshield washer anti-freeze must be used to prevent freeze up of the system.

Faulty components must be replaced including the motor and pump assembly. Problems usually result from incorrectly aimed nozzles, use of incorrect fluid, clogged nozzles, poor electrical connections, and the like.

Power Windows

Power windows are controlled by a single switch at each of the windows as well as a master set of switches at the driver's position. The master set allows the driver to operate all windows from one position.

The switches control a reversible electric motor at each window. The electric motor drives the window regulator mechanism forward or reverse, providing up-and-down window movement.

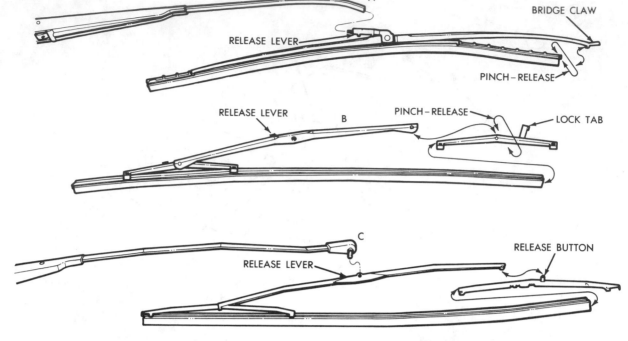

FIGURE 25-21. Various wiper blade attachment designs. *(Courtesy of Chrysler Corporation)*

System operation relies on properly adjusted windows and window channels to ensure freedom of movement in the channels without excessive friction or binding. Electric motor operation relies on proper system voltage ensured by good electrical connections and switch operation.

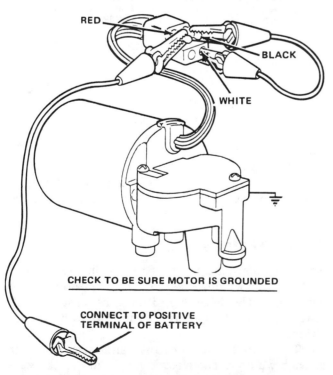

FIGURE 25-22. Testing wiper motor operation. *(Courtesy of American Motors Corporation)*

Power Seats

Both four-way and six-way power seats are used on many vehicles. Adjustment is provided in up to six different directions: up, down, forward, back, tilt forward, and tilt rearward. Four-way systems do not provide tilt adjustments.

The typical six-way power seat consists of a three-armature reversible motor (actually three motors in one), a control switch assembly, rack and pinion assemblies located in the seat tracks, and cables connecting the pinions to the motor assembly.

The horizontal drive consists of a rack and pinion on each track. The pinion housing and motor is attached to the movable section of the track. When the switch is actuated, the front armature is energized, and the horizontal drive units are activated. The seat is then moved forward or rearward by the pinion gears traveling in a rack in each lower track section.

In the vertical drive, worm gear planetary reducers and sector gear mechanisms are utilized. The drive units are located in the front and rear of the transmission case. When the switch is actuated, the center and rear armatures are simultaneously energized and the vertical drive units are activated. The seat is then moved up or down by the sector gears.

When the front tilt switch is actuated, the center armature drives the front vertical worm gear and moves the seat to the desired position. When the rear tilt switch is actuated, the rear armature drives

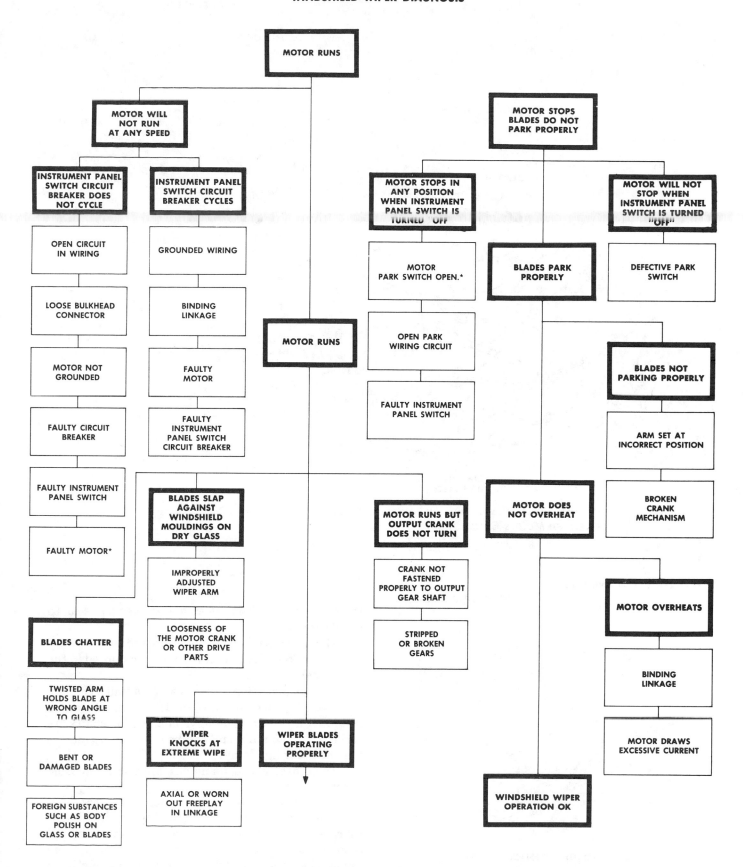

FIGURE 25-23. *(Courtesy of Chrysler Corporation)*

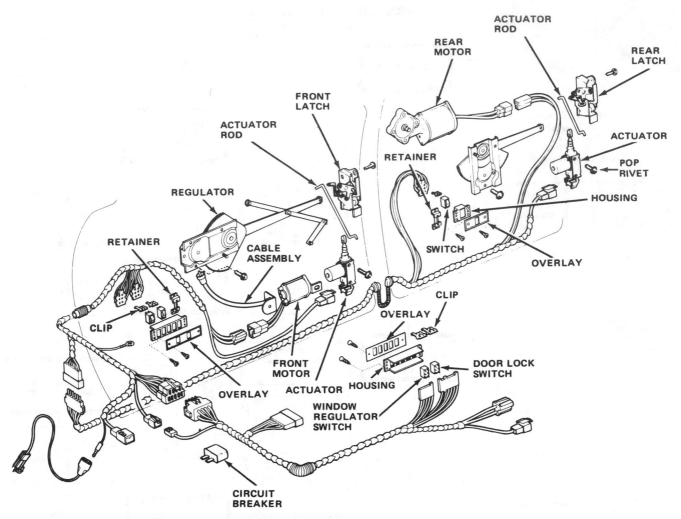

FIGURE 25-24. Power window components and wiring harness. *(Courtesy of American Motors Corporation)*

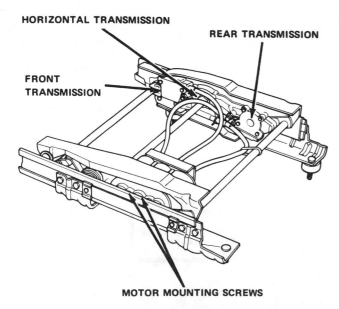

FIGURE 25-25. Power seat mechanism. *(Courtesy of American Motors Corporation)*

the rear vertical worm gear and moves the seat to the desired position.

The power seat circuit is protected by a 30-amp circuit breaker. The circuit breaker is mounted in the fuse panel.

The transmission is serviced as a unit. The motor assembly, which contains three armatures, is serviced only as an assembly. The flexible shafts are serviced individually and can be removed by removing the securing clamps.

The switch and housing assembly is serviceable separately.

System operation is dependent on the free movement of the seat through the full travel distances—up, down, forward, and back—without excessive friction or interference from articles placed under the seat. Electrical operation is relatively trouble free and is dependent on good electrical connections and proper switch function.

Power Door Locks

A switch-operated, two-position electric solenoid actuator is typically used in each door to electrically operate the door-locking mechanism. Usually, each door can be locked and unlocked individually, with either front door switch operating all four door locks. This allows the driver or the passenger to lock or unlock all four doors with one switch. If the electric locking mechanism fails, the manual system still works normally.

Other powered accessories include electric trunk or deck lid release, power radio antenna, electric fuel door or cap lock, power outside mirrors, clocks, and the like.

Speed Control

A speed control system provides the means to maintain a desired driving speed without maintaining throttle position by foot pressure on the accelerator pedal. Some variation in selected speed is normal when driving uphill or downhill. Most systems provide a "resume speed" function which causes the vehicle to resume the preselected speed on the driver's demand after the system has been disengaged. The system is disengaged by depressing the brake or clutch pedal. Speed is resumed when the resume speed switch is activated.

The system typically uses engine vacuum to operate a servo which controls throttle position. The servo receives a controlled amount of vacuum from a transducer to regulate throttle position.

A speedometer cable from the transmission drives the transducer, and a second speedometer cable from the transducer drives the speedometer. The cruise control transducer contains a low speed limit switch that prevents system engagement below a minimum speed—ranging between 25 and 40 mph (40 and 64 km/h) depending on the transducer used. The operation of the transducer unit is controlled by an engagement switch button located in the end of the directional signal lever and the off/on resume slide switch. To disengage the system, two release switches are provided. An electrical release switch mounted on the brake pedal bracket (clutch pedal bracket on cars equipped with manual transaxle) disengages the system electrically when the brake pedal (or clutch pedal) is depressed. A vacuum re-

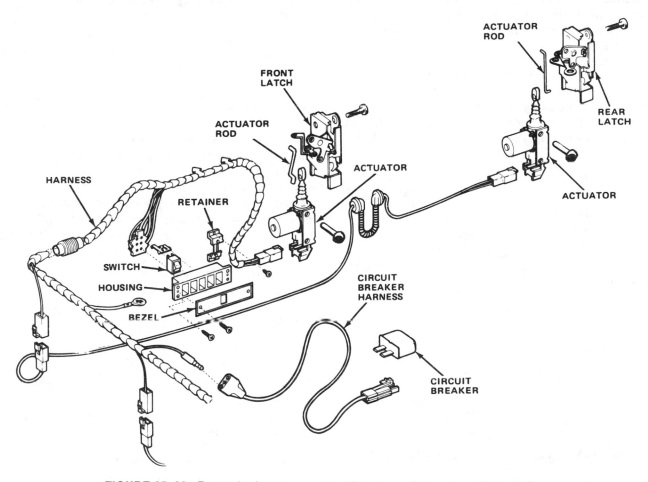

FIGURE 25-26. Power lock components. *(Courtesy of American Motors Corporation)*

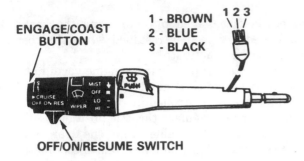

FIGURE 25-27. Speed control switch steering column mounted. *(Courtesy of General Motors Corporation)*

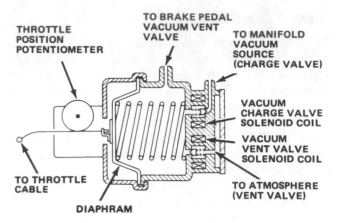

FIGURE 25-29. Details of speed control servo assembly. *(Courtesy of American Motors Corporation)*

lease valve, mounted on the brake pedal bracket, vents controlled vacuum to the atmosphere when the brake pedal is depressed, allowing the servo unit to quickly return the throttle to idle position.

Good vacuum and electrical connections, as well as proper servo-cable-to-throttle adjustment, are required for proper system operation.

The system is typically operated as follows.

(Warning: The use of "speed control" is not recommended when driving conditions do not permit maintaining a constant speed, such as heavy traffic or on roads that are winding, icy, snow covered, or slippery.)

1. *To Engage:* Move slide switch to the *on* position; attain desired speed, and then, momentarily depress and release *speed set* button, establishing speed memory and engaging system. Remove foot from accelerator. Speed will be maintained at this

level. Moving the slide switch from *off* to *on* while the vehicle is in motion establishes memory without system engagement at that speed.

2. *To Disengage:* Normal brake application, or a soft tap on the brake pedal, will disengage control unit without erasing speed memory. Moving the slide switch to the *off* position, or turning the ignition *off,* also disengages the system and erases the speed memory.

3. *To Resume:* Momentarily move slide switch to the *resume* position. Vehicle will resume the previously memorized speed.

4. *To Vary Speed Setting:* To increase speed, depress accelerator to desired speed and momentarily depress and release *speed set* button. When speed control unit is engaged, tapping *speed set* button may increase speed setting incrementally.

To decrease speed, tap brake pedal lightly, disengaging system. When desired speed has been obtained, depress and release *speed set* button. Decrease in speed can also be attained by holding set button depressed until desired speed is attained. Releasing the button engages the system at that speed.

5. *To Accelerate for Passing:* Depress accelerator as needed; when passing is completed, release accelerator and vehicle will return to previous speed setting.

Audible Warning Devices

Various types of tone generators, including buzzers, chimes, and voice synthesizers, are used to remind drivers of a number of vehicle conditions. Some of the most common are:

- Warning to fasten seat belts
- Door ajar warning
- Key left in ignition warning

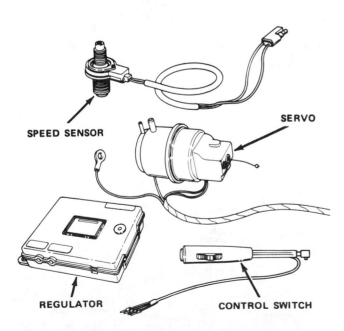

FIGURE 25-28. Typical speed control system components. *(Courtesy of American Motors Corporation)*

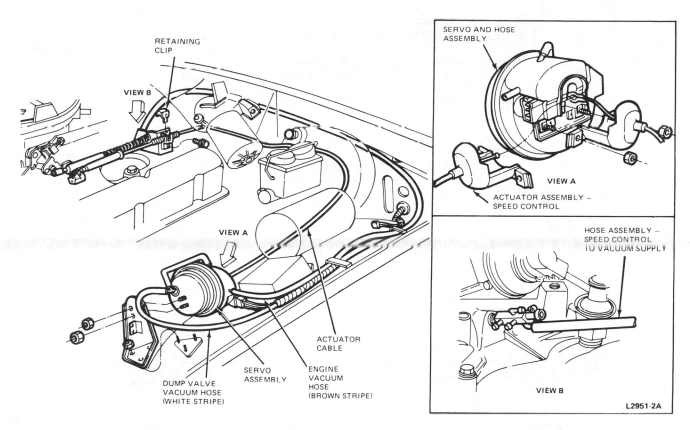

FIGURE 25–30. Typical speed control underhood component arrangement. *(Courtesy of Ford Motor Co. of Canada Ltd.)*

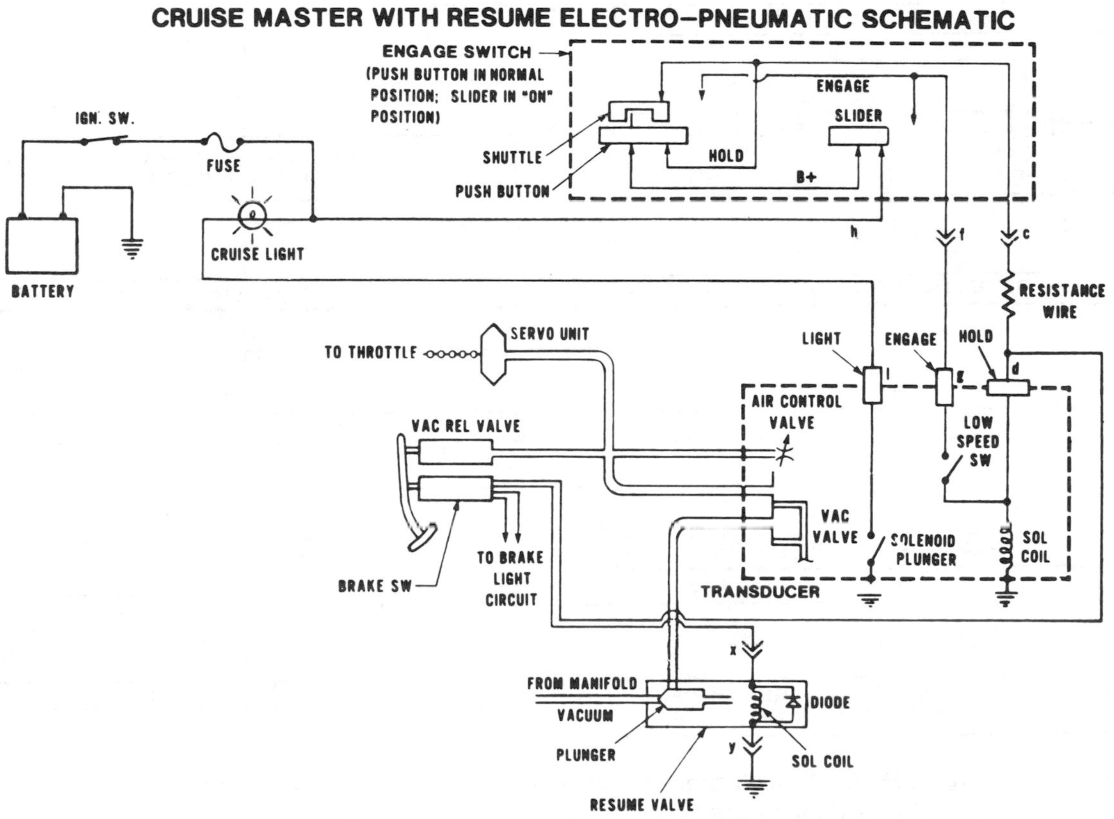

CRUISE MASTER WITH RESUME ELECTRO–PNEUMATIC SCHEMATIC

FIGURE 25–31. Wiring diagram and vacuum line routing for Cruise Master speed control system. *(Courtesy of General Motors Corporation)*

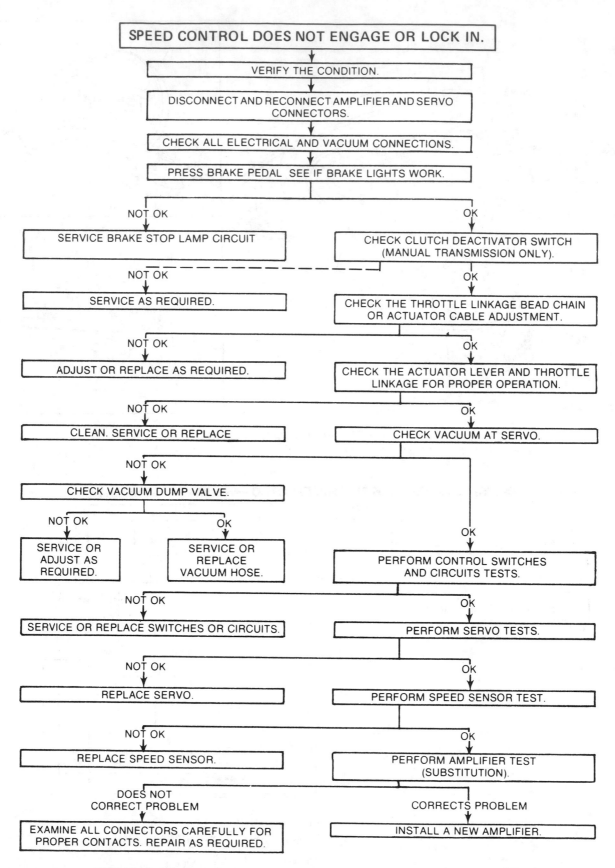

FIGURE 25–32. Typical speed control diagnostic procedure. *(Courtesy of Ford Motor Co. of Canada Ltd.)*

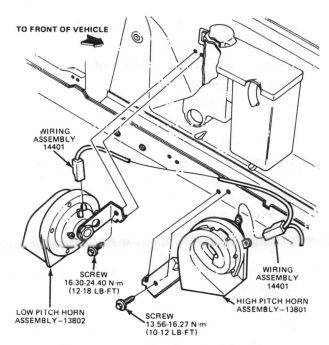

FIGURE 25-33. Typical dual horn mounting. *(Courtesy of Ford Motor Co. of Canada Ltd.)*

- Lights left on warning
- Low fluid level warning

All of these are designed to remind the driver to operate the vehicle in a safe manner.

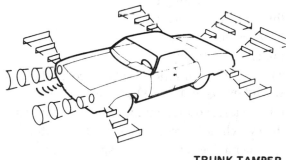

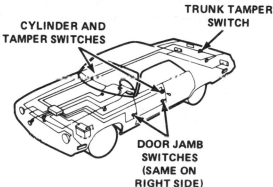

FIGURE 25-34. Theft deterrent system is actuated when tampered with. Lights flash and horns blow to scare off intruder. *(Courtesy of General Motors Corporation)*

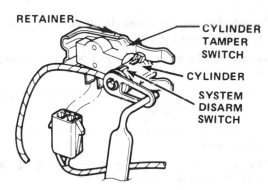

FIGURE 25-35. Details of lock cylinder and switch assembly for theft deterrent system shown in Figure 25-34. *(Courtesy of General Motors Corporation)*

Horns

Automotive horn operation makes use of an electromagnet, a set of points, a vibrator diaphragm, and a spiral sound amplifier or trumpet. Battery current energizes the electromagnet when the horn button or switch is depressed. The electromagnet attracts a metal disc, moving it slightly toward the electromagnet against spring measure. The metal disc is connected to the sound-producing diaphragm. As the disc is attracted to the electromagnet, the points are opened; this de-energizes the magnet and the diaphragm returns to its normal position, closing the points once again. This sequence of events is repeated very rapidly as long as the horn button is being depressed. The vibrating action of the diaphragm produces the sound which is amplified by the spiral trumpet. In most cases, a horn relay is used to reduce the current carried by the horn operating switch. The distance the diaphragm can move is adjustable on most horns and adjustment must be maintained within narrow limits in either direction for good sound, and proper operation in all ambient temperatures.

PART 4   SELF-CHECK

1. What is the purpose of the rheostat in the headlamp switch?
2. How many wire connections are required at the headlamps on a four-headlamp system?
3. How many filaments are there in each headlamp in a two-headlamp system?
4. How is horizontal and vertical headlight adjustment provided?
5. The hazard warning system is inoperative when the ignition switch is off. True or false?

6. Name the two common designs of electrical instrument panel gauges.

7. When an odometer disc turns one revolution, the disc to its left turns how far?

8. Most electric motors used to drive automotive accessories are of the _____ type.

9. How many electric motors are used in a six-way power seat?

10. Name the four major components of a speed control system.

PART 5   TEST QUESTIONS

1. The candlepower of a conventional headlamp is about:
   - (a) 750
   - (b) 7500
   - (c) 75,000
   - (d) 75

2. To aim headlamps, you should:
   - (a) calibrate the aiming equipment first
   - (b) check the vehicle suspension height
   - (c) inflate the tires, if necessary
   - (d) all of the above

3. Vertical headlight aiming adjustment is achieved by:
   - (a) a focusing screw
   - (b) an adjustment screw at the top
   - (c) an adjustment screw at the side
   - (d) none of the above

4. Automatic cancelling of signal lights is provided by:
   - (a) the signal lever
   - (b) the cancelling cam
   - (c) turning in the direction being signalled
   - (d) none of the above

5. A signal light flasher consists of:
   - (a) a set of contacts
   - (b) a heating coil
   - (c) a bimetal strip
   - (d) all of the above

6. Lighting system problems are usually the result of:
   - (a) a blown fuse
   - (b) a loose connection
   - (c) burned out bulbs
   - (d) a poor electrical path

7. A bimetal type of instrument panel gauge operates on the principle of:
   - (a) two magnetic coils
   - (b) magnetic force
   - (c) heat deflecting metal
   - (d) spring pressure against magnetism

8. The indicator needle on a speedometer is held to the zero position by:
   - (a) magnetic force
   - (b) the weight of the needle
   - (c) the speedometer cable
   - (d) a coiled spring

9. Power window systems use:
   - (a) permanent magnet motors
   - (b) reversible motors
   - (c) electric motors
   - (d) all of the above

10. The electropneumatic speed control system uses the following major components:
    - (a) electric motor, switch, solenoid, gear system
    - (b) switch, solenoid, servo, electric motor
    - (c) solenoid, electric motor, speed sensor, switch
    - (d) speed sensor, servo, switch, regulator

DIAGNOSIS AND PERFORMANCE TESTS

Chapter 26

Diagnostic and Performance Testing Procedures

Performance Objectives

After sufficient study of this chapter and adequate practice on the appropriate training models, and with the necessary tools, equipment, and shop manuals, you should be able to do the following:

1. Complete the self-check and test questions with at least 80 percent accuracy.
2. State the purpose of a good tune-up.
3. Follow the generally accepted safety precautions.
4. Properly diagnose engine and engine systems performance according to the diagnostic charts, procedures, and shop manuals provided.
5. Correctly identify and correct any problems in accordance with manufacturer's recommendations and specifications.
6. Retest the system to determine the success of the repairs completed.
7. Prepare the vehicle for customer acceptance.

PART 1   IDENTIFYING THE PROBLEM

Vehicle performance can be divided into several categories to help narrow down the possible problem area. However, it must be understood that many of the systems on the automobile are interrelated. The experienced technician will take advantage of all the skills and tools at his command. He can rely heavily on his past experience and knowledge of automotive systems. The less experienced must rely more heavily on the experience of others through charts and manuals. This is not to say, however, that the experienced technician does not also rely on the experience of others, on diagnostic charts, and on service manuals; he does, though to a lesser extent.

Let us take a look at the categories of vehicle systems diagnosis and at the skills needed to successfully diagnose automotive problems quickly and accurately.

Problems that are perceivable by the owner-operator-customer may be grouped as follows:

1. Engine performance
2. Noise
3. Vehicle control
4. Comfort

Although this chapter deals primarily with engine performance diagnosis and correction, a few words on the other three areas are in order here.

Noise

The noise category can be broken down into two areas—source of noise and type of noise. The noise may originate in any of the following areas:

1. Wind noise
2. Noise from loose body parts
3. Engine—external or internal
4. Exhaust—manifold, muffler, converter, pipes, etc.
5. Drive train—clutch, transmission, differential, drive shafts, axles
6. Running gear—wheels, bearings, tires
7. Brakes—discs, calipers, pads, drums, shoes, linings

The type of noise may be classified as:

- Tap
- Knock
- Rattle
- Squeak
- Squeal
- Whine

- Ring
- Click
- Clunk
- Thud
- Ping
- Chirp

The term used to describe a noise is open to interpretation by the owner/operator.

The technician or service writer is wise to use discretion in interpreting the customer's use of a word and the technician's use of the same word—they may not be the same. It is, therefore, important that the complaint be positively identified before corrective action is taken. Nothing is worse for the customer or more embarrassing to the technician and service department than spending a lot of the customer's money without correcting the problem which brought the customer in. Experience in customer relations and experience in identifying and locating noise problems are essential to success in this area. Refer to the appropriate section in the text for suspected areas.

Vehicle Control

The ability of the driver to control the vehicle is dependent on several systems operating properly. Areas of vehicle control problems are:

- Hard to steer—manual steering, power steering
- Wanders—jumps from side to side
- Leads to one side—when braking, when not braking
- Shimmies
- Vibrates
- Bounces
- Hard ride
- Hard to stop—poor braking
- Wheels lock

These problems are dealt with in the appropriate chapters in this text, and diagnostic charts are also provided.

Comfort

Passenger comfort, aside from quality of ride and seating comfort, includes: ventilation, heating, and air conditioning. These subjects are covered in Chapter 40 of this text.

Engine Performance

The general topic of engine performance may be divided into several areas such as:

- Won't start
- Poor idle
- Stalls
- Misses
- Lacks power
- Diesels when shut off
- Cuts out
- Hesitates
- Uses too much oil
- Noise—knocks, pings, rattles, squeaks, squeals, etc.
- Smoke from exhaust or under hood
- Overheats
- Smells—raw fuel, or exhaust odor
- Uses too much fuel

These are the kinds of problems that are perceivable by the owner, the operator, and the technician alike. The source or cause of these problems may be any one or more of a number of engine systems. Thorough knowledge of each system is essential to isolate such problems.

The appropriate diagnostic charts and procedures for performance problems may be found in this text as follows and will therefore not be repeated here.

- Lubrication system diagnosis—Chapter 7, Part 7
- Cooling system diagnosis—Chapter 8, Part 5
- Gasoline and diesel engine diagnosis—Chapter 9, Part 3
- Air supply system diagnosis—Chapter 10, Part 5
- Fuel system diagnosis—Chapter 12, Part 7
- Carburetor diagnosis—Chapter 13, Part 6
- Gasoline injection diagnosis—Chapter 14, Part 9
- Diesel fuel system diagnosis—Chapter 15, Part 6
- Exhaust system diagnosis—Chapter 16, Part 5
- Emission control diagnosis—Chapter 17, Parts 11, 12, 13
- Battery diagnosis—Chapter 18, Part 5
- Starting system diagnosis—Chapter 21, Part 4

• AC charging system diagnosis—Chapter 22, Part 3

• DC charging system diagnosis—Chapter 23, Part 3

• Ignition system diagnosis—Chapter 24, Part 7

The method selected and used for vehicle diagnosis will depend on the type of equipment available for the purpose; however, all shops are normally equipped with sufficient test equipment of one kind or another to enable the technician to perform an accurate diagnosis of the problem.

Some of the types of test equipment used are as follows:

1. Hand held test equipment (or mounted in portable stands) including:

• Voltmeter

• Ammeter

• Ohmmeter

• Vacuum gauge

• Tachometer

• Pressure gauge

• Compression tester

• Cylinder leak down test adapters

• Test light

• Jumper wire

• Test type circuit breaker

• Infrared exhaust analyzer

2. Oscilloscope—may be combined with programmed memory of all specifications for all makes and models and include print out capability of test results as well as infrared test equipment.

3. Computerized Digital Display Analyzers—compare pre-programmed vehicle specifications with test results and display both on the screen. Many have printout capability. Information on vehicle make, model, engine size, and the like is entered by the operator before the test sequence is begun.

4. Dynamometer—used in conjunction with oscilloscope or with test equipment listed in item 1 above.

PART 2   ON-BOARD DIAGNOSTIC SYSTEMS

Many vehicles have built-in, on-board diagnostic systems which may be used with or without other test instruments depending on design. The system is able to monitor the operation of many of the engine operating systems. A multiple terminal electrical connector provides the means for checking the various systems. This is called the diagnostic connector or the self-test terminal connector.

In general, it can be used to identify systems that are not functioning normally. The procedure is to either use a special tester connected to the diagnostic connector or to use a low reading voltmeter and jumper wire. When using the special tester, read out information appears on the tester in the test sequence specified by the vehicle and test equipment manufacturer. When using the jumper wire and voltmeter, specified terminals are grounded while the voltmeter is connected to other specified terminals in the diagnostic connector. Voltmeter needle readings are taken or pulsations are counted and compared to specifications. Others may use a test light to check at the diagnostic connector or may have instrument panel diagnostic read out results.

In every case it is essential to follow the vehicle and equipment manufacturer's recommendations as to:

• Equipment to use

• Test methods to use

• Test sequence to follow and

• Interpretation of test results

One typical General Motors example of the use of a diagnostic connector is to use a test light or voltmeter to check the following electrical components and wiring:

• Battery

• Generator

• Distributor, coil, and module

• Starter and solenoid

• Ignition switch

• Fusible links (both)

• Light switch

• Bulkhead connector

• Plugs and wires

The advantage of the diagnostic connector is that all checks can be made from the side of the car.

There is no need to remove components, raise the car, or crawl under the dash. When trying to solve an electrical problem, the frustration is compounded when much effort is made to check a component only to find out that it is not the cause of the problem.

The typical test terminals check the following systems:

Terminal 1: Battery-to-starter solenoid and fusible link

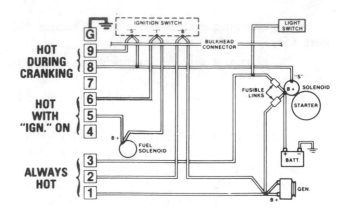

FIGURE 26-3. Wiring diagram (diesel). *(Courtesy of General Motors Corporation)*

DIAGNOSTIC CONNECTOR

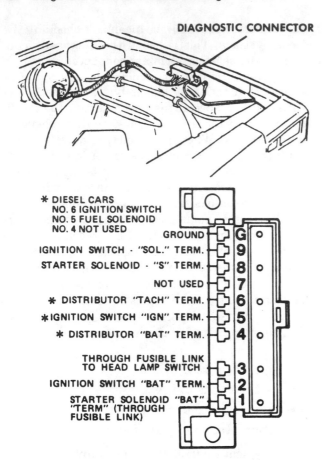

* DIESEL CARS
NO. 6 IGNITION SWITCH
NO. 5 FUEL SOLENOID
NO. 4 NOT USED

GROUND

IGNITION SWITCH - "SOL." TERM.

STARTER SOLENOID - "S" TERM.

NOT USED

* DISTRIBUTOR "TACH" TERM.

*IGNITION SWITCH "IGN" TERM.

* DISTRIBUTOR "BAT" TERM.

THROUGH FUSIBLE LINK
TO HEAD LAMP SWITCH

IGNITION SWITCH "BAT" TERM.

STARTER SOLENOID "BAT"
"TERM" (THROUGH
FUSIBLE LINK)

FIGURE 26-1. *(Courtesy of General Motors Corporation)*

Terminal 2: Battery-to-ignition switch

Terminal 3: Battery-to-headlight switch and fusible link

Terminal 4: Battery-to-distributor wiring (on gas engine applications)

Terminal 5: Ignition switch "I" terminal (fuel solenoid on diesel engine applications

Terminal 6: Distributor "tach" terminal (ign. of ignition switch on diesel engine)

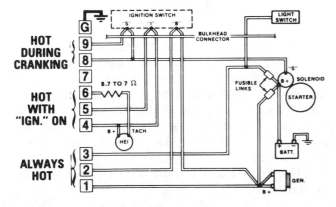

FIGURE 26-2. Wiring diagram (gas). *(Courtesy of General Motors Coporation)*

The wire to terminal six on gasoline engine applications is a resistance wire used to prevent damage to the coil in case of accidental grounding.

Terminal 7: Blank
Terminal 8: Starter solenoid "S" terminal
Terminal 9: Ignition switch "S" terminal of starter
Terminal "G" ground to body or chassis

The diagnostic connector provides an easy hook-up between terminals six and ground. When you are doing an HEI system analysis, you can make the tests without removing the coil and module from the distributor. (See Figures 26-1 and 26-2.)

PART 3 COMPRESSION TESTING— GASOLINE ENGINE

Cylinder compression tests are performed to determine cylinder compression pressures in comparison with each other and with specifications. Compression pressures may be lower than specified for the following reasons:

- Leakage past the valves
- Leakage past the rings
- Leakage past a cylinder head gasket particularly between adjacent cylinders
- Low cranking speed

Compression pressures considerably above specifications indicate carbon build-up in the combustion chamber and on the piston head.

To perform a compression test, proceed as follows with a tester capable of 200 psi (1300–1400 kPa).

1. Engine should be at operating temperature.

2. Battery and cranking system should be in good condition. Remove air cleaner.

3. Carefully remove spark plug wires from spark plugs. Do not pull on high-tension wire since this will damage wires. Grasp the plug boot by hand or with the appropriate tool. Twist and pull the boot from the plug.

4. Loosen all spark plugs one full turn only. Reconnect plug wires and start engine. Run the engine for a moment at about 1000 rpm. Then shut off the engine. Doing this will blow any dirt or carbon from the spark plugs and prevent entry of dirt into the cylinders when the plugs are removed.

5. Disconnect the primary lead from the coil. On HEI distributors disconnect the BAT terminal from the distributor. This prevents any sparks from occurring during compression testing and protects the ignition coil from damage.

6. Remove all spark plugs, keeping them in order so you know which plug came from each cylinder. This allows spark plugs to be analyzed to help determine cylinder condition. (See the chapter on ignition systems for analysis procedure).

7. Hold choke and throttle plates fully open during compression tests.

8. Starting with the number one cylinder, install "screw in" or "hold in" adapter into spark plug hole in a manner that will prevent any pressure leakage through the spark plug hole. Crank the engine through at least five compression strokes; note the highest compression reading and the number of strokes required to obtain the reading. Repeat the test on each of the remaining cylinders, cranking the engine the same number of strokes as were needed to obtain the highest reading on number one cylinder.

9. Record the results of each cylinder tested.

10. Analyze the results of the compression test as follows:

Normal—Compression builds up quickly and evenly to specified pressure on each cylinder.

Low Readings—Use three full squirts of SAE 30 engine oil squirted into cylinders that have a low reading and repeat the compression test for that cylinder. If compression pressure increases considerably as a result, leakage past the piston rings is the cause. If compression pressure does not increase appreciably, leakage past the valve is indicated.

Very Low Readings on Adjacent Cylinders—This would indicate a *blown* head gasket between the affected cylinders.

Excessively High Readings—This would indicate a build-up of carbon deposits in the combustion chamber. This condition is usually also evidenced by pinging on acceleration and may also cause pre-ignition and detonation. Carbon deposits should be removed only as specified by the vehicle manufacturer. While it is possible to remove carbon deposits with special top engine cleaners, severe damage and overheating of catalytic converters may be caused by this procedure.

Comparison Between Cylinders

In order for cylinders to produce relatively even power output, compression pressures should be similar within certain limits. The comparison of compression pressures between cylinders is just as important as actual compression pressures. Since engine temperature, oil, viscosity, and engine cranking speed all have a bearing on test results, some variation from specified pressures may be expected. However, compression pressures should be comparable between cylinders. Some manufacturers allow a maximum difference in pressures between cylinders of 20 percent. A greater than 20 percent difference requires repair to the affected cylinders.

Compression Testing—Diesel Engines

To perform a compression test on a diesel engine, proceed as follows with a tester capable of 500 psi (3450 kPa).

1. Engine should be at operating temperature.

2. Batteries and cranking system should be in good condition.

3. Remove air cleaner.

4. Disable the fuel system and glow plug system as specified by the vehicle manufacturer. This may require disconnecting a fuel solenoid lead on some models, as well as glow plug connections. Refer to service manual for procedure to follow.

5. Remove either glow plugs or injectors to allow installation of compression tester. Some engines are compression tested through the glow plug holes, while others are tested through the injector holes. Compression testers may be equipped with screw-in or clamp-in adapters, depending on application. Be sure to follow engine and equipment manufacturer's instructions for use of compression tester.

6. Install compression tester into number one cylinder.

7. Crank the engine through at least six compression strokes—note the highest compression reading and the number of strokes required to obtain the reading. Repeat the test on each of the remaining cylinders, cranking the engine the same number of strokes as were required to obtain the highest reading for number one cylinder.

8. Record the results from all cylinders.

9. Analyze the test results as follows:

Normal—Compression builds up quickly and evenly to specified compression pressure on all cylinders.

Piston Ring Leakage—Compression low on first stroke but tends to build up on following strokes. Does not reach normal cylinder pressure.

Caution—Due to high compression ratio of diesel engine and very small combustion chamber volume, do not add oil to any cylinder for compression testing. Extensive engine damage can result from this procedure.

A cylinder balance test is performed when using the scope in place of a compression test in some cases. The cylinder balance test compares cylinder power output with other cylinders on the same engine. The cylinder balance test does not isolate the cause of low cylinder output without further tests.

PART 4 CYLINDER LEAKAGE TESTING

Cylinder leakage tests are performed to determine whether compression pressures are able to leak past the rings into the crankcase, past the exhaust valves into the exhaust system, past the intake valves into the induction system, or past the head gasket into the engine coolant.

A simplified cylinder leakage test may be performed using a shop air line adapter made from a discarded spark plug of the appropriate type—10 mm, 14 mm, or 18 mm with tapered seat or gasket seat as required. A male shop air coupler is welded to the spark plug main body after the porcelain has been removed. This allows the adapter to be screwed into the spark plug hole and shop air to be coupled to the adapter.

Shop air pressure of 100 to 150 psi (700–1000 kPa) is required for this test.

To perform a cylinder leakage test proceed as follows:

1. Engine at operating temperature.

2. Carefully remove spark plug wires from spark plugs as outlined under compression test for gasoline engines.

3. Remove air cleaner. Disconnect battery ground cable at battery.

4. Perform steps 4, 6, and 7 as outlined under compression test for gasoline engines.

5. Install air line adapter into number one cylinder.

6. Remove crankcase oil dipstick, oil filler cap, and radiator cap.

7. Turn crankshaft to position number one piston at TDC position on the compression stroke. Make sure piston is exactly at TDC on the upstroke of the compression stroke. This is important for three reasons. First, the piston will be forced down by shop air if not exactly at the TDC position. Second, the piston rings should be at the bottom of their grooves for this test. Moving the piston up will do this. Third, both valves are closed with the piston in this position.

8. Now connect shop air to the adapter in number one cylinder.

9. Listen for air leakage into the exhaust system at the tailpipe. If present, this indicates exhaust valve leakage. Listen for air leakage at the carburetor air horn. If present, this indicates intake valve leakage. Listen for air leakage at the oil filler cap or dipstick tube. If present, this indicates leakage past the rings. Listen for leakage at spark plug holes of cylinders adjacent to the one being tested. If present, this indicates cylinder head gasket leak-

CONDITION	POSSIBLE CAUSE	CORRECTION
Air escapes through carburetor	Intake valve not seated properly.	Refer to valve reconditioning under cylinder head.
Air escapes through tailpipe	Exhaust valve not seated properly.	Refer to valve reconditioning under cylinder head.
Air escapes through radiator	Head gasket leaks or crack in cylinder block.	Remove cylinder head and inspect.
More than 50% leakage on adjacent cylinders	Head gasket leaks or crack in cylinder block or head between adjacent cylinders.	Remove cylinder head and inspect.
More than 25% leakage and air escapes through oil filler cap opening only	Stuck or broken piston ring(s); cracked piston; worn rings and/or cylinder wall.	Inspect for broken ring(s) or piston. Measure ring gap and cylinder diameter, taper, and out-of-round.

age between cylinders. Watch for air bubbles in coolant in radiator. If present, this indicates cylinder head gasket leakage to cooling system.

10. Disconnect shop air line from cylinder adapter and repeat test procedure for all cylinders.

PART 5 OSCILLOSCOPE TESTING

The oscilloscope, or "scope" as it is more commonly known, has been used for many years in the automotive service industry. It provides the means for a quick, comprehensive analysis of all the engine systems and indicates the mechanical condition of the engine as well. The scope is able to diagnose and pinpoint problems in the following systems:

- Battery and starting system
- Ignition system
- Charging system
- Cylinder balance
- Fuel system
- Induction system
- Combustion and exhaust emissions

The ability of the technician to use the scope effectively depends on several factors:

- Knowledge of the system being tested
- Knowledge of the equipment being used
- Skill, experience, and expertise of the technician.

A large part of the scope consists of a number of commonly used testers, such as voltmeter, ammeter, ohmmeter, tachometer, dwell meter, timing

DIAGNOSTIC INSPECTION REPORT

NAME			CAR MAKE		YEAR	MODEL	CAR NO.
ADDRESS			CITY		LICENSE NUMBER		MILEAGE
DATE	PHONE	TRANSMISSION ☐ AUTOM ☐ MAN	ENGINE CYL.	DISPL.	H.P.	CARB	ACCESSORIES ☐ PB ☐ PS ☐ AC

ALLEN PROGRAMMED DIAGNOSIS SEQUENCE

✱ VISUAL INSPECTION	GOOD	MARG	FAIL	NOTES
1. Battery & Cable Insp.				
2. Air Filter Condition				
3. Oil Level & Condition				
4. Transm. Fluid Cond.				
5. Steering Fluid Level				
6. Oil/Fluid Leakage				
7. Belt Tension & Cond.				
8. Cooling System				
A BATTERY & STARTING CIRCUIT				
9. Cranking Speed				
10. Starting Current				
11. Cranking Voltage				
12. Battery Recovery Voltage				
B PRIMARY CIRCUIT				
13. Ballast Resistor Circuit				
14. Ballast Resistor By-Pass				
C ALTERNATOR OUTPUT				
15. Alternator Output				
16. Battery Accepting the Charge				
D DISTRIBUTOR PRIMARY				
17. Average Dwell				
18. Point Resistance				
19. Dist. Ground				
20. Dwell Variations				
E IGNITION TIMING				
21. Initial Timing				
22. Centrifugal Advance				
23. Total Advance				
24. Vacuum Advance				

F IGNITION OUTPUT	GOOD	MARG	FAIL	NOTES
25. Coil Output				
26. Distr. Cap & Rotor Leakage				
27. Distributor Rotor Airgap				
28. Plug Firing Voltage				
KV 1 HI/LO, 2 HI/LO, 3 HI/LO, 4 HI/LO, 5 HI/LO, 6 HI/LO, 7 HI/LO, 8 HI/LO				
29. Plug Firing Accel. Check				
G CYLINDER BALANCE				
30. Engine Performance per Cylinder				
1 2 3 4 5 6 7 8 — Low speed / High speed / Cylinder F. O.				
31. Multi: Cylinder Test				
H CARBURETOR & COMBUSTION				
32. Adjust Idle – Jet Balance				
33. PCV System Operation *				
34. Exhaust Analysis (Idle)				
35. Acceleration Pump *				
36. Exhaust Analysis (Cruise)				
37. Power-Valve Operation *				
38. Carburetor Condition *				
39. Exhaust Emission Control *				
40. Dashpot Condition *				
I VOLTAGE REGULATOR				

RECOMMENDATION:

FIGURE 26-4.

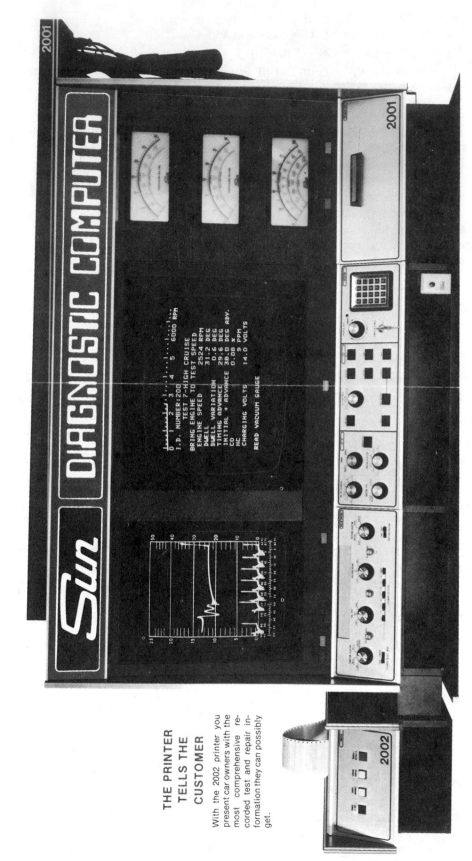

FIGURE 26-5. Typical oscilloscope used to test various engine systems. *Note:* Always follow the equipment manufacturer's directions for connections of leads and equipment use. *(Courtesy of Sun Equipment)*

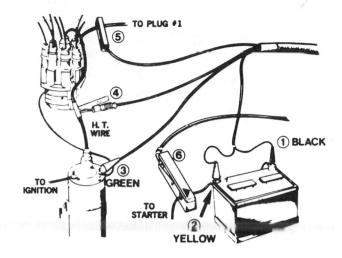

FIGURE 26-6. Typical underhood connections of oscilloscope leads. Note induction-type pickups at numbers 4, 5, and 6. (Courtesy of Ford Motor Co. of Canada Ltd.)

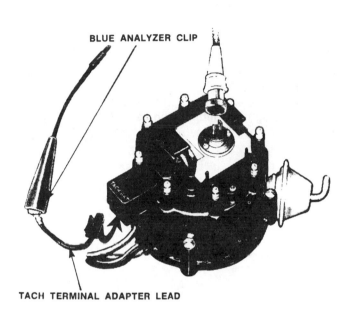

FIGURE 26-7. HEI ignition system requires special adapter of the type shown here for analyzer connections (oscilloscope).

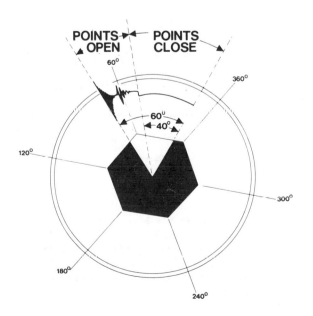

FIGURE 26-8. Relationship between the scope pattern and distributor operation. (Courtesy of Ford Motor Co. of Canada Ltd.)

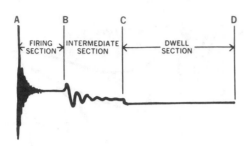

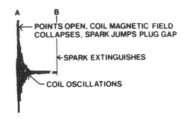

FIGURE 26-9. Normal primary scope pattern of a breaker point ignition system. *(Courtesy of Ford Motor Co. of Canada Ltd.)*

FIGURE 26-10. Firing section (A to B) of normal primary scope pattern. *(Courtesy of Ford Motor Co. of Canada Ltd.)*

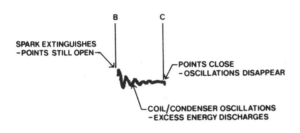

FIGURE 26-11. Intermediate section of normal primary scope pattern. Coil-condenser oscillations begin when there is insufficient voltage to maintain a spark across the spark-plug gap. Diminishing oscillations disappear when ignition points close. *(Courtesy of Ford Motor Co. of Canada Ltd.)*

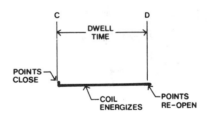

FIGURE 26-12. Dwell time of normal primary scope pattern. Points are closed when distributor shaft rotates from C to D. During this time the primary winding of the coil becomes fully energized. When points open at D the pattern repeats itself starting at A again, as in Figure 26-9. *(Courtesy of Ford Motor Co. of Canada Ltd.)*

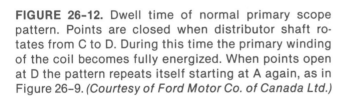

FIGURE 26-13. When the secondary pattern select button has been pushed, the scope secondary pattern as shown here will appear on the screen. It is divided into three sections, as was the primary pattern. *(Courtesy of Ford Motor Co. of Canada Ltd.)*

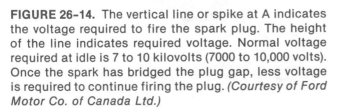

FIGURE 26-14. The vertical line or spike at A indicates the voltage required to fire the spark plug. The height of the line indicates required voltage. Normal voltage required at idle is 7 to 10 kilovolts (7000 to 10,000 volts). Once the spark has bridged the plug gap, less voltage is required to continue firing the plug. *(Courtesy of Ford Motor Co. of Canada Ltd.)*

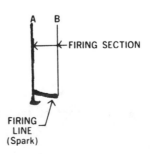

FIGURE 26-15. As soon as secondary voltage is inadequate to continue firing the plug, the coil-condenser oscillations begin. These oscillations represent the remaining energy bouncing back and forth until they are diminished at the point close signal. *(Courtesy of Ford Motor Co. of Canada Ltd.)*

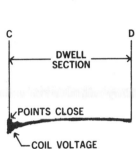

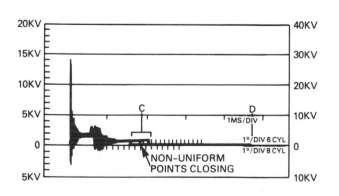

FIGURE 26-16. At C the points close resulting in some minor oscillations. The section C to D represents coil primary winding buildup time or dwell. At D the points open, and the cycle is repeated again, starting at A as in Figure 26-13. *(Courtesy of Ford Motor Co. of Canada Ltd.)*

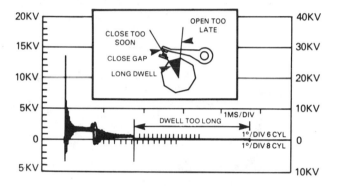

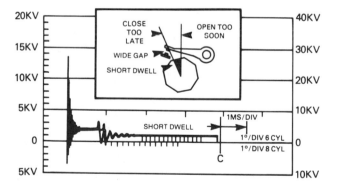

FIGURE 26-17. Primary patterns superimposed (all cylinder patterns shown at once, one on top of the other). Dwell time shown on pattern (in degrees of distributor shaft rotation) should correspond to vehicle manufacturer's specifications. *(Courtesy of Ford Motor Co. of Canada Ltd.)*

FIGURE 26-18. Primary pattern superimposed showing variations in dwell. Possible causes: uneven distributor cam lobes; bent distributor shaft; worn distributor shaft and bushing; worn timing chain or gears. *(Courtesy of Ford Motor Co. of Canada Ltd.)*

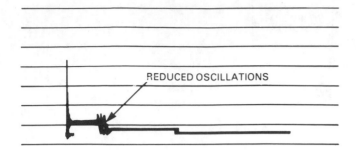

REDUCED OSCILLATIONS

FIGURE 26-19. Reduced oscillations on primary pattern indicate shorted condenser. Condenser must be replaced. Shorted or partly shorted condenser causes arcing at the points. *(Courtesy of Ford Motor Co. of Canada Ltd.)*

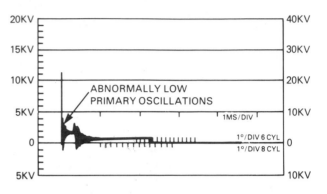

FIGURE 26-20. Abnormally low primary oscillations as shown here indicate excessive primary circuit resistance. *(Courtesy of Ford Motor Co. of Canada Ltd.)*

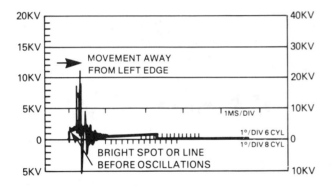

FIGURE 26-21. Primary oscillations shifted to the right indicate arcing at the points while they are open due to burned or pitted points or insufficient gap. *(Courtesy of Ford Motor Co. of Canada Ltd.)*

FIGURE 26-22. Bouncing points resulting from insufficient point spring tension will cause the primary oscillations shown at the points close signal. *(Courtesy of Ford Motor Co. of Canada Ltd.)*

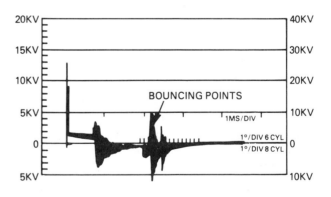

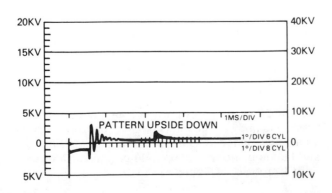

FIGURE 26-23. An upside-down secondary pattern indicates reversed coil polarity. Primary connections at coil must be corrected. *(Courtesy of Ford Motor Co. of Canada Ltd.)*

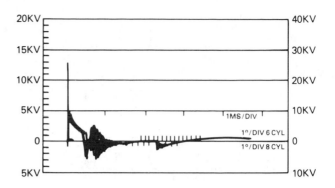

FIGURE 26-24. High external secondary resistance will show up as a line sloping down to the right from the firing spike. Superimposed pattern shown here indicates problem exists in secondary before it leaves the distributor. *(Courtesy of Ford Motor Co. of Canada Ltd.)*

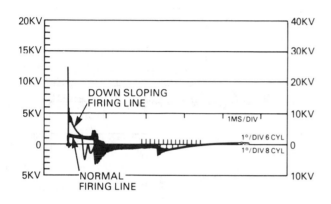

FIGURE 26-25. Superimposed secondary pattern showing only one cylinder with high secondary resistance. This indicates the problem exists in that portion of the secondary which feeds this particular cylinder. *(Courtesy of Ford Motor Co. of Canada Ltd.)*

FIGURE 26-26. High secondary internal resistance in one cylinder shown in this superimposed pattern. This indicates a possible wide plug gap, a lean fuel mixture, or excessive compression pressure due to carbon buildup in the cylinder. *(Courtesy of Ford Motor Co. of Canada Ltd.)*

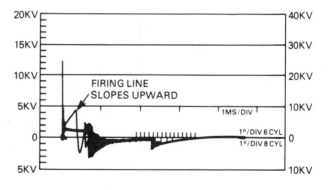

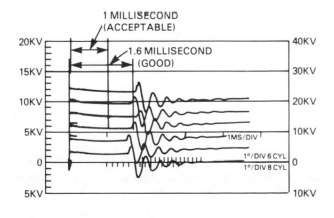

FIGURE 26-27. Some scopes have a *firing time* feature that measures firing time in milliseconds. When this test is selected, the firing line is shown in expanded form on the screen. Problems in the primary or secondary circuits of the ignition system can change the firing time of the plugs. *(Courtesy of Ford Motor Co. of Canada Ltd.)*

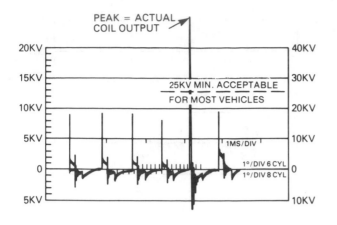

PEAK = ACTUAL COIL OUTPUT

25KV MIN. ACCEPTABLE
FOR MOST VEHICLES

FIGURE 26-28. Coil secondary voltage potential is measured by removing one spark-plug wire and holding it away from ground. *(Courtesy of Ford Motor Co. of Canada Ltd.)*

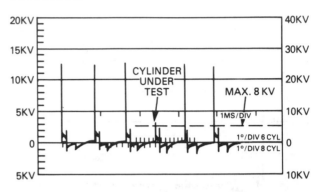

CYLINDER UNDER TEST

MAX. 8 KV

FIGURE 26-29. When that same spark plug wire is grounded, the height of the spike on the screen indicates the voltage required to jump the gap between the rotor and the distributor cap terminal. *(Courtesy of Ford Motor Co. of Canada Ltd.)*

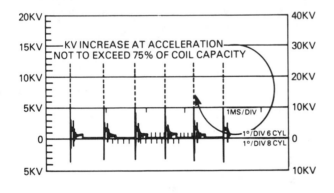

KV INCREASE AT ACCELERATION NOT TO EXCEED 75% OF COIL CAPACITY

FIGURE 26-30. Under acceleration, the secondary parade (showing all cylinders in sequence of firing order across the screen) pattern will show the increased voltage required to fire the plugs. This results from the increased pressure in the cylinders (increased resistance). *(Courtesy of Ford Motor Co. of Canada Ltd.)*

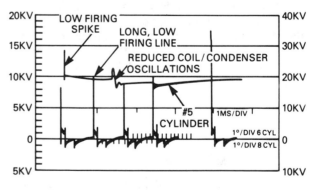

LOW FIRING SPIKE

LONG, LOW FIRING LINE

REDUCED COIL/CONDENSER OSCILLATIONS

#5 CYLINDER

FIGURE 26-31. Secondary cylinder select pattern (raised above superimposed pattern) shows a low firing spike and a long firing line resulting from a fouled plug, shorted plug, or a plug gap that is too small. *(Courtesy of Ford Motor Co. of Canada Ltd.)*

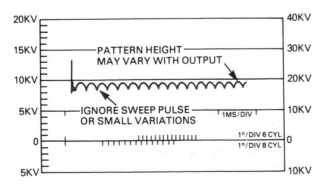

PATTERN HEIGHT MAY VARY WITH OUTPUT

IGNORE SWEEP PULSE OR SMALL VARIATIONS

FIGURE 26-32. Charging system select normal alternator pattern. *(Courtesy of Ford Motor Co. of Canada Ltd.)*

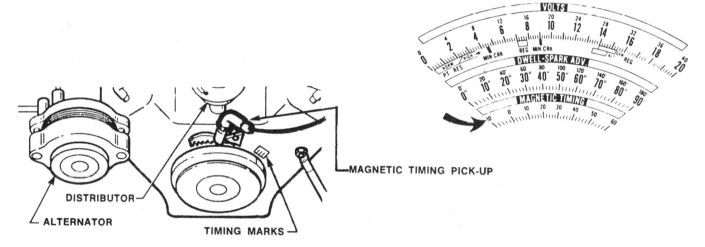

FIGURE 26-33. An open diode, open winding, or loose connector in the alternator will result in the pattern shown here. *(Courtesy of Ford Motor Co. of Canada Ltd.)*

FIGURE 26-34. A shorted diode results in the pattern shown here. *(Courtesy of Ford Motor Co. of Canada Ltd.)*

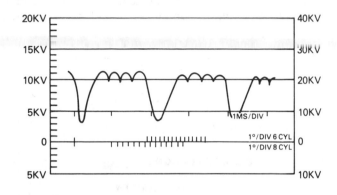

MAGNETIC TIMING PICK-UP

DISTRIBUTOR

ALTERNATOR

TIMING MARKS

FIGURE 26-35. Vehicles with electronically controlled timing have a magnetic timing probe that registers timing on the scale of the scope.

FIGURE 26-36. Ford and Bosch electronic primary ignition pattern. Although dwell line is shown here, dwell cannot be altered on electronic ignition.

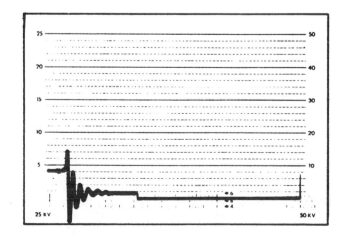

577

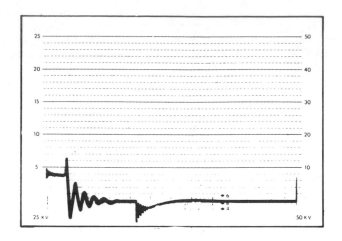

FIGURE 26-37. Ford and Bosch electronic ignition secondary pattern. Note 50-kilovolt scale, which accommodates high output potential of electronic ignition systems.

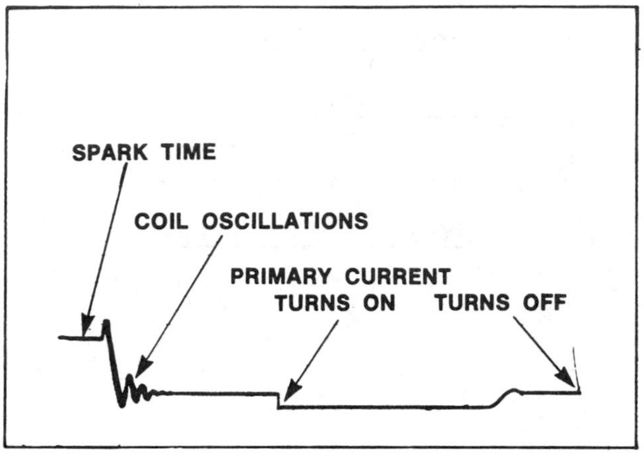

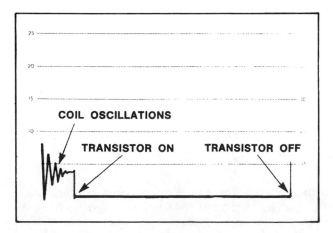

FIGURE 26-38. HEI, BID, and IHC primary electronic ignition pattern.

FIGURE 26-39. Secondary ignition pattern of HEI, BID, and IHC electronic ignition systems.

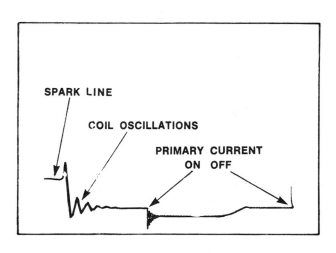

FIGURE 26-40. Chrysler's electronic ignition primary pattern.

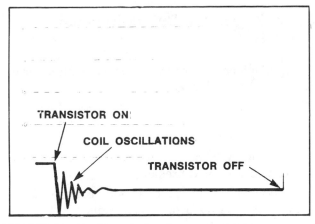

FIGURE 26-41. Chrysler's electronic ignition secondary pattern.

light, vacuum gauge. The unique feature of the scope is that it has a picture tube much like a television picture tube on which engine and engine system conditions are projected for analysis.

In general, it can be said that the height of the pattern on the screen is representative of the voltage output of the system or component being tested. The horizontal width of the projected pattern indicates the *duration* of electrical activity of the system or component being tested. The duration of the pattern is, of necessity, related to engine speed and therefore to distributor shaft speed, and is expressed in degrees of shaft rotation.

The voltage value shown on the screen is dependent on the kilovolt scale selected. For example, on a 50-kilovolt (50,000-volt) scope it is possible to select the 25- or the 50-kilovolt scale.

In addition, the scope is able to measure the quality of combustion by sampling and testing the exhaust gases for the following:

- Air-fuel ratio (rich or lean)
- Hydrocarbon emissions (HC)
- Carbon monoxide emissions (CO)

Analyzers use the infrared type of tester to measure the actual content of HC and CO present in the exhaust gases.

Vehicles equipped with a catalytic converter must have exhaust samples taken from a point between the catalyst and the engine in order to be an accurate indicator of exhaust gas quality. If sample testing is done after the catalyst, a false impression may be obtained since the catalyst will reduce HC and CO content even though it may be overloaded. Overloading the catalyst (with a too rich mixture) causes excessive heat in the catalyst and catalyst deterioration.

PART 6 EXHAUST GAS ANALYSIS

In order to tell how well the engine is performing, the exhaust gases must be analyzed. In this way, the type of combustion that is taking place in the cylinders can be determined. From this information, engine operation is indicated.

An exhaust gas analyzer of the infrared type is used to determine what is happening in the combustion chambers. An infrared analyzer accurately measures the hydrocarbon (HC) and carbon monoxide (CO) emissions from internal combustion engines. Hydrocarbon (HC) is measured as N-hexane in parts per million (PPM), and carbon monoxide (CO) is measured in percent (%).

Hydrocarbon present in the exhaust system represents unburned gasoline. An increase in the level of HC emission is a direct result of poor compression and/or misfiring. Just one spark plug not firing will raise the HC emission by many times the normal PPM reading.

Carbon monoxide is a by-product of fuel that has burned in the combustion chamber. An overrich mixture will cause a high reading of the CO meter.

Exhaust gas samples are continuously picked up by a probe inserted in the vehicle's tailpipe or probe plug hole ahead of the catalyst and are conveyed to the exhaust gas analyzer through a special hose. If the exhaust is sampled downstream from the catalyst, consideration must be given to the fact that the catalyst may be overworked and overheating if engine combustion is producing excessive emissions.

The infrared analyzing device determines the exact amount of hydrocarbon and carbon monoxide contained in the sample. This data is then converted into electrical signals and read out on the respective meters.

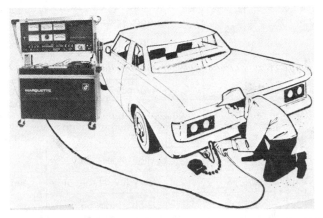

FIGURE 26-42. Using infrared analyzer to sample HC and CO content of exhaust gases.

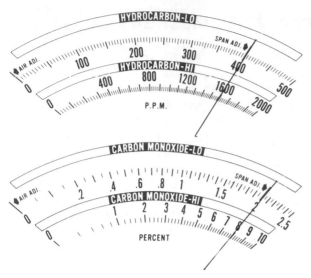

FIGURE 26-43. Typical HC and CO meters.

Visual Inspection Before Exhaust Analysis

1. Visually inspect the air cleaner filter for excessive dirt and clogged condition.

2. Visually inspect the carburetor for choke valve operation and for any sticking or binding of the choke or throttle linkage.

3. Visually inspect vacuum lines for loose connections, cracks, and breaks.

4. Visually inspect all emission control devices, and connections for proper operation.

Any component failing the visual inspection must be repaired or replaced before performing the operation tests.

The chart in Figure 26-44 may be used as a general guide to the test sequence for sampling exhaust gases and for diagnosis of basic problems. For additional diagnosis of systems identified as being faulty through exhaust gas analysis, refer to the diagnostic charts listed earlier in this chapter.

Emissions standards for past and future vehicle models are given at the end of this chapter.

	APPROX. SPEED					
	IDLE	1000 RPM	2000 RPM	TEST RESULTS	TYPICAL MALFUNCTIONS	RECOMMENDATIONS
CO 1				Normal	Poor point action. Open plug wire or fouled plug.	Recheck with scope.
HC	High	High	High	High all speeds		
CO 2				Normal	Vacuum leak affecting one cylinder.	Check for vacuum leak.
HC	High	High	High	Unsteady		
CO 3	Low	Low	Low	Low	General vacuum leak.	Check for general vacuum leak.
HC	High	High		High at low rpm	Should decrease at higher rpm.	
CO 4	High			High at idle	PCV valve restricted or carburetor idle mixture misadjusted.	Check the PCV valve or adjust the carburetor.
HC				Above normal		
CO 5	High	High	High	High at all rpm	Dirty air cleaner choke malfunction or carburetor malfunction.	Replace the air cleaner, service the choke, overhaul carburetor.
HC				Above normal		
CO 6	High	High		High at low speeds	Rich carburetor adjustment.	Adjust the carburetor to specification.
HC	High			High at idle		
CO 7				Normal	Ignition misfire at high speed or floating exhaust valves.	Recheck with scope.
HC			High	High at high rpm		
CO 8				Normal	Compression loss or vacuum leak.	Check compression and manifold vacuum.
HC	High			High at idle only		
CO 9	Low			Very low at idle only	Lean carburetor adjustment.	Adjust carburetor to specification.
HC	High			High at idle only		

FIGURE 26-44.

PART 7 DYNAMOMETER TESTING

Basic dynamometer operation is described in Chapter 5, Part 13 of this text. Depending on design, the chassis dynamometer, when used in conjunction with other test instruments (most notably the oscilloscope), can be used to test vehicle performance in the following areas:

- Engine operation
- Ignition system and electrical systems
- Fuel system
- Exhaust system
- Transmission and drive line
- Differential
- Brakes

Operating the vehicle on the chassis dynamometer involves simulating all possible road and load conditions the vehicle is likely to encounter when in daily use. This includes operation at idle, low speed, cruise, high speed, acceleration, deceleration, all gear positions, various loads in each operating mode, and braking. By observing vehicle operation and observing the test instruments, an accurate analysis of vehicle operation is obtained.

Most automotive shops (except for heavy duty vehicle shops) are not equipped with a chassis dynamometer.

The equipment manufacturer's recommended procedures should be followed when testing a vehicle on a dynamometer.

FIGURE 26-45. Typical dynamometer testing. *(Courtesy of Sun Equipment)*

PART 8 ROAD TESTING

Since many shops are not equipped with a dyna-mometer, road load engine performance must be determined during a road test when required.

In order to perform a valid road test that will accurately indicate engine performance, several prerequisites must be met by the person doing the road test. These include the following:

1. Thorough knowledge of all automotive systems such as engine, fuel, electrical, cooling, heating, air conditioning, drive train, braking, steering, and suspension systems.

2. The ability to select a section of road where road and traffic conditions will allow the vehicle to be safely operated in all different modes.

3. The ability to operate the vehicle during the road test in a manner that will not jeopardize anyone's safety.

4. The ability to duplicate all possible driver-induced operating modes normally encountered during vehicle operation.

5. The ability to identify which system is causing the problem.

Guidelines for Road Testing

A performance problem may be encountered in one or more vehicle operating modes. The technician performing the road test should be able to duplicate all vehicle operating modes and understand which systems are operational in each mode for the test to be meaningful and productive. The following points may be used as a guide:

1. At which engine operating temperature does the problem occur?

   (a) when cold?

   (b) during warmup?

   (c) at normal operating temperature?

2. During which operating modes does the problem occur?

   (a) at cruise?—if so at what speed?

   (b) on acceleration?—at light, heavy, WOT, or lift foot immediately after sudden acceleration?

   (c) when coasting?

   (d) during braking?—light or heavy?

   (e) when turning steering wheel?—right or left or both?

   (f) with A/C on or with A/C off?

   (g) with transmission in neutral, reverse, or forward gear positions?

   (h) with vehicle heavily loaded, pulling a trailer, or lightly loaded?

3. Other factors which must be considered when performing a road test and a fuel consumption test (using special fuel metering test equipment) are:

   (a) tire and wheel size (standard, over, or undersize)

   (b) tire inflation pressures (under, over, or unequal)

   (c) tire condition

   (d) road surface condition (paved, gravel, wet, dry)

   (e) weather conditions (wind speed and direction in relation to direction of vehicle movement—head, tail, or cross wind—rain or snow)

   (f) terrain (up or down hill)

   (g) driving habits (heavy acceleration and excessive use of brakes)

   (h) traffic conditions (heavy or light, highway or city driving)

PART 9 TUNE-UP PROCEDURE

What is a tune-up? The term tune-up does not necessarily mean the same thing to everyone. According to some, a tune-up includes such items as carburetor overhaul, valve adjustment, and distributor overhaul. According to others, a tune-up does not include overhaul of any unit, merely cleaning and adjusting of the various units.

If the engine is not mechanically sound, a tune-up will not restore its full potential. The principle of good tune-up is to determine whether the following four conditions are present in sufficient quantity and quality to ensure good performance and economy, and to meet emissions standards.

1. *Adequate compression:* Poor compression indicates a mechanically unsound engine, which should be corrected before a tune-up can be properly performed.

2. *Correct air/fuel ratio:* An air/fuel ratio that is too rich or too lean or of insufficient quantity will adversely affect performance, economy, and emissions.

3. *Adequate ignition at the spark plugs at the correct time:* The spark at the spark-plug gaps must be of sufficient intensity and duration to promote good combustion of the air-fuel mixture. The spark must occur at each spark plug at the correct time every time the piston is in a position to be fired.

EXHAUST EMISSIONS STANDARDS

CALIFORNIA AIR RESOURCES BOARD
NEW VEHICLE STANDARDS SUMMARY*

PASSENGER CARS—Exhaust Emissions Standards

The following California standards, up through 1979, and federal standards, up through 1974, apply only to gasoline-powered passenger cars (1). Federal standards for 1975 and later, and California standards for 1980 and later, apply to both gasoline and diesel-powered passenger cars.

Year	Standard	Test Procedure	Hydro-Carbons (HC)		Carbon Monoxide (CO)	Oxides of Nitrogen (NOx)	
Prior to controls	none	7-mode	850	ppm	3.4%	1000	ppm
		7-mode	11	g/mi	80 g/mi	4	g/mi
		CVS-75	8.8	g/mi	87.0 g/mi	3.6	g/mi
50,000 Mile Exhaust Emissions Standards							
1966–67	Calif.	7-mode	275	ppm	1.5%	no std.	
1968–69	Calif.	7-mode				no std.	
	federal	50–100 CID	410	ppm	2.3%	no std.	
		101–140 CID	350	ppm	2.0%	no std.	
		over 140 CID	275	ppm	1.5%	no std.	
(Grams Per Mile)							
1970	Calif.	7-mode	2.2		23	no std.	
	federal						
1971	Calif.	7-mode	2.2		23	4.0	
	federal	7-mode	2.2		23	no std.	
1972	Calif.	7-mode or	1.5		23	3.0	
	Calif.	CVS-72	3.2		39	3.2 (2)	
	federal	CVS-72	3.4		39	no std.	
1973	Calif.	CVS-72	3.2		39	3.0	
	federal	CVS-72	3.4		39	3.0	
1974	Calif.	CVS-72	3.2		39	2.0	
	federal	CVS-72	3.4		39	3.0	
1975–76	Calif.	CVS-75	0.9 (3)		9.0	2.0	
	federal	CVS-75	1.5		15	3.1	
1977–79	Calif.	CVS-75	0.41		9.0	1.5	
	federal	CVS-75	1.5		15	2.0	

*(Revised 9/30/82)

PASSENGER CARS — 50,000 Mile Exhaust Emissions Standards
CVS-75 Test Procedure
(Grams Per Mile)

Year	Standard	Hydrocarbons(4)		Carbon Monoxide (CO)	Oxides of Nitrogen (NOx)
		Non-Methane	Total HC		
1980	Calif.	0.39	(0.41)	9.0	1.0(8)
	federal	no std.	(0.41)	7.0	2.0
1981	Calif. (5) Option A	no std.	(0.41)	3.4	1.0(8)
	Calif. (5) Option B	0.39	(0.41)	7.0	0.7(8)
	federal	no std.	(0.41)	3.4	1.0
1982	Calif. (5) Option A	0.39	(0.41)	7.0	0.4(9)
	Calif. (5) Option B	0.39	(0.41)	7.0	0.7(9)
	federal	no std.	(0.41)	3.4	1.0
1983 & Subsequent	Calif.	0.39	(0.41)	7.0	0.4(10)
	Calif.	0.39	(0.41)	7.0	0.7(11)
	federal	no std.	(0.41)	3.4	1.0
California 100,000 Mile Exhaust Emissions Standards					
CVS-75 Test Procedure					
(Grams Per Mile)					
1980	(6) (7) Option 1	0.39	(0.41)	9.0	1.5
	(6) (7) Option 2	0.46	no std.	10.6	1.5
1981	(6) (7) Option 1	0.39	no std.	3.4	1.5
	(6) (7) Option 2	0.46	no std.	4.0	1.5
1982–83	(6) Option 1	0.39	(0.41)	7.0	1.5
	(6) Option 2	0.46	no std.	8.3	1.5
1984 & Subsequent	(6) Option 1	0.39	(0.41)	7.0	1.0
	(6) Option 2	0.46	no std.	8.3	1.0

(1) Passenger car as defined in Title 13 of the California Administrative Code means any motor vehicle designed primarily for transportation of persons having a capacity of 12 persons or less.

(2) Hot 7-mode test.

(3) Hydrocarbon emissions from 1975–76 limited production vehicles may not exceed 1.5 gm/mi.

(4) Hydrocarbon standards in parentheses indicate total hydrocarbons. When applicable, manufacturers may elect to certify vehicle to either the nonmethane or total hydrocarbon standards.

(5) For the 1981 model year, manufacturers may choose either Option A or B for their entire 50,000 mile certified product line. The option chosen in 1981 must be retained for the 1982 model year.

(6) 100,000 mile options: Option 1 standards refer to the projected 50,000 mile emissions for hydrocarbons and carbon monoxide, whereas Option 2 standards refer to the projected 100,000 mile emissions for these pollutants. NOx emissions standards for both options refer to the 100,000 mile projected emissions.

(7) For vehicles with evaporative emissions values below 1.0 g/test, an adjustment to the exhaust hydrocarbon emissions standard may be granted by the Executive Officer (100,000 mile option only).

(8) 1.5 g/mi NOx standard for small manufacturers subject to "in lieu" standards pursuant to Section 1960.2 of Title 13, California Administrative Code. Production passenger cars must meet a 1.0 g/mi cumulative corporate average NOx standard based upon a full year's production.

(9) 1.0 g/mi NOx standard for small manufacturers subject to "in lieu" standards pursuant to Section 1960.4 of Title 13, California Administrative Code. Production passenger cars must meet a 0.7 g/mi cumulative corporate average NOx standard for the full 1982 model year production.

(10) 0.7 g/mi NOx standard for the 1983 and 1984 model years for small manufacturers subject to "in lieu" standards pursuant to Section 1960.4 of Title 13, California Administrative Code. Production passenger cars must meet a 0.7 g/mi cumulative corporate average NOx standard for each production quarter. For 1985 and subsequent model years, a small manufacturer must meet a 0.4 g/mi NOx standard for the prototype vehicle certification and for production vehicles per engine family on a quarterly basis.

(11) A manufacturer may choose to certify to this optional set of standards provided that the conditions set forth in Section 1960.15, Title, 13, California Administrative Code are met. These conditions include a 7-year/75,000 mile recall provision for selected emissions control parts.

Additional Requirements

Beginning with the 1980 model-year, the maximum projected emissions of oxides of nitrogen measured on the federal Highway Fuel Economy Test shall be no greater than 1.33 times the applicable passenger car oxides of nitrogen standards shown above.

Effective 1978, evaporative emissions standards are 6.0 grams per SHED test for the 1978–79 model years and 2.0 grams per SHED test for 1980 and later model years.

SHED Test (Sealed Housing Evaporative Determination) - A method for measuring evaporative emissions from motor vehicles.

Previous evaporative emissions standards of 6.0 grams per test for 1970–71 and 2.0 grams per test for 1972 and later were based on the "carbon trap procedure," which became obsolete when the SHED test procedure was adopted for 1978 and subsequent model years.

Diesel-powered passenger cars are subject to the following 50,000 mile particulate exhaust emission standards: 0.6 g/mi for the 1982 through 1984 model years, 0.4 g/mi for the 1985 model year, 0.2 g/mi for the 1986 through 1988 model years, and 0.08 g/mi for 1989 and subsequent model years.

g/mi = grams per mile.
CVS-72 = constant volume sample cold start test.
CVS-75 = constant volume sample test which includes cold and hot starts.
7-mode = 137 second driving cycle test.
ppm = parts per million.

LIGHT-DUTY TRUCKS — Exhaust Emissions Standards

The following California standards, up through 1977, and federal standards, up through 1975, apply only to gasoline-powered light-duty trucks (1). Federal standards for 1975 and later and California standards for 1978 and later apply to both gasoline and diesel-powered light-duty trucks.

50,000 Mile Exhaust Emissions Standards

Year	Standard	Test Procedure	Hydro-Carbons (HC)	Carbon Monoxide (CO)	Oxides of Nitrogen (NOx)
1966–67	Calif.	7-mode	275 ppm	1.5%	no std.
1968–69	Calif.	7-mode			
	federal	50–100 CID	410 ppm	2.3%	no std.
		101–140 CID	350 ppm	2.0%	no std.
		over 140 CID	275 ppm	1.5%	no std.
			(Grams Per Mile)		
1970	Calif.	7-mode	2.2	23	no std.
	federal				
1971	Calif.	7-mode	2.3	23	4.0
	federal	7-mode	2.2	23	no std.
1972	Calif.	7-mode or	1.5	23	3.0
	Calif.	CVS–72	3.2	39	3.2 (2)
	federal	CVS–72	3.4	39	no std.

Year	Standard	Test Procedure	Hydro-Carbons (HC)	Carbon Monoxide (CO)	Oxides of Nitrogen (NOx)
1973	Calif.	CVS-72	3.2	39	3.0
	federal	CVS-72	3.4	39	3.0
1974	Calif.	CVS-72	3.2	39	2.0
	federal	CVS-72	3.4	39	3.0
1975	Calif.	CVS-75	2.0	20	2.0
	federal	CVS-75	2.0	20	3.1
1976–78	Calif.	CVS-75	0.9	17	2.0
	federal	CVS-75	2.0	20	3.1
1979	Calif. (3)	CVS-75	0.41	9.0	1.5 (6)
	Calif. (4)	CVS-75	0.50	9.0	2.0
	federal (5)	CVS-75	1.7	18	2.3

LIGHT-DUTY TRUCKS — 50,000 Mile Exhaust Emissions Standards
CVS-75 Test Procedure
(Grams Per Mile)

Year	Standard	Hydrocarbons (8)		Carbon Monoxide (CO)	Oxides of Nitrogen (NOx)
		Non-Methane	Total HC		
1980	Calif. (3)	0.39	(0.41)	9.0	1.5 (6)
	Calif. (4)	0.50	(0.50)	9.0	2.0
	federal	no std.	(1.7)	18.0	2.3
1981–82	Calif. (3)	0.39	(0.41)	9.0	1.0 (7)
	Calif. (4)	0.50	(0.50)	9.0	1.5
	federal	no std.	(1.7)	18.0	2.3
1983 & Subsequent	Calif. (3)	0.39	(0.41)	9.0	0.4 (11)
	Calif. (3)	0.39	(0.41)	9.0	1.0 (12)
	Calif. (4)	0.50	(0.50)	9.0	1.0
	federal	no std.	(1.7)	18.0	2.3

California 100,000 Mile Exhaust Emissions Standards
CVS-75 Test Procedure
(Grams Per Mile)

Year	Standard	Hydrocarbons		Carbon Monoxide (CO)	Oxides of Nitrogen (NOx)
1981–83	(3) Option 1 (9) (10)	0.39	(0.41)	9.0	1.5
	(3) Option 2 (9) (10)	0.46	no std.	10.6	1.5
	(4) (10)	0.50	(0.50)	9.0	2.0
1984 & Subsequent	(3) Option 1 (9)	0.39	(0.41)	9.0	1.0
	(3) Option 2 (9)	0.46	no std.	10.6	1.0
	(4)	0.50	(0.50)	9.0	1.5

(1) Light-duty trucks as defined by Title 13 of the California Administrative Code means any motor vehicle rated at 6,000 lbs. GVW or less, which is designed primarily for purposes of transportation of property or is a derivative of such vehicle, or is available with special features enabling off-street or off-highway operation and use.

(2) Hot 7-mode test.

(3) 0-3999 pounds equivalent inertia weight (curb weight plus 300 pounds).

(4) 4000–5999 pounds equivalent inertia weight.

(5) Effective 1979, federal LDT classification will be extended to 8500 pounds GVW.

(6) 2.0 g/mi NOx for four-wheel drive vehicles in this category.

(7) 1.5 g/mi NOx for small manufacturers subject to "in lieu" standards pursuant to Section 1960.3 of Title 13, California Administrative Code. Producrtion light-duty trucks meet a 1.0 g/mi cumulative corporate average NOx standard based upon a full year's production.

(8) Hydrocarbon standards in parentheses indicate total hydrocarbon. When applicable, manufacturers may elect to certify vehicles to either the non-methane or total hydrocarbon standards.

(9) 100,000 mile options: Option 1 standards refer to the projected 50,000 mile emissions for hydrocarbons and carbon monoxide, while Option 2 standards refer to the projected 100,000 mile emissions for these pollutants. NOx emission standards for both options refer to the 100,000 mile projected emissions.

(10) For 1981 model year vehicles with evaporative emissions values below 1.0 g/test, an adjustment to the exhaust hydrocarbon emissions standard may be granted by the Executive Officer (100,000 mile option only).

(11) 1.0 g/mi NOx standard for small manufacturers subject to "in lieu" standards pursuant to Section 1960.4 of Title 13, California Administrative Code. Production light-duty trucks must meet a 0.7 g/mi cumulative corporate average NOx standard for the full model year's production.

0.7 g/mi NOx standard for small manufacturers for the 1984 and 1985 model years. Production light-duty trucks must meet a 0.7 g/mi cumulative corporate average NOx standard for each production quarter.

For the 1986 and subsequent model years a small manufacturer must meet a 0.4 g/mi NOx standard for the prototype vehicle certification and for production vehicles per engine family on a quarterly basis.

(12) A manufacturer may choose to certify to this optional set of standards provided that the conditions set forth in Section 1960.15, Title 13, California Administrative Code are met. These conditions include a 7-year/75,000-mile recall provision for selected emissions control parts.

Additional Requirements

Beginning with the 1981 model year, the maximum projected emissions of oxides of nitrogen measured on the federal Highway Fuel Economy Test shall be no greater than 2.0 times the applicable light-duty truck oxides of nitrogen standards shown above.

Effective 1978, evaporative emissions standards are 6.0 grams per SHED test for 1978–79 model year and 2.0 grams per SHED test for 1980 and later model year.

SHED Test (Sealed Housing Evaporative Determination) - A method for measuring evaporative emissions from motor vehicles.

Previous evaporative emissions standards of 6.0 grams per test for 1970–71 and 2.0 grams per test for 1972 and later were based on the "carbon trap procedure" which became obsolete when the SHED test procedure was adopted for 1978 and subsequent model years.

Diesel-powered light-duty trucks are subject to the following 50,000 mile particulate exhaust emission standards: 0.6 g/mi for the 1982 through 1984 model years, 0.4 g/mi for the 1985 model year, 0.2 g/mi for the 1986 through 1988 model years, and 0.08 g/mi for 1989 and subsequent model years.

g/mi = grams per mile.
CVS-72 = constant volume sample cold start test.
CVS-75 = constant volume sample which includes cold and hot starts.
7-mode = 137 second driving cycle test.
ppm = parts per million.

MEDIUM-DUTY VEHICLES — Exhaust Emissions Standards

The following California standards, up through 1972, and federal standards, up through 1973, apply only to gasoline-powered medium-duty vehicles (1). California standards for 1973 and later year and federal standards for 1974 and later apply to both gasoline and diesel-powered medium-duty vehicles.

		Hydrocarbons (5)		Carbon Monoxide (CO)	Oxides of Nitrogen (NOx)
Year	Standard	Non-Methane	Total HC		
1969–77	Calif.	see heavy-duty standards			
1970–78	federal	see heavy-duty standards			

50,000 Mile Exhaust Emissions Standards
CVS-75 Test Procedure
(Grams Per Mile)

Year	Standard	Non-Methane	Total HC	Carbon Monoxide (CO)	Oxides of Nitrogen (NOx)
1978–79	Calif.	no std.	(0.9)	17	2.3
1979	federal	see light-duty truck standards			
1980	Calif.	0.9	(0.9)	17	2.3
	federal	no std.	(1.7)	18	2.3
1981–82	Calif. (2)	0.39	(0.41)	9.0	1.0 (8)
	Calif. (3)	0.50	(0.50)	9.0	1.5
	Calif. (4)	0.60	(0.50)	9.0	2.0
	federal	no std.	(1.7)	18.0	2.3
1983 & Subsequent	Calif. (2)	0.39	(0.41)	9.0	0.4 (9)
	Calif. (2)	0.39	(0.41)	9.0	1.0 (10)
	Calif. (3)	0.50	(0.50)	9.0	1.0
	Calif. (4)	0.60	(0.60)	9.0	1.5
	federal	no std.	(1.7)	18.0	2.3

California 100,000 Mile Exhaust Emissions Standards
CVS-75 Test Procedure

Year	Standard	Hydrocarbons (5)		Carbon Monoxide (CO)	Oxides of Nitrogen (NOx)
		Non-Methane	Total HC		
1981–82	(2) Option 1 (6) (7)	0.39	(0.41)	9.0	1.5
	(2) Option 2 (6) (7)	0.46	no std.	10.6	1.5
	(3)	0.50	(0.50)	9.0	2.0
	(4)	0.60	(0.60)	9.0	2.3
1983	(2) Option 1 (6)	0.39	(0.41)	9.0	1.5
	(2) Option 2 (6)	0.46	no std.	10.6	1.5
	(3)	0.50	(0.50)	9.0	2.0
	(4)	0.60	(0.60)	9.0	2.0
1984 & Subsequent	(2) Option 1 (6)	0.39	(0.41)	9.0	1.0
	(2) Option 2 (6)	0.46	no std.	10.6	1.0
	(3)	0.50	(0.50)	9.0	1.5
	(4)	0.60	(0.60)	9.0	2.0

(1) Medium-duty vehicles as defined in Title 13 of the California Administrative Code means heavy-duty vehicles having a manufacturer's gross vehicle weight rating of 8,500 pounds or less. (Manufacturers may elect to certify medium-duty vehicles up to 10,000 pounds GVW.)

(2) 0–3999 pounds equivalent inertia weight (curb weight plus 300 pounds).

(3) 4000–5999 pounds equivalent inertia weight.

(4) 6000–8500 (or 10,000) pounds equivalent inertia weight.

(5) Hydrocarbon standards in parentheses indicate total hydrocarbon. When applicable, manufacturers may elect to certify vehicles to either the non-methane or total hydrocarbon standards.

(6) 100,000 mile options: Option 1 standards refer to the projected 50,000 mile emissions for hydrocarbons and carbon monoxide, whereas Option 2 standards refer to the projected 100,000 mile emissions for these pollutants. NOx emissions standards for both options refer to the 100,000 mile projected emissions.

(7) For 1981 model year vehicles with evaporative emissions values below 1.0 g/test, an adjustment to the exhaust hydrocarbon emissions standard may be granted by the Executive Officer (100,000 mile option only).

(8) 1.5 g/mi NOx for small manufacturers subject to "in lieu" standards pursuant to Section 1960.3 of Title 13, California Administrative Code. Production medium-duty vehicles must meet a 1.0 g/mi cumulative corporate average NOx standard based upon a full year's production.

(9) 1.0 g/mi NOx standard for small manufacturers subject to "in lieu" standards pursuant to Section 1960.4 of Title 13, California Administrative Code. Production medium-duty vehicles must meet a 0.7 g/mi cumulative corporate average NOx standard for the full model year's production.

0.7 g/mi NOx standard for small manufacturers for the 1984 and 1985 model years. Production medium-duty vehicles must meet a 0.7 g/mi cumulative corporate average NOx standard for each production quarter.

For the 1986 and subsequent model years, a small manufacturer must meet a 0.4 g/mi NOx standard for the prototype vehicle certification and for production vehicles per engine family on a quarterly basis.

(10) A manufacturer may choose to certify to this optional set of standards provided that the conditions set forth in Section 1960.15, Title 13, California Administrative Code are met. These conditions include a 7-year/75,000-mile recall provision for selected emissions control parts.

Additional Requirements

Beginning with the 1981 model year, the maximum projected emissions of oxides of nitrogen measured on the federal Highway Fuel Economy Test shall be no greater than 2.0 times the applicable medium-duty vehicle oxides of nitrogen standards shown above.

Effective 1978, evaporative emissions standards are 6.0 grams per SHED test for the 1978–79 model years and 2.0 grams per SHED for 1980 and later model years.

SHED Test (Sealed Housing Evaporative Determination) - A method for measuring evaporative emissions from motor vehicles.

Previous evaporative emissions standards of 6.0 grams per test for 1970–71 and 2.0 grams per test for 1972 and later were based on the "carbon trap procedure" which became obsolete when the SHED test procedure was adopted for 1978 and subsequent model years.

Diesel-powered medium-duty vehicles are subject to the following 50,000 mile particulate exhaust emission standards: 0.6 g/mi for the 1982 through 1984 model years, 0.4 g/mi for the 1985 model year, 0.2 g/mi for the 1986 through 1988 model years, and 0.08 g/mi for 1989 and subsequent model years.

g/mi = grams per mile.
CVS-75 = constant volume sample test which includes cold and hot starts.

HEAVY-DUTY ENGINES AND VEHICLES — Exhaust Emissions Standards
(Diesel (1) and Gasoline)

The following is a summary of heavy-duty engine and vehicle (2) standards adopted by both the California Air Resources Board and federal Environmental Protection Agency, based on the 9-mode test procedures for gasoline engines and 13-mode test procedures for diesel engines. Also see footnote (5).

Year	Standard	Hydro-Carbons	Carbon Monoxide	Oxides of Nitrogen	Hydrocarbons & Oxides of Nitrogen
1969–71 (3)	Calif.	275 ppm	1.5%	no std.	no std.
1970–73 (4)	federal	275 ppm	1.5%	no std.	no std.
1972	Calif.	180 ppm	1.0%	no std.	no std.
		(Grams Per Brake-Horsepower-Hour)			
1973–74	Calif.	no std.	40	no std.	16
1973–78	federal	no std.	40	no std.	16
1975–76	Calif.	no std.	30	no std.	10
1977–78	Calif. or	no std.	25	no std.	5
	Calif.	1.0	25	7.5	no std.
1979 (6)	Calif. or	1.5	25	7.5	no std.
	Calif. or	no std.	25	no std.	5
	Calif.	1.0	25	7.5	no std.
1979–1983	federal or	1.5	25	no std.	10
	federal	no std.	25	no std.	5
1980–83	Calif. or	1.0	25	no std.	6.0
	Calif.	no std.	25	no std.	5
1984 &	Calif. or	0.5	25	no std.	4.5
later	Calif. (5)	1.3	15.5	5.1	no std.
	federal (5)	1.3	15.5	10.7	no std.

(1) The above standards apply to diesel engines and vehicles sold in California on or after January 1, 1973, and nationwide on or after January 1, 1974.

(2) These standards apply to motor vehicles having a manufacturer's GVW rating of over 6000 pounds, excluding passenger cars and 1978 and later medium-duty vehicles.

(3) Applies to vehicles manufactured on or after January 1, 1969.

(4) Applies to vehicles manufactured on or after January 1, 1970.

(5) These standards are based upon the new transient cycle test procedures.

(6) For 1979 only, manufacturer using heated flame ionization detection (HFID) method of measuring hydrocarbons must meet the 1.5 g/bhp-hr standard; whereas, manufacturers using non-dispersive infrared (NDIR) method of measuring hydrocarbons must meet the 1.0 g/bhp-hr standard. Both standards are equivalent in stringency. Manufacturers may use either HFID or NDIR in meeting the combined hydrocarbon and oxides of nitrogen standard of 5 g/bhp-hr. After 1979, manufacturers are required to use HFID.

Additional Requirements

Effective 1978, evaporative emissions standards are 6.0 grams per SHED test for the 1978–79 model years and 2.0 grams per SHED test for 1980 and later model years.

SHED Test (Sealed Housing Evaporative Determination) - A method for measuring evaporative emissions from motor vehicles.

Previous evaporative emissions standards of 6.0 grams per test for 1970–71 and 2.0 grams per test for 1972 and later were based on the "carbon trap procedure" which became obsolete when the SHED test procedure was adopted for 1978 and subsequent model years.

g/bhp-hr = grams per brake-horsepower-hour.
   ppm = parts per million.

MOTORCYCLES

The following is a summary of motorcycle (1) standards adopted by both the California Air Resources Board and the federal Environmental Protection Agency.

Year	Standard	Displacement (2) (4)	Hydrocarbons	Carbon Monoxide
1978–79	Calif. & federal	50–169	5.0 g/km	17 g/km
		170–749	5.0 + 0.0155 (D–170) g/km (3)	17 g/km
		750 or greater	14 g/km	17 g/km
1980–81	Calif.	All (50 or greater)	5.0 g/km	12 g/km
1980 & later	federal	All (50 or greater)	5.0 g/km	12 g/km
1982 & later	Calif.	50–279	1.0 g/km (5)	12 g/km
1982 and 1983		280 or greater	2.5 g/km	12 g/km
1984 and later		280 or greater	1.0 g/km	12 g/km

(1) Any motor vehicle other than a tractor having a seat or saddle for the use of the rider and designed to travel on not more than three wheels in contact with the ground and weighing less than 1500 pounds, except that four wheels may be in contact with the ground when two of the wheels function as a sidecar.

(2) Displacement shown in cubic centimeters.

(3) Motorcycle Hydrocarbon Formula

D = engine displacement in cubic centimeters
e.g., 300 cc engine; standard = (300–170) × .0155 + 5.0 = 7.0 g/km

(4) Federal classifications based on engine displacement are:

Class	Displacement (cc)
I	50–169
II	170–279
III	280–greater

(5) Small volume manufacturers (under 3,000 new units sold per year in California) can apply for a standard of up to 5.0 grams per kilometer hydrocarbon exhaust for 1982 model year Class I and II motorcycles only.

Additional Requirements

Effective 1983, evaporative emission standards for Classes I and II are 6.0 grams peer SHED test for 1983–84 model years, and 2.0 grams per SHED test for 1985 and later model years.

Effective 1984, evaporative emission standards for Class III are 6.0 grams per SHED test for 1984–85 model years, and 2.0 grams per SHED test for 1986 and later model years.

SHED Test (Sealed Housing Evaporative Determination) - A method for measuring evaporative emissions from motorcycles.

g/km = grams per kilometer

4. In addition, the tune-up must ensure the kind of operation that will allow the vehicle to *meet emissions standards.*

An orderly sequence of service operations to be performed is essential to systematic diagnosis and fault correction in any tune-up. The following order of tune-up procedures can be used to achieve good results. Always use fender covers and abide by the general precautions given in each chapter. Refer to the appropriate chapter for inspection and service of specified units.

Visual Inspection

1. Battery and cables.
2. Air cleaner, connections, and filter.
3. Fluid levels (power steering, crankcase, automatic transmission, coolant).
4. Fluid leaks and hoses.
5. Belts: condition, and tension.
6. Heat riser valve operation.
7. Vacuum hoses: routing, and leaks.
8. Wiring: routing and condition.
9. Exhaust system: leaks, restrictions.
10. Emission control system operation.

Analyzer

At this point, if an analyzer is to be used it should be connected and operated according to the equipment manufacturer's instructions. Various types of analyzers are in use, such as the oscilloscope, special analyzers that connect to diagnostic connectors in the vehicle wiring harness, special analyzers for electronic timing component testing and electronic fuel system testing, and so on. A very common analyzer is the oscilloscope or "scope" as it is commonly called. The use of this type of analyzer is discussed in part 5 of this chapter.

1. *Starter current draw and cranking voltage test.*

2. *Remove and service spark plugs* and high-tension wires. (Keep plugs in order for each cylinder for diagnosis before cleaning.)

3. *Compression test.* See part 3 of this chapter.

4. *Remove carburetor (if applicable):* Disassemble, clean, and inspect; replace faulty parts, assemble, adjust, and install.

5. *Remove distributor (if applicable):* Disassemble, clean, inspect, replace faulty parts, assemble, test, and adjust and install.

6. *Ignition timing:* Adjust base timing.

7. *Adjust idle mixture and speed.*

8. *Road test vehicle performance.*

9. *Prepare vehicle for customer acceptance.*

PART 10   SELF-CHECK

1. What four factors of engine operation must be restored in a good tune-up?

2. Why is a systematic approach to diagnosis and service necessary?

3. Describe the proper procedure to perform an engine compression test.

4. List six systems a "scope" type of analyzer is able to test.

5. What is meant by 50 kilovolts?

6. HC and CO are measured with the _____.

7. What are the three sections of the primary scope pattern called?

8. The height of the firing spike indicates _____ _____.

9. Define dwell time.

10. How is reverse coil polarity recognized on a scope pattern?

11. Internal resistance can be recognized on a scope pattern by the _____ slope of the firing line.

12. A normal AC charging system scope pattern consists of a series of _____ evenly spaced and of the same _____.

PART 11   TEST QUESTIONS

1. Overall vehicle performance can be grouped into the following areas:
   (a) engine performance, noise, vehicle control, comfort
   (b) comfort, noise, emissions, economy
   (c) economy, acceleration, noise, comfort
   (d) engine performance, emissions, economy, comfort

2. The technician's most important diagnostic tools include:
   (a) experience and knowledge of the systems
   (b) service manuals and diagnostic procedures
   (c) equipment and tools
   (d) all of the above

3. Compression pressures that are too low are the result of:
   (a) carbon build-up
   (b) excessive cranking speeds

(c) high compression ratios

(d) cylinder leakage

4. Cylinder leakage tests are performed to:

(a) check leakage past the rings

(b) check leakage past the valves

(c) check leakage past gaskets

(d) all of the above

5. A good tune-up restores good performance to the following systems:

(a) ignition, fuel

(b) induction, cooling

(c) emissions control, exhaust

(d) all of the above

6. The infrared analyzer measures the exhaust gases for content of:

(a) hydrocarbons and nitric oxides

(b) carbon monoxide and nitric oxides

(c) nitric oxides and hydrocarbons

(d) hydrocarbons and carbon monoxide

7. A very high firing spike on a scope pattern indicates:

(a) low resistance in the primary circuit

(b) high resistance in the primary circuit

(c) low resistance in the secondary circuit

(d) high resistance in the secondary circuit

8. The scope pattern consists of the following three sections:

(a) the primary, secondary, and intermediate

(b) the intermediate, secondary, and firing

(c) the firing, intermediate, and dwell

(d) the dwell, primary, and secondary

9. The dwell pattern on a scope indicates:

(a) points closing and opening

(b) points closed period

(c) points open period

(d) none of the above

10. Exhaust emissions levels are determined by:

(a) percentage of CO

(b) hydrocarbon ppm

(c) grams per mile

(d) all of the above

Section **6**

SUSPENSION, STEERING AND ALIGNMENT

Chapter 27

Suspension Systems

Performance Objectives

After thorough study of this chapter and sufficient practical work on the appropriate components, and with the appropriate shop manual, tools, and equipment, you should be able to do the following:

1. State the purpose of the suspension system.
2. Describe the construction and operation of the various front and rear suspension system designs.
3. Follow the accepted general precautions.
4. Accurately diagnose suspension system faults.
5. Remove and replace faulty front and rear suspension system components.
6. Perform the necessary checks to determine the success of the service performed.
7. Complete the self-check and test questions with at least 80 percent accuracy.
8. Complete all practical work with 100 percent accuracy.
9. Prepare vehicle for customer acceptance.

The suspension system is designed to provide the best combination of ride quality, directional control, ease of handling, safety, stability, and service life.

PART 1 FRAMES, SPRINGS, AND SHOCK ABSORBERS

Frames

The frame is the foundation upon which the entire vehicle is built. All other vehicle components are directly or indirectly attached to the frame. Holes and brackets are provided in the frame for this purpose.

Several types of frame construction are used by different vehicle manufacturers as illustrated. Frame side rails and crossmembers can have tubular, U-channel, or boxed crosssection construction. Unibody construction has short frame sections or no separate frame at all.

Bumpers

Bumpers are normally attached to the vehicle at the front and at the rear. Energy-absorbing bumpers of the hydraulic or energy-absorbing-metal type are used.

Springs

Several types of springs are used in suspension systems as illustrated. Springs are needed to absorb the shock of surface irregularities on the road. Tires and shock absorbers help the springs to do this job. All the weight supported by the springs is known as *sprung weight;* the weight of those components not supported by the springs is known as *unsprung weight.* The lower the proportion of unsprung weight in a vehicle, the better is the ride in general. Parts included in unsprung weight are wheels, tires, rear axle (but not always the differential), steering linkage, and some suspension parts.

Front and rear differentials on four-wheel-drive vehicles are sprung weight on some models and unsprung weight on others. Front-wheel-drive vehicles having two-wheel-drive use a transaxle in which the transmission and differential are sprung weight.

Springs are classified by the amount of deflec-

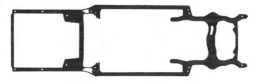

FIGURE 27-1. Perimeter-type frame assembly. *(Courtesy of General Motors Corporation)*

593

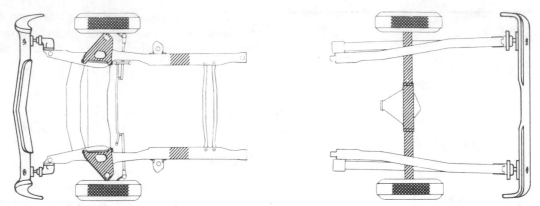

FIGURE 27-2. Stub-type frame as used with unibody construction. Note energy-absorbing bumper mounting. *(Courtesy of General Motors Corporation)*

tion under a given load. This is known as the *spring rate*. Hooke's law says that a *force applied to a spring will cause a spring to compress in direct proportion to the force applied*. When that force is removed, the spring returns to its original position if not overloaded.

Heavier vehicles require stiffer springs than do lighter vehicles. Springs are designed to carry the load of the vehicle adequately while still providing as soft or smooth a ride as possible.

Coil springs, leaf springs (both multiple and single leaf), and torsion bars are the most commonly used springs. Air-type springs are used on some vehicles. Springs are rubber-mounted to reduce noise and road shock.

Leaf springs have a spring eye at one end to attach to the frame and either a slipper mount or spring eye and shackle mount at the other end. The shackles or slipper is needed because the length of the spring varies as the spring is compressed and relaxed.

Single-leaf springs are usually of the tapered plate type with a heavy or thick center section tapering off to both ends. This provides a variable spring rate for a smooth ride and good load-carrying ability.

The multiple-leaf spring has a main leaf with

spring eyes at each end and a number of successively shorter leaves held together with a center bolt. The assembly is mounted to the axle housing with U-bolts, brackets, and rubber pads. The center bolt head fits in a hole in the mounting bracket of the axle housing. This prevents fore-and-aft movement of the axle, keeping it in proper alignment. Friction pads are often used between leaves to reduce friction, wear, and noise. Rebound clips are required to keep spring leaves in alignment with each other and to prevent leaf separation during rebound.

Shock Absorbers

Without shock absorbers, the continuing jounce (compression) and rebound (extension) of the spring are uncontrolled. This would be hard on the steering and suspension system, as well as provide a rough and unstable riding vehicle. The shock absorbers reduce the number and severity of these spring oscillations. Faulty shock absorbers can cause spring breakage.

Shock absorbers are mounted between the frame and the suspension by means of brackets and rubber bushings. The most common type of shock absorber is the direct acting, telescopic, hydraulic,

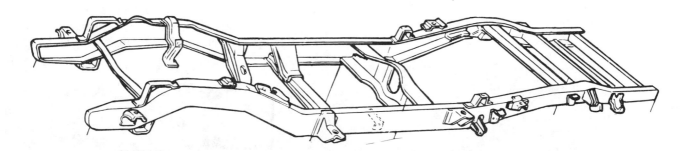

FIGURE 27-3. Ladder-type frame as two nearly parallel side rails with a number of crossmembers. *(Courtesy of Ford Motor Co. of Canada Ltd.)*

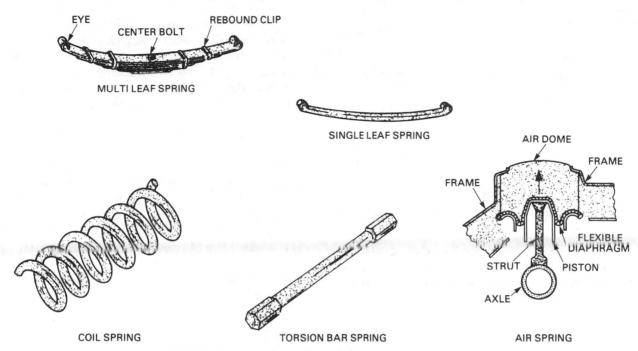

FIGURE 27-4. Various types of automotive springs.

double-acting type. This type of shock absorber is used with all types of suspension systems.

The shock absorber operates on the principle of forcing fluid through restricted openings (orifices) on both jounce (compression) and rebound (extension). Fluid is forced from one compartment in the shock absorber into another compartment by piston and cylinder movement. (See Figures 27–7 and 27–8.)

As the piston moves toward the compression head, the fluid must flow through two paths. One path is through the piston, and the other path is through the compression head into the reservoir.

Fluid passes through the restriction ports, under an O-ring, and through the carrier orifice. Increased velocity, which produces increased pressures, lifts the O-ring assembly against the bypass spring, permitting controlled flow of the fluid.

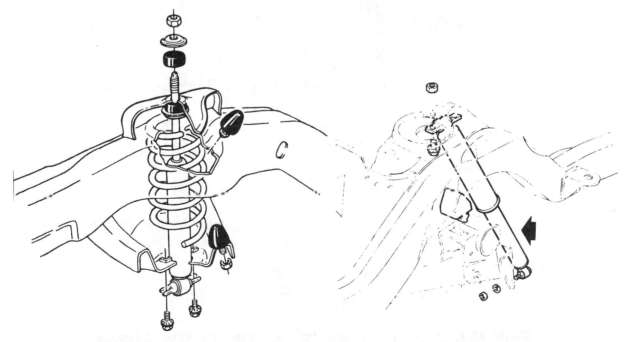

FIGURE 27-5. Typical front shock absorber mounting detail (left) and rear (right). (Courtesy of Ford Motor Co. of Canada Ltd.)

At the same time, the fluid volume displaced by the piston rod passes through the compression head orifice. As the piston velocity increases, the fluid is forced through the compression valve restriction, opening the valve against the valve spring. During extension, as the piston moves slowly toward the inner cylinder head, the fluid between piston and cylinder head is forced through the restriction ports and the recoil orifice. As the piston velocity increases and more fluid is forced through these passages, pressure on the recoil valve increases until the force overcomes the valve spring, passing fluid to the opposite side of the piston. At the same time, the piston rod is wiped clean by the piston rod seal. This wiped fluid is returned to the reservoir. Fluid from the reservoir flows into the inner cylinder below the piston through the replenishing valve. This fluid volume is exactly equal to the piston rod vol-

FIGURE 27-6. Series of spring oscillations occur as above when not controlled by shock absorber. Notice reduced number and severity of oscillations when controlled by shock absorber (below).

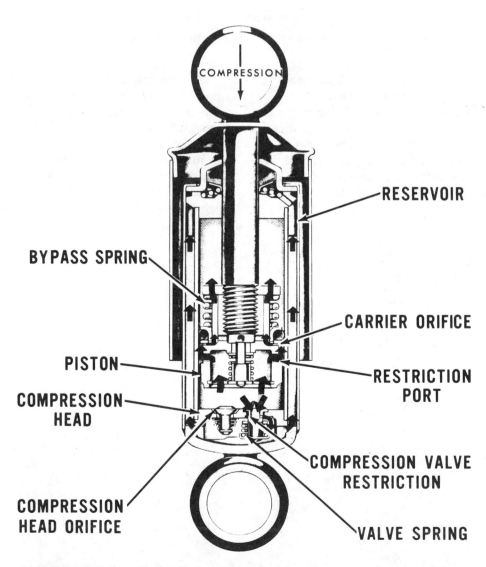

FIGURE 27-7. Shock absorber operation during the compression (jounce) phase. Arrows indicate direction of fluid flow through valves and restrictions. *(Courtesy of Ford Motor Co. of Canada Ltd.)*

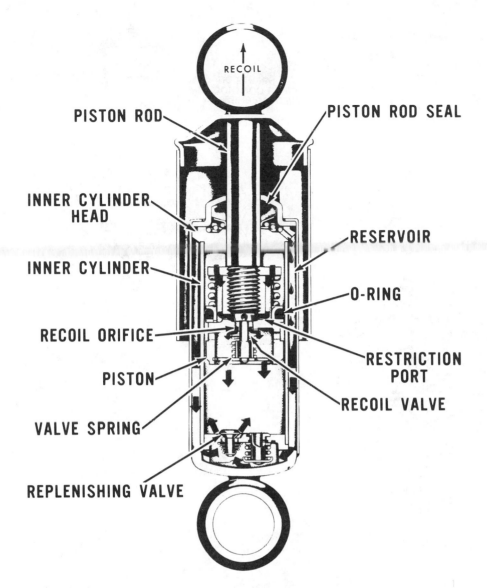

FIGURE 27–8. Shock absorber operation during recoil (rebound) phase. Arrows show direction of fluid flow. *(Courtesy of Ford Motor Co. of Canada Ltd.)*

ume that has passed through the inner cylinder head. During this entire stroke, the O-ring has been sealing the piston and inner cylinder, thus directing the fluid through the recoil control passages.

The recoil resistance of the shock absorber is controlled by the restriction ports, the recoil orifice, and the force of the recoil valve spring. Each of these may be varied independently so as to provide the damping resistance desired.

Shock absorbers are mounted vertically or at an angle. Angle mounting of shock absorbers is used to improve vehicle stability and to dampen accelerating and braking torque.

Air Shock Absorbers and Automatic Load-Leveling System

Air-adjustable rear shock absorbers are available as an option. These units help to maintain ride height when hauling heavy loads or towing trailers. Adjustment is accomplished by increasing or decreasing air pressure within the shock absorbers.

Two air shock systems are used: manually adjusted units that are inflated through air lines that connect the shocks to an air valve mounted at the rear of the automobile, and an automatic load-leveling system. On the automatic system the air shocks are inflated by an on-board compressor. Ad-

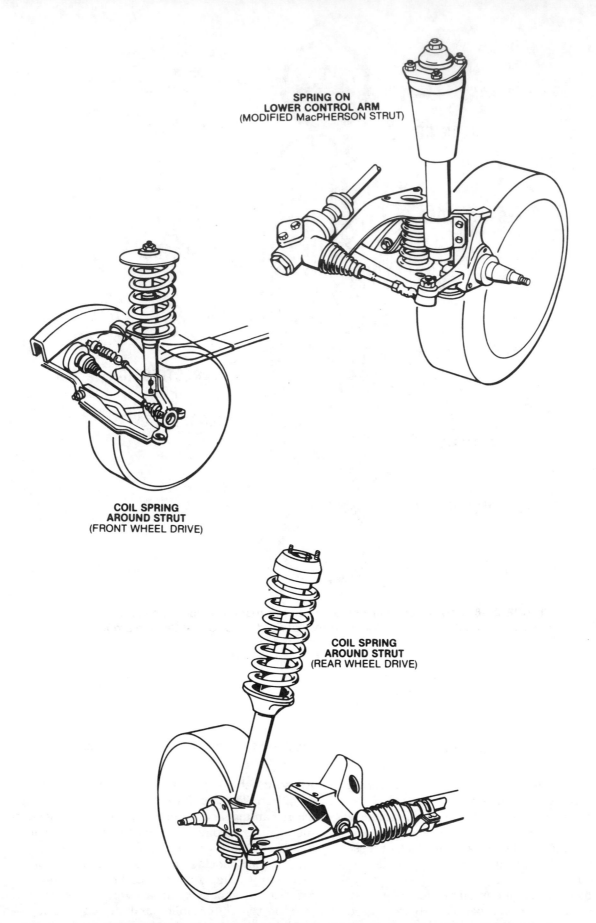

SPRING ON
LOWER CONTROL ARM
(MODIFIED MacPHERSON STRUT)

COIL SPRING
AROUND STRUT
(FRONT WHEEL DRIVE)

COIL SPRING
AROUND STRUT
(REAR WHEEL DRIVE)

FIGURE 27-9. Several designs of strut-type front suspension. *(Courtesy of Moog Automotive Inc.)*

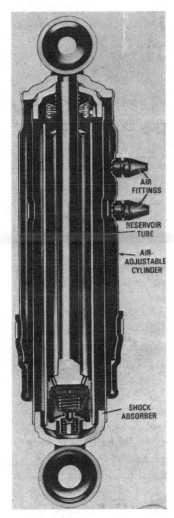

FIGURE 27-10. Air adjustable type of shock absorber used to maintain vehicle suspension height with increased load. *(Courtesy of General Motors Corporation)*

justment is accomplished by the compressor, which is mounted in the engine compartment. The compressor is manually controlled by a three-position switch located in the compressor mounting bracket. In the automatic mode, the compressor is operated by the height sensor and relay. An auxiliary air hose may be included with the system. This hose can be connected to an auxiliary air valve on the compressor and used to inflate tires, air mattresses, and other inflatable items. Maximum shock absorber inflation pressure is usually about 90 pounds per square inch, psi (621 kPa). Maximum allowable pressures should not be exceeded. Should the air boot leak, normal shock absorber action is not affected.

Spring Assist Shock Absorber

Spring assist shock absorbers are available for the front or rear suspension to increase the load-carrying capacity of the springs. These units consist of a conventional shock absorber with a coil spring fitted to

it in a manner that causes the spring to compress when the shock absorber compresses. An upper spring seat is attached to the upper shock tube and a lower spring seat is mounted on the lower shock tube with the spring mounted in between. The spring is under some tension in its normal curb height position.

Gas Pressure Shock Absorber

Gas pressure shock absorbers operate on the same principle as conventional shock absorbers—with hydraulic fluid. The difference is that there is no air in the gas pressure shock, which reduces fluid aeration. Instead of a fluid reservoir, which contains some air in the conventional shock absorber, the gas pressure shock absorber has a floating piston and valve assembly that serves as the bottom of the lower pressure chamber. As the operating piston moves up and down, the difference in fluid volume displacement above and below the operating piston due to piston rod displacement is compensated for by the floating piston and gas chamber. The gas is either freon or nitrogen gas under pressure of 100 psi (689.5 kPa) to 360 psi (2482.2 kPa). Getting rid of fluid aeration results in more consistent shock absorber operation.

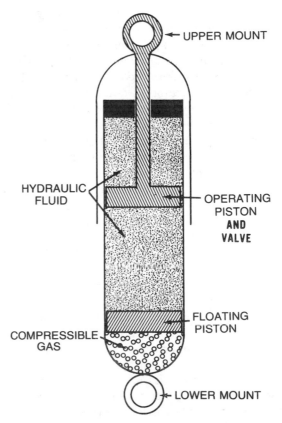

FIGURE 27-11. One type of gas-filled shock absorber with floating piston above gas chamber.

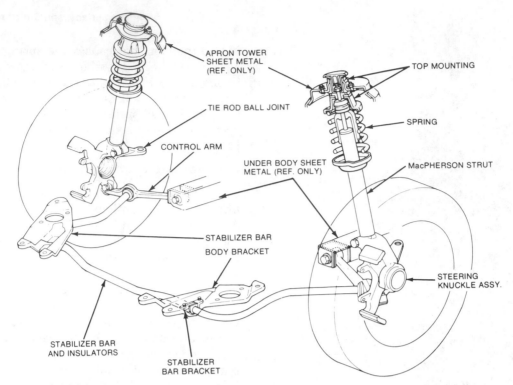

FIGURE 27-12. Stabilizer bar also serves as strut rod on this design. *(Courtesy of Ford Motor Co. of Canada Ltd.)*

Stabilizer

The stabilizer bar (sway bar) reduces sway and stabilizes the front suspension or rear suspension. It is basically a wide U-shaped bar with one end of the U attached to each of the lower control arms through rubber mounts or links. The center section of the U is mounted to the frame at two points with rubber mounts and can pivot at these points. It is made of spring steel, which gives it the elasticity to bend or deflect and then return to its relaxed position.

When the vehicle is stationary with both wheels at the same level, there is no tension on the bar. When one wheel or the other is raised or lowered, the opposite end of the bar held by the other wheel causes the bar to twist, thereby helping to maintain the vehicle in a more level position than it would otherwise be. Thus, vehicle sway or lean in a turn is reduced.

On some vehicles the stabilizer bar is designed to act as the radius rod or strut rod as well as to provide stabilizer action. Since the ends of the stabilizer bar must be attached to the outer end of the lower control arm in any case, a relatively minor design change allows this adaptation. Naturally this reduces production costs and vehicle weight.

Some front-wheel-drive vehicles use a beam-type trailing arm rear suspension system. In this design the two wheels connected to the axle beam by means of the trailing arms can move up or down in a semi-

independent manner. When this happens, the axle beam must twist. This provides the necessary stabilizer action as well as a degree of independent rear wheel movement.

Track Bar

The track bar is a bar usually used with coil springs; it is rubber mounted to the frame at one end and horizontally mounted to the rear axle at the other to prevent any sideways movement between the rear axle and the body.

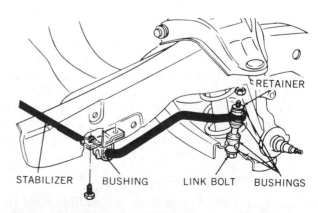

FIGURE 27-13. Stabilizer bar (left half shown) controls sway and stabilizes front suspension; also known as a sway bar. *(Courtesy of General Motors Corporation)*

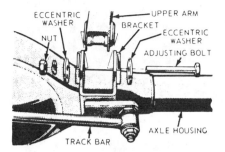

FIGURE 27-14. Track bar. Section shown is attached to rear axle housing, while other end is attached to car frame. The track bar keeps the body and rear axle in alignment.

PART 2 FRONT SUSPENSION

Front-suspension system design must provide good ride and stability characteristics. In addition, the front suspension must make provision for turning the front wheels to both right and left for turning corners. Straight ahead directional control is also provided for primarily by the front-suspension system. Because of weight transfer during braking, the front-suspension system absorbs most of the braking torque. All these factors result in the front-suspension system requiring more frequent servicing than the rear-suspension system.

Several types of front-suspension system designs must be considered. These are (1) long and short arm, (2) single control arm (strut type), (3) monobeam, and (4) twin I-beam. All these suspension systems are used by manufacturers and may be found on front-wheel-drive, rear-wheel-drive, or four-wheel-drive vehicles.

Long- and Short-Arm Suspension

This independent front-suspension system has one upper control arm and one lower control arm at each front wheel. These arms are attached to the frame at the inner end of the arm through bushings that

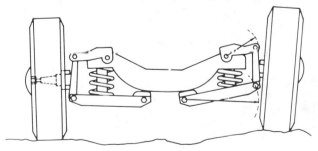

FIGURE 27-15. Coil-spring type independent front suspension. With independent suspension the up and down movement of one wheel does not affect the other wheel and reduces body movement as compared to solid axle suspension.

allow up and down movement of the outer ends of the arms. The outer ends of the arms are attached to a steering knuckle (spindle support) by means of ball joints. The ball joints allow the spindle to move up and down, as well as turn right and left as needed. Up-and-down movement is required to absorb road surface irregularities, whereas turning to right and left is required for vehicle directional control. The wheel-and-tire assembly is mounted to the spindle shaft with ball or roller bearings, a tanged washer, nut, and cotter pin.

The upper control arm is shorter than the lower arm in order to prevent the tire from scrubbing sideways during up-and-down movement of the suspension or body. This unequal arm length causes the top of the wheel to move in and out with suspension movement and prevents the tire from sliding or scrubbing sideways at the bottom, where it is in contact with the road surface. Each wheel can move up and down independently, reducing the amount of body tilt as bumps on the road are encountered.

A strut rod is used with the narrow type of lower control arm to prevent fore-and-aft movement of the outer end of the control arm. The wide A-frame type of lower control arm does not need the strut rod. One end of the strut rod is mounted to the outer end of the lower control arm. The other end of the rod is rubber-mounted to the frame and pivots at this point with control arm movement.

Coil springs or torsion bars are used with independent front suspension.

Ball joints provide the pivot or hinging action for up-and-down movement and turning movement of the front wheels. One ball joint acts as the load carrier on each side whereas the other is the idler. The load-carrying ball joint is the lower one when the spring is mounted on the lower arm and the upper one when the spring is mounted on the upper arm.

When the load tends to pull the stud out of the ball joint, it is known as a *tension* ball joint. When the load tends to push the stud into the ball joint, it is known as a *compression* ball joint.

Ball joint studs are tapered and fit into tapered holes in the steering knuckle. A castellated nut is threaded onto the stud and locked with a cotter pin. Ball joints are provided with either a lubrication fitting or a plug that can be removed to install a fitting.

Some ball joints are provided with a wear indicator; others must be measured for wear to determine if replacement is needed. Some ball joints are riveted to the control arm; others are bolted to or threaded into it; others are a press fit in the arm.

The spring action of leaf springs is provided by

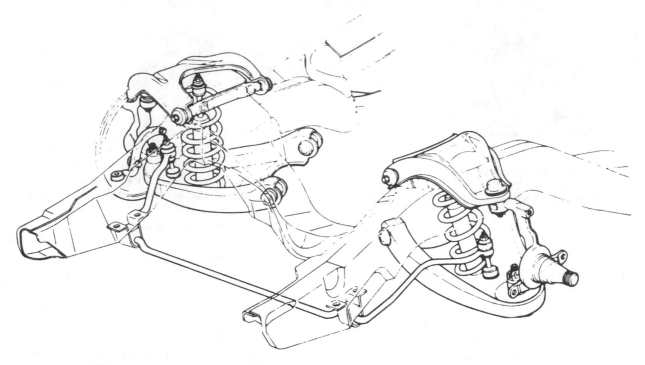

FIGURE 27-16. Coil-spring type of independent front suspension showing spring mounted in seat of lower control arm. Upper end of coil spring is located in a pocket in the frame. *(Courtesy of General Motors Corporation)*

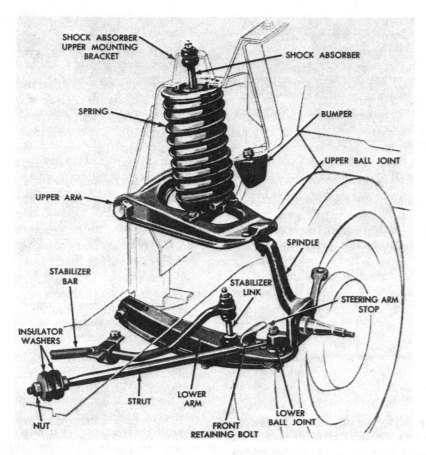

FIGURE 27-17. Coil spring mounted above upper control arm. Top end of spring is mounted inside a reinforced section of the body.

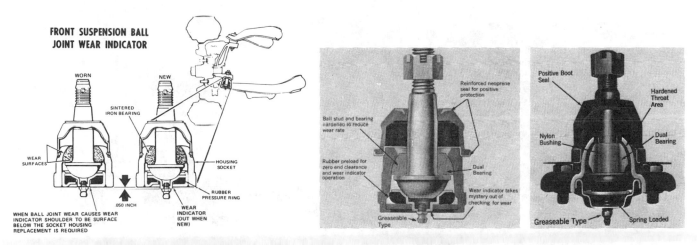

FIGURE 27-18. Wear indicator type of ball joint (left), spring-loaded self-adjusting type (middle), and permanently adjusted type (right).

the ability of the spring to bend and then return to its original position. On torsion bars, spring action is provided by twisting the torsion bar. When a load is applied, the bar is twisted or wound in one direction; when the load is removed, the bar unwinds and returns to its original position. When the load is applied to a coil spring, it is compressed; when the load is removed, the spring extends to its original position.

Two rubber bumpers on each side (one for jounce and one for rebound) prevent metal-to-metal contact when travel limit is reached on front suspension. On rear suspension, one bumper on each side prevents metal-to-metal contact when "bottoming out."

Single Control Arm Suspension (Strut Type)

The single control arm suspension system, also called the McPherson strut suspension system, is based on a triangle design. The strut shaft itself is a structural member that does away with the upper control arm and bushings and the upper ball joint required on the long- and short-arm suspension. Since the strut shaft is also the shock absorber shaft, it receives a tremendous amount of vertical and horizontal force due to the accelerating and braking torque forces.

Two types of strut suspensions are used. One type has the spring surrounding the strut whereas the other has the spring mounted on the control arm. The former is used on both front- and rear-wheel-drive vehicles whereas the latter is used only on rear-wheel-drive vehicles. When the strut has the spring mounted around the strut assembly, the shock absorber, spindle, and spring are sometimes a combined unit located at the top by the upper mount assembly and at the bottom by the ball joint and lower control arm. The ball joint on this system is a follower ball joint. When the spring is mounted on

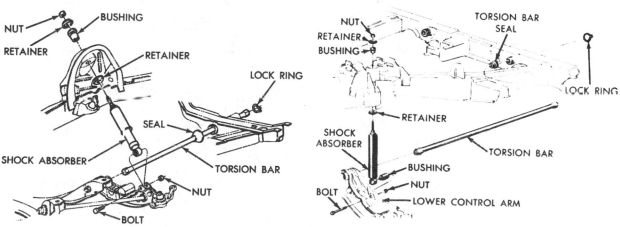

FIGURE 27-19. Torsion bar suspension system. Front torsion bar is mounted in hex socket at inner end of lower control arm. Rear of torsion bar is mounted in hex socket in frame crossmember.

603

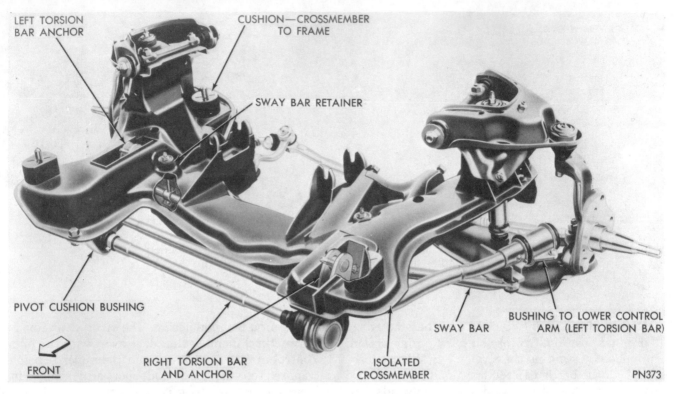

FIGURE 27-20. Transverse-mounted torsion bar front suspension. *(Courtesy of Chrysler Corporation)*

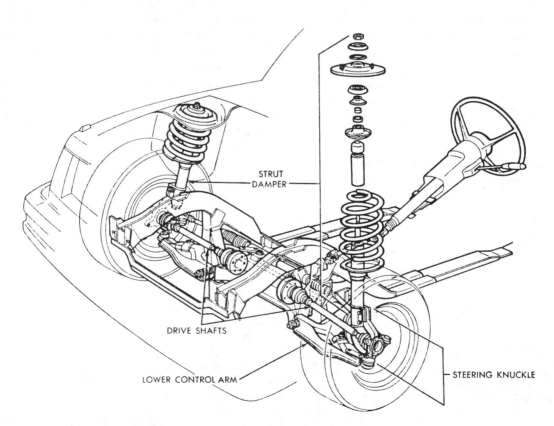

FIGURE 27-21(A). Strut type of suspension system. This sytem has only one control arm and is used on many compact cars. *(Courtesy of Chrysler Corporation)*

BEARING AND SEAL ASSY.
MUST BE SEATED INTO
THE SPRING SEAT

1 DUST CAP
18A179

2 NUT AND WASHER
N802050

3 UPPER MOUNT
18183

4 THRUST PLATE
3K048

5 BEARING AND SEAL
3B455

6 SPRING SEAT
5A324

7 NUT
N801310-S100 (2)

8 SPRING INSULATOR 5415

9 SPRING 5310

10 JOUNCE BUMPER, FRONT
18A085

11 SHOCK ABSORBER STRUT
18045

F3072-B

FIGURE 27-21(B).

the control arm, the ball joint is a load carrier. The lower arm may be of forged or stamped steel construction. The lower arm, if it is not an A-frame design, is located either by a strut rod (compression rod) or the stabilizer bar, which can function as a combined strut rod and stabilizer bar.

The shock absorber is built into the strut outer housing. The coil spring is held in place by a lower seat welded to the strut casing and an upper seat bolted to the shock absorber piston rod. The upper mount bolts to the vehicle body and is the load-carrying member through the use of a bearing or rubber bushings in most designs. In this case the coil spring and shock absorber turn right or left as the steering wheel is turned. Another design has the load-carrying bearing below the coil spring. In this case the spring does not turn when the steering wheel is turned.

Monobeam Suspension

The monobeam suspension is a single I-beam solid axle suspension used on trucks. It does not provide the riding comfort of independent suspension. The spindle is attached to the I-beam axle by means of a king pin (spindle bolt) and bushings. This provides for turning of the front wheels to right and left. The

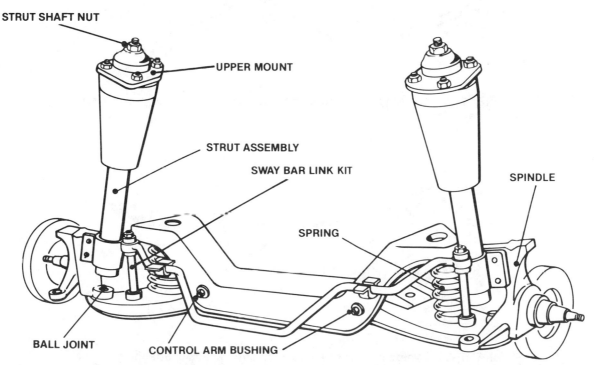

FIGURE 27-22. Modified strut front-suspension system used on rear-wheel-drive vehicle. *(Courtesy of Moog Automotive Inc.)*

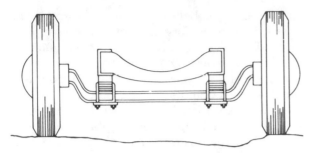

FIGURE 27-23. Solid axle (I-beam) front suspension with multiple-leaf springs. On this type of suspension, when one wheel rides on top of a bump, the entire vehicle is tilted much more than on independent suspension systems.

king pin is held in the axle by means of a lock bolt or pin. Two designs are used to attach the spindle to the axle: the Elliot and the reverse Elliot designs. The Elliot design has the yoke on the axle, whereas the reverse Elliot has the yoke on the spindle. The reverse Elliot is easier to service when replacing king pins and bearings.

Either leaf springs or coil springs are used with this axle. In the leaf spring design, the spring assemblies maintain fore-and-aft positioning of the wheels and transfer braking torque. The coil spring design requires radius arms or rods to position the wheels fore and aft and to transfer braking torque.

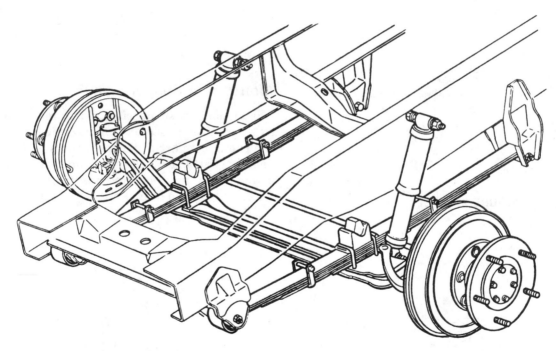

FIGURE 27-24. Truck-type of solid axle front suspension. *(Courtesy of General Motors Corporation)*

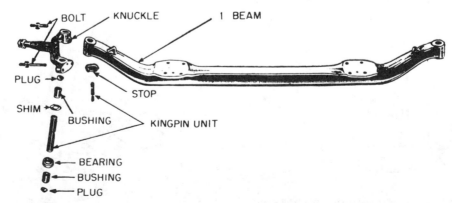

FIGURE 27-25. Exploded view of spindle (steering knuckle) attaching parts. When the yoke is on the spindle, as shown here, it is known as the Reverse Elliot type of axle. When the yoke is on the axle, it is called an Elliot type.

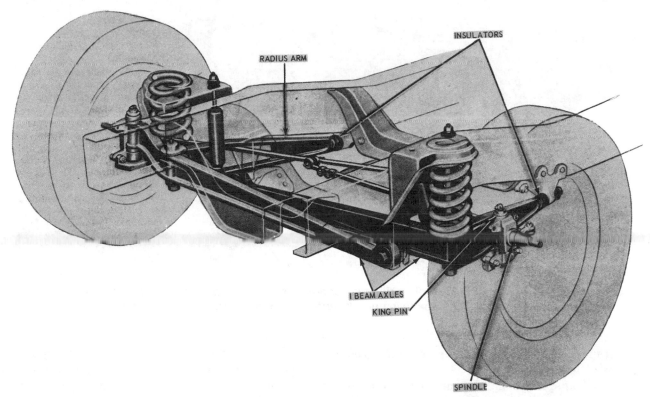

FIGURE 27-26. Twin I-beam type of front suspension as used on some Ford trucks. (*Courtesy of Ford Motor Co. of Canada Ltd.*)

Twin I-Beam Suspension

Twin I-beam suspension is a combination of the solid axle and fully independent suspension systems. Two I-beams are used with coil springs. Radius rods prevent fore-and-aft movement. On four-wheel-drive vehicles the I-beams are replaced by stamped steel axle housings, which act the same as twin I-beam suspension. One of the housings contains the differential. Either coil springs or leaf springs are used. When coil springs are used, radius rods or arms control fore-and-aft positioning of the wheels and transfer driving and braking torque. In the leaf spring design, the springs serve this function.

PART 3   REAR SUSPENSION

A variety of rear-suspension system designs are being used for both driving and nondriving rear axles. This includes both nonindependent and independent suspension types.

The driving axle types must provide the means for transmitting both driving and braking torque. The nondriving rear suspension must provide the means for braking torque only. All rear-suspension systems must provide for ride quality and vehicle stability.

Nonindependent Driving Rear Suspension

Nonindependent rear-suspension types with rear-wheel drive include the coil spring and control arm type, the coil spring, trailing arm and torque arm type, and the leaf spring type.

The coil spring and control arm type transmits driving and braking torque through three or four control arms depending on design. The control arms also control fore and aft positioning of the rear axle and wheels and in some cases lateral or side to side position of the rear axle and wheels in relation to the vehicle body. This requires two upper and two lower control arms. The lower control arms are positioned at ninety degrees to the rear axle and the upper arms at forty-five degrees to the rear axle. An eccentric mount at the front of the upper control arms provides the means for adjusting the drive shaft rear universal joint operating angle. Rubber bushings at each end of the control arms provide the necessary pivoting action and also help to insulate the vehicle body from road shock and noise. A track bar is used on some designs to maintain lateral alignment of the rear axle with the vehicle body. A stabilizer bar is also used on some models.

A variation of this design uses two lower trailing control arms and one long upper torque arm. The torque arm is mounted at the front to the rear of

607

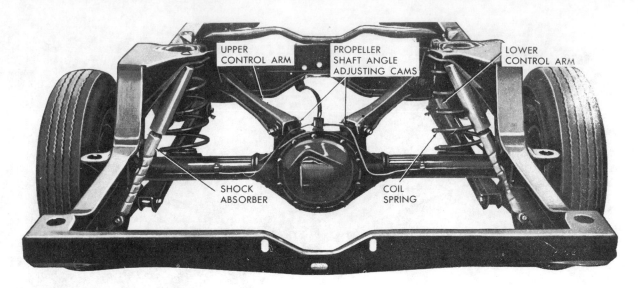

FIGURE 27-27. Coil-spring type of rear suspension. Two angled upper control arms control side movement. *(Courtesy of General Motors Corporation)*

the transmission extension housing, and at the rear to the differential housing.

The leaf spring nonindependent suspension system uses two single tapered plate or multi-leaf springs. The springs transmit driving and braking torque and provide the means for fore-and-aft as well as lateral positioning of the rear axle.

Independent Driving Rear Suspension

Several types of rear wheel drive independent suspension systems are used by different vehicle manufacturers. All of these have the differential mounted on a heavy frame crossmember. This reduces the amount of unsprung weight.

One design uses a trailing A frame type of arm and coil spring arrangement. The A frame is wide at the front where it is mounted to a heavy crossmember. This provides the means for maintaining both fore-and-aft and lateral positioning of the drive wheels. Rubber bushings at the front mount provide the pivoting action and help isolate the vehicle from road noise and shock. The A frame provides the lower seat for the coil spring. The upper seat is in a reinforced section of the body.

Another design uses a narrow trailing arm and a transverse multiple-leaf spring. The trailing arms control the fore-and-aft position of the wheels while two tie rods maintain lateral wheel position. Driving and braking torque are transmitted through the trailing arms. The control arms are mounted by means of rubber bushings at the front to provide

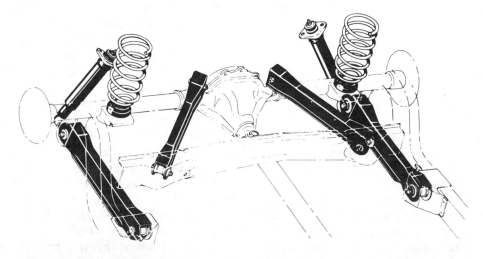

FIGURE 27-28. Location and mounting of control arms, shock absorbers, and springs in rear suspension.

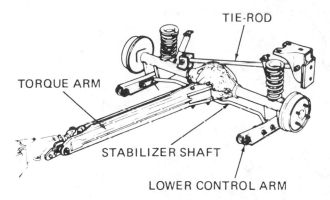

FIGURE 27–29. Solid-axle, coil-spring rear suspension with a long torque arm as used on rear-wheel-drive vehicle. *(Courtesy of General Motors Corporation)*

pivoting action and noise isolation. The tie rods are mounted at both ends by means of rubber bushings.

A variation of the trailing arm design uses transverse torsion bar springs. The trailing arm in this case is actually a spring plate. The front end of the spring plate arm is attached to cne end of a transverse torsion bar. The other end of the arm is attached to the wheel assembly. Driving and braking torque is transmitted through the arms.

A strut type of independent rear-suspension rear-wheel-drive system uses tranversely mounted A-frames and a McPherson strut type of coil spring and shock absorber unit. Driving and braking torque is transmitted through the A-frames and struts. Rubber bushings at all mounting points provide pivoting action and noise isolation.

Nonindependent Nondriving Rear Suspension

This type of rear suspension used on some front-wheel-drive cars uses a solid axle between the two wheels, attached to the body by means of two trailing arms. The trailing arms maintain fore-and-aft

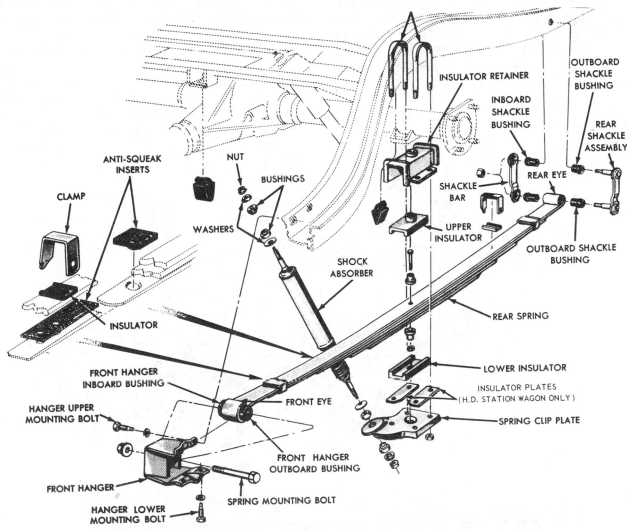

FIGURE 27–30. Attaching parts of rear suspension multiple-leaf spring. Note rubber bushings at front and rear of spring. *(Courtesy of Chrysler Corporation)*

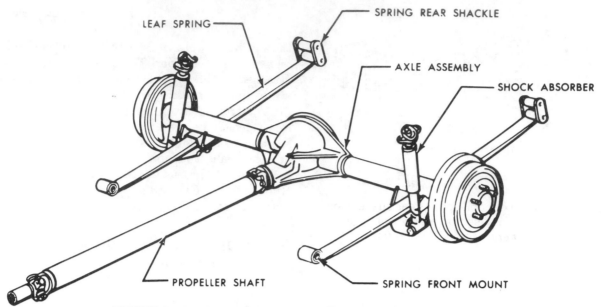

FIGURE 27-31. Single-leaf tapered plate spring rear suspension.

positioning of the rear axle while a track bar keeps the axle in lateral alignment with the vehicle body. Rubber bushings at the front of the trailing arms and at each end of the track bar provide the pivoting action and noise isolation. Braking torque is transmitted through the trailing arms. A stabilizer bar is used to improve vehicle stability.

Independent Nondriving Rear Suspension

This system uses two transverse arms, coil springs, strut-shock absorbers, and tie rods. The two arms control the lateral positioning of the wheels and provide the pivoting action. The shock absorber-strut assemblies are attached at the lower end to the spindle, which is also attached to the outer end of the transverse arm. The upper end of the shock-strut is attached to a reinforced section in the body. Tie rods attached at the rear to the spindle and at the front to the torque box on the body maintain fore-and-aft wheel positioning. Braking torque is transmitted through the struts and tie rods. Rubber bushings at all mounting points provide the pivoting action and noise insulation.

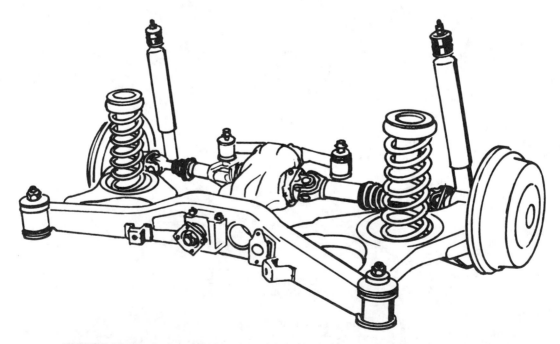

FIGURE 27-32. Independent trailing A-frame coil-spring rear suspension used on some rear-wheel-drive vehicles. Differential on this design is sprung weight. *(Courtesy of Moog Automotive Inc.)*

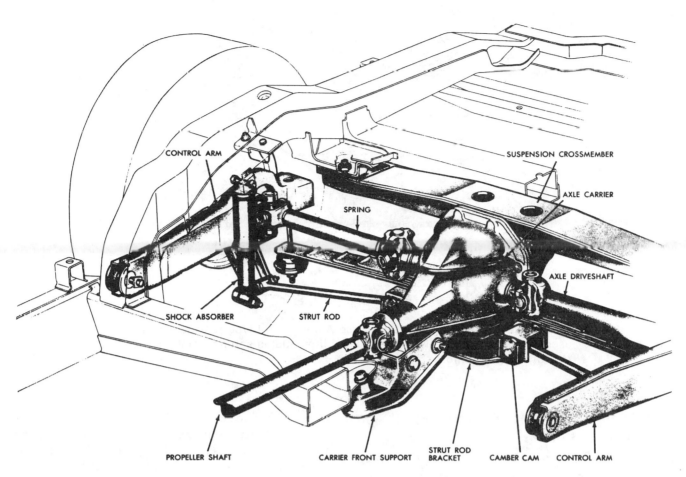

CONTROL ARM

SUSPENSION CROSSMEMBER

AXLE CARRIER

SPRING

AXLE DRIVESHAFT

SHOCK ABSORBER

STRUT ROD

PROPELLER SHAFT

CARRIER FRONT SUPPORT

STRUT ROD BRACKET

CAMBER CAM

CONTROL ARM

FIGURE 27-33. Independent rear suspension with multileaf transverse-mounted spring. *(Courtesy of General Motors Corporation)*

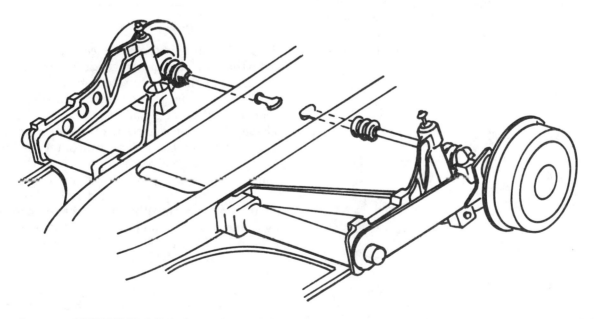

FIGURE 27-34. Independent trailing arm transverse torsion bar rear suspension used on some rear- wheel-drive vehicles. *(Courtesy of Moog Automotive Inc.)*

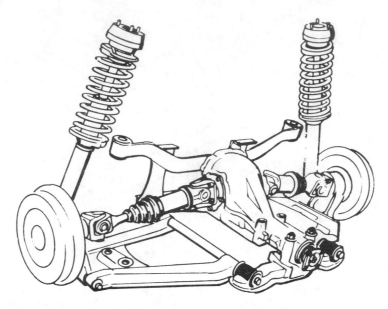

FIGURE 27-35. Independent transverse A-frame strut-type rear suspension used on some rear-wheel-drive vehicles. Differential is sprung weight. *(Courtesy of Moog Automotive Inc.)*

Semi-Independent Nondriving Rear Suspension

Many front-wheel-drive cars use this type of rear suspension. Two trailing arms attached at the front to an axle beam are used in this system. The arms and axle assembly are attached to the vehicle by mounting brackets and rubber bushings. Up-and-down movement of either wheel imparts a twisting action to the axle beam. This provides a stabilizer effect as well as allowing semi-independent wheel movement. A coil spring and shock absorber-strut assembly are attached at the bottom to the rear of the trailing arm and at the top of a reinforced sec-

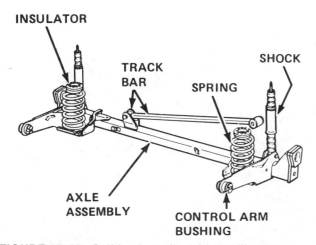

FIGURE 27-36. Solid-axle, coil-spring trailing arm suspension used on some front-wheel-drive vehicles. *(Courtesy of General Motors Corporation)*

tion of the body. Braking torque is transmitted through the trailing arms and struts. Pivoting action and noise isolation are provided by means of rubber bushings at all affected mounting points. Fore-and-aft and lateral positioning of the wheels is maintained by the trailing arms and the struts.

PART 4   SUSPENSION–RELATED CHARACTERISTICS

Scrub Radius

The scrub radius is the distance between the point where the projected steering axis pivot line contacts the road and the effective contact point of the tire on the road. It is determined by the steering axis inclination (SAI) angle and the camber angle of the vehicle. If the contact point of the steering axis pivot line is inside the actual tire contact point, it is referred to as a positive scrub radius. If the contact point of the steering axis pivot line is outside the actual tire contact point, it is referred to as negative scrub radius. On the other hand, if the steering axis pivot line contact point and the actual tire contact point were to intersect at the road surface, this would be zero scrub radius. This is neither desirable nor practical.

Both the positive and the negative scrub radius designs provide a pivot center, which allows the tire to roll around the pivot line contact point during steering. This reduces the amount of tire squirm and distortion during steering as compared to a zero

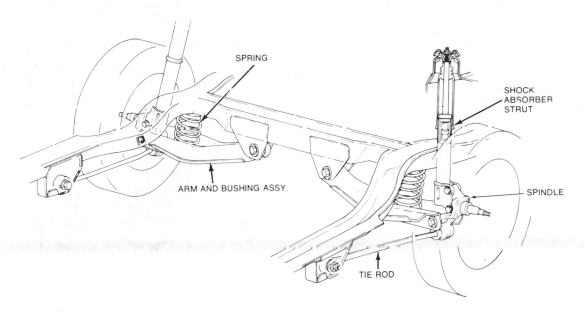

FIGURE 27–37. Independent transverse-arm, coil-spring rear suspension used on some front-wheel-drive vehicles. *(Courtesy of Ford Motor Co. of Canada Ltd.)*

scrub radius. An excessive amount of scrub radius, however, will increase steering effort and the effects of road shock to the steering and suspension systems. A good example of increased positive scrub radius is the use of offset wheels to accommodate wider-than-standard tires.

The effect of a positive scrub radius is to tend to turn the wheel outward (toe out) while driving and during braking on non-driving front wheels. On front-wheel-drive vehicles the effect is to tend to turn the wheel inward during driving and outward during braking. The effect of a negative scrub ra-

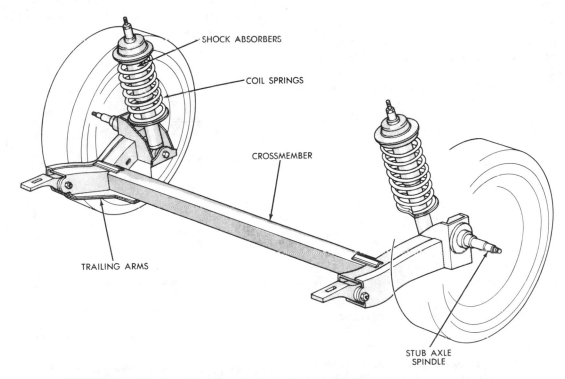

FIGURE 27–38. Semi-independent trailing-arm, strut-type rear suspension used on some front-wheel-drive vehicles. Axle crossmember twists to provide a measure of independent rear wheel action and also provides stabilizer bar benefits. *(Courtesy of Chrysler Corporation)*

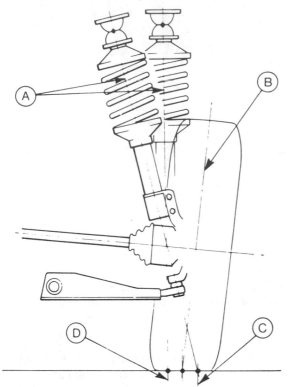

A — Suspension pivot center line
B — Center of tire
C — Pivot center outside contact point
(negative scrub radius geometry)
D — Pivot center inside contact point
(positive scrub radius geometry)

FIGURE 27-39. Suspension design determines whether a vehicle will have a negative or a positive scrub radius, as shown here. The scrub radius is the product of the steering axis inclination angle A and the wheel center line B where they intersect the road surface. A negative scrub radius is necessary on a front-wheel-drive vehicle with a diagonally split brake hydraulic system. *(Courtesy of Ford Motor Co. of Canada Ltd.)*

dius is to tend to turn the wheel inward during braking. This effect is used to offset the brake imbalance created by failure of one half of a diagonally split hydraulic system. A negative scrub radius also tends to turn the wheel outward during torque application (driving) on front-wheel-drive vehicles.

The vehicle manufacturer chooses a scrub radius design that provides the best possible handling characteristics, ride quality, and life expectancy of tires and steering and suspension system components in concert with other design factors of the vehicle. This combination of design objectives is, at best, a compromise among the various factors involved. Scrub radius is affected by suspension system curb height, curb weight, camber setting, steering axis inclination, wheel and tire diameter, and wheel mounting surface to rim offset.

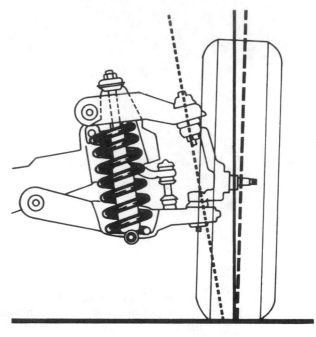

FIGURE 27-40. Positive scrub radius in long- and short-arm coil-spring front suspension used on rear-wheel-drive vehicle with a front-rear split brake hydraulic system. *(Courtesy of Moog Automotive Inc.)*

Instant Center

The angle of the upper and lower control arms in the at-rest position of the vehicle (curb height and weight) determines the instant center of the vehicle suspension design. When the inner pivot points of

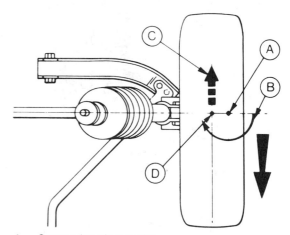

A — Suspension pivot center
B — Turning moment
C — Force being applied to tire
D — Effective contact point of tire
Broad tapered arrow shows direction of motion of vehicle

FIGURE 27-41. Effect of negative scrub radius during braking on vehicle with diagonally split brake hydraulic system. Force of friction at road surface (C) offsets pull during braking when one half of hydraulic system has failed. *(Courtesy of Ford Motor Co. of Canada Ltd.)*

the upper and lower control arms are closer together than the outer pivots (ball joints), the instant center is located inboard of the car. When the outer pivots are closer together than the inner pivots, the instant center is located outside the car. Some long- and short-arm suspension systems are the former design, whereas the latter design is used on other models.

The proportionate length and angle of the arms determine the amount and type of camber change and the amount of side slip that will occur during suspension jounce and rebound. When the vehicle is in a turn, the outer wheel is put into jounce position and the inner wheel into rebound position due to the transfer of weight caused by centrifugal forces (body roll).

On the design with the instant center outside the vehicle, the outer wheel will have positive camber and the inner wheel will have negative camber. It can be argued that this will reduce tire-to-road contact and therefore reduce good handling in a turn.

On the design with the instant center inside the vehicle, the tendency is to produce negative camber on the outer wheel and positive camber on the inner wheel in a turn. This tends to maintain good tire-to-road contact and therefore good vehicle control.

The instant center on the McPherson strut suspension tends to produce negative camber on the outer wheel and positive camber on the inner wheel when the vehicle is in a turn. In this type of suspension, the instant center is determined by the length and angle of the lower control arm and the length and angle of the strut assembly.

The single solid I-beam axle produces little camber change and relatively little side slip during jounce and rebound. This is due to the fact that there is a large radius arc produced by the up-and-down movement of the wheel. Twin I-beam axles have a somewhat increased side slip and camber change due to the reduced radius of the arc of wheel travel caused by the pivot point being closer to the wheel.

Side Slip

The amount of side slip or scuff of the tire on the road surface is a result of the camber change as the vehicle suspension moves during jounce and rebound. Side slip is a tire wear factor.

The design objective is a compromise between the effects of more and the effects of less side slip. Zero side slip would be best if tire wear were the only consideration. However, a limited amount of side slip helps dampen suspension action due to road surface irregularities.

Suspension design determines the amount of tire scuff or side slip. This is dependent on the relative length and angle of the control arms on long- and short-arm suspension and on the relative length and angle of the control arm and strut on strut-type suspension.

Wheelbase

The wheelbase of a vehicle is the distance between the exact rotating center of the front wheel and the exact center of the rear wheel (on the same side of the vehicle and with the wheels in a straight ahead position). The wheelbase of a vehicle has an effect on its ride quality and on its turning radius.

Generally speaking, a longer wheelbase makes for a better riding car—all other factors being equal. This is because the suspension and steering systems have more time to recover from the effects of bumps or holes in the road from the time the front wheels

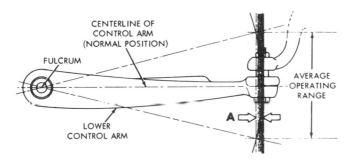

"SIDE-SLIP"—CONTROL ARM IN NORMAL POSITION

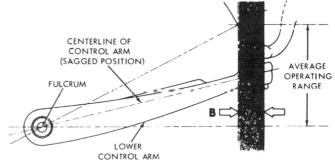

"SIDE-SLIP"—CONTROL ARM IN ABNORMAL POSITION DUE TO SAGGED COIL SPRING

FIGURE 27-42. Normal amount of tire side slip during suspension action with proper suspension height of vehicle shown at A on left. Excessive side slip at B on right as a result of sagged springs. (Courtesy of Moog Automotive Inc.)

have passed over the bump until the rear wheels pass over the same bump.

In general, the longer the wheelbase, the longer the turning radius required to turn the vehicle.

The wheelbase of a vehicle may not be exactly the same from one side of the vehicle to the other because of production tolerances and because of differences in front-wheel caster settings. A maximum difference of about 1/4 inch (6.35 millimeters) or as specified by the manufacturer is allowable.

Damage to the suspension system at the front or the rear, either through wear or through distortion, can change the wheelbase of the vehicle. Steering and handling will therefore be adversely affected. The wheelbase of the vehicle is determined by the manufacturer.

Track Width

The track width of a vehicle is the distance measured between the exact center of a tire where it contacts the road and the same point of the opposite tire on the other side of the vehicle. The track width of the front wheels and the rear wheels may be the same on some vehicles but may be different at the front as compared with the rear on others. Damage to suspension components will affect track width and vehicle handling.

Understeer and Oversteer

Understeer and *oversteer* are terms used to describe the difference between the direction in which the front wheels are pointed and the actual direction of vehicle movement during a turn.

Understeer is the condition whereby the vehicle is able to turn less than indicated by the turning position of the front wheels. Oversteer is the condition whereby a vehicle makes a sharper turn than indicated by the turning position of the front wheels.

Standard production automobiles are designed to provide some understeer. Since understeer results in slower vehicle response in a turn, it provides a degree of safety for the average driver.

Factors affecting the degree of steering in a vehicle are vehicle design, vehicle speed, body roll, and the ability of the tires to adhere to the road surface. The automotive technician has the most responsibility for this last factor.

Factors affecting the tire's ability to adhere to the road surface and to balanced adhesion among all four tires are correct size and type of tire on all four wheels; condition of tires on all four wheels; proper inflation pressures in all tires; and condition of suspension system including curb height and weight. However, the factor of vehicle speed is the respon-

sibility of the driver, who should take into consideration the condition of the road surface, traffic conditions, and legal speed limits to determine proper vehicle speed.

PART 5 SUSPENSION SYSTEM DIAGNOSIS AND SERVICE

General Precautions

Overhauling suspension systems should not be attempted without being fully aware of all the potential hazards involved. Injury to yourself and others can result if proper procedures and safety measures are not followed. Some of these factors are as follows.

- The vehicle must be properly supported at all times.
- Use only proper tools and supports in good condition, and use them as recommended.
- Do not disassemble any suspension parts without proper consideration of the consequences; a loaded spring packs a powerful punch.
- Always refer to the manufacturer's manual for proper procedures; then follow them.
- Never use suspension parts that have been heated, damaged, bent, or straightened.
- Avoid getting grease, solvent, brake fluid, or dirty fingerprints on brake discs, pads, linings, and drums.
- Always tighten all fasteners to specified torque.
- Always install new cotter pins properly locked wherever needed.

Suspension Height

The condition of the vehicle's suspension system, especially the springs, can be determined to some extent by measuring suspension height. This should be done in accordance with manufacturer's procedures and specifications.

In general, the procedure is as follows.

- Vehicle at curb weight (no passengers, no cargo, full tank of fuel, and spare tire in place)
- Vehicle on level floor
- Tire pressures corrected
- Tires of correct size and type
- Accumulations of mud or ice removed
- Measure at points specified by the manufacturer's manual

DIAGNOSTIC CHART: FRONT SUSPENSION

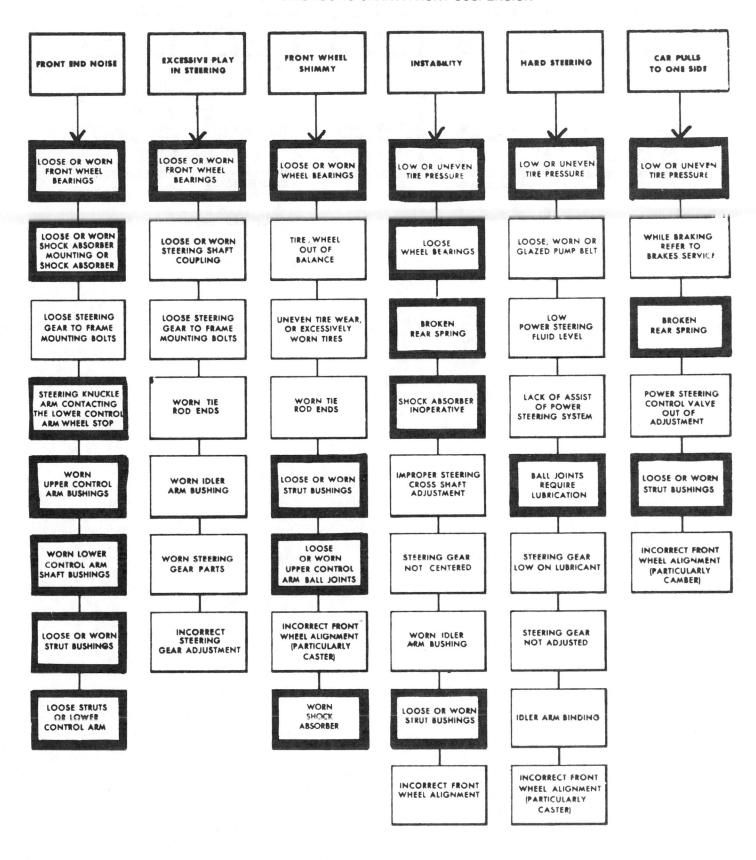

FRONT END NOISE
→ LOOSE OR WORN FRONT WHEEL BEARINGS → LOOSE OR WORN SHOCK ABSORBER MOUNTING OR SHOCK ABSORBER → LOOSE STEERING GEAR TO FRAME MOUNTING BOLTS → STEERING KNUCKLE ARM CONTACTING THE LOWER CONTROL ARM WHEEL STOP → WORN UPPER CONTROL ARM BUSHINGS → WORN LOWER CONTROL ARM SHAFT BUSHINGS → LOOSE OR WORN STRUT BUSHINGS → LOOSE STRUTS OR LOWER CONTROL ARM

EXCESSIVE PLAY IN STEERING
→ LOOSE OR WORN FRONT WHEEL BEARINGS → LOOSE OR WORN STEERING SHAFT COUPLING → LOOSE STEERING GEAR TO FRAME MOUNTING BOLTS → WORN TIE ROD ENDS → WORN IDLER ARM BUSHING → WORN STEERING GEAR PARTS → INCORRECT STEERING GEAR ADJUSTMENT

FRONT WHEEL SHIMMY
→ LOOSE OR WORN WHEEL BEARINGS → TIRE, WHEEL OUT OF BALANCE → UNEVEN TIRE WEAR, OR EXCESSIVELY WORN TIRES → WORN TIE ROD ENDS → LOOSE OR WORN STRUT BUSHINGS → LOOSE OR WORN UPPER CONTROL ARM BALL JOINTS → INCORRECT FRONT WHEEL ALIGNMENT (PARTICULARLY CASTER) → WORN SHOCK ABSORBER

INSTABILITY
→ LOW OR UNEVEN TIRE PRESSURE → LOOSE WHEEL BEARINGS → BROKEN REAR SPRING → SHOCK ABSORBER INOPERATIVE → IMPROPER STEERING CROSS SHAFT ADJUSTMENT → STEERING GEAR NOT CENTERED → WORN IDLER ARM BUSHING → LOOSE OR WORN STRUT BUSHINGS → INCORRECT FRONT WHEEL ALIGNMENT

HARD STEERING
→ LOW OR UNEVEN TIRE PRESSURE → LOOSE, WORN OR GLAZED PUMP BELT → LOW POWER STEERING FLUID LEVEL → LACK OF ASSIST OF POWER STEERING SYSTEM → BALL JOINTS REQUIRE LUBRICATION → STEERING GEAR LOW ON LUBRICANT → STEERING GEAR NOT ADJUSTED → IDLER ARM BINDING → INCORRECT FRONT WHEEL ALIGNMENT (PARTICULARLY CASTER)

CAR PULLS TO ONE SIDE
→ LOW OR UNEVEN TIRE PRESSURE → WHILE BRAKING REFER TO BRAKES SERVICE → BROKEN REAR SPRING → POWER STEERING CONTROL VALVE OUT OF ADJUSTMENT → LOOSE OR WORN STRUT BUSHINGS → INCORRECT FRONT WHEEL ALIGNMENT (PARTICULARLY CAMBER)

DIAGNOSTIC CHART: REAR SUSPENSION

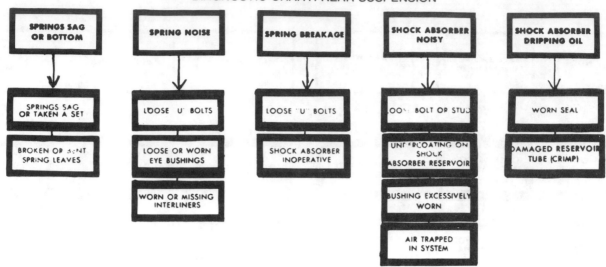

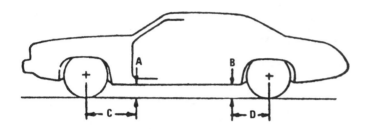

"A" Dim. — Ground to rocker panel at front.
"B" Dim. — Ground to rocker panel at rear.
"C" Dim. — Front wheel centerline to "A".
"D" Dim. — Rear wheel centerline to "B".

FIGURE 27-43. Typical body suspension height measuring points. Follow shop manual procedures for specific points since these may vary from one make or model to another. *(Courtesy of Moog Automotive Inc.)*

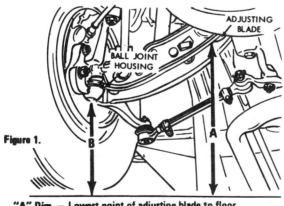

"A" Dim. — Lowest point of adjusting blade to floor.
"B" Dim. — Lowest point to steering knuckle arm
(at centerline) to floor.
"C" Dim. — Top of "Jacking Slot" in rear bumper to ground.

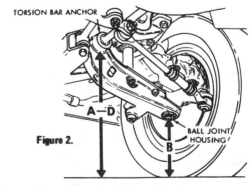

"A" Dim. — Bottom of front torsion bar anchor
at control arm, to floor.
"B" Dim. — Lowest point on ball joint housing to floor.
"C" Dim. — Top of "Jacking Slot" in rear bumper to ground.
"D" Dim. — Bottom of lower control arm inner pivot bushing to floor.

FIGURE 27-44. Typical height measuring points for torsion bar suspension used on some Chrysler vehicles. Refer to shop manual for specifications and procedures. *(Courtesy of Moog Automotive Inc.)*

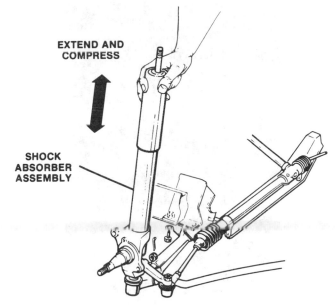

FIGURE 27–45. Checking shock absorber operation on strut-type suspension. *(Courtesy of Ford Motor Co. of Canada Ltd.)*

• Compare measurements to the manufacturer's specifications

• Repair or replace springs in axle pairs only as needed

• Replace suspension parts as needed and as recommended by the manufacturer

Shock Absorbers

A quick check of shock absorber action can be made by jouncing the vehicle as hard as possible at each corner. When the jouncing is stopped, the vehicle should come to rest almost immediately. If not, shock absorbers can be suspected. Visually inspect

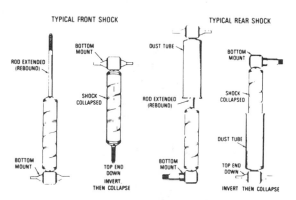

FIGURE 27–46. Air should be bled from new shock absorbers before installation. With shock in upright position (left, above), extend shock fully, then invert shock and collapse completely. Repeat this procedure until all air is bled from the shock. This can be felt when resistance is constant throughout shock piston travel. *(Courtesy of General Motors Corporation)*

the shock absorbers for proper mounting, physical damage, and leakage. A slight amount of fluid seepage is normal. Replace damaged or badly leaking shock absorbers in axle pairs. If mounting is faulty or bushings are deteriorated, replace bushings and mount properly. New shock absorbers should be properly bled to remove all air before installation. To prevent preloading of rubber bushings, tighten the shock absorber mounting with vehicle weight on springs.

Air Shock Leak Test

Inflate the shock absorbers to 90 psi (621 kPa) and apply a solution of soapy water to the fittings, lines, and shock absorbers and check for leaks. Leaks will cause the soapy water solution to form bubbles in or near the area of leakage. If a leak is detected, repair or replace the defective parts as necessary.

Ball Joints

Ball joint wear should be checked with the vehicle properly supported and ball joints unloaded. Position the dial indicator as recommended by vehicle manufacturer's manual. Grasp the wheel firmly with

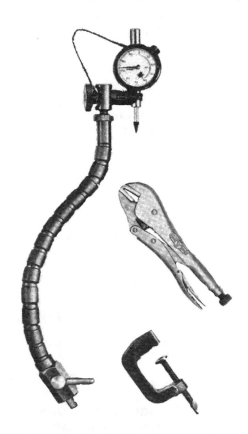

FIGURE 27–47. Special dial indicator with flexible mounting arm used to check ball joint wear. *(Courtesy of Moog Automotive Inc.)*

FIGURE 27-48. Axial check of ball joint. For an axial check, first position the dial indicator C-clamp on the control arm, then clean off the flat on the spindle next to the ball joint stud nut. Position the dial indicator on the spindle flat and depress the plunger approximately .250 of an inch. Turn lever to tighten indicator in place. Pry bar between floor and tire and record reading. *(Courtesy of Moog Automotive Inc.)*

one hand at the top of the wheel and the other at the bottom. Push in at the top and pull out at the bottom. Alternate this in-and-out movement vigorously and observe total dial indicator needle movement. Compare the reading with the manufacturer's specifications and replace the ball joint if specifi-

FIGURE 27-49. Radial check of ball joints. For radial check, attach dial indicator to the control arm of the ball joint being checked. Position and adjust plunger of dial indicator against edge of wheel rim nearest to ball joint being checked. Set dial ring to zero marking. Move the wheel in and out and note the amount of ball joint radial looseness registered on the dial. *(Courtesy of Moog Automotive Inc.)*

cations are exceeded. This check is for lateral (radial) movement only.

To check vertical movement, use a bar under the wheel assembly and pry upward; then release. With the dial indicator properly positioned, repeat this movement and observe total dial indicator needle movement. Compare the reading with the manufacturer's specifications and replace the ball joint if specifications are exceeded. Follow the manufactur-

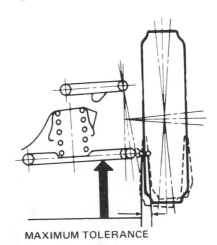
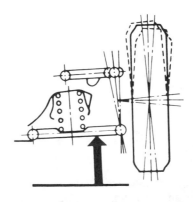

MAXIMUM TOLERANCE

FIGURE 27-50. Checking ball joint wear on suspension with coil on lower arm. Place jack under lower arm at arrow to unload ball joints fully. Measure vertical and lateral movement in ball joints with dial indicator. If movement exceeds the manufacturer's specifications on any ball joint, it should be replaced. On torsion bar suspension, ball joint wear is measured similarly.

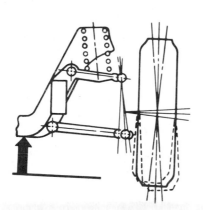 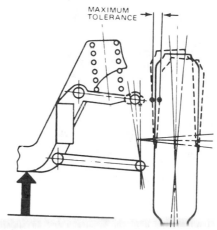

FIGURE 27-51. Checking ball joint wear on suspension with coil on upper arm. To unload ball joints, block upper arm between arm and frame. Place jack where indicated by arrow and proceed as in Figure 27-50.

er's manual for proper procedure for ball joint replacement. Some ball joints have wear indicators. Follow the manufacturer's directions to determine whether replacement is required.

Control Arms

While the vehicle is supported for checking ball joint wear, check for control arm bushing wear as well. When the wheel is moved laterally, the control arm that is not spring loaded can be checked. The spring-loaded control arm cannot be checked without spring removal except for visual inspection. Damaged or bent control arms must be replaced. Rubber bushings that have cracked must be replaced. Surface checks (very small cracks) are permissible.

Follow the general procedure for spring removal as well as the manufacturer's recommended procedures before removing the control arms. The control arms can then be removed for bushing or arm replacement both front and rear, as specified in shop manual.

Strut Rods

If the vehicle is equipped with a strut rod, inspect it for physical damage or distortion. Check bushings for cracks. Replace the rod and bushings as required when servicing control arms.

FIGURE 27-52. Ball joint wear checking procedure on strut suspension. *(Courtesy of Ford Motor Co. of Canada Ltd.)*

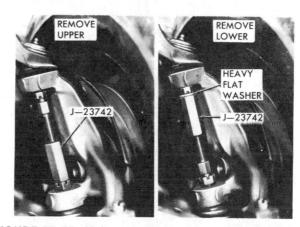

FIGURE 27-53. Using special tool to force tapered ball joint stud from spindle support. To perform this procedure, ball joint nut must be loosened until flush with end of ball joint stud. Follow the manufacturer's recommended procedures. *(Courtesy of General Motors Corporation)*

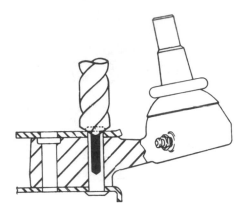

FIGURE 27-54. On some vehicles, ball joints are riveted to control arm. Rivets should be drilled at exact center to remove head, then drilled with a smaller drill to relieve rivet interference fit in hole. This makes it easier to drive it out of the hole with a pin punch. Replacement ball joint is bolted in.

FIGURE 27-55. Do not attempt to remove a coil spring until you are aware of the proper procedures and hazards involved. One method of removing a coil spring is shown here. The jack must be handled carefully and the vehicle properly supported to prevent serious injury.

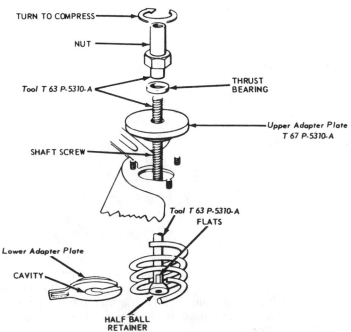

TURN TO COMPRESS

NUT

Tool T 63 P-5310-A

THRUST BEARING

Upper Adapter Plate
T 67 P-5310-A

SHAFT SCREW

Tool T 63 P-5310-A
FLATS

Lower Adapter Plate

CAVITY

HALF BALL
RETAINER

FIGURE 27-56. Spring compressor is used to compress spring before removal on suspension with coil on upper arm. Follow the manufacturer's procedures.

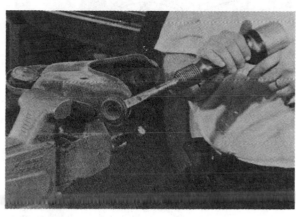

FIGURE 27-58. Removing rubber control arm bushing with air-operated tool and arm clamped in vise. *(Courtesy of Moog Automotive Inc.)*

FIGURE 27-57. Strut-suspension, spring-compressor tool for servicing strut suspension units. *(Courtesy of Moog Automotive Inc.)*

Springs

Springs should be replaced if suspension height determines springs to be at fault. Leaf springs can be removed and re-arched to restore them to the original position.

Sagging coil springs can be shimmed or coil jacks used to restore vehicle height, but this does nothing to restore the spring. Spring replacement is the only proper solution.

Springs should be replaced according to procedures given in the manufacturer's manual. All component parts required for spring mounting and installation should be inspected and faulty or damaged parts replaced. Tighten all rubber bushing mounting bolts with the vehicle weight on the springs to prevent preloading of bushings. Align the front suspension according to the general procedures in Chapter 30 and according to the manufacturer's manual after any suspension work.

The stabilizer bar and bushings can be serviced without spring removal. Replace a damaged or bent bar or linkage. Replace cracked rubber bushings as specified by the shop manual.

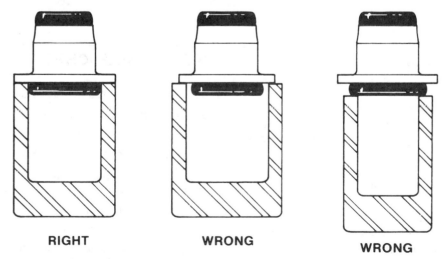

RIGHT   **WRONG**   **WRONG**

FIGURE 27-59. Proper procedure of pressing new suspension bushings into place. *(Courtesy of Moog Automotive Inc.)*

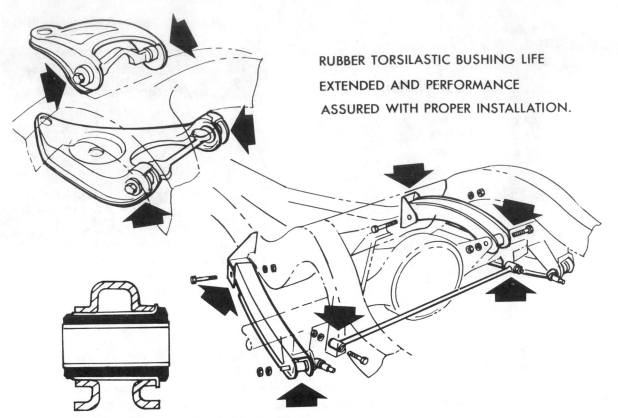

FIGURE 27-60. Rubber torsilastic suspension and steering bushings must be torqued only when the chassis is in its normal "loaded height" position. Rubber torsilastic bushings tightened while the car is on a lift and with wheels hanging free cause high stress, premature failure, and even temporary suspension height changes. Idler arm and center link bushings tightened while wheels are turned may cause the vehicle to pull to one side, hamper returnability, and cause premature failures of the bushings. This applies to all bushings, whether in the front or rear suspensions. Other bushings to consider are the track bar bushings found in various rear coil spring suspensions and front-rear bushings found in leaf springs. Neither should be tightened until the vehicle has been lowered to its normal "loaded height" position. When installing rubber torsilastic bushings, do not press on the rubber or the inner sleeve. Press only on the outer sleeve. *(Courtesy of Moog Automotive Inc.)*

RUBBER TORSILASTIC BUSHING LIFE EXTENDED AND PERFORMANCE ASSURED WITH PROPER INSTALLATION.

Wheel Bearings and Wheels

Inspect and service wheel bearings according to the manufacturer's specifications. Repackable wheel bearings require periodic maintenance, which includes removal, washing in solvent, blowing dry with compressed air, inspection, repacking with wheel-bearing grease, assembly, and adjustment. Factory-sealed bearings require no periodic maintenance.

Refer to Chapter 29, part 4 for wheel-bearing service. Always mount wheel assembly by tightening mounting nuts in proper sequence and to specified torque.

PART 6 SELF-CHECK

1. List three types of automotive frames.
2. List four types of automotive springs.
3. Define Hooke's law.
4. Define jounce and rebound.
5. What is the purpose of the shock absorber?
6. What is the purpose of the stabilizer bar?
7. What is the advantage of independent front suspension over solid axle front suspension?
8. Why is the upper control arm shorter than the lower control arm?

9. Which type of rear suspension uses control arms?

10. What is the purpose of the shackle on leaf springs?

11. Define curb weight.

12. What are the general procedures for checking suspension height? List eight points.

13. How is the amount of ball joint wear determined?

14. Always use_____cotter pins on all suspension parts.

15. Describe how to bleed air from a hydraulic shock absorber.

PART 7   TEST QUESTIONS

1. Four types of frames are the:
   (a) ladder, perimeter, "X," and stub
   (b) ladder, perimeter, channel, and stub
   (c) channel, perimeter, "X," and stub
   (d) perimeter, "X," ladder, and channel

2. Automotive suspensions use any of the following spring types:
   (a) coil, leaf, hydraulic, and air
   (b) air, torsion bar, hydraulic, and leaf
   (c) coil, air, hydraulic, and torsion bar
   (d) coil, leaf, air, and torsion bar

3. The short- and long-arm independent front suspension is designed to:
   (a) prevent tire scrubbing
   (b) improve ride characteristics
   (c) improve stability and directional control
   (d) all of the above

4. Front wheel shimmy is caused by:
   (a) loose wheel bearings
   (b) wheels out of balance
   (c) unevenly worn tires
   (d) any of the above

Chapter 28

Steering
Systems

Performance Objectives

After you have thoroughly studied this chapter and had sufficient practice on steering system components, you should be able to do the following.

1. Follow the accepted general precautions.
2. Correctly disassemble all steering system components.
3. Properly clean all steering system components.
4. Accurately inspect and measure all steering system components to determine their serviceability.
5. Properly replace all steering system components according to the manufacturer's specifications.
6. Perform the necessary inspection to determine the success of the steering system and component overhaul.
7. Properly prepare the vehicle for customer acceptance.
8. Complete the self-check and test questions with at least 80 percent accuracy.
9. Complete all practical work with 100 percent accuracy.
10. Prepare vehicle for customer acceptance.

The steering system is the means by which the driver of a vehicle is able to control the position of the front wheels. The system must provide ease of handling, good directional control, and stability. This is achieved by the steering system in conjunction with the suspension system.

PART 1 STEERING LINKAGE

The steering linkage includes the steering arms that are attached to (or are a part of) the steering knuckle, tie rods and tie rod ends, adjusting sleeves and clamps, a center link (relay rod or drag link), an idler arm, and a pitman arm. The arrangement of these parts is shown in Figure 28-1. Another type of linkage is shown in Figure 28-2. These are the two most common types of steering linkage on passenger cars.

Other types of linkage arrangements are used on older cars and on trucks. The wheel assembly, including the steering knuckle, pivots at the ball joints allowing the front wheels to turn to the right or to the left. The steering arms that are attached to the steering knuckle turn the wheels to right or left as the linkage moves from side to side.

The pivoting action in the linkage is provided by the tie rod ends. The outer ends of the tie rods are attached to the steering arms and the inner ends to the center link. Threaded adjusting sleeves between the outer tie rod end and tie rod connect the two and provide a means of adjusting tie rod length. Adjusting sleeves are split for ease of adjustment and are clamped at each end. The clamps provide a means of preventing the sleeves from turning on the rods during vehicle operation. The inner ends of the two tie rods are attached to the center link by means of tie rod ends.

The center link is supported at one end by the idler arm and at the other by the pitman arm. The pitman arm swings through an arc from side to side, as does the idler arm, when the steering wheel is turned from right to left and back.

The idler arm is bolted to the frame on the right side of left-hand-drive vehicles. The pitman arm is attached to the splined sector shaft of the steering gear with a nut and lock washer.

On rack-and-pinion steering two tie rods are used, one on each side. These rods are threaded at both ends. The inner end is attached to the rack and the outer end to the steering arm. Lock nuts hold the adjustment in place.

PART 2 MANUAL–STEERING GEARS

The steering gear provides the means of converting the turning of the steering wheel to side-to-side movement of the steering linkage. On some vehicles

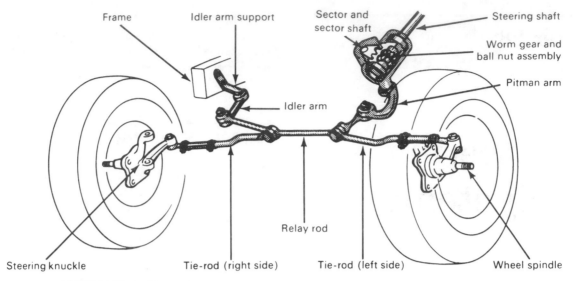

FIGURE 28-1. Manual or integral power-steering linkage components. This type of linkage is known as parallelogram linkage. This illustration shows a manual type of steering gear.

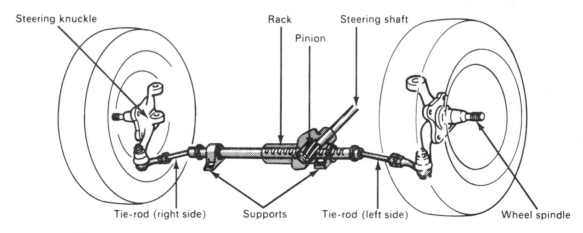

FIGURE 28-2. Rack-and-pinion type of steering linkage. Note that the steering knuckle arms are pointing forward instead of rearward as in Figure 28-1.

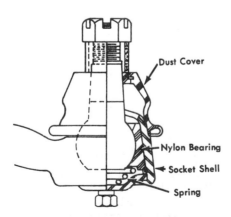

FIGURE 28-3. Tie rod end cross-sectional view showing spring-loaded ball and socket. Note dust boot and plug for grease fitting. Tapered stud fits into tapered hole of linkage and is fastened with castellated nut and cotter pin.

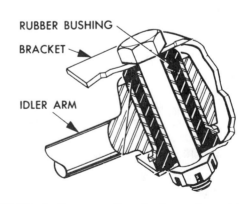

FIGURE 28-4. Cross-sectional view of an idler arm bushing. The outer metal shell is a press fit in the idler arm. The bolt passes through the inner metal shell and clamps it tight to prevent rotation. Linkage movement during steering simply deflects the rubber, which is bonded to the two metal shells.

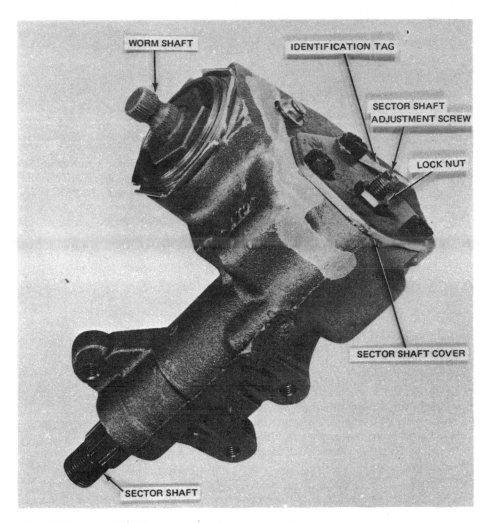

FIGURE 28-5. Outside view of recirculating ball type of manual steering gear. *(Courtesy of Ford Motor Co. of Canada Ltd.)*

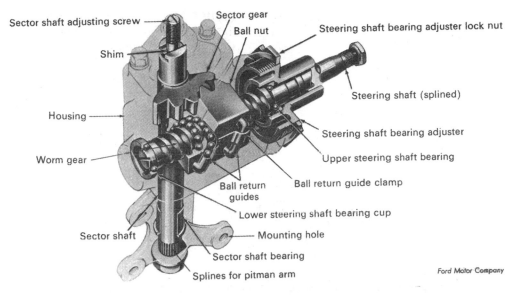

FIGURE 28-6. Phantom view of recirculating ball type of manual-steering gear showing names of major parts. Steering effort is reduced by using the worm-and-recirculating ball-nut design. *(Courtesy of Ford Motor Co. of Canada Ltd.)*

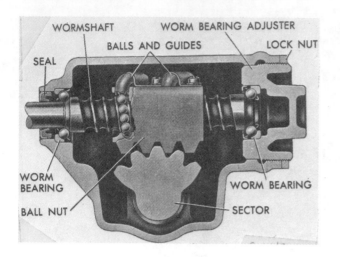

WORMSHAFT

WORM BEARING ADJUSTER

BALLS AND GUIDES

LOCK NUT

SEAL

WORM BEARING

BALL NUT

WORM BEARING

SECTOR

FIGURE 28-7. Steering gear ball nut and sector teeth shown in mesh. Note worm bearings supporting worm shaft and worm bearing adjuster and lock nut. There are two separate ball circuits. Balls do not pass from one guide to the other. (*Courtesy of Ford Motor Co. of Canada Ltd.*)

FIGURE 28-8. Constant-ratio and variable-ratio steering gear pitman shaft and rack piston teeth compared. The ratio of front-wheel turn to steering wheel movement remains constant throughout a complete turn right to left or left to right with the constant-ratio steering gear. The variable-ratio steering gear provides relatively little front-wheel movement during the first quarter of a turn to right or left from straight ahead. Front-wheel movement increases at a faster rate as the steering wheel is turned farther. The advantage is quicker maneuverability for parking. (*Courtesy of General Motors Corporation*)

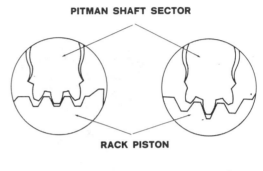

PITMAN SHAFT SECTOR

RACK PISTON

CONSTANT RATIO

VARIABLE RATIO

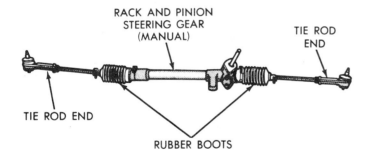

RACK AND PINION STEERING GEAR (MANUAL)

TIE ROD END

TIE ROD END

RUBBER BOOTS

FIGURE 28-9. Rack-and-pinion steering gear assembly incorporates gear and linkage as a unit. (*Courtesy of Chrysler Corporation*)

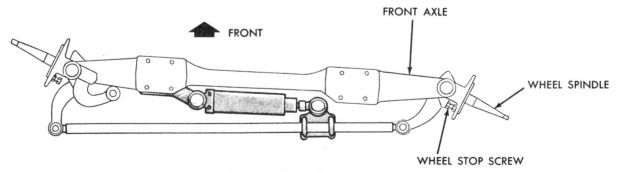

FRONT AXLE

FRONT

WHEEL SPINDLE

WHEEL STOP SCREW

FIGURE 28-10. Steering linkage damper controls wheel shimmy. Operation is similar to a shock absorber. The moveable piston rod is connected to the steering linkage while the cylinder is anchored at the axle in this illustration or to the frame in other applications. (*Courtesy of Chrysler Corporation*)

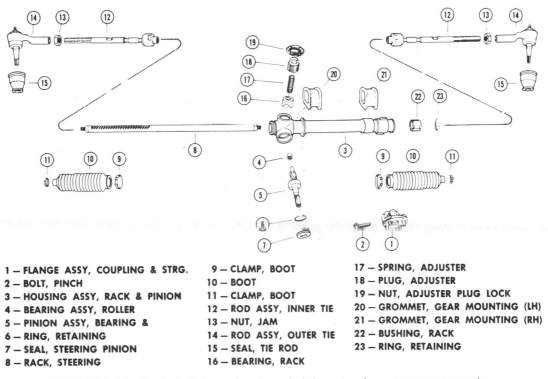

1 — FLANGE ASSY, COUPLING & STRG.	9 — CLAMP, BOOT	17 — SPRING, ADJUSTER
2 — BOLT, PINCH	10 — BOOT	18 — PLUG, ADJUSTER
3 — HOUSING ASSY, RACK & PINION	11 — CLAMP, BOOT	19 — NUT, ADJUSTER PLUG LOCK
4 — BEARING ASSY, ROLLER	12 — ROD ASSY, INNER TIE	20 — GROMMET, GEAR MOUNTING (LH)
5 — PINION ASSY, BEARING &	13 — NUT, JAM	21 — GROMMET, GEAR MOUNTING (RH)
6 — RING, RETAINING	14 — ROD ASSY, OUTER TIE	22 — BUSHING, RACK
7 — SEAL, STEERING PINION	15 — SEAL, TIE ROD	23 — RING, RETAINING
8 — RACK, STEERING	16 — BEARING, RACK	

FIGURE 28–11. Exploded view of rack-and-pinion steering gear components. *(Courtesy of General Motors Corporation)*

the steering gear converts the turning of the steering wheel to fore-and-aft movement of the pitman arm, which is then converted to side-to-side linkage movement by a specially shaped steering arm. The steering gear is bolted to the frame. The most common types of manual-steering gears are the recirculating-ball type and the rack-and-pinion type.

Turning the steering wheel on a vehicle equipped with a recirculating-ball type of steering gear turns the grooved wormshaft in the gear. Turning the grooved wormshaft causes the ball nut to thread its way up or down the worm. The teeth of the ball nut push against the sector shaft teeth as the wormshaft is turned. The sector shaft teeth and sector shaft are integral. As the sector shaft teeth move back and forth, the sector shaft is also forced to turn back and forth. This causes the pitman arm to move from side to side to actuate the linkage.

The steering gear also provides a gear reduction. This is needed to reduce the amount of effort required to turn the steering wheel, particularly when parking. During straight-ahead driving, this also reduces the possibility of oversteering. This gear reduction is known as steering gear ratio. Ratios vary considerably, depending largely on vehicle size and weight. Larger, heavier vehicles require a greater reduction in manual steering gears. The steering gear also absorbs much of the road shock, which tends to turn the front wheels right or left.

The rack-and-pinion type of steering mechanism is used on many smaller cars. A small toothed gear is connected to the bottom of the steering shaft through a flexible coupling or shaft. The toothed gear or pinion is in mesh with teeth either on a long horizontal bar or on a rack with teeth on one side. As the steering wheel is turned, the pinion turns, causing the rack to move from side to side. The ends of the rack are connected to the tie rods, which in turn are connected to the steering arms at the wheels. The rack-and-pinion assembly is enclosed in a housing and sealed at each end with a flexible rubber boot. It is also sealed at the pinion shaft. The entire assembly is attached to the vehicle frame or fire wall.

PART 3   POWER STEERING

The power steering unit is designed to reduce the amount of effort required to turn the steering wheel; it also reduces driver fatigue and increases safety by providing better control on rough road surfaces or during tire failure.

The system includes a pump driven by a belt from the crankshaft pulley. This pump provides the fluid pressure and flow needed to operate the system. Maximum pressure is controlled by a pressure-regulating valve in the pump. A pressure line and a return line connect the pump to the system. Three types of power-steering pumps are used. All operate

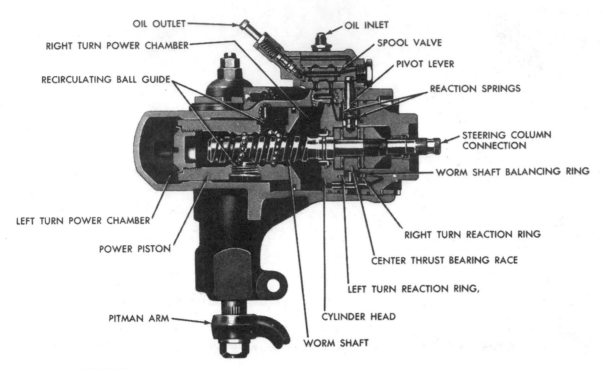

FIGURE 28-12. Cross-sectional view of spool-valve type of integral power steering gear showing major parts. *(Courtesy of Chrysler Corporation)*

similarly and differ mainly in rotor design. Some pumps have rollers; others have slippers or vanes.

The integral type of power-steering unit combines, all in a single assembly, the power piston and cylinder with the steering gear and flow control valve. Typical integral power-steering gear components are shown in Figure 28-12. System operation is shown and described in Figures 28-15 to 28-19.

Another type of power-steering system is the linkage booster type. Major components of this system are shown in Figures 28-23 and 28-24. System operation is shown in Figure 28-25.

Rack-and-pinion power steering incorporates the control valve, power piston, and gear in a single assembly. See Figure 28-22.

Power steering provides most of the force needed for steering. The remaining steering effort provides needed driver "feel" for good steering control.

Integral Rotary Valve Power Steering

An open center, three-position, rotary valve is used to control hydraulic assist. Pump supplied fluid enters the valve body through a pressure port in the gear housing. The valve then directs fluid to the rack piston through fluid passages in the housing.

The valve body, spool valve, torsion bar, and stub shaft (which is pinned to the torsion bar) are connected to the front wheels by a mechanical linkage.

Because of the pressure exerted on the front wheels by car weight, the wheels and valve body tend to resist any turning effort applied at the steering wheel. As front wheel resistance to turning effort increases, the torsion bar (which is pinned to the stub shaft) deflects. Since the spool valve is connected to the stub shaft by a locating pin, torsion bar deflection causes the spool valve to rotate within the valve body.

As the spool valve rotates, fluid directional passages in the valve are brought into alignment with matching passages in the valve body. When these passages are aligned, fluid at operating pressure from the pump is directed through the passages and against either side of the rack piston to provide hydraulic assist.

Torsion bar deflection provides the required amount of steering gear "road feel." If ever the bar should break, road feel would be lost but the steering system would still function due to auxiliary locking tabs on the stub shaft. In this situation, the gear would operate the same as a manual recirculating ball gear.

Rack and Pinion Power Steering

The power rack and pinion design combines the steering gear and linkage into one compact assembly.

The gear consists of a tube and housing containing the steering rack and piston, pinion shaft and valve body assembly, and adjuster plug assembly. Thrust bearings and bushings are used to support

ROLLER TYPE

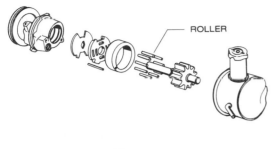

ROLLER

VANE TYPE

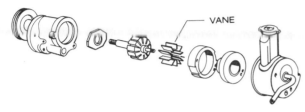

VANE

SLIPPER TYPE

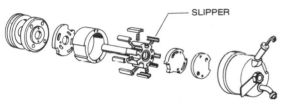

SLIPPER

FIGURE 28-13. Common power-steering pump designs. Operation of these pumps is similar even though the pumping elements (vanes, rollers, slippers) differ. *(Courtesy of Moog Automotive Inc.)*

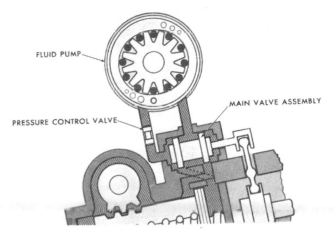

FLUID PUMP

MAIN VALVE ASSEMBLY

PRESSURE CONTROL VALVE

FIGURE 28-15. The power-steering pump (fluid pump) provides the hydraulic pressure for the power steering gear. Pressure is regulated by the pressure control valve and is directed to the rack piston by the main valve assembly. This provides power-assisted steering whenever the steering wheel is turned. *(Courtesy of Chrysler Corporation)*

the pinion shaft in the housing. A bushing and bulkhead assembly support the steering rack in the tube. The protective rubber boots, breather tube, and steering linkage components used with the power steering gear are similar to those used with manual rack and pinion steering gear assemblies.

The steering rack piston is attached to the rack and operates within the power cylinder section of the tube. The piston is positioned on the rack so it is centered between the oil line fitting bosses when

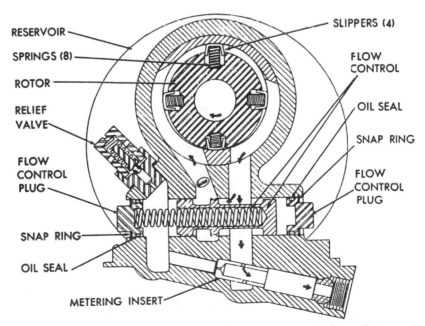

RESERVOIR

SPRINGS (8)

ROTOR

RELIEF VALVE

FLOW CONTROL PLUG

SNAP RING

OIL SEAL

METERING INSERT

SLIPPERS (4)

FLOW CONTROL

OIL SEAL

SNAP RING

FLOW CONTROL PLUG

FIGURE 28-14. Slipper-type power-steering pump operation. Flow-control valve controls flow to steering gear. Relief valve limits maximum pump pressure. *(Courtesy of Applied Power)*

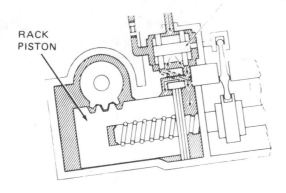

FIGURE 28-16. During straight-ahead driving, hydraulic pressure is directed equally to both sides of the rack piston. *(Courtesy of Chrysler Corporation)*

FIGURE 28-17. If a front wheel hits a bump or hole in the road, the front wheels are deflected to the right or left. This creates a tendency to self-steer to right or left. This action is transferred to the control valve as shown by arrows causing hydraulic pressure to offset the self-steering tendency. *(Courtesy of Chrysler Corporation)*

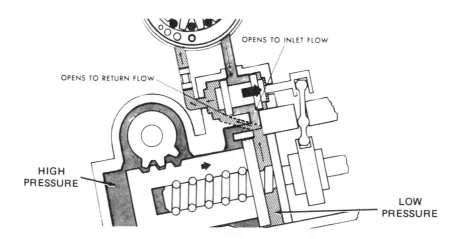

FIGURE 28-18. A left turn causes the worm shaft to thread into the rack piston, which pulls the piston up. A reaction on the pivot moves the control valve up, which directs hydraulic pressure to the bottom side of the rack piston. At the same time a return passage is opened from the chamber above the piston to allow fluid return and a pressure drop in this chamber. In effect, the pressure difference on the two sides of the piston assists the piston to move up which provides steering assist. *(Courtesy of Chrysler Corporation)*

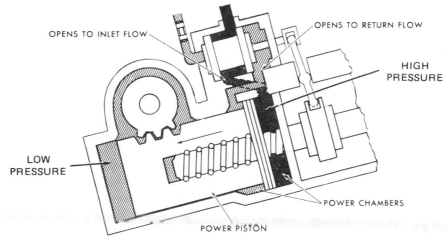

OPENS TO INLET FLOW   OPENS TO RETURN FLOW

HIGH PRESSURE

LOW PRESSURE

POWER CHAMBERS

POWER PISTON

FIGURE 28-19. During right turn the power piston moves down, creating an opposite reaction on the control valve as compared to Figure 28–18. The higher pressure above the piston helps move the piston down to the low-pressure area, providing steering assist. *(Courtesy of Chrysler Corporation)*

the wheels are straight ahead. A seal is used on the piston.

Operating pressure in the power cylinder is contained by a seal formed in the housing end of the power cylinder. An O-ring and lip-type seal with compression spring is located in the two-piece bulkhead assembly at the opposite end of the cylinder.

The externally mounted oil lines installed be-

tween tube and housing conduct power steering fluid from the valve body to the tube power cylinder section.

An open center, three-position, rotary-type valve body assembly is used. The valve body assembly consists of a stub shaft and torsion bar, spool valve and valve body, O-rings, and teflon rings. Locating lugs on the pinion shaft engage with locating

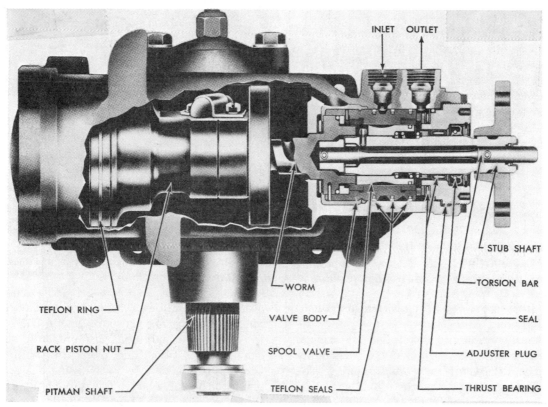

INLET   OUTLET

TEFLON RING

RACK PISTON NUT

PITMAN SHAFT

WORM

VALVE BODY

SPOOL VALVE

TEFLON SEALS

STUB SHAFT

TORSION BAR

SEAL

ADJUSTER PLUG

THRUST BEARING

FIGURE 28-20. Integral power steering with a torsion bar and different type of control valve assembly. *(Courtesy of General Motors Corporation)*

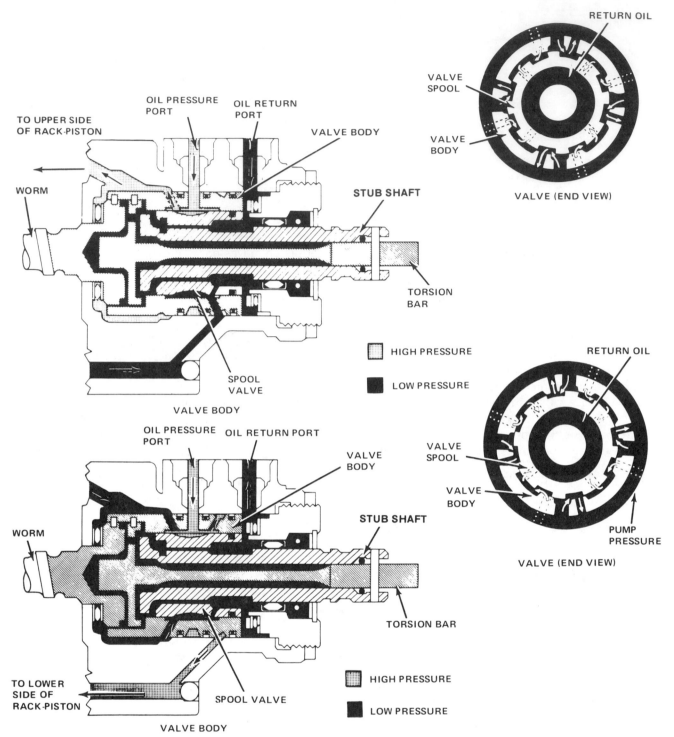

FIGURE 28-21. Rotary valve power steering operation. Left turn shown at top and right turn at bottom. *(Courtesy American Motors Corporation)*

slots in the stub shaft and torsion bar to connect the pinion shaft and valve body.

Pinion shaft preload is controlled by conical thrust bearing races. The adjuster plug assembly determines the degree of preload applied to the thrust bearings and also retains the pinion shaft and valve body in the housing. A preload spring maintains pinion bushing position and compensates for bushing wear. Seal rings on the valve body, lip-type seals in the adjuster, plus the housing, together maintain operating pressure within the housing.

The valve body controls hydraulic steering assist. In operation, fluid from the pump is routed through the inlet hose to the steering gear housing and into the valve body. The valve body directs fluid to either side of the power cylinder to provide hydraulic steering assist.

The valve body, spool valve, torsion bar, and

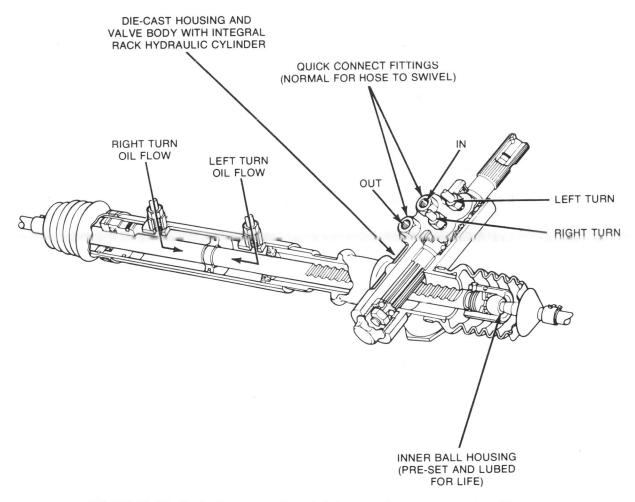

DIE-CAST HOUSING AND
VALVE BODY WITH INTEGRAL
RACK HYDRAULIC CYLINDER

QUICK CONNECT FITTINGS
(NORMAL FOR HOSE TO SWIVEL)

RIGHT TURN
OIL FLOW

LEFT TURN
OIL FLOW

IN

OUT

LEFT TURN

RIGHT TURN

INNER BALL HOUSING
(PRE-SET AND LUBED
FOR LIFE)

FIGURE 28–22. Typical power rack-and-pinion steering gear operation. *(Courtesy of Ford Motor Co. of Canada Ltd.)*

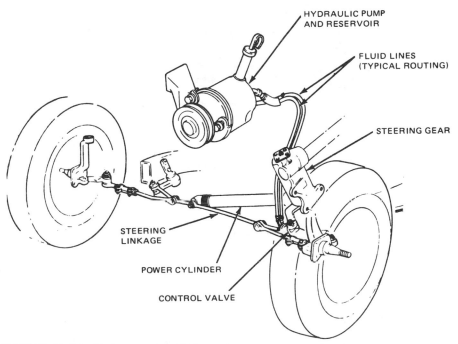

HYDRAULIC PUMP
AND RESERVOIR

FLUID LINES
(TYPICAL ROUTING)

STEERING GEAR

STEERING
LINKAGE

POWER CYLINDER

CONTROL VALVE

FIGURE 28–23. Major parts of linkage booster power steering. Note that the control valve, power cylinder, and steering gear are separate units. The power cylinder provides steering assist. *(Courtesy of Ford Motor Co. of Canada Ltd.)*

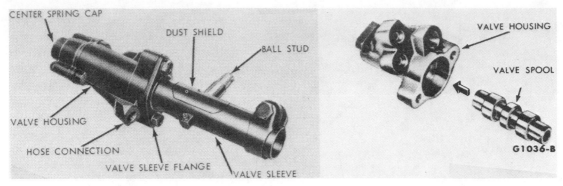

FIGURE 28-24. Major components of linkage booster power-steering control valve assembly. *(Courtesy of Ford Motor Co. of Canada Ltd.)*

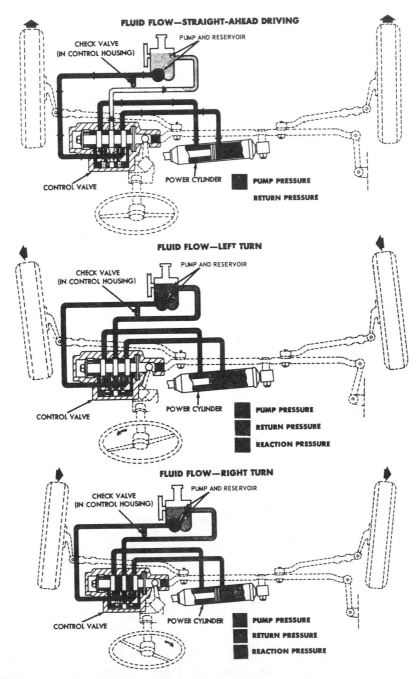

FIGURE 28-25. Operation of linkage booster type of power steering. *(Courtesy of Ford Motor Co. of Canada Ltd.)*

stub shaft that is pinned to the torsion bar are, in effect, attached to the front wheel through mechanical connections. Because of the pressure exerted on the front wheel by car weight, the wheel and valve body tend to resist any turning effort applied at the steering wheel. As resistance to turning by the wheel and valve body increases, the torsion bar that is pinned to the stub shaft deflects. Since the spool valve is connected to the stub shaft by a locating pin, torsion bar deflection causes the spool valve to rotate within the valve body. As the spool valve rotates, fluid directional passages machined into the valve are aligned with matching passages in the valve body. Fluid from the pump is then directed through the aligned passages and into either side of the power cylinder through one of the externally mounted oil lines.

PART 4   STEERING COLUMNS

The steering column connects the steering gear to the steering wheel by means of a shaft and one or more flexible couplings. The steering column shaft is enclosed in a tubular mast jacket that is collapsible on impact due to collision. The steering column shaft and gear shift control rod are also collapsible. The steering column assembly includes such items as the turn signal switch, headlight dimmer switch, windshield wiper switch, ignition switch, steering wheel lock, gear shift lever and rod, speed control switch, horn switch, and necessary electrical wiring. Brackets at the dashboard and the floor panel hold the assembly in position. Some steering columns can be tilted or telescoped to adjust the steering wheel position to the driver's preference.

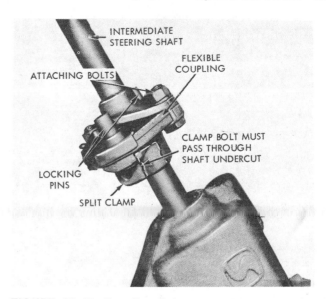

FIGURE 28-26. Details of flexible coupling between steering column shaft and steering gear shaft. A flexible coupling is required since the steering column shaft and steering gear shaft are not in alignment with each other. *(Courtesy of General Motors Corporation)*

PART 5   STEERING SYSTEM DIAGNOSIS AND SERVICE

General Precautions

When servicing steering systems or suspension systems, safe vehicle operation should always be ensured. Follow the manufacturer's specifications and recommendations. Some additional points to remember follow.

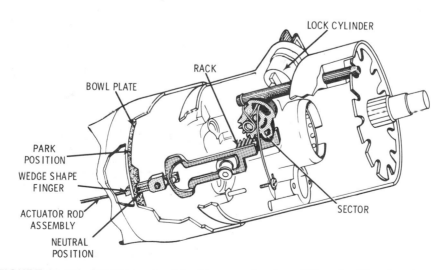

FIGURE 28-27. Steering wheel locking mechanism. When ignition key is removed, steering wheel is locked, which helps prevent theft of vehicle. *(Courtesy of General Motors Corporation)*

DIAGNOSTIC CHART

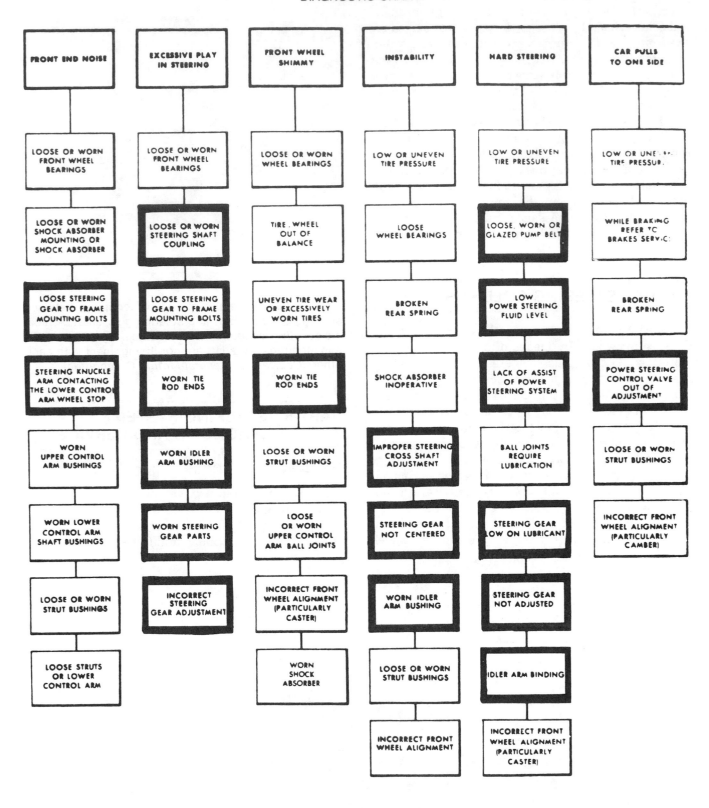

FRONT END NOISE	EXCESSIVE PLAY IN STEERING	FRONT WHEEL SHIMMY	INSTABILITY	HARD STEERING	CAR PULLS TO ONE SIDE
LOOSE OR WORN FRONT WHEEL BEARINGS	LOOSE OR WORN FRONT WHEEL BEARINGS	LOOSE OR WORN WHEEL BEARINGS	LOW OR UNEVEN TIRE PRESSURE	LOW OR UNEVEN TIRE PRESSURE	LOW OR UNEVEN TIRE PRESSURE
LOOSE OR WORN SHOCK ABSORBER MOUNTING OR SHOCK ABSORBER	LOOSE OR WORN STEERING SHAFT COUPLING	TIRE, WHEEL OUT OF BALANCE	LOOSE WHEEL BEARINGS	LOOSE, WORN OR GLAZED PUMP BELT	WHILE BRAKING REFER TO BRAKES SERVICE
LOOSE STEERING GEAR TO FRAME MOUNTING BOLTS	LOOSE STEERING GEAR TO FRAME MOUNTING BOLTS	UNEVEN TIRE WEAR OR EXCESSIVELY WORN TIRES	BROKEN REAR SPRING	LOW POWER STEERING FLUID LEVEL	BROKEN REAR SPRING
STEERING KNUCKLE ARM CONTACTING THE LOWER CONTROL ARM WHEEL STOP	WORN TIE ROD ENDS	WORN TIE ROD ENDS	SHOCK ABSORBER INOPERATIVE	LACK OF ASSIST OF POWER STEERING SYSTEM	POWER STEERING CONTROL VALVE OUT OF ADJUSTMENT
WORN UPPER CONTROL ARM BUSHINGS	WORN IDLER ARM BUSHING	LOOSE OR WORN STRUT BUSHINGS	IMPROPER STEERING CROSS SHAFT ADJUSTMENT	BALL JOINTS REQUIRE LUBRICATION	LOOSE OR WORN STRUT BUSHINGS
WORN LOWER CONTROL ARM SHAFT BUSHINGS	WORN STEERING GEAR PARTS	LOOSE OR WORN UPPER CONTROL ARM BALL JOINTS	STEERING GEAR NOT CENTERED	STEERING GEAR LOW ON LUBRICANT	INCORRECT FRONT WHEEL ALIGNMENT (PARTICULARLY CAMBER)
LOOSE OR WORN STRUT BUSHINGS	INCORRECT STEERING GEAR ADJUSTMENT	INCORRECT FRONT WHEEL ALIGNMENT (PARTICULARLY CASTER)	WORN IDLER ARM BUSHING	STEERING GEAR NOT ADJUSTED	
LOOSE STRUTS OR LOWER CONTROL ARM		WORN SHOCK ABSORBER	LOOSE OR WORN STRUT BUSHINGS	IDLER ARM BINDING	
			INCORRECT FRONT WHEEL ALIGNMENT	INCORRECT FRONT WHEEL ALIGNMENT (PARTICULARLY CASTER)	

- Perform only quality workmanship.

- Always support the vehicle safely when working under the vehicle.

- Use correct equipment and tools in good condition, and use them as recommended.

- Do not use heat on parts that are to be reused.

- Replace all damaged, bent, or worn parts.

- Always use a torque wrench to tighten fasteners to specified torque.

- Always use new cotter pins; never reuse any cotter pin.

- Always lubricate where needed, but never overlubricate.

Steering Linkage Service

Inspect all steering linkage for bent, damaged, or broken parts, including torn or ruptured seals and mounting bolts and nuts. If linkage appears to be in good condition, a further inspection must be made to determine wear. Tie rod ends and idler arm bushing wear should be checked and corrected as follows:

- Support the vehicle safely on jack stands.

- Grasp the tire firmly at front and back and move back and forth alternately (a short distance only). Do this vigorously.

- Observe whether there is any lateral movement in each tie rod end; if so, replace the tie rod end.

- To check idler arm wear, grasp the linkage at the idler arm and try to move it up and down. If

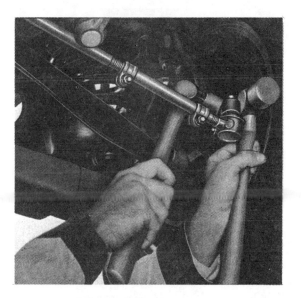

FIGURE 28-29. Another method of removing tie rod end stud from steering arm. *(Courtesy of Chrysler Corporation)*

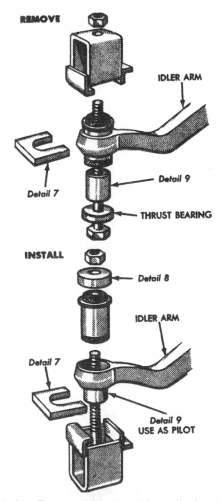

FIGURE 28-30. Removal (top) and installation (bottom) of one type of idler arm bushing using a special tool for the job. *(Courtesy of Chrysler Corporation)*

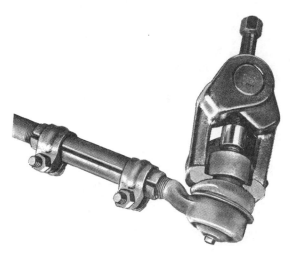

FIGURE 28-28. Using a special tool to remove tie rod end from steering arm after cotter pin and nut have been removed. After stud removal and after loosening clamp on adjusting sleeve, count the number of turns required to remove the tie rod end from the sleeve. Install the new tie rod end the same number of turns, and tighten clamp away from split in sleeve; then, adjust toe in. *(Courtesy of Chrysler Corporation)*

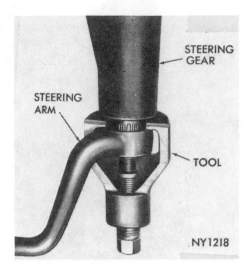

FIGURE 28-31. Using a puller to remove the pitman arm from the steering gear sector shaft after nut has been removed.

there is any movement up or down, replace the idler arm.

- Replace any bent or damaged parts.
- Tighten all bolts and nuts to specified torque and lock with new cotter pin. If holes do not line up, tighten to the next hole only; never loosen to line up cotter pin holes.

Manual-Steering Gear Service

The steering gear should be checked to determine if adjustment or repairs are needed. In general, if steering gear is suspected, proceed as follows.

- Check the lubricant level; if low, check for leaks and correct.
- Check mounting bolts; tighten to specifications or replace if damaged.
- Check whether there is any lost motion at the flexible coupling; correct as necessary.
- Check whether the pitman arm and nut are tight on sector shaft; tighten to specifications. If splines are worn, replace both pitman arm and sector shaft.
- Check whether there is any looseness (lost motion), roughness, or bind in the steering gear. If too loose or too tight, adjust to specifications. If adjustment does not correct the problem or if the gear is rough, overhaul the steering gear according to Figures 28-32 to 28-46, and to the manufacturer's specifications.

Power Steering Service

Power steering problems are usually evidenced by one of the following conditions:

- Hard to steer
- Erratic assist

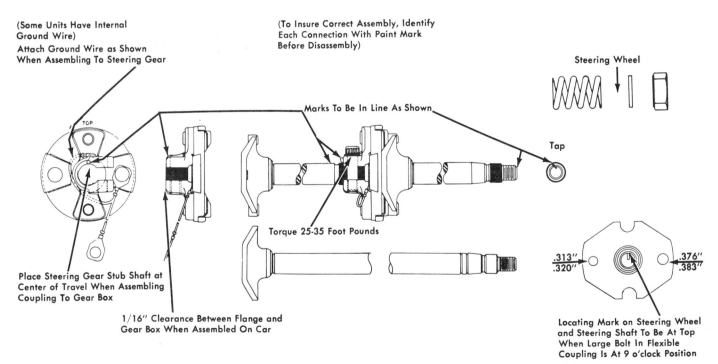

FIGURE 28-32. Special precautions must be observed before disassembly and during assembly to ensure correct assembly of steering column shaft and steering gear shaft connections. This is only one example; other makes and models require other procedures. *(Courtesy of General Motors Corporation)*

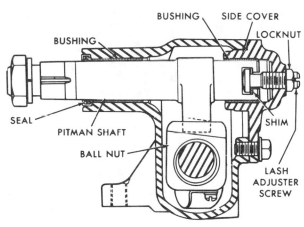

FIGURE 28-33. Cross-sectional view of manual steering gear. Note that sector shaft teeth and ball nut teeth are tapered. Note that the lash adjuster screw, when turned, moves the sector shaft endwise to adjust mesh. *(Courtesy of General Motors Corporation)*

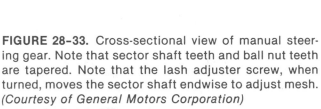

FIGURE 28-34. Removing sector shaft after side cover bolts have been removed. This is the first step in manual-steering gear disassembly. *(Courtesy of General Motors Corporation)*

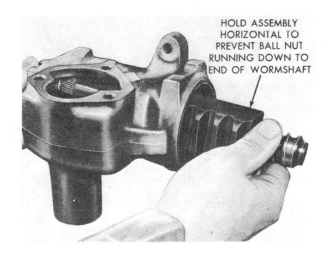

HOLD ASSEMBLY HORIZONTAL TO PREVENT BALL NUT RUNNING DOWN TO END OF WORMSHAFT

FIGURE 28-35. Removing wormshaft and ball-nut assembly after wormshaft bearing adjuster has been removed. *(Courtesy of General Motors Corporation)*

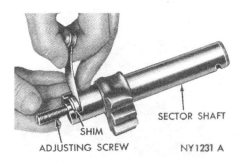

FIGURE 28-36. Checking lash adjusting screw head-to-sector shaft clearance with a feeler gauge. Excessive clearance at this point allows excessive sector shaft movement, which results in loose steering and vehicle wander. Use a thicker shim to restore correct clearance. *(Courtesy of Chrysler Corporation)*

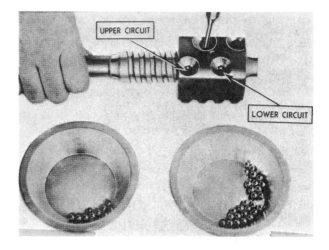

FIGURE 28-37. Installing balls into ball-nut assembly. Ball guides of this type (with holes for loading) make the job easy. A retainer covers the holes and keeps the ball guides in place after loading. Since there are two ball circuits, each circuit is loaded separately. Turning the wormshaft helps to load the circuits. *(Courtesy of General Motors Corporation)*

FIGURE 28-38. Assembling ball-nut assembly on unit that has no ball loading holes in ball guides. On this type of unit the wormshaft must not be turned during this procedure, since this will allow balls to escape from their circuit. *(Courtesy of General Motors Corporation)*

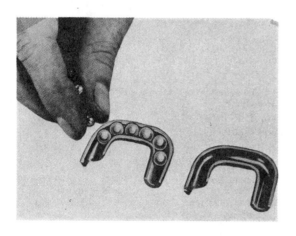

FIGURE 28-39. After loading ball nut with balls (Figure 28-37) ball guides must be loaded with balls as shown here. Use some steering gear lubricant to help keep balls in place during guide installation. *(Courtesy of General Motors Corporation)*

FIGURE 28-40. Installing loaded ball guide in previously loaded ball-nut assembly. A retainer plate holds both guides in place after installation. *(Courtesy of General Motors Corporation)*

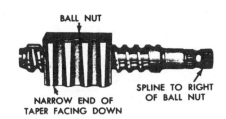

BALL NUT

SPLINE TO RIGHT OF BALL NUT

NARROW END OF TAPER FACING DOWN

FIGURE 28-41. Assembled ball nut and wormshaft should look like this. If wormshaft is installed in other end of nut, proper mesh and lash adjustment cannot be achieved. *(Courtesy of Ford Motor Co. of Canada Ltd.)*

WORMSHAFT AND BALL NUT ASSEMBLY

ND 468

FIGURE 28-42. During assembly, install wormshaft and ball nut in gear case first, as shown here. *(Courtesy of Chrysler Corporation)*

WORM SHAFT ADJUSTER

NK463

FIGURE 28-43. After wormshaft and ball nut are installed, adjust wormshaft bearing preload to manufacturer's specifications. *(Courtesy of Chrysler Corporation)*

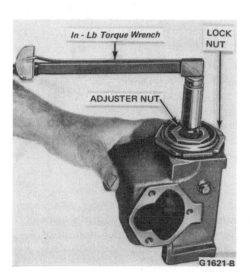

In - Lb Torque Wrench

LOCK NUT

ADJUSTER NUT

G1621-B

FIGURE 28-44. Wormshaft bearing preload is checked with a torque wrench as shown here. Too much preload causes early failure, while loose bearings cause loose steering as well as early failure. *(Courtesy of Ford Motor Co. of Canada Ltd.)*

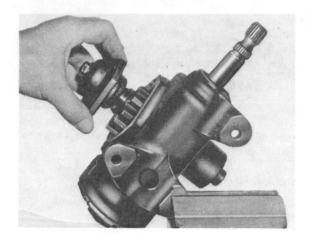

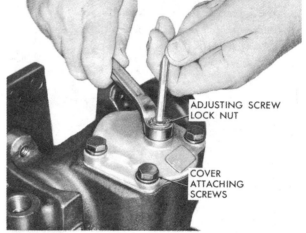

FIGURE 28-45. After correct worm bearing preload has been obtained, install sector shaft assembly. Make sure that lash adjuster is backed off to prevent teeth from binding when bolting down the cover. *(Courtesy of General Motors Corporation)*

FIGURE 28-46. Proper lash adjustment is achieved by loosening the lock nut and turning the adjusting screw. Wormshaft should be turned back and forth through midpoint of travel to obtain "feel" of "high point" and correct lash adjustment. Follow shop manual specifications for correct setting. *(Courtesy of General Motors Corporation)*

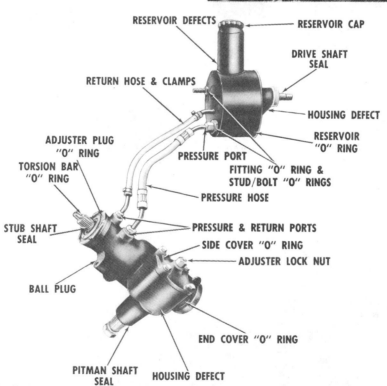

FIGURE 28-47. Points at which fluid leakage can occur on integral power steering units. Wipe area of suspected leakage clean, then check source of leakage. Fluid can run down onto adjacent parts and lead to incorrect diagnosis. *(Courtesy of General Motors Corporation)*

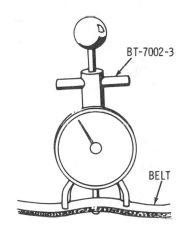

FIGURE 28-48. Checking belt tension on power steering with tension gauge. Incorrect tension can result in erratic steering assist, belt squeal, and early belt, bearing, and pulley failure. *(Courtesy of General Motors Corporation)*

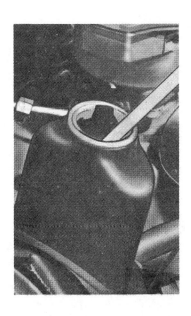

FIGURE 28-49. Power-steering fluid level should be checked with system at operating temperature and according to the manufacturer's specifications.

FIGURE 28-50. Checking power-steering system pressure is one method of problem diagnosis. This will determine if pressure is up to the manufacturer's specifications and whether the pump or steering gear unit is at fault.

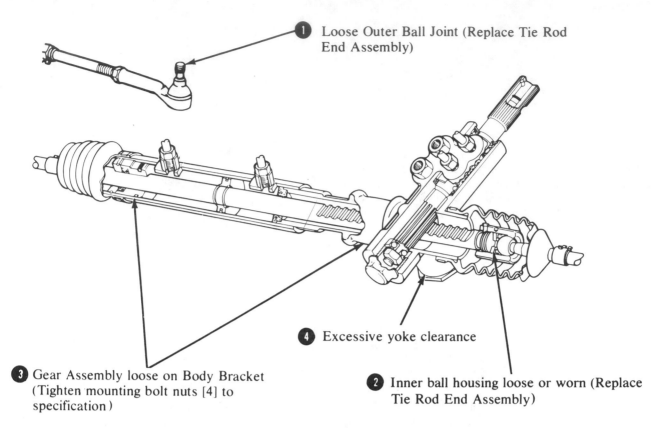

1 Loose Outer Ball Joint (Replace Tie Rod End Assembly)

4 Excessive yoke clearance

3 Gear Assembly loose on Body Bracket (Tighten mounting bolt nuts [4] to specification)

2 Inner ball housing loose or worn (Replace Tie Rod End Assembly)

FIGURE 28-51. Typical rack-and-pinion power-steering gear wander diagnosis procedure.

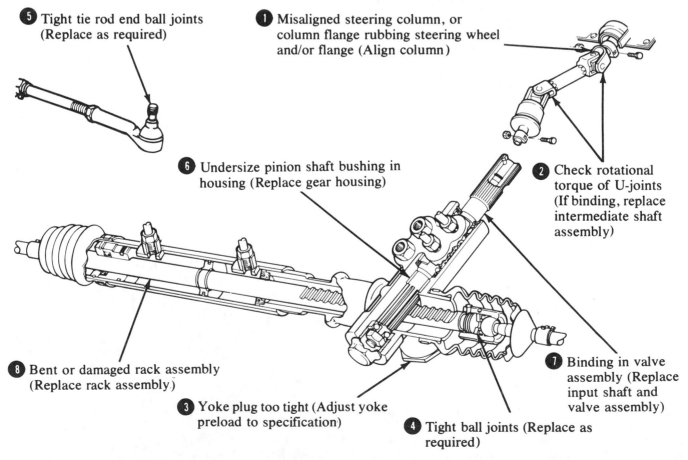

5 Tight tie rod end ball joints (Replace as required)

1 Misaligned steering column, or column flange rubbing steering wheel and/or flange (Align column)

6 Undersize pinion shaft bushing in housing (Replace gear housing)

2 Check rotational torque of U-joints (If binding, replace intermediate shaft assembly)

8 Bent or damaged rack assembly (Replace rack assembly)

7 Binding in valve assembly (Replace input shaft and valve assembly)

3 Yoke plug too tight (Adjust yoke preload to specification)

4 Tight ball joints (Replace as required)

FIGURE 28-52. Diagnosis procedure for poor returnability condition (stick feeling) for power rack-and-pinion steering gear. *(Courtesy of Ford Motor Co. of Canada Ltd.)*

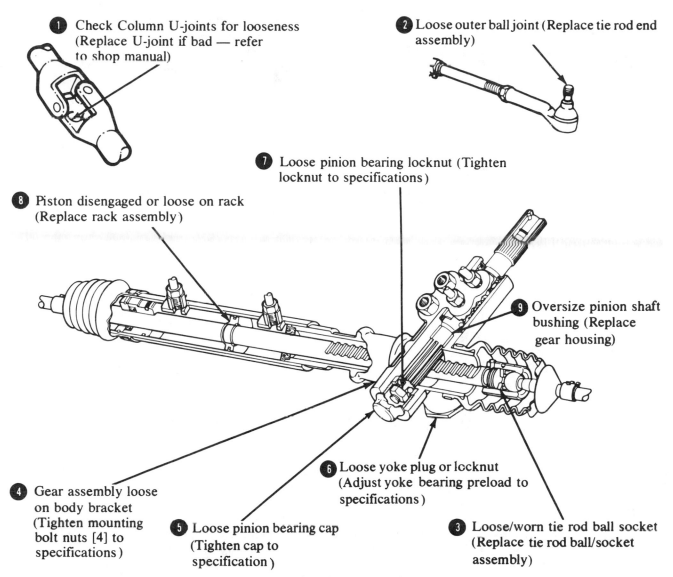

1 Check Column U-joints for looseness (Replace U-joint if bad — refer to shop manual)

2 Loose outer ball joint (Replace tie rod end assembly)

7 Loose pinion bearing locknut (Tighten locknut to specifications)

8 Piston disengaged or loose on rack (Replace rack assembly)

9 Oversize pinion shaft bushing (Replace gear housing)

4 Gear assembly loose on body bracket (Tighten mounting bolt nuts [4] to specifications)

6 Loose yoke plug or locknut (Adjust yoke bearing preload to specifications)

5 Loose pinion bearing cap (Tighten cap to specification)

3 Loose/worn tie rod ball socket (Replace tie rod ball/socket assembly)

FIGURE 28-53. Diagnosis procedure for steering feedback condition (rattle, chuckle, knocking noises in steering gear) on power rack-and-pinion steering gear. *(Courtesy of Ford Motor Co. of Canada Ltd.)*

• Noisy steering

• Pulling to one side (self-steering)

To determine the cause of problems in power steering, proceed as follows.

• Check the lubricant level. If low, check for leaks and correct.

• Check belt tension and condition; replace any glazed or damaged belt.

• Check pump and gear mounting bolts; correct as necessary.

• Check for lost motion at flexible coupling; correct as necessary.

• Check the pitman arm and nut for any looseness; if the pitman arm or sector shaft splines are worn, replace.

• Check for any looseness (lost motion), roughness, or bind in the steering gear; if too loose or too tight, adjust to specifications. If adjustment does not correct the problem or if gear is rough, overhaul according to the manufacturer's procedures and specifications.

• Jack the front of the car to raise front wheels off the floor; support the car on stands; position the steering wheel at the center of travel; start the engine; and, without touching the steering wheel, observe whether the wheel self-steers to right or left; if it does, adjust or repair as required by the manufacturer's manual.

• Check system pressure to determine if pressure developed meets specifications. If too low, pump must be serviced. If pressure is correct and all other checks have been completed, steering gear should be suspected. Remove and repair as needed.

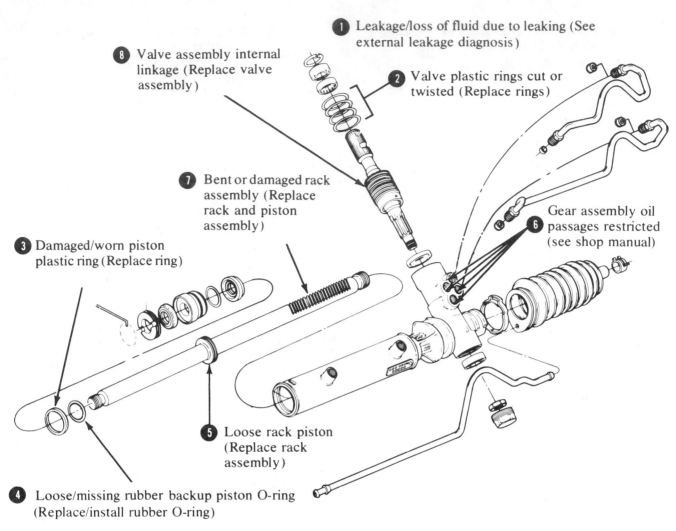

① Leakage/loss of fluid due to leaking (See external leakage diagnosis)

② Valve plastic rings cut or twisted (Replace rings)

⑧ Valve assembly internal linkage (Replace valve assembly)

⑦ Bent or damaged rack assembly (Replace rack and piston assembly)

⑥ Gear assembly oil passages restricted (see shop manual)

③ Damaged/worn piston plastic ring (Replace ring)

⑤ Loose rack piston (Replace rack assembly)

④ Loose/missing rubber backup piston O-ring (Replace/install rubber O-ring)

FIGURE 28–54. Diagnosis procedure for heavy steering effort condition (poor assist or loss of assist) for power rack-and-pinion steering gear. *(Courtesy of Ford Motor Co. of Canada Ltd.)*

PART 6   SELF-CHECK

1. What part of the steering linkage provides for linkage adjustment?

2. What is the purpose of the idler arm?

3. The outer tie rod ends are connected to the _____.

4. What is the purpose of using the recirculating ball-and-nut design in the manual steering gear?

5. The rack-and-pinion steering gear is an integral part of the _____.

6. List three types of power-steering pumps.

7. List three types of power-steering systems.

8. What is the purpose of the flexible coupling between the steering gear and steering column shaft?

9. List three causes of hard steering.

10. List four causes of excessive play in steering.

PART 7   TEST QUESTIONS

1. The center link is supported by the:
   (a) idler arm and steering arm
   (b) steering arm and pitman arm
   (c) pitman arm and linkage booster
   (d) idler arm and pitman arm

2. The pitman arm is splined to the:
   (a) center link
   (b) sector shaft
   (c) wormshaft
   (d) none of the above

3. The recirculating ball type of manual steering gear:
   (a) reduces steering effort
   (b) reduces wear
   (c) improves handling
   (d) all of the above

4. The rack and pinion steering is an integral part of the:
   (a) vehicle frame
   (b) steering linkage
   (c) steering box
   (d) none of the above

5. Power steering pump designs include the:
   (a) roller, slipper, and gear
   (b) vane, gear, and roller
   (c) slipper, vane, and gear
   (d) vane, roller, and slipper

Chapter 29

Wheels, Tires, and Balance

___ Performance Objectives ___

After thorough study of this chapter and sufficient practical work on the appropriate components, and with the appropriate shop manual, tools, and equipment, you should be able to do the following:

1. Complete the self-check and test questions with at least 80 percent accuracy.
2. Follow the accepted general precautions.
3. Accurately diagnose and correct wheel, tire, wheel bearing, and wheel balancing problems.
4. Perform all work to 100 percent accuracy.
5. Prepare the vehicle for customer acceptance.

The tire-and-wheel assemblies provide the only connection between the vehicle and the road. The tires, being air-filled and flexible, absorb much of the road shock from surface irregularities. This reduces the effects of such shock on steering and suspension system components as well as on passengers. In addition, the tires grip the road surface, providing traction for driving, braking, and turning the vehicle.

PART 1 WHEELS

Passenger car wheels consist of a stamped steel disc riveted or welded to a circular rim. Wheel mounting holes are provided in the disc. Mounting holes are tapered to fit tapered mounting nuts that center the wheel over the hub. The rim has a hole for the valve stem and a drop center area for ease of tire removal and installation. The drop center is offset to provide easier tire removal and installation. Other wheels are made of die-cast or forged aluminum or magnesium. Wheels and tires must have minimal radial run-out (out-of-round) and minimal lateral run-out (wobble).

Wheel size is designated as rim width and rim diameter. Rim width is determined by measuring across the rim between the rim flanges. Rim diameter is measured across the bead seating areas from top to bottom of the wheel.

PART 2 TIRES

Most automotive vehicles use the modern tubeless tire. Another type of tire uses an inner rubber tube. This is known as a tube-type tire.

A tubeless tire consists of a rubberized cord body attached to two circular beads. An airtight inner layer seals the air in the tire. The beads are seated at the outer edges of the wheel rim. A layer of rubber is bonded to the outside of the cord body. This layer of rubber is thickest at the outside circumference of the tire, forming the tire tread.

Tire tread designs include summer-and winter-tread types in many variations. Winter-tread tires are designed to grip the snow and be self-cleaning. Studded tires (steel studs inserted in holes in the tread rubber) provide traction on icy surfaces. Lug spacing is irregular in order to reduce noise as much as possible. Summer tires are designed to provide maximum traction in all conditions. Hydroplaning (tires running on top of water-surfaced road as if water skiing) is reduced by certain tread designs. When tires hydroplane, directional control of the vehicle is lost.

Radial-ply tires provide better traction than bias-ply or bias-belted tires in most circumstances. Radial tires have less rolling resistance and thereby decrease fuel consumption.

Tire sizes are determined by wheel rim diameter and tire width. The correct wheel and tire size combination must be used for any given vehicle. Tire and wheel types and sizes must not be mixed on the same vehicle. Mixing tire sizes with wheel sizes and types affects steering, ride, handling, control, and braking.

Basic Tire Construction*

Every bias-ply, belted-bias, and radial tire shares three basic components: the beads, cord body, and tread.

___
*Courtesy of Firestone Tire & Rubber Co.

(a)

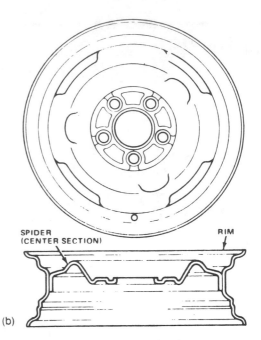

SPIDER
(CENTER SECTION)   RIM

(b)

FIGURE 29-1. Stamped-steel wheel construction detail (A) and cast aluminum wheel (B). ([A] *Courtesy of American Motors Corporation and* [B] *Courtesy of General Motors Corporation)*

Tire Beads

The beads in passenger car tires are made of high-tensile steel wires. The beads anchor the tire to the rim. As a tire rotates, the force of the tire spinning attempts to throw the tire off the rim. In order to keep the tire from being thrown off the rim, the plies of the tires are attached to rings made of high-tensile steel wire. These rings are designed to fit snugly against the automobile rim and anchor the tire to the rim; these wire rings are referred to as *beads.*

Air pressure in the casing of the tire forces the beads of the tire out against the rim and holds them securely in place. The bead is protected from chafing damage against the rim by a strip of rubber, known as a *chafer strip.*

Cord Body

The cord body is composed of plies. It retains air under pressure, which supports the load. Layers of fabric or other material laid on top of each other make up the *cord body* of a tire; they are bonded together in rubber to form one strong unit.

For example, in a conventional four-ply tire, the cords in each ply travel on a bias, or diagonally, from the bead on one side of the tire to the bead on the other side. Each layer of plies travels in alternating directions. This bias construction provides the tire with the strength to prevent unnecessary twisting or damage and also allows the cord body to remain flexible enough to absorb shock and provide a smooth, comfortable ride.

The cord angle of a tire is the degree at which the plies cross the center line of any given tire.

Cord body fabrics most commonly used are rayon, nylon, and polyester.

The cord angle in the conventionally constructed tire determines:

1. The degree of distortion that may occur at high speeds

2. Handling characteristics

3. Coolness of running

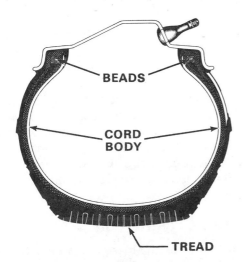

BEADS

CORD
BODY

TREAD

FIGURE 29-2. Tire cross section showing identification of tire components. *(Courtesy of Firestone Tire and Rubber Co.)*

654

The tread is applied over the cord body and is then molded into a specific design. The tread comes directly in contact with the road surface.

Separate components are used for the tread area and the sidewall of any tire.

1. *Tread rubber.* This is compounded, or mixed, to provide customers with a maximum of (a) traction, (b) cut resistance, and (c) long-wearing capabilities.

2. *Sidewall rubber.* In any given tire design, the sidewalls must be flexible and meet different performance requirements than the tread area. Therefore, a different compound is used to produce a suitable rubber for the sidewall area.

Every tire is designed to meet a specific need for performance and safety. All tread designs are developed through an extensive research, development, and testing program, providing quality tires for all types of vehicles and every type of driving—from the stop-and-go driving of the city to the high-speed driving of today's modern highways.

The design of the tread influences:

1. Mileage
2. Handling
3. Ride
4. Amount of road noise
5. Traction

Tread Design

The design of the tread pattern affects the overall performance of any given tire. Depending upon the type of performance required of a tire, the tread will vary in order to meet specific needs. A varying, zig-zag tread pattern that provides mileage and traction and reduces side slippage meets most driving requirements.

The tread is molded into a series of grooves and ribs. The ribs provide the traction edges necessary for gripping the road surface and the grooves provide an easy, fast escape for any foreign matter such as water on the road, and provide the tread edges with a direct, positive grip on the surface traveled on.

Tread rib is the area on which traction edges and sipes are designed. Grooves are the spaces between the adjacent tread ribs.

Sipes

In order to increase the traction ability of any tire and to increase the number of traction edges, small grooves, referred to as sipes, are molded into the ribs of the tread design.

As the tire flexes on the road surface, these sipes open and provide extra gripping action.

When studying a tread surface, the sipes look as though they are very shallow and only on the surface. The sipes travel the full depth of the tread, providing traction for the entire tread life of the tire.

The more grooves and sipes a tire has, the greater its wet pavement traction.

Construction Types

Three types of tire construction are in use. They are referred to as bias ply, bias-belted, and radial-ply construction. The description for each construction type is derived from the method used to position the tire body cord plies in relation to the centerline of the tread.

Conventional Bias Construction

Conventional bias construction may have two, four, or more plies placed on top of one another with cords running in alternating directions on the bias. The body-ply cords run from bead to bead, with:

SIPES

FULL DEPTH SIPING

FIGURE 29-3. Sipes in tire treads improve the tractive ability of a tire on wet surfaces. *(Courtesy of Firestone Tire and Rubber Co.)*

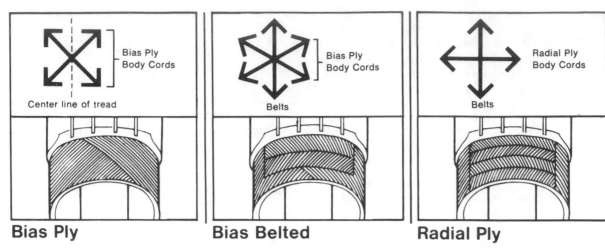

Bias Ply **Bias Belted** **Radial Ply**

FIGURE 29–4. The bias-ply tire has two or more layers of crisscrossed body cords. The bias-belted tire body is constructed the same as the bias-ply but with two or more circumferential belts added. The radial-ply tire has the body cords running from bead to bead across the tire at 90° to direction of tire travel, with two or more belts added.

Basic, simplified construction

Dependable traction and mileage performance

Handling stability and body strength in all directions

Belted-bias Construction

In belted-bias construction, the cord body is constructed in the conventional manner with the cord in the body plies running on a bias from bead to bead. Two or more bias belts are then applied on top of the body plies directly under the tread area. Adding these high-strength belts, regardless of the type of cord material used, to any conventional bias-ply tire gives greatly increased mileage.

The belts are located under the tread area only; they do not extend from bead to bead as the body plies do. Rayon, fibergalss, and steel cord are the most commonly used belt materials.

Features of belted-bias construction include:

Increased mileage. The belts restrict the stresses of the cord body and stabilize the tread area. This reduction in tread scrubbing on the highway surface results in tremendous mileage increases.

Road hugging ability. The stabilizer belts hold the tread flatter against the road surface providing increased traction and safety.

The tread belts increase resistance to punctures, cuts, and bruises.

Radial-ply Construction

In radial construction, the body-ply cords run in a straight line, parallel to one another, from bead to bead. Located on top of these body plies and directly under the tread area are two or more belts. The cords in these belts are on the bias and are referred to as stabilizer belts as they stabilize or hold firmly the tread area of the tire.

The features of radial-ply construction are a result of combining the flexible radial cord body and high-strength belts. Radial tires have the longest tread footprint in contact with the road surface of all tire constructions, giving more traction surface.

Less tread flexing results in greater mileage due to the stabilizer belts located under the tread area. These belts are more rigid than those used in belted-bias tires. Radial body plies exert less pulling, tugging forces on belts.

Other features are:

Greatest resistance to bruises and impacts in the tread area that contacts the road.

Savings in fuel costs due to a greater reduction in rolling resistance compared to bias or belted-bias tires.

Improved handling and cornering control. The flexible sidewalls of a radial tire lean into turns while the stiff belts hold the complete tread area in contact with the road.

Comparing Tire Designs

A *conventional bias tire* is made with two, four, or more cord body plies running at bias angles.

Belted-bias tires are built with a two- or four-ply cord body with plies running on the bias, plus a two- or more-ply belt directly under the tread area. The cord in these belt plies also runs at bias angles.

Radial construction has body-ply cords that run straight across the tire from bead to bead. Radial

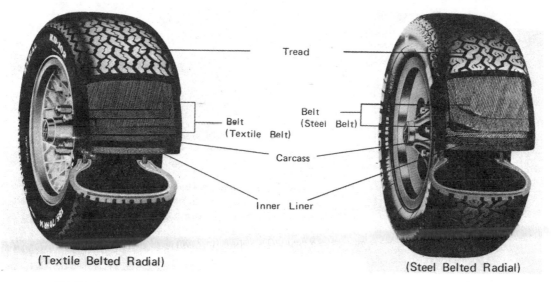

Tread

Belt
(Textile Belt)

Belt
(Steel Belt)

Carcass

Inner Liner

(Textile Belted Radial)

(Steel Belted Radial)

FIGURE 29-5. Two examples of radial tire construction. *(Courtesy of Bridgestone)*

tires also have two or more belt plies directly under the tread area. The cord in these belt plies runs at a bias angle.

Radial body plies do not set up diagonal stress in the footprint and expansion cycles like bias cord bodies. The radial cord body alone is extremely flexible and it sets up different types of stresses.

In cornering, radial cord body plies do not provide lateral stability; therefore, greater pressures are exerted on the belt plies under the tread area. This flexibility in a radial cord body means that the belt plies must both restrict the stresses in the footprint and give added lateral stability while cornering.

Every passenger tire, regardless of construction, goes through three stress cycles during one complete revolution of the wheel: the footprint or contraction cycle (A), the expansion cycle (B), and the normal stress cycle (C). See Figure 29-7.

Figure 29-8 illustrates the tread of a *conventional bias* construction tire as it goes through the three stress cycles in one revolution of a wheel. The top illustration shows a normal tread; the center illustration shows how the footprint or contraction cycle squeezes the tread together as the cord pulls at opposing angles; the bottom illustration shows how the tread design expands as the cord body reverses the direction of its pull in the expansion cycle. This opening and closing of the tread causes it to scrub on the pavement and is the major cause of tire wear.

The three cycles for a *belted-bias* construction tire, Figure 29-8 center, show that the addition of a belt under the tread area greatly reduces the pull of the cord body during the footprint cycle and minimizes the contraction. It also diminishes the reverse pull in the expansion cycle and reduces the expansion. This reduction in contraction and expansion results in less scrubbing on the pavement and is the reason that tires with belted-bias construction give longer mileage than conventional tires.

In *radial* tires the belt plies eliminate any contraction or expansion of the tread design, as illustrated in Figure 29-8. The absence of the scrubbing action, caused by contraction and expansion, makes radial tires the ultimate for long mileage. The unique flex action of the radial tire as it goes through the footprint cycle gives a longer footprint, as shown in the contraction cycle.*

Tread Wear Indicators

As a visible check of tire condition, tread wear indicators are molded into the bottom of the tread grooves. These indicators appear in the form of 1/2-inch (13 millimeters) wide bands across the tread when it is worn to a thickness of 1/16-inch (1.58 millimeters). The tire should be replaced when these indicator bands become visible. A number of states have statutes concerning minimum permissible tread depths and use these indicators as the tire wear limit.

Slip Angle

The slip angle of a tire is the difference between the direction in which a wheel is positioned and the direction in which it is actually moving. As the lateral load on a tire is increased during a turn, the slip angle increases. If the lateral load is increased sufficiently, the tire will actually slip sidewise.

Bias-ply tires have the greater slip angle. Bias-belted tires have a lower slip angle, and radial-ply tires have the lowest slip angle. As the slip angle

*Courtesy of Firestone Tire & Rubber Co.

657

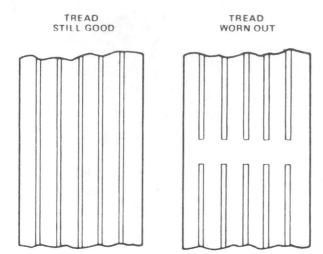

TREAD
STILL GOOD

TREAD
WORN OUT

FIGURE 29-6. Tread pattern on tires has several sections where grooves are not as deep as elsewhere. These sections are called *tread wear bars*. When tire tread is worn down to tread wear bars, tire should be replaced. *(Courtesy of American Motors Corporation)*

FIGURE 29-7. A car tire goes through three stress cycles during every revolution of the wheel: (A) contraction, (B) expansion, (C) normal stress. *(Courtesy of Firestone Tire and Rubber Co.)*

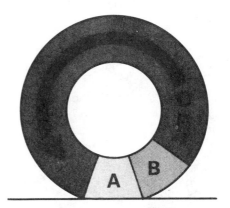

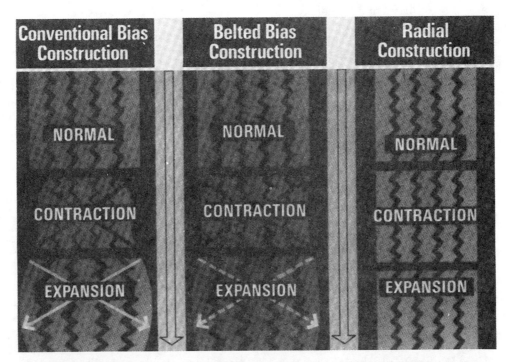

FIGURE 29-8. Effects of stress cycles on tire tread of tires of different construction. Radial tires show least effect. *(Courtesy of Firestone Tire and Rubber Co.)*

increases, control of the vehicle becomes more difficult. Adhesion of the tire to the road surface (coefficient of friction) is critical to vehicle control.

The rate of slip-angle increase (until the point of loss of control) is more gradual with bias-ply tires as compared with radial-ply tires. As higher speed and sharper turns increase the lateral force on the tires, the radial-ply tire suddenly loses adhesion with the road surface and sideslip results. A bias-ply tire, on the other hand, has a gradual increase in slip angle, which provides more warning time to the driver.

Factors affecting a tire's slip angle are lateral force on the tire, depending on vehicle speed; load and degree of turn; tire inflation pressure; tire temperature; type of tire rubber compound; type of tire construction (bias-ply, bias-belted, radial); tire condition (wear); type of road surface (pavement, gravel, etc.); and condition of road surface (wet, dry, icy).

It is extremely important that (a) a vehicle be equipped with the recommended tire type and size, (b) only tires in good condition be used, (c) proper inflation pressures be maintained, and (d) tire types and sizes not be mixed in order to maintain good vehicle handling and safety of directional control and braking.

Radial-tire Lead and Waddle

Lead is the tendency of the car to deviate from a straight path on a level road when there is no pressure on the steering wheel in either direction. Lead may be caused by improper alignment, uneven braking, or the tires.

An off-center belt in a radial tire can cause a tire to lead. This type of tire creates a side force on the vehicle resulting in lead. Also, if one side of a tire is smaller in diameter than the other side, the tire will cause the vehicle to lead. Front tires with unequal

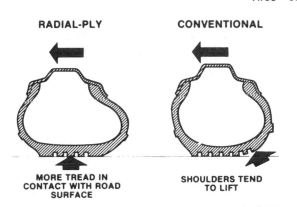

FIGURE 20-10. More flexible sidewalls and radial-ply construction improve tire adhesion to road surface as compared to conventional tire construction during a turn. This reduces the amount of slip angle. (*Courtesy of Ford Motor Co. of Canada Ltd.*)

tread wear can also cause lead. Tires must be of the same size, type, and condition on the front wheels to prevent tire lead. Rear tires do not cause lead; however, rear tires should also be of the same size, type, and condition to assure balanced braking and vehicle control.

Load Rating

The load-carrying ability of a tire is indicated by a letter designation on the sidewall of the tire. Letter ratings of A, B, C, D, etc., indicate progressively higher load ratings. The load-rating D tire is capable of carrying a greater load than a C load rating tire. Refer to the load-rating chart (Figure 29–16) for comparisons. Load ratings are given for specific inflation pressures only. However, maximum inflation pressures recommended by the tire manufacturer should not be exceeded. Tire failure resulting in accidents and injury can be the result.

Tire Inflation Pressures

Tire inflation pressures are stated in pounds per square inch (psi) or in kilopascals (kPa). Maximum inflation pressures are usually stated on the sidewall of the tire and are to be used when maximum

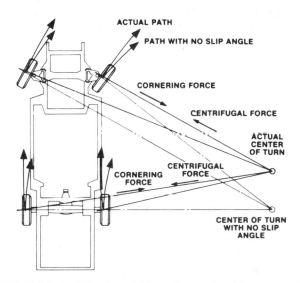

FIGURE 29-9. Effects of tire slip angle. (*Courtesy of Ford Motor Co. of Canada Ltd.*)

FIGURE 29-11. Effects of radial tire waddle on vehicle. (*Courtesy of General Motors Corporation*)

INFLATION PRESSURE CONVERSION CHART
(KILOPASCALS TO PSI)

kPa	psi	kPa	psi
140	20	215	31
145	21	220	32
155	22	230	33
160	23	235	34
165	24	240	35
170	25	250	36
180	26	275	40
185	27	310	45
190	28	345	50
200	29	380	55
205	30	415	60

Conversion: 6.9 kPa = 1 psi

FIGURE 29-12. Tire pressure conversion chart. *(Courtesy of General Motors Corporation)*

stated load on the same tire is to be carried. Lesser pressures may be used as recommended by the vehicle manufacturer with lighter loads. The pressure recommended for any model is carefully calculated to give a satisfactory ride, stability, steering, tread wear, tire life, and resistance to bruises.

Tire pressure should be checked with tires cold (after the car has sat for three hours or more or driven less than one mile), and checked monthly or before any extended trip and set to the specifications on the tire placard located on rear face of driver's door, door post, or glove compartment. Valve caps or extensions should be on the valves to keep dust and water out.

Tire pressures may increase as much as 40 kPa (6 psi) when hot. Higher-than-recommended pressure can cause

1. Hard ride
2. Tire bruising or carcass damage
3. Rapid tread wear at center of tire

Lower-than-recommended pressure can cause

1. Tire squeal on turns
2. Hard steering
3. Rapid and uneven wear on the edges of the tread
4. Tire rim bruises and rupture
5. Tire cord breakage
6. High tire temperatures
7. Reduced handling
8. High fuel consumption

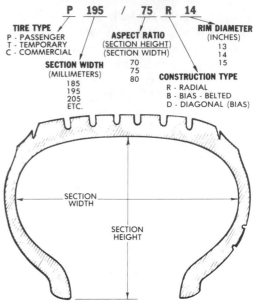

METRIC TIRE SIZES

P 195 / 75 R 14

TIRE TYPE
P - PASSENGER
T - TEMPORARY
C - COMMERCIAL

ASPECT RATIO
(SECTION HEIGHT)
(SECTION WIDTH)

RIM DIAMETER
(INCHES)
13
14
15

SECTION WIDTH
(MILLIMETERS)
185
195
205
ETC.

70
75
80

CONSTRUCTION TYPE
R - RADIAL
B - BIAS - BELTED
D - DIAGONAL (BIAS)

SECTION WIDTH

SECTION HEIGHT

FIGURE 29-13. Tire size designation found on tire sidewall is explained here. *(Courtesy of General Motors Corporation)*

Unequal pressure on the same axle can cause

1. Uneven braking
2. Steering lead
3. Reduced handling
4. Swerve on acceleration

Tire Sizes

Tire size designations are stated on the tire sidewall. Tire cross-sectional width and bead-to-bead diameter are the major size designations. Typical sidewall tire size and type markings are shown in Figures 29-13 and 29-15.

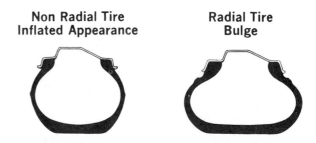

Non Radial Tire Inflated Appearance

Radial Tire Bulge

FIGURE 29-14. Tire profile of nonradial tire as compared to radial tire. Although the radial tire appears to be underinflated, it is not. This is normal appearance at proper inflation; do not overinflate. *(Courtesy of Bridgestone)*

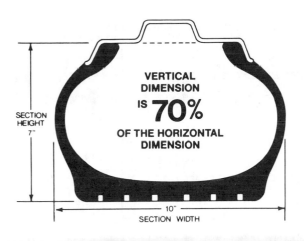 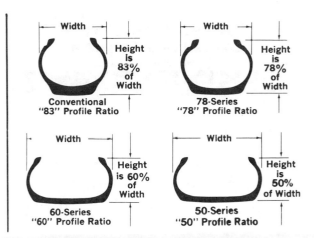

FIGURE 29-15. The aspect ratio (profile ratio) of a tire is its cross-sectional height compared to its cross-sectional width expressed in percentage figures.

Radial Tire Grading

Radial tires produced by the various tire manufacturers are classified according to their tread life, wet traction capability, and high-temperature capability. The high-temperature capability is directly related to the tire's high-speed capability. These ratings are moulded into the tire sidewall of some tires.

The tread wear rating is stated in numbers in increments of ten. Every ten points represents 3,000 miles (4800 km) of tread life expectancy. A rating of 100 for tread wear would therefore indicate a tread life expectancy of 30,000 miles (48,000 km). Traction ratings and temperature resistance ratings are stated in letter grades A, B and C, with A the best.

Compact Spare

The compact spare is designed to reduce weight and increase trunk space. It will perform well with the other tires on the car for the 1,600 to 4,800 km (1,000 to 3,000 miles) life of the tread. A narrow wheel is used. The compact spare tire should not be used with any other wheel. The compact spare wheel should not be used with standard tires, snow tires, wheel covers, or trim rings. If such use is attempted, damage to these items or other parts of the car may occur. The compact spare should only be used on cars that offered it as original equipment. Since it is smaller in diameter, it must not be used on cars equipped with a limited slip differential, because possible damage to the differential might occur. Inflation pressure should be periodically checked and maintained at recommended pressure. The compact spare is serviceable with present equipment and procedures.

The compact spare should be used only as recommended by the vehicle manufacturer.

PART 3   WHEEL BEARINGS

There are several types of wheel bearing arrangements for both driving and nondriving wheels, whether front-wheel drive, rear-wheel drive, or four-wheel drive. One design uses two opposed, tapered roller bearings with the inner bearing being the larger of the two. This arrangement usually provides for replacement of faulty bearings and allows periodic repacking of the bearings. In many applications of this design, a precise adjustment of the wheel bearings is required, while on other applications adjustment is automatically provided by tightening the retaining nut to specified torque.

Another design uses a preassembled, prelubricated, and sealed bearing and hub assembly. This design does not provide for periodic repacking of wheel-bearings; no wheel bearing adjustment is required or possible. A wheel-bearing problem requires replacement of the bearing and hub assembly.

A variation of the sealed type allows replacement of the sealed bearing without replacing the hub. The sealed unit may have roller bearings or ball bearings.

Many rear-wheel-drive axle bearings are of the straight roller bearing design. These usually use the drive axle shaft as the inner bearing race. Other rear-wheel-drive axle bearings are of the tapered roller bearing or ball bearing type. In these types a complete bearing is used rather than having the axle shaft serve as the inner race. Lubrication is provided from the differential lubricant in some cases, while other designs may require packing the bearing with wheel-bearing grease or multipurpose grease during assembly or a prelubricated, sealed bearing may be used.

For further details, see the wheel bearing diagnosis and service section following.

Tire Interchangeability and Load and Inflation Data

LOAD LIMITS (LBS. PER TIRE) FOR TIRES USED ON PASSENGER CARS, STATION WAGONS AND MULTI-PURPOSE PASSENGER VEHICLES

Load Range B (4 ply-rating) ———→
Load Range C (6-ply rating) ————————→
Load Range D (8-ply rating) ————————————————→

TIRE SIZE OR DESIGNATION

Conventional Bias Ply 1965-On	78 Series	70 Series	60 Series	50 Series	Metric	Radial Ply 78 Series	70 Series	20	22	24	26	28	30	32	34	36	38	40
6.00-13					165R13													
	A78-13	A70-13	A60-13			AR78-13	AR70-13	770	820	860	900	930	970	1010	1040	1080	1110	1140
								810	860	900	940	980	1020	1060	1090	1130	1160	1200
6.50-13	B78-13		B60-13	B50-13	175R13	BR78-13	BR70-13	890	930	980	1030	1070	1110	1150	1190	1230	1270	1300
	C78-13	C70-13	C60-13			CR78-13	CR70-13	950	1000	1050	1100	1140	1190	1230	1270	1320	1360	1400
7.00-13					185R13			980	1030	1080	1130	1180	1230	1270	1310	1360	1400	1440
	D78-13	D70-13	D60-13					950	1000	1050	1100	1140	1190	1230	1270	1320	1360	1400
								1010	1070	1120	1170	1220	1270	1320	1360	1410	1450	1490
					195R13			1060	1110	1170	1220	1280	1320	1370	1420	1470	1510	1560
6.45-14					155R14			780	820	860	900	940	970	1010	1040	1080	1110	1140
	B78-14					BR78-14		860	910	960	1000	1040	1080	1120	1160	1200	1240	1270
					165R14			870	930	980	1030	1070	1110	1150	1190	1230	1270	1300
								860	910	960	1000	1040	1080	1120	1170	1200	1240	1280
6.95-14	C78-14					CR78-14	CR70-14	950	1000	1050	1100	1140	1190	1230	1270	1310	1350	1390
					175R14			950	1000	1050	1100	1140	1190	1230	1270	1320	1360	1400
								950	1000	1050	1100	1140	1190	1230	1280	1320	1360	1400
	D78-14	D70-14	D60-14			DR78-14	DR70-14	1010	1070	1120	1170	1220	1270	1320	1360	1410	1450	1490
7.35-14					185R14			1040	1100	1160	1210	1260	1310	1360	1400	1450	1490	1540
	E78-14	E70-14	E60-14			ER78-14	ER70-14	1040	1100	1160	1210	1260	1310	1360	1410	1450	1500	1540
								1070	1130	1190	1240	1300	1350	1400	1440	1490	1540	1580
7.75-14					195R14			1150	1210	1270	1330	1390	1440	1500	1550	1600	1650	1690
	F78-14	F70-14	F60-14			FR78-14	FR70-14	1150	1210	1270	1330	1390	1440	1500	1540	1590	1640	1690
								1160	1220	1280	1340	1400	1450	1500	1550	1610	1650	1700
8.25-14					205R14			1250	1310	1380	1440	1500	1560	1620	1670	1730	1780	1830
	G78-14	G70-14	G60-14	G50-14		GR78-14	GR70-14	1250	1310	1380	1440	1500	1560	1620	1680	1730	1780	1830
								1250	1310	1380	1440	1500	1560	1620	1680	1730	1780	1830
8.55-14					215R14			1360	1430	1510	1580	1640	1710	1770	1830	1890	1950	2000
	H78-14	H70-14	H60-14	H50-14		HR78-14	HR70-14	1360	1430	1510	1580	1640	1710	1770	1830	1890	1950	2010
								1360	1440	1510	1580	1650	1710	1770	1830	1890	1950	2010
8.85-14								1430	1510	1580	1660	1730	1790	1860	1920	1990	2050	2100
	J78-14	J70-14	J60-14			JR78-14	JR70-14	1430	1500	1580	1650	1720	1790	1860	1920	1980	2040	2100
					225R14			1430	1510	1580	1660	1730	1790	1860	1920	1980	2040	2100
		L70-14	L60-14				LR70-14	1520	1600	1680	1750	1830	1900	1970	2040	2100	2170	2230
				M50-14				1610	1700	1780	1860	1940	2020	2090	2160	2230	2300	2370
				N50-14				1700	1790	1880	1970	2050	2130	2210	2280	2360	2430	2500
	A78-15	A70-15				AR78-15		810	860	900	940	980	1020	1060	1090	1130	1160	1200
			B60-15		165R15	BR78-15		870	910	960	1000	1050	1090	1130	1170	1200	1240	1280
								890	930	980	1030	1070	1110	1150	1190	1230	1270	1300
6.85-15	C78-15	C70-15	C60-15					950	1000	1050	1100	1140	1190	1230	1270	1320	1360	1390
					175R15			950	1000	1050	1100	1140	1190	1230	1270	1320	1360	1400
								950	1000	1050	1100	1140	1190	1230	1280	1320	1360	1400
	D78-15	D70-15					DR70-15	1010	1070	1120	1170	1220	1270	1320	1360	1410	1450	1490
7.35-15	E78-15	E70-15	E60-15			ER78-15	ER70-15	1070	1130	1180	1240	1290	1340	1390	1440	1480	1530	1570
								1070	1130	1190	1240	1300	1350	1400	1440	1490	1540	1580
					185R15			1070	1130	1180	1240	1290	1340	1390	1430	1480	1520	1570
7.75-15					195R15			1150	1210	1270	1330	1380	1440	1490	1540	1590	1640	1690
	F78-15	F70-15	F60-15			FR78-15	FR70-15	1160	1220	1280	1340	1400	1450	1500	1550	1610	1650	1700
8.15-15					205R15			1240	1300	1370	1430	1490	1550	1610	1660	1720	1770	1820
	G78-15	G70-15	G60-15			GR78-15	GR70-15	1250	1310	1380	1440	1500	1560	1620	1680	1730	1780	1830
8.25-15								1250	1310	1380	1440	1500	1560	1620	1670	1730	1780	1830
8.45-15					215R15			1340	1410	1480	1550	1620	1680	1740	1800	1860	1920	1970
								1340	1410	1480	1550	1620	1680	1740	1800	1860	1910	1970
	H78-15	H70-15	H60-15			HR78-15	HR70-15	1310	1400	1450	1520	1580	1640	1710	1760	1820	1880	1930
								1360	1440	1510	1580	1650	1710	1770	1830	1890	1950	2010
8.55-15								1360	1430	1510	1580	1640	1710	1770	1830	1890	1950	2000
8.85-15					225R15			1430	1510	1580	1650	1720	1790	1860	1920	1980	2040	2100
	J78-15	J70-15	J60-15			JR78-15	JR70-15	1430	1500	1580	1650	1720	1790	1860	1920	1980	2040	2100
9.00-15								1460	1540	1620	1690	1760	1830	1900	1970	2030	2090	2150
		K70-15					KR70-15	1460	1540	1620	1690	1770	1830	1900	1970	2030	2090	2150
9.15-15								1510	1600	1680	1750	1830	1900	1970	2030	2100	2160	2230
					235R15			1510	1600	1680	1750	1830	1900	1970	2040	2100	2170	2230
	L78-15	L70-15	L60-15			LR78-15	LR70-15	1520	1600	1680	1750	1830	1900	1970	2040	2100	2170	2230
						MR78-15	MR70-15	1610	1700	1780	1860	1940	2020	2090	2160	2230	2300	2370
	N78-15					NR78-15		1700	1790	1880	1970	2050	2130	2210	2280	2360	2430	2500
8.90-15								1700	1810	1880	1970	2050	2130	2210	2290	2360	2430	2500
6.00-16								1075	1135	1195	1250	1300	1350	1400	1450	1500		
6.50-16								1215	1280	1345	1405	1465	1525	1580	1635	1690	1740	1790
7.00-15								1310	1380	1450	1515	1580	1640	1700	1760	1820	1870	1930
7.00-16								1365	1440	1515	1585	1650	1715	1780	1840	1900		

Maximum inflation and load is that shown in the 32 psi column for Load Range B (4-ply rating) tires, 36 psi for Load Range C (6-ply rating) tires and 40 psi for Load Range D (8-ply rating) tires.

If you are considering replacing present tires with tires of a different size designation, be sure to check the automobile manufacturer's recommendations. Interchangeability is not always possible because of differences in load ratings, tire dimensions, wheel well clearances and rim sizes. Also, tires of different construction (bias, bias/belted, or radial) or different sizes should never be used together on the same axle. If radial tires are used with other tire types, the radials must be used on the rear axle only.

FIGURE 29-16. Tire size, load rating, and inflation pressure chart. *(Courtesy of Goodyear Canada Inc.)*

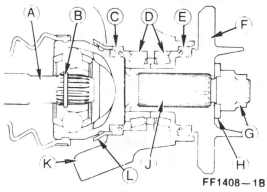

FF1408—1B

A—Intermediate   F—Hub
     Driveshaft   G—Retaining Nut
B—Clip   H—Washer
C—Grease Retainer   J—Outer Fix-Joint
D—Bearings   K—Spindle Carrier
E—Grease Retainer   L—Dust Shield

FIGURE 29-17. Nonadjustable tapered roller wheel bearing arrangement on one front-wheel-drive model. *(Courtesy of Ford Motor Co. of Canada Ltd.)*

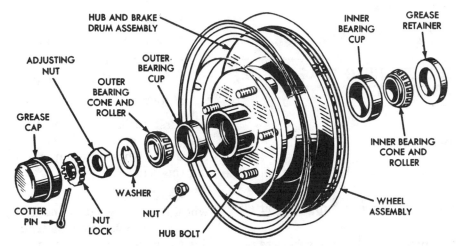

FIGURE 29-18. Exploded view of wheel hub and bearing assembly. *(Courtesy of Ford Motor Co. of Canada Ltd.)*

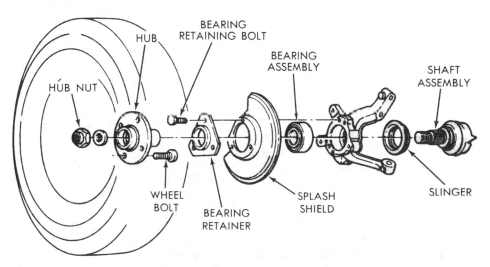

FIGURE 29-19. Sealed bearing type of front-wheel-drive and mounting arrangement. *(Courtesy of Chrysler Corporation)*

663

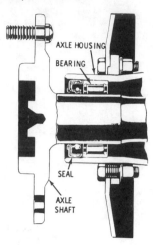

FIGURE 29-20. Straight roller type rear-axle bearing-and-seal arrangement. Notice the absence of a separate inner bearing race. Rollers run on axle shaft. *(Courtesy of General Motors Corporation)*

PART 4   WHEEL BEARING DIAGNOSIS AND SERVICE

General Precautions

- Raise the vehicle only at the contact points specified by the vehicle manufacturer.
- The vehicle must be properly supported at all times.
- Use only the proper tools and supports in good condition and use them as recommended.
- Do not disassemble any suspension parts without proper consideration of the consequences; a loaded spring packs a powerful punch.
- Always refer to the manufacturer's manual for proper procedures; then follow them.
- Never allow a wheel-and-tire assembly to bounce; keep the wheel under control at all times.
- Never depress the brake pedal when brake parts have been removed.
- Never mix parts from one wheel assembly with another.
- Never add grease to wheel bearings. Completely remove all old grease and use only new grease.
- Never use suspension parts that have been heated, damaged, bent, or straightened.
- Avoid getting grease, solvent, brake fluid, or dirty fingerprints on brake discs, pads, linings, and drums.

- Never allow suspension or brake parts to hang on brake hoses or constant velocity universal joints.
- Always use the correct size and type of fastener.
- Use new fasteners when recommended by the manufacturer.
- Always tighten all fasteners to specified torque.
- Always install new cotter pins properly locked wherever needed.

Wheel Bearing Removal

Front or Rear

The procedure for removal of wheel bearings will vary considerably depending on the following design differences:

- Front wheel, nondriving, disc brakes
- Front wheel, nondriving, drum brakes
- Front wheel, driving, drum brakes
- Rear wheel, nondriving, drum brakes
- Rear wheel, driving, drum brakes
- Rear wheel, driving, disc brakes

First position the vehicle in the shop where it is going to be serviced. Next remove the wheel covers and loosen wheel-retaining nuts one turn before raising the vehicle.

Caution: Never move or drive a vehicle with wheel nuts loosened; damage to wheels will result.

Raise the vehicle on a frame contact hoist to allow the wheels to hang from the suspension or jack the vehicle and place safety stands under the vehicle to achieve the same result. Mark one wheel stud and wheel stud hole to maintain wheel balance after assembly by maintaining original wheel-to-hub position. Chalk mark all wheels as to position on the vehicle—left front, right front, left rear, right rear—for proper reassembly.

Remove the wheels. On drum brake units mark the brake drums similarly, then remove the drums. This may require retracting the brake shoe adjustment. This can be done by holding the self-adjuster away from the star wheel adjuster and turning the adjuster in the correct direction. Access to the self-adjuster is made through a hole in the backing plate in most cases. On ratchet-type self-adjusters, pry the spring-loaded ratchet back to the release position.

On rear-wheel drum units the drum may be held by speed nut retainers on the wheel-mounting studs or by screws that hold the drum to the axle flange. These must first be removed to allow drum removal. Handle drums with care to prevent distortion. Do

Wheel bearing noise diagnosis procedure for Citation front-wheel-drive vehicle. In general the same procedure may be used for most drive-wheel noise problems, front or rear. (Courtesy of General Motors Corporation)

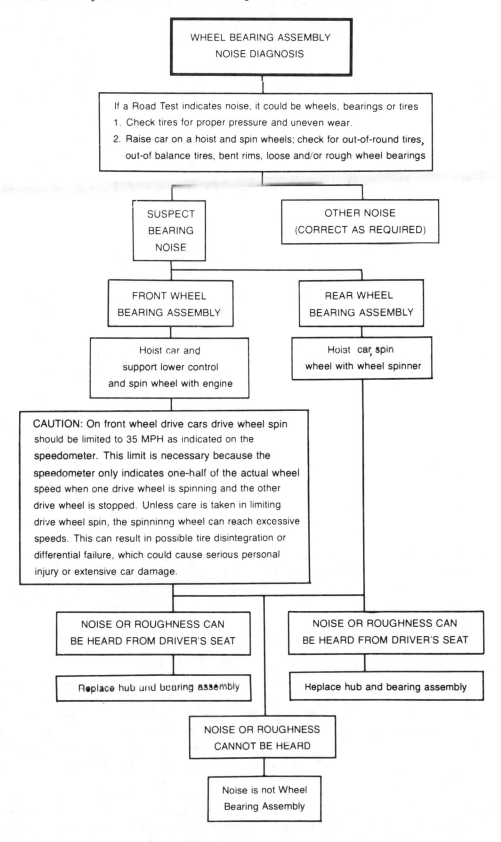

Typical sealed wheel bearing looseness diagnosis procedure for General Motors Citation. (Courtesy of General Motors Corporation)

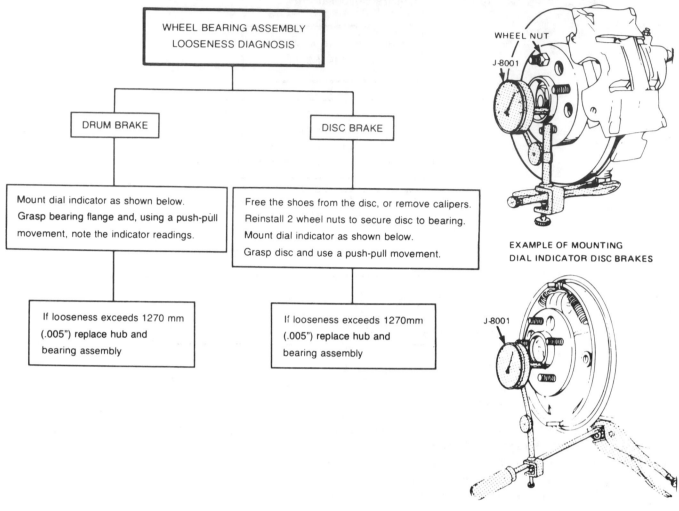

WHEEL BEARING ASSEMBLY LOOSENESS DIAGNOSIS

DRUM BRAKE

DISC BRAKE

Mount dial indicator as shown below. Grasp bearing flange and, using a push-pull movement, note the indicator readings.

Free the shoes from the disc, or remove calipers. Reinstall 2 wheel nuts to secure disc to bearing. Mount dial indicator as shown below. Grasp disc and use a push-pull movement.

If looseness exceeds 1270 mm (.005") replace hub and bearing assembly

If looseness exceeds 1270mm (.005") replace hub and bearing assembly

WHEEL NUT

J-8001

EXAMPLE OF MOUNTING DIAL INDICATOR DISC BRAKES

J-8001

EXAMPLE OF MOUNTING DIAL INDICATOR DRUM BRAKES

not use a hammer on the brake drums. If drums are tight, use the drum puller recommended for the purpose. However, incorrect use of the puller, such as applying too much force, can also distort the drum.

On disc brake units remove the caliper from the steering knuckle and support the caliper so that it will not hang by the flexible brake hose.

On many front-wheel units and some rear-wheel units, the dust cap must be removed to allow access to the retaining nut. The dust cap is a tight press fit into the wheel hub and should be removed with a special tool or pried off with a screwdriver to prevent damage to the dust cap.

Next remove the cotter pin by using a pair of side cutters. Grip the cotter pin head firmly with the side cutters and pry up. If the nut is staked to a groove in the spindle or axle shaft, carefully force the staked part of the nut up out of the groove with a special tapered narrow chisel-type tool. Lubricate the threads if dry and remove the nut. In most cases

this will allow the removal of the retaining washer and hub assembly from the spindle.

Next pry the inner seal from the hub and remove the bearing cone. Do the same with the outer seal if so equipped.

Repacking and Assembly

Wipe all excess grease from the spindle, hub, and bearings; then wash these parts in cleaning solvent. These parts must be absolutely clean of all old grease and dirt. Blow dry with compressed air but never spin bearings with compressed air. Spinning will damage the bearing; it may fly apart, causing injury and damage.

Examine all parts for wear or damage; if bearing cups in the hub are tight and in good condition, they may be used again. If not, replace them as shown in the illustrations.

Repack good used bearing cones with the rec-

WHEEL BEARING DIAGNOSIS

CONSIDER THE FOLLOWING FACTORS WHEN DIAGNOSING BEARING CONDITION:

1. GENERAL CONDITION OF ALL PARTS DURING DISASSEMBLY AND INSPECTION.
2. CLASSIFY THE FAILURE WITH THE AID OF THE ILLUSTRATIONS.
3. DETERMINE THE CAUSE.
4. MAKE ALL REPAIRS FOLLOWING RECOMMENDED PROCEDURES.

ABRASIVE ROLLER WEAR

PATTERN ON RACES AND ROLLERS CAUSED BY FINE ABRASIVES.

CLEAN ALL PARTS AND HOUSINGS. CHECK SEALS AND BEARINGS AND REPLACE IF LEAKING, ROUGH OR NOISY.

GALLING

METAL SMEARS ON ROLLER ENDS DUE TO OVERHEAT, LUBRICANT FAILURE OR OVERLOAD (WAGON S)

REPLACE BEARING -- CHECK SEALS AND CHECK FOR PROPER LUBRICATION.

BENT CAGE

CAGE DAMAGE DUE TO IMPROPER HANDLING OR TOOL USAGE.

REPLACE BEARING.

ABRASIVE STEP WEAR

PATTERN ON ROLLER ENDS CAUSED BY FINE ABRASIVES.

CLEAN ALL PARTS AND HOUSINGS. CHECK SEALS AND BEARINGS AND REPLACE IF LEAKING, ROUGH OR NOISY.

ETCHING

BEARING SURFACES APPEAR GRAY OR GRAYISH BLACK IN COLOR WITH RELATED ETCHING AWAY OF MATERIAL USUALLY AT ROLLER SPACING.

REPLACE BEARINGS -- CHECK SEALS AND CHECK FOR PROPER LUBRICATION.

BENT CAGE

CAGE DAMAGE DUE TO IMPROPER HANDLING OR TOOL USAGE.

REPLACE BEARING.

INDENTATIONS

SURFACE DEPRESSIONS ON RACE AND ROLLERS CAUSED BY HARD PARTICLES OF FOREIGN MATERIAL.

CLEAN ALL PARTS AND HOUSINGS. CHECK SEALS AND REPLACE BEARINGS IF ROUGH OR NOISY.

CAGE WEAR

WEAR AROUND OUTSIDE DIAMETER OF CAGE AND ROLLER POCKETS CAUSED BY ABRASIVE MATERIAL AND INEFFICIENT LUBRICATION.

CLEAN RELATED PARTS AND HOUSINGS. CHECK SEALS AND REPLACE BEARINGS.

MISALIGNMENT

OUTER RACE MISALIGNMENT DUE TO FOREIGN OBJECT.

CLEAN RELATED PARTS AND REPLACE BEARING. MAKE SURE RACES ARE PROPERLY SEATED.

667

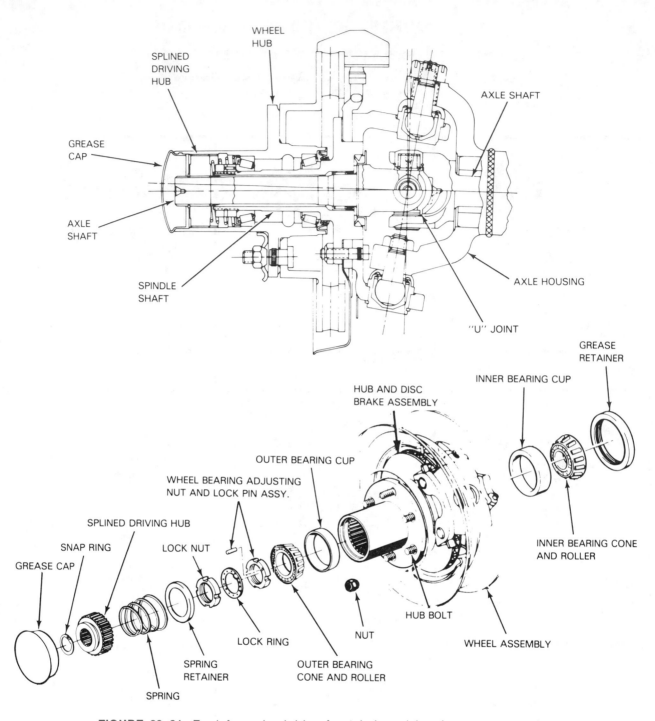

FIGURE 29-21. Ford four-wheel-drive front hub and bearing arrangement. *(Courtesy of Ford Motor Co. of Canada Ltd.)*

ommended grade of wheel bearing grease or multipurpose grease. Make sure that all rollers are completely surrounded with grease. This can be done by hand or with a bearing packer designed for the purpose. Also, apply a small layer of the same grease to the inside of the hub, to the spindle, and to the dust cap. This prevents rust and provides a reserve of lubricant.

Install the inner wheel-bearing cone and new

dust seal in the hub. Position the hub over the spindle without damaging the seal and install the outer bearing washer and retaining nut.

Follow the manufacturer's recommended procedure in the service manual for correct tightening of the nut. The general procedure for the adjustable type is to tighten the nut to specified torque to seat the bearings. Then back the nut off one turn. Next tighten the nut either finger-tight or to specified

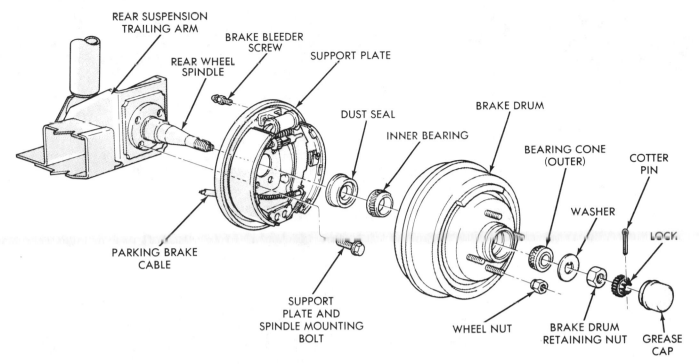

FIGURE 29-22. Trailing rear-axle wheel mounting and bearing arrangement. Two opposed tapered roller bearings are used, and bearings are adjustable. *(Courtesy of Chrysler Corporation)*

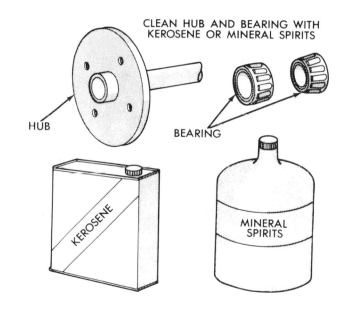

FIGURE 29-23. *(Courtesy of Chrysler Corporation)*

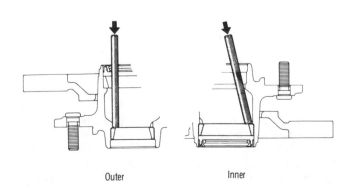

Outer   Inner

FIGURE 29-24. Removing wheel bearing outer races or cups from front-wheel hub or rear-wheel-drive vehicle. *(Courtesy of Chrysler Corporation)*

669

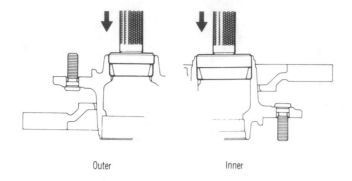

Outer   Inner

FIGURE 29-25. Using bearing driver to install front-wheel bearing cups into front-wheel hubs. Cups must be fully seated. *(Courtesy of Chrysler Corporation)*

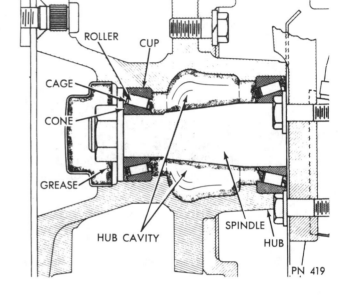

ROLLER   CUP

CAGE

CONE

GREASE

HUB CAVITY

SPINDLE

HUB

PN 419

FIGURE 29-26. Dark shaded area shows grease in hub, bearings, spindle, and dust cap on properly lubricated front wheel bearings. *(Courtesy of Chrysler Corporation)*

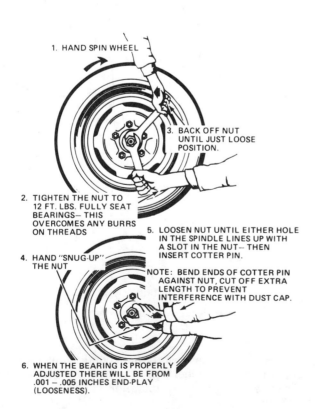

1. HAND SPIN WHEEL

3. BACK OFF NUT UNTIL JUST LOOSE POSITION.

2. TIGHTEN THE NUT TO 12 FT. LBS. FULLY SEAT BEARINGS— THIS OVERCOMES ANY BURRS ON THREADS

4. HAND "SNUG-UP" THE NUT

5. LOOSEN NUT UNTIL EITHER HOLE IN THE SPINDLE LINES UP WITH A SLOT IN THE NUT— THEN INSERT COTTER PIN.

NOTE: BEND ENDS OF COTTER PIN AGAINST NUT, CUT OFF EXTRA LENGTH TO PREVENT INTERFERENCE WITH DUST CAP.

6. WHEN THE BEARING IS PROPERLY ADJUSTED THERE WILL BE FROM .001 – .005 INCHES END-PLAY (LOOSENESS).

FIGURE 29-27. Typical wheel bearing adjustment procedure for one type of bearing arrangement. Procedures and specifications vary depending on design. Manufacturer's specifications and procedures must be followed. *(Courtesy of General Motors Corporation)*

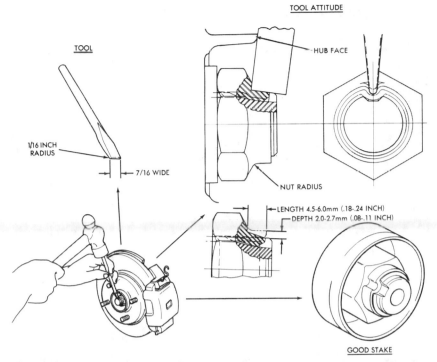

FIGURE 29-28. Procedure for staking (locking) one type of front-wheel bearing retaining nut. *(Courtesy of Chrysler Corporation)*

torque. This provides the necessary end play (no preload) for the bearings. Next install the cotter pin in the castellated type of nut. If the holes do not line up, the nut should be backed off to the first hole only; then install the cotter pin of the correct size and lock it securely. If a plain nut and nut lock are used, position the nut lock so that the cotter pin holes line up; install and lock the cotter pin. Now install the dust cap without distorting or denting it.

On drum brake units, preliminary adjustment of brake shoes may be required before drum installation (see the brake service section in this text).

Install the brake caliper or brake drum (depending on design) and tighten all bolts to specifica-

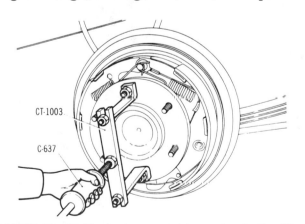

FIGURE 29-29. Removing rear drive axle shaft with a slide hammer type of puller after axle shaft retainer bolts or C-lock have been removed. *(Courtesy of Chrysler Corporation)*

tions. Install the wheels, taking note of the position markings, and tighten lug nuts in the proper sequence and to proper torque. This is critical to prevent disc or drum distortion and to assure lug nuts do not loosen. Undertightening and overtightening are equally undesirable. Depress the brake pedal several times to restore pedal reserve after all brake parts are reassembled.

Replacing Sealed Wheel Bearings

Front or Rear

Many front-wheel-drive vehicles have the sealed type of wheel bearings, which do not require periodic service or repacking with grease. These bearings are serviced only when a wheel bearing noise problem or roughness problem occurs, at which time the old bearings are removed and new bearings installed.

Disassembly of disc and drum brake units on these vehicles is similar to that of other repackable bearing designs. In some cases the hub-and-bearing assembly must be replaced as a unit. In others the sealed bearing can be replaced separately.

Most sealed bearing arrangements do not require any bearing adjustment other than tightening the retaining nut to specified torque and locking the nut either by staking or with a cotter pin. The manufacturer's recommended procedures and specifications must be followed when replacing sealed bearings.

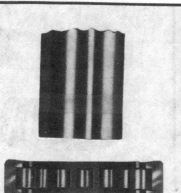

WEAR (MINOR)

LIGHT PATTERN ON RACES AND ROLLERS CAUSED BY FINE ABRASIVES.

CLEAN ALL PARTS AND HOUSINGS. CHECK SEALS AND REPLACE BEARINGS IF ROUGH OR NOISY.

WEAR (MAJOR)

HEAVY PATTERN ON RACES AND ROLLERS CAUSED BY FINE ABRASIVES.

CLEAN ALL PARTS AND HOUSINGS. CHECK SEALS AND REPLACE BEARINGS IF ROUGH OR NOISY.

INDENTATIONS

SURFACE DEPRESSIONS ON RACE AND ROLLERS CAUSED BY HARD PARTICLES OF FOREIGN MATERIAL.

CLEAN ALL PARTS AND HOUSINGS. CHECK SEALS AND REPLACE BEARINGS IF ROUGH OR NOISY.

SINGLE EDGE PITTING

FLAKING OF SURFACE METAL RESULTING FROM FATIGUE, USUALLY AT ONE EDGE OF RACE AND ROLLERS.

REPLACE BEARING -- CLEAN ALL RELATED PARTS.

DOUBLE EDGE PITTING

FLAKING OF SURFACE METAL RESULTING FROM FATIGUE, USUALLY AT BOTH EDGES OF RACE AND ROLLERS.

REPLACE BEARING -- CLEAN ALL RELATED PARTS.

BRINELLING

SURFACE INDENTATIONS IN RACEWAY CAUSED BY ROLLERS EITHER UNDER IMPACT LOADING OR VIBRATION WHILE THE BEARING IS NOT ROTATING.

REPLACE BEARING IF ROUGH OR NOISY.

MISALIGNMENT

REPLACE BEARING AND MAKE SURE RACES ARE PROPERLY SEATED.

REPLACE SHAFT IF BEARING OPERATING SURFACE DAMAGED.

FRETTAGE

CORROSION SET UP BY SMALL RELATIVE MOVEMENT OF PARTS WITH NO LUBRICATION.

REPLACE BEARING. CLEAN RELATED PARTS. CHECK SEALS AND CHECK FOR PROPER FIT AND LUBRICATION.

REPLACE SHAFT IF DAMAGED.

SMEARS

SMEARING OF METAL DUE TO SLIPPAGE. SLIPPAGE CAN BE CAUSED BY POOR FITS, LUBRICATION, OVERHEATING, OVERLOADS OR HANDLING DAMAGE.

REPLACE BEARINGS, CLEAN RELATED PARTS AND CHECK FOR PROPER FIT AND LUBRICATION.

REPLACE SHAFT IF DAMAGED.

Rear Axle Bearings and Seals

Rear-Wheel Drive

When a rear-axle bearing problem is suspected, a thorough diagnosis must be performed to determine the problem and identify the particular axle bearing causing the problem. Follow the problem diagnosis procedure at the beginning of this part and the vehicle manufacturer's diagnosis procedure.

Once the problem bearing has been identified, the bearing must be replaced. Follow the recommended jacking or hoisting procedure and use safety stands to support the vehicle. Remove the wheel after proper marking of the wheel and stud and proceed to disassemble the disc or drum brake unit as outlined earlier for wheel bearing service.

Rear-drive axle shafts are retained in the axle housing in one of several ways. Some are held in place by the axle bearing and a retainer plate at the outer end of the axle housing. Others are held in place by a C-shaped lock that fits into a groove on the axle shaft at the inner end of the shaft, inside the differential. This latter type requires draining the differential gear oil and removing the differential inspection cover. This provides access to remove the differential pinion gear shaft retaining screw or pin and pinion gear shaft. Removing the pinion gear shaft (sometimes called spider gear shaft) allows the axle shaft to be pushed in to expose the C-lock for removal.

The retainer plate at the outer end should then be removed. Retainer bolts are accessible through the hole in the axle drive flange. The axle shaft can then be removed with the appropriate slide hammer puller as illustrated.

There are two basic types of bearing mounting. One type has the complete bearing mounted by a press fit on the axle shaft and retained by a press fit retaining ring. The other type has the bearing mounted in the axle housing and the axle shaft machined surface serves as the inner bearing race.

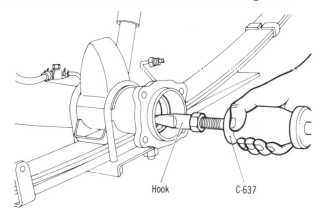

FIGURE 29-30. Removing inner axle shaft seal from axle housing with a slide hammer type of seal puller. *(Courtesy of Chrysler Corporation)*

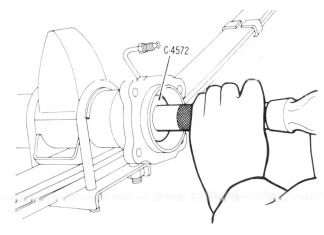

FIGURE 29-31. Installing inner axle shaft seal with proper seal driver. Seal must be installed proper side out and to correct depth in housing. Refer to shop manual for specifications. *(Courtesy of Chrysler Corporation)*

Remove and Install Axle Bearing and Seal (from axle shaft)

The rear-wheel bearing and bearing retainer ring both have a heavy press fit on the axle shaft. Because of this fit, they should be removed or installed separately. Both the retainer ring and the bearing must be removed to replace the seal.

1. Position and tighten the axle shaft in a vise at an angle so that the retainer ring rests on the vise jaws. Use a heavy chisel and hammer to crack the retainer ring. *Do not use heat to remove the retainer ring, as this may temper the axle shaft and result in axle shaft failure.*

2. Press the axle bearing off, using the recommended tools and equipment. Follow the equipment manufacturer's directions for setting up the axle and press to avoid damage to parts and equipment and to avoid injury to yourself and others.

3. Remove the axle shaft seal and retainer plate.

4. If necessary, install a new retainer plate and seal on the axle shaft, then install the bearing.

5. Press the bearing into place, using the recommended tools and equipment and following the manufacturer's instructions for setting up and operating the equipment. Make sure that the bearing is pressed fully against the shoulder or on the axle shaft.

6. Press the new bearing retainer on the axle shaft with the proper tool and make sure that the retainer is seated against the bearing.

7. If the axle housing has an inner seal, re-

move and replace it with a new seal. On this type, the axle bearing is either a sealed bearing or must be packed with wheel bearing grease.

8. Install the axle shaft in the housing and install and tighten the retaining plate bolts and nuts to specified torque.

9. Push the axle shaft in all the way and install the C-locks, pinion shaft, and lock if so equipped. Clean the differential inspection cover and mounting surface on the axle housing. Do not allow any foreign matter to enter the differential housing. Apply new gasket or RTV (room temperature vulcanizing) sealer to cover as recommended and install cover and bolts. Tighten bolts to specified torque and fill the differential to the proper level with the lubricant type specified by the vehicle manufacturer.

10. Install the drum or disc and wheel assembly as outlined earlier and tighten all bolts to specified torque. Damaged bolts and nuts should not be used.

Remove and Install Bearing and Seal
(from axle housing)

1. With the axle shaft removed, use a slide hammer puller to remove the seal and bearing from the axle housing.

2. Install a new bearing in the housing using the proper bearing driver. Make sure that the bearing is installed to the proper depth in the housing. Lubricate the bearing with wheel bearing grease.

3. Install a new seal with the sealing lip facing inward, using the proper size seal driver. Do not allow the seal to cock in the housing bore since this will damage the seal. Make sure that the seal is installed to the correct depth. Follow the manufacturer's instructions for this.

4. Lubricate the seal with wheel bearing grease.

5. Install the axle shaft (if in good condition), being careful not to damage the seal. Axle bearing and seal surfaces must be in good condition, the shaft must not be bent, splines must be in good condition, and the wheel mounting flange should not be bent. Install the retaining plate bolts and nuts and tighten to specified torque.

6. Push the axle shaft in all the way and install the C-locks, pinion shaft, and lock if so equipped. Clean the differential inspection cover and mounting surface on the axle housing. Do not allow any foreign matter to enter the differential housing. Apply new gasket or RTV sealer to cover as recommended and install cover and bolts. Tighten bolts to specified torque and fill the differential to the proper level with the lubricant type specified by the vehicle manufacturer.

7. Install the drum or disc and wheel assembly as outlined earlier and tighten all bolts to specified torque. Damaged bolts and nuts should not be used.

Wheel Lug Bolt Replacement

On flanged drive axles and on driving or nondriving wheel hubs where the lug bolts or studs are not swaged, the stud is removed with a C-clamp type of tool. Use of this type of tool prevents damage to the flange. The lug bolt should not be driven out with a hammer since this could distort the flange and cause excessive flange and wheel run out.

To install a new lug bolt place the bolt in the hole in the flange. Make sure that the serrations on the bolt and in the hole are aligned. Place enough flat washers on the bolt to cover half the bolt threads. Thread standard wheel nut on the lug bolt with the flat side of the nut against the washers. Tighten the nut until the bolt head is seated against the flange. Remove the nut and washers.

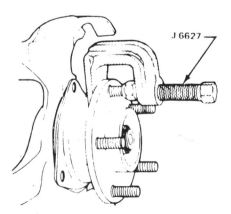

REMOVE WHEEL STUD

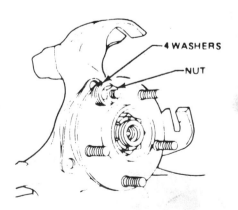

INSTALL WHEEL STUD

FIGURE 29-32. Removing and installing wheel mounting bolts. This method avoids damage to drive flange. *(Courtesy of General Motors Corporation)*

Swaged wheel studs must have the swaged stud material removed with the proper cutting tool before the stud is removed. The new stud is then installed and swaged with a special peening tool. Care must be exercised during this procedure not to damage the stud threads. On drum brake units the brake drum should be checked on a brake drum lathe to ensure drum concentricity. At least one light cut should be taken to determine concentricity. Refer to the section on brake system service for this procedure.

PART 5 WHEEL AND TIRE DIAGNOSIS AND SERVICE

General Precautions

- Avoid getting grease, solvent, brake fluid, or dirty fingerprints on brake discs, pads, linings, and drums.
- Always use safe jacking and vehicle support procedures.
- Always tighten all fasteners to specified torque.
- Do not allow inflated tires to drop; they will bounce.
- Follow all manufacturer's procedures and specifications.
- Do not exceed 275 kPa (40 psi) pressure when initially inflating any tire, including compact spares. If 275 kPa (40 psi) pressure will not seat beads, deflate, relubricate and reinflate. Overinflation may cause the bead to break and cause serious personal injury.
- Test the repair with water or soap suds.
- Never try to convert a tubeless tire to a tubed tire to remedy serious damage.
- Never try to repair tires worn below 1/16-inch (1.5 mm) tread depth.

Tire Roughness and Vibration*

General

Vibration, roughness, tramp, shimmy and thump may be caused by excessive tire or wheel run-out, worn or cupped tires, or wheel and tire unbalance. These problem conditions may also be caused by rough or undulating road surfaces. Driving the automobile on different types of road surfaces will in-

*The discussion of tire roughness and vibration and vibration in general is provided courtesy of American Motors.

dicate if the road surfaces are actually causing the problem.

Always road-test the automobile, preferably with the owner in the automobile, to determine the exact nature of the problem. The automobile should be driven at least 7 miles to warm the tires and remove flat spots that may have formed temporarily while the automobile was parked. Note tire condition and wear, and check and adjust tire inflation pressure before road testing.

Radial-Tire Performance Characteristics

Because of their unique construction, radial-ply tires produce ride, handling, and appearance characteristics noticeably different from conventional tires. Radial-ply tire ride quality and feel may seem harsh, particularly at low speeds. This is due to the stiff belts used in the construction of these tires. Harshness often leads to the assumption that the tires are overinflated. Inflate radial-ply tires to recommended levels only.

Radial-ply tires have a highly flexible sidewall, which produces a characteristic sidewall bulge, making the tire appear underinflated. This is a normal condition for radial-ply tires. Do not attempt to reduce this bulge by overinflating the tire. Always check tire inflation pressures, using an accurate gauge, and inflate the tires to recommended levels only.

Radial-ply tires also produce a side-to-side or waddle motion that is most noticeable at speeds of 15 miles per hour (mph) (24 km/h) or less. This motion is a normal characteristic of radial-ply tires and is a result of their unique construction. An objectionable waddle condition can sometimes be reduced by rotating the tires front-to-rear; however, do not attempt to correct a waddle condition by balancing.

Proper mounting and balancing of radial-ply tires is very important. Improper balancing or incomplete seating of the tire bead can produce a high frequency vibration noticeable throughout the automobile at speeds above approximately 45 mph (72 km/h). Improper bead seating can be checked by visually inspecting the tire. To correct unbalance, reseat the bead if necessary, and balance the tire using dynamic, two-plane balancing equipment. This type of balancing equipment is essential to solving radial-ply tire unbalance problems.

Tire Thump

Thump is a noise caused by the tire moving over irregularities in the road or by irregularities within the tire itself. The thump sound will coincide with each wheel revolution.

DIAGNOSTIC CHART

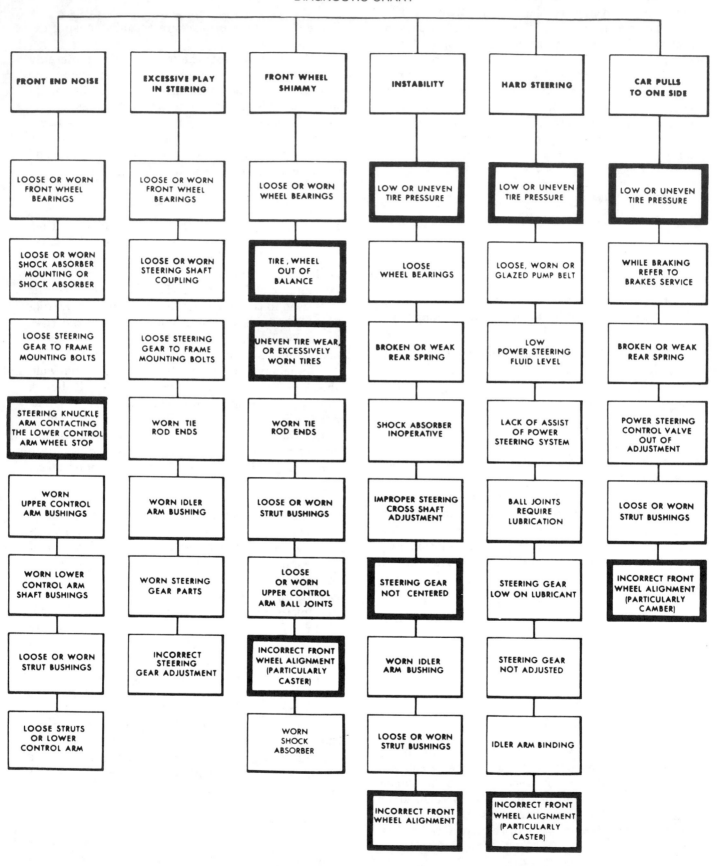

FRONT END NOISE	EXCESSIVE PLAY IN STEERING	FRONT WHEEL SHIMMY	INSTABILITY	HARD STEERING	CAR PULLS TO ONE SIDE
LOOSE OR WORN FRONT WHEEL BEARINGS	LOOSE OR WORN FRONT WHEEL BEARINGS	LOOSE OR WORN WHEEL BEARINGS	LOW OR UNEVEN TIRE PRESSURE	LOW OR UNEVEN TIRE PRESSURE	LOW OR UNEVEN TIRE PRESSURE
LOOSE OR WORN SHOCK ABSORBER MOUNTING OR SHOCK ABSORBER	LOOSE OR WORN STEERING SHAFT COUPLING	TIRE, WHEEL OUT OF BALANCE	LOOSE WHEEL BEARINGS	LOOSE, WORN OR GLAZED PUMP BELT	WHILE BRAKING REFER TO BRAKES SERVICE
LOOSE STEERING GEAR TO FRAME MOUNTING BOLTS	LOOSE STEERING GEAR TO FRAME MOUNTING BOLTS	UNEVEN TIRE WEAR, OR EXCESSIVELY WORN TIRES	BROKEN OR WEAK REAR SPRING	LOW POWER STEERING FLUID LEVEL	BROKEN OR WEAK REAR SPRING
STEERING KNUCKLE ARM CONTACTING THE LOWER CONTROL ARM WHEEL STOP	WORN TIE ROD ENDS	WORN TIE ROD ENDS	SHOCK ABSORBER INOPERATIVE	LACK OF ASSIST OF POWER STEERING SYSTEM	POWER STEERING CONTROL VALVE OUT OF ADJUSTMENT
WORN UPPER CONTROL ARM BUSHINGS	WORN IDLER ARM BUSHING	LOOSE OR WORN STRUT BUSHINGS	IMPROPER STEERING CROSS SHAFT ADJUSTMENT	BALL JOINTS REQUIRE LUBRICATION	LOOSE OR WORN STRUT BUSHINGS
WORN LOWER CONTROL ARM SHAFT BUSHINGS	WORN STEERING GEAR PARTS	LOOSE OR WORN UPPER CONTROL ARM BALL JOINTS	STEERING GEAR NOT CENTERED	STEERING GEAR LOW ON LUBRICANT	INCORRECT FRONT WHEEL ALIGNMENT (PARTICULARLY CAMBER)
LOOSE OR WORN STRUT BUSHINGS	INCORRECT STEERING GEAR ADJUSTMENT	INCORRECT FRONT WHEEL ALIGNMENT (PARTICULARLY CASTER)	WORN IDLER ARM BUSHING	STEERING GEAR NOT ADJUSTED	
LOOSE STRUTS OR LOWER CONTROL ARM		WORN SHOCK ABSORBER	LOOSE OR WORN STRUT BUSHINGS	IDLER ARM BINDING	
			INCORRECT FRONT WHEEL ALIGNMENT	INCORRECT FRONT WHEEL ALIGNMENT (PARTICULARLY CASTER)	

676

RADIAL TIRE LEAD DIAGNOSIS

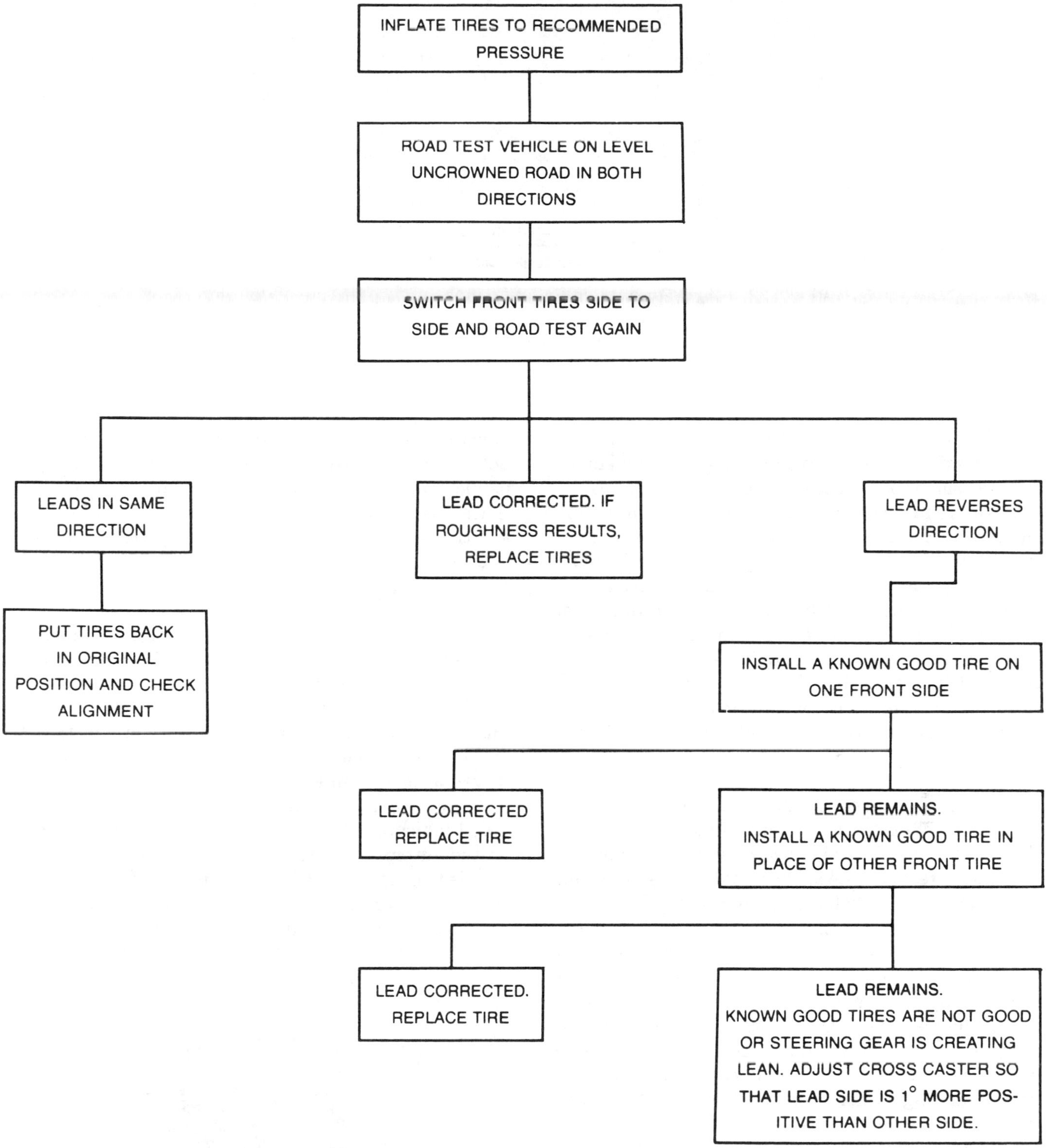

```
┌─────────────────────────────┐
│  INFLATE TIRES TO RECOMMENDED│
│           PRESSURE           │
└─────────────────────────────┘
               │
┌─────────────────────────────┐
│  ROAD TEST VEHICLE ON LEVEL  │
│  UNCROWNED ROAD IN BOTH      │
│          DIRECTIONS          │
└─────────────────────────────┘
               │
┌─────────────────────────────┐
│  SWITCH FRONT TIRES SIDE TO  │
│  SIDE AND ROAD TEST AGAIN    │
└─────────────────────────────┘
```

| LEADS IN SAME DIRECTION | LEAD CORRECTED. IF ROUGHNESS RESULTS, REPLACE TIRES | LEAD REVERSES DIRECTION |

PUT TIRES BACK IN ORIGINAL POSITION AND CHECK ALIGNMENT

INSTALL A KNOWN GOOD TIRE ON ONE FRONT SIDE

LEAD CORRECTED REPLACE TIRE

LEAD REMAINS.
INSTALL A KNOWN GOOD TIRE IN PLACE OF OTHER FRONT TIRE

LEAD CORRECTED. REPLACE TIRE

LEAD REMAINS.
KNOWN GOOD TIRES ARE NOT GOOD OR STEERING GEAR IS CREATING LEAN. ADJUST CROSS CASTER SO THAT LEAD SIDE IS 1° MORE POSITIVE THAN OTHER SIDE.

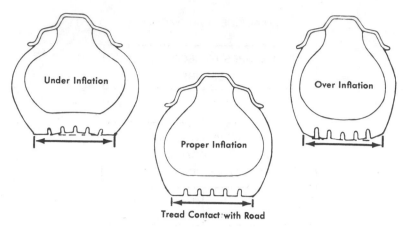

FIGURE 29-33. Effects of different inflation pressures on the tire's footprint. Handling, control, ride quality, and tire life are all affected by inflation pressures. Always inflate tires to recommended pressures only.

To determine which tire is causing thump, temporarily inflate all tires to 50 psi (345 kPa) and drive over the same roads. If this procedure eliminates the problem, reduce the air pressure in one tire at a time and repeat the road test. Perform this procedure until all tires have been tested and each test is made with three tires at high pressure and one tire at recommended pressure. When thump again develops, the tire just deflated to the recommended pressure is the defective tire and should be replaced. *Note:* Although the procedure for diagnosing tire thump is quite effective with conventional tires, it is considerably less effective with radial tires.

Tire Tramp

Tire tramp is caused by tire and wheel static unbalance or by excessive radial and lateral run-out of the tire or wheel. The most effective method for checking tire and wheel static balance is by using off-the-automobile balancing equipment.

Static balance is the result of an equal distribution of wheel and tire weight about the spindle in such a manner that the assembly lacks the tendency to rotate by itself when mounted on the arbor of a balancing machine. Static unbalance occurs when an unequal portion of weight is concentrated at one point on the tire and wheel. It causes a vibratory-type pounding action, which is referred to as tire tramp, wheel tramp, or wheel hop.

Dynamic balance is the result of an equal distribution of wheel and tire weight around the plane of rotation, which causes the wheel to rotate smoothly about the axis that bisects the wheel and tire centerline. Dynamic unbalance occurs when unequal forces are concentrated at opposing points on the tire circumference. It causes wheel shimmy and vibration at medium and high speeds.

The most effective method for balancing wheels and tires is by using equipment that will correct both static and dynamic balance conditions. Dynamic, two-plane balancing equipment is preferable. Since procedures vary with different machines, follow the equipment manufacturer's instructions explicitly.

Wheel and Tire Run-out

Excessive radial and lateral run-out of a wheel-and-tire assembly can cause roughness, vibration, tramp, tire wear, and steering wheel tremor.

Before checking run-out and to avoid false readings caused by temporary flat spots in the tires, check run-out only after the automobile has been driven at least 7 miles (11 km).

The extent of run-out should be measured with a dial indicator. All measurements should be made on the automobile with the tires inflated to recommended reduced load inflation pressures and with the wheel bearings adjusted to specifications.

Measure tire radial run-out at the center and outside ribs of the tread face. Measure tire lateral

FIGURE 29-34. Several tire wear indicator bars are located around the tire tread. When tread wear exposes these fully, there are only about 1.6 millimeters of tread remaining. Tire should then be replaced. *(Courtesy of Bridgestone)*

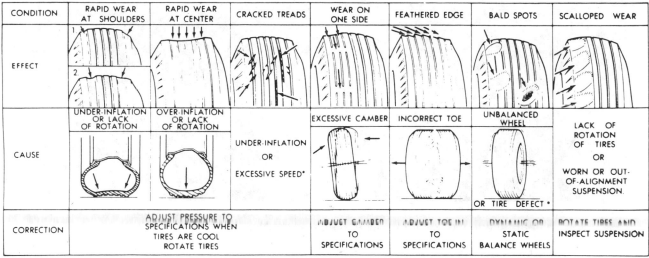

CONDITION	RAPID WEAR AT SHOULDERS	RAPID WEAR AT CENTER	CRACKED TREADS	WEAR ON ONE SIDE	FEATHERED EDGE	BALD SPOTS	SCALLOPED WEAR
EFFECT							
CAUSE	UNDER-INFLATION OR LACK OF ROTATION	OVER-INFLATION OR LACK OF ROTATION	UNDER-INFLATION OR EXCESSIVE SPEED*	EXCESSIVE CAMBER	INCORRECT TOE	UNBALANCED WHEEL OR TIRE DEFECT *	LACK OF ROTATION OF TIRES OR WORN OR OUT-OF-ALIGNMENT SUSPENSION.
CORRECTION	ADJUST PRESSURE TO SPECIFICATIONS WHEN TIRES ARE COOL ROTATE TIRES			ADJUST CAMBER TO SPECIFICATIONS	ADJUST TOE IN TO SPECIFICATIONS	DYNAMIC OR STATIC BALANCE WHEELS	ROTATE TIRES AND INSPECT SUSPENSION

*HAVE TIRE INSPECTED FOR FURTHER USE.

FIGURE 29-35. Tire wear conditions are stated across the top. The resulting effects are illustrated in the next column across. Causes of these conditions are shown next, with the appropriate corrective procedures across the bottom. *(Courtesy of Chrysler Corporation)*

run-out just above the buffing rib on the sidewall. Mark the high points of lateral and radial run-out for future reference. On conventional tires, radial run-out must not exceed 0.105 inch (2.66 millimeters) and lateral run-out must not exceed 0.100 inch (2.54 millimeters). On radial-ply tires, radial run-out must not exceed 0.080 inch (2.03 millimeters) and lateral run-out must not exceed 0.100 mch (2.54 millimeters).

If total radial or lateral run-out of the tire exceeds specified limits, it will then be necessary to check wheel run-out to determine whether the wheel or tire is at fault. Wheel radial run-out is measured at the wheel rim just inside the wheel cover retaining nibs. Wheel lateral run-out is measured at the wheel rim bead flange just inside the curved lip of the flange. Wheel radial run-out should not exceed 0.035 inch (0.89 millimeter) and wheel lateral run-

out should not exceed 0.045 inch (1.14 millimeters). Mark the high points of radial and lateral run-out for future reference.

If total tire run-out, either lateral or radial, exceeds the specified limit but wheel run-out is within the specified limit, it may be possible to reduce run-out to an acceptable level by changing the position of the tire on the wheel so that the previously marked high points are 180° apart.

Vibration

General

Vibration may be caused by tire/wheel unbalance or run-out, incorrectly adjusted wheel bearings, loose or worn suspension or steering components, worn or defective tires, incorrect universal joint angles, worn universal joints, excessive propeller shaft or yoke

FIGURE 29-36. Example of tread wear (feather-edge tread) due to excessive toe-in or toe-out at left. Two-sided wear can be the result of underinflation or high-speed cornering.

FIGURE 29–37. One-side wear at left indicates excessive camber. Cupped wear at right is the result of underinflation or imbalance.

run-out, rotor or brake drum run-out, loose engine or transmission supports, or engine-driven accessories.

Vibration Categories

Vibrations can be divided into two categories: mechanical and audible. Mechanical vibrations are felt through the seats, floorpan, or steering wheel and usually produce some visible motion in the rear-view mirror, front fenders, dash panel, or steering wheel.

Audible vibrations are heard or sometimes sensed above normal road and background noise and may be accompanied by a mechanical vibration. In some cases, they occur as a droning or drumming noise. In other cases, they produce a buffeting sensation felt or sensed by the driver rather than heard.

Vibration Sensitivity

Mechanical and audible vibrations are sensitive to changes in engine torque, automobile speed, or engine speed. They usually occur within one and sometimes two well-defined ranges in terms of automobile speed, engine revolutions per minute (rpm), and torque application.

Consider for correction only those items coded on the charts that are related to the problem con-

dition. Refer to the correction codes for a definition of the various correction procedures.

Vibration Diagnosis Chart Codes

TRR—Tire and wheel radial run-out. Not a cause of vibration below 20 mph (32 km/h). Speed required to cause vibration increases as run-out decreases. Automobile-speed-sensitive vibration.

WH—Wheel hop. Not a cause of vibration below 20 mph (32 km/h). Produces up-down movement in steering wheel and instrument panel along with mechanical vibration. Most noticeable between 20-40 mph (32-64 km/h). Caused by tires having radial run-out of more than 0.045 inch (1.14 millimeters). Do not attempt to correct by balancing; replace the tire. Automobile-speed-sensitive vibration.

TB—Tire balance. Static unbalance not a cause of vibration below 30 mph (48 km/h). Dynamic unbalance not a cause under 40 mph (64 km/h). Automobile-speed-sensitive vibration.

TLR—Tire and wheel lateral run-out. Not a cause of vibration below 55 mph (88 km/h) unless run-out is extreme. Automobile-speed-sensitive vibration.

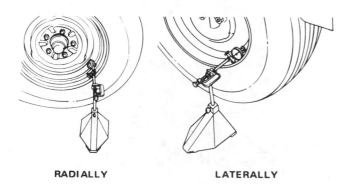

RADIALLY   LATERALLY

FIGURE 29–38. Using a dial indicator to measure wheel run-out. *(Courtesy of American Motors Corporation)*

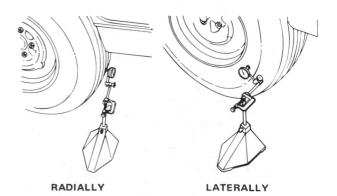

RADIALLY   LATERALLY

FIGURE 29–39. Using a dial indicator to measure tire run-out. *(Courtesy of American Motors Corporation)*

TW—Tire wear. Abnormal wear can cause vibration in 30 to 55 mph (48 to 88 km/h) range and may also generate whine at high-speed changing to growl at low speed. Automobile-speed-sensitive vibration.

W—Radial tire waddle. Normal condition with radial-ply tires. Unique construction causes side-to-side waddle motion at speeds up to 15 mph (24 km/h). Rotating tires front-to-rear may reduce condition. Replace tires if the condition cannot be reduced satisfactorily. Automobile-speed-sensitive vibration.

UJA—Universal joint angles. Incorrect angles may cause mechanical vibration below 20 mph (32 km/h) and mechanical or audible vibration at 35 to 55 mph (56 to 88 km/h). Torque-sensitive vibration.

UJ—Universal joints. If the ends of bearing crosses or bearing cups are galled, worn excessively, brinelled, or binding due to over-tightened U-bolts or clamp strap bolts, they will cause vibration at any speed. Torque-sensitive vibration.

PSY—Propeller shaft and yokes. Not a cause of vibration below 35 mph (56 km/h). Excessive run-out, unbalance, loss of balance weights, or undercoating on shaft will cause vibration at 35 mph (56 km/h) and above. Torque-sensitive vibration.

WB—Front wheel bearings. If loose, can cause automobile speed sensitive mechanical vibration at 35 mph (56 km/h) and above. If rough or damaged, can cause growl and grind noise at low speed or whine at high speed. Automobile-speed-sensitive vibration.

AN—Rear axle noise. Not a cause of vibration unless axle shaft is bent or shaft bearing has broken. Worn or damaged gears or bearings will cause noise in varying speed ranges in relation to amount of torque applied.

TEB—Transmission extension housing bushing. If worn or loose, can cause torque-sensitive mechanical vibration and oil leakage.

EA—Engine-driven accessories. Loose or broken air-conditioning compressor, power-steering pump, air pump, alternator, water pump, etc., can cause engine-speed-sensitive mechanical vibration. Usually apparent when transmission is placed in neutral and engine speed is increased.

ADB—Accessory drive belts. If excessively worn or loose, can cause engine-speed-sensitive audible vibration that sounds like droning, flutter, or rumbling noise.

DEM—Damaged engine mounts. If worn or broken, may allow engine or accessories to contact body, causing noise and vibration.

Wheel and Tire Service

Only small clean punctures should be repaired in tires. Repairs should be restricted to the safe repair area (Figure 29-41). Tire repair methods vary greatly and should be done according to the supplier's and vehicle manufacturer's procedures and recommendations.

Tire service life is greatly extended by periodic and systematic tire rotation. Follow the manufacturer's recommendations for best results. Wheel and tire radial and lateral run-out must be within specifications for good handling and tire life. Wheel-and-tire assemblies must also be properly balanced.

Always replace valve stems when replacing tubeless tires. Be sure that the rims are clean for proper bead sealing.

Inspection and Cleaning

The condition of the wheels should be checked periodically. Replace any wheel that is bent, cracked, severely dented, or has excessive run-out. Also check the condition of the tire inflation valve. Replace the valve if worn, cracked, loose, or leaking air.

When cleaning steel or aluminum wheels, use a mild soap and water solution only and rinse with clean water. Do not use any type of caustic solution or abrasive substance, especially on forged aluminum wheels. After cleaning aluminum wheels, apply a coating of protective wax to preserve the finish and retain the original luster.

The finned urethane inserts on styled wheels may be cleaned using a sponge or soft bristle brush. Do not press overly hard on the inserts to clean them. They are flexible to a degree but can be damaged if due care is not exercised.

Always mount wheel assembly by tightening mounting nuts in proper sequence and to specified torque.

Tire Removal

Remove the valve core to deflate the tire completely. Unseat tire beads from the wheel, using bead breaker. Mount the wheel assembly in holding equipment for demounting. Follow the equipment manufacturer's directions; procedures vary depending on available equipment. Remove the tire from the wheel.

Puncture Repair Procedures

After removing the tire from the rim, probe repairable tire injuries in order to remove a nail or other damaging material. Make sure that the area around the injury is thoroughly dry. Scrape the damaged

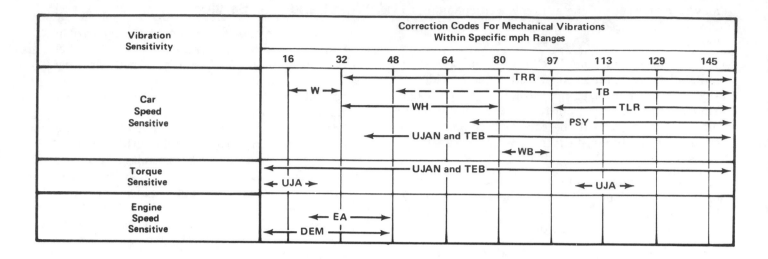

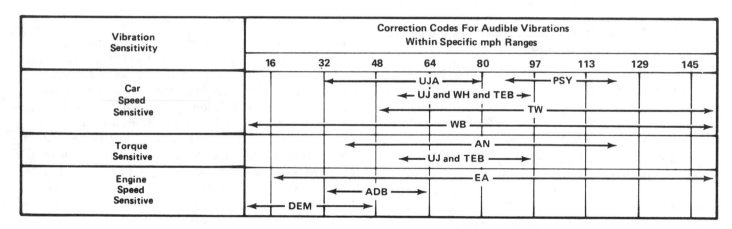

FIGURE 29-40. *(Courtesy of American Motors Corporation)*

area with a sharp-edged tool and buff. Take care not to damage the liner or expose any cords.

Lubricate the injury by pushing the snout of the vulcanizing fluid can into the injury from both sides of the tire. Also pour vulcanizing fluid on the inser-

tion tool and push it through with a twisting motion until it can be inserted and withdrawn easily.

Using a head-type or headless straight plug slightly larger than the size of the injury, place it in the eye of the insertion tool. When a headless

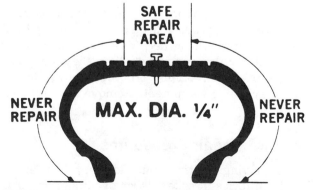

FIGURE 29-41. The area of safe tire repair is shown here.

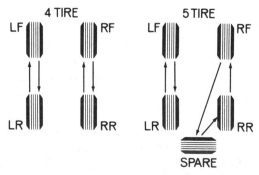

FIGURE 29-42. Proper sequence of tire rotation for radial tires. Tires should be rotated at 5,000-mile (8,000-kilometer) intervals or as recommended by manufacturer.

straight plug is used, always back it up with a patch. Wet both the plug and insertion tool with vulcanizing fluid. Always pour directly from the can so as not to contaminate the can's contents.

While holding and stretching the long end of the plug, insert the plug into the injury from *inside* the tire. Hold and stretch the long end of the plug as it is forced into the injury until one end extends through it.

Remove the insertion and cut off the plug 1/16 inch above the surfaces. Do not pull on the plug while cutting. Do not wash previously prepared surface with solvent prior to application of vulcanizing fluid.

When using a cold patch, carefully remove the backing from the patch. Center the patch base over the damaged area on which vulcanizing fluid has been spread and allowed to dry. Roll the patch down firmly with the roller tool, working from the center out.

When using a hot patch, cover the buffed area with a light coat of cement of the type specified for the patch and allow it to dry. Remove the backing from the patch. Center the patch over injury. Clamp—finger tighten only. Apply heat, cure, and allow to cool. Before remounting the tire, clean and deburr the rim carefully.

Mounting Tires

If a rim is dirty or corroded or if the tire is not centered on the rim, the tire bead may "bind" on the rim and refuse to seat. Allowing air pressure to build within the assembly in an attempt to seat the bead is a *dangerous practice*. Inflation beyond 40 psi (275 kPa) may break the bead (or even the rim) with explosive force. This can cause serious injury to the person inflating the tire. Injuries caused by such explosions include severed fingers, broken arms, broken jaws, and severe facial lacerations.

1. Be certain that rim flanges and bead ledge (especially hump and radius) areas are smooth and clean. Remove any oxidized rubber, dried soap solution, rust, heavy paint, etc., with a wire brush or a file.

2. Lubricate tire beads, rim flanges, and bead ledge areas with a liberal amount of thin vegetable oil soap solution or with an approved rubber lubricant. Start the mounting procedure with the narrow bead ledge of the rim up at all times.

3. Be sure that the assembly is securely locked down on the mounting machine.

4. *Use a tire mounting band.* The use of a tire mounting band (or bead expander) is helpful when inflating tubeless tires. This device constricts the tread center line of the tire, thereby helping to force the beads onto the bead seats of the rim. Follow these steps.

   a. When the tire is on the wheel, and before inflating, attach the bead expander around the center of the tread.

   b. Inflate the tire sufficiently (10 psi [69 kPa] or less) to move the tire beads out to contact bead seats of rim. Then, as a safety precaution, remove the expander. Never exceed 10 psi (69 kPa) pressure with the mounting band on the tire.

   c. Increase air pressure, as needed, up to 40 psi (275 kPa) to seat the tire beads fully on the rim.

   d. Check for leakage and, if none, adjust air pressure to recommended pressure. *Important:* On safety or hump-type rims, make sure that tire beads have moved over the hump on the rim and are fully seated.

5. Do not allow air pressure to exceed 40 psi (275 kPa) during the bead-seating process. If beads have not seated by the time pressure reaches 40 psi (275 kPa), deflate the assembly, reposition the tire on the rim, and relubricate and reinflate it to recommended operating pressure.

6. Make certain that the valve core is inserted in the valve stem. Worn valves should be replaced, using the valve designated by the manufacturer, since valves vary as to length and diameter. Valve caps should be screwed on finger-tight.

7. Use an extension gauge with clip-on chuck so that air pressure buildup can be closely watched and so that you can stand well back from the assembly during the seating process.

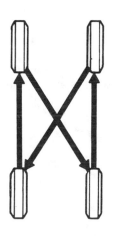
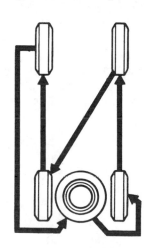

BIAS PLY TIRE
4 WHEEL ROTATION

BIAS PLY TIRE
5 WHEEL ROTATION

FIGURE 29-43. Four- and five-tire rotation sequence for bias-ply tires. *(Courtesy of General Motors Corporation)*

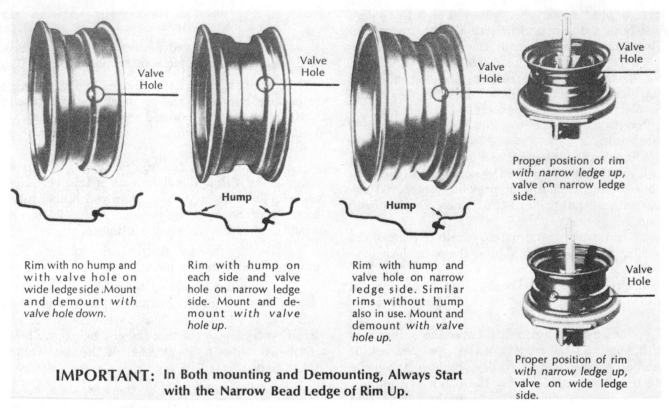

Valve Hole

Valve Hole

Valve Hole

Valve Hole

Hump

Hump

Proper position of rim *with narrow ledge up,* valve on narrow ledge side.

Rim with no hump and with valve hole on wide ledge side .Mount and demount *with valve hole down.*

Rim with hump on each side and valve hole on narrow ledge side. Mount and demount *with valve hole up.*

Rim with hump and valve hole on narrow ledge side. Similar rims without hump also in use. Mount and demount *with valve hole up.*

Valve Hole

Proper position of rim *with narrow ledge up,* valve on wide ledge side.

IMPORTANT: **In Both mounting and Demounting, Always Start with the Narrow Bead Ledge of Rim Up.**

FIGURE 29-44. Important wheel and tire service information that must be followed to service wheel-and-tire assemblies properly.

FIGURE 29-45. Several types of tubeless-tire valve stems. Stems come in different lengths and diameters for different-sized wheel stem holes.

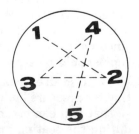

FIGURE 29-46. Always follow the above star pattern when tightening wheel bolts or lug nuts. This prevents misalignment and distortion.

PART 6 WHEEL–BALANCING PROCEDURE

Procedure

• Clean all dirt and foreign matter from the wheels and remove all wheel weights.

• Clean larger stones from tire tread.

• Check and correct tire and wheel run-out in excess of specifications.

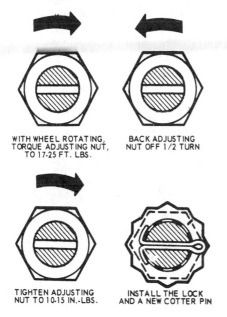

WITH WHEEL ROTATING, TORQUE ADJUSTING NUT, TO 17-25 FT. LBS.

BACK ADJUSTING NUT OFF 1/2 TURN

TIGHTEN ADJUSTING NUT TO 10-15 IN.-LBS.

INSTALL THE LOCK AND A NEW COTTER PIN

FIGURE 29–47. Example of wheel-bearing nut adjustment sequence and properly installed lock and cotter pin. Follow the manufacturer's specifications whenever servicing wheel bearings. *(Courtesy of Ford Motor Co. of Canada Ltd.)*

• Correct tire inflation pressure.

• For off-the-car balancing, mount the wheel as recommended.

• For on-the-car balancing, position jacks and wheel spinner safely and mount attachments as recommended.

• Stay clear of the plane of tire rotation when spinning tire and wheel assembly (flying stones can injure).

• Attach all balancing weights securely.

• If the wheel was removed for balancing, install and tighten to proper torque after balancing.

• Replace hub cap or wheel cover using a rubber mallet around the edges.

Balancing Drive Wheels on the Car

Standard Differential

• Jack up one side only and block the other wheel.

• *Caution:* The wheel speed is double that of the speedometer reading. Do not overspeed; damage to the differential may result. Maximum speed is 35 mph (60 km/h).

• Prepare the wheel for balancing as indicated and balance the wheel assembly.

• Repeat the procedure for the other side.

Limited Slip Differential

• Jack up both rear wheels and support with jack stands; block the front wheels.

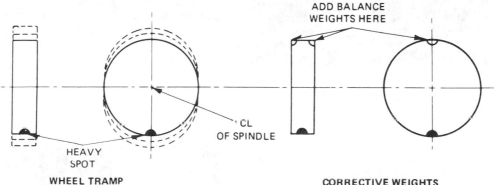

ADD BALANCE WEIGHTS HERE

CL OF SPINDLE

HEAVY SPOT

WHEEL TRAMP

CORRECTIVE WEIGHTS

FIGURE 29–48. A wheel assembly must be statically in balance to prevent wheel tramp. A wheel that is not statically in balance has a heavy spot. To bring the wheel into static balance, place two equal-sized weights 180° from the heavy spot, one on each side of the wheel rim. The combined weight of the two balance weights must equal the weight of the heavy spot. A statically balanced wheel has equal weight distribution radially around the axis of rotation. *(Courtesy of General Motors Corporation)*

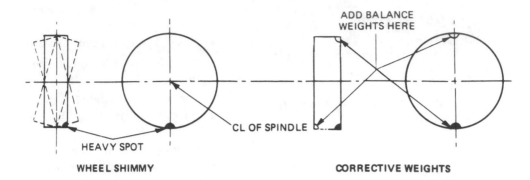

WHEEL SHIMMY   CORRECTIVE WEIGHTS

FIGURE 29-49. A wheel must also be in dynamic balance to prevent wheel shimmy. A wheel that is not in dynamic balance has a heavy spot to one side of the center of the plane of tire rotation. To bring the wheel into dynamic balance, the combined weight of the two balance weights placed as above must equal the heavy spot. A dynamically balanced wheel has equal weight on each side of the wheel center line or plane of rotation. *(Courtesy of General Motors Corporation)*

FIGURE 29-50. Static balancer. This type of balancer does not balance a wheel dynamically. Placing an equal amount of weight on each side of the rim opposite to and equal to the heavy spot will leave dynamic balance unaffected.

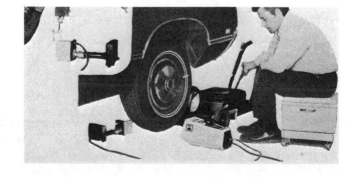

FIGURE 29-51. Strobe-light type of on-a-car balancer balances entire wheel and brake disc or drum assembly as a unit. *(Courtesy of Hunter Engineering Co.)*

FIGURE 29–52. Electronic computerized wheel balancer balances wheels both statically and dynamically. *(Courtesy of Sun Electric Corporation)*

• Remove one rear wheel.

• Prepare the other wheel (on the car) for balancing as indicated and proceed to balance.

• The speedometer reading is actual wheel speed on limited slip differential vehicles when balancing.

• Follow the manufacturer's recommendations for procedures and speeds.

PART 7 SELF-CHECK

1. What three materials are used for wheel construction?

2. How is wheel size determined or designated?

3. What is the purpose of the wheel rim drop center?

4. Why are tire beads required?

5. List three types of tire construction.

6. What is the purpose of tire tread sipes?

7. Define the slip angle of a tire.

8. What causes radial tire lead?

9. How is tire load rating designated?

10. How should wheel and tire radial and lateral run-out be checked?

11. Do not exceed _____ air pressure when inflating an automobile tire.

12. Tire repairs should not be attempted on sidewalls. True or false?

13. What is the purpose of a tire-mounting band?

14. Define static wheel balance.

15. List four different types of wheel and axle bearings.

16. Why is it necessary to mark wheels and wheel studs before wheel removal?

17. Describe the basic method of cleaning and repacking nondriving front- or rear-wheel bearings.

18. What is the proper procedure for wheel bearing adjustment?

19. Describe the proper method for tightening wheel mounting nuts.

20. To remove a damaged wheel lug bolt, just drive it out with a hammer. True or false?

21. When installing a new wheel lug, the serrations should be lined up. True or false?

22. Define dynamic wheel balance.

23. How should a wheel and tire be prepared for balancing?

PART 8   TEST QUESTIONS

1. The purpose of tire sipes is to:
   (a) increase tread life
   (b) decrease noise level
   (c) provide a softer ride
   (d) increase traction

2. A radial tire is one which has:
   (a) bias ply body cords
   (b) bias ply belts
   (c) radial ply body cords
   (d) radial ply belts

3. Tire tramp is caused by:
   (a) dynamic unbalance
   (b) static unbalance
   (c) axial run-out
   (d) shimmy

4. Mechanical and audible vibrations are sensitive to:
   (a) changes in engine speed
   (b) changes in engine torque
   (c) changes in automobile speed
   (d) any of the above

5. To prepare a wheel and tire for balancing they should be:
   (a) cleaned
   (b) checked for run-out
   (c) inflated to correct pressure
   (d) all of the above

Chapter 30

Wheel Alignment

The purpose of proper wheel alignment and balance is to provide maximum safety, ease of handling, stability, and directional control of the vehicle. This requires that each of the steering angles (steering geometry) be adjusted to the specifications recommended by the vehicle manufacturer. Different makes and models of vehicles require different settings. Follow the specific shop manual for each vehicle. The wheels must also be in proper dynamic and static balance to achieve these purposes.

PART 1 STEERING GEOMETRY

Tracking

For proper tracking, all four wheels must be parallel to the frame. This requires that the wheelbase be equal on both sides of the vehicle. The four wheels should be positioned to form a rectangle.

Camber

Camber is the inward or outward tilt of the wheel at the top. Inward tilt is negative camber and outward tilt is positive camber. The tilt of the wheel (camber) is measured in degrees and is adjustable on many vehicles. Camber is needed for the following purposes:

1. To bring the point of load more nearly to the center of the tire where it contacts the road

2. To reduce steering effort by putting more of the load at the inner end of the spindle on the larger bearing

3. To reduce tire wear

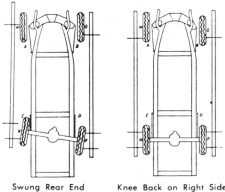

Swung Rear End   Knee Back on Right Side

FIGURE 30-1. Rear wheels must follow front wheels properly for good steering, handling, and vehicle stability. This is called *tracking*, which occurs if all four wheels are parallel to the frame. This illustration shows the method for checking tracking by using a track bar (sometimes called *tramming*). When track bar pointers are set to contact wheels on one side of a vehicle, they should contact wheels at same points on the other side. If they do not, there is possibly a shifted frame or suspension parts.

Performance Objectives

After study of this chapter and adequate occasion to practice wheel alignment and balance, you should be able to do the following.

1. Follow the accepted general precautions.
2. Accurately perform all prealignment checks.
3. Accurately measure and correct all alignment factors to the manufacturer's specifications.
4. Properly prepare the wheel assemblies for balancing.
5. Accurately balance the wheel assemblies both statically and dynamically.
6. Perform the necessary checks to determine the success of the alignment and balance procedures.
7. Complete the self-check and test questions with at least 80 percent accuracy.
8. Complete all practical work with 100 percent accuracy.
9. Properly prepare the vehicle for customer acceptance.

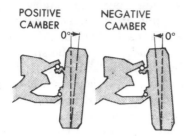

FIGURE 30-2. Camber is the inward or outward tilt of the wheel at the top. If the wheel is absolutely vertical, there is zero camber. *(Courtesy of Chrysler Corporation)*

Incorrect camber settings can cause the following:

1. Excessive wear to suspension parts

2. Excessive wheel bearing wear

3. Excessive tire wear (excess positive camber, outside tire-tread wear; excess negative camber, inside tire-tread wear)

4. Excessive unequal camber will cause the car to pull to one side

5. Excessive negative camber on the right wheel will cause pull to the left

6. Excessive positive camber on the right wheel will cause pull to the right

7. Excessive negative camber on the left wheel will cause pull to the right

8. Excessive positive camber on the left wheel will cause pull to the left

Caster

Caster is the forward or backward tilt of the spindle or steering knuckle at the top when viewed from the side. Forward tilt is negative caster and backward

**WHEEL WITH NEGATIVE CAMBER
TENDS TO ROLL UPHILL**

FIGURE 30-3. Effect of negative camber on directional control. If there is a difference in camber from one front wheel to the other, the vehicle will tend to pull to the side with the most positive camber. *(Courtesy of Bear)*

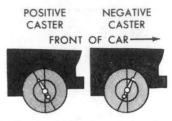

FIGURE 30-4. Caster is the forward or backward tilt of the spindle (steering knuckle) at the top as viewed from the side. When the spindle support is vertical, there is zero caster. *(Courtesy of Chrysler Corporation)*

tilt is positive caster. Caster is measured in the number of degrees that it is forward or backward from true vertical and is adjustable on many vehicles. Caster is needed for the following purposes:

1. To aid in directional control by helping to keep wheels in straight-ahead position on some models

2. To help return the wheel to straight ahead after a turn

3. To offset the effects of road crown by setting the left side ¼° to ½° more negative (or less positive)

Incorrect caster can result in the following:

1. Wander (too little caster)

2. Hard steering (too much caster)

3. Road shock and shimmy (too much caster)

Steering Axis Inclination

Steering axis inclination is the inward tilt of the steering knuckle at the top. Steering axis inclination is measured in degrees and is not adjustable. If incorrect, suspension parts are at fault and must be replaced. Steering axis inclination is needed for the following purposes:

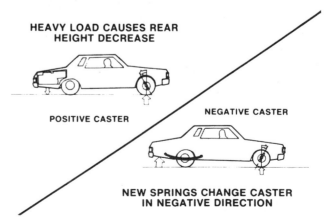

FIGURE 30-5. Caster is affected by vehicle load and by sagged springs. *(Courtesy of Ford Motor Co. of Canada Ltd.)*

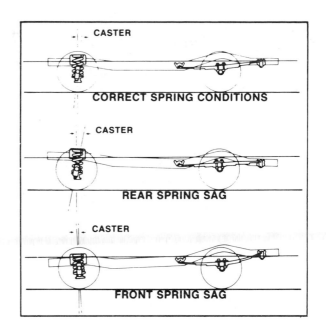

FIGURE 30-6. Steering angles are adversely affected by incorrect suspension height. Sagged springs are a common cause of this condition. *(Courtesy of Ford Motor Co. of Canada Ltd.)*

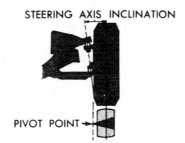

STEERING AXIS INCLINATION

PIVOT POINT

FIGURE 30-7. Steering axis inclination is the inward tilt of the spindle support at the top. *(Courtesy of Chrysler Corporation)*

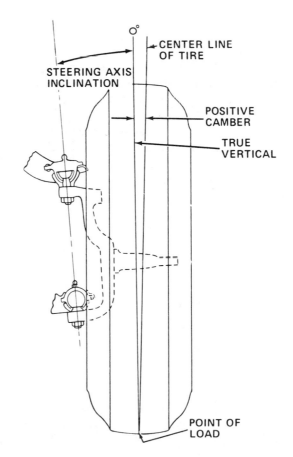

FIGURE 30-8. Relationship of steering axis inclination to camber. One of the effects of these two angles is to place the point of vehicle load at the center of the tire on the road surface. *(Courtesy of General Motors Corporation)*

691

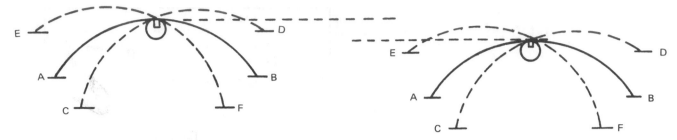

FIGURE 30-9. The effect of steering axis inclination on the travel of the outer end of spindle as shown by the line A to B when front wheels are turned from right to left. Since the spindle cannot in fact push the wheel into the road surface, the result is that the car is raised when turned to right or left. This helps return front wheels to straight ahead after a turn and aids directional stability. The line A to B represents a zero caster setting, the line C to D a negative caster setting, and the line E to F a positive caster setting. A car will lead to the side with the most negative or least positive caster. The figure on the left represents a zero camber setting; the figure on the right shows the result of a positive camber setting. The effect is that it tries to lower the outer end of the spindle.

1. To place the weight of the vehicle more nearly under the center of the tire where it contacts the road

2. To reduce steering effort, because of item 1

3. To provide good directional control (Figure 30-10).

Incorrect steering axis inclination will affect all the preceding and may prevent being able to set camber properly.

Toe-In

Toe-in occurs when the front wheels are slightly closer together at the front than at the rear. Toe-in is measured in inches, millimeters, or degrees. A limited amount of toe-in or toe-out is needed to allow for the fact that the wheels spread apart or come together slightly at the front when driving down the road, depending on vehicle design. This provides a zero running toe and no tire scuffing.

Incorrect toe-in or toe-out is the most frequent

cause of rapid tire-tread wear. Toe setting is the last adjustment to be made when performing a wheel alignment. On most front-wheel-drive vehicles, toe-out setting is required to provide a zero running toe. This is because the driving front wheels are trying to go around the SAI pivot point with a negative scrub radius.

Toe-Out on Turns

Toe-out on turns is the different turning radius of the two front wheels. When the car is in a turn, the inner wheel is turned more than the outer wheel, resulting in toe-out on turns. This is caused by the steering arms being bent inward where they connect to the steering linkage. It is needed to prevent tire scuffing (dragging sideways) during a turn. Since the inner wheel follows a smaller circle than the outer wheel when in a turn, toe-out on turns is necessary. Toe-out on turns is not adjustable and is corrected by replacing steering arms.

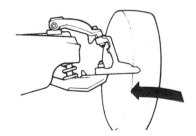

KING PIN INCLINATION
ANGLE HELPS WHEELS TO RETURN
WHEN COMING OUT OF TURNS

FIGURE 30-10. Another effect of steering axis inclination is shown here. *(Courtesy of Chrysler Corporation)*

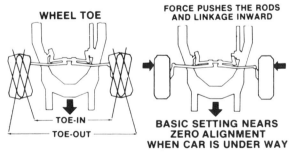

FIGURE 30-11. The objective in setting toe is to have the front wheels running straight ahead (zero running toe). To achieve this, a small amount of static toe-in must be present. Driving force deflects steering parts enough to result in zero running toe. Some cars with a negative scrub radius may require a toe-out setting. *(Courtesy of Ford Motor Co. of Canada Ltd.)*

DIAGNOSTIC CHART

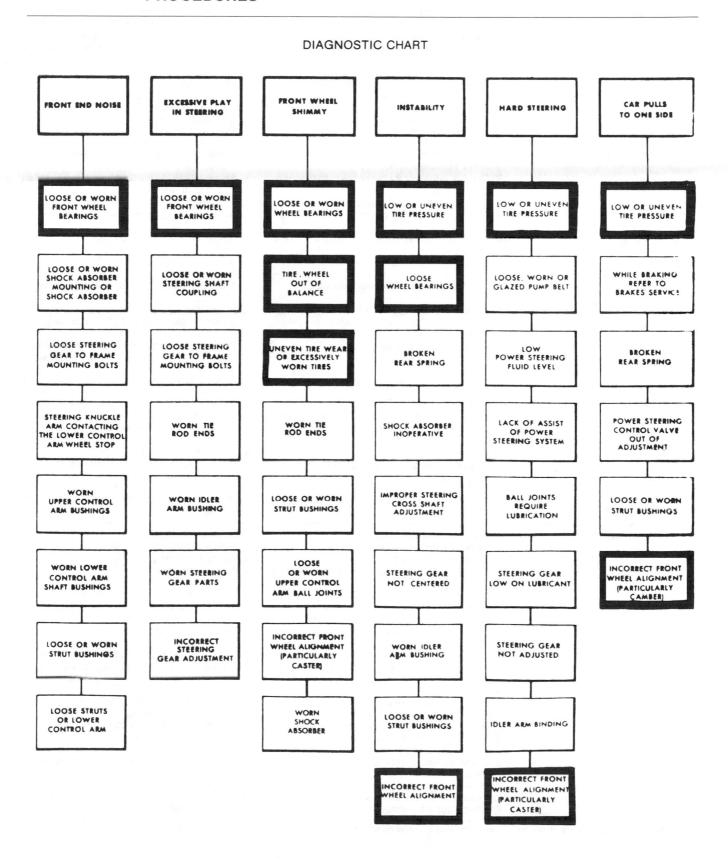

DIAGNOSTIC CHART

PROBLEM	CAUSE	CORRECTION
Hard steering	1. Ball joints require lubrication. 2. Low or uneven tire pressure. 3. Low power-steering fluid level. 4. Lack of assist of power-steering system. *5. Incorrect front-wheel alignment (particularly caster) resulting from a bent control arm, steering knuckle, or steering knuckle arm. 6. Steering gear low on lubricant. 7. Steering gear not adjusted. 8. Idler arm binding.	1. Lubricate ball joints. 2. Inflate tires to recommended pressures. 3. Fill pump reservoir to correct level. 4. Inspect, test, and service the power-steering pump and gear as required. 5. Replace bent parts and adjust the front-wheel alignment. 6. Fill gear to correct level. 7. Adjust steering gear. 8. Free up idler arm.
Car pulls to one side.	*1. Low or uneven tire pressure. 2. Front brake dragging. 3. Grease, lubricant, or brake fluid leaking onto brake lining. 4. Loose or excessively worn strut bushings. 5. Power-steering control valve out of adjustment. *6. Incorrect front-wheel alignment (particularly camber). 7. Broken or weak rear spring.	1. Inflate tires to recommended pressure. 2. Adjust brakes. 3. Replace brake shoe and lining as necessary and stop all leaks. 4. Tighten or replace strut bushings. 5. Adjust steering gear control valve. 6. Adjust front-wheel alignment. 7. Replace spring.
Excessive play in steering.	1. Worn or loose front-wheel bearings. 2. Incorrect steering gear adjustment. 3. Loose steering gear-to-frame mounting bolts. 4. Worn ball joints or tie rod. 5. Worn steering gear parts. 6. Worn upper or lower ball joints.	1. Adjust or replace wheel bearings as necessary. 2. Adjust steering gear. 3. Tighten steering gear to frame bolts. 4. Replace ball joints or tie rods as necessary. 5. Replace worn steering gear parts and adjust as necessary. 6. Replace ball joints.
Front-wheel shimmy.	*1. Tire, wheel out of balance. 2. Uneven tire wear or excessively worn tires. 3. Worn or loose wheel bearings. 4. Worn tie rod ends. 5. Strut mounting bushings loose or worn. *6. Incorrect front-wheel alignment (particularly caster). 7. Worn or loose upper control arm ball joints.	1. Balance wheel and tire assembly. 2. Rotate or replace tires as necessary. 3. Replace or adjust wheel bearings as necessary. 4. Replace tie rod ends. 5. Replace strut mounting bushings. 6. Adjust front-wheel alignment. 7. Inspect ball joints and replace where required.
Front-end noise.	1. Ball joint needs lubrication. 2. Shock absorber and bushings worn. 3. Worn strut bushings. 4. Loose struts, lower control arm bolts and nuts 5. Loose steering gear on frame. 6. Worn upper control arm bushings. 7. Worn lower control arm shaft bushings. 8. Worn upper or lower ball joint. 9. Worn tie rod ends. 10. Loose or worn front-wheel bearings. *11. Steering knuckle arm contacting the lower control arm, strut, or wheel stop.	1. Lubricate ball joint. 2. Replace bushings or shock. 3. Replace bushing. 4. Tighten all bolts and nuts. 5. Tighten the steering gear mounting bolts. 6. Replace worn bushings. 7. Replace worn bushings. 8. Replace ball joint. 9. Replace tie rod end. 10. Adjust or replace bearings as necessary. 11. Smooth off the contacting area and lubricate with a water-resistant grease.
Instability.	*1. Low or uneven tire pressure. 2. Loose wheel bearings. 3. Improper steering cross-shaft adjustment. 4. Steering gear not centered. 5. Worn idler arm bushing. 6. Loose or excessively worn front strut bushings. 7. Weak or broken rear spring. *8. Incorrect front-wheel alignment. 9. Shock absorber inoperative.	1. Inflate tires to correct pressure. 2. Adjust wheel bearing. 3. Adjust steering cross shaft. 4. Adjust steering gear. 5. Replace bushing. 6. Tighten nuts on strut rods or replace bushings. 7. Replace spring. 8. Measure and adjust front-wheel alignment. 9. Replace shock absorber.

*Wheel alignment problems. However, when diagnosing alignment problems, other related items must also be considered.

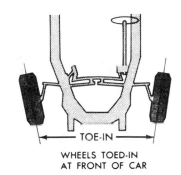

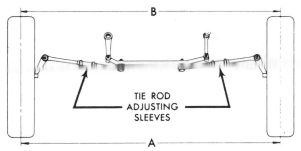

FIGURE 30–12. When front wheels have toe-in, they are closer together at the front wheels than at the rear. Dimension A is less than dimension B. *(Courtesy of General Motors Corporation and Chrysler Corporation)*

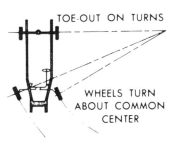

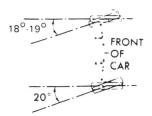

FIGURE 30–13. Toe-out on turns (turning radius) is needed to reduce tire scuffing when turning a corner. Since all four wheels turn around a common center, the inner front wheel must be turned sharper, as shown above. This is accomplished by steering arm design. Steering arms are angled inward where they attach to the steering linkage. *(Courtesy of General Motors Corporation and Chrysler Corporation)*

PART 3 WHEEL ALIGNMENT PROCEDURE

General Precautions

Customer and vehicle safety depend on the technician's ability to follow proper procedures and specifications. To achieve this, the following factors should be included.

- Perform all prealignment checks properly to determine extent of repairs required.
- The vehicle's steering and suspension system, including tires, should be in good condition before attempting alignment.
- Use all alignment equipment as recommended by manufacturer.
- Tighten all fasteners to specified torque.
- Install cotter pins wherever required.
- Observe all safety precautions when positioning the vehicle on the alignment machine.

Prealignment Checks

The following checks should be made before attempting wheel alignment. Correct any abnormal conditions before alignment.

1. Check tire size (tires should be the size and type recommended by the manufacturer).
2. Check tire wear (badly worn tires will affect steering and handling).
3. Correct all tire pressures.
4. Check wheels and tires for radial and lateral run-out. See Chapter 29 for the procedure.
5. The vehicle should be at curb weight (all accessories in place, full tank of fuel, spare tire in place, no passengers or additional weight).
6. Check the suspension system condition front and rear. See Chapter 27 for the procedure.
7. Check the steering linkage and gear condition. See Chapter 28 for the procedure.
8. Lubricate all lubrication points on the steering and suspension systems.
9. Balance all wheels. See Chapter 29 for the procedure.

Adjustment Methods

Adjustment methods vary considerably from one vehicle to another. Some use shims; others use eccentrics, slotted hole adjustments, or adjustable rods. Camber, caster, and toe-in are adjustable on

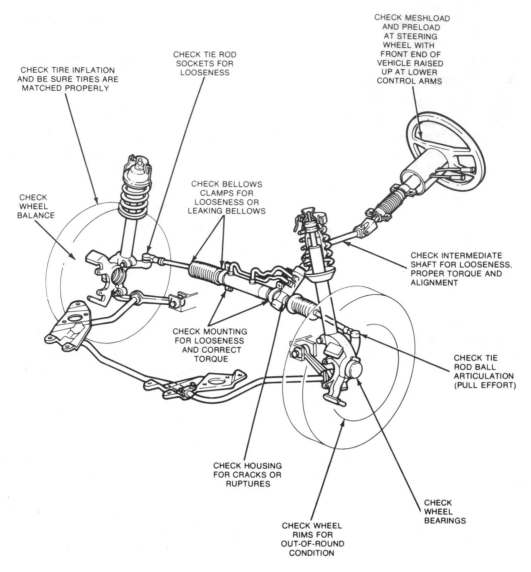

CHECK TIRE INFLATION AND BE SURE TIRES ARE MATCHED PROPERLY

CHECK TIE ROD SOCKETS FOR LOOSENESS

CHECK MESHLOAD AND PRELOAD AT STEERING WHEEL WITH FRONT END OF VEHICLE RAISED UP AT LOWER CONTROL ARMS

CHECK WHEEL BALANCE

CHECK BELLOWS CLAMPS FOR LOOSENESS OR LEAKING BELLOWS

CHECK INTERMEDIATE SHAFT FOR LOOSENESS, PROPER TORQUE AND ALIGNMENT

CHECK MOUNTING FOR LOOSENESS AND CORRECT TORQUE

CHECK TIE ROD BALL ARTICULATION (PULL EFFORT)

CHECK HOUSING FOR CRACKS OR RUPTURES

CHECK WHEEL BEARINGS

CHECK WHEEL RIMS FOR OUT-OF-ROUND CONDITION

FIGURE 30-14. Checks required before performing wheel alignment on strut suspension with rack-and-pinion steering. *(Courtesy of Ford Motor Co. of Canada Ltd.)*

FIGURE 30-15. Typical wheel alignment machine mounted above the floor. *(Courtesy of Hunter Engineering Co.)*

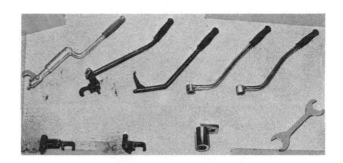

FIGURE 30-16. A number of special tools are required for wheel alignment, such as those illustrated here. *(Courtesy of Hunter Engineering Co.)*

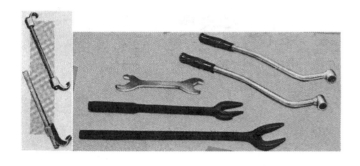

FIGURE 30-17. Tools such as these are used for adjusting tie rod sleeves. A pipe wrench should not be used. *(Courtesy of Hunter Engineering Co.)*

FIGURE 30-18. Wheel and tire run-out indicator measures wheel and tire radial and lateral run-out. *(Courtesy of Hunter Engineering Co.)*

FIGURE 30-19. Steering wheel holder keeps steering wheel centered for adjusting toe. *(Courtesy of Hunter Engineering Co.)*

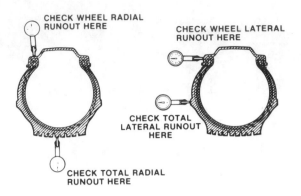

FIGURE 30-20. Points at which run-out indicator should be positioned for checking radial and lateral run-out of both tire and wheel. *(Courtesy of Ford Motor Co. of Canada Ltd.)*

FIGURE 30-21. Brake pedal depressor is used to keep brakes applied while checking and adjusting caster. *(Courtesy of Hunter Engineering Co.)*

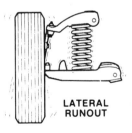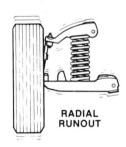

LATERAL RUNOUT

RADIAL RUNOUT

FIGURE 30-22. Effects of lateral and radial run-out are transmitted to suspension parts and the entire vehicle. *(Courtesy of Ford Motor Co. of Canada Ltd.)*

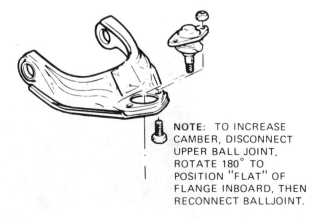

NOTE: TO INCREASE CAMBER, DISCONNECT UPPER BALL JOINT, ROTATE 180° TO POSITION "FLAT" OF FLANGE INBOARD, THEN RECONNECT BALLJOINT.

FIGURE 30-23. Camber adjustment is provided at the upper ball joint on some vehicles. *(Courtesy of General Motors Corporation)*

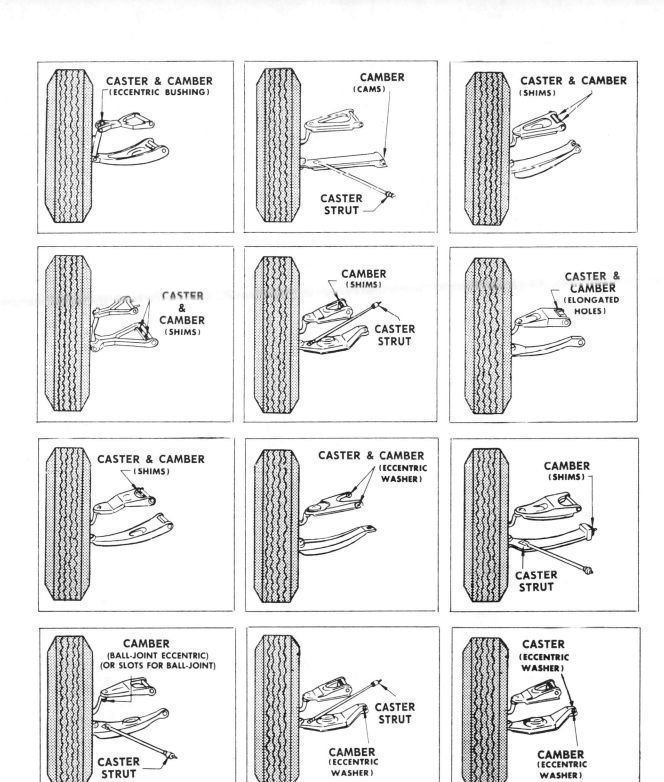

FIGURE 30–24. Different suspension designs showing various locations for adjusting caster and camber. *(Courtesy of Snap-on Tools Corporation)*

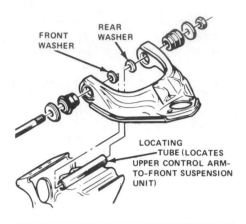

SERVICE CHANGE		
FRONT	REAR	NET CHANGE
3MM	9MM	+1°
9MM	3MM	−1°

FIGURE 30-25. Changing selective thickness washers on upper control arm shaft changes caster as used on some vehicles. *(Courtesy of General Motors Corporation)*

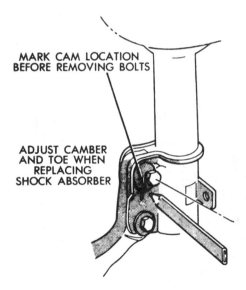

FIGURE 30-26. Some strut-suspension systems use a cam adjustment for setting camber as shown here. *(Courtesy of Chrysler Corporation)*

Some vehicles equipped with McPherson struts have no means for adjusting caster and camber and if alignment specs are wrong, tires wear excessively. Installation of the KF-39 Caster-Camber Adjusting Kit is made only once and alignment is a very simple adjustment — from under the hood — any time thereafter.

The strut is loosened so a plate can be bolted thru the existing holes in the inner fender. The strut is returned to its original position and held in place by the two plates. The vehicle is now ready for alignment.

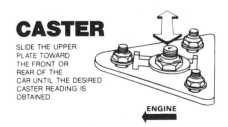

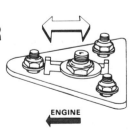

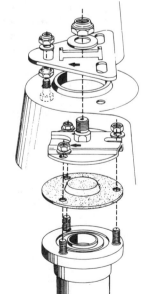

FIGURE 30-27. *(Courtesy of Moog Automotive Inc.)*

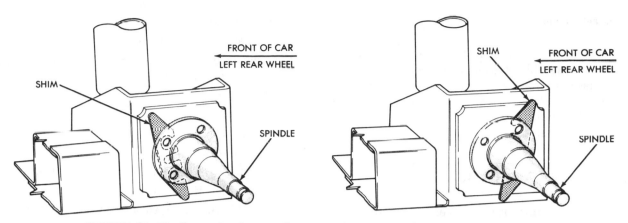

FIGURE 30-28. Rear-wheel toe adjustment by means of shims as used on some front-wheel-drive vehicles. *(Courtesy of Chrysler Corporation)*

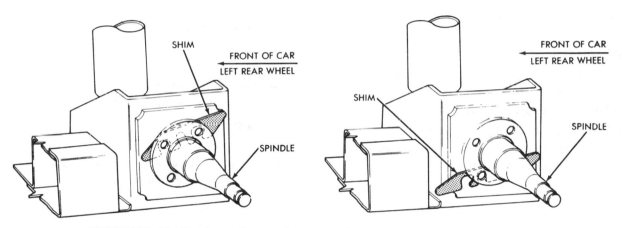

FIGURE 30-29. Camber adjustment on rear wheels by means of shims as used on some front-wheel-drive vehicles. *(Courtesy of Chrysler Corporation)*

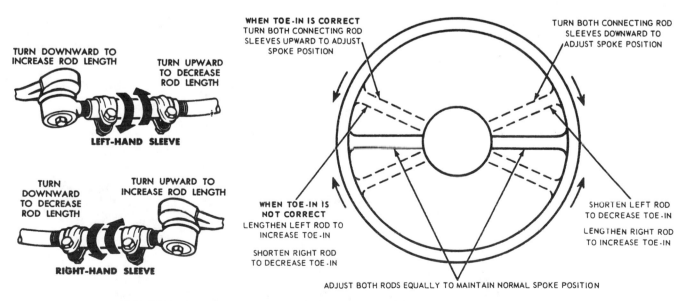

FIGURE 30-30. How to center steering wheel (left) and adjust steering linkage (toe-in, right). *(Courtesy of Ford Motor Co. of Canada Ltd.)*

most vehicles. Conversion kits are available for many nonadjustable strut suspension systems to allow adjustment for caster and camber correction. Steering axis inclination and toe-out on turns are not adjustable. A number of different points of adjustment are illustrated.

PART 4 SELF-CHECK

1. What is the purpose of wheel alignment?
2. What six alignment factors must be checked and corrected for proper alignment?
3. List three effects of incorrect camber.
4. Give three reasons why caster is needed.
5. How is incorrect steering axis inclination corrected?
6. What is the result of excessive toe-in or toe-out?
7. List eight prealignment checks that should be made before wheel alignment.
8. What is the cause of wheel tramp?
9. What is the cause of wheel shimmy?
10. List three methods of adjusting camber on strut-suspension systems.

PART 5 TEST QUESTIONS

1. Positive camber means that the wheel is tilted:
   (a) inward at the top
   (b) outward at the top
   (c) forward at the top
   (d) rearward at the top
2. Negative caster means that the steering knuckle at the top is tilted:
   (a) inward
   (b) outward
   (c) forward
   (d) rearward
3. The purpose of steering axis inclination is to:
   (a) aid directional control
   (b) aid in returning to straight ahead after a turn.
   (c) place vehicle weight more nearly under the center of the tire where it contacts the road.
   (d) all of the above
4. Incorrect turning radius of a car can be corrected by:
   (a) adjusting toe-in
   (b) adjusting camber and caster
   (c) adjusting steering axis inclination
   (d) none of the above
5. A properly balanced wheel is in balance:
   (a) statically
   (b) dynamically
   (c) neither statically nor dynamically
   (d) both statically and dynamically

Section 7

BRAKE SYSTEMS

Chapter 31

Automotive Brakes

Performance Objectives

After sufficient study of this chapter and the appropriate training models, you should be able to:

1. Complete the self-check and test questions with at least 80 percent accuracy.
2. State the purpose of all the brake systems and their components described in this chapter.
3. Describe the basic construction and operation of all the brake systems and their components covered in this chapter.

The brake system is one of the most important safety systems on the automobile. The ability of the brake system to bring a vehicle to a safe controlled stop is absolutely essential in preventing accidental vehicle damage, personal injury, and loss of life.

To identify and to correct a brake system problem, as well as to restore that system to its maximum effectiveness, requires considerable knowledge of the system's construction and operation. This includes the friction devices at each of the vehicle's wheels and the mechanical and hydraulic control systems that control the action of these friction devices. A good basic understanding of the principles of mechanical devices, hydraulic systems, and friction devices is essential.

PART 1   HYDRAULIC AND BRAKING PRINCIPLES

Pressure, Force, and Motion

A hydraulic system uses a liquid to transmit pressure, force, and motion. When force is applied to a confined liquid, a pressure is produced and exerted undiminished throughout the system. This pressure acts at right angles to all surfaces in the system and with equal force on equal areas. This is known as Pascal's law and is basic to all hydraulic systems.

Pressure is stated in pounds per square inch or in kilopascals. Force is the amount of force produced by the output piston as the input piston is moved. If there is only one input piston and only one output piston, both with the same reaction area, they will travel an equal distance. For example, if a hydraulic system has an input piston with a reaction area of 1 square inch (645.2 square millimeters) and an output piston of 1 square inch (645.2 square millimeters), the output piston will move 1 inch (25.4 millimeters) if the input piston is moved 1 inch (25.4 millimeters). At the same time, if a force of 50 pounds (222.4 newtons) is applied to the input piston, the available force at the output piston will also be 50 pounds (222.4 newtons). Output force can be increased by increasing the size of the output piston. If, for instance, the output piston had a reaction area of 2 square inches, the available output force would be 50 pounds per square inch multiplied by the square inches of the piston, or 100 pounds of force. However, the distance traveled by the output piston would be reduced by 50 percent. The hydraulic system's efficiency depends to a great extent on the total absence of air or vapor in the system. If air or vapor is present in the system, the compressibility of these gases causes a loss in pressure, force, and motion.

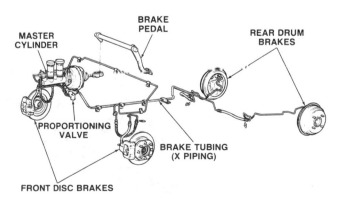

FIGURE 31-1. Service brake, power disc, and drum type. *(Courtesy of Ford Motor Co. of Canada Ltd.)*

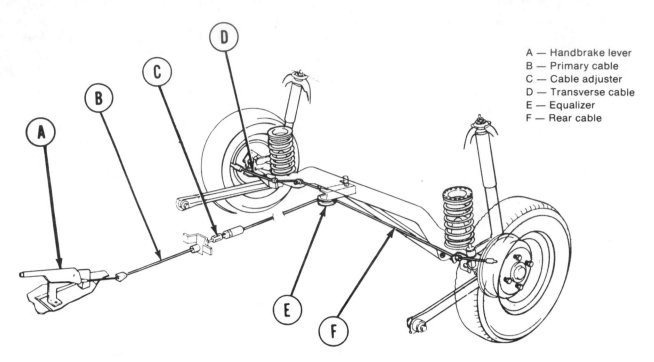

FIGURE 31–2. Parking brake control mechanism for one make of front-wheel-drive vehicle. *(Courtesy of Ford Motor Co. of Canada Ltd.)*

Friction

The brake system depends on the principle of *friction* for operation. *Sliding friction* (kinetic friction) is the rubbing action of one object sliding on the surface of another, such as a brake disc on a brake pad or a brake drum on a brake lining. *Static friction* is the resistance to the sliding of one object on the surface of another. In a brake system, when the brakes are applied there is sliding friction between the shoe and drum or the disc and pad, as long as the wheels are still turning, and there is static friction between the tire and the road surface. Upon severe braking, the wheels become locked, at which time there is a sliding friction between the tire and the road and static friction between the shoe and drum or disc and pad.

The most effective braking takes place just before wheel lock-up occurs. The amount of *pressure* applied to the surfaces in contact determines the amount of friction present. More pressure means

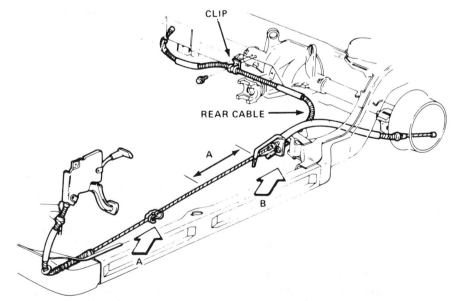

FIGURE 31–3. Parking brake, foot operated. *(Courtesy of General Motors Corporation)*

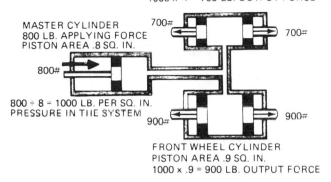

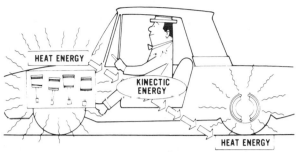

FIGURE 31-4. This schematic shows how a hydraulic system transmits force and motion. By varying output piston size, the available output force can be either increased or decreased as illustrated.

FIGURE 31-6. Energy conversion. The fuel's heat energy is converted to mechanical energy by the engine. The engine's mechanical energy is used to put the vehicle in motion (kinetic energy). The kinetic energy of the moving vehicle is converted to heat energy by the brake system to bring the vehicle to a stop. *(Courtesy of Ford Motor Co. of Canada Ltd.)*

more friction; less pressure, less friction. If, for example, it takes a 60-pound pull to slide a 100-pound object over a dry, stationary surface, the resultant *coefficient of friction* would be 60/100 or 0.60. It would therefore take only 30 pounds of pull to slide 50 pounds of the same material over the same surface. Less weight, which has resulted in less pressure between the two surfaces, results in less friction.

Heat

Friction produces *heat*. More friction produces more heat. In the brake system, the energy (momentum or kinetic energy) of the moving vehicle is converted to heat energy by the friction in the brake system. This heat energy or heat must be dissipated by the brake drum and linings or rotor and pad. Repeated severe braking results in excessive heat buildup in brake parts and causes *brake fade*. Brake fade is a

condition that the driver recognizes as requiring excessive brake pedal pressure, which results in little or no braking. This condition is caused by the change in the coefficient of friction between lining and drum or disc and pad. Pads and linings become glazed, while drum and disc surfaces become hardened.

The ability of a brake system to dissipate heat depends on brake design. The size of the surface area of the friction elements, pads, discs, linings, and drums is a factor. Since disc brake friction surfaces are more exposed to atmosphere, they dissipate heat more effectively than drum brakes of similar size. Since about 60 percent (more on front-wheel-drive vehicles) of braking is done by the front brakes (due to forward weight transfer during braking), disc brakes are usually used in the front, and drum brakes, at the rear. The stopping distance of a vehicle depends on driver reaction time, weight of the vehicle, and speed. If a vehicle's weight is doubled,

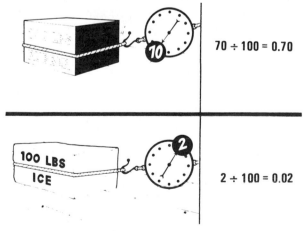

$$70 \div 100 = 0.70$$

$$2 \div 100 = 0.02$$

FIGURE 31-5. Coefficient of friction is calculated by dividing the weight of the object into the number of pounds of pull required to move the subject. *(Courtesy of Ford Motor Co. of Canada Ltd.)*

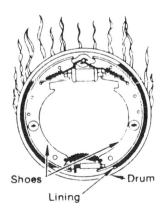

Shoes   Drum
Lining

FIGURE 31-7. Heat energy produced by the brakes must be dissipated to the atmosphere. *(Courtesy of Ford Motor Co. of Canada Ltd.)*

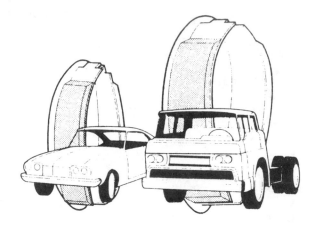

FIGURE 31-8. The larger or heavier the vehicle, the greater the friction area required to dissipate the heat generated by the brakes. *(Courtesy of Ford Motor Co. of Canada Ltd.)*

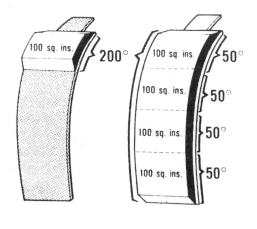

FIGURE 31-9. The larger the friction area in the brake system, the less heat is generated per square inch. *(Courtesy of Ford Motor Co. of Canada Ltd.)*

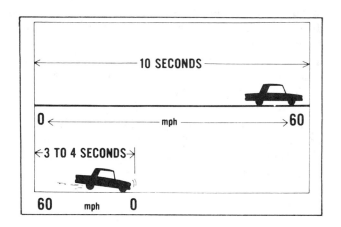

FIGURE 31-10. A vehicle that can accelerate from 0 to 60 mph in 60 seconds with a 100-horsepower engine is expected to come to a stop in as little as 3 to 4 seconds. This requires the brakes to dissipate approximately 1,500 horsepower of heat energy in 3 to 4 seconds. *(Courtesy of Ford Motor Co. of Canada Ltd.)*

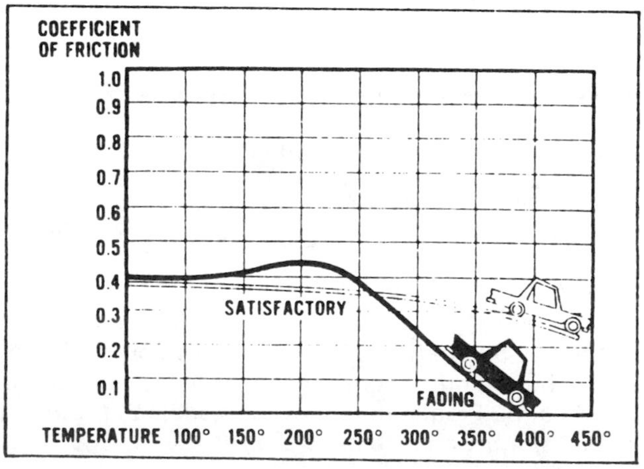

FIGURE 31-11. This table shows approximate stopping distance required to bring a vehicle to a stop at various speeds. Note the great increase in distance travelled as speed is increased.

VEHICLE SPEED M.P.H.	DISTANCE TRAVELED DURING DRIVER'S REACTION TIME	DISTANCE TRAVELED AFTER APPLICATION OF BRAKES	TOTAL STOPPING DISTANCE
20	22 FT.	22 FT.	44 FT.
30	33 FT.	50 FT.	83 FT.
40	44 FT.	88 FT.	132 FT.
50	55 FT.	138 FT.	193 FT.
60	66 FT.	200 FT.	266 FT.

FIGURE 31-12. Severe braking can cause brakes to fade due to overheating. Overheating causes the characteristics of the friction surfaces to change so there is less friction. Little or no braking can result even with heavy pedal pressure. This is called *brake fade*.

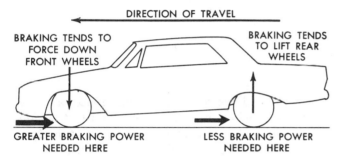

FIGURE 31-13. This shows why greater braking power is required at the front wheels of the car.

the stopping distance required is doubled. If both weight and speed are doubled, approximately eight times the stopping distance is required.

PART 2   BRAKE HYDRAULIC SYSTEM

Master Cylinder (Front-Rear Split System)

When the driver pushes down on the brake pedal, the master cylinder pushrod pushes the primary piston into the master cylinder. This in turn forces the secondary piston deeper into the master cylinder. Fluid is forced out of the primary system through steel and flexible lines to the front brakes and from the secondary system through separate lines to the rear brakes. As the level of fluid in the reservoir rises and falls, the diaphragm flexes, since the cover is vented to atmosphere.

In normal operation, the secondary piston is actuated hydraulically. Should a fluid leak develop in the primary system, the primary piston pushes

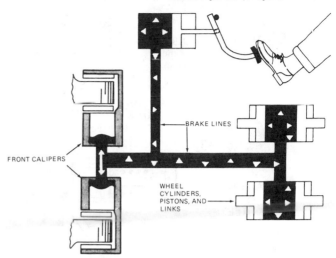

FIGURE 31-14. Hydraulic brake system operation with rear drum brakes and front disc brakes.

against the secondary piston since hydraulic pressure in the primary piston is lost. Should a leak develop in the secondary system, the secondary piston "bottoms out" in the master cylinder, and the primary system still operates normally. In either case the brake pedal will be somewhat lower than normal, and the brake warning light will go on when the pedal is pushed down.

When the brake pedal is released, the brake shoe

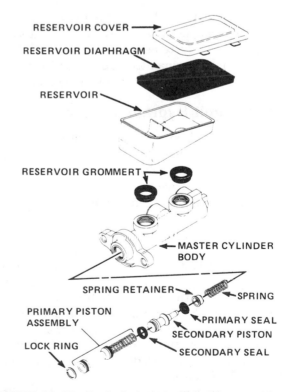

FIGURE 31-15. Exploded view of tandem master cylinder. (Courtesy of General Motors Corporation)

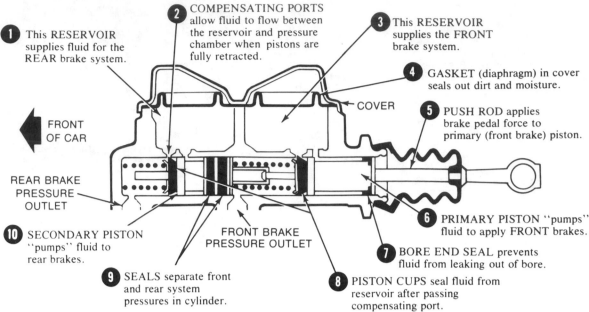

- Separate reservoirs, cylinders and pistons for front and rear systems.

① This RESERVOIR supplies fluid for the REAR brake system.

② COMPENSATING PORTS allow fluid to flow between the reservoir and pressure chamber when pistons are fully retracted.

③ This RESERVOIR supplies the FRONT brake system.

④ GASKET (diaphragm) in cover seals out dirt and moisture.

⑤ PUSH ROD applies brake pedal force to primary (front brake) piston.

FRONT OF CAR

COVER

REAR BRAKE PRESSURE OUTLET

⑩ SECONDARY PISTON "pumps" fluid to rear brakes.

⑨ SEALS separate front and rear system pressures in cylinder.

FRONT BRAKE PRESSURE OUTLET

⑥ PRIMARY PISTON "pumps" fluid to apply FRONT brakes.

⑦ BORE END SEAL prevents fluid from leaking out of bore.

⑧ PISTON CUPS seal fluid from reservoir after passing compensating port.

FIGURE 31-16. Cutaway view of tandem master cylinder with parts identified. *(Courtesy of Ford Motor Co. of Canada Ltd.)*

return springs force fluid from the wheel cylinders back through the lines to the master cylinder. When pressure in the system drops to approximately 8 to 18 psi (55 to 124 kPa), the check valve closes and fluid flow stops. This residual or static pressure helps seal piston cups in the wheel cylinders.

Disc brake systems do not have check valves since disc brake caliper pistons have a different seal. Some drum brake systems use mechanical wheel cylinder piston cup expanders and thereby eliminate the need for static pressure in the system.

Diagonally Split Hydraulic System

This system is used on vehicles where the weight distribution is such that the greater proportion of weight acts on the front wheels. This is the case with front-engine, front-wheel-drive vehicles with a high degree of weight transfer from the rear to the front during braking.

With a diagonally split system, the left front wheel and the right rear wheel would be linked hydraulically to one half of the master cylinder while the right front wheel and left rear wheel would be linked hydraulically to the other half of the master cylinder. Each of the two halves of the diagonally split hydraulic system operates independently of the other half, just as in the front-rear dual hydraulic system, and provides a high degree of safety in case of partial brake failure.

In this design, when one half of the system fails, the other half would still provide braking at one front wheel and one rear wheel. This creates a brake imbalance, which would result in a pull to the side of the vehicle where the front brake is still functioning. However, to offset this imbalance, a negative scrub radius is designed into the front suspension system. This negative scrub radius also compensates for any difference in tire-to-road adhesion during braking caused by differences in road surface conditions between front wheels, i.e., ice, gravel, etc. (See Chapter 27, Part 4.)

Quick Take-Up Master Cylinder

This master cylinder is used in a diagonal split system. It incorporates the functions of the standard dual master cylinder plus a warning light switch and proportioners. It incorporates a quick take-up feature that provides a large volume of fluid to the wheel brakes at low pressure with the initial brake application. The low-pressure fluid quickly provides the fluid displacement requirements of the system created by the seals retracting the pistons into the front calipers and retraction of rear drum brake shoes. The quick take-up master cylinder operates as follows.

1. With the initial brake application, more fluid is displaced in the primary piston low-pressure chamber than in the high-pressure chamber since the low-pressure chamber has a larger diameter. The additional fluid is forced around the outside diameter of the primary piston lip seal, into the high-pressure

710

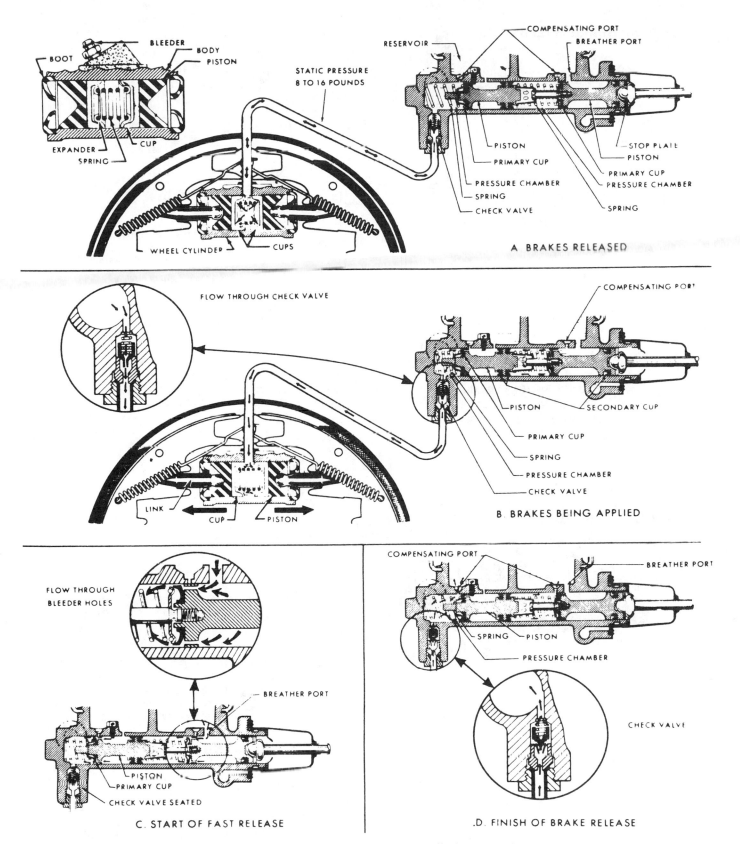

FIGURE 31-17. Dual (tandem) master cylinder operation.

711

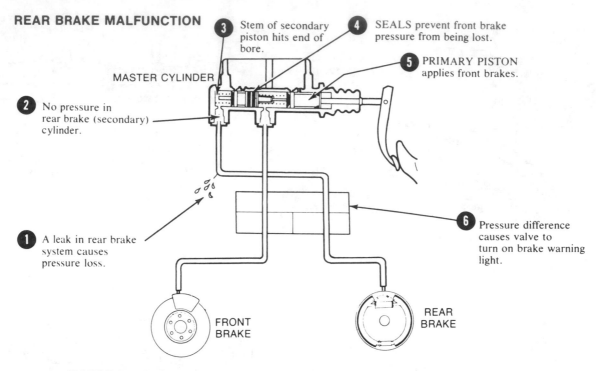

REAR BRAKE MALFUNCTION

3 Stem of secondary piston hits end of bore.

4 SEALS prevent front brake pressure from being lost.

5 PRIMARY PISTON applies front brakes.

MASTER CYLINDER

2 No pressure in rear brake (secondary) cylinder.

1 A leak in rear brake system causes pressure loss.

6 Pressure difference causes valve to turn on brake warning light.

FRONT BRAKE

REAR BRAKE

FIGURE 31–18. This shows what happens in the master cylinder when there is a leak in the secondary hydraulic system, such as in the rear brake lines or rear-wheel cylinders. *(Courtesy of Ford Motor Co. of Canada Ltd.)*

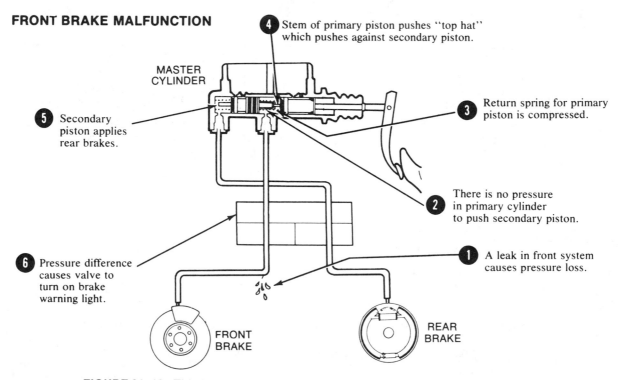

FRONT BRAKE MALFUNCTION

4 Stem of primary piston pushes "top hat" which pushes against secondary piston.

MASTER CYLINDER

5 Secondary piston applies rear brakes.

3 Return spring for primary piston is compressed.

2 There is no pressure in primary cylinder to push secondary piston.

6 Pressure difference causes valve to turn on brake warning light.

1 A leak in front system causes pressure loss.

FRONT BRAKE

REAR BRAKE

FIGURE 31–19. This illustration shows how the dual master cylinder operates when there is a hydraulic leak in the primary system, such as in the lines to the front brakes or in the front-wheel calipers. *(Courtesy of Ford Motor Co. of Canada Ltd.)*

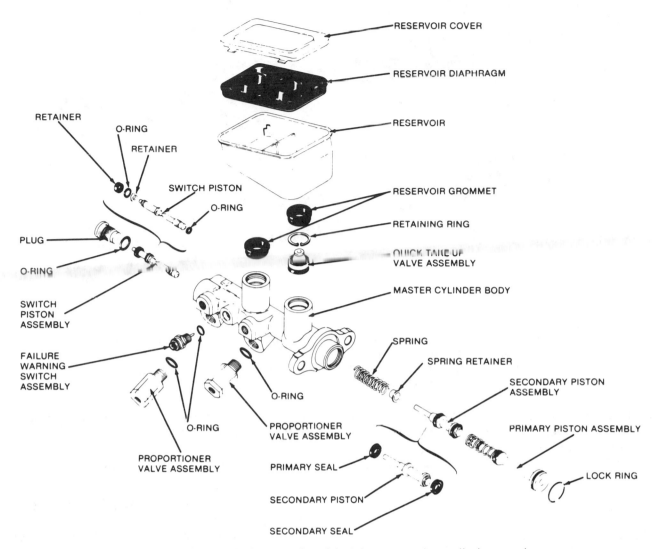

FIGURE 31-20. Exploded view of quick take-up master cylinder used on diagonally split hydraulic system on front-wheel-drive vehicle. (*Courtesy of General Motors Corporation*)

chamber, and onto the wheel brake units. Since equal pressure and displacement must be maintained in both primary and secondary systems, the primary piston moves a shorter distance than the secondary piston to compensate for the larger volume of fluid moved from the low-pressure area of the primary piston to the high-pressure area.

2. As the low-pressure displacement requirements are met, pressure will increase in the primary piston low-pressure chamber until the spring-loaded ball check valve in the quick take-up valve opens. This allows fluid to flow into the reservoir.

3. After the quick take-up phase of the cycle is completed, the pistons function in the same manner as in a conventional dual master cylinder.

4. With the release of the brakes, the master cylinder springs will return the master cylinder pistons faster than fluid can flow back through the sys-

tems. This would tend to create a vacuum on both the low-pressure and high-pressure chambers of the pistons if proper compensation were not provided.

5. The primary piston is compensated by fluid flowing from the reservoir through the small diameter holes of the quick take-up valve around the outside diameter of the quick take-up lip seal through the bypass hole and compensating port and into the low- and high-pressure chambers of the primary piston. The secondary piston is compensated by fluid flowing from the reservoir through the bypass hole and compensating port into the high- and low-pressure areas.

6. Expansion and contraction of brake fluid are handled by fluid passing directly from the master cylinder bore through the bypass hole and compensating port to the reservoir in a conventional dual bore master cylinder. The secondary piston in the

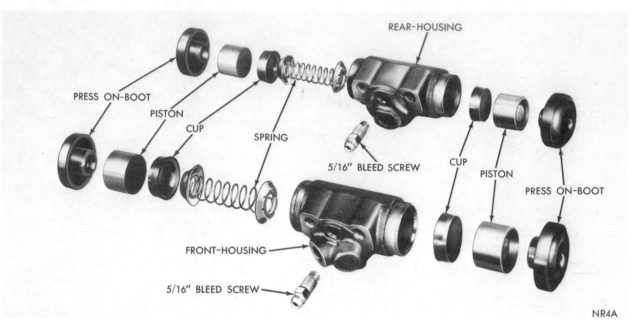

FIGURE 31–21. Exploded view of rear drum brake wheel cylinder (top) and front drum brake wheel cylinder (bottom). Note the difference in piston diameters resulting in more output at the front brakes, which do most of the braking. *(Courtesy of Chrysler Corporation)*

quick take-up master cylinder functions in this same manner. However, the primary piston must work through the quick take-up valve; thus a bypass groove is used to account for the fluid flow from or to the primary piston chambers.

Wheel Cylinders

Wheel cylinders are used in drum brakes to force the brake shoes against the drum. Front-wheel cylinders are usually larger in diameter than rear-wheel cylinders since most of the braking is done at the front wheels. Each wheel cylinder is fitted with a spring, cups, pistons, pushrods, and dust boots. A fitting is provided to which the brake line is attached, and a bleeder is used to bleed air from the system. When brakes are applied, the pistons are forced outward to push the shoes against the drum. On brake release, the brake shoe return springs force the fluid out of the wheel cylinder by pushing

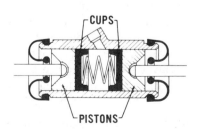

FIGURE 31–22. Cutaway view of assembled wheel cylinder. Note piston cups must face spring to seal hydraulic fluid pressure properly. *(Courtesy of Ford Motor Co. of Canada Ltd.)*

the pistons into the cylinder. Wheel cylinders are mounted to the backing plate.

Wheel Cylinder Design and Operation

Wheel cylinder designs include dual-piston, single-bore cylinders; dual-piston, step-bore cylinders; and single-piston cylinders.

The dual-piston, single-bore wheel cylinder is used with the dual-servo drum brake design. The step-bore, dual-piston wheel cylinder may be used with some nonservo drum brake designs. The larger diameter piston acts on the secondary or trailing shoe to increase apply force since self-energization has a tendency to resist hydraulic apply force on this design.

The single-piston wheel cylinder is used on some dual-servo design brakes and on some nonservo double-leading shoe drum brakes.

The spring in the wheel cylinder holds the rubber cup against the piston and the piston against the push rod or brake shoe, depending on design. The sealing edge of the rubber cup is flared (larger in diameter than the wheel cylinder bore) to help prevent fluid leakage and entry of air.

Usually, residual hydraulic pressure in the system or metal disc cup expanders or both increase the sealing pressure of the cup against the cylinder bore. When the brakes are applied, increased hydraulic pressure increases the sealing pressure of the cup lip against the cylinder bore to prevent any escape of fluid. Obviously, if the rubber cup were to be installed the wrong way, this action would not

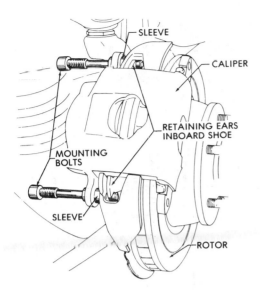

FIGURE 31-23. Caliper, guide pins, and bushings shown positioned over the rotor (disc). *(Courtesy of General Motors Corporation)*

take place and fluid would be forced past the cup out of the hydraulic system.

The cylinder bore area between the rubber cups is subject to corrosion and rust especially if brake fluid becomes contaminated. As the brake linings wear, the distance between the cups increases and the possibility for corrosion in a larger area of the cylinder bore is obvious. Should the brake shoes or linings be installed without servicing the wheel cylinders, the wheel cylinder piston cups would be pushed back and would be forced to operate on the rusted or corroded area of the cylinder bore. This would soon result in cup damage and hydraulic fluid leakage with resultant brake failure.

Wheel cylinders are equipped with dust boots or seals. In some designs the boot fits around the outside of the wheel cylinder whereas on others the boot fits on the inside of the end of the wheel cylinder bore. The dust boot prevents dirt and moisture from entering the wheel cylinder bore area, where the piston must travel back and forth.

If the operation of the wheel cylinders and the brake hydraulic system are properly understood the reasons for good service procedures are also understood and can be better explained to the customer or vehicle owner.

Calipers

The disc brake caliper is attached to the disc brake adapter (anchor plate). The caliper consists of a housing and cylinder with a piston and seal in the cylinder. The disc brake pads are also mounted in the calipers. The floating caliper usually has only one piston on the inboard side and acts on the disc or rotor like a C-clamp tightening on it. The caliper can move slightly in or out, thereby exerting equal

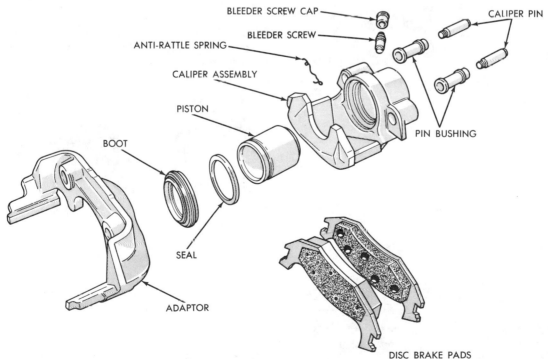

FIGURE 31-24. Exploded view of single-piston caliper showing parts identification. *(Courtesy of Chrysler Corporation)*

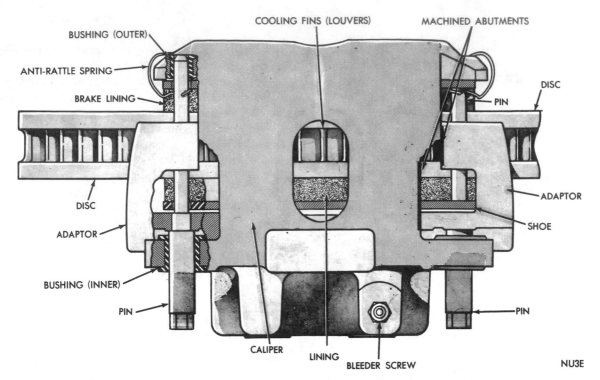

COOLING FINS (LOUVERS)   MACHINED ABUTMENTS

BUSHING (OUTER)

ANTI-RATTLE SPRING

BRAKE LINING

DISC

PIN

DISC

ADAPTOR

ADAPTOR

SHOE

BUSHING (INNER)

PIN

PIN

CALIPER   LINING   BLEEDER SCREW   NU3E

FIGURE 31-25. Another view of the single-piston caliper and pads (shoe and lining). *(Courtesy of Chrysler Corporation)*

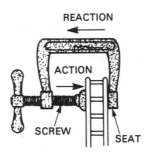

REACTION

ACTION

SCREW   SEAT

FIGURE 31-26. Single-piston floating caliper acts like a C-clamp exerting equal pressure on both sides of disc when brakes are applied.

FIGURE 31-27. C-clamp action of floating disc brake caliper.

UNAPPLIED   APPLIED

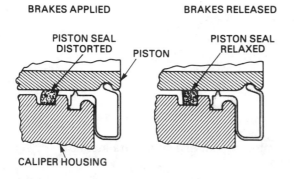

BRAKES APPLIED   BRAKES RELEASED

PISTON SEAL DISTORTED   PISTON   PISTON SEAL RELAXED

CALIPER HOUSING

FIGURE 31-28. Piston seal distorts when brakes are applied and resumes normal relaxed position, retracting the piston, when brakes are released. This provides proper pad-to-rotor clearance.

pressure to both sides of the disc. The caliper either floats on pins and rubber bushings or slides on metal guides. When the brakes are applied, the fluid forces the piston out, pushing the pad against the disc. The reaction on the caliper causes it to move the other pad inward slightly, applying equal pressure to the other side of the disc. On brake release the piston seal resumes its normal relaxed shape, thus pulling the piston back slightly. The piston maintains proper pad-to-disc clearance by moving out as the pads wear, thereby providing the self-adjusting feature. A connection for the brake line and a bleeder are also provided.

PART 3   DRUM BRAKES

Drum Brake Units

On the typical dual-servo drum brakes the entire braking assembly is mounted on a backing-plate. This backing plate is bolted to the axle housing at the rear and to the steering knuckle at the front.

The shoe anchor is attached to the backing plate and must absorb all the braking torque developed as the shoes are applied to the drums.

The shoes are mounted to the backing plate by hold-down pins and springs and are able to slide back and forth slightly on the backing plate ledges. A star-wheel adjuster is positioned between the shoes at the bottom, and return springs hold the shoes against the anchor at the top. A wheel cylinder is mounted to the backing plate just below the anchor to push the shoes against the drum during braking. The entire assembly is enclosed with a brake drum that is attached to the wheel hub or axle flange. Two types of self-adjusters are in use: a cable-operated type and a lever-operated type. When the brakes are applied while the car is backing up, the rear brake shoe is pulled away from the anchor. This actuates the cable or levers, which in turn move the star-wheel adjuster. This happens when enough lining wear has taken place to provide enough shoe

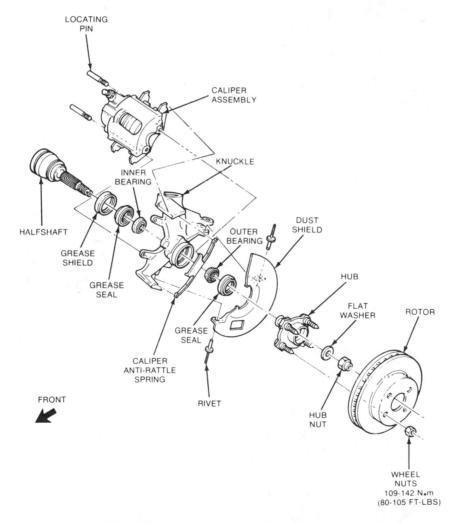

FIGURE 31-29. Front-wheel-drive disc brake components. *(Courtesy of Ford Motor Co. of Canada Ltd.)*

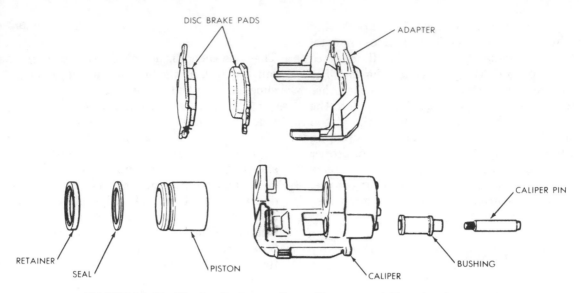

FIGURE 31-30. Single-pin type caliper. *(Courtesy of Chrysler Corporation)*

FIGURE 31-31. Backing plate mounted on front-wheel steering knuckle.

FIGURE 31-32. At the rear wheels, backing plates are mounted on flanges at the ends of the axle housing.

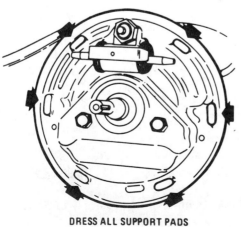

DRESS ALL SUPPORT PADS

FIGURE 31-33. Backing plate ledges or platforms keep the shoes in proper alignment with the backing plate and brake drum.

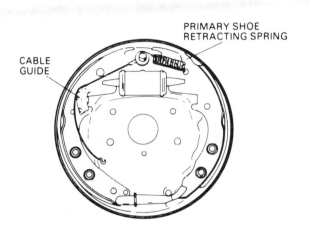

FIGURE 31-34. A hydraulic wheel cylinder is mounted on the backing plate. When the brake pedal is pushed down, hydraulic pressure inside the wheel cylinder forces the two pistons to move outward slightly, pushing against the pushrods and forcing the shoes against the drum.

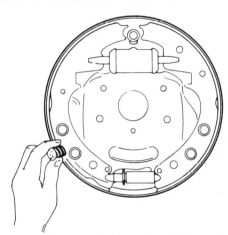

FIGURE 31-35. The shoe assembly is positioned on the backing plate and secured with hold-down pins, springs, and cups. The assembly is able to slide back and forth slightly on the backing plate. Retracting springs hold the shoes against the anchor.

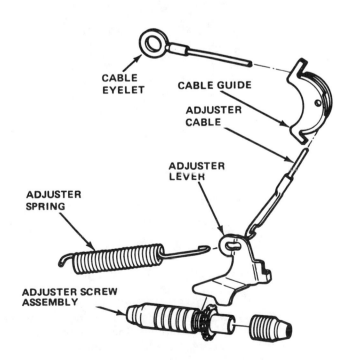

FIGURE 31-36. Star-wheel self-adjuster is lengthened or shortened by turning the adjusting screw to provide proper shoe-to-drum clearance. Adjusters for the left side are not interchangeable with adjusters for the right side of the vehicle.

719

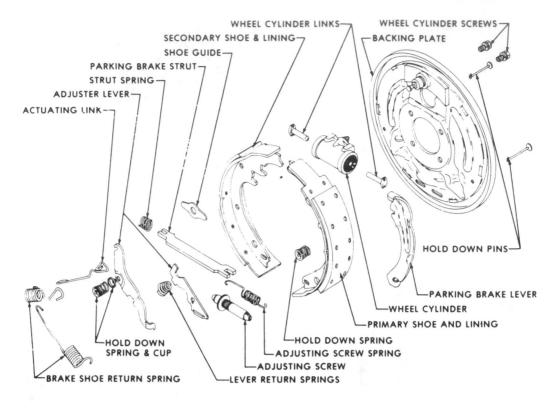

WHEEL CYLINDER LINKS
WHEEL CYLINDER SCREWS
SECONDARY SHOE & LINING
BACKING PLATE
SHOE GUIDE
PARKING BRAKE STRUT
STRUT SPRING
ADJUSTER LEVER
ACTUATING LINK

HOLD DOWN PINS
PARKING BRAKE LEVER
WHEEL CYLINDER
PRIMARY SHOE AND LINING

HOLD DOWN SPRING & CUP
HOLD DOWN SPRING
ADJUSTING SCREW SPRING
ADJUSTING SCREW
BRAKE SHOE RETURN SPRING
LEVER RETURN SPRINGS

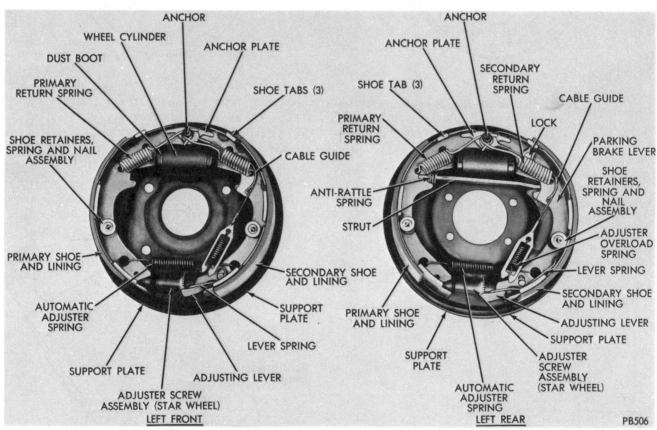

ANCHOR
WHEEL CYLINDER
DUST BOOT
PRIMARY RETURN SPRING
ANCHOR PLATE
SHOE TABS (3)
SHOE RETAINERS, SPRING AND NAIL ASSEMBLY
CABLE GUIDE
PRIMARY SHOE AND LINING
AUTOMATIC ADJUSTER SPRING
SUPPORT PLATE
ADJUSTING LEVER
ADJUSTER SCREW ASSEMBLY (STAR WHEEL)
LEVER SPRING
SUPPORT PLATE
SECONDARY SHOE AND LINING
SUPPORT PLATE
LEFT FRONT

ANCHOR
ANCHOR PLATE
SECONDARY RETURN SPRING
SHOE TAB (3)
PRIMARY RETURN SPRING
LOCK
CABLE GUIDE
PARKING BRAKE LEVER
SHOE RETAINERS, SPRING AND NAIL ASSEMBLY
ANTI-RATTLE SPRING
STRUT
ADJUSTER OVERLOAD SPRING
LEVER SPRING
SECONDARY SHOE AND LINING
ADJUSTING LEVER
SUPPORT PLATE
PRIMARY SHOE AND LINING
SUPPORT PLATE
AUTOMATIC ADJUSTER SPRING
ADJUSTER SCREW ASSEMBLY (STAR WHEEL)
LEFT REAR
PB506

FIGURE 31–37. Different types of self-adjusting mechanisms and their application. Operation is similar on all. As the vehicle moves in reverse and the brakes are applied, the secondary shoe moves away from the anchor. This actuates the self-adjusting linkage. When lining wear allows sufficient linkage movement, the adjuster will move one notch. This adjusts the shoes closer to the brake drum. *(Courtesy of General Motors Corporation and Chrysler Corporation)*

720

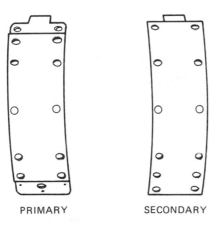

FIGURE 31-38. Primary shoe with shorter lining is mounted at front position while longer lining secondary shoe is mounted at rear position of each wheel.

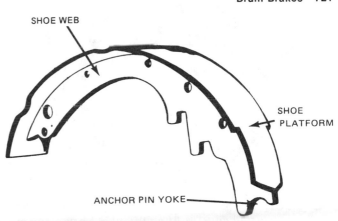

FIGURE 31-40. Typical brake shoe before lining has been attached.

movement to move the star wheel adjuster one notch.

The front brake shoe is known as the *primary shoe* and the rear shoe on the same wheel is known as the *secondary shoe*. The primary shoe usually has a shorter lining, often of a different material than the secondary lining, because the secondary shoe must do most of the braking. Since the shoe-and-lining assembly are floating and self-centering in the drum, the primary shoe pushes against the secondary shoe through the adjuster. When the brakes are applied, the primary shoe tends to bite deeper into the drum and wants to rotate with the drum, thereby pushing the secondary shoe much tighter against the drum. The tendency for the shoe to bite deeper into the drum is called self-energizing. The primary shoe pushing against the secondary shoe is called servo-action.

Brake linings either are bonded to the shoe under heat and pressure or are riveted to the shoe. Many standard brake linings are organic and contain a large amount of asbestos with a number of additives for bonding and stabilizing. Heavy-duty

linings are usually metallic. Under severe braking, temperatures may reach 500° F. (260° C.) or more. Metallic brake linings are better able to withstand higher temperatures. Brake linings can crack and separate from the shoe under severe braking conditions, such as descending a mountain. The brake shoe itself is made of metal and is very rigid since it must maintain its shape under high pressures.

The secondary shoe at the rear wheels has a parking lever attached to it that is actuated by the parking brake cable. A parking brake link or strut is positioned between this lever and the primary shoe. The link is also equipped with an anti-rattle spring.

Brake drums are cast iron with a steel disc or web. Many drums are finned for better cooling and some have spring-type vibration dampers. Drums can become out-of-round, distorted, bell-mouthed, or barrel-shaped due to wear and abuse.

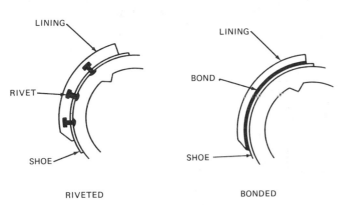

FIGURE 31-39. Methods of attaching brake linings to brake shoes. Rivet holes in riveted linings are countersunk about two-thirds of lining thickness. Tubular rivets are used. Bonded linings are glued to the shoe, clamped in place, then cured in an oven.

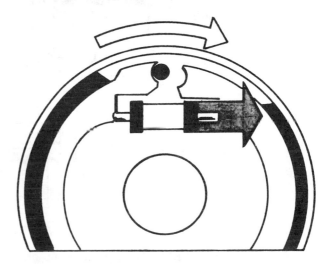

FIGURE 31-41. Wheel cylinder forces primary shoe against drum. Drum rotation pulls primary shoe away from anchor. Drum rotation also causes primary shoe to bite deeper into drum (self-energizing).

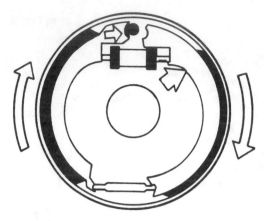

FIGURE 31-42. Self-energizing action of primary shoe pushes against secondary shoe through the adjuster at the bottom (servoaction). As a result, the secondary shoe does more of the braking. Secondary shoe rotation is prevented by the anchor at the top.

FIGURE 31-43. Heavier cars often use finned brake drums to aid in cooling the brakes.

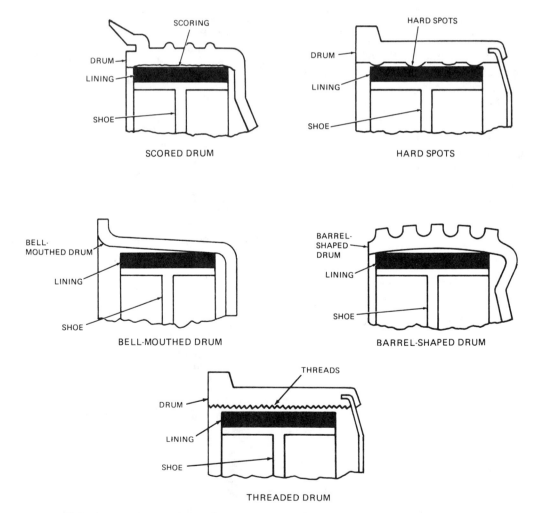

FIGURE 31-44. Scored drums are caused by worn-out linings or dirt. Hard spots are caused by overheating. Bell-mouthed and barrel-shaped drums result from shoe misalignment and worn-out drums. A threaded drum results from incorrect machining.

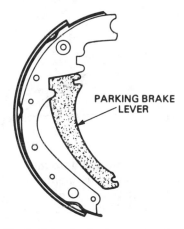

FIGURE 31–45. Parking brake lever attached to the secondary shoe. Lever pivots at its attaching pin and is held in place by a horseshoe-type retainer.

Drum Brake Design

Several different drum brake designs have been used. These are:

1. The dual-servo brake
2. The uniservo brake
3. The nonservo brake

Some minor variations exist in each of these designs such as wheel cylinder position, fixed or floating wheel cylinder, anchor mounting (on backing plate or direct to plate suspension component), anchor location on backing plate, type of adjuster, and type of shoe mounting.

Dual-Servo Design

The dual-servo drum brake design uses one "dual-piston" wheel cylinder and two brake shoes, a primary shoe in the front position and a secondary shoe

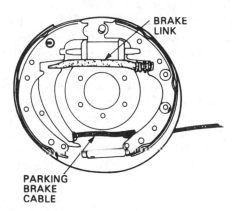

FIGURE 31–46. Parking brake cable is connected to the parking brake lever at the bottom. As the lever is pulled forward by the cable, it causes the link to push the primary shoe against the drum. Reaction at the lever pivot pushes the secondary shoe against the drum. When the parking brake is released, a spring on the cable pushes the lever back to its release position.

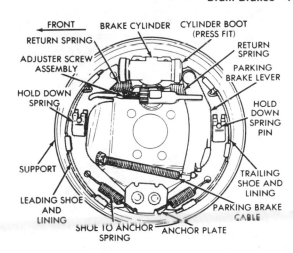

FIGURE 31–47. Nonservo rear drum brake unit with manual brake shoe adjuster used by one manufacturer on a front-wheel-drive vehicle.

at the rear position. In this design the self-energizing action of the primary shoe pushes against the secondary shoe through the adjuster to increase braking apply force. The secondary shoe attempts to rotate until it contacts the anchor where braking torque is transmitted to the backing plate and the suspension system.

Uniservo Design

The uniservo drum brake design is the same as the dual-servo design with one exception. It uses a single-piston wheel cylinder instead of a dual-piston wheel cylinder. The wheel cylinder is mounted so that brake apply force from the wheel cylinder acts on

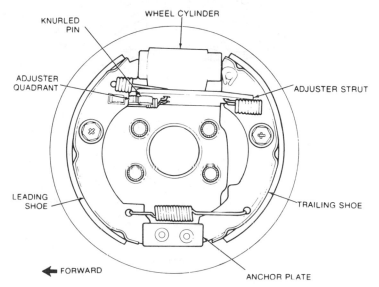

FIGURE 31–48. Nonservo rear drum brake unit with ratchet type of self-adjuster used by one manufacturer on a front-wheel-drive vehicle. *(Courtesy of Ford Motor Co. of Canada Ltd.)*

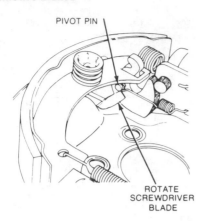

FIGURE 31-49. Backing off the brake adjustment with a screwdriver on the type of brake shown in Figure 31-48. *(Courtesy of Ford Motor Co. of Canada Ltd.)*

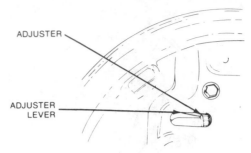

FIGURE 31-51. Access hole through backing plate allows backing off brake adjustment to facilitate drum removal on brake unit shown in Figure 31-50. *(Courtesy of Ford Motor Co. of Canada Ltd.)*

the primary shoe only. Self-energization and servo-action increase braking force in the same manner as in the dual-servo design.

Nonservo Design

The nonservo drum brake design has the brake shoes operating entirely independently from each other. There is no servo-action. Depending on design, there may or may not be self-energization.

On the leading-trailing shoe design, a dual-piston wheel cylinder is used to apply both shoes independently since each shoe is separately anchored. This arrangement does not provide any servo-action. Self-energization takes place on the leading shoe only when brakes are applied during forward motion and on the trailing shoe only when brakes are applied during reverse vehicle movement. Braking torque is transmitted to the anchor from one shoe and to the wheel cylinder from the other.

On the two leading shoe designs each shoe is actuated by a separate single piston-wheel cylinder. The wheel cylinders are mounted to provide self-energization of both shoes upon brake application during forward movement of the vehicle. There is no self-energization when brakes are applied while the vehicle is moving in a reverse direction. Since each shoe is separately anchored, there is no servo-action. Braking torque is transmitted to the two anchors during forward motion braking.

Drum Brake Adjustment

Shoe-to-drum clearance adjustment is provided in some designs by a star wheel screw-type adjuster between the two shoes and may be adjusted automatically, manually, or both. A ratchet cam and strut arrangement is also used in some designs for both manual and automatic adjustment. A direct acting cam or manually adjusted eccentric is also used on some vehicles. Periodic adjustment of lining-to-drum clearance is necessary to maintain pedal reserve. If the lining-to-drum clearance is excessive, the brake pedal may bottom out before the linings contact the brake drum. This condition is dangerous.

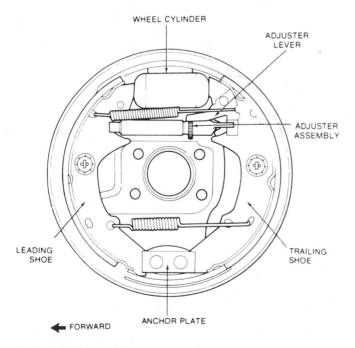

FIGURE 31-50. Nonservo rear drum brake unit used on front-wheel-drive vehicle by one manufacturer. This unit has a ratchet type of self-adjuster. *(Courtesy of Ford Motor Co. of Canada Ltd.)*

PART 4 DISC BRAKE UNITS

The disc brake unit consists of caliper, disc or rotor, pads, and splash shield. The caliper, described earlier in this chapter, is the unit that applies the brake pads against the disc. Earlier disc brakes used mul-

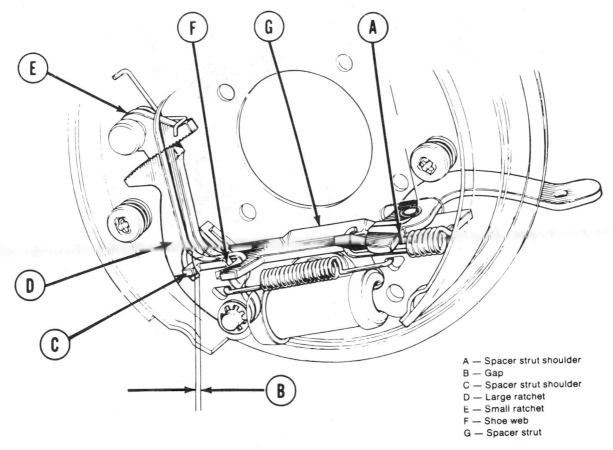

A —	Spacer strut shoulder
B —	Gap
C —	Spacer strut shoulder
D —	Large ratchet
E —	Small ratchet
F —	Shoe web
G —	Spacer strut

FIGURE 31–52. Ratchet type of self-adjuster used on front-wheel-drive rear drum brake by one vehicle manufacturer. *(Courtesy of Ford Motor Co. of Canada Ltd.)*

tipiston fixed calipers. Current disc brakes are mostly of the sliding or floating caliper single-piston type.

The most common application of disc brakes is on the front wheels, with drum brakes provided for the rear wheels. Some cars use four-wheel disc brakes. Calipers are bolted to a support bracket, which in turn is bolted to the steering knuckle. When braking during forward motion, braking torque at-

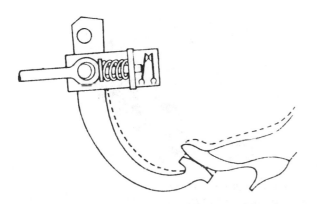

FIGURE 31–53. Pedal-actuated brake stop light switch completes electrical circuit to rear brake lights when pedal is depressed.

tempts to push the upper end of the knuckle forward. The steering knuckle therefore must absorb all the braking torque developed at the front wheels.

Discs or rotors are either the solid or finned type. The finned type has better cooling and therefore is usually used on heavier cars. Disc brake surfaces, like drum brake surfaces, are highly machined and must remain smooth and parallel for effective braking. The disc is made of cast iron, which has proved to be the best friction material for both discs and drums. The minimum thickness for discs is often stamped in the disc. Brake drums also have maximum allowable diameters stamped on them. Disc brake pads are either bonded or riveted to a metal shoe. Pads are usually backed with a stick-on anti-rattle material on the metal shoe side and are often mounted with anti-rattle clips. Disc brakes are not self-energizing and therefore have large pistons to produce the necessary force for high apply pressures. This generates more heat than do drum brakes, but disc brakes are better able to dissipate the heat produced. The result is less *brake fade* than with drum brakes. Brake fade occurs when friction surfaces become so hot that their coefficient of friction drops so low that even the application of severe pedal pressure can result in little actual braking.

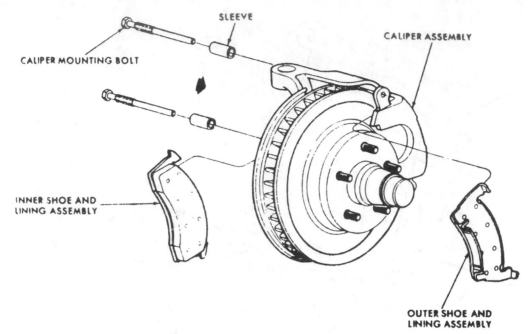

FIGURE 31-54. Floating caliper disc brake components.

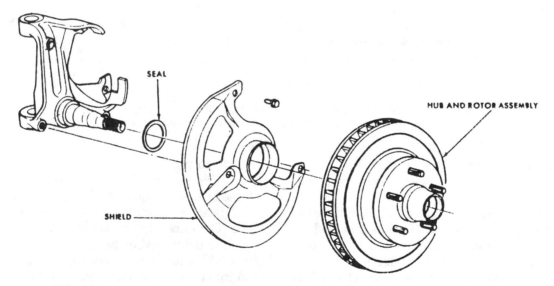

FIGURE 31-55. Steering knuckle, splash shield, and finned rotor for disc brake.

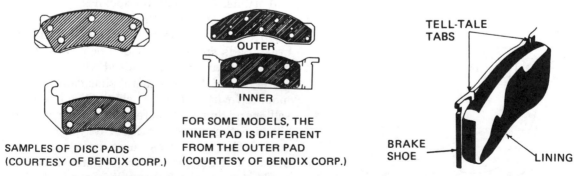

SAMPLES OF DISC PADS
(COURTESY OF BENDIX CORP.)

FOR SOME MODELS, THE
INNER PAD IS DIFFERENT
FROM THE OUTER PAD
(COURTESY OF BENDIX CORP.)

FIGURE 31-56. Various types of disc brake pads. When linings are worn down to telltale tabs, they cause a noise to be heard, reminding the driver that the brakes need attention. Friction materials used on pads are organic compounds, combination organic and metallic compounds, and metallic compounds.

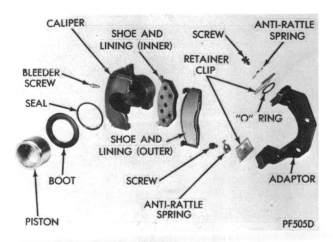

FIGURE 31-57. Disc brake caliper, exploded view. Anti-rattle clips for brake pads are also shown. (*Courtesy of Chrysler Corporation*)

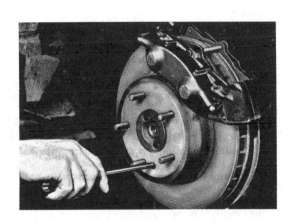

FIGURE 31-58. Using a screwdriver to adjust the parking brake shoe to drum clearance on the rear wheel of one type of four-wheel disc brake. See internal parts of this unit in Figure 31-59. (*Courtesy of General Motors Corporation*)

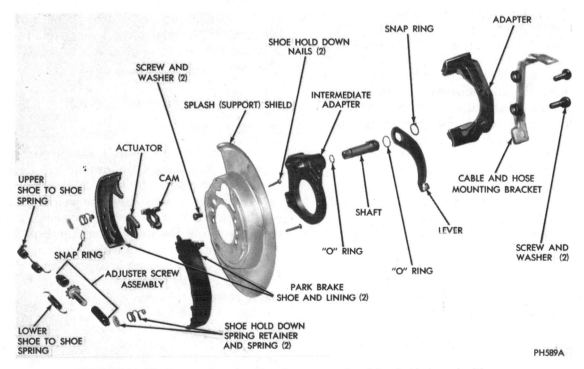

FIGURE 31-59. Internal expanding shoe type of parking brake used with some four-wheel disc brakes. The rear disc incorporates a small brake drum for the parking brake. (*Courtesy of Chrysler Corporation*)

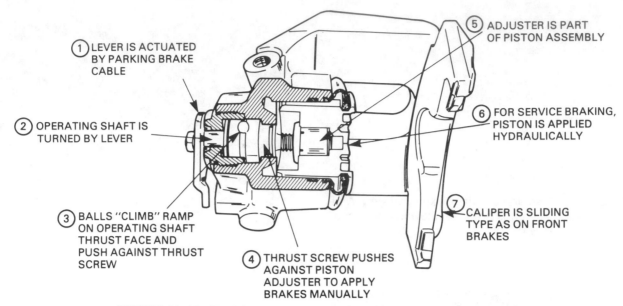

① LEVER IS ACTUATED BY PARKING BRAKE CABLE

② OPERATING SHAFT IS TURNED BY LEVER

③ BALLS "CLIMB" RAMP ON OPERATING SHAFT THRUST FACE AND PUSH AGAINST THRUST SCREW

④ THRUST SCREW PUSHES AGAINST PISTON ADJUSTER TO APPLY BRAKES MANUALLY

⑤ ADJUSTER IS PART OF PISTON ASSEMBLY

⑥ FOR SERVICE BRAKING, PISTON IS APPLIED HYDRAULICALLY

⑦ CALIPER IS SLIDING TYPE AS ON FRONT BRAKES

FIGURE 31-60. Ford four-wheel disc brake parking brake operation.

Four-Wheel Disc Brakes

Disc brakes are used on some vehicles on all four wheels because of the advantage disc brakes have over drum brakes. Rear-wheel disc brakes are similar in design to front-wheel disc brakes and they operate in essentially the same manner. The same type of components are used—calipers, pads, rotors—and the hydraulic system is the same. The major difference is that a parking brake is required at the rear wheels.

Some manufacturers use an internal expanding shoe and drum type of parking brake. The usual type of parking brake control mechanism is used to operate the parking brake. This unit consists of a backing plate on which two shoes are mounted in a similar manner as the duo-servo drum brake arrangement and a brake drum that is an integral part of the brake disc. A screw-type adjuster is used to provide proper shoe-to-drum clearance.

Another type of rear-wheel disc brake uses the disc brake as the parking brake. This is accomplished by using a modified caliper assembly that allows mechanical application of the pads against the rotor. A lever-operated ramp-and-ball arrangement forces the caliper piston to move to apply the brakes manually (see Figure 31-60).

PART 5   BRAKE LINES, SWITCHES, VALVES AND FLUID

Brake Lines

Seamless steel brake lines carry the brake fluid from the master cylinder to a brake warning light switch or to a combination valve. From there, additional steel lines carry the fluid to the front wheel openings and to the rear of the frame or body. At the rear, a high-pressure flexible line connects the steel line to other steel lines in the rear axle, which lead to the rear-wheel cylinders. High-pressure flexible lines are also used at each front-wheel cylinder or caliper. Only recommended steel and flex lines should be used for replacement.

Two types of steel line flared ends are used. One type is the double lap flare and the other type is the ISO flare. Fittings for these two types are also of different design and should never be mixed or interchanged. Never use copper or aluminum lines; they can fail due to the high pressure developed in the brake system.

Pressure Differential Switch

(Warning Light)

A brake warning light switch is used with the dual braking system. When a hydraulic leak develops in either system and the brake pedal is applied, a pressure difference is sensed by the switch completing the electrical circuit to the light and causing it to go on. This warns the driver that the brake system needs attention. An additional function for this brake light on many cars is to warn the driver that the parking brake is applied and should be released before starting to drive.

Metering Valve

Cars equipped with disc brakes for the front-rear split system sometimes have a metering valve in the front-brake hydraulic system. This prevents the front brakes from applying until the rear brakes are

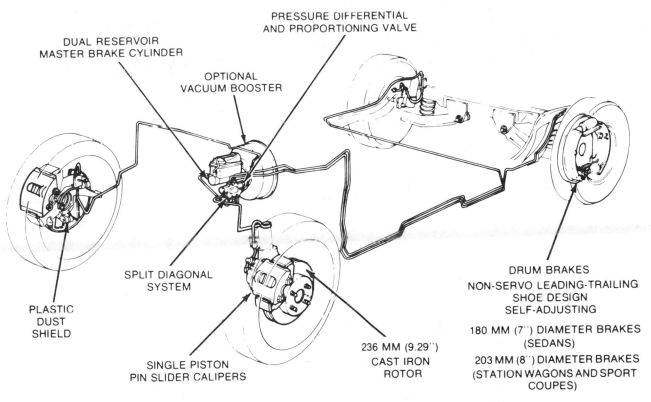

FIGURE 31-61. Brake lines on a front-wheel-drive vehicle with a diagonally split hydraulic system. This system requires two brake lines to the rear of the vehicle. *(Courtesy of Ford Motor Co. of Canada Ltd.)*

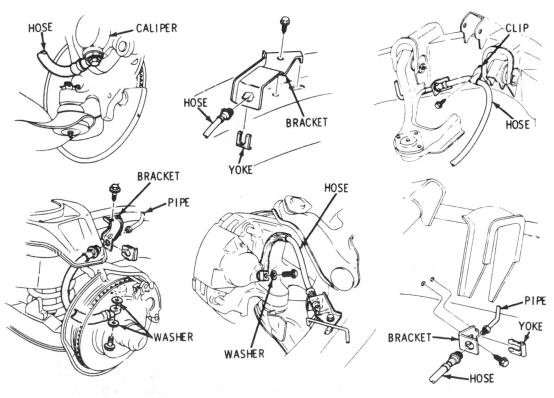

FIGURE 31-62. Typical examples of front-wheel brake line mounting methods. *(Courtesy of General Motors Corporation)*

729

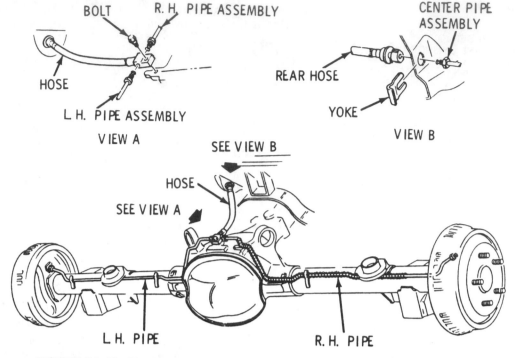

VIEW A

VIEW B

SEE VIEW B

HOSE

SEE VIEW A

L.H. PIPE

R.H. PIPE

FIGURE 31-63. Typical brake line routing on a rear axle of a front-rear split hydraulic brake system. *(Courtesy of General Motors Corporation)*

applying at approximately 90 to 180 psi (620.55 kilopascals to 1241.1 kilopascals). Since front disc brakes have no brake shoe return springs for the hydraulic pressure to overcome, they would apply too soon and could cause loss of directional control of the car. The diagonally split system requires two metering valves.

Proportioning Valve

During severe braking, more of the car weight is transferred to the front wheels. As a result, the front wheels do most of the braking. Without a proportioning valve, the rear wheels, having relatively little traction, would skid. The proportioning valve

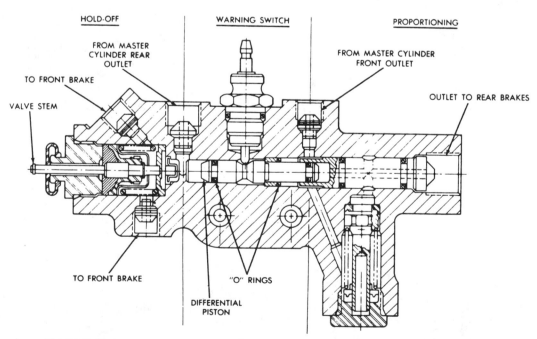

FIGURE 31-64. A combination brake valve for a front-rear split hydraulic system includes a hold-off (metering) valve, a brake warning light switch (pressure differential switch), and a proportioning valve. Many cars equipped with disc and drum brakes use this valve.

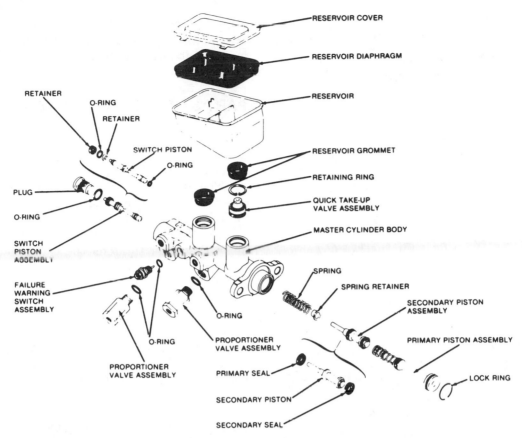

FIGURE 31-65. Quick take-up master cylinder assembly for a diagonally split hydraulic brake system used on a front-wheel-drive vehicle. Note two separate proportioning valves (one for each rear wheel), differential switch piston, and failure switch. *(Courtesy of General Motors Corporation)*

reduces hydraulic pressure buildup to the rear wheels as compared to pressure buildup at the front wheels after a specified pressure has been reached (approximately 350 psi or 2,413.25 kilopascals). In the diagonal split system, two proportioners are required—one for each system.

Combination Valve

The combination valve combines the brake warning light switch, metering valve, and proportioning valve into one unit. Many cars with the front-rear split system use this type of valve.

Brake Fluid

The fluid used in the hydraulic brake system is a special fluid, and only brake fluid of high quality should be used. Mineral oil, hydraulic oil, automatic transmission fluid, power steering fluid, or other oils should *never* be used in a hydraulic brake system.

High-quality brake fluid has a number of char-

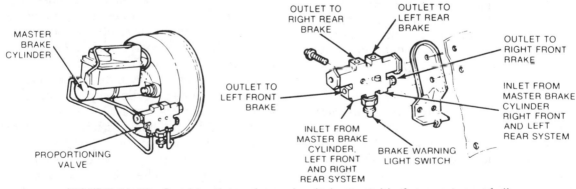

FIGURE 31-66. Combination valve-and-switch assembly for one type of diagonally split brake hydraulic system. This unit includes the pressure differential valve and switch and proportioning valves. *(Courtesy of Ford Motor Co. of Canada Ltd.)*

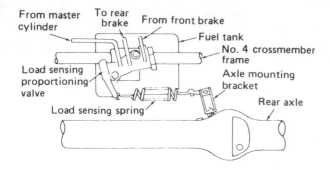

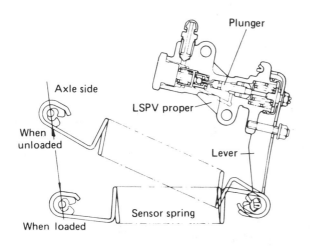

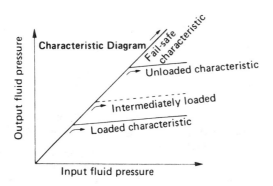

FIGURE 31-67. Load sensing proportioning valve for light truck senses vehicle load and proportions braking between front and rear brakes in proportion to load variations and degree of rear to front weight transfer during braking. *(Courtesy of Chrysler Corporation)*

acteristics. It is able to absorb moisture and therefore should never be left open to atmosphere, since the atmosphere contains moisture. It has a high boiling point to prevent evaporization, which would result in loss of braking effectiveness. A boiling point of 550°F. (287.8°C.) or higher is needed for present brake systems. Good brake fluid is noncorrosive, has good lubricating qualities, remains stable over a long period of time, and is compatible with

other high-quality brake fluids. Brake fluid must be kept absolutely clean and in airtight containers to maintain its effectiveness.

PART 6   PARKING BRAKES

Parking brake mechanisms for rear-wheel drum brake units and rear-wheel disc brake units are described in this chapter, Parts 3 and 4 respectively.

The parking brake may be operated by a separate foot pedal or by a hand-operated lever. The lever or pedal operates a cable system linked to the rear brakes and applies them mechanically. Pushing down the pedal tightens the cable and forces the shoes against the drum or the pads against the rotor. Some cars use a vacuum motor to release the parking brake automatically as soon as the car starts. In four-wheel disc brakes two different types of parking brake are used, as described earlier. Older cars and some trucks use a drum mounted at the rear of the transmission for the parking brake. See Figures 31–2, 31–3, and 31–68.

PART 7   POWER BRAKES

Many cars are equipped with power brakes. Power brakes reduce the amount of force the driver needs to apply to the brake pedal. Two types of power brakes are in use. The vacuum-operated power brake is the most common. The other type of power brake is hydraulically operated from power steering pump pressure. This unit is commonly called Hydro-Boost or Hydro Max.

Vacuum Power Brake

The vacuum-suspended power brake uses the engine intake manifold vacuum. A vacuum booster is mounted between the master cylinder and the firewall. The brake pedal pushes against the booster pushrod, which in turn operates a valve assembly. The valve assembly closes off the vacuum to the rear chamber of the booster and admits atmospheric pressure to that side. This causes the piston to move toward the master cylinder. The piston pushes against the master cylinder pushrod, thereby providing braking assistance. Most of the apply force is provided by the booster; however, a *reaction* assembly allows part of the apply pressure to be felt by the driver, giving the driver needed pedal *feel*.

The booster can be in the *released, apply,* or *hold* position. In the released position the atmospheric valve is closed and the intake manifold vacuum is present on both sides of the piston, allowing the piston return spring to hold the piston in the release

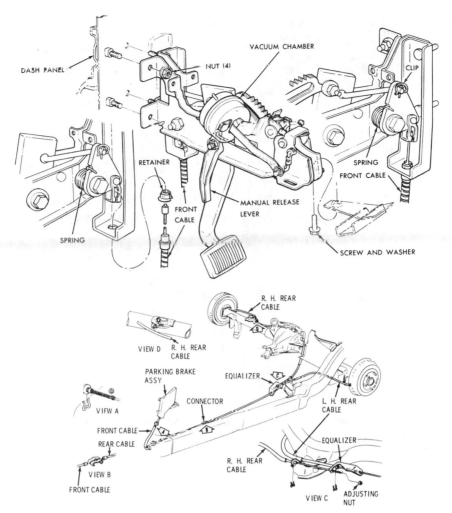

FIGURE 31-68. Parking brake linkage. The equalizer provides equal apply force to both rear wheels. Also shown is a vacuum-operated parking brake automatic release. *(Courtesy of General Motors Corporation)*

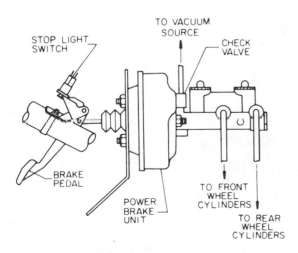

FIGURE 31-69. Power brake and master cylinder mounting arrangement. *(Courtesy of General Motors Corporation)*

position. When the brake pedal is depressed, the booster is in the apply position. The vacuum port to the rear booster chamber is closed, and the atmospheric port is opened. This allows atmospheric pressure to push the piston forward, applying the brakes. As soon as the pedal movement stops, the booster is in the hold position. In this position the piston has caught up with pedal and pushrod movement, causing the atmospheric port to close. Since the vacuum port is already closed, the booster holds the apply position desired by the driver. As soon as the pedal is released, the atmospheric port closes and the vacuum port opens, allowing the spring to return the booster piston to the release position.

The vacuum power brake stores sufficient vacuum for several brake applications should the engine fail to provide vacuum. Heavier cars use a dual-piston booster for added braking assist.

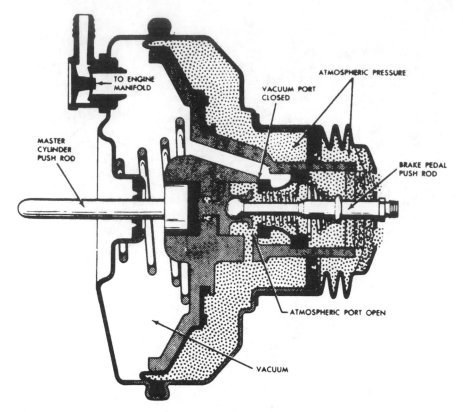

FIGURE 31-70. Vacuum brake booster in apply position. Vacuum port is closed and atmospheric port is open.

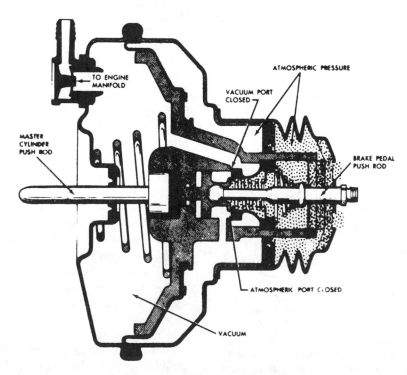

FIGURE 31-71. Booster in hold position. Both ports are closed.

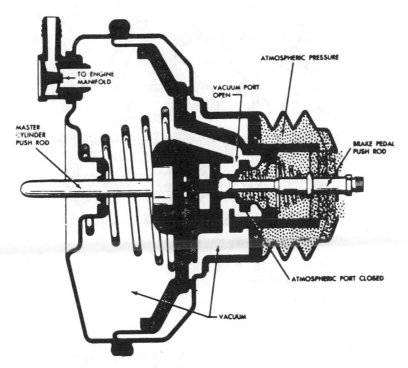

FIGURE 31-72. Booster in released position. Vacuum port is open and atmospheric port is closed.

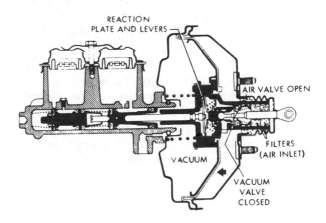

FIGURE 31-73. Delco-Moraine lever-type reaction mechanism.

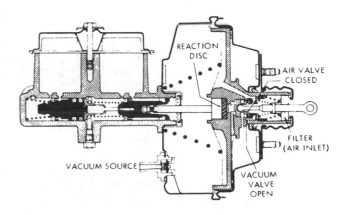

FIGURE 31-74. This Bendix booster uses a disc-type reaction.

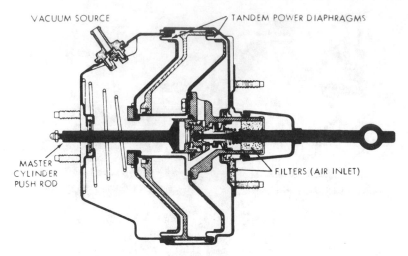

FIGURE 31-75. This tandem power diaphragm booster is used on larger cars requiring more apply pressure, since a heavier car requires more braking effort to bring it to a stop.

Hydro-Boost Power Brake

The addition of emission-control devices to the engine reduced the available intake manifold vacuum, and in some cases there was insufficient vacuum to operate a vacuum power brake. A hydraulic brake booster called Hydro-Boost was used to overcome this problem. This unit uses power-steering pump hydraulic pressure to assist in applying the brakes.

When the brake pedal is depressed, a control valve in the Hydro-Boost unit allows power-steering pump pressure to act on a piston, which in turn pushes on the master cylinder pushrod. The amount of assist depends on pedal pressure and the position of the control valve. In the hold position the valve shuts off any additional hydraulic pressure from the power-steering pump to the booster. On release, the valve dumps apply pressure as the piston is returned to the release position.

An accumulator is added to store sufficient hydraulic pressure for several brake applications should the power-steering pump fail. After that, the brakes operate normally but without power assist.

PART 8 SKID CONTROL SYSTEMS

Systems Operation

Braking is most effective while the wheels are still rotating just before a skid or wheel lock-up takes place. A skid control system is designed to prevent skid or wheel lock-up. The system consists of a speed

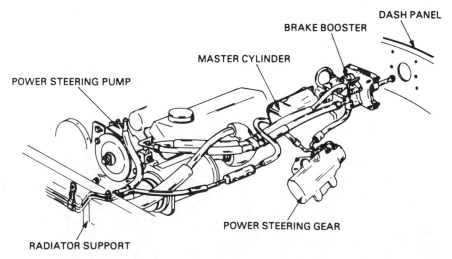

FIGURE 31-76. Hydro-Boost power brake system layout. *(Courtesy of Ford Motor Co. of Canada Ltd.)*

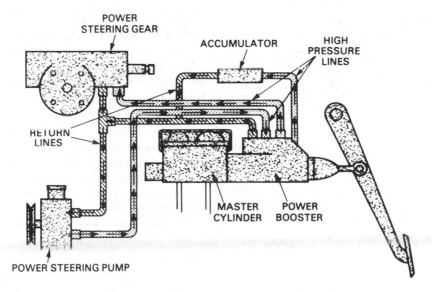

FIGURE 31-77. Hydro-Boost fluid flow diagram.

sensor at each wheel, which sends an electric signal to a control modulator, which reduces hydraulic pressure to the wheel, which signals an impending skid. The system does not affect normal brake operation except during an impending skid.

PART 9 ELECTRIC BRAKES

Electric brakes are most commonly used on trailers. The friction components are basically the same as for hydraulic brakes; however, instead of using a hydraulic system to actuate the brakes, an electrical system is used. A foot- or hand-operated rheostat is used to control the amount of electrical current to

an electromagnet. The electromagnet operates a cam, which in turn pushes the shoes against the drum. When current stops, the cam and brake shoes are returned to the release position by springs. The severity of braking increases with increased current.

A variation of the hand- or foot-operated rheostat is one sensitive to brake hydraulic system pressure. As pedal pressure is increased, hydraulic pressure actuates the rheostat to increase current to the electromagnet. Another type uses an inertia weight to uncover a light. As the vehicle slows, the weight or pendulum in the control device moves forward, exposing a light-sensitive diode to more of the light beam and thereby increasing current to the electromagnet in the trailer brake.

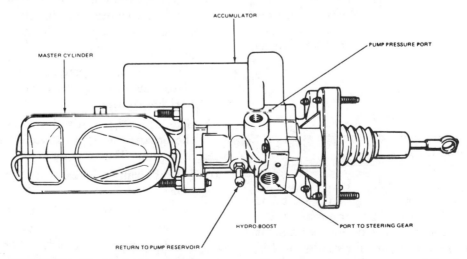

FIGURE 31-78. Hydro-Boost with master cylinder attached. *(Courtesy of Ford Motor Co. of Canada Ltd.)*

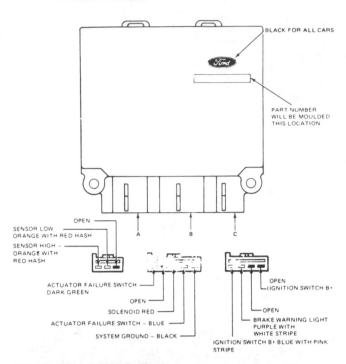

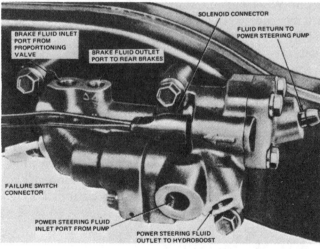

FIGURE 31-79. Control module multiple connectors (above) and actuator assembly (below) for Ford Sure-Track Brake System. *(Courtesy of Ford Motor Co. of Canada Ltd.)*

PART 10   AIR BRAKES

Air brake operation is similar to hydraulic brake operation except that compressed air is used to actuate the brakes instead of hydraulic pressure. Air brakes are used on heavier trucks and equipment. Typical system components are illustrated in Figure 31-81.

When the brakes are applied by operating a foot valve or a hand-operated valve, air pressure is applied directly to the brake shoes through a diaphragm in the brake chamber through mechanical linkage.

The engine-driven compressor provides air pressure to the pressure tanks at approximately 100 to 130 psi (689.5 to 896.35 kPa). When pressure reaches approximately 130 psi (896.35 kPa), the governor cuts out the compressor operation. When the brakes are applied, pressure drops. When pressure drops to approximately 100 psi (689.5 kPa), the governor again cuts in the compressor to raise system pressure. A warning buzzer warns the driver when system pressure drops to about 60 psi (413.7 kPa).

Compressor and governor operation are illustrated in Figure 31-82. The brake-actuating mechanism is either a wedge or a cam. The cam type is shown in Figure 31-83. Brake chamber and parking brake operation are shown in Figure 31-84. Quick-release valves are located near the brake chambers to exhaust air rapidly for quick brake release.

PART 11   SELF-CHECK

1. Wheel brake units are either the _____ type or the _____ type.
2. Two types of power brakes in use are the _____ type and the _____ type.
3. Electric brakes are most commonly used on _____.
4. Heavier trucks and highway transports are normally equipped with _____ brakes.
5. Hydraulic brakes operate on the principle that liquids are not _____.
6. Force and motion can be transmitted through a hydraulic system, which can also multiply force through varying cylinder sizes. True or false?
7. Single-piston caliper braking action can be compared to that of a _____.
8. When the brake pedal is released, the caliper piston and brake pad are returned to the release position by the _____.
9. Self-adjusting on disc brakes only occurs when the brakes are applied while the car is moving in reverse. True or false?
10. During brake application, the power brake unit has:
    (a) vacuum on one side and atmospheric pressure on the other side of the diaphragm
    (b) vacuum on both sides of the diaphragm
    (c) atmospheric pressure on both sides of the diaphragm

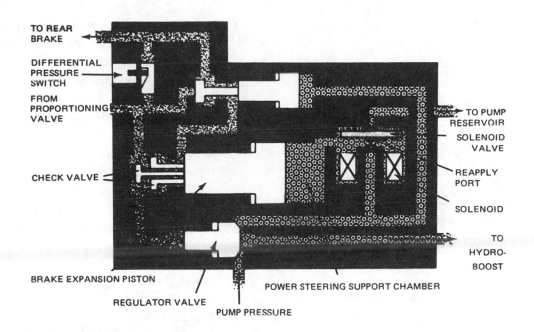

TO REAR BRAKE

DIFFERENTIAL PRESSURE SWITCH

FROM PROPORTIONING VALVE

CHECK VALVE

TO PUMP RESERVOIR

SOLENOID VALVE

REAPPLY PORT

SOLENOID

TO HYDRO-BOOST

BRAKE EXPANSION PISTON

REGULATOR VALVE

PUMP PRESSURE

POWER STEERING SUPPORT CHAMBER

Schematic—Actuator In Normal Position

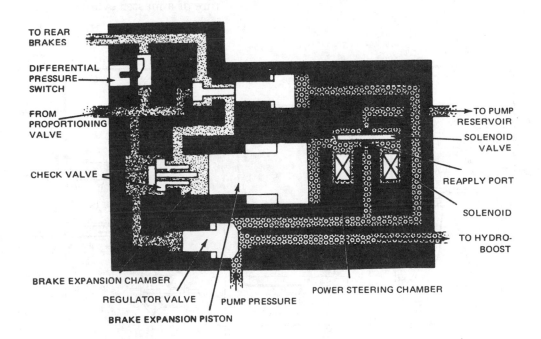

TO REAR BRAKES

DIFFERENTIAL PRESSURE SWITCH

FROM PROPORTIONING VALVE

CHECK VALVE

TO PUMP RESERVOIR

SOLENOID VALVE

REAPPLY PORT

SOLENOID

TO HYDRO-BOOST

BRAKE EXPANSION CHAMBER

REGULATOR VALVE

PUMP PRESSURE

POWER STEERING CHAMBER

BRAKE EXPANSION PISTON

Schematic—Actuator In Activated Position

FIGURE 31-80(A). Actuator operation in normal position (above) and in activated position (below). (*Courtesy of Ford Motor Co. of Canada Ltd.*)

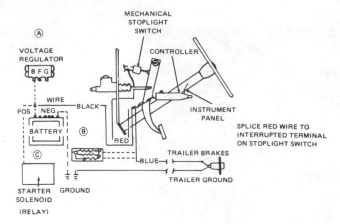

FIGURE 31-80(B). A typical electric trailer brake control system. A rheostat is located inside the controller, and it varies current flow to trailer brakes.

11. Air flow into the vacuum power brake unit accomplishes which of the following:

   (a) releases the brakes

   (b) applies the brakes

   (c) keeps brakes in hold position

12. In vacuum power brakes, the pressures on both sides of the control valve are:

   (a) equal at all times

   (b) equal in the hold position

   (c) equal in the apply position

   (d) equal in the release position

13. Hydro-Boost power brake units use _____ pressure from the _____ pump.

14. Hydro-Boost power brakes allow for several power brake applications due to _____ pressure being stored in the _____.

15. What method is used to compensate for brake pull when one half of a diagonally split brake system fails?

16. What is the purpose of the "quick take-up" feature of a master cylinder?

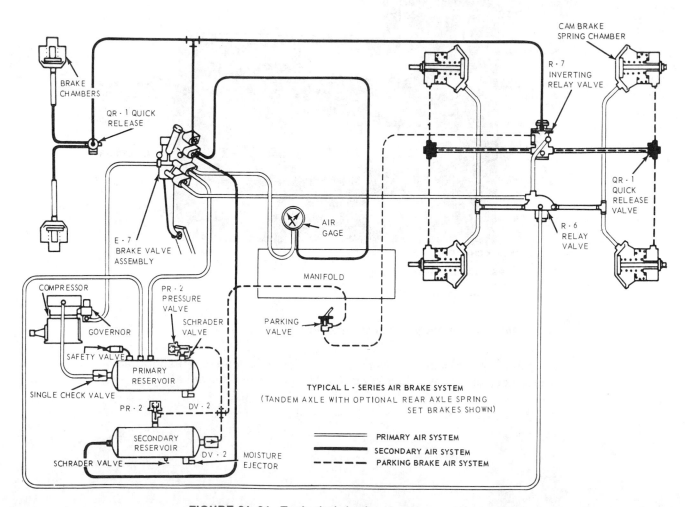

FIGURE 31-81. Typical air brake system components.

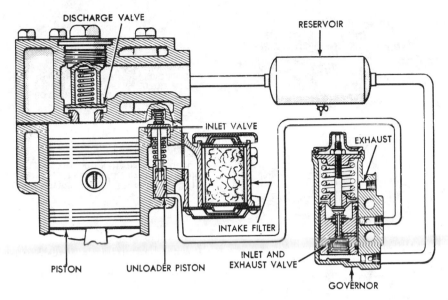

FIGURE 31-82. Compressor and governor operation. The engine-driven compressor produces the compressed air while the governor tells the compressor when to do it.

PART 12 TEST QUESTIONS

1. The brake hydraulic system is designed to transmit:
   (a) pressure
   (b) force
   (c) motion
   (d) all of the above

2. The coefficient of friction between lining and drum is altered by:
   (a) heat
   (b) moisture
   (c) dirt
   (d) all of the above

3. Brake fade is:
   (a) loss of pedal

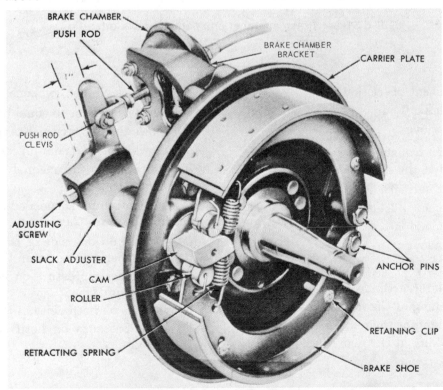

FIGURE 31-83. Cam-type air brake actuating mechanism.

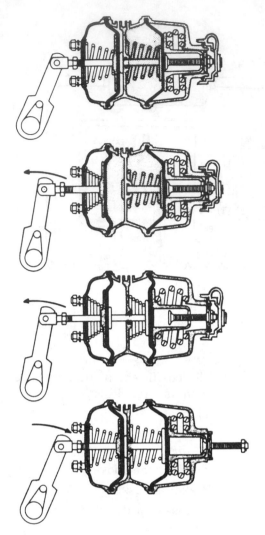

NORMAL DRIVING

A SAFE LEVEL OF AIR PRESSURE WITHIN THE SYSTEM HOLDS SPRING BRAKES RELEASED, BUT ALWAYS READY FOR PARKING OR EMERGENCY APPLICATION.

NORMAL SERVICE BRAKE

WITH THE SEPARATION OF THE TWO UNITS, THE SPRING BRAKE CANNOT INTERFERE WITH THE OPERATION OF THE NORMAL SERVICE BRAKE.

PARKING BRAKES

A FINGER-TIP CONTROL IN THE CAB TO EXHAUST AIR PRESSURE WITHIN THE SPRING BRAKE GIVES THE DRIVER FOOLPROOF AND POSITIVE PARKING BRAKES.

EMERGENCY BRAKES

THE SPRING BRAKES ARE INSTALLED TO OPERATE AUTOMATICALLY UPON LOSS OF AIR PRESSURE.

MANUAL RELEASE

THE BUILT-IN MANUAL RELEASE ALLOWS EASY RELEASE TO RELINE BRAKES OR MOVE THE VEHICLE IN THE ABSENCE OF AIR PRESSURE.

FIGURE 31-84. Brake chamber and parking brake operation.

(b) loss of coefficient of friction

(c) loss of hydraulic fluid

(d) none of the above

4. Because of weight transfer, the ratio of braking at the front and at the rear wheels is:

(a) 50% at front and 50% at rear

(b) 50% at front and 40% at rear

(c) 40% at front and 60% at rear

(d) none of the above

5. The proportioning valve is designed to:

(a) increase braking at the front wheels

(b) decrease braking at the front wheels

(c) increase braking at the rear wheels

(d) decrease braking at the rear wheels

6. The master cylinder compensating port:

(a) compensates for unequal braking

(b) allows fluid to return after pedal is released

(c) allows fluid to maintain residual pressure

(d) compensates for unequal primary and secondary pressures

7. When the vacuum suspended power brake is in the hold position there is:

(a) vacuum on one side of the diaphragm and atmospheric pressure on the other side

(b) atmospheric pressure on both sides of the diaphragm

(c) vacuum on both sides of the diaphragm

(d) equal pressure on both sides of the diaphragm

Chapter 32

Brake System Diagnosis and Service Procedure

Performance Objectives

After you have thoroughly studied the chapter on brakes and have had sufficient practice work on the various brake system components, you should, with the aid of a shop manual and the proper tools and equipment, be able to do the following:

1. Follow the accepted general precautions while servicing brakes.
2. Correctly disassemble all brake system components.
3. Properly clean all brake system components as recommended.
4. Accurately inspect and measure all brake system components to determine their serviceability.
5. Machine and recondition all brake system components accurately to the manufacturer's specifications.
6. Properly assemble and correctly adjust all brake system components.
7. Successfully bleed all air from a brake hydraulic system.
8. Perform the necessary inspection and testing procedures to determine the success of the brake system overhaul.
9. Complete the self-check and test questions with at least 80 percent accuracy.
10. Complete all practical work with 100 percent accuracy.
11. Prepare the vehicle for customer acceptance.

PART 1 GENERAL PRECAUTIONS

1. Areas where brake work is done should be set aside if possible, and entrances should be posted with an asbestos exposure sign as follows:

- Asbestos
- Dust Hazard
- Avoid Breathing Dust
- Wear Assigned Protective Equipment
- Do Not Remain in Area Unless Your Work Requires It
- Breathing Asbestos Dust May Be Hazardous To Your Health
- Dispose of asbestos contaminated waste in recommended manner.

2. The importance of high-quality workmanship on brake repairs cannot be overemphasized. The lives of the driver, the passengers, and other people on the road depend on the ability of the car's brake system to bring it to a safe, controlled stop. Shoddy or inferior workmanship can cause injury and loss of life.

3. Safe procedures must also be followed when raising a car on a hoist or on stands to do brake work. Never work on a car supported only on a jack. Place the car on a hoist or place stands where recommended by the vehicle manufacturer.

4. Absolute cleanliness must be observed when servicing hydraulic brake parts. Hydraulic parts must be properly cleaned in recommended brake cleaning fluid and kept clean. During assembly, these parts should be lubricated with clean, new brake fluid or other recommended assembly lubricant. Friction surfaces such as brake linings, pads, drums, and discs must not have any grease, oil, or brake fluid in contact with them. Contamination of this kind destroys their frictional characteristic and can cause grab and pull.

5. When lubricating brake mechanisms inside the brake drum unit, such as backing plates and adjusters, do not overlubricate. Overlubrication can cause contamination of linings and drums and result in grab or pull. Use only recommended high-temperature lubricant.

6. Brake fluid should not be allowed to come in contact with painted surfaces since it is a very effective paint remover. If fluid is accidentally spilled onto a painted surface, it should immediately be washed thoroughly with water.

PROBLEM	CAUSE	CORRECTION
Pedal bottoms out; no brakes	1. Fluid leak. 2. Air in system. 3. Lining worn. 4. Low fluid level. 5. Linkage disconnected. 6. Automatic shoe adjusters not functioning. 7. Vaporized fluid.	1. Repair source of leak. 2. Bleed system. Repair source of air entry. 3. Adjust or reline. 4. Fill and bleed system. 5. Connect. 6. Replace adjusters. Adjust shoes. 7. Install super-heavy-duty fluid and bleed.
Spongy pedal	1. Air in system. 2. Drums too thin. 3. Soft hose. 4. Shoe lining wrong fit. 5. Cracked brake drum. 6. Brake shoes distorted.	1. Bleed system. Repair source of air entry. 2. Replace drums. 3. Replace hose. 4. Install correct lining. 5. Replace drum. 6. Replace shoes.
Hard pedal; little braking	1. Incorrect lining. 2. Linings contaminated. 3. Primary and secondary shoes reversed. 4. Brake linkage binding. 5. Master or wheel cylinder pistons frozen. 6. Linings hard and glazed. 7. Lining ground to wrong radius. 8. Brake line or hose clogged or kinked. 9. Power booster unit defective. 10. No vacuum to power booster. 11. Engine fails to maintain proper vacuum to booster.	1. Install proper lining. 2. Replace or reline shoes. Repair source of leak. 3. Install shoes in correct location. 4. Free and lubricate. 5. Rebuild or replace cylinder. 6. Replace linings. 7. Grind lining as specified. 8. Replace. 9. Replace power booster. 10. Replace clogged, soft lines. Repair leaks. 11. Tune or overhaul engine.
Pedal fade	1. Excessive use of brakes. 2. Poor brake fluid. 3. Improper lining to drum contact. 4. Thin brake drums. 5. Dragging brakes. 6. Riding the brake pedal.	1. Use lower gears, reduce speed, load, etc. 2. Flush. Install super-heavy-duty fluid. 3. Adjust shoes or grind to correct radius. 4. Install new drums. 5. Adjust or repair other cause of dragging. 6. Keep foot from brake unless needed.
Pulsating pedal	1. Brake drums out of round. 2. Excessive disc run-out. 3. Loose wheel bearings. 4. Drums loose. 5. Rear axle bent.	1. Turn drums in pairs. 2. Replace disc or recondition. 3. Adjust. 4. Tighten wheel lugs. 5. Replace axle.
Brakes grab	1. Grease or brake fluid on lining. 2. Lining charred. 3. Lining loose on shoe. 4. Loose wheel bearings. 5. Defective wheel bearings. 6. Loose brake backing plate. 7. Defective drum. 8. Sand or dirt in brake shoe assembly. 9. Wrong lining. 10. Primary and secondary shoes reversed.	1. Install shoes, correct leak. 2. Reline. 3. Replace. 4. Adjust. 5. Replace. 6. Torque fasteners. 7. Turn drum. Turn drum on opposite side also to same size. 8. Disassemble and clean. 9. Install correct lining. 10. Install correctly.
Car pulls to one side, brakes applied	1. One wheel grabbing. 2. Different lining on one side or shoes reversed on one side. 3. Plugged line or hose. 4. Uneven tire pressure. 5. Front end alignment out. 6. Sagged, weak, or broken spring. Weak shock absorber.	1. See "Brakes grab." 2. Replace lining or install shoes in proper position. 3. Replace. 4. Correct pressures. 5. Align front end. 6. Install new spring or shocks.
Brakes drag	1. Parking brake too tight. 2. Clogged hose or line.	1. Adjust. 2. Replace.

PROBLEM	CAUSE	CORRECTION
	3. No pedal free travel.	3. Adjust pedal free travel so that compensating port will be open when brake is released.
	4. Brakes adjusted too tight.	4. Adjust.
	5. Master cylinder or wheel cylinder cups soft and sticky.	5. Rebuild or replace cylinders. Flush system.
	6. Loose wheel bearing.	6. Adjust.
	7. Parking brake fails to release.	7. Clean and lubricate parking brake linkage and adjust.
	8. Shoe retracting springs weak or broken.	8. Replace.
	9. Out-of-round drum.	9. Turn drum in pairs.
	10. Defective power booster.	10. Replace booster.
Brakes chatter	1. Weak or broken shoe retracting springs.	1. Replace.
	2. Defective power booster.	2. Replace booster.
	3. Loose backing plate.	3. Tighten.
	4. Loose or damaged wheel bearings.	4. Adjust or replace bearings.
	5. Drums tapered or barrel shaped.	5. Turn drum in pairs.
	6. Bent shoes.	6. Replace shoes.
	7. Dust on lining.	7. Clean.
	8. Lining glazed.	8. Replace.
	9. Drum dampener spring missing.	9. Install dampener spring.
	10. Grease or fluid on linings.	10. Reline brakes and correct leak.
	11. Shoes not adjusted properly.	11. Adjust.
Brakes squeal	1. Glazed or charred lining.	1. Replace.
	2. Lining rivets loose.	2. Replace.
	3. Wrong lining.	3. Replace with correct lining.
	4. Shoe hold-downs weak or broken.	4. Replace.
	5. Drum damper spring missing.	5. Install spring.
	6. Shoes improperly adjusted.	6. Adjust to specifications.
	7. Shoes bent.	7. Replace.
	8. Bent backing plate.	8. Replace plate.
	9. Shoe retracting springs weak or broken.	9. Replace springs.
	10. Drum too thin.	10. Replace drum.
	11. Lining saturated with grease or brake fluid.	11. Replace linings.
Brake shoes click	1. Shoe is pulled from backing plate by following tool marks in drum.	1. Machine drum properly, in pairs.
	2. Shoe bent.	2. Replace.
	3. Shoe support pads on backing plate grooved.	3. Smooth and lubricate pads or replace.

DIAGNOSIS CHART: SURE-TRACK BRAKE SYSTEM

PROBLEM	CAUSE	CORRECTION
Brake warning light comes on immediately and stays on after key is turned to run position.	1. Check sure-track 4-amp fuse. 2. Differential valve shuttled. 3. Short in brake warning light ground circuit. 4. Open B+ lead to module. 5. Shorted B+ lead to module.	1. Replace fuse. 2. Refer to hydraulic brake system diagnostic procedure. 3. Remove plug C from module. Turn ignition to *run*. If light comes on, locate and repair short. 4. Check B+ wiring and connectors for open circuit and repair as required. 5. Check B+ wiring and connectors for short circuit and repair as required. Perform solenoid test and repair as required.
Brake warning light flashes and then comes on and stays on 4 to 6 seconds after ignition key is turned to run position.	1. Open speed sensor, circuit connections, and/or circuitry. 2. Open actuator failure switch, circuit connections, and/or circuitry. 3. Closed actuator differential failure switch in actuator. 4. Open actuator solenoid, circuit connections, and/or circuitry. 5. Incorrect computer module is installed.	1. Check sensor, harness connections at computer module, in trunk, and at sensor, and repair as required. 2. Check failure switch, connections at actuator, computer module, and in engine compartment. Repair as required (perform failure switch test). 3. Perform failure switch test. Perform hydraulic brake system diagnostic procedure. 4. Check solenoid plus connectors at computer module in passenger compartment and at actuator. Repair as required (perform solenoid test). 5. Replace black (white on Granada and Monarch) case.
Brake warning light does not flash and go out as soon as the key is turned to run position and: (a) Brake warning light comes on when the key is turned to start. (b) Brake warning light does not come on when key is turned to start.	1. Loose or missing skid control ground wire. 2. Connectors loose or not connected to skid control module. 3. Skid control module not installed. 4. Burned out brake warning light bulb. 5. Loose or broken wire in brake warning light circuit.	1. Repair ground wire (perform system ground test). 2. Replace and/or repair connectors. 3. Install skid control module. 4. Replace bulb. 5. Replace or repair wire.
Brake warning light operates normally (flashes) and skid control system cycles during rough road conditions or normal braking.	1. Loose ground connection. 2. Loose sensor connection. 3. Worn or damaged sensor or sensor rotor. 4. Loose B+ and failure light connector at computer module.	1. Perform system ground test procedure. 2. Check sensor connection at computer module in trunk, and at sensor. Repair as required. 3. Perform sensor test. 4. Check plug C and repair as required.
Brake warning light operates normally (flashes) and actuator cycles slowly or not at all during maximum braking condition.	1. Shorted sensor circuit or worn or damaged sensor or rotor. 2. Plugged actuator filter.	1. Perform sensor test. 2. Replace actuator.

If the corrections listed do not correct the observed condition, it may be necessary to replace the computer module.

AIR BRAKE SYSTEM DIAGNOSTIC CHART

TRUCKS, TRACTORS, BUSES

Insufficient Brakes
Brakes need adjusting, lubrication, or relining.
Wrong type brake lining.
Poor fit between lining and drum.
Low air pressure (below 80 psi) (551.6 kPa).
Brake valve defective; not delivering pressure.
Incorrect angle between slack adjuster and brake chamber push
   rod.

Brakes Apply Too Slowly
Brakes need adjusting or lubricating.
Low air pressure in the brake system (below 80 psi) (551.6 kPa).
Brake valve delivery pressure below normal.
Excessive leakage when brakes applied.
Restricted tubing or hose line.
Binding in camshaft or anchor pins.
Binding in brake linkage.

Brakes Release Too Slowly
Brakes need adjusting or lubricating.
Brake valve not returning to fully released position.
Restricted tubing or hose line.
Exhaust port of brake valve or quick-release valve restricted or
   plugged.
Defective brake valve or quick-release valve.
Binding in camshaft or anchor pins.
Binding in brake linkage.

Brakes Grab
Grease on brake lining; reline brakes.
Brake drum out of round.
Defective brake valve.
Brake rigging binding.
Wrong type brake lining.

Uneven Brakes
Brakes need adjusting, lubricating, or relining.
Grease on lining.
Brake shoe return spring or brake chamber spring weak or
  broken.
Brake drum out of round.
Leaking brake chamber diaphragm.

TRAILERS

Insufficient Brakes
Same as for trucks except may also be caused by defective relay-
   emergency valve.
Restricted tubing (service line).

Brakes Apply Too Slowly
Same as for trucks.
Excessive air leakage with brakes applied.

Brakes Release Too Slowly
Same as for trucks.
Exhaust port of relay-emergency valve restricted or plugged.

Brakes Do Not Apply
Brake system not properly connected to brake system of tractor.
Tractor protection valve malfunctioning.
No air pressure.
Plugged tubing or hose.

Brakes Do Not Release
Brake system not properly connected to towing vehicle.
Relay-emergency valve in emergency position.
Tractor protection valve malfunctioning.

Brakes Grab
Same as for trucks.
Defective relay emergency valve.

Uneven Brakes
Same as for trucks.

HYDRO-BOOST DIAGNOSIS GUIDE

PROBLEM	CAUSE	CORRECTION
Excessive brake pedal effort (poor power steering assist in both directions also) at idle speed.	1. Loose or broken steering pump belt. 2. Power-steering fluid reservoir low or empty. 3. Power-steering hose leaking. 4. Leaking at tube fittings: power steering or booster connections. 5. Low idle speed. 6. Restriction in pressure hose to booster. 7. Low power-steering pump pressure.	1. Tighten or replace belt. 2. Fill reservoir and check for leaks. 3. Replace hose. 4. Tighten fitting. If it still leaks, check tube flare. Replace hose if flare is damaged. Check tube seat; repair if damaged. 5. Adjust idle speed to specification. 6. Replace hose. 7. Perform pump pressure test.
Excessive brake pedal effort (power steering normal in both directions at idle speed).	1. Binding in pedal and/or pedal linkage. 2. Contamination. 3. Nicked or burred spool valve.	1. Repair and lubricate as required. 2. Hold steering wheel against stop (maximum 5 seconds) and apply brake pedal sharply several times. If contamination is dislodged, flush system. 3. Replace Hydro-Boost.
Slow or incomplete brake pedal return.	1. Binding in the pedal and/or pedal linkage. 2. Restriction in return line from booster to pump reservoir. 3. Internal restriction in the Hydro-Boost fluid return system.	1. Repair and lubricate as required. 2. Replace return hose. 3. Replace the Hydro-Boost.
Brake pedal chatter, pulsation.	1. Power-steering pump belt slipping. 2. Power-steering pump reservoir fluid low. 3. Power-steering pump pressure erratic. 4. Spool valve faulty.	1. Tighten belt. 2. Fill reservoir, check for leaks. 3. Repair pump. 4. Replace Hydro-Boost.
Oversensitive braking.	1. Binding in the pedal and/or pedal linkage. 2. Faulty spool action.	1. Repair and lubricate as required. 2. Replace Hydro-Boost.
Noise.	1. Power-steering pump fluid low or empty. 2. Power-steering fluid aerated. 3. Power-steering pump belt loose. 4. Restriction in hoses.	1. Fill reservoir. 2. Bleed system. 3. Tighten belt. 4. Replace hose.

PART 3   BRAKE SYSTEM INSPECTION

Each of the components of the brake system must be in good working condition if the brakes are to function efficiently.

The use of the inspection procedures presented here, together with the diagnostic charts, will assist in determining the condition of the complete brake system and the need for service. Brake inspection should conclude with a written report on conditions.

A. *Brake Pedal*

1. Apply and release brake pedal several times (with engine running for power brakes) and check for noise and friction. Pedal movement should be smooth and return fast, with no noise.

2. Move brake pedal from side to side to check movement. Excessive side movement indicates worn pedal mounting parts.

3. Apply heavy foot pressure to pedal (with engine running for power brakes) and check for sponginess and pedal reserve. Pedal should feel firm; foot pad should be a minimum of 2" from floor for manual brakes or 1" for power brakes.

4. Hold pedal depressed with medium foot pressure (25 to 35 pounds) for 15 seconds; pedal should not drop under steady pressure.

B. *Stop Light*

1. Apply and release brake pedal several times and check stop light operation. Stop lights should come on each time pedal is depressed and go off each time pedal is released.

C. *Master Cylinder*

1. Inspect exterior of master cylinder. Presence of brake fluid indicates an external leak.

2. Remove reservoir cover or cap and check brake fluid. Fluid level should not be below specified level (about 1/4 inch from top). Also, brake fluid should be clean—no residue in bottom of reservoir or other evidence of contamination.

3. Check vent holes in reservoir cover or cap; vent holes should be clean and open.

4. Check reservoir diaphragm; diaphragm should not have holes or other damage.

5. Watch fluid in reservoir (front reservoir of dual system master cylinder) while an assistant depresses brake pedal 1/4 inch to 1/2 inch. A spurt or agitation should be visible in the brake fluid. This indicates closing of the compensating port.

6. Depress brake pedal and release; then open a wheel cylinder bleeder screw slightly and close quickly to prevent air from entering hydraulic system. There should be a small spurt of brake fluid when the bleeder screw is opened; this indicates that the residual pressure check valve is maintaining residual pressure in the line.

Note: Residual pressure check valves are not used in the line to disc brakes. Many automobiles do not have a check valve in the line to the drum brakes.

D. *Power Brakes*

1. With engine off, depress and release pedal several times. Then hold pedal depressed with light pressure (15 to 25 pounds) and start engine. Pedal should drop slightly when engine starts and then hold firm.

2. Run engine to medium speed and turn off. Wait 90 seconds and apply brakes several times. Two or more applications should be power assisted. Pedal should get firmer (indicating no power assist) after four or five applications.

3. Check vacuum hose from power brake to intake manifold. Hose should not be kinked, collapsed, split, or torn.

E. *Brake Lines and Hoses*

1. Inspect brake lines and brake warning light switch. Lines should not be kinked, dented, or damaged, and there should be no leakage.

2. Inspect brake hoses. Hoses must be flexible and free from leaks, cuts, cracks, and bulges.

3. Check back side of brake backing plates on drum brakes. Backing plates should be free from brake fluid and grease.

F. *Parking Brake*

1. Apply heavy pressure to parking brake. Pedal or lever should not move more than 2/3 of full travel.

2. Check parking brake cables, equalizer, and linkage. Cables should not be frayed or damaged and should move freely in both directions (apply and release).

G. *Disc Brakes*

1. Remove wheel and tire assembly and inspect pad and plate assemblies. Pads should not be below minimum thickness and should not be contaminated with grease or brake fluid.

2. Inspect caliper assembly and caliper mounting. Caliper should not be leaking or damaged; mounting bolts must be tight.

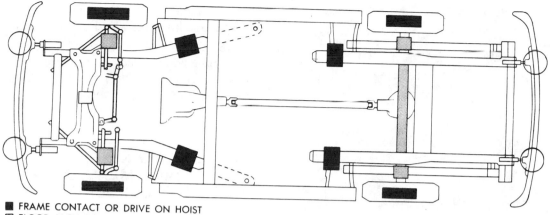

■ FRAME CONTACT OR DRIVE ON HOIST
▨ FLOOR JACK OR HOIST
○ BUMPER JACK (AT BUMPER SLOT ONLY)

FIGURE 32–1. Hoisting or jacking points are shown for one particular type of vehicle. Other vehicles may have different lift points.

3. Inspect rotor and check thickness variation (parallelism) and side-to-side wobble (lateral run-out). Rotor must not have cracks, excessive ridges, or grooves, and must not exceed thickness variation and run-out limits.

H. *Drum Brakes*

1. Remove and inspect brake drum. Drum should not be cracked, out of round, bellmouthed, or have excessive scores, heat checks, or hard spots.

2. Check condition and thickness of lining. Lining should not be glazed, soiled with grease or brake fluid, or otherwise damaged. There should be a minimum of 1/32 inch of usable lining remaining (above rivet heads on riveted type) at the thinnest point.

Note: Some local inspection laws may specify a minimum lining thickness different from the above. Therefore, check local inspection laws and follow them.

3. Inspect the brake shoes. Shoes should not be distorted, cracked, or have broken welds.

4. Check wheel cylinder by pulling back edge of a dust boot. There should be no accumulation of brake fluid inside boot.

5. Inspect shoe holddown parts and springs. Shoe holddown pins, springs, and cups, and shoe return springs must be properly installed and be neither damaged nor weak.

6. Inspect automatic brake adjuster parts. Adjuster parts must not be damaged or excessively worn and must be properly installed and operate freely.

PART 4 DISASSEMBLY PROCEDURE (TYPICAL DISC-DRUM BRAKES)

1. Place the car on stands. Position stands safely where recommended by the manufacturer. If work is to be done with the car on a hoist, position the car on the hoist and lift at the points recommended by the vehicle manufacturer. Mark wheel to drum and drum to axle position.

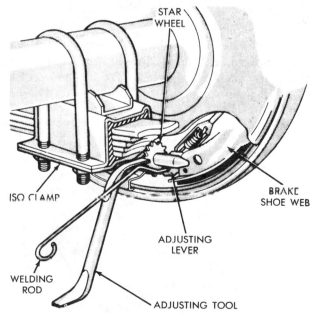

FIGURE 32–2. Manual adjustment on self-adjusting brakes. This must be backed off for drum removal when drums are worn.

749

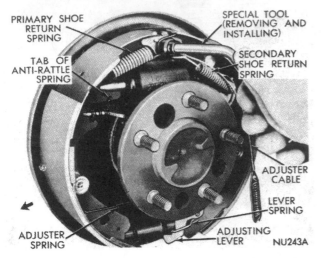

FIGURE 32-3. Removing brake shoe retracting springs with special tool.

2. Remove wheel mounting studs or nuts. (Some older cars have left-hand thread on the left side.) Mark the wheels for proper assembly. Remove 2/3 of fluid from master cylinder.

3. Remove the brake drums. Some drums have speed nut retainers or a small screw holding drum to axle flange or hub. If the drum is worn, the brake shoe adjustment will have to be backed off for the drum to clear the brake shoes. Do not force the drum or distort it. Do not allow the drum to drop.

4. Remove caliper mounting bolts, brake line, calipers, and pads.

5. Remove front-wheel dust cap, cotter pin, and a wheel bearing nut from the front wheels. See Chapter 29, Part 4 for wheel bearing service.

6. Remove brake shoe return springs, hold-down springs and pins, adjuster, and brake shoes from rear-wheel backing plates. Do not distort or overstretch the springs.

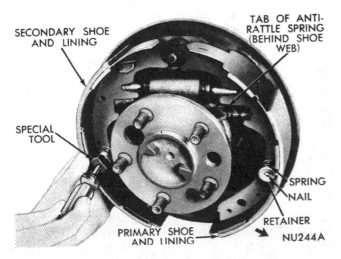

FIGURE 32-4. Removing brake shoe hold-down springs.

7. Remove the wheel cylinders by disconnecting brake line and wheel cylinder mounting bolts.

8. Remove the master cylinder (first disconnect the brake pedal linkage on nonpower brakes). Then disconnect brake lines, master cylinder mounting nuts, and master cylinder.

PART 5   CLEANING, INSPECTION, AND MEASURING PROCEDURE

1. Check *rear axle seals* for leakage. If leaking differential oil, axle shafts must be removed, seals and bearings replaced, and axle shafts installed. (See Chapter 29, Part 4).

2. Clean *backing plates* with vacuum cleaner and solvent. Blow dry with compressed air. Inspect ledges for wear. If not much wear is present, sand ledges smooth. Inspect anchor pin for wear. Inspect backing plate for damage. Plate should not be bent or physically damaged.

3. Inspect *brake shoe and linings*. Uneven lining wear can indicate improperly mounted parts, drum distortion, or wear. Linings should be replaced before lining wear allows metal rivets or brake shoe metal to contact the drum. Some disc brake pads have a wear indicator telling the driver or mechanic when they should be replaced. New linings must be fitted to the drum with 0.006- to 0.010-inch (0.1524 to 0.254 millimeter) heel-and-toe clearance on most drum brakes. If linings do not have this kind of heel-and-toe clearance, they must be re-arced to fit. (See item 2, Part 6.)

4. Clean and inspect all *springs, linkages,* and *adjusters* for wear or distortion. Springs should not be discolored from overheating and should not be stretched or distorted. Adjuster threads and sockets should be cleaned and lubricated with a good-grade brake lubricant. Replace any faulty parts.

5. Measure *drums* for wear and out-of-round. If drum wear exceeds the manufacturer's limit, drums must be replaced. In most cases, for car brake drums the maximum allowable oversize after machining is 0.060 inch (1.524 millimeter) over standard drum diameter. The manufacturer's specifications must be followed for maximum safe tolerances. If wear is within limits, drums should be machined to recondition the friction surface. If machining the drums removes enough material to increase drum diameter beyond the manufacturer's specifications, the drum must be replaced. Brake drums should not have excessive run-out (wobble) or out-of-round. Follow the manufacturer's specifications.

DRUM R&I AND COMPONENTS

1. REMOVE AND INSTALL BRAKE DRUM.

REMOVE	INSTALL
1. HOIST CAR AND MARK RELATIONSHIP OF WHEEL TO AXLE. REMOVE WHEEL.	NOTICE: SEE NOTICE AT THE BEGINNING OF THIS SECTION.
2. MARK RELATIONSHIP OF DRUM TO AXLE AND REMOVE DRUM.	1. ALIGN MARKS ON DRUM AND AXLE. INSTALL DRUM.
	2. ALIGN MARKS ON WHEEL AND AXLE. INSTALL WHEEL. TORQUE LUG NUTS TO 140 N·m (102 FT. LBS.).

2. REMOVE AND INSTALL BRAKE COMPONENTS.

REMOVE

1. REMOVE COMPONENTS AS SHOWN AND A, B, C, D AND E FOLLOWING.

NOTICE: IF ANY PARTS ARE OF DOUBTFUL STRENGTH OR QUALITY DUE TO DISCOLORATION FROM HEAT, OVER-STRESS, OR ARE WORN, THE PART(S) SHOULD BE REPLACED.

INSTALL

NOTICE: SEE NOTICE AT THE BEGINNING OF THIS SECTION.

1. INSTALL COMPONENTS AS SHOWN AND A, B, C, D AND E FOLLOWING.

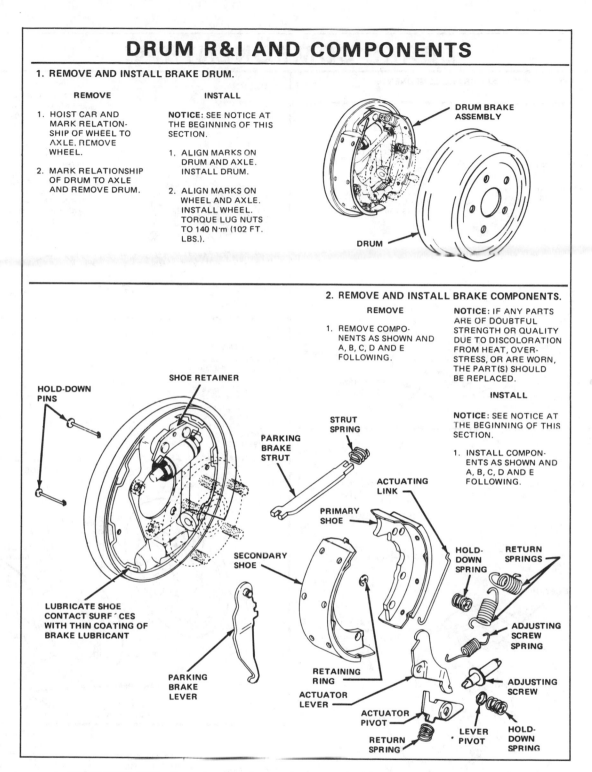

FIGURE 32–5(A). Rear drum brake service on typical front-wheel-drive vehicle. *(Courtesy of General Motors Corporation)*

6. Inspect *discs* for scoring and wear. Severe scoring requires disc replacement. Minor scoring can be corrected by machining. Measure the discs for thickness. Discs should not be less than manufacturer's stated thickness limit usually stamped on disc. Minimum thickness refers to rotor or disc thickness after machining. The discs should also be measured for run-out, surface parallelism, and thickness variation. Usual tolerance is 0.0005 inch (0.0127 millimeter) for parallelism and thickness variation and .002 inch (.051 millimeter) to .005 inch (.127 millimeter) for run-out. Follow the manufacturer's recommendation. Front-wheel hubs should be cleaned thoroughly after the bearings are removed.

751

BRAKE COMPONENT R&I

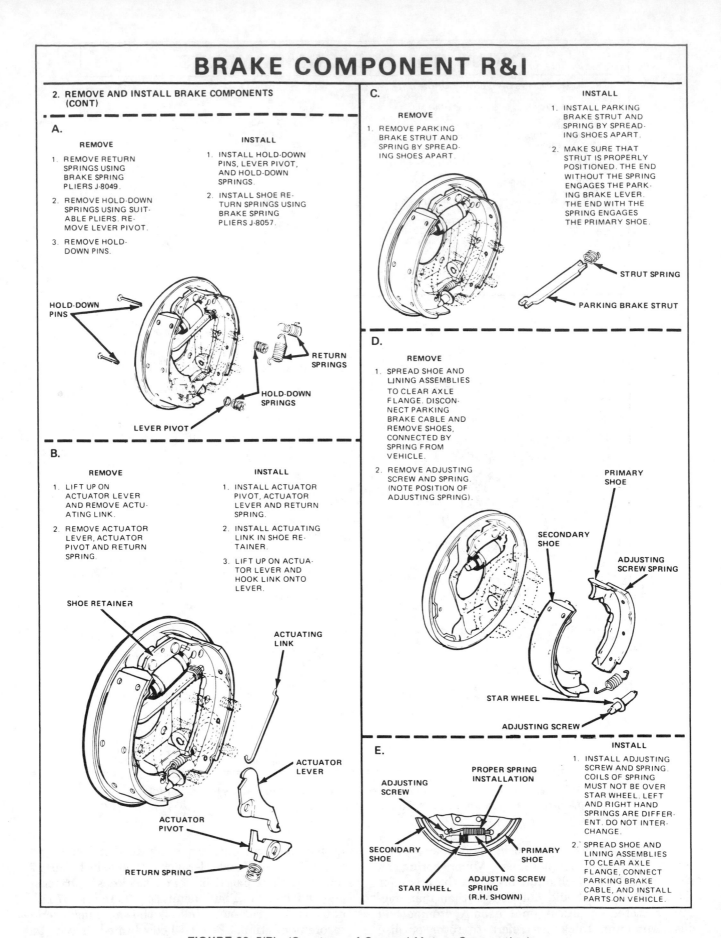

2. REMOVE AND INSTALL BRAKE COMPONENTS (CONT)

A.

REMOVE

1. REMOVE RETURN SPRINGS USING BRAKE SPRING PLIERS J-8049.
2. REMOVE HOLD-DOWN SPRINGS USING SUITABLE PLIERS. REMOVE LEVER PIVOT.
3. REMOVE HOLD-DOWN PINS.

INSTALL

1. INSTALL HOLD-DOWN PINS, LEVER PIVOT, AND HOLD-DOWN SPRINGS.
2. INSTALL SHOE RETURN SPRINGS USING BRAKE SPRING PLIERS J-8057.

HOLD-DOWN PINS
RETURN SPRINGS
HOLD-DOWN SPRINGS
LEVER PIVOT

B.

REMOVE

1. LIFT UP ON ACTUATOR LEVER AND REMOVE ACTUATING LINK.
2. REMOVE ACTUATOR LEVER, ACTUATOR PIVOT AND RETURN SPRING.

INSTALL

1. INSTALL ACTUATOR PIVOT, ACTUATOR LEVER AND RETURN SPRING.
2. INSTALL ACTUATING LINK IN SHOE RETAINER.
3. LIFT UP ON ACTUATOR LEVER AND HOOK LINK ONTO LEVER.

SHOE RETAINER
ACTUATING LINK
ACTUATOR LEVER
ACTUATOR PIVOT
RETURN SPRING

C.

REMOVE

1. REMOVE PARKING BRAKE STRUT AND SPRING BY SPREADING SHOES APART.

INSTALL

1. INSTALL PARKING BRAKE STRUT AND SPRING BY SPREADING SHOES APART.
2. MAKE SURE THAT STRUT IS PROPERLY POSITIONED. THE END WITHOUT THE SPRING ENGAGES THE PARKING BRAKE LEVER. THE END WITH THE SPRING ENGAGES THE PRIMARY SHOE.

STRUT SPRING
PARKING BRAKE STRUT

D.

REMOVE

1. SPREAD SHOE AND LINING ASSEMBLIES TO CLEAR AXLE FLANGE. DISCONNECT PARKING BRAKE CABLE AND REMOVE SHOES, CONNECTED BY SPRING FROM VEHICLE.
2. REMOVE ADJUSTING SCREW AND SPRING. (NOTE POSITION OF ADJUSTING SPRING).

PRIMARY SHOE
SECONDARY SHOE
ADJUSTING SCREW SPRING
STAR WHEEL
ADJUSTING SCREW

E.

ADJUSTING SCREW
PROPER SPRING INSTALLATION
SECONDARY SHOE
PRIMARY SHOE
STAR WHEEL
ADJUSTING SCREW SPRING
(R.H. SHOWN)

INSTALL

1. INSTALL ADJUSTING SCREW AND SPRING. COILS OF SPRING MUST NOT BE OVER STAR WHEEL. LEFT AND RIGHT HAND SPRINGS ARE DIFFERENT. DO NOT INTERCHANGE.
2. SPREAD SHOE AND LINING ASSEMBLIES TO CLEAR AXLE FLANGE, CONNECT PARKING BRAKE CABLE, AND INSTALL PARTS ON VEHICLE.

FIGURE 32-5(B). *(Courtesy of General Motors Corporation)*

752

WHEEL CYLINDER R&I

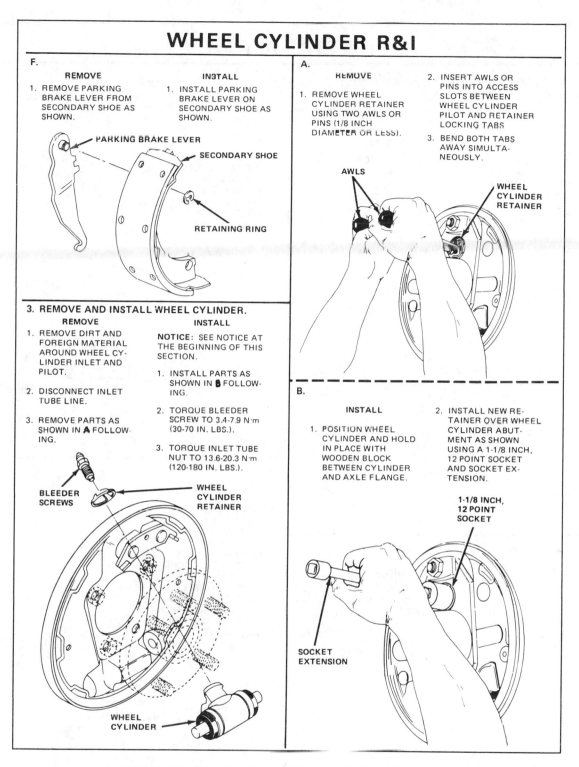

F.

REMOVE

1. REMOVE PARKING BRAKE LEVER FROM SECONDARY SHOE AS SHOWN.

INSTALL

1. INSTALL PARKING BRAKE LEVER ON SECONDARY SHOE AS SHOWN.

PARKING BRAKE LEVER

SECONDARY SHOE

RETAINING RING

A.

REMOVE

1. REMOVE WHEEL CYLINDER RETAINER USING TWO AWLS OR PINS (1/8 INCH DIAMETER OR LESS).

2. INSERT AWLS OR PINS INTO ACCESS SLOTS BETWEEN WHEEL CYLINDER PILOT AND RETAINER LOCKING TABS

3. BEND BOTH TABS AWAY SIMULTANEOUSLY.

AWLS

WHEEL CYLINDER RETAINER

3. REMOVE AND INSTALL WHEEL CYLINDER.

REMOVE

1. REMOVE DIRT AND FOREIGN MATERIAL AROUND WHEEL CYLINDER INLET AND PILOT.

2. DISCONNECT INLET TUBE LINE.

3. REMOVE PARTS AS SHOWN IN **A** FOLLOWING.

INSTALL

NOTICE: SEE NOTICE AT THE BEGINNING OF THIS SECTION.

1. INSTALL PARTS AS SHOWN IN **B** FOLLOWING.

2. TORQUE BLEEDER SCREW TO 3.4-7.9 N·m (30-70 IN. LBS.).

3. TORQUE INLET TUBE NUT TO 13.6-20.3 N·m (120-180 IN. LBS.).

BLEEDER SCREWS

WHEEL CYLINDER RETAINER

WHEEL CYLINDER

B.

INSTALL

1. POSITION WHEEL CYLINDER AND HOLD IN PLACE WITH WOODEN BLOCK BETWEEN CYLINDER AND AXLE FLANGE.

2. INSTALL NEW RETAINER OVER WHEEL CYLINDER ABUTMENT AS SHOWN USING A 1-1/8 INCH, 12 POINT SOCKET AND SOCKET EXTENSION.

1-1/8 INCH, 12 POINT SOCKET

SOCKET EXTENSION

FIGURE 32-5(C). *(Courtesy of General Motors Corporation)*

7. Clean and inspect *front-wheel bearings* as described in Chapter 29. Wash bearings in solvent and blow dry with compressed air. *Caution:* Do not spin bearings with compressed air. This can damage bearings, and they may fly apart, causing injury. Inspect bearing rollers for damage or discoloration. Bearing roller cage should not be distorted or bent.

Bearing cups should show a normal, dull-gray wear pattern. Replace damaged, worn, or rough bearings.

8. Disassemble the wheel cylinder. Inspect the cylinder bore for minor damage. If the cylinder bore is not excessively corroded, rusted, or worn, it can be honed and a new kit installed if recommended by manufacturer. Check piston-to-bore clearance after

CALIPER R&I

1. REMOVE AND INSTALL CALIPER ASSEMBLY. SEE A, B, C AND D BELOW.

A.

REMOVE

1. REMOVE 2/3 OF BRAKE FLUID FROM MASTER CYLINDER ASSEMBLY.

2. HOIST CAR AND REMOVE WHEEL.

3. POSITION C-CLAMP AS SHOWN AND TIGHTEN UNTIL PISTON BOTTOMS IN BORE.

4. REMOVE C-CLAMP.

INSTALL

NOTICE: SEE NOTICE AT THE BEGINNING OF THIS SECTION.

1. INSTALL WHEELS AND LOWER CAR.

2. FILL MASTER CYLINDER TO PROPER LEVEL.

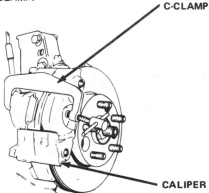

C-CLAMP

CALIPER

B.

REMOVE

1. REMOVE BOLT HOLDING INLET FITTING AS SHOWN. (IF ONLY SHOE AND LINING ARE BEING REPLACED, DO NOT REMOVE INLET FITTING.)

INSTALL

NOTICE: SEE NOTICE AT THE BEGINNING OF THIS SECTION.

1. INSTALL INLET FITTING AS SHOWN AND TORQUE TO 24-40 N·m (18-30 FT. LBS.).

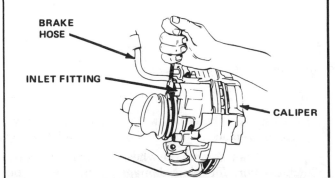

BRAKE HOSE

INLET FITTING

CALIPER

C.

REMOVE

1. REMOVE ALLEN HEAD MOUNTING BOLTS, AS SHOWN.

2. INSPECT MOUNTING BOLTS FOR CORROSION. IF CORROSION IS FOUND, USE NEW BOLTS WHEN INSTALLING CALIPER.

INSTALL

NOTICE: SEE NOTICE AT THE BEGINNING OF THIS SECTION.

1. INSTALL MOUNTING BOLTS AS SHOWN AND TORQUE TO 28-47 N·m (21-35 FT. LBS.).

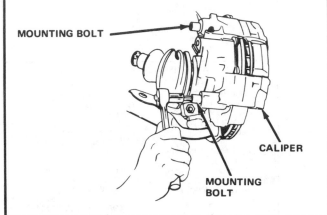

MOUNTING BOLT

CALIPER

MOUNTING BOLT

D.

REMOVE

1. IF ONLY SHOE AND LININGS ARE BEING REPLACED, REMOVE CALIPER FROM ROTOR AND SUSPEND WITH A WIRE HOOK FROM SPRING AS SHOWN. REFER TO STEP 2 FOR REMOVAL AND INSTALLATION OF SHOE AND LINING ASSEMBLIES.

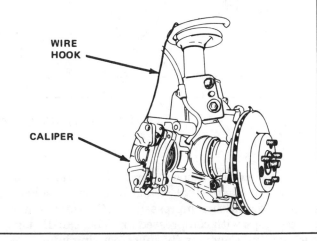

WIRE HOOK

CALIPER

FIGURE 32-6(A). Typical front-wheel-drive disc brake service. (*Courtesy of General Motors Corporation*)

SHOE AND LINING R&I

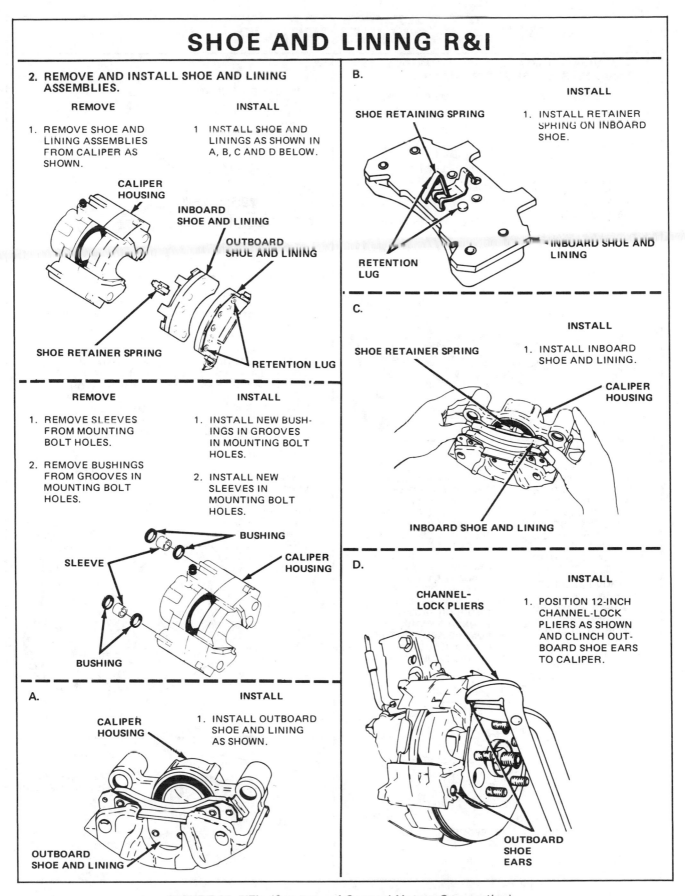

2. REMOVE AND INSTALL SHOE AND LINING ASSEMBLIES.

REMOVE

1. REMOVE SHOE AND LINING ASSEMBLIES FROM CALIPER AS SHOWN.

INSTALL

1. INSTALL SHOE AND LININGS AS SHOWN IN A, B, C AND D BELOW.

CALIPER HOUSING

INBOARD SHOE AND LINING

OUTBOARD SHOE AND LINING

SHOE RETAINER SPRING

RETENTION LUG

REMOVE

1. REMOVE SLEEVES FROM MOUNTING BOLT HOLES.

2. REMOVE BUSHINGS FROM GROOVES IN MOUNTING BOLT HOLES.

INSTALL

1. INSTALL NEW BUSHINGS IN GROOVES IN MOUNTING BOLT HOLES.

2. INSTALL NEW SLEEVES IN MOUNTING BOLT HOLES.

BUSHING

SLEEVE

CALIPER HOUSING

BUSHING

A.

INSTALL

1. INSTALL OUTBOARD SHOE AND LINING AS SHOWN.

CALIPER HOUSING

OUTBOARD SHOE AND LINING

B.

INSTALL

1. INSTALL RETAINER SPRING ON INBOARD SHOE.

SHOE RETAINING SPRING

RETENTION LUG

INBOARD SHOE AND LINING

C.

INSTALL

1. INSTALL INBOARD SHOE AND LINING.

SHOE RETAINER SPRING

CALIPER HOUSING

INBOARD SHOE AND LINING

D.

INSTALL

1. POSITION 12-INCH CHANNEL-LOCK PLIERS AS SHOWN AND CLINCH OUTBOARD SHOE EARS TO CALIPER.

CHANNEL-LOCK PLIERS

OUTBOARD SHOE EARS

FIGURE 32-6(B). *(Courtesy of General Motors Corporation)*

CALIPER REPAIR

3. REMOVE AND INSTALL SEAL, PISTON, DUST BOOT AND BLEEDER SCREW

REMOVE

1. REMOVE PARTS AS SHOWN.

2. CLEAN ALL PARTS, NOT INCLUDED IN REPAIR KIT, IN CLEAN, DENATURED ALCOHOL. USE DRY, FILTERED COMPRESSED AIR TO DRY PARTS AND BLOW OUT ALL PASSAGES IN THE CALIPER HOUSING AND BLEEDER VALVE.

INSTALL

1. INSTALL PARTS AS SHOWN.

2. TORQUE BLEEDER SCREW TO 9-16 N·m (80-140 IN. LBS.).

B.

REMOVE

1. REMOVE DUST BOOT AS SHOWN, BEING CAREFUL NOT TO SCRATCH THE HOUSING BORE.

C.

REMOVE

1. REMOVE PISTON SEAL FROM GROOVE IN CALIPER BORE WITH A PIECE OF WOOD OR PLASTIC. DO NOT USE A METAL TOOL OF ANY TYPE AS DAMAGE TO BORE MAY RESULT.

2. INSPECT CALIPER BORE FOR SCORING, NICKS, CORROSION OR WEAR. USE CROCUS CLOTH TO POLISH OUT ANY LIGHT CORROSION. REPLACE CALIPER HOUSING IF BORE WILL NOT CLEAN UP USING CROCUS CLOTH.

INSTALL

NOTICE: SEE NOTICE AT THE BEGINNING OF THIS SECTION.

1. LUBRICATE NEW SEAL WITH CLEAN BRAKE FLUID.

2. INSTALL PISTON SEAL IN CALIPER BORE GROOVE, MAKING SURE SEAL IS NOT TWISTED.

A.

REMOVE

1. USE CLEAN SHOP TOWELS TO PAD THE INTERIOR OF THE CALIPER AND REMOVE THE PISTON BY DIRECTING COMPRESSED AIR INTO THE CALIPER INLET HOLE.

2. REMOVE BLEEDER SCREW.

3. INSPECT PISTON FOR SCORING, NICKS, CORROSION AND WORN OR DAMAGED CHROME PLATING. REPLACE PISTON IF ANY OF THE ABOVE DEFECTS ARE FOUND.

NOTICE: USE JUST ENOUGH AIR TO EASE THE PISTON OUT OF THE BORE. IF PISTON IS BLOWN OUT—EVEN WITH PADDING PROVIDED, IT MAY BE DAMAGED.

CAUTION: DO NOT PLACE THE FINGERS IN FRONT OF THE PISTON IN AN ATTEMPT TO CATCH OR PROTECT IT WHEN APPLYING COMPRESSED AIR. THIS COULD RESULT IN SERIOUS INJURY.

D.

INSTALL

1. INSTALL DUST BOOT ON PISTON AS SHOWN.

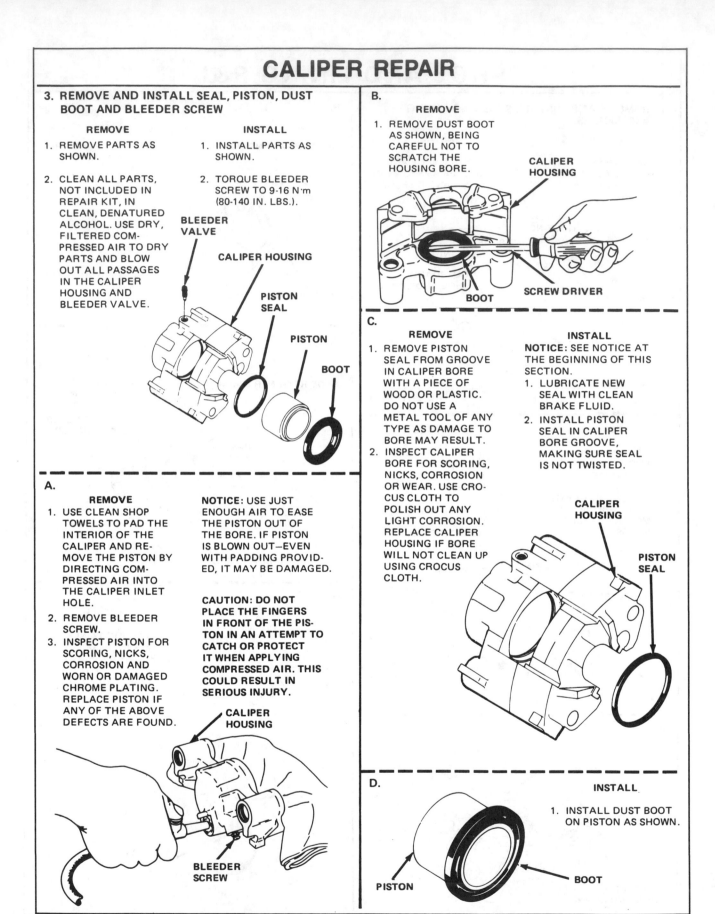

FIGURE 32-6(C). *(Courtesy of General Motors Corporation)*

FIGURE 32-7. Removal of typical sliding caliper. *(Courtesy of Chrysler Corporation)*

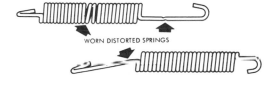

FIGURE 32-8. Worn or distorted springs should be replaced.

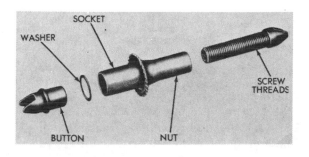

FIGURE 32-9. Star-wheel adjuster exploded view.

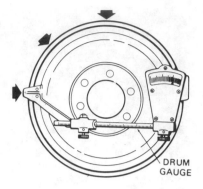

FIGURE 32-10. Brake drum must be measured at several points for wear and out of round.

FIGURE 32-11. Most brake drums show the maximum allowable drum diameter stamped on the drum.

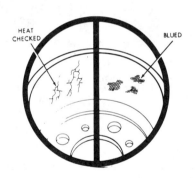

FIGURE 32-12. Drums that are overheated show heat checks and blued spots that have become hardened. This may prevent machining.

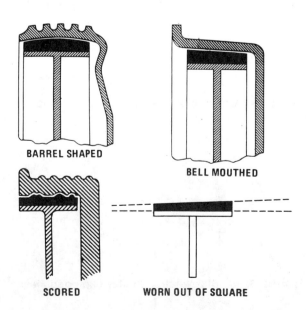

BARREL SHAPED

BELL MOUTHED

SCORED

WORN OUT OF SQUARE

FIGURE 32-13. Other drum conditions that may require machining or drum replacement.

FIGURE 32-14. Rotor showing minimum thickness marking stamped on the disc.

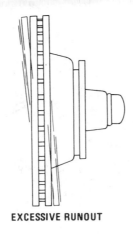

EXCESSIVE RUNOUT

FIGURE 32-15. Rotor run-out causes piston "knock back" with resultant loss of pedal reserve, as well as a pulsating brake pedal.

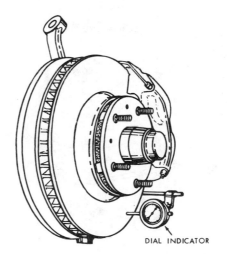

DIAL INDICATOR

FIGURE 32-16. Using a dial indicator to measure rotor run-out.

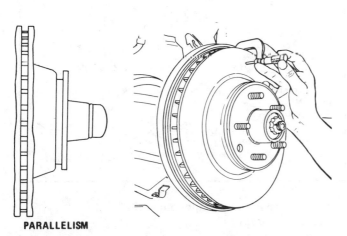

PARALLELISM

FIGURE 32-17. Measuring rotor thickness and parallelism with a micrometer.

1. REMOVE AND INSTALL POWER MASTER CYLINDER.

REMOVE

1. DISCONNECT ELEC- TRICAL LEAD AND FOUR HYDRAULIC LINES.
2. REMOVE TWO ATTACHING NUTS.
3. REMOVE MASTER CYLINDER AS SHOWN.

INSTALL

NOTICE: SEE NOTICE AT THE BEGINNING OF THIS SECTION.

1. INSTALL MASTER CYLINDER AS SHOWN AND TORQUE ATTACHING NUTS TO 30-40 N·m (22-30 FT. LBS.).
2. ATTACH ELECTRICAL LEAD AND FOUR HYDRAULIC LINES. TORQUE TUBE NUTS TO 13.6-20.3 N·m (120-180 IN. LBS.).

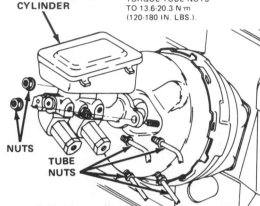

POWER MASTER CYLINDER

NUTS

TUBE NUTS

2. REMOVE AND INSTALL RESERVOIR COVER AND DIAPHRAGM.

REMOVE

1. REMOVE RESERVOIR COVER AND DIA- PHRAGM AS SHOWN.
2. DISCARD ANY BRAKE FLUID IN RESER- VOIR.
3. INSPECT RESERVOIR COVER AND DIA- PHRAGM FOR CUTS, CRACKS OR DEFOR- MATION. REPLACE DAMAGED OR DEFECTIVE PARTS.

INSTALL

NOTICE: SEE NOTICE AT THE BEGINNING OF THIS SECTION.

1. INSTALL RESERVOIR DIAPHRAGM IN RESERVOIR COVER.
2. INSTALL ASSEMBLY ON RESERVOIR.

RESERVOIR COVER

RESERVOIR DIAPHRAGM

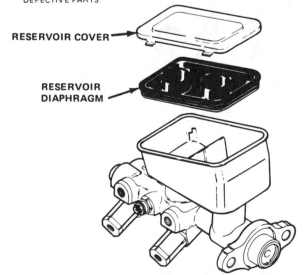

3. REMOVE AND INSTALL PROPORTIONERS AND FAILURE WARNING SWITCH.

REMOVE

1. REMOVE PARTS AS SHOWN.
2. FAILURE WARNING SWITCH O-RING IS OPTIONAL ON ORIGI- NAL EQUIPMENT.

INSTALL

NOTICE: SEE NOTICE AT THE BEGINNING OF THIS SECTION.

1. INSTALL NEW O-RINGS ON PRO- PORTIONERS AND FAILURE WARNING SWITCH.
2. INSTALL PROPOR- TIONERS AND TORQUE TO 24.1-41.0 N·m (18-30 IN. LBS.).
3. INSTALL FAILURE WARNING SWITCH AND TORQUE TO 1.7-5.6 N·m (15-50 IN. LBS.).

FAILURE WARNING SWITCH

O-RINGS

PROPORTIONERS

4. REMOVE AND INSTALL PRIMARY AND SECONDARY PISTONS.

REMOVE

1. DEPRESS PRIMARY PISTON AND RE- MOVE LOCK RING.
2. DIRECT COMPRESS- ED AIR INTO ONE OF THE OUTLETS AT THE BLIND END OF THE BORE AND PLUG THE OTHER THREE OUTLETS TO REMOVE PRIMARY AND SECONDARY PISTONS.
3. DISASSEMBLE SECONDARY PISTON AS SHOWN IN **A** BELOW.
4. INSPECT MASTER CYLINDER BORE FOR CORROSION. IF BORE IS CORRODED, RE- PLACE MASTER CY- LINDER. NO ABRA- SIVES SHALL BE USED ON BORE.

INSTALL

NOTICE: SEE NOTICE AT THE BEGINNING OF THIS SECTION.

1. ASSEMBLE SECOND- ARY PISTON AS SHOWN IN **A**.
2. INSTALL SPRING, SPRING RETAINER AND SECONDARY PISTON IN CYLINDER.
3. INSTALL PRIMARY PISTON, DEPRESS, AND INSTALL LOCK RING.

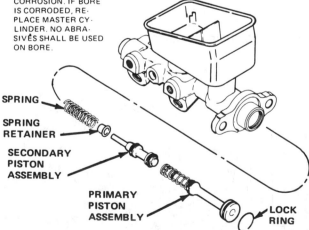

SPRING

SPRING RETAINER

SECONDARY PISTON ASSEMBLY

PRIMARY PISTON ASSEMBLY

LOCK RING

FIGURE 32-18(A). Quick take up master cylinder service for diagonally split hydraulic system. *(Courtesy of General Motors Corporation)*

MASTER CYLINDER REPAIR-B

4. CONT

REMOVE	INSTALL
1. REMOVE SEALS AS SHOWN.	1. INSTALL NEW SEALS, POSITIONING AS SHOWN.

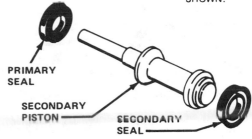

PRIMARY SEAL

SECONDARY PISTON

SECONDARY SEAL

5. REMOVE AND INSTALL SWITCH PISTON ASSEMBLY

REMOVE	INSTALL
1. REMOVE ALLEN HEAD PLUG.	**NOTICE:** SEE NOTICE AT THE BEGINNING OF THIS SECTION.
2. REMOVE SWITCH PISTON ASSEMBLY WITH NEEDLE NOSE PLIERS.	1. INSTALL NEW O-RINGS AND RETAINERS ON SWITCH PISTON AS SHOWN.
3. DISASSEMBLE SWITCH PISTON ASSEMBLY AS SHOWN.	2. INSTALL SWITCH PISTON ASSEMBLY AS SHOWN.
	3. ASSEMBLE NEW O-RING ON PLUG AND INSTALL. TORQUE PLUG TO 4.5-16 N·m (40-140 IN. LBS.).

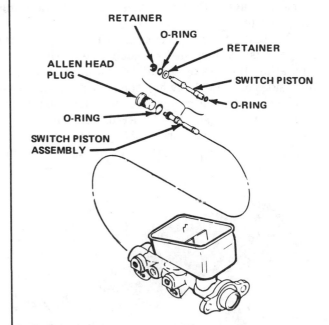

RETAINER

O-RING

RETAINER

ALLEN HEAD PLUG

SWITCH PISTON

O-RING

O-RING

SWITCH PISTON ASSEMBLY

6. REMOVE AND INSTALL RESERVOIR

REMOVE	INSTALL
1. REMOVE RESERVOIR AS SHOWN IN A BELOW.	1. INSTALL RESERVOIR AS SHOWN IN B BELOW.

A.

REMOVE

1. CLAMP MASTER CYLINDER IN VISE AS SHOWN—DO NOT CLAMP ON MASTER CYLINDER BODY— AND USE PRY BAR TO REMOVE RESERVOIR.

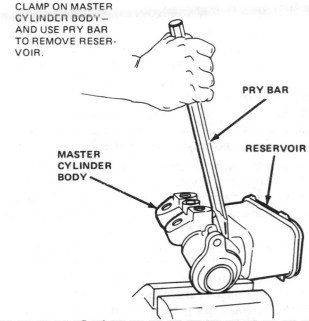

PRY BAR

RESERVOIR

MASTER CYLINDER BODY

B.

INSTALL

1. LAY RESERVOIR ON FLAT, HARD SURFACE AS SHOWN. PRESS ON MASTER CYLINDER BODY USING ROCKING MOTION.

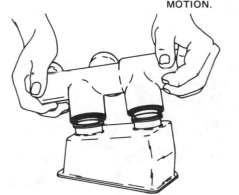

FIGURE 32–18(B). *(Courtesy of General Motors Corporation)*

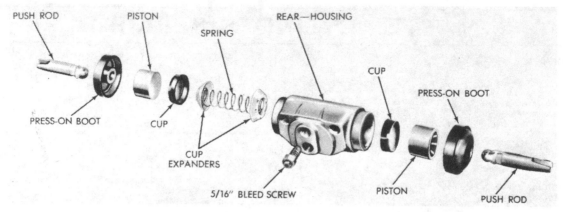

FIGURE 32-19. Exploded view of common type of wheel cylinder.

honing. Clearance should not exceed the manufacturer's specifications, usually 0.003 to 0.004 inch (0.0762 to 0.1016 millimeter). Wash the cylinder thoroughly in brake cleaning fluid and assemble with parts from new kit. Parts should be lubricated with lubricant provided with the kit or with clean, new brake fluid. Make sure that the bleeder screw is free, clear, and in good condition.

9. Disassemble the *master cylinder* by removing the primary piston retainer snap ring or screw and the secondary piston stop screw (if so equipped). The secondary piston stop screw is located inside the reservoir on some master cylinders. Remove the pistons and springs. Examine the cylinder bore condition. Minor damage can be polished out with crocus cloth or with a brake cylinder hone. If corrosion or rust is excessive, the master cylinder must be replaced. During honing no more than just a few thousandths of an inch should be removed from the cylinder to maintain proper piston-to-bore clearance. Measure with a feeler gauge between piston and bore. Follow the manufacturer's specifications for maximum allowable clearance. Honing is not recommended for some types of master cylinders. After honing and after checking piston-to-bore clearance, thoroughly wash the master cylinder in brake cleaning fluid and assemble with the new master cylinder kit. A rebuild kit usually contains the primary and the secondary parts, as well as residual check valves and seats where applicable. Lubricate all internal parts with clean, new brake fluid. The master cylinder is then ready for installation.

10. *Lines, switches,* and *valves* should be inspected for damage. Flex lines should not be cracked or swollen. Steel lines should be checked for dents and rust. Severely damaged lines should be replaced with seamless steel brake lines of the same diameter. Lines must be bent to fit with the proper bending tool to avoid kinking or restricting the line. The metering valve can be tested by installing a pressure gauge between the valve and the front disc brakes. By operating the brake pedal, the opening pressure of the metering valve can be observed. An alternate method of testing the metering valve is to depress the brake pedal carefully. A slight "bump" should be felt as the brake pedal passes the first inch of pedal travel. This indicates that the metering valve is working.

To test the proportioning valve, a pressure gauge must be installed on each side of the valve. Operating the brake pedal will show pressure on both sides of the valve when the *split* point has been reached. When the gauge between the master cylinder reads 500 psi (3,447.5 kPa), the other gauge should read approximately 350 psi (2,413.25 kPa). If the brake warning light stays on, it may be be-

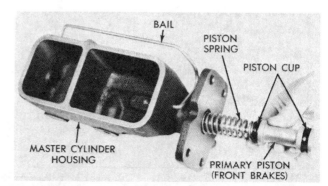

FIGURE 32-20. Removal or installation of secondary piston in dual master cylinder.

FIGURE 32-21. Removal or installation of master cylinder primary piston in dual master cylinder.

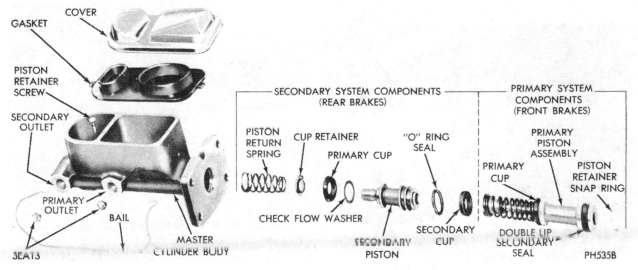

FIGURE 32–22. Exploded view of tandem master cylinder component parts disassembled.

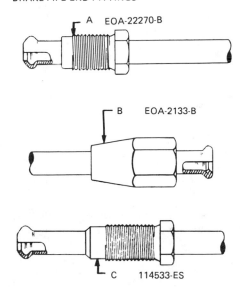

BRAKE PIPE END FITTINGS

A   EOA-22270-B

B   EOA-2133-B

C   114533-ES

FIGURE 32–23. Several types of brake line fittings. Note double-lap flared tubing at center and ISO-type tubing at top and bottom.

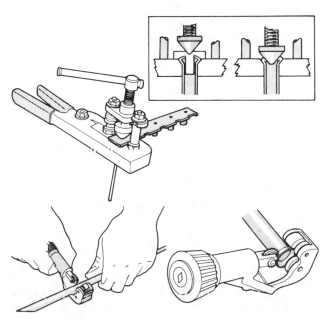

FIGURE 32–24. Sequence for flaring steel lines with a double-lap flare. *(Courtesy of Chrysler Corporation)*

763

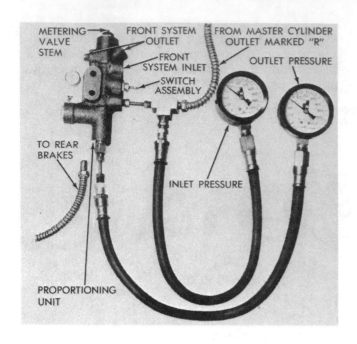

FIGURE 32-25. Gauge connections for testing proportioning valve operation. At 500 psi, master cylinder pressure proportioning valve output pressure should be approximately 350 psi. If defective, valve must be replaced.

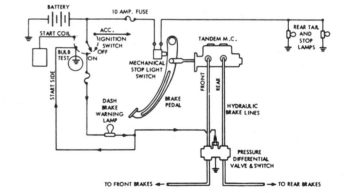

FIGURE 32-26. Hydraulic system schematic showing pressure differential switch and brake warning light.

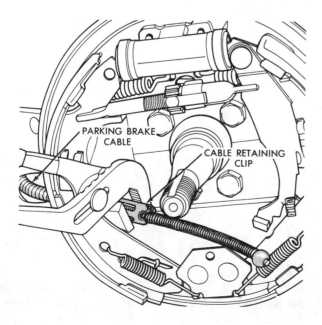

FIGURE 32-27. To remove parking brake cable from backing plate, squeeze retaining clip with pliers and slide cable through plate. (Courtesy of Chrysler Corporation)

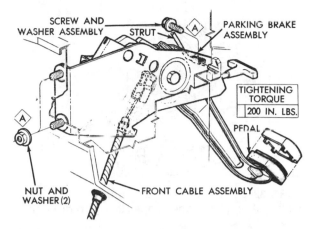

FIGURE 32-28. Parking brake pedal mechanism showing cable connection. *(Courtesy of Chrysler Corporation)*

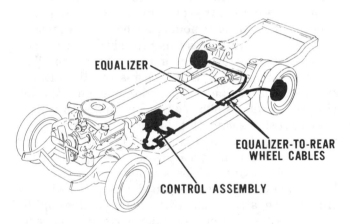

FIGURE 32-29. Location of parking brake equalizer. Adjustment is usually made at this point. *(Courtesy of Ford Motor Co. of Canada Ltd.)*

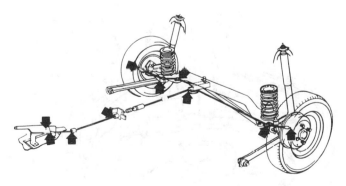

FIGURE 32-30. Lubrication points for typical parking brake control mechanism. *(Courtesy of Ford Motor Co. of Canada Ltd.)*

cause the switch is not the self-centering type. This often happens after bleeding brakes. To correct this condition, bleed the side opposite to the one that was bled last. For example, if the primary side was bled last, bleed the secondary side until the light just goes off. This will center the switch and turn the light off. To check if the bulb is working, watch the warning light when the ignition switch is turned to the start position; it should light. If not, replace the bulb or check the circuit.

11. Inspect the *parking brake* linkage and cables for damage. Damaged parts should be replaced. Cables and linkage should operate freely and be properly lubricated to assure continued good operation. Adjust the parking brake according to the manufacturer's specifications. This is usually done at the equalizer between the front and rear cables, after the service brake adjustment.

PART 6   MACHINING AND RECONDITIONING PROCEDURE

1. Brake drums and discs must be machined to restore balanced and effective braking. Always machine drums and discs in axle pairs. When machining drums, start with the one showing the most wear. If it cleans up properly before the maximum allowable diameter is reached, it can be used again. Machine the other drum to within 0.010 inch (0.254 millimeter) of this diameter to prevent pull to one side. Follow the machine manufacturer's instructions for mounting and machining procedures. On front wheel drive vehicles, discs are often machined without removal from the vehicle. Brake discs need not be machined to the same thickness, since a thickness difference in two front discs will not cause uneven braking or pull. When machining discs, re-

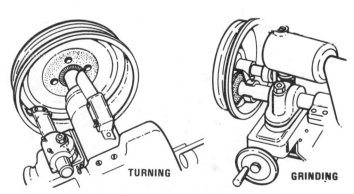

FIGURE 32-31. Brake drum mounted for machining on two different types of machines.

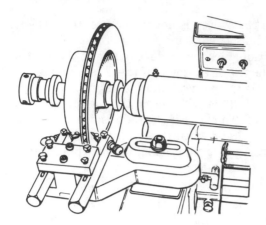

FIGURE 32-32. Disc brake rotor mounted in machine for resurfacing.

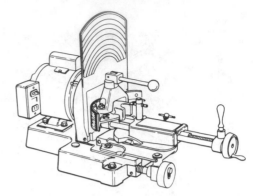

FIGURE 32-33. Brake shoe contour grinding is sometimes required to provide proper lining to drum-fit.

move as little as possible and still achieve the desired friction surfaces. Discs should be replaced if they do not recondition by the time minimum thickness has been reached. Follow the equipment manufacturer's instructions for mounting discs on the machine and for machining. Always machine in pairs.

2. Brake shoe linings must be fitted to the new or reconditioned drum to provide full lining-to-drum contact during braking and to avoid squeal and chatter. This requires arcing or radius grinding of the lining to provide from 0.006-to 0.010-inch (0.1524 to 0.254 millimeter) heel-and-toe clearance when the shoe is held in the drum by hand. It is good practice to chalk the entire lining surface before radius grinding. This makes it easier to see when the entire surface has been ground. Remove as little material as possible when radius grinding and still achieve the desired fit. Follow the equipment manufacturer's instructions for mounting shoes in machine and

for proper adjustment and grinding procedure. Follow local and federal regulations regarding the control of asbestos dust and use of masks.

3. *Wheel cylinder, master cylinder,* and *caliper piston bores* are reconditioned in a similar manner. Minor nicks, scratches, and burrs should be dressed with crocus cloth. Anything more serious requires caliper replacement or honing of the cylinder, where the manufacturer allows this procedure. If the bore diameter is increased more than the permissible amount before the cylinder cleans up, the master cylinder, wheel cylinder, or caliper must be replaced. Honing is usually followed by polishing with crocus cloth to ensure a smooth cylinder surface and to prevent damage to cups and seals. Thorough cleaning of these parts is necessary after honing to insure that no abrasive particles are allowed to enter the hydraulic system. Pistons can also be polished with crocus cloth, after which they should be thoroughly cleaned. All new internal rubber parts, pistons, and bores should be thoroughly lubricated with clean, new brake fluid or recommended special assembly lubricant during assembly. Avoid using screwdrivers on rubber seals and boots to prevent puncturing or cutting. A wooden or plastic tool will avoid this.

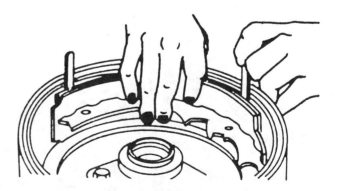

.010' CLEARANCE AT BOTH ENDS OF LINING

FIGURE 32-34. Checking heel-and-toe clearance with feeler gauges.

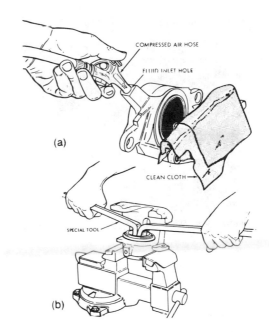

FIGURE 32-35. Removing caliper piston with air pressure (A) and with special tool (B).

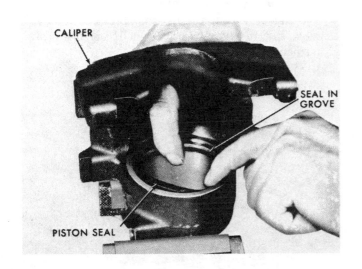

FIGURE 32-36. Installing the piston seal in caliper piston bore.

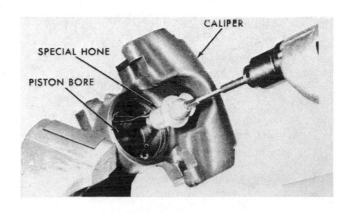

FIGURE 32-37. Honing a caliper piston bore.

FIGURE 32–38. Installing the caliper piston boot after seal and piston have been installed.

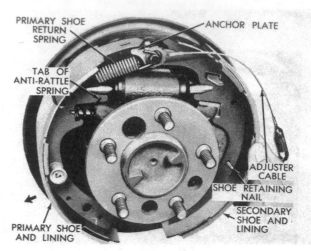

FIGURE 32–40. Drum brake assembly nearly completed. Primary (short) lining must be at front of assembly. Primary and secondary return springs must not be interchanged.

PART 7   ASSEMBLY AND ADJUSTMENT PROCEDURE

Drum Brake Unit

To assemble the drum brake unit, proceed as follows.

• Lubricate the parking brake at all points recommended in the service manual.

• Mount the backing plate on the spindle at the front and the axle flange at the rear. Install the rear axle seal and axle shaft.

• Lubricate the shoe platforms on the backing plate. Use a good-quality, high-temperature lubricant that will not run, and use it sparingly to prevent lining contamination.

• Mount the assembled wheel cylinder and attach the brake line.

• Attach the parking brake cable to the secondary shoe lever at the rear.

• Mount the shoes, hold-downs, parking brake link, and adjuster mechanism.

• Make sure that the parking brake is fully released so that it will not interfere with service brake adjustment.

• Make sure that the primary and secondary shoe retracting springs are not interchanged.

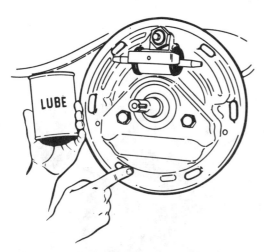

FIGURE 32–39. Lubricating backing plate ledges with special lubricant. Avoid overlubrication.

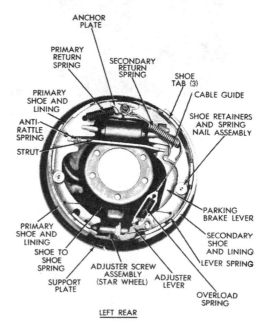

FIGURE 32–41. Completed assembly before drum installation should be checked for free movement on backing plate. Self-adjuster operation can be checked by tightening cable by hand. When cable is released, the adjuster should turn, slightly expanding the brake shoes.

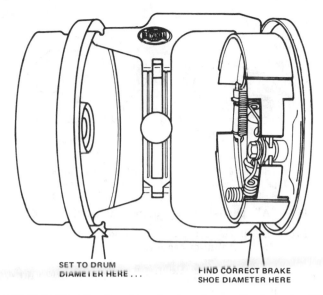

SET TO DRUM
DIAMETER HERE...

FIND CORRECT BRAKE
SHOE DIAMETER HERE

FIGURE 32-42. Checking brake shoe adjustment with gauge. By using this method, proper lining-to-drum clearance can be achieved without "dragging" brakes. *(Courtesy of Ford Motor Co. of Canada Ltd.)*

• The completed shoe assembly should float or slide freely on the backing plate.

• Use the gauge to determine proper shoe adjustment and adjust shoes to drum size.

• Install the brake drum and drum retainer if used.

• Install wheel and torque bolts or nuts in proper sequence to specifications.

• Repack wheel bearings with wheel bearing grease as described in Chapter 29, Part 4.

Caution: Be sure not to touch the drum or disc friction surface with grease, greasy hands, or brake fluid. Friction surfaces must remain clean and dry.

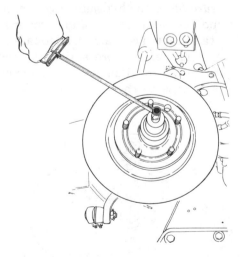

FIGURE 32-43. Using a torque wrench to adjust wheel bearings. Usual procedure is to tighten nut to specifications; then back off nut a specified amount and lock with cotter pin.

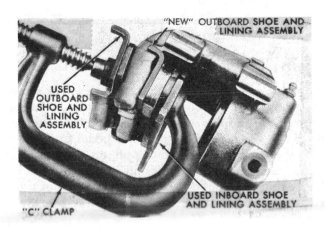

"NEW" OUTBOARD SHOE AND LINING ASSEMBLY

USED OUTBOARD SHOE AND LINING ASSEMBLY

"C" CLAMP

USED INBOARD SHOE AND LINING ASSEMBLY

FIGURE 32-44. Installing brake pad in caliper with C-clamp. Antirattle materials and clips must be installed properly with pads.

Disc Brake Unit

After wheel bearings have been repacked and the disc installed, proceed as follows.

• Install new disc brake pads on a new or reconditioned caliper.

• Make sure that any anti-rattle clips and materials are in place with pads.

• The caliper piston must be forced back into the caliper to provide sufficient room between the pads to fit over the disc. Use a spreader between the pads or a C-clamp to do this.

• Mount the caliper over the disc.

• Make sure that all attaching parts, bushings, clips, and retainers are properly positioned. Tighten mounting bolts to specified torque. Connect the brake line.

FIGURE 32-45. Tightening wheel nuts must be done to specified torque and in proper sequence to avoid drum or disc distortion.

• Attach the wheel and torque to specifications in proper sequence.

Master Cylinder

Attach the master cylinder to the firewall or power brake unit. Be sure that the master cylinder piston returns to the fully released position. This requires proper pushrod adjustment. If no pedal free play is provided, the master cylinder piston will keep the compensating port covered and brakes will not release, since hydraulic system pressure cannot drop. Bleed the master cylinder and connect the brake lines.

PART 8   BLEEDING HYDRAULIC SYSTEM

Bleeding the brake hydraulic system is necessary after reconditioning or if air has entered the system. Air in the system results in spongy pedal feel and action; since air in the system is compressible, reduced pressure and force result in poor braking action when the brakes are applied.

Two methods of bleeding brakes are normally used: manual bleeding and pressure bleeding.

To bleed the brakes manually, proceed as follows.

• Close all bleeder screws.

• Fill the master cylinder with clean brake fluid.

• Use a bleeder drain tube and jar to drain fluid from each wheel.

• Have an assistant push down the brake pedal.

• Attach the bleeder drain to the right rear-wheel bleeder.

• While the pedal is down, open the bleeder screw about a three-quarter turn.

WITH VALVE BUTTON
Type "A" — Push-in Only

WITH VALVE STEM
Type "A" — Push-in
Type "B" — Pull-out

Type "A", push-in: 12 - 25 pounds spring load.

Type "B", pull-out: 22 - 35 pounds spring pull, 0.060 inch minimum travel.

FIGURE 32-47. Metering valve must be held open during bleeding of brakes.

• Close the bleeder screw when the flow stops.

• Release the pedal.

• Repeat this procedure until all air has been removed and a stream of fluid with no bubbles flows when the bleeder is opened. Keep the master cylinder full.

• Repeat this procedure next at the left rear wheel, then the right front wheel, and finally the left front wheel.

• If brakes were properly adjusted and bled, there should be a firm pedal feel with no more than half the total pedal movement required (pedal reserve).

• On brakes equipped with a metering valve, the valve may have to be held open during the bleeding process.

To *pressure bleed* the hydraulic system, a pressure tank and special master cylinder cover are required. The tank should contain an adequate supply of good brake fluid and be pressurized to approximately 25 psi (172.375 kPa). A quick coupler connects the tank hose to the master cylinder cover.

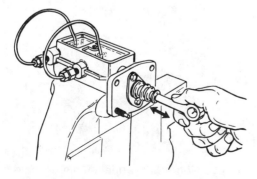

FIGURE 32-46. Bench bleeding of master cylinder is done as illustrated.

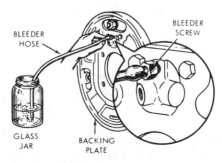

FIGURE 32-48. Bleeder hose and jar used for bleeding brakes.

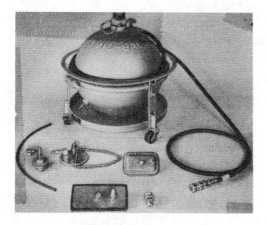

FIGURE 32–49. Pressure bleeding equipment with special covers for different types of master cylinders.

With all the bleeders closed, the pressure tank valve is opened, pressurizing the brake system and keeping the master cylinder full of fluid. If brakes are equipped with a metering valve, the valve must be held open during bleeding. No pedal operation is required. Bleeding is then accomplished by opening the bleeder screw at each wheel in the same manner and sequence as in manual bleeding until all air is removed. Then the pressure tank valve is closed and the pressure bleeder disconnected. Replace the master cylinder cover and check pedal feel and reserve.

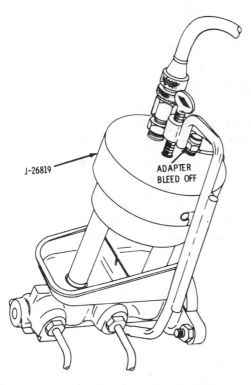

J-26819

ADAPTER
BLEED OFF

FIGURE 32–50. Typical master cylinder pressure bleeder adapter for plastic reservoir master cylinder. *(Courtesy of General Motors Corporation)*

PART 9   POWER BRAKE SERVICE PROCEDURE

Vacuum Power Brake

The general practice is to determine the booster's condition by performing a functional test; if the booster fails this test; it is repaired or replaced with a new or rebuilt unit.

Functional Test

1. With the engine stopped, depress the brake pedal three or four times to eliminate all vacuum in the booster.

2. Hold the brake pedal down and start the engine. When the engine starts, the brake pedal should move down slightly, indicating power assist.

3. Release the brake pedal. Stop the engine and let it stand for 15 to 30 minutes. After this period of time there should be sufficient vacuum in the unit for several power-assisted brake applications. If no vacuum is present at this time, there is a leak in the vacuum booster check valve.

4. Loss of brake fluid from the master cylinder reservoir can sometimes be traced to a fluid leak from the master cylinder into the booster. Such a leak is not visible externally but may be detected by traces of brake fluid in the vacuum booster line to the intake manifold. This requires master cylinder repairs and cleaning or replacement of the booster.

Hydro-Boost Power Brake

The malfunction must be diagnosed to determine whether the booster unit itself is defective or if the problem is in the pressure supply system from the power steering unit. After proper diagnosis, if the Hydro-Boost unit is found to be faulty, it must be repaired or replaced. Follow the procedures outlined in the diagnosis guide.

PART 10   FINAL INSPECTION AND TESTING PROCEDURE

After the brake system has been overhauled, a final inspection should be performed as follows.

1. Depress the brake pedal firmly to pressurize the system. Check for hydraulic fluid leaks while the system is pressurized.

2. The pedal should remain firm and not move

down while constant pressure is applied. There should be adequate pedal reserve.

3. Check the parking brake operation. Brakes should hold firmly when the parking brake is applied and release completely when released.

4. The brake warning light should be on when the parking brake is applied but should not be on when service brakes are applied.

5. Rear brake lights should go on when brakes are applied.

6. Road test the vehicle to determine whether brakes operate properly. There should be no pull to either side when braking; no excessive front-end dive or rear-wheel lock-up; no squeal, rattle, or chatter from the brakes; and no brake drag (brakes not fully releasing).

7. As with any service job, customer acceptance of a vehicle is very important. It does not matter how good a job has been done on the vehicle if grease, oil, and smudges appear on the windows, doors, steering wheel, and upholstery; the customer will not be happy. A job well done leaves the car with no such evidence that it has been serviced.

PART 11 SELF-CHECK

1. Brake system service should not be attempted without a thorough knowledge of proper repair procedures. True or false?

2. The lives of drivers, passengers, and pedestrians are literally dependent on the technician's ability to do a good brake job. True or false?

3. Rotor thickness should not vary more than _____ inch.

4. Rotor run-out must be checked with a _____.

5. Rotor parallelism in disc brakes must be checked with _____.

6. Power brakes that are hard to apply while the engine is running could have which of the following:

(a) a leaking master cylinder
(b) a leaking wheel cylinder
(c) a vacuum problem
(d) air in hydraulic system

7. List four causes of brake pedal bottoming out.

8. Name three reasons for a pulsating brake pedal.

9. List three reasons for slow release of air brakes.

10. Brake drum hard spots are caused by _____.

PART 12 TEST QUESTIONS

1. The maximum oversize limit for brake drums is usually:
   (a) 0.060 inch (1.524 mm)
   (b) 0.120 inch (3.048 mm)
   (c) 0.012 inch (0.3048 mm)
   (d) 0.60 inch (15.24 mm)

2. Rotor parallelism is checked with a:
   (a) micrometer
   (b) straight edge
   (c) dial indicator
   (d) caliper

3. Brake fade may be caused by:
   (a) overheated drums
   (b) glazed linings
   (c) overheated discs
   (d) any of the above

4. A pulsating brake pedal is caused by:
   (a) low fluid level
   (b) air in hydraulic system
   (c) contaminated linings
   (d) out of round drums or excessive rotor run-out

5. The cause of a car pulling to one side when braking is:
   (a) one wheel grabbing
   (b) a seized caliper piston
   (c) incorrect wheel alignment
   (d) all of the above

DRIVE TRAIN

Chapter 33

Front-Wheel-Drive Axles and Drive Shafts

Performance Objectives

After sufficient study of this chapter, the necessary practical experience on the appropriate training models, and the necessary tools, equipment, and shop manuals, you should be able to:

1. Complete the self-check and test questions with at least 80 percent accuracy.
2. Describe the purpose, construction, and operation of:
   (a) The front-wheel-drive axles
   (b) The rear-wheel-drive shaft
3. Diagnose drive line and drive axle problems accurately.
4. Correctly service, remove, repair, replace, and adjust drive line, drive axle, and components to manufacturer's specifications.
5. Adequately test the drive lines and drive axle to determine the success of the services performed.
6. Prepare the vehicle for customer acceptance.

PART 1 OPERATING REQUIREMENTS (FRONT–WHEEL–DRIVE AXLES)

The primary purpose of the front-wheel-drive half-shaft is to transfer engine torque from the transaxle to the front wheels. The universal joints used must be capable of operating at varying angles and provide a means for shaft length changes to allow for vertical suspension (wheel) and engine movement.

These requirements are satisfied by using constant velocity (CV) joints at the inboard (differential) end and outboard (wheel) end of the halfshaft. Some designs use a tripod type of joint at the inner end. A constant velocity joint is a mechanism for transferring uniform torque and rotary motion while operating through its angle range. The inboard joint is a sliding-type joint which provides for shaft length changes. The outboard CV joint has a higher angle capability than the inboard joint to accommodate wheel turning angles.

The front-wheel-drive joints and halfshaft assemblies rotate at approximately 1/3 the speed of conventional rear-wheel-drive driveshafts and do not contribute to rotational vibration disturbances. Proper operation of the drive axle joint is dependent on proper suspension height. Suspension height determines CV joint operating angles.

PART 2 DESIGN (FRONT–WHEEL–DRIVE AXLES)

The joints are connected by an interconnecting shaft. The interconnecting shafts (left-hand and right-hand) are splined at both ends and are retained in the inboard and outboard joints by circlips. Halfshafts are of solid steel or tubular steel construction. When one shaft is considerably longer than the other, the longer shaft is of tubular steel for greater strength and rigidity, whereas the shorter shaft is made of solid steel.

The inboard joint stubshaft is splined and held in the differential side gear by a circlip. The outboard CV joint stubshaft is splined to accommodate a splined hub, which is pressed on and secured with a staked nut. The joints are lube-for-life with a special CV joint grease; they require no periodic lubrication. The CV joint boots are designed to exclude dirt and moisture and retain the lubricant. If damaged or ruptured, rapid joint deterioration will be the result.

The halfshaft design for automatic and manual transaxle applications differs only slightly.

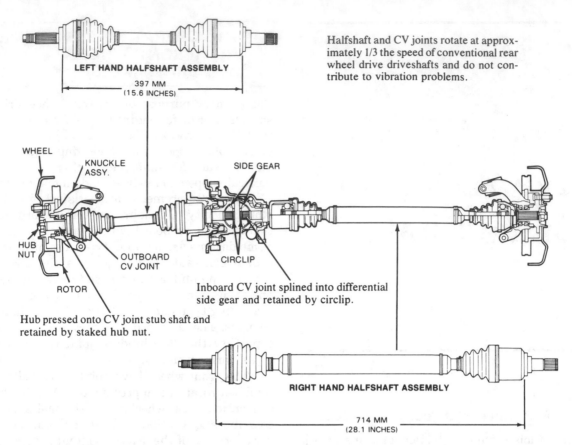

LEFT HAND HALFSHAFT ASSEMBLY

397 MM
(15.6 INCHES)

Halfshaft and CV joints rotate at approximately 1/3 the speed of conventional rear
wheel drive driveshafts and do not contribute to vibration problems.

WHEEL

KNUCKLE
ASSY.

SIDE GEAR

HUB
NUT

OUTBOARD
CV JOINT

CIRCLIP

ROTOR

Inboard CV joint splined into differential
side gear and retained by circlip.

Hub pressed onto CV joint stub shaft and
retained by staked hub nut.

RIGHT HAND HALFSHAFT ASSEMBLY

714 MM
(28.1 INCHES)

FIGURE 33-1. Front-wheel-drive shafts for Ford ATX transaxle. Note left shaft
(short) is solid steel whereas longer right side shaft is tubular type. *(Courtesy
of Ford Motor Co. of Canada Ltd.)*

PART 3 DIAGNOSIS AND SERVICE (FRONT-WHEEL-DRIVE AXLES)

Since front-wheel-drive axles operate at a much
slower speed than the drive shaft for rear-drive-front
engine vehicles, service requirements are less. No
periodic service is required. If the CV joint boot is
punctured or damaged, it should be replaced immediately; loss of lubricant and entry of dirt and
moisture will soon damage the joint.

Service procedures include the following:

1. Replace the CV joint boot and lubricate joint
2. Replace outer CV joint
3. Replace inner CV joint
4. Replace entire shaft assembly

Each of these operations requires the following
general disassembly and reassembly procedures, as
well as the manufacturer's service manual. Support
vehicle on hoist or stands.

1. In some cases, it may be necessary to remove
the right side shaft first before the left shaft can be
removed, or the other way around depending on design. On some models, either shaft may be removed
without being affected by the other. Follow service
manual sequence.

2. Remove drive wheel hub nut (staked or cotter pinned). For staked nut removal procedure, see
Chapter 29, Part 4.

3. Separate the steering knuckle from the suspension arm. Support the drive axle with wire tied
to it and tied to some part of the vehicle. Slide the
wheel hub and steering knuckle assembly from the
outer stub shaft. Be sure not to put excessive strain
on the flexible brake line during this procedure.

4. Disconnect the inner end of the drive axle
from the transaxle in one of the following ways depending on design.

(a) simply slide the stub shaft out of the
transaxle

(b) remove retaining flange bolts and slide
stub shaft from transaxle

(c) remove access cover from transaxle; push
stub shaft into transaxle to gain access to
retaining circlip, and remove circlip; then,
slide shaft out of transaxle

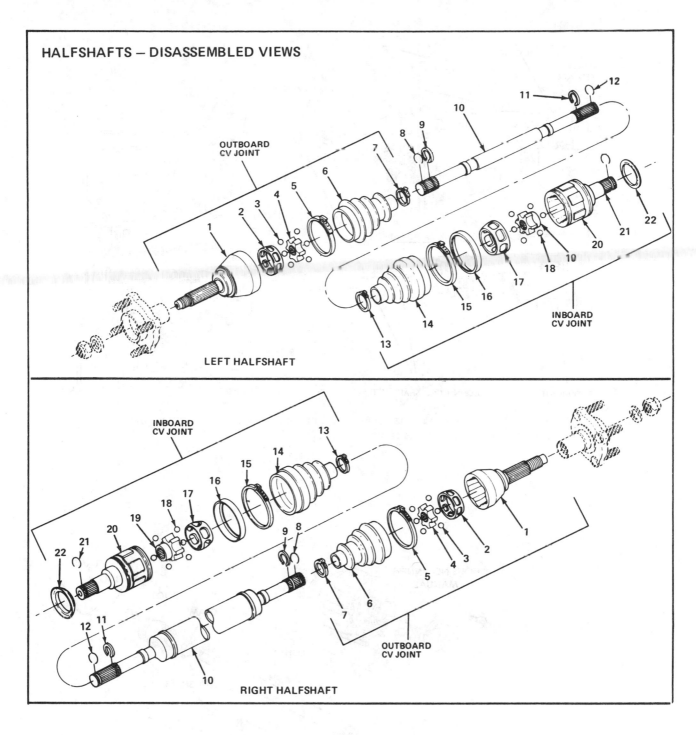

HALFSHAFTS — DISASSEMBLED VIEWS

OUTBOARD CV JOINT

INBOARD CV JOINT

LEFT HALFSHAFT

INBOARD CV JOINT

OUTBOARD CV JOINT

RIGHT HALFSHAFT

LEGEND:

1. OUTER BEARING RACE AND STUB SHAFT ASSEMBLY
2. BEARING CAGE
3. BALL BEARINGS (6)
4. INNER BEARING RACE
5. BOOT CLAMP (LARGE)
6. BOOT
7. BOOT CLAMP (SMALL)
8. CIRCLIP
9. STOP RING
10. INTERCONNECTING SHAFT
11. STOP RING
12. CIRCLIP
13. BOOT CLAMP (SMALL)
14. BOOT
15. BOOT CLAMP (LARGE)
16. BEARING RETAINER
17. BEARING CAGE
18. BALL BEARINGS (6)
19. INNER BEARING RACE
20. OUTER BEARING RACE AND STUB SHAFT ASSEMBLY
21. CIRCLIP
22. DUST DEFLECTOR

FIGURE 33–2. Front-wheel-drive axle components. *(Courtesy of Ford Motor Co. of Canada Ltd.)*

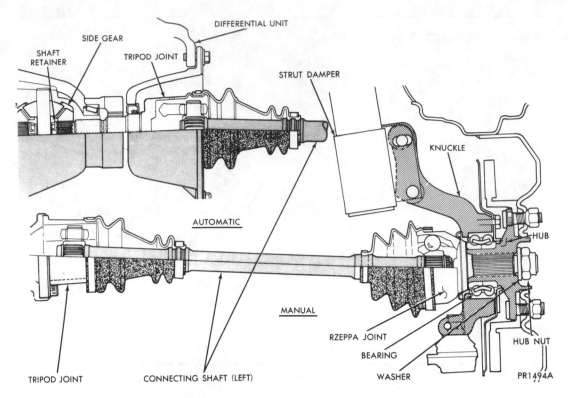

FIGURE 33-3. Cross-sectional view of front-wheel-drive axle components. *(Courtesy of Chrysler Corporation)*

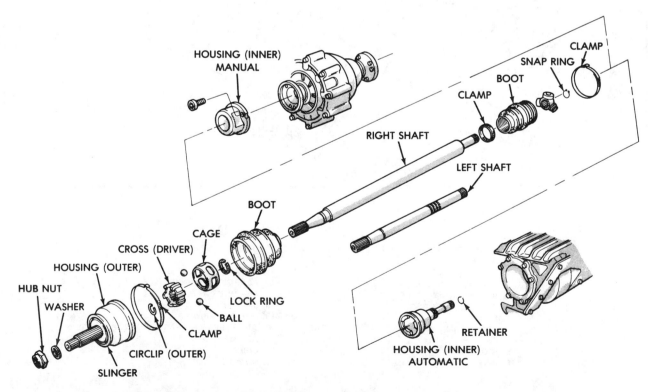

FIGURE 33-4. Front-wheel-drive axle assembly components using two universal joints of different types. *(Courtesy of Chrysler Corporation)*

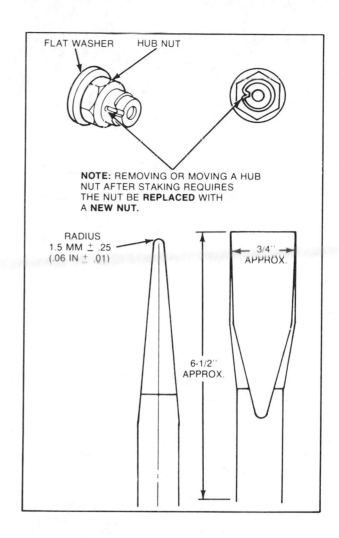

NOTE: REMOVING OR MOVING A HUB NUT AFTER STAKING REQUIRES THE NUT BE **REPLACED** WITH A **NEW NUT.**

FIGURE 33-5. Drive axle hub nut staking method. *(Courtesy of Ford Motor Co. of Canada Ltd.)*

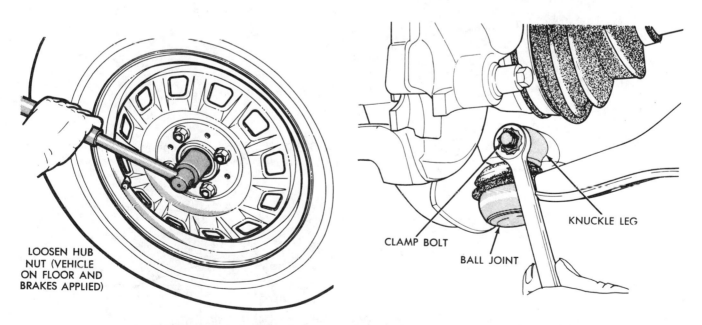

FIGURE 33-6. Loosening hub nut (left) and disconnecting control arm (right) from steering knuckle prior to drive axle removal. *(Courtesy of Chrysler Corporation)*

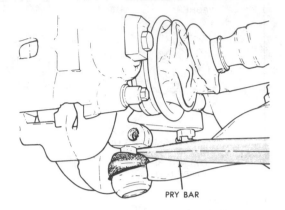

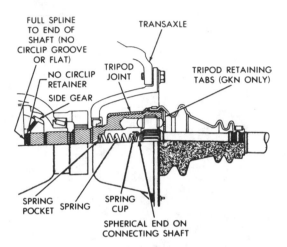

FIGURE 33-7. Using a pry bar to disconnect steering knuckle from control arm. *(Courtesy of Chrysler Corporation)*

FULL SPLINE
TO END OF
SHAFT (NO
CIRCLIP GROOVE
OR FLAT)

TRANSAXLE

NO CIRCLIP
RETAINER

TRIPOD
JOINT

SIDE GEAR

TRIPOD RETAINING
TABS (GKN ONLY)

SPRING
POCKET

SPRING

SPRING
CUP

SPHERICAL END ON
CONNECTING SHAFT

FIGURE 33-8. Spring-loaded type of inner tripod joint can be removed by prying stub shaft from transaxle. See Figure 33-9. *(Courtesy of Chrysler Corporation)*

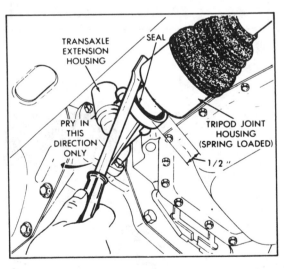

TRANSAXLE
EXTENSION
HOUSING

SEAL

PRY IN
THIS
DIRECTION
ONLY

TRIPOD JOINT
HOUSING
(SPRING LOADED)

1/2"

FIGURE 33-9. Prying back spring-loaded tripod joint from transaxle. *(Courtesy of Chrysler Corporation)*

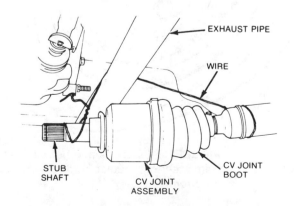

EXHAUST PIPE

WIRE

STUB
SHAFT

CV JOINT
ASSEMBLY

CV JOINT
BOOT

FIGURE 33-10. Using wire to support CV joint and shaft during removal. *(Courtesy of Ford Motor Co. of Canada Ltd.)*

780

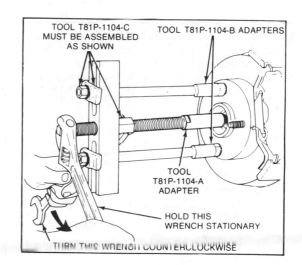

FIGURE 33-11. Using a puller to separate outboard CV joint and stub shaft from wheel hub. *(Courtesy of Ford Motor Co. of Canada Ltd.)*

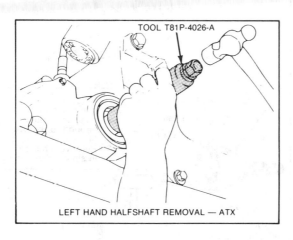

FIGURE 33-12. Using special driver to drive out left hand shaft from Ford automatic transaxle after right side shaft has been removed. *(Courtesy of Ford Motor Co. of Canada Ltd.)*

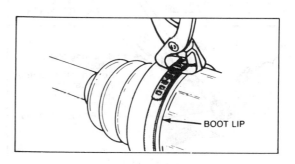

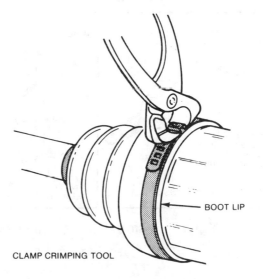

FIGURE 33-13. Removing (top) and installing (bottom) CV joint boot clamps. *(Courtesy of Ford Motor Co. of Canada Ltd.)*

781

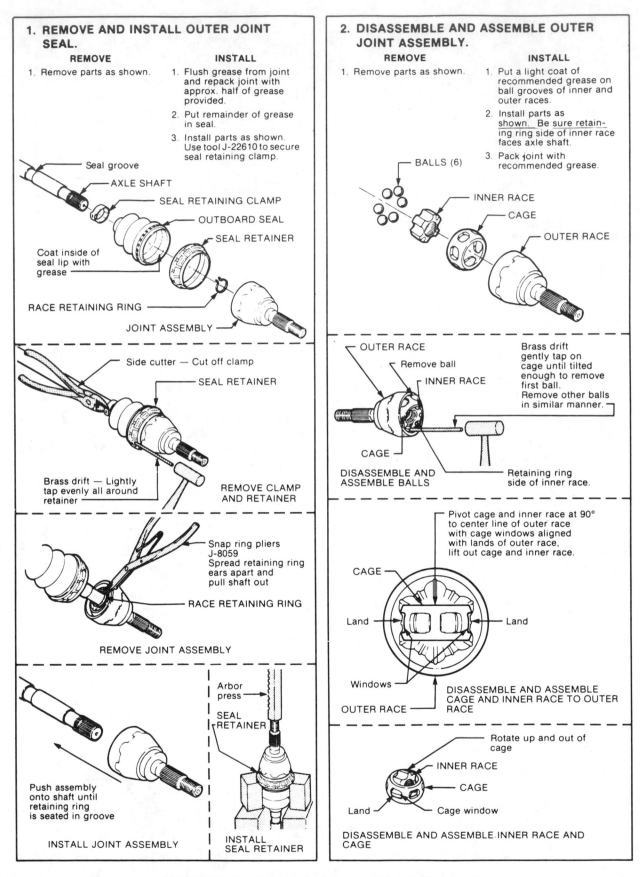

1. REMOVE AND INSTALL OUTER JOINT SEAL.

REMOVE

1. Remove parts as shown.

INSTALL

1. Flush grease from joint and repack joint with approx. half of grease provided.
2. Put remainder of grease in seal.
3. Install parts as shown. Use tool J-22610 to secure seal retaining clamp.

Seal groove

AXLE SHAFT

SEAL RETAINING CLAMP

OUTBOARD SEAL

SEAL RETAINER

Coat inside of seal lip with grease

RACE RETAINING RING

JOINT ASSEMBLY

Side cutter — Cut off clamp

SEAL RETAINER

Brass drift — Lightly tap evenly all around retainer

REMOVE CLAMP AND RETAINER

Snap ring pliers J-8059 Spread retaining ring ears apart and pull shaft out

RACE RETAINING RING

REMOVE JOINT ASSEMBLY

Push assembly onto shaft until retaining ring is seated in groove

INSTALL JOINT ASSEMBLY

Arbor press

SEAL RETAINER

INSTALL SEAL RETAINER

2. DISASSEMBLE AND ASSEMBLE OUTER JOINT ASSEMBLY.

REMOVE

1. Remove parts as shown.

INSTALL

1. Put a light coat of recommended grease on ball grooves of inner and outer races.
2. Install parts as shown. Be sure retaining ring side of inner race faces axle shaft.
3. Pack joint with recommended grease.

BALLS (6)

INNER RACE

CAGE

OUTER RACE

OUTER RACE

Remove ball

INNER RACE

Brass drift gently tap on cage until tilted enough to remove first ball. Remove other balls in similar manner.

CAGE

DISASSEMBLE AND ASSEMBLE BALLS

Retaining ring side of inner race.

Pivot cage and inner race at 90° to center line of outer race with cage windows aligned with lands of outer race, lift out cage and inner race.

CAGE

Land

Land

Windows

OUTER RACE

DISASSEMBLE AND ASSEMBLE CAGE AND INNER RACE TO OUTER RACE

Rotate up and out of cage

INNER RACE

CAGE

Land

Cage window

DISASSEMBLE AND ASSEMBLE INNER RACE AND CAGE

FIGURE 33-14. *(Courtesy of General Motors Corporation)*

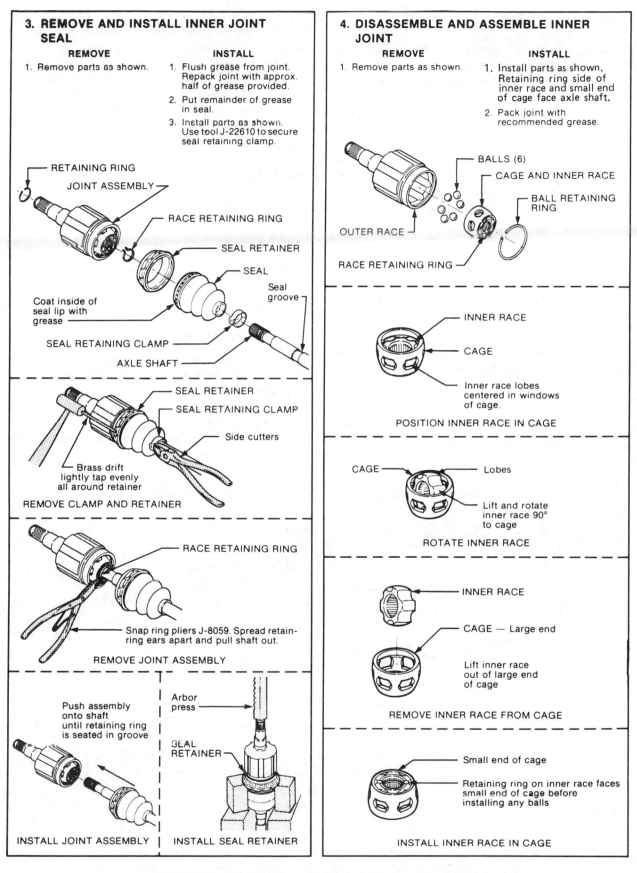

3. REMOVE AND INSTALL INNER JOINT SEAL

REMOVE

1. Remove parts as shown.

INSTALL

1. Flush grease from joint. Repack joint with approx. half of grease provided.
2. Put remainder of grease in seal.
3. Install parts as shown. Use tool J-22610 to secure seal retaining clamp.

- RETAINING RING
- JOINT ASSEMBLY
- RACE RETAINING RING
- SEAL RETAINER
- SEAL
- Seal groove
- Coat inside of seal lip with grease
- SEAL RETAINING CLAMP
- AXLE SHAFT

- SEAL RETAINER
- SEAL RETAINING CLAMP
- Side cutters
- Brass drift lightly tap evenly all around retainer

REMOVE CLAMP AND RETAINER

- RACE RETAINING RING
- Snap ring pliers J-8059. Spread retaining-ring ears apart and pull shaft out.

REMOVE JOINT ASSEMBLY

Push assembly onto shaft until retaining ring is seated in groove

Arbor press

SEAL RETAINER

INSTALL JOINT ASSEMBLY | **INSTALL SEAL RETAINER**

4. DISASSEMBLE AND ASSEMBLE INNER JOINT

REMOVE

1. Remove parts as shown.

INSTALL

1. Install parts as shown. Retaining ring side of inner race and small end of cage face axle shaft.
2. Pack joint with recommended grease.

- BALLS (6)
- CAGE AND INNER RACE
- BALL RETAINING RING
- OUTER RACE
- RACE RETAINING RING

- INNER RACE
- CAGE
- Inner race lobes centered in windows of cage.

POSITION INNER RACE IN CAGE

- CAGE
- Lobes
- Lift and rotate inner race 90° to cage

ROTATE INNER RACE

- INNER RACE
- CAGE — Large end
- Lift inner race out of large end of cage

REMOVE INNER RACE FROM CAGE

- Small end of cage
- Retaining ring on inner race faces small end of cage before installing any balls

INSTALL INNER RACE IN CAGE

FIGURE 33–15. *(Courtesy of General Motors Corporation)*

In each case, loss of lubricant either through the shaft hole or through the inspection cover may be expected. Use a clean pan to catch any escaping lubricant.

Special tools may be required to push or drive out the splined stub axle either from the wheel hub or from the transaxle.

To reassemble, follow the above procedure in reverse order. Typical CV joint disassembly and reassembly is shown in Figures 33–14 and 33–15. Recheck the lubricant level and add some if necessary.

PART 4   DRIVE SHAFTS

The drive line (drive shaft or propeller shaft) must be able to transfer driving torque from the transmission output shaft to the differential under all operating conditions. It should do this smoothly and without any appreciable loss of torque.

Drive Shaft

The one-piece tubular-steel drive shaft with two cross and roller universal joints (one at each end)

mounted in phase is the most common type of shaft in use. The rear-wheel-drive vehicles with the engine mounted in front and an unsprung rear axle known as Hotchkiss drive use this type of drive line.

The torque tube drive used on some older vehicles had an enclosed drive line with a single universal joint at the transmission end of the drive shaft inside a torque ball. This allows the torque tube to pivot with up and down movement of the drive axle assembly. The torque tube encloses the solid-steel drive shaft and is attached solidly to the rear axle without a universal joint.

A two-piece tubular drive shaft with a rubber element pressed between the two tubes, which reduces torsional vibrations, is used on some vehicles.

Four-wheel-drive vehicles use two drive shafts—one to drive the rear axle and one to drive the front axle. Front and rear drive shafts are similar in design.

Universal Joints

Universal joints are required in a drive line for two reasons: (1) the transmission output shaft and the differential pinion shaft are not in a direct line, and (2) the differential on most rear-wheel-drive vehicles moves up and down in relation to the vehicle transmission. If the transmission and differential were in

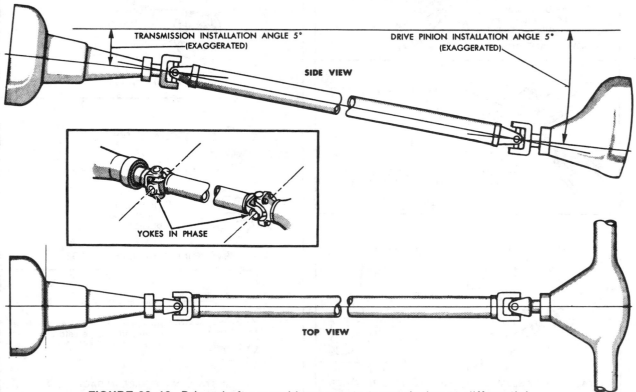

FIGURE 33–16. Drive shaft assembly connects transmission to differential. Note that differential center line and transmission center line are parallel (top) as viewed from the side and in line (bottom) as viewed from above. Note U joint yokes are in "phase" (center) which makes unit deliver torque at constant velocity. *(Courtesy of Ford Motor Co. of Canada Ltd.)*

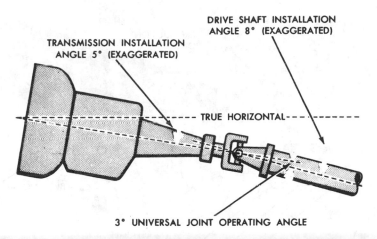

TRANSMISSION INSTALLATION
ANGLE 5° (EXAGGERATED)

DRIVE SHAFT INSTALLATION
ANGLE 8° (EXAGGERATED)

TRUE HORIZONTAL

3° UNIVERSAL JOINT OPERATING ANGLE

FIGURE 33-17. The difference between the transmission installation angle and the drive shaft installation angle is the universal joint operating angle. At the other end of the drive shaft, the universal joint operating angle is the difference between the drive shaft installation angle and the differential installation angle. *(Courtesy of Ford Motor Co. of Canada Ltd.)*

exact alignment with each other and were to remain in this fixed position, driving torque could be transmitted without universal joints.

Drive line universal joints consist of a cross and roller arrangement mounted between two yokes. The drive shaft tube has a yoke at each end. The front of the shaft is connected to an internally splined slip yoke by means of a U joint. The slip yoke is able to slide fore and aft on the transmission output shaft in order to allow rear axle and differential movement to take place.

The rear yoke of the drive shaft is connected to the companion flange (drive flange) of the differential by means of another U joint. A double Cardan

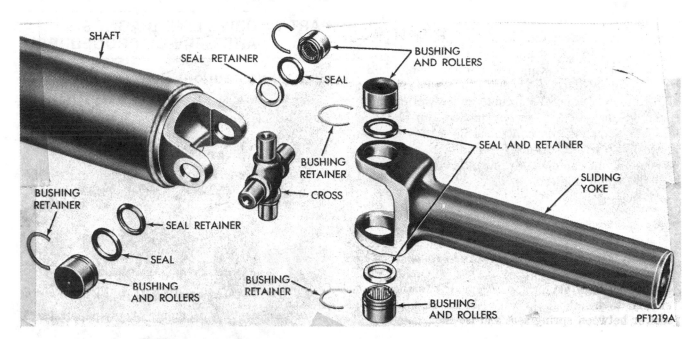

FIGURE 33-18. Typical universal joint components at transmission end of drive shaft. Note sliding slip yoke, which allows effective length of drive shaft to change as rear-drive wheels move up and down in relation to vehicle body. The effective length of the drive shaft also changes because of the effects of driving and braking torque on the rear axle. As the vehicle accelerates, driving torque will cause the front of the differential to rise, while braking torque reaction will cause the front of the differential to dip down. The slip yoke accommodates the changes in drive length required as a result of this action. *(Courtesy of Chrysler Corporation)*

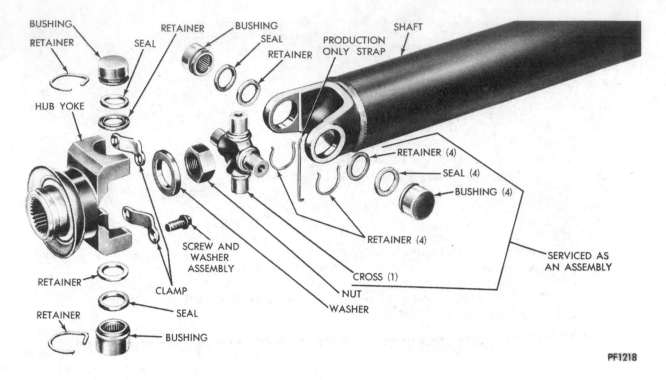

FIGURE 33-19. Typical universal joint components at differential end of drive shaft. *(Courtesy of Chrysler Corporation)*

or double cross and roller universal joint is used on some vehicles to accommodate a more severe U-joint operating angle, (constant velocity joint).

The correct operating angle of a universal joint must be maintained in order to prevent drive line vibration and damage. Shimming of leaf springs and control arms (on coil spring suspension) and adjustable eccentrics on control arms allows for adjustment to specifications. Shimming at the transmission mount can also be done on some vehicles to change U-joint angles.

PART 5 DRIVE LINE DIAGNOSIS AND SERVICE PROCEDURE

General Precautions

• Place vehicle safely on stands or hoist for under-vehicle work.

• Make sure problem is in drive line before proceeding with drive line removal.

• Do all in-shop drive line diagnosing (vehicle running) with vehicle at normal curb weight and

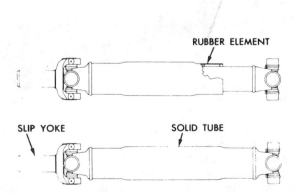

FIGURE 33-20. Drive shaft with rubber element between two connecting tubes (above) and one-piece tubular shaft (bottom). *(Courtesy of General Motors Corporation)*

FIGURE 33-21. Constant velocity universal joint is able to operate at a more severe angle than single cross and roller U joint. *(Courtesy of General Motors Corporation)*

PROBLEM	CAUSE	CORRECTION
Leak at front slip yoke. (An occasional drop of lubricant leaking from splined yoke is normal and requires no attention.)	1. Rough outside surface on splined yoke. 2. Defective transmission rear oil seal.	1. Replace seal if cut by burrs on yoke. Minor burrs can be smoothed by careful use of crocus cloth. Replace yoke if outside surface is rough or burred badly. 2. Replace transmission rear oil seal. Bring transmission oil up to proper level after correction.
Knock in drive line, clunking noise when car is operated under floating condition in high gear or neutral at low speeds.	1. Worn or damaged universal joints. 2. Differential noise.	1. Replace universal joints or yokes as needed. 2. Correct as required.
Ping, snap, or click in drive line. (Usually occurs on initial load application after transmission has been put into gear, either forward or reverse.)	1. Loose or worn U joints.	1. Replace.
Roughness usually at low speeds, light load, 15 to 35 mph.	1. Improper joint angles. Usually rear joint angle is too large. 2. Improperly adjusted front joint angle.	1. Check rear trim height at curb weight. Check rear joint angle and correct. 2. Correct by shimming transmission support.
Scraping noise.	1. Slinger, pinion flange, or end yoke rubbing on rear axle carrier.	1. Straighten slinger to remove interference.
Roughness above 35 mph felt and/or heard.	1. Tires unbalanced or worn. 2. Bent drive shaft.	1. Balance or replace as required. 2. Replace drive shaft.
Squeak.	1. Lack of lubricant in universal joint.	1. Replace universal joint.
Shudder on acceleration, low speed.	1. Incorrectly set front joint angle.	1. Shim transmission support mount to correct front joint angle.
Vibration in drive line.	1. Worn transmission extension housing bushing.	1. Replace bushing and yoke as needed.

height. (Vehicle should be supported under axle housing.) Consult vehicle manufacturer's manual for proper lift points and diagnostic procedures.

• Be careful of oil running out of transmission when slip yoke is removed, or gear oil when differential drive flange is removed. Correct fluid levels after repairs have been made.

• Never distort drive shaft by clamping in vise and overtightening.

• Never collapse or distort universal joint yokes while removing or installing U-joint bearing cups. Use proper support for yoke during this operation.

• Beware of needle bearings dropping out of place during assembly and preventing bearing cups from being properly installed.

• Be sure bearing cups are inside of alignment lugs on differential drive flange yoke before tightening clamp bolts.

• Always lubricate yoke externally and internally on splines with recommended lubricant before assembly.

• Tighten all bolts to specifications.

Checking Drive Shaft Run-out

If a noise or vibration is present at high speed, which might be caused by a bent shaft, or if a shaft has been damaged through rough handling or a collision, it may be checked for straightness as follows:

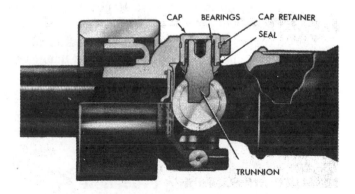

FIGURE 33–22. Inertia ring or torsional damper ring absorbs torsional vibration. Note absence of bearing retaining snap rings. Bearings are held in place by injection-molded plastic at cap retainer. *(Courtesy of General Motors Corporation)*

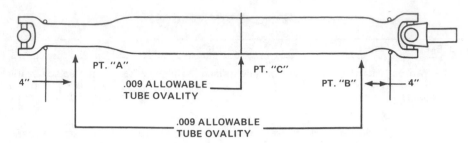

FIGURE 33-23. Points at which drive shaft run-out should be checked with dial indicator. Refer to appropriate service manual for run-out limits for any specific vehicle. *(Courtesy of General Motors Corporation)*

1. Raise vehicle on a twin post hoist so that the rear is supported on the rear axle housing with wheels free to rotate.

2. Mount a dial indicator on a movable support that is high enough to permit contact of the indicator button with the propeller shaft, or mount dial indicator to a magnetic base and attach to a suitable smooth place on the underbody of the vehicle. Readings are to be taken at points indicated in Figure 33-23.

3. With transmission in neutral, check for run-out by turning a rear wheel so the propeller shaft will rotate.

Notice: For different cars there may be different drive shafts used. Specifications for run-out are different on different shafts. See service manual for specifications. Care must be taken not to include indicator variation caused by ridges, flat spots, or other surface variations in the tube.

4. If run-out exceeds specifications, rotate the shaft 180° at companion flange and reinstall. Check run-out again.

5. If run-out is still over specifications at one or more locations, replace the drive shaft, but only after checking vibration or noise. Replacement shaft must be rechecked for run-out also.

6. If the new drive shaft run-out is still over specifications, check for a bent companion flange or slip yoke. Refer to balancing procedure if noise or vibration persists.

Run-out specifications vary depending on vehicle make and model from approximately .020 inch (0.50 mm) to .045 inch (1.27 mm).

Drive Shaft Balancing Procedure

Hose Clamp Method

1. Place the car on a twin post hoist so that the rear of the car is supported on the rear axle housing and the rear wheels are free to rotate. Remove both rear tire and wheel assemblies and reinstall wheel lug nuts with flat side next to drum.

2. Mark and number propeller shaft at four (4) points 90 degrees apart at rear of shaft just forward of balance weight.

3. Install two (2) hose clamps on the rear of the propeller shaft, and slide them rearward until the clamps stop at the nearest balance weight welded to the tube. Align both clamps to any one of the four marks made on shaft in Step 2. Tighten the clamps (see Figure 33-24). Be sure sufficient clearance is maintained so that clamp heads do not contact floor pan of car when axle is in contact with rebound bumper in frame. In order to gain sufficient clearance, it may be necessary to position the clamps over the balance weights.

4. Run the car through the speed range to 50-55 mph. (81-89 km/h). Note amount of unbalance. *Caution:* Never run car higher than 55 mph (89 km/h). Also, all personnel should stay clear of driveline.

5. Loosen clamps and rotate clamp heads 90 degrees to the next mark on shaft. Tighten clamps and repeat Step 4.

6. Repeat Step 5 until car has been run with clamp heads located at all four marks on shaft.

7. Position clamps at point of minimum unbalance. Rotate the clamp heads away from each other 45 degrees. (One each way from the point of minimum unbalance.) Run the car and note if unbalance has improved. In some cases, it may be necessary to use one clamp or possibly three clamps in order to obtain a good balance. Replace shaft if three hose clamps do not improve the imbalance.

8. Continue to rotate the clamps apart in smaller angular increments until the car feel for unbalance is best. Do not run car on hoist for extended periods due to danger of overheating the transmission or engine.

9. Reinstall tire and wheel assemblies and road test the car for final check of balance. Vibration felt

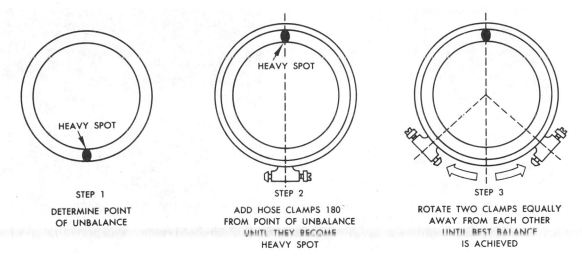

STEP 1
DETERMINE POINT
OF UNBALANCE

STEP 2
ADD HOSE CLAMPS 180°
FROM POINT OF UNBALANCE
UNTIL THEY BECOME
HEAVY SPOT

STEP 3
ROTATE TWO CLAMPS EQUALLY
AWAY FROM EACH OTHER
UNTIL BEST BALANCE
IS ACHIEVED

FIGURE 33-24. Typical method of positioning screw-type hose clamps to achieve drive shaft balance. *(Courtesy of General Motors Corporation)*

in the car on the hoist may not show up in a road test, which is the final determining factor.

Removal of Drive Shaft

Warning: Do not pound on original propeller shaft yoke ears as injection joints may fracture.

There are two methods of attachment of the rear of the drive shaft to the differential pinion flange or end yoke.

1. Raise vehicle on hoist. Mark relationship of shaft to pinion flange and disconnect the rear universal joint by removing straps or U-bolts. If bearing cups are loose, tape together to prevent dropping and loss of bearing rollers.

2. Withdraw propeller shaft slip yoke from transmission by moving shaft rearward, passing it under the axle housing. Do not allow drive shaft to drop or allow universal joints to bend to an extreme

angle, as this might fracture the joint internally. Support propeller shaft during removal.

Disassembly of Universal Joints

1. Position propeller shaft and press adapter in press equipped with base plate and ram adapter. Remove all bearing retaining snap rings.

2. Actuate the pump to force the spider and bearing out. (On injection-moulded joints this will cause the plastic to shear.) Remove the bearing.

3. Release pump valve; rotate propeller shaft 1/2 revolution and install spider guide into yoke bore of removed bearing and onto the journal end of the spider.

4. Position propeller shaft as before and use spider press and power ram hydraulic pump to shear

FIGURE 33-25. Removing U-joint bearing cups in an arbor press. *(Courtesy of General Motors Corporation)*

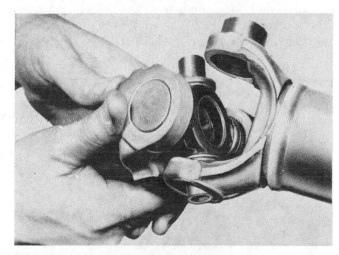

FIGURE 33-26. Removing or installing universal joint and yoke assembly. *(Courtesy of General Motors Corporation)*

789

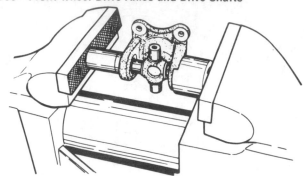

FIGURE 33-27. Installing U-joint bearing using a bench vise and socket. *(Courtesy of Chrysler Corporation)*

the nylon injection ring; remove the opposite bearing.

The above procedures should also be used to disassemble the front universal joint.

Once a production universal joint of the injection-moulded type is disassembled, it cannot be reassembled as there are no snap ring grooves provided in the bearing cap. A replacement kit must be used.

This procedure can also be done in a properly supported vise and using the required adapters. Appropriate sized sockets can sometimes be used as adapters. The following procedure can be used similarly for assembly in a bench vise.

Assembly of Universal Joints

When reassembling a propeller shaft, install complete universal joint repair kits which include a spider, four bearing assemblies, spacers, seals, and shields. The four bearings come equipped with snap rings.

1. Make certain the shields and seals are in firm position and not damaged on the spider and install the spider in the yoke. The spider may face in either direction if there is no grease fitting.

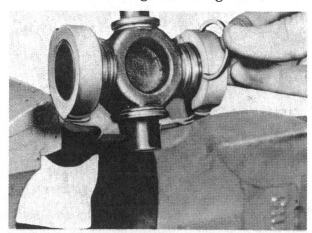

FIGURE 33-28. Typical U-joint retaining clip installation. *(Courtesy of General Motors Corporation)*

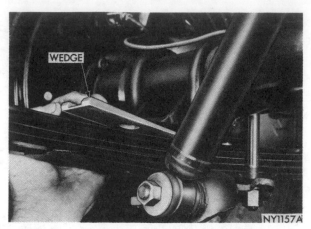

FIGURE 33-29. Tapered wedge can be used between rear leaf spring and axle housing to correct rear universal joint operating angle. *(Courtesy of Chrysler Corporation)*

2. Install spider guide into one yoke bore and position spider journal into the guide. Push guide in far enough for opposite journal to extend slightly above yoke bore. Spider journals and bearings must be free of dirt and foreign material.

3. Place the propeller shaft and yoke assembly in position in the press. Inspect bearing cup to see that all needle bearings are in place and properly lubricated. Make certain the plastic washer is in place against the needle bearings. Position bearing straight over yoke bore and onto spider journal. Failure to pilot the spider journal into the bearing could cause the bearing needles to become dislodged during installation of the bearing cup.

With the pump, force the bearing into the yoke. As the bearing nears the end of its required travel it will cause the spider to push the guide outward without damage to the seal or shield. The bearing cup is properly positioned in the yoke when the snap ring groove is exposed enough to install the snap ring. When the bearing is correctly positioned in the yoke, turn the assembly over, remove the guide, and again place bearing over the bore in the yoke.

Carefully slide the spider partially out of the previously seated bearing and start it carefully into the bearing being installed. This prevents the bearing needles from burring the edge of the spider journal if forced over journal other than straight. Even slight burring of the journal can cause premature failure.

While pressing the bearings into position, move the spider back and forth to make certain that the spider journals engage the bearings squarely. This avoids damage and binding. If binding exists, remove the bearings and spider and examine for dislodged rollers or damaged journals.

If excessive resistance is encountered, the bearings should be removed as this is an indication that one or more of the needles are out of place.

4. While observing the previous precautions, install the balance of the bearings necessary to complete the assembly and install snap rings.

5. Strike the yoke firmly with a hammer to fully seat the snap rings against the yoke. Turn the spider to make certain that it is free.

Installation of Drive Shaft

The propeller shaft must be supported carefully during handling to avoid jamming or bending any of the parts.

1. Inspect outer diameter of splined yoke to ensure that it is not burred, as this will damage transmission seal. Inspect splines of slip yoke for damage.

2. Apply engine oil to all splined propeller shaft yokes; then, slide yoke and drive shaft assembly onto transmission output shaft.

Notice: Do not drive the propeller shaft into place with a hammer. Check for burrs on transmission output shaft spline, twisted slip yoke splines, or possibly the wrong U-joint yoke. Make sure that the splines agree in number and fit. To prevent trunnion seal damage, do not place any tool between yoke and splines.

When making rear shaft connections, be sure to align mark on pinion flange or end yoke with mark on drive shaft.

3. Position rear universal joint to rear axle pinion flange; make sure bearings are properly seated in pinion flange yoke.

4. Install rear joint fasteners and tighten evenly to torque specified.

Notice: The propeller shaft to pinion flange or end yoke fasteners are important attaching parts in that they may affect the performance of vital components and systems, which may result in major repair expense. They must be replaced with one of the same part number or with an equivalent part, if replacement becomes necessary. Do not use a replacement part of lesser quality or substitute design. Torque values must be used as specified during reassembly to assure proper retention of these parts.

PART 6   SELF-CHECK

1. State the purpose of front-wheel drive axles.
2. Front-wheel drive axles do not change their effective length during operation. True or false.
3. What type of universal joints are used in front-wheel drive axles?
4. What is the purpose of a rear-wheel drive slip yoke?
5. What factors determine rear-wheel drive shaft U-joint operating angle?
6. Describe briefly how to balance a rear-wheel drive shaft with hose clamps.

PART 7   TEST QUESTIONS

1. Mechanic A says the drive line slip yoke is designed to slip when overloaded. Mechanic B says the slip yoke allows the shaft to change its effective length. Who is right?
   (a) Mechanic A
   (b) Mechanic B
   (c) both A and B
   (d) neither A nor B

2. Front-drive axle CV joints must accommodate the following:
   (a) changes in effective length of drive axle
   (b) changes in steering wheels left to right
   (c) changes in suspension height
   (d) all of the above

3. The front-drive axle is connected to the drive wheel hub by means of:
   (a) splines
   (b) a woodruff key
   (c) a cotter pin
   (d) all of the above

4. CV joint boots:
   (a) are designed to contain lubricant
   (b) prevent entry of dirt
   (c) must be replaced when punctured
   (d) all of the above

5. Rear-wheel drive shaft vibration may be caused by:
   (a) a bent shaft
   (b) a worn universal joint
   (c) an unbalanced shaft
   (d) all of the above

Chapter 34

Differentials

Performance Objectives

After sufficient study of this chapter, the necessary practical experience on the appropriate training models, and with the necessary tools, equipment, and shop manuals, you should be able to do the following:

1. Complete the self-check and test questions with at least 80 percent accuracy.

2. Describe the purpose, construction, and operation of: (a) the standard differential, (b) the limited slip differential.

3. Diagnose differential problems accurately.

4. Correctly service, remove, repair, replace, and adjust differentials and components to manufacturer's specifications.

5. Adequately test differential to determine the success of the service performed.

6. Prepare the vehicle for customer acceptance.

PART 1 COMPONENTS AND OPERATING REQUIREMENTS

A differential is needed between any two drive wheels whether in a rear-wheel-drive axle, a front-wheel-drive transaxle, or the front-drive axle on a four-wheel-drive vehicle. The reason it is needed is because the two drive wheels must turn at different speeds when the vehicle is in a turn.

A differential is a set of gears arranged to divide the driving torque between the two drive axle shafts. It also includes a gear reduction between the drive shaft and the axle shafts.

The standard differential consists of a drive pinion and ring gear, a differential case or cage, differential pinions and shaft, and side gears or axle gears. The entire arrangement is enclosed in a differential carrier (housing).

The ring gear is bolted to the flange of the differential case, which is supported in the carrier by two side bearings. The drive pinion drives the ring gear and case. A small shaft mounted in the case supports two pinion gears. The pinion gears are in mesh with the two side or axle gears, and the axle gears are splined to the axle shafts.

In operation, the rotating differential case causes the small pinion shaft and pinion gears to rotate end over end with the case. Since the pinion gears are in mesh with the side gears, the side gears and axle shafts are also forced to rotate. This is what happens during straight-ahead vehicle motion when both wheels have adequate traction.

When the vehicle turns a corner, the inner wheel travels a shorter distance (smaller circle) than the outer wheel. When this happens the inner wheel axle gear is forced to slow down. This causes the small

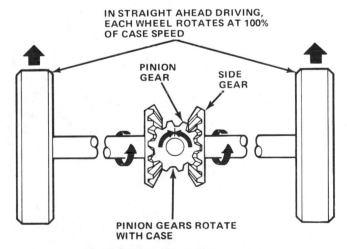

IN STRAIGHT AHEAD DRIVING, EACH WHEEL ROTATES AT 100% OF CASE SPEED

PINION GEAR

SIDE GEAR

PINION GEARS ROTATE WITH CASE

FIGURE 34–1. Differential action in straight ahead driving. (*Courtesy of American Motors Corporation*)

793

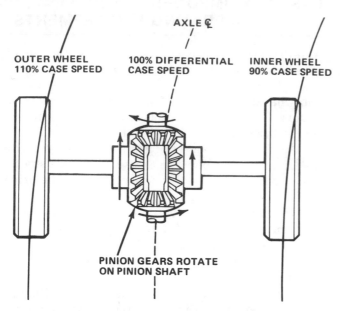

FIGURE 34-2. Differential action when turning a corner. *(Courtesy of American Motors Corporation)*

differential pinion gears to "walk" around the slower turning axle gear. This results in these pinion gears rotating on the pinion shaft. This rotational torque is transmitted to the outer wheel side gear, causing

it to turn faster, but still providing equal torque to both wheels.

When one of the driving wheels has little or no traction, the torque required to turn the wheel without traction is very low. The wheel with good traction is in effect "holding" the axle gear on that side stationary. This causes the pinions to walk around the stationary side gear and drive the other wheel at twice the normal speed but without any vehicle movement.

With one wheel stationary, the other wheel turns at twice the speed shown on the speedometer. Excessive spinning of one wheel can cause severe damage to the differential. The small pinion gears can actually become welded to the pinion shaft or differential case.

There are two types of solid axle housings: the removable carrier type and the integral type. The removable carrier type has a differential carrier assembly that is removable from the front of the housing. The integral type of drive axle assembly consists of a housing and differential carrier assembly that are integral (carrier not removable). On this unit the differential is removed from the rear of the housing. In the transaxle assembly, the differential and final drive are enclosed in the same housing as the transmission or in a separate housing bolted to the transaxle housing.

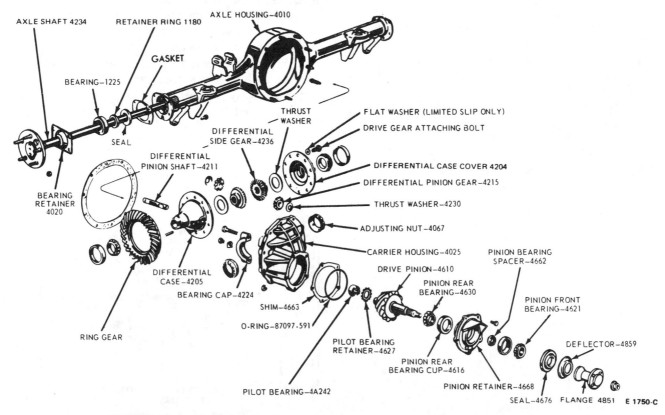

FIGURE 34-3. Exploded view of removable carrier type of rear axle assembly. *(Courtesy of Ford Motor Co. of Canada Ltd.)*

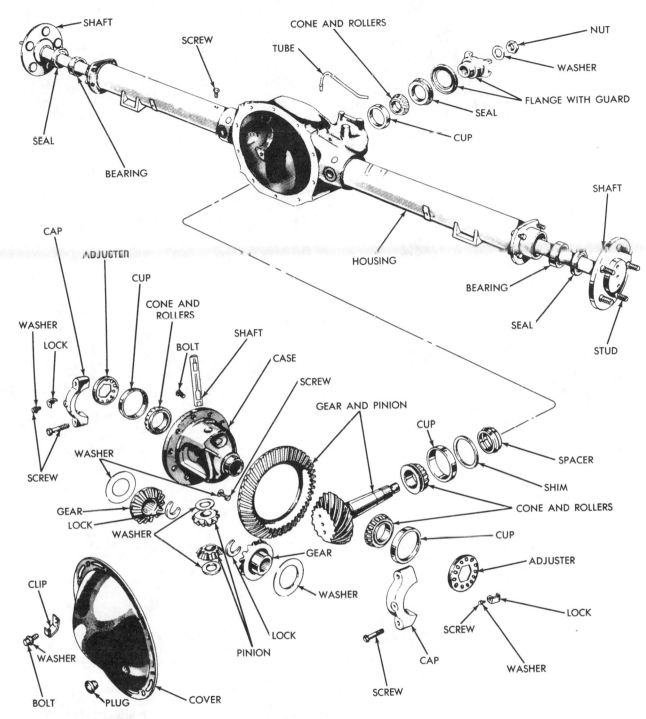

FIGURE 34-4. Integral carrier type of rear axle (exploded view). *(Courtesy of Chrysler Corporation)*

PART 2   DIFFERENTIAL GEARS

The differential drive pinion or gear and ring gear are a matched set and should not be interchanged with gears from another set. There are two types of differential gears: spiral bevel gears and hypoid gears.

The *spiral bevel gear* has the drive pinion center line intersect with the center line through the ring gear. The hypoid gearset has the pinion mounted well below the center line of the ring gear. The *hypoid gearset* is the most common type of differential gearing used in passenger cars.

Hypoid gears are quiet running, allow several teeth to absorb the driving force, and allow a lower hump in the floor of the vehicle body. The teeth are curved, causing a wiping action during meshing. The inner end of the teeth on the ring gear is known as the *toe* and the outer end of the teeth as the *heel* of

795

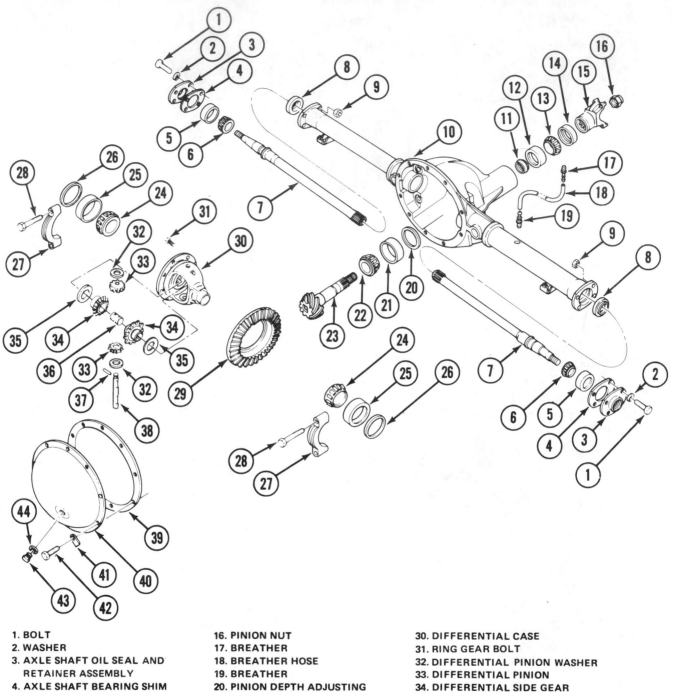

1. BOLT
2. WASHER
3. AXLE SHAFT OIL SEAL AND RETAINER ASSEMBLY
4. AXLE SHAFT BEARING SHIM
5. AXLE SHAFT BEARING CUP
6. AXLE SHAFT BEARING
7. AXLE SHAFT
8. AXLE SHAFT INNER OIL SEAL
9. NUT
10. AXLE HOUSING
11. COLLAPSIBLE SPACER
12. PINION BEARING CUP-FRONT
13. PINION BEARING-FRONT
14. PINION OIL SEAL
15. UNIVERSAL JOINT YOKE

16. PINION NUT
17. BREATHER
18. BREATHER HOSE
19. BREATHER
20. PINION DEPTH ADJUSTING SHIM
21. PINION REAR BEARING CUP
22. PINION BEARING-REAR
23. PINION GEAR
24. DIFFERENTIAL BEARING
25. DIFFERENTIAL BEARING CUP
26. DIFFERENTIAL BEARING SHIM
27. DIFFERENTIAL BEARING CAP
28. DIFFERENTIAL BEARING CAP BOLT
29. RING GEAR

30. DIFFERENTIAL CASE
31. RING GEAR BOLT
32. DIFFERENTIAL PINION WASHER
33. DIFFERENTIAL PINION
34. DIFFERENTIAL SIDE GEAR
35. DIFFERENTIAL SIDE GEAR THRUST WASHER
36. DIFFERENTIAL PINION SHAFT THRUST BLOCK
37. DIFFERENTIAL PINION SHAFT PIN
38. DIFFERENTIAL PINION SHAFT
39. AXLE HOUSING COVER GASKET
40. AXLE HOUSING COVER
41. AXLE IDENTIFICATION TAG
42. BOLT
43. AXLE HOUSING COVER FILL PLUG
44. WASHER

FIGURE 34-5. Integral carrier type rear axle and differential components. *(Courtesy of American Motors Corporation)*

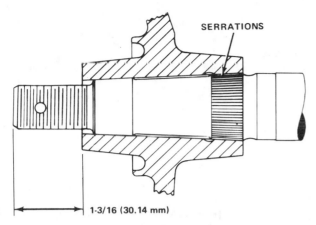

SERRATIONS

1-3/16 (30.14 mm)

FIGURE 34-6. Drive wheel hub and axle shaft mounting detail for rear axle shown in Figure 34-5. *(Courtesy of American Motors Corporation)*

the teeth. The *drive* side of the teeth is curved in a convex shape, while the *coast* side of the teeth is concave.

While engine torque is being applied to the drive pinion, the pinion teeth exert pressure on the drive or convex side of the ring gear teeth. During coast or engine braking, the concave side of the ring gear teeth exerts pressure on the drive pinion. When there is no torque being applied either in drive or in coast, the condition is known as *float.*

Upon heavy acceleration the drive pinion attempts to climb up the ring gear and raises the front of the differential. A rubber bumper between the car body and differential prevents metal-to-metal contact on heavy acceleration or when the vehicle is heavily loaded and accelerated. Normally, the leaf springs or the torque arms on coil spring suspension absorb the torque.

The drive pinion is commonly mounted in either of two ways: (1) straddle mounted or (2) over-hung mounted. The *straddle-mounted pinion* has two opposed tapered roller bearings close together with a short spacer between the inner races ahead of the pinion gear and a third bearing, usually a straight roller bearing, supporting the rear of the pinion gear.

The *overhung mounted pinion* has two opposed tapered roller bearings somewhat farther apart than the bearings on the straddle-mounted type but no third bearing. The two roller bearings must be farther apart to provide adequate pinion support since there is no third bearing behind the pinion gear.

A *collapsible spacer* is used between the two large tapered roller bearings to provide for proper pinion bearing preload. Some differentials use a solid noncollapsible spacer with selective thickness shims to adjust pinion bearing preload. When the pinion shaft nut is tightened, pressure is exerted by the pinion drive flange against the inner race of the front pinion bearing. This applies pressure against the

spacer and the rear bearing, which cannot move because it is located against the drive pinion. When the nut is tightened to specifications, a slight load is placed on the two pinion bearings. This assures that there will be no pinion shaft end play.

During drive the angle on the gear teeth attempts to move the pinion forward, and during coast it tries to move to the rear. If there is any pinion shaft end play, the result is a "walking" pinion (fore and aft moving pinion) and rapid gear and bearing wear.

Differential gears are also classified as *nonhunting, partial nonhunting,* and *hunting gears.* During assembly the nonhunting and partial nonhunting gears must be assembled with the timing marks properly aligned. The reason for this is that during manufacture they have been *lapped,* and since specified teeth on the pinion will always meet specific teeth on the ring gear (owing to the gear ratios), a noisy gear will result if not properly timed.

All ratios ending in .00 (3.00:1, 4.00:1) are nonhunting gears and must be timed. All ratios with a .50 ending (3.50:1, 4.50:1) are partial nonhunting gears and must also be timed. All gear ratios that do not fall into the above categories are called hunting gears and need not be timed.

The *differential case* is supported in the carrier by two tapered roller side bearings. This assembly can be adjusted from side to side to provide (1) the proper backlash between the ring gear and pinion and (2) the required side bearing preload. This adjustment is achieved by threaded bearing adjusters on some units and selective shims and spacers on others.

Transaxle Final Drive Gears and Differential

The transaxle final drive gears provide the means for transmitting transmission output torque to the differential section of the transaxle. The final drive gears include the drive pinion connected to the transmission output and the differential drive gear attached to the differential case. The drive pinion and drive gear provide a gear reduction from approximately 3 to 1 to 3.8 to 1, depending on design.

Final drive gear designs include the helical type, the spiral bevel type, and the chain drive. The angled teeth of both gear designs provide the wiping action of meshing gear teeth that results in quiet operation.

The differential section of the transaxle has the same components as the differential gears described earlier and operates in a similar manner. On some models, the differential and final drive gears operate

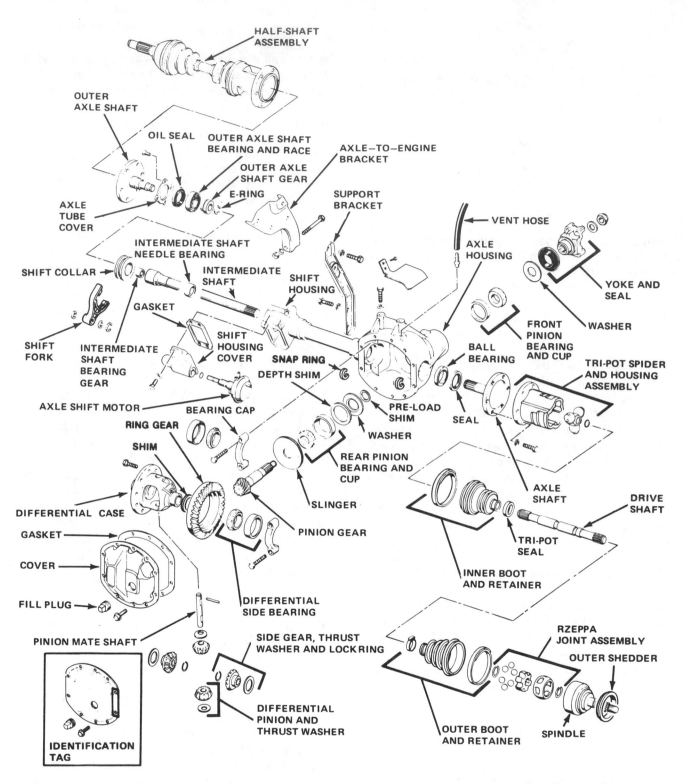

FIGURE 34-7. Select drive system front axle and differential components used on American Motors four-wheel drive. Note shift motor and shift mechanism to engage and disengage front drive. *(Courtesy of American Motors Corporation)*

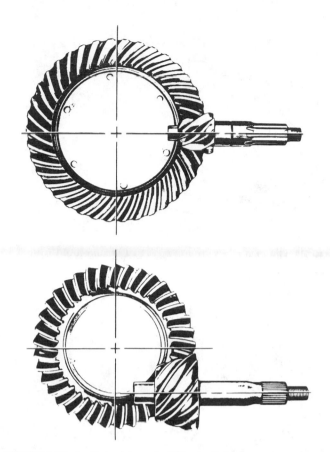

FIGURE 34-8. Spiral bevel differential gears (top) and hypoid gears (bottom). *(Courtesy of Ford Motor Co. of Canada Ltd.)*

in the same lubricant as the transmission section of the transaxle. On other designs, the differential section is separately enclosed and operates in different lubricant than does the transmission section. Adequate sealing is provided between the differential and transmission sections to contain the different lubricants. Seals between the differential and the drive axles are provided to prevent lubricant leakage past the drive axles.

For more information on manual transaxles, see Chapters 36 and 37; for automatic transaxles, see Chapters 38 and 39.

PART 3 LIMITED SLIP DIFFERENTIALS

The limited slip unit performs an additional function over standard differentials; that is, it provides more driving force to the wheel with traction when one wheel begins to spin. Therefore, it modifies load-equalizing action with certain amounts of speed-equalizing action to enhance vehicle capability and operation.

With a standard differential, if one wheel is on a slippery surface, such as ice, snow, or mud, and the other wheel is on dry ground, the wheel on the slippery surface would spin and the other would not drive the car. A limited slip unit would drive the wheel with traction and reduce the possibility of becoming immobile.

Limited slip differentials fall into two categories: those with clutch plates and those with clutch cones. Both units perform the same task. The differential cases are similar to standard cases except for a large internal recess in the area of each side gear. This recess accepts either a clutch pack or a clutch cone depending on design.

The clutch pack consists of clutch discs and plates. The clutch discs are splined to the side gear, and the clutch plates are tanged and fit into the case. The discs rotate with the side gear and the plates with the differential case. In the other unit, the cone is splined to the axle shaft, and it rotates with the side gear only.

A preload spring or springs provide the necessary clutch apply pressure to provide drive to both axles and wheels during unequal traction on the drive wheels. The spring tension is low enough to allow clutch slippage on the inner drive axle when turning corners.

Drive Axle Shafts and Bearings

On solid drive axles the inner end of the axle shafts is splined to the axle side gears of the differential and the outer end of the shaft has a flange to mount the wheel. The inner end of the shaft is supported through the side gear in the differential case, and the outer end is supported by a bearing between the axle and axle housing. A seal and retaining plate prevent lubricant leakage.

The axle endwise movement is controlled by a C-type retainer on the inner end of the axle shaft or by a bearing retainer and retaining plate at the outer end of the axle shaft. Axle bearing types include ball bearings, tapered roller bearings (both with an inner race), and a straight roller bearing that uses the axle shaft as the inner race.

Transaxle drive axles usually have two universal joints to allow independent front wheel movement and steering of the wheels. These U joints also allow for lengthening and shortening of the axle drive shafts as the wheels move up and down. See Chapter 29, Parts 3 and 4 and Chapter 34 for more on drive axles.

Differential Lubricants

Hypoid gears require hypoid gear lubricant of the extreme pressure type. Gear lube viscosity is generally SAE 75 to 90. Limited slip differentials require special limited slip lubricant, which provides

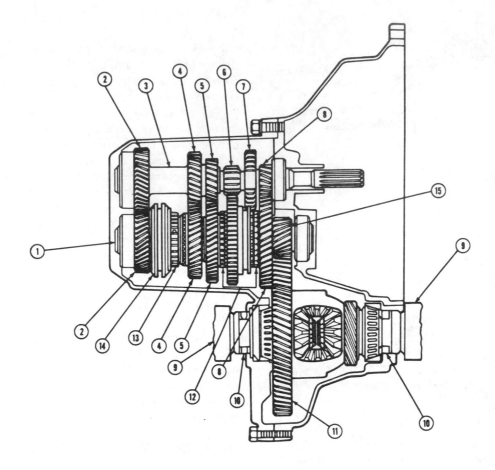

LEGEND:

1. MAINSHAFT
2. 4TH SPEED GEARS
3. INPUT CLUSTER
4. 3RD SPEED GEARS
5. 2ND SPEED GEARS
6. REVERSE GEAR
7. REVERSE IDLER GEAR
8. 1ST SPEED GEARS

9. HALF SHAFTS
10. DIFFERENTIAL OIL SEALS
11. FINAL DRIVE RING GEAR
12. 1ST/2ND SPEED SYNCHRONIZER
    BLOCKER RINGS
13. 3RD/4TH SPEED SYNCHRONIZER HUB
14. 3RD/4TH SPEED SYNCHRONIZER SLEEVE
15. PINION GEAR – PART OF MAINSHAFT

FIGURE 34-9. Manual transaxle and differential gear component relationship. Bottom section shows differential. *(Courtesy of Ford Motor Co. of Canada Ltd.)*

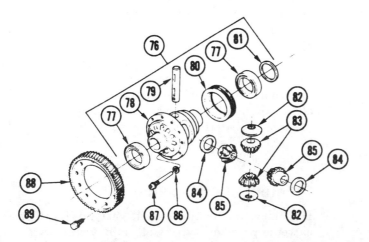

76. **DIFFERENTIAL ASSEMBLY**
77. **BEARING ASSEMBLY,** Differential
78. **CASE,** Differential
79. **SHAFT,** Differential Pinion
80. **GEAR,** Speedo Drive
81. **SHIM,** Differential Bearing Adjustment
82. **WASHER,** Pinion Thrust
83. **GEAR,** Differential Pinion
84. **WASHER,** Side Gear Thrust
85. **GEAR,** Differential Side
86. **LOCKWASHER**
87. **SCREW,** Pinion Shaft
88. **GEAR,** Differential Ring
89. **BOLT**

FIGURE 34-10. Transaxle differential components. *(Courtesy of General Motors Corporation)*

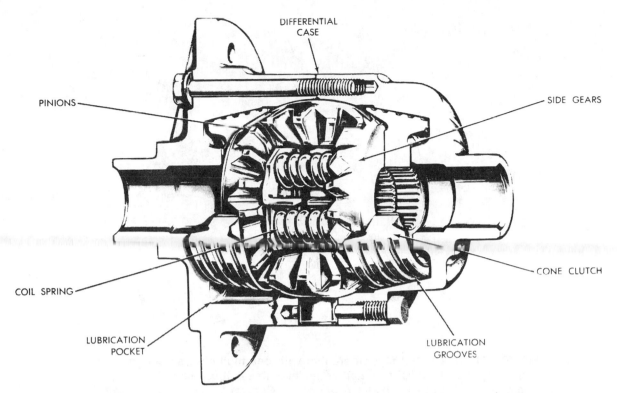

FIGURE 34–11. Cone type of limited slip differential using coil type of preload springs. *(Courtesy of Chrysler Corporation)*

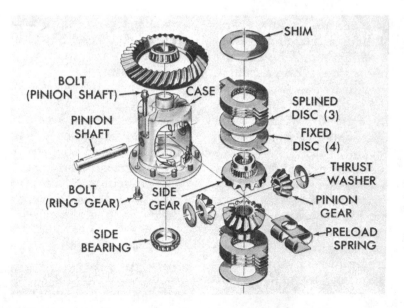

FIGURE 34–12. Limited slip differential with two multiple-disc clutch packs and wave type of preload spring. *(Courtesy of General Motors Corporation)*

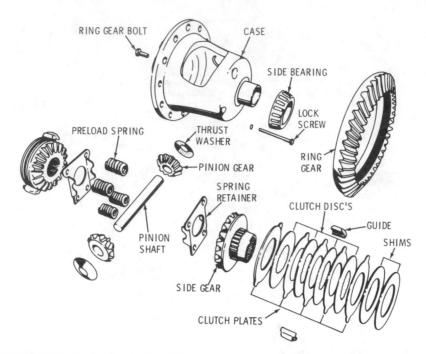

RING GEAR BOLT

CASE

SIDE BEARING

LOCK SCREW

PRELOAD SPRING

THRUST WASHER

PINION GEAR

RING GEAR

SPRING RETAINER

CLUTCH DISC'S

GUIDE

SHIMS

PINION SHAFT

SIDE GEAR

CLUTCH PLATES

FIGURE 34-13. Limited slip differential with one multiple-disc clutch pack and coil-type preload springs. Earlier model of this unit used a Belleville type of preload spring (dished plate). *(Courtesy of General Motors Corporation)*

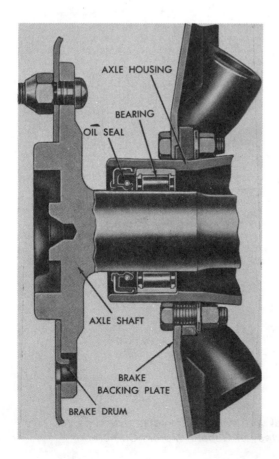

AXLE HOUSING

BEARING

OIL SEAL

AXLE SHAFT

BRAKE BACKING PLATE

BRAKE DRUM

FIGURE 34-14. Typical drive axle bearing and seal arrangement. Note bearing rollers operate directly on axle shaft surface. Axle shaft is held in place by C lock at inner end of axle shaft. *(Courtesy of General Motors Corporation)*

FIGURE 34-15. Removing pinion shaft lock screw and pinion shaft from differential. This must be done before C locks can be removed from inner end of drive axles. *(Courtesy of General Motors Corporation)*

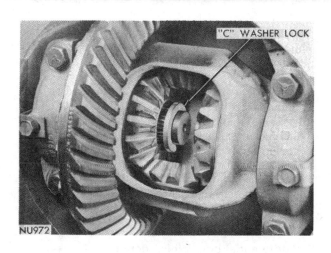

FIGURE 34-16. Drive axle shaft has been pushed into differential far enough to allow removal of C lock from axle shaft. *(Courtesy of Chrysler Corporation)*

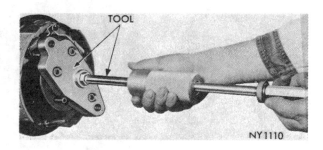

FIGURE 34-17. Removing drive axle shaft with slide-hammer type of puller. *(Courtesy of Chrysler Corporation)*

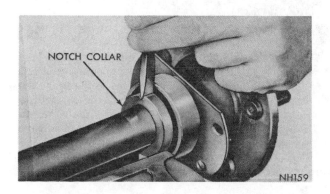

FIGURE 34-18. Removing axle bearing retainer from axle shaft to allow removal of axle bearing and axle retaining plate. *(Courtesy of Chrysler Corporation)*

803

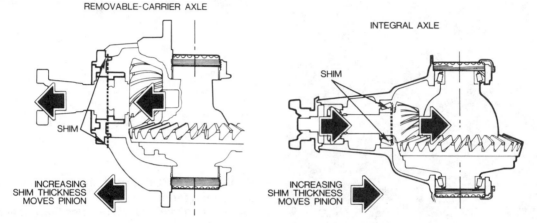

FIGURE 34-19. Using dial indicator to measure axle shaft end play. End play must be adjusted to specifications. *(Courtesy of General Motors Corporation)*

REMOVABLE-CARRIER AXLE

INTEGRAL AXLE

SHIM

SHIM

INCREASING SHIM THICKNESS MOVES PINION

INCREASING SHIM THICKNESS MOVES PINION

FIGURE 34-20. Typical methods of adjusting differential drive pinion depth. *(Courtesy of Ford Motor Co. of Canada Ltd.)*

PAINT MARKING INDICATES POSITION IN WHICH GEARS WERE LAPPED   E 1722-A

FIGURE 34-21. Timing marks on nonhunting type of differential gears. *(Courtesy of Ford Motor Co. of Canada Ltd.)*

FIGURE 34-22. Drive pinion marking indicates production tolerance and amount of shim increase or decrease required for correct pinion depth. *(Courtesy of General Motors Corporation)*

the required coefficient of friction for the clutch discs or cones, as well as proper gear lubrication. Transaxles may require separate lubricants for the transmission and differential. Always refer to manufacturer's recommendations for lubricants and frequency of change for every unit.

PART 4   DIFFERENTIAL DIAGNOSIS AND SERVICE PROCEDURE (REAR-WHEEL DRIVE AND FOUR-WHEEL DRIVE TYPE)

Differential service includes periodic inspection for leaks, lubrication, diagnosis and correction of noise problems (some differential gear noise is acceptable), limited slip differential diagnosis, drive axle bearing and seal replacement. The diagnostic chart will give general direction to the most common problems. Manufacturer's manuals should be consulted for specific units and specific problems.

Trailer towing will require more frequent lubrication service of the differential and drive axle assembly, including changing of the lubricant at specified mileage intervals.

For manual transaxle service see Chapter 37; for automatic transaxle service, see Chapter 39.

Figures 34-23 through 34-28 show the normal sequence of checks and measurements required during overhaul. All specifications must meet tolerances specified by the vehicle manufacturer, including pinion depth, pinion bearing preload, side bearing preload, gear backlash, ring gear run-out, gear tooth contact pattern, axle shaft end play, and so on.

General Precautions

Follow all the normal personal and shop general precautions as well as the following:

• Avoid getting lubricant or other contamination on brake linings, drums, discs, or pads.

• Be sure all axle mounting components are in good condition and are properly attached.

• Observe all precautions specified by manufacturer on limited slip differentials as well as standard differentials.

• Always use new seals and gaskets when overhauling.

• Be sure all metal filings are removed from entire axle housing if present.

Service Procedure

This section defines various possible rear axle conditions and describes tests for identifying the cause and the repair procedure. The four rear axle conditions that will be reviewed are:

• Noise conditions
• Leakage conditions
• Vibration conditions
• Inoperative conditions

The diagnosis material also deals with problem analysis; that is, uncovering the original cause of a problem so that you can avoid repeat service. However, the purpose of this section is to provide tips on service steps of special importance.

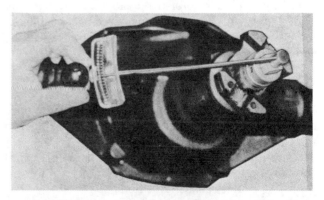

FIGURE 34-23. Measuring differential pinion bearing preload with a torque wrench. Pinion bearing preload must be as specified to prevent endwise movement of pinion during operation. *(Courtesy of General Motors Corporation)*

PROBLEM	CAUSE	CORRECTION
Noise in drive and coast.	1. Road noise. 2. Tire noise. 3. Front wheel bearing noise. 4. Front or rear U-joint angle incorrect.	1. No correction. 2. Correct tire inflation pressure or replace tires. 3. Correct as needed, lubricate or replace. 4. Correct angle.
Similar noise is produced with car standing and driving.	1. Engine noise. 2. Transmission noise.	1. Inspect and correct as required 2. Inspect and correct as required
Vibration.	1. Rough rear wheel bearing. 2. Unbalanced or damaged propeller shaft. 3. Tire unbalance. 4. Worn universal joint in propeller shaft. 5. Front or rear U-joint angle too great.	1. Replace. 2. Replace. 3. Balance tires. 4. Replace. 5. Correct angle.
Noise most pronounced on turns.	1. Differential side gear and pinion. 2. Axle bearing.	1. Replace. 2. Replace.
Drive noise, coast noise.	1. Ring and pinion gear.	1. Replace.
Clunk on acceleration or deceleration.	1. Worn differential cross shaft in case. 2. Worn U-joint. 3. No grease in propeller shaft slip yoke.	1. Replace as needed. 2. Replace. 3. Lubricate.
Groan in "Forward" or "Reverse".	1. Wrong lube in differential.	1. Drain and fill with proper lubricant.
Chatter on turns.	1. Wrong lube in differential. 2. Clutch plates worn.	1. Drain and fill with proper lubricant. 2. Repair differential as needed.

Noise Acceptability

A gear driven unit (especially an automotive drive axle) will produce a certain amount of noise. Some noise is acceptable and may be audible at certain speeds or under various driving conditions (for example, on a newly paved blacktop road). The slight noise is in no way detrimental to operation of the rear axle and must be considered normal.

With the traction-lock limited slip differential axle, slight chatter noise on slow turns after extended highway driving is considered acceptable and has no detrimental effect on the locking axle function.

Road Test

A road test is a must for any complaint of noise and/or vibration that is not eliminated by the on-hoist check of chassis components.

The diagnosis check has four operating conditions or modes in which some axle noises come and go: drive, cruise, coast, and float.

It is important to a good diagnosis check to operate in all four modes and check off those in which the noise occurs. It is important that rear axle noise complaints be evaluated with the transmission in direct drive and not in overdrive. Transmission noise can be mistaken for rear axle noise when in overdrive.

Follow the diagnosis charts to isolate rear axle noise.

Axle Noise

1. Gear noise is the typical "howling" or "whining" of the ring gear and pinion due to an improper gear pattern, gear damage, or improper bearing preload. It can occur at various speeds and driving conditions, or it can be continuous.

2. "Chuckle" is a particular rattling noise that sounds like a stick against the spokes of a spinning bicycle wheel. It occurs while decelerating from 40 mph and usually can be heard all the way to a stop. The frequency varies with the speed of the car.

3. "Knock" is very similar to chuckle, though it may be louder and occurs on acceleration or deceleration. The teardown will disclose what has to be corrected.

4. "Clunk" may be a metallic noise heard when the automatic transmission is engaged in reverse or drive, or it may occur when throttle is applied or released. It is caused by backlash somewhere in the driveline; it is "felt" or heard in the axle.

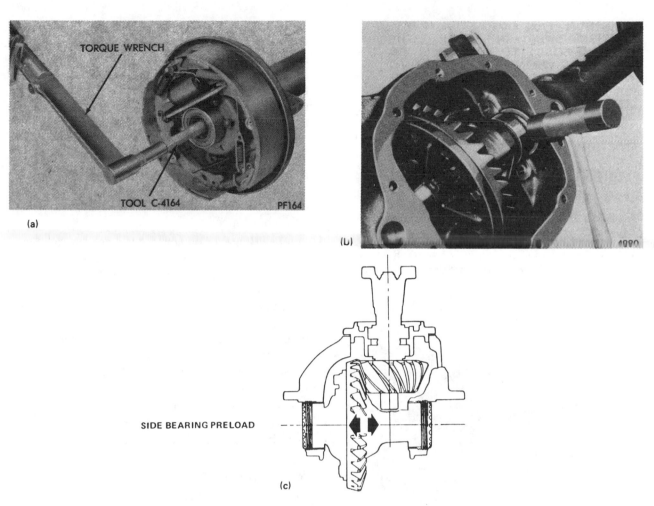

FIGURE 34-24. Three different methods (A, B, and C) of adjusting differential side bearing preload and gear backlash. *(Courtesy of Chrysler Corporation and Ford Motor Co. of Canada Ltd.)*

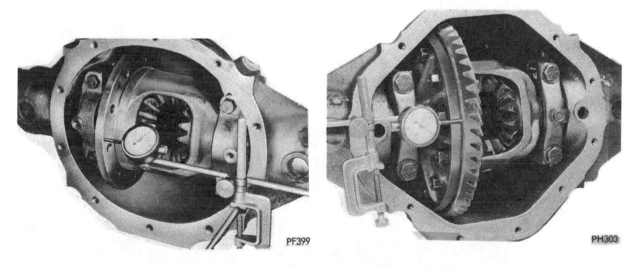

FIGURE 34-25. Measuring differential case run-out (left) and ring gear run-out (right). *(Courtesy of Chrysler Corporation)*

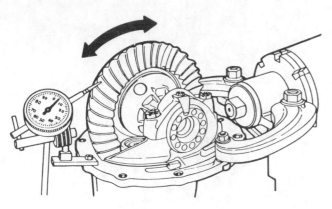

FIGURE 34-26. Measuring ring gear backlash while pinion is stationary. *(Courtesy of Ford Motor Co. of Canada Ltd.)*

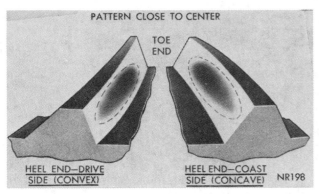

FIGURE 34-27. Ideal tooth contact pattern. *(Courtesy of Chrysler Corporation)*

5. Bearing "whine" is a high-pitched sound similar to a whistle. It is usually caused by malfunctioning pinion bearings that are operating at driveshaft speed. Roller wheel bearings may whine the same way if they run completely dry. Bearing noise occurs at all driving speeds, distinguishing it from gear whine, which usually comes and goes as speed changes.

6. Bearing "rumble" sounds like marbles being rumbled. This condition is usually caused by a malfunctioning wheel bearing. The lower pitch is because the wheel bearing turns at only about 1/3 of driveshaft speed.

7. "Chatter" on corners is a condition where the whole rear end vibrates only when the car is moving. The vibration is as plainly felt as it is heard. In conventional axles, extra differential thrust washers cause a condition of partial lockup that creates this chatter. Chatter noise on Traction Lok axles can usually be traced to erratic movement between adjacent clutch plates and can be corrected with a lubricant change and the addition of a friction modifier available for the purpose.

8. "Click" at engagement is a condition on axles of a slight noise, distinct from a "clunk," that happens in reverse or drive engagement.

Non-Axle Noise

There are a few other conditions that can sound just like axle noise and have to be considered in prediagnosis. The four most common are exhaust, tires, roof racks, and trim moldings.

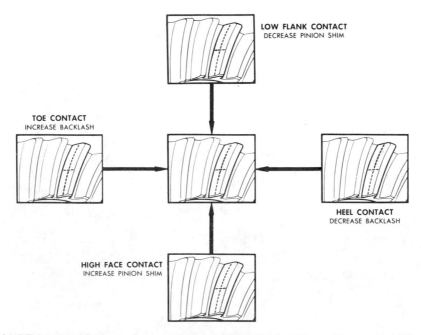

FIGURE 34-28. Method of correcting tooth contact pattern. *(Courtesy of General Motors Corporation)*

1. In certain conditions, the pitch of the exhaust may sound very much like gear whines. At other times, it can be mistaken for a wheel bearing rumble.

2. Tires (especially snow tires) can have a high-pitched tread whine or roar similar to gear noise. Radial tires, to some degree, have this characteristic. Also, any non-standard tire with an unusual tread construction may emit a roar or whine-type noise.

3. Roof racks on station wagons may, because of an airfoil effect, make roaring or rumbling sounds which appear to come from the "rear end."

4. Trim and mouldings also can cause a whistling or whining noise.

Therefore, be sure that none of these is the cause of the noise before proceeding with an axle teardown and diagnosis.

Cleaning and Inspection— Inspection Before Disassembly

Integral Carrier

The differential case assembly and drive pinion should be inspected before they are removed from the carrier casting. These inspections help to find the cause of the trouble and to determine the correction needed. Drain lubricant and remove cover, then proceed as follows:

1. Wipe the lubricant from the internal working parts and visually inspect the parts for wear and/or damage.

2. Rotate the gears to see if there is any roughness to indicate defective bearings or gears.

3. Check the ring gear teeth for signs of scoring, abnormal wear, or nicks and chips.

4. Set up a dial indicator and check ring gear backlash and ring gear backface run-out.

5. Do not check for gear tooth contact pattern. A contact pattern is not an acceptable guide to check for noise. Proper gear set assembly must be checked using the pinion depth gauge tool, which shows correct pinion shim required to assure acceptable running condition.

Disassembly Procedure

Integral Carrier

1. Remove axle shafts.

2. Mark bearing retainer caps for correct assembly later.

3. Remove bearing caps.

4. Use housing spreader if required, or pry differential out as required. Be careful unit does not

drop—it is heavy. Keep right and left bearing cups separate to install in same location later. Keep all shims for right and left sides separate for reference and later assembly.

5. Remove drive shaft.

6. Remove differential pinion nut and drive flange.

7. Remove drive pinion and pinion bearings and cups.

Inspection After Disassembly of Carrier

Replace all parts that do not pass inspection.

Thoroughly clean all parts. Synthetic seals must not be cleaned, soaked, or washed in cleaning solvents. Always use clean solvent when cleaning bearings. Oil the bearings immediately after cleaning to prevent rusting. Inspect the parts for defects. Clean the inside of the carrier before rebuilding it. When a scored gear set is replaced, the axle housing should be washed thoroughly and steam cleaned. This can only be done effectively if the axle shafts and shaft seals are removed from the housing. Inspect individual parts as outlined below.

Gears

Examine the pinion and ring gear teeth for scoring or excessive wear. Extreme care must be taken not to damage the pilot bearing surface of the pinion. Worn gears cannot be rebuilt to correct a noisy condition. Gear scoring is the result of excessive shock loading or the use of an incorrect lubricant. Scored gears cannot be reused. Examine the teeth and thrust surfaces of the differential gears. Wear on the hub of the differential gear can cause a checking noise known as chuckle when the vehicle is driven at low speeds. Wear of splines, thrust surfaces, or thrust washers can contribute to excessive driveline backlash.

Bearing Cups and Cone and Roller Assemblies

Check bearing cups for rings, scores, galling, or excessive wear patterns. Pinion cups must be solidly seated. Check for seating by attempting to insert a 0.0015 inch (0.0381 mm) feeler gauge between these cups and the bottoms of their bores.

When operated in the bearing cups, cone and roller assemblies must turn without roughness. Examine the large roller ends for wear. If the original blend radius has worn to a sharp edge, the cone and roller assembly should be replaced.

If inspection reveals either a worn bearing cup or a worn cone and roller assembly, both parts should be replaced to avoid damage.

Universal Joint Flange

Be sure that the surfaces of the flange have not been damaged in removing the driveshaft or in removing the flange from the axle. The end of the flange that contacts the front pinion bearing inner race, as well as the flat surface of the pinion nut counterbore, must be smooth. Polish these surfaces if necessary. Roughness aggravates backlash noises and causes wear of the flange and pinion nut, with a resultant loss in pinion bearing preload. Flange seal surface must be smooth and not grooved due to wear from seal contact.

Carrier Housing

Make sure that the differential bearing bores are smooth and the threads are not damaged. Remove any nicks or burrs from the mounting surfaces of the carrier housing.

Differential Case

Make sure that the hubs where the bearings mount are smooth. Carefully examine the differential case bearing shoulders, which may have been damaged when the bearings were removed. The bearing assemblies will fail if they do not seat firmly against the shoulders. Check the fit (free rotation) of the differential side gears in their counterbores. Be sure that the mating surfaces of the two parts of the case are smooth and free from nicks or burrs.

Traction-Lok Differential Parts

Inspect the clutch plates for uneven or extreme wear. The dog-eared clutch plates must be free from burrs, nicks, or scratches, which could cause excessive or erratic wear to the internally splined clutch plates. The internally splined clutch plates should be inspected for condition of the material and wear. Replace the plates if their thickness is less than specified or if the material is scored or badly worn. Inspect the plate internal teeth for wear. Replace them if excessive wear is evident. Plates should be replaced as a set only. Examine all thrust surfaces and hubs for wear. Abnormal wear on these surfaces can contribute to a noisy axle.

Assembly

1. Assemble differential case, clutches (if applicable), ring gear, and bearings.

2. Install pinion bearing cups.

3. Install drive pinion spacer and bearings as outlined in service manual using pinion depth setting gauge to ensure proper pinion depth adjustment.

4. Install pinion seal and drive flange.

5. Install drive pinion nut to specified torque to ensure correct pinion bearing preload.

6. Install differential case assembly by following specifications regarding shim packs at each side to provide correct side bearing preload and gear backlash.

7. Install bearing retaining caps and bolts to specified torque.

8. Recheck ring gear backlash and run-out to make sure they remain within specifications.

9. If desired, a tooth pattern check may be made at this point. Follow manufacturer's service manual for procedure.

10. Install axle shafts, differential pinions, shaft, and shaft retainer as required. Install wheels.

11. Install differential cover using gasket or recommended sealer. Tighten bolts to specifications.

12. Fill unit to specified level with lubricant specified by manufacturer.

13. Install drive shaft.

PART 5   SELF-CHECK

1. Trace the power flow through the standard differential by naming all the parts involved in proper sequence from the drive line to the drive wheels.

2. In the standard differential, when one wheel is stationary the other wheel turns at _____ the speed shown on the speedometer.

3. What is the main difference between spiral bevel gears and hypoid gears?

4. How is the straddle-mounted pinion different from the overhung-mounted pinion?

5. Hunting and nonhunting differential gears must be timed during assembly. True or false?

PART 6   TEST QUESTIONS

1. Side bearing preload and gear backlash is determined by:
   (a) ring gear to pinion position
   (b) side bearing shim thickness
   (c) side bearing threaded adjusters
   (d) all of the above

2. The type of differential gear that must be timed during assembly is the:

(a) hypoid

(b) spur and bevel

(c) hunting

(d) nonhunting

3. The hypoid rear axle is designed to:

(a) lower the body profile

(b) provide more tooth contact

(c) provide quieter operation

(d) all of the above

4. The overhung-mounted pinion has how many bearings?

(a) one

(b) two

(c) three

(d) four

5. The collapsible sleeve between the pinion bearings in the differential controls:

(a) pinion depth

(b) backlash

(c) tooth contact pattern

(d) pinion bearing preload

6. What is the purpose of the limited slip feature in a differential?

Chapter 35

Clutches

Performance Objectives

After sufficient study of this chapter and the necessary practice on the appropriate training models, and with the proper tools, equipment, and shop manuals, you should be able to do the following:

1. Complete the self-check and test questions with at least 80 percent accuracy.
2. Describe the purpose, construction, and operation of the clutch assembly and its components.
3. Diagnose clutch problems according to the diagnostic chart provided.
4. Recondition and replace faulty clutch components according to manufacturer's procedures and specifications.
5. Test the vehicle to determine the success of the services performed.
6. Prepare the vehicle for customer acceptance.

PART I CLUTCH FUNCTION AND CAPACITY

Clutch Function

The clutch in an automotive vehicle provides a means of connecting and disconnecting the engine from the transmission. The application of engine power to the load must be gradual to provide smooth engagement and to lessen the shock on the driving parts. After engagement, the clutch must transmit all the engine power to the transmission without slipping. Further, it is desirable to disconnect the engine from the power train during the time the gears in the transmission are being shifted from one gear ratio to another.

The transmission of power through the clutch is accomplished by bringing one or more rotating drive members secured to the crankshaft into gradual contact with one or more driven members secured to the unit being driven. These members are either stationary or rotating at different speeds. Contact is established and maintained by strong spring pressure controlled by the driver through the clutch pedal and suitable linkage.

When the full spring pressure is applied, the speed of the driving and driven members is the same. All slipping has stopped, and there is, in effect, a direct connection between the driving and driven parts. Some slight slippage or clutch creep may occur.

The clutch is located between the engine flywheel and the transmission on rear-wheel-drive vehicles. On front-wheel-drive vehicles it is located in the transaxle assembly between the engine flywheel and transmission section of the transaxle.

Clutch Capacity

The ability of a clutch to transmit torque depends on several factors:

1. Applied pressure (springs and centrifugal devices).

2. Coefficient of friction of clutch frictional surfaces.

3. Surface area of frictional surfaces (square inches or square centimeters).

4. Internal and external diameter of driven disc.

The clutch is designed with sufficient overcapacity to allow for deterioration due to normal wear. The clutch is also designed to prevent flying apart or bursting. High performance vehicles are usually equipped with a scatter shield or blanket designed to contain flying parts should the clutch assembly fly apart at high speeds.

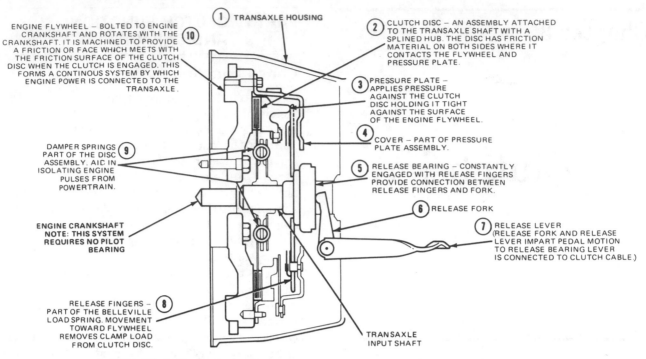

FIGURE 35-1. Typical clutch component operation in transaxle assembly. (*Courtesy of Ford Motor Co. of Canada Ltd.*)

Figure labels:

① TRANSAXLE HOUSING

② CLUTCH DISC – AN ASSEMBLY ATTACHED TO THE TRANSAXLE SHAFT WITH A SPLINED HUB. THE DISC HAS FRICTION MATERIAL ON BOTH SIDES WHERE IT CONTACTS THE FLYWHEEL AND PRESSURE PLATE.

③ PRESSURE PLATE – APPLIES PRESSURE AGAINST THE CLUTCH DISC HOLDING IT TIGHT AGAINST THE SURFACE OF THE ENGINE FLYWHEEL.

④ COVER – PART OF PRESSURE PLATE ASSEMBLY.

⑤ RELEASE BEARING – CONSTANTLY ENGAGED WITH RELEASE FINGERS PROVIDE CONNECTION BETWEEN RELEASE FINGERS AND FORK.

⑥ RELEASE FORK

⑦ RELEASE LEVER (RELEASE FORK AND RELEASE LEVER IMPART PEDAL MOTION TO RELEASE BEARING LEVER IS CONNECTED TO CLUTCH CABLE.)

⑧ RELEASE FINGERS – PART OF THE BELLEVILLE LOAD SPRING. MOVEMENT TOWARD FLYWHEEL REMOVES CLAMP LOAD FROM CLUTCH DISC.

⑨ DAMPER SPRINGS PART OF THE DISC ASSEMBLY. AID IN ISOLATING ENGINE PULSES FROM POWERTRAIN.

⑩ ENGINE FLYWHEEL – BOLTED TO ENGINE CRANKSHAFT AND ROTATES WITH THE CRANKSHAFT. IT IS MACHINED TO PROVIDE A FRICTION OR FACE WHICH MEETS WITH THE FRICTION SURFACE OF THE CLUTCH DISC WHEN THE CLUTCH IS ENGAGED. THIS FORMS A CONTINOUS SYSTEM BY WHICH ENGINE POWER IS CONNECTED TO THE TRANSAXLE.

ENGINE CRANKSHAFT NOTE: THIS SYSTEM REQUIRES NO PILOT BEARING

TRANSAXLE INPUT SHAFT

PART 2   CLUTCH OPERATION

The driving members of a clutch usually consist of two flat surfaces machined to a smooth finish. One of these surfaces is the rear face of the engine flywheel, and the other is a heavy flat ring with one side machined. This part is known as the *pressure plate*. It is fitted into a steel cover, which is bolted to the flywheel. The entire assembly is carefully balanced to prevent vibration.

The driven member is a disc with a splined hub that is free to slide along the splines of the clutch shaft (transmission input shaft), but which drives the shaft through these same splines. Grooves on both sides of the clutch-driven disc lining prevent sticking of the disk to the flywheel and pressure plate on engaging.

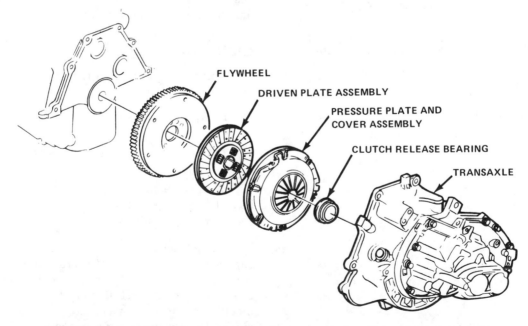

FIGURE 35-2. Typical transaxle clutch components. (*Courtesy of General Motors Corporation*)

Figure labels: FLYWHEEL, DRIVEN PLATE ASSEMBLY, PRESSURE PLATE AND COVER ASSEMBLY, CLUTCH RELEASE BEARING, TRANSAXLE

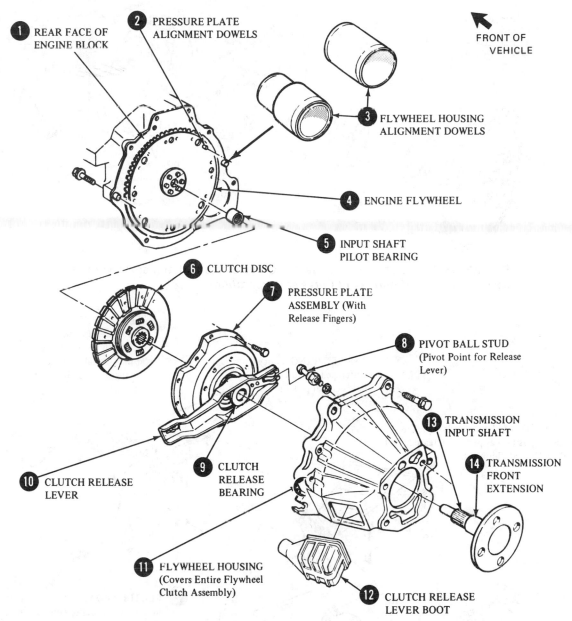

FIGURE 35-3. Typical components of clutch assembly for rear-wheel-drive vehicle. *(Courtesy of Ford Motor Co. of Canada Ltd.)*

The clutch disc is made of spring steel in the shape of a single flat disc consisting of a number of flat segments. Suitable frictional facings are attached to each side of the disc by means of brass rivets. These facings are heat resistant since friction produces heat. The most commonly used facings are made of cotton and asbestos fibers woven or molded together and impregnated with resins or similar binding agents. Very often, copper wires are woven or pressed into material to give it additional strength. To make clutch engagement as smooth as possible and eliminate chatter, the steel segments attached to the splined hub are slightly twisted, which causes the facings to make gradual contact as the disc flattens out.

The clutch disc is provided with a flexible center to absorb the torsional vibration of the crankshaft, which would be transmitted to the power train unless it were eliminated. The flexible center has steel compression springs placed between the hub and the steel disc. The springs permit the disc to rotate slightly with relation to its hub. The slight backward and forward rotation permitted by the springs allows the clutch shaft to rotate at a more uniform rate than the crankshaft, thereby eliminating some of the torsional vibration from the crankshaft.

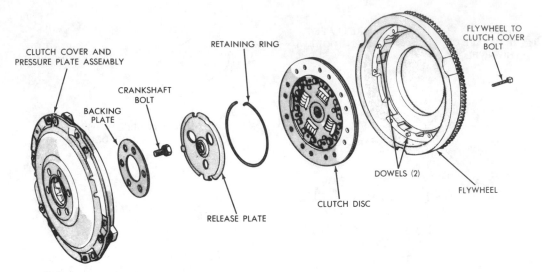

FIGURE 35-4. Clutch components for Chrysler manual transaxle with recessed flywheel. *(Courtesy of Chrysler Corporation)*

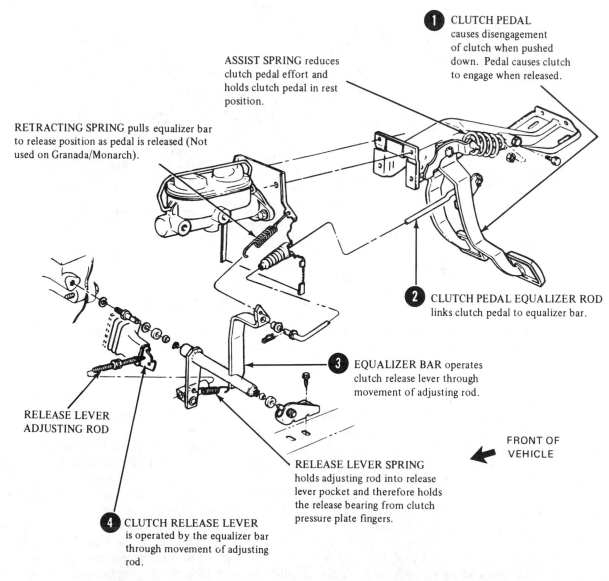

ASSIST SPRING reduces clutch pedal effort and holds clutch pedal in rest position.

RETRACTING SPRING pulls equalizer bar to release position as pedal is released (Not used on Granada/Monarch).

1 CLUTCH PEDAL causes disengagement of clutch when pushed down. Pedal causes clutch to engage when released.

2 CLUTCH PEDAL EQUALIZER ROD links clutch pedal to equalizer bar.

3 EQUALIZER BAR operates clutch release lever through movement of adjusting rod.

RELEASE LEVER ADJUSTING ROD

FRONT OF VEHICLE

RELEASE LEVER SPRING holds adjusting rod into release lever pocket and therefore holds the release bearing from clutch pressure plate fingers.

4 CLUTCH RELEASE LEVER is operated by the equalizer bar through movement of adjusting rod.

FIGURE 35-5. Clutch linkage component operation (rod-and-lever type mechanical linkage shown). *(Courtesy of Ford Motor Co. of Canada Ltd.)*

The driving and driven members are held in contact by spring pressure. This pressure may be exerted by a one-piece diaphragm spring or by a number of small helical springs located around the outer portion of the pressure plate. In the diaphragm design clutch, the throw-out bearing moves forward against the spring fingers, forcing the diaphragm spring to pivot around the inner pivot ring, dishing the fingers toward the flywheel. The outer circumference of the spring now lifts the pressure plate away from the driven disc through a series of retracting springs placed around the outer circumference of the pressure plate. In the helical-spring clutch, a system of levers pivoted on the cover forces the pressure plate away from the driven disc and against the pressure of the springs, thus performing the same function as the dish-shaped diaphragm spring.

PART 3   CLUTCH CONTROLS

The clutch release or (throw-out) bearing is a ball-thrust bearing contained in the clutch release bearing housing or collar, mounted on the front bearing retainer of the transmission case. The release bearing is connected through linkage to the clutch and is moved by the release yoke to engage the release levers and move the pressure plate to the rear, thus separating the clutch driving members from the driven member when the clutch pedal is depressed by the driver. A pedal return spring preloads clutch linkage, removing looseness due to wear. The clutch free pedal travel will increase with linkage wear and decrease with driven disc wear.

Two basic types of clutch linkages are used—the mechanical and the hydraulic control. The mechanical linkage consists of a series of rods and levers or a flexible cable connecting the clutch pedal to the clutch release fork. The hydraulic control consists of a hydraulic master cylinder operated by a push-rod connected to the brake pedal, and a slave cylinder, which operates the clutch release fork. The master cylinder and slave cylinder are connected hydraulically by a steel tube. The advantage of the hydraulic control is that force multiplication is easily achieved hydraulically, and the need for complicated linkage is eliminated.

Clutch linkage may be designed to provide clearance between the release bearing and release fingers when the clutch is fully applied (pedal in return position). Other units are designed to provide continuous running of the release bearing.

Clutch linkage adjustment is extremely important in either case. Without proper linkage adjustment, full clutch engagement may not be achieved or full clutch release may not be possible. Clutch life and transmission shifting are adversely affected if linkage is not properly adjusted. Some linkage systems are designed to be self-adjusting.

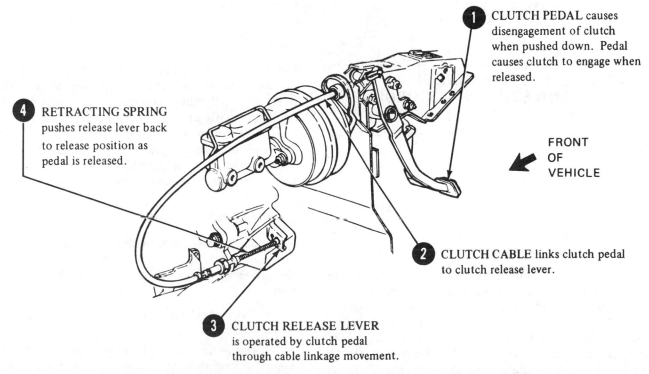

4 RETRACTING SPRING pushes release lever back to release position as pedal is released.

1 CLUTCH PEDAL causes disengagement of clutch when pushed down. Pedal causes clutch to engage when released.

FRONT OF VEHICLE

2 CLUTCH CABLE links clutch pedal to clutch release lever.

3 CLUTCH RELEASE LEVER is operated by clutch pedal through cable linkage movement.

FIGURE 35-6. Cable type of mechanical clutch linkage operation. (Courtesy of Ford Motor Co. of Canada Ltd.)

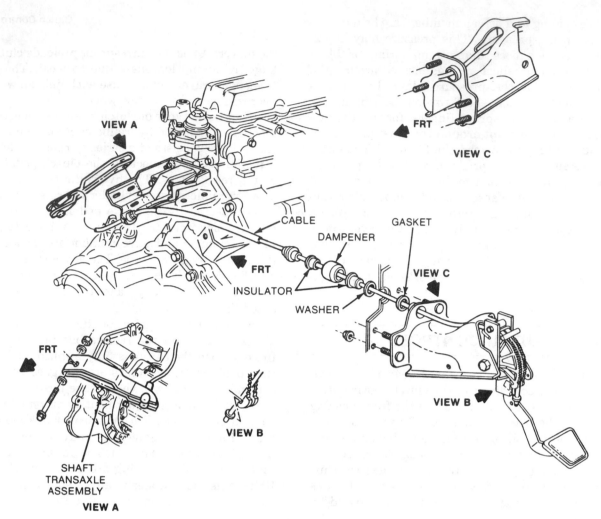

FIGURE 35–7. Transaxle clutch cable type linkage. *(Courtesy of General Motors Corporation)*

PART 4   CLUTCH DIAGNOSIS AND SERVICE PROCEDURE

Clutch problems can generally be grouped under the following headings:

- No disengagement
- Noise
- Chatter
- Slippage
- Vibration

Most of the causes and corrections for these conditions are shown in the diagnostic chart.

If adjustment does not correct a clutch problem, the normal procedure is to replace the faulty part or parts. It is not general practice to reface clutch-driven discs or to overhaul clutch pressure plates. If either of these units is faulty, the accepted practice is to replace both the driven disc and the pressure plate assembly with matched units. If

the flywheel shows signs of overheating and surface cracks, it should be resurfaced or replaced. If there is excessive flywheel run-out, the cause should be determined (flywheel web bent, crankshaft flange bent, bolts loose, and so on) and corrected. If housing bore and face alignment are not within specifications, the housing should be realigned to ensure proper transmission-to-clutch alignment.

General Precautions

For procedures on any vehicle, the appropriate service manual should be used and followed. However, the general precautions that follow should also be observed.

- Avoid getting burned by hot clutch or exhaust parts.
- Disconnect battery to avoid accidental cranking of the engine during clutch or transmission work.
- Support vehicle safely before doing any work under vehicle. Use hoist or safety stands (do not

818

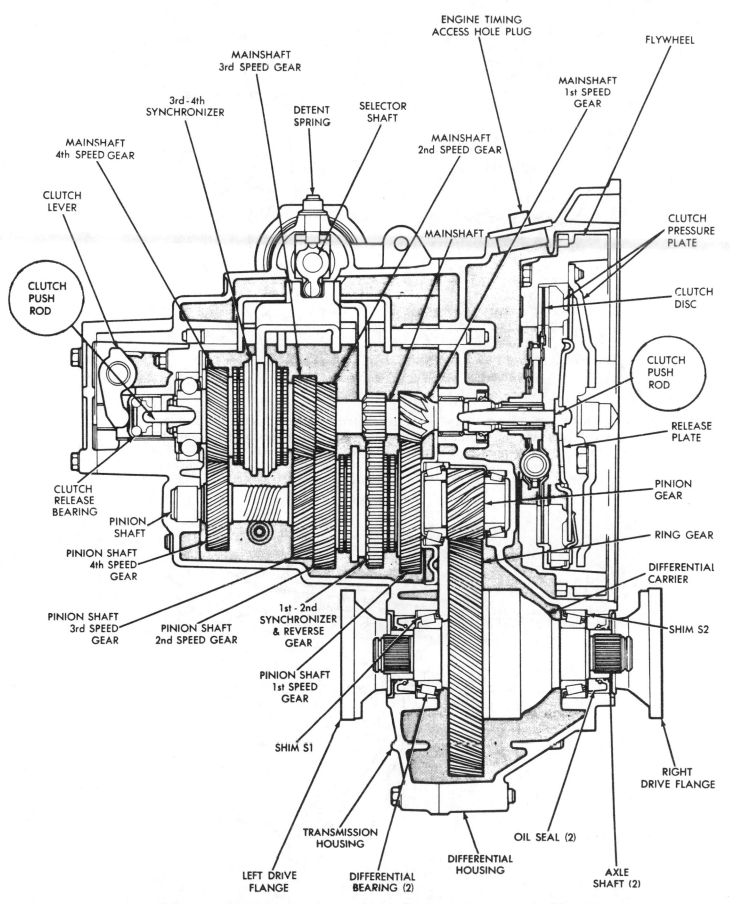

FIGURE 35–8. Note clutch operating push rod passes through center of mainshaft in this transaxle. *(Courtesy of Chrysler Corporation)*

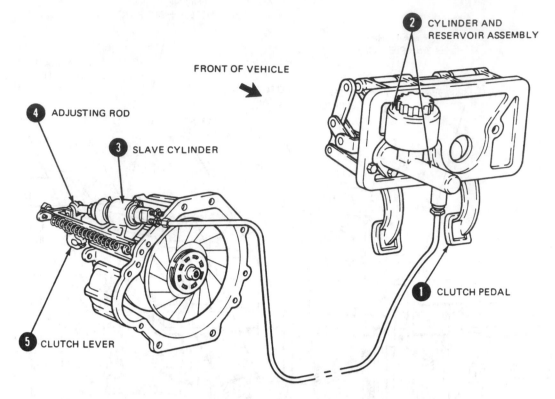

FIGURE 35-9. Hydraulically operated clutch linkage. When the clutch pedal (1) is depressed, it pushes fluid from the cylinder and reservoir assembly (2) to the slave cylinder (3) activating the adjusting rod (4) which moves the clutch lever (5) for clutch disengagement. When the pedal is released, the clutch is applied. *(Courtesy of Ford Motor Co. of Canada Ltd.)*

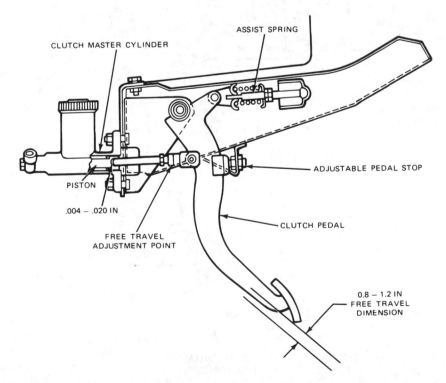

FIGURE 35-10. Hydraulic clutch master cylinder and pedal arrangement. *(Courtesy of Ford Motor Co. of Canada Ltd.)*

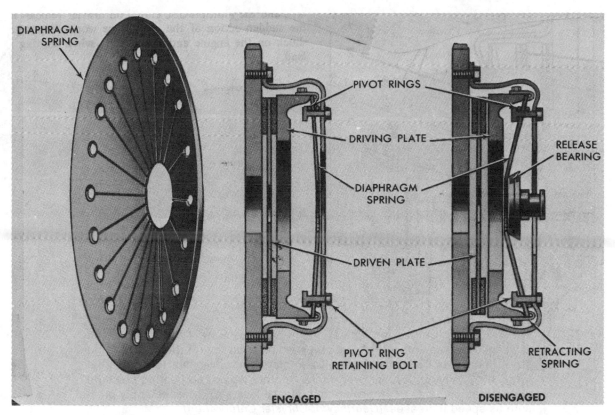

FIGURE 35-11. Diaphragm type of clutch pressure plate showing diaphragm spring operation. Note clearance on both sides of clutch-driven plate (disc) in diagram on right when clutch is in the disengaged position (pedal depressed). *(Courtesy of General Motors Corporation)*

work under vehicle supported by hydraulic jacks or bumper jacks).

- Support engine properly before transaxle, transmission, or cross-member removal.

- Use proper transmission or transaxle jack for removal procedure.

- Always make sure heavy clutch parts and flywheel do not drop during removal (injury and damage could result).

- Support transmission or transaxle properly to prevent clutch plate damage during removal and installation. Transmission must move straight back from flywheel during removal to disengage clutch shaft from clutch. Allowing weight of transmission to hang on input shaft and clutch disc will damage clutch disc.

- Do not use compressed air to blow out clutch housing. Asbestos dust (from clutch facing) can cause cancer if inhaled. Use proper vacuum cleaner. Use filter for breathing protection.

- Do not allow any grease, oil, or other contamination to come in contact with clutch friction surfaces. Even dirty hands can damage the coefficient of friction and cause clutch problems.

Clutch Replacement Procedure

Clutch disc, pressure plate, flywheel, pilot bearing, release bearing, and clutch fork replacement require transmission or transaxle removal as outlined in Chapter 36. Refer to this section and to the appropriate manufacturer's shop manual for safe and proper procedures for transmission or transaxle removal. For transaxle halfshaft removal, see Chapter 33, Part 3.

After transmission removal, proceed as follows to remove the clutch pressure plate and driven disc.

- Remove release bearing assembly.

- Mark both flywheel and pressure plate cover with a center punch to ensure correct reassembly if pressure plate is to be used again.

- Loosen pressure plate attaching bolts progressively a little at a time until all spring pressure has been relieved.

- Remove bolts (be sure to have a firm grip on the heavy assembly); then remove pressure plate and clutch disc.

- Inspect flywheel for damaged ring gear teeth, heat spots, cracks, scoring, and wear. Replace or re-

821

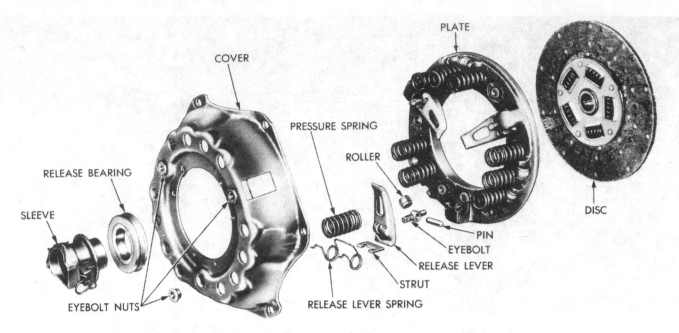

FIGURE 35-12. Coil spring type of clutch pressure plate. Note roller, which is wedged between pressure plate cover and plate during rotation. As rotating speed increases, roller wedges between plate and cover due to centrifugal force, increasing clutch apply pressure. Another type of coil spring pressure plate assembly uses counterweighted release levers to increase apply pressure as speed increases. *(Courtesy of Chrysler Corporation)*

surface flywheel if badly damaged. If flywheel is serviceable, clean with fine emery cloth to remove glazed finish. If ring gear teeth are badly damaged, replace ring gear as outlined in service manual.

• Inspect clutch pressure plate friction surface for heat spots, cracks, scoring, and wear. Inspect

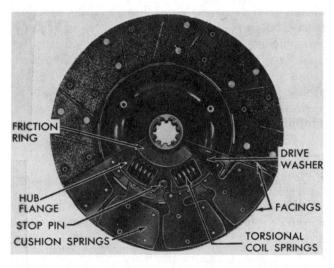

FIGURE 35-13. Clutch-driven disc construction. Cushion springs cushion clutch apply and reduce the tendency to chatter. Cushion springs are wavy in shape. As the clutch is applied, the wavy cushion springs flatten out. Torsional coil springs are positioned between driven disc and disc hub in such a way that torque is transmitted from the disc to the hub through the springs. This cushions torsional vibrations. *(Courtesy of General Motors Corporation)*

springs for damage due to overheating. Springs show burned paint or discoloration if overheated due to slippage. Inspect cover for damage or warpage. Check drive lugs and drive lug holes for wear. Replace pressure plate if damaged. Usual procedure is to replace release bearing, pressure plate, and clutch disc as a matched assembly, if one or the other requires replacement.

• Inspect clutch disc friction material for overheating, cracks, glazing, or oil contamination. Check to make sure attaching rivets are tight and that enough lining (about 2/3 of original thickness) remains. Check wave springs and metal disc; they should not be cracked or warped. Check torsional springs and drive pins. Springs should not be loose or broken. Drive pins and washers should be tight. Replace disc if required.

• Replace pilot bushing (if required) and lubricate as recommended.

• Check and correct clutch housing alignment (bell housing) if required.

• Use a clutch aligning arbor or suitable dummy shaft to assemble clutch disc and pressure plate to flywheel. (Make sure proper side of disc faces flywheel.) Tighten bolts progressively to specified torque.

• Inspect release bearing for roughness or looseness. Replace if required.

• Install release bearing (lubricate interior of sleeve if recommended).

DIAGNOSTIC CHART

PROBLEM	CAUSE	CORRECTION
Fails to release	1. Improper linkage adjustment. 2. Improper pedal travel. 3. Loose linkage. 4. Faulty pilot bearing. 5. Faulty driven disc. 6. Fork off ball stud. 7. Clutch disc hub binding on clutch gear spline. 8. Clutch disc warped or bent.	1. Adjust linkage. 2. Trim bumper stop and adjust linkage. 3. Replace as necessary. 4. Replace bearing. 5. Replace disc. 6. Install properly. 7. Repair or replace clutch gear and/or disc. 8. Replace disc.
Slipping	1. No pedal free play. 3. Oil-soaked driven disc. 3. Worn facing or facing torn from disc. 4. Warped pressure plate or flywheel. 5. Weak diaphragm spring.	1. Adjust linkage to provide 1- to 1½-inch pedal free play. 2. Install new disc and correct leak at its source. 3. Replace disc. 4. Replace pressure plate or flywheel. 5. Replace pressure plate.
Grabbing (chattering)	1. Oil on facing. Burned or glazed facings. 2. Worn splines on clutch gear. 3. Loose engine mountings. 4. Warped pressure plate or flywheel.	1. Install new disc and correct leak. 2. Replace transmission clutch shaft. 3. Tighten or replace mountings. 4. Replace pressure plate or flywheel.
Rattling transmission click	1. Weak retracting springs. 2. Throw-out fork loose on ball stud or in bearing groove. 3. Driven plate damper spring failure.	1. Replace pressure plate. 2. Check ball stud and retainer. 3. Replace driven disc.
Throw-out bearing noise with clutch fully engaged	1. No pedal free play. 2. Throw-out bearing binding on transmission bearing retainer. 3. Insufficient tension between clutch fork spring and ball stud. 4. Fork improperly installed. 5. Weak return spring.	1. Adjust linkage to provide 1- to 1½-inch pedal free play. 2. Clean, relubricate, check for burrs, nicks, etc. 3. Replace fork. 4. Install properly. 5. Replace spring.
Noisy throw-out bearing during clutch engagement or disengagement	1. Worn throw-out bearing. 2. Fork off ball stud (heavy clicking).	1. Replace bearing. 2. Install properly and lubricate fork fingers at bearing.
Pedal stays on floor when disengaged	1. Bind in linkage or release bearing. 2. Springs weak in pressure plate.	1. Lubricate and free up linkage and release bearing. 2. Replace pressure plate.
Hard pedal effort	1. Bind in linkage.	1. Lubricate and free up linkage.

DIAGNOSIS OF SUSPECTED RELEASE BEARING NOISE — CONTINUOUS RUNNING TYPE

Chirp, squeak, and clatter, with clutch pedal up, can be caused by insufficient bearing pre-load, out-of-plane pressure plate fingers or transmission, or a worn or damaged release bearing. The following procedures will isolate the cause:

ACTION	RESULT	CONCLUSION	NEXT STEP
With engine idling and transaxle in neutral, depress clutch pedal to the floor.	Still noisy	Release bearing is damaged or worn	Replace bearing
	Noise gone	Release bearing is OK	Proceed to next action
Disconnect clutch cable from release lever and move lever away from cable to disengage bearing from pressure plate fingers.	Still noisy	Noise is from transaxle	Refer to section on transaxle diagnosis
	Noise gone	Transmission is OK	Proceed to next action
Apply 5 lb. load to release lever at cable junction in direction of cable—pull to pre-load bearing.	Still noisy	Binding release lever pivot	Lube/free pivot/bushing
		Pressure plate fingers out of plane	Note I
	Noise gone	Clutch control system damaged	Note II

I. Binding pivots will reduce bearing pre-load, resulting in possible scrubbing between pressure plate fingers and bearing face. Out-of-plane fingers will cause oscillation of the release lever, resulting in noise if pivot is dry. Lever plane is affected by pressure plate mounting bolt torque. Assure bolts are properly tightened.
II. Service/replace as necessary any sticky or binding clutch control components.

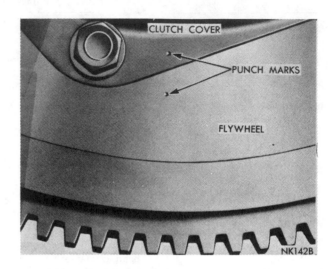

FIGURE 35-14. Installing a clutch release bearing on a release bearing sleeve. *(Courtesy of Chrysler Corporation)*

FIGURE 35-15. Punch marks assure correct assembly of pressure plate (clutch cover) to flywheel. *(Courtesy of Chrysler Corporation)*

FIGURE 35-16. Using slide hammer puller to remove clutch pilot pushing or bearings. *(Courtesy of Ford Motor Co. of Canada Ltd.)*

FIGURE 35-17. Installing new clutch pilot bushing with bushing driver. *(Courtesy of Ford Motor Co. of Canada Ltd.)*

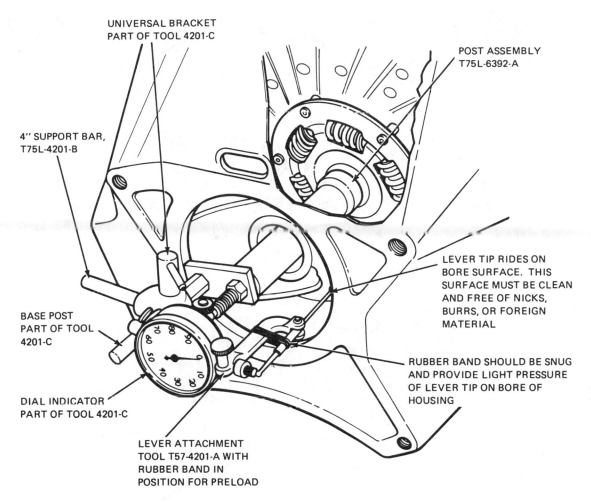

UNIVERSAL BRACKET
PART OF TOOL 4201-C

POST ASSEMBLY
T75L-6392-A

4" SUPPORT BAR,
T75L-4201-B

LEVER TIP RIDES ON
BORE SURFACE. THIS
SURFACE MUST BE CLEAN
AND FREE OF NICKS,
BURRS, OR FOREIGN
MATERIAL

BASE POST
PART OF TOOL
4201-C

DIAL INDICATOR
PART OF TOOL 4201-C

RUBBER BAND SHOULD BE SNUG
AND PROVIDE LIGHT PRESSURE
OF LEVER TIP ON BORE OF
HOUSING

LEVER ATTACHMENT
TOOL T57-4201-A WITH
RUBBER BAND IN
POSITION FOR PRELOAD

FIGURE 35-18. Measuring clutch housing bore run-out with dial indicator. Housing bore, clutch shaft, pilot bearing, and transmission must be in concentric alignment for proper clutch operation. *(Courtesy of Ford Motor Co. of Canada Ltd.)*

• Install transaxle or transmission, cross member, and drive line or halfshafts as applicable.

• Adjust pedal height, clutch linkage, and transmission linkage as specified in manufacturer's manual.

• Check transmission lubricant level and correct if required.

• Road test performance of the clutch, making sure there is sufficient pedal travel and free play for proper clutch apply and release and good transmission shifting.

• Prepare vehicle for customer acceptance.

PART 5   SELF-CHECK

1. State the purpose of the clutch.
2. What factors determine clutch capacity?
3. Why is clutch pedal free travel required on non-continuous running release bearing clutches?

4. List three types of clutch operating controls.
5. How is clutch application cushioned?
6. What types of pressure plates are used in clutch design?

PART 6   TEST QUESTIONS

1. Clutch capacity is determined by:
   (a) linkage length, clutch diameter, surface area, apply pressure, and coefficient of friction.
   (b) clutch diameter, pedal leverage, surface area, apply pressure.
   (c) apply pressure, clutch diameter, surface area, coefficient of friction.
   (d) coefficient of friction, surface area, pedal pressure, and clutch diameter.

2. Clutch assembly driven members are the:
   (a) disc and clutch shaft

825

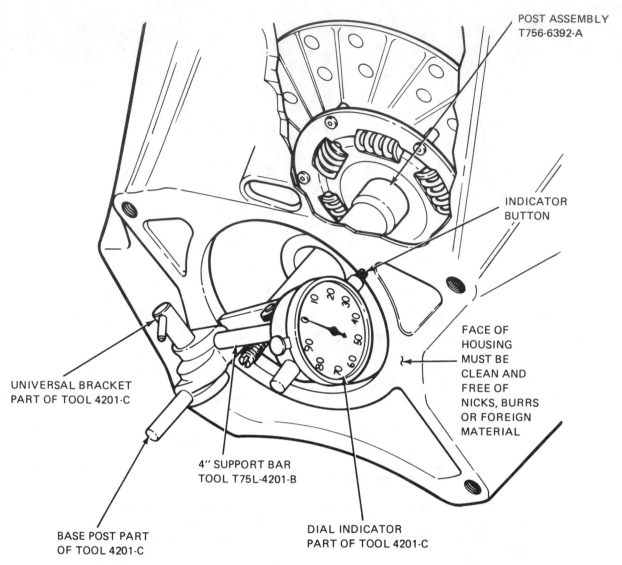

POST ASSEMBLY
T756-6392-A

INDICATOR
BUTTON

FACE OF
HOUSING
MUST BE
CLEAN AND
FREE OF
NICKS, BURRS
OR FOREIGN
MATERIAL

UNIVERSAL BRACKET
PART OF TOOL 4201-C

4" SUPPORT BAR
TOOL T75L-4201-B

BASE POST PART
OF TOOL 4201-C

DIAL INDICATOR
PART OF TOOL 4201-C

FIGURE 35–19. Measuring clutch housing face run-out. Transmission mounting surface must be at 90 degrees to clutch shaft center line for proper shaft and clutch alignment. *(Courtesy of Ford Motor Co. of Canada Ltd.)*

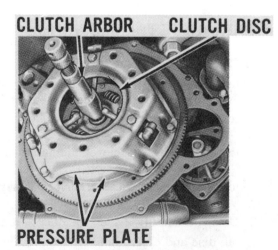

CLUTCH ARBOR CLUTCH DISC

PRESSURE PLATE

FIGURE 35–20. Using clutch aligning arbor to align clutch disc before tightening pressure plate attaching bolts. A discarded transmission input shaft (of the type that fits the vehicle) can also be used for this purpose. Unless the clutch disc is centered over the pilot bushing in the crankshaft, the transmission cannot be installed. *(Courtesy of Ford Motor Co. of Canada Ltd.)*

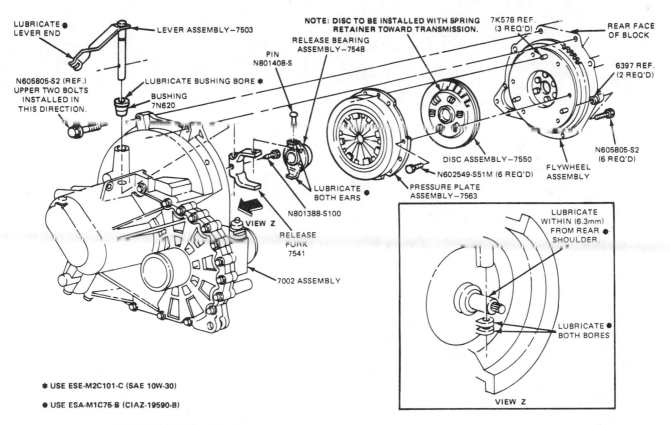

FIGURE 35-21. Clutch service points for Ford MTX transaxle. *(Courtesy of Ford Motor Co. of Canada Ltd.)*

(b) pressure plate and clutch shaft

(c) flywheel and clutch shaft

(d) pressure plate and flywheel

3. The clutch is operated by:

(a) a cable

(b) a system of rods

(c) a hydraulic system

(d) any of the above

4. Clutch slippage may be caused by:

(a) no pedal free play

(b) weak clutch springs

(c) contaminated clutch disc

(d) any of the above

5. A clutch failing to release may be caused by:

(a) incorrect linkage adjustment

(b) weak clutch springs

(c) no pedal free play

(d) faulty pilot bearing

Chapter 36

Manual Transmissions and Transaxles

Performance Objectives

After sufficient study of this chapter and the necessary practice on the appropriate training models, you should be able to do the following:

1. Complete the self-check and test questions with at least 80 percent accuracy.
2. Describe the purpose, construction, and operation of the manual transmission and transaxle and their components.

An internal conbustion engine cannot develop appreciable torque at low speeds to drive the vehicle in direct drive. Also, the crankshaft of an engine must always rotate in the same direction. The transmission or transaxle provides the mechanical advantage that enables the engine to propel the vehicle under various loads. It also furnishes the driver with a selection of vehicle speeds while the engine is held at speeds within the effective torque range. It allows disengaging and reversing the power flow from the engine to the wheels. The purpose of the transmission is (1) to provide the operator with a selection of gear ratios between engine and wheels so that the vehicle can operate at best efficiency under a variety of driving conditions and loads, (2) to provide reverse, and (3) to allow engine braking.

PART 1 PRINCIPLES OF GEAR OPERATION

Gear Terminology

What is a gear? Simply stated, a gear is a series of levers around a common center.

Gears are normally mounted on a shaft. The shaft may drive the gear, the gear may drive the shaft, or the gear may be free to turn on the shaft and simply act as an idler gear (depending on application).

Gears can be used to: transfer torque unchanged, multiply torque and decrease speed, and increase speed and decrease torque.

Drive Gear (Input)

A drive gear is a gear that drives another gear or causes another gear to turn.

Driven Gear (Output)

A driven gear is a gear that is driven or forced to turn by a drive gear, by a shaft, or by some other rotating device.

Rotation and Direction of Rotation

Rotation is simply a term used to describe the fact that a gear, shaft, or other device is turning.

The direction of rotation is described by comparing it to the rotation of the hands of a clock. All clocks that have hands rotate the hands in the same direction. In order to tell what time it is, one must face the front of the clock. As time progresses the hands of the clock move in a "clockwise" direction. This can also be described as turning in a right-hand direction (as "right-hand" threads on a bolt or nut).

Rotation in the opposite direction is described as "counterclockwise" rotation or turning to the left (as in "left-hand" threads on a bolt or nut).

When considering the power flow through the gear system of a transaxle or transmission, it is important that everyone use the same terminology.

To determine the direction of rotation of gears in a transmission, you must face the front of the transmission. The front of the transmission is that end which is attached to the engine, whether mounted in a transverse (crosswise) manner or in a longitudinal manner. The direction of rotation of all transmission gears and shafts is therefore determined by viewing the end of the transmission that is attached to the engine.

The abbreviation of the term clockwise is CW, and for counterclockwise, it is CCW.

Another term for clockwise rotation is forward rotation. Other terms used for counterclockwise ro-

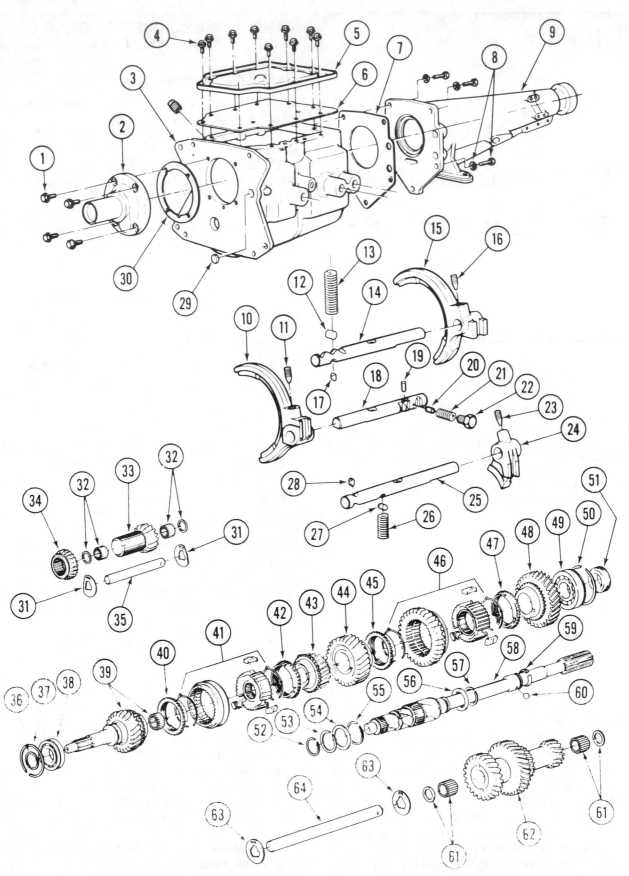

FIGURE 36–1(A). Exploded view of four-speed overdrive transmission. *(Courtesy of Ford Motor Co. of Canada Ltd.)*

1. INPUT SHAFT BEARING RETAINER ATTACHING BOLT
2. INPUT SHAFT BEARING RETAINER
3. TRANSMISSION CASE
4. COVER ATTACHING BOLT
5. COVER
6. COVER GASKET
7. EXTENTION HOUSING GASKET
8. EXTENTION-TO-CASE BOLT AND LOCKWASHER
9. EXTENTION HOUSING ASS'Y.
10. 3RD-OVERDRIVE SHIFT FORK
11. SET SCREW
12. DETENT PIN
13. LONG SPRING
14. 1ST-2ND SPEED SHIFT RAIL
15. 1ST 2ND SPEED SHIFT FORK
16. SET SCREW
17. INTERLOCK DETENT PIN
18. 3RD-OVERDRIVE SHIFT RAIL
19. INTERLOCK PIN
20. PIN
21. DETENT SPRING
22. SIDE DETENT BOLT
23. SET SCREW
24. REVERSE SHIFT FORK
25. REVERSE SHIFT RAIL
26. DETENT PIN SPRING
27. REVERSE DETENT PIN
28. DETENT PIN
29. EXPANSION PLUG
30. RETAINER GASKET
31. THRUST WASHER
32. BEARINGS AND 3/4" FLAT WASHER

33. REVERSE IDLER GEAR
34. REVERSE SLIDING GEAR
35. REVERSE IDLER GEAR SHAFT
36. SNAP RING
37. SNAP RING
38. INPUT SHAFT BEARING
39. INPUT SHAFT GEAR AND BEARINGS
40. BLOCKING RING
41. 3RD-OVERDRIVE SYNCHRONIZER ASS'Y.
42. BLOCKING RING
43. OVERDRIVE GEAR
44. SECOND SPEED GEAR
45. BLOCKING RING
46. 1ST-2ND SYNCHRONIZER ASS'Y.
47. BLOCKING RING
48. 1ST SPEED GEAR
49. OUTPUT SHAFT BEARING
50. SNAP RING
51. SPEEDOMETER DRIVE GEAR
52. SNAP RING
53. SNAP RING
54. THRUST WASHER
55. SNAP RING
56. THRUST WASHER
57. SNAP RING
58. OUTPUT SHAFT
59. SNAP RING
60. SPEEDOMETER GEAR DRIVE BALL
61. BEARINGS AND 7/8" FLAT WASHER
62. COUNTERSHAFT GEAR CLUSTER
63. THRUST WASHER
64. COUNTERSHAFT

FIGURE 36-1(B). Key for Figure 36-1(A). *(Courtesy of Ford Motor Co. of Canada Ltd.)*

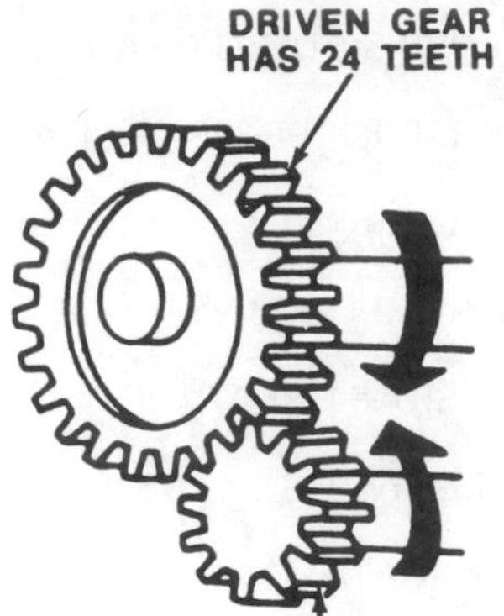

DRIVEN GEAR
HAS 24 TEETH

DRIVING GEAR
HAS 12 TEETH

FIGURE 36-2. Small gear driving large gear.

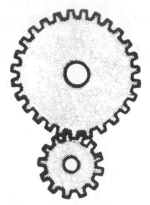

FIGURE 36-4. Large gear driving small gear equals more speed but less torque.

tation are backward rotation, turning backwards, or turning in a reverse direction.

Speed of Rotation

The term "speed" is used to describe the rotating frequency of gears of shafts. When used to describe engine speed, it refers to the number of turns or revolutions the engine crankshaft makes in one minute (stated in "revolutions per minute" or rpm).

When used to describe the rotation of transmission parts, the word *speed* is used in a more general way to compare the rotating speed of one part to that of another. Terms used to describe speed comparisons include: faster, slower, increased speed, decreased speed, direct drive (same speed) or one to one, and overdrive (output faster than input).

Axis (of Rotation)

The axis is the center line around which a gear or part rotates.

External Gears

An external gear is a gear that has the gear teeth arranged around the outer circumference.

Internal Gear

An internal gear is a ring-type gear with the teeth arranged around the inner circumference of the ring.

Straight Spur Gears

A straight spur gear has teeth that are parallel to the axis of rotation of the gear.

Helical Gears

A helical gear has gear teeth that are at an angle to the axis of rotation of the gear. Advantages of helical gears include the fact that more than one tooth is doing the driving at all times, which is not the case with straight spur gears. Helical gears also run quieter since they create a wiping action as they engage and disengage the teeth on another gear. A disadvantage is that helical teeth on a gear cause the gear to move fore or aft on a shaft (depending on the direction of the angle of the gear teeth). This

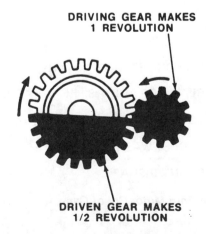

DRIVING GEAR MAKES
1 REVOLUTION

DRIVEN GEAR MAKES
1/2 REVOLUTION

FIGURE 36-3. Two-to-one gear ratio.

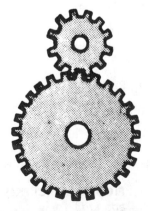

FIGURE 36-5. Small gear driving larger gear equals less speed but more torque.

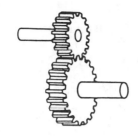

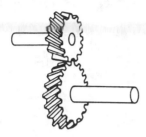

FIGURE 36-6. Straight cut (top) and helical cut (bottom).

axial thrust must be absorbed by thrust washers and other transmission gears, shafts, or the transmission case.

Drive and Coast

The drive side of gear teeth is the side that is in contact with teeth of another gear while torque is being applied. This is the side of gear teeth that is subject to the most wear. The coast side of gear teeth is the opposite side from the drive side. This side of the teeth is in contact when the drive wheels are driving the engine (e.g., during deceleration).

Constant Mesh

The term *constant mesh* refers to gears that remain in mesh with each other and are not engaged or disengaged from each other by transmission or driver action when shifting gears. Synchronizers are used to engage or disengage constant mesh gears.

Backlash

Backlash is the term used to describe the amount one gear is able to move when the gear with which it is in mesh is held stationary. All gears have some backlash to allow for expansion of metal due to heat and for proper lubrication. Excessive backlash is an indication of gear tooth wear.

Bottoming

The condition known as "bottoming" occurs when the teeth of one gear touch the lowest point between teeth of a mating gear. Bottoming does not occur in

a two-gear drive combination but can occur in multiple-gear drive combinations. A simple two-gear drive combination always tends to force the two gears apart; therefore, bottoming cannot occur in this arrangement.

Climbing

Climbing is a gear problem caused by excessive wear in gears, bearings, and shafts whereby the gears move sufficiently apart to cause the apex (or point) of the teeth on one gear to climb over the apex of the teeth on another gear with which it is meshed. This results in a loss of drive until other teeth are engaged; it also causes rapid destruction of the gears.

A general understanding of the terms described here will help to understand gear operation in the transaxle and transmission.

Gear Mounting

Gears are mounted on shafts in transaxles and transmissions in several ways. Gears that drive shafts or are driven by shafts are splined or keyed to the shaft or connected to the shaft by means of a synchronizer. In the latter case, the gear is free to turn independently from the shaft when not engaged by the synchronizer. Another method used is to cast gears in multiple gear combinations (cluster gear or countergear) where several gears operate on a shaft as a unit. A gear can also be an integral part of the shaft, as in the case of a transmission input shaft or clutch shaft.

PART 2 TYPES OF TRANSMISSIONS AND TRANSAXLES

Some of the more common transmissions used are as follows:

1. Three speed; third speed being direct drive, all forward speeds synchronized.

2. Four speed; fourth speed being direct drive, all forward speeds synchronized.

3. Four speed; third speed being direct drive and fourth speed being an overdrive.

4. Five speed; fourth speed being direct drive and fifth speed being overdrive.

Gear ratios vary considerably depending on the vehicle and engine size, axle ratio, and wheel and tire size. When a small gear drives a larger gear, the result is a gear reduction. A gear reduction provides an increase in torque and a decrease in speed. When a small gear is driven by a larger gear, the result is a decrease in torque and an increase in speed.

If a gear with 15 teeth is used to drive a gear with 30 teeth, the ratio is 2:1. This is calculated by dividing the number of teeth on the drive gear into the number of teeth on the driven gear: driven/drive. In this example, 30/15:1 or 2:1.

When power flows through a series of gears, the ratio can be calculated in a similar manner. For example, if a 20-tooth drive gear drives a 24-tooth cluster gear, and the second speed cluster gear has 16 teeth driving a 20-tooth second speed driven gear, the result would be a 1.5:1 ratio. This is calculated as follows:

$$\frac{\text{Driven}}{\text{Drive}} \times \frac{\text{Driven}}{\text{Drive}} \text{ or } \frac{24}{20} \times \frac{20}{16} = 1.5{:}1$$

which is an acceptable second gear ratio.

Synchromesh Transmission or Transaxle

The synchromesh transmission or transaxle is a constant mesh design. Components of these units are the case, which houses the gears and shaft; the control cover, which may house the shifter mechanism; and the various shafts and gears. The input shaft has an integral main drive gear and rotates with the clutch-driven plate (disc); that is, the shaft rotates all the time the clutch is engaged and the engine is running. The input shaft is supported in the case by a ball bearing and at the front end by an oil-impregnated bushing mounted in the engine crankshaft. The drive gear is in constant mesh with the countershaft drive gear. Since all gears in the countershaft cluster are integral, they also rotate at the time the clutch is engaged. The countergear is carried on roller bearings at both ends, and thrust is absorbed by thrust washers located between the countergear and thrust bosses in the case. An anti-lash plate (on some models) at the front face of the countergear provides a constant spring tension between the countergear and the main drive gear to reduce torsional vibrations. The transmission main-shaft is held in line with the input shaft by a pilot bearing at its front end, which allows it to rotate or come to rest independently of the input shaft. It is carried at the rear by a ball bearing mounted in the front face of the extension housing.

Helical gears are incorporated throughout, sometimes including reverse gear. The mainshaft gears are free to rotate independently on the mainshaft and are in constant mesh with the countershaft gears. The reverse idler gear is carried on a bearing or bushing, and thrust is taken on the thrust bosses of the case.

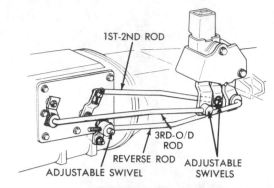

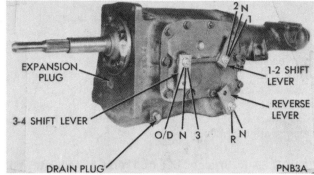

FIGURE 36-7. External view of typical manual transmission (four speed) and shift linkage arrangement (console shift). *(Courtesy of Chrysler Corporation)*

Synchronizers

Transmissions and transaxles are usually fully synchronized in all forward speeds; however, reverse gear is not. The synchronizer assemblies consist of a hub, sleeve, two blocking rings, two key springs, and three synchronizer keys. The synchronizer hubs are splined to the mainshaft and retained by snap rings. These assemblies permit gears to be selected without clashing by synchronizing the speeds of mating parts before they engage.

The sleeve is splined to the hub but can slide fore and aft on the hub. The shift fork engages a groove in the sleeve and controls sleeve position.

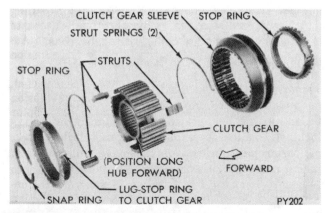

FIGURE 36-8. Exploded view of a typical synchronizer assembly as used in many transmissions. *(Courtesy of Chrysler Corporation)*

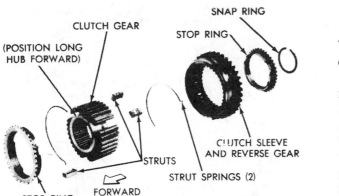

FIGURE 36-9. Exploded view of first-to-second synchronizer assembly with reverse driven gear integral with the sleeve. In a transmission using this arrangement, the sliding reverse idler gear is shifted into mesh with the reverse driven gear shown here. *(Courtesy of Chrysler Corporation)*

When a particular gear is selected, the sleeve slides on the splined hub toward the driven gear required.

Movement of the sleeve pushes the blocking ring into contact with a cone on the driven gear. Friction between the two parts brings them to the same rotating speed. At this point the sleeve is able to move into full engagement with the synchronizer teeth on the driven gear. This prevents clashing of gears during shifting. Since equalization of speed of rotating parts is required for engagement, sufficient time, during shifting, is required for this to occur. Force shifting can damage synchronizers and gears.

Gear Selection

Gearshift levers on manual transaxles or transmissions are located either on the steering column or on

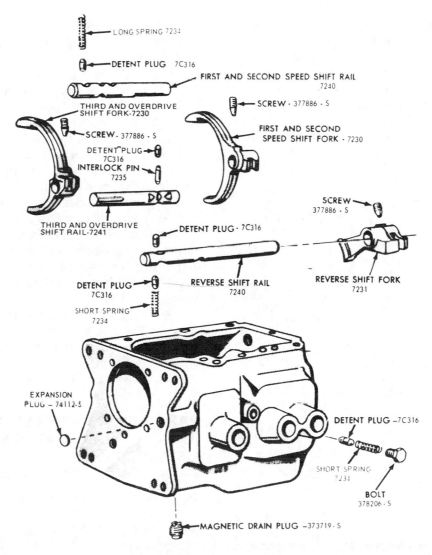

FIGURE 36-10. Exploded view of shift rails, forks, detents, and interlock. *(Courtesy of Ford Motor Co. of Canada Ltd.)*

the floor. Regardless of location, the lever performs two operations: It selects the gear or synchronizer assembly to be moved, and moves it either forward or backward into the desired gear position. The action is the same whether a floor-type shift lever or a steering-column shift lever is used. When the shift lever is moved, the movement is carried by linkage to the transmission. This linkage (cable or control rods) is connected to levers that are mounted on shafts that extend through the transmission case and are connected to levers inside the transmissions. The other ends of these shafts inside the transmission are the shift forks. On other transmissions, however, the external linkage is connected to a selector shaft located inside the transmission with ends extending through the case, which operates the shift forks.

Shift Mechanism

Gear shifting is done by means of forks that are positioned in grooves in synchronizer sleeves or sliding gears. The forks are connected to sliding shift rails or shaft operated cams. The shafts or cams are operated by cable or rod type linkage connected to the gear shift lever; the gear shift lever may, in some instances, actuate the shift rails directly, without any linkage. In this latter case, the shift lever is mounted directly to the transmission case.

The gear shift lever is mounted so that it is able

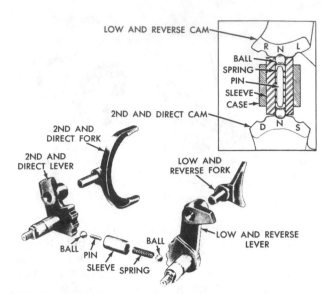

FIGURE 36–12. Cam-and-lever-type shift system showing interlock pin and detent balls and spring. (*Courtesy of Chrysler Corporation*)

to select the desired shift rail or shift cam; then, the shift is completed by moving the lever forward or pulling back.

Shift rails or shafts are equipped with spring-loaded balls that snap into notches in the shift rail—one for each gear position and neutral position. This device, known as a detent, helps keep the synchronizer or gear in the position selected. An interlock device is also provided, which makes it impossible to shift the transmission into two gears at once. The interlock in the shift rail system is usually a plate or pin located in the case between two shift rails or plates. The pin or plate is able to slide toward either rail. Notches in the rail are arranged so that the pin is pushed into a notch in the stationary rail or selector plate as the other rail is shifted. This prevents shifting of more than one shift rail at any time.

A similar interlock pin is provided between two cams on the cam and shaft arrangement. A spring-loaded detent is used to hold the shift cam in the selected position.

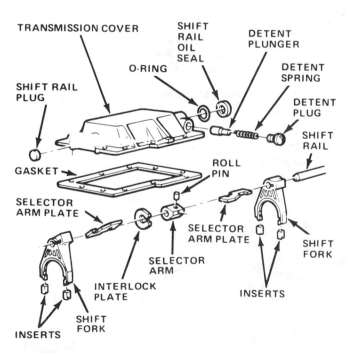

FIGURE 36–11. Single-rail-type shift cover showing forks, selector plates, interlock, and detent. (*Courtesy of American Motors Corporation*)

PART 3   REAR–WHEEL–DRIVE TRANSMISSIONS

Three-Speed Transmission (Typical)

In the typical three-speed manual transmission, four of the transmission gears constitute the countergear. These are the driven gear, second-speed gear, first-speed gear, and reverse gear. The engine-driven main gear drives the countergear through a constant mesh counter. The countergear rotates in a di-

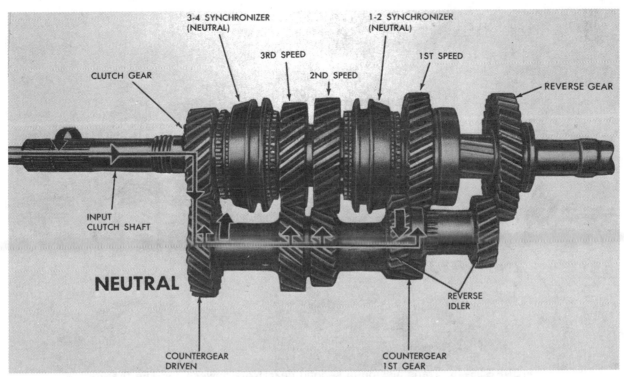

FIGURE 36-13. Internal parts of a four-speed transmission showing rotating parts when the engine is running, clutch engaged, and transmission in neutral. The reverse gear is splined to the output shaft. These two parts do not rotate unless the vehicle is moving. *(Courtesy of General Motors Corporation)*

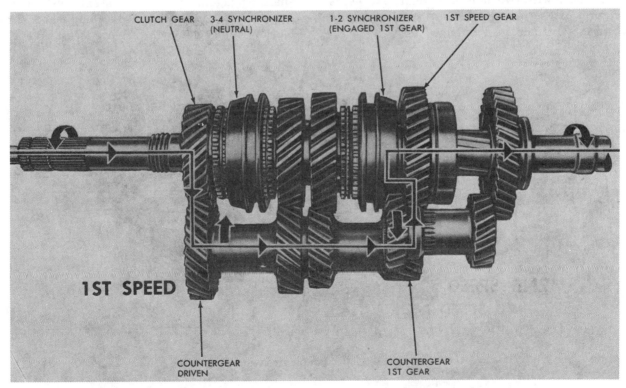

FIGURE 36-14. Power flow through transmission in first gear. The first-to-second synchronizer has been shifted to the rear of the transmission connecting the first-speed gear to the output shaft. This results in a speed reduction and an increase in torque. *(Courtesy of General Motors Corporation)*

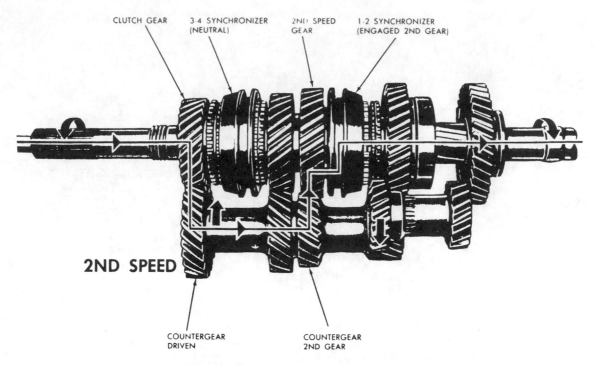

FIGURE 36-15. Transmission in second gear. Note power flow. The first-to-second synchronizer sleeve has been shifted forward to connect the second-speed gear to the output shaft. *(Courtesy of General Motors Corporation)*

rection opposite to the rotation of the main gear. Forward-speed gears on the countergear remain in constant mesh with two nonsliding mainshaft gears, giving first and second speed. Third speed is a direct drive with the main gear engaged directly to the mainshaft. Forward gears are engaged through two sliding synchronizer sleeves mounted on the mainshaft. Engagement of the constant mesh mainshaft gears to the mainshaft is accomplished through blocker ring-type synchronizers described earlier.

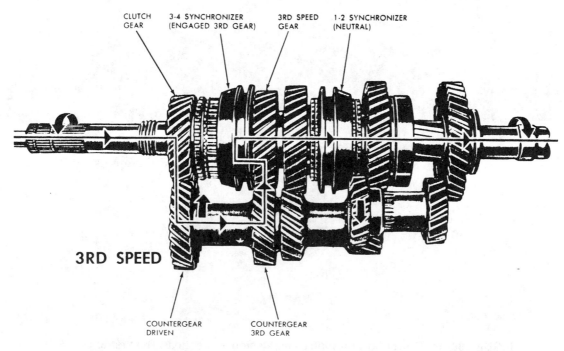

FIGURE 36-16. Power flow in third gear. The third-to-fourth synchronizer sleeve has been shifted to the rear to connect the third-speed gear to the output shaft. *(Courtesy of General Motors Corporation)*

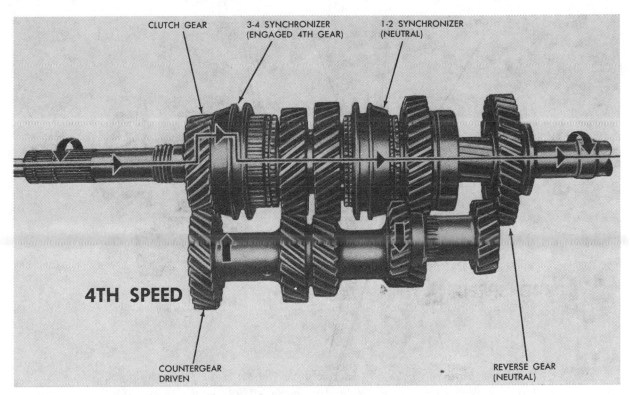

FIGURE 36-17. Power flow in fourth gear. The third-to-fourth synchronizer sleeve has been shifted forward. This connects the input shaft to the output shaft, which provides direct (1:1) drive. *(Courtesy of General Motors Corporation)*

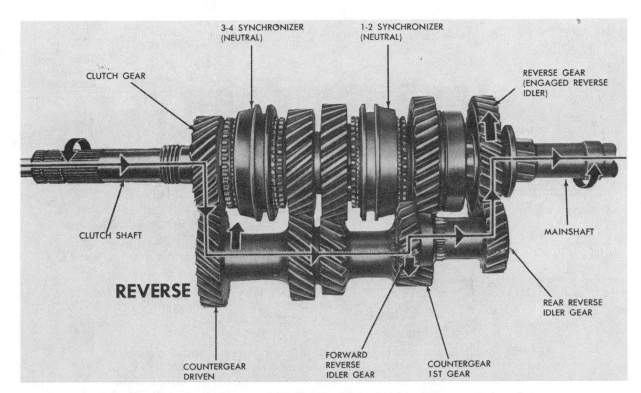

FIGURE 36-18. Power flow in reverse. The reverse sliding gear has been shifted forward to engage the reverse idler gear, providing reverse. *(Courtesy of General Motors Corporation)*

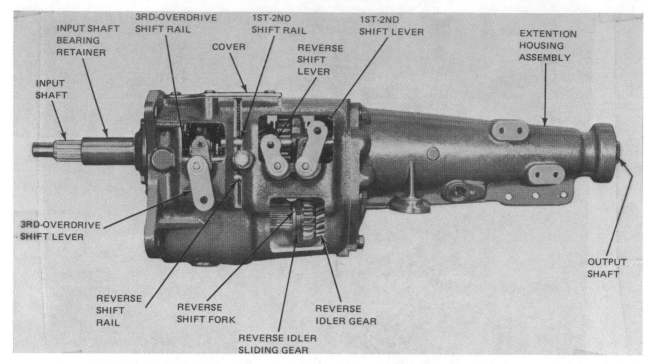

FIGURE 36-19. Typical four-speed overdrive transmission. Note sliding reverse idler gear. *(Courtesy of Ford Motor Co. of Canada Ltd.)*

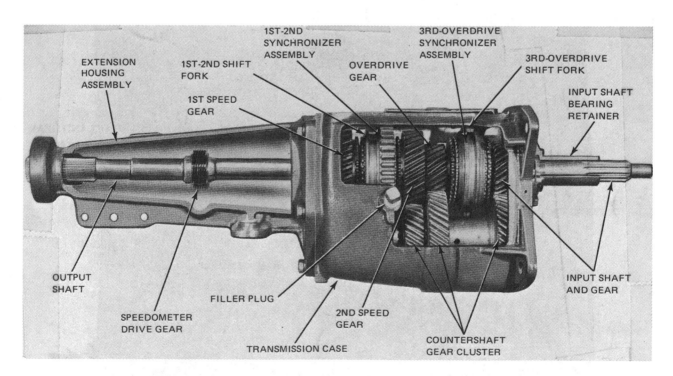

FIGURE 36-20. Four-speed overdrive transmission cutaway showing gear arrangement. In this transmission, third gear is direct (1:1) drive. Overdrive is provided by moving the third and overdrive synchronizer sleeve to the rear to connect the overdrive driven gear to the output shaft. Power flow is from the input shaft gear to countergear to overdrive gear and output shaft. *(Courtesy of Ford Motor Co. of Canada Ltd.)*

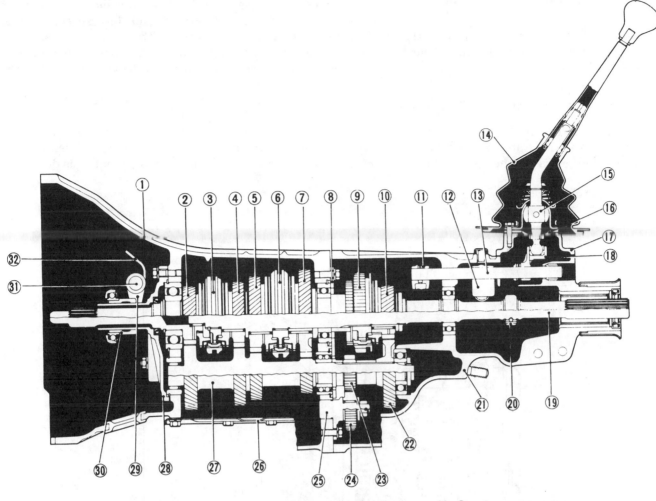

1. Transmission case
2. Main drive pinion
3. Synchronizer assy. (3–4 speed)
4. 3rd speed gear
5. 2nd speed gear
6. Synchronizer assy. (1–2 speed)
7. 1st speed gear
8. Rear bearing retainer
9. Synchronizer assy. (overdrive)
10. Overdrive gear
11. Control finger
12. Neutral return finger
13. Control shaft
14. Control lever cover
15. Control lever assy.
16. Stopper plate
17. Control housing
18. Change shifter
19. Mainshaft
20. Speedometer drive gear
21. Extension housing
22. Counter overdrive gear
23. Counter reverse gear
24. Reverse idler gear
25. Reverse idler gear shaft
26. Case cover
27. Counter gear
28. Front bearing retainer
29. Clutch shift arm
30. Release bearing carrier
31. Clutch control shaft
32. Return spring

FIGURE 36–21. Typical five-speed overdrive transmission for rear-wheel-drive vehicle. *(Courtesy of Chrysler Corporation)*

Reverse is accomplished by moving the external toothed synchronizer-reverse sliding gear assembly into mesh with the reverse idler.

Four-Speed Transmission (Typical)

The engine-driven main drive gear drives the countergear through a constant mesh countershaft gear. Forward-speed gears on the countergear remain in constant mesh with three nonsliding mainshaft gears giving first, second, and third speeds. Fourth speed is a direct drive with the gear engaged directly to the mainshaft. Forward gears are engaged through two sliding synchro sleeves mounted on the mainshaft.

Engagement of the mainshaft gears to the mainshaft is accomplished through blocker ring-type synchronizers. The only sliding gear used is reverse gear splined to the mainshaft. When reverse gear is slid forward into engagement, it is driven by

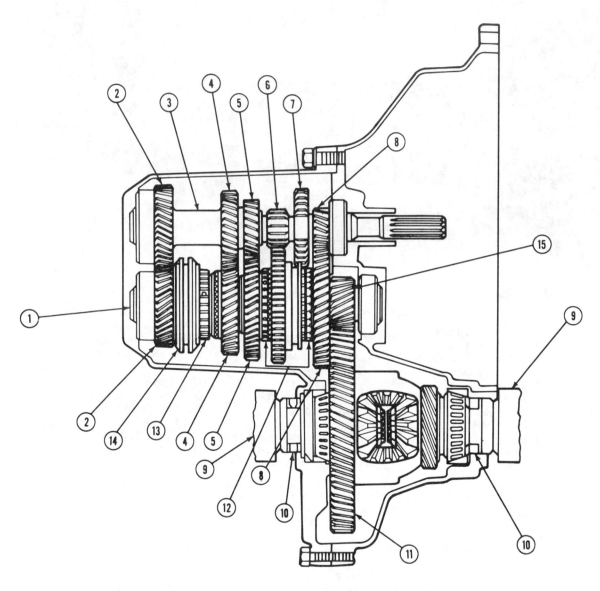

1. MAINSHAFT
2. 4TH SPEED GEARS
3. INPUT CLUSTER
4. 3RD SPEED GEARS
5. 2ND SPEED GEARS
6. REVERSE GEAR
7. REVERSE IDLER GEAR
8. 1ST SPEED GEARS
9. HALF SHAFTS
10. DIFFERENTIAL OIL SEALS
11. FINAL DRIVE RING GEAR
12. 1ST/2ND SPEED SYNCHRONIZER
    BLOCKER RINGS
13. 3RD/4TH SPEED SYNCHRONIZER HUB
14. 3RD/4TH SPEED SYNCHRONIZER SLEEVE
15. PINION GEAR – PART OF MAINSHAFT

FIGURE 36–22. Four-speed manual transaxle cutaway view. *(Courtesy of Ford Motor Co. of Canada Ltd.)*

the reverse idler gear. The reverse idler gear is in constant mesh with the countergear.

On some models, the first-second gear synchronizer sleeve has gear teeth on its outside circumference, enabling it to serve as reverse gear. Reverse gear is obtained by engaging the sliding reverse idler and reverse gear on the countergear. Except for this difference, power flow is essentially the same for both transmissions.

Knowing mechanical power flow assists in proper transmission trouble diagnosis. Typical four-

speed-power flow is shown in Figures 36–13 to 36–18.

Five-Speed Overdrive Transmission (Figure 36-21)

The engine-driven main drive gear drives the countergear through a constant mesh countershaft gear. Forward-speed gears on the countergear remain in

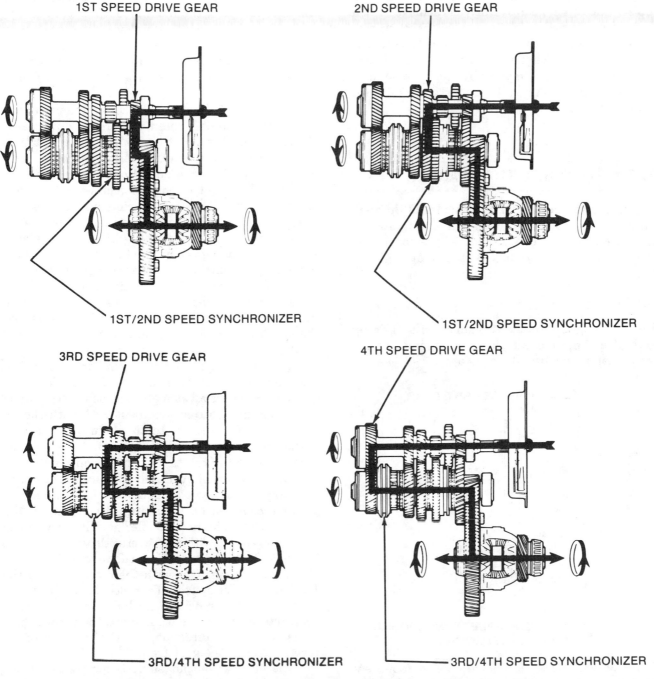

FIGURE 36–23. Power flow in forward speeds for four-speed manual transaxle. *(Courtesy of Ford Motor Co. of Canada Ltd.)*

constant mesh with four non-sliding mainshaft gears giving first, second, and third speeds. Fourth speed is a direct drive with the gear engaged directly to the mainshaft with the third and fourth speed synchronizer connecting the input and output shafts to each other. Forward gears are engaged through sliding synchro sleeves mounted on the mainshaft.

Engagement of the mainshaft gears to the mainshaft is accomplished through blocker ring-type synchronizers. The only sliding gear used is reverse gear splined to the mainshaft through the synchronizer hub. Fifth-gear overdrive is achieved when the overdrive synchronizer connects the overdrive gear to the output shaft when it is moved to the rear for engagement. When reverse gear is slid forward into engagement, it is driven by the reverse idler gear. The reverse idler gear is in constant mesh with the countergear.

PART 4 MANUAL TRANSAXLES

Transaxles combine the transmission and differential assemblies in one unit. Both four- and five-speed overdrive designs are used. The five-speed overdrive unit provides increased fuel economy at highway speeds.

Four-Speed Transaxle

Power is brought into the transmission section by means of an input shaft that corresponds to the cluster gear or countershaft in a conventional in-

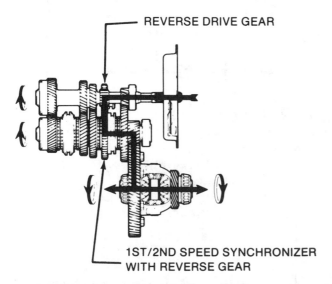

REVERSE DRIVE GEAR

1ST/2ND SPEED SYNCHRONIZER WITH REVERSE GEAR

FIGURE 36-24. Power flow in reverse in four-speed manual transaxle. *(Courtesy of Ford Motor Co. of Canada Ltd.)*

stallation. This input shaft is splined to accept the clutch hub and is made in one piece with the cluster gear. It is supported in the case on two ball bearings.

The mainshaft or output shaft that meshes with the input shaft is one piece with the pinion or drive gear that meshes with the axle drive gear (corresponding to the ring gear in a conventional type axle). All the remaining gears of the main or output shaft assembly float on the shaft like those in other constant-mesh transmissions. Only the synchronizer hubs are splined to the shaft. They are locked in position with snap rings as other transmissions of this type. Thus, the main or output shaft is driven in all speeds by the sliding synchronizer sleeves and hubs as the sliding sleeves are moved by the selector forks. Synchronizer assemblies are similar in design to those used in other four-speed transmissions.

Operation of the synchronizers minimizes gear clash when changing speed upward or downward. They act as both a clutch and a brake in regulating the gear speed during shifting. As an example, when shifting upward, the selector fork moves the synchronizer sleeve out of engagement with the lower speed gear and its blocking ring and moves the higher speed blocking ring against the conical face of the higher speed gear. The blocking ring then acts as a brake, bringing the input shaft gear train down to the output shaft speed. Further movement of the synchronizer sleeve then positively locks the selected higher speed gear to the main-shaft through the internal splines on the synchronizer sleeve and the synchronizer hub that is splined to the mainshaft.

The reverse gear train is similar to the conventional four-speed transmission design. The three gears involved are all straight-cut, since the reverse idler must slide into engagement with both the reverse drive gear and the teeth cut into the outside of the 1st and 2nd speed synchronizer sleeve in order to reverse the rotation of the output shaft.

The sequence of events in shifting to reverse is as follows. Both synchronizers are held in neutral position, centered on their respective hubs by the selector forks. The reverse idler gear is then moved into engagement with the reverse drive gear on the input shaft; at the same time the reverse idler gear slides into engagement with the teeth cut into the 1st and 2nd gear synchronizer sleeve. As the sleeve is splined to the synchronizer hub, which is in turn splined to the main or output shaft, the output shaft turns in a reverse direction, due to the action of the reverse idler in the gear train.

The main or output shaft is supported at the outer end by a ball bearing and at the inner end by a roller bearing in this example.

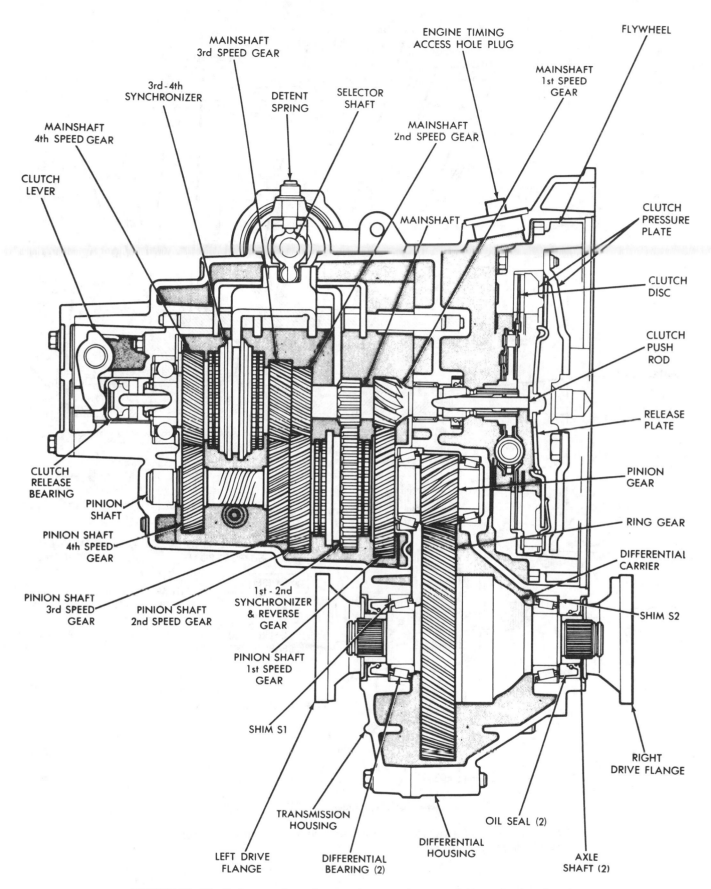

FIGURE 36-25. Cutaway view of manual transaxle assembly as used on front-wheel drive. Note location of clutch and differential. (*Courtesy of Chrysler Corporation*)

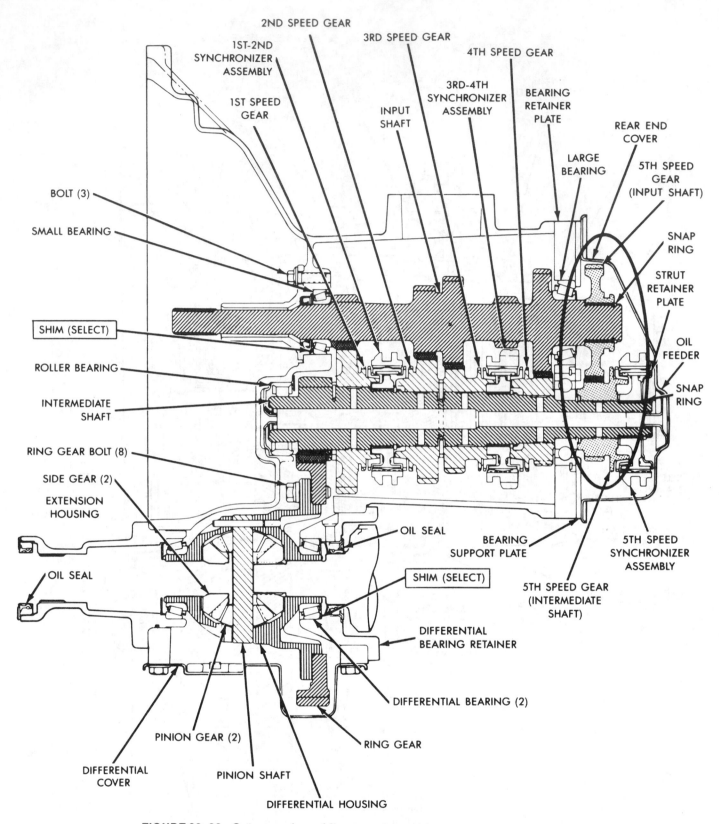

FIGURE 36-26. Cutaway view of five-speed overdrive manual transaxle. (*Courtesy of Chrysler Corporation*)

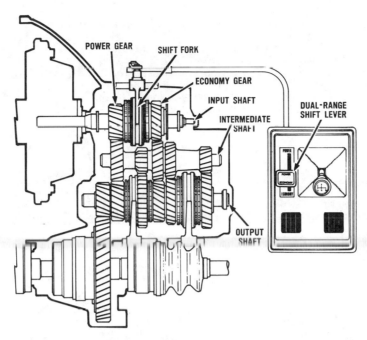

FIGURE 36-27. Dual-range transaxle provides four speeds in each range for a total of eight forward speeds. Low range for power and high range for economy. Note two shift levers. *(Courtesy of Chrysler Corporation)*

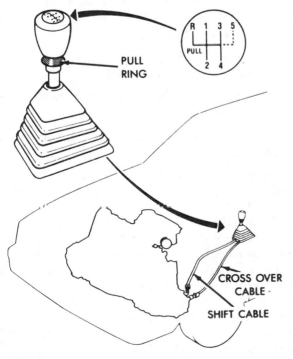

FIGURE 36-28. Shift linkage for five-speed overdrive transaxle. *(Courtesy of Chrysler Corporation)*

Transaxle Differential Section

Excepting the helical-cut axle drive gear, the differential assembly is basically similar to those used in front-engine, rear drive cars. It is a two-pinion type with conventional side gears into which the constant-velocity joints are locked by means of snap rings. Because of the helical-cut gearing, all the time-consuming adjustments required on conventional ring gear and pinion are eliminated. As on the differential side bearings in a conventional axle, this differential is held in position by preload shims.

Power is brought into the differential drive assembly by means of the drive pinion, which is an integral part of the transmission main or output shaft. The drive pinion meshes with the drive gear which is in turn bolted to the differential case or housing. Driving torque is then transmitted through the differential side gears to the constant-velocity joints that are splined to the side gears. The constant-velocity joints then transmit the power to the front wheels through the axle shafts and the outer constant-velocity joints.

The differential assembly is positioned in the case by two tapered roller bearings similar to con-

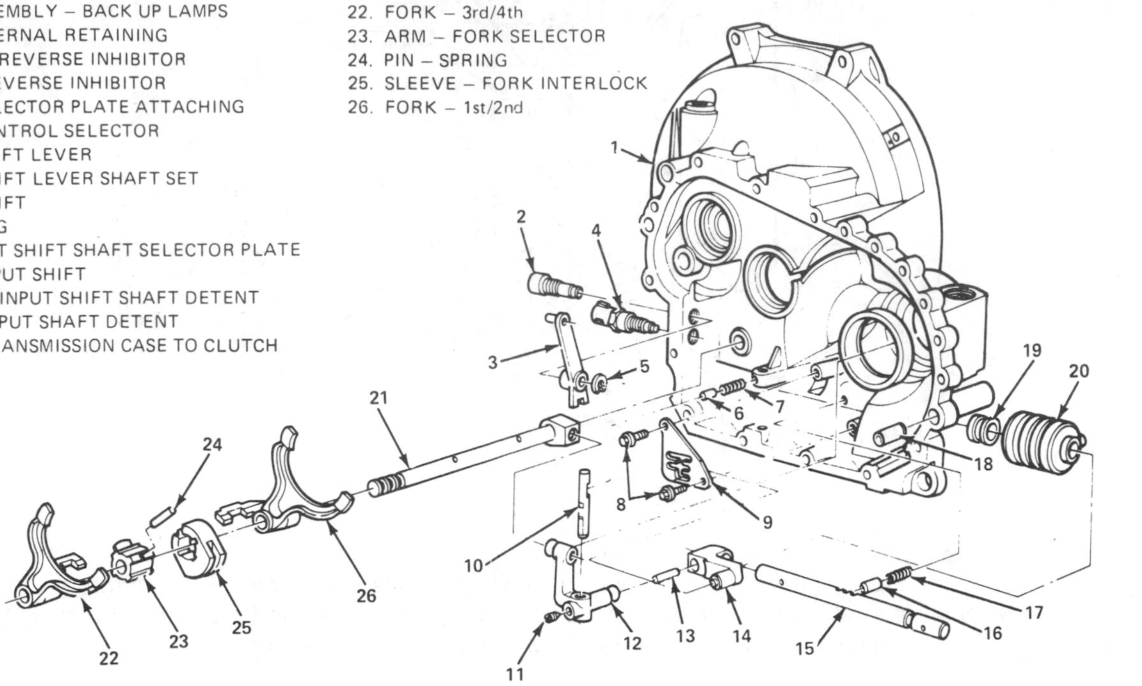

1. CASE – CLUTCH HOUSING
2. PIN – REVERSE RELAY LEVER PIVOT
3. LEVER – REVERSE RELAY
4. SWITCH ASSEMBLY – BACK UP LAMPS
5. RING – EXTERNAL RETAINING
6. PLUNGER – REVERSE INHIBITOR
7. SPRING – REVERSE INHIBITOR
8. BOLTS – SELECTOR PLATE ATTACHING
9. PLATE – CONTROL SELECTOR
10. SHAFT – SHIFT LEVER
11. SCREW – SHIFT LEVER SHAFT SET
12. LEVER – SHIFT
13. PIN – SPRING
14. ARM – INPUT SHIFT SHAFT SELECTOR PLATE
15. SHAFT – INPUT SHIFT
16. PLUNGER – INPUT SHIFT SHAFT DETENT
17. SPRING – INPUT SHAFT DETENT
18. DOWEL – TRANSMISSION CASE TO CLUTCH HOUSING
19. SEAL ASSEMBLY – SHIFT CONTROL SHAFT OIL
20. BOOT – SHIFT CONTROL SHAFT
21. SHAFT – MAIN SHIFT CONTROL
22. FORK – 3rd/4th
23. ARM – FORK SELECTOR
24. PIN – SPRING
25. SLEEVE – FORK INTERLOCK
26. FORK – 1st/2nd

FIGURE 36–29. Typical internal shift mechanism for four-speed manual transaxle. *(Courtesy of General Motors Corporation)*

ventional mountings. Shims are used to exert a constant pressure or preload on the side bearings.

The speedometer drive gear is mounted on the differential case and held in position by the side bearing.

Oil seals surround the constant-velocity joint shafts where they enter the housing.

Dual-Range Transaxle

The dual-range four-speed transaxle is a three-shaft type: input, intermediate, and output. The output of the transaxle is through a conventional differential. This transaxle has two gears on the input shaft—"economy" and "power"—with a synchronizer assembly. Drivers have a choice of gear ratios; they select either the power mode or the economy mode by shifting the dual-range lever. Selection can be made while in any gear by clutching and shifting the dual-range lever, which is a separate lever from the gear selector lever.

PART 5 FOUR-WHEEL DRIVE

Four-wheel drive systems are designed to provide both two-wheel drive and four-wheel drive as needed or desired. Four-wheel drive provides extra traction by driving all four wheels instead of only two. When four-wheel drive is not needed, two-wheel drive can be selected to provide normal economy driving.

The four-wheel drive system, in addition to the conventional rear two-wheel drive, requires the following additional components:

• Transfer case (mounted at the rear of automatic or manual transmission)

• Front drive differential and axles

• Front drive shaft

• Front drive wheel locking hubs (automatic or manual locking)

Two basic types of four-wheel drive designs are used—part time and full time. Part time four-wheel drive delivers equal and constant power to the front and rear axles without any differential action between the two drive shafts. The transfer case does not provide differential action. In this design, the driver must get out of the vehicle to lock or unlock the front-wheel drive hubs. Normal highway driving on dry, hard surfaces in part time four-wheel drive is not recommended since adverse handling, vehicle stability, excessive tire wear, and inter-axle conflict would result.

Full time four-wheel drive uses a transfer case with differential action between the two drive

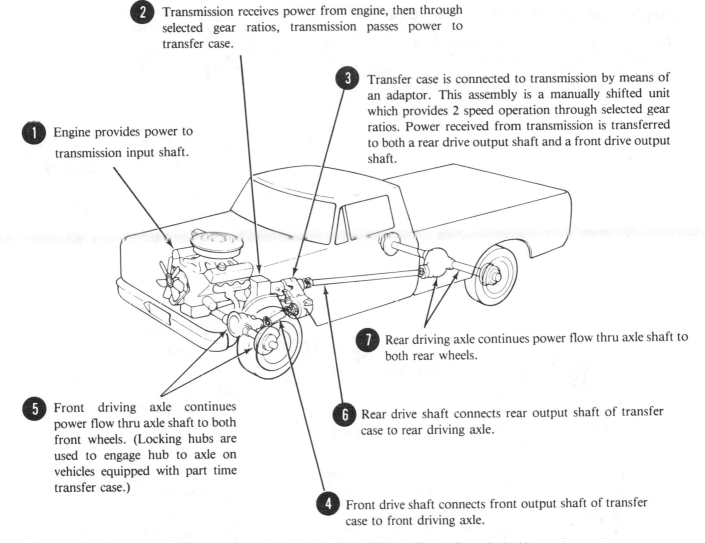

2 Transmission receives power from engine, then through selected gear ratios, transmission passes power to transfer case.

3 Transfer case is connected to transmission by means of an adaptor. This assembly is a manually shifted unit which provides 2 speed operation through selected gear ratios. Power received from transmission is transferred to both a rear drive output shaft and a front drive output shaft.

1 Engine provides power to transmission input shaft.

7 Rear driving axle continues power flow thru axle shaft to both rear wheels.

5 Front driving axle continues power flow thru axle shaft to both front wheels. (Locking hubs are used to engage hub to axle on vehicles equipped with part time transfer case.)

6 Rear drive shaft connects rear output shaft of transfer case to rear driving axle.

4 Front drive shaft connects front output shaft of transfer case to front driving axle.

FIGURE 36-30. *(Courtesy of Ford Motor Co. of Canada Ltd.)*

shafts. This allows driving forces to be continually transferred to the front and rear axles as conditions dictate. The differential in the transfer compensates for the difference in front and rear axle speeds that can occur when turning a corner or as a result of varying road conditions. The conventional full time four-wheel drive transfer case differential operates in the same way as a drive axle differential. With full time four-wheel drive, the driver can select two- or four-wheel drive from the driver's seat since front drive hubs are automatic. Some transfer case designs use a planetary gear differential, whereas another design uses planetary gears to provide high and low speed ranges. High and low ranges are provided by two sets of helical gears with a synchronizer used to select either range in another design.

Various driving modes are possible depending on design. Some of these modes include four-wheel drive high, four-wheel drive low, neutral, and two-wheel drive for part time units. Full time four-wheel drive modes include high and low differentiated four-wheel drive, high and low locked four-wheel drive, neutral, and two-wheel drive. Transfer case design includes both gear drive and chain drive types. Some designs include a limited slip unit in the differential section of the full time transfer case. This is a sealed silicone fluid viscous clutch unit.

Manual Transmission and Transaxle Lubricants

It is important to follow the vehicle manufacturer's recommendations as to the type and viscosity of lubricant to use in a specific transmission. Some manufacturer's recommend using an extreme pressure gear oil of 75W to 80W viscosity for year-round use; others may recommend the use of automatic transmission fluid in their transmissions.

The shift characteristics, transmission noise,

NEW PROCESS 205 PART TIME TRANSFER CASE

This manually-shifted unit provides two-speed 4 wheel drive operation by means of a constant-mesh helical gear train. Speeds are changed by using sliding clutch gears. A single shift lever controls the integrated shift linkage system.

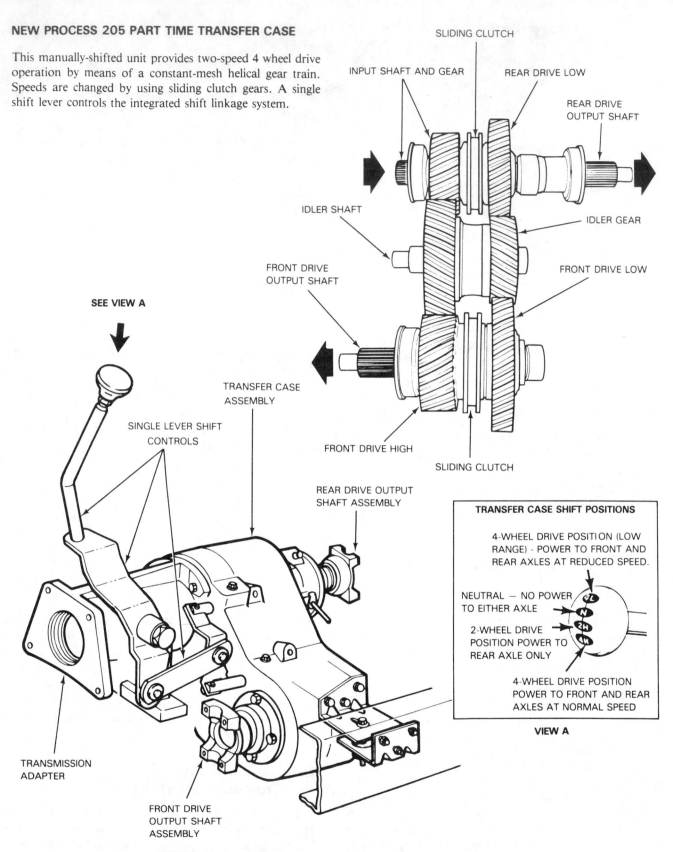

SLIDING CLUTCH

INPUT SHAFT AND GEAR

REAR DRIVE LOW

REAR DRIVE OUTPUT SHAFT

IDLER SHAFT

IDLER GEAR

FRONT DRIVE OUTPUT SHAFT

FRONT DRIVE LOW

FRONT DRIVE HIGH

SLIDING CLUTCH

SEE VIEW A

SINGLE LEVER SHIFT CONTROLS

TRANSFER CASE ASSEMBLY

REAR DRIVE OUTPUT SHAFT ASSEMBLY

TRANSMISSION ADAPTER

FRONT DRIVE OUTPUT SHAFT ASSEMBLY

TRANSFER CASE SHIFT POSITIONS

4-WHEEL DRIVE POSITION (LOW RANGE) - POWER TO FRONT AND REAR AXLES AT REDUCED SPEED.

NEUTRAL — NO POWER TO EITHER AXLE

2-WHEEL DRIVE POSITION POWER TO REAR AXLE ONLY

4-WHEEL DRIVE POSITION POWER TO FRONT AND REAR AXLES AT NORMAL SPEED

VIEW A

FIGURE 36-31. *(Courtesy of Ford Motor Co. of Canada Ltd.)*

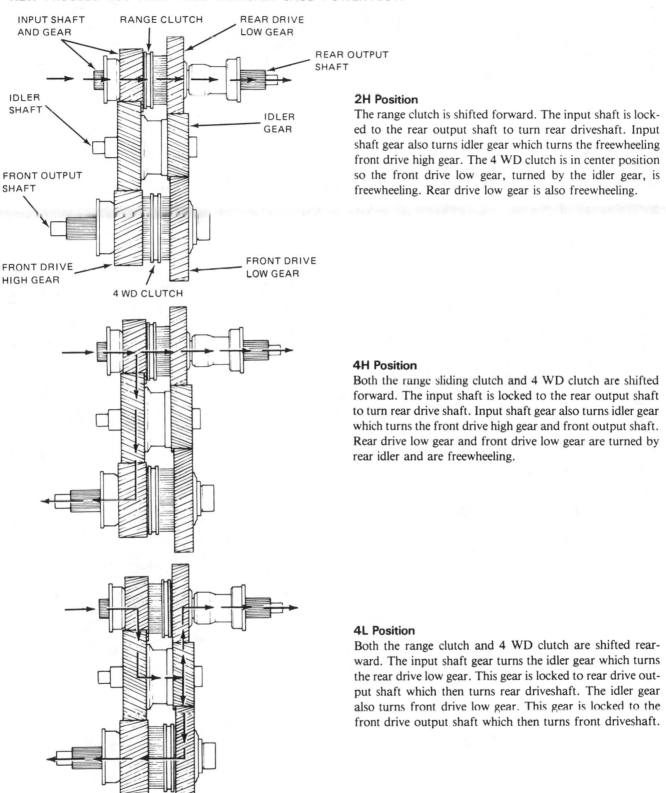

2H Position

The range clutch is shifted forward. The input shaft is locked to the rear output shaft to turn rear driveshaft. Input shaft gear also turns idler gear which turns the freewheeling front drive high gear. The 4 WD clutch is in center position so the front drive low gear, turned by the idler gear, is freewheeling. Rear drive low gear is also freewheeling.

4H Position

Both the range sliding clutch and 4 WD clutch are shifted forward. The input shaft is locked to the rear output shaft to turn rear drive shaft. Input shaft gear also turns idler gear which turns the front drive high gear and front output shaft. Rear drive low gear and front drive low gear are turned by rear idler and are freewheeling.

4L Position

Both the range clutch and 4 WD clutch are shifted rearward. The input shaft gear turns the idler gear which turns the rear drive low gear. This gear is locked to rear drive output shaft which then turns rear driveshaft. The idler gear also turns front drive low gear. This gear is locked to the front drive output shaft which then turns front driveshaft.

FIGURE 36-32. *(Courtesy of Ford Motor Co. of Canada Ltd.)*

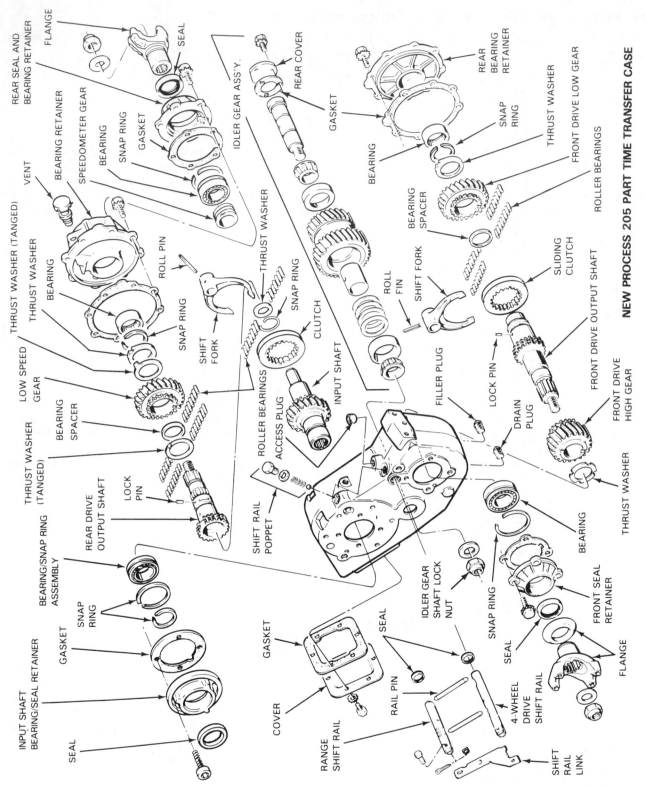

FIGURE 36-33. *(Courtesy of Ford Motor Co. of Canada Ltd.)*

NEW PROCESS 205 PART TIME TRANSFER CASE

REAR SEAL AND BEARING RETAINER

FLANGE

SEAL

REAR COVER

REAR BEARING RETAINER

GASKET

THRUST WASHER

FRONT DRIVE LOW GEAR

SNAP RING

ROLLER BEARINGS

BEARING

BEARING SPACER

SLIDING CLUTCH

ROLLER BEARINGS

FRONT DRIVE OUTPUT SHAFT

FRONT DRIVE HIGH GEAR

THRUST WASHER

BEARING

FRONT SEAL RETAINER

SEAL

FLANGE

SHIFT RAIL LINK

4-WHEEL DRIVE SHIFT RAIL

RAIL PIN

IDLER GEAR LOCK SHAFT NUT

SNAP RING

SEAL

RANGE SHIFT RAIL

COVER

GASKET

SEAL

DRAIN PLUG

LOCK PIN

FILLER PLUG

SHIFT FORK

ROLL PIN

SHIFT RAIL POPPET

ACCESS PLUG

ROLLER BEARINGS

INPUT SHAFT

CLUTCH

SNAP RING

THRUST WASHER

SHIFT FORK

SNAP RING

ROLL PIN

BEARING

LOW SPEED GEAR

BEARING SPACER

THRUST WASHER (TANGED)

THRUST WASHER (TANGED)

VENT

BEARING RETAINER

SPEEDOMETER GEAR

BEARING

SNAP RING

GASKET

IDLER GEAR ASS'Y.

REAR DRIVE OUTPUT SHAFT

LOCK PIN

BEARING/SNAP RING ASSEMBLY

SNAP RING

GASKET

INPUT SHAFT BEARING/SEAL RETAINER

SEAL

852

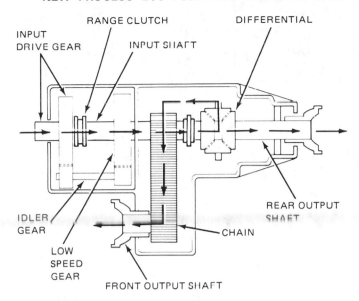

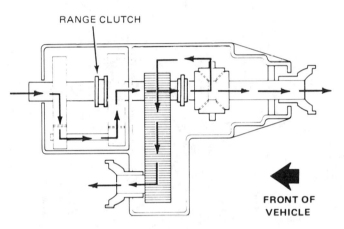

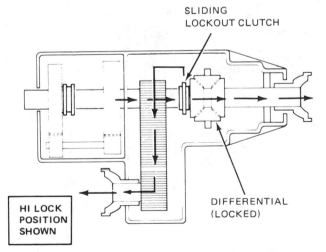

HI Position

The range clutch is shifted forward. The input drive gear is locked to the input shaft assembly which transfers power through the differential to the chain sprockets and chain. The chain turns the front output shaft which turns front driveshaft. The input shaft assembly also transfers power through the differential to the rear output shaft which turns the rear driveshaft. The input drive gear is also turning the idler gear which then turns the freewheeling low speed gear.

Lo Position

The range clutch is shifted rearward. The input drive gear is turning the idler gear which then turns the low speed gear. The low speed gear is now locked to the input shaft assembly by the sliding clutch in the rearward position. The input shaft assembly transfers power through the differential to both the chain sprocket and rear output shaft, which then power the front driveshaft and rear driveshaft respectively.

Hi Lock and Lo Lock Positions

The shift to either HI LOCK or LO LOCK position moves the sliding lockout clutch rearward to lock-up the differential. This prevents the front and rear axle from rotating independently of each other. In HI LOCK, the range clutch is shifted forward and power flow is the same as HI except the differential action is not part of the flow. In LO LOCK, the range clutch is shifted rearward and the power flow is the same as LO except the differential action is not part of the flow.

FIGURE 36-34. *(Courtesy of Ford Motor Co. of Canada Ltd.)*

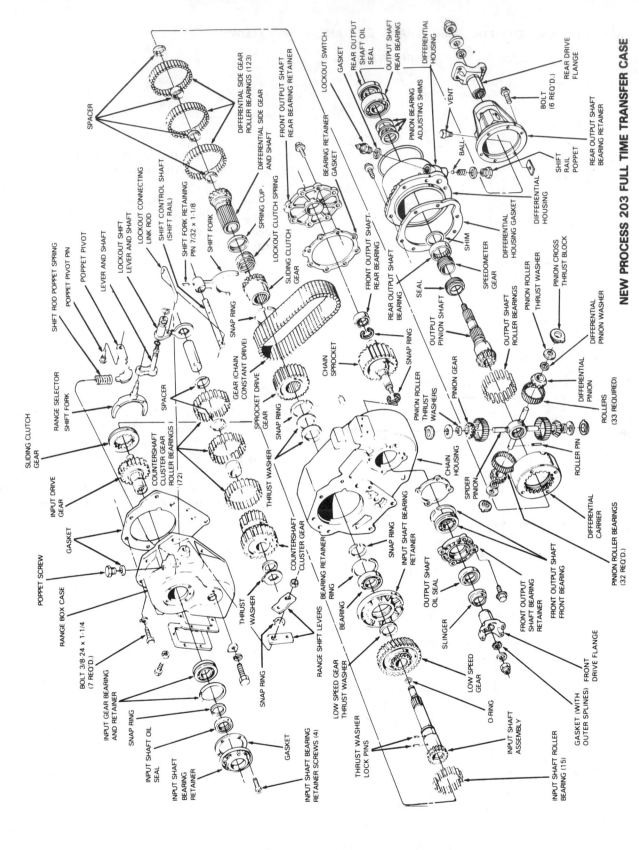

NEW PROCESS 203 FULL TIME TRANSFER CASE

FIGURE 36-35. *(Courtesy of Ford Motor Co. of Canada Ltd.)*

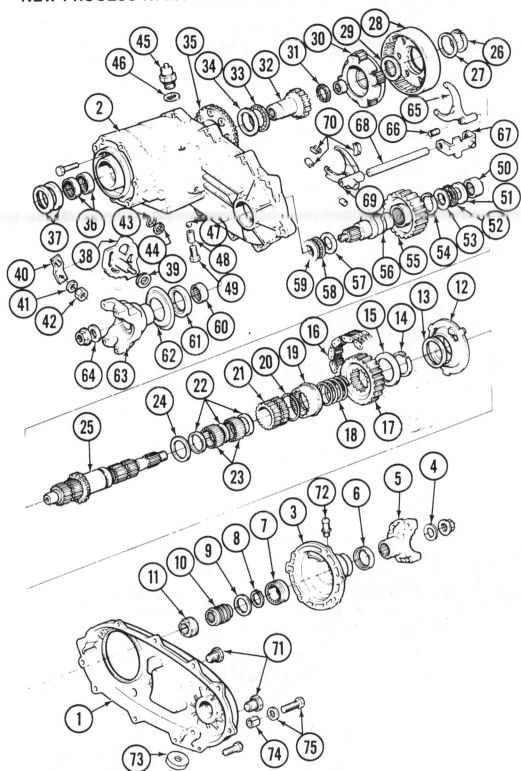

FIGURE 36-36(A). *(Courtesy of Ford Motor Co. of Canada Ltd.)*

1. COVER
2. CASE
3. REAR OUTPUT SHAFT BEARING RETAINER
4. FIBRE WASHER
5. REAR OUTPUT SHAFT YOKE
6. OIL SEAL
7. REAR OUTPUT SHAFT BALL BEARING
8. SNAP RING
9. RETAINER RING
10. SPEEDOMETER DRIVE GEAR
11. OIL PUMP GEAR
12. OIL PUMP HOUSING
13. OIL PUMP SEAL
14. SNAP RING
15. THRUST WASHER
16. DRIVE CHAIN
17. DRIVE SPROCKET
18. SLIDING CLUTCH SHIFT SPRING
19. 4-WHEEL DRIVE SLIDING CLUTCH
20. RETAINING SNAP RING
21. DRIVE SPROCKET CARRIER GEAR
22. SEPARATOR RINGS (3)
23. NEEDLE BEARINGS (120)
24. THRUST WASHER
25. REAR OUTPUT SHAFT
26. SNAP RING
27. THRUST WASHER
28. ANNULUS GEAR
29. THRUST WASHER
30. PLANETARY GEAR ASSEMBLY
31. THRUST BEARING
32. INPUT SHAFT ASSEMBLY
33. THRUST BEARING
34. THRUST WASHER
35. ANNULUS GEAR LOCKING PLATE
36. INPUT SHAFT NEEDLE BEARINGS (2)
37. INPUT SHAFT OIL SEALS (2)
38. SHIFT CAM
39. SPACER WASHER
40. SHIFT LEVER
41. WASHER
42. NUT
43. "O" RING
44. RETAINER
45. 4-WHEEL DRIVE INDICATOR SWITCH
46. WASHER
47. DETENT BALL
48. DETENT SPRING
49. DETENT SCREW
50. FRONT OUTPUT SHAFT INNER SUPPORT NEEDLE BEARING
51. THICK SPACER WASHER
52. THRUST BEARING
53. THIN SPACER WASHER
54. SNAP RING
55. DRIVEN SPROCKET
56. FRONT OUTPUT SHAFT
57. THIN SPACER WASHER
58. THRUST BEARING
59. THICK SPACER WASHER
60. FRONT OUTPUT SHAFT NEEDLE BEARING
61. FRONT OUTPUT SHAFT SEAL
62. OIL SLINGER
63. FRONT OUTPUT SHAFT YOKE
64. FIBRE WASHER
65. 4-WHEEL DRIVE SHIFT FORK
66. SHIFT FORK SPRING
67. SHIFT FORK HOLDER
68. SHIFT RAIL
69. SPEED SELECTION SHIFT FORK ASSEMBLY
70. WEAR PADS (3)
71. FILL AND DRAIN PLUGS
72. BREATHER VENT
73. MAGNETIC CHIP COLLECTOR
74. ALIGNMENT SLEEVE (2)
75. LONG BOLTS & WASHERS (2)

FIGURE 36–36(B). Key to Figure 36–36(A). *(Courtesy of Ford Motor Co. of Canada Ltd.)*

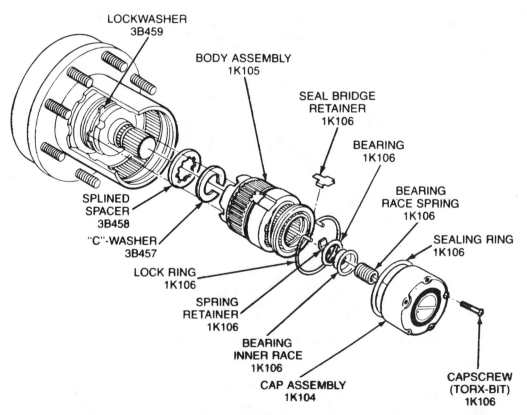

FIGURE 36–37. Automatic locking front-wheel-drive hub for four-wheel drive. *(Courtesy of Ford Motor Co. of Canada Ltd.)*

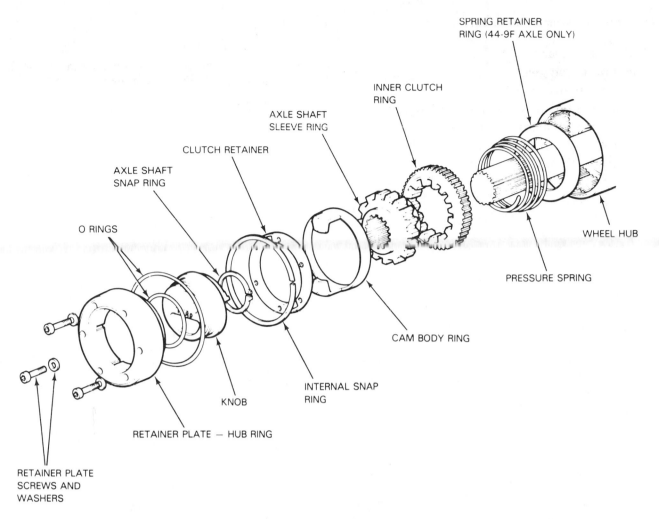

SPRING RETAINER
RING (44-9F AXLE ONLY)

INNER CLUTCH
RING

AXLE SHAFT
SLEEVE RING

CLUTCH RETAINER

AXLE SHAFT
SNAP RING

O RINGS

WHEEL HUB

PRESSURE SPRING

CAM BODY RING

INTERNAL SNAP
RING

KNOB

RETAINER PLATE — HUB RING

RETAINER PLATE
SCREWS AND
WASHERS

FIGURE 36–38. Front-wheel-drive hub for four-wheel drive (manually locking type). *(Courtesy of Ford Motor Co. of Canada Ltd.)*

and wear, can all be affected by the type of lubricant being used. Use only the lubricant recommended by the vehicle manufacturer.

PART 6   SELF–CHECK

1. Describe synchronizer operation.
2. How is the front of the mainshaft supported?
3. How is the front of the input shaft supported?
4. The input shaft is splined to the _____.
5. What is the purpose of the shift interlock?
6. The synchronizer clutch gear hub is splined to the _____.
7. The gear ratio in second gear of a transmission with a 16-tooth drive gear, a 12-tooth cluster drive gear, a 15-tooth second-speed cluster gear, and an 18-tooth second-speed driven gear is _____.

PART 7   TEST QUESTIONS

1. The number of gears on a fully synchronized three-speed transmission mainshaft is:
   (a) two
   (b) three
   (c) four
   (d) five
2. The second- and third-speed synchronizer hub is splined to the:
   (a) clutch shaft
   (b) mainshaft
   (c) cluster gear
   (d) input shaft
3. The only gear not turning when the three-speed fully synchronized transmission is in neutral with the engine running and the clutch applied is the:
   (a) clutch gear

(b) cluster gear

(c) low driven gear

(d) reverse driven gear

4. The transmission section of the four-speed transaxle has how many forward driven gears?

(a) three

(b) four

(c) five

(d) none of the above

5. The five-speed transmission for rear-wheel drive vehicles has how many synchronizers?

(a) three

(b) four

(c) five

(d) six

Chapter 37

Manual Transmission and Transaxle Diagnosis and Service Procedure

Performance Objectives

After sufficient study of this chapter and the necessary practice on the appropriate training models, and with the proper tools, equipment, and shop manuals, you should be able to do the following:

1. Complete the self-check with at least 80 percent accuracy.
2. Diagnose manual transmission and transaxle problems according to the diagnostic chart provided.
3. Recondition and replace faulty transmission and transaxle components according to manufacturer's procedures and specifications.
4. Test the vehicle to determine the success of the service performed.
5. Prepare the vehicle for customer acceptance.

Most of the common manual transmission problems and the possible causes and corrections for these problems are listed in the Diagnostic Chart in this section. Some transmission problems can be corrected without transmission removal. Some problems that may at first appear to be transmission problems may in fact be clutch, drive shaft, differential or axle shaft problems.

It is good practice to determine whether the problem is external or internal before removing the transmission. If the problem is internal, the transmission must be removed in most cases and either replaced or overhauled.

PART 1 GENERAL PRECAUTIONS

For procedures on any vehicle, the appropriate service manual should be used and followed. However, the general precautions that follow should also be observed.

• Avoid getting burned by hot clutch or exhaust parts.

• Disconnect battery to avoid accidental cranking of the engine during clutch or transmission work.

• Support vehicle safely before doing any work under vehicle. Use hoist or safety stands. (Do not work under a vehicle supported by hydraulic jacks or bumper jacks.)

• Support engine properly before removal of transaxle, transmission, or cross-member.

• Use proper transmission or transaxle jack for removal procedure.

• Always make sure heavy clutch parts and flywheel do not drop during removal. Injury and damage could result.

• Support transmission or transaxle properly to prevent clutch plate damage during removal and installation. Transmission must move straight back from flywheel during removal to disengage clutch shaft from clutch. Allowing weight of transmission to hang on input shaft and clutch disc will damage clutch disc.

If the clutch is to be serviced, observe the following:

• Do not use compressed air to blow out clutch housing. Asbestos dust (from clutch facing) can cause cancer if inhaled. Use proper vacuum cleaner. Use filter for breathing protection.

• Do not allow any grease, oil, or other contamination to come in contact with clutch friction surfaces. Even dirty hands can damage the coefficient of friction and cause clutch problems.

See Chapter 35 for clutch service information.

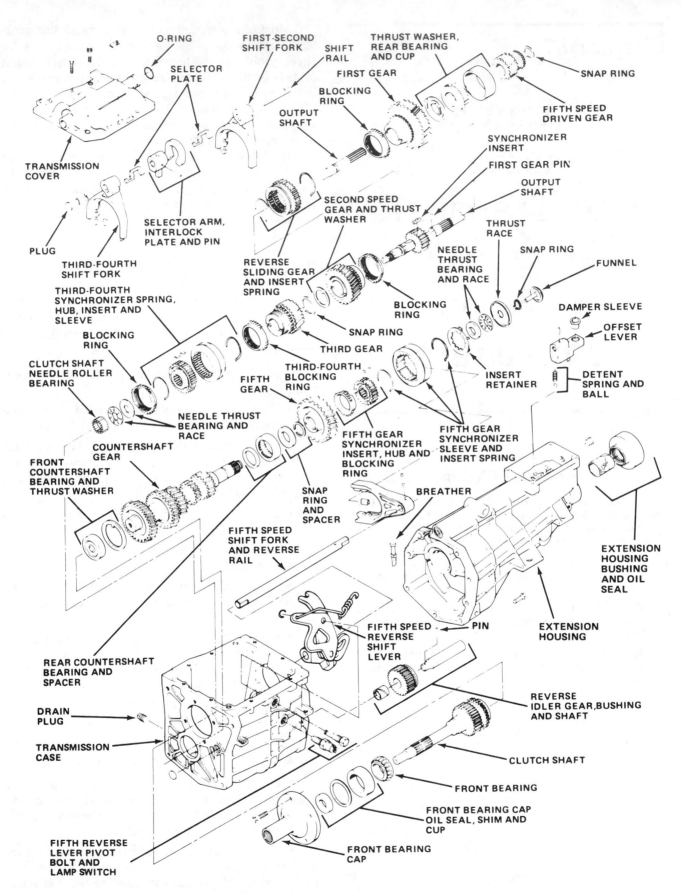

FIGURE 37-1. Five-speed overdrive manual transmission parts, all of which should be inspected for wear or damage (see Part 4). *(Courtesy of American Motors Corporation)*

PART 2   PROBLEM DIAGNOSIS CHART

PROBLEM	CAUSE	CORRECTION
Transmission shifts hard	1. Clutch adjustment incorrect 2. Clutch linkage binding 3. Shift rail binding	1. Adjust clutch 2. Lubricate or repair as necessary 3. Check for mispositioned selector arm roll pin, loose cover bolts, worn shift rail bores, worn shift rail, distorted oil seal, or extension housing not aligned with case. Repair as necessary.
	4. Internal bind in transmission caused by shift forks, selector plates, or synchronizer assemblies 5. Clutch housing misalignment 6. Incorrect lubricant	4. Remove, disassemble, and inspect transmission. Replace worn or damaged components as necessary. 5. Check run-out at rear of clutch housing. Correct run-out. 6. Drain and refill transmission.
Gear clash when shifting from one gear to another	1. Clutch adjustment incorrect 2. Air in hydraulic system 3. Clutch linkage or cable binding 4. Clutch housing misalignment 5. Lubricant level low or incorrect lubricant 6. Gearshift components or synchronizer assemblies worn or damaged	1. Adjust clutch. 2. Bleed hydraulic control system. 3. Lubricate or repair as necessary. 4. Check run-out at rear face of clutch housing. Correct run-out 5. Drain and refill transmission and check for lubricant leaks if level was low. Repair as necessary. 6. Remove, disassemble, and inspect transmission. Replace worn or damaged components as necessary.
Will not shift into one gear	1. Gearshift selector plates, interlock plate, or selector arm, worn, damaged, or incorrectly assembled 2. Shift rail detent plunger worn, spring broken, or plug loose 3. Gearshift lever worn or damaged 4. Synchronizer sleeves or hubs damaged or worn	1. Remove, disassemble, and inspect transmission cover assembly. Repair or replace components as necessary. 2. Tighten plug or replace worn or damaged components as necessary. 3. Replace gearshift lever. 4. Remove, disassemble, and inspect transmission. Replace worn or damaged components.
Locked in one gear—cannot be shifted out of that gear	1. Shift rail(s) worn or broken, shifter fork bent, setscrew loose, center detent plug missing or worn. 2. Broken gear teeth on countershaft gear, clutch shaft, or reverse idler gear. 3. Gearshift lever broken or worn, shift mechanism in cover incorrectly assembled or broken, worn or damaged gear train components	1. Inspect and replace worn or damaged parts. 2. Inspect and replace damaged part. 3. Disassemble transmission. Replace damaged parts or assemble correctly.
Jumps out of gear	1. Clutch housing misalignment 2. Offset lever nylon insert worn or lever attached nut loose 3. Gearshift mechanism, shift forks, selector plates, interlock plate, selector arm, shift rail, detent plugs, springs, or shift cover worn or damaged 4. Clutch shaft or roller bearings worn or damaged 5. Gear teeth worn or tapered, synchronizer assemblies worn or damaged, excessive end play caused by worn thrust washers or output shaft gears 6. Pilot bushing worn	1. Check run-out at rear face of clutch housing. 2. Remove gearshift lever and check for loose offset lever nut or worn insert. Repair or replace as necessary. 3. Remove, disassemble, and inspect transmission cover assembly. Replace worn or damaged components as necessary. 4. Replace clutch shaft or roller bearings as necessary. 5. Remove, disassemble, and inspect transmission. Replace worn or damaged components as necessary. 6. Replace pilot bushing.
Transmission noisy	1. Lubricant level low or incorrect lubricant 2. Clutch housing-to-engine, or transmission-to-clutch housing bolts loose 3. Dirt, chips, or foreign material in transmission 4. Gearshift mechanism or transmission gear, or bearing components worn or damaged 5. Clutch housing misalignment	1. Drain and refill transmission. If lubricant level is low, check for leaks and repair as necessary. 2. Check and correct bolt torque as necessary. 3. Drain, flush, and refill transmission. 4. Remove, disassemble, and inspect transmission. Replace worn or damaged components as necessary. 5. Check run-out at rear face of clutch housing. Correct run-out.

PROBLEM DIAGNOSIS CHART (*continued*)

PROBLEM	CAUSE	CORRECTION
Leaks lubricant	1. Excessive amount of lubricant in transmission	1. Drain to correct level.
	2. Loose or broken main drive gear bearing retainer	2. Tighten or replace retainer.
	3. Main drive gear bearing retainer gasket damaged	3. Replace gasket.
	4. Side cover loose or gasket damaged.	4. Tighten cover or replace gasket.
	5. Rear bearing retainer oil seal leaks	5. Replace seal.
	6. Countershaft loose in case	6. Replace case.
	7. Shift lever seals leak	7. Replace seal.

PART 3   TRANSMISSION AND TRANSAXLE REMOVAL PROCEDURE

The following general procedure can be used for manual transmission removal. Variations to this procedure may be necessary for some models, such as transaxle assemblies. Always refer to manufacturer's manual for specific procedures.

- Disconnect battery.
- Support vehicle on hoist or safety jack stands.
- Drain transmission lubricant.
- Scribe mark drive line to flange connection at rear.
- Disconnect rear-wheel-drive drive line at rear and tape U-joint bearings in place to prevent loss of bearings or entry of dirt.
- Slide drive line from transmission output shaft. Inspect as outlined in Chapter 33, Part 5.

- Remove front-wheel-drive axles from transaxle. (Chapter 33, Part 3.)
- Disconnect all transmission linkages, speedometer cable, and any electrical connections.
- Support engine as required.
- Remove cross member (if required). Note location of any alignment shims and identify for later assembly.
- Support transmission on transmission jack.
- Remove transmission attaching bolts.
- Move transmission straight out of clutch assembly; avoid any binding in clutch to prevent clutch damage.
- Place transmission on work bench for overhaul.

PART 4   CLEANING AND INSPECTION GUIDELINES

Cleaning

1. Wash all parts (except the sealed ball bearings and seals) in a suitable cleaning solvent. Brush or scrape all foreign matter from the parts. Be care-

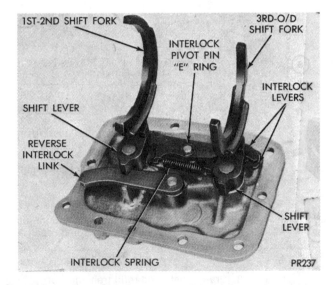

FIGURE 37-2. Typical four-speed shift fork and cover arrangement, showing interlock feature that prevents accidentally engaging two gears at once. (*Courtesy of Chrysler Corporation*)

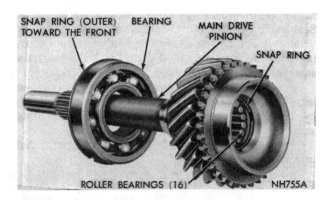

FIGURE 37-3. Details of transmission input shaft and support bearing. Roller bearings inside of input shaft gear support front of output shaft (mainshaft). (*Courtesy of Chrysler Corporation*)

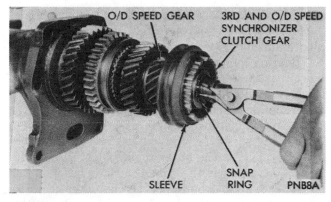

FIGURE 37-4. Transmission parts mounted on output shaft (mainshaft) of four-speed overdrive transmission. Note smaller overdrive driven gear. *(Courtesy of Chrysler Corporation)*

ful not to damage any parts with the scraper. Do not clean, wash, or soak transmission seals in cleaning solvents. Dry all parts with compressed air.

2. Rotate the non-sealed ball bearings in a cleaning solvent until all lubricant is removed. Hold the bearing assembly to prevent it from rotating and dry it with compressed air.

3. Lubricate the bearings with approved transmission lubricant and wrap them in a clean, lint-free cloth or paper until ready for use.

4. Clean the magnet in the bottom of the case with kerosene or mineral spirits.

Inspection

1. Inspect the transmission case for cracks, worn or damaged bearing bores, damaged threads, or any other damage that could affect the operation of the transmission.

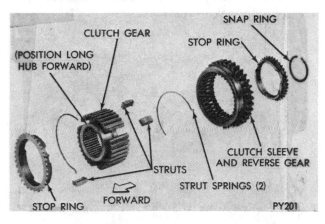

FIGURE 37-5. Exploded view of first-to-second synchronizer assembly with reverse driven gear integral with the sleeve. In a transmission using this arrangement, the sliding reverse idler gear is shifted into mesh with the reverse driven gear shown here. *(Courtesy of Chrysler Corporation)*

2. Inspect the front face of the case for small nicks or burrs that could cause misalignment of the transmission with the flywheel housing. Remove all small nicks or burrs with a fine stone on cast iron cases or with a fine file on aluminum cases.

3. Replace any cover that is bent or distorted. Make sure that the vent hole is open.

4. Check the condition of the shift levers, forks, shift rails, and the lever and shafts.

5. Inspect the ball bearings as per instructions under ball bearing inspection, below.

6. Replace roller bearings that are broken, worn, or rough, and check their respective races.

7. Replace the countershaft (cluster) gear if the teeth are chipped, broken, or worn. Replace the countershaft if it is bent, scored, or worn.

8. Replace the reverse idler gear or sliding gear if the teeth are chipped, worn, or broken. Replace the idler gear shaft if bent, worn, or scored.

9. Replace the input shaft and gear if the splines are damaged or if the teeth are chipped, worn, or broken. If the roller bearing surface in the bore of the gear is worn or rough, or if the cone surface is damaged, replace the gear and the gear rollers.

10. Replace all other gears that are chipped, broken, or worn.

11. Check the synchronizer sleeves for free movement on their hubs. Make sure that the alignment marks (if present) are properly indexed.

12. Inspect the synchronizer blocking rings for widened index slots, rounded clutch teeth, and smooth internal surfaces (must have machined grooves). With the blocker ring on the cone the distance between the face of the blocker ring and the clutch teeth on the gear must not be less than 0.020 inches (0.5 mm).

13. Replace the speedometer drive gear if the teeth are stripped or damaged. Make certain to install the correct size replacement gear.

14. Replace the output shaft if there is any evidence of wear or if any of the splines are damaged.

15. Inspect the bushings and the seal in the extension housing, and replace if worn or damaged. The bushing and/or seal should be replaced after the extension housing has been installed on the transmission.

16. Replace the seal in the input shaft bearing retainer.

17. Replace the seals on the cam and shafts.

Inspection—Ball Bearing

1. *Inner Ring Raceway*. While holding the outer ring stationary, rotate the inner ring at least three revolutions. Examine the raceway of the inner ring from both sides for pits or spalling. A bearing assembly should be replaced when thus damaged. Light particle indentation is acceptable.

2. *Outer Ring Raceway*. While holding the inner ring stationary, rotate the outer ring at least three revolutions. Examine the raceway of the outer ring from both sides as with the raceway of the inner ring. If the raceway is spalled or pitted, replace the bearing assembly.

Bearing External Surfaces

The bearing must be replaced if damage is found in any of the following areas:

1. Radial cracks on front and rear faces of the outer or inner rings.

2. Cracks on outside diameter or outer ring (particularly around snap ring groove).

3. Deformation or cracks in ball cage (particularly around rivets).

Spin Test

1. Lubricate the bearing raceways with a slight amount of clean oil. Turn the bearing back and forth slowly until the raceways and balls are coated with oil.

2. Hold the bearing by the inner ring in a vertical position. Vertical movement between the inner and outer rings is acceptable. Spin the outer ring several times by hand (do not use an air hose). If roughness or vibration is noticeable or the outer ring stops abruptly, the bearing should be replaced.

PART 5 TRANSMISSION TRANSAXLE DISASSEMBLY AND REASSEMBLY PROCEDURE

Disassemble transmission or transaxle according to manufacturer's manual. Procedures vary considerably in different models; therefore, it is important to follow the recommended sequence. In some cases the countershaft must be removed before input and mainshaft removal. In some cases the mainshaft is removed with the extension housing; in others it is removed through the shift cover opening. To avoid difficulty in disassembly follow the recommended sequence.

Clean all parts and inspect for damage. Bearings should not have rough feel while rotating. Replace damaged or worn parts.

Bearing removal and installation procedures require that the force applied to remove or install the bearing should always be on the tight race. In some cases the inner race is the one that is tight on the shaft. In this instance the force to remove or install the bearing should be applied to this race. In other applications it is the outer race that is tight in its bore. Where this is the case the removal or installation force should be aplied to the outer race. Serious damage to the bearing can result if this practice is not followed.

Use only a soft-faced hammer if some tapping is required or use a brass drift and ball peen hammer. Never use excessive force.

During assembly of the transmission, never attempt to "squeeze" parts into place by tightening front bearing retainer bolts or extension housing bolts. All parts must be fully in place before tightening any bolts. Check for free rotation and shifting.

New gaskets and seals should always be used.

PART 6 TRANSMISSION/TRANSAXLE INSTALLATION PROCEDURE

To install the transmission, proceed as follows:

• If required, check clutch parts and perform required service as outlined in Chapter 35 before installing transmission.

• Apply a coat of high-temperature lubricant to such areas as the pilot bushing, release bearing hub or transmission bearing retainer extension, and clutch release fork, as recommended.

• Place transmission or transaxle securely on transmission jack.

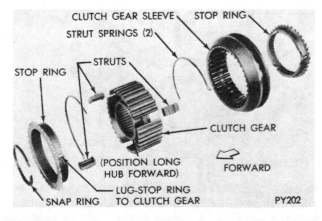

FIGURE 37-6. Exploded view of a typical synchronizer assembly as used in many transmissions. *(Courtesy of Chrysler Corporation)*

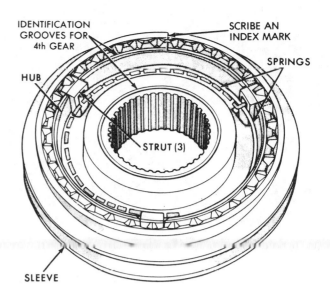

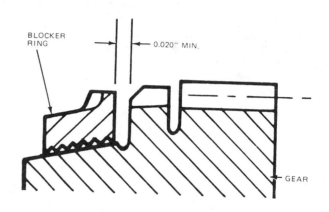

FIGURE 37-7. Synchronizer sleeve to hub position should be scribe marked for proper reassembly (top). Clearance between blocking ring and synchronizer gear teeth on mating gear should not be less than 0.020 inch (0.50 mm). (*Courtesy of Chrysler Corporation* [top] *and Ford Motor Co. of Canada Ltd.* [bottom])

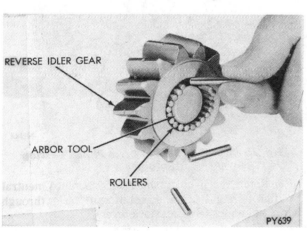

FIGURE 37-8. Reverse idler gear needle-type roller bearings. Some reverse idler gears use a bushing instead of the rollers. Others (sliding type) are splined to a sleeve. (*Courtesy of Chrysler Corporation*)

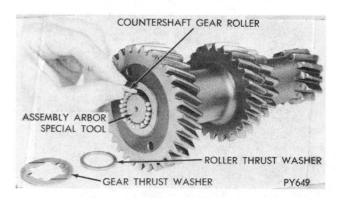

FIGURE 37-9. Needle bearing and thrust washer arrangement of typical countergear assembly. (*Courtesy of Chrysler Corporation*)

865

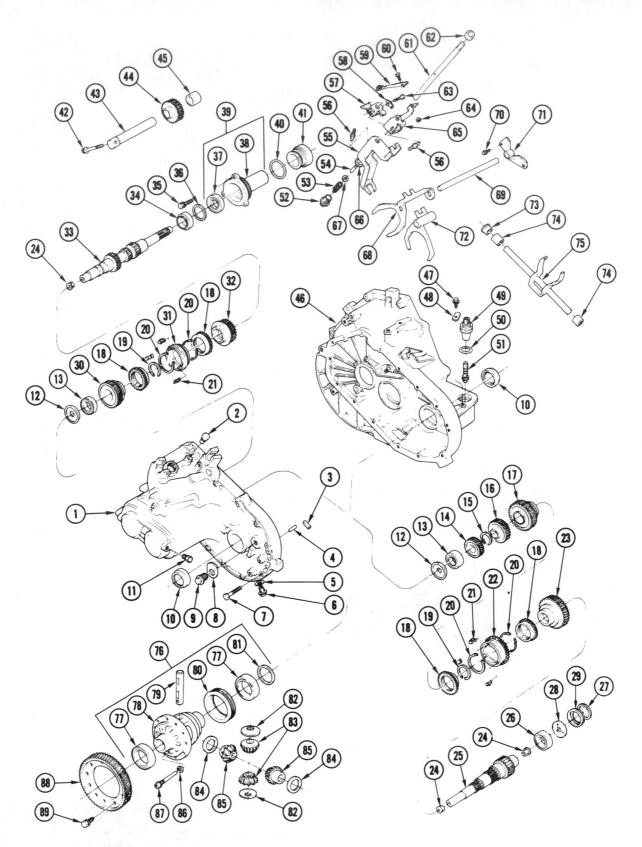

FIGURE 37-10(A). All parts must be individually inspected (see Part 4) for damage. Four-speed transaxle shown. *(Courtesy of General Motors Corporation)*

1. CASE ASSEMBLY
2. VENT ASSEMBLY
3. MAGNET
4. PIN
5. WASHER, Drain Screw
6. SCREW, Drain
7. BOLT
8. WASHER, Fill Plug
9. PLUG, Fill
10. SEAL ASSEMBLY, Axle Shaft
11. PLUG
12. SHIELD, Oil
13. BEARING ASSEMBLY
14. GEAR, 4th Speed Output
15. RING, 3rd Speed Output Gear Retaining
16. GEAR, 3rd Speed Output
17. GEAR, 2nd Speed Output
18. RING, Synchronizer Blocking
19. RING, Synchronizer Retaining
20. SPRING, Synchronizer Key Retaining
21. KEY, Synchronizer
22. SYNCHRONIZER ASSEMBLY
23. GEAR, 1st Speed Output
24. SLEEVE, Oil Shield
25. GEAR, Output
26. BEARING ASSEMBLY, Output
27. SHIM, Output Gear Bearing Adjustment
28. SHIELD, Output Bearing Oil
29. RETAINER, Output Gear Bearing Oil Shield
30. GEAR, 4th Speed Input
31. SYNCHRONIZER ASSEMBLY
32. GEAR, 3rd Speed Input
33. GEAR, Input Cluster
34. BEARING ASSEMBLY, Input
35. SCREW
36. SHIM, Input Gear Bearing Adjustment
37. SEAL ASSEMBLY, Input Gear
38. RETAINER, Input Gear
39. RETAINER ASSEMBLY, Input Gear Bearing
40. SEAL, Input Gear Bearing Retainer
41. BEARING ASSEMBLY, Clutch Release
42. SCREW & WASHER, Reverse Idler

43. SHAFT, Reverse Idler
44. GEAR ASSEMBLY, Reverse Idler
45. SPACER, Reverse Idler Shaft
46. HOUSING ASSEMBLY, Clutch & Differential
47. SCREW
48. RETAINER, Speedo Gear Fitting
49. SLEEVE, Speedo Driven Gear
50. SEAL, Speedo Gear Sleeve
51. GEAR, Speedo Driven
52. SEAT, Reverse Inhibitor Spring
53. SPRING, Reverse Inhibitor
54. PIN
55. LEVER, Reverse Shift
56. STUD, Reverse Lever Locating
57. LEVER ASSEMBLY, Detent
58. WASHER, Lock Detent Lever
59. SPRING, Detent
60. BOLT
61. SHAFT, Shift
62. SEAL ASSEMBLY, Shift Shaft
63. BOLT
64. NUT
65. INTERLOCK, Shift
66. SHIM, Shift Shaft
67. WASHER, Reverse Inhibitor Spring
68. FORK, 3rd & 4th Shift
69. SHAFT, Shift Fork
70. SCREW
71. GUIDE, Oil
72. FORK, 1st & 2nd Shift
73. SEAL ASSEMBLY, Clutch Fork Shaft
74. BEARING, Clutch Fork Shaft
75. SHAFT ASSEMBLY, Clutch Fork
76. DIFFERENTIAL ASSEMBLY
77. BEARING ASSEMBLY, Differential
78. CASE, Differential
79. SHAFT, Differential Pinion
80. GEAR, Speedo Drive
81. SHIM, Differential Bearing Adjustment
82. WASHER, Pinion Thrust
83. GEAR, Differential Pinion
84. WASHER, Side Gear Thrust
85. GEAR, Differential Side
86. LOCKWASHER
87. SCREW, Pinion Shaft
88. GEAR, Differential Ring
89. BOLT

FIGURE 37-10(B). Key to Figure 37-10(A). *(Courtesy of General Motors Corporation)*

• Install guide pins in bell housing to align transmission during installation. (Install shims if any were present during removal.)

• Slide transmission/transaxle into place without using undue force. Make sure input shaft splines and clutch disc hub splines are aligned.

• With transmission firmly against engine or bell housing, install attaching bolts and tighten to specified torque.

• Install cross member (replace any shims that were removed) and mount.

• Remove jack and engine support.

• Install drive axle shafts or drive line (lubricate slip yoke before sliding into transmission) as per scribe marks.

• Reconnect and adjust linkage; connect speedometer cable and electrical connections.

• Fill transmission with recommended lubricant to proper level.

• Lower vehicle to floor and check for leaks.

• Road test vehicle for proper performance of transmission/transaxle.

• Inspect for possible leakage.

• Prepare vehicle for customer acceptance.

PART 7   SELF-CHECK

1. List four causes of hard shifting.

2. Name four reasons why a transmission would jump out of gear.

3. A noisy transaxle may be caused by:

   (a) _____

   (b) _____

   (c) _____

   (d) _____

4. Bearing failure may be caused by _____.

5. Why is clearance between the blocking ring and synchronizer teeth important?

PART 8   TEST QUESTIONS

1. To spin test a bearing:

   (a) use the air hose to spin the outer race

   (b) spin the inner race by hand

   (c) hold the outer race by hand

   (d) hold the inner race and spin the outer race by hand

2. Guide pins should be used during transmission installation to:

   (a) prevent damage to the pressure plate

   (b) prevent damage to the release bearing

   (c) prevent damage to the clutch disc

   (d) all of the above

3. If a transmission can be shifted into two gears at once, the cause could be:

   (a) worn countershaft bearings

   (b) worn second and third gears

   (c) worn synchronizers

   (d) faulty interlock

4. If a transaxle does not stay in the gear selected, look for:

   (a) worn synchronizer teeth

   (b) faulty detent

   (c) worn bearings

   (d) any of the above

5. An excessively high lubricant level may cause:

   (a) foaming

   (b) lubricant loss

   (c) seal failure

   (d) any of the above

Chapter 38

Automatic Transmissions and Transaxles

Performance Objectives

After sufficient study of this chapter and the appropriate training models, you should be able to perform the following tasks successfully at the request of your instructor.

1. Define the terms *pressure* and *force* as they apply to hydraulic fluids.

2. Define Pascal's law.

3. Define force multiplication by hydraulic means and give an example of force multiplication by means of hydraulics.

4. Define the relationship between force and motion transmitted by hydraulic means, and give an example of this relationship.

5. Describe briefly the various types of automatic transmission hydraulic fluids and their properties.

6. State the purpose of the hydraulic pump in the automatic transmission.

7. Describe the basic construction and operation of the three types of hydraulic pumps discussed in this chapter, including the causes and effects of pump wear.

8. Describe the basic construction and operation of the following types of valves and flow control devices:

    (a)   ball check valve
    (b)   poppet valve
    (c)   spool valve
    (d)   pressure relief valve
    (e)   pressure-regulating valve
    (f)   orifice
    (g)   accumulator
    (h)   governor valve
    (i)   shift valves

Automatic transmissions are used on many rear-wheel drive and four-wheel-drive vehicles. Automatic transaxles which combine the transmission and differential functions in one assembly are used in many front-wheel drive vehicles.

Automatic upshifts and downshifts are a convenience for the driver because a foot-operated clutch is not required to shift gears and because the vehicle can be brought to a stop without the use of a clutch and without shifting the transmission into neutral. This is especially useful in urban traffic where frequent stops are necessary.

Transaxle differentials are covered in Chapters 34 and 36 and will therefore not be discussed in this chapter.

The automatic transmission or transaxle provides the necessary gear ratios to operate the vehicle under a wide range of speeds and loads. It does this with a minimum amount of effort on the part of the driver. Upshifts occur smoothly and automatically, as do downshifts. Depending on the range selected by the driver, the transmission freewheels or provides engine braking during deceleration.

A common type of automatic transaxle or transmission for passenger cars has three forward speeds, reverse, neutral, and park positions. In addition, provision is made for the manual selection of low and intermediate gear positions. Four speed automatic transmissions with fourth gear overdrive are also used by several manufacturers.

A number of multiple-disc clutches, one-way roller clutches, bands, a compound planetary gear set, and a hydraulic control system provide the means for the various gear ratios.

The transmission is driven from the engine through a three-member hydrodynamic unit called a *torque converter*. There is no mechanical connection between the engine and the transmission drive mechanism except in the case of a *lock up* torque converter or overdrive transmission.

Engine torque is transmitted to the transmission by means of high-velocity hydraulic fluid.

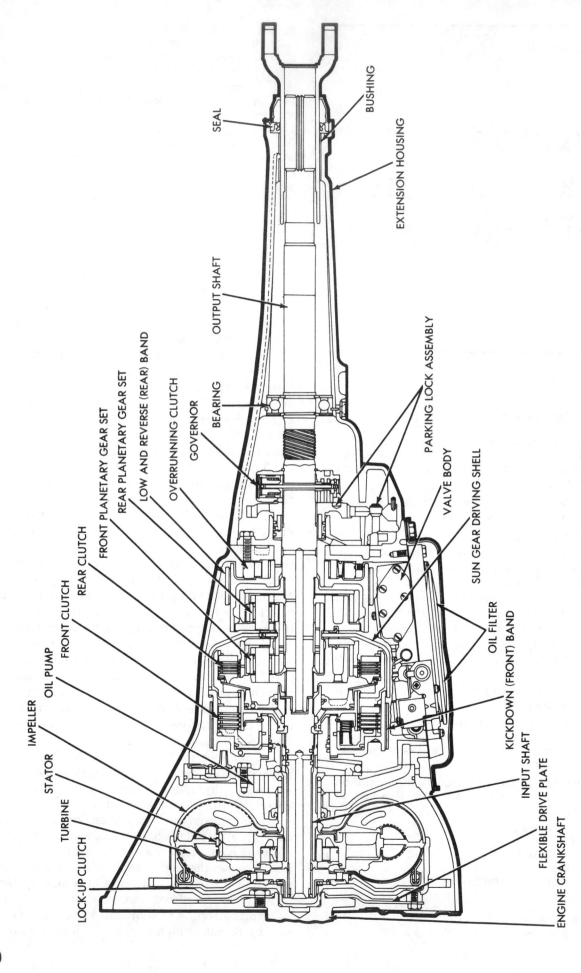

SEAL

BUSHING

EXTENSION HOUSING

OUTPUT SHAFT

LOW AND REVERSE (REAR) BAND

REAR PLANETARY GEAR SET

FRONT PLANETARY GEAR SET

OVERRUNNING CLUTCH

GOVERNOR

BEARING

PARKING LOCK ASSEMBLY

REAR CLUTCH

FRONT CLUTCH

OIL PUMP

IMPELLER

STATOR

TURBINE

LOCK-UP CLUTCH

VALVE BODY

SUN GEAR DRIVING SHELL

OIL FILTER

KICKDOWN (FRONT) BAND

INPUT SHAFT

FLEXIBLE DRIVE PLATE

ENGINE CRANKSHAFT

FIGURE 38-1. Cross-sectional view of typical automatic transmission. This transmission is also equipped with a torque converter lock-up clutch to ensure that there is no slippage in direct drive. *(Courtesy of Chrysler Corporation)*

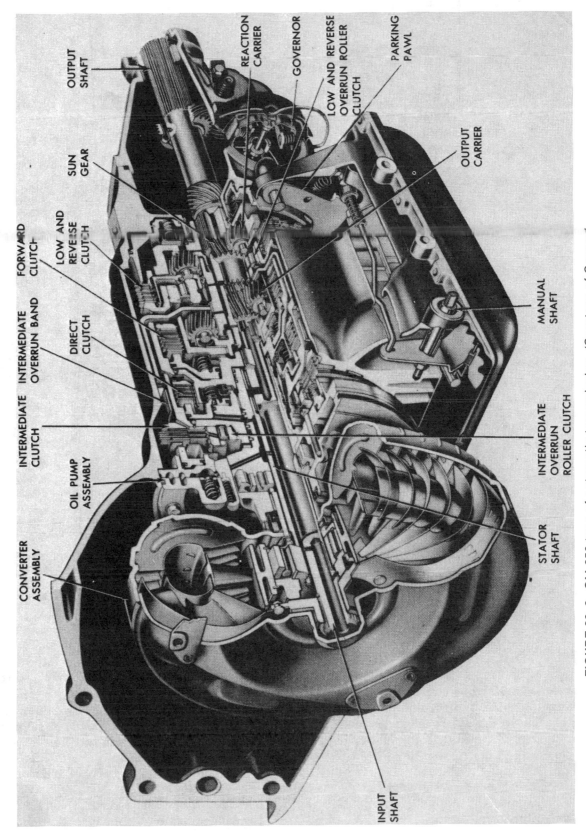

OUTPUT SHAFT

REACTION CARRIER

GOVERNOR

LOW AND REVERSE OVERRUN ROLLER CLUTCH

PARKING PAWL

SUN GEAR

FORWARD CLUTCH

LOW AND REVERSE CLUTCH

INTERMEDIATE OVERRUN BAND

INTERMEDIATE CLUTCH

DIRECT CLUTCH

OIL PUMP ASSEMBLY

CONVERTER ASSEMBLY

OUTPUT CARRIER

MANUAL SHAFT

INTERMEDIATE OVERRUN ROLLER CLUTCH

STATOR SHAFT

INPUT SHAFT

FIGURE 38-2. GM 350 type of automatic transmission. (*Courtesy of General Motors Corporation*)

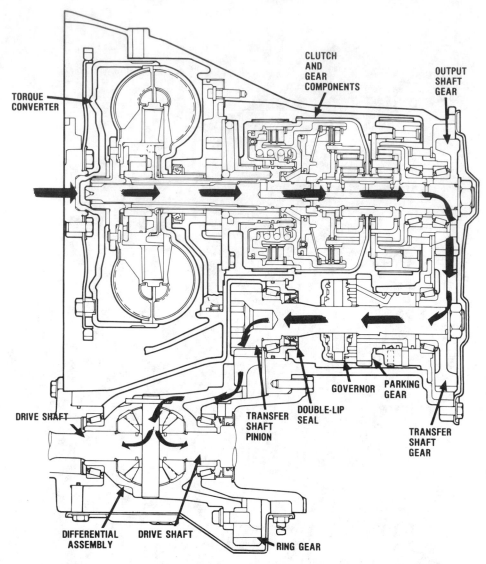

FIGURE 38-3. Automatic transaxle assembly used in front-wheel-drive vehicle includes transmission and differential. (*Courtesy of Chrysler Corporation*)

PART 1   TORQUE CONVERTERS

The three-member torque converter consists of the impeller, the turbine, and the stator. The entire assembly is enclosed in a steel shell and is full of transmission fluid at all times. The steel shell or housing of the converter is bolted to a flex plate that is attached to the engine crankshaft. Inside the shell the rear portion contains a series of vanes known as the impeller. Whenever the crankshaft turns, this part of the converter turns with it.

The turbine is located in this same shell and is splined to the transmission input shaft. The turbine is free to rotate independently from the impeller. The turbine is similar in appearance to the impeller but has curved vanes.

When the engine is running, the rotating impeller causes fluid to be "thrown" toward the turbine vanes. When this occurs with sufficient force to overcome the resistance to rotation, the turbine begins to turn, turning the transmission input shaft. Without a stator between the impeller and the turbine, the fluid flow leaving the turbine would be in a direction opposite to impeller rotation and would resist impeller rotation.

The stator vanes redirect the fluid flow back to the same direction as impeller rotation, thereby assisting impeller rotation. This fluid flow, from the impeller to the turbine, to the stator, and back to the impeller is called *vortex flow*. The circular fluid flow is called *rotary flow*.

The vortex flow of the fluid in the torque con-

872

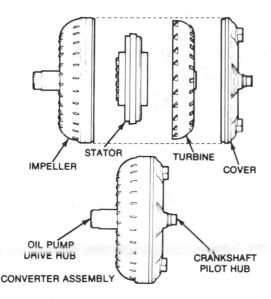

FIGURE 38-4. Torque converter components. *(Courtesy of Ford Motor Co. of Canada Ltd.)*

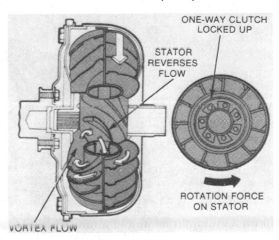

FIGURE 38-6. Fluid flow from turbine is redirected by stator vanes (during torque multiplication) to same direction as impeller. This aids impeller rotation. This flow is called *vortex flow*. *(Courtesy of Ford Motor Co. of Canada Ltd.)*

verter results in torque multiplication. In other words, the impeller is turning faster than the turbine, and fluid striking the stationary vanes is redirected to aid in impeller rotation.

The stator consists of a series of vanes surrounding a one-way clutch. The one-way clutch hub is splined to an extension of the transmission hydraulic pump, which is bolted to the transmission case. This extension is referred to as a *stator shaft* (although it is tubular) or *reaction shaft*, and it cannot rotate.

The one-way clutch prevents the stator vane assembly from rotating counterclockwise (opposite to impeller rotation) but allows clockwise rotation.

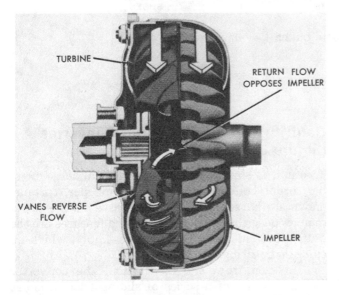

FIGURE 38-5. Fluid flow from impeller to turbine (turbine is splined to transmission input shaft). *(Courtesy of Ford Motor Co. of Canada Ltd.)*

When turbine speed increases to the point where it approaches impeller speed (approximately nine tenths), fluid leaving the turbine vanes begins to strike the reverse side of the stator vanes, causing the stator to rotate in the same direction as the impeller and the turbine. This is called the *coupling stage*, which provides almost a 1:1 ratio through the torque converter.

As long as the engine is transmitting torque, the impeller is the drive member and the turbine is the driven member. An infinite series of ratios is possible between the two because of the hydro-dynamic connection (transfer of torque through hydraulic fluid).

The range of drive ratios through the converter is from approximately 2.2:1 to almost 1:1.

During deceleration the vehicle's momentum (kinetic inertia) causes the turbine to drive the impeller hydraulically. This tends to drive the engine. Since the engine is trying to return to idle speed, "engine braking" helps slow down vehicle speed.

PART 2 LOCKUP TORQUE CONVERTERS

The lockup design feature used in many torque converters provides a direct mechanical drive connection between the engine and the transmission. This feature provides better torque converter efficiency during certain operating conditions, which, in turn, results in better fuel economy.

Vehicle manufacturers use several different methods to provide some means of mechanical drive

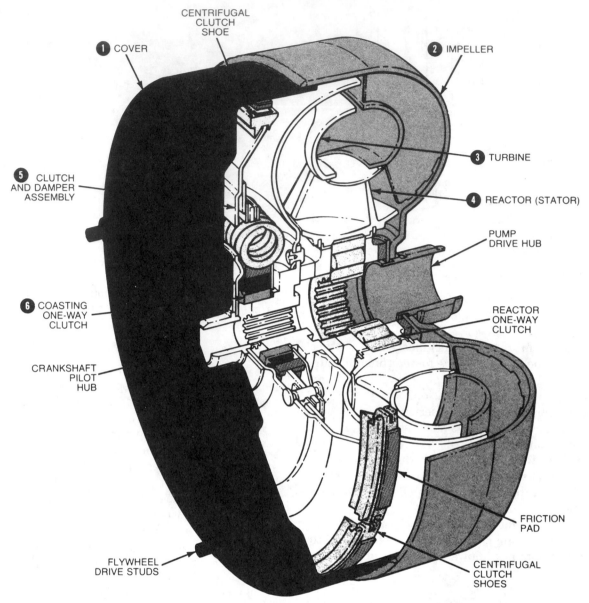

FIGURE 38-7. Cutaway view of centrifugal clutch lock-up converter. *(Courtesy of Ford Motor Co. of Canada Ltd.)*

through the torque converter. A centrifugal clutch and damper assembly is used by one manufacturer to lock the turbine to the converter cover, thereby providing a mechanical drive connection.

A hydraulically operated disc-type clutch and damper is another method used by several manufacturers to connect the turbine to the torque converter cover. A third method is to incorporate a simple planetary gearset into the converter to provide varying degrees of mechanical drive under various operating conditions. A fourth method is to use a direct driveshaft and damper assembly splined to the converter cover in addition to the usual turbine shaft.

Centrifugal Clutch Lockup Converter (Figure 38-7)

This unit is similar to the conventional three-member torque converter. It has the impeller, turbine, and stator assembly, which operate in the usual manner described earlier. The added features are the centrifugal clutch and damper assembly, which includes a coasting one-way clutch.

As seen from the illustration, the converter clutch consists of a series of sliding friction shoes arranged around the circumference of the damper assembly. As the speed of the turbine increases, the friction shoes slide outward due to increased cen-

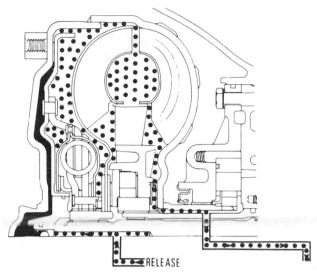

FIGURE 38-8. Fluid flow in converter clutch release position. *(Courtesy of General Motors Corporation)*

trifugal force. When the friction shoes are fully applied against the converter cover, power flows from the converter cover to the damper clutch through the torsional springs to the turbine hub and turbine shaft, thereby providing mechanical drive through the converter. Torsional shocks are dampened by the torsional springs.

The centrifugal clutch is designed to provide some slippage as torque demand from the engine increases. Consequently, when the vehicle is under load there may be a split between mechanical drive and hydraulic drive through the converter.

The factors determining whether the centrifu-

gal clutch will be applied, and the degree of application, are rotating speed and vehicle load. During mechanical drive, the clutch and damper assembly drive the turbine and turbine shaft through the one-way clutch assembly. During coasting conditions, the one-way clutch freewheels or overruns.

Hydraulically Controlled Lockup Clutch Converters

This type of torque converter is similar in design and operation to the conventional three-member torque converter. The difference is in the addition of a hydraulically operated single-plate direct-drive clutch.

The basic function of the General Motors lockup converter and the Chrysler lockup converter (also used by American Motors) is similar. Both designs use a clutch apply piston or pressure plate assembly, which is splined to the turbine. This unit is equipped with a series of torsional springs through which torque is transmitted from the clutch to the turbine shaft. The purpose of the torsional springs is to dampen the effects of engine power impulses and the shock of clutch lockup.

The clutch piston or pressure plate is applied and released by hydraulic pressure from the transmission hydraulic system. Clutch friction material is attached to the inside of the converter cover. When applied, mechanical power flow is from the converter cover through the clutch to the torsional springs, the pressure plate hub, and the turbine shaft.

The Chrysler lockup converter operates as any three-element converter in all gears except third or direct. In third gear, the clutch is applied at approximately 25 to 40 mph (40 to 64 km/h), depending on vehicle engine size and drive axle ratio. On a forced downshift (kickdown), whether part throttle or full throttle, the torque converter clutch releases; normal hydrodynamic torque converter operation transfers torque to the transmission planetary gears.

The General Motors torque converter clutch may apply in second, third, and fourth gears, or in third or fourth on four-speed transmissions (depending on vehicle model) and in third gear only on three-speed transmissions. A number of factors other than gear position determine whether the converter clutch will be applied or released.

On vehicles not equipped with computer command control, the following items control the converter clutch.

1. *Brake release switch.* To avoid stalling the engine when braking, any time the brakes are applied, the converter clutch is released.

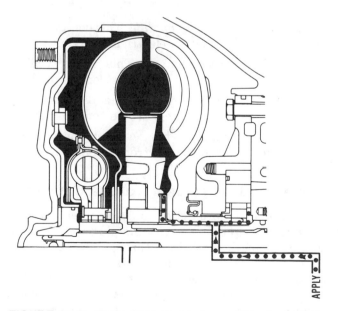

FIGURE 38-9. Fluid flow in apply position in lock-up clutch converter. *(Courtesy of General Motors Corporation)*

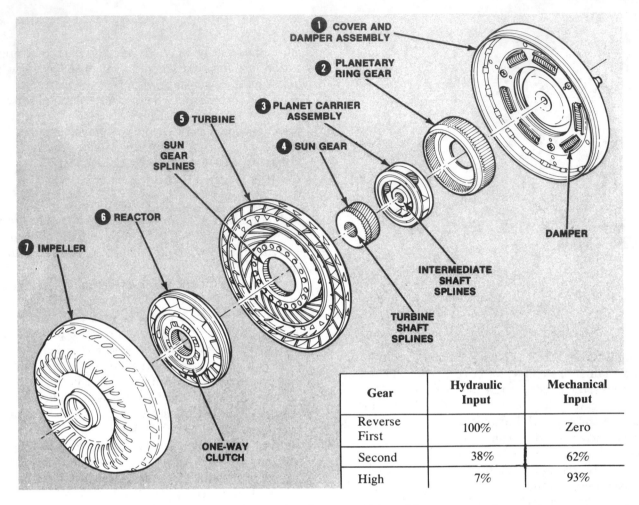

Gear	Hydraulic Input	Mechanical Input
Reverse First	100%	Zero
Second	38%	62%
High	7%	93%

FIGURE 38-10. Exploded view of splitter gear type of torque converter used in Ford transaxle. *(Courtesy of Ford Motor Co. of Canada Ltd.)*

2. *Thermal vacuum valve.* It prevents the converter clutch from applying until the engine coolant temperature has reached 130°F.

3. *Engine vacuum switch.* It releases the converter clutch when engine vacuum drops to approximately 1.5 to 3 inches of mercury (5 to 10 kPa) during moderate acceleration, prior to a part-throttle to detent downshift.

4. *Vacuum delay valve.* This slows the vacuum switch response to vacuum changes.

5. *Ported vacuum.* The source of vacuum to vacuum switch, it opens the vacuum switch to release the clutch during a closed vacuum coastdown.

Vehicles equipped with computer command control have the following items controlling the converter clutch:

1. *Brake release switch.* To avoid stalling the engine when braking, any time the brakes are applied, the converter clutch is released.

2. *Electronic control module.* This energizes and grounds the transmission electrical system.

3. *Vehicle speed sensor.* This sends vehicle speed information to the electronic control module.

4. *Throttle position sensor.* It sends throttle position information to the electronic control module.

5. *Vacuum sensor.* This sends engine vacuum (load) information to the electronic control module.

Planetary Splitter Gear Torque Converter

The Ford ATX automatic transaxle uses a torque converter equipped with a single planetary gearset to provide mechanical drive through the converter. This unit is sometimes referred to as a splitter gear since it splits or divides engine torque transmission between mechanical and hydraulic means in second and third gears.

In second gear, the turbine supplies 38 percent of the torque hydraulically; 62 percent is transmit-

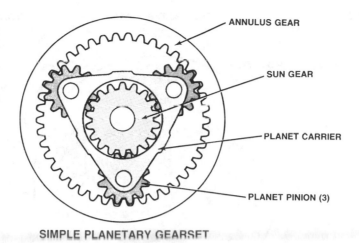

SIMPLE PLANETARY GEARSET

FIGURE 38-11. Planetary gear components. Annulus gear is also called an *internal* gear or *ring* gear. Planet carrier is also called a *cage.* Planetary gears transmit torque when one of the three members is the drive member, one is the held member, and the other is the driven member. *(Courtesy of Chrysler Corporation)*

ted mechanically. In third gear, the planetary gear mechanical torque output is increased to 93 percent with only 7 percent torque transmitted hydraulically.

Operation of the unit is dependent on the interaction between the torque converter and the planetary gear train in the transmission. Understanding the operation of this unit may require studying planetary gear operation and power flow.

Construction of this converter includes a torsional spring damper assembly riveted to the inside of the converter cover. The planetary ring gear (internal gear) is splined into the damper assembly so that these parts always turn at engine speed. The planet pinion carrier is splined to the transmission intermediate shaft and the pinions are, of course, in mesh with the ring gear. The sun gear, which is in mesh with the planet pinions, is splined to the turbine hub and to the turbine shaft.

Mechanical transmission of torque through the torque converter is dampened by the torsional springs located between the converter cover and planetary ring gear. The degree of mechanical transmission of torque is dependent on gear position and the interaction between the transmission planetary gear train and the torque converter.

Ford Automatic Overdrive Torque Converter

The torque converter used with the Ford automatic overdrive transmission is a conventional three-member torque converter with a damper assembly attached to the inside of the converter cover. It has the usual turbine shaft power output and an additional direct-drive converter output shaft.

In operation, this unit has the usual turbine-driven turbine shaft (transmission input shaft) for hydraulic transmission of torque. In reverse, first, and second gears, hydraulic drive only through the turbine and turbine shaft transmits engine torque to the transmission.

In third gear, torque is split between the turbine shaft (40 percent) and a direct-drive shaft splined to the hub of the torsional damper in the converter cover (60 percent).

In fourth gear (overdrive), the direct-drive shaft only is transmitting engine torque mechanically. Torsional pulsations are dampened by the damper assembly.

Action by the various clutches and band in the transmission (determined by gear position) causes the converter to deliver torque as described.

PART 3 PLANETARY GEAR PRINCIPLES

A simple planetary gearset consists of three components: a sun gear, a carrier (with pinion gears mounted in it), and an internally toothed ring gear.

Power transmission through a planetary gearset is possible only if one of the three members is held (prevented from rotating) or if two members are locked together. A number of ratios, forward, reverse, and neutral are possible depending on which member is the drive, driven, or held unit.

Planetary gears are compact and are in constant mesh (no shifting of gears required). Clutches are used to connect or disconnect planetary gear

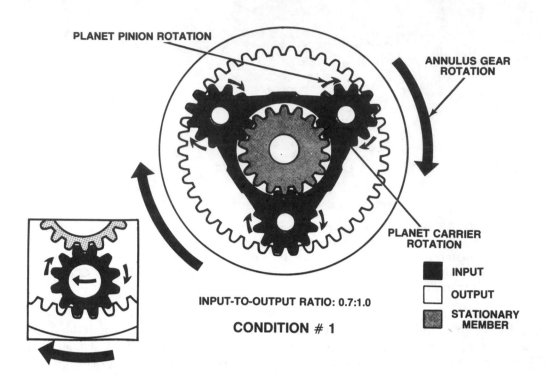

SPEED INCREASE   FORWARD ROTATION   TORQUE REDUCTION

PLANET PINION ROTATION

ANNULUS GEAR ROTATION

PLANET CARRIER ROTATION

INPUT

OUTPUT

STATIONARY MEMBER

INPUT-TO-OUTPUT RATIO: 0.7:1.0

CONDITION # 1

FIGURE 38–12. In this condition the drive (input) member is the carrier, the sun gear is being held (stationary), and the ring (annulus) gear is the driven member providing an overdrive. In this condition, the pinions "walk" around the stationary sun gear, forcing the carrier to rotate. This arrangement is used in automatic transmissions. *(Courtesy of Chrysler Corporation)*

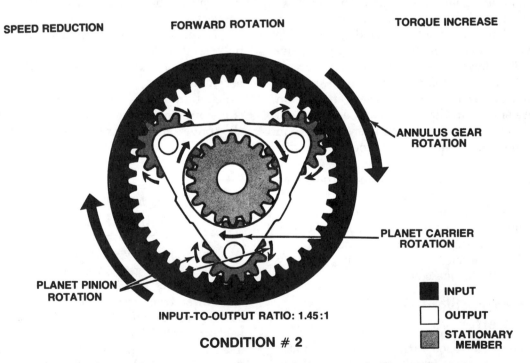

SPEED REDUCTION   FORWARD ROTATION   TORQUE INCREASE

ANNULUS GEAR ROTATION

PLANET CARRIER ROTATION

PLANET PINION ROTATION

INPUT

OUTPUT

STATIONARY MEMBER

INPUT-TO-OUTPUT RATIO: 1.45:1

CONDITION # 2

FIGURE 38–13. In this condition, the drive member is the ring gear, the sun gear is held, and the carrier is the driven member providing a gear reduction. In this condition, the pinions "walk" around the stationary sun gear, forcing the carrier to rotate. This arrangement is used in automatic transmissions to achieve second gear. *(Courtesy of Chrysler Corporation)*

878

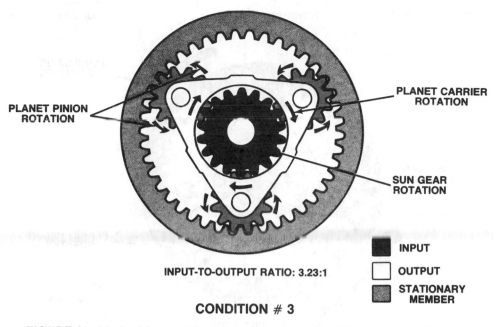

INPUT	■
OUTPUT	□
STATIONARY MEMBER	▨

INPUT-TO-OUTPUT RATIO: 3.23:1

CONDITION # 3

FIGURE 38-14. In this condition, the sun gear is the drive member, the ring gear is held, and the carrier is the driven member. In this condition, the pinions "walk" around the stationary ring gear, forcing the carrier to rotate. This arrangement is not used in automatic transmissions. *(Courtesy of Chrysler Corporation)*

SPEED INCREASE   **FORWARD ROTATION**   **TORQUE REDUCTION**

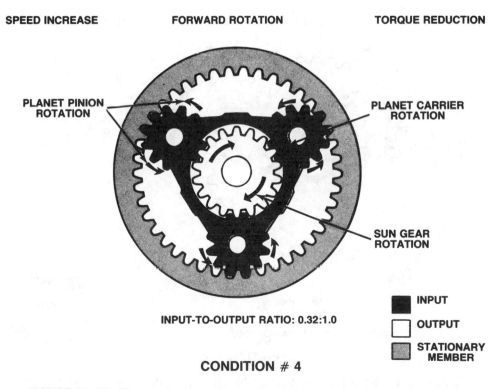

INPUT	■
OUTPUT	□
STATIONARY MEMBER	▨

INPUT-TO-OUTPUT RATIO: 0.32:1.0

CONDITION # 4

FIGURE 38-15. The carrier is the input, the ring gear is held, and the sun gear is the output member. In this condition, the pinions "walk" around the stationary ring gear, forcing the carrier to rotate. This arrangement is not used in automatic transmissions. *(Courtesy of Chrysler Corporation)*

SPEED INCREASE   REVERSE ROTATION   TORQUE REDUCTION

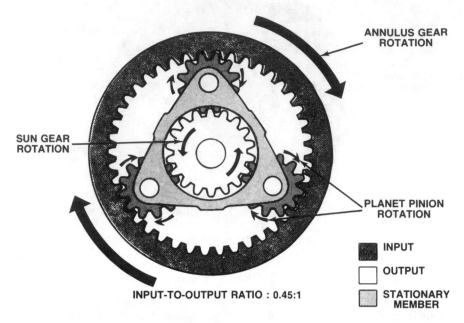

ANNULUS GEAR
ROTATION

SUN GEAR
ROTATION

PLANET PINION
ROTATION

■ INPUT

□ OUTPUT

▨ STATIONARY
MEMBER

INPUT-TO-OUTPUT RATIO : 0.45:1

CONDITION # 5

FIGURE 38–16. Here the ring gear is the drive gear, the carrier is held, and the sun gear is the driven gear. In this case, the pinion gears simply act as idlers, reversing the direction of rotation. Since this is an overdrive, it is not practical to use this arrangement for reverse. *(Courtesy of Chrysler Corporation)*

SPEED REDUCTION   REVERSE ROTATION   TORQUE INCREASE

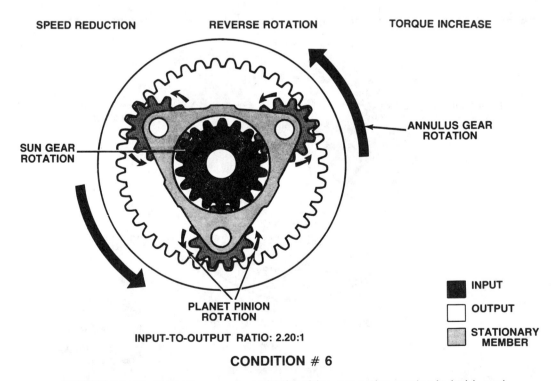

ANNULUS GEAR
ROTATION

SUN GEAR
ROTATION

PLANET PINION
ROTATION

■ INPUT

□ OUTPUT

▨ STATIONARY
MEMBER

INPUT-TO-OUTPUT RATIO: 2.20:1

CONDITION # 6

FIGURE 38–17. Here the sun gear is the drive gear, the carrier is held, and the ring gear is the driven gear. In this condition, the pinion gears simply act as idlers, reversing the direction of rotation. This arrangement is commonly used to achieve reverse in automatic transmissions. *(Courtesy of Chrysler Corporation)*

members to the input shaft. Clutches or bands are used to hold planetary gear members.

In a simple planetary gearset with a sun gear that has 30 teeth and a ring gear that has 90 teeth, the *effective number* for the carrier is 120 teeth. This is calculated by adding the number of teeth on the sun gear to the number of teeth on the ring gear: 30 + 90 = 120. In other words, S + R = C.

To calculate the gear ratio through this gearset, simply divide the number of teeth of the drive member into the number of teeth on the driven member: driven/drive.

For example, if the sun gear is the drive member, the ring gear is the driven member, and the carrier is being held, the ratio would be

$$\frac{90}{30} : \text{or } 3:1$$

If the carrier is the drive member and the ring gear is the driven member with the sun gear being held, the ratio would be

$$\frac{90}{120} : 1 \text{ or } 0.75:1$$

There are eight possible conditions that can be used with a simple planetary gearset. Six of these are shown in Figures 38–12 to 38–17. The other two conditions are (1) direct drive when two members are locked to each other, and (2) neutral when there is no drive member or no held member.

When two planetary gear members are locked together, the entire planetary gearset rotates as an assembly for direct drive.

PART 4 COMPOUND PLANETARY GEARS—SIMPSON GEARSET

To provide three forward speeds and reverse, it is necessary to use a compound planetary gearset. The most common compound planetary gearset consists of two simple planetary gearsets with a common sun gear, which connects the two gearsets. This is known as the Simpson compound planetary gearset.

In this unit the forward gearset ring gear and the sun gear can be connected to the transmission input shaft by means of two separate multiple-disc clutches.

The sun gear and the rear gearset carrier can be held. The sun gear can be held by a band (intermediate or kickdown band) on some transmissions. Other transmissions use a multiple-disc clutch to lock the sun gear to the transmission case.

In manually selected low gear, the rear carrier is held by a band in some transmissions while others use a multiple-disc holding clutch. In both cases there is also a one-way clutch that prevents backward rotation of the carrier but allows forward rotation. When the drive position has been selected,

the one-way clutch only does the holding while in low gear.

The forward gearset carrier and the rear gearset ring gear are splined to the transmission output shaft. This is accomplished by the output shaft extending through the hollow sun gear to reach the forward gearset carrier.

For the power flow and typical ratios in each gear position study Figures 38–18 to 38–22.

PART 5 RAVIGNEAUX PLANETARY GEARS

The Ravigneaux compound planetary gear train consists of two sun gears, one planet pinion carrier containing two sets of pinions, and one ring gear. The discussion of this gearset is confined to the three-speed and four-speed overdrive arrangements and does not include the older two-speed version.

The Ravigneaux planetary gear system is used in several domestic and import automatic transmissions. Among these are Ford's FMX, automatic overdrive, and ATX transaxle; General Motors' (MD3) 180; BMW's 3HP22; Mitsubishi's Borg-Warner; Volvo's Borg-Warner; and others.

This discussion will use the Ford FMX three-speed, Ford automatic overdrive four-speed, and ATX transaxle arrangements to explain the operation of this gearset.

Components and Construction (FMX)

In the three-speed arrangement of this planetary gearset there are two sun gears, one behind the other and each free to turn separately. The front sun gear is slightly larger than the rear sun gear.

The rear sun gear is in mesh with one set of short pinions. These short pinions are in mesh with a set of long pinions mounted in a single carrier. The long pinions are in mesh with the front or larger sun gear and also with the ring gear or internal gear. This completes the physical arrangement of these gears.

The ring gear also has external teeth on it, which are used to provide the park position for this gearset. All gears have helical teeth for quiet operation and are highly finished high-grade steel for toughness and durability.

The gearset is controlled by two multiple-disc clutches, two bands, and a one-way clutch.

Operation

The selector lever has six positions: park, reverse, neutral, drive, 2, and 1.

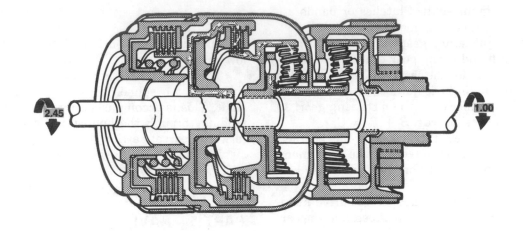

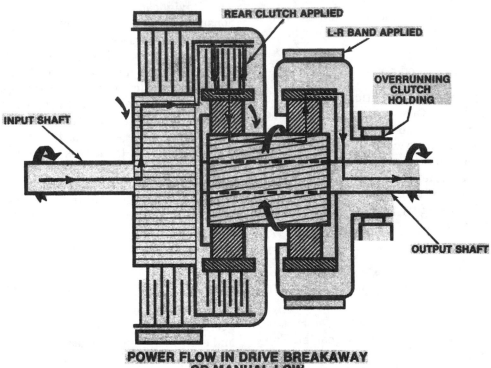

POWER FLOW IN DRIVE BREAKAWAY

REAR CLUTCH APPLIED

L-R BAND APPLIED

OVERRUNNING CLUTCH HOLDING

INPUT SHAFT

OUTPUT SHAFT

POWER FLOW IN DRIVE BREAKAWAY OR MANUAL LOW

FIGURE 38–18. In drive low the low and reverse band is not applied. In manually selected low, the l and r band is applied for extra holding power and to provide engine braking during deceleration. (Some transmissions use a low and reverse holding clutch instead of a low and reverse band; see Figure 38–2.) *(Courtesy of Chrysler Corporation)*

In park, the ring gear and output shaft are held stationary by a park pawl, which engages the external teeth on the ring gear. The park pawl is anchored to the transmission case.

In reverse, the rear (reverse and high) clutch is applied to drive the front or secondary sun gear in a clockwise direction. The secondary sun gear drives the secondary (long) pinions counterclockwise. The counterclockwise-turning secondary pinions drive the ring gear and output shaft in a counterclockwise direction for reverse. The low and reverse holding clutch is applied to prevent the carrier from turning in a forward direction. It tries to do this since there is a resistance to motion of the ring gear and output shaft due to vehicle load.

In neutral no clutches or bands are applied.

In the drive position, the transmission starts in low and shifts automatically to second and to third.

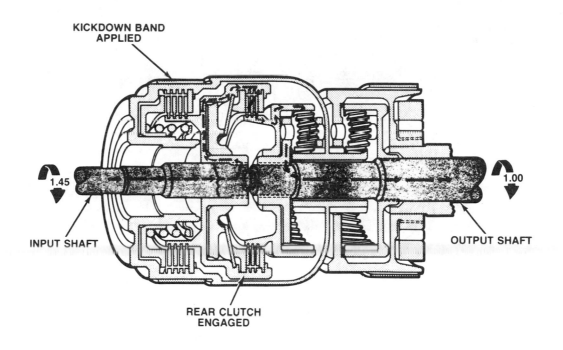

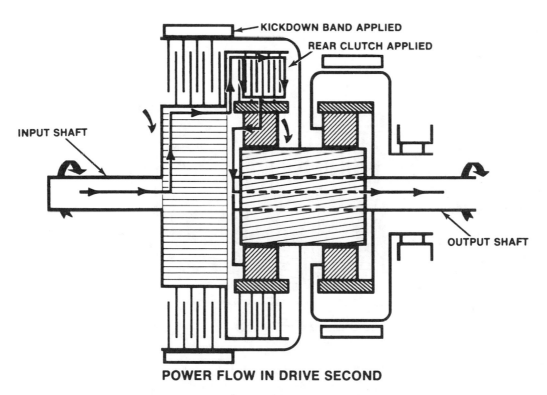

POWER FLOW IN DRIVE SECOND

FIGURE 38–19. When the transmission has shifted from low to second (with lever in D position), the kickdown band (intermediate band) is applied and the rear clutch is still applied as it was in low. *(Courtesy of Chrysler Corporation)*

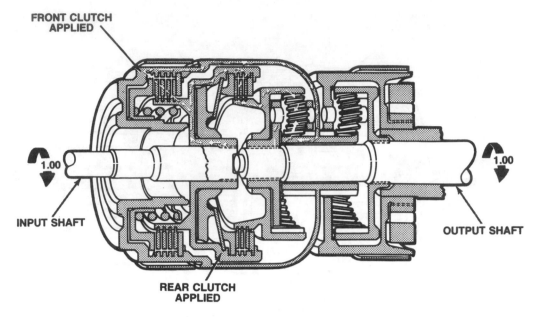

FRONT CLUTCH
APPLIED

1.00

INPUT SHAFT

1.00

OUTPUT SHAFT

REAR CLUTCH
APPLIED

**POWER FLOW IN DRIVE POSITION—
DIRECT**

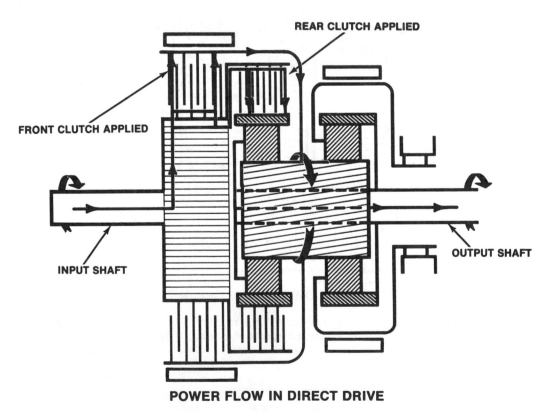

REAR CLUTCH APPLIED

FRONT CLUTCH APPLIED

INPUT SHAFT

OUTPUT SHAFT

POWER FLOW IN DIRECT DRIVE

FIGURE 38-20. When the transmission shifts automatically from second to third, the intermediate band releases and the front clutch is applied. The rear clutch is also still applied providing direct drive. (The entire gear train is locked together and rotates as a unit.) *(Courtesy of Chrysler Corporation)*

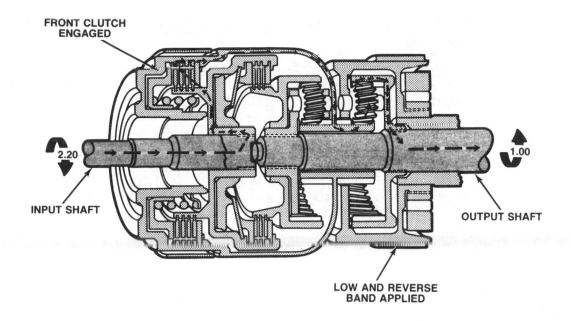

FRONT CLUTCH
ENGAGED

2.20

INPUT SHAFT

OUTPUT SHAFT

LOW AND REVERSE
BAND APPLIED

1.00

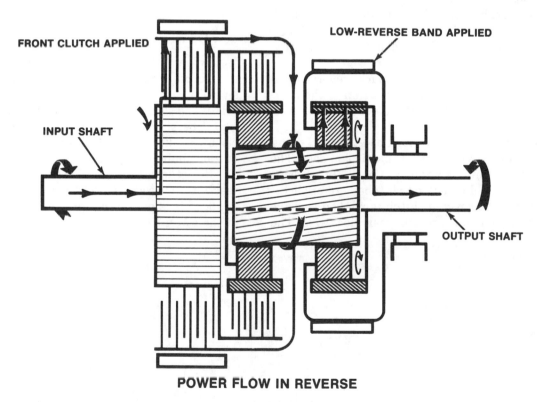

FRONT CLUTCH APPLIED

LOW-REVERSE BAND APPLIED

INPUT SHAFT

OUTPUT SHAFT

POWER FLOW IN REVERSE

FIGURE 38-21. In reverse only the rear half of the gearset is in use. The front clutch is applied driving the sun gear. The low and reverse band is applied holding the rear carrier. *(Courtesy of Chrysler Corporation)*

LOW (D) (Breakaway) 2.45:1	LOW (1) (Manual) 2.45:1	SECOND 1.45:1	DIRECT 1.0:1	REVERSE 2.20:1
REAR CLUTCH DRIVES FRONT ANNULUS GEAR	**REAR CLUTCH** DRIVES FRONT ANNULUS GEAR	**REAR CLUTCH** DRIVES FRONT ANNULUS GEAR	**REAR CLUTCH** DRIVES FRONT ANNULUS GEAR	**FRONT CLUTCH** DRIVES SUN GEAR
OVERRUNNING CLUTCH HOLDS REAR PLANET CARRIER	**LOW AND REVERSE BAND** HOLDS REAR PLANET CARRIER	**KICKDOWN BAND** HOLDS SUN GEAR	**FRONT CLUTCH** DRIVES SUN GEAR	**LOW AND REVERSE BAND** HOLDS REAR PLANET CARRIER

FIGURE 38–22(A). Summary of clutch and band applications in all gear positions. *(Courtesy of Chrysler Corporation)*

Ford Automatic Overdrive (Four-Speed)

The Ford automatic overdrive four-speed transmission uses four multiple-disc clutches, two one-way clutches, two bands, and two input shafts to control a Ravigneaux-type planetary gear system. A tubular turbine shaft is used, allowing a direct-drive shaft to be located inside the turbine shaft. The direct-drive shaft is spring-dampened in the torque converter.

Selector lever positions are park, reverse, neutral, drive, 3, and 1. The drive position is the overdrive position, and the 3 position locks out the overdrive.

In the park position the park pawl locks the ring gear and output shaft to the transmission case. The low and reverse band is applied in park but no drive condition is possible since no clutches are applied.

In reverse the reverse clutch is applied to drive the reverse (front, larger) sun gear clockwise. The low and reverse band holds the carrier to prevent it from turning forward. This allows the clockwise-turning reverse sun gear to drive the long pinions counterclockwise. The long pinions drive the ring gear and output shaft in reverse (counterclockwise).

In neutral no clutches or bands are applied.

Low Gear

In low gear the forward clutch is applied to cause the turbine shaft to drive the forward (rear or smaller) sun gear in a clockwise direction. This drives the short pinions in a counterclockwise direction. The short pinions drive the long pinions in a clockwise direction, which drives the ring gear and output shaft forward or clockwise for low gear.

Resistance to motion of the ring gear creates a reaction on the carrier, which attempts to turn backward. This is prevented by a one-way clutch just as in the FMX three-speed transmission.

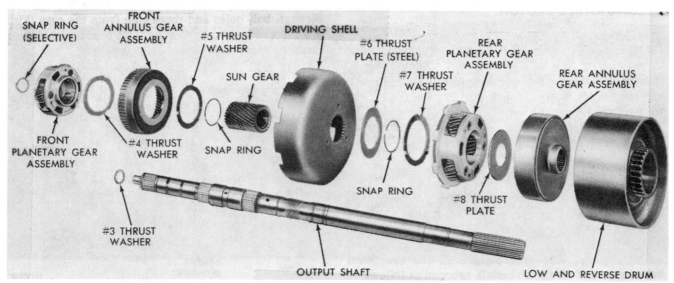

FIGURE 38–22(B). Exploded view of compound planetary gearset (Simpson type) and output shaft. *(Courtesy of Chrysler Corporation)*

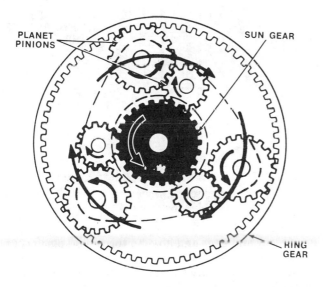

FIGURE 38-23. Ravigneaux single-carrier, dual-pinion, single-ring-gear, dual-sun-gear, compound-planetary-gear set used in Ford FMX and automatic overdrive transmissions.

On deceleration the one-way clutch overruns, providing no engine braking.

In manual low the low and reverse band is applied to prevent carrier rotation and provide engine braking on deceleration.

Second Gear

In second gear the intermediate holding clutch is applied to lock the outer race of the intermediate one-way clutch to the transmission case. This prevents the reverse (larger) sun gear from turning counterclockwise. This is the case during engine torque application. During deceleration the intermediate one-way clutch overruns, resulting in a freewheeling–no engine braking condition.

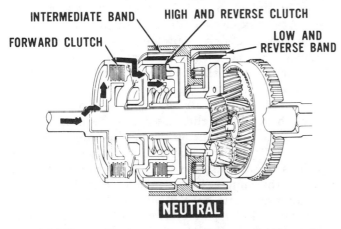

FIGURE 38-24. In neutral, no clutches or bands are applied; therefore, no power is transmitted to the output shaft in this Ravigneaux three-speed gearset. (Courtesy of Ford Motor Co. of Canada Ltd.)

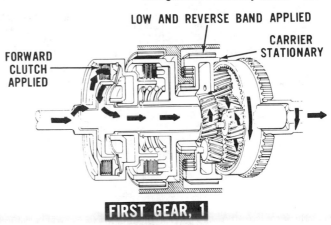

FIGURE 38-25. In first gear at selector lever position 1, the pinion carrier is held against rotation by the low and reverse band. (Courtesy of Ford Motor Co. of Canada Ltd.)

In second gear, then, the reverse sun gear is held by the intermediate holding clutch and one-way clutch. Since the forward clutch is still applied, drive is from the turbine shaft to the forward clutch to the forward (small) sun gear driving it clockwise. The forward sun gear drives the short pinions counterclockwise. The short pinions drive the long pinions clockwise. The long pinions are forced to walk around the stationary reverse sun gear, causing the carrier to rotate and driving the ring gear and output shaft at an increased speed compared to low gear.

The intermediate holding clutch remains applied in third and fourth gear but has no effect since the entire gear train is turning in a clockwise direction in third and fourth. The fact that the interme-

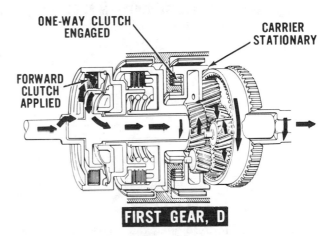

FIGURE 38-26. In first gear at selector lever position D, the pinion carrier is held against rotation by the one-way clutch instead of the low and reverse band. First gear in D is the only gear that uses the one-way clutch. (Courtesy of Ford Motor Co. of Canada Ltd.)

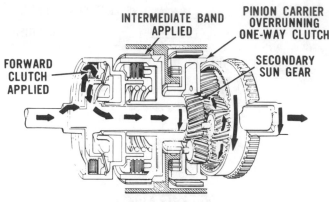

INTERMEDIATE BAND APPLIED

PINION CARRIER OVERRUNNING ONE-WAY CLUTCH

FORWARD CLUTCH APPLIED

SECONDARY SUN GEAR

SECOND GEAR

FIGURE 38-27. Second-gear ratio is obtained by driving the primary sun gear and holding the secondary sun gear. The primary pinions drive the secondary pinions, causing them to "walk" around the secondary sun gear and to carry the internal gear and output shaft around with them. *(Courtesy of Ford Motor Co. of Canada Ltd.)*

diate clutch remains applied in third and fourth results in smoother 3-2 downshifts.

There is no manually selected second gear in this transmission. However, if the selector lever is moved to the 1 or manual low position when car speed is above 25 mph (40 km/h), the transmission will operate in second gear until vehicle speed drops below that speed.

Third Gear (Direct)

To upshift from second gear to third gear, the direct clutch must be applied. The direct clutch is driven by the direct-drive shaft (not the turbine shaft) and when applied drives the carrier at engine speed.

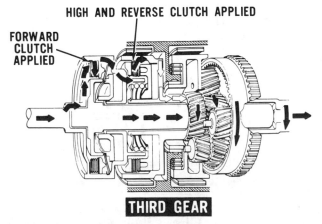

HIGH AND REVERSE CLUTCH APPLIED

FORWARD CLUTCH APPLIED

THIRD GEAR

FIGURE 38-28. In third gear, the primary and secondary sun gears are locked together and driven as a unit. Therefore, the pinions cannot rotate and the entire planetary train revolves as a unit, which causes the output shaft to rotate at the same speed as the turbine shaft. *(Courtesy of Ford Motor Co. of Canada Ltd.)*

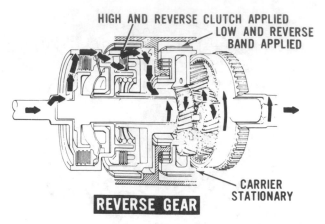

HIGH AND REVERSE CLUTCH APPLIED

LOW AND REVERSE BAND APPLIED

CARRIER STATIONARY

REVERSE GEAR

FIGURE 38-29. Reverse gear is obtained by driving the secondary sun gear and holding the pinion carrier. The secondary pinions drive the internal gear in the reverse direction. The primary sun gear and the primary pinions rotate freely and have no effect on the gear train. *(Courtesy of Ford Motor Co. of Canada Ltd.)*

Since the forward clutch is still applied, driving the forward sun gear, and the carrier is driven through the direct clutch, the entire gear train is forced to turn at engine speed, or 1:1. The direct clutch transmits about 60 percent of the drive while the forward clutch transmits the other 40 percent.

However, although the gear train is locked up and rotates as a unit for all practical purposes, there is some converter slip in direct drive, causing the planet pinions to turn on their shafts to a very small degree. As mentioned, the intermediate holding clutch remains applied but has no effect on third-gear operation since the entire gear train is turning clockwise and the intermediate one-way clutch therefore overruns.

Fourth Gear (Overdrive)

As the transmission automatically shifts from third gear direct to fourth gear overdrive, the overdrive band is applied to hold the reverse sun gear stationary. At the same time the forward clutch is released while the direct-drive clutch is still left applied. The transmission is now driven through the direct-drive shaft only, bypassing the turbine and turbine shaft and thereby eliminating converter slip.

Power flow is from the direct-drive shaft, through the direct clutch, driving the carrier clockwise. Since the overdrive band is holding the reverse sun gear stationary, carrier rotation causes the long pinions to walk around the reverse sun gear. This causes the pinions to turn on their shafts, forcing the ring gear and output shaft to turn faster than the carrier in overdrive. The result is an overdrive ratio of 0.667:1. The intermediate clutch, though still applied, has no effect on overdrive operation since all gear components are turning clockwise and the intermediate one-way clutch therefore overruns.

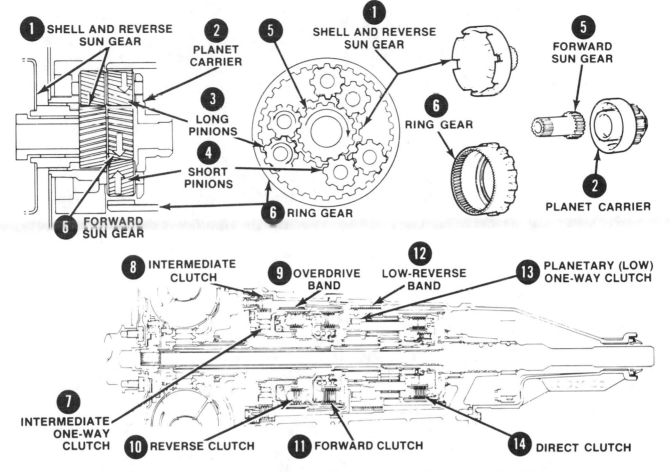

FIGURE 38–30. Ford automatic overdrive gear train. *(Courtesy of Ford Motor Co. of Canada Ltd.)*

Ford ATX Automatic Transaxle

Ford's ATX automatic transaxle is a three-speed automatic transmission and final drive assembly used on front-wheel-drive Ford cars.

A unique three-element torque converter with a simple planetary splitter gear is used to transmit engine torque to the Ravigneaux gear train in the transmission. As described earlier this torque converter has two output shafts: the turbine shaft, which transmits torque converter hydraulic torque output, and the intermediate shaft, which transmits engine torque hydraulically and mechanically through a torsional damper assembly. Both shafts are tubular, with the intermediate shaft inside the turbine shaft. A third shaft inside the intermediate shaft is used to drive the transmission hydraulic pump, which is located at the opposite end of the transmission from the torque converter. The pump drive shaft is splined to the torque converter cover. The turbine shaft is splined to the sun gear in the converter. The sun gear is splined to the turbine. The intermediate shaft is splined to the splitter gear car-

rier in the converter. The ring gear is splined to the converter damper and cover assembly.

ATX Gear Train Components and Operation

The ATX Ravigneaux planetary gear train consists of two sun gears, one carrier, and one ring gear: the reverse sun gear and a larger foward sungear; the carrier; and two sets of pinions—the short pinions in mesh with the low and reverse sun gear and the long pinions; the long pinions in mesh with the short pinions, the forward sun gear, and the ring gear.

This gearset is controlled by a one-way clutch, three multiple-disc clutches, and a band. The input members of this gear train are the low and reverse sun gear and the ring gear. The gear train members that can be held are the ring gear and the forward sun gear. The carrier serves as the output member and is splined to the final drive gear.

The clutches and band act as follows:

• One-way clutch allows the turbine shaft to drive the reverse sun gear.

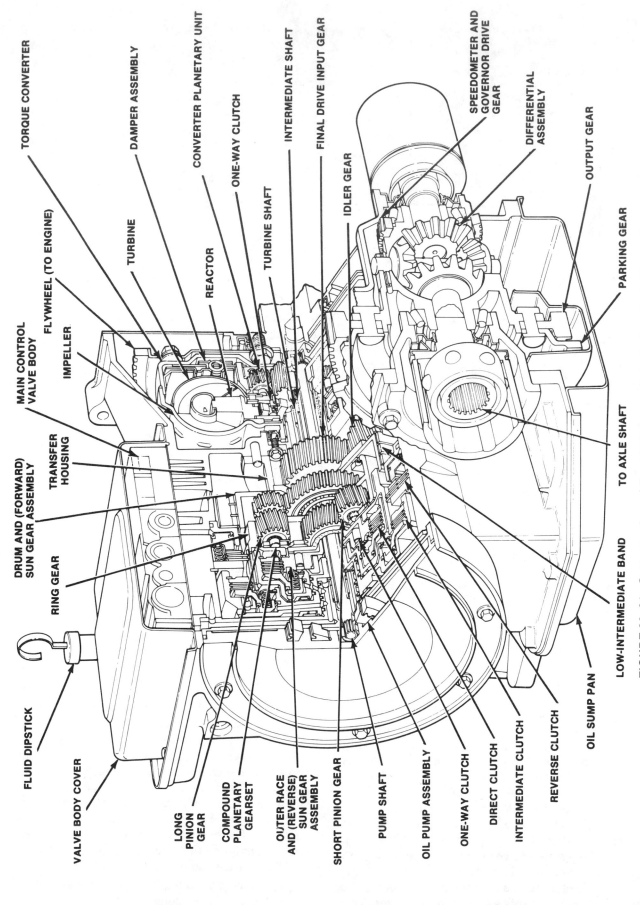

FLUID DIPSTICK

VALVE BODY COVER

MAIN CONTROL VALVE BODY

FLYWHEEL (TO ENGINE)

IMPELLER

DRUM AND (FORWARD) SUN GEAR ASSEMBLY

TRANSFER HOUSING

RING GEAR

TORQUE CONVERTER

DAMPER ASSEMBLY

CONVERTER PLANETARY UNIT

TURBINE

REACTOR

ONE-WAY CLUTCH

INTERMEDIATE SHAFT

TURBINE SHAFT

FINAL DRIVE INPUT GEAR

IDLER GEAR

SPEEDOMETER AND GOVERNOR DRIVE GEAR

DIFFERENTIAL ASSEMBLY

OUTPUT GEAR

PARKING GEAR

TO AXLE SHAFT

LOW-INTERMEDIATE BAND

OIL SUMP PAN

REVERSE CLUTCH

INTERMEDIATE CLUTCH

DIRECT CLUTCH

ONE-WAY CLUTCH

OIL PUMP ASSEMBLY

PUMP SHAFT

SHORT PINION GEAR

OUTER RACE AND (REVERSE) SUN GEAR ASSEMBLY

COMPOUND PLANETARY GEARSET

LONG PINION GEAR

FIGURE 38-31. Cutaway view of Ford ATX transaxle including final drive and differential gears. *(Courtesy of Ford Motor Co. of Canada Ltd.)*

- Direct clutch allows the turbine shaft to drive the reverse sun gear without any freewheeling.

- Intermediate clutch allows the intermediate shaft to drive the ring gear.

- Reverse clutch allows the ring gear to be held stationary.

- Band allows the forward sun gear to be held stationary.

Selector lever positions for this transmission are:

P—park,

R—reverse,

N—neutral,

D—drive,

2—intermediate,

1—manual low.

- Park. All transmission components are in neutral with clutches and band released. Although the turbine is driving the low-reverse sun gear, no torque is being transmitted through the transmission since there is no reaction or held member. The differential case is locked to the transmission case by a park pawl, preventing drive wheel movement.

- Reverse. The ring gear is held stationary by applying the reverse clutch. Drive is from the turbine shaft, the direct clutch that is applied, and the low and reverse sun gear in a clockwise direction. The low and reverse sun gear drives the short pinions counterclockwise, which in turn drive the long pinions clockwise. The clockwise-turning long pinions are forced to walk around the stationary ring gear, forcing the carrier and output to turn counterclockwise in reverse reduction of 1.97:1. Reverse gear drive through the torque converter is 100 percent hydraulic from the turbine and turbine shaft only.

- Neutral. Neutral is the same as park as far as action in the transmission gear train is concerned; however, in neutral the park pawl is not engaged and the vehicle is able to roll freely.

- Drive. In the drive range the transmission starts in low and shifts automatically to second and then to third or direct.

- In drive low the band is applied to hold the forward sun gear stationary. Drive is from the turbine shaft through the one-way clutch to the low and reverse sun gear in a clockwise direction. The low and reverse sun gear drives the short pinions counterclockwise, which drive the long pinions clockwise. The clockwise-turning long pinions are forced to walk around the stationary forward sun gear in a clockwise direction taking the carrier and output forward in a first-gear reduction of 2.79:1 ratio. All torque in first gear is transmitted hydraulically to the turbine shaft and low-reverse sun gear. On deceleration, while the transmission is in drive low, the one-way clutch will overrun, which results in no engine braking.

- Intermediate (drive range). In intermediate the band remains applied just as in drive low to hold the forward sun gear stationary. The intermediate clutch applies to drive the planetary ring gear.

- Manual Low. In manually selected low gear the only difference from drive low is that the direct clutch is applied to connect the low-reverse sun gear solidly to the turbine shaft. Power flow is exactly the same as in drive low but freewheeling does not occur and engine braking on deceleration takes place.

Power flow is now split in the converter. The turbine provides the hydraulic drive torque to the intermediate shaft since the turbine is splined to the converter sun gear. The converter cover provides the mechanical drive to the intermediate shaft since the ring gear is splined to the damper assembly in the converter cover. This means that two members of the splitter gear are being driven—one hydraulically and the other mechanically—driving the third member, the carrier, at relatively the same speed. There is, of course, some hydraulic slip in the converter. Torque input to the intermediate shaft in second gear is 38 percent hydraulic and 62 percent mechanical.

To continue the power flow in the transmission gear train, the intermediate shaft drives the intermediate clutch and planetary ring gear clockwise. This drives the long pinions clockwise and forces them to walk around the stationary forward sun gear. This causes the output carrier to turn forward in a reduction ratio of 1.61:1.

- Manual second. In manually selected second gear, power flow is exactly as in first and second in the drive range. However, no upshift to third is possible since the 2–3 upshift circuit is locked out.

- Third (Direct). In third or direct drive, the band is released, the intermediate clutch remains applied, and the direct clutch is applied. Applying the direct clutch allows the turbine shaft to drive the low and reverse sun gear. The intermediate shaft is still driving the ring gear through the intermediate clutch. Driving these two planetary members forces the carrier to turn at the same speed. For all practical purposes the entire planetary unit is locked together and turns as a unit in direct drive in a virtual 1:1 ratio.

There is, of course, still some hydraulic slip in the converter, allowing some minor rotation of pinions on their axes. This is insignificant, however, since input torque in direct is 93 percent mechanical and only 7 percent hydraulic, resulting in virtually 100 percent mechanical drive if we consider a 10 percent slip in the 7 percent hydraulic torque input. Since the direct clutch is applied, the one-way clutch cannot overrun, allowing engine braking in third gear.

PART 6 OVERDRIVE TRANSMISSIONS

THM 325-4L Four-Speed Overdrive

The THM 325-4L Turbo Hydra-Matic transmission is a four-speed overdrive transmission with a three-element lockup torque converter for use in front-wheel-drive vehicles. It consists of the common Simpson compound planetary gear drive train chain driven from the overdrive planetary gearset and torque converter.

The advantages of overdrive include reduced engine speed (in relation to road speed) and therefore less fuel consumption and less wear on engine parts and accessories.

The lockup torque converter and Simpson gear train operate as described earlier. The addition of a simple planetary gearset between the torque converter and the Simpson gear train allows the transmission input shaft to be driven at either turbine shaft speed or at overdrive speed, which is 0.67:1 (turbine shaft to transmission input shaft ratio). The overdrive planetary gear unit is controlled by two multiple-disc clutches and a one-way roller clutch.

Overdrive is achieved when the carrier is driving, the sun gear is held, and the ring gear is the driven member. The ring gear has external teeth to engage the drive link or chain.

The overdrive carrier is splined to the turbine shaft of the converter. The carrier is attached to the outer race of the one-way roller clutch. The sun gear is attached to the inner race of the roller clutch.

Because of the resistance to rotation of the ring gear (because of vehicle load), the carrier and pinions try to turn the sun gear faster than the carrier. This causes the one-way clutch to lock up, turning the carrier, sun gear, and ring gear all at the same speed. This is the condition any time engine torque is being applied. When the driver releases the accelerator pedal, the vehicle drive wheels try to drive the engine through the transmission and overdrive unit.

However, under these conditions the one-way clutch releases and overruns, allowing the sun gear to turn faster than the carrier. This results in no en-gine braking when the selector lever is in the drive position. In manually selected first, second, or third, the overrrun clutch applies, locking the sun gear to the carrier, which prevents the one-way clutch from overdrive running. This allows engine compression to be used for engine braking when going downhill.

Overdrive occurs with the selector lever in the drive (D) position when the transmission has shifted into fourth gear (overdrive). In fourth-gear overdrive the fourth clutch applies to hold the overdrive sun gear. The torque converter drives the carrier, which in turn drives the overdrive ring gear at an increased speed.

The clockwise-turning carrier forces the pinions to walk around the stationary sun gear, which causes the ring gear to turn faster than the carrier.

Torque converter lockup occurs in drive-range second, third, and fourth only.

THM 700-R4 Four-Speed Overdrive

The THM 700-R4 Turbo Hydra-Matic transmission is a four-speed overdrive unit with a lockup torque converter. The planetary gear train resembles the Simpson gearset but operates differently. The torque converter locks up in drive-range second, third, and fourth only.

The planetary gearset consists of two simple planetary gearsets similar to the Simpson component gear train. However, in the 700-R4 transmission the two sun gears are able to operate independently as necessary, which is not the case with the common Simpson gearset. In this transmission five multiple-disc clutches, two roller clutches, and one band control operation of the gearset.

Overdrive is achieved when the selector lever is in the drive-range and the transmission has up-shifted into fourth-gear overdrive. The rear or reaction planetary gearset produces overdrive when the 2-4 band prevents the reaction sun gear from turning.

The 3-4 clutch is applied to drive the front ring gear. The front ring gear is splined to the rear carrier, which is now driven at turbine speed.

With the 2-4 band on, the rear sun gear cannot turn. This forces the pinions in the rear carrier to walk around the stationary sun gear and causes the rear ring gear to turn faster than the carrier. The rear ring gear is splined to the transmission output shaft. This produces an overdrive ratio between turbine shaft and transmisison output shaft of approximately 0.70:1.

First Gear

In first gear the forward clutch and input roller clutch are applied to drive the input or front sun gear clockwise. The input or front ring gear is prevented

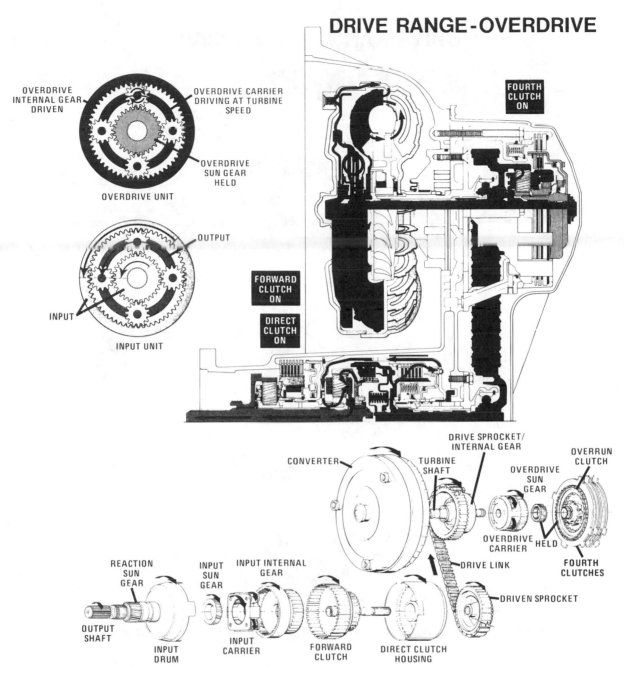

FIGURE 38-32. GM 325-4L overdrive operation. (*Courtesy of General Motors Corporation*)

from turning in a counterclockwise direction by a one-way low roller clutch.

Driving the sun gear clockwise causes the pinions in the front carrier to walk around the stationary front ring gear. This forces the carrier and output shaft (to which it is splined) to turn at reduced speed for low gear. This is the condition when the transmission is in low gear and the selector lever is in the drive, 3, or 2 position. This condition does not provide any engine braking since the low roller clutch will overrun on deceleration.

In the manually selected low or 1 position the only difference is that the low and reverse multiple-disc clutch is applied to prevent the front ring gear from turning and the low roller clutch from overrunning. This position provides engine braking. No automatic upshifts occur since all the hydraulic upshift circuits are locked out in this selector lever position.

Second Gear

To shift from first gear to second gear, the 2-4 band is applied to hold the reaction or rear sun gear. The forward clutch is still on, which still drives the front

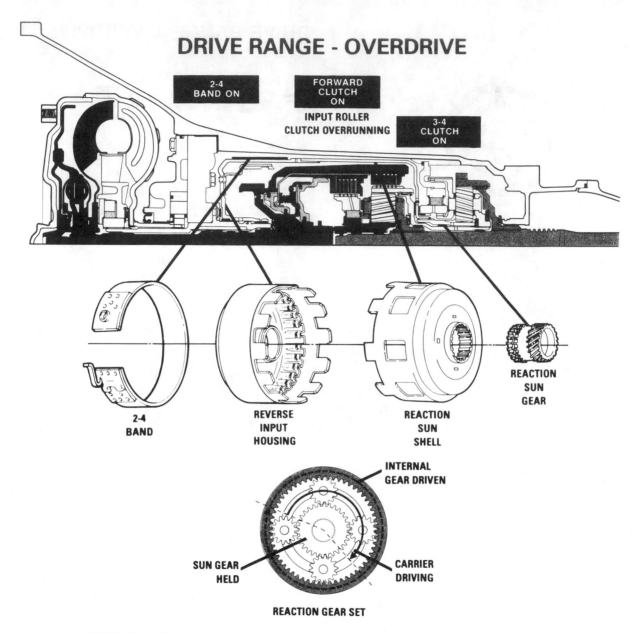

DRIVE RANGE - OVERDRIVE

2-4 BAND ON

FORWARD CLUTCH ON

INPUT ROLLER CLUTCH OVERRUNNING

3-4 CLUTCH ON

REACTION SUN GEAR

2-4 BAND

REVERSE INPUT HOUSING

REACTION SUN SHELL

INTERNAL GEAR DRIVEN

SUN GEAR HELD

CARRIER DRIVING

REACTION GEAR SET

FIGURE 38-33. GM 700 R4 overdrive operation. *(Courtesy of General Motors Corporation)*

or input sun gear through the input roller clutch in a clockwise direction.

In low gear the front or input ring gear was stationary, providing a 3.06:1 sun-gear-to-carrier reduction.

In second gear the front or input ring gear is forced to turn in a forward or clockwise direction since the rear sun gear is being held by the 2-4 band. Holding the rear sun gear, which was turning counterclockwise in low gear, causes the front or input ring gear to turn in a forward to clockwise direction. This increases the speed of the input carrier and output shaft to a second gear speed of approximately 1.63:1. This arrangement does not provide any en-

gine braking since the input roller clutch overruns when decelerating.

In manually selected second the transmission starts in low and automatically upshifts to second. Further upshifts are prevented.

However, in manual second the overrun clutch is applied, locking the input sun gear to the turbine shaft and effectively eliminating any overrun of the one-way clutch on deceleration. This provides engine braking in manually selected second gear.

Third Gear

To shift into third gear the 2-4 band is released and the 3-4 clutch is applied.

Applying the 3–4 clutch connects the front or input ring gear to the turbine shaft. Since the forward clutch and roller clutch are still on, the input sun gear is also being driven by the turbine shaft. Driving these two members of the planetary gearset causes the front carrier and output shaft to be driven at turbine shaft speed. This is direct drive, or 1:1. Engine braking is not possible since the input roller clutch will overrun when decelerating.

In the manually selected third position the transmission shifts from first to second and from second to third as it does in the drive range. However, no 3–4 upshift takes place. In addition, the overrun clutch is applied just as in manual second. This prevents the input roller clutch from overrunning when decelerating, thereby providing engine braking.

Reverse

Reverse is provided in the 700-R4 transmission by applying the reverse input clutch and the low and reverse holding clutch. Applying the reverse input clutch causes the turbine shaft to drive the rear or reaction sun gear in a clockwise direction. Applying the low and reverse holding clutch prevents the reaction carrier from turning.

The clockwise-turning sun gear drives the pinions counterclockwise. The pinions drive the ring gear and output shaft (to which it is splined) in a counterclockwise or reverse direction at a reduction of about 2.30:1.

General Motors 200 4R four-speed overdrive uses a simple planetary gearset at the rear of the three-speed Simpson gearset to provide fourth-gear overdrive.

The Ford automatic overdrive is described in Part 5 of this chapter.

PART 7   CLUTCHES AND BANDS

Multiple-Disc Clutches

Automatic transmissions use multiple-disc-type clutches to connect a planetary gear member to the transmission input shaft. Many automatic transmissions also employ one or more multiple-disc clutches as holding devices to prevent the rotation of one or more planetary gear members.

The simplest Simpson compound three-speed planetary gear arrangement uses two multiple-disc clutches to connect the input shaft to the planetary gear system. One of these clutches is called the forward clutch since it is applied in all three forward speeds; the other is known as the reverse and high clutch since it is applied in high gear and reverse

only. Some shop manuals refer to these clutches as the rear clutch and the front clutch because of physical position in the transmission.

The forward clutch in this arrangement connects the ring gear of the forward half of the planetary gearset to the transmission input shaft when it is applied. The reverse and high clutch connects the common sun gear to the input shaft when the clutch is applied.

The transmission input shaft (turbine shaft), the reverse and high (front) clutch hub, and the forward (rear) clutch cylinder (drum) rotate as an assembly. The clutch pack consists of an alternately stacked arrangement of externally toothed or tanged steel plates and internally toothed friction surface plates. The external tangs of the steel plates engage grooves in the clutch drum and therefore rotate with the drum. The internal teeth of the friction plate engages splines or grooves on the clutch hub and therefore rotate with the hub.

When a clutch is applied, the hub, steel plates, friction plates, and drum rotate as a unit. When the clutch is released, one set of plates may be stationary while the other set is turning or the steel plates and friction plates in the same clutch may be turning in opposite directions, depending on planetary gear operation and the drive range in which the transmission is operating. Precise clutch pack clearance is critical to proper clutch apply and release.

A hydraulic piston in the clutch cylinder applies the clutch while a pressure plate and retaining ring on the other side of the clutch pack provide the reaction. Synthetic rubber seals between the piston and cylinder prevent fluid leakage and loss of apply pressure. A dished-plate–type Belleville spring, a heavy coil spring, or a series of small coil springs is used to return the piston to the release position when hydraulic apply force is removed. A Belleville spring is used only in the forward clutch since fast release is required only in the reverse and high clutch during a part throttle or full throttle downshift. In many cases the clutch pack also includes a snap ring type of wave spring or in some cases one or more dished steel plates to cushion clutch application for smoother shifts.

A ball type of check valve is located in the clutch piston. The check ball controls a fluid exhaust passage. Fast clutch release is required to provide smooth rapid shifts and prevent unwanted friction in the clutch. The rapidly spinning clutch assembly deposits residual fluid between the piston and cylinder base circumference, which attempts to continue clutch apply. Centrifugal force unseats the fluid exhaust check ball and allows fluid to exhaust, preventing this condition. When the clutch is once

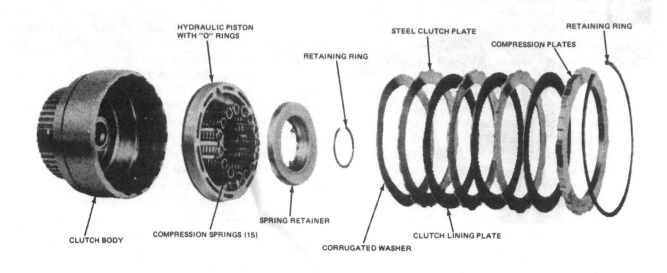

- CLUTCH BODY
- COMPRESSION SPRINGS (15)
- HYDRAULIC PISTON WITH "O" RINGS
- SPRING RETAINER
- RETAINING RING
- CORRUGATED WASHER
- CLUTCH LINING PLATE
- STEEL CLUTCH PLATE
- COMPRESSION PLATES
- RETAINING RING

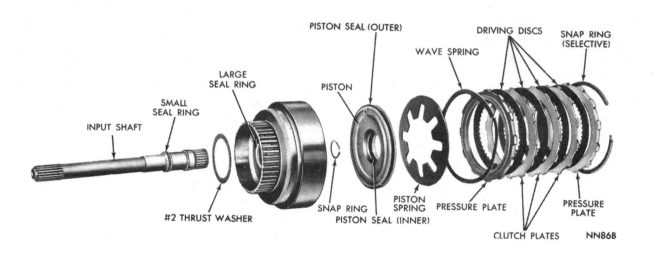

- INPUT SHAFT
- SMALL SEAL RING
- LARGE SEAL RING
- #2 THRUST WASHER
- SNAP RING
- PISTON SEAL (INNER)
- PISTON SEAL (OUTER)
- PISTON
- PISTON SPRING
- WAVE SPRING
- PRESSURE PLATE
- DRIVING DISCS
- CLUTCH PLATES
- PRESSURE PLATE
- SNAP RING (SELECTIVE)
- NN86B

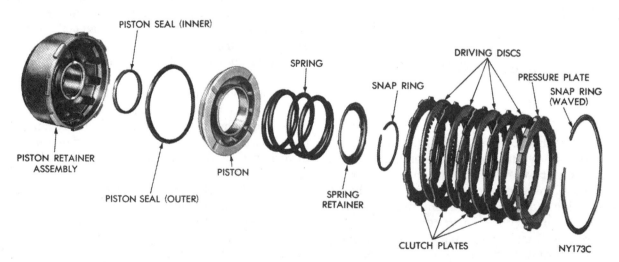

- PISTON RETAINER ASSEMBLY
- PISTON SEAL (INNER)
- PISTON SEAL (OUTER)
- PISTON
- SPRING
- SPRING RETAINER
- SNAP RING
- DRIVING DISCS
- CLUTCH PLATES
- PRESSURE PLATE
- SNAP RING (WAVED)
- NY173C

FIGURE 38-34. Typical multiple-disc drive clutches. Note difference in release springs. *(Courtesy of Ford Motor Co. of Canada Ltd.)*

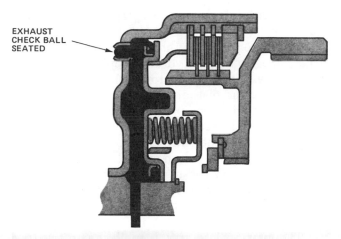

FIGURE 38–35. Clutch check ball seats when hydraulic pressure applies clutch, preventing escape of fluid. *(Courtesy of General Motors Corporation)*

again applied, hydraulic pressure seats the check ball and seals off the exhaust orifice.

Clutch Plates

Steel clutch discs are stamped from steel stock and are finished with a dull surface to facilitate proper break-in with new friction discs. After proper break-in, steel discs become polished.

Friction discs are steel plates with friction material bonded to both sides. Friction material may be organic or metallic, depending on friction characteristics required.

Metallic material is usually a sintered or powdered copper and graphite mix with bonding agents. Semi-metallic materials include asbestos powders. Non-metallic organic friction materials are normally

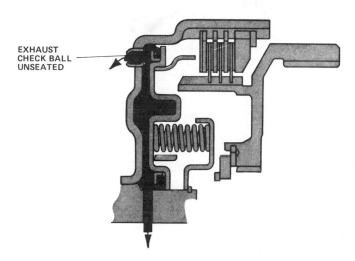

FIGURE 38–36. When hydraulic pressure is released, centrifugal force unseats check ball and causes fluid to be exhausted through check ball port. This prevents partial clutch application during clutch release. *(Courtesy of General Motors Corporation)*

a paper type sometimes combined with asbestos and the proper bonding agents.

The friction characteristics of these materials are modified by the type of fluid used and by grooving of the friction discs. The slip-lockup characteristics of multiple-disc clutches are critical to shift quality. Due to the nature of the frictional characteristics of the clutch plates, new and old plates should never be mixed, since glazing could occur.

Clutch Torque Capacity

The maximum torque capacity of the multiple-disc clutch is determined by the following factors:

1. Clutch diameter
2. Frictional surface area (number of plates)
3. Hydraulic pressure
4. Surface area acted on by hydraulic pressure
5. In the case of a Belleville-spring–type clutch, the mechanical advantage gained by the lever action of the spring

The diameter of the clutch is limited by the room available in the transmission case. The frictional surface area can be increased or decreased by the number of plates used in the clutch pack. Increasing hydraulic apply pressure will, of course, increase the torque capacity of a clutch and also will result in harsher shifts. The surface area against which the hydraulic pressure acts (piston size) is also limited by the available room in the clutch cylinder.

Engine size and vehicle design are factors that influence the design and balance of torque capacity factors utilized by the vehicle manufacturer.

Multiple-Disc Holding Clutch

Many transmission designs utilize multiple-disc holding clutches in place of bands and servos. The clutch pack and piston are located in the same bore whereas a band requires a separate servo to operate the band. The multiple-disc holding clutch uses the transmission case as the clutch cylinder.

A hydraulically applied and spring-released piston is used. Steel and friction plates stacked alternately comprise the clutch pack. The externally tanged steel plates engage corresponding grooves in the transmission case. The internally toothed friction plates engage grooves on a drum attached to the planetary gear member to be held. A heavy pressure plate and snap ring absorb clutch apply reaction pressure. A wave spring may be used to help cushion clutch application.

Typical examples of transmissions using multiple-disc clutches as holding devices are the General Motors Turbo Hydra-Matics and the Ford C6 transmissions.

Bands and Servos

Many automatic transmission designs use the hydraulic-servo–operated wrap-around band as a holding device to control planetary gear operation. The band does not increase the diameter of the gear train as much as a multiple-disc clutch does but requires room for a servo to operate the band.

Hydraulic Servo

A hydraulic servo converts hydraulic force to mechanical force. The servo consists of a piston operating in a bore in the transmission case or in a separate servo cylinder bolted to the transmission case. A piston rod is used to act directly on the band or through a lever and link assembly. The lever usually is used to increase apply force. Reaction force is applied to an anchor at the other end of the band.

The anchor is attached to or part of the transmission case.

The piston in a low and reverse band servo is usually single acting. Hydraulic apply force is available on one side of the piston with a spring on the other side of the piston to return the piston to the release position when apply pressure is removed. A piston plug in the servo piston may be used to cushion servo apply. The two piston return springs are located between the piston and a land on the piston plug and between the piston and spring retainer. Band adjustment may be provided at the lever or the anchor to maintain proper operating clearance between the band and the drum.

The intermediate servo usually has a two-land piston and is double acting. The servo bore and piston are stepped—the small end of the piston operating in the smaller diameter bore and the larger diameter of the piston in the larger bore. A piston rod and return spring are located inside the piston. A piston return spring is used between the piston and piston rod guide, which is held in the bore by means of a snap ring.

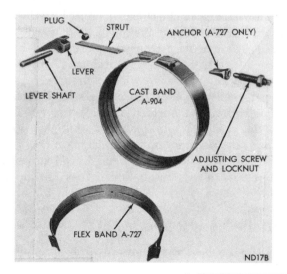

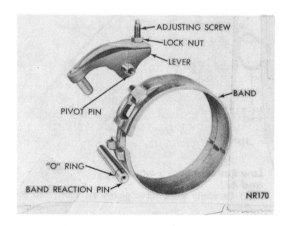

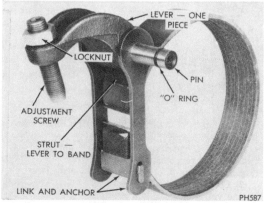

FIGURE 38-37. Several types of bands used in automatic transmissions. Bands are lined with friction material ranging from fiber to sintered metal. *(Courtesy of Chrysler Corporation)*

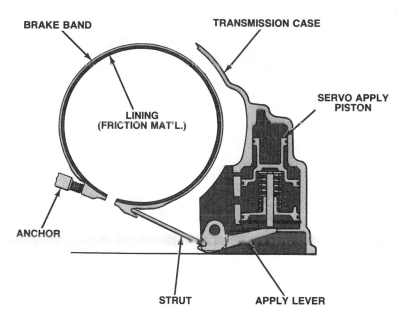

FIGURE 38-38. Details of band and servo operation showing band-adjusting anchor screw. *(Courtesy of Chrysler Corporation)*

Hydraulic pressure applied between the piston and piston bore applies the intermediate band on a 1-2 upshift or a 3-2 downshift. Spring pressure returns the piston to the release position on a 2-1 downshift. On a 2-3 upshift, hydraulic pressure introduced to the release side of the piston plug spring pressure forces the piston back against apply pressure to release the band for third gear. During a 3-2 downshift, intermediate servo release pressure is dumped. Since apply pressure is still present, the intermediate band applies for second-gear operation.

During a part-throttle or full-throttle 3-2 downshift, it is essential that the intermediate band be applied immediately as the direct clutch is released in order to prevent excessive engine speed increase. The intermediate servo piston rod may be direct acting on the band or it may act on the band through a lever and link or strut. Reaction force is absorbed by the other end of the band through an anchor in the transmission case.

Proper operating clearance may be adjusted to some transmissions by means of an anchor screw adjustment. Other transmissions may use selective length band actuating rods or may have no adjustment. Proper band-to-drum clearance is required to prevent drag on the drum when the band is in the

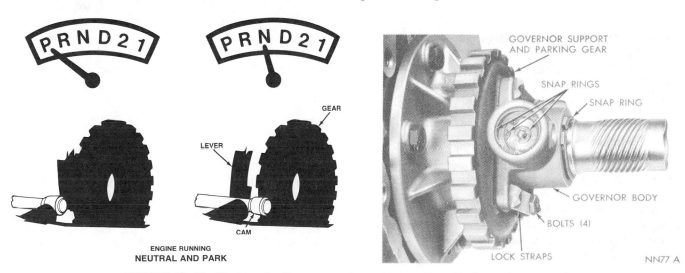

FIGURE 38-39. Parking brake gear and pawl operation. Park pawl mounted in transmission case locks output shaft and drive wheels when engaged in parking gear. Parking gear is splined to the transmission output shaft. *(Courtesy of Chrysler Corporation)*

released position and to assure full band application before the servo piston bottoms in its bore to prevent slippage.

Bands

Transmission bands may be of the rigid or flexible type. The rigid type is also flexible to the extent that it will contract during band application and expand on band release. The flexible type when removed from the transmission does not retain its circular shape to fit the drum. Bands are either single wrap or double wrap. The double-wrap design increases the effects of self-energization when the band is applied. Self-energizing is the tendency of a band to tighten around a drum during drum rotation.

The double-wrap band design is used for low and reverse where greater holding force is required due to the high torque of low and reverse gear operation. Bands have either a relatively hard metallic friction lining or a softer organic friction material.

The metallic materials are generally more abrasive than the organic materials. For this reason they are usually used only on the low and reverse band since this band is usually applied to a static or slow-turning drum.

The softer organic materials, usually a paper-based compound, are used on bands required to operate on fast-turning drums. Metallic lined bands used on these drums would result in much more rapid drum wear.

Drum material is also a factor in the slip-lockup characteristics of band operation. The proper combination of drum material, drum surface finish, and band frictional material is designed to provide the required slip-lockup characteristics for smooth positive shifts without causing premature band and drum wear or glazing.

Band frictional linings are usually grooved to control the escape of transmission fluid. This helps in providing the desired band application characteristics.

To ensure proper operation of the bands, the fluid specified by the transmission or vehicle manufacturer must be used. Using incorrect fluid results in a change of the coefficient of friction of all friction devices (clutches and bands) and consequent changes in shift characteristics. Harsher, more severe shifts or "mushy" delayed shifts can be the result of using improper fluid in the transmission.

Torque Capacity of Bands

The torque capacity of a transmission band must be great enough to hold the desired reaction member under all appropriate operating conditions. Torque capacity is determined by the friction characteristics of the band and drum (band friction lining and drum material); surface finish of the drum, drum and band diameter; servo piston diameter; hydraulic pressure to the servo piston; ratio of lever used to apply the band; and whether the servo is positioned to take advantage of the self-energizing effect of drum rotational direction when the band is applied. In the case of a low and reverse band, of course, the held member attempts to rotate counterclockwise in low and clockwise in reverse. It is therefore impossible to have self-energizing benefits in both directions. Higher hydraulic pressures are sometimes used in reverse to offset the difference there would otherwise be in torque capacity.

Higher hydraulic apply pressures are also used in reverse on transmissions equipped with a multiple-disc low and reverse holding clutch. This is required since the reaction force on the held member is greater in reverse than in low. In reverse, only the rear half of the planetary gearset provides the gear reduction while in low gear, reduction is achieved through both the front and rear section of the gear train. In the band and servo design, the self-energizing effect will work against hydraulic servo apply pressure, requiring even greater hydraulic pressure in reverse.

One-Way Clutches

Automatic transmissions use one or more one-way clutches to control planetary gear operation. A one-way clutch is also used in the torque converter stator.

One-way clutches can be used to allow rotation of a unit in one direction and prevent rotation of that unit in the other direction. The stator one-way clutch is a good example of this application. This unit prevents counterclockwise rotation of the stator during torque multiplication and allows clockwise rotation of the stator during the coupling phase of converter operation.

The one-way clutch can also be used to drive a unit in one direction and allow the unit to overrun the drive member under certain conditions. The turbine shaft driving the low-reverse sun gear through a one-way clutch in low-gear in the Ford ATX transaxle is a good example of this application.

A common application of a one-way roller clutch in the planetary gear train is the use of the clutch as a reaction or holding device in drive-range low gear. While engine torque is being applied to the gearset, the one-way clutch prevents counterclockwise rotation of one member of the planetary gearset. The particular planetary gear member acting as the reaction member depends on transmission de-

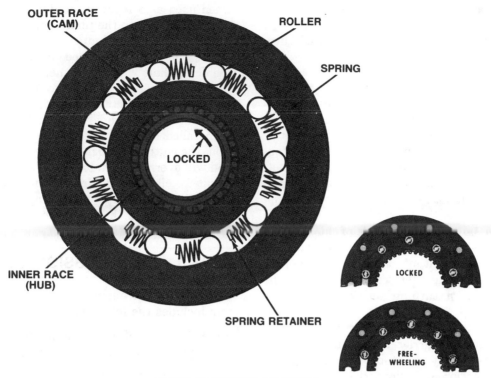

OVER RUNNING CLUTCH

FIGURE 38-40. Details of roller-type one-way clutch operation. This type of one-way clutch is used in the torque converter stator as well as in the planetary gear train. *(Courtesy of Chrysler Corporation)*

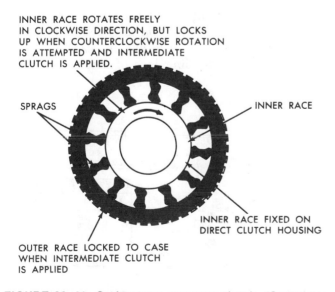

FIGURE 38-41. Spring-type one-way clutch. *(Courtesy of General Motors Corporation)*

sign. In the common Simpson three-speed automatic transmission gear train it is the rear carrier. In the Ravigneaux three-speed automatic arrangement it is the carrier.

Another application of the one-way roller clutch is its use in drive-range second gear on some transmissions, notably the THM 350. This allows freewheeling in drive-range second gear while still providing instant reaction through the intermediate roller clutch and sun gear when engine torque is applied to the gear train. In the manual second or L2 position, the intermediate band applies to render intermediate roller clutch overrun ineffective and provide engine braking by holding the sun gear.

In the THM 700-R4 four-speed overdrive transmission, a one-way roller clutch is used to drive the input sun gear. Other applications of the one-way clutch can be found by studying the power flow through the different makes and models of automatic transmissions.

Advantages of One-Way Clutches

One-way clutches have some distinct advantages that make them desirable for use in automatic transmissions. Automatic transmissions change gears by applying and releasing clutches and bands that control the drive and reaction in a planetary gearset. Precise timing of the application and release of these units is critical to smooth shifts. The one-way clutch acts and reacts instantly to application of torque and torque reversal. A good example of this is in the three-speed Simpson gear train. In drive low the one-way clutch provides instant reaction when engine torque is applied to the gear train, preventing the reaction carrier from turning backward (counterclockwise).

As soon as the transmission shifts from first to second, the reaction carrier must turn forward (clockwise). The one-way clutch provides instant capability for this action and allows the reverse to occur on a 2–1 downshift.

The one-way clutch is compact in design and requires no mechanical linkage or hydraulic devices for operation. This results in normally troublefree operation for the life of the transmission.

One-Way Clutch Construction and Operation

There are two types of one-way clutches: the sprag clutch and the roller clutch. Both rely on a wedging action for clutch lockup.

The sprag clutch consists of a sprag and cage assembly positioned between an inner and outer race. The roller clutch consists of an inner race, an outer race, and a series of spring-loaded rollers positioned between the two races.

The sprag clutch relies on wedging the larger diameter of the sprags between the inner and outer race for lockup and by tilting the sprags slightly on release, positioning the smaller diameter of the sprags between the two races. Spring action on the sprags and the direction of torque application to the race determine when the sprag clutch locks up or overruns.

The roller clutch relies on wedging rollers between the high part of the cams on the outer race and the inner race for lockup. Energizing springs tend to keep the rollers close to the high part of the cam. Torque application wedges the rollers firmly between the inner and outer race for lockup. Torque reversal causes the rollers to roll down the cam against spring action for freewheeling action.

In both of these designs one race is bolted, riveted, splined, or clutched to the transmission case when used as a reaction holding device. The other race is attached to the planetary gear member serving as the reaction member. When used as a driving device one race is clutched or attached directly to the drive shaft while the other race is connected to the planetary gear member to be driven.

It is critical to transmission operation that one-way clutches be properly assembled and installed. If installed in the opposite way to normal installation, the clutch will lock up when it should overrun and will overrun when it should lock up. This would result in either a no-drive condition or complete transmission lockup, depending on the type of transmission and the drive range selected.

PART 8   TRANSMISSION CONTROLS

The automatic transmission hydraulic control system includes the following:

- A source of hydraulic pressure
- Hydraulic pressure regulation
- Manual controls
- Throttle valve
- Governor valve
- Shift valves
- Shift timing and shift quality control valves
- Fluid types

Hydraulic Principles

When pressure is applied to a confined liquid, it is transmitted equally (pounds per square inch or kilopascals) in all directions throughout the entire system. Since fluid is virtually incompressible, motion can be transmitted without loss.

Force can be multiplied by using an output piston that is larger in reaction area than the input piston. However, the resultant increase in force produces a corresponding loss of motion (Figures 38–42 and 38–43).

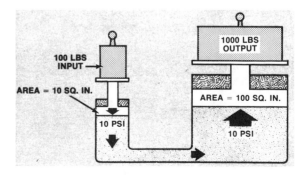

FIGURE 38–42. Principle of force multiplication using hydraulic pressure. *(Courtesy of Chrysler Corporation)*

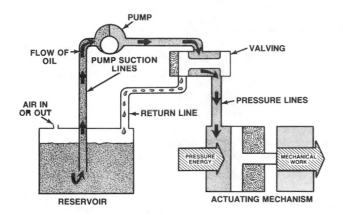

FIGURE 38-43. Basic hydraulic system. *(Courtesy of Chrysler Corporation)*

The automatic transmission uses these hydraulic principles to apply and release clutches and bands and to control their apply and release automatically.

Pressure Source

A gear or rotor type of positive displacement hydraulic pump is used to produce fluid flow and pressure. For the pump to be able to produce pressure, the fluid must be confined. The automatic transmission hydraulic control system is virtually a closed system except for minor fluid leakage past valves and the like, and for lubrication. The pump is driven by notches or lugs on the torque converter hub.

Pressure Regulation

A pressure regulator valve controls maximum system pressure (line pressure) and usually also torque converter, lubrication, and cooling circuit pressures. As pressure builds up in the system, the spool type of pressure regulator valve is forced back against spring pressure. When pressure reaches a predetermined maximum (determined by spring pressure), the valve moves far enough to allow some fluid to bypass the valve and return to the sump.

Manual Controls

A steering column or console-mounted shift-selector lever is connected by means of linkage to the manual valve in the transmission valve body. Hydraulic pressure or line pressure is fed to the manual valve. When the shift selector lever is moved to any of the gear positions, line pressure is directed to the appropriate clutches, bands, and valves to provide the drive through the transmission.

Fluid flow is provided for the torque converter, transmission cooler, and the transmission lubrication circuit whenever the engine is running, including Park and Neutral positions.

Park Position

When this position is selected, the park pawl engages the park gear on the transmission output shaft, preventing it from turning. Clutches and bands are not applied.

Reverse Position

When reverse is selected, line pressure is directed to the reverse and high driving clutch and the low and reverse band (or low and reverse holding clutch).

Neutral Position

No clutches or bands are applied; therefore, there is no drive through the transmission.

Drive Position

On most transmissions when this position is selected the vehicle starts in low gear, automatically

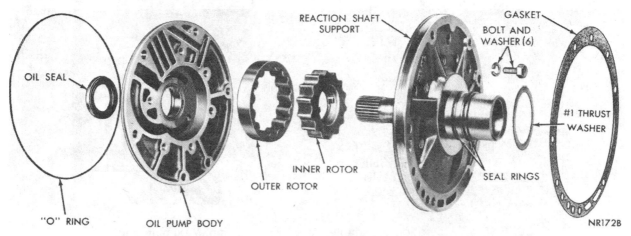

FIGURE 38-44. Disassembled view of rotor type of automatic transmission hydraulic pump. *(Courtesy of Chrysler Corporation)*

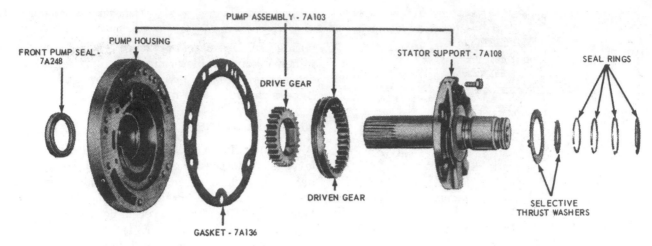

FIGURE 38–45. Gear type of transmission hydraulic pump. *(Courtesy of Ford Motor Co. of Canada Ltd.)*

shifts to second, and then automatically shifts to third.

Drive Position Low. Hydraulic pressure is directed to the forward-speed clutch, the throttle or modulator valve, the governor valve, and the first-to-second and second-to-third shift valves in most cases.

Drive Position Second. When the vehicle has reached sufficient road speed for governor pressure

acting on the first-to-second shift valve to overcome combined spring pressure and throttle pressure on the other end of the shift valve, the first-to-second shift valve upshifts. This directs hydraulic pressure to the intermediate band (intermediate holding clutch on some models) servo applying the band. The forward-speed clutch remains applied.

Drive Position Third (or Direct). As vehicle road speed increases further, governor pressure acting on

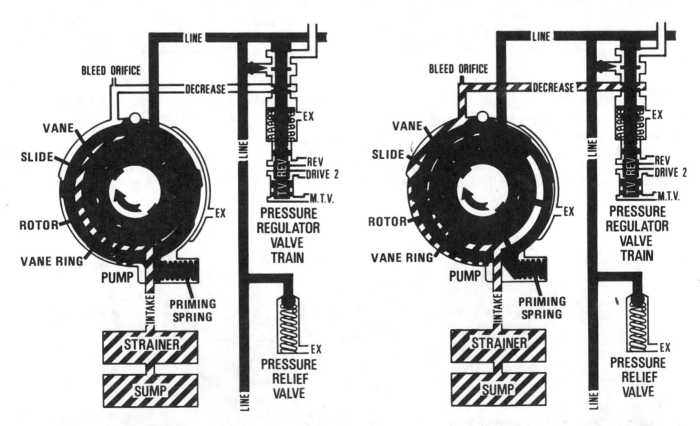

FIGURE 38–46. Operation of variable capacity vane pump. Maximum output on left and minimum output on right. *(Courtesy of General Motors Corporation)*

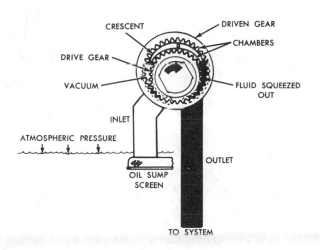

FIGURE 38-47. Gear-type pump operating principle. *(Courtesy of Ford Motor Co. of Canada Ltd.)*

the second-to-third shift valve overcomes combined spring pressure and throttle pressure on the other end of the shift valve and causes the transmission to upshift into third or direct. This directs hydraulic pressure to the release side of the intermediate band servo causing the band to release. At the same time, hydraulic pressure applies the low and reverse driving clutch. Since this locks two planetary gear members to the input shaft, direct drive is the result. This condition remains until the vehicle slows down sufficiently for governor pressure to drop below throttle pressure, allowing the shift valves to downshift.

Another way for the transmission to downshift is by suddenly depressing the accelerator pedal. This causes a sudden increase in throttle pressure, and if road speed is not too high a forced downshift will occur either from third to second or from third to first. If road speed is high enough for governor pressure to equal line pressure, no downshift will occur.

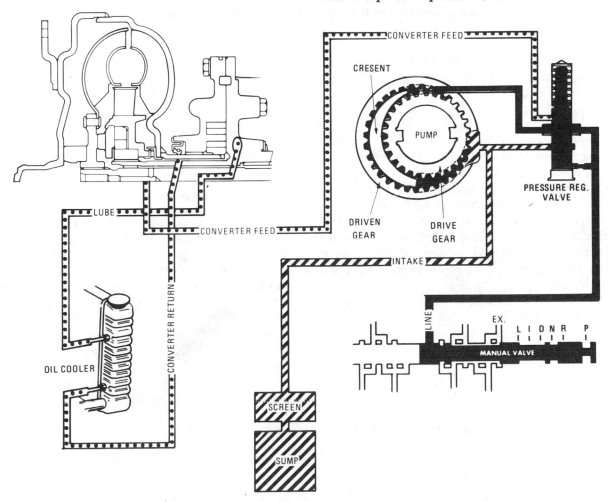

FIGURE 38-48. Hydraulic pressure system of an automatic transmission. This portion of the hydraulic system includes pressure production and regulation, torque converter feed, lubrication and cooling circuits, and the manual shift valve, which is controlled by the shift selector lever. *(Courtesy of General Motors Corporation)*

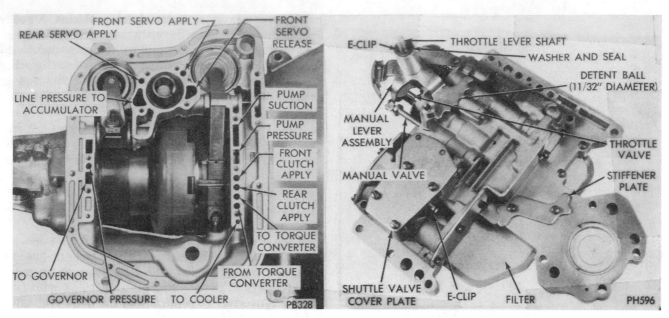

FIGURE 38-49. Typical hydraulic circuit passages in the transmission case (left). The control valve body (right) is bolted to the transmission case to connect the case passages to the valve body. *(Courtesy of Chrysler Corporation)*

Most transmissions provide for both a part-throttle downshift (kickdown) and a full-throttle downshift (kickdown).

Second Position

When second position is selected, some transmissions are designed to start in low and automatically upshift to second and stay in second. Others are designed to start in second and remain in second. In the latter case, no governor pressure is required since there is no automatic shift provided for. In this situation line pressure is directed to the forward clutch and to the intermediate band servo (or intermediate holding clutch in some models) and the throttle valve.

In the former situation, where second-gear lever position is selected, line pressure is directed to the forward clutch, the governor valve, and the throttle valve. The transmission starts off in low and upshifts automatically to second just as in the D selector position. However, in the second selector position the second-to-third shift valve is prevented from operating, effectively keeping the transmission in second until a coasting downshift or a forced downshift occurs.

The torque increase provided in second gear is useful for mountain driving and trailer towing where heavy loading may occur. Engine braking is also a useful feature of manually selected second gear.

Manual Low Position

When this position is selected, line pressure is directed to the forward clutch, the low and reverse band servo (or low and reverse holding clutch), and the throttle valve. Line pressure is not directed to the governor valve. Consequently, no governor pressure is produced, resulting in no automatic upshifts (transmission remains in low). Manually selected low is useful for pulling heavy loads and for heavy engine braking when going downhill with heavy loads.

Throttle Valve

The throttle valve is mechanically operated through the accelerator linkage or vacuum operated by a vacuum diaphragm modulator connected to intake manifold vacuum. In either case, the throttle valve modifies line pressure to produce throttle pressure. The value of throttle pressure is directly proportional to carburetor throttle opening in the linkage-operated model and directly proportional to the level of intake manifold vacuum in the case of the vacuum-modulator-operated throttle valve.

As throttle opening increases, throttle pressure increases. Throttle pressure is directed to one end of the first-to-second and second-to-third shift valves and is a force that tries to keep these valves in the downshifted position. Throttle pressure is aided by spring pressure in both shift valves.

Governor Valve

The governor valve provides a modified line pressure known as governor pressure in direct proportion to vehicle road speed. As vehicle speed increases, governor pressure also increases.

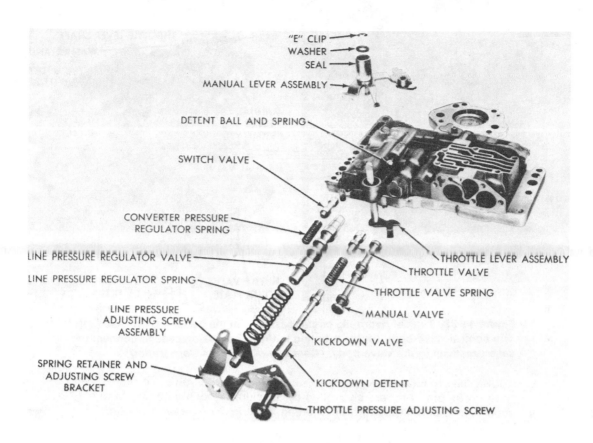

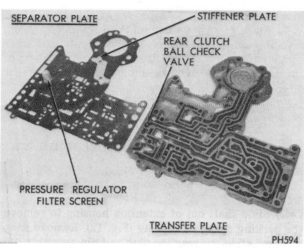

FIGURE 38-50. Typical control valves and control valve body passages (only a few of the valves are shown here). *(Courtesy of Chrysler Corporation)*

Governor pressure is directed to the first-to-second and second-to-third shift valves in opposition to the throttle pressure acting on the shift valves. When vehicle speed has reached a point where governor pressure acting on the shift valve is greater than throttle pressure and spring pressure acting on the same shift valve, an upshift takes place.

First-to-Second and Second-to-Third Shift Valves

The shift valves respond to governor pressure and throttle pressure to provide the automatic upshifts and downshifts at the desired speeds. These valves are simply on–off valves controlling the flow of line pressure to the first-to-second shift circuit and the second-to-third shift circuit.

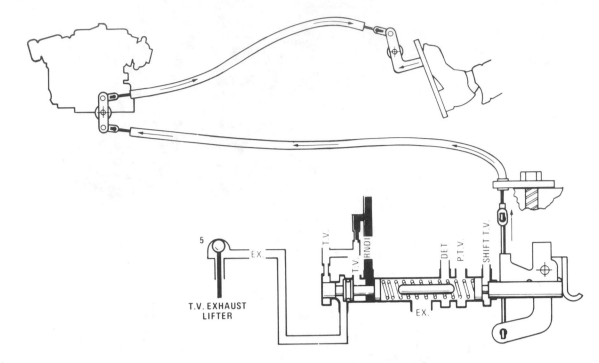

FIGURE 38-51. Example of a linkage-operated throttle valve. Throttle valve (and throttle pressure) are controlled by accelerator pedal position in direct proportion to carburetor throttle opening. *(Courtesy of General Motors Corporation)*

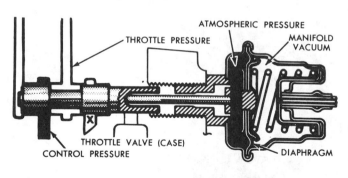

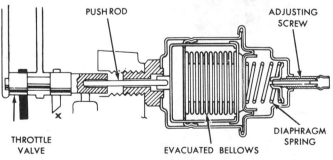

FIGURE 38-52. Examples of transmission vacuum modulators. Lower modulator is altitude compensated to maintain shift characteristics at all altitudes. Pressure-sensitive evacuated bellows provide compensation for various atmospheric pressures. The modulator controls the throttle valve (and therefore throttle pressure) in direct proportion to engine intake manifold vacuum. Throttle pressure is directed to one end of the first-to-second and second-to-third shift valves, and governor pressure is directed to the other end of the shift valves. *(Courtesy of Ford Motor Co. of Canada Ltd.)*

Shift Timing and Quality

Several different devices are used in automatic transmissions to control shift timing and quality. Application of clutches and bands is cushioned by such devices as an orifice or an accumulator piston or valve. An orifice restricts apply pressure for a short period until pressure is built up "downstream" from the orifice. An accumulator in the apply circuit is used with a spring-loaded valve or piston. The piston or valve is forced to move against spring pressure during clutch or band engagement, thereby absorbing some of the apply pressure and cushioning the shift.

Similar devices are used to control the timed sequence of band and clutch apply and release. For example, during a second-to-third upshift the reverse and high clutch must not be fully applied before the intermediate band (or intermediate holding clutch) is released. If the apply and release of these units was not properly timed, a braking effect would result. A downshift valve controls forced downshifts.

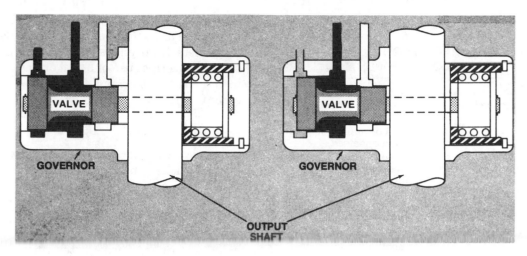

FIGURE 38–53. The governor valve assembly modifies line pressure to produce governor pressure. Governor pressure is directed to one end of the shift valves. When road speed has increased enough to produce sufficient governor pressure, the shift valve is forced to move to the upshifted position. The figure at left shows the governor valve blocking line pressure at the passage closest to the output shaft. Governor pressure in the middle passage is exhausted at the left passage. This is the condition when the output shaft and vehicle are stationary. When the vehicle and output shaft begin to move, the weights to the right of the shaft move away from the shaft (due to centrifugal force) and pull the valve closer to the shaft. This closes the governor exhaust passage and opens the line pressure passage to the governor passage, producing governor pressure in direct proportion to output shaft speed. When output shaft speed is great enough to move the valve to its wide-open position, governor pressure is equal to line pressure. *(Courtesy of Chrysler Corporation)*

PART 9 SEALS AND FLOW CONTROL SEAL RINGS

Sealing hydraulic pressures and fluids in an automatic transmission is a big job. Confining hydraulic pressures is critical to proper transmission operation.

The automatic transmission has several gaskets and many seals of different shapes and materials. Some are used between parts that do not move against each other while others are used to seal between a stationary part and a moving part.

This section deals with some of the more common types of seals and seal materials used in automatic transmissions.

Static Seals

A static seal is one that seals between two parts that do not move in relation to each other. Gaskets are perhaps the most common type of static seal. The automatic transmission uses gaskets in such places as between the hydraulic pump and the transmission case, between the oil pan and the case, between the extension housing and the case, and between some parts of the valve body.

Gasket materials include cork and paper compounds. Sometimes gaskets are used with a sealing compound. However, using a sealer on automatic transmissions may result in clogged hydraulic passages if not done properly. A gasket can do its job properly only if the right gasket is used, if it is installed as recommended, and if proper tightening (tightening sequence and correct torque) of fasteners is done.

Other static seals include O rings and lathe-cut or rectangular or square cross-sectional seal rings. These are usually made from synthetic rubber materials. Typical O-ring use is between the selector shaft and transmission case. Lathe-cut seals are often used between the hydraulic pump and the transmission case.

Both O-ring and lathe-cut static seals must be of the correct cross-sectional dimensions as well as the correct total diameter for the particular application in order to do their job properly since they fit in grooves in the parts that they seal. Seals of too small cross-sectional dimension do not provide

SUMMARY OF HYDRAULIC CONTROL SYSTEMS
(TYPICAL OF C5 FORD)

SYSTEM	FUNCTION
Main control pressure	Regulates line (control) pressure
Converter and cooler	Feeds converter, cools fluid, and lubricates transmission
Throttle pressure	Engine load input; delays upshift and forces downshift (torque demand)
Forward clutch	Engages transmission in forward gears
Governor	Road speed input; causes upshifts
Control pressure cutback	Reduces line pressure at increased road speeds
1–2 and 2–3 shift valves	Control upshifts and downshifts
1–2 accumulator	Controls 1–2 upshift feel
Reverse and high clutch/ servo release	Applies reverse and high clutch and releases intermediate servo together
2–3 backout	Prevents clutch-band tie-up on 2–3 shift
3–2 timing valve	Times 3–2 downshift to prevent tie-up or buzz-up
Kickdown	Causes downshift with accelerator through-detent or WOT upshift
Manual 2/first-gear lockout	Causes front servo application in range 2 and prevents downshift to first
Line pressure boost	Increases line pressure at low TV pressure in ranges 1 and 2
Third-gear lockout	Prevents 2–3 shift valve from moving to upshift position in ranges 1 and 2
Second-gear lockout	Prevents 1–2 shift valve and drive 2 valve from moving to upshift position in range 1
Low-reverse	Applies rear servo in manual low and R
1–2 transition	Prevents band-to-band tie-up on manual 1–2
Reverse pressure boost	Causes maximum line pressure in R

for any compression. This results in lack of static pressure between parts to be sealed. Seals of too small a total diameter stretch, reducing cross-sectional dimensions, while too large a total diameter results in cutting and damage to the seal.

Transmission overhaul gasket and seal packages may contain seals and gaskets for several different models of the same transmission. There may be duplicate seals or gaskets with slight differences not noticeable unless closely examined. It is essen-tial that the correct gaskets and seals be selected for the transmission being serviced. Selecting seals or gaskets from packages must be done carefully since an incorrect use of a seal or gasket could result in the transmission not functioning properly or in early failure.

Dynamic Seals

Dynamic seals are used to seal between a moving and a stationary part or between two moving parts. Dynamic seal designs include the O-ring type, the lathe-cut type, and the lip type of synthetic rubber construction. Other types include Teflon, nylon, and cast-iron, square or rectangular cross-section circular seal rings. These latter rings may be of the butt-end design, the tapered-end, or locking type.

Lip-type and lathe-cut seals are used to seal between clutch pistons and clutch cylinders as well as servo pistons and piston bores. Lip-type seals are always installed with the edge of the lip facing the fluid or pressure to be confined. Hydraulic pressure pushes the lip against the bore surface to increase the sealing ability of the seal.

Cast-iron seal rings are often used on accumulator pistons and on transmission shafts. Seal rings of synthetic materials such as Teflon are used in these areas by some transmission makers.

These seal rings are positioned in grooves on the parts to be sealed and must be of exact cross-sectional size as well as the proper diameter to function effectively. The use of an incorrect seal ring or its improper installation may result in early transmission failure or an inoperative transmission after overhaul.

Flow Control Rings (Oil Transfer Rings)

Flow control rings are dynamic seal rings. However, they are part of a hydraulic passage. These rings allow hydraulic flow and pressure to be transferred

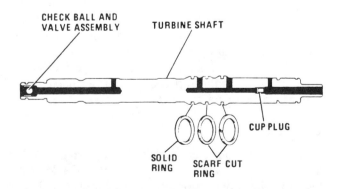

FIGURE 38-54. Typical application of oil transfer rings on turbine shaft. *(Courtesy of General Motors Corporation)*

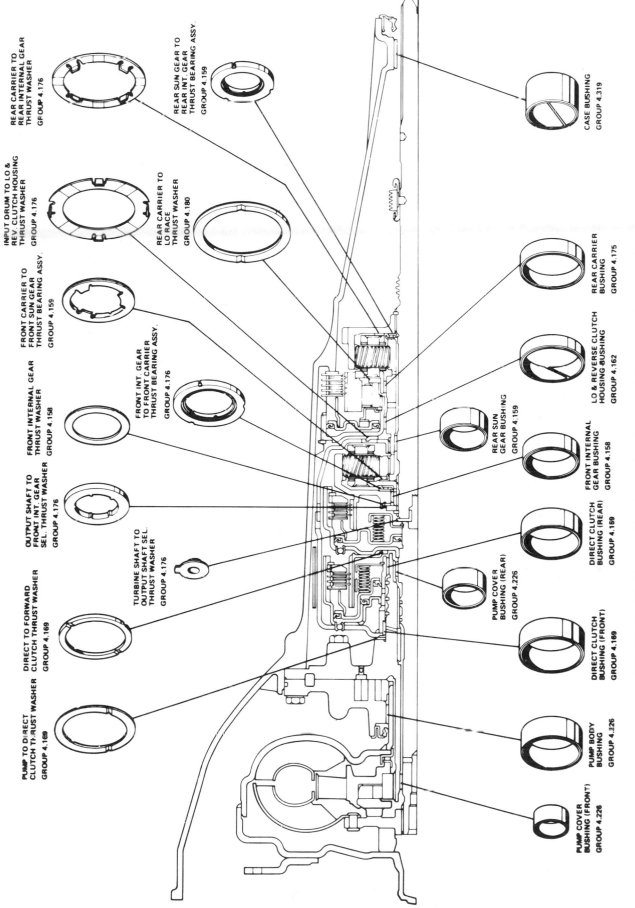

REAR CARRIER TO
REAR INTERNAL GEAR
THRUST WASHER
GROUP 4.176

REAR SUN GEAR TO
REAR INT. GEAR
THRUST BEARING ASSY.
GROUP 4.159

CASE BUSHING
GROUP 4.319

INPUT DRUM TO LO &
REV. CLUTCH HOUSING
THRUST WASHER
GROUP 4.176

REAR CARRIER TO
LO RACE
THRUST WASHER
GROUP 4.180

REAR CARRIER
BUSHING
GROUP 4.175

FRONT CARRIER TO
FRONT SUN GEAR
THRUST BEARING ASSY.
GROUP 4.159

LO & REVERSE CLUTCH
HOUSING BUSHING
GROUP 4.162

FRONT INTERNAL GEAR
THRUST WASHER
GROUP 4.158

FRONT INT. GEAR
TO FRONT CARRIER
THRUST BEARING ASSY.
GROUP 4.176

REAR SUN
GEAR BUSHING
GROUP 4.159

FRONT INTERNAL
GEAR BUSHING
GROUP 4.158

OUTPUT SHAFT TO
FRONT INT. GEAR
SEL. THRUST WASHER
GROUP 4.176

TURBINE SHAFT TO
OUTPUT SHAFT SEL.
THRUST WASHER
GROUP 4.176

DIRECT CLUTCH
BUSHING (REAR)
GROUP 4.169

PUMP COVER
BUSHING (REAR)
GROUP 4.226

DIRECT TO FORWARD
CLUTCH THRUST WASHER
GROUP 4.169

DIRECT CLUTCH
BUSHING (FRONT)
GROUP 4.169

PUMP TO DIRECT
CLUTCH THRUST WASHER
GROUP 4.169

PUMP BODY
BUSHING
GROUP 4.226

PUMP COVER
BUSHING (FRONT)
GROUP 4.226

FIGURE 38-55. Types of bushings, bearings, and thrust washers used in a typical automatic transmission. Selective thickness thrust washers control gear train end play. *(Courtesy of General Motors Corporation)*

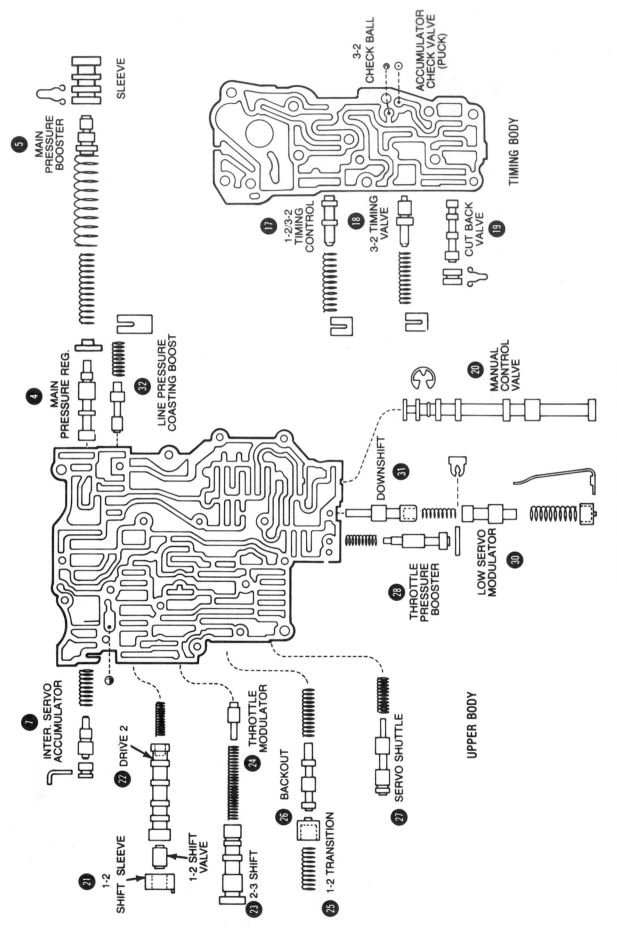

FIGURE 38-56. Valve body exploded view.

SLEEVE

5 MAIN PRESSURE BOOSTER

4 MAIN PRESSURE REG.

32 LINE PRESSURE COASTING BOOST

17 1-2/3-2 TIMING CONTROL

18 3-2 TIMING VALVE

19 CUT BACK VALVE

3-2 CHECK BALL

ACCUMULATOR CHECK VALVE (PUCK)

TIMING BODY

20 MANUAL CONTROL VALVE

DOWNSHIFT

31

28 THROTTLE PRESSURE BOOSTER

30 LOW SERVO MODULATOR

UPPER BODY

7 INTER. SERVO ACCUMULATOR

21 1-2 SHIFT SLEEVE

1-2 SHIFT VALVE

22 DRIVE 2

23 2-3 SHIFT

24 THROTTLE MODULATOR

26 BACKOUT

25 1-2 TRANSITION

27 SERVO SHUTTLE

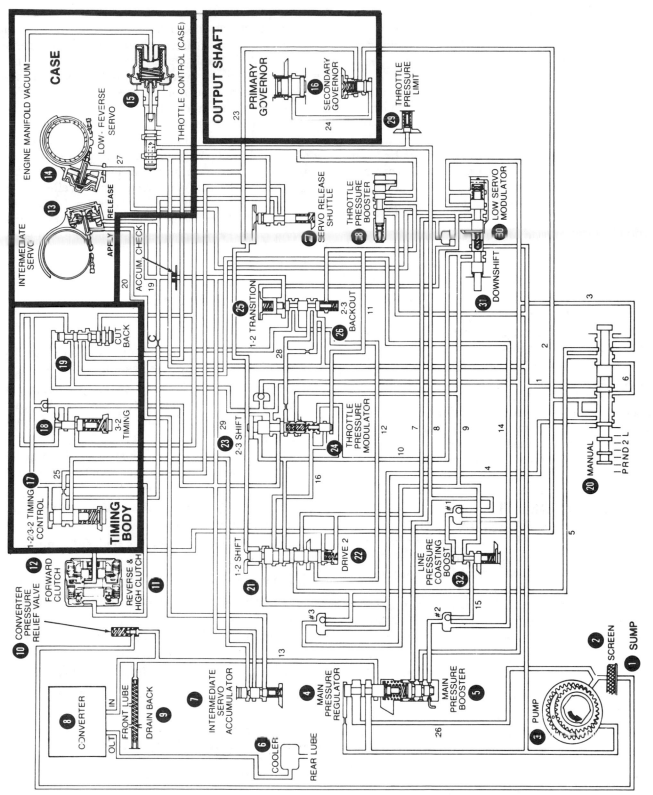

FIGURE 38-57. C5 hydraulic system schematic.

913

uninterrupted from a stationary part to a moving or rotating part and from a rotating part such as a shaft to a stationary part.

They fit into grooves in either the stationary part or the moving part. One example of the use of flow control rings is in directing hydraulic pressure from the pump housing to the forward clutch. Seal rings in the grooves of the stationary pump housing seal against the inner circumference of the rotating clutch drum. Fluid from a passage in the pump housing is directed between the two seal rings to a passage in the clutch drum leading to the area between the clutch piston and clutch drum.

Sealing between the outer circumference and the rotating drum is the result of mechanical pressure of the ring against the drum. Hydraulic pressure pushes the rings apart to seal against the sides of the grooves in the pump housing.

Materials used for flow control seal rings include cast iron and synthetic materials such as Teflon. Ring ends may of the butt-end, tapered-end, or locking type.

Precise cross-sectional size and diameter are critical to the proper function of flow control seal rings. The use of an incorrect seal ring or its improper installation can result in faulty operation of the transmission and early transmission failure.

PART 10   AUTOMATIC TRANSMISSION FLUID

In 1968 when high horsepower engines had almost reached their peak, improvements to transmission fluids were again realized. Ford's fluid was identified by a new Ford fluid designation number but continued to be known as Type F. General Motors' new improved fluid was designated as Dexron fluid. Chrysler and American Motors also specified Dexron fluid for their vehicles. The current Dexron II-D designation identifies the latest improved Dexron fluid.

In 1977 the Ford Motor Company introduced a new type of fluid designated CJ fluid for use in several Ford transmission designs, including their automatic overdrive transmission. Ford's C5 transmission with the centrifugal clutch lockup converter requires a special fluid designated Type H.

Although some original factory-fill transmission fluids may not be dyed red, most replacement fluids are red. The red dye aids in distinguishing oil leaks from the transmission from engine oil leaks.

Automatic transmission clutches and bands are designed to provide the correct coefficient of friction for good shifting and long service life only if the

correct transmission fluid is used. The slip-lock-up characteristics of different transmission fluid is not the same. If the incorrect fluid is used, the transmission will not shift properly and its service life will be reduced. In every case, make sure that the correct transmission fluid is used as recommended by the vehicle manufacturer.

Transmission fluids can become extremely hot if the transmission is abused (excessive rocking when stuck). Overheating of transmission fluid causes rapid oxidation of the fluid and shortens life expectancy drastically. Towing heavy trailers with cars not properly equipped with a trailer towing package (which includes a proper auxiliary transmission cooler) can cause serious damage and early failure of the transmission.

PART 11   SELF-CHECK

1. Define Pascal's law.
2. Explain how force multiplication can be achieved in a hydraulic system.
3. Explain why the distance moved by a servo piston is less than that of the pump piston in a simple force multiplication type of hydraulic system.
4. Why is it necessary to use only the fluid specified by the transmission manufacturers in their automatic transmissions?
5. Name the three types of hydraulic pumps used in automatic transmissions.
6. What is the advantage of a hydraulic pump capable of variable delivery capacity?
7. What is the purpose of a pressure relief valve?
8. What is the purpose of a pressure regulator valve?
9. What is the difference in purpose between a static seal and a dynamic seal?
10. What is the purpose of flow control seal rings?
11. List the three types of seal ring end designs.

PART 12   TEST QUESTIONS

1. The torque converter turbine drives the:
   (a) impeller
   (b) stator
   (c) turbine shaft
   (d) one-way clutch
2. A simple planetary gearset consists of:
   (a) ring gear, annulus gear, and sun gear
   (b) sun gear, pinions, and carrier

(c) carrier, ring gear, and annulus gear

(d) ring gear, sun gear, and carrier

3. The transmission band is tightened around a drum by a:

(a) hydraulic servo

(b) accumulator

(c) shift valve

(d) governor

4. Transmission line pressure cannot exceed a specified maximum due to the action of the:

(a) shift control valve

(b) governor valve

(c) accumulator

(d) regulator valve

5. Which of the following are holding devices?

(a) multiple-disc clutch

(b) one-way clutch

(c) band

(d) park pawl

(e) any of the above

6. Governor pressure acts on the:

(a) accumulator

(b) servo

(c) shift valves

(d) one-way clutch

Chapter 39

Automatic Transmission Diagnosis and Service

- • Remove valve body and perform air pressure tests.
- • Service hydraulic servos.
- • Adjust bands.
- • Service the governor.
- • Road test and interpret results.

6. Follow all the required safety procedures and general precautions required for the safe and successful removal, overhaul, and installation of automatic transmissions.

7. Clean, disassemble, inspect, determine the serviceability of, overhaul, assemble, install, and adjust all automatic transmission subassemblies and components designated by the instructor.

8. Adequately test the transmission to determine the success of the service performed.

9. Complete all service work to 100 percent accuracy (manufacturer's specifications).

10. Prepare the vehicle for customer acceptance.

Performance Objectives

After adequate study of this chapter and sufficient practical experience on the appropriate training models, and with the necessary tools, equipment, and shop manuals, you should be able to do the following:

1. Complete the self-check and test questions with at least 80 percent accuracy.

2. Follow the general precautions given in this chapter.

3. Diagnose correctly the cause of specific automatic transmission problems by following the accepted systematic approach to problem diagnosis given in this chapter, in the appropriate service repair manual, and by the instructor.

4. Perform the appropriate diagnostic tests; interpret the test results correctly; make the necessary adjustments.
   - • Check fluid level and condition.
   - • Adjust manual shift linkage to specifications.
   - • Adjust throttle linkage to specifications.
   - • Check and adjust vacuum modulator system and vacuum lines to specifications.
   - • Check and adjust engine idle speed to specifications.
   - • Perform stall test; record and interpret results.
   - • Perform hydraulic pressure tests; record and interpret results.
   - • Perform road test and interpret results.

5. Perform the following in-vehicle service checks and adjustments.
   - • Change the oil and filter.

The proper diagnosis of automatic transmission problems requires a thorough understanding of transmission operation and it requires a systematic, step-by-step approach. A hit-or-miss, shot-in-the-dark approach is dangerous and open to creating more problems and wasting of valuable time.

This chapter presents a systematic, step-by-step approach to problem diagnosis that is generally applicable to all types of automatic transmissions. Diagnostic procedures and a chart are included for some of the more common automatic transmissions. Also included are the more common external and internal in-vehicle checks, adjustments, and service procedures.

The successful automatic transmission technician is one who has learned to apply knowledge of the transmission and its operating characteristics to a quick and accurate diagnosis of transmission problems. When a transmission problem is presented, the competent technician immediately considers all the possible causes and pursues the diagnostic procedure with these in mind.

The diagnostic procedures then are used to verify one or more of the possible causes suspected, and the appropriate corrections are then made. The road test is used to validate the corrections and assure proper transmission operation.

The following diagnostic and service procedures are general in nature and do not cover the wide range of specific procedures and specifications that apply to different types and installations of automatic transmissions and transaxles. For specific testing, removal, disassembly, and reassembly procedures and specifications refer to the appropriate manufacturer's service manual for the unit being serviced.

PART 1   GENERAL PRECAUTIONS

All the usual personal safety factors, such as proper clothing, work habits, and shop practice, should be observed when working on automatic transmissions. Proper tools and equipment should be used in the correct manner as outlined by the equipment manufacturer.

Particular attention should be given to proper hoisting and jacking methods. No one should be under a vehicle that is being raised or lowered, and no one should be under a vehicle supported only by a jack. Safety stands properly positioned must be used when working under a vehicle raised by a jack.

A clean, uncluttered work area is also essential to safe shop practice. Jack handles, electrical cords and hoses, or tools and equipment left lying around on the shop floor are open invitations to accidents and injury. Dirt and oil on shop floors are similarly hazardous.

Some additional points to remember follow.

- Disconnect the battery when not actually required for test procedures.
- Be careful of hot engine, exhaust, and transmission parts.
- Be careful of hot transmission fluid. Fluid temperatures may be hot enough to cause severe burns.
- Transmissions are heavy. Use only the proper equipment to remove and install.
- Handle all parts carefully. Many transmission parts are machined to very close tolerances and are easily damaged, requiring replacement.
- Never drop transmission parts. Place all parts so that they will not roll off workbenches.
- Absolute cleanliness of all parts for assembly is essential. Even a small particle of dirt or lint can cause transmission problems.
- Make sure that whatever you are doing will not result in consequences that can cause personal injury or damage to parts or vehicles.

PART 2   DIAGNOSTIC PROCEDURES, TESTS, AND ADJUSTMENTS

Successful accurate diagnosis of automatic transmission problems is not difficult or complicated. However, it can only be achieved if transmission operation is thoroughly understood and if a logical step-by-step procedure is followed. This approach soon tells the technician what is working properly in the transmission and what is not working properly.

Preliminary Diagnosis Procedure

1. Vehicle not drivable. Check for broken or disconnected throttle linkage to transmission. Check for disconnected shift linkage. Check the fluid level and condition. Check and correct leaks and fluid level. Raise the vehicle on a hoist, start the engine, and place the transmission in gear. If the drive shaft turns, the problem is in the differential.

If propeller shafts do not turn and the transmission is noisy, stop the engine, remove the oil pan, and check for debris. If debris is not found, remove the transmission and check for a broken drive plate or drive-plate-to-converter bolts, broken converter hub, broken input or output shaft, broken oil pump, or stripped torque converter turbine hub splines. If propeller shafts do not turn and the transmission is not noisy, perform the hydraulic pressure test to determine if the problem is a malfunction of a hydraulic or mechanical component.

2. Vehicle driveable. Proceed with checks and adjustments outlined in the following groups 1 and 2.

It is important that the checks and procedures in group 1 be performed first, then those in group 2, and then those in group 3. Unless this is done, some of the tests in group 2 may not be valid. Of course, it would not make much sense to remove the transmission to effect a repair or adjustment that can be made in group 1 or group 2 without transmission removal.

The following procedures are general and should be used in conjunction with service manuals for specific transmissions.

Group 1. Those that can be done without any disassembly of the transmission.

Group 2. Those that can be done by partial transmission disassembly but without transmission removal.

Group 3. Those that require transmission removal.

PART 3 TORQUEFLITE DIAGNOSIS CHART: GENERAL

POSSIBLE CAUSE

No.	Possible Cause
1	Stuck switch valve.
2	Stuck lock-up valve.
3	Engine idle speed too high.
4	Hydraulic pressures too low.
5	Low-reverse band out of adjustment.
6	Valve body malfunction or leakage.
7	Low-reverse servo, band or linkage malfunction.
8	Low fluid level.
9	Incorrect gearshift control linkage adjustment.
10	Oil filter clogged.
11	Faulty oil pump.
12	Worn or broken input shaft seal rings.
13	Aerated fluid.
14	Engine idle speed too low.
15	Incorrect throttle linkage adjustment.
16	Kickdown band out of adjustment.
17	Overrunning clutch not holding.
18	Output shaft bearing and/or bushing damaged.
19	Governor support seal rings broken or worn.
20	Work or broken reaction shaft support seal rings.
21	Governor malfunction.
22	Kickdown servo band or linkage malfunction.
23	Worn or faulty front clutch.
24	High fluid level.
25	Breather clogged.
26	Hydraulic pressure too high.
27	Kickdown band adjustment too tight.
28	Faulty cooling system.
29	Insufficient clutch plate clearance.
30	Worn or faulty rear clutch.
31	Rear clutch dragging.
32	Planetary gear sets broken or seized.
33	Overrunning clutch worn, broken or seized.
34	Overrunning clutch inner race damaged.

CONDITION key

- C1 – Harsh engagement from neutral to D or R
- C2 – Delayed engagement from neutral to D or R
- C3 – Runaway upshift
- C4 – No upshift
- C5 – 3-2 kickdown runaway
- C6 – No kickdown or normal downshift
- C7 – Shifts erratic
- C8 – Slips in forward drive positions
- C9 – Slips in reverse only
- C10 – Slips in all positions
- C11 – No drive in any position
- C12 – No drive in forward drive positions
- C13 – No drive in reverse
- C14 – Drives in neutral
- C15 – Drags or locks
- C16 – Grating, scraping growling noise
- C17 – Buzzing noise
- C18 – Hard to fill, oil blows out filler tube
- C19 – Transmission overheats
- C20 – Harsh upshift
- C21 – Delayed upshift

Diagnosis matrix (X = possible cause applies to the condition)

Cause	C1	C2	C3	C4	C5	C6	C7	C8	C9	C10	C11	C12	C13	C14	C15	C16	C17	C18	C19	C20	C21
1	X																				
2															X						
3	X																	X	X		
4		X	X	X			X	X	X	X	X	X	X						X	X	X
5									X				X								
6	X	X	X	X	X	X	X	X	X	X	X	X	X	X		X				X	X
7		X	X						X	X			X								
8		X	X	X									X			X				X	
9		X	X	X	X		X	X					X	X							
10		X	X				X	X		X	X						X				
11		X					X	X	X	X			X								
12		X					X	X	X	X		X									
13		X	X	X			X	X	X	X						X	X				
14		X	X																		
15			X	X	X	X	X	X												X	X
16					X							X			X				X		X
17							X				X										
18																X					
19				X			X												X		X
20			X	X	X		X	X				X							X		X
21					X	X	X														X
22			X	X	X	X	X														X
23			X	X	X	X	X	X				X									X
24																	X	X			
25																	X	X			
26	X																		X	X	
27															X				X		
28																			X		
29														X				X	X		
30	X	X						X				X	X	X							
31														X							
32											X	X	X		X	X					
33								X			X	X		X	X						
34																X					

Diagnostic Procedures

Step 1 Verify the Complaint

If the shop where you are working allows direct contact with the customer, discuss the problem with the owner of the vehicle. This can help in identifying the problem later during a road test. If customer contact is not allowed, discuss the complaint with those responsible for customer contact in your shop. Determine whether any recent transmission service or fluid change has been performed.

Step 2 Check Fluid Level and Condition

The following conditions should apply when checking the fluid level.

1. Transmission fluid is at operating temperature 185°F (85°C).

2. The vehicle is in a level position.

3. The parking brake is fully applied.

4. With the engine running at idle, move the selector lever through all gear positions.

5. Leave the engine running at idle (most vehicles) and place the selector lever in the position specified by the vehicle manufacturer (usually park or neutral). Many vehicles show a different fluid level in park from that in neutral; therefore it is important to place the selector lever in the specified position.

6. Use a clean, lintfree, preferably white cloth. Pull the dipstick and wipe the blade clean. Insert the dipstick, making sure that it is fully seated. Remove the dipstick and check the fluid level and condition (color, smell, contamination). The car should not be road tested while the fluid level is too low or too high since further damage to the transmission is possible. Fluid level must be corrected first.

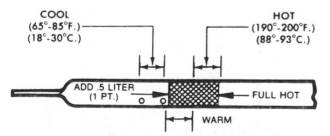

DO NOT OVERFILL. IT TAKES ONLY ONE PINT TO RAISE LEVEL FROM "ADD" TO "FULL" WITH A HOT TRANSMISSION.

FIGURE 39-1. Typical General Motors transmission dipstick. *(Courtesy of General Motors Corporation)*

A fluid level that is too low can result in air in the hydraulic system, which in turn can cause insufficient apply pressure to friction elements. Clutch and band slippage can cause overheating and serious transmission damage. Varnish forms on internal transmission parts; it can cause valve malfunctions. Delayed engagement and mushy shifts can also be caused by low fluid levels.

The cause for the low fluid level should be determined and the problem corrected (see the section on leak diagnosis in this chapter). A fluid level that is too high can cause similar damage. The fluid is churned up by the rotating gear train, causing fluid aeration and foam. Foaming allows air to get into the hydraulic system. This causes clutch and band slippage, wear, overheating, and varnish deposits. Foaming can also result in fluid being forced out of the transmission vent or filler tube, which may be mistaken for a fluid leak.

Fluid Condition. Transmission fluid colors range from an almost clear fluid to a deep red. Some fluids tend to discolor and darken somewhat after use. This should be taken into account when checking fluid condition.

The transmission oil pan should be removed for further diagnosis of fluid and deposits if the following conditions are present in the fluid:

• Very dark, colored fluid, which has a pungent, burned smell

• Presence of metallic particles and particles of friction material from bands or clutches

• Milky colored fluid, which indicates a coolant leak into the transmission fluid via the fluid cooler in the radiator

• Varnish deposits on the dipstick and fluid that is dark brown in color

Depositing several drops of fluid from the dipstick onto a clean white cloth helps determine fluid condition and the presence of metal or friction particles. The fluid should feel smooth and slippery when rubbed between the finger and thumb. If there is a gritty feel to the fluid, further diagnosis is required. Make sure that hands are clean for this test.

If further verification of fluid and transmission condition is required, the transmission oil pan should be removed and the fluid and deposits examined.

Oil Pan Removal and Inspection. Remember that the oil pan and the fluid in it may be hot enough to cause severe burns.

To remove the pan, use a large drain pan to catch the transmission fluid when the pan is removed. First, loosen all the oil pan bolts a turn or two. Remove all the bolts from the three sides of the pan, which will allow the pan to drop slightly to drain the fluid.

Loosen the remaining bolts an additional few turns to allow the other side of the pan to drop some more. When all the fluid has drained, remove the remaining bolts and the pan.

Carefully pour the remaining fluid out of the oil pan. Before disturbing the deposits in the pan, examine them for type and quantity. Metallic particles are shiny. Friction material deposits are very dark or black. A small amount of deposit is normal. Any larger deposits indicate that a transmission overhaul is required.

Fluid contaminated by engine coolant (water or antifreeze) appears milky and requires repair of the leak, reverse flushing of the cooler and lines, a complete draining of the transmission and torque converter, replacement of the filter, and filling with new fluid.

Step 3 External Checks and Adjustments

The number and types of possible external checks and adjustments vary slightly among the various makes and models of automatic transmissions. Those included here cover the majority of makes and models.

1. Manual shift linkage. It is essential to proper transmission operation that the selector lever position and the manual valve position in the transmission be synchronized. In other words, when the driver selects reverse, for example, it is essential that the manual valve in the valve body also be in the reverse position.

The position of the selector lever in each range is determined by gates in the shift mechanism. The position of the manual shift valve in each range is held in place by detents. Synchronization of selector lever position and manual valve position is determined by adjustment of the linkage between the two.

A typical linkage adjustment involves loosening or disconnecting the linkage at the transmission shift lever bracket. The selector lever is then placed in park against the gate, and the shift valve lever is placed in the park detent position. With these in position, the clamp on the sliding adjustment is tightened to maintain this relationship. On the threaded type of linkage adjustment, the connection is lengthened or shortened as required to make the connection.

A further check is required by selecting all gear positions and making sure that the engine will start in the park and neutral positions but not in any other positions. Some vehicles may require a neutral start switch adjustment to be made after the linkage adjustment has been corrected.

Incorrect manual shift linkage adjustment can cause delayed engagement, slippage, overheating, and shift problems. Manual shift linkage types include those using rods and those with a cable.

2. Throttle linkage. There are two types of throttle linkage: the type that controls only the downshift valve (these transmissions are equipped with a vacuum modulator to control the throttle valve) and the type that controls both the downshift valve and the throttle valve (these transmissions do not have a vacuum modulator). Linkage design includes the rod and lever type and the cable type. Some of these linkage systems are not adjustable.

The importance of throttle valve linkage adjustment stems from the fact that throttle pressure rises proportionately with increased carburetor throttle opening. If TV (throttle valve) linkage adjustment is incorrect, it can result in:

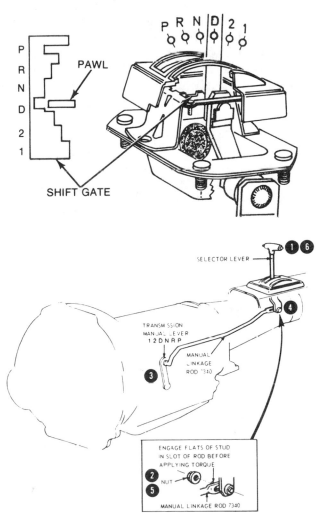

FIGURE 39–2. Manual linkage adjustment requires synchronization of shift lever, pawl, gate, and detent. *(Courtesy of Ford Motor Co. of Canada Ltd.)*

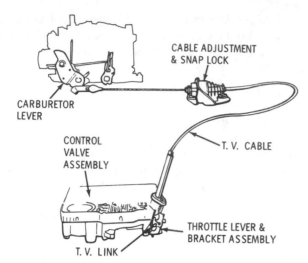

FIGURE 39-3. Throttle valve cable and linkage. *(Courtesy of General Motors Corporation)*

(a) Throttle pressure that is too high in relation to carburetor throttle opening. This results in harsh upshifts and delayed upshifts. Part-throttle (to detent) and WOT (through detent) downshifts will occur earlier than normal. Part-throttle downshifts can occur at a relatively small increase in throttle opening. This can be annoying in city traffic and on the highway.

(b) Throttle pressure that is too low in relation to carburetor throttle opening. This results in up-

shifts occurring too early and "mushy" upshifts and may result in slippage of bands and clutches. Greater than normal carburetor throttle opening will be required to effect forced downshifts.

Procedures for adjusting throttle valve and downshift linkage vary considerably. Since transmission operating characteristics and transmission life are affected by TV and downshift linkage, it is important that procedures and specifications given in the appropriate service repair manual are followed for every unit being serviced. Differences in specifications may exist, for example, for the same model and year of transmission on a car equipped with a six-cylinder engine as compared to the same unit on a car equipped with an eight-cylinder engine. Some examples of linkage adjustment are shown in the illustrations.

3. Vacuum modulator system. The vacuum modulator system has the same effect on the transmission hydraulic control system as the throttle valve linkage system. Engine intake manifold vacuum varies with engine speed and load and is related to carburetor throttle opening. Any leakage in the vacuum system will have the effect of reducing vacuum. This results in higher than normal throttle (or modulator, GM) pressure with the same effect on transmission operation as described in the preceding item 2, throttle linkage, section a.

The general procedure for checking the vacuum modulator system requires checking the vacuum at the line removed from the modulator. If vacuum

ADJUSTING SELF-ADJUSTING TYPE T.V. CABLE
GAS ENGINE MODEL ONLY

Stop engine.

LOCK TAB (UNLOCKED)

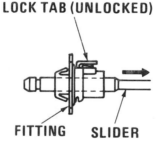

FITTING   SLIDER

Depress lock tab and hold. Move slider back through fitting in direction away from throttle body or pump lever until slider stops against fitting.

LOCK TAB (LOCKED)

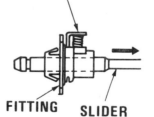

FITTING   SLIDER

Release lock tab.

CARBURETOR LEVER

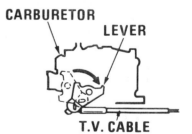

T.V. CABLE

Open carburetor lever to "full throttle stop" position to automatically adjust T.V. cable. Release Carburetor lever.

FIGURE 39-4. *(Courtesy of General Motors Corporation)*

ADJUSTING MANUAL TYPE T.V. CABLE
GAS ENGINE MODEL ONLY

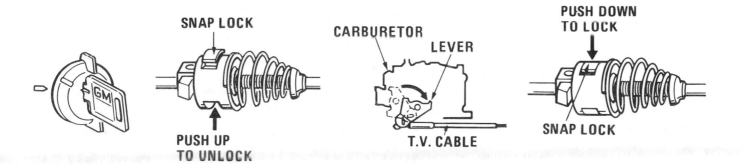

Stop engine.

Unlock T.V. cable "snap-lock" button.

Rotate carburetor lever by hand to wide open throttle and hold open.

Engage T.V. cable "snap-lock" button.

FIGURE 39-5. *(Courtesy of General Motors Corporation)*

readings taken at this point are normal, there are no vacuum leaks in the line and the engine condition is assumed to be satisfactory. If any transmission fluid is noticeable when the vacuum line is disconnected at the modulator, the vacuum diaphragm in the modulator is leaking and the engine is consuming some transmission fluid through the vacuum line to the intake manifold. The vacuum modulator must be replaced. If the vacuum source, vacuum lines, and vacuum modulator are in good condition but shift characteristics indicated a vacuum modulator system problem, the vacuum modulator may have to be adjusted. This requires removing the modulator from the transmission. Special modulator wrenches are required to remove some screw-in–type units since there is very little room between the transmission case and the modulator body in some cases. The push-in–type modulator has a clamp and cap screw holding it in place. The cap screw and clamp must be removed and the modulator can then be pulled out. In some cases it may have to be pried out. Whenever a vacuum modulator is removed from a transmission have a pan ready to catch any fluid that may drain from the transmission (about 1 quart or 1 liter).

The modulator should be removed carefully in order not to lose the actuating pin, which may drop during modulator removal. After removal, the modulator can be bench tested with the use of a vacuum pump and gauge and with the use of special gauge pins in some cases. If adjustment is required, this

should only be done as specified in the appropriate service manual.

Some examples of testing and adjusting procedures for vacuum modulators are shown in the accompanying illustrations. A new O-ring seal should be used.

4. EGR (exhaust gas recirculation) system. Since EGR system operation affects engine intake manifold vacuum and manifold vacuum affects transmission operation, this system should be checked. If not operating properly, the necessary corrections should be made.

A quick check can be made as follows:

• Check the engine at operating temperature and at idle speed.

• Locate and observe movement of the EGR valve stem as engine speed is increased to at least 1,700 rpm.

If no movement is evident, check the EGR vacuum source. If OK, the EGR valve is stuck and requires service as specified in the service manual.

5. Engine idle speed. The engine fast-idle and hot-idle speed should be adjusted to specifications. Too high an engine idle speed results in harsh engagement of clutches in both forward and reverse. This is perceived by the customer as a clunk during engagement. A harsh closed throttle (coasting) downshift may also be caused by too high an engine idle speed.

ADJUSTING MANUAL TYPE T.V. CABLE
DIESEL ENGINE MODEL ONLY

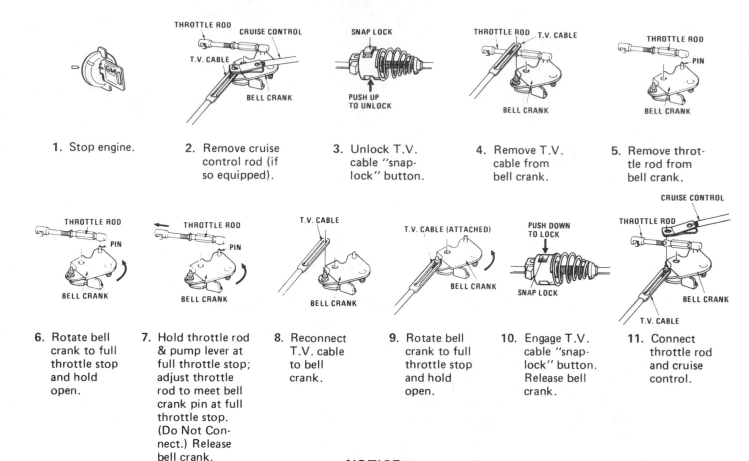

1. Stop engine.

2. Remove cruise control rod (if so equipped).

3. Unlock T.V. cable "snap-lock" button.

4. Remove T.V. cable from bell crank.

5. Remove throttle rod from bell crank.

6. Rotate bell crank to full throttle stop and hold open.

7. Hold throttle rod & pump lever at full throttle stop; adjust throttle rod to meet bell crank pin at full throttle stop. (Do Not Connect.) Release bell crank.

8. Reconnect T.V. cable to bell crank.

9. Rotate bell crank to full throttle stop and hold open.

10. Engage T.V. cable "snap-lock" button. Release bell crank.

11. Connect throttle rod and cruise control.

NOTICE

If bell crank full throttle stop is not obtained when accelerator pedal is completely depressed, all full throttle adjustments must be made by completely depressing the accelerator pedal instead of rotating the bell crank by hand.

FIGURE 39-6. *(Courtesy of General Motors Corporation)*

Use a tachometer and adjust both the fast idle and hot idle to the manufacturer's specifications. These are usually stated on the underhood emission sticker.

6. WOT check. With the engine off, check to make sure that pressing the accelerator pedal to the floor does in fact position the carburetor throttle valves to the wide-open position. If not, adjust the linkage to achieve this condition. Through detent (WOT), downshift operation is affected by incorrect adjustment.

Step 4   Stall Testing

1. *Caution:* Perform a stall test only on vehicles when the manufacturer recommends a stall test. Follow all safety precautions required during a stall test.

Depending on the make and model of the

transmission being tested, the following tests may be made during a stall test:

D position—forward clutch, one-way clutch in transmission, stator one-way clutch, engine power output

2 position—forward clutch, one-way clutch in transmission, stator one-way clutch, intermediate band and servo (some models only), engine power output

1 position—forward clutch, one-way clutch in converter, engine power output

R position—reverse and high clutch, low and reverse band and servo or low and reverse holding clutch, stator one-way clutch

2. Procedure and safety precautions. Since a stall test is performed at wide-open throttle, the fol-

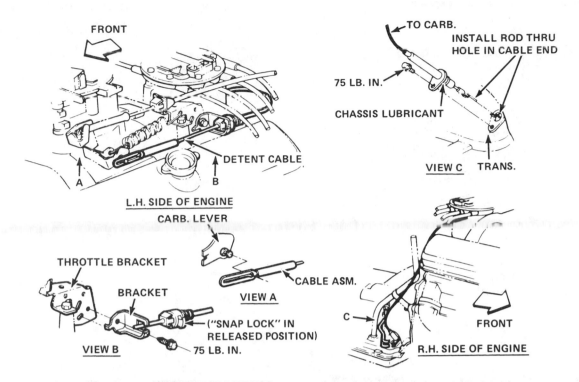

FRONT

TO CARB.
INSTALL ROD THRU HOLE IN CABLE END

75 LB. IN.

CHASSIS LUBRICANT

VIEW C — TRANS.

DETENT CABLE

A B

L.H. SIDE OF ENGINE

CARB. LEVER

THROTTLE BRACKET

BRACKET

CABLE ASM.

VIEW A

("SNAP LOCK" IN RELEASED POSITION)

VIEW B — 75 LB. IN.

C

FRONT

R.H. SIDE OF ENGINE

DETENT CONTROL CABLE ADJUSTMENT PROCEDURE
1. AFTER INSTALLATION TO TRANSMISSION, AND CLIP IF SPECIFIED, INSTALL DETENT CONTROL CABLE IN CONTROL CABLE BRACKET WITH "SNAP LOCK" DISENGAGED (DETENT CABLE SHOULD BE FREE TO SLIDE THROUGH "SNAP LOCK" TO ALLOW FOR ADJUSTMENT).
2. INSTALL DETENT CONTROL CABLE TO CARBURETOR LEVER.
3. OPEN CARBURETOR LEVER TO "FULL THROTTLE STOP" AND HOLD IN THIS POSITION.
4. CARBURETOR LEVER <u>MUST BE TIGHT AGAINST FULL THROTTLE STOP</u>, THEN PUSH "SNAP LOCK" UNTIL IT IS FLUSH WITH THE REST OF THE DETENT CABLE FITTING.
5. RELEASE CARBURETOR LEVER.

FIGURE 39-7. *(Courtesy of General Motors Corporation)*

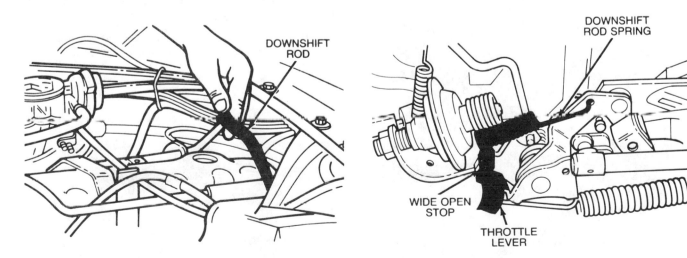

DOWNSHIFT ROD

DOWNSHIFT ROD SPRING

WIDE OPEN STOP

THROTTLE LEVER

FIGURE 39-8. Checking downshift rod for binding. *(Courtesy of Ford Motor Co. of Canada Ltd.)*

FIGURE 39-9. Wide-open throttle check. *(Courtesy of Ford Motor Co. of Canada Ltd.)*

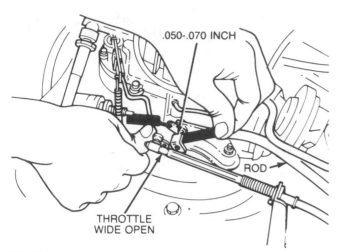

FIGURE 39-10. Downshift rod adjustment. *(Courtesy of Ford Motor Co. of Canada Ltd.)*

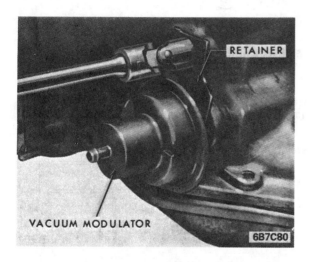

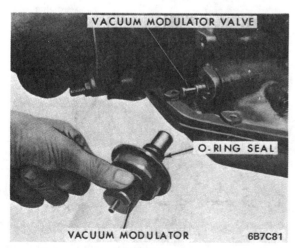

FIGURE 39-11. Removing vacuum modulator—push-in type. *(Courtesy of General Motors Corporation)*

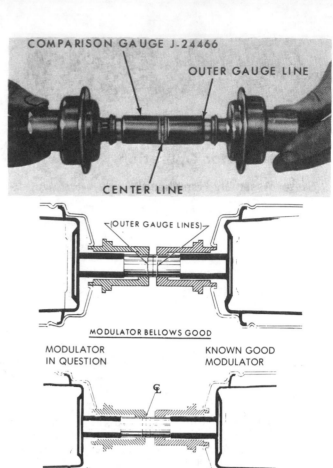

FIGURE 39-12. Checking vacuum modulator with special gauge. *(Courtesy of General Motors Corporation)*

lowing procedure and safety precautions should be rigidly observed during a stall test. Perform a stall test only if recommended by the vehicle manufacturer.

(a) Connect the tachometer to the engine. You must know your power flow for this test to be meaningful. This will tell you which clutch, band, or servo is being tested in each case.

(b) The engine cooling system should be in good condition and engine and transmission fluid levels correct.

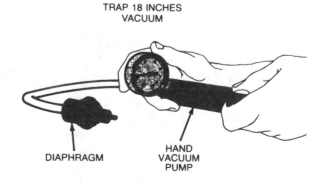

FIGURE 39-13. Diaphragm leak test. *(Courtesy of Ford Motor Co. of Canada Ltd.)*

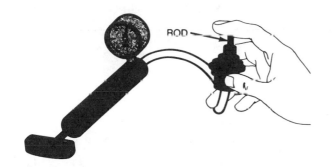

FIGURE 39-14. Checking diaphragm rod for binding. *(Courtesy of Ford Motor Co. of Canada Ltd.)*

(c) The engine and transmission should be at normal operating temperature. This requires approximately 15 minutes of operation.

(d) Block vehicle wheels for safety front and back.

(e) Parking brake and service brakes must be fully applied during the stall test.

(f) No one should be in front of the vehicle or behind the vehicle during stall tests.

(g) Never hold the throttle at the wide-open position for more than 5 seconds at a time.

(h) After each 5-second test, place the selector lever in neutral and run the engine at 1,000 to 1,500 rpm for at least 15 seconds to cool the converter before making the next test.

(i) If specified engine speed is exceeded during any specific test, release the accelerator pedal immediately since clutch or band slippage is indicated. Continued testing in this position would result in further transmission damage.

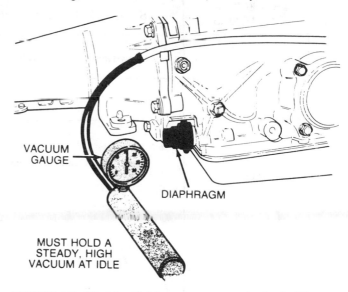

FIGURE 39-16. Manifold vacuum supply test. *(Courtesy of Ford Motor Co. of Canada Ltd.)*

(j) Place the selector lever in each specified position in turn and make the test. Record engine rpm in each case.

3. Stall test results. All stall test results should be compared with those given in the appropriate service repair manual. Some variation in readings should be allowed for possible reduced engine power output and for higher altitudes.

• Stall speed above normal = clutch or band slippage.

• Stall speed slightly below normal = engine power output below normal; engine requires tuneup or mechanical repair.

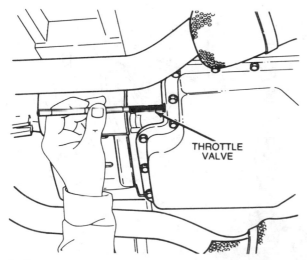

FIGURE 39-15. Checking throttle valve. *(Courtesy of Ford Motor Co. of Canada Ltd.)*

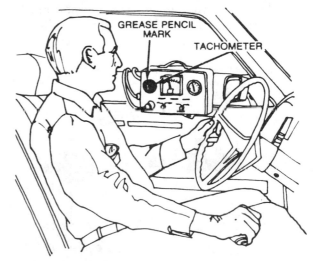

FIGURE 39-17. Stall testing transmission. *(Courtesy of Ford Motor Co. of Canada Ltd.)*

SELECTOR POSITIONS	STALL SPEED(S) HIGH (SLIP)	STALL SPEEDS LOW
D only	Low (Planetary) One-Way Clutch	
D, 2 and 1	Forward clutch	1. Does engine misfire or bog down under load? Check Engine for Tune-Up. If OK . . .
All Driving Ranges	Perform Control Pressure Test	2. Remove torque converter and bench test for reactor one-way clutch slip.
R Only	Reverse and High Clutch or Low-Reverse Band or Servo	

FIGURE 39-18. Stall test results diagnosis. (Courtesy of Ford Motor Co. of Canada Ltd.)

• Stall speed well below (about 2/3) normal = stator one-way clutch in converter not holding. Fluid leaving the turbine is acting against impeller and engine rotation, which reduces engine speed. Poor low-speed acceleration is evident since the converter is acting as a simple fluid coupling.

Step 5   Road Testing

A road test is performed to obtain the following information about transmission operation: *what is normal* about the transmission and *what is abnormal* about transmission operation.

Caution: Transmission fluid level, engine oil level and coolant level should be corrected before road testing. The engine and transmission must be at operating temperature for a road test to be valid.

Caution: Traffic conditions and consideration for others on the road are prime safety considerations during road testing procedures. Unexpected maneuvers can cause accidents. Select a section of road where speed limits and traffic conditions will allow safe road testing.

Look for the following points during a road test:

1. Proper engagement as the selector lever is moved to each gear position including park. Things to look for are delayed or harsh engagement.

2. Proper transmission operation in all forward ranges. This includes:

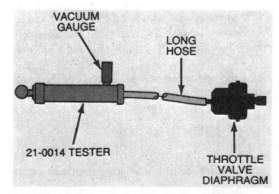

FIGURE 39-19. Vacuum supply for governor test. (Courtesy of Ford Motor Co. of Canada Ltd.)

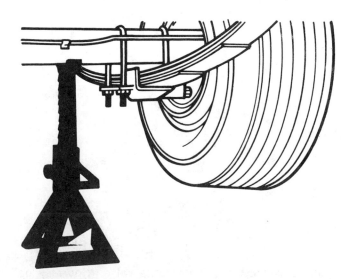

FIGURE 39-20. Raising vehicle for governor test.

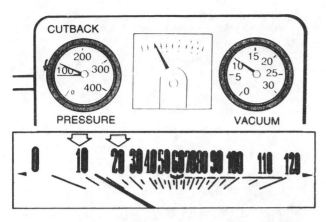

FIGURE 39-21. Governor light load test indicated by line pressure cutback at specified vacuum and road speed. *(Courtesy of Ford Motor Co. of Canada Ltd.)*

heavy throttle operation. Shifts should be firmer and have a more positive feel with no engine flare-up or run-up during upshifts. Compare to specifications.

3. To detent (part throttle or torque demand) downshift operation. Downshifts and downshift pattern should correspond to those given for the particular vehicle make, model, engine, and differential ratio combination. Tire size will also have a bearing on shift speed patterns.

4. Through detent (WOT downshift or kickdown) operation. Compare to specifications in item 3.

5. Coasting downshift (closed-throttle downshift) operation. Brakes can be used to retard vehicle for this check. Note downshift speed and quality and compare with specifications.

6. Noisy operation. Note any abnormal noise (this may require a window to be open) and note the gear position in which noise occurs. If disassembly is required later, this will help pinpoint the problem if you know the power flow patterns.

(a) The 1–2, 2–3, 3–4 upshifts and converter lockup during light throttle operation. Shifts should be smooth, yet noticeable, with no engine flare-up or run-up during shifts. Upshifts should occur at proper speeds.

(b) The same shifts during medium and

RANGE	CHECK FOR	CONDITION (OK OR NOT OK)
1	Engagement	
	Should be **no** 1-2 upshift	
	Engine braking in low gear	
	Shifts 3-2 and then 2-1 coming out of D at cruise	
	No slipping	
2	Engagement/Starts in second gear	
	Should be **no** 2-3 upshift	
	Shifts 3-2 coming out of D at cruise	
	No slipping	
D	Engagement/Starts in first gear	
	Upshifts not mushy or harsh	
	Upshifts and downshifts at specified speeds	
	● Minimum Throttle 1-2	
	● Minimum Throttle 2-3	
	● Minimum Throttle 3-2	
	● Minimum Throttle 2-1	
	● To-detent (heavy throttle) 1-2	
	● To-detent (heavy throttle) 2-3	
	● To-detent (heavy throttle) 3-2	
	● Through-detent (W.O.T.) 1-2	
	● Through-detent (W.O.T.) 2-3	
	● Through-detent (W.O.T.) 3-2	
	● Through-detent (W.O.T.) 3-1 or 2-1	
R	Engagement	
	Back up without slip	

FIGURE 39-22. Road test check chart. *(Courtesy of Ford Motor Co. of Canada Ltd.)*

7. Manually selected downshifts. While driving in third or fourth gear at approximately 35 mph (56 km/h), manual selection of second- or first-gear position can help determine intermediate band (or clutch) operation, both apply and release.

Some typical conclusions that can be drawn from abnormal transmission operation during a road test include the following:

• Forward clutch slippage, causing delayed engagement in all forward gears, poor acceleration.

• Direct clutch (reverse and high clutch) Slippage, causing delayed engagement in reverse, delayed 2–3 upshift, engine speedup (neutral feel) during 2–3 upshift, and poor acceleration in third or direct.

• Intermediate band or clutch slippage, causing delayed 1–2 upshift, engine speedup (neutral feel) during 1–2 upshift, and poor acceleration in second gear.

• Leaking vacuum modulator or vacuum supply line, causing delayed or no upshift.

• Governor sticking, possibly causing delayed or no upshift or early upshift regardless of throttle opening.

• Worn hydraulic pump, causing delayed engagement and slippage in all gear positions if severe wear present.

• Stator one-way clutch not holding, causing very poor low-speed acceleration.

For more detailed and more specific problems, refer to the diagnostic charts and procedures in the appropriate service manual.

Step 6   Hydraulic Pressure Testing

Although road testing provides the means to identify which area in the transmission is causing a problem, hydraulic pressure testing may be required to verify the diagnosis and isolate the problem further. If road testing yields conclusive results, pressure testing is not required.

The number of hydraulic circuits that can be tested varies between different makes and models of transmissions. Generally, all transmissions can be tested for proper line (or control) pressures, including proper line pressure increase and decrease in the various modes of transmission operation. From this it can easily be seen that pressure testing may be required to solve a shift timing or shift quality problem since pressure changes affect both.

Pressure testing will indicate whether the following systems are operating properly:

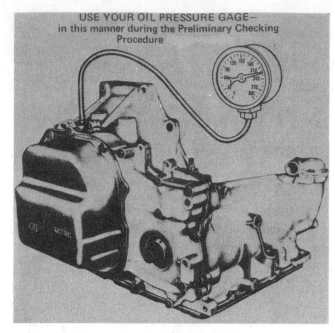

USE YOUR OIL PRESSURE GAGE— in this manner during the Preliminary Checking Procedure

FIGURE 39–23. GM-125C pressure test hookup. *(Courtesy of General Motors Corporation)*

• The pressure supply system—pump and pressure regulator valve

• The throttle pressure system—throttle valve and vacuum modulator system (if so equipped)

• The governor pressure system—the governor valve, weights, and springs

The following equipment is required to perform a hydraulic pressure test:

• A tachometer (capable of being read from the driver's position).

• One or two hydraulic pressure gauges (depending on the transmission being tested) with fittings and hoses long enough to hang gauges inside the vehicle for the driver to observe. Gauges should be capable of at least 400 psi (2,800 kPa).

• A vacuum gauge (for those transmissions equipped with a vacuum modulator) with a long hose capable of reaching the driver's position for easy reading.

• A vacuum supply pump, possibly needed to provide adequate vacuum in some cases to verify accurately and distinguish between transmission-caused problems and engine-caused transmission problems.

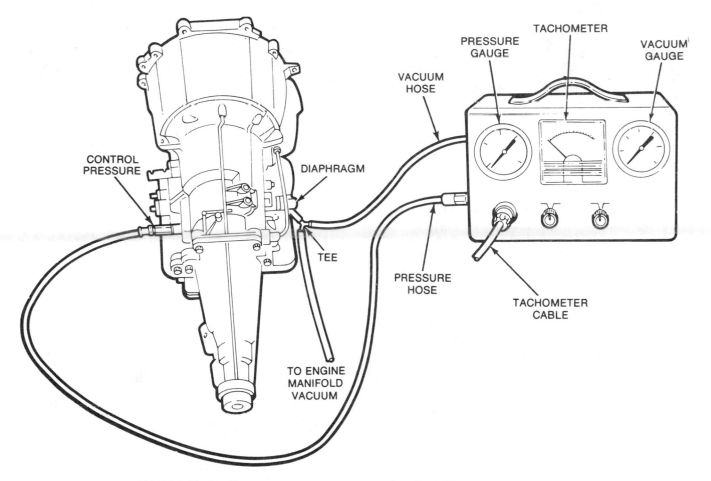

FIGURE 39-24. Pressure test connections for Ford C3 transmission. *(Courtesy of Ford Motor Co. of Canada Ltd.)*

Many automatic transmission testers provide all the required equipment in one portable unit, which makes it easier to use than individual gauges.

Some transmissions have more than one plugged pressure tap. The specific problem encountered in the transmission and the step-by-step diagnostic procedure in the manual will decide by process of elimination how many pressure taps must be used. The tap plug is removed and the pressure gauge fitting screwed into the threaded opening. Make sure that you have the correct fitting with the correct size and type of thread. The fitting should screw easily into the hole by hand at least several turns; then tighten it with a wrench.

The vacuum gauge is connected to the vacuum line at the modulator with a T-fitting. The vacuum gauge is necessary to determine whether specified hydraulic pressures are achieved at specified vacuum values.

All hydraulic pressure test results, both vacuum and hydraulic pressures, should be recorded for tests in order to be valid and for accurate comparison and analysis with the manufacturer's specifi-

cations. Use the appropriate chart from the service manual for comparison analysis.

Checking for External Fluid Leakage

When checking for transmission fluid leaks, it is important to be able to distinguish between transmission fluid, engine oil, power steering fluid, and antifreeze. Once it has been determined that it is in fact transmission fluid that is leaking, the suspected area should be cleaned and wiped dry. The transmission should then be operated, and the point of leakage determined by close examination of new leakage.

Areas of transmission leakage are as follows:

- Torque converter.
- Front pump seal or gasket.
- Transmission case, oil pan gaskets, servo cover gaskets, and extension housing gasket and seal.
- Speedometer cable adapter.
- Filler tube O ring.

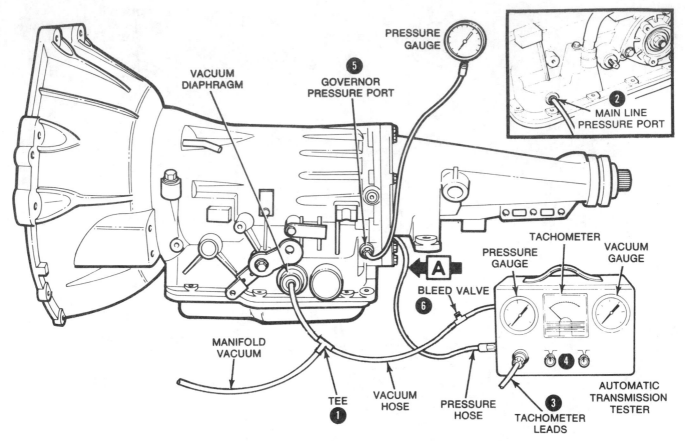

FIGURE 39–25. Pressure test connections for Ford Jatco transmission. *(Courtesy of Ford Motor Co. of Canada Ltd.)*

- Shift linkage shafts and O rings.

- Vacuum modulator (engine vacuum can draw fluid into engine through ruptured modulator diaphragm; to check, remove vacuum line from modulator; there should be no evidence of fluid in modulator or vacuum line).

- Vent or filler tube leakage can result from overfilling of transmission with fluid.

If transmission has been operated with a low fluid level sufficiently to cause internal damage, both the internal damage and the leak must be corrected.

PART 4 TRANSMISSION AND TRANSAXLE REMOVAL AND INSTALLATION

No automatic transmission should be removed unless a thorough systematic diagnosis has definitely established that removal and overhaul are required. Automatic transmissions are designed to provide 100,000 miles (16,000 km) or more of normal service

life. Malfunctions may require only minor in-vehicle adjustment or service. Removing and overhauling a transmission unnecessarily is costly and unfair to the customer as well as damaging to the reputation of the technician and the repair shop.

Severe automatic transmission service may be defined as any one or more of the following:

1. Driving in heavy city traffic

2. Operating regularly in ambient temperatures of 90°F (32°C) or higher

3. Driving in hilly or mountain areas

4. Frequent or heavy trailer towing

5. Use as a taxi, police car, or delivery service vehicle

More frequent service may be required under these operating conditions.

Transmission Identification

In order to obtain the correct parts and the proper specifications for any automatic transmission, it is necessary to identify the unit positively.

Transmission identification includes the following:

1. Make of the transmission (vehicle make)
2. Model year of the vehicle
3. Transmission number

The transmission number may be stamped on the side of the pan mounting flange on either the right or left side on some units. On others, it is found on a tag attached with one of the valve body attaching screws or it may be stamped or painted on the transmission converter housing. Refer to the appropriate manufacturer's service repair manual to help locate and identify the transmission number.

General Precautions

1. Be careful of hot transmission fluid and hot exhaust parts. (Fluids may reach 350°F [177°C].)

2. Follow all normal personal safety habits: no loose clothing; no smoking; no jewelry; cleanliness; face mask; and the like.

3. Use only a soft hammer and light tapping blows in order to prevent damage to transmission parts.

4. Follow all normal shop safety procedures: proper jacking and hoisting of vehicle; clean floor and tools; proper routing of electrical cords and air hoses; no jack handles sticking out; proper shop ventilation; proper use of transmission jack; and the like.

A good practice to develop and to follow is to anticipate hazardous conditions and to prevent accident and injury from happening. The competent technician has developed the skill of anticipating the consequences of actions into a sixth sense, which avoids unsafe and dangerous habits almost without conscious effort.

5. Parts that are machined to very close tolerances and are highly polished are used in automatic transmissions. Parts should be handled so as to prevent nicking and scoring. Do not drop any parts. Do not allow parts to bump and scrape against each other. Do not place parts where they can roll off and drop on the floor with the slightest jar.

6. Never remove the transmission attaching bolts until both the engine and the transmission are properly supported.

7. Always use a block of wood between the jack and the oil pan in a manner that will prevent any damage to the pan or the transmission.

8. It is good practice to leave the hood open during removal and installation of the transmission

in order to prevent damage to it when raising the engine slightly.

9. Always disconnect the battery to prevent anyone from cranking the engine accidentally and to prevent electrical shorts during transmission overhaul.

These are a few reminders to help avoid injury and damage. It is possible for individuals not thinking of the consequences of their actions to proceed in any number of unpredictable and unsafe practices. It is critical for you as a technician to avoid this kind of action.

Removal and Installation

1. Open the hood and place fender protectors on both sides.

2. Disconnect the negative battery cable for safety reasons.

3. Remove the air cleaner if clearance to the fire wall is limited. Lowering the rear of the engine during transmission removal may cause interference or damage if the air cleaner is not removed.

4. Remove the transmission dipstick. If left in, damage could result due to limited clearance during transmission removal.

5. Disconnect the throttle valve linkage or cable as needed.

6. Raise the car on a hoist.

7. Mark the drive shaft with scribe marks or spray paint for assembly in the same position. Remove the drive shaft or transaxles shafts.

8. Remove the starter if required. The starter must be removed if any starter mounting bolts are attached to the converter housing.

9. Remove any steering linkage or drive axles (transaxles) that may interfere with transmission removal.

10. Disconnect the manual shift linkage and throttle linkage from the transmission. Use pliers to push rods out of plastic grommets.

11. Disconnect the speedometer cable at the transmission.

12. Disconnect the vacuum line at the vacuum modulator if so equipped.

13. Disconnect all electrical connections at the transmission.

14. Disconnect or remove any exhaust system components that may interfere with transmission removal and lowering.

15. Remove transmission rear mount bolts. Re-

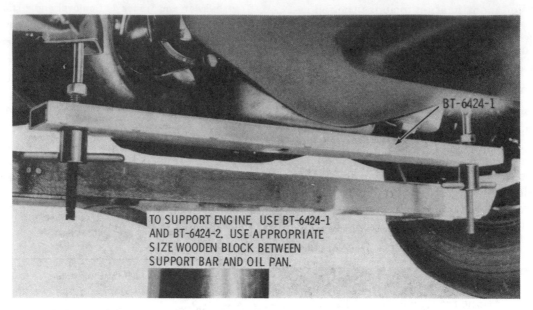

FIGURE 39–26. Typical engine support bracket required for automatic transmission removal. Similar bracket can be fabricated. *(Courtesy of General Motors Corporation)*

move crossmember bolts if the crossmember is to be moved for transmission clearance.

16. Remove the converter housing cover plate and mark the converter to drive plate position with scribe marks or spray paint for proper assembly later.

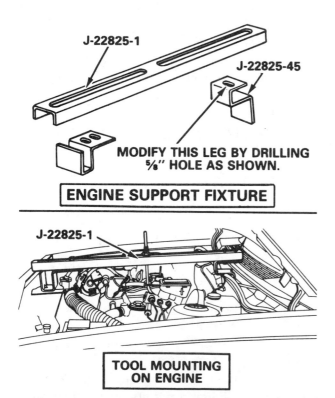

J-22825-1

J-22825-45

MODIFY THIS LEG BY DRILLING
⅝" HOLE AS SHOWN.

ENGINE SUPPORT FIXTURE

J-22825-1

**TOOL MOUNTING
ON ENGINE**

FIGURE 39–27. Engine support fixture used for transaxle removal. *(Courtesy of General Motors Corporation)*

17. Remove the torque converter from the flexplate attaching bolts or nuts. You may have to use a socket wrench at the crankshaft pulley bolt at the front of the engine in order to turn the converter for access to all bolts. The converter and transmission must always be removed or installed as an assembly. This prevents converter or drive plate damage. The weight of the transmission or converter must never hang on the drive plate.

18. Disconnect the oil cooler lines from the transmission. Cap all openings.

19. Install the engine holding fixture if required. Some engines must be properly supported with a holding fixture to prevent damage to the radiator, shroud, radiator hoses, and the like during

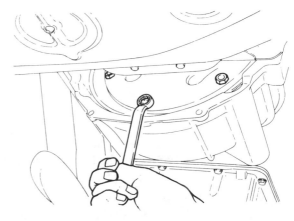

FIGURE 39–28. Removing torque converter drive bolts prior to transmission removal. *(Courtesy of Chrysler Corporation)*

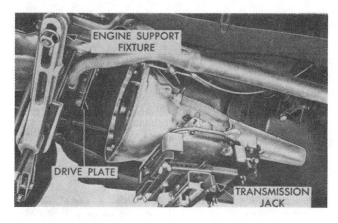

FIGURE 39-29. Removing or installing transmission and converter assembly. *(Courtesy of Chrysler Corporation)*

transmission removal or installation. In many cases the engine is balanced well enough on its mounts not to require a holding fixture. In both cases, however, due care and attention must be given to prevent the fan from damaging the radiator or fan shroud and the radiator hoses from being overstretched.

20. Position a transmission jack under the transmission and install the hold-down chain to secure the transmission to the jack. Tilt the jack contact pad to fit the transmission properly. Raise the jack enough to raise the engine slightly.

21. Remove the previously disconnected crossmember (if necessary), keeping all alignment shims in place for proper reassembly.

22. Remove the converter housing to engine attaching bolts.

23. Install the converter retaining tool to prevent the converter from moving forward during transmission removal.

24. Carefully lower the transmission. *Caution:* It may be necessary to wiggle the transmission from side to side at the rear to break it loose from the dowel pins. Do this carefully so as not to upset the jack when the transmission lets go. This requires having the jack at the correct height for enough support on the transmission, without raising the engine.

25. Carefully and slowly lower the transmission jack to maneuver the transmission clear of any wiring, tubing, or linkage. Do not damage or bend any of these during transmission removal.

26. Remove the transmission from the jack. *Caution:* The transmission is heavy and you should have help for this. Place the transmission in the

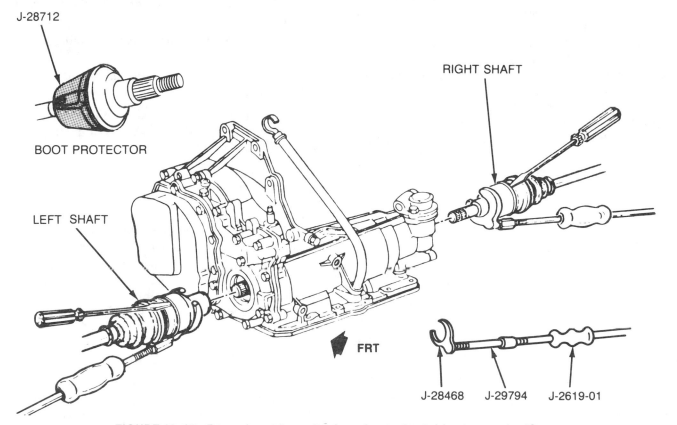

FIGURE 39-30. Removing drive axles from front-wheel-drive transaxle. *(Courtesy of General Motors Corporation)*

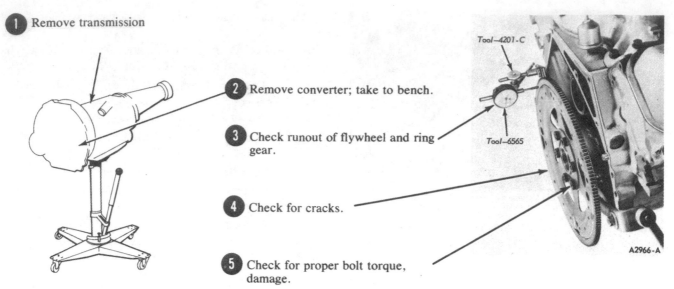

1. Remove transmission

2. Remove converter; take to bench.

3. Check runout of flywheel and ring gear.

4. Check for cracks.

5. Check for proper bolt torque, damage.

Tool–4201-C

Tool–6565

A2966-A

FIGURE 39-31. *(Courtesy of Ford Motor Co. of Canada Ltd.)*

clean-up area and clean all exterior dirt from the transmission. Be sure that all openings remain capped during this cleaning process.

27. Place the transmission on the repair bench.

28. At this point, a careful inspection of the converter flex plate will determine if replacement is required. Inspect for starter gear tooth wear or damage, cracks, worn converter attaching holes, and worn or damaged converter hub pilot hole. If transmission diagnosis established that there is a vibration problem in the converter area or if there is front seal leakage, it is good practice to check the flex plate run-out if otherwise in good condition. A flex plate that does not run true can cause vibration and rapid front seal and pump bushing wear, which results in oil leakage. Check the flex plate run-out with a dial indicator and compare to specifications. Maximum allowable run-out is approximately 0.060 inch (1.50 mm).

Cooler and Cooler Line Flushing

In a major transmission failure, where particles of metal have been carried with the oil throughout the units of the transmission, it will be necessary to flush out the oil cooler and connecting lines. To flush the oil cooler and lines, use the following procedures.

1. With both cooler lines from the transmission disconnected:

2. Place a hose over the end of the cooler inlet line (from the bottom of the cooler) and insert the hose into an empty container.

3. Flush clean solvent through the return line (from the top of the cooler) using an oil suction gun

until clean solvent comes out of the hose. This will back-flush the cooler.

4. Remove the hose from the inlet cooler line and place it on the return line.

5. Flush clean solvent through the inlet line until clean solvent comes out the return line. Remove the remaining solvent from cooler with compressed air applied to the return line and flush with transmission fluid.

Caution: Maximum air pressure should not exceed 50 psi (345 kPa).

6. Reconnect oil cooler lines and torque nuts to specified torque.

This procedure can also be done with converter flushing equipment. Follow the equipment manufacturer's instructions for procedures and pressures to use.

Oil Cooler Lines

If replacement of transmission steel tubing cooler lines is required, use only double-wrapped and brazed steel tubing. Under no condition use copper or aluminum tubing to replace steel tubing. Those materials do not have satisfactory fatigue durability to withstand normal car vibrations. Steel tubing should be flared using the double-flare method and the proper fittings.

Transmission Installation

The transmission and torque converter must be installed as an assembly. This requires that the torque converter fully engage the drive gear of the hydraulic pump. If full engagement of the torque converter is not assured, pump damage will occur when

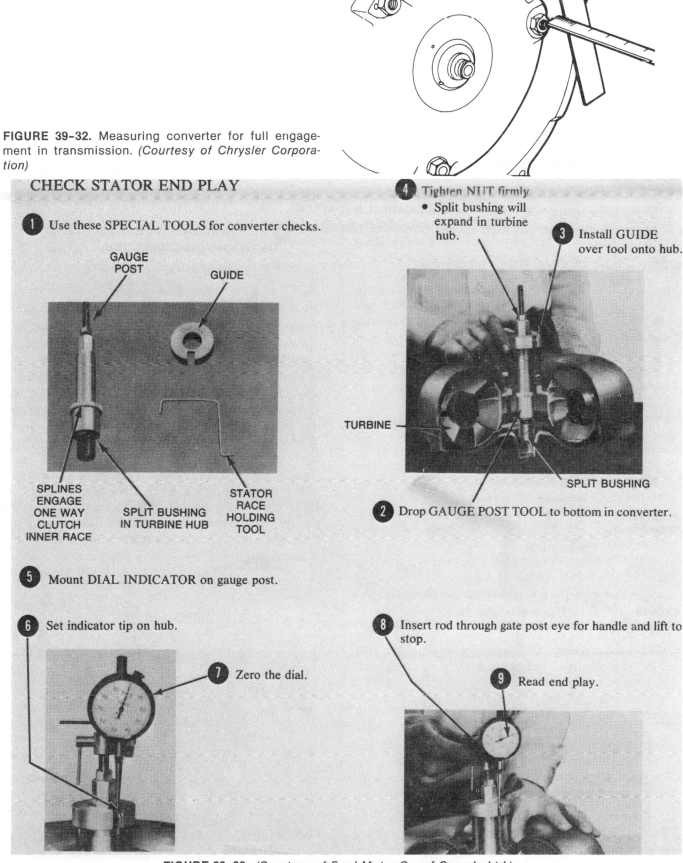

FIGURE 39-32. Measuring converter for full engagement in transmission. *(Courtesy of Chrysler Corporation)*

CHECK STATOR END PLAY

1 Use these SPECIAL TOOLS for converter checks.

GAUGE POST

GUIDE

SPLINES ENGAGE ONE WAY CLUTCH INNER RACE

SPLIT BUSHING IN TURBINE HUB

STATOR RACE HOLDING TOOL

2 Drop GAUGE POST TOOL to bottom in converter.

3 Install GUIDE over tool onto hub.

4 Tighten NUT firmly
- Split bushing will expand in turbine hub.

TURBINE

SPLIT BUSHING

5 Mount DIAL INDICATOR on gauge post.

6 Set indicator tip on hub.

7 Zero the dial.

8 Insert rod through gate post eye for handle and lift to stop.

9 Read end play.

FIGURE 39-33. *(Courtesy of Ford Motor Co. of Canada Ltd.)*

the transmission is installed and the mounting bolts tightened.

To assure full engagement, a measurement is taken between the mounting surface of the converter bell housing and the converter to the flex plate mounting surface. If this dimension is less than specified, the converter is not fully engaged. Once the converter is fully engaged, the converter holding bracket (you can make your own from a suitable piece of flat iron) should be installed to maintain converter engagement during transmission installation.

To install the transmission, lubricate the converter pilot hub. Then install the transmission by reversing the removal procedure. Clean and lubricate all bolts and tighten to specified torque. Bolts not lubricated may destroy aluminum threads.

When the transmission is raised into position, guide it over the dowel pins and push it toward the engine until mating surfaces are flush. Check to see that there is no interference between the converter and the converter drive plate. If there is, the converter may not be fully engaged with the hydraulic pump. Proceeding under these circumstances would damage the pump. If the converter is properly installed and the correct dimensions obtained between the converter face and the bell housing face, there should be no problem. Install all the mounting bolts by hand, then tighten to specified torque. Install the cross member, remove the jack and engine support, and complete the assembly. Make sure that the torque converter is aligned with marks made during removal. Tighten attaching bolts or nuts to specifications. Lower the vehicle. Apply the parking brake securely.

Put in 2, 3, or 4 quarts (or liters) of the specified fluid in the transmission and start the engine. Let the engine idle; do not accelerate. With the engine idling, add the remaining fluid to the cold level or add-oil level on the dipstick.

Caution: Do not fill above this level at this time. Move the selector lever through all gear ranges and place it in the specified position (P or N); add oil if needed to bring fluid level to cold level mark or add-oil mark on the dipstick.

During this procedure note if the transmission has the proper engagement feel.

Run the engine until transmission reaches a normal operating temperature (about 175°F, 80°C), recheck the fluid level, and add fluid if necessary.

Caution: Do not overfill. If accidentally overfilled, the fluid level must be corrected by draining until the proper level is reached.

PART 5 DISASSEMBLY AND ASSEMBLY GUIDELINES

After the transmission has been removed, the exterior cleaned and placed on the work bench, the overhaul should proceed in an organized and systematic manner.

The sequence of operations includes the following.

First all subassemblies are removed from the transmission, generally in the following order:

- Torque converter
- Oil pan and filter
- Valve body
- Hydraulic pump
- Clutch units, gear train, and bands
- Extension housing
- Governor
- Output shaft

End-play measurements are taken and recorded before and during disassembly. These measurements are used to determine selection of proper thrust washer thickness during assembly. Thrust washer thickness determines end-play requirements for the transmission. Excessive end play indicates excessive wear internally and allows clutch drums to move back and forth excessively in the transmission case. Assembled end-play measurements should be between minimum and maximum specifications with preference being at the low end of specifications since end play will increase as the transmission is put in service. Refer to the appropriate shop manual for specifications and for information on the proper procedure for end-play measurements.

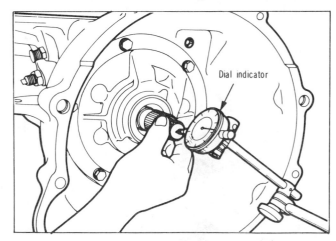

FIGURE 39-34. Measuring turbine shaft end play. *(Courtesy of Chrysler Corporation)*

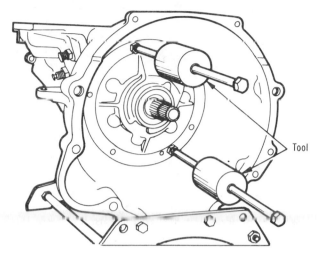

FIGURE 39–35. Using slide hammer pullers to remove hydraulic pump after pump attaching bolts have been removed. *(Courtesy of Chrysler Corporation)*

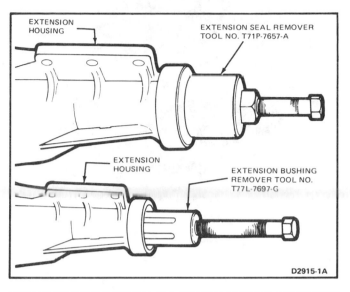

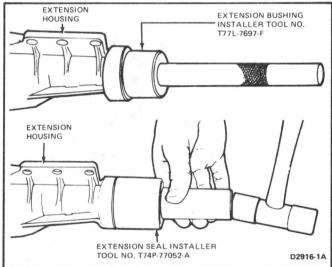

FIGURE 39–36. *(Courtesy of Ford Motor Co. of Canada Ltd.)*

After end-play measurements have been recorded and all subassemblies removed, the procedure is to disassemble, clean, inspect, measure (where required), repair, and assemble the various units. When all units have been properly reconditioned, the transmission is assembled and installed. Although there are differences in the number of clutches and bands and the design of clutches, bands, servos, valve bodies, governors, and planetary gears, the general procedure for servicing these units is similar for all transmissions.

Cleaning and Inspection Guidelines

1. Follow the disassembly sequence and procedure given in the appropriate service repair manual and this text.

2. Remove all old gasket material from metal surfaces with a suitable scraper. Avoid scoring or gouging the metal since this can cause fluid leakage.

3. Replace all old gaskets and seals with those supplied in the gasket and seal kit.

4. Replace oil transfer rings and metal seal rings if worn. Gasket and seal kits do not normally contain replacement oil transfer rings. Overhaul kits (which are more expensive) usually contain all gaskets, seals, oil transfer rings, check balls, and in some cases servo pistons.

5. Use only filtered, moisture free compressed air regulated at 50 psi (345 kPa) maximum for cleaning passages, etc.

6. Do not use solvents, detergents, or vapor degreasers on composition clutch plates, bands, synthetic seals, and check balls.

7. Use only lint free cloth for any wiping of parts. Lint can cause valves to stick and oil to leak.

8. Do not over expand snap rings. Damaged snap rings must be replaced.

9. Do not overstretch seals and seal rings. Fluid leaks and malfunction are caused by stretched and distorted seals and seal rings.

10. Ends of angle-cut (scarf-cut) seal rings must be installed with angled cuts facing each other.

11. Hooked cast-iron seal rings must be properly hooked and flush with no step in hooked ends when installed.

12. Use only the recommended type of transmission fluid for lubrication during assembly.

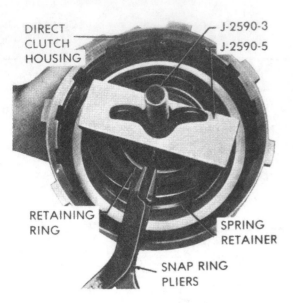

DIRECT CLUTCH HOUSING

J-2590-3
J-2590-5

RETAINING RING

SPRING RETAINER

SNAP RING PLIERS

FIGURE 39-37. Using clutch spring compressor to allow removal of snap ring and spring retainer, THM 350. *(Courtesy of General Motors Corporation)*

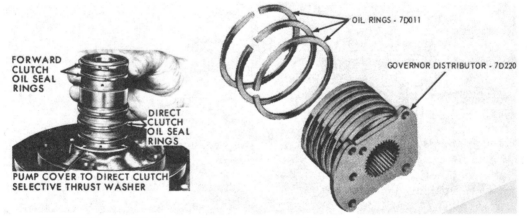

FORWARD CLUTCH OIL SEAL RINGS

DIRECT CLUTCH OIL SEAL RINGS

PUMP COVER TO DIRECT CLUTCH SELECTIVE THRUST WASHER

OIL RINGS - 7D011

GOVERNOR DISTRIBUTOR - 7D220

FIGURE 39-38. Oil flow control rings are used to transfer hydraulic pressure between rotating and stationary transmission parts. Cast iron, Teflon, and other materials are used in these rings. *(Courtesy of Ford Motor Co. of Canada Ltd. and General Motors Corporation)*

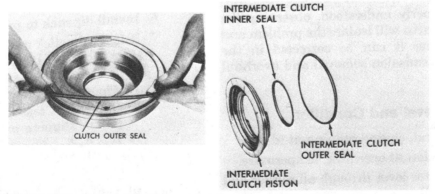

CLUTCH OUTER SEAL

INTERMEDIATE CLUTCH INNER SEAL

INTERMEDIATE CLUTCH OUTER SEAL

INTERMEDIATE CLUTCH PISTON

FIGURE 39-39. Hydraulic pistons (clutch and servo) use various types of piston seals, such as lip-type and lathe-cut (rectangular cross section) seals, for clutch pistons, and cast iron, Teflon, or lip-type synthetic rubber seals on servo pistons. Static-ring seals are used to seal between parts where there is no relative motion. *(Courtesy of General Motors Corporation)*

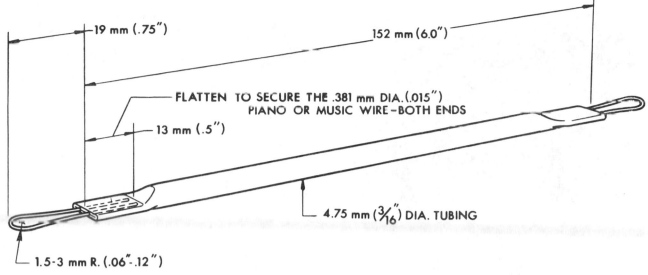

FIGURE 39-40. Piston and seal installing tool can be fabricated as above. *(Courtesy of General Motors Corporation)*

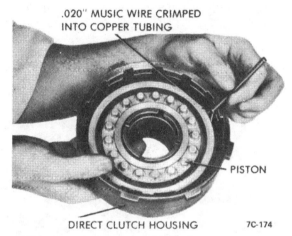

FIGURE 39-41. Using tool to install clutch piston. Lips of seals must not fold back or be damaged during installation. *(Courtesy of General Motors Corporation)*

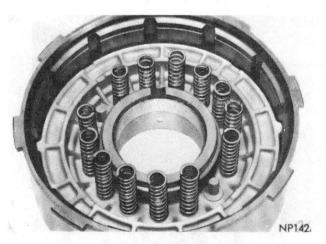

FIGURE 39-42. Location of front clutch piston springs in 727 Torqueflite transmission. *(Courtesy of Chrysler Corporation)*

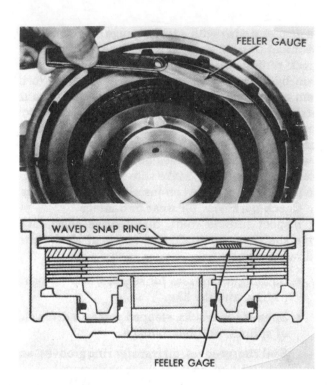

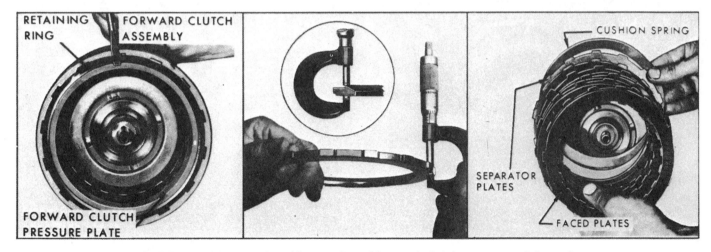

FIGURE 39-43. Measuring front clutch pack clearance on Torqueflite transmission. *(Courtesy of Chrysler Corporation)*

FIGURE 39-44. Removal and inspection of forward clutch pressure plate and clutch pack, THM 350. *(Courtesy of General Motors Corporation)*

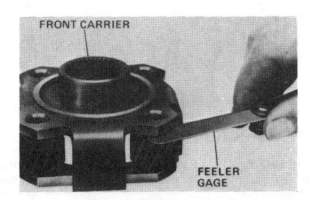

FIGURE 39-45. Measuring pinion end play on GM 200 transmission. *(Courtesy of General Motors Corporation)*

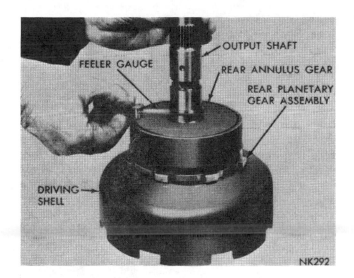

FIGURE 39-46. Measuring planetary gear train end play on Torqueflite transmission. *(Courtesy of Chrysler Corporation)*

FIGURE 39-47. Checking pump-body-to-gear-face clearance, GM 200. *(Courtesy of General Motors Corporation)*

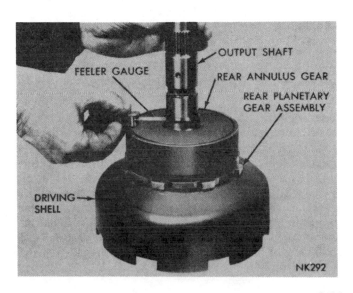

FIGURE 39-48. Assembling pump with aligning tool, Torqueflite. *(Courtesy of Chrysler Corporation)*

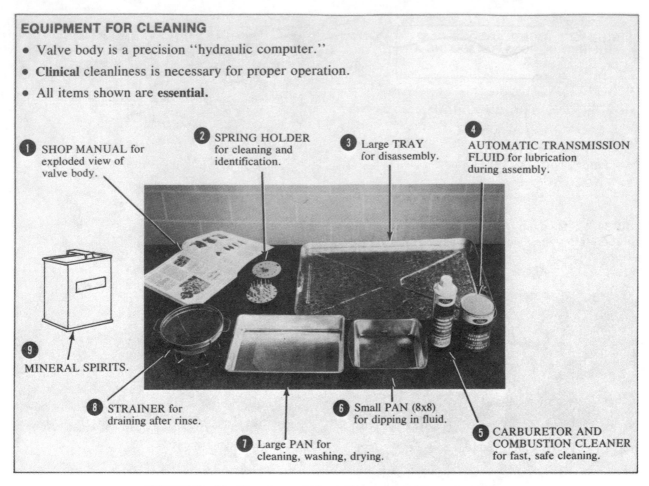

EQUIPMENT FOR CLEANING

- Valve body is a precision "hydraulic computer."
- **Clinical** cleanliness is necessary for proper operation.
- All items shown are **essential.**

1 SHOP MANUAL for exploded view of valve body.

2 SPRING HOLDER for cleaning and identification.

3 Large TRAY for disassembly.

4 AUTOMATIC TRANSMISSION FLUID for lubrication during assembly.

9 MINERAL SPIRITS.

8 STRAINER for draining after rinse.

7 Large PAN for cleaning, washing, drying.

6 Small PAN (8x8) for dipping in fluid.

5 CARBURETOR AND COMBUSTION CLEANER for fast, safe cleaning.

FIGURE 39-49. *(Courtesy of Ford Motor Co. of Canada Ltd.)*

Petroleum-jelly (Vaseline) type of lubricant can also be used. In some cases a lubricant such as Door Ease® may be useful in keeping a clutch seal in place for assembly. Never use any high temperature lubricant such as white grease. It will clog oil passages since it is not compatible with transmission fluids.

13. Every passage in every component must be free and clear of all obstructions.

14. Where fasteners of unequal length are used, be sure that each fastener is installed in the correct location. Installing a shorter fastener in place of the normal length will destroy the threads when it is tightened. Tighten all fasteners to specifications with a torque wrench.

15. Install all paper gaskets dry. The cork pan gasket should also be installed dry with dry mating surfaces. Oily, greasy, or slippery sealant surfaces cause cork gaskets to crack at bolt holes and squish out as fasteners are tightened to specified torque. A little petroleum jelly may be used on paper gaskets to help keep the gasket in place during assembly.

16. Always maintain the original position of parts to be reused.

PART 6   SELF-CHECK

1. Why is a systematic approach to problem diagnosis necessary?

2. Describe how to check the fluid level and condition in a vehicle of your choice.

3. What problems can maladjusted manual shift linkage cause?

4. What effect does throttle linkage adjustment have on shift timing and on shift quality?

5. What effect does a vacuum leak in the modulator diaphragm have on transmission operation?

6. What is the purpose of a stall test?

7. Why should fluid level and linkage adjustments be checked and adjusted before road testing?

8. What is the purpose of air pressure checks?

9. What effect does improper band adjustment have on transmission operation?

10. Describe how to perform a stall test.

11. Slippage in all forward gears could be caused by _____.

12. A malfunctioning governor could cause _____
_____.

13. Define severe automatic transmission service.

14. List as many general precautions as you can that apply to automatic transmission overhaul procedures.

15. Why should you not remove the transmission first and then the torque converter?

16. Why is full engagement of the torque converter required prior to and during transmission installation?

17. What is the importance of taking end play measurements during transmission disassembly?

18. List the checks required to determine the serviceability of a torque converter.

19. Why must clutch pack clearance not be over or under specifications?

20. List four causes of burned clutch discs.

21. How is clutch pack clearance corrected?

22. What happens if the low-gear one-way clutch is installed backwards?

23. Excessive pump rotor or gear clearance will cause reduced pump _____and _____.

24. How is front unit (turbine shaft) end play corrected?

25. How should minor nicks and scratches be removed from spool valves?

26. Spool valves are available as replacement parts for rebuilding valve bodies. True or false?

27. State two reasons why a turbine shaft would not be able to be turned after tightening hydraulic pump mounting bolts.

PART 7   TEST QUESTIONS

1. The hydraulic pump should be measured for:
   (a) pump cover warpage
   (b) tooth or rotor tip clearance
   (c) gear or rotor to cover clearance
   (d) all of the above

2. Overfilling an automatic transmission can cause:
   (a) excessive lubrication
   (b) excessive converter pressure
   (c) insufficient clutch apply pressure
   (d) insufficient cooling

3. A harsh upshift may be caused by:
   (a) incorrect throttle linkage adjustment
   (b) excessive hydraulic pressure
   (c) neither (a) nor (b)
   (d) both (a) and (b)

4. Slipping in all gear positions may be caused by:
   (a) hydraulic pressure too low
   (b) low fluid level
   (c) neither (a) nor (b)
   (d) both (a) and (b)

5. Harsh engagement into drive or reverse may be caused by:
   (a) idle speed too low
   (b) hydraulic pressure too low
   (c) neither (a) nor (b)
   (d) both (a) and (b)

6. A condition that allows the engine to be started in any gear position may be caused by:
   (a) incorrect gearshift linkage adjustment
   (b) incorrect throttle linkage adjustment
   (c) incorrect back-up switch adjustment
   (d) incorrect neutral switch adjustment

7. Excessive cluch pack clearance can cause:
   (a) too much clutch apply pressure
   (b) poor clutch release
   (c) too little shift lag time
   (d) insufficient clutch application

8. Precise band adjustment is required to ensure:
   (a) full band application when needed
   (b) full band release when needed
   (c) both (a) and (b)
   (d) neither (a) nor (b)

9. A governor valve stuck in the closed or at rest position can cause:
   (a) no downshifts
   (b) no upshifts
   (c) both (a) and (b)
   (d) neither (a) nor (b)

10. Gear train end play can be corrected with the use of:
    (a) selective gear sizes
    (b) oversize shafts
    (c) selective carrier sizes
    (d) selective thrust washers

VENTILATING, HEATING AND AIR-CONDITIONING SYSTEMS

Chapter 40

Heating and Air-Conditioning Systems

The comfort of the driver and passengers in a vehicle is partially dependent on the quality and temperature of air in the vehicle. Three interrelated systems are used to provide the desired air temperature and quality. These are:

- The ventilating system
- The heating system
- The air conditioning system.

Depending on climatic conditions in which the vehicle operates, these systems may also be required to prevent windows from fogging or frosting up. An electric grid type of heated rear window may also be used.

PART 1   HEATING AND VENTILATING SYSTEM

Ventilating System

The ventilating system on most vehicles is designed to supply outside air to the passenger compartment through upper or lower air vents or both. Outside air enters the vehicle through openings in the front grille area or through a louvered cowl opening at the base of the windshield. Outside air entry is usually controlled by air flow control valves, doors, or windows.

Air circulation is the result of ram air caused by vehicle movement and by a blower driven by an electric motor. Blower speed is controlled at several possible speed selections depending on design. This blower and motor assembly is the same one that provides circulation of warm air by the heating system.

Plastic or fiber air distribution ducts conduct air from the outer air inlet to the openings inside the vehicle. Doors or valves in the air distribution system allow the selection of four modes of air circulation.

- Fresh air entry only
- Fresh air heated by the heating system
- A mix of fresh and heated air
- No fresh air entry

Depending on system design, the air flow may be directed to provide upper level circulation, lower level circulation, or both. Air flow control doors or valves may be manually operated by control cables or by vacuum motors controlled by a vacuum switch.

Heating System

The heating system is designed to operate in conjunction with the air ventilating system to provide

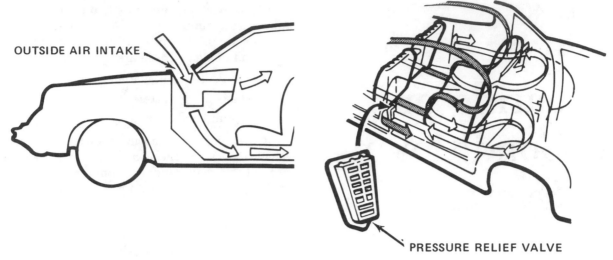

OUTSIDE AIR INTAKE

PRESSURE RELIEF VALVE

FIGURE 40-1. Typical air flow heating system. Note pressure relief valve (in rear quarter pillar or under rear seat) that vents stale air from passenger compartment. *(Courtesy of General Motors Corporation)*

the desired air temperature. The heating system uses heated engine coolant delivered to a heater core (similar in design to radiator construction) located in the air distribution system. Rubber hoses connect the heater core inlet and outlet to the engine coolant circulation system. The engine's water pump provides movement of heated coolant through the heater core. Circulation of heated coolant through the heater core can be controlled by a flow control valve located in the heater inlet hose. This valve can

be manually operated by a cable control or by a vacuum motor, depending on design. The valve controls the volume of heated coolant allowed to circulate through the heater core thereby controlling the temperature of air passing through the heater core.

Most automobiles use the blend air type of heating system. In this system, outside air passes through a plenum chamber to the heater core. A temperature control door at the heater core directs incoming air through the heater core or through the

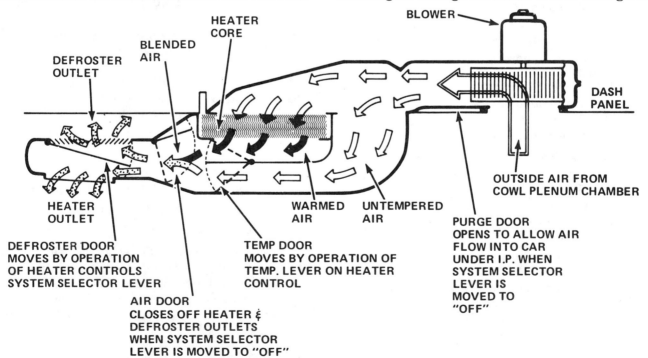

DEFROSTER OUTLET

BLENDED AIR

HEATER CORE

BLOWER

DASH PANEL

HEATER OUTLET

WARMED AIR

UNTEMPERED AIR

OUTSIDE AIR FROM COWL PLENUM CHAMBER

DEFROSTER DOOR MOVES BY OPERATION OF HEATER CONTROLS SYSTEM SELECTOR LEVER

AIR DOOR CLOSES OFF HEATER & DEFROSTER OUTLETS WHEN SYSTEM SELECTOR LEVER IS MOVED TO "OFF"

TEMP DOOR MOVES BY OPERATION OF TEMP. LEVER ON HEATER CONTROL

PURGE DOOR OPENS TO ALLOW AIR FLOW INTO CAR UNDER I.P. WHEN SYSTEM SELECTOR LEVER IS MOVED TO "OFF"

FIGURE 40-2. Air flow through heater housing. Temperature door position determines air flow path—through heater core or bypassing heater core. *(Courtesy of General Motors Corporation)*

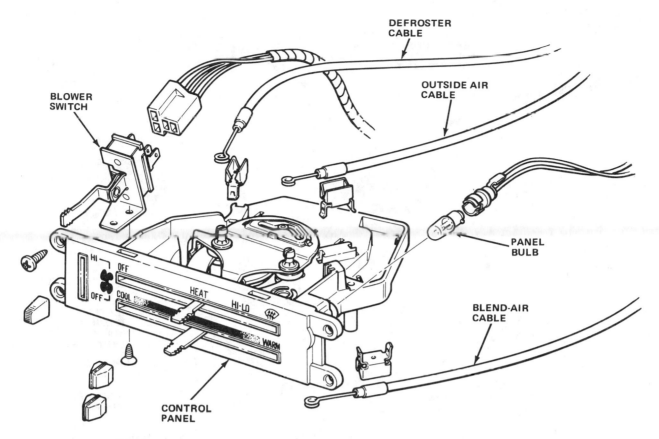

FIGURE 40-3. Typical heating system controls. Cables control flow control doors and switch controls blower speed. *(Courtesy of American Motors Corporation)*

heater core bypass. The amount of "blend air" (mix of heated air and non-heated air) is governed by the position of the blend air door. The temperature control on the instrument panel operates the blend air door. The discharge of air to the floor outlets, upper level vent outlets, or defrost outlets at the windshield is controlled by the heater/defroster control on the instrument panel.

A blower switch controls the speed of the blower motor and therefore the velocity of air being discharged. The switch usually incorporates a resistor block consisting of two helically wound wire resistors connected to terminals attached to a small panel. The blower switch selectively connects one, two, or none of the resistors in series to the blower motor, thereby providing three blower speeds.

A summary of components and their function follows:

• Motor and fan assembly (blower)—Provides and regulates air flow from the air inlet for further processing and/or distribution.

• Heater core—Transfers heat from engine coolant to inlet air, thus heating the inlet air.

• Temperature valve—Regulates the amount of air passing through the heater core, thus controlling the temperature and mix of heated and ambient air.

• Mode (defroster) valve—Regulates the flow and distribution of processed air to the distribution (heater or defroster) ducts.

• Vent valve—Regulates the flow of nonprocessed (outside) air into the passenger compartment.

• Plenum and ducts—Conduct air from inlets to heater or defroster outlets.

PART 2 DIAGNOSIS AND SERVICE PROCEDURE

General Precautions

All the normal personal and shop safety precautions outlined in Chapter 1 should be followed as well as those in Chapter 8 regarding cooling system service and Chapter 18 regarding the electrical system.

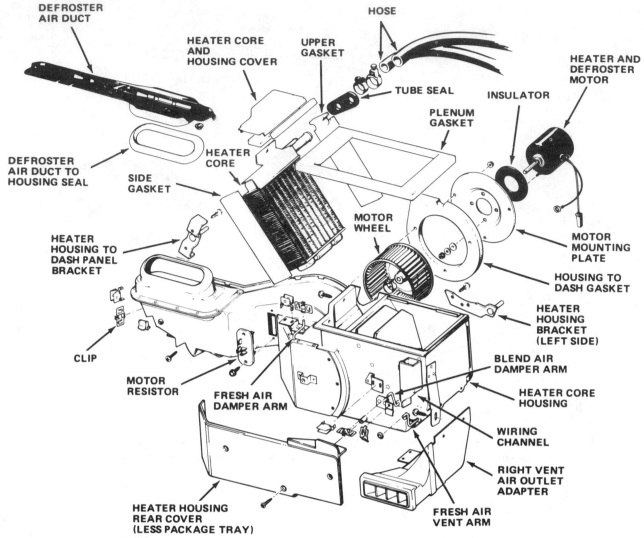

FIGURE 40-4. Components of car heating system. *(Courtesy of American Motors Corporation)*

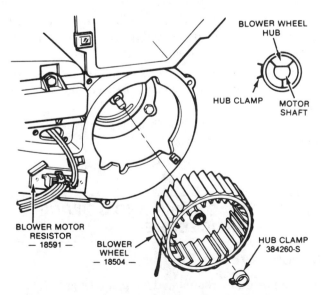

FIGURE 40-5. Drum-type heater blower and blower retaining clamp. *(Courtesy of Ford Motor Co. of Canada Ltd.)*

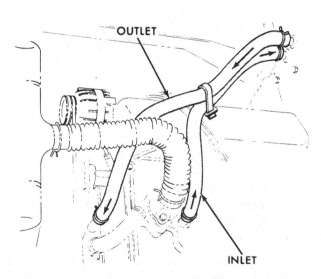

FIGURE 40-6. Typical heater hose installation. Hot coolant from engine flows to heater core. Return line goes to water pump for positive circulation. *(Courtesy of Chrysler Corporation)*

PROBLEM	CAUSE	CORRECTION
1. Insufficient heat	Slow warming in car	1. Incorrect operation of controls. Advise operator of proper operation of heater controls. Explain operation of vents and controls. 2. Low coolant level. 3. Faulty thermostat. 4. Check control cable and blower operation.
	Objectionable engine or exhaust fumes in car	1. Check for seal between engine compartment and plenum. 2. Check for proper sealing between air inlet duct assembly and dash. 3. Locate and seal any other air leaks.
	Cold drafts on floor	1. Check operation and adjustment of vent cables. 2. Advise operator of proper operation of heater system. 3. Advise operator to use blower to force air to rear seat area. 4. Check to be sure front floor mat is under floor mat retainer at dash.
	Insufficient heat to rear seat	1. Obstruction on floor: possibly wrinkled or torn insulator material between front seat and floor. 2. Advise operator to use HI blower speed.
	Low engine coolant level—drop in heater air temperature at all blower speeds	1. Check radiator and cooling system for leaks; correct and fill to proper level. Run engine to clear any air lock.
	Failure of engine cooling system to warm up	1. Check engine thermostat. Replace if required. 2. Check coolant level.
	Kinked heater hoses	1. Remove kink or replace hose.
	Foreign material obstructing water flow through heater core	1. Remove foreign material if possible. Otherwise, replace core; can usually be heard as squishing noise at core.
	Temperature door (valve) improperly adjusted. Air doors do not operate	1. Adjust cable. 2. Check installation and/or adjustment of air control or air-defrost cable.
2. Too much heat	Temperature door improperly adjusted	1. Adjust temperature cable.
	Incorrect operation of controls	1. Advise operator of proper operation of heater system.
3. Inadequate defrost	Air door does not open Defroster door does not open fully	1. Check cable operation.
	Air door does not open	1. Check installation and/or adjustment of air control or air-defrost cable.
	Temperature door does not open	1. Check and adjust temperature control cable if necessary.
	Obstructions in defroster outlets at windshield	1. Remove obstruction. Look for and fix loose instrument panel pad cover at defroster outlet.
	Blower motor not connected	1. Connect wire; check ground.
	Inoperative blower motor	1. Check heater fuse and wiring. Replace motor if necessary.
	Series blower motor operates whenever Ignition switch is ON or in RUN	1. Check connectors, switch, and wiring.
	Inoperative blower motor switch.	1. Replace switch if necessary.
4. Insufficient air circulation	Blown fuse	1. Replace fuse.
	Open circuit	1. Repair circuit between ignition switch, blower switch, and blower motor.
	Inoperative blower motor switch	1. Replace faulty switch.
	Shorted or open blower resistor	1. Check blower motor resistor.
	Inoperative motor	1. Replace motor.

The causes and correction for some miscellaneous problems that may be encountered are:

CAUSE	CORRECTION
Blown fuses caused by short in electrical system	1. Locate and correct short.
Front floor mat wet under heater caused by improperly sealed windshield or leaking heater core	1. Reseal windshield. 2. Repair (if possible) or replace heater core. 3. Check for proper seal to dash and for leak at hose connection on heater core. 4. Hose leaking into the heater case is often misdiagnosed as leaking core.
Heater gurgle or whine	1. Check engine coolant level in radiator; check for obstruction in core and/or hoses.

Refer to the appropriate manufacturer's service manual for procedure to follow before performing corrections listed above; design differences result in a variety of procedural differences.

Problem Diagnosis and Correction Chart

Heating and ventilating system problems can be grouped into several basic areas of malfunction as follows on non-air-conditioned vehicles.

1. Insufficient heat
2. Too much heat
3. Inadequate defrost
4. Insufficient air circulation.

PART 3   AIR CONDITIONING

The tremendous popularity of automotive air conditioning has created a relatively large service market. When air conditioning is mentioned, the first thought that comes to mind is cool, refreshing air. Actually, the automotive air-conditioning system not only cools the air but also cleans, dehumidifies, and circulates it for the health and comfort of the passengers. It does this by working in conjunction with the heating and ventilating systems described earlier.

Refrigeration Principles

The principle of *refrigeration* is the principle of removal of heat. Cold is the absence of heat. There is always some heat in everything, even if it is cold. The complete absence of heat is at approximately $-273°C$ ($-523.4°F$).

The temperature of the car's interior rises to an uncomfortable level owing to a number of factors, as shown in Figure 40-7. The air-conditioning system removes this heat by providing a substance (refrigerant) that is recirculated from the car's interior (the evaporator) to the car's exterior (the condenser). The refrigerant absorbs heat while it is in the evaporator and dispells it while in the condenser.

Intensity of Heat

The *intensity* of heat is measured by a thermometer. The intensity of heat is the degree of heat you are able to feel. This is called *sensible* heat. The higher the temperature, the hotter it feels.

Humidity

The effect of *humidity* on the intensity of heat is that the higher the relative humidity the more uncomfortable you feel. For example, a person should feel comfortable at a 75°F (23.89°C) temperature and a 40 percent relative humidity level, but would feel uncomfortably hot at the same temperature with the relative humidity at 95 percent. The reason is that the air is almost saturated with moisture, and the body cannot dispose of perspiration nearly as fast. The heat of the body therefore will not be removed as quickly. The process of dehumidifying is

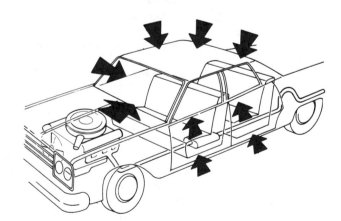

FIGURE 40-7. When vehicle interior temperatures rise above approximately 22°C or 72°F passengers become uncomfortable. This heat comes from several sources, such as the sun, underhood engine heat, exhaust heat including catalytic converters, heat from other vehicles in heavy slow-moving traffic, and heat from road surfaces and passengers in the vehicle. (*Courtesy of Ford Motor Co. of Canada Ltd.*)

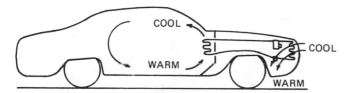

FIGURE 40-8. Heat from the car's interior is transferred to the evaporator of the AC system. Heat absorbed by the evaporator is transferred to the condenser at the front of the car by the refrigerant. The refrigerant in the condenser is cooled by outside air and then returned to the evaporator. As soon as cooling is required, this process goes on continuously.

therefore an essential function of the automotive air conditioner along with the removal of heat and impurities.

Quantity of Heat

The amount or quantity of heat removed from the car interior is measured in British thermal units (Btu or joules). One Btu (1055 joules) is the amount of heat required to change the temperature of 1 pound (0.4536 kg) of liquid water 1°F (0.55°C). This is the average amount required throughout the 32° to 212°F (0° to 100°C) range of liquid water. The amount required varies somewhat with water temperature. One Btu (1055 joules) is also equal to 778 pound feet of mechanical energy or 252 calories.

The capacity of an automotive air conditioner is stated in Btu per hour. The average capacity ranges from 12,000 to 24,000 Btu per hour.

Transfer of Heat

Heat always passes from a warm substance to a cold substance. To change the temperature of 1 pound (0.4536 kg) of water at 32°F (0°C) to 212°F (100°C) at sea level requires 180 Btu of heat. To change that 1 pound (0.4536 kg) of 212°F (100°C) liquid to vapor requires the addition of another 970 Btu of heat. However, the temperature of the vapor (before dispersal) is still at 212°F (100°C). The vaporization process has the ability to absorb heat without a change in the intensity (temperature) of the heat. This added heat is call *latent* heat. Latent heat is to be distinguished from sensible heat, which can be felt and measured with a thermometer. Latent heat is not sensible and cannot be felt. This is called the *latent heat of vaporization.*

To change the state of 1 pound of water vapor at 212°F back to a liquid state requires the removal of 970 Btu of heat. This leaves the liquid water at 212°F in spite of the removal of 970 Btu of heat. This is called the *latent heat of condensation.*

A similar process takes place with the refriger-

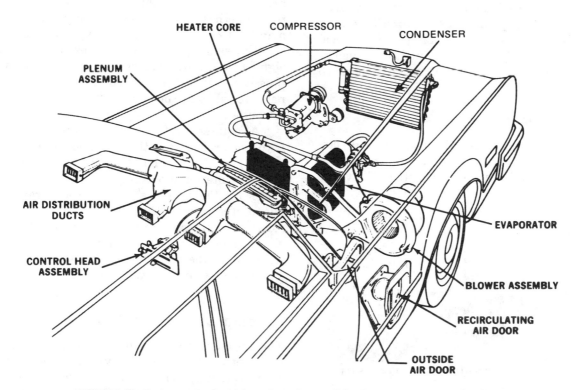

FIGURE 40-9. Layout of automotive air-conditioning components in the vehicle. *(Courtesy of Ford Motor Co. of Canada Ltd.)*

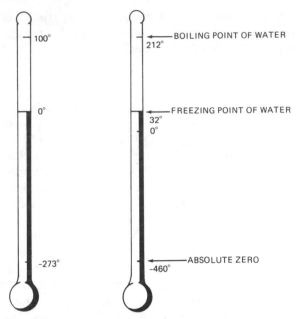

FIGURE 40-10. The intensity of heat is measured with a thermometer. This diagram shows the comparison between Celsius and Fahrenheit temperatures.

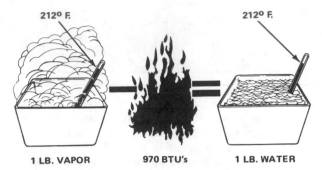

FIGURE 40-12. Latent heat of condensation. A similar process takes place with the refrigerant in the condenser of the automotive AC system. *(Courtesy of Ford Motor Co. of Canada Ltd.)*

ant (R12) Freon in the automotive air-conditioning (AC) system. However, R12 has a vaporization (boiling) point of −21.7°F at sea level. It can be said that fluids give off heat when changed from a vapor to a liquid and absorb heat when changed to a vapor (Figure 40-13). Refrigerant R12 requires 79 Btu of latent heat of condensation to change it from a vapor to a liquid, and 79 Btu of latent heat of vaporization to change one pound of R12 from a liquid to a vapor.

Super-Heated Vapor

It has been found that, when the evaporator is cooling at maximum capacity, the last refrigerant vaporizes just before the evaporator outlet. The vapor

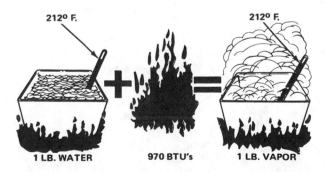

FIGURE 40-11. Hidden (latent) heat of vaporization. Basically, this is what happens to the refrigerant in the evaporator. *(Courtesy of Ford Motor Co. of Canada Ltd.)*

absorbs a small amount more heat and leaves the evaporator superheated 10 degrees.

The expansion valve is designed to compare the temperature and pressure at the evaporator outlet and meter just enough refrigerant to maintain 10 degrees superheat.

If the evaporator begins to starve, the gas is overheated with respect to its pressure, and the expansion valve increases flow. If the evaporator starts to flood, there is some refrigerant liquid at the outlet, and the vapor remains in the saturated state. Thus, the temperature is low with respect to the pressure, and the expansion valve decreases flow.

This action is the basis of the temperature-pressure test of expansion valve operation. Incorrect superheat indicates that the expansion valve may be flooding or starving the evaporator.

The expansion valve receives its temperature signals from a thermal bulb or tube; it receives its pressure signals from the equalizer tube. Both signals are taken at the suction line near the evaporator outlet.

A requirement for an automotive air conditioner is to use a refrigerant that has a low boiling (vaporization) point. This enables it to absorb heat from the car's interior at a lower refrigerant temperature. Lowering the pressure on the refrigerant in the evaporator assists the vaporization process, and raising the pressure in the condensor helps change the refrigerant back to a liquid. R12 will not react with any of the materials in the AC system and is compatible with the AC lubricant.

Automotive Air Conditioning

The automotive air-conditioning system consists of three separate interrelated systems. They are (1) the refrigeration system, (2) the air circulation system, and (3) the control system. Control systems can be either manual temperature control, automatic temperature control or semi-automatic control.

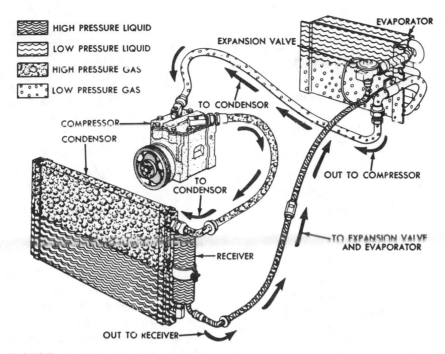

FIGURE 40-13. Lowering pressure in the evaporator helps vaporize the refrigerant, which absorbs heat (latent heat of vaporization). Raising pressure in the condenser helps the process of condensation, which releases heat (latent heat of condensation). *(Courtesy of Ford Motor Co. of Canada Ltd.)*

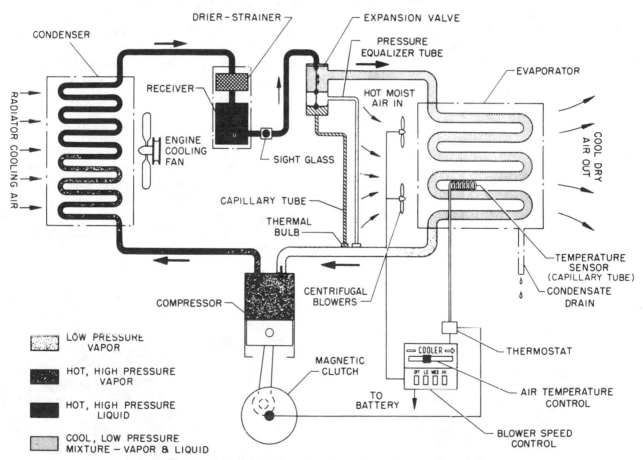

FIGURE 40-14. The AC system transfers heat from inside the vehicle to the atmosphere outside the vehicle. In this process the air in the vehicle is cooled and dehumidified (dried). The blower fans circulate the air over the evaporator and the car's interior. The entire system includes a refrigeration system, an air circulation and distribution system, and a control system.

PART 4   REFRIGERATION SYSTEM

The refrigeration system includes the compressor, condenser, evaporator, receiver-dryer, and connecting lines, as well as one or more of the following depending on system design: expansion valve, orifice tube, ST (Suction Throttling) valve, POA (Positive Operating Absolute) valve, EPR (Evaporator Pressure Regulator) valve, thermal sensor, cycling compressor clutch, and high pressure cut-off switch.

Compressor

The compressor separates the low-pressure side from the high-pressure side of the system. The compressor pumps the refrigerant through the refrigeration system. It draws the refrigerant vapor from the evaporator, compresses it and discharges it to the condenser.

There are several types of compressors, all serving the same purpose. Some of these are the axial six-cylinder reciprocating, two-cylinder reciprocating V type, two-cylinder in-line type, and the four- or five-cylinder radial type.

The compressor has a reservoir or sump that must contain the correct amount of the proper lubricant. One-way valves control the direction of refrigerant flow. Compressors are belt driven from the engine crankshaft. The compressor drive includes an electromagnetic clutch to engage and disengage the compressor.

Condenser

The condenser consists of a long tube curved back and forth to fit in front of the car's radiator or on the roof of some light trucks and recreational vehi-

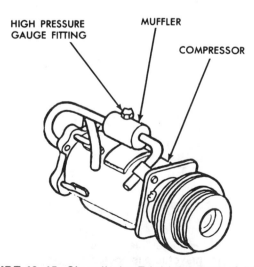

FIGURE 40–15. Six-cylinder Frigidaire type of AC compressor. *(Courtesy of General Motors Corporation)*

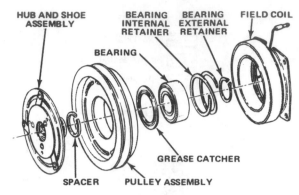

FIGURE 40–16. Exploded view of the electromagnetic compressor drive clutch. *(Courtesy of Ford Motor Co. of Canada Ltd.)*

cles. Fins attached to the tubes aid in the dissipation of heat from the high-pressure refrigerant in the condenser. Air flowing across the fins absorbs the latent heat of condensation from the conversion of the high pressure vapors to a liquid and dissipate it to the atmosphere. Air is caused to flow across the condenser by ram air while driving and by the action of the engine fan or electric fan.

Receiver-Drier

The receiver-drier filters and dries the refrigerant as it passes through the filter pads and dessicant (moisture-absorbing material) contained in the unit. It may include a sight glass to observe whether air is present in the refrigerant during operation.

Accumulator-Dryer Operation

Oil-laden refrigerant from the evaporator enters through the fitting at the top. It flows against an umbrella-shaped diverter cup so that liquid drips down onto the bottom of the housing. Vapor rises and enters the vapor return tube and then flows down the tube to the compressor suction line.

An oil bleed hole near the bottom of the housing allows compressor oil and some liquid refrigerant to

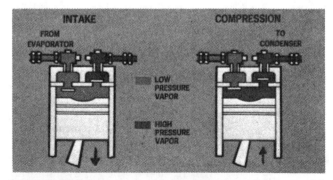

FIGURE 40–17. Valve action and piston travel in the AC compressor during operation. *(Courtesy of Ford Motor Co. of Canada Ltd.)*

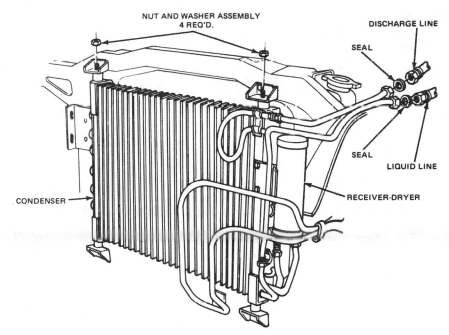

FIGURE 40-18. The AC condenser is normally mounted as above just in front of the cooling system radiator where it is exposed to ambient (outside) air flow. *(Courtesy of Ford Motor Co. of Canada Ltd.)*

flow to the compressor at a controlled rate. A fine mesh filter screen surrounds the bottom of the tube to prevent contamination from plugging the bleed hole.

The suction service access gauge port valve is mounted on the inlet fitting. This valve can be used

for pressure testing and for servicing the refrigerant.

Another Schrader-type valve is installed directly in the accumulator housing to provide a pressure signal and mounting for the clutch cycling pressure switch.

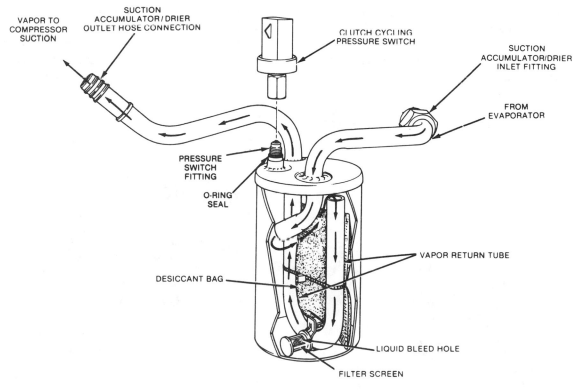

FIGURE 40-19. Accumulator-dryer cross section and connections. *(Courtesy of Ford Motor Co. of Canada Ltd.)*

DEHYDRATOR AND RECEIVER

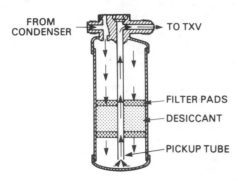

FIGURE 40-20. Receiver-dryer filters and dries refrigerant (TXV, Thermostatic Expansion Valve). *(Courtesy of Ford Motor Co. of Canada Ltd.)*

Expansion Valve

The thermostatic expansion valve is mounted at the inlet side of the evaporator. It controls the pressure in the evaporator by metering the flow of refrigerant to the evaporator. This drops the pressure on the refrigerant in the evaporator. A sensing device called a capillary tube signals the diaphragm in the expansion valve to vary the orifice size. This modulates, meters, and regulates refrigerant flow to the evaporator.

The temperature sensing bulb is located at the evaporator outlet. The bulb and connecting capillary tube are filled with a gas, which may be refrigerant or carbon dioxide. This gas expands and acts on one side of a diaphragm in the expansion valve.

On systems designed with an evaporator freeze

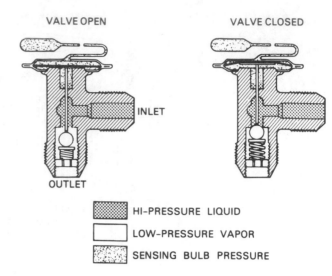

FIGURE 40-21. Expansion valve reduces and regulates system pressure to evaporator to ensure complete vaporization of refrigerant and control the amount of cooling. *(Courtesy of Ford Motor Co. of Canada Ltd.)*

control valve (STV, POA, or EPR), an equalizer line connects the freeze control valve pressure to the expansion valve. Freeze control valve pressure acts on the expansion valve diaphragm in opposition to gas pressure in the capillary tube.

Methods of Evaporator Freeze Control

Moisture from the air of the car's interior condenses on the cooler evaporator surface. If evaporator pressure drops below a certain value (approximately 28 psi [193.06 kp]), this moisture freezes and builds up to restrict air flow through the evaporator coils. This results in little cooling taking place. To prevent this, several methods are in use.

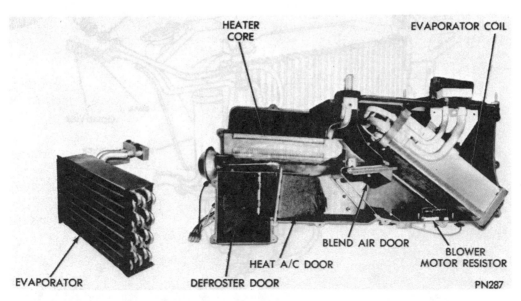

FIGURE 40-22. Tube and fin type of evaporator (left) and its location in housing. *(Courtesy of Chrysler Corporation)*

EVAPORATOR

- Functions as a "heat exchanger".

- Cools the air stream as it flows through the evaporator housing.

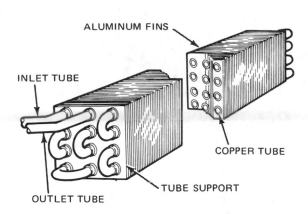

ALUMINUM FINS

INLET TUBE

COPPER TUBE

TUBE SUPPORT

OUTLET TUBE

1 Evaporator is constructed of several "runs" of tubing with cooling fins attached.

(Used with Thermostatic De-Icing Switch)

2 Or in latest designs of aluminum stampings brazed together.

(Used with STV)

3 As air passes through the evaporator, it is cooled by the fins, which are cooled by refrigerant evaporating inside the coils.

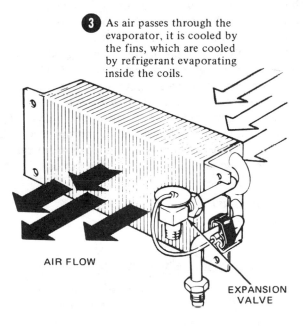

AIR FLOW

EXPANSION VALVE

NOTE:

Removing moisture (humidity) from the air uses up cooling capacity. On humid days, best cooling is achieved by operating the system for "recirculating" cooling.

4 As the air is cooled, moisture condenses on the evaporator core . . .

5 Drips off into a drain pan under the core.

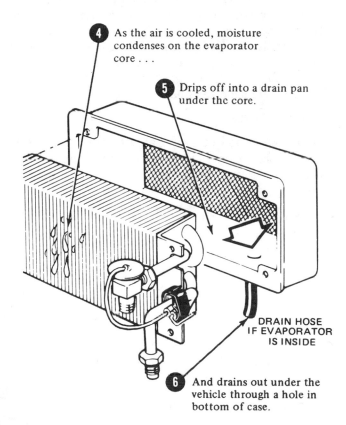

DRAIN HOSE IF EVAPORATOR IS INSIDE

6 And drains out under the vehicle through a hole in bottom of case.

FIGURE 40-23. Typical evaporator types (top) and operation (bottom). *(Courtesy of Ford Motor Co. of Canada Ltd.)*

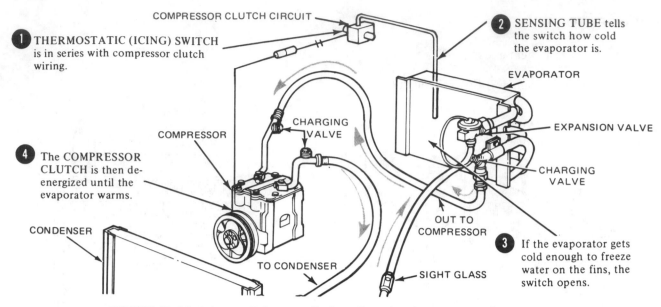

FIGURE 40-24. Icing switch controlled cycling clutch evaporator freeze protection system. *(Courtesy of Ford Motor Co. of Canada Ltd.)*

Cycling Compressor Clutch

The electromagnetic compressor clutch is controlled by a thermostatic switch. This switch senses evaporator pressure or temperature. When evaporator temperature nears the freezing point, the compressor clutch is disengaged, halting the refrigerant cycle. As the temperature rises to a predetermined value, the switch energizes the compressor clutch and refrigeration resumes.

Control Valves

Another method of evaporator freeze control is to control the refrigerant flow from the evaporator to the compressor. This controls the pressure (and therefore evaporator temperature) of the refrigerant in the evaporator. This is done by installing a valve in the line from the evaporator to the compressor. Several types of valves are used. The pilot (or positive) operated absolute (POA) valve, the evaporator pressure regulator (EPR), and the suction throttling valve (STV) are some of these. A signal from the evaporator refrigerant pressure controls the valve.

As pressure in the evaporator drops, the control valve restricts refrigerant flow to the compressor. As evaporator pressure increases, the valve allows a greater flow of refrigerant to the compressor. This controls evaporator pressure and therefore temperature to prevent freeze up. Another function of this

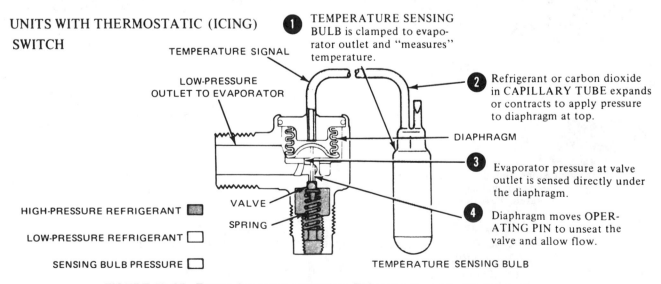

FIGURE 40-25. Expansion valve operation. This type is used with the system in Figure 40-24. *(Courtesy of Ford Motor Co. of Canada Ltd.)*

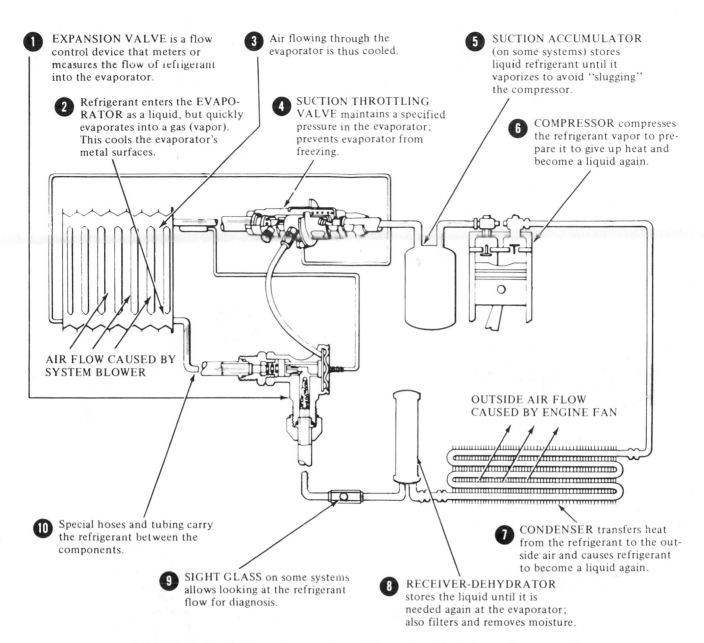

1. EXPANSION VALVE is a flow control device that meters or measures the flow of refrigerant into the evaporator.

2. Refrigerant enters the EVAPORATOR as a liquid, but quickly evaporates into a gas (vapor). This cools the evaporator's metal surfaces.

3. Air flowing through the evaporator is thus cooled.

4. SUCTION THROTTLING VALVE maintains a specified pressure in the evaporator; prevents evaporator from freezing.

5. SUCTION ACCUMULATOR (on some systems) stores liquid refrigerant until it vaporizes to avoid "slugging" the compressor.

6. COMPRESSOR compresses the refrigerant vapor to prepare it to give up heat and become a liquid again.

AIR FLOW CAUSED BY SYSTEM BLOWER

OUTSIDE AIR FLOW CAUSED BY ENGINE FAN

10. Special hoses and tubing carry the refrigerant between the components.

7. CONDENSER transfers heat from the refrigerant to the outside air and causes refrigerant to become a liquid again.

9. SIGHT GLASS on some systems allows looking at the refrigerant flow for diagnosis.

8. RECEIVER-DEHYDRATOR stores the liquid until it is needed again at the evaporator; also filters and removes moisture.

FIGURE 40-26. Refrigeration system with suction throttling valve type of evaporator freeze protection. *(Courtesy of Ford Motor Co. of Canada Ltd.)*

valve is to assist in temperature control in automatic temperature control AC systems.

Evaporator

The evaporator is similar in construction to the condenser and is located in the AC housing, either in the passenger compartment or just outside the fire wall under the hood. Evaporator pressure and temperature are controlled as outlined earlier (approximately 28 psi [193.06 kpa]) (30°F −1°C). Air is forced to flow over the evaporator coils, which remove the latent heat of vaporization, moisture, and impurities from the air. Condensed moisture with the impurities from the evaporator drip into a tray and are drained to the outside of the vehicle.

Summary of Evaporator Control Systems

1. Expansion valve actuated by a thermal bulb and capillary tube. The thermal bulb is located at the evaporator outlet. Expanding gas in the thermal bulb and capillary tube acts on one side of the diaphragm in the expansion valve to regulate pressure into the evaporator outlet temperature and controls the cycling clutch compressor for freeze control. Figure 40-24 and 40-25.

2. Expansion valve actuated by a thermal bulb and capillary tube (as in 1 above). An evaporator outlet control valve (STV, POA, or EPR valve) con-

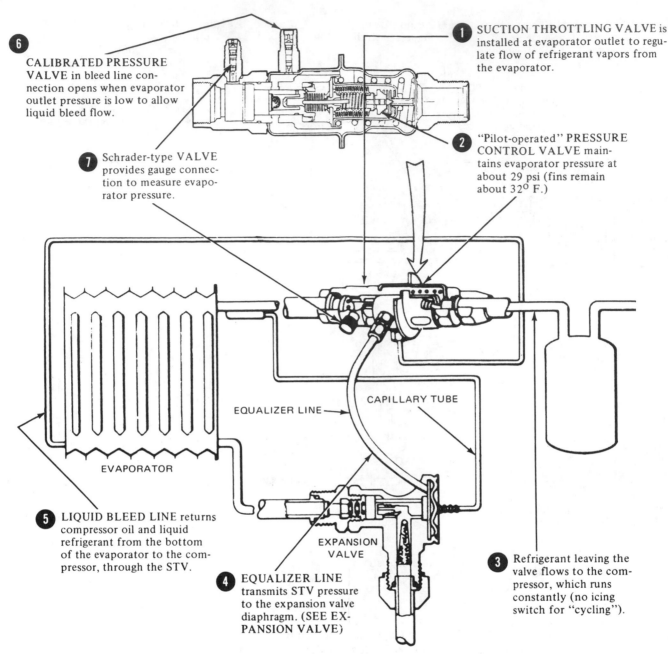

6 CALIBRATED PRESSURE VALVE in bleed line connection opens when evaporator outlet pressure is low to allow liquid bleed flow.

1 SUCTION THROTTLING VALVE is installed at evaporator outlet to regulate flow of refrigerant vapors from the evaporator.

7 Schrader-type VALVE provides gauge connection to measure evaporator pressure.

2 "Pilot-operated" PRESSURE CONTROL VALVE maintains evaporator pressure at about 29 psi (fins remain about 32° F.)

EQUALIZER LINE

CAPILLARY TUBE

EVAPORATOR

5 LIQUID BLEED LINE returns compressor oil and liquid refrigerant from the bottom of the evaporator to the compressor, through the STV.

EXPANSION VALVE

4 EQUALIZER LINE transmits STV pressure to the expansion valve diaphragm. (SEE EXPANSION VALVE)

3 Refrigerant leaving the valve flows to the compressor, which runs constantly (no icing switch for "cycling").

FIGURE 40-27. Refrigeration system with STV and POA valve. *(Courtesy of Ford Motor Co. of Canada Ltd.)*

trols minimum evaporator pressure (and, therefore, evaporator temperature). STV outlet pressure is routed to the expansion valve and acts on the opposite side of the diaphragm from capillary tube pressure. This provides evaporator freeze control. Figure 40-26 to 40-28.

3. Orifice tube controls pressure and expansion of refrigerant into evaporator. A pressure sensitive switch in the evaporator outlet operates the cycling clutch on the compressor for evaporator freeze control. Figure 40-29 and 40-30.

Lines and Fittings

High-pressure lines and fittings connect the various components to each other to complete the refrigerant flow circuit. Both flexible and rigid lines are used with special fittings that provide leakproof connections when properly tightened.

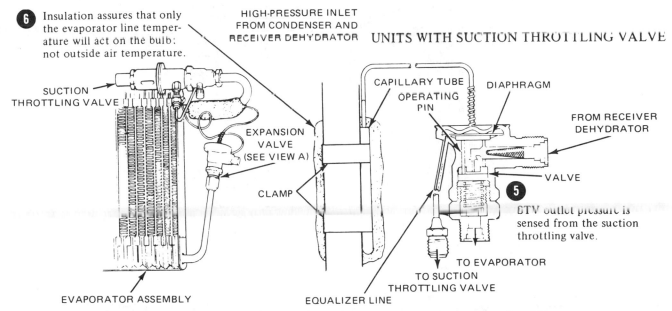

6 Insulation assures that only the evaporator line temperature will act on the bulb; not outside air temperature.

HIGH-PRESSURE INLET FROM CONDENSER AND RECEIVER DEHYDRATOR

UNITS WITH SUCTION THROTTLING VALVE

SUCTION THROTTLING VALVE

CAPILLARY TUBE

OPERATING PIN

DIAPHRAGM

FROM RECEIVER DEHYDRATOR

EXPANSION VALVE (SEE VIEW A)

VALVE

CLAMP

5 STV outlet pressure is sensed from the suction throttling valve.

TO EVAPORATOR

TO SUCTION THROTTLING VALVE

EVAPORATOR ASSEMBLY

EQUALIZER LINE

FIGURE 40-28. Details of expansion valve on system using suction throttling valve. *(Courtesy of Ford Motor Co. of Canada Ltd.)*

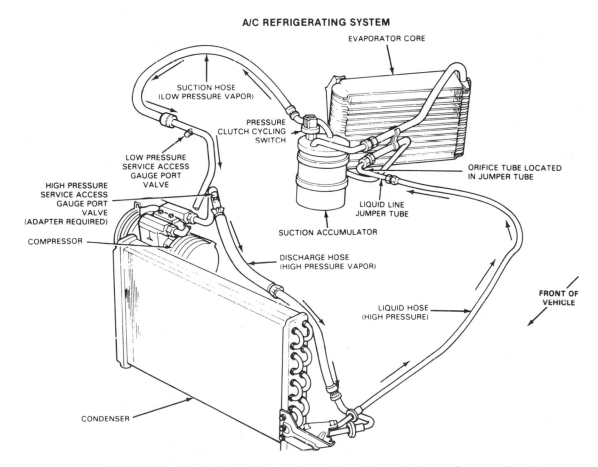

A/C REFRIGERATING SYSTEM

EVAPORATOR CORE

SUCTION HOSE (LOW PRESSURE VAPOR)

PRESSURE CLUTCH CYCLING SWITCH

ORIFICE TUBE LOCATED IN JUMPER TUBE

LOW PRESSURE SERVICE ACCESS GAUGE PORT VALVE

LIQUID LINE JUMPER TUBE

HIGH PRESSURE SERVICE ACCESS GAUGE PORT VALVE (ADAPTER REQUIRED)

SUCTION ACCUMULATOR

COMPRESSOR

DISCHARGE HOSE (HIGH PRESSURE VAPOR)

FRONT OF VEHICLE

LIQUID HOSE (HIGH PRESSURE)

CONDENSER

FIGURE 40-29. Refrigeration system with orifice tube type of expansion control and cycling clutch freeze control. *(Courtesy of Ford Motor Co. of Canada Ltd.)*

965

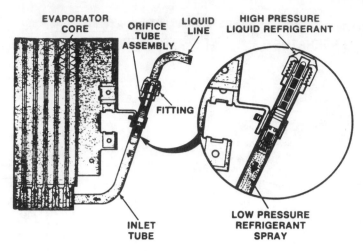

FIGURE 40-30. Details of orifice tube type of evaporator expansion control. *(Courtesy of Ford Motor Co. of Canada Ltd.)*

PART 5   CONTROL SYSTEMS

Air Distribution and Circulation System

A blower or blowers force outside air or air from the car interior to pass through the evaporator coils for cleaning, cooling, and dehumidifying. This air is then distributed by a housing and duct system including directionally controlled louvred outlets to various levels and areas in the vehicle. Dashboard and floorboard outlets are used for good flow distribution. Blower fans can be operated at various speeds either by a manually operated switch or automatic temperature controls.

An electrical control system and a vacuum control system are used to control the air flow system.

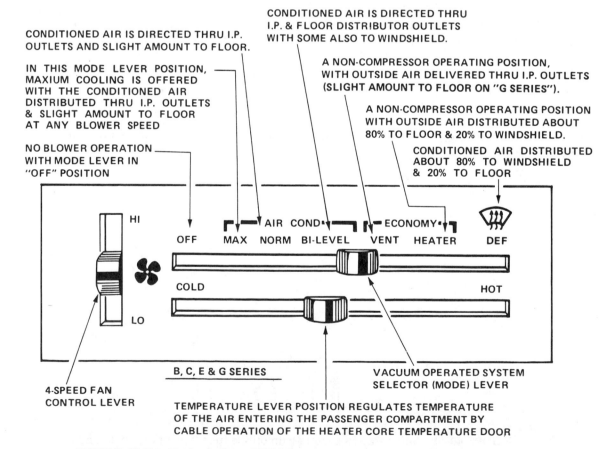

FIGURE 40-31. Typical air-conditioning controls. *(Courtesy of General Motors Corporation)*

REFRIGERANT — 12
PRESSURE — TEMPERATURE
RELATIONSHIP

The table below indicates the pressure of Refrigerant — 12 at various temperatures. For instance, a drum of Refrigerant at a temperature of 80°F (26.6°C) will have a pressure of 84.1 PSI (579.9 kPa). If it is heated to 125°F (51.6°C), the pressure will increase to 167.5 PSI (1154.9 kPa). It also can be used conversely to determine the temperature at which Refrigerant — 12 boils under various pressures. For example, at a pressure of 30.1 PSI (207.5 kPa), Refrigerant — 12 boils at 32°F (0°C).

(°F)(°C)		(PSIG)(kPa)		(°F)(°C)		(PSIG)(kPa)	
−21.7	−29.8C	0(ATMOSPHERIC PRESSURE)	0(kPa)	55	12.7C	52.0	358.5
				60	15.5C	57.7	397.8
−20	−28.8C	2.4	16.5	65	18.3C	63.7	439.2
−10	−23.3C	4.5	31.0	70	21.1C	70.1	482.7
−5	−20.5C	6.8	46.9	75	23.8C	76.9	530.2
0	−17.7C	9.2	63.4	80	26.6C	84.1	579.9
5	−15.0C	11.8	81.4	85	29.4C	91.7	632.3
10	−12.2C	14.7	101.4	90	32.2C	99.6	686.7
15	−9.4C	17.7	122.0	95	35.0C	108.1	745.3
20	−6.6C	21.1	145.5	100	37.7C	116.9	806.0
25	−3.8C	24.6	169.6	105	40.5C	126.2	870.2
30	−1.1C	28.5	196.5	110	43.3C	136.0	937.1
32	0C	30.1	207.5	115	46.1C	146.5	1010.1
35	1.6C	32.6	224.8	120	48.8C	157.1	1083.2
40	4.4C	37.0	255.1	125	51.6C	167.5	1154.9
45	7.2C	41.7	287.5	130	54.4C	179.0	1234.2
50	10.0C	46.7	322.0	140	60.0C	204.5	1410.0

FIGURE 40-32. The effects of pressure and temperature on the boiling (vaporization) point of R12 refrigerant. *(Courtesy of General Motors Corporation)*

The vacuum system operates a number of doors in the air flow system to control direction of air flow and mixing of air. Manual, automatic and semi-automatic temperature control systems are used.

Air flow may be directed to the defroster outlets, the instrument panel outlets and the floor outlets.

Blend Air Method of Temperature Control

The temperature control device controls the position of the temperature blend door.

The temperature control is connected by cable to the temperature blend door. When the lever is set at *cool*, the door is positioned so that it shuts off the passage of air through the heater core and bypasses it directly to the plenum chamber, unheated. When the lever is moved toward the *warm* setting, the control cable moves the temperature blend door from minimum to full heat position to modulate the air flow through and/or around the heater core. At full *warm* position, the bypass is shut off and all air passes through the heater core to provide maximum heat.

On some designs, the temperature control also controls a water valve in the coolant line to the heater core.

On automatic temperature control systems, the blend air door is controlled automatically to maintain the desired temperature.

Thermostatic Method of Temperature Control

The temperature control lever on the instrument panel operates a thermostatic switch for temperature selection.

The thermostatic switch controls the evaporator temperature by controlling the compressor magnetic clutch. When the points in the switch are closed, the compressor clutch is energized and the

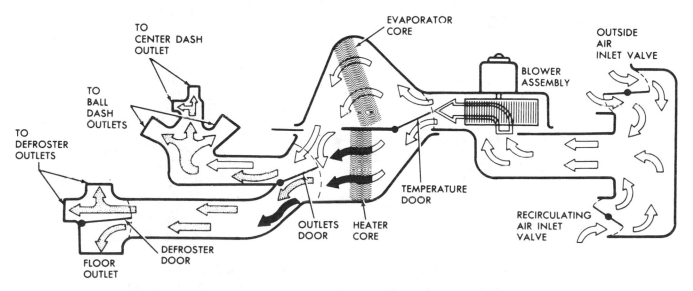

FIGURE 40-33. Typical air flow system for heating and air-conditioning systems. *(Courtesy of General Motors Corporation)*

compressor operates; with the points open, the compressor stops.

The position of the temperature selector lever determines the switch setting. If the selector is set at *off*, the contact points are open. In the cooling range, the switch can be set to regulate the evaporator temperature between 30° and 60°F (−1° and 15.6°C).

Opening and closing of the points is controlled by a power element attached to the evaporator fins. The element is gas filled—a temperature rise causes pressure to increase, whereas a temperature drop causes pressure to decrease. When the control is first placed in the cooling range, the points close and start the compressor. When the evaporator temperature reaches the switch setting, the points open and stop the compressor. The control works on a 6° F (3°C) differential. This means the evaporator must warm up that much before the points close again to start the compressor.

Of course, the control could be designed to let the evaporator cool far below 30 degrees because the refrigerant will boil all the way down to −21.7°F (−29.8°C). But if the evaporator gets too cold, water

that is condensed out of the air freezes and blocks air flow. So the minimum temperature of the evaporator is 30°F (−1°C) at 28.5 psi (196.5 kPa).

This system is used in many non-factory air-conditioning systems, as well as older automotive air conditioning units.

PART 6   AIR-CONDITIONING DIAGNOSIS AND SERVICE PROCEDURE

General Precautions

The following general precautions should be observed before and during AC system service.

- Store refrigerant where its temperature will not rise above 125°F (51.67°C).

- Avoid skin contact with refrigerant; instant freezing results from contact.

- AC system is highly pressurized. Follow recommended procedure to depressurize and disconnect components.

- Always wear eye protection.

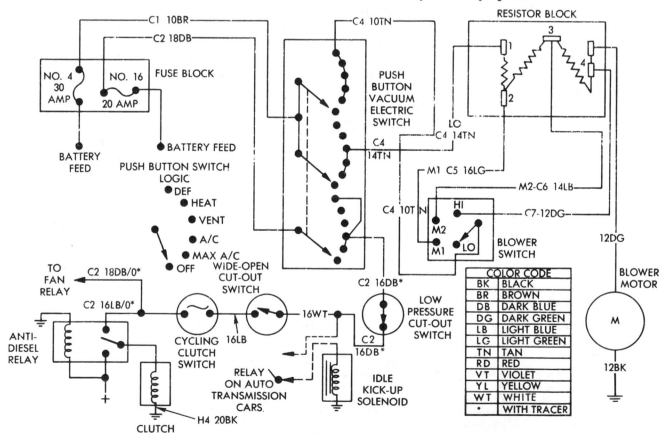

FIGURE 40-34. Wiring diagram for air-conditioning system with cycling clutch switch, idle speed kick-up solenoid, and wide-open throttle compressor cut out switch. Some systems also have a compressor cut out switch for high pressure power steering conditions. *(Courtesy of Chrysler Corporation)*

• Open flame in contact with refrigerant creates poisonous phosgene gas.

• Disconnect battery when servicing electrical components.

• Connect exhaust system to vent fumes outside when running engine to performance test AC system.

Testing Procedure

Visual Testing

Before any performance testing is conducted, the system should first undergo a thorough visual inspection. Check for the following:

1. Belt drives are tightened within specifications. They should not be worn or frayed and should line up with other pulleys. A belt-tension gauge, of which several are available, eliminates guesswork in tightening the compressor belt.

2. Compressor brackets and braces tight and not cracked or broken.

3. Hoses and lines worn or leaking.

4. The compressor seal leaking. This is indicated by an oily streak across the underside of the engine compartment hood.

5. The condenser is clean and properly mounted. Bugs and dirt clog the condenser and impair air movement through the fins, interfering with proper condensing action. Bug screens in front of the condenser will prevent bugs from clogging the condenser but at the same time will prevent full air passage to the condenser coils. Any interference with full air flow over the condenser coils must be corrected to allow proper condensing action of the system.

6. All ducts, louvers, and air-distribution mechanisms are operating smoothly without binding and sticking.

7. The evaporator is free from accumulations of dust.

8. Blower motor is operating correctly. Operate blower motor at all speeds. If the blower operates in some speed settings, but not others, check the blower resistor for a short circuit.

9. Air filters are clean.

10. There are visual leaks. An oily spot usually indicates a refrigerant leak as oil is carried out with the escaping refrigerant.

Procedure for Connecting the Manifold Gauge Set

If the system has hand shutoff valves, the following procedure should be followed:

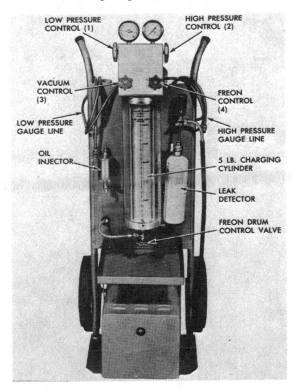

FIGURE 40-35. Portable air-conditioning system testing station. *(Courtesy of General Motors Corporation)*

1. Put on safety glasses.

2. Protect car finish by using fender covers.

3. Remove protective caps from service valves.

4. Slowly remove acorn caps from service valves, ensuring that no refrigerant is leaking past the service valve.

5. Close both manifold gauge valves.

6. Connect low side manifold hose (blue) to the intake (suction) port of the compressor.

7. Connect high-pressure gauge to the port on the discharge side of the compressor.

8. Ensure that manifold valves are closed before proceeding.

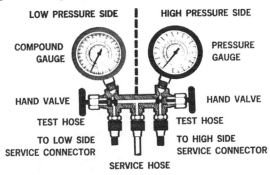

FIGURE 40-36. Two-gauge-type test connections. *(Courtesy of Ford Motor Co. of Canada Ltd.)*

PROBLEM	CAUSE	CORRECTION
System produces no cooling.	*Electrical* 1. Blown fuse. 2. Broken or disconnected electrical wire. 3. Broken or disconnected ground wire. 4. Clutch coil or solenoid burned out or disconnected. 5. Electrical switch contacts in thermostat burned excessively, or sensing element defective. 6. Blower motor disconnected or burned out.	1. Replace fuse. 2. Check all terminals for loose connections; check wiring for hidden breaks. 3. Check ground wire to see if loose, broken, or disconnected. 4. Check current flow to clutch or solenoid; replace if inoperative. 5. Replace thermostat. 6. Check current flow to blower motor; repair or replace if inoperative.
	Mechanical 1. Loose or broken drive belt. 2. Compressor partially or completely frozen. 3. Compressor reed valves inoperative. 4. Expansion valve stuck in open position.	1. Replace drive belts and/or tighten to specifications. 2. Remove compressor for service or replacement. 3. Service or replace compressor reed valves. 4. Replace expansion valve.
	Refrigeration 1. Broken refrigerant line. 2. Fusible plug blown (does not apply to all units). 3. Leak in system. 4. Compressor shaft seal leaking. 5. Clogged screen or screens in receiver dehydrator or expansion valve; plugged hose or coil. *Note:* After completing repairs of any above, system *must* have dehydrator replaced, purged, evacuated, and charged.	1. Examine all lines for evidence of breakage by external stress or rubbing wear. 2. Examine fusible plug; if blown, replace with correct plug. 3. Evacuate system, apply static charge, leak test system, and repair leak as necessary. 4. Replace compressor shaft seal. 5. Repair as necessary.
System will not produce sufficient cooling.	*Electrical* 1. Blower motor sluggish in operation.	1. Remove blower motor for service or replacement.
	Mechanical 1. Compressor clutch slipping. 2. Obstructed blower discharge passage. 3. Clogged air intake filter. 4. Outside air vents open. 5. Insufficient air circulation over condenser coils; fins clogged with dirt or bugs. 6. Evaporator clogged. 7. Evaporator pressure regulator, hot gas bypass valve, suction throttling valve, or selectrol defective or improperly adjusted.	1. Remove clutch assembly for service or replacement. 2. Examine entire discharge passage for kinks, waddings, or failure to open passage. Correct as necessary. 3. Remove air filter screens and service or replace, whichever is necessary. 4. Close air vents (adjust controls if necessary). *Note:* Some owners must be instructed on keeping air vents closed when air-conditioning unit is in operation. 5. Clean engine radiator and condenser. 6. Loosen, pull down, and clean with compressed air. Use cleaning solvent to remove cigarette tars. *Caution:* Protect floor mats. 7. Repair or adjust as necessary.
	Refrigeration 1. Insufficient refrigerant in system. 2. Clogged screen in expansion valve. 3. Expansion valve thermal bulb has lost charge. 4. Clogged screen in receiver. 5. Excessive moisture in system. 6. Air in system.	1. Test for leaks. Repair as necessary. Recharge system until bubbles disappear and gauge readings stabilize to specifications. 2. Purge system, remove screen, clean and replace, or replace expansion valve. 3. Purge system; replace expansion valve. 4. Purge system; replace receiver. 5. Evacuate and recharge system. 6. Purge, replace filter-drier, evacuate, and charge system with new refrigerant.

System cools intermittently	Electrical	
	1. Defective circuit breaker, blower switch, or blower motor.	1. Remove defective part for service or replacement.
	2. Partial open, improper ground, or loose connection in compressor clutch coil or solenoid.	2. Check connections or remove clutch coil or solenoid for service or replacement.
	Mechanical	
	1. Compressor clutch slipping.	1. Slippage will require that clutch be removed for service; may require readjustment for proper spacing.
	Refrigeration	
	1. Unit icing up may be caused by excessive moisture in system, incorrect superheat adjustment in expansion valve.	1. Replace expansion valve if excess moisture present. Purge, evacuate, recharge.
	2. Stuck suction throttle valve.	2. Purge and evacuate and replace dehydrator to remove moisture. Replace STV valve.
Excessively noisy system	**Electrical**	
	1. Defective winding or improper connection in compressor clutch coil or solenoid.	1. Replace or repair as necessary.
	Mechanical	
	1. Loose or excessively worn drive belts.	1. Tighten or replace as required.
	2. Noisy clutch.	2. Remove clutch for service or replacement as necessary.
	3. Compressor noisy.	3. Check mountings and repair; remove compressor for service or replacement.
	4. Loose panels on car.	4. Check and tighten all panels; hose hold-down clamps or rubbing or vibrations of hoses or pipes.
	5. Compressor oil level low.	5. If oil level low, determine cause of loss. If correction made, fill with specified oil.
	6. Blower fan noisy; excessive wear in blower motor.	6. Remove blower motor for service or replacement as necessary.
	7. Idler pulley and bearing defective.	7. Replace bearing; inspect idler and pulley as may be worn excessively.
	Refrigeration	
	1. Excessive charge in system.	1. Discharge excess Freon until high-pressure gauge drops within specifications.
	2. Low charge in system.	2. Check system for leaks; charge system.
	3. Excessive moisture in system.	3. Replace dehydrator; purge, evacuate, and charge system.
	4. High-pressure service valve closed.	4. Open valve immediately.

If the system is equipped with *Schrader valves,* the following procedure should be followed.

1. Put on safety glasses.

2. Protect car finish by using fender covers.

3. Slowly remove acorn caps from the low and high side service ports, ensuring that no refrigerant is leaking past a defective Schrader valve.

4. Ensure that the service hoses are equipped with a Schrader valve depressing pin.

5. Close hand shutoff valves.

6. Connect high side and low side hoses to correct service valves: *low side hose (blue) to low side valve and high side hose (red) to high side valve.* Ensure that high side valve is tight.

Purging Hoses

1. Crack low side service valve on the manifold. Wait a few seconds and close.

TEMPERATURE		HEAD PRESSURE		SUCTION PRESSURE			
				(STV or PAO)			
°F.	°C.	psi	kPa	psi	kPa	psi	kPa
60	15.5	120–170	827.4 –1172.1	28–31	193.06–213.745	7–15	48.26–103.42
70	21.1	150–250	1034.25–1723.75	28–31	193.06–213.745	7–15	48.26–103.42
80	26.6	180–275	1241.1 –1896.12	28–31	193.06–213.745	7–15	48.26–103.42
90	32.2	200–310	1379.0 –2137.45	28–31	193.06–213.745	7–15	48.26–103.42
100	37.7	230–330	1585.85–2275.35	28–35	193.06–241.32	7–30	48.26–206.85
110	43.3	270–360	1861.65–2482.2	28–38	193.06–262.01	7–35	48.26–241.32

1. Low suction pressure, head pressure normal.	1. Thermostat defective. 2. Screen in expansion valve clogged. 3. Restriction between receiver and expansion valve. 4. Moisture in system. 5. Expansion valve closed if low-pressure gauge reads a vacuum.
2. High suction pressure, head pressure normal.	1. Improper operation of expansion valve. 2. Sensing element of expansion valve defective or making improper contact.
3. High suction pressure, low head pressure.	1. Compressor defective. 2. Compressor reed valve defective. 3. Compressor head gasket blown. 4. Possible loss of vacuum POA capsule. Bellows or valve piston stuck closed.
4. Excessive head pressure.	1. Excessive charge of refrigerant in system. 2. Condenser air passages clogged. 3. Restriction in condenser, dehydrator, filter, or any high-pressure line. 4. Excessive oil in compressor. 5. Engine overheating.
5. Low head pressure, low evaporator.	1. Refrigerant lost or low. 2. Expansion valve diaphragm discharged.

2. Crack high side service valve on the manifold. Wait a few seconds and close.

3. Air should now be purged from the service hoses.

Testing the System Using Gauges

Now that the gauges are properly connected, the system can be effectively tested.

Approximate Gauge Pressure Readings

For specific pressure readings, refer to manufacturer's manuals.

The above pressures are obtained with the following procedures:

1. Engine speed 2000 rpm.

2. Fan in front of condenser.

3. AC control in MAX cold.

4. Hi blower.

5. Open hood and front doors.

6. Open all AC outlets.

Interpreting Gauge Readings. It is not practical to list low- and high-pressure readings. This is

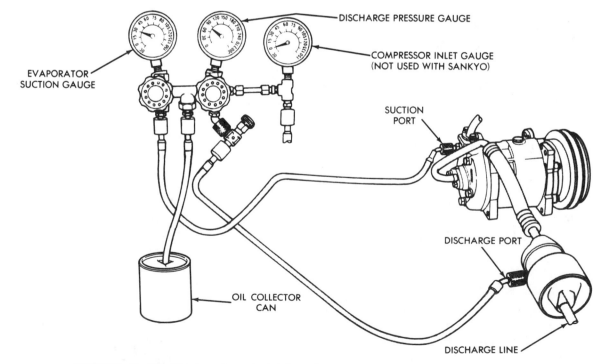

FIGURE 40-37. Discharging the AC system (depressurizing the system). *(Courtesy of Chrysler Corporation)*

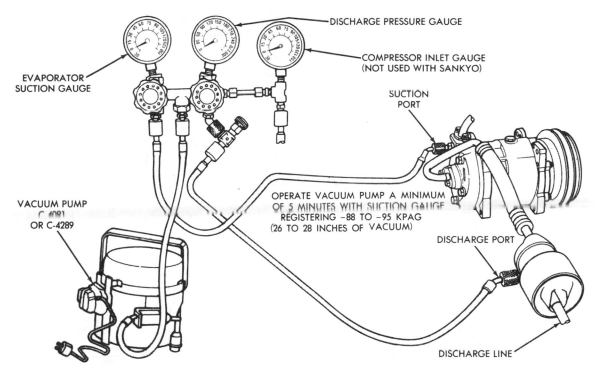

FIGURE 40-38. Evacuating the AC system (removing all refrigerant, air, and moisture with the use of a vacuum pump). The vacuum pump and gauge can also be used to check the system for leaks. *(Courtesy of Chrysler Corporation)*

because the pressures will vary according to ambient temperature, relative humidity, atmospheric pressure, and the components used on the system. For specific performance specifications, see manufacturer's manual.

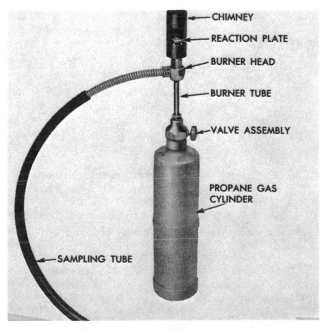

FIGURE 40-39. After the AC system has been charged, it must be tested for leaks. One type of leak detector is shown above. *(Courtesy of Ford Motor Co. of Canada Ltd.)*

PART 7   SELF-CHECK

1. What is the purpose of the automotive air-conditioning system? List three functions.
2. What is the principle of refrigeration, simply stated?
3. What equipment is used to measure the intensity of heat?
4. The quantity of heat is measured in _____.
5. The thermometer is used to measure latent heat. True or false?
6. What type of refrigerant is used in automotive air conditioners?
7. List the six major components of the refrigeration system.
8. State two functions of the compressor.
9. Refrigerant pressure is higher in the evaporator than in the condenser. True or false?
10. List six general precautions that should be followed when servicing air-conditioning systems.

PART 8   TEST QUESTIONS

1. The heating system includes the following major components:

   (a) evaporator, condenser, controls, hoses, blower

973

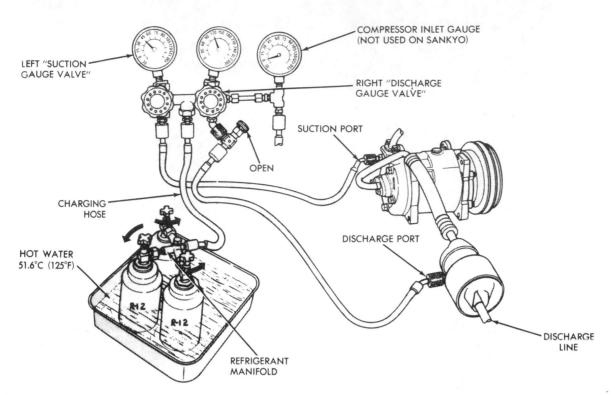

FIGURE 40-40. Charging the AC system (installing the specified amount of refrigerant and pressurizing the system). This must be done according to manufacturer's specifications. Charging the system includes performance testing the system with the gauges attached. *(Courtesy of Chrysler Corporation)*

(b) hoses, heater core, controls, blower

(c) controls, heater core, condenser, hoses, blower

(d) evaporator, heater core, hoses, controls, blower

2. Temperature control in the heating system is achieved by:

(a) mixing cold and hot coolant in the heater core

(b) mixing heated and non-heated air

(c) controlling the condenser

(d) controlling the evaporator

3. Heater control systems may be:

(a) cable operated

(b) vacuum operated

(c) cable and vacuum operated

(d) any of the above

4. The intensity of heat is measured in:

(a) British Thermal Units

(b) degrees Fahrenheit or Celsius

(c) calories

(d) watts

5. The quantity of heat is measured in:

(a) British Thermal Units

(b) degrees

(c) temperature

(d) percentage

6. Heat transfer takes place by:

(a) conduction

(b) convection

(c) radiation

(d) all of the above

7. Latent heat is:

(a) sensible heat

(b) hidden heat

(c) measured with a thermometer

(d) none of the above

8. The air conditioning system is designed to:

(a) cool, clean, dry, and circulate the air

(b) cool, dry, and circulate the air

(c) cool, clean, and circulate the air

(d) cool and circulate the air

9. The refrigerant must be handled with care since it can cause:

(a) dangerous phosgene gas

(b) instant skin freezing

(c) permanent eye damage

(d) all of the above

Appendix

REFERENCE
CHARTS

GM TABLE OF FREQUENTLY USED UNITS (U.S.) **GM**
SI (SYSTEME INTERNATIONAL d'UNITES)

Multiply	by	to get equivalent number of:
LENGTH		
Inch	25.4	millimetres (mm)
Foot	0.304 8	metres (m)
Yard	0.914 4	metres
Mile	1.609	kilometres (km)
AREA		
Inch²	645.2	millimetres² (mm²)
	6.45	centimetres² (cm²)
Foot²	0.092 9	metres² (m²)
Yard²	0.836 1	metres²
VOLUME		
Inch³	16 387.	mm³
	16.387	cm³
	0.016 4	litres (l)
Quart	0.946 4	litres
Gallon	3.785 4	litres
Yard³	0.764 6	metres³ (m³)
MASS		
Pound	0.453 6	kilograms (kg)
Ton	907.18	kilogram
Ton	0.907	tonne (t)
FORCE		
Kilogram (force)	9.807	newtons (N)
Ounce	0.278 0	newtons
Pound	4.448	newtons

Multiply	by	to get equivalent number of:
ACCELERATION		
Foot/sec²	0.304 8	metre/sec² (m/s²)
Inch/sec²	0.025 4	metre/sec²
TORQUE		
Pound-inch	0.112 98	newton-metres (N·m)
Pound-foot	1.355 8	newton-metres
POWER		
Horsepower	0.746	kilowatts (kW)
PRESSURE OR STRESS		
Inches of mercury	3.38	kilopascals (kPa)
Pounds/sq. in.	6.895	kilopascals
ENERGY OR WORK		
BTU	1 055.	joules (J)
Foot-pound	1.355 8	joules
Kilowatt-hour	3 600 000 or 3.6x10⁶	joules (J = W·s)
LIGHT		
Footcandle	10.764	lumens/metre² (lm/m²)
FUEL PERFORMANCE		
Miles/gal	0.425 1	kilometres/litre (km/l)
Gal/mile	2.352 7	litres/kilometre (l/km)
VELOCITY		
Miles/hour	1.609 3	kilometres/hr. (km/h)

TEMPERATURE

Degree Fahrenheit (°F-32) ÷ 1.8 = degree Celsius (°C)

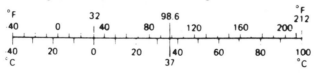

Left Column is units of 10, (0, 10, 20, 30 etc.);
Top Row is in units of one (0, 1, 2, 3, etc).

EXAMPLE: Feet to Inches Conversion Chart

feet	0	1	2	3	4	5	6	7	8	9	feet
	inches	inches	inches	inches	inches	inches	inches	inches	inches	inches	
..		12	24	36	48	60	72	84	96	108	..
10	120	132	144	156	168	180	192	204	216	228	10
20	240	252	264	276	288	300	312	324	336	348	20
30	360	372	384	396	408	420	432	444	456	468	30
40	480	492	504	516	528	540	552	564	576	588	40
50	600	612	624	636	648	660	672	684	696	708	50

12 feet equals 144 inches. Read across from 10 and down from 2.
6 feet equals 72 inches. Read down from 6.

FEET TO METERS

ft	0	1	2	3	4	5	6	7	8	9	ft
	m	m	m	m	m	m	m	m	m	m	
..		0.305	0.610	0.914	1.219	1.524	1.829	2.134	2.438	2.743	..
10	3.048	3.353	3.658	3.962	4.267	4.572	4.877	5.182	5.486	5.791	10
20	6.096	6.401	6.706	7.010	7.315	7.620	7.925	8.230	8.534	8.839	20
30	9.144	9.449	9.754	10.058	10.363	10.668	10.973	11.278	11.582	11.887	30
40	12.192	12.497	12.802	13.106	13.411	13.716	14.021	14.326	14.630	14.935	40
50	15.240	15.545	15.850	16.154	16.459	16.764	17.069	17.374	17.678	17.983	50
60	18.288	18.593	18.898	19.202	19.507	19.812	20.117	20.422	20.726	21.031	60
70	21.336	21.641	21.946	22.250	22.555	22.860	23.165	23.470	23.774	24.079	70
80	24.384	24.689	24.994	25.298	25.603	25.908	26.213	26.518	26.822	27.127	80
90	27.432	27.737	28.042	28.346	28.651	28.956	29.261	29.566	29.870	30.175	90
100	30.480	30.785	31.090	31.394	31.699	32.004	32.309	32.614	32.918	33.223	100

METERS TO FEET

m	0	1	2	3	4	5	6	7	8	9	m
	ft	ft	ft	ft	ft	ft	ft	ft	ft	ft	
..		3.2808	6.5617	9.8425	13.1234	16.4042	19.6850	22.9659	26.2467	29.5276	..
10	32.8084	36.0892	39.3701	42.6509	45.9318	49.2126	52.4934	55.7743	59.0551	62.3360	10
20	65.6168	68.8976	72.1785	75.4593	78.7402	82.0210	85.3018	88.5827	91.8635	95.1444	20
30	98.4252	101.7060	104.9869	108.2677	111.5486	114.8294	118.1102	121.3911	124.6719	127.9528	30
40	131.2336	134.5144	137.7953	141.0761	144.3570	147.6378	150.9186	154.1995	157.4803	160.7612	40
50	164.0420	167.3228	170.6037	173.8845	177.1654	180.4462	183.7270	187.0079	190.2887	193.5696	50
60	196.8504	200.1312	203.4121	206.6929	209.9738	213.2546	216.5354	219.8163	223.0971	226.3780	60
70	229.6588	232.9396	236.2205	239.5013	242.7822	246.0630	249.3438	252.6247	255.9055	259.1864	70
80	262.4672	265.7480	269.0289	272.3097	275.5906	278.8714	282.1522	285.4331	288.7139	291.9948	80
90	295.2756	298.5564	301.8373	305.1181	308.3990	311.6798	314.9606	318.2415	321.5223	324.8032	90
100	328.0840	331.3648	334.6457	337.9265	341.2074	344.4882	347.7690	351.0499	354.3307	357.6116	100

MILES TO KILOMETERS

mile	0	1	2	3	4	5	6	7	8	9	mile
	km	km	km	km	km	km	km	km	km	km	
..		1.609	3.219	4.828	6.437	8.047	9.656	11.265	12.875	14.484	..
10	16.093	17.703	19.312	20.921	22.531	24.140	25.750	27.359	28.968	30.578	10
20	32.187	33.796	35.406	37.015	38.624	40.234	41.843	43.452	45.062	46.671	20
30	48.280	49.890	51.499	53.108	54.718	56.327	57.936	59.546	61.155	62.764	30
40	64.374	65.983	67.593	69.202	70.811	72.421	74.030	75.639	77.249	78.858	40
50	80.467	82.077	83.686	85.295	86.905	88.514	90.123	91.733	93.342	94.951	50
60	96.561	98.170	99.779	101.39	103.00	104.61	106.22	107.83	109.44	111.04	60
70	112.65	114.26	115.87	117.48	119.09	120.70	122.31	123.92	125.53	127.14	70
80	128.75	130.36	131.97	133.58	135.19	136.79	138.40	140.01	141.62	143.23	80
90	144.84	146.45	148.06	149.67	151.28	152.89	154.50	156.11	157.72	159.33	90
100	160.93	162.54	164.15	165.76	167.37	168.98	170.59	172.20	173.81	175.42	100

KILOMETERS TO MILES

km	0	1	2	3	4	5	6	7	8	9	km
	mil	mil	mil	mil	mil	mil	mil	mil	mil	mil	
..		0.621	1.243	1.864	2.486	3.107	3.728	4.350	4.971	5.592	..
10	6.214	6.835	7.457	8.078	8.699	9.321	9.942	10.562	11.185	11.805	10
20	12.427	13.049	13.670	14.292	14.913	15.534	16.156	16.776	17.399	18.019	20
30	18.641	19.263	19.884	20.506	21.127	21.748	22.370	22.990	23.613	24.233	30
40	24.855	25.477	26.098	26.720	27.341	27.962	28.584	29.204	29.827	30.447	40
50	31.069	31.690	32.311	32.933	33.554	34.175	34.797	35.417	36.040	36.660	50
60	37.282	37.904	38.525	39.147	39.768	40.389	41.011	41.631	42.254	42.874	60
70	43.497	44.118	44.739	45.361	45.982	46.603	47.225	47.845	48.468	49.088	70
80	49.711	50.332	50.953	51.575	52.196	52.817	53.439	54.059	54.682	55.302	80
90	55.924	56.545	57.166	57.788	58.409	59.030	59.652	60.272	60.895	61.515	90
100	62.138	62.759	63.380	64.002	64.623	65.244	65.866	66.486	67.109	67.729	100

GALLONS (U.S.) TO LITERS

U.S. gal	0	1	2	3	4	5	6	7	8	9	U.S. gal
	L	L	L	L	L	L	L	L	L	L	
..		3.7854	7.5709	11.3563	15.1417	18.9271	22.7126	26.4980	30.2834	34.0638	..
10	37.8543	41.6397	45.4251	49.2105	52.9960	56.7814	60.5668	64.3523	68.1377	71.9231	10
20	75.7085	79.4940	83.2794	87.0648	90.8502	94.6357	98.4211	102.2065	105.9920	109.7774	20
30	113.5528	117.3482	121.1337	124.9191	128.7045	132.4899	136.2754	140.0608	143.8462	147.6316	30
40	151.4171	155.2025	158.9879	162.7734	166.5588	170.3442	174.1296	177.9151	181.7005	185.4859	40
50	189.2713	193.0568	196.8422	200.6276	204.4131	208.1985	211.9839	215.7693	219.5548	223.3402	50
60	227.1256	230.9110	234.6965	238.4819	242.2673	246.0527	249.8382	253.6236	257.4090	261.1945	60
70	264.9799	268.7653	272.5507	276.3362	280.1216	283.9070	287.6924	291.4779	295.2633	299.0487	70
80	302.8342	306.6196	310.4050	314.1904	317.9759	321.7613	325.5467	329.3321	333.1176	336.9030	80
90	340.6884	344.4738	348.2593	352.0447	355.8301	359.6156	363.4010	367.1864	370.9718	374.7573	90
100	378.5427	382.3281	386.1135	389.8990	393.6844	397.4698	401.2553	405.0407	408.8261	412.6115	100

LITERS TO GALLONS (U.S.)

L	0	1	2	3	4	5	6	7	8	9	L
	gal	gal	gal	gal	gal	gal	gal	gal	gal	gal	
..		0.2642	0.5283	0.7925	1.0567	1.3209	1.5850	1.8492	2.1134	2.3775	..
10	2.6417	2.9059	3.1701	3.4342	3.6984	3.9626	4.2267	4.4909	4.7551	5.0192	10
20	5.2834	5.5476	5.8118	6.0759	6.3401	6.6043	6.8684	7.1326	7.3968	7.6610	20
30	7.9251	8.1893	8.4535	8.7176	8.9818	9.2460	9.5102	9.7743	10.0385	10.3027	30
40	10.5668	10.8310	11.0952	11.3594	11.6235	11.8877	12.1519	12.4160	12.6802	12.9444	40
50	13.2086	13.4727	13.7369	14.0011	14.2652	14.5294	14.7936	15.0577	15.3219	15.5861	50
60	15.8503	16.1144	16.3786	16.6428	16.9069	17.1711	17.4353	17.6995	17.9636	18.2278	60
70	18.4920	18.7561	19.0203	19.2845	19.5487	19.8128	20.0770	20.3412	20.6053	20.8695	70
80	21.1337	21.3979	21.6620	21.9262	22.1904	22.4546	22.7187	22.9829	23.2470	23.5112	80
90	23.7754	24.0396	24.3037	24.5679	24.8321	25.0962	25.3604	25.6246	25.8888	26.1529	90
100	26.4171	26.6813	26.9454	27.2096	27.4738	27.7380	28.0021	28.2663	28.5305	28.7946	100

GALLONS (IMP.) TO LITERS

IMP gal	0	1	2	3	4	5	6	7	8	9	IMP gal
	L	L	L	L	L	L	L	L	L	L	
..		4.5460	9.0919	13.6379	18.1838	22.7298	27.2758	31.8217	36.3677	40.9136	..
10	45.4596	50.0056	54.5515	59.0975	63.6434	68.1894	72.2354	77.2813	81.8275	86.3732	10
20	90.9192	95.4652	100.0111	104.5571	109.1030	113.6490	118.1950	122.7409	127.2869	131.8328	20
30	136.3788	140.9248	145.4707	150.0167	154.5626	159.1086	163.6546	168.0005	172.7465	177.2924	30
40	181.8384	186.3844	190.9303	195.4763	200.0222	204.5682	209.1142	213.6601	218.2061	222.7520	40
50	227.2980	231.8440	236.3899	240.9359	245.4818	250.0278	254.5738	259.1197	263.6657	268.2116	50
60	272.7576	277.3036	281.8495	286.3955	290.9414	295.4874	300.0334	304.5793	309.1253	313.6712	60
70	318.2172	322.7632	327.3091	331.8551	336.4010	340.9470	345.4930	350.0389	354.5849	359.1308	70
80	363.6768	368.2223	372.7687	377.3147	381.8606	386.4066	390.9526	395.4985	400.0445	404.5904	80
90	409.1364	413.6824	418.2283	422.7743	427.3202	431.8662	436.4122	440.9581	445.9041	450.0500	90
100	454.5960	459.1420	463.6879	468.2339	472.7798	477.3258	481.8718	486.4177	490.9637	495.5096	100

LITERS TO GALLONS (IMP.)

L	0	1	2	3	4	5	6	7	8	9	L
	gal	gal	gal	gal	gal	gal	gal	gal	gal	gal	
..		0.2200	0.4400	0.6599	0.8799	1.0999	1.3199	1.5398	1.7598	1.9798	..
10	2.1998	2.4197	2.6397	2.8597	3.0797	3.2996	3.5196	3.7396	3.9596	4.1795	10
20	4.3995	4.6195	4.8395	5.0594	5.2794	5.4994	5.7194	5.9394	6.1593	6.3793	20
30	6.5593	6.8193	7.0392	7.2592	7.4792	7.6992	7.9191	8.1391	8.3591	8.5791	30
40	8.7990	9.0190	9.2390	9.4590	9.6789	9.8989	10.9189	10.3389	10.5588	10.7788	40
50	10.9988	11.2188	11.4388	11.6587	11.8787	12.0987	12.3187	12.5386	12.7586	12.9786	50
60	13.1986	13.4185	13.6385	13.8585	14.0785	14.2984	14.5184	14.7384	14.9584	15.1783	60
70	15.3983	15.6183	15.8383	16.0582	16.2782	16.4982	16.7182	16.9382	17.1581	17.3781	70
80	17.5981	17.8181	18.0380	18.2580	18.4780	18.6980	18.9179	19.1379	19.3579	19.5779	80
90	19.7978	20.0178	20.2378	20.4578	20.6777	20.8977	21.1177	21.3377	21.5576	21.7776	90
100	21.9976	22.2176	22.4376	22.6575	22.8775	23.0975	23.3175	23.5374	23.7574	23.9774	100

POUNDS TO KILOGRAMS

lb	0	1	2	3	4	5	6	7	8	9	lb
	kg	kg	kg	kg	kg	kg	kg	kg	kg	kg	
..		0.454	0.907	1.361	1.814	2.268	2.722	3.175	3.629	4.082	..
10	4.536	4.990	5.443	5.897	6.350	6.804	7.257	7.711	8.165	8.618	10
20	9.072	9.525	9.979	10.433	10.886	11.340	11.793	12.247	12.701	13.154	20
30	13.608	14.061	14.515	14.969	15.422	15.876	16.329	16.783	17.237	17.690	30
40	18.144	18.597	19.051	19.504	19.958	20.412	20.865	21.319	21.772	22.226	40
50	22.680	23.133	23.587	24.040	24.494	24.948	25.401	25.855	26.308	26.762	50
60	27.216	27.669	28.123	28.576	29.030	29.484	29.937	30.391	30.844	31.298	60
70	31.751	32.205	32.659	33.112	33.566	34.019	34.473	34.927	35.380	35.834	70
80	36.287	36.741	37.195	37.648	38.102	38.555	39.009	39.463	39.916	40.370	80
90	40.823	41.277	41.730	42.184	42.638	43.092	43.545	43.998	44.453	44.906	90
100	45.359	45.813	46.266	46.720	47.174	47.627	48.081	48.534	48.988	49.442	100

KILOGRAMS TO POUNDS

kg	0	1	2	3	4	5	6	7	8	9	kg
	lb	lb	lb	lb	lb	lb	lb	lb	lb	lb	
..		2.205	4.409	6.614	8.818	11.023	13.228	15.432	17.637	19.842	..
10	22.046	24.251	26.455	28.660	30.865	33.069	35.274	37.479	39.683	41.888	10
20	44.092	46.297	48.502	50.706	52.911	55.116	57.320	59.525	61.729	63.934	20
30	66.139	68.343	70.548	72.752	74.957	77.162	79.366	81.571	83.776	85.980	30
40	88.185	90.389	92.594	94.799	97.003	99.208	101.41	103.62	105.82	108.03	40
50	110.23	112.44	114.64	116.84	119.05	121.25	123.46	125.66	127.87	130.07	50
60	132.28	134.48	136.69	138.89	141.10	143.30	145.51	147.71	149.91	152.12	60
70	154.32	156.53	158.73	160.94	163.14	165.35	167.55	169.76	171.96	174.17	70
80	176.37	178.57	180.78	182.98	185.19	187.39	189.60	191.80	194.01	196.21	80
90	198.42	200.62	202.83	205.03	207.23	209.44	211.64	213.85	216.05	218.26	90
100	220.46	222.67	224.87	227.08	229.28	231.49	233.69	235.89	238.10	240.30	100

POUNDS PER SQUARE INCHES TO KILOPASCALS

lb/in²	0	1	2	3	4	5	6	7	8	9	lb/in²
	kPa	kPa	kPa	kPa	kPa	kPa	kPa	kPa	kPa	kPa	
..	0.0000	6.8948	13.7895	20.6843	27.5790	34.4738	41.3685	48.2663	55.1581	62.0528	..
10	68.9476	75.8423	82.7371	89.6318	96.5266	103.4214	110.3161	117.2109	124.1056	131.0004	10
20	137.8951	144.7899	151.6847	158.5794	165.4742	172.3689	179.2637	186.1584	193.0532	199.9480	20
30	206.8427	213.7375	220.6322	227.5270	234.4217	241.3165	248.2113	255.1060	262.0008	268.8955	30
40	275.7903	282.6850	289.5798	296.4746	303.3693	310.2641	317.1588	324.0536	330.9483	337.8431	40
50	344.7379	351.6326	358.5274	365.4221	372.3169	379.2116	386.1064	393.0012	399.8959	406.7907	50
60	412.6854	420.5802	427.4749	434.3697	441.2645	448.1592	455.0540	461.9487	468.8435	475.7382	60
70	482.6330	489.5278	496.4225	503.3173	510.2120	517.1068	524.0015	530.8963	537.7911	544.6858	70
80	551.5806	558.4753	565.3701	572.2648	579.1596	586.0544	592.9491	599.8439	606.7386	613.6334	80
90	620.5281	627.4229	634.3177	641.2124	648.1072	655.0019	661.8967	668.7914	675.6862	682.5810	90
100	689.4757	696.3705	703.2653	710.1601	717.0549	723.9497	730.8445	737.7393	744.6341	751.5289	100

KILOPASCALS TO POUNDS PER SQUARE INCHES

kPa	0	1	2	3	4	5	6	7	8	9	kPa
	lb/in²	lb/in²	lb/in²	lb/in²	lb/in²	lb/in²	lb/in²	lb/in²	lb/in²	lb/in²	
..		.1450	.2901	.4351	.5801	.7252	.8702	1.0153	1.1603	1.3053	..
10	1.4504	1.5954	1.7404	1.8855	2.0305	2.1556	2.3206	2.4656	2.6107	2.7557	10
20	2.9007	3.0458	3.1908	3.3359	3.4809	3.6259	3.7710	3.9160	4.0610	4.2061	20
30	4.3511	4.4961	4.6412	4.7862	4.9313	5.0763	5.2213	5.3664	5.5114	5.6564	30
40	5.8015	5.9465	6.0916	6.2366	6.3816	6.5267	6.6717	6.8167	6.9618	7.1068	40
50	7.2518	7.3969	7.5419	7.6870	7.8320	7.9770	8.1221	8.2671	8.4121	8.5572	50
60	8.7022	8.8473	8.9923	9.1373	9.1824	9.4274	9.5724	9.7175	9.8625	10.0076	60
70	10.1526	10.2976	10.4427	10.5877	10.7327	10.8778	11.0228	11.1678	11.3129	11.4579	70
80	11.6030	11.7480	11.8930	12.0381	12.1831	12.3281	12.4732	12.6182	12.7633	12.9083	80
90		13.1001	13.2424	13.4884	13.6335	13.7785	13.9236	14.0686	14.2136	14.3587	90
100	14.5037	14.6487	14.7938	14.9388	15.0000				16.0010	16.8000	100

POUND FEET TO NEWTON-METERS

ft-lb	0	1	2	3	4	5	6	7	8	9	ft-lb
	N·m	N·m	N·m	N·m	N·m	N·m	N·m	N·m	N·m	N·m	
..		1.3558	2.7116	4.0675	5.4233	6.7791	8.1349	9.4907	10.8465	12.2024	..
10	13.5582	14.9140	16.2698	17.6256	18.9815	20.3373	21.6931	23.0489	24.4047	25.7605	10
20	27.1164	28.4722	29.8280	31.1838	32.5396	33.8954	35.2513	36.6071	37.9629	39.3187	20
30	40.6745	42.0304	43.3862	44.7420	46.0978	47.4536	48.8094	50.1653	51.5211	52.8769	30
40	54.2327	55.5885	56.9444	58.3002	59.6560	61.0118	62.3676	63.7234	65.0793	66.4351	40
50	67.7909	69.1467	70.5025	71.8584	73.2142	74.5700	75.9258	77.2816	78.6374	79.9933	50
60	81.3491	82.7049	84.0607	85.4165	86.7724	88.1282	89.4840	90.3898	92.1956	93.5514	60
70	94.9073	96.2631	97.6189	98.9747	100.3305	101.6863	103.0422	104.3980	105.7538	107.1096	70
80	108.4654	109.8213	111.1771	112.5329	113.8887	115.2445	116.6003	117.9562	119.3120	120.6678	80
90	122.0236	123.3794	124.7353	126.0911	127.4469	128.8027	130.1585	131.5143	132.8702	134.2260	90
100	135.5818	136.9376	138.2934	139.6493	141.0051	142.3609	143.7167	145.0725	146.4283	147.7842	100

NEWTON METERS TO POUND FEET

N·m	0	1	2	3	4	5	6	7	8	9	N·m
	ft-lb	ft-lb	ft-lb	ft-lb	ft-lb	ft-lb	ft-lb	ft-lb	ft-lb	ft-lb	
..		.7376	1.4751	2.2127	2.9502	3.6878	4.4254	5.1692	5.9005	6.6381	..
10	7.3756	8.1132	8.8507	9.5883	10.3258	11.0634	11.8010	12.5385	13.2761	14.0136	10
20	14.7512	15.4888	16.2264	16.9639	17.7015	18.4390	19.1766	19.9142	20.6517	21.3893	20
30	22.1269	22.8644	23.6020	24.3395	25.0771	25.8147	26.5522	27.2898	28.0274	28.7649	30
40	29.5025	30.2400	30.9776	31.7152	32.4527	33.1903	33.9279	34.6654	35.4030	36.1405	40
50	36.8781	37.6157	38.3532	39.0908	39.8283	40.5659	41.3035	42.0410	42.7786	43.5162	50
60	44.2537	44.9913	45.7288	46.4664	47.2040	47.9415	48.6791	49.4167	50.1542	50.8918	60
70	51.6293	52.3669	53.1045	53.8420	54.5796	55.3171	56.0547	56.7923	57.5298	58.2674	70
80	59.0050	59.7425	60.4801	61.2176	61.9552	62.6928	63.4303	64.1679	64.9055	65.6430	80
90	66.3806	67.1181	67.8557	68.5933	69.3308	70.0684	70.8060	71.5435	72.2811	73.0186	90
100	73.7562	74.4938	75.2313	75.9689	76.7064	77.4440	78.1816	78.9191	79.6567	80.3943	100

DIMENSION AND TEMPERATURE CONVERSION CHART

Inches	Decimals	Milli-meters	Inches to millimeters		Millimeters to inches		Fahrenheit & Celsius			
			Inches	mm	mm	Inches	°F	°C	°C	°F
1/64	.015625	.3969	.0001	.00254	0.001	.000039	-20	-28.9	-30	-22
1/32	.03125	.7937	.0002	.00508	0.002	.000079	-15	-26.1	-28	-18.4
3/64	.046875	1.1906	.0003	.00762	0.003	.000118	-10	-23.3	-26	-14.8
1/16	.0625	1.5875	.0004	.01016	0.004	.000157	-5	-20.6	-24	-11.2
5/64	.078125	1.9844	.0005	.01270	0.005	.000197	0	-17.8	-22	-7.6
3/32	.09375	2.3812	.0006	.01524	0.006	.000236	1	-17.2	-20	-4
7/64	.109375	2.7781	.0007	.01778	0.007	.000276	2	-16.7	-18	-0.4
1/8	.125	3.1750	.0008	.02032	0.008	.000315	3	-16.1	-16	3.2
9/64	.140625	3.5719	.0009	.02286	0.009	.000354	4	-15.6	-14	6.8
5/32	.15625	3.9687	.001	.0254	0.01	.00039	5	-15.0	-12	10.4
11/64	.171875	4.3656	.002	.0508	0.02	.00079	10	-12.2	-10	14
3/16	.1875	4.7625	.003	.0762	0.03	.00118	15	-9.4	-8	17.6
13/64	.203125	5.1594	.004	.1016	0.04	.00157	20	-6.7	-6	21.2
7/32	.21875	5.5562	.005	.1270	0.05	.00197	25	-3.9	-4	24.8
15/64	.234375	5.9531	.006	.1524	0.06	.00236	30	-1.1	-2	28.4
1/4	.25	6.3500	.007	.1778	0.07	.00276	35	1.7	0	32
17/64	.265625	6.7469	.008	.2032	0.08	.00315	40	4.4	2	35.6
9/32	.28125	7.1437	.009	.2286	0.09	.00354	45	7.2	4	39.2
19/64	.296875	7.5406	.01	.254	0.1	.00394	50	10.0	6	42.8
5/16	.3125	7.9375	.02	.508	0.2	.00787	55	12.8	8	46.4
21/64	.328125	8.3344	.03	.762	0.3	.01181	60	15.6	10	50
11/32	.34375	8.7312	.04	1.016	0.4	.01575	65	18.3	12	53.6
23/64	.359375	9.1281	.05	1.270	0.5	.01969	70	21.1	14	57.2
3/8	.375	9.5250	.06	1.524	0.6	.02362	75	23.9	16	60.8
25/64	.390625	9.9219	.07	1.778	0.7	.02756	80	26.7	18	64.4
13/32	.40625	10.3187	.08	2.032	0.8	.03150	85	29.4	20	68
27/64	.421875	10.7156	.09	2.286	0.9	.03543	90	32.2	22	71.6
7/16	.4375	11.1125	.1	2.54	1	.03937	95	35.0	24	75.2
29/64	.453125	11.5094	.2	5.08	2	.07874	100	37.8	26	78.8
15/32	.46875	11.9062	.3	7.62	3	.11811	105	40.6	28	82.4
31/64	.484375	12.3031	.4	10.16	4	.15748	110	43.3	30	86
1/2	.5	12.7000	.5	12.70	5	.19685	115	46.1	32	89.6
33/64	.515625	13.0969	.6	15.24	6	.23622	120	48.9	34	93.2
17/32	.53125	13.4937	.7	17.78	7	.27559	125	51.7	36	96.8
35/64	.546875	13.8906	.8	20.32	8	.31496	130	54.4	38	100.4
9/16	.5625	14.2875	.9	22.86	9	.35433	135	57.2	40	104
37/64	.578125	14.6844	1	25.4	10	.39370	140	60.0	42	107.6
19/32	.59375	15.0812	2	50.8	11	.43307	145	62.8	44	112.2
39/64	.609375	15.4781	3	76.2	12	.47244	150	65.6	46	114.8
5/8	.625	15.8750	4	101.6	13	.51181	155	68.3	48	118.4
41/64	.640625	16.2719	5	127.0	14	.55118	160	71.1	50	122
21/32	.65625	16.6687	6	152.4	15	.59055	165	73.9	52	125.6
43/64	.671875	17.0656	7	177.8	16	.62992	170	76.7	54	129.2
11/16	.6875	17.4625	8	203.2	17	.66929	175	79.4	56	132.8
45/64	.703125	17.8594	9	228.6	18	.70866	180	82.2	58	136.4
23/32	.71875	18.2562	10	254.0	19	.74803	185	85.0	60	140
47/64	.734375	18.6531	11	279.4	20	.78740	190	87.8	62	143.6
3/4	.75	19.0500	12	304.8	21	.82677	195	90.6	64	147.2
49/64	.765625	19.4469	13	330.2	22	.86614	200	93.3	66	150.8
25/32	.78125	19.8437	14	355.6	23	.90551	205	96.1	68	154.4
51/64	.796875	20.2406	15	381.0	24	.94488	210	98.9	70	158
13/16	.8125	20.6375	16	406.4	25	.98425	212	100.0	75	167
53/64	.828125	21.0344	17	431.8	26	1.02362	215	101.7	80	176
27/32	.84375	21.4312	18	457.2	27	1.06299	220	104.4	85	185
55/64	.859375	21.8281	19	482.6	28	1.10236	225	107.2	90	194
7/8	.875	22.2250	20	508.0	29	1.14173	230	110.0	95	203
57/64	.890625	22.6219	21	533.4	30	1.18110	235	112.8	100	212
29/32	.90625	23.0187	22	558.8	31	1.22047	240	115.6	105	221
59/64	.921875	23.4156	23	584.2	32	1.25984	245	118.3	110	230
15/16	.9375	23.8125	24	609.6	33	1.29921	250	121.1	115	239
61/64	.953125	24.2094	25	635.0	34	1.33858	255	123.9	120	248
31/32	.96875	24.6062	26	660.4	35	1.37795	260	126.6	125	257
63/64	.984375	25.0031	27	690.6	36	1.41732	265	129.4	130	266

DECIMAL EQUIVALENTS AND TAP DRILL SIZES

DRILL SIZE	DECIMAL	TAP SIZE	DRILL SIZE	DECIMAL	TAP SIZE	DRILL SIZE	DECIMAL	TAP SIZE
1/64	.0156		17	.1730		Q	.3320	3/8-24
1/32	.0312		16	.1770	12-24	R	.3390	
60	.0400		15	.1800		11/32	.3437	
59	.0410		14	.1820	12-28	S	.3480	
58	.0420		13	.1850	12-32	T	.3580	
57	.0430		3/16	.1875		23/64	.3594	
56	.0465		12	.1890		U	.3680	7/16-14
3/64	.0469	0-80	11	.1910		3/8	.3750	
55	.0520		10	.1935		V	.3770	
54	.0550	1-56	9	.1960		W	.3860	
53	.0595	1-64, 72	8	.1990		25/64	.3906	7/16-20
1/16	.0625		7	.2010	1/4-20	X	.3970	
52	.0635		13/64	.2031		Y	.4040	
51	.0670		6	.2040		13/32	.4062	
50	.0700	2-56, 64	5	.2055		Z	.4130	
49	.0730		4	.2090		27/64	.4219	1/2-13
48	.0760		3	.2130	1/4-28	7/16	.4375	
5/64	.0781		7/32	.2187		29/64	.4531	1/2-20
47	.0785	3-48	2	.2210		15/32	.4687	
46	.0810		1	.2280		31/64	.4844	9/16-12
45	.0820	3-56,4-32	A	.2340		1/2	.5000	
44	.0860	4-36	15/64	.2344		33/64	.5156	9/16-18
43	.0890	4-40	B	.2380		17/32	.5312	5/8-11
42	.0935	4-48	C	.2420		35/64	.5469	
3/32	.0937		D	.2460		9/16	.5625	
41	.0960		E, 1/4	.2500		37/64	.5781	5/8-18
40	.0980		F	.2570	5/16-18	19/32	.5937	11/16-11
39	.0995	5-40	G	.2610		39/64	.6094	
38	.1015	5-44	17/64	.2656		5/8	.6250	11/16-16
37	.1040	6-32	H	.2660		41/64	.6406	
36	.1065		I	.2720	5/16-24	21/32	.6562	3/4-10
7/64	.1093		J	.2770		43/64	.6719	
35	.1100		K	.2810		11/16	.6875	3/4-16
34	.1110	6-36	9/32	.2812		45/64	.7031	
33	.1130	6-40	L	.2900		23/32	.7187	
32	.1160		M	.2950		47/64	.7344	
31	.1200		19/64	.2968		3/4	.7500	
1/8	.1250		N	.3020		49/64	.7656	7/8-9
30	.1285		5/16	.3125	3/8-16	25/32	.7812	
29	.1360	8-32, 36	O	.3160		51/64	.7969	
28	.1405	8-40	P	.3230		13/16	.8125	7/8-14
9/64	.1406		21/64	.3281		53/64	.8281	
27	.1440					27/32	.8437	
26	.1470					55/64	.8594	
25	.1495	10-24				7/8	.8750	1-8
24	.1520					57/64	.8906	
23	.1540					29/32	.9062	
5/32	.1562					59/64	.9219	
22	.1570	10-30				15/16	.9375	1-12,14
21	.1590	10-32				61/64	.9531	
20	.1610					31/32	.9687	
19	.1660					63/64	.9844	
18	.1695					1	1.000	
11/64	.1719							

PIPE THREAD SIZES

THREAD	DRILL	THREAD	DRILL
1/8-27	R	1 1/2-11 1/2	1 47/64
1/4-18	7/16	2-11 1/2	2 7/32
3/8-18	37/64	2 1/2-8	2 5/8
1/2-14	23/32	3-8	3 1/4
3/4-14	59/64	3 1/2-8	3 3/4
1-11 1/2	1 5/32	4-8	4 1/4
1 1/4-11 1/2	1 1/2		

Index